Sports Law

FOURTH EDITION

Sports Law

FOURTH EDITION

Simon Gardiner, BA (Hons), MA

John O'Leary, LLB (Hons), M Phil

Roger Welch, LLB (Hons), LLM, PhD

Simon Boyes, LLB (Hons), LLM

Urvasi Naidoo, LLB (Hons), LLM

Routledge
Taylor & Francis Group

LONDON AND NEW YORK

Fourth edition first published 2012
by Routledge
2 Park Square, Milton Park, Abingdon, Oxon, OX14 4RN

Simultaneously published in the USA and Canada
by Routledge
711 Third Avenue, New York, NY 10017

Routledge is an imprint of the Taylor & Francis Group, an informa business

© 2012 Simon Gardiner, John O'Leary, Roger Welch, Simon Boyes
and Urvasi Naidoo

Previous editions published by Cavendish Publishing Limited
First edition   1998
Third edition   2006

British Library Cataloguing in Publication Data
A catalogue record for this book is available from the British Library

Library of Congress Cataloging in Publication Data
    Sports law / Simon Gardiner ... [et al.]. – [4th ed.]
        p. cm.
    Includes bibliographical references and index.
    ISBN 978-0-415-59184-3 (hbk : alk. paper) – ISBN 978-0-415-59183-6
    (pbk. : alk. paper) -- ISBN 978-0-203-18088-4 (ebk) 1. Sports–Law and
    legislation–Great Britain. I. Gardiner, Simon.
    KD3525.S69 2011
    344.41'099–dc23   2011020137

ISBN: 978–0–415–59184–3 (hbk)
ISBN: 978–0–415–59183–6 (pbk)
ISBN: 978–0–203–18088–4 (ebk)

Typeset in Joanna
by RefineCatch Limited, Bungay, Suffolk

Printed and bound in Great Britain by the MPG Books Group

To all our families. Thank you for all your support, and in particular for Alexander, Maighraed, Niamh and Orfhlaith — the sports lawyers of tomorrow.

Contents

About the Authors   xi
Foreword   xiii
Preface   xv
Acknowledgements   xx
Table of Cases   xxiii
Table of Statutes   xxxv
Table of Statutory Instruments   xxxix
Table of EU Conventions and Treaties   xli
Table of EU Secondary Legislation   xliii

PART 1   THE REGULATION AND GOVERNANCE OF SPORT   1
1   Cultural, Historical and Organisational Perspectives on UK
         Regulation of Sport   3
         Introduction   4
         What is a Sport?   4
         History of Sport   13
         Historical Perspectives on Sports Regulation   16
         The Victorian Age: Origins of Modern Sport   22
         The Contemporary Significance of Sport   24
         Sociology of Sport   26
         Framework of Sport in Britain   30
         Conclusion   42
         Key Points   42
         Key Sources   42

2   Theoretical Understanding of the Regulation of Sport   43
         Introduction   44
         The Normative Rule Structure of Sport   45
         Adjudicative Officials and Playing Rules   51
         Challenging the Rules: Cheating and Sportsmanship   55
         The Contemporary Regulation of Sport   70
         Juridification of Sport: The Role of Law   73
         Globalisation of Sports Law   77
         Viva Sports Law – Sport and the Law RIP   83
         Conclusion   86
         Key Points   87
         Key Sources   87

3 **The Legal Regulation of Sports Governing Bodies** 88
  Introduction 89
  Sport and Self-Regulation 90
  Access to the Courts: Actions Against Sports Governing Bodies 93
  Sports Governing Bodies: The Contractual Relationship 105
  Economic Regulation: Restraint of Trade and Competition Law 114
  Substantive Rights Against Sports Governing Bodies 117
  Alternatives to Litigation: Sports Governing Bodies and Alternate
    Dispute Resolution 138
  Evaluation 142
  Key Points 143
  Key Sources 144

4 **Sport and the Law of the European Union** 145
  Introduction 146
  Establishing the Relationship Between European Union Law and Sport 147
  Bosman: The Application of European Union Law to Sport 151
  The Applicability of EU Competition Law to Sport 176
  The Application of EU Competition Law to Sport 181
  Sports Broadcasting and EU Law 196
  The Modern Era: The Path to Lisbon, the EU Reform Treaty and Beyond 199
  Conclusions 205
  Key Points 206
  Key Sources 206

PART 2 **LEGAL PROTECTION OF THE COMMERCIAL INTEGRITY OF SPORT** 207
5 **Sport and Money: Accountability and Regulation** 209
  Introduction 210
  Professionalisation and the End of Amateurism 212
  Commercialisation of Sport 219
  The Economics of Sport 220
  Characteristics of Sport Business 222
  Commodification 225
  Models of Regulation 227
  Football Task Force 230
  Effective Sports Governance 241
  Competition and Broadcasting 245
  Other Competition Law Intervention into UK Sport 254
  Conclusion 257
  Key Points 257
  Key Sources 257

6 **Sport, Match Fixing and Corruption** 258
  Introduction 259
  Football: Bungs and Brown Paper Bags 259
  Regulation of Sports Agents 265
  Ethics and Hosting of Major Sports Events 270
  Match Fixing in Sport 272
  Gambling and Sport 290

Developments in Fighting Match Fixing and Sports-Related Gambling 297
Conclusion 301
Key Points 301
Key Sources 301

7 The Exploitation and Protection of Olympic Commercial Rights 302
Introduction 303
Sponsorship 304
Licensing 310
Ticketing 312
Intellectual Property Rights 318
Ambush Marketing 329
Looking into the Future 355
Conclusions 357
Key Points 359
Key Sources 360

PART 3 LEGAL ISSUES IN THE SPORTS WORKPLACE 361
8 The Regulation of Doping in Sport 363
Introduction 364
Anti-Doping Institutions 369
The World Anti-Doping Code 371
The Future 390
Key Points 391
Key Sources 392

9 Sport and Contracts of Employment 393
Introduction 394
Who is an Employee? 394
Formation and Terms of a Contract of Employment 397
Performance of the Contract 402
Judicially Implied Terms 404
Restraint of Trade 409
Termination of Contracts of Employment in Sport 418
Remedies for Wrongful Dismissal 423
Unfair Dismissal 426
Procedural Fairness 435
The *Bosman* Case and the Transfer System 441
Conclusions 457
Key Points 458
Key Sources 459

10 Sports Participants and the Law of Discrimination 460
Introduction 461
Unlawful Discrimination 465
Unlawful Harassment 477
Discrimination and European Law 483
Key Points 496
Key Sources 497

11 Safety and Participants in Sport 498

Introduction 499

What is Sports Violence? 500

Civil Law Liability for Sports Participant Violence 500

Potential Defendants 503

Criminal Liability for Sports Participant Violence 515

Prosecutorial Discretion – the Solution? 520

Risk Management and Extreme Sports 526

Child Protection: Sports Coaches and Child Athletes 533

Conclusion 540

Key Points 541

Key Sources 542

12 Sports Venues and the Law 543

Introduction 544

Parliamentary Enquiries 544

Stadium Liability Issues 552

Spectators 564

Crowd Management 567

Football Hooliganism 574

Spectator Racism in Sport 579

Key Points 589

Key Sources 589

Index 590

About the Authors

All the five co-authors are keen sports fans and all try to continue to compete on a recreational level in a number of sports. Fandom is, of course, an important part of participation within the sports world. Those of you who know us will be well aware of our sporting allegiances: football dominates but, since the last edition, the fortunes of our respective teams (very sadly on my part) have fluctuated. Premier League representation lies solely with John, 'a true blue' Chelsea supporter. Lower league devotion can be found with Roger and his adored Pompey. Having 'lived the dream', and then the nightmare, I look forward to better times with the finest United in England – Leeds of course! The other Simon provides foundational and inspirational support for us all – dreaming about the future glories of Scarborough Athletic.

During the summer what is there to do – no football! Cricket provides a welcome juxtaposition. While we all enjoy the improving performance of the England team and the winning of the Ashes, a healthy form of north–south rivalry exists between the two Simons and their allegiance to the mighty White Rose of Yorkshire and the softy southerners Roger and John, who follow Essex and Middlesex respectively. Last, but certainly not least, Vasi sets aside her professional involvement with many of the leading cricket issues over the last few years, and cheers on the South African team.

We hope the foci of our sporting devotion are not too obvious in our respective commentaries. Enjoy.

Simon Gardiner
Bishop's Stortford
May 2011

Author Biographies

Simon Boyes is a Senior Lecturer at Nottingham Law School, Nottingham Trent University. He teaches on Nottingham Law School's LLM Sports Law, as well as its Sports Law module on the undergraduate law programme. His primary research interests are in the self-regulatory aspects of sport and their relationship with the law. He also has an interest in the relationship between sport and the European Union. Most of his recent published work is in this area, including, 'One Size Fits All? The Myth of a Homogenous European Sports Law' (2006) 1–2 *International Sports Law Journal* 16 and 'Caught Behind or Following-On? Cricket, the European Union and the "Bosman Effect"' (2005) 3 *Entertainment and Sports Law Journal*.

Simon Gardiner is a Reader in Sports Law at Leeds Metropolitan University and Senior Research Fellow at the Asser International Sports Law Centre. His particular research interests include sports governance, racism and the construction of national identity in sport. He has published widely in a number of areas of sports law. He is co-editor of *EU, Sport, Law and Policy: Regulation, Re-regulation and Representation*, 2nd edn (Cambridge: CUP, 2009, with Parrish, R and Siekmann, R.), and author of 'UK Sports Law' in Blanpain, R and Hendrickx, F (eds) *International Encyclopaedia of Sports Law* (The Hague: Kluwer, 2008). He is editor of the *Sport and the Law Journal* and on the editorial board of the *International Sports Law Journal*.

Urvasi Naidoo is a sports lawyer who previously worked for the Salt Lake Olympic and Paralympic Winter Games 2002 in the Brand Protection Department and the International Cricket Council as their In House Lawyer. She is currently employed as the Chief Executive Officer of the International Federation of Netball Associations. She is a Trustee to Sporting Equals, the only organisation working across the UK to promote opportunities for black and ethnic minorities in sport and physical activity, and sits on the Commission for the Future of Women's Sports. She has published a number of sports law articles and is a regular speaker/guest lecturer on her specialist topics: Ambush Marketing, Brand Protection, Constitutional and Regulatory Matters, Dispute Resolution, Disciplinary Measures, Anti Corruption, Sport and Corporate Social Responsibility and Contract. Her interest in the Olympic movement saw her volunteer at Athens 2004 and Vancouver 2010 and she is down to volunteer again at London 2012.

John O'Leary is a Senior Lecturer in Law and member of the International Law Unit at Anglia Ruskin University. He has written extensively and published widely in the areas of doping, stadium safety and sports contracts. He acts as a consultant to sports governing bodies, was co-author of a report on doping for the European Commission and has advised UK Anti-Doping on legal aspects of anti-doping regulation. He is editor of *Drugs and Doping in Sport: Socio-Legal Perspectives* (London: Cavendish, 2000).

Roger Welch is a visiting research fellow at the University of Portsmouth. His research interests are primarily in the areas of employment law, trade union rights and sports law, and he has published widely in these areas. His publications in sports law include: 'A Snort and a Puff: Recreational Drugs and Discipline in Professional Sport', in O' Leary, J (ed), *Drugs and Doping in Sport* (London: Cavendish, 2001); 'Player Mobility, the FIFA Transfer Rules and Freedom of Movement', *International Sports Law Review*, 2006; 'The Contractual Dynamics of Team Stability Versus Player Mobility: Who Rules "The Beautiful Game"'? *Entertainment and Sports Law Journal*, 2007 (with S Gardiner); 'Football, Racism and the Limits of "Colour Blind" Law Revisited', in Burdsey, D (ed), *Ethnicity and Football: Persisting Debates and Emergent Issues* (Routledge, 2011) (with S Gardiner); 'Bosman – There and Back Again: the Legitimacy of Playing Quotas under European Union Sports Policy', *European Law Journal*, 2011 (with S Gardiner).

Foreword

As this leading textbook reveals, the playing field of sports law has become far more than a pleasant relief from the cares of the world. Given the attention that the global public lavishes on sports, the related issues are of fundamental significance in civil society around the world. In response, an impressive growth of academic courses, publications, programmes and specialised law practice attests to the development of sports law in recent years.

It is difficult to imagine a reliable and comprehensive survey of this burgeoning field of law without the expertise that the well-respected editors of this text have provided under Simon Gardiner's leadership. Now in its fourth edition, the book, with its particular attention to British and European law, is bound to remain essential in both classrooms and professional offices.

I am honoured and pleased to have this opportunity not only to recommend the text, but also to take note of a few of the fresh contributions to this edition. These range from updates on the jurisprudence of the Court of Arbitration for Sport, the World Anti-Doping Agency Code and the related UNESCO Convention, to reforms of the transfer system in team sports and the extraordinarily difficult issues of discrimination that have emerged in recent years. Readers of previous editions of this book will also note a succinct reorganisation of the material into three core parts: The Regulation and Governance of Sport, Legal Protection of the Commercial Integrity of Sport, and Legal Issues in the Sports Workplace. May the benefits of this book, old and new, begin!

James A.R. Nafziger
Thomas B. Stoel Professor of Law and Director of International Programs,
Willamette University College of Law
Honorary President, International Association of Sports Law
Salem, Oregon
August 2010

Preface

The fourth edition of *Sports Law* reflects the continued growth of the subject of sports law in Britain as an important area of academic inquiry. This growth over the thirteen years since the first edition was published corresponds to the growth in the legal practice of sports law – significant numbers of lawyers spend a considerable amount of their professional time on sports-related legal issues, with some firms having dedicated sports law practices. During the 1990s the subject has grown in stature. The creation of the British Association for Sport and the Law in 1992 was an important development. There are now a significant number of undergraduate modules in sports law in UK law degrees and it has become an important part of the curriculum in the plethora of sports studies courses that have developed in Britain in recent years. A number of postgraduate courses have also developed in UK Universities.

In addition, the sports law literature has expanded considerably. Books such as Craig Moore's *Sports Law Litigation*, David Griffith-Jones's *Law and the Business of Sport*, Michael Beloff *et al's Sports Law*, Richard Verow *et al's Sport, Business and the Law*, and Adam Lewis and Jonathan Taylor's *Sport: Law and Practice*, the latter two titles both in their second editions, are focused primarily at practitioners. Steve Greenfield and Guy Osborne's edited collection, *Law and Sport in Contemporary Society*, William Stewart's edited collection, *Sport and the Law – The Scots Perspective*, and, more recently, Mark James's *Sports Law* and Jack Anderson's *Modern Sports Law: a Textbook*, are focused primarily on a wider academic examination; and of course the late Edward Grayson's *Sport and the Law* provides his uniquely detailed and dense account of the development of sports law.

Specialisms have also developed: David McArdle's *From Bootman to Bosman: Football, Society and Law*, John O'Leary's edited collection, *Drugs and Doping in Sport: Socio-Legal Perspectives*, and Hazel Hartley's two books, *Exploring Sport and Leisure Disasters: A Socio-legal Perspective* and *Sport, Physical Recreation and the Law* are examples. European sports policy and regulation has been a specific focus, with Richard Parrish's *Sports Law and Policy in the European Union* and the edited collection by Simon Gardiner, Richard Parrish and Robert Siekmann, *EU, Sport, Law and Policy: Regulation, Re-regulation and Representation*. A number of UK-based sports law journals provide updated information and commentary: *World Sports Law Report*, *Sport and the Law Journal*, *Sports Law Administration and Practice* and the *International Sports Law Journal*. This all provides a significant body of literature that has supported the growing maturity of sports law as an academic discipline. It has intellectual rigour and there are intellectually challenging issues with which to engage.

In the preface to the first edition of this book in 1998 it was stated: 'There is clearly a growing interest in the academic study of the legal regulation of sport and now is the time to produce a book that attempts to not only provide an exposition of the growing sports law jurisprudence, but provide a full analysis and critical evaluation of its operation, reflecting the growing maturity of this legal subject.' The publication provided the first rigorous academic analysis of the role that law has in sport in Britain. This fourth edition continues this mission.

The approach has been to develop a text and materials book with extensive extracts from primary and secondary sources. We provide detailed analysis of this material and the major issues in sports law. This analysis will be of value to sports lawyers, sports administrators and students at sub-degree, undergraduate and postgraduate level; and studying sports law or sports studies.

The fourth edition of *Sports Law* updates the issues covered in the third edition. To fully understand the issues and complexities of sports law, it is vital that a thorough theoretical examination informs practice and vice versa. The two approaches are intertwined, but it is vital that a rigorous theoretical underpinning of sports law practice is made explicit. Sport has immense cultural significance. Its future regulation is increasingly subject to external legal norms. If lawyers are to play an increasingly influential role as the custodians of sport, they need to take on this responsibility in an informed and dependable way.

For sport, as for society in general, legal regulation and litigation are a reality of modern life. The law has expertise and values that can contribute to the running and organisation of modern sport. However, there is still debate over the legitimacy and extent to which the law should be involved with sport. What role should the law have in the 'regulatory space' surrounding sport? The recent debate concerning the future development and application of European Union policy concerning sport is an example of where the intervention of the law is contested: should sport have a special exemption or should it be subject to the general regulation of European law?

In the preface to the first edition of this book, it was stated that a major issue was whether this subject of legal inquiry should be labelled 'sports law' or merely 'sport and the law'. This debate may still linger among some individuals, who see the area as merely the application of traditional legal principles to the sports industry. To others it may be seen as essentially an abstract esoteric argument. However, in Britain the speedy emergence of a recognisable and distinct set of principles and doctrine concerning the legal regulation of the sports world that can be designated as a distinct legal area can be discerned. As with other legal disciplines – for example, information technology law and entertainment law – the same argument applies. It was no accident that this book is entitled *Sports Law*. The publication of subsequent texts with similar titles may not only reflect the notion that 'imitation is truly the sincerest form of flattery'. Sports law has now arrived as a legitimate legal subject. As a generic term, more publications will appear in the area of sports law. Law has a crucial role to play in contemporary sport and the growing body of statutory and case law specific to sport is a testimony to this fact. Similar to the growth of a *lex mercatoria* in the Middle Ages, a *lex sportiva* is fast developing.

This book provides an analysis of the legal regulation of sport clearly within the socio-cultural and political context of contemporary sport. The focus is, inevitably, on elite professional sport, although it should not be forgotten that the vast majority of participation in sport is on an amateur and recreational level. Football also tends to dominate the analysis of legal issues. It is, of course, Britain's primary national sport, but every attempt has been made to cover as wide a range of sports as possible.

A primary focus has been to highlight the contingencies as to how certain areas of law are developing in sport. The areas of uncertainty have been highlighted in the hope that this will lead to further research and enquiry in these areas. Sports law is an area where different types of legal research methodology, ranging from traditional library based methods to socio-legal empirical approaches, are possible. The book attempts to explain quite technical and formal bodies of law and also to put the development of sports law into a socio-economic context, in order to help understand the reasons for the increasing role of the law in regulating sport. The term regulation is used throughout the book, typifying the reality that law plays a role alongside other normative rules within a regulatory framework of sport.

This book has been a co-operative effort with a number of contributors. As with the top sports teams, the personnel shift over a period of time: the team for this edition is comprised of myself, John O'Leary, Roger Welch, Simon Boyes and Urvasi Naidoo. We all bring our own particular areas of expertise to this fourth edition. All have been involved in the growth of the academic study of sports law in Britain. A major strength of the book is that it represents the work of a research-active group who have applied their individual interests and areas of expertise to their respective areas of sports law.

Additionally, as the discipline develops, the structure of books such as this should evolve. A major development over the period since the third edition has been the emergence of self-regulatory mechanisms, as exemplified in the growing influence of the Court of Arbitration for

Sport in resolving a range of sports disputes, and additionally the World Anti-Doping Agency. Also, some of the more practice-orientated material from the third edition has been removed – excellent practitioner-based books such as that of Adam Lewis and Jonathan Taylor are admirable in this regard. This fourth edition is divided into three sections, each of which is sub-divided into chapters, which has the aim of providing a coherent and unfolding account of the dominant issues in sports law. Due to the differing nature of the subjects involved, each chapter differs in the amount of case law and statutory law discussed and the use of extracts of primary and secondary sources.

Part 1: The Regulation and Governance of Sport

This section provides a context within which sports law is located. It is vital to have a full understanding of the cultural and historical significance of sport in attempting to understand the contemporary role that law has in regulating sport. Regulation is a key word. As with other 'social fields', how best to regulate is a complex question. This section also provides a number of national, European and international perspectives on the role that the law has in supporting and, in some ways, enforcing effective governance in sport and the resolution of sporting disputes.

Simon Gardiner writes Chapter 1, entitled 'Cultural, Historical and Organisational Perspectives on UK Regulation of Sport'. It provides an introduction to the historical and socio-cultural role that law has had in regulating sport. Some foundational material attempts to explain how sport is defined, particularly necessary in the context of arguments supporting the need for a legal definition of sport. The history of the law's greater involvement in sport regulation is explored.

Simon Gardiner also writes Chapter 2, entitled 'Theoretical Understanding of the Regulation of Sport'. It considers the reasons why law is increasingly used as a primary form of regulating sport. The relationship between law and the other normative rules, primarily the internal rules of the sport itself, are explored. Basic models of regulation are examined. An attempt is made to provide a theoretical framework for understanding the role of law in modern sport, premised largely, but not exclusively, on the reality of the commercialised nature of much of contemporary professional sport. The wider globalisation of sport and the development of an international sports law are also examined.

Simon Boyes writes Chapter 3, entitled 'The Legal Regulation of Sports Governing Bodies'. On a UK national basis, the role that the courts have in reviewing the operation and decisions of sports governing bodies is critically evaluated. Grounds for such examination, such as restraint of trade and natural justice, are considered. In addition, alternative dispute mechanisms in sport are examined, primarily the Court of Arbitration in Sport.

Simon Boyes also writes Chapter 4, entitled 'Sport and the Law of the European Union'. The increasing role that the European Commission has as a form of 'supervised autonomy' in the regulation of sport and the development of a recognisable European Union sports policy are discussed. The impact of the European Union, and specifically the European Court of Justice and the relevant jurisprudence, on sport is also evaluated. The Lisbon Treaty has finally provided the EU with a formal, albeit soft, competence on sport. Article 149 TFEU states that 'the union shall contribute to the promotion of European sporting issues, while taking account of the specific nature of sport, its structures based on voluntary activity and its social and educational function'.

Part 2: Legal Protection of the Commercial Integrity of Sport

Sport at the professional and elite level is clearly big business. The sports industry accounts for over 3 per cent of world trade. The role of the law in sport can be premised on the argument that, as law regulates business, it therefore must regulate sport in a similar way. However, it is clear that sport is not like any other business – it has a number of very specific characteristics.

Simon Gardiner writes Chapter 5, entitled 'Sport and Money: Accountability and Regulation'. The regulation of financial dealings in sport is examined and competing models of sports business are compared. A comparative examination is taken of the ways in which sport can be regulated through competition law provisions. There is a particular focus on the issues surrounding the sale of broadcasting rights and the monopoly position that many sports governing bodies hold. The move to professionalisation in a greater number of sports and in expanding parts of the world is also discussed.

Simon Gardiner also writes Chapter 6, entitled 'Sport, Match Fixing and Corruption', which examines the clash between the values associated with financial probity generally found in business and the idiosyncratic way that financial dealings and transactions have traditionally been carried out in sport. There is a primary focus on match fixing in a number of sports including football, cricket and tennis.

Urvasi Naidoo writes Chapter 7, entitled 'The Exploitation and Protection of Olympic Commercial Rights'. An examination is carried out of the various forms of intellectual property rights, including trade marks, and how these can protect event organisers in the organisation of major sports events such as the Olympics. Additionally, the range of legal measures which can be deployed as part of a brand protection policy are examined, particularly in the context of ambush marketing.

Part 3: Legal Issues in the Sports Workplace

The dynamics of the employment of sports athletes is complex. Not only is their working life usually quite short, but their contractual position is often unclear – are they an employee or an independent contractor? The power relations between sports governing bodies and sports athletes have often led to highly inequitable situations. The impact of *Bosman* on team sports has challenged many of the restraints that have been found within the sporting world. A number of discriminatory practices have also begun to be challenged. In the early 1990s, this was a primary focus of sports law in the UK, particularly in the aftermath of the Hillsborough disaster in 1989. A specific regulatory approach to ensuring safety in sports stadiums has developed, with an emphasis on risk assessment and management. In addition, the law has intervened increasingly in terms of potential liability between participants in sporting activities.

John O'Leary writes Chapter 8, entitled 'The Regulation of Doping in Sport'. The focus is on the major issue of how national and international sports governing bodies should regulate doping in sport. The regulation of drugs in sport is highly contentious, as it is generally in society. An evaluation is made of the impact of the World Anti-Doping Agency and the effectiveness of internal sport anti-doping procedures and the role of the law in re-enforcing and challenging these procedures.

Roger Welch writes Chapter 9, entitled 'Sport and Contracts of Employment'. The role that employment law has in sport and in the formation and termination of sporting employment contracts and the rights that sports athletes enjoy is the focus of this chapter. The contractual terms of sports athletes have in the past reflected the unequal position they have with club owners and sports promoters. This relationship has been subject to increased legal challenge under concepts such as restraint of trade. The 1995 decision of the European Court of Justice in *Bosman* is analysed at length. Participation in sport at elite levels is always precarious in the context of the never-ending spectre of career-breaking or ending injuries. Loss of form is always around the corner too. Disciplinary rules in a number of sports are evaluated and the dynamics of how contracts come to an end is discussed.

Roger Welch also writes Chapter 10, entitled 'Sports Participants and the Law of Discrimination'. The primary issues discussed are discrimination in terms of sex, race and disability. A major social aim of sport during the recent past has been the promotion of equal opportunities for participation in sport: 'sport for all' policies. However, much of the structural discrimination found generally in the workplace is also found in sport and the effectiveness of the legal remedies that exist is analysed. Additionally, sport-specific programmes to counter discrimination are evaluated.

Simon Gardiner writes Chapter 11, entitled 'Safety and Participants in Sport'. The focus is on the relationship between the law and the internal rules within sport regulating physical force and the interaction between sports athletes that is an essential part of much sport. Excessive force can often be characterised as 'sports violence' and has come to be regarded as one of the major problems in contemporary sport. How should criminal law liability be constructed in such circumstances? Additionally, the civil law application to sports injuries and the case law that has developed in this area of liability is evaluated. The distinction between legitimate and illegitimate, legal and illegal play within sport is a vital issue in terms of how liability is determined for participants, coaches and officials. Liability in extreme sports will also be examined, including boxing. Lastly, the crucial issues of providing a safe environment for children participating in sport will be examined.

John O'Leary and Simon Gardiner write Chapter 12, entitled 'Sports Venues and the Law'. The focus is on the legal regulation of sports stadiums and spectating. Sporting events attract large numbers of people and, as with any congregation of people, their regulation and control needs to be carefully managed. One of the major events in recent sporting history in Britain was the Hillsborough tragedy, which led to the Taylor Report. The subsequent regulatory framework for safety is analysed in depth. The role of the civil and criminal law is evaluated in how it directs relationships among sports spectators, participants, the police and sports organisers, particularly in the context of football hooliganism.

Acknowledgements

Grateful acknowledgement is made to all the authors and publishers of copyright material which appears in this book, and in particular for permission to reprint material from the sources indicated.

Acreman, L, 'Tackling ticket touting in sport with criminal legislation' (2009) 7(2) World Sports Law Reports

Bale, J, *Landscapes of Modern Sport* (1994), Leicester: Leicester UP. Printed with permission from the Continuum International Publishing Company. Bale, J © 1994

Barnes, J, *Sports and the Law in Canada* (1996), Toronto: Butterworths. Reproduced with permission of the publisher LexisNexis Canada Inc.

Beloff, M, Kerr, T and Demetriou, M, 'Sports Law' (1999), Oxford: Hart Publishing

Birley, D, *Sport and the Making of Britain* (1993), Manchester: Manchester UP

Bitel, N, 'Ambush marketing' (1997) 5(1) Sport and the Law Journal

Blake, A, *The Body Language: The Meaning of Modern Sport* (1996), London: Lawrence and Wishart

Boyes, S, 'The regulation of sport and the impact of the Human Rights Act 1998' [2000] 6(4) EPL 517

Brackenridge, C, *Spoilsports: Understanding and Preventing Sexual Exploitation in Sport* (2001), London: Routledge

Brearly, M, 'Cricket: Atherton Affair: the dirt that is in all our pockets', *The Observer*, 31 July 1994. Copyright Guardian News & Media Ltd 1994

Brown, WM, 'Paternalism, drugs and the nature of sport' (1994) XI Journal of the Philosophy of Sport

Cagier, A and Gardiner, S, *Professional Sport in the EU: Regulation and Re-regulation* (2000), The Hague: Asser

Cashmore, E, *Making Sense of Sports* (1996), London: Routledge

Chaudhary, V, 'Asians can play football, too' *The Guardian*, 17 August 1994. Copyright Guardian News & Media Ltd 1994

Chaudhary, V, 'This decision will allow a police state to bask in reflected glory', *The Guardian*, 14 July 2001. Copyright Guardian News & Media Ltd 1994

Coakley, J, 'Sport in Society: Issues and Controversies' (1994), St Louis: Moseby

Couchman, N, 'IP rights in website content' (2000) 7 Sports and Character Licensing

De Knop, P, 'Globalization, Americanization and localization in sport' (2000) 2 International Sports Law Journal 20, pp. 20–21. London: Sweet and Maxwell

Deloitte & Touche, *Annual Review of Football Finances*, August 2000

Downes, S and Mackay, D, *Running Scared: How Athletics lost its Innocence* (1996), Edinburgh: Mainstream

Duthie, M and Giles, C, 'Anti-Ticket Touting: The Campaign Continues' (2006) 4 (12) World Sports Report

Fitzsimons, P, *The Rugby War* (1996), Sydney: HarperSports

Foster, K, 'Developments in sporting law', in Allison, L (ed), *The Changing Politics of Sport* (1993), Manchester: Manchester UP

Foster, K, 'How sport can be regulated', in Greenfield, S and Osborn, G (eds), *Law and Sport in Contemporary Society* (2000), London: Frank Cass

Fraser, D, Cricket and the Law: *The Man in White is Always Right* (1993), Sydney: Institute of Criminology

Gardiner, S, 'The law and hate speech: "Ooh aah Cantona" and the demonstration of "the other" ', in Brown, A (ed), *Fanatics! Power, Identity and Fandom in Football* (1998), London: Routledge

Goldman, B and Klatz, R, *Death in the Locker Room 2* (1992), Chicago: Elite Sports Medicine Publications.

Gray, A, 'Swimming and Child Protection: the story so far' (1999) 2 (2) Sports Law Bulletin, London: Sweet and Maxwell

Grayson, E, *Sport and the Law* (1994), 2nd edn, London: Butterworths

Greenfield, S and Osborn, G, 'Regulating sport: finding a role for the law?', Sport in Society 13 (2010), London: Routledge

Haigh, G, *Cricket War: The Inside Story of Packer's World Series Cricket* (1993), Melbourne: Text Publishing Company

Hargreaves, J, *Sport, Power and Culture: A Social and Historical Analysis of Popular Sports in Britain* (1986), Cambridge: Polity

Henderson, P, 'Hosting: City of Vancouver Olympic regulatory framework' (2010) 8 (6) World Sports Law Review

Holt, R, *Sport and the British: A Modern History* (1989), Oxford: Clarendon

Lazic, V, 'Conference on ADR in sports disputes' (2001) 5/6 International Sports Law Journal 35

Leaman, O, 'Cheating and fair play in sport', in Morgan, W (ed), *Sport and the Humanities: A Collection of Original Essays* (1981), Educational Research and Service, University of Tennessee

Long, J, Tongue, N, Spacklen, K and Carrington, B, *What's the Difference? A Study of the Nature and Extent of Racism in Rugby League* (1995), School of Leisure and Sports Studies, Leeds Metropolitan University

Longmore, A, 'Absurd cup rule obscures football's final goal' *The Times*, 1 February 1994. Copyright News International 1994

Mason, T, *Sport in Britain* (1988), London: Faber & Faber

McVicar, J, 'Violence in Britain: the sporting life of crime' *The Guardian*, 19 September 1995. Copyright Guardian News & Media Ltd 1995

Miettinen, S, & Parrish, R 'Nationality Discrimination in Community Law' (2007), 5(2) Entertainment and Sports Law Journal

Monnington, T, 'Politicians and sport: uses and abuses', in Allison, L (ed), *The Changing Politics of Sport* (1992), Manchester: Manchester UP

Morris, P and Little, G, 'Challenging sports bodies' determinations' (1998) 17 Civil Justice Quarterly

Murphy, M, 'Participation Rules: Pistorius Case: Implications of His Successful IAAF Challenge', World Sports Report 6 (2008), London: Cecile Park Publishing

Nelson, G, *Left Foot Forward* (1995), London: Headline

Redhead, S, *Unpopular Culture: The Birth of Law and Popular Culture* (1995), Manchester: Manchester UP

Reid, F, 'Combating traditional and "new age" ambush marketing' (2001) 4 (4) Sports Law Bulletin

Reid, R, 'Report of the FA Premier League Seminar', 8 January 1996, British Association for Sport and Law

Robins, D, 'Sport and Crime Prevention: The Evidence of Research' (1996), Criminal Justice Matters 26, London: Routledge

Ryan, J, *Little Girls in Pretty Boxes* (1995), New York: Warner

'Shamateurism's end: taking the money and running', *The Guardian*, 28 August 1995. Copyright Guardian News & Media Ltd 1994

Sheard, K, 'Aspects of boxing in the Western civilising process' (1997) 32(1) International Review for the Sociology of Sport, Sage 1997

Stephens, K, 'British Horseracing Board (BHB) v. William Hill (WH): The race is never lost, till won' (2005) Institute of Trade Mark Attorneys Review

Summerhayes, J, 'Injury Liability: Off-the-ball player attacks: club liability' (2008), 6 (7) World Sports Law Report

Sutcliffe, P, 'The noble art?', *Total Sport*, February 1996, EMAP

Verow, R, Lawrence, C and McCormick, P, *Sport, Business and the Law* (1999), Bristol: Jordan

Welch, R. 'Player Mobility, The FIFA Transfer Rules & Freedom of Movement' (2006), 83 International Sports Law Review, London: Sweet and Maxwell

Williams, J, 'Support for all?', 121 When Saturday Comes, March 1997. Published with kind permission of WSC Magazine.

Thanks to HarperCollins Australia for permission to reproduce extracts from Brasch, R, How Did Sports Begin? (1986)

The Centre for Crime and Justice Studies, 2 Langley Lane, London SW8 1GB; email: info@ crimeandjustice.org.uk; website: http://www.crimeandjustice.org.uk for permission to reproduce extracts from Robins, D, 'Sport and crime prevention: the evidence of research' (1996) 23 Criminal Justice Matters

Virgin Publishing Ltd for permission for the extract taken from Football Babylon® Russ Williams (1996)

'Anzla News Ltd's Super League Appeal Success', Anzla Newsletter Update, January 1997

We would like to thank the Court of Arbitration for Sport, the Council of Europe, the European Commission, the English Football Association, the International Cricket Council, the International Olympic Committee, the Organisers of 'The Rules of the Game' – Europe's first conference on the Governance of Sport and the UK Sports Dispute Resolution Panel for reproduction of materials.

There are many people to thank who have provided formal and informal comments on ideas and issues that have become part of this book. We are particularly grateful to John Barnes, Michael Beloff QC, Adam Brown, Brian Doyle, Ken Foster, Andy Gibson, James Gray, Hazel Hartley, Barrie Houlihan, Vicki Latta, Dave McArdle, Paul McCutcheon, Steve Morrow, Richard Parrish, Nades Raja, Fraser Reid, Robert Siekmann, Janwillem Soek, Sue Taylor, Michelle Verroken, Emile Vrijman, Stephen Weatherill and John Wolohan for the support they have provided. A number of materials have been included from these writers, especially from contributions to the Sport and the Law Journal and Sports Law Bulletin. We would like to thank colleagues at Routledge for their patience and continued support.

We would also like to thank all the undergraduate and postgraduate students who we have taught over the last few years who have always been prepared to enter a dialogue and have provided many useful insights to the whole range of sports law issues.

We thank those who have allowed the inclusion of their work. Every effort has been made to trace all the copyright holders but if any have been inadvertently overlooked the publishers will be pleased to make the necessary arrangement at the first opportunity.

Table of Cases

A

A v B [2003] QB 195 ... 137

ACF Chemiefarma v Commission (Case 41/69) [1970] ECR 661 ... 178

AEK Athens and Slavia Prague v UEFA (CAS 98/2000) award of 20 August 1999 ... 142, 190

Aberavon & Port Talbot RFC v WRU Ltd [2003] EWCA Civ 584 ... 118

Abercromby v Town Commissioners of Fermoy [1900] 1 IR 302 ... 12

Adams v Cape Industries plc [1990] 2 WLR 657 ... 553

Adidas-Salomon AG v Draper [2006] EWHC 1318 (Ch) ... 117

Agar v Hyde (2000) 173 ALR 665; [2000] CLR 201 ... 510, 512

Alcock v Chief Constable of South Yorkshire [1991] 4 All ER 907; [1991] 1 WLR 814 ... 544, 572, 573

American Cyanamid v Ethicon [1975] AC 396 ... 401

An Agreement between the FA Premier League and BskyB, Re [2000] EMLR 78. ... 197

Arsenal Football Club plc v Matthew Reed (Case C-206/01) [2003] ECWA Civ 696, [2003] 3 All ER 865, CA, Reversing [2002] EWHC 2695 (Ch), Ch D ... 321, 327, 331

Arsenal Football Club plc v Reed (Case C-206/1) [2003] All ER (EC) 1, ECJ; Referred from [2001] RPC 922, Ch D ... 321, 327

Ashworth Hospital Authority v MGN Ltd [2002] 1 WLR 2033 ... 137

Aston Cantlow and Wilmcote with Billesley Parochial Church Council v Wallbank [2003] UKHL 37 ... 103

Attorney General v Corke [1933] Ch 89 ... 555

Attorney General's Reference (No 6 of 1980) [1981] QB 715; 2 All ER 1057 ... 6

Attorney General's Reference (No 3 of 1999), Re British Broadcasting Corpn [2009] UKHL 34 ... 136

B

B v Chief Constable of Avon and Soerset Constabulary [2001] 1 WLR 340 ... 578

BBC v TalkSport (2001) Fleet Street Reports 53 ... 320

BMW Belgium v Commission (Case 32/78) [1979] ECR 2435 ... 178

Badeck v Hessischer Ministerpresident [2000] IRLR 432 ... 473

Bain v Gillespie 357 NW 2d 47 (1984) ... 52

Baker v Jones [1954] 2 All ER 553 ... 105, 118

Beck v Lincoln City FC (IT Case 2600760/98) unreported ... 433

Bennett v Football Association (1978) unreported (CA) ... 473

Bilka-Kaufhaus GmbH v Weber von Hartz [1987] ICR 110 ... 448, 470

Blackpool and Fylde Aero Club v Blackpool Borough Council [1990] 3 All ER 25 ... 110

Bliss v Hall (1838) 4 Bing NC 183 ... 560

Bolam v Friern Hospital Management Committee [1957] 1 WLR 582 ... 512

Bolton v Stone and Others [1951] 1 All ER 1078 ... 556, 558, 560

Bookmakers Afternoon Greyhound Services Ltd v Wilf Gilbert (Staffordshire) Ltd [1994] FSR 723, Ch D ... 551

Bosman v Commission (Case C-117/91) [1991] ECR I-3353 ... 152

Bosman, See Union Royale Belge des Socéitiés de Football ASBLv Jean-Marc Bosman—

Boston Athletic Association v Mark Sullivan (1989) 867 F 2d 22 (1st Cir 1989) ... 322, 332

Boxing Australia v AIBA (CAS 2008/O/1455) award of 16 April 2008 ... 142

Boyo v Lambeth LBC [1995] IRLR 50 ... 425

Bradley v The Jockey Club [2004] EWHC 2164 (QB); [2005] EWCA Civ 1056 ... 104, 112, 113, 117, 119, 120, 287, 288, 369

Brady v Sunderland Football club (1998) unreported ... 500, 513

Brasserie de Haecht v Wilkin and Wilkin [1968] CMLR 26 ... 448

Breach v Epsylon Industries Ltd [1976] IRLR 180 ... 405

British Home Stores v Burchell [1980] ICR 303 ... 437

British Horseracing Board (BHB) and the Jockey Club v William Hill Organisation Ltd [2001] EWHC 517; ECJ (Case C-203/02) [2004] ECR I-10415 ... 325, 326, 329

British Leyland (UK) Ltd v Swift [1981] IRLR 91 (CA) ... 431

Brown v Lewis (1896) 12 TLR 455 ... 545, 552

Bundesgericht (Kevin Miller) (6B 298/2007) (unreported, 24 October 2007) (Switzerland) ... 524

Burton v De Vere Hotels Ltd [1997] ICR 1 ... 481

Butcher v Jessop 1989 SLT 593 ... 517

C

CRE v Dutton [1989] QB 783 ... 466

Caldwell v Maguire and Fitzgerald [2001] All ER (D) 363; [2001] EWCA Civ 1054; [2001] PIQR 45 ... 502, 503, 566

Calvin v Carr and others [1979] 2 All ER 440; [1980] AC 574 ... 131, 133, 380

Cambridge Water v Eastern Counties Leather plc [1994] 1 All ER 53 ... 556

Campbell v MGN Ltd [2004] 2 WLR 1232 ... 137

Canadian Olympic Committee v International Skating Union (ISU) CAS OG 06/006 ... 54

Caparo Industries v Dickman [1990] 1 All ER 568 ... 502, 556

Carlgarth, The [1927] P 93 (CA) ... 554

Carlton Communications plc (2) Granada Media plc v Football League [2002] EWHC 1650 (Comm), LTL 1/8/2002 (unreported elsewhere) ... 238

Carmichael v National Power [1998] ICR 1167 ... 395

Castle v St Augustines Links Ltd and Another (1922) 38 TLR 615 ... 556

Chambers v British Olympic Association [2008] EWHC 2028 (QB) ... 116, 120, 126, 127, 369

Chapman v Lord Ellesmere and Others [1932] 2 KB 431 ... 391

Chessington World of Adventures v Reed [1998] ICR 97 ... 476

Chief Constable of Greater Manchester v Wigan Athletic AFC Ltd [2007] EWHC 3095 (Ch), CA; Reversing (2008) SLJR 3 ... 551

Chief Constable of the Lincolnshire Police v Stubbs and Others [1999] ICR 547 ... 480

Clark v Welch (unreported) ... 504

Club Atlético Peñarol v Carlos Heber Bueno Suarez, Cristian Gabriel Rodriguez Barrotti & Paris Saint-Germain (TAS 2005/A/983 & 984) ... 163

Colgan v Kennel Club (2001) unreported, 26 October, QBD ... 288

Collett v Smith [2008] EWHC 1962 (QB); ISLR. 2008, 4, SLR 125–45 ... 515

Collier v Sunday Referee Publishing Co Ltd [1940] 2 KB 647 ... 405

Collins v Willcock [1984] 1 WLR 1172 ... 501

Comitato Olimpico Nazionale Italiano (CONI) (CAS 2000/C/255) 16 June 2000 ... 142

Commission v France (Case 167/73) [1974] ECR 359 ... 155

Commission v Italy (Case C-283/99) [2001] ECR I-4363 ... 492

Commission v Volkswagen AG (Case C-74/04 P) [2006] ECR I-06585 ... 178

Condon v Basi [1985] 1 WLR 866; [1985] 2 All ER 453 ... 499, 502, 504

Couch v British Board of Boxing Control (Case No 2304231/97) (1997) unreported ... 472

Council of Civil Service Unions v Minister for Civil Service [1985] AC 375 ... 94, 127

Credit Suisse & Asset Management Ltd v Armstrong [1996] IRLR 450 ... 405

Croft v Royal Mail Group Plc [2003] IRLR 592, CA ... 476

Crystal Palace FC Ltd v Bruce (2002) QBD, unreported ... 405

D

DHN Food Distributors Ltd v Tower Hamlets LBC [1976] 1 WLR 852 ... 553

Dallas Cowboys Cheerleaders Inc v Pussycat
    Cinema Ltd [1979] 604 F 2d 200, 204–05
    (2nd Cir 1979) ... 322
Davenport v Farrow [2010] EWHC 550 (QB) ...
    514
Davis v Carew-Pole [1956] 1 WLR 833 ... 106,
    107, 118
Dawkins v Department of the Environment
    [1993] IRLR 284 ... 466
De Francesco v Barnum [1890] 45 Ch 430 ...
    398
De Souza v Automobile Association [1986] IRLR
    103 (CA) ... 479
Dekker v VJV Centrum [1991] IRLR 27 ... 483
Deliège v Liège Ligue Francophone de Judo et
    Disciplines Associées ASBL (Cases C-51/96
    and C-191/97) judgment 11 April 2000;
    [2002] ECR I-2549 ... 44, 168, 169, 172,
    176, 184, 185, 204, 243, 256, 369
Deutscher Handballbund eV v Maros Kolpak
    (Case C-438/00) [2003] ECR I-4135 ... 172,
    173, 184, 491, 492, 496
Dietman v Brent LBC [1987] IRLR 259 ... 424
Dimes v Grand Junction Canal (1852) 3 HLC
    759 ... 132
Dimskal Shipping v ITWF [1992] IRLR 78 ...
    401
Director General of Fair Trading v the
    Proprietary Association of Great Britain and
    the Proprietary Articles Trade Association
    Judgment of 21 Secember 2000 ... 380
Director of Public Prosecution v Stoke on Trent
    Magistrates' Court [2004] 1 Cr App R 4 ...
    584, 585
Distribution of Package Tours during the 1990
    World Cup (Cases IV/33384 and IV/33378)
    OJ L 326, 12.11.92, Decision 92/521/EEC of
    27 October 1992 ... 177
Doherty (T) v Consignia plc: Doherty (M) v
    Consignia plc (2001) Case No 2204805/00,
    (2001) Case No 2205635/00 ... 435
Don Revie Case, See Revie v Football Association—
Donà v Mantero (Case 13/76) [1976] 2 CMLR
    578; [1976] ECR 1333 ... 147, 150, 151,
    153, 155, 184, 486, 488
Donoghue v Stevenson [1932] AC 562 ... 501,
    556
Doyle v White City Stadium Ltd [1935] 1 KB 520
    ... 398

Duffy and Others v Newcastle United Football
    Club (2000) The Times, 7 July; (2000) 3(5)
    Sports Law Bulletin 6 ... 223
Dunk v George Waller & Son [1970] 2 All ER 630
    ... 398

E

EBU/Eurovision System (Case IV/32.150)
    (OJ 1993 L 179) ... 197
Eastham v Newcastle United Football Club
    Ltd [1963] 3 All ER 139; [1964] 1
    Ch 413 ... 115, 121, 122, 410, 411, 441,
    458
Edwards v BAF [1998] 2 CMLR 363; [1997]
    EuLR 721 ... 116
Elliott v Saunders and Liverpool FC (1994)
    unreported ... 500, 501, 504, 521
Enderby Town Football Club v The Football
    Association Ltd [1971] 1 Ch 591 ... 97, 103,
    106, 114, 128, 129, 132, 139
Erven Warnink BV v J Townend & Sons (Hull) Ltd
    [1979] AC 731 ... 320
Essam El-Hadaray v FIFA & Al-Ahly Sporting Club
    CAS 2009/A/1880 ... 453
Eurovision (Case IV/32.150) (OJ 2000
    L 151) ... 197

F

FIA and Formula One (Case COMP/36.638)
    IP/01/1523, 30/10/2001 ... 192
FIFA and UEFA v Commission (Cases T-385/07,
    T-55/08 and T-68/08) Judgments of 17
    February 2011 ... 199, 251
FSS Travel & Leisure Systems v Johnson [1998]
    IRLR 382 ... 405
Falkirk Council v Whyte [1997] IRLR
    560 ... 469
Fallon v Horseracing Regulatory Authority
    [2006] EWHC 2030 (QB) ... 113, 119, 120,
    288
Ferguson v Normand [1995] SCCR 770 ... 517,
    523
Finch v Betabake (Anglia) Ltd [1977] IRLR
    470 ... 398
Finnigan v NZRFU (No 1) [1985] 2 NZLR
    159 ... 111, 114
Fitch v Rawling (1795) 2 H Bl 393 ... 12
Fitzgerald v Hall, Russell & Co Ltd [1970] AC
    984 ... 428

Fixtures Marketing Ltd v Organismos Prognostikon Agonon Podosfairou (Case C-444/02) [2004] ECR I-10549 ... 329

Fixtures Marketing Ltd v Oy Veikkaus AB (Case C-46/02) [2004] ECR I-10365 ... 329

Fixtures Marketing Ltd v Svenska Spel AB (Case C-338/02) [2004] ECR I-10497 ... 329

Flaherty v National Greyhound Racing Club [2005] EWCA Civ 1117 ... 113, 133, 364

Flood v Kuhn 407 US 258 (1972) ... 221

Football Association Premier League Ltd and Others v QC Leisure & Others: Karen Murphy v Media Protection Services Ltd (Cases C-403/08, C-429/08) Judgment of the Court, 4 October 2011 ... 198

Football Association Rule K Arbitration, Re; Leeds United 2007 Ltd v The Football League Ltd (Arbitration Tribunal 1 May 2008) [2008] BCC 701 ... 240

Football Dataco Limited v Brittens Pools and Yahoo! [2010] EWHC 841 (Ch); [2010] WLR (D) 104. ... 329

Football Dataco v Stan James' (2010) 18 (6) WSLR ... 329

Ford v AUEW [1969] 2 QB 303 ... 399

Ford v Warwickshire CC [1983] ICR 273 (HL) ... 428

Fowles v Bedfordshire County Council [1995] ELR 51 ... 514

Francis v Cockerell (1870) LR 5 QB 501 ... 545, 552

G

G v International Equestrian Federation (FEI) (CAS 92/63) (10 September 1992) ... 141

Gannon v Rotherham MBC (1991) unreported ... 514

Gardner v National Netball League [2001] FMCA 50 ... 484

Gasser v Stinson and Another (1988) unreported, 15 June QBD ... 116, 124, 143, 374

Gaynor v Blackpool FC [2002] CLY 3280 ... 505

German Ceramic Tiles Discount Agreement, Re [1971] CMLR D6 ... 448

Gilham Case ... 433

Gilsenan v Gunning (1982) 137 DLR (9sd) 252 ... 505

Goldman v Hargrave [1967] AC 645 ... 559

Goodwin v UK [2002] IRLR 664 ... 476

Goold Ltd v McConnell [1995] IRLR 516 ... 429

Gottrup Klim v DLG (Case C-250/92) [1994] ECR I-5461 ... 181

Gough v Chief Constable of Derbyshire [2002] 2 All ER 985 ... 578, 579

Grant v South-West Trains Ltd [1998] ICR 449 ... 474

Gravil v Carroll and Redruth Rugby Football Club [2008] EWCA Civ 689 ... 505

Greig v Insole; World Series Cricket Pty Ltd v Insole [1978] 3 All ER 449; [1978] 1 WLR 302 ... 115, 123, 216–18

Grinstead v Lywood [2002] EWHC 1743 (QB) ... 514

Grobbelaar (Bruce) v News Group Newspapers Ltd and Another [2001] 2 All ER 437 ... 272

Gundel v FEI (1993) Swiss Federal Tribunal, 15 March ... 141

H

Haddon v Van Den Burgh Foods [1999] ICR 1150 (EAT) ... 432

Hall v Brooklands Auto Racing Club [1993] 1 KB 205 ... 564, 565

Hall v Holker Estate Company Ltd [2008] EWCA Civ 1422 ... 554

Hall v New South Wales Trotting Club (1977) 1 NSWLR 378 ... 133

Hambrook v Stokes Bros [1925] 1 KB 141 ... 572

Hannan v Bradford Corporation [1970] 1 WLR 937 ... 133

Harris v Sheffield United Football Club [1988] QB 77; [1987] 2 All ER 838 ... 550, 551, 567

Hearn v Rugby Football Union (2003) The Times, 15 September ... 126

Hendry v World Professional Billiards and Snooker Association [2002] ECC 8 ... 117, 126, 180, 181, 194

Hertz v Aldi Marked [1991] IRLR 31 ... 483

Hilder v Associated Portland Cement Manufacturers Ltd [1961] 1 WLR 1434 ... 557, 558

Hilti v Commission (Case C-53/92 P) [1991] ECR I-667. ... 180

Höffner and Elser (Case C-41/90) [1993] I ECR 1979 ... 177

Holmes v Home Office Case ... 469

Home Box Office Inc v Showtime the Movie Channel 56 USLW 2336 4 USPQ 2D Nov 3 (1987) ... 331

Horkulak v Cantor Fitzgerald International [2003] EWHC 1918 (QB) ... 407

Hotson v East Berkshire AHA [1987] 3 WLR 232 ... 571

Hughes v Western Australian Cricket Association [1986] 69 ALR 660 ... 124

Hunter and Others v Canary Wharf Ltd; Hunter and Others v London Docklands Development Corporation [1997] NLJ 634 ... 556

Hussaney v Chester City FC and Kevin Ratcliffe (IT Case 2102426/97) unreported ... 478, 480

I

Iceland Frozen Foods Ltd v Jones [1982] IRLR 439 ... 431, 432

Igbo v Johnson Matthey [1986] IRLR 215 (CA) ... 419

Initial Services Ltd v Putterill [1968] 1 QB 396 (CA) ... 408

International News Service v Associated Press 248 US215, 63 L Ed 211, 39, SCt 68 (1918) ... 303

International Olympic Committee et al v San Francisco Arts and Athletics et al (1982) 219 USPQ (BNA) 982 (1982) ... 358

Irvine v TalkSport Limited [2002] 1 WLR 2355 ... 321

J

JJB Sportsplc v OFT [2004] CAT 17 ... 255

James v Eastleigh BC [1990] ICR 554 ... 467

Jockey Club v Buffham and BBC [2003] QB 462; [2002] EWHC 1866 (QB) ... 137, 287

Johnson v IAAF (1997) unreported 25 July, Ontario Court (General Division) ... 124

Jones v Tower Boot Co [1997] IRLR 168; [1995] IRLR 529, EAT ... 480

Jones v University of Manchester [1993] IRLR 218 ... 469, 471

Jones v Welsh Rugby Football Union (1997) The Times, 6 March; (1998) The Times, 6 January ... 131, 132, 134

Jones v Wright [1991] 1 All ER 353 ... 572

K

Keck and Mithouard (Cases C-267, 268/91) [1993] ECR I-6097, [1995] 1 CMLR 101 ... 158

Kennaway v Thompson [1981] QB 88 (CA) ... 562, 563

Korda v ITF [1999] All ER (D) 84; [1999] All ER (D) 337, CA ... 140, 141

Korean Olympic Committee (KOC) v International Skating Union (ISU) OWG 02/007 ... 53–5

L

Lacey v Parker and Bingle (1994) 2(3) Sport and the Law Journal 9 ... 561

Lance Armstrong v Times Newspapers Ltd, David Walsh, Alan English [2005] EWCA Civ 1007 ... 391

Langston v AUEW [1974] ICR 180 ... 405

Lausutina v IOC and FIS (2003) Swiss Federal Tribunal, 27 May ... 141

Law v National Greyhound Racing Club Ltd [1983] 3 All ER 300; [1983] 1 WLR 1302 (CA (Civ Div)) ... 94, 95, 97, 99, 369

Laws v London Chronicle Ltd [1959] 2 All ER 285 (CA) ... 419

Leatherland v Edwards (1999) unreported (HC) ... 505

Lee v Showman's Guild of Great Britain [1952] 2 QB 329 ... 365

Lehtonen (Jyri) & Castors Canada Dry Namur-Braine v Fédération Royale Belge des Sociétés de Basketball ASBL (Belgiam Basketball Federation) (Case C-176/96) 96, [2000] ECR I-2681 ... 44, 170–2, 176, 184, 204, 243, 415

Lestina v West Bend Mutual Insurance Co 176 Wis 2d 901, 501 NW 2d 28 (1993) ... 502

Letang v Cooper [1965] 1 QB 232; [1964] 2 All ER 929 ... 501

Lewis v Blackpool Golf Club 1993 SLT (Sh Ct) 43 ... 505

Lewis v Motorworld Garages Ltd [1986] 1CR 157, CA ... 422

Lister v Hesley Hall Ltd [2002] 1 AC 215; [2001] UKHL 22; [2001] 2 WLR 1311 ... 505

Lister v Romford Ice and Cold Storage Co Ltd [1957] All ER 125 ... 407

London Underground Ltd v Edwards (No 2) [1998] IRLR 364 ... 470

Luke Michael v Australian Canoeing (CAS 2008/A/1549) award of 4 June 2008 ... 142

Lumley v Gye (1853) 2 E & B 216 ... 401, 424

Lustig-Prean and Beckett v United Kingdom [1999] IRLR 734 (European Court of Human Rights) ... 474

M

McCord v Swansea City AFC Ltd (1997) The Times, 11 February ... 504, 505

McDermid v Nash Dredging Ltd [1987] AC 906 ... 570

Macdonald v Attorney-General for Scotland; Pearce v Governing Body of Mayfield School [2004] 1 All ER 339; [2003] ICR 937 ... 474, 480, 481

McDyer v The Celtic Football and Athletic Co Ltd [2000] SC 379 ... 544

McHale v Watson (1996) 115 CLR 199 ... 557

McInnes v Onslow-Fane [1978] 3 All ER 211; [1978] 1 WLR 1520 ... 129, 130, 369

McKeown v British Horseracing Authority [2010] EWHC 508 (Admin). ... 113

McLoughlin v O'Brian [1983] AC 410 ... 572

Macari v Celtic Football and Athletic Association (Case 0/309/98) (Court of Session) ... 419–21, 433

Machin v Football Association (1973) The Times, July 20 ... 52

Majrowski v Guy's and St Thomas' NHS Trust [2006] UKHL 34, [2007] 1 AC 224, [2006] 4 All ER 395 ... 481

Malaja v French Basketball Federation (2000), Court Administrative d'Appel de Nancy, 3 February (See The Observer, 6 February 2000) ... 173

Malik v BCCI [1997] IRLR 462 ... 407

Mandla v Dowell Lee [1983] ICR 385, HL ... 465

Massey v Crown Life Insurance Co [1978] ICR 509 (CA) ... 395

Matheson v Northcote College Board of Governors [1957] 2 NZLR 106 ... 556

Matuzalem/Shaktar Donetsk/Real Zaragoza/FIFA CAS 2008/A/1519-1520 ... 453, 454

Meca-Medina and Majcen v Commission (Case T-313/02) [2004] ECR II-3291. ... 44, 182, 183, 205

Meca-Medina and Majcen v Commission (Case C-519/04 P) [2006] ECR I-6991; [2006] 5 CMLR 18 ... 185, 188, 205, 243, 365, 368, 369, 390, 454, 457, 495

Meggeson v Burns [1972] 1 Lloyd's Rep 223 ... 118

Mendy v Association Internationale de Boxing Amateur (AIBA), CAS ad hoc Division, Atlanta, OG 96/006 ... 53, 55

Mercer v Denne [1904] 2 Ch 553 ... 12

Métropole Télévision SA (M6), Antena 3 de Televisión, SA, Gestevisión Telecinco, SA and SIC – Sociedade Independente de Comunicação, SA v Commission of the European Communities (Joined Cases T-185/00, T-216/00, T-299/00 and T-300/00) [2002] ECR II-3805 ... 197

Metropole Télévision SA and Reti Televisive Italiane SpA and Gestevisión Telecinco SA and Antena 3 de Televisión v Commission (Case T-528/93) [1996] ECR II-649 ... 197

Middlesborough Football & Athletic Co v Liverpool Football & Athletic Grounds plc [2002] EWCA Civ 1929 ... 425

Midtjylland v FIFA (CAS 2008/A/1485 FC) ... 541

Miller v Jackson [1977] 3 All ER 338 (CA) ... 559, 562, 563

Modahl v British Athletic Federation Ltd 2001 WL 1135166 ... 364, 365, 379

Modahl v British Athletic Federation Ltd (No 2) [2002] 1 WLR 1192 ... 106, 107, 113, 118, 131, 133, 241

Morris Communications Corporation v PGA Tour Inc [2002] 235 F Supp 2d 1269 (MD Fla 2002); 364 F 3d 1288 Eleventh Circuit Court of Appeals 2004 ... 329

Morris v Ford Motor Co [1973] QB 792 ... 407

Mosely v News Group Newspapers Ltd [2008] EWHC 1777 (QB) ... 137

Motosykleistiki Omospondia Ellados Npid v Elliniko Dimosio (MOTOE) (Case C-49/07) [2008] ECR I-4863 ... 191–3

Mountford v Newlands School and Another [2007] EWCA Civ 21 ... 507

Mullins v McFarlane [2006] EWHC 986 (QB) ... 113

Murphy v Southend United Football Club (1999) unreported ... 426

Murray and Another v Harringay Arena Ltd [1951] 2 KB 529 ... 565, 567

Mutu (Adrian) v Chelsea Football Club Ltd (unreported) 31 July 2009 (CAS) ... 391, 404

N

NWL Ltd v Woods [1979] ICR 867 ... 401

Nabozny v Barnhill, 334 NE 2d 258 (Ill App Ct 1975) ... 502

Nagle v Feilden [1966] 1 All ER 689; [1966] 2 QB 633 ... 93, 109–12, 114, 365, 369

National Basketball Association and NBAProperties Inc v Motorola Inc and Stats Inc [1997] 105 F 3d 841, 2nd Cir 1997 ... 329

National Football League v Governor of Delaware et al 195 USPQ Aug 11 (1977) ... 332

National Football League Properties Inc v New Jersey Giants Inc [1986] 637 F Supp 507 (DNJ 1986) ... 322

National Football League Properties Inc v Wichita Falls Sportswear Inc [1982] 532 F Supp 651 (WD Wash 1982) ... 322

National Hockey League v Pepsi Cola Canada Ltd 2 BCLR 3rd 3 1995 Feb 17 (1995). ... 332

Nettleship v Weston [1976] 2 QB 691; [1971] 3 All ER 581 ... 557

Newport Association Football Club v Football Association of Wales [1995] 2 All ER 87 ... 124, 127

Neykova v International Rowing Federation (FISA) & International Olympic Committee Arbitration CAS OG Sydney 2000/12 Digest Vol 2, p 674 ... 53, 54

Nordenfelt v Maxim Nordenfelt Guns and Ammunition Co [1894] AC 535 ... 114

North East Coast Shiprepairers v Secretary of State for Employment [1978] IRLR 149 ... 398

Nowatske v Osterloh (1996) 534 NW 2d 256 ... 512

O

O'Reilly v Mackman [1983] 2 AC 237 ... 94, 95, 113

Olinger v United States Golf Association, 55 F Supp 2d 926 ... 69

Olympique Lyonnais SASP v Olivier Bernard and Newcastle United (Case C-325/08) [2010] ECR I-2177 ... 174, 175, 204, 205, 494

Omilaju v Waltham forest LBC [2005] ICR 481, CA. ... 422

Oulmers Case, See SA Sporting Pays du Charleroi and G-14 Groupement des Clubs de Football Européens v FIFA (Case C-243/06)—

Overseas Tankship (UK) Ltd v Miller SS Co Pty (The Wagon Mound (No 2)) [1967] 1 AC 617; [1966] 2 All ER 709 (PC) ... 558, 572

Overseas Tankship (UK) Ltd v Morts Dock and Engineering Co Ltd (The Wagon Mound (No 1)) [1961] UKPC 1 ... 515

P

P v S and Cornwall CC [1996] ICR 795 ... 475

PGA Tour, Inc v Martin (00-24) 532 US 661 (2001) 204 F 3d 994, ... 68, 69, 477

Page One Records Ltd v Britton [1968] 1 WLR 157 ... 423

Page v Smith [1995] 1 WLR 644 ... 572

Panesar v Nestlé [1980] ICR 144 ... 466

Peabody Donation Fund v Parkinson [1985] AC 210 ... 556

Pearson v Lightning [1998] 95 (20) LSG ... 504

Pepper v Webb [1969] 2 All ER 216 ... 419

Perera v Civil Service Commission [1983] ICR 428 ... 469

Petty v British Judo Association [1981] ICR 660 ... 472

Pharmaceutical Society of Great Britain v Dickson [1970] AC 403 (HL) ... 115

Phillips v Whiteley Ltd [1938] 1 All ER 566 ... 557

Piau v Commission (Case T-193/02) [2005] ECR II-209 ... 177, 188, 189

Piau v Commission (Case C-171/05) [2006] ECR I-37 ... 189

Pistorius v IAAF (Arbitration CAS 2008/A/1480) award of 16 May 2008 ... 67, 68, 142

Pitcher v Huddersfield Town FC [2001] All ER (D) 223 (Jul) ... 505

Pittsburgh Athletic Co et al v KVQ Broadcasting Company (1937) 24 F Supp 490 (WD Pa 1938). ... 246, 303

Polkey v AE Dayton Services Ltd [1988] ICR 142 (HL) ... 438, 441

Poppleton v Trustees of the Portsmouth Youth Activities Centre [2008] EWCA Civ 646 ... 554

Porter v Magill [2002] 2 AC 494 ... 132

Post Office v Foley; HSBC Bank plc v Madden [2000] IRLR 827 ... 432, 437

Post Office v Liddiard, 7 June 2001 (CA) ... 435

Proactive Sports Management Limited v (1) Wayne Rooney (2) Coleen Rooney (formerly McLoughlin) (3) Stoneygate 48 Limited (4) Speed 9849 Limited [2010] EWHC 1807 (QB) ... 410

Provident Financial Group plc v Hayward [1989] ICR 160 (CA) ... 405

Q

Quigley v UIT CAS 94/129 ... 374

R

R v Barnes [2004] EWCA Crim 3246 ... 90, 518, 520–3

R v Billinghurst [1978] Crim LR 553 ... 517

R v Birkin [1988] Crim LR 854 ... 517

R v Bishop (1986) Unreported ... 517

R v Blissett (1992) The Independent, 4 December ... 517, 518

R v Bradshaw (1878) 14 Cox CC 83 ... 499, 516

R v Brown [1993] 2 All ER 75; [1993] 2 WLR 556; [1994] 1 AC 212 ... 6, 519, 525, 526

R v Calton [1999] 2 Cr App R(S) 64; (1998) Yorkshire Post, 29 September ... 517

R v Cantona (1995) The Times, 25 March. ... 516

R v Cey (1989) 48 CCC (3d) 480 ... 520

R v Chapman (1989) 11 Cr App R(S) 93 ... 517

R v Ciccarelli (1989) 54 CCC (3d) 121 ... 520

R v City Panel on Takeovers and Mergers, ex p Datafin plc [1987] 1 All ER 564; [1987] QB 815 ... 95–102, 104

R v Civil Service Appeal Board, ex p Cunningham [1991] 4 All ER 310 ... 130

R v Davis [1991] Crim LR 70 ... 517

R v Derbyshire County Council, ex p Noble [1990] ICR 808 ... 97

R v Diouf (2005) unreported ... 517

R v Disciplinary Committee of the Jockey Club, ex p Aga Khan [1993] 1 WLR 909 (CA (Civ Div)) ... 369

R v Disciplinary Committee of the Jockey Club, ex p Massingberd-Mundy [1993] 2 All ER 207 ... 98–100

R v Football Association, ex p Football League Ltd [1993] 2 All ER 833 ... 100, 101, 104

R v Football Association of Wales, ex p Flint Town United Football Club [1991] COD 44 ... 97, 98

R v Gingell (1980) 2 Cr App R (S) 198; [1980] Crim LR 661 ... 517

R v Gough [1993] AC 646 ... 379, 380

R v Hardy (1994) The Guardian, 27 July; (1994) The Daily Telegraph, 19 September ... 500

R v Higher Education Funding Council, ex p Institute of Dental Surgery [1994] 1 WLR 242 ... 130

R v Home Secretary, ex p Doody [1993] 1 WLR 154 ... 130

R v Independent Television Commission, ex p TVDanmark 1 Ltd [2000] 1 WLR 1604 ... 251, 253

R v Inner West London Coroner, ex p Dallaglio [1994] 4 All ER 139 ... 380

R v Jobidon (1991) 2 SCR 714 ... 520

R v Jockey Club, ex p Aga Khan [1993] 1 WLR 909 ... 102–5, 136

R v Jockey Club, ex p RAM Racecourses [1993] 2 All ER 225 ... 99, 101

R v Johnson (1986) 8 Cr App R(S) 343 ... 517

R v Kamara (1988) The Times, 15 April ... 516

R v Kite, R v Stoddart, R v OLL Ltd (1994) Unreported, 9 December, Winchester Crown Court. ... 533

R v Leclerc (1991) 67 CCC (3d) ... 520

R v Lincoln (1990) 12 Cr App R 250 ... 517

R v Lloyd [1989] Crim LR 513; (1989) 11 Cr App R(S) 36 ... 517

R v Manchester Crown Court, ex p McCann [2001] 1 WLR 1084 ... 578

R v McHugh (1998) unreported (See 2(4) SLB 2) ... 517

R v Mills (2005) unreported ... 517

R v Moore (1898) 15 TLR 229 ... 499, 516

R v Moss [2000] 1 Cr App R(S) 64 ... 517

R v Oxfordshire County Council and Others, ex p Sunningwell Parish Council [1999] 3 WLR 160 ... 11, 12

R v Secretary of State for Education and Employment, ex p Portsmouth FC [1988] COD 142 ... 489

R v Shervill (1989) 11 Cr App R(S) 284 ... 517

R v Stein (1983) unreported ... 517

R v Suffolk County Council, ex p Steed (1995) 70 P& CR 487 ... 12

R v Sussex Justices, *ex p* McCarthy [1924] 1 KB 256 ... 133, 380

R v Winkler [2004] EWCA Crim 1590; (2004) 168 JPN 720, CA (Crim Div) ... 578

R (on the application of Brown) v Inner London Crown Court (2003) LTL 15/12/2003 (unreported elsewhere) ... 576

R (on the application of Catt) v Brighton and Hove CC [2006] EWHC 1337 (Admin) ... 544

R (on the application of Hasan) v Secretary of State for Trade and Industry [2008] EWCA Civ 1312 ... 130

R (on the application of Mullins) v The Jockey Club Appeal Board (No 1) [2005] EWHC 2197 (Admin); (2005) *The Times*, 24 October (QBD (Admin)) ... 103, 104, 113, 136, 369

R (on the application of Pamela Beresford) v Sunderland City Council [2004] 1 All ER 160 ... 12

RFU and Nike v Cotton Traders Ltd [2002] EWHC 467 (Ch) ... 320

Raguz v Sullivan (2000) 50 NSWLR 236 ... 141

Ratcliffe v McConnell [1999] 1 WLR 670 ... 554

Read v J Lyons [1947] AC 156 ... 556

Reading Festival Ltd v West Yorkshire Police Authority [2006] EWCA Civ 524; [2006] 1 WLR 2005 ... 551

Ready Mixed Concrete (South East) Ltd v Minister of Pensions and National Insurance [1968] 2 QB 497; [1968] 1 All ER 433 ... 395

Reckitt & Coleman Products Ltd v Borden Inc [1990] RPC 341 ... 320

Revie v Football Association (1979) *The Times*, 14 December ... 133

Reynolds v Times Newspapers Ltd [2001] 2 AC 127 ... 391

Roberts v Grey [1913] 1 KB 520 ... 398

Roe v Minister of Health [1954] 2 QB 661 ... 557

Rogers v Bugden and Canterbury-Bankstown (1993) ATR 81–246 ... 501

Rootes v Shelton [1968] ALR 33 ... 502

Rubython v Federation Internationale De L'Automobile (2003) (unreported) 6 March, QBD ... 136

Ruddiman v Smith (1889) 60 LT 708 ... 505

Russell v Duke of Norfolk [1949] 1 All ER 109, CA; *affirming* [1948] 1 All ER 488 ... 127, 128

Rylands v Fletcher (1868) LR 3 HL 330; [1861–73] All ER Rep 1 ... 555

S

S, A Barrister, Re [1981] QB 670 ... 133

S (A Child) (Identification: Restrictions on Publication), Re [2004] UKHL 47 ... 136

S v FINA (CAS 2005/A/830) award of 15 July 2005 ... 142

SA Sporting Pays du Charleroi and G-14 Groupement des Clubs de Football Européens v FIFA (Case C-243/06) (OJ C 212, 2 September 2006) (Oulmers Case) ... 190, 454, 457, 496, 511

Sagen v Vancouver Organizing Committee for the 2010 Olympic and Paralympic Winter Games [2009] BCSC 942 (Sup Ct (BC)) ... 464

Salomon v Salomon & Co Ltd [1897] AC 22 (HL) ... 552

San Francisco Arts and Athletics Inc (SFAA) v USOC 483 US 522 107 S Ct, 2971, 97 L Ed 2d 427 (US 1987) ... 323, 359

Sankofa & Charlton Athletic v Football Association [2007] EWHC 78 (Comm) ... 140

Saunders v Richmond BC [1977] IRLR 362 ... 467, 474

Segura v International Amateur Athletic Federation (IAAF) CAS OG Sydney 2000/13 Digest Vol 2:680:17 ... 53

Seide v Gillette Industries [1980] IRLR 427 ... 466

Sheffield United FC Ltd v West Ham United Football Club plc [2008] EWHC 2855 (Comm), [2009] 1 Lloyd's Rep 167, [2008] All ER (D) 293 (Nov) ... 140

Shelfer v City of London Electric Lighting Co [1895] 1 Ch 287 ... 562

Sims v Leigh Rugby Club [1969] 2 All ER 923 ... 568, 570

Simutenkov (Igor) v Ministerio de Educación y Cultura (Case C-265/03) [2005] ECR I-2579 ... 172, 491

Sinclair v Cleary (1946) St R Qld 74 ... 52

Singh v The Football Association Ltd, The Football League Ltd & Others (2001) ET Case Number 5203593/99 ... 395, 397, 428, 467

Smith v Gardner Merchant Ltd [1996] IRLR 342; [1998] IRLR 510 ... 474

Smith v Littlewoods Organisation [1987] AC 241 ... 507, 556

Smith v Scott [1973] Ch 314 ... 556

Smoldon v Nolan and Whitworth [1997] ELR 249; (1997) The Times, 18 December ... 52, 500, 506–508, 514

Société Technique Miniere v Maschinbau Ulm (Case 56/65) [1966] ECR 235. ... 178

Sport Lisboa e Benfica Futebol SAD v UEFA & FC Porto Futebol SAD (CAS 2008/A/1583) ... 142

Sterling v Leeds Rugby League Club and Others (2000) (Case 1802453/00) (ET), See (2000) Sports Law Bulletin 3 ... 468

Stevenage Borough Football Club v Football League Ltd (1996) The Times, 1 August ... 125, 127

Stoker v Lancashire CC [1992] IRLR 75 (CA) ... 438

Stransky v Bristol Rugby Ltd (2002) unreported 11 December ... 397, 426

Stretch v Romford FC (1971) 115 Sol Jo 7461 ... 555, 563

Stretford v Football Association Ltd [2007] EWCA Civ 238, [2006] EWHC 479 (Ch) ... 141, 269

Sturges v Bridgman (1879) 11 Ch D 892 ... 560

Subaru Tecnica International Inc v Burns & Others (2001) unreported, Ch D ... 423

T

TTF Liebherr Ochsenhausen v ETTU (CAS 2007/A/1363) ... 142

Tele Danmark (Brandt-Nielson) Case [2001] IRLR 853 ... 483

Terry v Persons Unknown [2010] EWHC 119 (QB) ... 137

Tetley v Chitty [1986] 1 All ER 663 ... 563

Theakston v MGN Ltd [2002] EMLR 22 ... 137

Tibor Balog v ASBL Royal Charleroi Sporting Club (Case C-264/98) ... 162, 173, 190, 454

Timeplan Education Group Ltd v NUT [1997] IRLR 457 ... 424

Tolley v Fry [1931] All ER 131; [1931] AC 333 (HL) ... 64, 321

Tomlinson v Congleton Borough Council [2003] UKHL 47 ... 554

Torpedoes Sportswear Pty Ltd v Thorpedo Enterprises Pty Ltd [2003] FCA 901 (Australia) (27 August 2003) ... 321

Towcester Racecourse Ltd v Racecourse Association [2002] EWHC 2141 ... 118

Tracey v Zest Equipment Co [1982] IRLR 268 ... 419

Trebor Bassett Ltd v The Football Association (FA) Ltd [1997] FSR 211 Ch D ... 320, 331

U

Union Royale Belge des Socéitiés de Football ASBLv Jean-Marc Bosman (Cases C-415/93, C-340/90, C-269/92) [1995] ECR I-4192; [1996] 1 CMLR 645; 15 December 1995 ... 78, 80, 115, 146, 150–2, 156, 157, 159–61, 163, 165, 168, 169, 171–3, 176–9, 182, 184, 191, 196, 197, 205, 206, 222, 224, 228, 229, 368, 411, 441–51, 458, 485, 488–96, 580

United Brands v Commission (Case 27/76) [1978] ECR 207 ... 179

Universe Tankship Inc of Monrovia ITWF [1982] ICR 262 ... 401

US Dist and San Francisco Arts and Athletics Inc et al v USOC et al 483 US 522 (1987) ... 358

V

Van Den Bergh Foods v Haddon, See Haddon v Van Den Bergh Foods—

Van Open v Clerk to the Trustees of the Bedford Charity (Harpur Trust) (1988) The Times, 9 August ... 514

Venables v News Group Newspapers Ltd [2001] 2 WLR 1038 ... 137

Victoria Park Racing and Recreation Grounds Co Ltd v Taylor and Others (1937) 58 CLR 479 ... 246, 303

Vitória Sport Clube de Guimarães v UEFA & FC Porto Futebol SAD (CAS 2008/A/1584) award of 15 July 2008 ... 142

Vowles v Evans and the Welsh Rugby Union Ltd [2003] EWCA Civ 318 ... 52, 507, 508

W

Wagon Mound, The (No 1), See Overseas Tankship (UK) Ltd v Morts Dock and Engineering Co Ltd—

Wagon Mound, The (No 2), See Overseas Tankship (UK) Ltd v Miller SS Co Pty—

Walker v Crystal Palace Football Club [1910] 1 KB 87 (CA) ... 394, 395

Wallace v CA Roofing Services Ltd [1996] IRLR 435 ... 398

Walrave and Koch v Association Union Cycliste Internationale (Case 36/74) [1974] ECR 1405; [1975] 1 CMLR 320 ... 147, 148, 150, 151, 155, 172, 184, 187, 488

Warner Brothers Pictures Inc v Nelson [1937] KB 209 ... 423

Warren v Mendy [1989] 1 WLR 853; [1989] ICR 525 ... 423, 424

Watson and Bradford City FC v Gray and Huddersfield Town FC (1998) unreported ... 500, 505

Watson v British Boxing Board of Control [2001] QB 1134; [2001] 1 WLR 1256, CA; *Affirming* (1999) The Law Times, 24 September; [2001] ISLR 170 ... 500, 508–11, 571

Wattleworth v Goodwood Road Racing Company Ltd, Royal Automobile Club Motor Sports Association Ltd and Federation Internationale De L'Automobile [2004] EWHC 140 (QB) ... 509, 571

Wayde v New South Wales Rugby League Ltd [1985] 59 ALJR 798 ... 91

West Bromwich Albion Football Club Ltd v El-Safty, Court of Appeal (Civil Division) [2007] PIQR 7 ... 513

Western Excavating Ltd v Sharp [1978] ICR 221 (CA) ... 421

Wheat v Lacon [1966] 1 All ER 582 ... 553

White and Other v Chief Constable of South Yorkshire Police and Others [1999] 1 All ER 1 ... 574

White v Blackmore [1972] 2 QB 651 ... 554

White v Bristol Rugby Club [2002] IRLR 204 ... 398

White v Jameson (1874) LR 18 Eq 303 ... 563

Whitehouse v Jordan [1981] 1 All ER 267, HL ... 557

Wigan Athletic FC/Heart of Midlothian/Webster CAS 2007/A/1298/1299/1300 ... 452–4, 457

Wilander v Tobin [1997] 2 Lloyd's Rep 293; (1996) The Times, 8 April ... 124

Wilander v Tobin (No 2) [1997] 2 CMLR 346 ... 117, 369

Williams v Reason [1988] 1 All ER 262; [1988] 1 WLR 96 (CA) ... 64

Wilson v Racher [1974] IRLR 114 (CA) ... 419

Wise v Filbert Realisations Respondent (Formerly Leicester City Football Club) (In Administration) (2004) EAT/0660/03, 9 February ... 438

Withers v Flackwell Heath Football Supporters Club [1981] IRLR 307 ... 396

Woods v W/M Car Services [1981] ICR 666 ... 406

Wooldridge v Sumner [1963] 2 QB 43 ... 502, 503, 514, 565–7, 569

Woolfson v Strathclyde Regional Council 1978 SLT 159 ... 553

WWf – World Wide Fund for Nature (Formerly World Wildlife Fund) (1); (2) World Wildlife Fund Inc v World Wrestling Federation Entertainment Inc (2002) IPD 25023 ... 8

X

X v Y [2004] EWCA Civ 662, CA ... 475

Y

Yang v Hamm CAS 2004/A/704 ... 53

Young and Woods Ltd v West [1980] IRLR 201 (CA) ... 395

Table of Statutes

Note: Jurisdiction is given in brackets after the
name of the Act

A

Activity Centres (Young Persons' Safety) Act 1995
(UK) ... 533, 552
Amateur Sports Act (US) ... 359
Americans with Disabilities Act 1990 (US)—
Title II ... 68
Arbitration Act 1996 (UK) ... 139
ss 67–69 ... 139

B

Betting Act 1853 (UK) ... 292
Betting, Gaming and Lotteries Act 1963 (UK) ...
295
s 24 ... 98
Broadcasting Act 1996 (UK) ... 198, 251
s 97 ... 199

C

Charter of Rights and Freedoms (Canada)—
s 15(1) ... 464
Children Act 1989 (UK) ... 499, 533
Civil Liability Act 2003 (Qld) ... 512
s 22 ... 512
Commons Registration Act 1965 (UK) ... 11, 12
s 13(b) ... 11
s 22(1) ... 11, 12
s 22(1)(c) ... 12
Communications Act 2003 (UK) ... 249
Competition Act 1998 (UK) ... 176, 248, 249,
254–6, 327
Ch I ... 116, 248
Ch II ... 116, 248
Comprehensive Internet Gambling Prohibition
Act 2002 (US)—
s 3006 ... 297
Constitutional Reform Act 2005 (UK) ... 94
Copyrights, Designs and Patents Act 1988 (UK)
... 324

Counterfeit Law 2003 (Brazil) ... 356
Criminal Justice and Immigration Act 2008
(UK)—
s 74 ... 588
Criminal Justice and Public Order Act 1994 (UK)
... 76, 314–17, 576
s 154 ... 581
s 166 ... 313, 314, 316, 317
s 166A ... 313
Criminal Justice (Scotland) Act 2003 (UK) ...
589
s 74 ... 588, 589
Criminal Procedure (Scotland) Act 1995 (UK)—
s 12 ... 523

D

Data Protection Act 1998 (UK) ... 298, 539
Decree 75.572 (Brazil) ... 356
Decree 90.129 (Brazil) ... 356
Disability Discrimination Act 1995 (UK) ... 434,
465

E

Elite Sports Act (2005) (Denmark) ... 391
Employment Act 1982 (UK) ... 401
Employment Protection (Consolidation) Act
1978 (UK) ... 394, 426
Employment Relations Act 1999 (UK)—
ss 10–15 ... 399
s 23 ... 396
Employment Rights Act 1996 (UK) ... 394, 426,
427, 466, 473, 484
ss 1–3 ... 397
s 13(1) ... 439
s 95(1) ... 429
s 98 ... 430, 431
s 98(1) ... 431
s 98(1)(b) ... 431
s 99 ... 484
s 114 ... 440
s 115 ... 440

s 119 ... 440
s 123(1) ... 441
s 123(4) ... 441
s 212 ... 428
s 212(3) ... 428
s 230 ... 394
Enterprise Act 2002 (UK) ... 248
Equal Pay Act 1970 (UK) ... 484, 485
Equality Act 2006 (UK) ... 465
Equality Act 2010 (UK) ... 399, 461, 465,
    471–3, 475–7, 479, 480, 482, 484, 485,
    496
s 4 ... 461
s 6 ... 476
s 7 ... 475, 476
s 7(1) ... 475
s 9 ... 465, 466
s 10 ... 466
s 12(1) ... 475
s 13 ... 465
s 13(1) ... 467
s 14 ... 466
s 15 ... 477
s 18 ... 484
s 19 ... 469
s 20 ... 477
s 40 ... 480
s 40(2) ... 481
s 40(3) ... 481
ss 64–70 ... 484
s 83(1) ... 466
s 109 ... 480
s 135 ... 467
s 159 ... 473
s 195 ... 471, 472, 476, 496
s 195(3) ... 472, 473
s 195(4) ... 473
Extradition Act (Singapore) ... 65

F

Federal Constitution 1988 (Brazil) ... 356
Federal Trademark Act 1946 (15 USC) (The
    Lanham Act) (US) ... 322, 331, 335
s 43(a) ... 331, 335
s 114 ... 322
FIFA World Cup South Africa Special Measures Act
    (2010) (South Africa) ... 342
Fire Safety and Safety of Places of Sport Act 1987
    (UK) ... 549, 551, 555

s 19 ... 549
s 27 ... 551
s 27(1) ... 555
Football Disorder Act 2000 (UK) ... 72, 517,
    576–9
Football (Offences) Act 1991 (UK) ... 72, 75,
    552, 576, 581, 583, 588
s 3 ... 581, 583, 584, 588
s 3(2) ... 581
s 3(2)(b) ... 585
Football (Offences and Disorder) Act 1999 (UK)
    ... 72, 576, 577, 584
s 9 ... 584
Football Spectators Act 1989 (UK) ... 72, 75,
    555, 575, 576, 578
s 14B ... 578
Pt III ... 552
Sch 1 ... 577
Fraud Act 2006 (UK) ... 299, 315–17
s 1(3) ... 316
s 2 ... 299, 316
s 2(2) ... 316
s 2(4) ... 316
s 2(5) ... 316

G

Gambling Act 2005 (UK) ... 286, 298–300
s 42 ... 298, 299
s 42(1) ... 298, 299
s 42(2) ... 299
s 42(3) ... 299
Gender Recognition Act 2004 (UK) ... 476
s 19 ... 476
Glasgow Commonwealth Games Act 2008 (UK)
    ... 315–17
s 17 ... 317

H

Health and Safety at Work Act 1974 (UK)
    ... 570
s 2 ... 570
s 3 ... 570
Human Rights Act 1998 (UK) ... 103, 134–8,
    269, 380, 409, 474
s 2 ... 134, 135
s 3 ... 134
s 4 ... 134
s 6 ... 103, 134–6, 474
s 6(1) ... 135, 136

s 6(3)(a) ... 135
s 6(3)(b) ... 135–137
s 12 ... 137

I

Immigration Act 1971 (UK) ... 489
Immigration Act 1988 (UK) ... 489
Industrial Property Act 1996 (Brazil) ... 356
Industrial Property Law, 14/05/1996, No 9.279
  (Brazil) ... 356
  Art 124 ... 356
  Art 195 ... 356, 357
Insolvency Act 1986 (UK) ... 240

L

Law Reform (Contributory Negligence) Act 1945
  (UK) ... 514
Licensing Act 1988 (UK) ... 75
London Olympic Games and Paralympics Games
  Act 2006 (UK) ... 31, 315–17, 319,
  336–40
  s 31 ... 315–17
  s 31(6) ... 315
  Sch 4 ... 337, 339
  Sch 4, para 3(1) ... 339

M

Medicines Act 1968 (UK)—
  s 58(2) ... 375
Merchandise Marks Amendment Act 2002 (South
  Africa) ... 341, 342
Misuse of Drugs Act 1971 (UK) ... 375, 381
  s 28(2) ... 375
  Sch 2 ... 381
Municipal Enabling and Validating Act
  (No. 3) British Columbia 2009 (Canada)
  ... 352

N

National Labor Relations Act 1982 (29 USC)
  (US) ... 267
  s 159(a)–(e) ... 267
National Lottery etc Act 1993 (UK)—
  s 23(2) ... 31

O

Occupiers' Liability Act 1957 (UK) ... 508,
  553–5, 565, 568
  s 2 ... 509, 553

s 2(1) ... 554
s 2(2) ... 554
s 2(5) ... 569
Occupiers' Liability Act 1984 (UK) ... 553, 554
  s 3(a) ... 554
Offences Against the Person Act 1861 (UK)—
  s 18 ... 517
  s 20 ... 516, 518, 526
  s 47 ... 518
Olympic and Amateur Sports Act 1978 (36 USC)
  (Ted Stevens Act) (US) ... 322, 323
  s 380 ... 323
Olympic and Paralympic Act 2007 (c 25)
  (Canada) ... 336
  s 4(1) ... 336
  s 4(2) ... 336
  Sch 3 ... 336
Olympic Arrangements Act 2000 (NSW) ... 335
Olympic Symbol etc (Protection) Act 1995 (UK)
  ... 319, 336–9

P

Pele Law 1998 (Brazil) ... 356
Police Act 1964 (UK)—
  s 15(1) ... 567
Police Act 1996 (UK)—
  s 25 ... 551
Police Act 1997 (UK) ... 538, 539
Police, Public Order and Criminal Justice
  (Scotland) Act 2006 (UK) ... 589
Prevention and Combating of Corrupt Activities
  Act (No 12 of 2004) (South Africa) ... 299
Proceeds of Crime Act 2002 (UK) ... 314–17
  s 328 ... 317
  s 329 ... 316
  s 334 ... 317
Professional and Amateur Sports Protection Act
  1992 (28 USC) (US)—
  s 3702 ... 297
Protection from Harassment Act 1997 (UK) ...
  481, 482
  s 1 ... 481
  s 3 ... 481
Public Disclosure Act 1998 (UK) ... 408
Public Order Act 1986 (UK) ... 581
  s 4 ... 517, 523, 581
  s 4A ... 581
  s 5 ... 517, 581
  Pt 3A ... 588

R

Race Relations Act 1976 (UK) ... 465, 466, 473, 479, 480, 482
  s 1 ... 468
  s 12 ... 468
  s 32 ... 480
  s 32(3) ... 480
  s 39 ... 471
Restrictive Trade Practices Act 1976 (UK) ... 247, 248, 408
Road Traffic Code (Greece)—
  Art 49 ... 191, 193

S

Safety of Sports Grounds Act 1975 (UK) ... 546, 548, 549, 554
  s 1 ... 549
  s 1(1) ... 554
  s 1(3) ... 554
  s 2 ... 551, 554
  s 2(2) ... 549
  s 2(2)(a) ... 549
  s 2(2)(b) ... 549
  s 2(2)(c)(iii) ... 549
  s 10 ... 554, 555
  s 13(1) ... 555
Senior Courts Act 1981 (UK)—
  s 31 ... 94, 95
Sex Discrimination Act 1975 (UK) ... 465, 473–5, 480, 484
  s 1(1)(b) ... 469
  s 1(1)(b) ... 470
  s 7 ... 473
  s 44 ... 472, 473
  s 63A ... 467
  Sch 9 ... 473
Sex Offenders Act 1997 (UK) ... 539
Sherman Act 1890 (US) ... 248
Sporting Events (Control of Alcohol etc) Act 1985 (UK) ... 546, 547
  s 1 ... 546, 547

  s 1(2)(a) ... 547
  s 2 ... 546
  s 2(1)(a) ... 546, 547
  s 2(1)(b) ... 547
  s 2(2) ... 547
  s 2(3) ... 547
Sports Broadcasting Act 1961 (US) ... 247
Street Betting Act 1906 (UK) ... 290, 292

T

Television Act 1954 (UK) ... 198
Theft Act 1968 (UK) ... 299, 316
Theft Act 1978 (UK) ... 299
Tobacco Advertising and Promotion Act 2002 (UK) ... 220
Trade Disputes Act 1906 (UK) ... 401
Trade Marks Act 1994 (UK) ... 319
  s 1(1) ... 319
Trade Practices Act No 76 of 1976 (South Africa) ... 340, 341
Trade Union and Labour Relations Act 1974 (UK) ... 401
Trade Union and Labour Relations (Consolidation) Act 1992 (UK)—
  s 179 ... 399
  s 207A ... 429

U

United States Constitution (US)—
  Art 1 ... 69
Unfair Contract Terms Act 1977 (UK) ... 508, 554
  s 2(1) ... 318, 554
  s 2(2) ... 554

V

Violent Crime Reduction Act 2006 (UK) ... 313, 314, 576, 577

W

Wages Act 1986 (UK)—
  s 1(1) ... 439

Table of Statutory Instruments

A

Additonal Parental Leave Regulations 2010 (SI 2010/1055) ... 484

C

Civil Procedure Rules 1998 (SI 1998/3132) ... 103
Pt 54 ... 103
r 54.1(2) ... 103

E

Employment Act 2002 (Dispute Resolution) Regulations 2004 (SI 2004/752) ... 429
Employment Equality (Religion or Belief) Regulations 2003 (SI 2003/1600) ... 479
Employment Equality (Sexual Orientation) Regulations 2003 (SI 2003/1661) ... 475, 479

F

Fixed-Term Employees (Prevention of Less Favourable Treatment) Regulations 2002 (SI 2002/2034) ... 429

Football Spectators (Prescription) (Amendment) Order 2006 (SI 2006/761) ... 314

P

Part-Time Workers (Prevention of Less Favourable Treatment) Regulations 2000 (SI 2000/1551) ... 396, 470
Paternity and Adoption Leave Regulations 2002 (SI 2002/2788) ... 484

R

Race Relations Act 1976 (Amendment) Regulations 2003 (SI 2003/1626) ... 479
Rules of the Supreme Court—
Ord 53 ... 94

S

Sex Discrimination (Indirect Discrimination and Burden of Proof) Regulations 2001 (SI 2001/2660) ... 467

W

Working Time Regulations 1998 (SI 1998/1833) ... 396

Table of EU Conventions and Treaties

A

Amsterdam Declaration ... 204

C

Council of Europe Convention ... 370

E

EU Constitutional Treaty ... 199
European Agreement between Slovakia and the
    EU ... 491
    Art 38 ... 491
European Convention on the Protection of
    Human Rights and Fundamental
    Freedoms ... 119, 134–7, 373, 448, 474,
    578
    Art 4 ... 136
    Art 6 ... 136, 137, 141, 380, 578
    Art 8 ... 136, 137, 287, 391, 434, 474, 578
    Art 8(2) ... 578
    Art 10 ... 136, 137, 409
    Art 11 ... 154
European Convention on the Protection of
    Human Rights and Fundamental Freedoms,
    Protocol IV—
    Art 2 ... 448
    Art 3 ... 448
EC Treaty (Pre and Post Treaty of Amsterdam) ...
    146, 165, 168, 171, 185, 187, 191, 192,
    203, 366, 402, 448, 495
    Art 2 ... 365
    Art 39 ... 146, 185, 187, 365, 366, 368, 442,
    450, 455, 489
    Art 39(3) ... 492
    Art 48 ... 152, 170–2, 442, 443, 447–9, 485,
    487, 489
    Art 48(3) ... 486
    Art 49 ... 146, 183–5, 187, 188, 365, 366,
    369
    Art 81 ... 146, 183–5, 187, 188, 190, 366–8,
    442, 448
    Art 81(1) ... 183, 187, 188, 367, 368

Art 81(3) ... 189
Art 82 ... 146, 183–5, 187–92, 195, 366, 442
Art 85 ... 152, 162, 177, 442, 448
Art 86 ... 152, 191, 442
Art 90 ... 250
Art 128 ... 163
Art 138 ... 456
Art 139 ... 456
Art 141 ... 448, 484
Art 230 ... 183, 189
Art 234 ... 494
EEC Treaty (Treaty of Rome) 1957 ...
    146–8, 150, 151, 153, 154, 158, 169, 170,
    442
    Art 2 ... 148
    Art 3(c) ... 149
    Art 6 ... 170
    Art 7 ... 148–50
    Art 30 ... 158
    Arts 48–51 ... 148
    Art 48 ... 146, 147, 149, 150, 152–5, 157,
    158, 160, 170
    Art 48(2) ... 156
    Art 48(3) ... 155
    Art 52 ... 158
    Arts 59–66 ... 148, 169
    Art 59 ... 146, 147, 149, 150, 169, 170
    Art 85 ... 146, 152, 160, 169, 170, 194
    Art 85(1) ... 194
    Art 86 ... 146, 152, 160, 169, 170
    Art 119 ... 448
    Art 173 ... 152
    Art 177 ... 147

I

International Agreements on Trade Related
    Aspects on Intellectual Property Rights 1994
    ... 356
International Covenant on Civil and Political
    Rights 1966—
    Art 12 ... 448

N

Nairobi Treaty on the Protection of the Olympic
    Symbol, 1981 ... 319, 356
Nice Declaration ... 199

P

Paris Convention for the Protection of Intellectual
    Property 1975 Decree ... 356

T

Treaty of Accession ... 147
Treaty of Amsterdam 1997 ... 164, 204
    Art 13 ... 474
Treaty of Lisbon (Reform Treaty) ... 146, 203, 204
Treaty of Nice ... 204
Treaty on the Functioning of the European Union
    ... 146, 203, 204, 206, 254, 442
    Art 45 ... 146, 152, 154, 228, 442, 449, 450,
        458, 485, 491, 492
    Art 56 ... 146, 183, 188, 189
    Art 101 ... 116, 146, 152, 176–9, 181, 188,
        197, 228, 248, 254, 255, 442
    Art 101(1) ... 176, 177, 179, 183, 188, 198
    Art 101(1)(e) ... 177
    Art 101(2) ... 177, 179
    Art 101(3) ... 177, 179, 181, 190, 197
    Art 102 ... 116, 146, 152, 176, 179, 181, 188,
        190, 228, 248, 254, 255, 417, 442, 450
    Art 157 ... 484, 485
    Art 165 ... 146, 203, 204, 206
    Art 165(1)–(4) ... 203
    Art 263 ... 152, 183, 189
    Art 267 ... 147, 442

U

UNESCO International Convention Against
    Doping in Sport ... 369, 370
    Art 1 ... 369
    Art 2 ... 369
    Art 3 ... 369, 370
United Nations Universal Declaration of Human
    Rights 1948 (UN)—
    Art 13 448

Table of EU Secondary Legislation

Directives

Council Directive (73/148/EEC)—
 Art 1 578
 Art 2 578
Council Directive (75/117/EEC) (Equal Pay) 484
Council Directive (76/207/EEC) (Equal Treatment) 448, 474, 483
 Art 2 483
Council Directive (89/104/EEC) (Trade Marks Directive) 319
Council Directive (89/552/EEC) (Television Without Frontiers) 250
 Art 3(a) 199, 251
 Art 3A 250
Art 3A(1)–(3) 250
Council Directive (96/34/EC) (Parental Leave) 484
Council Directive (97/81/EC) (Part-Time Workers) 470
Council Directive (97/900/EC) (Burden of Proof) 467
Council Directive (99/70/EC) (Fixed-Term Work) 429
Council Directive (2000/43/EC) (Equal Treatment) 474, 475, 479
Council Directive (2000/78/EC) (General Framework for Equal Treatment) 474, 479
Council Directive (2010/13/EU) (Audiovisual Media Services Directive) 199
 Art 13 199

Decisions

Commission Decision (92/521/EEC of 27 October 1992) Relating to a Proceeding under Article 85 of
 the EEC Treaty 194
Commission Decision (2003/778/EC of 23 July 2003) Relating to a Proceeding Pursuant to Article 81
 of the EC Treaty and Article 53 of the EEA Agreement 197

Regulations

Council Regulation (1612/68)—
 Art 4 156
 Art 4(1) 155
 Art 7(4) 149

Part 1

The Regulation and Governance of Sport

1   Cultural, Historical and Organisational
    Perspectives on UK Regulation of Sport   3

2   Theoretical Understanding of the
    Regulation of Sport   43

3   The Legal Regulation of Sports
    Governing Bodies   88

4   Sport and the Law of the European Union   145

Chapter 1

Cultural, Historical and Organisational Perspectives on UK Regulation of Sport

Chapter Contents

Introduction	4
What is a Sport?	4
History of Sport	13
Historical Perspectives on Sports Regulation	16
The Victorian Age: Origins of Modern Sport	22
The Contemporary Significance of Sport	24
Sociology of Sport	26
Framework of Sport in Britain	30
Conclusion	42
Key Points	42
Key Sources	42

Introduction

Compared with most other European countries, the British state's formal involvement in sport has been fairly minimal. Sports bodies are treated as autonomous independent bodies and self-regulation has been the tradition. The state has played a passive role even when promoting and effectively 'managing' sport. Within Europe a distinction can be made between northern countries, which share this approach, and southern 'Mediterranean' countries, where there is a tradition of specific regulation.[1] As will be stressed below, there has been a long history of legal prohibition of certain types of sport in Britain. Additionally in recent years, there has been a steady move to greater regulatory involvement.[2]

The lack of recent success in Britain's national sporting teams and the sporadic accomplishment of its individual sportsmen and women have intensified the debate concerning the effective role that the state can play in sport. Increasing pressure has been brought to bear upon the state to provide greater financial and material assistance to British sport through national lottery funding, for example.

Sport is going through significant changes: the context within which law has assumed an increasingly important role in regulating sport will be analysed during this chapter. The chapter is divided into four sections. First, a question will be posed, namely 'What is a sport?' This will be answered by both looking at various social definitions of sport and the historical origins of its development and identification. Second, the historical regulatory environment of sport in Britain will be examined. Third, the cultural and political significance of sport will be evaluated together with a discussion of various sociological theories that have developed to explain the role that sport plays in society. Sport is a truly global phenomenon. As a social activity, whether it is in terms of participation as a recreational pastime, competitive playing at amateur levels, the elite and mainly professional level or in terms of spectating, sport assumes immense cultural significance.[3] Fourth and last, a consideration will be made of the framework through which the state may intervene in British sport. Such intervention can be through various methods including financial support and the promotion of sport as an activity that has health and social benefits. The use of sport as a form of social policy to fight crime and social exclusion will also be considered, and the role of bodies such as the Sports Councils will be briefly discussed.

What is a Sport?

This is a fundamental question that needs to be posed to help demarcate the disciplinary area of sports law. A good starting point is to see sport as a human activity that exists somewhere along the continuum from work to play. There is a need to demarcate sport from recreational activities in general and games and play specifically. But an attempt at a definition reveals the dynamic and changing nature of sport. In modern elite sport, professionalisation has led to an increasing transformation of sport into a type of work with the world of 'amateur play' seemingly contracting quickly.[4] There are also a number of anomalies in the way participation in sport is described. Some sports such as football, rugby and golf are seen as being 'played', and the participants are 'players'.

---

1   See Council of Europe, *Study of National Sports Legislation in Europe* (1999); see details of a number of European countries including Michel, A, 'Sports policy in France', in Chalip, L, Johnson, A and Stachura, L (eds), *National Sports Policies: An International Handbook* (1996), Westport, CT: Greenwood.
2   See Lewis, A and Taylor, J (eds), *Sport: Law and Practice*, 2nd edn (2008), Haywards Heath: Tottel, pp 1–53.
3   For an examination of many of the cultural issues concerning sport see Tomlinson, A (ed), *The Sports Studies Reader: Sport, Culture and Society* (2001), London: Routledge; Cashmore, E (ed), *Sports Culture: An A–Z Guide* (2000), London: Routledge; and *Making Sense of Sport*, 3rd edn (2000), London: Routledge.
4   This can be illustrated by the move away from the distinction between amateurs and gentlemen in cricket shortly after the Second World War and the recent professionalisation of rugby union during the 1990s.

These are the sports most akin to work. There are other sports where it is uncommon to talk of those involved as being players; with fishing, archery and hunting the sport is not 'played' but, in contrast to the former group, it is closer to play and leisure than work.

There are positive reasons for needing to provide definitional clarity. An activity defined as a sport has a number of financial and legal advantages. Where are the lines going to be drawn between sport, games, recreation, leisure, work and play?

Social definition

A historical examination of the development and meaning of sport provides a powerful view of what we mean by sport and its social import. This will be addressed shortly. However, the historical perspective also needs a clear social context. The use of the term sport in its expansive meaning is one that is a product of modernity. The definitional problems are alluded to by Slusher when he analogises between sport and religion:

> Basically sport, like religion defies definition. In a manner it goes beyond definitive terminology. Neither has substance which can be identified. In a sense both sport and religion are beyond essence.[5]

There is a considerable body of sociological and cultural literature concerning the definition of sport.[6] Coakley believes:

> Sports are institutionalised competitive activities that involve vigorous physical exertion or the use of relatively complex physical skills by individuals whose participation is motivated by a combination of intrinsic and extrinsic factors.[7]

Singer similarly sees sport as:

> . . . a human activity that involves specific administrative organisations and historical background of rules which define the objective and limit the pattern of human behaviour; it involves competition and/or challenge and a definite outcome primarily determined by physical skill.[8]

An exact definition of sport seems to be impossible, but some common elements of the existence of a recognisable organisational structure, rules, physical exertion and competition need to be present. It is important to have clear definitions of the concepts that are being studied. In the sociology of sport a good working definition helps an understanding of the role that sport has as a part of social life. Similarly, the study of sport and the law needs the same definitional clarity.

One approach to a clear definition of sport is to look at the level of the sporting activity. Are games or individual pursuits at elite level more likely to be termed sport than kids playing on a patch of wasteland? Do we want to develop a definition of sport that differentiates it from mere physical recreation, aesthetic and conditioning activities and informal games? There are considerable problems in attempting to provide answers. For example, what of activities such as mountain climbing, which has been developed as an indoor competitive 'sport' of wall climbing, and

5   Slusher, H, Men, Sport and Existence: A Critical Analysis (1967), Philadelphia: Lea and Febiger.
6   See Loy, J, 'The nature of sport: a definitional effort', in Loy, J and Kenyon, G (eds), Sport, Culture and Society: A Reader on the Sociology of Sport (1969), New York: Macmillan; Coakley, J, Sport in Society: Issues and Controversies (1994), 5th edn, St Louis: Mosbey; Sprietzer, E, Social Aspects of Sport (1967), Englewood Cliffs, New Jersey: Prentice Hall; Mandel, R, Sport: A Cultural History (1981), Oxford: Clarendon; and Dunning, E (ed), The Sociology of Sport: A Selection of Readings (1971), Oxford: Blackwell.
7   Coakley, J, Sport in Society: Issues and Controversies (1994), St Louis: Mosbey; p 21.
8   Singer, R, Physical Education: Foundations (1976), New York: Holt, Rinehart and Winston.

mountain biking, an activity that takes place within a continuum from the use of bikes being purely about mobility, through their use for recreational leisure, to involvement in highly competitive national and international competitions such as the Tour de France. It may also be important to consider the subjective intention and motivation of the participant; this may distinguish between involvement in sport rather than mere play or entertainment.

Using the above guidelines, can we define activities such as jogging as a sport? What about synchronised swimming, darts, fox hunting, skin diving, chess? What about hybrid sports[9] and those that are more likely to be viewed as forms of recreation and entertainment?[10] One common claim is that sport needs some notion of being a physical activity, in that there is 'the use of physical skill, physical prowess or physical exertion'.[11] Chess and other board games clearly need a minimal amount of physical effort either in terms of complex physical skills or vigorous exertion; the skills required are essentially cognitive.[12] The international federation of chess has been recognised by the IOC and the sport has complied with anti-doping requirements under the World Anti-Doping Code. However, it has not yet been officially classified as an Olympic sport.

Such a definitional approach emphasising physical effort could potentially include all physical activities, including sex, as a sport! In R v Brown,[13] a case involving the legality of consensual sado-masochistic homosexual activity, an argument was expressed that the participants might have gained protection and exemption from criminal liability under the law of assault if they could be seen as being involved 'in the course of properly conducted games or sports'.[14] The application of 'rules of play', which evidence showed often existed in sadomasochistic sex, and the 'policing' by a referee were suggested as characteristics of a would-be sport.

To distinguish sport from recreational activity, it is necessary to consider the context or condi-tions of the physical activity and to determine whether it needs to take place in some institutional-ised situation. This can help distinguish between formally organised competitive activities compared with those carried out in an ad hoc unstructured form; for example, the distinction between a Premier League football match and a number of children kicking a football in a park. Elements that characterise the former are perhaps standardised rules, official regulatory agencies, the importance of organisational and technical aspects and the learning of strategies, skills and tactics by partici-pants.

This process can be applied to the codification of the two branches of football, rugby and association, in the late nineteenth century. It can also be illustrated with the emergence and institutionalisation of body-building, which has developed from an activity based on aesthetics and health objectives to one open to competitions and being considered a sport. Such an approach produces an essentially objective understanding of a sport. Meier argues that subjective perceptions of participants are irrelevant in determining the nature of sport.[15] Some writers, however, have considered that the motivations of the participants in the sport help determine its meaning. Coakley claims that a 'play spirit' based on the internal motivations of the participant is an important element in determining whether the activity in question can be termed as a sport.[16] Huizinga describes play as:

---

9   For example, bicycle polo, octopush – a form of underwater hockey – and horseball, an amalgam of rugby, basketball and horse riding. See 'Horsing around with a ball', *The Times*, 21 April 1997.
10 Note also World Wrestling Entertainment (WWE, formerly the WWF) professional wrestling, ballroom dancing and dragon boat racing.
11 Op. cit., fn 7, Coakley (1994), p 13.
12 See 'Chess – a sport or just a game' (1999) 2(2) SLB 16.
13 [1993] 2 All ER 75.
14 This exemption from liability short of grievous bodily harm (serious injury) that was consented to factually during a sporting activity was laid down in *Attorney General's Reference (No 6 of 1980)* [1981] 2 All ER 1057.
15 Meier, K, 'On the inadequacies of sociological definitions of sport' (1981) 16(2) International Review of Sports Sociology 79.
16 Op. cit., fn 7, Coakley (1994), p 16.

... a free activity standing quite consciously outside 'ordinary' life as being 'not serious' but at the same time absorbing the player intensely and utterly ... it proceeds within its own proper boundaries of time and space according to fixed rules and in an orderly manner.[17]

Stone argues that sports are composed of two types of behaviour which he characterises as 'play' and 'dis-play'.[18] Play is where the participant's motivations are concerned with that individual's relationship with the activity. Dis-play, on the other hand, is participation being essentially concerned with spectators to the activity – the notion of a spectacle becomes more important than the sport. External motivations such as money and fame, especially if they replace the internal motivations for participating in the activity, lead to this danger. The dangers of increased commercialisation and commodification of sport together with the spectacularisation of contemporary sport are clear. Two sports where such dangers arise are boxing and wrestling:

Michener, J, *Sports in America*

In 1946, boxing and wrestling and roller derbies were taken seriously but when they began to grab the nearest dollar, the quickest laugh, the most grotesque parody of violence, their credibility was destroyed. When enough people begin laughing at the exaggerations of any sport, it is doomed.[19]

Stone, G, 'American sports: play and dis-play'

Play and dis-play are precariously balanced in sport and, once that balance is upset, the whole character of sport in society may be affected. Furthermore, the spectacular element of sport may, as in the case of American professional wrestling, destroy the game. The rules cease to apply and the 'cheat' and the 'spoilsport' replace the players. Yet even here counter forces are set in motion. If we may discontinuously resume our analysis of wrestling, we would note that there is always the 'hero' who attempts to defeat the 'villain' within the moral framework of the rules of the game. It is a case of law versus outlaw, cops and robbers, the 'good guys' versus the 'bad guys'. Symbolically the destruction of the game by the spectacle has called into existence forces of revival that seek to re-establish the rules, but these forces are precisely symbolic – representative. They are seldom able to destroy the spectacular components of the display. They are part of the spectacle itself.

The point may be made in another way. The spectacle is predictable and certain; the game, unpredictable and uncertain. Thus spectacular display may be reckoned from the outset of the performance. It is announced by the appearance of the performers – their physiques, costumes and gestures. On the other hand, the spectacular play is solely a function of the uncertainty of the game. The spectacular player makes the 'impossible catch' – 'outdoes himself'. He is out of character. The 'villains' and 'heroes' of the wrestling stage are in character. They are the *dramatis personae* of a pageant – an expressive drama. Consequently their roles have been predetermined. The denouement of the contest has been decided at its inception and the hero is unlikely to affect the course of events.[20]

This can be illustrated by the disintegration of the professional boxing regulatory organisations and the emergence of a plethora of world governing bodies offering their own world titles.[21] In

---

17 Huizinga, J, *Homo Ludens – A Study of the Play-Element in Culture* (1955), Boston: Beacon.
18 Stone, G, 'American sports: play and dis-play' (1965) 9 Chicago Review 83; and see also Dunning, E (ed), *The Sociology of Sport: A Selection of Readings* (1971), London: Frank Cass, p 47.
19 Michener, J, *Sports in America* (1976), New York: Fawcett, p 540.
20 Op. cit., fn 18, Stone (1965), p 59.
21 For example, see the World Boxing Association (WBA), the World Boxing Council (WBC), the World Boxing Organisation (WBO) and the International Boxing Federation (IBF).

professional wrestling, the emergence of World Wrestling Entertainment (WWE), formerly the World Wrestling Federation (WWF),[22] has clearly demarcated itself from amateur wrestling still mainly played for Stone's internal reasons. WWE has become purely a spectacle where characters such as 'The Undertaker' and 'The Rock' present a slick entertainment televised throughout the world in artificially created championships, 'The Royal Rumble', 'The King of the Ring' and 'Wrestle Mania', a paradigm example of the spectacularisation of sport – content and values such as 'uncertainty of outcome' have been sacrificed for image.[23]

Hargreaves, J, *Sport, Power and Culture*

The extent to which a given cultural formation is enabled to feed the power network also depends crucially on its own particular character, that is on those autonomous features which distinguish it from others as a specific type of cultural formation. The realm of sport encompasses a bewildering diversity of radically different kinds of activity, which defies a watertight definition – from the local hunt and pub darts match, village cricket, inter-collegiate rowing and little league football, to professionalised mass entertainment like the Football League, the Wimbledon Tennis Championships, heavyweight boxing and horse racing. Some of this activity plainly has little, if any, connection with power. Despite the complexity, in our view sufficient distinguishing characteristics can be identified, which enable us to analyse how, in specific conditions, the sport–power relation may be constituted. First, sports to one or other degree embody an irreducible element of play. Play is a type of activity having no extrinsic purpose or end and as such it is a form of activity which enjoys a universal appeal. Sports play is not always unalloyed by other motives or considerations – financial gain, prestige, etc – and in specific instances (politicised and professional sport for example) play may be by no means the most important element. But the ludic impulse is, nevertheless, always present to some degree at least, existing in tension with disciplined organised aspects of sporting activity.

Secondly sports play tends to be highly formalised: in many cases it is governed by very elaborate codes or statutes. Sports play in this sense is far from being spontaneous: it is by convention rule orientated and to have no rules would be a contradiction in terms. Whether the rules are, in fact, being followed, is therefore an ever present issue in the conduct of sports and in this sense we could say that not only are sports rule orientated – they can be rule-obsessed. Rule-structured play, like play in general, 'suspends reality' but in this case through the acceptance of formal codes ordering the use of space, time and general behaviour. In choosing to structure their activity thus, both participants and onlookers are indulging in a form of 'play acting'and in this respect the activity can be said to be 'unserious' or set aside from normal life. Play acting is also involved in sporting activity when 'display' before an audience is one of the objectives. In addition, many sports were associated historically with the great festivals and to varying extents are still conducted in a spirit of festivity, a spirit which, by 'turning the world upside down', suspends while simultaneously challenging reality.

Thirdly, sports involve some element of contest between participants. The rules which structure sporting contests, however, unlike those that structure competition and conflict in the real world, deliberately set out to equalise conditions of participation, that is, they are intended to be neutral, so that no one party to the contest has an advantage over the other(s). Since a contest within neutral rules makes the outcome inherently uncertain and in principle unpredictable, the very point of the activity is negated when either the rules are biased in favour

---

22 See litigation that led to name change: (1) *WWF – World Wide Fund For Nature (Formerly World Wildlife Fund)*; (2) *World Wildlife Fund Inc v World Wrestling Federation Entertainment Inc.* (2002) IPD 25023.
23 See cultural resistance to the sometime gratuitous violence 'Singapore Broadcasting Authority blasts WWF', 17 May 2001, www. sportbusiness.com.

of one or other party or when the contestants are matched unevenly, for then the outcome does indeed become predictable. The uncertainty of the contest's outcome and the attendant tension it creates lends a unique excitement to sports, compared with other activities involving play, and it is probably one of the main reasons why sports become so often the subject of intense interest and emotion. Paradoxically, the deep commitment which sports often arouse also makes them deadly serious affairs as well as unserious ones.

Three other attributes of sporting activity which have received much less attention are crucial in any consideration of the sport–power relation. The play acting, contest and uncertainty elements ensure that sports are an intrinsically dramatic means of expression and an audience in addition transforms them into a form of theatre. We argue that sports fall within the province of 'the popular' and in so far as they take on the attribute of a dramatic performance they can be said to constitute a form of popular theatre, arguably the most popular contemporary form of theatre.[24]

Fundamental characteristics of sport

An attempt has been made to demarcate the parameters of what we might understand as the social practice of sport. This takes place both at a recreational level and competitively at both an amateur level and elite professional level. For this sporting activity to have integrity it must exhibit a range of inherent characteristics. Undertaking the sport with reference to an agreed set of rules within an accepted playing culture required to achieve the values associated with 'Fair Play', is required at all levels of participation. This will be discussed further in Chapter 2. The European Union has listed the following general sporting characteristics:

> The European Council hopes in particular that the cohesion and ties of solidarity binding the prac-
> tice of sports at every level, fair competition and both the moral and material interests and the
> physical integrity of those involved in the practice of sport, especially minors, may be preserved.[25]

The focus is on ensuring the integrity of sport. The term integrity has no fixed meaning but is an amalgam of a range of values that need to be supported so as to have integrity in any given sporting activity. Although the focus is on both recreational and professional sport, it is the latter where crucial issues around competitive balance become important. The following characteristics, which are not necessarily exhaustive or exclusive of each other, need to be noted:

1.   Unpredictability or uncertainty of outcome – competition is a fundamental prerequisite for sport and any factors which negatively impact upon this, for example unequal distribution of resources such as financial strength and playing talent between teams within the same professional league, may distort that competition and allow one or more clubs to dominate, so that the unpredictability of sporting competition is compromised. Many of the contemporary issues around the regulation of sporting competition that will be examined later in this book attempt to engage with this problem.

2.   Level Playing Field – sporting competition should not be based on a participant having an unfair advantage over another through the use of 'artificial aids' such as the use of prohibited drugs.

3.   Compliance with the external legal environment – this is of course the central focus of the discipline of sports law.

---

24 Hargreaves, J, *Sport, Power and Culture: A Social and Historical Analysis of Popular Sports in Britain* (1986), Cambridge: Polity, pp 9–10.
25 Declaration on the specific characteristics of sport and its social function in Europe, of which account should be taken in implementing common policies (2000), http://ec.europa.eu/sport/information-center/doc/timeline/doc244_en.pdf.

Recognition procedure in sport

In the UK, the Sports Councils have a set of recognition criteria for sports. These criteria can be divided into two basic groups: those that are to demarcate a physical sport from a recreation, hobby or pastime and those that are based on safety and ethical considerations together with the legitimate structure of the sports organisation.

They have a number of statutory duties that require them to identify sports, deciding on those sports that should be associated with and developed; to advise local authorities and other bodies on the activities they should promote; to advise on safety in sport; to evaluate the competence of organising and supervising sporting bodies; and to evaluate the financial support to be given to a sport by the Council. The process of recognition is twofold. First, the sporting activity is recognised, and then the sport's organisational structure needs to be recognised in terms of competency to administer any government funds it may receive. The sport's governing body must maintain and demonstrate an agreed level of management and financial accountability. The Sports Councils have modified the criteria used over a period of time. A clear notion of physicality is required. For new activities seeking recognition this has been characterised as requiring 'physical skills, physical effort, and physical challenge'. Other criteria include whether the activity: is unique; is accessible; has established rules and organised competition; includes strategy and tactics as elements for success; and has a minimum of regular participants in the UK.

The emphasis has moved to a need for recognised sports activities to have recognisable and sustainable governing bodies.

Guidelines on the Recognition of English Governing Bodies by Sport England (2008)

Recognised Sporting Activity

The sporting activity, which the governing body is claiming to govern, must already be included on the recognised sporting activity list.

Uniqueness

There is no other governing body operating in England (recognised or unrecognised) that could better govern and develop the sport.

Sustainability

The governing body has been established for a minimum of two years and can demonstrate this by forwarding a copy of its signed constitution and its Annual General Meeting minutes and accounts for the preceding two years. (Where the body is a new organisation formed by the merger of two or more already established governing bodies, Sport England will not normally insist on this criteria being met. However, they will expect to see evidence of a properly constituted merger and plans in place to ensure the new body can continue to govern its sport.)

International Affiliation

The governing body can demonstrate it is affiliated or is in the process of affiliating to the GB/UK governing body where one exists and, where appropriate, the international governing body for the sport.

Governance Structure

An appropriate constitution and statement on anti doping, child protection and equity are in place and have been formally adopted by the governing body.

Membership and Participation

The governing body seeking recognition has demonstrated significant membership in terms of affiliated membership, club structures, participation, etc.

Influence and Control

The governing body can demonstrate that it has reasonable influence in the context of the sport controlled, e.g. in terms of governing the rules of the sporting activity within the jurisdiction, the training and education of coaches and officials.[26]

In the context of eligibility for National Lottery funding, the Sports Councils have been looking at the definition and recognition of sports. In the past, camping and caravanning were recognised but they have been deselected – however model aircraft flying, folk dancing, skipping, rambling, caving and lifesaving continue to be recognised sports. Some controversy was caused when darts was derecognised and effectively deselected as a sport.[27] Recognition also has other financial implications including exemption from VAT. In the past, the Sports Council considered that darts involved insufficient physical activity by the participants. The British Darts Organisation (BDO) believed they had been singled out due to snobbery:

> They wrote to us and said that they do not simply decide what is and is not a sport but 'identify sports and governing bodies with which they want to be associated'. They are really saying that they do not want to be associated with fat blokes with fags in their mouth but that is such an outdated image of the sport.[28]

In 2005, however, Sport England reselected darts as a sport under the auspices of the BDO.[29] So can we conclude on a working dentition of sport that can be used in terms of legal proceedings? The European Sports Charter provides this definition:

> 'Sport' means all forms of physical activity which, through casual or organised participation, aim at expressing and improving physical fitness and mental well-being, forming social relationships, or obtaining results in competition levels.[30]

A legal definition of sport

There is no precise legal definition of sport in English law.[31] Nevertheless, it has been necessary in cases to provide a view of whether a sporting activity is taking place. In *R v Oxfordshire County Council and Others ex p Sunningwell Parish Council*,[32] there was an appeal by the local parish council from the decision of the Court of Appeal refusing leave to apply for judicial review against the decision of the respondent council not to register the glebe (village green) in their village as common land, under s 13(b) of the Commons Registration Act 1965. Section 22(1) of the Act contains a three-part definition of a town or village green:

> . . . (a) land which has been allotted by or under any Act for the exercise or recreation of the inhabitants of any locality or (b) on which the inhabitants of any locality have a customary right

---

26 Guidelines on the Recognition of English Governing Bodies by Sport England (2008), www.sportengland.org.

27 See 'When octopush comes to shove ha'penny, it isn't "croquet" ', *The Observer*, 18 February 1996; 'When is a sport not a sport?' *The Daily Telegraph*, 27 February 1996.

28 'Darts swept from the board' *The Guardian*, 14 February 1996.

29 'Bull's-eye! Darts achieves sporting recognition', *The Guardian*, 25 March 2005.

30 The Council of Europe, *The European Sport Charter* (2001), www.coe.int/t/dg4/sport/sportineurope/charter_en.asp.

31 See Gardiner, S, 'Sport: a need for a legal definition?' (1996) 4(2) SATLJ 31, for a fuller discussion. There is no definition in the Act of a lawful sport in the Commons Registration Act 1965, which provides registration for land which can be used by local inhabitants to indulge in 'lawful sports and pastimes'; see Samuels, A, 'Getting greens registered' (1995) SJ 948.

32 *R v Oxfordshire County Council and Others ex p Sunningwell Parish Council* [1999] 3 WLR 160.

to indulge in lawful sports and pastimes or (c) on which the inhabitants of any locality have indulged in such sports and pastimes as of right for not less than 20 years.

The issue was whether under s 22(1)(c) of the Act, the phrase 'as of right' was to be construed as meaning that the right to indulge in sports and pastimes on the green must be exercised in the belief that it was a right enjoyed by the inhabitants of the village to the exclusion of all other people. The respondent argued *inter alia* that the nature of the activities on the glebe did not include anything which could properly be called a 'sport' as required by the definition in the 1965 Act.

R v Oxfordshire County Council and Others ex p Sunningwell Parish Council

Lord Hoffmann: The first point concerned the nature of the activities on the glebe. They showed that it had been used for solitary or family pastimes (walking, tobogganing, family games) but not for anything which could properly be called a sport. Miss Cameron said that this was insufficient for two reasons. First, because the definition spoke of 'sports and pastimes' and therefore, as a matter of language, pastimes were not enough. There had to be at least one sport. Secondly, because the 'sports and pastimes' in class c had to be the same sports and pastimes as those in respect of which there could have been customary rights under class b and this meant that there had to be some communal element about them, such as playing cricket, shooting at butts or dancing round the maypole. I do not accept either of these arguments. As a matter of language, I think that 'sports and pastimes' is not two classes of activities but a single composite class which uses two words in order to avoid arguments over whether an activity is a sport or a pastime. The law constantly uses pairs of words in this way. As long as the activity can properly be called a sport or a pastime, it falls within the composite class. As for the historical argument, I think that one must distinguish between the concept of a sport or pastime and the particular kind of sports or pastimes which people have played or enjoyed at different times in history. Thus in *Fitch v Rawling* (1795) 2 H Bl 393, Buller J recognised a custom to play cricket on a village green as having existed since the time of Richard I, although the game itself was unknown at the time and would have been unlawful for some centuries thereafter: see *Mercer v Denne* [1904] 2 Ch 538–39, 553. In *Abercromby v Town Commissioners of Fermoy* [1900] 1 I R 302 the Irish Court of Appeal upheld a custom for the inhabitants of Fermoy to use a strip of land along the river for their evening passeggiata. Holmes LJ said, at p 314 that popular amusement took many shapes: 'legal principle does not require that rights of this nature should be limited to certain ancient pastimes'. In any case, he said, the Irish had too much of a sense of humour to dance around a maypole. Class c is concerned with the creation of town and village greens after 1965 and in my opinion sports and pastimes includes those activities which would be so regarded in our own day. I agree with Carnwath J in *R v Suffolk County Council ex p Steed* (1995) 70 P & CR 487, 503, when he said that dog walking and playing with children were, in modern life, the kind of informal recreation which may be the main function of a village green. It may be, of course, that the user is so trivial and sporadic as not to carry the outward appearance of user as of right. In the present case, however, Mr Chapman found 'abundant evidence of use of the glebe for informal recreation' which he held to be a pastime for the purposes of the Act.[33]

The appeal was allowed and Oxfordshire County Council directed to register the glebe as a village green.[34]

---

33 Ibid, per Lord Hoffmann, pp 171–72.
34 Also see *R (on the application of Pamela Beresford) v Sunderland City Council* [2004] 1 All ER 160.

History of Sport

The term 'sport' derives from the French-determined Middle English verb *sporten*, to divert,[35] and also the Latin term *desporto*, literally 'to carry away'. The emphasis is therefore on it being a distraction, something that gives pleasure. Throughout the Middle Ages sport in England meant mainly hunting of a variety of animals. Archery, bowls and horse racing can be seen as early sports dating from the sixteenth century.[36] One of our main cultural and historical identifications with sport is with the original Greek Olympics believed to have been held in 686 BC.[37] Going further back in time, the earliest evidence of boxing's existence is recorded in Ethiopian hieroglyphics around 4000 BC. The world's oldest ball game is thought to have been played as early as 1400 BC in Mexico.[38]

Hunting can be seen as the precursor of much of modern sport. The fact that forms of hunting still persist today indicates its longevity. It is likely that as a sport it originally grew out of a form of play that early man took part in, especially in childhood, as a training for the reality of life: that being a 'hunter gatherer' included the killing of animals to survive:

Brasch, R, *How Did Sports Begin?*

In the beginning, sport was a religious cult and a preparation for life. Its roots were in man's desire to gain victory over foes seen and unseen, to influence the forces of nature and to promote fertility among his crops and cattle. Sport, as a word, is an abbreviation: the shortened form of disport, a diversion and an amusement. Rooted in Latin, it literally means 'carry away' (from *desporto*). In our time millions of people, whether spectators or participants, amateurs or professionals, are carried away by the sport they love from the cares of their daily toil, their anxieties and frustrations, to a world of relaxation and emulation, excitement and thrill. However, going back to the very beginning of sport as such, we find that far from being restricted, it started as part of man's history and is bound up closely with his very being. Sport was not merely a diversion or pastime but an essential feature of man's existence. An inborn impulse and a basic need caused primitive man to play games, even though it might be only hitting a stone with a branch. It eased his tension, helped him to get aggressiveness out of his system and, altogether, served as an innocuous outlet for otherwise harmful urges. After all, to hit an object was so much better than to hit a friend. Thus sport fulfilled a primary want of man and, spontaneously taken up, games catered to it, giving satisfaction and a sense of achievement and overcoming.

Sport was a natural result of a universal love of play and man's innate desire to compete with and to excel, if not dominate, others. Another mainspring of sport was man's need effectively to defend himself, his tribe and, later on, his country. In panic and fear when escaping from danger, he learned to run, jump and swim. To avoid defeat or to subdue opponents, he invented archery, judo and karate. And in order to be ready for combat, at all times he practised them and new sports evolved out of his martial training. Even football and baseball carry vestiges of battles between tribes. Muscular strength and alertness served well in the repulse or conquest of foes. Sports taught man endurance and courage, essential qualities in a fighter, and man was a fighter from the very beginning. However, in some parts of the world where the severity of the elements and a low protein diet endangered his life, man's healthy instinct led him to create sports for yet another reason. In cold climates, games provided vital exercise, making the blood course through the veins and keeping man warm and resistant to the hazards

---

35 *Webster's New Collegiate Dictionary* (1995), New York: Webster.
36 Grayson, E, former President of the British Association for Sport and Law, in his inaugural presidential address (1993) 1(1) SATLJ 36.
37 See Toohey, K and Veal, A, *The Olympic Games: A Social Science Perspective* (2000), New York: Cabi.
38 'When did sport begin?' (1998) 1(3) SLB 12.

of nature and the harshness of the weather. Man's wish to survive, in this world and the next, explains the origin of a majority of sports. They were not deliberately invented but arose, almost inevitably, out of man's quest to exist and to overcome the countless enemies that threatened him: natural and supernatural, man and beast. He had to ward them off everywhere. Most of all, sports began as fertility magic, to ensure birth, growth and the return of spring. Therefore sport to begin with was mainly a magical rite. It tried to attain human survival by supernatural means. Numerous examples of this are at hand in ancient records and the practices of primitive races. For instance, for the Zunis, a Mexican tribe that lived in arid zones, rain was the prime necessity for life. Droughts were frequent and it was because of them that the Zunis first played games. They were convinced that these would magically bring rain for the crops.

Other primitive tribes established a fraternity of rain-making priests. The sole task of this first team of professional players was to join in games of chance, which, they believed, would force nature to precipitate rain. With the approach of the whaling season, Mach Indians played a primitive type of hockey, using whalebone for ball and bat, the latter symbolising the war god's club. A hill tribe in Assam, India, arranged a regular tug of war to expel demons. The ceremony – it was not then a sport – took place at a fixed time each year. Two bands of men (the original teams) stood on opposite banks of a river, each tugging at the end of a rope stretched across the water. One team represented the forces of evil, the other those of increase in nature. On the result of the struggle depended whether trouble would haunt the tribe or the sun would shine, literally. Wrestling bouts were practised in southern Nigeria. They took the form also of a religious act to strengthen the growth of the crop by sympathetic magic. In suspense, huge crowds watched the contestants. They were not reluctant to interfere should either of the fighters show weakness, anger or fatigue, lest these deficiencies cause any ill-effect on the reproductive forces of nature. Games were highly important in winter and at the coming of spring. They were considered essential to hasten the return of the sun and ensure a fruitful season. Some of the games took place between groups of single men and women, representing the unprolific and married people, symbolising fecundity. The Wichita tribe, on the Red River of Oklahoma, conducted a sporting event very similar to modern field hockey. This, too, enacted symbolically a contest between winter and spring, to assist in the renewal of life and the conquest of the evil forces of winter. For a similar reason, some Eskimos had seasonal games. In spring, the players used a kind of cup and ball – to catch the sun. In the autumn, when the sun was going south, a sort of cat's cradle of seal gut was used to enmesh the sun and delay its departure.

Sport thus assumed even cosmic significance. Definite rules in primitive ball games were religiously observed to direct the winds, the bringers of life. The two teams represented earth and sky and as no one would dare to cheat the gods, an umpire was unnecessary. No wonder that primitive man believed that sport, if not divine itself, was a gift of the gods. He was firmly convinced that 'to play the game' meant to accelerate the revival of nature and the victory of vegetation. The association of games with religious worship continued from prehistoric times well into the classical period. The Olympic Games were centred on the magnificent temple of Zeus at Olympia and were played in his honour. The Python Games were closely linked with the oracle of Apollo and his shrine at Delphi. It was from those magical roots of primitive faith that our sports mainly grew. With the passing of time and frequent repetition of games, their original purpose was forgotten and people enjoyed the contests for their own sake, discovering in them a source of excitement, amusement and strength. All these pursuits can be called 'natural' sports, as they 'naturally' evolved from early rites, training for warfare and defence against threats of nature, whether of the animate or inanimate kind. Equally prominent in this class are sports now taken up for mere pleasure, which developed out of man's search for sustenance: hunting for food, catching fish, rowing and sailing across rivers and the sea. In the practice of these skills, he acquired as well a liking for them, independent of their primary aim, and pursued them even after their original purpose no longer applied. A means to an end here became an end in itself. And that is how hunting, angling, yachting and shooting became sports. There is no doubt that the present day probing of outer space sooner or later will create a modern twentieth (or twenty-first) century sport, perhaps called cosmonauts. Finally, of course, there are those sports which do not constitute relics of man's previous preoccupation with his fate or which are not the by-products of vital tasks. They were artificially created and from the very beginning designed as sports and nothing else. New technological advance may account for the origin of such sports as car racing and flying. Mostly, the motive was to present a new type of exercise, demanding different skills and a novel kind of recreation when older games could not be played or, for one reason or another, had lost their appeal. In one case, however, ten pin bowling, a new sport was devised simply as a legal subterfuge. And yet, unconsciously, even the latest of sports continues to answer some of the identical needs that had urged our ancestors in the dim past to play games.

Some of the earliest statutes emphasised the power and agility of man. Sporting pictures adorned the walls of Egyptian temples. The Pharaohs and their nobles enjoyed sport, not merely as spectators but as participants. A hieroglyphic inscription lauds Pharaoh Amenophis II as a perfect athlete – 'strong of arm', 'long of stride', 'a skilled charioteer', an efficient oarsman and a powerful archer. Gradually, sport soon became part and parcel of man's social life. Even the Bible, though interested mainly in the spiritual aspect of existence, could not ignore sporting activities altogether. Hebrew Scripture mentions the use of the sling and the bow. Some authorities have even suggested that it contains certain allusions to weightlifting, either as a test of strength or a means to toughen one's muscles (Zechariah XII: 3). Contests and tournaments were known and with them, the selection of champions. The New Testament abounds in references to games and St Paul, especially, aware of how much they belonged to everyday life, makes frequent metaphorical use of them. In the Epistle to the Corinthians, for instance, he recalls the spirit of contest to illustrate the strenuous and glorious issue of the Christian fight. Foot races, boxing and wrestling alike supplied him with memorable phrases to express essential lessons. Paul thus speaks of man's wrestling against the powers of darkness, his fighting the good fight and finishing the race. Describing his mission and the task of the faithful Christian, he could say: 'I do not run aimlessly, I do not box as one beating the air but I pommel my body to subdue it.' A notable passage in the Epistle to the Hebrews compares the vast multitude of men and women who have borne testimony to their faith in God, to the enormous crowd of spectators at a foot race in which the contestant discards all unnecessary encumbrance. He needs patience to go forward perseveringly and to gain the prize conferred by the umpire, who judges all. The terminology of sports has its own story. The word 'game' recalls an Old English and Teutonic term that referred to 'participation' and a 'gathering' for fun. The scoring of points is linked with primitive methods of counting and recording. 'Score' is derived from an Old Norse word for 'notch'. Notches made on a stick served to register the correct number of hits, wins or killings. Score also came to indicate units of 20. In earliest days, dents were cut into pieces of wood to mark every 20, possibly, first of all, when sheep were being counted. Originally, 'umpire' – from the Latin *non par* – described an 'odd' man who was called upon to settle differences. Amateurs (from the Latin *amare*, 'to love') played for the love of the game. Civilisation has been defined as what man does with his leisure time. Its wise use for the practice of sports has had its beneficial effect not only on his physical health and the promotion of numerous skills but on his moral character. All sports, irrespective of their origin, developed in man faculties that have enriched his life manifold. They trained him in endurance, hard work and vigorous self control, gave him stamina and the will to do his best, no matter what. Some of the greatest lessons of life have come out of the world of sport. They have taught man to be undaunted by any challenge. Athletics, from the Greek, embodies the 'prize' (*athlon*) awarded to the winning contestant. Yet, failing to gain it, the true sportsman also knows how to take defeat. He will always be ready to try again and strive to attain what has never before been achieved. Sports, not least, have had their impact on the social ethics of man. Not accidentally do we speak of 'playing the game', it 'not being cricket', to 'abide by the rules of the game' or 'hitting below the belt' and being a 'spoilsport'.[39]

Historical Perspectives on Sports Regulation

David Birley, in his two volumes on the history of British sport, *Sport and the Making of Britain*[40] and *Land of Sport and Glory – Sport and British Society 1887–1910*,[41] believes that the Celts who came to Britain around 1000 BC developed boar hunting as a form of military sport. This could be seen as the birth of hunting as a recognisable sport. Birley also speculates that the Romans brought with them ball games and chariot racing. During the Dark Ages until the Norman Conquest, he provides some scant evidence of other developing sports: swimming, running, archery and horse racing. He also chronicles early prohibition of sport: hunting was limited to the ruling classes and certain areas of land; the Church tried to control the misuse of holy days; for example, in AD 747 the Council of Clofeshoh in the North of England forbade sports and horse racing on Rogation Days (the three preceding days before Ascension Day, itself 40 days after Easter, which should be set aside for prayer).

Below are a number of extracts from *Sport and the Making of Britain*, which chart both the origins and development of recognisable sports and their control and prohibition by the state. Greater state control appeared with the coming of the Normans:

> In Normandy bloodthirsty fights between barons and knights had long been a menace that defied control . . . But the melees and skirmishes that were rife on the continent were held in check by the force of William and his judicious distribution of largesse (clemency).[42]

Restrictions on hunting that had been in force before the Norman Conquest continued, especially amongst the 'lower orders', with only the rabbit and the wolf open to 'hunting for all'. The law has consistently controlled hunting rights on private land up to the modern age. Formal jousting, however, became a common event. With the first meaningful urbanisation occurring towards the end of the twelfth century, new sporting forms developed as sporting activity became not only exclusive to rural life and:

> Shrove Tuesday, the great carnival before Lent, was a special day for schoolboys. In the morning, on receipt of his cock-penny, the master would cancel lessons so that his pupils could match the fighting cocks they had trained for the occasion. This educational custom survived for many years and its passing was bemoaned by traditionalists. Cock fighting itself remained a fashionable and popular diversion, declining in reputation as the squeamish middle classes grew in influence but still an attraction to the raffish, rich and poor alike, in the nineteenth century.
>
> For the medieval students of London and their counterparts in industry the holiday was not over. After lunch they went to play 'the famous game of Ball' (*ad ludum Pilae celebrem*) on a level ground near the city (probably Smithfield). Scholars from every place of learning and workers in the various occupations of the town played their own games of Ball, whilst older men, fathers and rich men from the city on horseback, watched the young men's contests, being young along

---

39 Brasch, R, *How Did Sports Begin?* (1986), Sydney: Angus and Robinson, pp 1–5.
40 Birley, D, *Sport and the Making of Britain* (1993), Manchester: Manchester University Press.
41 Birley, D, *Land of Sport and Glory: Sport and British Society 1887–1910* (1995), Manchester: Manchester University Press.
42 Op. cit., fn 40, Birley (1993), p 16.

with them in their own way, showing a natural excitement at so much action and sharing in the uninhibited pleasures of youth.

We are told no more about these games but they may have included football, which was so prominent in the later history of Shrove Tuesday sport. Annual tussles, village against village with the ball being captured and carried home in triumph or married versus single, with the ball provided by newlyweds, were part of ancient manorial custom. They were tolerated and even encouraged by parish clergy, some of whom provided the ball, as part of the pre-Lenten carnival, a good way of letting off steam. Lords of the manor were often hosts at the celebrations, and later, in more urban communities, Shrove Tuesday football matches were sponsored by the various craft guilds with special reference to the initiation of apprentices.[43]

Control of urban sporting activity began in the thirteenth century:

London needed special attention. In 1285 after years of political dissidence, corruption and violent crime Edward I manoeuvred the civic authorities into a situation where he could impose direct rule on the city. He immediately banned tournaments and swordplay . . . The other main category of prohibitions was that of games *ad pilam manualem, pedalem et baculoream, et cambucam*: handball, football, dub ball and cam buck. This last, also called cammock, may have been, as a contemporary commentator believed, a game in which a small wooden ball was propelled forward with a curved stick or mallet (and thus an ancestor of golf, pall mall and croquet), or, equally likely, an early form of hockey, also known as bandy, shinty, hurling and camogie, games that were played with the bent or knobbed stick from which cammock got its name. From the law enforcement point of view, of course, it did not matter if the categories were overlapping: overlap was better than underlap. Thus *pila baculorea*, club ball or stickball, could also refer to the hockey group of games. Club ball, however, was the term later used to denote the rounders-type game illustrated in early manuscripts and believed by Strutt (but not his later editors) to be the source of cricket.

The two remaining games in the prohibition were to cause the authorities great concern over the years. Football, *pila pedalis*, was banned, as Strutt put it 'not, perhaps from any particular objection to the sport in itself but because it cooperated, with other favourite amusements, to impede the progress of archery'. Handball, *pilamanualis*, no doubt took many forms about which the same could be said. The kind that caused most trouble later, however, was the French game *jeu de paume*, later known as tennis, played in an open quadrangular space, making use of surrounding roofs, buttresses and grilles.[44]

In the late fourteenth century, hunting restrictions increased:

Parliament had been given a fright and clamped down even harder on the peasants. In 1388 hunting laws were introduced which applied not just in the royal forest but throughout the land. Noting that 'artificers and labourers and servants and grooms' were in the habit of keeping 'greyhounds and other dogs' and that 'on holy days, when good Christian people be at Church' they went hunting 'in parks, warrens and coneyries of lords and others, to the very great destruction of the same', the new law forbade, on pain of a year's imprisonment, laymen with holdings worth less than forty shillings and clerics with benefices less than ten pounds a year to keep greyhounds or other hunting dogs or to use 'ferrets, hayes, rees, hare pipes, cords and other engines to take or destroy the deer, hares or coneys'. The legislation also renewed the ban on

---

43 Ibid, pp 20–21.
44 Ibid, pp 35–37.

'importune games' with particular reference to the servant and labourer class, forbidding all ball games whether handball or football, together with quoits, dice and casting the stone.[45]

Henry IV and V regularly renewed Edward III's ban on popular sports, with new Acts in 1401, 1409, 1410 and 1414 and they tried to apply the same disciplinary standards to the upper classes of society as to the lower orders.[46]

During the reign of Henry VIII, with the war against France continuing, prohibitions against sport were made in 1526 in order to boost the war effort:

Two years later with peace restored Wolsey introduced a revised measure which whilst equally draconian was more socially selective. It gave the county commissioners appointed under his 1526 legislation power to enter private houses in search of illicit crossbows and handguns and to enter hostelries, inns and alehouses to 'take and burn' tables, dice, cards, bowls, cloches, tennis balls and other instruments of the devil. Tennis was forbidden only if courts were not properly conducted: similarly bowls was condemned 'because the alleys are in operation in conjunction with saloons or dissolute places' which denied it the status of a true sport.[47]

Animal sports continued to be popular:

The death of Henry VIII left a power vacuum. Then the pendulum swung between the extreme Protestantism of the boy Edward VI (1547–53), who completed his father's asset stripping of the Roman church by dissolving the chantries, and the avenging Catholicism of his equally pious half-sister Mary, who burnt at the stake some 300 enemies of the faith. There was no apparent conflict between religious belief and personal cruelty.

At Christmas 1550 the saintly Edward had publicly rebuked Mary for popish practices like 'conjured bread and water': then after dinner on the feast of the Epiphany he watched a bear baiting with the 17-year-old Princess Elizabeth. When, as Queen, Mary was persuaded by her devious Philip of Spain to visit Elizabeth at her country house at Hatfield she was treated to a bear baiting, with which 'their highnesses were right well content'. And when Elizabeth herself became Queen in 1558 it was natural entertainment she offered to foreign ambassadors would include bear baiting.

The royal family had its own private bear gardens but there were public bear gardens in London of which the most famous was behind the Globe Theatre, Bankside. Because of their cost bears were usually kept alive (it was the dogs that died) but as they grew battle-scarred they could expect no mercy; as a German visitor pointed out: 'to this entertainment there often follows that of whipping a blind bear, which is performed by five or six men, standing in a circle with whips, which they exercise upon him without any mercy'.

Bulls were more readily available and expendable, though if they fought well they too might be retained for further service. They could do a lot of damage with their fearsome horns and the trick was for the bulldog to get in underneath and grab the muzzle, the dewlap or 'the pendant glands'. If it got a hold it clung on and either tore the flesh away and fell or had to be pulled off, with the aid of flour blown up the nostrils to make it let go. This tenacity so inspired the populace that the bulldog became an emblem of the British character. There was a convenient superstition that bulls needed to be baited to improve the taste of beef and in some parts of the country bylaws required this to be done.[48]

---

45 Ibid, p 38.
46 Ibid, p 41.
47 Ibid, pp 56–57.
48 Ibid, pp 62–64.

The masses were excluded from gentleman's sports:

> Tudor licensing laws were much concerned with keeping out 'men of base condition' from fashionable games like tennis and bowls. In 1592 Thomas Bedingfield, seeking permission to keep houses in London and Westminster for dice, cards, tables, bowls and tennis, proposed exemplary rules: no play before noon on weekdays or during hours of religious service on Sundays, no swearing or blaspheming and 'none but noblemen, gentlemen and merchants or such as shall be entered in the Book of Subsidies at £10 in land or goods'.[49]

In the late sixteenth century, common concerns on how the working masses spent their leisure time became prominent:

> Yet it was old religious allegiances that brought sport to the centre of the political stage, requiring the intervention of the King himself. There was a new twist to the old concern about the way the lower orders spent their leisure time. Now that archery practice had ceased to be thought desirable they were supposed to spend it reading the Bible or thinking improving thoughts. Catholic magistrates generally allowed games-playing after divine service but this was thought outrageous and provocative in Puritan circles, which were widening all the time. In Edinburgh games 'sic as gof' had been banned all day on the Sabbath since 1592. On a tombstone at Llanfair Church, South Wales, appeared the warning:
>
> > 'Who ever hear on Sunday, will practice playing at Ball. It may be before Monday, the Devil will *have* you all.'
>
> In 1607 young men of Aberdeen were arraigned for profaning the Sabbath by 'drinking, playing football, dancing and roving from parish to parish'. At Guisborough, Yorkshire, in 1616 a man was charged with 'making a banquet for football players' on a Sunday.
>
> The question for Puritans, as expressed by Stubbes, was whether 'the playing at foot ball, reding of mery bookes and such like delectations' profaned the Sabbath day. They had only one answer. But Puritanism was essentially a middle-class movement. A day of quiet contemplation each week was all very well for those who had leisure on weekdays for more exciting activities but a bit hard on the average man in the fields. Matters came to a head in Lancashire, a county of extremes. Many of the aristocracy and their rustic followers clung obstinately to the old faith but Puritanism was also strong. Sunday sport was an inevitable source of conflict. In 1616 the Manchester justices banned 'piping, dancing, bowling, bear and bull baiting' or any other 'profanation' at any time on the Sabbath and similar restrictions were imposed in surrounding districts.
>
> The following year as James was returning from Scotland a party of Lancashire villagers met him at Myerscough with a petition complaining about the attempt to ban their customary amusements. The King made an impromptu speech promising them protection. They took him at his word and the following Sunday there were complaints from churchgoers in the vicinity that their worship had been disturbed by music, piping, dancing, shouting and laughter outside. The outcome was a declaration drawn up on the King's instructions by the local bishop to be read from pulpits throughout Lancashire. It was a rambling document but it answered the purpose, which was compromise. The King rebuked certain 'Puritans and precise people' for interfering with the people's 'lawful recreations' and ordained that after divine service on Sundays and other holy days piping, dancing, archery, 'leaping and vaulting and other harmless

---

49 Ibid, p 68.

recreations were to be allowed'. Yet he maintained existing legislation which forbade bear and bull baiting and interludes on Sundays and bowling 'for the meaner sort of people' at all times. James was so impressed by the success of his Solomon-like judgment in Lancashire that in 1618 he ordered an expanded version to be read in every pulpit in England and Scotland, adding approval of May games, Whitsun ales, Morris dances and the like 'in due and convenient time' to his bounty. James's Book of Sports, as it came to be known, was a setback for extreme Puritanism. Its arguments, taken at face value, were hard to counter – the people would turn from the church if it allowed them no amusement; they would be 'less able for war'; if denied sport they would spend more time in the alehouse. Most telling of all, when would 'the common people have leave to exercise if not upon Sundays and holy days, seeing they must apply their labour and win their living in all working days?'[50]

In the seventeenth century, a more moderate approach to team sports and games seemed to be supported:

It was 1667 before new laws 'for the better observation of the Lord's Day' were enacted and they were not specifically directed at sport ... Indeed when in 1664 a law was passed against 'deceitful, disorderly and excessive gaming' the preamble declared that, properly used, games were innocent and moderate recreations: it was when they were misused that they promoted idleness and dissolute living and circumventing, deceiving, cozening and debauchery of many of the younger set.[51]

Violence against animals continued to be sport:

Bears, which had higher social status and did not toss dogs about, were in shorter supply. Bulls were therefore the standard fare, not only for baits but for rustic variants such as the traditional bull running at Stamford and the bizarre goings on at Tutford. The lowest level of baiting was of badgers, all that could be afforded in some country districts. The connoisseur's sport was cock fighting. Charles Cotton grew lyrical:

Cocking is a great sport or pastime so full of delight and pleasure that I know not any game ... to be preferred before it and since the Fighting Cock hath gained so great an estimation among the gentry in respect of this noble recreation I shall here propose it before all the other games of which I have afore succinctly dismissed.

Fighting cocks had metal spurs tied to their heels, often of silver, fashioned by expert craftsmen, proud to engrave their name on each pair. Cockspur Street in London took its name from this sophisticated craft. Huge sums were wagered on choice birds by the highest in the land.[52]

Public demonstrations of violence against the criminal classes were very violent and very visible and this was reflected in continued enjoyment of blood sports during the early eighteenth century:

Hanging and whipping were greatly enjoyed as public spectacles and what the literary set saw as cruelty in sport enthusiasts saw as a desirable emblem of virility. Thus cock fighting was proclaimed a valuable way of diverting the English gentry from effeminate dancing, whoring

---

50 Ibid, pp 79–80.
51 Ibid, p 91.
52 Ibid, p 94.

and drinking, 'which are three evils grown almost epidemical', and a more manly occupation than 'to run whooting after a poor, timorous hare'. Its ancient lineage was generally cited in its favour and at least one writer, a Scottish fencing master, cited Aristotle, with salacious intent.[53]

The distinction between the way football and cricket were viewed by the state was clear:

> . . . opposition to football grew, not only for its lack of decorum but for fear of what it bred, idleness, and what it could conceal, subversives. In England, football was sometimes a symbol of resistance to authority or to change . . . In East Anglia, which had its own popular variant, campball, it frequently marked objections to Fenland drainage schemes or enclosures . . . Amidst this turmoil cricket was better suited both to gambling and to the preservation of the social order.[54]

Field sports were going through a period of transition in the mid-eighteenth century, with shooting becoming more popular. Grouse, pheasants and the like began to be protected:

> The notion of game as property fitted well into the modern scheme of things. Thirty-two game laws were enacted in George III's reign and gamekeepers proliferated. Despite this – or perhaps because of it – poaching was rife. When the law made it illegal to buy and sell game both poachers and gamekeepers found it profitable to sell a few brace on the side. Animal predators, as ever, were a serious problem. Farmers' enemies, especially if they were edible like hares and rabbits, were more likely to be snared than shot but for bigger nuisances, like the fox, either shooting or stopping up their earths and digging them out was common.[55]

The preceding extracts show that the state has been involved in regulating sport for centuries.[56] Historically this has revolved around a number of issues. The control of land and the rights to hunting has been a perennial issue dividing clearly on class grounds between the aristocracy, landowners and the masses. The needs of war dictated the legitimacy of many sporting activities until the late Middle Ages. The maintenance of order has been a major concern, both in nationalistic terms, with alarm over foreign influence being attained by certain sports, and in the disorder implicit in many team sports. The spectre of the mob, the uncontrollable rabble, was a constant fear. The dysfunctional effects of gambling on sport have also clearly been an increasing concern.

It is certainly possible to speculate which of the above continue to be current concerns: the debate about fox hunting and the use of land;[57] the influx of 'foreign players' in a number of sports continues;[58] the regulation of sports crowds especially in the context of football hooliganism; restriction on sports gambling; to name just a few.

---

53 Ibid, p 106.
54 Ibid, p 115.
55 Ibid, p 131.
56 For other historical perspectives on sport, particularly of the nineteenth and twentieth centuries, see Holt, R, *Sport and the British: A Modern History* (1989), Oxford: Clarendon; Mangan, J, *Athleticism in the Victorian and Edwardian Public School* (1981), Cambridge: CUP; Mason, T, *Sport in Britain* (1988), London: Faber & Faber; Mason, T (ed), *Sport in Britain: A Social History* (1989), Cambridge: CUP; and Vamplew, W, *Pay up and Play the Game* (1989), Cambridge: CUP. On specific sports, see Vamplew, W, *The Turf: A Social and Economic History of Horse Racing* (1976), London: Frank Cass; Walvin, J, *The People's Game: A Social History of British Football* (1975), London: Allen Lane; Murray, B, *Football: A History of the World Game* (1994), London: Scholar; Taylor, R and Ward, A, *Kicking and Screaming: An Oral History of Football in England* (1995), London: Robson and the BBC television series of same name (1995); Brookes, C, *English Cricket: The Game and Its Players Through the Ages* (1978), London: Frank Cass; *The People's Century: Sporting Fever*, BBC Television (1996); Birley, D, *A Social History of English Cricket* (2000), London: Aurum; and Smith, S, *The Union Game: A Rugby History* (1999), London: BBC Books.
57 See Gardiner, S et al, *Sports Law*, 3rd edn (2006), London: Routledge Cavendish, Chapter 3, pp 122–28.
58 See Chapter 10 in this book, pp 492–6.

The Victorian Age: Origins of Modern Sport

The early years of Queen Victoria's reign began a period of the modernising of sport in a number of ways, including the regulation of blood sports:

Birley, D, *Sport and the Making of Britain*

Cock fighting became illegal in 1849 but it continued nevertheless, especially outside the range of the metropolitan police. In the capital there were two compensatory vogues in the sporting inns. One was ratting. Perhaps the most famous rat pit was that of Jeremy Shaw, an ex-pugilist, where the turnover was between 300 and 700 rats a week, and where handling rats dead and alive was a mark of virility. The dogs pitted against them were often little bigger than the rats: Henry Mayhew, the journalist, described the two-pound wonder, Tiny, who wore a lady's bracelet as a collar and had killed 200 rats. Another London attraction was dog fighting; in some hostelries there were contests every night and for some it was the sole topic of conversation. George Borrow recalled the scorn of a dog fancier when the topic of religion came up: 'Religion, indeed! If it were not for the rascally law my pit would fill better on Sundays than any other time. Who would go to church when they could come to my pit? Religion! Why the parsons themselves come to my pit'.[59]

During the Victorian era sport became increasingly codified and the formal rules of the major British sports were initiated. National governing bodies that exist today in their original or modified form were originated.[60] Team sports became an important part of social life, both in terms of playing and of spectating. The first concerns about spectator hooliganism, particularly in football, were raised. Concern also continued about the propensity of gambling and betting on sport.

Barnes, J, *Sports and the Law in Canada*

In the late eigheenth century, Britain began to change into the urban industrial society that would eventually produce modern organised sport. Before this time, sport bore the badges of 'Merrie Englande': landed society had its field sports, horse racing and cricket; the common people had rural folk games; and both classes patronised prize fights for their attractive combination of gore and gambling. The initial phase of the Industrial Revolution was then accompanied by a campaign against the lower class traditions as Puritanism affected the urban middle class. From the 1780s to the 1840s, state intervention in popular play was usually 'penal and restrictive'. The traditional folk sports were associated with taverns and with seasonal fairs and holidays; typical events included local versions of riotous football, smock races, greasy poles, pugilism and animal baiting. These customary festivities had pagan roots and brought associated problems of disorder, gambling and intemperance but they enjoyed the patronage of rural squires. Their slow decline occurred as public land was lost to enclosure and as authorities responded to the demands of evangelicals and industrial employers. The new morality called for personal salvation, seriousness, domesticity and a disciplined workforce. Such recreation as respectable reformers allowed had to be self-improving and 'rational'. Local magistrates and national legislators moved to ban fairs, street football and lower class cruel sports and sought to promote Sunday observance; employers meanwhile cut the number of holidays. Many traditional forms of play nevertheless survived and popular interest remained to be recaptured by the controlled and standardised sports of a later generation.

---

59 Op. cit., fn 40, Birley (1993), p 208.
60 These include the Amateur Boxing Association in 1880, the Amateur Athletics Association in 1880, the Football Association in 1863, the Rugby Football Union in 1871, the Amateur Swimming Association in 1886, the English Football League in 1888, the Scottish Football League in 1891 and the Rugby League in 1894.

By the 1850s, the stage was set for the Victorian reconstruction of sport. A positive games ethic first developed in the elite public schools, which had recently undergone moral renewal through the supposed influence of Thomas Arnold of Rugby. The reformed schools catered to the new upper middle class by assimilating their sons into the gentlemanly traditions of the aristocracy. Arnold's successors first promoted organised games to discipline boys' spare time and instil the manly virtues of courage, fair play and character but games soon became an end in themselves. The athletic culture then spread because it appealed to those shades of dominant Victorian opinion that saw sports as an effective means of preparing leaders. Educators and 'Sparto-Christians' found a favourable link with the ancient Greeks. Traditionalists and the Tory establishment saw sports as patriotic activities imbued with heroism and chivalry and serving as a training ground for military service and empire building. Social Darwinians and the commercial middle class appreciated the notional 'equality' of sports, where success goes to the healthy, industrious competitor who struggles for the survival of the fittest. The Victorians found the ultimate attraction in sport's capacity to distinguish the social classes and separate the sexes. Sport was useful in class conciliation but aristocratic patronage and the new code of amateurism ensured exclusivity. Medical myths, aesthetics and decency limited womens' exercises to appropriate feminine pursuits. In codifying games, the society pursued goals that were also central to the movement to restructure criminal law: the new sports and the new criminal law both sought to instil character and responsibility and looked to maintain disciplinary controls based on age, class and sex.

Conditions were now right for the growth of approved sports. Legitimate physical recreation emerged as cities provided parks and facilities and as 'muscular Christians', driven by an ideal of public service, began to incorporate lower-class participation. These social missionaries had their greatest conversion when working men adopted the newly codified version of football (soccer). Rule structures and elite governing bodies began to emerge in the 1860s and 1870s: the Football Association in 1863, the Amateur Athletic Club in 1865, boxing's Queensbury Rules in 1867, the Rugby Union in 1871 and the Wimbledon Lawn Tennis Tournament in 1877. Cricket was revitalised as a spectacle during the 1870s by the county championship and the exploits of WG Grace. The new games were suited to urban constraints of time and space and were seen as useful remedies for the problems of 'health, morality and discipline that affected city life'. They also conformed to the Victorian tendency to measure, regulate, structure and improve. Playing and watching were made possible by advances in transportation and by the more regular pattern of work and leisure time in industrial society. General interest in standardised sports was spread through the new system of public education and through communications technology and the popular press. By the 1880s, sports became important forms of mass entertainment. Soccer, in particular, emerged as a commercial spectacle played by professionals and offering a regular schedule of games through the Football League.

British traditions of class, religion and commerce thus found a way to tame and approve popular sports. The final vision of terraces packed with spectators was not exactly what the early reformers had had in mind but sports were now at least incorporated into the moral order: they had shifted from being the crimes of the idle to become well-drilled, respectable recreation that safely preserved class distinctions. The rationalised sports were capable of worldwide diffusion, so that they came to transcend all cultures. The British duly spread their games and in the 1890s an Anglophile French aristocrat revived the Olympics. North America in the nineteenth century offered especially strong possibilities: with their serious, clean, profitable Protestantism, sports seemed American to the core.[61]

61 Barnes, J, *Sports and the Law in Canada* (1996), Toronto: Butterworths, pp 4–7.

The importance of sport in society grew considerably during this period. The concept of 'muscular Christianity' became a powerful cipher of the time: sport could be used as a means of purifying the body by participation in rational recreation. This form of Christian socialism and social engineering was used as a mechanism of social control. A useful comparison can be made between the codification of sport during this period and the attempts that were made to increasingly codify areas of common law into statutory form as a more formal and legalistic form of societal control.

The Contemporary Significance of Sport

Moving to contemporary times, sport is a truly global phenomenon. As a social activity, whether it is in terms of participation as a recreational pastime, competitive playing at amateur levels, the elite and mainly professional level or in terms of spectating, sport assumes immense cultural significance.[62] The process of professionalisation in a number of sports will be considered in Chapter 5.

Sport is going through significant changes: the context within which law has assumed an increasingly important role in regulating sport will be analysed during this book. Sport is very much a part of popular culture and our consumption of it is increasingly mediated through television, radio, newspapers and a myriad of 'new technologies'. In Britain, more sport is shown on television than ever before. Satellite television, primarily in the guise of Rupert Murdoch's Sky TV with numerous dedicated sports channels and, to a lesser extent, the other terrestrial and cable channels, has had an immense impact upon the financial contours of contemporary elite sport. Sport is a major element on both national and local radio. Sport has also become a major part of the circulation battle between national newspapers, and the number of lavish magazines on sport and recreation has multiplied. Sport books are often in the best-sellers list and a number have clear literary merit.[63] The academic study of sport has mushroomed in the last 30 years with many university centres focusing on the scientific, philosophical, sociological, historical and legal study of sport; and there is a huge associated volume of work.

Blake, A, *The Body Language: The Meaning of Modern Sport*

. . . sport is very much part of popular culture. Many people participate in it, either as amateurs or professionals, and many people observe it as spectators inside stadia or by listening to the radio or watching television. At any rate, sport is continuously visible elsewhere in the world. Indeed, as this book will argue, sport is a crucial component of contemporary society, one very important way through which many of us understand our bodies, our minds and the rest of the world. This is true not only because of mass participation and observation: sport saturates the language that surrounds us. Sporting activity is reported in every newspaper; it forms an important part of the wider literary culture of magazines and books. Take the annual American journal of record, the *Britannica Yearbook for 1994*. In the section devoted to reviewing the previous year's events, Sports and Games form by far the longest entry. Forty pages are devoted to reports of events from the world of sport and a further 28 pages give 'the sporting record' of performance statistics (winners, newly broken records, times and distances); both national and global events are covered, from archery through gymnastics and rodeo to wrestling. By contrast,

---

62 For an examination of many of the cultural issues concerning sport see Tomlinson, A (ed), *The Sports Studies Reader: Sport, Culture and Society* (2006), London: Routledge; Cashmore, E (ed), *Sports Culture: An A–Z Guide* (2000), London: Routledge; and *Making Sense of Sport*, 4th edn (2005), London: Routledge.

63 Football books include Hopcraft, A, *The Football Man: People and Passions in Football* (1968), London: Penguin; Davies, H, *The Glory Game* (1972), London: Weidenfeld & Nicolson; Davies, P, *All Played Out – The Full Story of Italia '90* (1990), London: Mandarin; Hornby, N, *Fever Pitch* (1992), London: Indigo; Hamilton, I, *Gazza Agonistes* (1993), London: Granta; Winner, D, *Brilliant Orange: The Neurotic Genius of Dutch Football* (2000), London: Bloomsbury. A cricket masterpiece is James, CR, *Beyond a Boundary* (1996), London: Serpent's Tail. On boxing see Remnick, D, *The King of the World* (2000), London: Picador; and Michell, K, *War Baby* (2001), London: Random House.

there are only 20 pages on economic affairs and coverage of the arts is far thinner, with only four pages each on dance, music (covering both classical and popular) and publishing.

Sport is also perpetually audible and visible through the electronic media. Television and radio devote a great deal of time to sport. There are whole departments of most networks devoted to sport as current affairs, providing everything from the brief reporting of results on news programmes to the saturation coverage of events like the Olympics, World Cups and national championships in team sports on both mainstream and dedicated programmes and channels. Sport is arguably one of the most powerful presences within broadcasting. Both on television and radio, the principle of live coverage is often taken to mean that sporting events have priority over others. As well as driving other programming from the screen at certain times of the year, sport can instantly reshape television in a way which can only be matched by political crises or disasters involving loss of life. Unexpectedly rearranged fixtures or, more routinely, late finishing matches, disrupt published broadcast schedules, to the distress of people who do not wish to stay up late or people who have programmed their video recorders to record scheduled programmes. This prioritised saturation coverage means that even those uninterested in sport, or hostile to it, cannot escape its nagging presence, as an ongoing part of the 'background noise' of contemporary culture.[64]

Another perspective on the cultural significance of sport presents a theory of the relationship between sport and culture in the context of power relations:

Hargreaves, J, *Sport, Power and Culture*

When we refer to culture in the substantive sense, then, we mean first those activities, institutions and processes that are more implicated in the systematic production and reproduction of systems of meaning and/or those not concerned mainly or immediately with economic or political processes but which instead encompass other kinds of vital activities. We are referring here to major institutions, such as religion, education, science, the arts, the media of communication, the family, leisure and recreation, as well as sports – and, in fact, to much of the routine practice of everyday life. Secondly we find it useful to employ the ethnographer's substantive sense of culture as a 'whole way of life' of a particular group of people. Culture here refers to the way different threads of similarly placed individuals' lives – work, leisure, family, religion, community, etc. are woven into a fabric or tradition, consisting of customs, ways of seeing, beliefs, attitudes, values, standards, styles, ritual practices, etc. giving them a definite character and identity. It is thus we speak here of working-class culture, men's and women's culture, black culture, bourgeois culture and youth culture. Cultures in this sense are profound sources of power, reproducing social divisions here, challenging and rebelling against them there, while in many ways accommodating subordinate groups to the social order. We will be at pains to develop the theme throughout this study that the function and significance of sports varies with the type of culture in question and even does so within cultures. We will be arguing that it is precisely because sport plays different roles in relation to different cultures that it is able to reproduce power relations.

We contend that, in addition, the linkages between sport and power cannot be elucidated without reference to two other forms of culture – popular culture and consumer culture. As the term implies, popular culture engages 'the people' and although, therefore, it is not the product or possession of any one specific group, popular culture does overlap to a perplexing degree with working-class culture and the culture of subordinate groups as a whole. While expressing in its content and idiom the experience of those whom it engages, like its political counterpart

64 Blake, A, *The Body Language: The Meaning of Modern Sport* (1996), London: Lawrence & Wishart, pp 11–12.

'populism', it does so ambivalently, facing simultaneously in a radical and in a conservative direction – for popular culture as we know expresses a certain critical penetration of the power structure, while also manifesting a complicity in it. The long historical association between sports and popular culture, culminating in sport becoming a major component of the national popular culture is, we argue, highly significant for the character of sport. Accordingly, one of our major themes will be the ambivalent relation between sport and power, exemplified best perhaps, in that mixture of respectable family entertainment, violence, rebellion and chauvinism that characterises modern day professional football.

Consumer culture, by which we mean the way of life associated with and reproduced through the operations of consumer capitalism, clearly in many ways also overlaps with working-class and popular culture, to the extent that many aspects of the latter, notably sports, seem to have been in effect appropriated by consumer culture. We will be exploring the significance of the increasing tendency of sport to become one more commodity and attempting to specify the extent to which sporting activity, as an aspect of working-class and of popular culture, remains autonomous. In particular we are rather sceptical of the notion that sport has been absorbed into a manipulated form of culture supposedly exercising a uniformly conservative influence over 'the masses'; and we will be attempting to pinpoint ways in which, as far as commodified sport is concerned, it also exhibits an ambivalent tendency to, on the one hand, accommodate subordinate groups and on the other hand, to stimulate resistance and rebellion in certain ways.[65]

Sociology of Sport

The role of sport in society needs explanation. Traditional sociological theories develop competing perspectives:

Coakley, J, *Sport in Society: Issues and Controversies*

Sociology provides a number of theoretical frameworks that can be used to understand the relationship between sport and society and each takes us in a different direction . . . we focused on four of those frameworks: functionalism, conflict theory, critical theory and symbolic inter-actionism. The purpose of this chapter was to show that each framework has something to offer, helping us understand sport as a social phenomenon. For example functionalist theory offers an explanation for positive consequences associated with sport involvement in the lives of both athletes and spectators. Conflict theory identifies serious problems in sports and offers explanations of how and why players and spectators are oppressed and exploited for economic purposes. Critical theory suggests that sports are connected with social relations in complex and diverse ways and that sports change as power and resources shift and as there are changes in social, political and economic relations in society. Social interactionism suggests that an understanding of sport requires an understanding of the meanings, identities and interaction associated with sport involvement.

It is also useful to realise that each theoretical perspective has its own weaknesses. Functionalist theory leads to exaggerated accounts of the positive consequences of sports and sport participation; it mistakenly assumes that there are no conflicts of interests between groups within society; and it ignores powerful historical and economic factors that have influenced social events and social relationships. Conflict theory is deterministic, it overemphasises the importance of economic factors in society and it focuses most of its attention on top-level

---

65 Hargreaves, J, *Sport, Power and Culture: A Social and Historical Analysis of Popular Sports in Britain* (1986), Cambridge: Polity, pp 9–10.

spectator sports, which make up only a part of sport in any society. Critical theory provides no explicit guidelines for determining when sports are sources of opposition to the interests of powerful groups within society and it is only beginning to generate research on the everyday experiences of people involved in struggles to define and organise sport in particular ways. Symbolic interactionism does a poor job relating what goes on in sports with general patterns of social inequality in society as a whole and it generally ignores the body and physical experiences when it considers the self and issues of identity . . . Which theory or theoretical framework will lead us to the truth about sports?[66]

Coakley identifies the main theoretical perspectives as functionalism,[67] conflict theory,[68] critical theory[69] and symbolic interactionism.[70] There is not enough space to discuss any of these in detail. They all have some validity in understanding sport as a social phenomenon, and particular theoretical perspectives are used as the basis of research methodology for individual researchers' own projects within this discipline.[71]

Figurational theory

Legal positivism is the dominant ideology in Western jurisprudence. This perceives law as being autonomous and separate from political values. This could easily be located within a functionalist theoretical perspective. One applied theoretical position within a functionalist paradigm, which has been massively influential on the British sociology of sport movement, is that of 'Figuration', as espoused by Norbert Elias and developed by Eric Dunning.[72] Elias argues that British society since the late Middle Ages has become increasingly codified, with rules and norms gradually being introduced to govern human activity. This process can be identified with the codification process of sport in the Victorian era.

Blake, A, *The Body Language: The Meaning of Modern Sport*

Since the 1950s the so-called 'figurative sociology', the work of Norbert Elias and his followers, has become influential. Elias has always been interested in sports and his theories have always been applied to sports as much as to other aspects of society. The argument involves a particular interpretation of history. Here is the outline of the argument. Elias and friends argue that since the Middle Ages, western society has become more 'civilised', by which they mean better behaved, more temperate and less violent. Medieval sport was a violent part of a violent society: aristocratic tournaments, wild boar hunting and quarterstaff fighting could all involve the serious injury, even death, of the participants. They claim that new forms of public discipline, which were first practised at medieval courts, spread down the social scale. First the ruling elite became less military and more political and learned. In Britain, castles were gradually replaced by magnificent, but indefensible, country houses, as the ruling classes gave up the

---

66 Ibid, Coakley, fn 7 (1994), pp 49–50.
67 See Uschen, G, 'The interdependence of sport and culture', in Loy, J et al (eds), *Sport, Culture and Society* (1981), Philadelphia: Lea and Febiger; Wohl, A, 'Sport and social development' (1979) 14(3) IRSS 5–18.
68 See Hammond, D, *Foul Play: A Class Analysis of Sport* (1993), London: Ubique.
69 See op. cit., fn 65, Hargreaves (1986); Messner, M, *Power at Play: Sports and the Problem of Masculinity* (1992), Boston: Beacon; Donnelly, P (ed), 'British cultural studies and sport' (1992) 9(2) Special Issue of Sociology of Sport Journal.
70 Coakley, J and White, A, 'Making decisions: gender and sport participation amongst British adolescents' (1992) 9(1) Sociology of Sport Journal 20.
71 For both general reading and explanation of both general and specific theories see Hargreaves (1986); Jarvie, G and Maguire, J, *Sport and Leisure in Social Thought* (1994), London: Routledge, p 179; op. cit., fn 3, Cashmore (2005).
72 See Elias, N, *The Civilising Process* (1939), Oxford: Blackwell; and Dunning, E, *Sport Matters: Sociological Studies of Sport, Violence and Civilisation* (1999), London: Routledge.

civil wars and rebellions which had been routine in high politics before their apex, the seventeenth-century civil war. After this point, disagreements amongst gentlemen increasingly tended to take the form of parliamentary debate. At the same time, the gentlemanly elite began to set up the first nationally organised sports, cricket and horse racing. Then the middle classes sought to emulate the aristocracy and gentry, by gaining a classical education; sure enough the school system expanded massively during the nineteenth century and sure enough the universities set up the next wave of nationally organised sports, the newly rationalised games such as soccer and rugby. The values expressed in the ways that these games were taught and played – values such as public restraint and fair play within the rules – then spread to those who took up the team sports with such enthusiasm, the skilled working class . . . Sport is an example of the 'civilising process' in two ways. As well as providing a very necessary public arena for the display of public emotions, it displays, or demonstrates, the containing and disciplining of public violence. However violent they appear, Elias and followers argue, the new team sports show how high the threshold of public toleration of resistance has risen since the time of the Roman gladiatorial arena or the medieval tournament, in which people quite routinely killed others in front of cheering crowds.[73]

Elias presents a historical view of sport having increasingly become codified, regulated and a part of civil society. This presents a very specific view of history and one that can be contended. As Blake argues:

Elias and company offer a vision of 'progress' that is deeply Eurocentric, elitist (claiming that change spreads from the top of the social scale downwards) and masculinised. Many people would argue that the replacement of public confrontation and uprising by parliamentary discourse has merely disempowered people. In other words, by following rules, which conveniently protected the lives and property of an elite, we have gravely damaged the potential for radical social change.[74]

Elias uses the term 'sportisation' to refer to a process in the course of which the framework of rules applying to sport becomes stricter, including those rules attempting to provide for fairness and equal chances to win for all. The rules become more precise and explicitly differentiated, and the supervision of rule-observance becomes more efficient. In the course of the same process, self-control and self-discipline reach a new level, while in the games contests themselves a balance is established between the possibility of attaining a high level of 'combat-tension' and reasonable protection against injury. Rules are therefore a development to attain competition – seen, of course, as an integral part of sport.

Critical analysis

Figurational theory is therefore useful to apply to the contemporary regulation of sport. The increasing presence of 'regulatory law' could be argued as being a continuation of the codifying and 'civilising process'.[75] Sport has clearly become more rule-bound and is now augmented (and indeed challenged) by the rules of law. Conversely, can the law's involvement oppose the claim of increased civilisation of sport as supported by figurational theory, especially in areas such as sports violence and drug abuse, which can in fact be best explained by conflict or critical theories

---

73 Op. cit., fn 64, Blake (1996), pp 48–49.
74 Ibid, pp 49–50.
75 See Agozino, B, 'Football and the civilizing process: penal discourse and the ethic of collective responsibility in sports law', (1996) 24 International Journal of the Sociology of Law 163–88.

supporting law being used as a mechanism of control? These competing theoretical models will help underpin a theoretical model of sports law developed in Chapter 2.

These alternative sociological theoretical perspectives listed above are applied to the study of the sociology of law as they are to the sociology of sport. This book explicitly assumes a view of the law as a political instrument. Law is not value free; it is not democratic in terms of its construction. Law reflects the dynamic of power relations in society and changes as social, political and economic relations shift. Law is not a neutral mechanism, separate from societal values.

The use of law in regulating sport needs therefore to be understood in the context and recognition of its being used in a contingent and ideological way. Critical theory in sports sociology is probably the theoretical perspective, which is the most plausible in the subsequent theoretical explanation of law's intervention in sport. The concept of 'hegemony', largely introduced by the Italian Marxist, Antonio Gramsci,[76] and developed in the sport context by John Hargreaves, is central to this theoretical view.[77] What it characterises 'is the achievement of consent or agreement' to dominant ideologies in society, those determined by the groups who hold social, economic and political power and promoted as being in the interests of the whole of society. Sport, as an immensely powerful cultural institution, is seen as helping to carry out this process.

Feminist and race theories of sport

Men have historically monopolised sports participation in all capacities. In recent years, however, the involvement of women has increased despite many forms of resistance. Coakley recognises feminist theories as a form of critical theory which are becoming more important in the study of sport:

Coakley, J, *Sport in Society: Issues and Controversies*

Feminists describe sports as 'gendered' activities. The fact that organised sports were developed to emphasise competition, efficiency and performance ranking systems and to devalue supportiveness and caring contributes to the 'gendered' character. To say that sports are 'engendered' activities and to say that sports organisations are 'gendered' structures means that they have been socially constructed out of the values and experiences of men.[78]

Jarvie, G and Maguire, J, *Sport and Leisure in Social Thought*

It might be suggested that some or all of the following concerns have been central to many feminist accounts of sport and leisure: (a) to consider the structures which have historically exploited, devalued and often oppressed women; (b) to consider various strategies which are committed to changing the condition of women; (c) to adopt a critical perspective towards intellectual traditions and methods which have ignored or justified women's oppression; (d) to explain women's involvement in and alienation from different sport and leisure contexts and practices; and (e) to highlight the engendered nature of sport and leisure organisation, bureaucracies and hierarchies.[79]

Although there are many varieties of feminist methodology – liberal, radical, black and postmodern – the focus has been on why women are devalued in sport.[80] Areas of inquiry include levels of

---

76 Gramsci, A, *The Prison Notebooks* (1971), London: Lawrence & Wishart.
77 See earlier, pp 8–9.
78 Op. cit., fn 7, Coakley (1994), p 38.
79 Op. cit., fn 71, Jarvie and Maguire (1994), p 179.
80 See a good discussion in Scraton, S and Flintoff, A, *Gender and Sport Reader* (2001), London: Routledge.

participation in sport; legitimate use of the female body; barriers to participation and consumption; and biological myths surrounding performance.[81] The law has provided some provision for challenging gender discrimination in sport and this will be considered in Chapter 10, looking at issues such as the right of women to be professional boxers and the right of pregnant women to participate in elite competitive sport.

Similarly concerning issues of sports and race, the work of a number of theorists, notably Hylton,[82] has made calls for a sports-specific version of Critical Race Theory (CRT) to emerge from the sports and leisure studies movement. Hylton views CRT 'as a framework from which to explore and examine the racism in society that privileges whiteness as it disadvantages others because of their blackness.'[83] In the context of the law's role in engaging with racism in sport, these theoretical positions support challenges to dominant ideas about, for example, the fetishism with criminal law intervention and consequential punishment as the formal response to spectator racism.[84]

Framework of Sport in Britain

Until the Second World War, other than acts of prohibition of some sporting activity, there was virtually no direct state involvement in the framework and organisation of sport. All that existed were a number of private federations for particular sports, tracing their origins from the end of the nineteenth century. These organisations were, on the whole, controlled by establishment figures with close connections to the politically powerful. One significant development was the creation of what is now the Sport and Recreation Alliance (SRA), formerly the Central Council of Physical Recreation (CCPR) in 1935: this was initiated as a non-governmental voluntary organisation, an 'umbrella body' of sporting organisations funded from private sources.

In 1957 the CCPR appointed a committee to report on 'the future of sporting administration in promoting the general welfare of the community'. The subsequent Wolfenden Report in 1960 concluded with 57 paragraphs of recommendations. It indirectly led to other key developments in the state intervention of sport: the appointment of a Minister of Sport in 1962 and the birth of the Sports Council in 1966. Today the Sport and Recreation Alliance and the multiple Sports Councils are the main organisations enforcing sports policy in Britain.[85] They operate alongside the Department for Culture, Media and Sport (DCMS), the government department which has primary responsibility for sports policy and distributes central funding to the Sports Councils.

Three main approaches concerning state involvement in sport can be identified in the UK, namely direct intervention, indirect intervention and persuasion

Direct state intervention

There are many examples of direct intervention by means of legislation and/or other regulatory mechanisms. These areas will be explored in subsequent chapters. They include the issues of public safety and order at sports events. Direct state (albeit delayed) intervention in British sport was made in response to a number of stadium disasters (almost all concerning football) that occurred during the last 65 years. There were official reports after the 1946 disaster at Bolton (33 deaths), the 1972

---

81 See Tomlinson, A (ed), *Gender, Sport and Leisure* (1995), Brighton: University of Brighton; Hargreaves, J, *Sporting Females: Critical Issues in the History and Sociology of Women's Sport* (1994), London: Routledge; Humberstone, B (ed), *Researching Women and Sport* (1997), London: Macmillan.

82 Hylton, K, *'Race' and Sport: Critical Race Theory* (2009) Abingdon: Routledge.

83 Ibid, p 22.

84 See later Chapter 12, pp 580–9, also see Gardiner, S and Welch, R, 'Bosman – There and Back Again: the Legitimay of Playing Quotas under European Union Sports Policy', (2011) 17(6) *European Law* 828–49.

85 See Hargreaves, J, *Sport, Power and Culture* (1986), London: Polity, for an analysis of the operation of these bodies and state intervention in general.

disaster at Ibrox in Glasgow (66 deaths), the Bradford fire in 1985 (55 deaths), and most notably the 1989 Taylor Report on the Hillsborough disaster where 96 died. It was not until this last report that the British Government positively acted to legislate for sports stadium safety.[86] Legislation concerning engagement with football hooliganism is another example.[87] Additionally restrictions on tobacco advertising and sponsorship in sport[88] and provisions requiring certain sports events to be shown on 'free-to-air' television are examples.[89]

In the context of the London 2012 Olympics, the passing of the London Olympic Games and Paralympics Games Act 2006 is a clear example of legislative intervention which has set up the necessary infrastructure required for the hosting of this major sports event.[90]

Indirect state intervention

This occurs through various mechanisms and organisations.

The Sports Councils

The concept of the 'Sports Council' has gone through a number of changes since its inception in 1966. In contrast to the SRA, they are publicly funded official advisory bodies to the government. In 1972, the structure was muddied by the creation of the Great Britain Sports Council and three additional Councils for the other parts of the United Kingdom (Scotland, Wales and Northern Ireland) with extended powers. At the end of 1996, The Great Britain Sports Council was divided into the UK Sports Council (now 'UK Sport') and the English Sports Council (now 'Sport England'), with the three other home country Sports Councils continuing unchanged (Sport Northern Ireland, Sport Wales and Sport Scotland). They are all national, non-departmental public bodies (sometimes known as quangos), which receive funding from, and are accountable to, the Department of Culture, Media and Sport. UK Sport, Sport England and Sport Wales are all distributing bodies for the purposes of the National Lottery Distribution Fund.[91] There is a Secretary of State for this Department and a Parliamentary Under-Secretary of State, known as the Minister for Sport. The House of Commons scrutinises the work of UK Sport and Sport England via the relevant Select Committee and Public Accounts Committee.

UK Sport

UK sport (formerly the UK Sports Council) has a small staff and acts as a co-ordinating body for the four home country Sports Councils (England, Northern Ireland, Scotland and Wales).[92] It deals with areas of common interest at UK level. These include:

Performance

UK Sport is the strategic lead body for high-performance sport in the UK. It invests Exchequer and National Lottery funds in Britain's best Olympic and Paralympic sports and athletes to maximise their chances of success on the world stage. For London and beyond, a third stream of private sector funding – Team 2012 – complements this public investment.

Using a 'No Compromise' philosophy which targets investment at those most likely to deliver medals at Olympic and Paralympic level, UK Sport works with each sport to provide the

---

86 See Chapter 12 for a fuller discussion.
87 See Chapter 12, pp 574–9.
88 See Chapter 5, pp 219–20.
89 See Chapter 5 for a fuller discussion.
90 See Chapter 7 for a fuller discussion.
91 See the National Lottery etc Act 1993 s 23(2).
92 See *Sport and Legislation in the UK* (1996), 2nd edn, London: UK Sports Council.

best possible support for athletes, providing everything they need from world-class coaches to cutting edge research and innovation, talent identification and Performance Lifestyle support.

Major Events

UK Sport co-ordinates the bidding and staging of major international sporting events in the UK. Working in partnership with national governing bodies, cities and regions and home country agencies, over 120 events of World and European status have been supported through the World Class Events Programme since 1997.

Around £16 million will be invested in the 09–12 programme which has been specifically developed to help prepare the UK for hosting the Olympic and Paralympic Games in 2012. This programme will not only provide British athletes with valuable experience of competing on home soil ahead of London 2012, but will also help build up a network of suitably qualified volunteers and technical officials.

International

UK Sport's Mission

UK Sport works in partnership to lead sport in the UK to world-class success. UK Sport works with National Governing Bodies and other partner organisations to help them build positive working relationships with International Federations and other international bodies. This helps ensure Britain has a voice on the world stage by assisting with the appointment of individuals into key roles at such organisations.[93]

Sport England

As with the other Sports Councils from the home countries, in recent years the emphasis has increasingly been on the grass roots development of sport.

Sport England – 'What we do'

Sport England is the government agency responsible for building the foundations of sporting success, by creating a world-leading community sport system of clubs, coaches, facilities and volunteers. We want to create a vibrant sporting culture working in partnership with national governing bodies, our national partners, the HE/FE sector, local government and community organisations. Our focus is around three outcomes – growing and sustaining the numbers of people taking part in sport and improving talent development to help more people excel.[94]

The work of Sport England includes the promotion of women in sport, sport for people with disabilities and sustainable sport in the countryside. UK Sport is now the main focus for elite sport and the promotion of excellence. Since the mid-1990s, there has been a shift towards promoting excellence in sport, with the government indicating a more proactive role in sport.[95] The Coalition Government has indicated that it intends to combine UK Sport and Sport England after London 2012.[96]

93 See www.uksport.gov.uk.
94 See www.sportengland.org
95 See the latest policy position in *A Sporting Future for All* (2001), London: HMSO; Sporting Britain (2004) DCMS, www.culture.gov.uk.
96 'Government to merge work of UK Sport and Sport England', BBC Sport, 26 July 2010, http://news.bbc.co.uk/sport1/hi/front _page/8855543.stm.

The Sports and Recreation Alliance

The SRA, as the representative body of many British sports governing bodies, identifies its modern role as being:

The Sports and Recreation Alliance – What do we do?

(1) the umbrella organisation for the National Governing and Representative Bodies of sport and recreation in the UK;

(2) speaks and acts to promote, protect and develop the interests of sport and physical recreation at all levels;

(3) at the forefront of sports politics, providing support and services to those who participate in and administer sport and recreation;

(4) completely independent of any form of government control;

(5) having no responsibility for allocating funds;

(6) strictly non-party and will support or oppose proposed measures only on the basis of their perceived value to sport and recreation. [97]

There are a number of other bodies that are worthy of mention. A British Sports Forum has been in existence since the early 1990s. There are organisations such as Sports Coach UK (formerly the National Coaching Foundation), which provides educational and advisory services for coaches in all sports. In addition to the many sports organisations under the umbrella of the SRA, there is the British Olympic Association, founded in 1905, which is the National Olympic Committee for Britain.

Sport and social inclusion

The Labour Government which came into power in 1997 with a declared policy aim to encourage the involvement of those individuals whose participation in mainstream society had been restricted. Such groups included women, the elderly, those from lower socio-economic categories such as the long-term unemployed, and those from certain ethnic minorities. A Social Exclusion Unit located at the Cabinet Office was created. Sport has been identified as a social activity that can be used to help fight social exclusion.[98] Claims have been made that sport can help 'to tackle the issues around social exclusion' and that it can also help 'cut crime [and] improve health, education and employment prospects in deprived communities through teamwork, discipline, responsibility and creative expression'.[99]

Many initiatives are taking place. The increasing social policy claims made for sport are reflected in the rhetoric of the European Commission:

European Commission, *The Development and Prospects for Community Action in the Field of Sport*

Sport is unique in that it performs five functions:

(1) An education function: active participation in sport is an excellent way of ensuring balanced personal development for all age groups;

(2) A public health function: physical activity offers an opportunity to improve people's health; it is an effective means of combating certain illnesses such as heart disease and cancer and helps to maintain good health and quality of life among the elderly;

---

97 www.sportandrecreation.org.uk
98 See Collins, M, *Sport and Social Exclusion* (2001), London: Routledge.
99 Department of Culture Media and Sport 'A Sporting Future for All' (2000), London: DCMS.

(3) A social function: sport is a suitable tool for promoting a more inclusive society and for combating intolerance, racism, violence, and alcohol and drug abuse; sport can also assist in the integration of people excluded from the labour market;

(4) A cultural function: sport gives people an additional opportunity to put down roots, to get to know an area better, to integrate better and to protect the environment to a greater degree;

(5) A recreational function: sporting activity is an important leisure occupation and provides personal and collective entertainment. Employed in the correct way, sport is therefore a particularly effective weapon in the fight against intolerance, racism, violence, and alcohol and narcotics abuse. It is therefore particularly affected by the development of voluntary work as an expression of social solidarity.[100]

Claims are frequently made for sport as an effective tool for fighting crime and juvenile delinquency. This is, however, a contested issue: some argue that sport can positively influence and decrease anti-social acts; others argue that sports' impact upon social behaviour is far more limited.

McVicar, J, 'Violence in Britain: this sporting life of crime'

Despite this upsurge of concern about violence in sport, playing these games continues to be seen as character building; an assumption reinforced by John Major's recent governmental commitment to promoting excellence in sport. Doubtless he wants to incorporate it in his English vision of village greens and early morning mists. Yet one of the most glaring links between sport and violence is the way so many in organised crime began as useful sportsmen and continue to show an avid interest in sport throughout their criminal career.

This connection receives scant attention from social scientists, lawyers, sports administrators or government officials; yet go into any prison gymnasium and who is in the thick of the action? Not rapists – except Mike Tyson – but robbers, gangsters and others who figure in the criminal pecking order. Similar observations can be made at any big fight or in the stands at Highbury where north London's leading criminal family and their favoured hit man can be seen cheering on Arsenal. I was reminded of all this by two recent books by our great men of crime. In *Memoirs of a Life of Crime*, Mad Frankie Fraser talks about his lifelong obsession with boxing and football (he played park football into his 50s). Now in his mid 70s, Frank is a regular at Highbury and is ringside at all the big fights. And this love and involvement in sport is virtually the norm among heavy-duty professional criminals. Take the latest piece of – forgive me for mentioning the name – Kray memorabilia, *The Krays' Lieutenant* by Albert Donaghue. In this, one of the twins' old henchmen talks about Ronnie and Reggie being like 'two hunting dogs' as they sniffed out victims for their brainless mayhem; but their taste and capacity for violence had been honed during their long careers as amateur and professional boxers.

Obviously, an apprenticeship in sport is neither sufficient nor necessary for graduating into organised crime. But, given other factors, a solid grounding in sport can and often does make crime an attractive proposition. What factors? Well, first, this relationship applies almost solely to males: organised crime, like physical sport, is virtually a male preserve. Secondly sport and crime tend to coalesce only at the bottom of society. Sportsmen from higher up the social scale often develop for example, through playing rugby – a hyper-masculine identity but other circumstantial factors, such as family background, education and their social networks, militate against this being conducive to a life of crime. Finally, the sporting apprenticeship should not be too successful, as that is likely to catapult the athlete into a sporting career, diverting him from the temptations of crime. If Ronnie and Reggie Kray had been champion

---

100 Commission Staff Working Paper, *The Development and Prospects for Community Action in the Field of Sport* (1998).

boxers, they would almost certainly not have become murderers, nor, as a consequence, spent most of their lives in prison.

What is it about physical sports, though, that helps equip the young plebeian male for a life of crime? What qualities does it impart that make him better at crime and more likely to choose it as a career? (Incidentally, career criminals are nothing to do with the stage army of petty criminals who clog the courts and overcrowd the prisons. These inadequates invariably have disturbed upbringings that render them incapable of playing anything organised or disciplined; they are neither good at sport nor crime.) Contact sports, which are premised on mock war or combat, are not solely about orchestrating warrior virtues but the latter are clearly by-products of boxing, rugby, football and so on. Even if some don't teach a youngster how to look after himself, they all increase his strength and speed, his physical prowess. Males from the lowest level of society, though, find such qualities far more useful than their more socially privileged peers because violence, and its threat, figures far more in the regulation of their social life than it does on other social levels. Violent skills, even familiarity with violence, fitness, strength and so on, are also functional in the commission of crime. They confer, as it were, occupational advantages on the career criminal. Moreover, a capacity or potential for violence is also important in regulating relationships between criminals. Career criminals are enmeshed in a network of criminal relationships, the integrity of which rests upon their nature and content being hidden from the police. Thus all enduring criminal groups develop a prohibition against cooperating with law enforcement officials and others, such as journalists, who would be likely to pass on information to the police. This is the cornerstone of the criminal way of life.[101]

Robins, D, 'Sport and crime prevention: the evidence of research'

The idea that engaging in sports and outdoor activities has a morally redemptive quality was very popular with Victorian social reformers. Bold claims are sometimes made today. But how effective are sports and outdoor pursuits in crime prevention?

Mistaken assumptions

The assumption that participation in sport, or the provision of sports facilities affects levels of delinquency, is made in the absence of any supporting evidence. Coalter (1987), in his review of the literature on the subject commissioned by the Scottish Sports Council felt 'unable to conclude a correlation between high level of sports participation/low level of delinquency holds good in the UK'. Mason and Wilson alluded to the myriad of variables that have to be taken into account before the relation between sport and delinquency can be ascertained. My own (1990) study concluded that there is no sound theoretical basis for the use of sport and outdoor adventure activities to combat or prevent juvenile crime.

The view that participation in sport has little effect is shared by many of those who work professionally with offenders. Many are deeply sceptical of sport as prevention. But the power of the sports lobby is strong. Not for the first time, the findings of the researchers and the experiences of the practitioners are at odds with the decisions of the policy makers.

Sport as prevention

The use of sports, games and rigorous PE sessions are just as much the core feature of today's young offender institutions as they were of the borstals. The use of outdoor adventure in treatment programmes for youth at risk is also commonplace. Considerable amounts of public

---

101 McVicar, J, 'Violence in Britain: this sporting life of crime' *The Guardian*, 19 September 1995, p 6.

funds and private charitable donations are deployed in this direction. When asked to propose solutions for young offenders who for the most part are destined to spend their lives trying to survive in the jungles of the cities, politicians of all political persuasions will evoke windswept rock faces and speak of Challenges Overcome and Lessons Learnt. Even Britain's leading expert on young offenders, Professor David Farrington of Cambridge University, has invoked the supporting, and discredited, safety valve theory expounded by the Victorians by suggesting that 'if offending is linked to boredom, excitement seeking and impulsiveness then it might be reduced by some kinds of community or recreational programmes that provide socially approved opportunities for excitement and risk-taking'. For your average tearaway a socially approved 'buzz' is a contradiction in terms. This sort of thinking also implies that the best way to handle hyped up, manic and self-destructive kids, is to give them more and better opportunities to 'act out'.

The belief in 'sport as prevention' also occurs in community development capital programmes aimed at improving sport and recreational facilities in deprived areas. This approach aims to reduce delinquency rates by encouraging a positive use of leisure time. There is of course nothing objectionable about greater investment in sport and recreational provision in these areas. But it cannot be stressed enough that there is no evidence of concomitant reductions in juvenile crime following such developments. On the contrary, gleaming sports centres have become the foci for young people's negative projections and the targets for violent attacks.

In October 1990 the French high rise suburb of Vaulx en Velins was engulfed in a week of bloody clashes between police and local youths, during which new community facilities were set on fire and destroyed. Immediately before the disturbances a brand new sports centre, including a gymnasium and a swimming pool, had been opened in a euphoric mood of self-congratulation. A climbing wall inaugurated a few days earlier had been seen as the culmination of a successful programme based on the idea of providing constructive sports pursuits for people with time on their hands. At the height of the disturbances, several hundred riot police had to be deployed to protect the sports centre.

Some new treatment programmes attempt to blend the joys of sport and outdoor adventure with group confrontation therapy techniques. Sending 'bad boys' up mountains to find themselves, confronting childhood trauma with more trauma in group therapy: these are the alternatives to the customary verbal beating by the magistrate followed by the custodial sentence. I have found that advocates of such programmes are often propelled by a sort of aggressive optimism which acts as a defence against the hopelessness felt when confronting the destructive nihilism of criminalised youth. (Of course this is preferable to the attitude adopted by the present Home Secretary, Mr Michael Howard. He appears to be driven purely by a need to punish children.)

Policy makers and criminal justice professionals need to be reminded of the essential futility of sports and outdoor pursuits, the fact that they make no direct contribution to the wealth of the community, or to a fairer society. At the risk of sounding old fashioned, to privilege such programmes is to denigrate more cerebral activities. Intellectual qualities – a sceptical, questioning attitude towards authority and convention, broadening horizons, acquiring a more educated view of society – are not required. The old socialist belief in the educational, and intellectual, advance of working-class youth has been abandoned.

There is no evidence that participation in physical endeavour based programmes, whether punitive or 'liberal', prevents criminality. But another incontrovertible fact is that sports and games are massively popular. A staggering three million people play football on a regular basis. Every youth worker and prison officer knows that football is a priceless lowest common denominator of activity designed to hold the attention of young men who are otherwise uncooperative, and who have successfully resisted the lessons of the classroom. The sad consequence of the failure to find real educational solutions for young offenders is that the purely instrumental aspects of sport become the main rationale for provision.[102]

The view that sport can be the magical cure for juvenile crime is naive. Participation in sporting endeavour can of course be a positive channelling of energies and can help teach positive life values; however, it is unlikely to have a significant impact upon the underlying social reasons for criminality. The causes of crime are highly complex and contested. Sport has a role to play in helping fight crime, but one must be realistic about its limitations.

Government uses authority to persuade

This third function of state involvement is perhaps more problematic and can be pejoratively identified as political interference in the operation of sport. However, it of course reflects the reality that sport involves competing political values and conflicts of interest are inevitable. In Chapter 2, the ongoing pressure that the government has brought on English football, the national game, will be analysed including a specific examination of the operation of the Football Taskforce from 1997 to 1999. This government pressure has to be understood within the highly commercialised environment of a great deal of elite professional sport.

Another significant area within which government has brought pressure to bear concerns sporting contact and competition with nations where political regimes are involved with abuses of human rights. The political nature of organisations such as the International Olympic Committee (IOC)[103] and major international sports federations such as the Fédération Internationale de Football Associations (FIFA)[104] are more influential than many countries. The selection process of host cities for the summer and winter Olympics has created some disquiet for many years, and this will be considered in Chapter 6. Not only has the selection procedure been exposed as corrupt,[105] it represents the interstices of complex political interests of the bidders, the IOC and other nation states. The choice for the host city for the 2008 summer Olympics is a good example. Beijing, after narrowly losing out in the past, developed another bid and was successful. The human rights record in China came under the spotlight, and the 'practicalities' of deciding how relevant an issue this should be in the IOC's determination was vigorously contested.

Chaudhary, V, 'This decision will allow a police state to bask in reflected glory'

The decision to award Beijing the 2008 Olympic Games was greeted with concern and criticism from around the world, particularly over how China might exploit the games to cover up its poor human rights record and maintain a totalitarian regime. The American Government, which has tense relations with China, said its athletes would compete in Beijing and that the decision about where the games take place was up to the International Olympic Committee.

102 Robins, D, 'Sport and crime prevention: the evidence of research', (1996) 23 Criminal Justice Matters 26. Also see Coalter, F, *Sport and Delinquency* (1987), unpublished; Mason, G and Wilson, P, *Sport Recreation and Juvenile Crime* (1988), Canberra: Australian Institute of Criminology; Robins, D, *Sport as Prevention* (1990), Oxford: Centre for Criminal Research; Farrington, D, 'Implications of criminal career research for the prevention of offending' (1990) 13 Journal of Adolescence 93; Jones, V, 'Football and crime prevention' and Dulop, D, 'Can sport reduce crime amongst young people?' both (1996) 23 Criminal Justice Matters 24; Nichols, G and Crow, I, 'Measuring the impact of crime reduction interventions involving sports activities for young people' (2004) 43(3) Howard Journal of Criminal Justice, 267–83.
103 For a discussion of the role of FIFA, see Yallop, D, *How They Stole the Game* (1999), London: Poetic Products; Duke, V and Crolley, L, *Football Nationality and the State* (1996), Harlow: Longman; Sugden, J and Tomlinson, A, *FIFA and the Contest for World Football* (1998), London: Polity; and 'Who rules the people's game? FIFA versus UEFA in the struggle for control of world football', in Brown, A (ed), *Fanatics! Power, Identity and Fandom in Football* (1998), London: Routledge.
104 For a discussion of the role of the IOC, see Jennings, A, *The New Lords of the Rings* (1996), London: Pocket Books; *The Great Olympic Swindle: When the World Wanted Its Games Back* (2000), London: Simon & Schuster; Tomlinson, A; Whannel, G (eds), *Five Ring Circus – Money, Power and Politics at the Olympic Games* (1984), London: Pluto; and Hill, C, *Olympic Politics* (1992), Manchester: Manchester UP.
105 See later, pp 270–2 on the investigation of IOC corruption.

Condoleezza Rice, George Bush's national security adviser, said: 'We understand that this was a decision for the IOC to take. What we do know is that American athletes are going to go there, and they're going to compete and hopefully bring home lots of gold medals.' President Bush was said to be neutral on the issue. Ms Rice said the US remained concerned about the state of human rights in China. She said: 'The President has made very clear that human rights will be on the agenda. We have a human rights agenda with China, I think the Chinese expect it and we'll continue to pursue that in our bilateral relationship.' A spokesman for the British Government said: 'We very much hope that the Olympics will play a positive role in China.'

The island state of Taiwan, which is not officially recognised by China, said it hoped that the decision to award Beijing the games would decrease tension in the region. The Tibetan Government in exile, which is based in India, criticised the IOC for awarding the games to Beijing. China has been accused of carrying out widespread human rights abuses in Tibet after invading the region in 1950.

Kalon TC Tethong, spokesman for the exiled Tibetan Government, said the Olympic Games would mean more repression, referring to 'the suffering that will be unleashed on ordinary people by a totalitarian one-party state which will assume that it has received international permission for its horrendous repression'.

While officially western governments remained tight-lipped, individual politicians said the IOC was wrong to choose Beijing. In Washington, Tom Lantos, the house international relations committee's leading Democrat, said: 'It truly boggles the mind. This decision will allow the Chinese police state to bask in the reflected glory of the Olympic Games despite having one of the most abominable human rights records in the world.'

In Europe, the French were most critical of China's human rights record and the IOC's decision. François Loncle, the head of parliament's foreign affairs committee, said: 'Following the example of Nazi Germany in 1936 and the Soviet Union in 1980, communist China will use the games as a powerful propaganda instrument destined to consolidate its hold on power.'[106]

Although the focus of this book is on the regulation of British sport, it has already been stated that this cannot be understood purely in national terms. The wider supra-national and international regulatory environment needs to be considered and, as will be discussed later, the process of globalisation as it applies to sport is a crucial factor. Football is probably the one true global sport:

Gardiner, S and Felix, A, 'Juridification of the football field: strategies for giving law the elbow'

The cultural significance of football is enormous. Its ubiquity as the world's premier sport provides it with a unique position. Kitchen has called football the only 'global idiom' apart from science. It is truly a global sport with the majority of the world's nations members of the Fédération Internationale de Football Association (FIFA). The influence of FIFA should not be understated. From its Geneva headquarters it has direct contacts with many heads of state. It has in the past applied for observer status at the United Nations. The President, Joao Havelange, has largely been responsible for elevating the influence of FIFA and accommodating external pressures such as television. He was nominated for the Nobel Peace Prize in 1988. Bill Shankly's often quoted belief that football is not just a matter of life or death – it is more important – may seem an exaggeration of reality but for many its influence is as profound as any fundamentalist religion. For example in 1964, during a match between Peru and Argentina in Lima, it was estimated that 318 people died in rioting that was initiated largely due to the result.

---

106 Chaudhary, V, 'This decision will allow a police state to bask in reflected glory' *The Guardian*, 14 July 2001.

The murder of the Colombian player, Andres Escobar, after his own-goal in the 1994 World Cup, displays the extreme response that can be engendered by failure.

What cannot be refuted, however, is the growth of football as the global game and essentially in most countries as an important element of working-class culture. As with other mass participation and spectator sports, football is highly significant in popular discourse. Both in national and international contexts, football personifies the sectarianism of class, regional and national rivalry. The mass media play a crucial role in its representation, magnifying the significance of these competitive elements. Football has undergone many changes. Commercialisation has brought incremental change. Today it is increasingly commodified and developing as an integral part of the leisure industry . . . In England the emergence of the Premier league or 'Premiership' as a 'whole new ball game' reflects the view of football's potential as a big money maker. Players have also been the winners with incomes changing the financial contours of the game.[107]

Within both the national and the international community, the relationship between sport and formal politics is complex.[108] The argument that sport is apolitical in the sense of being neutral and value-free in terms of cultural values is often promulgated. Is sport really separate from formal politics? There are many examples where sport has become a part of the political arena and has been 'used' for political ends. Sporting boycotts have been used many times in recent history – it is a question of conjecture how effective they have been:

Monnington, T, 'Politicians and sport: uses and abuses'

The characteristic forceful intervention of Mrs Thatcher in policy implementation, which was much in evidence during the passage of the Football Spectators Bill, had been similarly apparent earlier in her administration in 1980, again in the sports arena. The major debate in international politics in 1980 was the Soviet Union's actions in Afghanistan. It was not only the intervention of that country in the domestic affairs of another sovereign state, but also the reported atrocities perpetrated there that aroused international concern. Direct action was impossible by either the British or American governments. In an endeavour to cause as much embarrassment to the Soviet Government as possible the Carter administration in the USA implemented a boycott of the forthcoming Olympic Games in Moscow that summer. Mrs Thatcher intervened personally in support of the American Games boycott and called on British athletes and the British Olympic Association to boycott the Games also.

The very limited success of this British boycott is again well-documented history, but its significance less so. The real diplomatic value of the American boycott in influencing the government of the USSR, according to a study by JH Frey, was minimal. He revealed that analysis of top-level contacts between the USA and USSR governments around the time of the Moscow Games made no reference to the boycott. The use of sport in this context was more for media and public consumption.

The consequence for the British political scene was not only an early indication of Thatcher's tendency to become involved directly in a wide range of policy matters, but also her willingness to ride roughshod over the heads of her ministers. The then Minister for Sport, Hector Munroe, was not even called to speak in the House of Commons debate on the Moscow Olympics, held in March 1980.

For Mrs Thatcher her intervention into the sporting arena proved to be a political disaster. Although she was not prepared to go as far as Jimmy Carter in withdrawing the British

---

107 Gardiner, S and Felix, A, 'Juridification of the football field: strategies for giving law the elbow' (1995) 5(2) MSLJ 189, p 191.
108 See Arnaud, P and Riordan, J, *Sport and International Politics: Impact of Fascism and Communism on Sport* (1998), London: Routledge.

competitors from the Games, she did consider seizing the passports of British competitors until advised as to the likely illegality of such an action. Attempts to persuade the British Olympic Association to refuse to send a team met with a frosty response.

Threats of dismissal were even made to members of the British team who were public employees if they chose to take their holidays at a time that would allow them to travel to Moscow for the Games. Several of the athletes faced with this threat resigned from their jobs rather than acquiesce to this overt pressure. In the end, with only a limited number of enforced absences, a British team attended the Games, competing under the Olympic flag. For the British Government and Mrs Thatcher in particular the entire incident was an embarrassment, an example of political naivety and a failed attempt to bring British sport into the Cold War political arena. Five years later, when the Heysel Stadium incident was debated in Cabinet, it was Mrs Thatcher and her senior ministers who were involved, not [Minister for Sport] Colin Moynihan. Moynihan had, as Macfarlane suggested, 'become a member of the smallest and most unimportant trade union in the House, the Trade Union of Ministers with special responsibility for Sport'.

The forceful diplomatic stand that Mrs Thatcher took with respect to the Soviet intervention into Afghanistan and her support for the American boycott of the Moscow Olympics contrasts with her position on South Africa. She maintained the support of the British Government for the Gleneagles Agreement signed by Callaghan in 1977, which discouraged sporting links with South Africa. But she has often been criticised as selective in her isolation policy with respect to that country by maintaining diplomatic and trade links. Sport was apparently an easy public policy weapon, without any real diplomatic or political recoil, to express the British Government's opposition to another country's conduct in its domestic affairs.

Mrs Thatcher's reluctance to take such a firm stand over sporting contacts with South Africa as she had with respect to the USSR in 1980, along with her obvious eagerness to avoid bringing South Africa to its knees through the imposition of economic sanctions, alienated many of the member nations of the British Commonwealth. The policy consequence for many of these nations was the boycott of the 1986 Commonwealth Games in Edinburgh. Mrs Thatcher was held to be personally responsible for their absence from the Games.

There are several other areas where sport has experienced the consequences of 'Thatcherism'. These have occurred when reforms such as compulsory competitive tendering, local management of schools, the 'opting-out' of schools from local authority control and actual local authority restructuring have been implemented. In addition, the current debate over the national curriculum in physical education bears the imprint of Thatcherism. But it is important to appreciate a subtle, yet important, difference here. Sport is affected in these instances as a consequence of policy, rather than being used as an instrument of policy implementation.

A final consideration must be the relationship of Mrs Thatcher to the Sports Council. She came to power with a 'New Right' ideological belief that government 'quangos' (quasi-autonomous non-governmental organisations) should be curtailed in power and number. The reality was that after 11 years in office the importance of such bodies was not significantly reduced. In particular, the Sports Council remained in existence, with an enhanced role and a much increased grant from government. However, it too did not remain isolated from the tentacles of Thatcherism. Increasingly, the Council was subjected to 'clientism' as successive Ministers for Sport, closely directed by Mrs Thatcher, more rigidly interpreted the Council's Royal Charter and regarded the body as an 'executive arm of government'. In particular the Council increasingly mirrored the government's stance on the role of sport in the maintenance of public order. A coincidental policy match or an example of the guiding hand of government? Have the most appropriate policy initiatives for sport that the Sports Council should have been pursuing been compromised or stifled as a result of government interference?

The hand of Thatcher with respect to sport, despite her apparent indifference to the activity itself, was clearly evident during her premiership. Sport was used and perhaps abused in a very

distinctive manner. The jury remains out, however, still considering its verdict on the consequences of her policies for sport.

Thus two highly visible politicians, Margaret Thatcher and Ronald Reagan, have in their
own particular manner utilised sport as a valuable medium to further their own political objectives. They both left office when their finest hours were perhaps already behind them. But they
have left a political legacy that is both significant in terms of policy successes as well as failures, and also in terms of style. The 'Gipper' and the 'Iron Lady' have assured themselves a
place in the annals of both political, as well as sporting, history.[109]

Gardiner, S and Felix, A, 'Juridification of the football field: strategies for giving law the elbow'

The relationship between sport and formal politics is, however, conversely best categorised as
one that 'lacks invisibility'. Although sport in general, and football in particular, have been
projected as autonomous from political values, they have been used both in terms of liberation
and the soliciting of legitimacy. The role of sport in the war against apartheid in South Africa
cannot be overstated. Conversely there are a number of examples of the role sport has played
in deception and distortion of political reality. The Brazilian national football team has been
used to symbolise harmony and well-being in general life. The 'beautiful game' can be easily
used to promote the beautiful life. In 1970 the winning of the World Cup was used to distract
concern away from the injustices of military rule. Today similarly the exploits of Romario,
Babeto et al and the winning of another World Cup (in 1994) have been used to attempt to
deflect national and international concern away from the infanticide being practised by the
'Justiceros' vigilante squads. Ironically, one sure way for street kids to escape the likelihood of
an early death is to excel at football.[110]

Largely due to sport's immense cultural importance, politicians are prone to see sport as a powerful
political tool. Of course this does not always have negative connotations. Sport can be used to
support very positive values of community and co-operation. It can also powerfully show disapproval. Many influential commentators have argued that the sports boycott of South Africa during
the apartheid era played an important role within the general political and economic boycott.[111]
The Gleneagles Agreement adopted by the Commonwealth heads of government was intended:

> . . . [to urge member governments] to combat the evil of apartheid by withholding any form of
> support for, and by taking every practical step to discourage contact or competition by their
> nationals with sporting organizations, teams or sportsmen from South Africa.[112]

More recently, the government applied pressure on the England and Wales Cricket Board to cancel
Zimbabwe's planned 2009 tour of England,[113] although they explicitly avoided ordering the ECB
not to allow it.[114]

---

109 Monnington, T, 'Politicians and sport: uses and abuses', in Allison, L (ed), *The Changing Politics of Sport* (1992), Manchester:
Manchester UP, p 128.
110 Op. cit., fn 107, Gardiner and Felix (1995), pp 194–95.
111 See Osborne, P, *Basil D'Oliveira: Cricket and Controversy* (2004), London: Little Brown.
112 The Gleneagles Agreement on Sporting Contacts with South Africa (1981), London. See Nafziger, J, *International Sports Law*,
2nd edn (2004), New York: Transnational; Booth, D, *The Race Game: Sport and Politics in South Africa* (1998), London: Frank Cass, for a
discussion on the effects of the agreement and other moves by the United Nations.
113 Brown seeks ban on Zimbabwe cricket tour, *The Guardian*, 3 January 2008, www.guardian.co.uk/politics/2008/jan/03/
politicalnews.uk.
114 'ECB cancel Zimbabwe's 2009 cricket tour and seek replacement for England', *Telegraph*, 25 June 2009, www.telegraph.co.uk/sport/
cricket/international/zimbabwe/2304059/ECB-cancel-Zimbabwes-2009-cricket-tour-and-seek-replacement-for-England.html.

Conclusion

This introductory chapter provides a historical and cultural context for the regulation of modern sport. The state has had a long-standing role in sport: historically this intervention has been very much about prohibition of activities seen as inappropriate and vulgar. The contemporary role of the state in sport continues to have prohibitionary characteristics but it is also very much about guidance and facilitating elite and recreational sport.

Key Points

- Sport has an immense cultural significance within society in terms of participation and spectating.
- The UK can be compared with other European countries, especially in Southern Europe, which have a significantly greater interventionist approach to regulating sport.
- Government intervenes in three main ways: direct state intervention, e.g. legislation; indirect state intervention, e.g. the Sports Councils; and persuasion, e.g. supporting sporting boycotts.
- Sport is used as a form of social policy to engage with, among other things, fighting crime and promoting health.
- Sporting activities have been regulated by the state for many hundreds of years.
- Historically in the UK, many forms of sporting activity have been prohibited, e.g. early forms of football.
- A number of sports were codified with a formal set of rules in the second half of the nineteenth century during the Victorian era.
- There are competing sociological theories of sport, most notably the competing functionalist 'figurational' theory and Marxist-based conflict theory.
- Sport can be demarcated from non-physical games and entertainment spectacles such as WWE wrestling.
- There is a formal 'recognition procedure' for sport in the UK which enables such sports to be eligible to financial benefits including lottery funding.

Key Sources

Burley, D, *Sport and the Making of Britain* (1993), Manchester: Manchester University Press.
Cashmore, E, *Making Sense of Sport* (2005), 4th edn, London: Routledge.
Grayson, E, *Sport and the Law* (2000), 3rd edn, London: Butterworths.
Houlihan, B, *Sport and Society: A Student Introduction* (2007), 2nd edn, Newcastle: Sage.
McArdle, D, *From Boot Money to Bosman: Football, Society and Law* (2000), London: Cavendish Publishing.

Chapter 2

Theoretical Understanding of the Regulation of Sport

Chapter Contents

Introduction	44
The Normative Rule Structure of Sport	45
Adjudicative Officials and Playing Rules	51
Challenging the Rules: Cheating and Sportsmanship	55
The Contemporary Regulation of Sport	70
Juridification of Sport: The Role of Law	73
Globalisation of Sports Law	77
Viva Sports Law – Sport and the Law RIP	83
Conclusion	86
Key Points	87
Key Sources	87

Introduction

The concern of the chapter will be to examine the normative rule structure concerning sport. There is clearly a structure or hierarchy of such normative rules. The term 'normative' indicates that they are designed to be prescriptive and are concerned with 'ought (not) may (not) or can (not), in relation to behaviour'.[1] Sport as a social practice is highly rule-bound. Individual sports are regulated by their own dedicated constitutional rulebooks and adjudication machinery. The volume of rules varies between different sports. Some are particularly multifarious. Rules in sport exist for both its organisation and playing (so-called 'game rules'). Additionally, there have been relatively new developments in the form of explicit codes of ethics, which are largely informal but written normative statements. Sport is also surrounded by strategies and practices that are not explicitly stated and recorded but partly amount to the 'working' or 'playing culture' of particular sports. The interaction of sports' internal rules and the influence of the law are also important; the internal rules of sport need to be examined before the role of the law in sport can be fully evaluated.

A key issue is to what extent should the internal rules and norms be superseded by external legal norms? Put more bluntly, to what extent do sports bodies need to comply with the law? The courts, particularly the European Court of Justice, have made some distinctions between internal rules of sport that can be considered 'sporting rules' and those that are open to external legal examination and compliance with legal provisions – invariably those that have an economic impact.[2] As has been stated earlier, sports law decreasingly can be understood merely in national (UK) terms – European and international regulation is increasingly pervasive.[3]

The first section of the chapter will provide a short history of the development of internal sporting rules so as to better understand the dynamics and structure of these rules. The process and motivations for rule changes will be considered. Both sport's informal and formal rules are subject to frequent change, creating a dynamic relationship with new tactics being developed by sports coaches and participants which become the 'playing culture' within a particular sport.[4] Excesses in this playing culture are challenged by policies such as codes of ethics introduced by administrators.

The application of game rules within sporting contests by adjudicating officials is very much one of the key dynamics of sport. The decisions of umpires, referees and other match officials are key matters of discussion during and after sporting contests. There seems to have been an increasing movement towards these decisions being subject to appraisal by tribunals and the courts, and this reflects greater external regulation. The reluctance of these forums of adjudication to intervene in 'field of play' disputes will be evaluated.

The third and main section of the chapter will focus on the variety of practices within sport that can be considered to be unethical. There are complex dynamics surrounding infringement and 'bending of the rules' within playing cultures. A major question is determining when these activities are unethical. It is generally accepted that where sporting advantage is gained through taking prohibited performance-enhancing drugs, fixing match results and excessive violence, unethical conduct is involved. These activities are wrong because they are considered to be a form of cheating. They are the corollary of those inherent sporting values considered in Chapter 1.[5] But what of the situations where sports participants use technological advancements to improve their performance or to re-balance a disability? What about faking an injury so as to exploit a rule in a sport concerning

---

1 Twining, W and Miers, D, *How to do Things With Rules*, 4th edn (1999), London: Butterworths, p 123. This is a good starting point in terms of examining the rule as the basic 'working tool' of the law.

2 See later, Chapter 4 and notably Cases C-51/96 and C-191/97 *Deliège v Liège Ligue Francophone de Judo*, judgment of 11 April 2000 and Case C176/96 *Lehtonen & Castors Canada Dry Namur-Braine v FRBSB (Belgian Basketball Federation)*, Judgment of 13 April 2000; however see later Case C-519/04 P, *Meca-Medina & Majcen v. Commission*, Judgment of 18 July 2006.

3 See Gardiner, S, Parrish, R and Siekmann, R (eds), *Professional Sport in the European Union: Representation, Regulation and Re-regulation*, 2nd edn (2009), Cambridge: CUP.

4 See 'Do not change the balls or tinker with the rules please', *The Times*, 6 July 1994.

5 See p 9.

substitution, as with the notorious 'Bloodgate' scandal discussed below.[6] What about purposively damaging equipment such as the ball in a game of cricket so as to gain a tactical advantage?[7] When do these activities amount to 'cheating'?

The fourth section will evaluate the process of juridification – that is, that sporting relations are increasingly viewed as essentially legally constructed. Recourse to litigation to secure legal remedies increasingly becomes the primary course of action, and therefore the discourse of the law becomes the language employed. This has arguably happened with doping in sport – no longer have disputes surrounding drug use essentially been constructed as sporting ones around concepts such as fair play. These disputes have gone through a process over the years of being professionalised – initially becoming a medical issue, with drug testing procedures becoming endemic, they are now fundamentally legal disputes to be resolved in relevant tribunals and courts. This may be good news for lawyers, but a vital question is whether it is in the long-term interests of sport. There are many ethical issues to be determined in sport, and the law has a role to play in helping provide solutions. There are competing perspectives on the reason for the contemporary involvement of law in sport beyond the obvious commercial reasons for law's greater presence, which have already been briefly noted. It may be too simplistic to see law's intervention as being purely due to increasing commercialisation; doing so may hide some of the other causal reasons for the greater role of the law in sport.

The fifth section will provide an examination of the international and global nature of sport and the consequential reality that where disputes occur, principles of international sports law have been developed. The Court of Arbitration for Sport and its jurisprudence has an ever-increasing role in the development of this sports-specific jurisprudence. Lastly, this section will evaluate what some may think is an abstract and esoteric argument. Is the concern in this legal discipline one that is best termed 'Sports Law' or 'Sport and the Law'? The preface to this book has clearly indicated what the authors' position is on this issue. The resolution of this debate is important within the recognition of Sports Law as an intellectually rigorous and increasingly mature legal discipline. If the many problematic issues that currently face sport are to be effectively challenged and the law is to have a well-reasoned and appropriate role within the general regulatory framework, sports lawyers and administrators need to have a sound theoretical understanding of the backgrounds, reasons and implications of law's involvement. The chapter will conclude by arguing that a sports law or lex sportiva is fast developing – indeed, a legal discipline that can be seen as analogous to a lex mercatoria – that needs to be understood not only in national legal terms but, perhaps more importantly when it comes to the regulation of sport, also in supra-national (European) and international terms.

The Normative Rule Structure of Sport

History of the rules of sport

Sport as an area of social life is extremely 'rule-bound'. An examination of the rule structure of sport is therefore required. This is the context within which the legal rules operate. The consequential tripartite amalgam of normative rules – sporting rules, sports' playing culture, and the law – potentially leads to many issues of demarcation. Rules are needed for specific sports to be played. The historical development of the 'codification' of sport and the creation of formal rule structures has been outlined in Chapter 1. They can generally be divided into those having the goal of ensuring safety and those regulating the dynamics of play.

In boxing, the rules developed to codify prize fighting in the eighteenth century were motivated by safety:

6   See later, p 64.
7   See later, pp 60–4.

That a square of a Yard be chalked in the middle of the Stage; and on every fresh set-to after a fall or being parted from the rails, each Second is to bring his Man to the side of the square and place him opposite to the other and till they are fairly set-to at the Lines, it shall not be lawful for one to strike at the other.[8]

These are the first crude rules set down in print to govern boxing, written by Jack Broughton in 1743, two years after he had killed George Stevenson in a prize-ring in Tottenham Court Road. They are couched in language that reflects the peculiarly 'muscular decency' of the times. These rules were further codified in 1867 under the auspices of the Marquis of Queensberry. As noted earlier, the late 1800s saw the formal codification of many sports.[9]

The combinations of safety rules and the rules determining the mechanics of play can be termed as any particular sport's 'constitutive rules':

Simon, R, *Fair Play: Sports, Values and Society*

If players were unaware of such rules or made no attempt to follow them they logically could not be playing basketball (although minimal modifications might be acceptable in informal play or other special contexts). Constitutive rules should be distinguished sharply from rules of strategy such as 'dribble only if there is no faster way of advancing the ball up the court'. Rules of strategy are general suggestions as to how to play the game well; constitutive rules determine what counts as a permissible move within the game itself.[10]

The increasing conformity of playing rules

So the formal rules of sport (of the variety that have been discussed) have developed very much as a product of modernity. As John Bale argues, they have produced an increasingly uniform activity:

Bale, J, *Landscapes of Modern Sport*

It is a plausible claim that 'the first laws ever to be voluntarily embraced by men *(sic)* from a variety of cultures and backgrounds are the laws of sports' and these laws are crucial to the contents of this book. Without laws which were accepted over large areas, inter-regional competition was difficult if not impossible and the laws of sports were drawn up to make competition between geographically dispersed teams more meaningful. To enforce these laws, national (or in large countries, regional) bureaucracies (i.e. sports associations) were set up. In western nations the cumulative frequency curves for the growth of such associations display a pattern of initially slow but subsequently rapid (late nineteenth century) growth, characteristic of many cultural innovations.

As sports diffused internationally the formation of national governing bodies was followed by similar global organisations but western sports did not simply take root in virgin soil; they were often firmly implanted – sometimes ruthlessly by imperialists, while in other cases indigenous elites sought to imitate their masters in order to gain social acceptance. Such sports colonisation was at the expense of indigenous movement cultures and as cultural imperialism swept the globe, sports played their part in westernising the landscapes of the colonies – tennis courts and golf courses, race tracks and football pitches becoming permanent features of the cultural environment while evidence of indigenous games often became relict features of the landscape. The laws drawn up by the sports bureaucracies almost always included the spatial parameters within which

---

8 'Sportsview: why they can't close school of hard knocks', *The Observer*, 29 October 1995, p 10.
9 See Chapter 1, p 22.
10 Simon, R, *Fair Play: Sports, Values and Society* (1991), Boulder: Westview, pp 14–15.

the sporting action was to take place. It is this explicitly spatial character of the globally applied rules of sport which has such an important impact on the sports environment since it facilitates global 'body trading', permitting people from different cultures to make sense of the sports landscape by encouraging 'sameness' wherever it might be in the world. Although the 'globalisation' of culture is not the same as its 'homogenisation', the globally enforced rules of sport encourage sameness, homogenisation and placelessness to an extent not so commonly found in such global common denominators as tourism, leisure or work. Even if one was to accept the rather unconventional view that modern sport is essentially the same as its antecedents in that each are 'the ritual sacrifice of physical energy', the modernity of sport (in the sense that word is used in this book) is demonstrated by its standardised spatial and environmental forms. Today, a squash court or a running track is essentially the same whether it is in London or in Lagos. Sports, therefore, are versions of what Appadurai calls 'technoscapes', each having roots in a number of multinational organisations (sports' governing bodies) which, with the help of modern technology insist on certain standardised landscapes within which sport is allowed to take place.[11]

Bale shows how sport has become more uniform wherever it is played through the development of rules regarding play and the increasingly standardised spatial dimensions of play; for example, football pitches need to be within certain size limits, international boxing rings need to meet a number of criteria on surface and size, and environmental factors such as wind velocity need to be inside certain parameters for the validity of international records in athletics. He also shows how certain sports facilities are increasingly regulating environmental factors. Examples include the Wembley Stadium with its retractable roof, and flooring that absorbs radiant heat at Melbourne Park (home of the Australian Open Tennis tournament).[12] He uses the terms 'placelessness' to describe this process of increasing standardisation of the places that sport is played. As he says:

> The modern sports landscape can be described as tending towards placelessness in its geographical sense of places looking and feeling alike with 'dictated and standardized values'.[13]

Interestingly, this is one of the complaints concerning the introduction of all-seater football stadia since the Taylor Report after the Hillsborough disaster – grounds have become too soulless, without recognisable ends and lacking the atmosphere of old. There have been recent calls for a return of a limited amount of standing 'terracing' areas at Premier League grounds.[14] In his geographical examination of sport, Bale highlights the greater than ever importance of the rule framework of sport.

Rule changes

Another issue is to what extent and frequency the rules of games should be modified. One argument is that changes are merely tinkering and are often carried out with the aim of short-term expediency.[15] This is often to placate external pressures such as sponsors and television, for example the introduction of the back-pass rule in football to speed the game up; or to curb the excellence of particular participants, for example the changes since 2005 to the rules of Formula One motor racing largely to

---

11 Bale, J, *Landscapes of Modern Sport* (1994), Leicester: Leicester University Press.
12 See Gardiner, S 'Sports Participation in Extreme Environmental Conditions' (2007), 15(3) *Sport and the Law Journal* 7–8.
13 Ibid, pp 94–5.
14 'Calls grow for return of terraces', BBC News, 14 March 2007, http://news.bbc.co.uk/go/pr/fr/-/sport1/hi/football/6444083.stm.
15 'Do not change the balls or tinker with the rules please', *The Times*, 6 July 1994, p 42; 'Law-makers struggle to keep pace with the law-breakers', *The Guardian*, 16 September 1994; 'Scots urge IB to speed up game', *The Guardian*, 4 October 1994; 'The dangers of playing for time-out', *The Independent on Sunday*, 9 April 1995; 'FIFA to hit taller keepers by moving the goalpost', *The Guardian*, 3 January 1996.

curb the dominance of Michael Schumacher and the Ferrari team from 2000 to 2004 and to create a better balance between the skill of the driver and the technology of the cars; and similarly the constant changes in cricket to the short-pitch delivery rules have been carried out to control fast bowlers, particularly the dominance of the West Indian bowlers during the 1980s and 1990s.[16]

The opposing argument is that rule changes are needed to secure the integrity of modern sport in the context of the commodification and globalisation of sport. New variants of a traditional sport are periodically introduced, such as one-day cricket in 1963 and 'Twenty20' (T20) cricket in 2003. Coaches and players are under increasing pressure to succeed and therefore exploit the limitations of existing rules. Rule changes are then required to try to re-establish the vitality and balance in a particular sport. New skills and strategies then develop to confront the new rules. This allows the sport to be dynamic and reflects the character of rules as being both certain and pliant.

Rules certainly do have an elasticity and, together with the participants' 'playing culture', are only part of the regulation of the sport. Without this acknowledgement and the ability to modify rules, sport is subject to predictability and ossification. But in most sports, rule changes have significantly accelerated in the last thirty years. Increasing external pressures may well be the cause. Too many changes can be counterproductive and can damage the balance of particular sports. Some sports, such as American Gridiron football, have numerous and complex rules. Others, such as football, have a simplicity that is derived from a small number of rules. Coherent rule changes are made for these reasons: to promote safety, to assist the fluidity of the game and to allow the skilful to shine. Some are not fundamental changes in the rules, but different interpretations of existing ones. There is, however, a danger that many rule changes in sport are developing an increasingly sanitised game for mass global consumption.

Some rule creations and changes, as with the law itself, can also be clearly dysfunctional and sometimes utterly bizarre:

Longmore, A, 'Absurd cup rule obscures football's final goal'

The law, they say, is an ass and more of an ass in sport than most walks of life but not even the bigwigs at the Football Association could have concocted a rule so daft that both sides ended a competitive cup match attacking their own goals, the farcical situation that occurred at the end of a recent match between Barbados and Grenada in the final group match of the Shell Caribbean Cup.

Needing to beat Grenada by two clear goals to qualify for the finals in Trinidad and Tobago, Barbados had established a 2–0 lead midway through the second half and were seemingly well in control of the game. However, an own goal by a Bajan defender made the score 2–1 and brought a new ruling into play, which led to farce. Under the new rule, devised by the competition committee to ensure a result, a match decided by sudden death in extra time was deemed to be the equivalent of a 2–0 victory. With three minutes remaining, the score still 2–1 and Grenada about to qualify for the finals in April, Barbados realised that their only chance lay in taking the match to sudden death. They stopped attacking their opponents' goal and turned on their own. In the 87th minute, two Barbadian defenders, Sealy and Stoute, exchanged passes before Sealy hammered the ball past his own goalkeeper for the equaliser.

The Grenada players, momentarily stunned by the goal, realised too late what was happening and immediately started to attack their own goal as well to stop sudden death. Sealy, though, had anticipated the response and stood beside the Grenada goalkeeper as the Bajans defended their opponents' goal. Grenada were unable to score at either end, the match ended 2–2 after 90 minutes and, after four minutes of extra time, Thorne scored the winner for Barbados amid scenes of celebration and laughter in the National Stadium in Bridgetown.

---

16 'Bouncer law is changed', *The Guardian*, 7 July 1994.

James Clarkson, the Grenadian coach, provided an unusual variation on the disappointed manager's speech: 'I feel cheated,' he said. 'The person who came up with these rules must be a candidate for the madhouse. The game should never be played with so many players on the field confused. Our players did not even know which direction to attack. Our goal or their goal. I have never seen this happen before. In football, you are supposed to score against the opponents to win, not for them,' he added. Nobody should tell the organising committee of the World Cup. They might get ideas.[17]

Playing culture

Rules of strategy are therefore separate from the constitutive rules of the game or sport. They may be formally written in coaching manuals, etc. or they may be informal rules. In addition, conventions and customs also have a powerful normative impact on play in a number of sports. These types of norms are informal and rarely defined except in very wide terms.[18] In fact there are numerous informal and unwritten rules in sports that guide athletes in how they play the game. For example, in rugby, there is a convention to tackle an opponent 'hard and low' early in a game to achieve a consequential advantage. It also includes 'psyching out' an opponent. As David Fraser says of 'sledging' (the practice of talking to or at a batsman in derogatory terms in cricket), 'while it is almost certainly illegal, sledging is a current and "accepted" ethical practice in some cricket circles'.[19] There is a view that there is more intimidation between opposing players in international cricket than ever before.[20] These actions can be defined as the 'working' or 'playing culture' of sport.

These playing cultures develop to gain an advantage within the formal rule structure. This behaviour challenges the formal playing rules and the adjudication of the referee or umpire in that it may be illegal. Indeed, certain practices that are contrary to the playing rules may be followed so frequently that it becomes 'customary' to break the law of the game. On a wider philosophical level, probably the most powerful value within liberal democracies and legal liberalism is the 'Rule of Law'. The duty to follow the law and not break it is seen as fundamental. On the contrary, however, theories of civil disobedience provide support for breaking the law in circumstances of injustice and, in fact, in certain circumstances, a 'moral duty' to so act.[21] Similarly in sport, violating the rules may be considered the right thing to do. Ice hockey can be used as an example:

Fraser, D, *Cricket and the Law: The Man in White is Always Right*

There are some sport sociologists who argue that no violation of the rules should be encouraged or permitted, just as there are jurists who argue that there is neither a right nor a duty to engage in acts of civil disobedience. An example of such formalism can be found in the recent soccer World Cup, for example, where FIFA instructed referees to issue a red card (expel) to any player committing a 'professional foul'.

On the other hand, our experience of sport indicates that rule-violating behaviour like the 'professional foul' is directly and intentionally integrated into the existential norms of participants and others who interpret the particular sport/text. Studies of ice hockey violence in Canada, for example, demonstrate that while fist-fights are illegal, they are accepted by all participants as an important and integral part of the game. Indeed, to refuse to fight, i.e., to refuse to break the rules, will lead to ostracism and shaming by peer and other reference groups (e.g. parents).

17 Longmore, A, 'Absurd cup rule obscures football's final goal', *The Times*, 1 February 1994, p 44.
18 See Chapter 11.
19 Fraser, D, *Cricket and the Law: The Man in White is Always Right* (1993), Sydney: Institute of Criminology, p 185.
20 See 'Lord's cracks down on appeals', *The Guardian*, 22 November 2000, and 'Cork's dumb insolence proves costly', *The Guardian*, 8 June 2001.
21 See Waldron, J, *The Law* (1990), London: Routledge.

Moreover, as other studies show, some rule-violating behaviour may be functional as a deterrent to other more serious rule-breaking. Again, the example of ice hockey violence indicates that there is a clear distinction between legitimate (although illegal) fighting (fist-fights) and illegitimate (and still illegal) violence (using the stick as a weapon). Not only is a player who uses his stick as a weapon ostracised and stigmatised as a 'cheap shot artist', but using a stick can cause serious, career-ending injury. Participants in the sport, and spectators and fans, see fist-fighting as legitimate not only because it functions to physically intimidate opponents (a skill or attribute which is honoured and legitimated when it occurs within the rules), thereby making it easier to win in a 'collision' sport, but it is also legitimate because it prevents the occurrence of more violent and dangerous instances of illegality by providing a relatively harmless outlet for aggression. Just as in the world of criminal law and criminological theory, in sport not all illegal acts can be simply lumped into a single category. More specificity and detail are required than simply and simplistically labelling an act 'illegal', if we are truly to understand the act and its place in a complex whole.[22]

This relationship between the formal rules and informal 'playing (or working) culture' of the sport can help determine when the law intervenes:

Gardiner, S, 'The Law and the Sports Field'

The reality is that in contact sports there is a continued risk of injury. The rules of sport are designed to avoid serious injury. They are a crucial guide in determining criminal liability. In the absence of proof of intent or recklessness to injure, participants who cause injury within the reasonable application of the rules of the sport can rely on the victim's consent to potential harm. An injury caused due to an illegal tackle that amounts to a foul within the rules of the sport is also likely to be seen as consensual. It may be contrary to the rules of the game but may well be inside the . . . 'working culture' of the sport. Consent is not limited solely by the formal rules in contact sports.[23]

The informality of the playing culture of sport can be exploited illegitimately, especially perhaps in the context of the winner-takes-all mentality of modern sport. The spectre of cheating is raised.[24] But playing cultures are pervasive in all sports.

Ethics in sport

Codes of ethics have become widespread in sport, and act as a counterpoint to the concept that the playing culture can be seen as enabling sportsmen to exploit the limitations of the playing rules. Such codes may be of general educative guidance of appropriate behaviour, or they may be specifically implied in the contractual terms of professional sportsmen who are employees.

Increasingly in sport, codes or charters of ethical behaviour and fair play have been developed, stressing the need to play fairly.[25] The focus on ethics in sport has grown in recent years, largely due to the wide range of ethical dilemmas faced in sport, including the use of violence, drug abuse and exploitation of young athletes. These codes target not only sports participants but also administra-

---

22 Op. cit., fn 19, Fraser (2005), p 28. On ice hockey and the culture of physical force, see Whitson, D and Gruneau, R, *Hockey Nights in Canada* (1993), Toronto: Garamond.

23 Gardiner, S, 'The law and the sports field' [1994] Crim LR 514. This will be looked at further concerning liability for participant violence; see Chapter 11.

24 See later, p 55, for some examples.

25 See Parry, S and McNamee, M, *Ethics and Sport* (1998), London: Routledge; Malloy, D, Ross, S and Zakus, D, *Sports Ethics: Concepts and Cases in Sport and Recreation*, 2nd edn (2003), Toronto: Thompson Education; McNamee, M (ed), *The Ethics of Sports: a Reader* (2010), London: Routledge; and for some additional resources, the Canadian Centre for Ethics in Sport at www.cces.ca.

tors, coaches, spectators and others. In terms of sports participants, though, they encourage ethical behaviour within the general context of the sport being played. Codes of ethics are able to challenge the playing culture, which in elite professional sport has invariably developed to circumvent the rules of play to the advantage of the athletes.

Two examples can be provided by way of illustration. The Council of Europe's 'Fair Play Charter' is essentially an attempt to provide an ethical context for the enjoyment and pursuit of sport. It supports the cultural importance of sport, but acknowledges that the pressures that are the reality of contemporary sport can undermine notions of fair play and sportsmanship.[26] Individual sports have their own codes of ethics and a second example comes from the world of surfing.[27] The surfing code is more specifically about risk management – engaging with what is inherently a dangerous sport.[28] The sport of surfing has needed to respond to how an increasing number of participants can share what is a physical and scarce resource, namely waves, and how inappropriate behaviour, including 'surf rage' between those competing for this resource, can be managed. The emergence of more 'extreme sports' makes the development of these types of codes increasingly important.

Adjudicative Officials and Playing Rules

There is a complex interaction between the playing rules and the officials who enforce them. At particular points in time, governing bodies instruct referees or umpires to enforce the rules more or less strictly.[29] This can lead to disquiet from players and more – or fewer – formal infringements and fouls during the game.[30] The statistics may indicate a fall or increase in foul play but it is unlikely to be primarily about changes in the style of play; that it is becoming more violent, for example. It is much more about officials' attitudes towards actual and potential perpetrators during the game.[31]

Increasingly, the human vulnerability of officials is being questioned. A number of sports are using various forms of technology to aid officials in coming to decisions. In sports such as horse racing and athletics, cameras have been used for many years. In tennis, line decisions are determined electronically by the 'Hawk-Eye' system. The use of video cameras as an aid to the officials on the field of play or as a guide to the 'third umpire' as the final arbiter have been used in sports such as cricket and rugby league in Britain for some years. There are interesting issues concerning whether this undermines the officials' authority, and makes a game too clinical, or whether human error needs to be minimised as much as possible when a wrong decision may have an enormous financial cost.[32] Where does justice lie in terms of adjudicating sporting performance? It reflects the debate concerning judging within the law – whether disputes should be treated consistently with the minimum of discretion, the notion of formal justice or formalism (prioritising the

---

26 Council of Europe, *Code of Sports Ethics: Fair Play – The Winning Way* (adopted by the Committee of Ministers on 24 September 1992): www.coe.int/t/dg4/epas/resources/texts/Rec(92)14rev_en.pdf. Also see Council of Europe, *Fair Play – The Winning Way Code of Sports Ethics* (1996), Sports Council leaflet.
27 British Surfing Association, *Code of Conduct for Surfers*. Although the BSA is no longer active, the code of conduct can still be found online at http://www.memory4teachers.co.uk/channels/presentations/British_Surfing_Association/code.html.
28 For more on safety and regulation of surfing, see Fitzgerald, B and Harrison, J (2003) 77 'Law of the Surf', *Australian Law Journal* 116, http:// eprints.qut.edu.au/9114/1/1194.pdf
29 'World Cup 2010: Fifa cautions referees to get tough in knockout rounds', *The Guardian*, 27 June 2010, www.guardian.co.uk/football/2010/jun/26/world-cup-2010-fifa-referees.
30 'Referees must go with the flow' *The Observer*, 18 September 1994, p 6.
31 Op. cit., fn 19, Fraser (2005), makes some interesting comparisons between umpires (officials) and judges; see Chapter 6, 'The man in white is always right: umpires, judges and the rule of law'. The comparison between styles of umpiring, being interventionist or not, frequently (using discretion) reflects the theorising of the jurist, Karl Llewellyn, concerning his formal and grand style of judging; see Twining, W, *Karl Llewellyn and the Realist Movement* (1973), London: Weidenfeld & Nicolson.
32 See Gardiner, S, 'The third eye: video adjudication in sport' (1999) 7(1) SATLJ 20.

unquestioned application of law), or whether the individual issues of the case should be considered specifically, the notion of substantive justice.[33]

National law courts have provided very limited opportunities for individuals to challenge decisions of adjudicative officials for on-field decisions. A major issue has been what legal standing an action might have. Actions in breach of contract, administrative law or in the law of tort are possible alternatives, insofar as analogies can be found in case law concerning other non-sporting matters.[34] Others argue that decisions within sport involving so-called 'game-rules' are 'virtually certain to be held non-reviewable by the courts . . . so obvious is the above proposition that one ought not to need authority to support it; it simply goes without saying'.[35] Arguing that this view is simplistic, Steve Cornelius states that 'as with all other matters, judicial remedies may be suitable and available in certain cases, yet unsuitable and unavailable in others,'[36] and concludes,

Cornelius, S, 'Liability of Referees (Match Officials) at Sports Events'

[T]hat the question of whether judicial or other intervention in decisions taken by officials at a sports events is possible, is more complex than a simple 'yes' or 'no' would permit . . . officials who act reasonably and in good faith should not have to fear legal action. However, it is equally clear that officials who act in bad faith or in a way that is grossly unreasonable may have to answer to the courts.[37]

In the United Kingdom, although case law has developed in the connected area of referee liability in negligence for injury caused to participants,[38] there are no authorities concerning successful challenges of officials' decisions concerning play. Any arguments along these lines have been given short shrift. In *Machin v Football Association*,[39] Lord Denning MR highlighted the dangers of the court second-guessing a decision taken by the referee. In the Australian case of *Sinclair v Cleary*,[40] an action in negligence failed when it was brought by the owner of a horse against a horse racing official on the grounds of the failure to place his horse as winner. The judge held that the plaintiff was contractually bound to accept the official's decision, the official was independent, and no wrongdoing was found on his part. In the US case of *Bain v Gillespie*,[41] a vendor of team merchandising apparel brought an action against the umpire in a basketball match for an alleged wrong decision contributing to a victory by the opponent team and consequential loss of business for the vendor. The judge commented: 'Heaven knows what uncharted morass a court would find itself in if it were to hold that an athletic official subject himself to liability every time he makes a questionable call . . . the possibilities are mind boggling.'[42]

This reluctance to intervene in decisions of sports adjudicative officials is also evident within the jurisprudence of the Court of Arbitration for Sport (CAS), where decisions of match officials will not be questioned when they take place within their specific jurisdiction of play. In essence, CAS recognizes subsidiarity as far as match officials are concerned.[43] Cases in this area have generally been heard as appeals during Olympic tournaments when CAS is sitting in its ad hoc

33 See Gardiner, S, 'Adjudicative Technology In Sport: Legal Challenges, Fair Play and the Reification Of Certainty', in Nafziger, J and Ross, S (eds) *International Handbook on Sports Law* (2011) Cheltenham: Edward Elgar.
34 Cornelius, S, 'Liability of Referees (Match Officials) at Sports Events' (2004) ISLJ 2.
35 Beloff, M, Kerr, T and Demetriou, M (1999) *Sports Law*, Oxford: Hart Publishing, p 107.
36 Op. cit., fn 34, Cornelius (2004), p 65.
37 Ibid, p 61.
38 *Smoldon v Nolan and Whitworth* [1997] *The Times* 18 December (2007); *Vowles v Evans and the Welsh Rugby Union Ltd* [2003] EWCA Civ 318.
39 *Machin v Football Association, The Times*, July 20, 1973, p 21, Court of Appeal.
40 *Sinclair v Cleary* (1946) St R Qld 74, discussed in Kelly, GM (1987), *Sport and the Law*, Sydney: Law Book Company, p 183.
41 *Bain v Gillespie* 357 NW 2d 47 (1984).
42 Ibid.
43 Oschutz, F (2006), 'The Arbitrability of Sports Disputes and the Rule of the Game', in Blackshaw, I, Siekmann, R and Soek, J, *The Court of Arbitration for Sport 1984–2004*, The Hague: Asser Press.

jurisdiction.[44] It has been consistently ruled that decisions made on the field of play should not be questioned and this is premised on the understanding that 'any contract that the player has made in entering the competition is that he or she should have the benefit of honest 'field of play' decisions, not necessarily the correct ones.'[45]

In *Mendy v Association Internationale de Boxing Amateur (AIBA)*,[46] CAS ruled that it would not review an allegation that an official had made a wrong ruling, in this case disqualifying a boxer who had hit his opponent 'below the belt'. The tribunal reasoned that it was 'less well placed to decide than the referee in the ring or the ring judges'.[47]

Mendy v Association Internationale de Boxing Amateur (AIBA)

[T]raditionally, doctrine and judicial practice have always deemed that game rules, [i.e. technical field of play rules] in the strict sense of the term, should not be subject to the control of judges, based on the idea that 'the game must not be constantly interrupted by appeals to the judge'[48] . . . [And further] in comparative law the game rule is not shielded from the control of judges, but their power of review is limited to that which is arbitrary or illegal . . .[49]

In another case,[50] CAS stated that before it would review a field of play decision, there must be

Korean Olympic Committee (KOC) v International Skating Union (ISU)

. . . evidence, which generally must be direct evidence, of bad faith. If viewed in this light, each of those phrases, such as 'arbitrary', 'breach of duty' and 'malicious intent', means that there must be some evidence of preference for, or prejudice against, a particular team or individual. CAS accepts that this places a high hurdle that must be cleared by any applicant seeking to review a field of play decision. However, if the hurdle were to be lower, the flood-gates would be opened and any dissatisfied participant would be able to seek the review of a field of play decision.[51]

In this case and others, however, this autonomy of adjudicating officials is clearly not a policy of 'complete abstention' but rather one of 'self-restraint'. Technical rules can be reviewed where there were actions that could be characterised as being 'arbitrary', 'a breach of duty' and of 'malicious intent', that is involving some corruption on part of official.[52] Essentially there needs to be some evidence of preference for, or prejudice against, a particular team or individual and 'decisions are taken in violation of . . . social rules or general principles of law'.[53] CAS arbitrators do not review the determinations made on the playing field by judges, referees, umpires or other officials as they are not, 'unlike on-field judges, selected for their expertise in officiating the particular sport'.[54]

CAS has also produced instructive guidance on the issue of challenging technology-based decisions. In *Neykova v International Rowing Federation (FISA) & International Olympic Committee*[55] the applicant was a participant in the women's single sculls event final during the Sydney Olympics. Following a

---

44 For a general analysis of this areas see Nafziger, J, *International Sports Law*, 2nd edn (2004), New York: Transnational Publishers, pp 109–18 and Foster, K, 'Lex Sportiva and Lex Ludica: The Court of Arbitration for Sports Disputes', in Blackshaw, I, Siekmann, R, Soek, J, *The Court of Arbitration for Sport 1084-2004* (2006), The Hague: Asser Press.

45 *Yang v Hamm* CAS 2004/A/704, 37, award dated 21 October 2004.

46 *Mendy v Association Internationale de Boxing Amateur (AIBA)*, CAS ad hoc Division, Atlanta, OG 96/006.

47 Ibid, para 13.

48 Ibid, para 5.

49 Ibid, para 11.

50 *Korean Olympic Committee (KOC) v International Skating Union (ISU)*, OWG 02/007 award of 23 February 2002.

51 Ibid, para 16.

52 Ibid, para 17.

53 *Mendy v Association Internationale de Boxing Amateur (AIBA)*, CAS ad hoc Division, Atlanta, OG 96/006. N. 34, para 13.

54 *Segura v International Amateur Athletic Federation (IAAF)* (CAS OG Sydney 2000/13 Digest Vol 2, p 680, para 17.

55 *Neykova v International Rowing Federation (FISA) & International Olympic Committee* Arbitration CAS ad hoc Division (OG Sydney) 00/012.

photo finish, the first place for the women's single sculls was awarded to Karsten from Belarus (time 7:28.141) and second place to Neykova from Bulgaria (time 7:28.153) on the basis of evidence produced by the official 'Scan'o'vision' photo finish system using two special Swatch photo finish cameras fixed permanently to the structural steel frame of the finish tower. The Bulgarian Olympic Committee challenged the result based on video evidence provided by television cameras. These cameras were set up in an approximate manner for the television audience and served no official purpose. So the question facing the panel was to what extent video evidence that has been presented as contradicting the official photographic technology might be used to override the stated result.

Essentially, *Neykova* concerned a challenge to the accuracy of the official technical equipment that determined placings in the race. Because the panel found that on this question, the applicant had not proved that the technical equipment was deficient, it dismissed the application. The case had not been based on evidence questioning the reliability of the official photographic equipment, but rather on the basis of images produced by TV cameras primarily positioned to produce pictures for viewers. In fact expert evidence argued that the TV cameras were

Neykova v International Rowing Federation (FISA) & International Olympic Committee

... located 10 centimetres ahead of the finish line. When this 10 centimetre discrepancy is projected across the 200 metre width of the course, it is not surprising that the television camera's perspective is different to that of the Scan'o'vision photo finish. This was therefore different to that of a typical official's field of play decision.[56]

The limitations of video imagery from single or multiple cameras is highlighted by the fact that

... it is obvious that a camera can only show what it sees from its particular angle. What it shows will depend upon where it was in relation to the particular incident when that incident took place. A different camera showing the same incident from a different position may well give an entirely different perspective of the same incident.[57]

In the subsequent case of *Canadian Olympic Committee v International Skating Union (ISU)*,[58] the Canadian Olympic Committee (COC) filed an application with the CAS AHD the day after the final of the ladies' short track speed skating. The COC requested CAS to order the ISU to instruct its referee to review the videotape of the race. The COC was seeking determination of whether a 'kicking out' infraction was committed by the winner of the race, Radanova, a Bulgarian skater. Possible disqualification of Radanova would have resulted in Canadian athletes advancing to the second and third places. The view of the panel was that,

Canadian Olympic Committee (KOC) v International Skating Union (ISU)

... there is a more fundamental reason for not permitting trial, by television or otherwise, of technical, judgmental decisions by referees. Every participant in a sport in which referees have to make decisions about events on the field of play must accept that the referee sees an incident from a particular position, and makes his decision on the basis of what he or she sees. Sometimes mistakes are made by referees, as they are by players. That is an inevitable fact of life and one that all participants in sporting events must accept. But not every mistake can be reviewed. It is

56 CAS OG Sydney 2000/12 Digest Vol 2, p 674, para 13.
57 *Korean Olympic Committee (KOC) v International Skating Union (ISU)*, OWG 02/007 award of 23 February 2002, para 11; also see Gardiner, S, 'The Third Eye: Video Adjudication in Sport' (1999) 7(1) Sport and the Law Journal 20.
58 CAS OG 06/006 Canadian Olympic Committee v ISU.

for that reason that CAS jurisprudence makes it clear that it is not open to a player to complain about a 'field of play' decision simply because he or she disagrees with that decision.[59]

The view of CAS continues to be that decisions by officials, irrespective of whether or not technology is involved, will only be reviewed in narrow circumstances where there is evidence helping to evaluate the decision which can be characterised as being clearly in bad faith, however that might be constructed within the specific case.[60]

Challenging the Rules: Cheating and Sportsmanship

In the above example on page 48, are the actions of the Barbadian team an example of cheating? The issue of cheating and its regulation in perhaps the two main sporting contexts – violence and drugs – will be discussed later in the book. Two examples can be used to illustrate where sportsmanship and cheating appear to converge.

It's just not cricket

In a one-day cricket international between the West Indies and Australia in Bridgetown, Barbados in April 1999, crowd disturbances, which included bottles thrown from the stand, caused the match to be stopped. The disturbances were initiated when West Indies opener and local hero Sherwin Campbell was given run out, after colliding with bowler Brendon Julian as the West Indies chased Australia's score of 252 runs. Julian appeared to body-check non-striker Campbell as he went for a quick single and, with the batsman left lying on the floor complaining, Michael Bevan completed the run-out.

Australian captain Steve Waugh led his players from the field and attempts were made to restore calm. After a long delay while the outfield was cleared of broken glass, match referee Raman Subba Row decided, at the suggestion of the Australians, that the game could continue as long as Campbell was reinstated. Under a revised total it was declared that West Indies needed 58 runs to win from 11 overs. Subba Row said: '. . . the Australians have very graciously said they would like Campbell to be brought back to continue his innings. We feel it was six of one and half a dozen of the other.' News of Campbell's reinstatement was greeted with cheers from fans in the Kensington stand where the trouble broke out.

Discretion was clearly used in a tense situation in deciding to reinstate Campbell and continue the game. The cricketing rules are silent about how the umpires should react when there is bodily contact between a fielder and an opposing batsman, although s 7 of Law 42 states that 'it shall be considered unfair if any fieldsman wilfully obstructs a batsman in running'. The umpire in such a situation should call a dead ball. The video replay of the incident indicated that this was no accident but an intentional body-check. The West Indies went on to win the match.

Sportsmanship in football

A similar event testing the match official's discretion occurred in the fifth round FA Cup tie between Arsenal and Sheffield United in the 1999–2000 season. A Sheffield United player kicked the ball out of play so that an injured teammate could receive medical attention. As the ball was thrown back to a Sheffield player, an Arsenal player chased on to it and crossed the ball for a goal. At the time the game was a draw – this goal put Arsenal into the lead. The referee did not disallow the goal. There is a convention in football that when a player is injured the ball is kicked out of play so that the

59 See *Korean Olympic Committee (KOC) v International Skating Union (ISU)*, OWG 02/007 award of 23 February 2002, para 11 – 'arbitrary', 'a breach of duty' and 'malicious intent'. Also see Charlish, P, 'Marathon Mugging: Athens 2004': [2006] ISLR.
60 *Mendy v Association Internationale de Boxing Amateur (AIBA)*, CAS ad hoc Division, Atlanta, OG 96/006.

game can be stopped and the player can receive medical help. From the throw-in, the ball is then returned to the opposing team who were previously in possession. This is constructed as 'good sportsmanship' or 'fair play'.

Arsenal subsequently won the match but the Arsenal manager, Arsène Wenger, offered to replay the match. He stated: 'It was the only answer to a difficult situation.' The English FA supported the move. FIFA, perhaps correctly, stalled on giving their full blessing to the rematch; a meeting of its International Board, football's law makers, highlighted that although the ball was not given back, a rule was not broken, merely a convention, and replaying a game in such circumstances created a problematic precedent.[61]

In both these incidents, if discretion had not been exercised the aggrieved party may well have attempted to seek a legal remedy. They highlight the gaps within the playing rules; just as with law, there will always be *casus omissus* – gaps in the rules of the sport. A response by the cricket law-makers to the type of incident between the West Indies and Australia has been to introduce a ruling concerning the 'Spirit of Cricket'. The core principle is:

The Laws of Cricket (2000 Code, 4th Edition – 2010) – 'The Preamble, the Spirit of Cricket'

Cricket is a game that owes much of its unique appeal to the fact that it should be played not only within its Laws but also within the Spirit of the Game. Any action which is seen to abuse this spirit causes injury to the game itself. The major responsibility for ensuring the spirit of fair play rests with the captains.[62]

Infringement of this ethical code can be used to support disciplinary action.[63] It can also provide guidance where sportsmen attempt to exploit the gaps in the rules identified above. Two further examples from cricket can be compared. In the shortened version of cricket, T20, players have developed many innovative strategies in batting, bowling and fielding to be more competitive. In batting, the switch-hitting of players such as Kevin Pietersen is an example.[64] Similarly, a proposal for bowlers to deliver a ball aiming for it to bounce twice, rather than normal deliveries that will either bounce once or not at all (a full toss), has been outlawed in English cricket. It is in this context that the Law of Cricket provides that:

The Laws of Cricket (2000 Code 4th Edition – 2010) Law 24(6)

Ball bouncing more than twice or rolling along the ground.
The umpire at the bowler's end shall call and signal No ball if a ball which he considers to have been delivered, without having previously touched the bat or person of the striker, either (i) bounces more than twice or (ii) rolls along the ground before it reaches the popping crease.[65]

In June 2010, the England and Wales Cricket Board (ECB) 'confirmed that the practice of bowling a ball that bounces twice should be disallowed with immediate effect. It is considered inappropriate for the image and spirit of our game.'[66] The idea to use the double-bouncer was the brainchild of Warwickshire bowling coach Graeme Welch. Although the ECB's decision would have thwarted

61 For more on this incident, see Demetriou, G, 'In the spirit of football?' (1999) 2(3) SLB 2.
62 The Laws of Cricket (2000 Code 4th Edition – 2010) – 'The Preamble, the Spirit of Cricket', MCC, www.ecb.co.uk.
63 See 'Jacobs banned for three games', *The Guardian*, 6 July 2001. West Indian wicketkeeper Ridley Jacobs was found to have transgressed the spirit of the game by indulging in 'cheating or any sharp practice' when he stumped Virender Sehwag without the ball in his gloves in a one-day international against India. Also see 'Speed urges better behaviour', BBC Sport, 18 July 2001, http://news.bbc.co.uk/sport1/hi/cricket/1445370.stm, on demands from past ICC Chief Executive, Malcolm Speed, for better compliance with rules by players.
64 www.lords.org/data/files/paper-on-switch-hit-for-website-10193.pdf
65 The Laws of Cricket (2000 Code, 4th Edition – 2010).
66 'ECB outlaws Warwickshire's idea to start bowling double-bouncing deliveries', *The Telegraph*, 9th June 2010, http://www.telegraph.co.uk/sport/cricket/counties/7814553/ECB-outlaws-Warwickshires-idea-to-start-bowling-double-bouncing-deliveries.html.

Welch's plans, he received encouragement from the MCC, the guardian of the laws of the game, which declared the delivery legitimate. As a result, the delivery can potentially be used in tournaments like the Indian Premier League or the World T20, over which the ECB has no control. Keith Bradshaw, the chief executive of the MCC, was quoted as saying, 'We don't think it is against the Spirit of Cricket or contrary to the Laws of the game . . . we see it as the same as the switch-hit and unless it changes the balance between the bat and ball we see no reason to change our view.'[67]

A comparison can be made with the incident that led to the introduction of the other action prohibited under the subsection of Law 24(6), namely that the delivery of the ball by rolling it down the pitch must be determined as a no-ball. In a one-day international between Australia and New Zealand in 1981, the Kiwis needed six off the last ball to tie the match. The Australian player Trevor Chappell was ordered by the captain, his brother Greg Chappell, to bowl the last ball of the match underarm, rolling the ball along the ground to prevent the New Zealand batsman from being able to hit the winning runs. Richie Benaud, the esteemed ex-cricketer and commentator, stated that the delivery was 'the most gutless thing I have ever seen on a cricket field'.[68]

What is cheating?

Whereas the first bowling incident has been disapproved of as not within the spirit of cricket, but is a strategy which may be legitimised in the future in other countries and competitions, the second incident was summarily seen to constitute a form of cheating and a rule change ensued. But what do we mean by 'cheating'? It is invariably seen as actions that are contrary to the rules of the sport; but can it be reconciled with the playing culture of the sport; when does the law have a role to play in regulating it? Leaman has attempted to define cheating:

Leaman, O, 'Cheating and fair play in sport'

It is not as easy as it might initially be thought to define cheating in sport and it is just as difficult to specify precisely what is wrong morally with such behaviour and why fair play should be prized. In this article I intend to try to throw some light on the notions of both cheating and fair play and to suggest that stronger arguments than those so far produced in the literature are required to condemn the former and approve the latter.

Let us try to deal first with the definitional problem of what sorts of behaviour constitutes cheating and come to the ethical issue later. Gunther Luschen boldly starts his essay on cheating in sport with this definition:

> Cheating in sport is the act through which the manifestly or latently agreed upon conditions for winning such a contest are changed in favour of one side. As a result, the principle of equality of chance beyond differences of skill and strategy is violated.

A problem with this definition is that it omits any consideration of intention. After all, if a player unwittingly breaks the rules and thereby gains an unfair advantage he will not necessarily have cheated. For example, if a boxer has a forbidden substance applied to bodily damage without his knowledge, then he has not cheated even though the rules have been broken to his advantage. Were he to be penalised or disqualified, it would not be because of his cheating but due to the rules having been broken by those who attend to him in the intervals.

A superior account of cheating is then provided by Peter McIntosh, who claims that:

> Cheating . . . need be no more than breaking the rules with the intention of not being found out . . . Cheating, however, implies an intention to beat the system even although the penalty, if the offender is found out, may still be acceptable.

---

67 Ibid.
68 Quoted in op. cit., fn 19, Fraser (2005), p 148.

But McIntosh next claims that:

> This definition, however, is too simple. It is not always the written or even the unwritten rule that is broken; tacit assumptions which one contestant knows that the other contestant acts upon may be rejected in order to gain an advantage.

McIntosh's adaptation of Luschen's account makes possible the useful distinction between intending to deceive, which he calls cheating, and breaking the rules without having that intention. He concludes that 'Cheating is an offence against the principles of justice as well as against a particular rule or norm of behaviour'.

> If people undertake to play a game, then they may be taken to have understood and agreed to the rules of the game and the principle upon which any fair victory in the game must rest . . . Yet what are 'the rules of the game' to which players supposedly commit themselves when they enter a game? If we look at the ways in which some sports are played it becomes evident that the rules of the game involve following the formal rules in so far as it is to the advantage of one's own side and breaking them when that is perceived, perhaps wrongly, to be to the side's advantage, where the possibility of suffering a penalty is taken into account. The existence of an authority in games enshrines cheating in the structure of the game; the authority is there to ensure that cheating does not interfere with the principle of fairness in a game. He is there to regulate cheating so that it does not benefit one side more than the other except where one side is more skilful at cheating than the other and to see that the amount of cheating which takes place is not so great as to change the general form of a particular game. That is, the formal rules of the game must in general be adhered to by all players since other-wise in a clear non-moral sense the game is not being played. But if we are profitably to discuss the notion of the rules of the game and of cheating and fair play, we must address ourselves to the ways in which players and spectators perceive those rules rather than to an abstract idea of the rules themselves. The next step is to determine what notion of fair play is applicable within the context of the ways in which players actually participate in sporting activities. An injection of realism into philosophical discussions of cheating and fair play in sport is long overdue.[69]

Cheating is therefore a complex philosophical phenomenon.[70] Four more examples from the cricket world will be used to illustrate this concept.

Bodyline

Holt, R, *Sport and the British: A Modern History*

All this brings us to 1932 and the 'bodyline' tour. The bones of the business can be set out quite simply. After being soundly beaten by Australia in England in 1930 mainly as a result of the remarkable batting of Bradman, whose 334 at Headingley broke the existing Test record, England had to find a way to contain the 'Don' and win back the Ashes. The England captain, Douglas Jardine, for all his Oxford amateurism, was a grim competitor. Like some of his Australian critics, he did not believe simply in 'playing the game for its own sake' and being a 'good loser'. Jardine had only one advantage in comparison to Bradman's Australia. He had a formidable pace attack at his disposal in the form of Larwood, Voce, Bowes and Allen. To be able to draw upon four fast

69 Leaman, O, 'Cheating and fair play in sport', in Morgan, W (ed), *Sport and the Humanities: A Collection of Original Essays* (1981), Educational Research and Service, University of Tennessee, pp 25–30.
70 See Luschen, G, 'Cheating in sport', in Landers, D (ed), *Social Problems in Athletics* (1977), Urbana: University of Illinois; McIntosh, P, *Fair Play: Ethics in Sport and Education* (1994), London: Heinemann; Meier, W and K (eds), 'Part IV – fair play, sportsmanship and cheating', in *Philosophical Inquiry in Sport*, 2nd edn (1995), Champaign: Human Kinetics; Simon, R, *Fair Play: Sports Values and Society* (1991), Boulder: Westview.

bowlers was extremely rare in the days when spin was still regarded as essential for a balanced side. The fact that Harold Larwood was possibly the fastest bowler of all time gave Jardine a potentially strong hand to play. It was the way he played that hand which caused the trouble.

Bradman had proved a magnificent player of spin bowling. If he had any weakness at all it was perhaps a tendency to play too much off the back foot and to hook the high fast ball on the line of the body. Whether the 'bodyline' assault was coldly premeditated by Jardine or it was Larwood himself who hit upon it while bowling to a momentarily nervous Bradman during the 1930 series may never be fully resolved. What is more important is that both captain and bowler were determined to use intimidatory bowling to unsettle Bradman. Larwood always claimed it was a fair tactic but it was precisely the legitimacy of playing this way which was at the heart of the controversy. Though he was slightly built, mentally Larwood was a tough professional, an ex-miner, who believed the batsmen who got the glory had to be able to take punishment and show courage when it was needed. Jardine also felt intimidatory bowling was legitimate. He set a leg-side field and waited for a simple catch as the batsman tried to protect himself from a sharply bouncing ball aimed at the upper body and an unprotected head. In brief, the tactic seemed to work. Bradman's test average slumped from over a hundred to a mere 50 – still well ahead of the rest – but England regained the Ashes.

The real trouble came in the third Test at Adelaide when the Australian captain was felled by a short pitched but straight ball from Larwood. What really incensed the crowd was Jardine's switch to a full leg-field immediately after the accident. Later the Australian wicket keeper Oldfield was struck on the head, again from a straight delivery from Larwood, and the crowd roared angry abuse at the England team. Jardine, who was believed to loathe Australians and to enjoy baiting them by his supercilious attitude, silk handkerchief and Harlequin cap, was the main target. When drinks were brought out, a voice from the crowd was heard to shout, 'Don't give him a drink, let the bastard die of thirst.' Jardine had been barracked in the earlier 1928–29 tour of Australia and was said to have deeply resented it. He had even requested that spectators be forbidden to attend net sessions. At the end of the day's play the England manager, 'Plum' Warner, who had been born in Australia and captained several successful pre-war tours, went to enquire about the injuries after the game and received what has since become the best-known rebuke in the history of the game: 'Of two teams out there,' said Woodfull, 'one is playing cricket, the other is making no effort to play cricket.' There are several versions of the precise form of words he used but the message was unmistakable and Warner left deeply hurt. Privately he urged Jardine to desist from the tactic but without success. 'Not cricket?' roared the Australian popular press and matters became much worse when the Australian Cricket Board surprisingly made public a telegram they sent to the MCC which read 'Bodyline bowling has assumed such proportions to menace the best interests of the game . . . in our opinion it is unsportsmanlike.' To have been a fly on the wall of the Long Room at Lord's when this arrived would have been a rare treat. The MCC have diplomatically 'lost' the records of their discussions but their icy reply insisting the 'unsportsmanlike' be withdrawn and offering to cancel the tour is well known. By implication the Australian cricketing authorities and public were questioning the good faith of the British in the common morality that bound them together . . . the MCC could not contemplate the public humiliation of accepting that their side was 'not playing the game'. So the MCC had to stick by its man for the duration of the series and the Australians withdrew the word 'unsportsmanlike'. But in the time-honoured traditions of the British establishment Jardine was quietly ditched despite his success and Larwood was never selected for England again. At this time in the 1930s this style of bowling was labelled as cheating. It would be interesting to see whether it would be viewed in the same way in modern cricket.[71]

---

71 Holt, R, *Sport and the British: A Modern History* (1989), Oxford: Clarendon, p 233, by permission of OUP. See Le Quesne, L, *The Bodyline Controversy* (1983), London: Macmillan; and op. cit., fn 19, Fraser (2005), for further discussion of the bodyline strategy.

Ball tampering I: dirt in the pocket

The second example comes from a Test match against South Africa in 1994, when the England cricket captain, Mike Atherton, was fined £1,000 by the Test and County Cricket Board (forerunner of the England and Wales Cricket Board), after he admitted not telling the whole truth over 'ball tampering' allegations. Atherton was seen on television putting his hands in his pockets and apparently rubbing something on the ball. Atherton said that he had dirt in his pockets, which he was using to dry his fingers on a clammy day. There is nothing wrong with this – but it would be illegal to use it on the ball, contrary to the Laws of Cricket and Law 42(5):

The Laws of Cricket 1980 Code – Law 42, Fair and Unfair Play

(5) Any member of the fielding side may polish the ball provided that such polishing wastes no time and that no artificial substance is used. No one shall rub the ball on the ground or use any artificial substance or take any action to alter the condition of the ball. In the event of a contravention of this Law, the Umpires, after consultation, shall change the ball for one of similar condition to that in use prior to the contravention. This Law does not prevent a member of the fielding side from drying a wet ball or removing mud from the ball.[72]

On the face of it the act was the time-honoured behaviour of a man doing something illegal to make the ball swing. However, Atherton, when challenged by the match referee Peter Burge to explain his actions, said he was drying his hands in his pockets and did not mention the dirt in there. With reference to the rule, a number of questions were left unanswered. Did Atherton rub dirt on the ball? What is an artificial substance? This raised interesting issues of interpretation:

Fraser, D, 'Balls, bribes and bails: the jurisprudence of Salim Malik'

The case of Michael Atherton with its legal, interpretative difficulties may well be more accurately classified as a case of 'perjury' or 'perversion of the course of justice' rather than as a case of 'ball tampering'. Nonetheless it remains true that it originally started off as what appeared to be a clear-cut case of 'ball tampering' and remains classified as such by many observers of the game. Whatever jurisprudential taxonomy one decides to apply in this case, however, it is clear that it was treated by all concerned, almost from the outset, as something different from a 'Pakistani ball tampering case'. It serves as a classic example of the way in which the apparently neutral discourses and practices surrounding the legal and ethical issues in question actually serve to establish a dual system of legal rules and ultimately of 'justice'. This epistemological and juridical duality is confirmed by recent events.[73]

Fraser goes on to recount how Atherton's misdemeanours were largely forgotten when he batted for almost 15 hours to save the Test against South Africa at Johannesburg in the return series in 1995. 'Atherton was treated as a hero of the great colonial struggles of yore.'[74]

Brearley, M, 'Cricket: Atherton affair: the dirt that is in all our pockets'

'Unfamiliar action', as the Test and County Cricket Board statement put it, it certainly was. I had never heard of a cricketer pocketing dirt to dry his hands. What is less clear is whether, in the same statement's second quaint phrase, 'there was nothing untoward'; this strange little incident contains, concealed in pockets about its person, several dubious psychological substances.

---

72 The Laws of Cricket, 1980 Code, MCC.
73 Fraser, D, 'Balls, bribes and bails: the jurisprudence of Salim Malik' (1995), Law and Popular Culture Research Group working papers, Manchester Metropolitan University, p 12.
74 Ibid, p 12.

The poets were right to see 'a world in a grain of sand' and 'fear in a handful of dust'! These issues touch us all. Are we not all inclined, to some degree, to be both over-suspicious and naive; to be self-righteous and to turn a blind eye? Do we not all have deep-seated responses to the possible downfall of the Great and the Good, ranging from horror to salacious triumph? This pocketful of dirt – does it epitomise the dirt we all carry, usually hidden, however white our gear?

In a society where cricket is supposedly synonymous with fair play, is the burden of expectation on England's captain too great? What, too, is the role of the cricket Establishment? Have they done all they could to be seen to be both fair and stringent? Do we have one standard for our own and another for others? (And this can work both ways: we can condemn our own man, like Caesar's wife, simply for being suspected – which in a world of lascivious suspiciousness may be simply unjust – or we may refuse to believe that one of us is dishonest while assuming dishonesty in, say, a Pakistani bowler.) And what, exactly, was Michael Atherton up to? If dishonest, he seemed so unconcerned; if honest, so disinclined to come clean.

First, the evidence; and then, as the Michelin guides have it, a little history. I start with the sequences shown on television news on Monday. To my eyes, Atherton looks like a man taking a little pinch of snuff from his pocket; instead of sniffing it, he appears to drop it on the ball. The stuff looks like fine, grey dust. He then polishes the ball and hands it to the bowler, Gough, who takes it with finger and thumb, presumably touching only the seam, gingerly, as if the rest of the ball were made of china. When questioned about what had happened, Atherton at first failed to mention the dirt in his pocket. Later he said that he had used it to dry his hands but that he didn't apply it to the ball. The umpires stated that the condition of the ball had not been altered. Later, Illingworth fined him £1,000 for doing whatever he was doing with the ball and £1,000 for not coming clean about the dirt with the match referee. I gather that Atherton had picked up the dust from the footholes not long before.

Now for the history. In England the traditional way of interfering with the ball has been to raise its seam with the nail. This practice is not, I think, endemic but it is certainly not rare. Seam picking goes on because English pitches often permit movement and the slightly raised seam makes such movement slightly more likely. Most professionals would tend to shrug their shoulders at a minor degree of seam raising. They would also be angered by the few who have gone further and more substantially and systematically altered the seam. From time to time umpires are instructed to check the condition of the ball frequently. Such spot checks eradicate the habit for the time being. Overseas the ball moves off the seam less and the likelier form of minor cheating has been to put skin cream or lip salve on the ball and thereby heighten the polish. This helps orthodox swing, that is, swing where the bowler delivers the ball with its shiny half on the side from which the ball is to swing; this shinier side meets less resistance and travels faster through the air. Sweat, a natural substance, is permitted for this purpose.

More recently, in Pakistan, where the ball tends to get roughened by the bare ground quicker than elsewhere, a new technique – reverse swing – has been developed. Apparently the essential requirement for this is an oldish ball whose non-shiny side is kept dry; hence the need for dry hands. For some reason reverse swing usually means in-swing. In Gough, England now have a bowler capable of doing this. Reverse swing can transform the game, since, as the innings goes on, it can make batting suddenly much harder rather than, as one would usually expect, easier. It also means that there is less need for spin bowlers, who usually do most of their work with the old ball. I first encountered this sharp, old ball in-swing batting against Sarfraz Nawaz in Karachi in 1972 but had no idea how he did it. Keeping the rough side dry is not the only aid to reverse swing. Bowlers have been accused of lifting the quarter-seam and scuffing and gouging the rough side. This, if practised, is ball tampering writ large. But I find it hard to understand why regular spot checks don't rule out such practices.

If I am right, that Atherton put a pinch of dust on the ball, then it is not true that he was using it only to dry his hands. (And wouldn't he need to dry both hands, not only his right hand?

Why not two pockets of dirt?) However, the umpires say the ball's condition was not altered and I see no reason to doubt this. The fine dust was probably used only to dry sweat from the ball. Moreover, the law does not say that no substances may be applied to the ball, only artificial ones. Presumably the intention was to rule out all substances except sweat; but dust, though perhaps artificial in contrast to sweat, is not artificial in contrast to sun cream. Nowadays, the ball may not be rubbed in the dirt but the laws don't explicitly rule out dirt being rubbed in the ball. (As far as gravediggers are concerned, the man going to the water is a different matter from the water coming to the man: *Hamlet* Act V Scene 1.)[75]

This particular Cricket Law in the new 2000 Code has been expanded considerably to attempt to address this perceived problem. As with the law generally, are more sporting rules necessarily going to be 'good laws' and provide better regulation? They often create very specific problems of interpretation. As will be seen below in the third example of alleged cricket ball tampering, a reading and interpretation of the Law below can be problematic.[76]

The Laws of Cricket (2000 Code 4th Edition – 2010)– Law 42, Fair and Unfair Play

3. The match ball – changing its condition
    (a)   Any fielder may
        (i)   polish the ball provided that no artificial substance is used and that such polishing wastes no time;
        (ii) remove mud from the ball under the supervision of the umpire;
        (iii) dry a wet ball on a towel.
    (b)   It is unfair for anyone to rub the ball on the ground for any reason, interfere with any of the seams or the surface of the ball, use any implement, or take any other action whatsoever which is likely to alter the condition of the ball, except as permitted in (a) above.
    (c)   The umpires shall make frequent and irregular inspections of the ball.
    (d)   In the event of any fielder changing the condition of the ball unfairly, as set out in (b) above, the umpires after consultation shall
        (i)   change the ball forthwith. It shall be for the umpires to decide on the replacement ball, which shall, in their opinion, have had wear comparable with that which the previous ball had received immediately prior to the contravention;
        (ii) inform the batsmen that the ball has been changed;
        (iii) award 5 penalty runs to the batting side. See 17 below;
        (iv) inform the captain of the fielding side that the reason for the action was the unfair interference with the ball;
        (v) inform the captain of the batting side as soon as practicable of what has occurred;
        (vi) report the occurrence as soon as possible to the Executive of the fielding side and any Governing Body responsible for the match, who shall take such action as is considered appropriate against the captain and team concerned.
    (e)   If there is any further instance of unfairly changing the condition of the ball in that innings, the umpires after consultation shall
        (i)   repeat the procedure in (d)(i), (ii) and (iii) above;
        (ii) inform the captain of the fielding side of the reason for the action taken and direct him to take off forthwith the bowler who delivered the immediately preceding ball. The bowler thus taken off shall not be allowed to bowl again in that innings;

---

75 Brearley, M, 'Cricket: Atherton affair: the dirt that is in all our pockets', *The Observer*, 31 July 1994, p 10; also see 'Cheating art that's not just cricket', *The Observer*, 31 July 1994.
76 See later, p 64.

(iii) inform the captain of the batting side as soon as practicable of what has occurred;

(iv) report this further occurrence as soon as possible to the Executive of the fielding side and any Governing Body responsible for the match, who shall take such action as is considered appropriate against the captain and team concerned.[77]

Ball tampering II: in the High Court

The legitimacy of ball tampering has become an ongoing debate within the cricket world.[78] The third example, the libel action by ex-English test cricketers Ian Botham and Allan Lamb, against the accusations of the ex-Pakistani test cricketer Imran Khan, had a complex underlying narrative concerning cheating. The dispute which resulted in the costly High Court action can be traced back to the summer of 1992, when the Pakistan cricket team arrived in England with allegations of cheating being made against them. The 1992 series, which Pakistan won 2–1, was described in court as savage and ugly, with accusations of cheating being made by the tabloid press against Pakistan's two fast bowlers, Wasim Akram and Waqar Younis. There were headlines like 'Paki cheats' and claims that the two Pakistan bowlers had regularly been tampering with the ball, by either picking the seam or scratching it on one side, to make it swing more than it should. Some even suggested that this had contributed to their World Cup win against England months earlier.[79]

The controversy resurfaced in 1994 when Imran admitted in a biography that he had scratched a ball with a bottle top while playing for Sussex in a county match. Imran claimed in court that he was merely trying to highlight the unacceptable face of ball tampering which he claimed had gone on in English cricket for years. Picking the seam with your fingers or applying a bit of grease to one side of the ball was 'tacitly accepted', but using outside agents like bottle tops was overstepping the limit. 'That is what I would call cheating,' Imran confessed while giving evidence during the trial.

Lamb and Botham responded swiftly to the Imran biography. In May 1994, Lamb contributed an article to *The Sun* newspaper in which Imran was accused of cheating and teaching Younis and Akram how to tamper with the ball. This was followed by an article in the *Daily Mirror* in which Botham called for a full investigation into Imran's ball tampering and demanded his resignation from the International Cricket Conference. Less than a week later, Imran, who by now had retired from Test Cricket and was concentrating on building a cancer hospital in his native Lahore, responded by giving an interview to *The Sun*. Under the headline 'World's greatest bowlers have all doctored the ball', he once again claimed that ball tampering was an accepted part of English cricket.

With England–Pakistan cricket relations at an all-time low, matters deteriorated when extracts from an interview given by Imran to *India Today* magazine appeared in the British press. He was quoted as calling Botham and Lamb racists, claiming that their approach to the whole issue of ball tampering was 'irrational' because they were 'lower-class and uneducated'. It was this interview that led Botham and Lamb to bring their libel action against Imran, while Botham alone was suing him for the *Sun* article, claiming that Imran had called him a cheat. At the trial a material issue discussed at some length concerned technical details of what happens to a cricket ball when it is scratched, has its seam picked or lip salve is applied. The issue of what constitutes cheating in cricket became crucial and the darker side of cricket was publicly exposed, with successive players, including England captain Mike Atherton and ex-test cricketer and television commentator Geoffrey Boycott, admitting that ball tampering was part and parcel of the game. At the end of the day it was a tussle between three cricket giants with egos to match who refused to back down once heated words were exchanged over what is cheating in their sport.

---

77 The Laws of Cricket, 2000 Code – Law 42, Fair and Unfair Play – see www.ecb.co.uk.
78 Khan, I, 'ICC need to come to grips with laws', *The Daily Telegraph*, 24 January 1996.
79 Also note the ball-tampering allegations that led to the early end of the Test match between England and Pakistan in 2006, see p 64.

This was the second time Lamb had been in a libel action. He was fined £5,000 by the Test and County Cricket Board after accusing Pakistani bowlers of ball tampering in 1992. The following year he was sued for libel by former Northamptonshire and Pakistani paceman Sarfraz Nawaz. The case was settled out of court but effectively ended his England career after 79 Tests, three as captain.[80]

Ball tampering III: Oval 2006

On the fourth day of the fourth Test match between England and Pakistan in August 2006, the match was ruled to have been forfeited and was awarded to England. This was because the Pakistan team returned to the ground around 30 minutes late after the scheduled tea break, after Umpire Darrell Hair had ruled that a member of the Pakistan team had tampered with the ball. After consultation with his colleague, Umpire Billy Doctrove, Pakistan were penalised five runs and the England batsmen were able to select another ball. The view of the Pakistan team was that the condition of the ball was that which would have been expected after the use of the elapsed 56 overs, and there was no evidence of deliberate scuffing.

Subsequently, as a result of disciplinary proceedings, the Pakistan captain, Inzamam-ul-Haq was cleared of ball tampering by the ICC but banned for four matches for bringing the game into disrepute. At a meeting of the ten Test-playing nations in November 2006, the ICC said they had 'lost confidence' in Hair, and that he would be excluded from the umpires list until his contract expired in March 2008. Hair subsequently initiated an action of racial discrimination, after being dropped from the elite umpires list. Hair claimed that while he – a white Australian – had been severely punished for the episode, Doctrove – a black West Indian – had escaped all censure. He said his competence as an umpire had never been questioned, and racism was the only possible explanation for his suspension. However, Hair dropped his claim after one week of proceedings before the employment tribunals and soon retired from umpiring.[81]

In 2008, the ICC formally changed the result to a draw. However, a second change was made in 2009 when the ICC board decided to reverse that decision and to reinstate an England win in the match. ICC chief executive Haroon Lorgat was reported as saying that the decision ensured 'the integrity of the game ... after reconsidering that match, taking into account the views of the MCC, some of the legal opinions we've got, the board was pretty unanimous in upholding the original umpires' decision'.[82]

Plethora of cheating incidents

In contemporary sport, examples of sharp practice seem to be regular stories in the sports pages.

Beloff, MJ, 'Editorial'

Now is the autumn of our discontent. Sport is submerged in a sea of scandal, ranging from the crime (Crashgate) to the ridiculous – the literal (for once a word correctly used) moving of the goalposts by Kim Christensen of IFK Gothenberg, caught on the all seeing video eye and constituting a misdemeanor so exotic that the rules of the game don't cater for it. A case for an implied offence maybe?

Flavio Briatore (a sometime client of mine while with Benneton) conceived a dangerous scheme to put his star driver Fernando Alonso in pole position (but midway through the race) at the Singapore Grand Prix 2008 by instructing another driver, Nelson Piquet Jr, to crash his car into a

---

80 See 'Judge raises finger to expansive Boycott', *The Guardian*, 27 July 1996, p 3, and 'Botham libel case: an exercise in futility', *The Guardian*, 1 August 1996, p 9. For other sporting libel cases see *Tolley v Fry* [1931] AC 333 (HL) and *Williams v Reason* [1988] 1 WLR 96 (CA) (both concerning allegations of shamateurism).

81 'Hair ends ICC discrimination case', BBC News, 9 October 2007, http://news.bbc.co.uk/sport1/hi/cricket/7035551.stm.

82 'Result U-turn for 2006 Oval Test', BBC News, 1 February 2009, http://news.bbc.co.uk/go/pr/fr/-/sport1/hi/cricket/7863464.stm.

barrier. Although Briatore is not directly subject to FIA jurisdiction, the effect of the FIA's ruling is to make him a motor sport leper, with whom no one subject to that jurisdiction can safely do business.

Whether what he did constitutes a crime under Singapore law (damage to property) has not been much discussed. But the Singapore Extradition Act lists 'acts done with the intention of endangering vehicles' and (more conventionally) 'malicious or wilful damage to property' as extradition crimes, so Briatore, like Roman Polanski, should take care where he travels to.

Two aspects of the reaction to the incident call for comment.

First the suspended sentence given to Team Renault seems not merely unduly lenient [such as would attract an Attorney General's reference to the Court of Appeal (Criminal Division) if meted out by a Crown Court judge], but contrasts strongly with the multi-million-pound fine imposed on McClaren last year for illicit acquisition of their rival's designs.

Secondly, Bernie Ecclestone's suggestion that Briatore's punishment was too harsh was particularly bizarre coming as it did from a member of the Commission that determined that sanction. Proportionality, consistency, the concept that justice should not only be done but be seen to be done are hallmarks of a mature system of domestic disciplinary law as well as of the law of the land. The sooner the FIA abdicates its self-contained jurisdiction and subscribes to the jurisdiction of the Court of Arbitration for Sport, as FIFA, UEFA and the IAAF have all done within the last decade, the more likely it is that the eccentricities I have described will be purged from this major global sport.

Bloodgate – the faking of a blood injury by Harlequins wing Tom Williams in order to justify the bringing onto the pitch of a proven goal kicker in the Heineken cup quarter final – led to a three years' ban for the legendary forward and club Director of Rugby, Dean Richards – like Briatore the brains behind the scam. As with long-term bans for doping offences in track and field – and other sports – issues about unreasonable restraint of trade are immediately engaged. Richard's own brief, the well-known sports lawyer Mark Gay, went public with the opinion that the sentence on his client was 'savage and excessive'; Hugh McIlvanney, the doyen of British sports journalists, took the opposite view, describing what Deano did as a 'larcenous enterprise'.

What is notable about Crash'gate and Bloodgate (Richard Nixon has a lot to answer for: the description of his hotel-bugging crime has become a lazy cliché, abused by those who do not even know its origins) is that the persons at the sharp end (in the Bloodgate case also literally), Nelson Piquet Jr and Tom Williams, walked virtually scot free. Williams reaped the benefits of whistle blowing, although – if press reports are accurate – it seems that his candour was a quality lately discovered and only when his efforts to strike a lucrative bargain with the club for his silence failed.

Eduardo's dive (or was it?) in a Champions' League match procured a penalty for Arsenal against Celtic rather than a yellow card for the player. It resulted in some characteristically eloquent words from Arsène Wenger (who, like the first of the three monkeys, sees no evil – at any rate where a Gunner is involved) about the charges brought against his player, and some twists and turns by UEFA ultimately overturning the original match ban, when the video evidence proved inconclusive, especially as to whether there was intent, mens rea as well as actus reus (in the end even the most sophisticated technology cannot provide definitive answers to issues such as whether a player cheated). But the real issue was possible disparity of prosecution. Players dive week in week out without attracting the attention that Eduardo's case did. There may indeed be a case for exemplary sentences to discourage this type of cheating, but it should be pre-announced and applied without discrimination.

All these cases provoked agonized debate about the corruption of sporting morals by money and the death of the Corinthian ideal. But all had legal dimensions. Brian Moore, who has triple qualifications as a distinguished player, a former solicitor and a journalist, put his finger on the nub of the matter in his column in the Daily Telegraph: 'laws must be well thought out, clear, well known, and consistently exercised '. And so say all of us.

In none of these incidents was the result of the game changed. Alonso might not have won the race but for Piquet's crash; or Arsenal have defeated Celtic despite the referee's hash. Harlequins went out of the Heineken Cup but for Williams's gash. In such situations the law is incapable of rewriting outcomes.

A different position obtains where the winner is not the beneficiary of some irregularity or breach of rule, but actually ineligible to compete. The saddest summer story was that of the South African athlete Caster Semenya, whom I watched win, in emphatic style, the 800m for women at the World Track and Field Championships in Berlin. Doubts have now been raised about whether she was indeed, by the controversial tests applied for gender identification, a woman at all. The athlete ran in all innocence. The outcome of investigation into her gender remains at the time of writing uncertain. What is certain, however, according to the IAAF is that she will retain her gold medal. But if she was ineligible to complete, why should this be so? Harsh cases can make bad law.[83]

The two highly publicised events listed above were the so-called 'Crashgate' and 'Bloodgate'.[84] One key issue is the application of disciplinary procedures and relative punishments, including playing bans and fines, applied to individuals for different types of sporting infringement.[85]

Evaluating cheating

In which types of situations can cheating be identified? Are the actions cheating when institution-alised over a period into the playing culture of the particular sport?[86] Are the intentions of the perpetrator a salient issue — cheating only occurs with a clear cognition on the part of the athlete?[87] What about the legitimacy and impact of sports psychology in modern sport, where sportsmen are taught how to psyche out opponents to gain a narrow but important advantage?[88]

Do the examples above illustrate the inadequacies of the internal rules of sport and maybe the need for the law to intervene, or do they in fact identify the flexibility of rules and the real problems of precise interpretation? This would seem to present a good example of 'rule scepticism', a concept which is identified with the jurisprudential movement, the American Realists, who were most prominent in the first half of the twentieth century. This concept emphasises the inherent problem of reducing law into a precise form of a set of rules, as the American Realists argued it is not possible to make exact interpretations of rules, be they legal or non-legal. The Atherton example is a good illustration of this problem. If we accept the validity of rule scepticism this suggests we need to be cautious in regarding the law as being able to provide exact solutions to the problems of sport.

Technological doping

The paradigm example of the construction of cheating in sport today is doping. The discussion on this will be expanded later.[89] Connected to this is so-called 'technological doping', with the use of new technology in terms of equipment and increasing sports science expertise that is pushing the boundaries of the physiological capabilities of the human body. An example is the banning of new swimsuits, which it is claimed provide an unfair advantage to those who use them, diluting the impact of the human talent and distorting competitive balance.[90]

---

83 ISLR 2009, 4, 67–8;

84 For more on Bloodgate see James, M and Gillett, M, 'The medical and legal implications of "Bloodgate"', (2010) SLA &P, Feb, 15–16; Cutting, S, 'Cheating: Feigning of Blood Injuries in Rugby Union: Implications' (2010) WSLR 8(1).

85 See Findlay, R, 'Harmonising punishment for cheats: issues & challenges' (2010) WSLR 8(3) 11–13.

86 See Greenberg, M and Gray, J, 'The legal aspects of the Tonya Harding figure skating eligibility controversy' (1994) 2(2) SATLJ 16.

87 Note the debate surrounding the concept of 'strict liability' in anti-doping controls; see later, Chapter 8.

88 See Bailey, D, 'Reappraising the strategic approach to regulating sporting conduct' (2009) SLA&P, Oct, 4–7.

89 See Chapter 8.

90 See for example Heshka, J and Lines, K, ' Swimming – Credibility Crisis or Tempest in a Teapot?' (2008) SATLJ 16 (3); also see Advisory opinion CAS 2000/C/267 Australian Olympic Committee (AOC), 1 May 2000 and Arbitration CAS 2009/A/1917 *Amaury Leveaux & Aurore Mongel v Fédération Internationale de Natation* (FINA), order of 29 July 2009.

Another example involves the South African athlete, Oscar Pistorius, a double-amputee. Pistorius, aka 'the Blade Runner', argued before the International Association of Athletics Federations (IAAF) that he should be eligible to compete in the able-bodied Olympics in Beijing in 2008 using his prosthetic limbs. In 2007, the IAAF prohibited the use of 'any technical device that incorporates springs, wheels or any other element that provides a user with an advantage over another athlete not using such a device'. The IAAF sought to bar him on the grounds that the technology of his prosthetics may have given him an unfair advantage over sprinters using their natural legs. Tests carried out by the IAAF on Pistorius running with his carbon fibre limbs concluded that he would have an unfair advantage when competing with the so-called able-bodied athletes. The tests concluded that his prosthetic limbs, essentially carbon fibre transtibial artificial limbs (fitting below the knee), would give him an unfair advantage over runners competing with non-prosthetic legs. Rather than bring him up to the norm, it was suggested that Pistorius's prosthetic legs would enhance his capacity to run. The prosthetic legs, it is argued, make him taller and give him a longer stride than he would have had with his natural legs, thereby giving him an unfair advantage when using them to compete against those without such prosthetics.

But the issue is not just one of advantage but of an 'unfair' advantage. Critiques of enhancement aids in the context of athletic performance typically rely upon two claims: first, that achievement has not been earned; and secondly, that the use of aids is unfair because not all athletes have equal access to them. In May 2008, however, the Court of Arbitration for Sport ruled that there was insufficient evidence to prove that Pistorius's flexible prosthetic legs gave him an advantage.[91]

Murphy, M, 'Participation Rules: Pistorius case: implications of his successful IAAF challenge'

The scientific evidence placed before the court did not prove conclusively that Pistorius was advantaged against other competitors when approached in this way and weighed with the evidence and opinions of the scientists who assisted Pistorius and who prepared a report described by the CAS as the 'Manhattan Report'. The IAAF bore the risk of non persuasion and this proved crucial. After assessing all the evidence, including that provided by the experts who assisted Pistorius, the CAS was not persuaded, the IAAF council should not have been persuaded and the appeal succeeded. A mountain of work was clearly done by all of the scientists involved and those representing the parties (and especially Pistorius) and the effect of that on the outcome cannot be understated. But have their efforts and Pistorius' challenge taught any lessons beyond the confines of this case?

It appears, at a first reading, that the CAS did not think so. Towards the end of the CAS award written by Professor Martin Hunter, there are a number of cautionary notes making the point that it is 'important to clarify what the result of this appeal does not decide. Firstly, the panels' decision applies to Mr Pistorius while using the particular model of Cheetah Flex-Foot prostheses that was the subject of the Cologne tests and shown to the panel as exhibits during the hearing in Lausanne. It is not a general licence for Mr Pistorius to use any further developments of the Cheetah Flex-Foot that might be found to provide him with an overall net advantage.

'Secondly, the panel does not exclude the possibility that, with future advances in scientific knowledge, at a testing regime designed and carried out to the satisfaction of both parties, the IAAF might in future be in a position to prove that the existing Cheetah Flex-Foot model provides Mr Pistorius with an overall net advantage over other athletes.

'Thirdly, the panel's decision in this appeal has absolutely no application to any other athlete, or other type of prosthetic limb. Each case must be considered by the IAAF on its own merits. The ruling does not grant a blanket licence to other single or double amputees in

---

91 Arbitration CAS 2008/A/1480 *Pistorius v/ IAAF*, award of 16 May 2008.

IAAF-sanctioned events using Cheetah Flex-Foot prosthetics, or indeed any other type of pros-
thesis. Each amputee athlete must collaborate with the IAAF to have his or her eligibility under
Rule 144.2(e), as interpreted by this panel, established on an individual basis. The panel hopes
that this will not impose a substantial new burden on the IAAF, because of the unique nature of
Mr Pistorius' case. However, if it does create an additional burden, it must be viewed as just one
of the challenges of twenty-first-century life.'[92]

Also of course the spectre of genetic engineering, with manipulation of the human genome – the
creation of the super athlete – will present immense ethical dilemmas in the sports world in the
coming years.[93]

Similarly, the use of various forms of equipment that will aid those who are physically challenged
in some way to compete with able-bodied athletes can be construed as a form of cheating. One example
is that of Casey Martin, a professional golfer with a birth defect in his right leg known as Klippel-
Trenaunay-Weber Syndrome. In order to walk, Casey has to wear a strong support stocking to keep the
swelling down. His right leg is two sizes too small and his doctors have told him there is a good chance
he will lose the leg in the near future. He claimed that he should be able to use a golf cart or buggy to
allow him to compete on a level playing field with able-bodied golfers and that, in prohibiting him
from using this aid, the PGA Tour, which organises major golf tournaments in the USA, would be acting
in a discriminatory manner under Title III of the Americans with Disabilities Act (ADA).[94]

The PGA Tour's arguments were that firstly, as the governing body, it should always have the
ability to make its own rules and regulations and the use of golf carts was forbidden. Second, it was
argued that walking is an integral part of the game and should not be lost. This is predicated on the
grounds that fitness and stamina are an important part of the game of golf and that by making an
exception to the tour's walking-only rule, it would change the nature of the game and, under
certain conditions, give Martin an unfair advantage over the rest of the field. At trial, the court found
in Martin's favour. The case finally ended on appeal at the US Supreme Court.

PGA Tour, Inc v Martin (00–24) 532 US 661 (2001) 204 F 3d 994, affirmed

Allowing Martin to use a golf cart, despite petitioner's walking requirement, is not a modification that would 'fundamentally alter the nature' of petitioner's tours or the third stage of the
Q-School. In theory, a modification of the tournaments might constitute a fundamental
alteration in these ways: (1) It might alter such an essential aspect of golf, e.g., the diameter of
the hole, that it would be unacceptable even if it affected all competitors equally; or (2) a less
significant change that has only a peripheral impact on the game itself might nevertheless give
a disabled player, in addition to access to the competition as required by Title III, an advantage
over others and therefore fundamentally alter the character of the competition. The Court is
not persuaded that a waiver of the walking rule for Martin would work a fundamental alteration
in either sense. The use of carts is not inconsistent with the fundamental character of golf, the
essence of which has always been shot-making. The walking rule contained in petitioner's
hard cards is neither an essential attribute of the game itself nor an indispensable feature of
tournament golf.[95]

---

92 Murphy, M, 'Participation Rules: Pistorius case: implications of his successful IAAF challenge', (2008) WSLR 6(9); also see
Charlish, P and Riley, S, 'Should Oscar Run?' (2008) Fordham Intell Prop Media & Ent LJ 18 929.

93 See Miah, A, 'The engineered athlete: human rights in the genetic revolution' (2000) 3(3) Culture, Sport and Society; Miah, A,
Genetically Modified Athletes: Biomedical Ethics, Gene Doping and Sport (2004), Abingdon: Routledge.

94 The potential relevance of the Pistorius and Martin cases to disability discrimination law in Britain is considered in Chapter 10
pp 476–7.

95 *PGA Tour, Inc v Martin* (00–24) 532 US 661 (2001) 204 F 3d 994, affirmed.

This ruling in favour of Martin was based on an overruling of the PGA Tour's view of the essential nature of the walking rule. There was a dissenting judgment, however, given by Justice Scalia, known for the conservative nature of his rulings.

Scalia, J, dissenting, *PGA Tour, Inc v Martin*

If one assumes, however, that the PGA Tour has some legal obligation to play classic, Platonic golf – and if one assumes the correctness of all the other wrong turns the Court has made to get to this point – then we Justices must confront what is indeed an awesome responsibility. It has been rendered the solemn duty of the Supreme Court of the United States, laid upon it by Congress in pursuance of the Federal Government's power '[t]o regulate Commerce with foreign Nations, and among the several States,' US Const., Art. I, §8, cl. 3, to decide What Is Golf. I am sure that the Framers of the Constitution, aware of the 1457 edict of King James II of Scotland prohibiting golf because it interfered with the practice of archery, fully expected that sooner or later the paths of golf and government, the law and the links, would once again cross, and that the judges of this august Court would some day have to wrestle with that age-old jurisprudential question, for which their years of study in the law have so well prepared them: Is someone riding around a golf course from shot to shot really a golfer? The answer, we learn, is yes. The Court ultimately concludes, and it will henceforth be the Law of the Land, that walking is not a 'fundamental' aspect of golf.

Either out of humility or out of self-respect (one or the other) the Court should decline to answer this incredibly difficult and incredibly silly question. To say that something is 'essential' is ordinarily to say that it is necessary to the achievement of a certain object. But since it is the very nature of a game to have no object except amusement (that is what distinguishes games from productive activity), it is quite impossible to say that any of a game's arbitrary rules is 'essential'. Eighteen-hole golf courses, 10-foot-high basketball hoops, 90-foot baselines, 100-yard football fields – all are arbitrary and none is essential. The only support for any of them is tradition and (in more modern times) insistence by what has come to be regarded as the ruling body of the sport – both of which factors support the PGA Tour's position in the present case. (Many, indeed, consider walking to be the central feature of the game of golf – hence Mark Twain's classic criticism of the sport: 'a good walk spoiled'.) I suppose there is some point at which the rules of a well-known game are changed to such a degree that no reasonable person would call it the same game.

The various courts which heard this case were clear that under the ADA cases should be decided on their own merits and no decisions would create a precedent for the future. Subsequently, in *Olinger v United States Golf Association*[96] the claimant argued he needed to use a golf cart because his disability, bilateral avascular necrosis, impaired his ability to walk. It was held, however, that the use of the golf cart would fundamentally alter and be an unreasonable modification of the game.

To conclude this section, in comparison to the use of prohibited drugs in sport and the issues around fixing of the results of matches in exchange for financial reward, both of which strike directly at the integrity of sport and will be examined in detail later, the incidents that have been discussed above are more subtle attempts to exploit and subvert the gaps in the playing rules and the wider playing culture for sporting advantage. The key question is: can these issues be resolved within this rule structure or is there a need for wider regulatory mechanisms to come into play? Legal intervention can attempt to at least protect the rights and interests of athletes, when the sporting rules fail. As Beloff *et al* claim, '. . . more lawyers in sport does not necessarily mean more justice in sport, but it may do, and it should do. The growth of legalism in sport is borne of a desire for higher standards of justice.'[97]

---

96 *Olinger v. United States Golf Association*, 55 F Supp 2d 926 (ND Ind, 20 May 1999).
97 Beloff, M, Kerr, T and Demetriou, M, *Sports Law* (1999), Oxford: Hart, p 6.

The Contemporary Regulation of Sport

In the UK, the law's role in playing a key part in the regulation of sport has become ever more significant in recent years. The second half of this chapter will chart that development and attempt to understand the different role that the law plays. This could not be done without mentioning the work of Edward Grayson, acknowledged as the 'founding father' of British sports law. He has strongly supported the involvement of law in the operation of sport over this period. His early writings, culminating in the book *Sport and the Law*, the first edition of which was published in 1988,[98] have been crucial in identifying and recognising this area of law. Grayson argues:

> . . . the law can and should come to the help of sport; and indeed . . . sport with its high profile and image can come to the help of the law. For sport without rules and their control creates chaos. Society without laws and their enforcement means anarchy.[99]

Similarly he believes:

> The rule of law in sport is as essential for civilisation as the rule of law in society generally. Without it generally anarchy reigns. Without it in sport, chaos exists.[100]

Supporting Corinthian values, Grayson argues that:

> . . . if sport and its rulers cannot or will not try to preserve that Corinthian tradition, which the citations throughout . . . and the inspiration for this book demonstrate is an ideal realistically recognised and capable of attainment to aim for, if not always achieved, then the courts can and will do it for them, through the law of the land at both criminal and civil levels and certainly if adequate compensation is required.[101]

Grayson regards the essential amateur Corinthian values as the epitome of sportsmanship and expresses concern about the increasingly dissipating ethos of modern professional sport. Corinthianism can be seen as a historical attempt to introduce a specific form and version of ethical behaviour. However, the view that these were in fact the dominant values in British sporting history has already been questioned. Much of sport in the past has been violent, secular, partisan and competitive. Sportsmanship is clearly a positive virtue as far as participation in sport is concerned. Players of the post-war era such as footballers Bobby Charlton, Gary Lineker and David Beckham and cricketers Denis Compton,[102] David Gower and Michael Vaughan embody that ethos.[103] Grayson uses pre-Second World War cricketers such as GO Smith and CB Fry and the Corinthian cricket and football teams to support the view that sport was played with absolute adherence to the letter and spirit of the rules.[104] The one fact that these sportsmen and teams shared in the early 1900s was their upper-class background of public school education and privilege. Grayson believes it was their background and professional lives as 'doctors, lawyers [sic] and schoolmasters' that provide them

---

98 Grayson, E, *Sport and the Law* (1988), London: Butterworths; also see *Police Review*, 19 November 1969; 'On the field of play' [1971] NLJ 413; 'The day sport died' [1988] NLJ 9; 'Keeping sport alive' [1990] NLJ 12.

99 Grayson, E, *Sport and the Law*, 2nd edn (1994), London: Butterworths, p vii.

100 Grayson, E, former President of the British Association for Sport and Law, in his inaugural presidential address, (1993) 1(1) SATLJ.

101 Ibid, p xxxvi.

102 On Compton's death in 1997, see 'Cricketing cavalier who dazzled a nation', *The Daily Telegraph*, 24 April 1997.

103 Also see 'Professional touch from the last Corinthian', *The Daily Telegraph*, 26 April 1997 on the rugby player, Lawrence Dallaglio.

104 See Grayson, E, *Corinthians and Cricketers: And Towards a New Sporting Era* (1996), Harefield: Yore. Also see Grayson, E, 'Sports and the law: a return to Corinthian values?', Inaugural professorial lecture, Lord's Cricket Ground, 15 January 1998, and 'Casuals stroll on defiantly', *The Observer*, 19 January 1997.

with this outlook on sport. He presents a view of the past where sport was purely played for the love of participation.

Gamesmanship and 'shamateurism' (sportsmen who were reified as amateurs and participating in sport merely for the love of the game but were in fact involved in paid work) in sports history have existed for many years. For example, the 'amateur' cricketer, WG Grace, earned £8,835 in 1895 and an estimated £120,000 during his lifetime, equivalent today to millions of pounds.[105] Corinthian values such as fair play and the joy of participation are still powerful values in contemporary sport – but limited largely to recreational and amateur levels. The commercial reality of contemporary sport is that participation has other motivations and, especially at the elite level, the nature of sport is much more complex. Grayson clearly supports the argument that modern sporting bodies cannot be trusted to uphold these Corinthian values (perhaps better stated as being the custodians of ethical positions) and that the rule(s) of law is needed. Commenting on the reasons for writing *Sport and the Law*, he once again stresses that dispute resolution should not be left to sports administrators:

Grayson, E, *Sport and the Law*

Many within both sport and the law could not see any need for bringing the law into sport believing, with the author, that it ought always to be enjoyed for fun and, at times, as a spectators' entertainment. Indeed they were generally hostile to such a position. For whatever the true meaning and the position of sport in society may be, if ever all of its elements can be defined, too many thought that sport was cocooned in a world of its own, sealed off from reality and the rule of law. The vagaries and limitations upon human conduct and contact, however, preclude such idealism in an ever-growing intensively competitive and commercially orientated sporting climate. Thus the creation of a book which explored that theme required justification, notwithstanding the existence for over a century of intervention by the courts and of Parliament, in relation to specific sporting issues. I was placed in a defensive position six years ago in 1988 in order to justify the subject of sport and the law. That defence was against a combination of abuse, ignorance, ridicule and hostility linked to the arrogance of feudalism based on an absence of awareness of the past which has permeated so much of sporting administration and still lingers again. The intervening six years, however, have changed all that. Indeed, anyone who seeks to challenge the need for law to partner sport for the benefit of each discipline in 1994 should examine his or her conscience . . . today no one can argue that the subject of sport and law does not exist.[106]

Wither sport and the law: what direction should sport take today? Whatever route is taken, the rule of law, on and off the field, alone can and must guide it within a rapidly revolving social setting whose pace can hardly match the kaleidoscopic changes daily imposed upon the public mind and eye.[107]

Whether it is a loss of the Corinthian values in sport or not, in many people's eyes there is a dissatisfaction with what sport has become in the modern world. Some detect a loss of innocence, a fading away of the essential spirit and values of sport that has been replaced by cynicism, gamesmanship and commercial excess.[108] It may well be, however, that past generations have had this same view of the deterioration of what they understand as sport, and nostalgia for a lost notion of true sport and sportsmanship. This is not just a British phenomenon. For example, in the United

---

105 Not only was he paid very well for his services, he was infamous for his tactics of gamesmanship; see Midwinter, E, *WG Grace: His Life and Times* (1981), London: Frank Cass; Holt, R, *Sport and the British: A Modern History* (1989), Oxford: Clarendon; and Sandiford, K, *Cricket and the Victorians* (1994), London: Frank Cass.
106 Op. cit., fn 99, Grayson (1994), pp xxxi–xxxii.
107 Ibid, p 418.
108 See 'The corruption of our sporting life', *The Sunday Times*, 18 December 1994, pp 2–20; 'Hijacking of our dreams', *The Observer*, 9 April 1995; 'Every little breeze seems to whisper new sleaze', *The Observer*, 19 March 1995.

States a number of disputes, notably the baseball strike that wiped out the second half of the 1994 season and the World Series, led to widespread spectator disillusionment.[109]

In Britain, sport has been subject to numerous sporting scandals during the 1990s and into the new millennium: drug use, cheating, corruption and others. The national game, football, seems to have been the most scandal-bound.[110] This can be combined with a lack of success of British sports teams and individual athletes on the world stage, perhaps crystallised with the small number of medals won at the Atlanta Olympic Games in 1996.[111] In comparison, the relative success at recent summer and winter Olympics, and the high expectations of London 2012, has boosted the 'feelgood factor' that sport has the power to create.[112]

Any cursory review of the daily newspapers reveals an increasing propensity of the law to be involved in the regulation of sport. This is not an absolutely new phenomenon: as we have seen, the state has been involved in regulating sporting activity for centuries, largely on grounds of policy-driven aims of prohibition. But today the law is intervening in sport in increasingly diverse ways and reaching into all the interstices of the sporting world.[113] Of course the general law that regulates social activities and relations in all areas of social life is involved in sport, in spheres such as the regulating of contracts of employment and services, revenue law taxing sport as a business and personal injuries law. But not only has there been the emergence of sports-specific legislation;[114] sports law-related litigation is widespread. This may of course reflect a more litigious society generally,[115] but over the last few decades a number of lawyers have begun to spend a considerable amount of their professional time on sports-related legal issues and a number of firms have sizeable sports law workloads.[116]

This leads to the question: does the law have a legitimate role to play in sport? This is a contentious issue. Clearly there are areas of sport where the law needs to intervene in terms of facilitating commercial dealings and supporting sports athletes' rights – here its role is uncontroversial. However, there are areas where this intervention is contested. At various points in the book, this issue will be highlighted. It needs to be remembered that in opposition to the view of Grayson that, 'the rule of law in sport is as essential for civilisation as the rule of law in society generally. Without it generally anarchy reigns. Without it in sport, chaos exists',[117] the law may not always be the saviour of sport and the most effective form of regulation.

The causes of this greater role of the law will be evaluated. In Chapter 5 and at other points in the book, the increasingly commercialised nature of sport, particularly at the elite level, will be examined. Legal issues concerning sport are, however, not solely concerned with commercial law – a wide variety of sports law issues have become a part of the general discourse of sport. The next section will attempt to put this expansion of sports law within a theoretical context of why it

---

109 For details, see 'America's field of bad dreams', *The Times*, 12 March 1995; 'Baseball strikes in the field of nightmares', *The Independent on Sunday*, 26 March 1995; 'Why sports don't matter anymore', *The New York Times Magazine*, 2 April 1995, p 50; Cosell, H, *What's Wrong with Sports* (1991), New York: Pocket Books; Weiller, P, *Levelling the Playing Field* (2000), Cambridge, MA: Harvard UP.

110 See 'How soccer sold its soul', *The Observer*, 3 December 1995; 'Football's drug crisis', *The Guardian*, 17 June 2001; 'Men behaving badly in version of the Mad Hatter's tea party', *Daily Telegraph*, 21 September 1996.

111 See 'Our athletes under cloud at Olympics', *The Sunday Times*, 4 August 1996; 'Troubled legacy of blighted games', *The Observer*, 4 August 1996.

112 See 'Success at Sydney', *The Times*, 30 September 2000.

113 See Grayson, E, *Sport and the Law*, 3rd edn (2000), London: Butterworths; Moore, C, *Sports Law Litigation* (1997), Birmingham: CLT; Griffith-Jones, D, *The Law and Business of Sport* (1997) London: Butterworths; Verow, R, Lawrence, C and McCormick, P, *Sport, Business and the Law* (1999), London: Jordan: Beloff, M, Kerr, T and Demetriou, M, *Sports Law* (1999), Oxford: Hart; and Stewart, WJ (ed), *Sport and the Law: The Scots Perspective* (2000), Edinburgh: Butterworths, focused primarily at practitioners. Greenfield, S and Osborn, G (eds), *Law and Sport in Contemporary Society* (2000), London: Frank Cass; Caiger, A and Gardiner, S (eds), *Professional Sport in the European Union: Regulation and Re-regulation* (2000), The Hague: Asser, are focused primarily on a wider academic examination. More focused books have appeared too – McArdle, D, *From Bootman to Bosman: Football, Society and Law* (2000), London: Cavendish; O'Leary, J (ed), *Drugs and Doping in Sport: Socio-Legal Perspectives* (2000), London: Cavendish. There are two UK-based sports law journals that provide updated information and commentary: *Sports Law Administration and Practice* and the *International Sports Law Review*.

114 Most notably in football, ie Football Spectators Act 1989, Football (Offences) Act 1991, Football (Offences and Disorder) Act 1998, Football Disorder Act 2000.

115 But see Armstrong, N, 'The litigation myth' (1997) 147 NLJ 1058.

116 See 'Legal eagles have landed', *The Observer*, 25 September 1995.

117 Op. cit., fn 100, Grayson (1993).

is happening and how best we can understand it, and will consider whether there is an area of self-regulation and 'sporting autonomy' into which outside regulation and the law should not intrude.

Juridification of Sport: The Role of Law

As expounded above, sport is internally governed and subject to a complex interaction of normative rules: playing and administrative rules; unwritten conventions and values that have developed informally; sports' complex playing cultures that develop to gain advantage and circumvent the formal rules (that may or not be constructed as cheating); and the engagement of codes of ethics to challenge perceived deficiencies in the behaviour regulated by this normative structure.[118] Also it is claimed that the dynamics of internal policing of and adjudication over sport's internal regulatory structure are inconsistent. If this internal regulation of sport is ineffective, does the law of the land have a role to play? If yes, when? How does it fit into this already crowded normative rule structure? An attempt will be made to provide an answer in the following section. It is clear that a complex 'normative rule milieu' now exists, with the rules of sport being supplemented and overridden by national, supra-national (European Union) and international law.

A major issue attending the intervention of law into new 'sporting arenas' is juridification: what were intrinsically social relationships between humans within a 'social field' (here sport) become imbued with legal values and are understood as constituting legal relationships – thus social norms become legal norms.[119] If a dispute then befalls the parties, a legal remedy is seen as the primary remedy. This invariably changes the nature and perception of the dispute and the relational connection between the parties.

Foster, K, 'Developments in sporting law'

> Juridification . . . at a simple level, it merely reproduces the traditional idea of private and public realms, with private areas increasingly being subject to public or judicial control, a move from voluntarism to legalism. But it offers also a more complex version which stresses the interaction as legal norms are used to reorder the power relations within the social arena.[120]

The debate around the juridification of sport has been characterised by the view held by Grayson that 'the law of the land never stops at the touchline'.[121] Although the quote arises from a study of the specific area of criminal liability for foul play on the sports field, it is a metaphor for a wider project that Grayson provides for law. The opposing view, held by this book's authors, among others, is that juridification is not automatically beneficial to sport and needs careful analysis.

Sport is not alone in being a social field that has increasingly become legally regulated. The 'private area' of the family, for example, has increasingly become regulated by the law; examples include the development of remedies for domestic violence, particularly against women; the recognition of child abuse as a real social problem; and the initiation of the Child Support Agency to bring to account errant fathers. There may be criticism of how the law actually works in these and connected areas, but few would argue that the family should not be subject to this 'public' legal regulation. The argument that law should never be involved in regulating sport is clearly absurd. The question is when and to what extent it should be involved.

---

118 It may be that the influence of ethics increasingly means that the informal playing culture is an amalgam of (il)legitimate strategy and codes of ethics.
119 See Bourdieu, P, 'The force of law: towards a sociology of the juridical field' (1987) 38 Hastings Law Review 814.
120 Foster, K, 'Developments in Sporting Law', in Allison, L (ed), *The Changing Politics of Sport* (1993), Manchester: Manchester UP, p 108.
121 Grayson, E and Bond, C, 'Making Foul Play a Crime' (1993) Solicitors Journal 693.

An important part of this process is the ability of lawyers to develop new areas of work. The involvement of lawyers in sport can be compared with their involvement in other environments where their participation is contested. As Bankowski and Mungham argue, concerning tribunals of both a legal and a wider quasi-legal nature, 'the creation and maintenance of legal problems by lawyers follows a . . . pattern . . . when "proper" becomes synonymous with "legal" and "paid" then there is created a pressure to abandon extra-legal means of dispute settlement in favour of legal ones.'[122] Similarly, Flood and Caiger, in their examination of lawyers' rivalry with non-lawyers to control arbitration mechanisms in the construction industry, argue, 'Lawyers are in a strong position to effect colonisation because of their power over the discourse of legalism. They have the power of appropriation.'[123]

The danger is that the law too easily becomes the primary regulatory mechanism to be used to provide remedies. However, it is increasingly argued that law is best understood in contemporary society, not in the classic formulation of English jurisprudence as a collection or model of rules but as a form of 'governance' or regulation. Alan Hunt stresses that this occurs not only through law but other quasi-legal and non-legal mechanisms:

Hunt, A, 'Law as a constitutive mode of regulation'

The model of law as regulation can be seen as a shift towards public law that focuses on the varied means whereby extensive fields of social life are made subject to regulatory intervention . . . we should recognise the diversity of legal phenomena and avoid falling into the presumption of a unitary entity 'the law' . . . on the one hand law exists as an increasingly detailed and particularistic regulation of ever more specific situations and relations in which any boundary between law and non-law is difficult if not impossible to identify. On the other hand this important recognition of the diversification and pluralisation of law and regulation should not lead us to forget about the role that law plays as the medium of an ever-expanding State.[124]

This view fits in with the interaction of law with internal sporting rules. The reluctance of the courts to judicially review sporting bodies' internal rule-based decisions perhaps indicates the contrary view that sports should govern themselves and are separate from the law of the land. Law's increased intervention in sport in recent years provides a mix of legal and quasi-legal regulation.

Hunt uses the work of the French philosopher Michel Foucault as the basis of his study of the sociology of governance.[125] He sees Foucault's contention that, although law was important in the pre-modern world as a form of control, in modern society (from the end of the eighteenth century) law has largely given way to 'governance' and 'policing', a more complex multidimensional form of regulation. One of Foucault's most persistent influences on political philosophy is his ideas on discipline and surveillance, in that increasingly the state uses bodies of knowledge to intervene as a form of power. As Hunt says, 'the picture that he is taken to have painted is of ever extending and ever more intrusive mechanisms of power that insert themselves into every nook and cranny of social and personal life'.[126]

One aim of this for Foucault is the stated aim for increasing 'normalisation' and the search for new sites of disciplinary intervention. Can sport be seen as one of these sites needing regulation? Of course, some of the sociological perspectives discussed earlier see sport itself as a form of social control. In a wider context, Steve Redhead sees the law's intervention in popular culture generally (sport being a significant part of this culture) as closely associated with the regulation of social

---

122 Bankowski, Z and Mungham, G, *Images of Law* (1976), London: Routledge, p 62.
123 Flood, J and Caiger, A, 'Lawyers and arbitration: the juridification of construction disputes' (1993) 56(3) MLR 412.
124 Hunt, A, 'Law as a constitutive mode of regulation', in *Explorations in Law and Society: Towards a Constitutive Theory of Law* (1993), London: Routledge, p 307.
125 Foucault, M, *Discipline and Punish: The Birth of the Prison* (1977), London: Penguin.
126 Op. cit., fn 124, Hunt (1993), p 288.

activities that are considered to be morally reprehensible, a threat to social order.[127] The earlier historical extracts showed how this has occurred particularly concerning team sports, especially those seen as the wrong type, notably football and the concomitant control of the crowd. Redhead sees the regulation of football as a clear example.[128] The work of Geoffrey Pearson is pertinent with his focus on the state's control of football and surrounding culture by its construction as something that was a threat and should be feared, what Pearson calls 'respectable fears'.[129] This construction of social problems has also been termed 'moral panics'.[130] Although football has persistently been subject to such condemnation, Redhead sees that much of popular culture has been censured since the end of the nineteenth century:

Redhead, S, *Unpopular Culture: The Birth of Law and Popular Culture*

The whole field of 'law and popular culture' (or law and 'play' to coin another phrase) is of increasing scholarly interest in the field of legal, social and cultural studies, not least in the massive body of regulatory instruments (court cases and statutes, local authority bylaws) now in place which require interpretation and application. In Britain, for instance, such laws seem to be literally everywhere. For example, consider the following Bills: the Entertainment (Increased Penalties) Act 1990 (dubbed the 'Bright' Bill or 'Acid House' Bill in the press) and its attack on the organisation of what have been called pay parties or legal or illegal 'raves'; the Football Spectators Act 1989 and its abortive compulsory identity card scheme to combat soccer hooliganism with its introduction of new measures to stop soccer fans travelling abroad and ban convicted offenders attending designated matches; the Football (Offences) Act 1991 with its attempt to outlaw racist abuse, pitch invasions and other 'hooligan' activity at domestic soccer matches; the strengthening of licensing laws to close down certain clubs through the Licensing Act 1988; the calls for changes in the environmental and other laws to curb the noise of all-night dance parties and the nuisance of the 1990s folk devils such as 'New Age travellers' and 'ravers' in various parts of town and countryside . . . the moral panics about ecstasy (MDMA), LSD, cannabis and other 'recreational' (as defined by users) drug taking amongst large swathes of late twentieth-century global youth.

These regulatory regimes all exhibit familiar features of the relationship between law, market and the state in the 1990s and illustrate contemporary attempts to regulate, discipline and police popular culture in the late twentieth century which apply generally to many countries outside the national boundaries from where specific examples are drawn. Indeed such boundaries are part of the problem, as technologies and other changes make control on such borders/lines almost impossible. But these aspects of legal discourse are for some commentators plainly what might be termed more or less 'repressive' in that they are seen to be part of a larger network of what many theorists persist, even in the 1990s, in calling 'social control' through criminal justice and penal systems which have in the past been theorised as part of the 'law and order control culture'. In the cruder, over-simplified versions of this conception, the State, through law, is seen as capable only of acting negatively – or repressively – against a group, class or individual. Power is conceived in much of this mode of theorising as a thing, an instrument, which is wielded by one group, class or individual against another . . . such theorisation of legal discourse and agency is often unsatisfactory – though Foucauldian alternative theorisations of the productivity of power can be equally problematic – especially when it is focusing on new instances of folk devils, moral panics or law and order campaigns.[131]

---

127 Also see Stanley, C, *Urban Excess and the Law: Capital Culture and Desire* (1996), London: Cavendish.
128 Also see the calls to have legislative intervention to regulate crowds at cricket matches in (2001) 4(4) Sports Law Bulletin 3.
129 See Pearson, G, *Hooligan: A History of Respectable Fears* (1983), London: Macmillan.
130 See Cohen, S, *Folk Devils and Moral Panics: The Creation of Mod Rockers* (1972), London: MacGibbon & Kee, for an explanation and analysis of moral panics.
131 Redhead, S, *Unpopular Culture: The Birth of Law and Popular Culture* (1995), Manchester: Manchester UP, pp 7–8.

Moral panics can therefore be seen as having justified some legal intervention in sport. Their creation in popular culture and sport arises from a complex amalgam of social pressures, the media having a central role in their amplification. Recent social examples are the allegations of satanic abuse, dangerous dogs, and the perceived widespread problem of road rage. Redhead presents a number of issues that have justified state intervention in regulating popular culture. In sport, football – and specifically football hooliganism – has been the most prone to this effect and this will be discussed at some length later in the book.[132] The consequence is 'panic law' that is invariably bad law in being ineffective and feckless. It fits in with the wider regulatory view of law colonising new social fields and expanding its sphere of influence.

There is a wider jurisprudential debate concerning the role of law within this complex regulatory milieu. There are those who see 'autonomous law' increasingly replaced by a bureaucratic regulation;[133] there are also those who see a positive development in this diversification of legal regulation.[134] What is clear, however, is that the boundaries between formal law and other normative rules are increasingly blurred.

This development reflects the jurisprudential theory of 'legal pluralism', associated with the work of writers such as Boaventura de Sousa Santos:

Santos, B, 'On modes of production of law and social power'

The legal regulation of social relations is not the exclusive attribute of any [one] form of normative order, it is rather the end result of a combination of the different forms of law and the modes of production thereof.[135]

In social contexts or social fields such as sport, legal pluralism seems credible and illuminating in terms of that area's regulation. The work of Stewart Macaulay on the non-contractual and therefore non-legal forms of business relations is an example of such a 'specific context'.[136] On sport, Macaulay has said:

Macaulay, S, 'Non-contractual relations in business: a preliminary study'

There is an official law, but there are complementary, overlapping, and conflicting private legal systems as well ... spectator sports offer versions of law that differ from that found in law schools. They also offer alternative resources from which people fashion their own understandings of what is necessary, acceptable and just.[137]

There is a complex interaction between the rules of sport and the rules of law that are increasingly intervening within a complex regulatory framework of various types of rules and quasi-law. Legal pluralism provides us with a theoretical context to make sense of this complex setting. It also provides

---

132 See Greenfield, S and Osborn, G, 'Criminalising football supporters: ticket touts and the Criminal Justice and Public Order Act 1994' (1995) 3(3) Sport and the Law Journal 36; Greenfield, S and Osborn, G, 'After the Act: the (Re)construction and regulation of football fandom' (1996) 1(1) Journal of Civil Liberties 7; Greenfield, S and Osborn, G, 'When the whites go marching in? Racism and resistance in English football' (1996) 6(2) Marquette Sports Law Journal 315; Gardiner, S, 'The law and hate speech: "Ooh aah Cantona" and the demonstration of "the other"', in Brown, A (ed), *Fanatics! Power, Identity and Fandom in Football* (1998), London: Routledge.

133 See Hayek, F, *Law, Legislation and Liberty* (1973–79), three volumes, London: Routledge; Posner, R, 'The decline of an autonomous discipline' (1987) 100 Harvard Law Review 761.

134 See Luhmann, N, *A Sociological Theory of Law* (1985), London: Routledge; Teubner, G (ed), *Dilemmas of Law in the Welfare State* (1986), New York: Walter de Gruyter.

135 Santos, B, 'On modes of production of law and social power' (1985) 13 International Journal of the Sociology of Law 299, 307; also see Teubner, G, 'Legal Pluralism in the World Society', in Teubner, G (ed), *Global Law Without a State* (1997), Andover: Dartmouth.

136 Macaulay, S, 'Non-contractual relations in business: a preliminary study' (1963) 28 American Sociological Review 55.

137 Macaulay, S, 'Images of law in everyday life: the lessons of school, entertainment, and spectator sports' (1987) 21 Law and Society Review 185.

us with a theoretical position with which to support the view that the interventionist role of the law in sport is too pervasive and to highlight the importance of other non-legal forms of regulation.

It must be stressed that this intervention of law in sport has come in many forms. In the UK, the traditional forms of both primary and secondary legislation have been enacted in specific areas and case law has emerged across a wide area. European Union law has had an increasing regulating influence on professional sport. Additionally reflecting the international nature of sporting competition and organisation, it is not surprising that an embryonic international sports law can be identified. Lastly, arbitration mechanisms, and most notably the Court of Arbitration for Sport, are providing supplementary sources of quasi-legal judgments.

Much of the material in this book is based on national law. A significant amount is based on the legal provisions that have emerged from the developing European Union policy in sport, which will be focus of Chapter 4. The wider international nature of sports law regulation will now be the focus.

Globalisation of Sports Law

Sports law issues are increasingly international in nature. There are a number of international sports bodies that have been noted: the Fédération Internationale de Football Association (FIFA), the International Olympic Committee (IOC) and the International Association of Athletics Federations (IAAF). Sports disputes often involve relationships between individual athletes and national and international bodies. Arbitration and mediation mechanisms, most notably the Court of Arbitration for Sport in Switzerland, are dedicated to resolving sports disputes, which often involve international issues. Issues of jurisdiction therefore become vital. The development of an 'international sports law' is becoming a practical necessity. As was highlighted in the previous chapter, sport is a practice that has developed from being largely localised and uncodified in its earliest forms, to the current position where many sports have a universal code of laws and regulations and are regulated by organisations that purport to influence their sports wherever they might be played.

De Knop, P, 'Globalization, Americanization and localization in sport'

Introduction

Today's world is tomorrow's village. As a consequence of increased mobility, new communication technologies, exploding information networks, mass media and the all-embracing economy, we are now experiencing globalization in numerous areas. We are living in a world where national borders are becoming ever more porous and in which different globalization processes are occurring (Horseman and Marshall, 1996). Sport, too, is going through this globalization, which has great impact on the way it is managed.

Definitions

'Globalization can be defined as the intensification of world-wide social relations which link distant localities in such a way that local happenings are shaped by events occurring many miles away and vice versa. This is a dialectical process because such local happenings may move in an obverse direction from the very distanciated relations that shape them. Local transformation is as much a part of globalization as the lateral extension of social connections across time and space' (Giddens, 1990, p 64).

Results – Globalization

That sport is going through a globalization process may be concluded from the facts enumerated hereunder.

1. A universalization of western sports, eastern combat sports, etc is taking place. Research in twenty different countries world-wide (De Knop *et al*, 1996) has found that there are hardly any major sports practised today which are exclusive to the youth of one (or only some) countries.

2. There is a marked presence of international 'sports heroes' such as Lewis, or Jordan, who are seen as universal role models. Some forms of sport contribute to globalization, not by contributing to the development of a metaculture, but rather through a fragmented and segmented culture, which regroups individuals independently from the national level. Such is the case, to a certain extent, for high-performance athletes whose identities are linked more to a network of training and competition than to any element of their national heritage, such as language or religion (Harvey and Houle, 1994).

3. (World) trade in sportswear and equipment is flourishing. Especially the large multinationals and sport brands such as Nike, Adidas and Reebok have stood to gain from the increased significance of sport. These three brands are undoubtedly the largest distributors of sports-wear and sports shoes. It is striking, however, that the majority of people buying these brands never or hardly ever engage in sport of any kind. Sports goods have become world-wide fashion articles through world-wide promotional campaigns and sponsoring.

4. Due to ever increasing specialization, the manufacture of products has become fragmented. Reich (1991) provides an example of economic, technological, and industrial globalization and interdependence in connection with sport: 'Precision hockey equipment is designed in Sweden, financed in Canada, and assembled in Cleveland and Denmark for distribution in North America and Europe, respectively, out of alloys whose molecular structure was researched and patented in Delaware and fabricated in Japan' (p 112). The sports goods industry does not only aim at growing segments of a global market but also adopts global strategies of production, such as delocalization. A growing portion of the population in developing countries is engaged in the production of goods for the reproduction of the lifestyles of those living in developed countries.

5. The power of the international sports organizations (IOC, AGFI, FIFA, etc) has increased. This is illustrated by, for example, the fact that the IOC decides the allocation of the Games to the Olympic cities, but also the Olympic recognition of a sport and thereby, indirectly, its popularity. According to the Olympic Charter a sport must comply with the following criteria in order to be an Olympic sport: it must be widely practised by men in at least seventy-five countries and on four continents and by women in at least forty countries and on three continents.

6. Public sports policy is discussed in a number of international structures, e.g., in the Council of Europe.

7. International (European) legislation has come to play an important role in sports, some-times with major consequences (eg, the *Bosman* case).

8. The Olympic Games, the Commonwealth Games, various world championships, and other uni- or multi-sports tournaments at a global level have gained in economic and political importance . . .

Conclusion

To sum up, it may be concluded that there is clearly a globalizing trend in sport. At the same time we notice a growing apart, a polarization of, on the one hand, the ever more commercial top-class sports and, on the other, the revival of local recreational sports and local traditions. The revival of local popular sports, such as folk games or traditional games are examples of this.

So, globalization versus localization. This phenomenon was described by Featherstone (1990) as the 'paradox of culture', or, in other words, seemingly contradicting tendencies going hand in hand. Both globalization and localization are manifestations of an ever increasing differentiation in sport, which has great impact on the organization of sport.[138]

A paradox of sport can therefore be identified in terms of both its characteristics of 'globalisation' and 'localisation'.[139] However, it is clear that regional and international sports federations regulate by cutting across traditional boundaries.[140] In effect it is often the case that these global regulators can override domestic sporting regulators, and even state authorities themselves, to effectively regulate activity within their 'jurisdiction'.

Nafziger, JAR, *International Sports Law*

Domestic law – local, state or federal – may . . . be affected significantly by a variety of forces outside of the control of any of the local decision makers involved. Global forces may encourage new forms of economic and legal harmonisation across legal and economic systems.[141]

Indeed, the International Olympic Committee has been likened to a specialised body of the United Nations.[142] It appears that sports' regulations can tolerate a certain amount of latitude in terms of their interpretation and application, relative to the local cultural, economic, social and legal context of their conduct. This is characterised in the jargon of globalisation as 'resistance'. However, where that 'resistance' imposes a difference so great that the theoretical 'level playing field' becomes unworkable, two possible outcomes arise. In the first instance, where the resistant 'locale' is relatively weak, it appears that the global regulator will in effect be able to ignore that resistance, and the locale will either have to accept the imposition of the global standard or accept isolation from the world system. This, it appears, has often been the case as global sporting standards have been absorbed by domestic systems of law and regulation. However, globalisation is not just a homogenising process; it also works in other ways.

Ougaard, M, 'Approaching the global polity'

Much attention has been given to internationalisation's impact on domestic policy and institutions, but the discourses on 'two levelness' point to the reverse process: domestic forces and processes are increasingly penetrating international politics. A process of *mutual interpenetration* between the domestic and the international is underway. The dual nature of this phenomenon is important. If you focus solely on the first side, you get a picture of domestic forces being subjected to a powerful, actorless process of internationalisation. If you focus on the other side, an element of *empowerment* appears: individuals, political parties, interest groups, etc, can influence events in the outside world, including the politics of harmonisation.[143]

Thus, according to Ougaard, the second scenario is one where the local or regional resistance has sufficient sway to influence the operation of the global system as a whole. This second scenario can be seen very clearly in relation to the re-regulation of football's transfer system. Though the EU was

---

138 De Knop, P, 'Globalization, Americanization and localization in sport' (2000) 2 International Sports Law Journal 20. Literature cited includes De Knop, P and Standeven, J, *Sport and Tourism: International Perspectives* (1999), Champaign, IL: Human Kinetics; Reich, Horseman and Marshall, in Donnelly, P, 'The local and the global; globalization in the sociology of sport' (1996) 11 Sociology of Sport Journal 239; Wagner, E, 'Sport in Asia and Africa: Americanisation or mundialization?' (1990) 7 Sociology of Sport Journal 399.
139 See Maguire, J, *Global Sport: Identities, Societies, Civilizations* (1999), Cambridge: Polity.
140 Note the work of Wallerstein, I. *The Modern World System* (1974), New York: Academic Press.
141 Nafziger, JAR, *International Sports Law* (1988), New York: Transnational, p 3.
142 Aman, A (Jr), 'Indiana Journal of Global Legal Studies: an introduction' (1993) 1(1) Indiana Journal of Global Legal Studies.
143 Ougaard, M, 'Approaching the global polity', Working Paper No 42/99, Centre for the Study of Globalisation and Regionalisation, p 14; emphasis in original. Available at www.csgr.org.

concerned with – and indeed has jurisdiction limited to – activities taking place within EU Member States, the changes implemented in the transfer system have been applied not only in respect of EU territories, but also across the footballing world.[144]

The situation should not be seen as being a question of either the local or the global taking precedence. In truth, the issue is not quite so polarised; the shape of sporting regulation is the result of a complex web of values and incentives, each pulling in a different direction. The case of football's transfer system may, on the face of it, appear to be a clear victory for 'local' EU law over the autonomy of the global regulator, FIFA. However, continuing suggestions that even the new transfer system may be contrary to EU law indicate that the new rules are in effect a compromise between the two, representing not so much a 'victory' for EU law over FIFA autonomy as a shift in the power dynamic toward EU law.[145]

This issue has clear implications for accountability and legal regulation of sports governing bodies. If these global regulators are not subject to law as such, but can effectively 'bargain' with state actors to determine the scope of their powers, how are individuals to effectively secure their rights as against these bodies? One way is through the use of domestic law, though it is clear that domestic courts may not always be able, or in any case willing, to strictly impose domestic law on global actors. In relation to football, FIFA has given clear indications recently that it will not tolerate state interference with the operation of the game's regulation.[146] Though EU law has proven to be a potent weapon where economic rights require protection, it is only in exceptional cases that this has impacted upon the global system through the action of an individual.[147] The impact of globalising tendencies on the ability of individuals to seek redress is emphasised in the following extract:

Devetak, R and Higgot, R, *Justice Unbound? Globalisation, States and the Transformation of the Social Bond*

The language of globalisation . . . has failed to recognise the manner in which the internationalisation of governance can also exacerbate the 'democratic deficit'. States are not only problem solvers, their policy élite are also strategic actors with interests of, and for, themselves. Collective action problem solving in international relations is couched in terms of effective governance. It is rarely posed as a question of responsible or accountable government, let alone justice.[148]

Increasing internationalisation, indeed 'globalisation', of sporting activity clearly raises concerns as to the accountability of the bodies that organise and regulate such activities. While many see this challenge as one to be addressed by domestic and transnational law,[149] others believe the solution to lie with a novel approach to the problem of globalisation:

Weatherill, S, 'After *Bosman*: tracking a sporting revolution'

Should the 'law' of international sporting bodies be treated as an autonomous system worthy of protection from disruption by state law or the law of transnational entities such as the EC? The intellectual case could be made that this is an internally coherent system, which responds to the

---

144 See later, Chapter 9 for full discussion on reform of the transfer system in international football.
145 For further discussion see Boyes, S, 'Globalisation, Europe and re-regulation of sport', in Caiger, A and Gardiner, S (eds) *Professional Sport in the European Union: Regulation and Re-regulation* (2000), The Hague: Asser Press.
146 'FIFA asks Greek Government to refrain from interfering with football', FIFA media release, 20 March 2001; 'Guinea FA suspension maintained, national team excluded from 2002 FIFA World Cup', FIFA media release, 19 March 2001; 'FIFA suspends Football Association of Albania', FIFA media release, 27 November 1996: all available from www.fifa.com.
147 The obvious example is Case C-415/93 *URBSFA v Jean-Marc Bosman* [1996] 1 CMLR.
148 Devetak, R and Higgot, R, *Justice Unbound? Globalisation, States and the Transformation of the Social Bond*, Working Paper No 29/99, Centre for the Study of Globalisation and Regionalisation, p 10; available at www.csgr.org.
149 See below, Chapter 3.

special interests of sport, and which should not be invaded by differently motivated, alien systems. To treat decisions of sporting associations as 'law' in their own right, rather than as private acts subordinate to 'real law', would argue for a differently conceived 'sports law' and would bring to mind questions surrounding choice of which legal order to apply in case of conflict.[150]

It has been suggested that such an approach might be furthered by the development of a 'World Sport Body', to oversee the regulation of sport at a global level.[151] While such an approach might be desirable, it appears that it is politically unlikely, particularly in the eyes of the IOC. However, this does support contentions that the manner in which sport is regulated needs to be conceived of in global terms, even if it is not organised in such a manner.

International Sports Law or Global Sports Law?

As the globalisation of sport has accelerated, the regulation of sport is increasingly in the hands of international sports federations. In turn the regulation of these ISFs has been variously described as both an international sports law and as a global sports law.

James Nafziger is perhaps the leading authority on the international law aspects of sport.

Nafziger, J, *International Sports Law*

The term 'international sports law' refers to a process that comprises a more or less distinctive body of rules, principles, institutions and procedures to govern important consequences of transnational sports activity. As a body of international law, it draws upon the general sources of law that are identified in the most widely accepted checklist, Article 38 of the Statutes of the International Court of Justice. The process of international sports law thus includes provisions of international agreements, international custom, as evidence of general principles accepted as law; general principles (including equity and general principles articulated in the resolutions of international organizations); and as subsidiary sources, judicial decisions (including those of both international and national tribunals) and scholarly writings.[152]

Ken Foster makes the distinction between international sports law and global sports law:

Foster, K, 'Is there a global sports law?'

International sports law can be applied by national courts. Global sports law by contrast implies a claim of immunity from national law. Some authors have used the concept '*lex sportiva*' in a superficial manner to describe what is happening with the globalisation of sports law. I argue that '*lex sportiva*' should be equated to 'global sports law'. To define it thus as 'global sports law' highlights that it is a cloak for continued self-regulation by international sports federations. It is a claim for non-intervention by both national legal systems and by international sports law. It thus opposes a rule of law in regulating international sport.[153]

Both writers view international sports law as universal principles of law that cannot be ignored by ISFs and believe this law can and should be enforced by any available legal institution that has jurisdiction. This would include principles such as those of fair hearings and the doctrine of proportionality. A significant source is the Olympic Charter, 'which codifies general principles,

---

150 Weatherill, S, 'After *Bosman*: tracking a sporting revolution', Sportzaken, Oktober 1999, 75–80.
151 Blackshaw, I, 'Regulating sport globally: a challenge for the twenty-first century' (2000) NLJ 617.
152 Nafziger, J, *International Sports Law* (2004), Transnational: New York, p 1; also see Nafziger, J, 'Globalizing sports law' (1999) 9(2) MSLJ 225; see ICJ website for further details: www.icj-cij.org.
153 Foster, K, 'Is there a global sports law?' (2003) 2(2) Entertainment Law.

custom and authoritative decisions applicable to international sports competition . . . from the normative foundation of international sports law.'[154]

They also agree that the Court of Arbitration for Sport is the source of these principles of a *lex sportiva* (sports law). The basis and role of CAS will be analysed later at length, and, setting aside claims about its lack of independence and flawed procedural issues that question the 'objectivity' of its decision making, it may be inappropriate to talk about an emerging *lex sportiva* anyway. The term *lex specialis*, a less specific body of law, may be a more appropriate term at this stage in the development of international sports law. But even on this point, Nafziger strikes a note of caution, in that 'the *lex sportiva* is the product of only a few hundred arbitral decisions within a limited range of disputes over a historically short period of time. It is more of a *lex ferenda* (future law) than a mature *lex specialis*.'[155]

Although there may be some debate about its significance, I think it is right to talk of a *lex sportiva* fast emerging as the influence of CAS in international sport disputes increases in a range of areas including anti-doping, eligibility for sporting competition and a wide range of commercial issues. An analogy has been made with *lex mercatoria*, a body of trading principles used by merchants throughout Europe in the Middle Ages and the basis of what has become contemporary international commercial law.

Mitten, MJ and Opie, H, 'Sports Law: Implications for the Development of International, Comparative, and National Law and Global Dispute Resolution'

For legal theorists, the evolving body of *lex sportiva* established by CAS awards is an interesting and important example of global legal pluralism without states arising out of the resolution of Olympic and international sports disputes between private parties. It is an emerging body of international law with some similarities to *lex mercatoria*, a much older and well-established body of international commercial law that has developed in the essentially private domain of commercial activity based on custom and arbitration awards.[156]

The growing jurisprudence of CAS as a *lex sportiva* is one element of international sports law, but increasingly a substantial if not the foremost element. This significance of CAS in contemporary sport will be further analysed in Chapter 3.

Foster identifies *lex sportiva* as a global sports law and as such it needs to be carefully distinguished from international sports law:

Foster, K, 'Is there a global sports law?'

. . . a transnational autonomous legal order created by the private global institutions that govern international sport. Its chief characteristics are first that it is a contractual order, with its binding force coming from agreements to submit to the authority and jurisdiction of international sporting federations and second that it is not governed by national legal systems.[157]

He goes on to claim that:

This clear distinction between international and global sports law shows that they are different concepts, which need careful analysis. To conflate the two concepts into a single concept, called *lex sportiva*, is misleading. In particular to describe what is happening with the globalisation of

---

154 Op. cit., fn 152, Nafziger (2004), p 2.
155 Ibid, p 49; *lex ferenda* can be seen as what the law ought to be in a particular area with norms in process of ripening into law.
156 Mitten, MJ and Opie, H, ' "Sports Law": Implications for the Development of International, Comparative, and National Law and Global Dispute Resolution' (2010) Tulane Law Review.
157 Op. cit., fn 153, Foster (2003).

sports law as *lex sportiva* is to imply that international sporting federations are legally immune from regulation by national legal systems. This allows the private regimes of international sporting federations, such as the IOC or FIFA, to be legally unaccountable except by arbitration systems established and validated by those very same private regimes.[158]

Foster's understanding of 'global sports law' is understood as a guise or cloak for continued self-regulation by ISFs. This perceptive distinction has been one largely ignored by other writers in the area.[159] However, it is a crucial distinction that needs to be examined further in terms of whether the growing influence of CAS is in the best interests of justice within sport.

Viva Sports Law – Sport and the Law RIP

In the context of the increasing body of law that has been specifically developed for sport generally, and sports such as football in particular, the penultimate section in this chapter will consider whether there is any identifiable legal subject which should be known as 'sports law' or whether it is more accurate to talk of merely a relationship of 'sport and the law'. The view of two practitioners first:

Grayson, E, *Sport and the Law*

No subject exists which jurisprudentially can be called sports law. As a soundbite headline, shorthand description, it has no juridical foundation; for common law and equity creates no concept of law exclusively relating to sport. Each area of law applicable to sport does not differ from how it is found in any other social or jurisprudential category . . . When sport hits the legal and political buffers, conventional and ordinary principles affecting the nature of the appropriate sporting issue concerned including parliamentary legislation are triggered into action.[160]

Woodhouse, C, 'The lawyer in sport: some reflections'

I have often said there is no such thing as sports law. Instead it is the application to sport situations of disciplines such as contract law, administrative law (disciplinary procedures), competition law, intellectual property law, defamation and employment law . . . I hope the next generation of sports lawyers will enjoy it as much as I have over the past 25 years. But do remember there is no such thing as sports law.[161]

Legal academics not surprisingly have a wider and more reasoned analysis:

Barnes, J, *Sports and the Law in Canada*

Sports law deals with State interests and the resolution of conflicts according to general legal norms. Sports maintain internal rules and structures to regulate play and organise competition. In sports law, the wider legal system impinges on this traditionally private sphere and

---

158 Op. cit., fn 153, Foster (2003). Foster cites the distinction that Houlihan makes between 'internationalised sport', which, 'like international law, is firmly based on nation states'. Teams are defined by their country of origin. This sporting culture prefers national or regional competitions to global or Olympic games. 'Internationalised sport is often funded by state subsidy and has a national framework of regulation.' 'Globalised sport' by contrast has nationally ambiguous or rootless teams, 'sport without a state', as in professional road cycling or Formula One motor racing where teams are named after corporate sponsors. Globalised sport has a uniform pattern of sport that diminishes national traditions and local diversity. Sports rely on commercial sponsorship rather than state funding; also see Houlihan, B, *Sport, Policy and Politics: A Comparative Analysis* (1997), London: Routledge.

159 For example, Beloff, M, Kerr, T and Demetriou, M, *Sports Law* (1999), Oxford: Hart; op. cit., fn 145, Caiger and Gardiner (2000).

160 Grayson, F, *Sport and the Law* (1999), London: Butterworths, p xxxvii.

161 Woodhouse, C, 'The lawyer in sport: some reflections' (1996) 4(3) Sport and the Law Journal 14.

subjects the politics of the sports game to the politics of the law game. The result is a double drama as the deep human concern for play combines with the concern for social justice. Sports law addresses basic ethical issues of freedom, fairness, equality, safety and economic security. The subject matter of sports law includes state control and subsidy of sport, rights of access, disciplinary powers and procedures, commercial and property rights, employment relations and compensation for injuries. Sports law is grounded in the material dimensions of sport and includes a study of the life and times of its heroic practitioners.

State interest in sport and recreation has a long history and there are early Canadian instances of civil litigation and prosecutions for violent play but the flowering of sports law dates from the 1970s when a 'daily barrage of socio-legal crises' began to fill newspaper sports pages. Law, politics and finance have since become prominent features of sports culture and various factors explain this trend: sports now offer lucrative commercial rewards so that participants look to protect their economic interests through legal and industrial relations processes; governments have addressed social problems in sport and have been involved in sports administration; and sports have been affected by emancipation movements seeking wider recognition of legal and constitutional rights. Sports management has always relied on legal power to control the enterprise and retain the prime slice of the pie. Conflict has grown as the underpaid, the injured and the excluded have acquired remedies and gained the organisational strength necessary to further claims. The legal profession has been happy to appropriate this conflict.

The most familiar court battles occurred in the North American professional sports leagues. Some disputes involved the community interests affected by the establishment or relocation of team franchises but most cases dealt with the rights and freedoms of players. Litigation in the United States has partly emancipated professional athletes from restraints that limit them in selling their services to the highest bidder. The formation of rival leagues first offered alternative markets and anti-trust actions and collective bargaining then brought further mobility and prosperity. These developments inevitably affected Canadian members of American-based leagues and the new freedoms served as models for Canadian athletes. Litigation has not, however, been limited to the major leagues. Sports organisations at all levels in Canada have been forced to respond to members who are more willing to seek judicial remedies and question restrictive regulations and disciplinary powers.

After a quarter century of intense conflict, litigation fatigue may now have set in and there is some yearning to revert to a lost 'pre-legal' ideal. The dissatisfaction with sports law reveals itself in public impatience over labour disputes and the lofty levels of professional salaries but a more concrete threat comes from the excesses of the war on drugs. Some feel that general legal principles should not intrude unduly into the sports world and that athletes' rights can only go so far.[162]

Opie, H, 'Sports associations and their legal environment'

'Sports law' is one of those fields of law which is applied law as opposed to pure or theoretical law. Rather than being a discipline with a common legal theme such as criminal law, equity or contract law, sports law is concerned with how law in general interacts with the activity known as sport. Hence, the label applied is law. Yet there is an increasing body of law which is specific to sport. This produces debate among scholars over whether one should use the term sports law, which indicates a legal discipline in its own right, or 'sport and law', which reflects the multifarious and applied nature of the field. No doubt the general public would regard this as one of those sterile debates which are so attractive to inhabitants of ivory towers – if the public bothered to think about it!

---

162 Barnes, J, *Sports and the Law in Canada* (1996), Toronto: Butterworths, pp 2–3.

Sport and the law is not the only field of law to be debated in this way. As new fields of law emerge it is almost customary for them to undergo this debate until they have been around long enough to establish themselves. This leads to an important observation: namely systematic attention to sport and law is a relatively new phenomenon in Australia. It is certainly something which has occurred only during the last 15 years. It is rare to find any seminar papers or learned articles on the topic prior to that period. Those which existed were regarded or presented almost as curiosities at their time of publication. There seem to have always been court cases concerning sport but these were isolated and are insignificant compared with the variety and volume of court proceedings that are to be observed today. A contributing factor to this prior inactivity is that in some fields of law the courts pursued a policy of non-intervention by holding that sport disputes were private matters which did not raise justiciable issues. Any informed observer will realise that the position is vastly different today. What has produced this change?[163]

These four accounts present alternative views on this issue: sport and the law or sports law? Grayson believes there is no such identifiable area of sports law. Woodhouse agrees. This view must be subject to challenge given the significant changes that have taken place in the regulation of sport.

Although they come from arguably more advanced jurisdictions in terms of sports law, Canada and Australia respectively, Barnes suggests that the proliferation of sports legislation, litigation and arbitral decisions has led to some 'special doctrine' and Opie believes that it is possible to see a recognisable sports law, an 'applied' area of law. He notes the debate concerning whether an 'identifiable legal subject' exists has occurred in other developing and burgeoning areas.

In the UK, more progressive practitioner observers have acknowledged the importance of recognition of sports law. Michael Beloff and his co-authors consider that:

Beloff, M, Kerr, T and Demetriou, M, *Sports Law*

. . . the law is now beginning to treat sporting activity, sporting bodies and the resolution of disputes in sport differently from other activities or bodies. Discrete doctrines are gradually taking shape in the sporting field . . . English courts are beginning to treat decisions of sporting bodies as subject to particular principles.[164]

Similarly, Adam Lewis and Jonathan Taylor contend that although their book seeks not to address this distinction, as it 'is an issue of academic rather than practical interest', they do:

Lewis, A and Taylor, J, *Sport: Law and Practice*

. . . share the belief of many writers in the field that in at least some areas, for example where international institutions such as the Court of Arbitration for Sport review the decisions of sports governing bodies, a separate and distinct body of law-inspired general principles of law common to all states is in the process of development. Equally the extent of the adaptation by the English courts of existing principles of challenge to address the particular circumstances of sports governing bodies' decisions is well on the way to construction of a model of review of such decisions analogous to the public law model, where previously there was much greater uncertainty.[165]

---

163 Opie, H, 'Sports associations and their legal environment', in McGregor-Lowndes, M, Fletcher, K and Sievers, S (eds), *Legal Issues for Non-Profit Associations* (1996), Sydney: LBC, pp 74–94.

164 Op. cit., fn 159, Beloff *et al* (1999), p 3.

165 Lewis, A and Taylor, J (eds) *Sport: Law and Practice* (2003) London: Butterworths, preface.

The emergence of legal disciplines

The development of this subject area of law's involvement in sport is part of a process that has happened to all legal areas in the past. Labour or employment law is a subject area that has only achieved relatively recent recognition. It has its origins in contract law in the employment context, but no one would doubt that with the plethora of legislation during the post-war era regulating the workplace, particularly from the 1960s onwards, it has become a subject area in its own right. Passing through various incarnations such as industrial law, it is now a mature legal subject.

Sports Law falls into the 'applied law' classification that Opie describes. The development of legal areas, which involves essentially the application of pure legal areas in the context of a human activity, in this case sport, has moved from a loose association such as sport and the law to a more recognisable body of law such as sports law. At the national level, it is true to say that it is largely an amalgam of interrelated legal disciplines involving such areas as contract, taxation, employment, competition and criminal law, but dedicated legislation and case law have developed specific sports law-related doctrines and principles and will continue increasingly to do so. As will be examined later, the development of a European Union Sports Policy and the application of EU law to sport have provided a significant body of law. There is an identifiable international sports law, a sub-component being a specific lex sportiva reflecting the growing influence of CAS. As an area of academic study and extensive practitioner involvement, the time is right to accept that a new legal area has been born and is thriving in the 'bloom of its youth' – viva sports law.

Conclusion

This chapter has provided an examination of the normative rule milieu that surrounds the regulation of contemporary sport. The emerging role of law has been analysed. To conclude, this chapter has shown that, in Britain and elsewhere, there are a number of reasons for law's intervention in sport. The commercialisation of sport presents a palpable need for legal regulation. The legal regulation of sport reflects the general increase of regulation of new social contexts or fields. In the regulation of sport there is evidence of pluralism with the interaction between different levels of normative rules. Sports law is an area on the periphery of the legal domain and, as such, the law's role in regulating sport is open to continual analysis, debate and evaluation. The debate concerning the appropriate regulatory model for English professional football that will be examined in the next chapter is a good illustration.

Many 'problems' in sport, such as drug use and violence, are presented as 'moral panics' in need of legal regulation. Supporting the rights of sportsmen has also become an important area. None of these interventions are unproblematic. A link needs to be made between this discussion and the two theoretical sociological models presented in Chapter 1. They may not necessarily be oppositional and can be potentially complementary. Applying the first model, the law's involvement, in addition to the internal constitutive sports rules, is an extension along the road of the civilising process in sport. The law is providing a functional role in the context of the modern commercial complexity of sport. This fits in with a figurational perspective on sport and society. Applying the second model from a critical Marxist position, the law as a form of regulatory power and control over sport, intervention is often legitimised in the context of the creation of moral panics.

Which is the most persuasive? As stated already, sports law cannot be understood exclusively, nor even primarily, in purely national terms and this regulatory debate needs to be located within a European and indeed wider international context. Professional sport needs to be increasingly understood internationally with the substantial power that international sports federations have in determining how sports are organised and played. In addition, it is a specific commodity that has developed complex and symbiotic relationships within the global media complex and sports marketing industry. This will be examined in the context of the very commercialised sport of English football in the next chapter.

Key Points

- Playing rules in sport involving both ensuring safety and improving the dynamics of play have become increasingly standardized.
- Rules are supplemented by a sport's informal playing culture.
- Codes of ethics have become increasingly visible in sport.
- Decisions by match officials will only be reviewed by the Courts of the Court of Arbitration for Sport, where these are actions that could be characterised as being 'arbitrary', a 'breach of duty' and involving 'malicious intent', that is involving some corruption on the part of an adjudicating official.
- Cheating is a complex phenomenon in sport, and increasingly leads to disciplinary intervention and potential additional legal actions.
- Cheating is identified as not only challenging the sporting integrity of sport but also the commercial integrity and willingness of external bodies to financially invest in sport.
- Law's greater involvement in contemporary sport brings with it the process of jurifidification.
- A distinct 'Sports Law' can be identified with a specific set of legal principles and authorities.
- In addition to the involvement of national law, the role of European Law and an emerging international sports law needs to be noted.
- A distinction can be made between international sports law and a global sports law, comprised of decisions of the increasingly influential Court of Arbitration for Sport.

Key Sources

Foster, K, 'Is there a global sports law?' (2003), 2(2) *Entertainment Law.*
Fraser, D, *Cricket and the Law: The Man in White is Always Right* (2005), London: Routledge.
McNamee, M (ed) *The Ethics of Sports (a Reader)* (2010), London: Routledge.
Nafziger, J, *International Sports Law* (2004), New York: Transnational.
Nafziger, J and Ross, S (eds.) *International Handbook on Sports* Law (2011), Cheltenham: Edward Elgar.

Chapter 3

The Legal Regulation of Sports Governing Bodies

Chapter Contents

Introduction	89
Sport and Self-Regulation	90
Access to the Courts: Actions Against Sports Governing Bodies	93
Sports Governing Bodies: The Contractual Relationship	105
Economic Regulation: Restraint of Trade and Competition Law	114
Substantive Rights Against Sports Governing Bodies	117
Alternatives to Litigation: Sports Governing Bodies and Alternate Dispute Resolution	138
Evaluation	142
Key Points	143
Key Sources	144

Introduction

The activities of the regulatory bodies that control sporting activities have become, and are becoming, increasingly entwined with the law and with lawyers.[1] With the rise in commercial and economic interests there have been ever greater incentives for those adversely affected by the rules and decisions of sports governing bodies to make a challenge in law. Equally, the regulatory processes of the sports governing bodies have themselves become increasingly legalistic and legalised, as legal professionals play an increasing role, on behalf of both regulated parties and the governing bodies themselves.

Such scrutiny is plainly important in light of the significant impact on livelihood and reputation that sports regulators can have upon actors within their jurisdiction and, indeed, upon parties outside of any formal contractual relationship.

In the relatively recent past the functions of sports regulators might have appeared relatively mundane and narrow; the emergence of sport as a justiciable field in the mid to late twentieth century was dominated by cases concerning the fairness of disciplinary hearings and the nature of employment relationships. These aspects retain their importance today, but the spectrum of activity, and thus the activities falling to be considered by the courts, has broadened significantly. Not only do sports regulators lay down rules that affect the on-field conduct of participants, but they also affect the commercial transactions which they may conduct, their employment relationships, personal behaviour and drug use. Governing bodies engage in licensing of playing facilities, sponsorship arrangements, control of safety standards and regulation of corruption and cheating, often overlapping with the activities of law enforcement agencies. Many of these activities are those that would ordinarily be performed by the state or its agents – yet it must be remembered that, for the most part, sports governing bodies are private associations.

These private, self-regulating associations generally grew up during the late nineteenth century as sport developed out of disparate and localised games into the codified and uniform packages that exist today. While government may have been generally supportive of the regulation of sports, because of the increased orderliness and control it brought to them, it took no significant part in the evolution of the regulatory process. It seems sport was simply not important enough for the state to involve itself in through either significant legislation or litigation.[2] Should the question arise now it seems that the outcome could be quite different. Now government shows an increasing interest and involvement in sport, whether it be in controlling doping, lottery funding for sport, the development of national stadia, bidding for the right to host international events such as the 2012 Olympic Games or 2018 FIFA World Cup, the availability of sport on television, the behaviour of spectators, the form of football's transfer system, or simply the price and availability of entry to sporting events.[3]

Much of this state interest in sport is driven by its increasingly global nature. Sports regulation and regulators increasingly transcend traditional national boundaries and operate on a transnational, global level.[4] This, in turn, provides new problems and challenges for domestic legal systems seeking to exert authority and control. This new legal and regulatory environment has been further transformed by the emergence of sport's own alternative mechanisms of resolving disputes, notably the Court of Arbitration for Sport, which, while offering new avenues of potential redress for aggrieved parties, also demand new and innovative responses from the courts to ensure that these mechanisms are themselves effective and legitimate.

---

1   See generally, Hoult, P 'The beautiful game' (2004) 101(12) LSG 26.
2   See Birley, D, *Sport and the making of Britain* (1993) Manchester: Manchester UP.
3   On interventionist and non-interventionist approaches see Lewis, A and Taylor J (eds) *Sport: Law and Practice*, 2nd edn (2008), London: Butterworths, pp 4–7.
4   See eg Maguire, J, *Global Sport: Identities, Societies, Civilizations* (1999), Cambridge: Polity; Giulianotti, R, *Football : a sociology of the global game* (1999), Cambridge: Polity.

The immense significance of sport, both to its participants, at whatever level, and to wider society is in little doubt. Thus the capacity to effectively scrutinise and challenge the rules and decisions of sports regulators is highly significant. This chapter considers the extent to which satisfactory scrutiny exists, taking into account the nature of sport's self-regulatory governing bodies. The purpose of this chapter is to examine the accountability of these bodies through domestic courts. It also addresses broader questions as to the desirability of the present situation and critically analyses sport's self-regulatory basis.[5]

Sport and Self-Regulation

In search of an appropriate relationship between sport and the courts

It has already been noted that the self-regulatory bodies that govern sport have the capacity to act governmentally while still possessing the institutional and legal structures and interests of private bodies. These quasi-public characteristics pose challenging issues for resolution by the law.

Self-regulation is perceived as having many benefits, most significantly that the costs of the regulation are largely internalised, thus reducing the burden on the public purse. Additionally, there are a number of perceived technical advantages in the utilisation of self-regulatory techniques in relation to expertise and efficiency. This much was noted in the Court of Appeal:

R v Barnes

In determining what the role of the courts should be, the starting point is the fact that most organized sports have their own disciplinary procedures for enforcing their particular rules and standards of conduct. As a result, in the majority of situations there is not only no need for criminal proceedings, it is undesirable for there to be criminal proceedings.[6]

Expertise

Certain regulatory functions may require the exercise of expert judgement where a decision-maker has to consider competing options or values and come to a balanced judgment on incomplete and shifting information. Then the regulator may claim legitimacy and support on the basis of expertise or specialist knowledge:[7]

Sinclair, D, 'Self-regulation versus command and control: beyond false dichotomies'

[E]ven with the best of intentions, regulators are often not in a strong position to determine the technical practicalities of regulating complex industrial processes. This is compounded in sectors where technology is rapidly changing, or with the advent of new, previously unregulated industrial activities, or with the discovery of previously unknown negative . . . impacts . . . It is in both government and industry's interests, therefore, for industry to constructively participate in the development of appropriate and effective regulatory strategies.[8]

This is certainly the case with sport in the United Kingdom. In 2003 the then Foreign Secretary, Jack Straw, indicated, in relation to a controversial proposed tour of Zimbabwe by the England cricket

---

5   See generally, Weatherill, S 'Do sporting associations make law or are they merely subject to it?' (1999) 13 Am Cur 24.
6   [2004] EWCA Crim 3246, per Lord Woolf CJ, at para 5
7   Baldwin, R and Cave, M, *Understanding Regulation: Theory Strategy and Practice* (1999), Oxford: OUP, p 80.
8   Sinclair, D, 'Self-regulation versus command and control: beyond false dichotomies' (1997) Law and Policy 545–46.

team, that the state had no role to play in these self-regulatory matters.[9] Self-regulation usually has the ability to command higher levels of relevant expertise and technical knowledge than is possible with independent or state regulation. This knowledge includes an understanding of that which the regulated parties will perceive as a reasonable regulatory burden. The role of the sector in setting its own standards engenders a close sense of ownership, meaning rules are more likely to be both acceptable and effective based on the expert knowledge of those actively involved in the area.[10] The potential for flexibility in a rapidly changing domain is enhanced. *Wayde v New South Wales Rugby League Ltd*[11] involved a challenge to a decision by the New South Wales Rugby League (NSWRL) to restructure its league format, which had the effect of excluding the claimant from the competition. The following extracts from the judgment further emphasise the importance of expertise in self-regulation:

Wayde v New South Wales Rugby League Ltd

Given the special expertise and experience of the Board, the *bona fide* and proper exercise of the power in pursuit of the purpose for which it was conferred and the caution which the court must exercise . . . the appellants faced a difficult task in seeking to prove that the decisions in question were unfairly prejudicial to [the Club] and therefore not in the interests of the members as a whole.[12]

Brennan J went on to emphasise the specialist nature of such bodies:

The directors had to make a difficult decision in which it was necessary to draw upon the skills, knowledge and understanding of experienced administrators of the game. There is nothing to suggest . . . that reasonable directors with the special qualities possessed by specialist administrators would have decided that it was unfair to exercise their power as the League's directors did.[13]

However, where matters of important policy are concerned, it may be that state organs will be less willing to cede regulatory territory to private actors. Thus, in these specific areas regulatory arrangements might look different to those where mundane, narrow or technical matters are concerned and the state may be willing to bow to the greater expertise of those involved in the sphere of activity. Conceptions of high policy are thus extremely important in this regard: these rarely remain settled as political agendas shift and change. Notably, the entry of new actors, possibly inter- or supra-national bodies, can play a role in the compilation of political priorities.[14]

In the context of sport this is most notable where sports regulators have imposed economic restrictions upon participants or other stakeholders as a part of their regulatory schemes. This is certainly evident from the case analysis in this chapter and that relating to the European Union.

Efficiency

Self-regulators generally have easy access to those under control, and experience low costs in acquiring the information necessary to formulate and set standards, with consequently low

---

9   See Jarvie, G, *Sport, Social Justice and the Public Intellectual* (2009) available from https://dspace.stir.ac.uk/dspace/
    bitstream/1893/747/1/SPORT%20SOCIAL%20CHANGE%20AND%20THE%20PUBLIC%20INTELLECTUAL(irssrevised).pdf.
10 Black, J, *Rules and Regulators* (1997) Oxford: Clarendon, pp 103, 219.
11 (1985) 59 ALJR 798.
12 [1985] 59 ALJR 798, per Mason ACJ, Wilson, Deane and Danson JJ, p 801.
13 Ibid.
14 Hancher, L and Moran, M, 'Organising regulatory space', in Baldwin, R, Scott, C and Hood, C (eds), *A Reader on Regulation* (1998),
    Oxford: OUP, p 162; Collins, H, *Regulating Contracts* (1999) Oxford: OUP, pp 63–64, 66.

monitoring and enforcement costs.[15] They are able to adapt their regimes to changes in individual conditions in a flexible manner, because of the relative informality of their procedures.[16] As outlined above, conceptions of policy priorities may affect when high-cost regulation will be considered acceptable.

However, criticisms relating to the adoption of self-regulatory strategies focus upon the issues of mandate, accountability and procedural fairness.[17]

Mandate

Because of their very nature, self-regulatory objectives can be drawn up by bodies with no or little democratic legitimacy. It is often hard to justify actions that affect parties outside of the association's membership structure – or to argue that the public interest is being served.[18] Indeed it is difficult to justify the impact of self-regulation on the members of an association itself, where the decision-making procedures of such an organisation are not founded upon internal democratic processes. It is often argued that self-regulatory bodies have a particularly poor record in protecting the public interest in the enforcement of standards.[19]

In the context of sport, criticisms of lack of legitimacy, and associated accountability, have been levelled with increasing frequency against, in particular, global regulators such as FIFA and the International Olympic Committee.[20] Indeed, in many sports it has become increasingly difficult to identify for whom the 'self'-regulation is conducted; the regulatory process is now dominated by powerful economic actors, principally highly commercialised sports clubs and teams, leagues, the broadcast media and, to a lesser extent, a small number of elite athletes. In many cases other stake-holders have little choice but to resort to litigation to ameliorate the adverse impact of supposed 'self'-regulation.

Accountability

Critics often perceive the existence of self-regulatory systems as being the manifestation of the capture of power by groups that are not accountable through normal democratic demands.[21] Many democratic models make the assumption that legitimate authority to exercise public power can only flow from a command of popular and legislative majorities.[22] On this basis, regulation should be subject to the scrutiny and effective control of the organs of the (democratic) state as a matter of necessity.

Regulation inevitably involves the exercise of public power, yet it seems that this is not always subject to the scrutiny and control that is demanded by constitutionalists.[23] The key, where self-regulating organisations are not underpinned by any legislative mandate, is the extent to which the courts can hold these associations to account, ensuring transparency and accountability. This is particularly so where bodies can often have an impact upon those outside of any legal relationship with the regulator. This would suggest that, in relation to sport at least, such self-regulatory bodies

15 Braithwaite, J, *Restorative Justice and Responsive Regulation* (2002) Oxford: OUP, p 247.
16 Op. cit., fn 7, Baldwin and Cave (1999), p 127.
17 Ibid, p 126.
18 Ogus, A, 'Rethinking self-regulation' (1995) OJLS 97, p 99.
19 Op. cit., fn 7, Baldwin and Cave (1999), p 129.
20 See eg Jennings, A, *The New Lords of the Rings* (1996) London: Pocket; Sugden, J and Tomlinson, A, *FIFA and the Contest for World Football: Who Rules the People's Game?* (1998) Cambridge: Polity.
21 Graham, G, 'Self-regulation', in Richardson, G and Genn, H, *Administrative Law and Government Action: The Courts and Alternative Mechanisms of Review* (1994), Oxford: Clarendon, p 190.
22 Op. cit., fn 14, Hancher and Moran (1998), p 150.
23 Black, J, 'Constitutionalising self regulation' (1996) 59 MLR 24.

ought to be subject to effective scrutiny by the courts in order to meet the requirements of democratic legitimacy. This much has been recognised in the context of sports governing bodies. In *Nagle v Feilden* – a case involving the licensing of race horse trainers by the Jockey Club – Lord Denning accepted that the right to work combined with capricious or arbitrary behaviour constituted sufficient grounds for intervention by the courts:

Nagle v Feilden

When an association, who have the governance of a trade, take it upon themselves to license persons to take part in it, then it is at least arguable that they are not at liberty to withdraw a man's licence – and thus put him out of business – without hearing him. Nor can they refuse a man a licence – and thus prevent him from carrying on his business – in their uncontrolled discretion.[24]

He then stated:

When authorities exercise a predominant power over the exercise of a trade or profession, the courts may have jurisdiction to see that this power is not abused . . . If a practice in this respect is invalid as being contrary to public policy, there is ground for thinking that the court has jurisdiction to say so.[25]

Procedural fairness

Self-regulatory schemes tend to be prone to criticisms of unfairness in so far as non-members may be affected by regulatory decisions to which they have had poor or no proper access. Typically they will not have been involved in the negotiations that established the regulation in the first place. Courts may act so as to ameliorate this; however, they have generally proven to be reluctant to do so.[26] Nevertheless, there are areas such as sport which are traditionally self-regulatory that have become sufficiently important to warrant great concern over the extent to which their regulation is subject to scrutiny. These sectors of activity, of which sport should be considered a foremost example, have, in effect, changed their nature to the extent that their activities can now be regarded as truly 'public' in practice and thus of constitutional significance.[27]

Access to the Courts: Actions Against Sports Governing Bodies

Judicial review

The traditional means by which public bodies are held to account through the courts in England is the claim for judicial review. The procedure operates in such a way that public bodies are required to exercise their powers in a lawful manner. Under this procedure the court does not hear an appeal against state measures or consider the merits of a decision; instead it undertakes a review of the capacity of the body to make the decision and the legality of the decision-making process. Where a decision has been made illegally it will not be allowed to stand. The court will not impose

---

24 [1966] 2 QB 633.
25 Per Lord Denning MR, p 647.
26 Op. cit., fn 7, Baldwin and Cave (1999), p 132
27 On regulation generally and for an assessment of different regulatory techniques see Better Regulation Task Force, *Imaginative Thinking for Better Regulation* (2003). See also Webb, K, 'Government, Private Regulation and the Role of the Market', Chapter 12 in MacNeil, M, Sargent, M and Swan P (eds) *Law, Regulation and Governance* (2002) Oxford: OUP.

a decision of its own, but will require the decision-maker to repeat the process in a lawful fashion. The parameters of judicial review were set out by Lord Diplock:

Council of Civil Service Unions v Minister for Civil Service

To qualify as a subject for judicial review a decision must have consequences which affect some person (or body of persons) other than the decision maker, although it may affect him too. It must affect such other person either (a) by altering rights or obligation of that person which are enforceable by or against him in private law; or (b) by depriving him of some benefit or advantage which either (1) he had in the past been permitted by the decision maker to enjoy and which he can legitimately expect to be permitted to continue to do until there has been communicated to him some rational grounds for withdrawing it on which he has been given an opportunity to comment; or (2) he has received assurance from the decision maker that will not be withdrawn without him giving him first an opportunity of advancing reasons for contending that they should not be withdrawn . . .

For a decision to be susceptible to judicial review the decision maker must be empowered by public law (and not merely, as in arbitration, by agreement between the private parties) to make decisions that, if validly made, will lead to administrative action or abstention from action by an authority endowed by law with executive powers, which have one or other of the consequences mentioned in the preceding paragraph. The ultimate source of the decision making power is nearly always nowadays a statute or subordinate legislation made under the statute; but in the absence of any statute regulating the subject matter of the decision the source of the decision making power may still be common law itself, i.e. that part of the common law that is given by lawyers the label of 'the prerogative'. Where this is the source of the decision making power, the power is confined to executive officers of central as distinct from local government and in constitutional practice is generally exercised by those holding ministerial rank.[28]

The rules pertaining to judicial review were consolidated in a package of measures, Order 53 of the Rules of the Supreme Court, which was in turn endorsed by s 31 of the then Supreme Court Act 1981.[29] These measures had the effect of bundling together the prerogative writs along with private law remedies so that they could be obtained by way of a unified process then known as application for judicial review, now a claim for judicial review. The reforms were instigated in order to streamline the public law process; however, new issues were also raised.

The case of O'Reilly v Mackman[30] established the concept of procedural exclusivity – the restriction that application for relief by way of private law process would not be permitted in situations where there lay a claim for judicial review.

A further important question raised by these reforms was whether the types of body subject to judicial review had been expanded. This was particularly pertinent in relation to sporting bodies, as they had traditionally been seen as excluded from the category of body subject to the prerogative writs.

Judicial review: *Law v National Greyhound Racing Club*

The issue was addressed soon afterwards in the seminal case of *Law v National Greyhound Racing Club Ltd*.[31] Law was a greyhound trainer, suspended after a dog in his charge was found to have been

---

28 *Council of Civil Service Unions v Minister for Civil Service* [1985] AC 375, pp 408–09.
29 The Supreme Court Act 1981 has since been renamed the Senior Courts Act 1981 by the Constitutional Reform Act 2005.
30 [1983] 2 AC 237.
31 [1983] 1 WLR 1302.

doped, contrary to the National Greyhound Racing Club (NGRC) rules. Law brought a private law action claiming a declaration that the NGRC had breached an implied contractual term that all actions taken to deprive him of his licence would be reasonable and fair and made on reasonable grounds and that the decision was *ultra vires* and therefore void. The NGRC sought to strike out the motion, relying on *O'Reilly v Mackman* and claiming that the action ought to have been brought by way of an application for judicial review as the claimant was alleging an abuse of power. Lawton LJ dismissed the suggestion that the power to suspend a licence had any public element, even though such a decision may affect the public.

Law v National Greyhound Racing Club Ltd

In my judgment, such powers as the stewards had to suspend the claimant's licence were derived from a contract between him and the defendants. This was so for all who took part in greyhound racing in stadiums licensed by the defendants. A steward's inquiry under the defendants' Rules of Racing concerned only those who voluntarily submitted themselves to the stewards' jurisdiction. There was no public element in the jurisdiction itself. Its exercise, however, could have consequences from which the public benefited, as, for example, by the stamping out of malpractices, and from which individuals might have their rights restricted . . . Consequences affecting the public generally can flow from the decisions of many domestic tribunals. In the past the courts have always refused to use the orders of certiorari to review the decisions of domestic tribunals.[32]

Lawton LJ also rejected any suggestion that the 1977 reforms had broadened the scope of the judicial review process:

The purpose of section 31 is to regulate procedure in relation to judicial reviews, not to extend the jurisdiction of the court . . . It did not purport to enlarge the jurisdiction of the court so as to enable it to review the decisions of domestic tribunals.[33]

The finding of the Court of Appeal in *Law* has proved to be an important one. The contractual relationship between Law and the NGRC served to exclude the application for judicial review and emphasised that the scope of judicial review had not been extended to domestic tribunals (that is, those founded in contract, not on the basis of statute or the Royal prerogative) such as sports governing bodies.

Judicial review: *Datafin* and beyond

The change in the law that prompted the National Greyhound Racing Club to make this argument appeared then to be clear. However, the position of sports bodies in judicial review developed through a number of decisions following the case of *R v City Panel on Take-overs and Mergers ex p Datafin*.[34] This case dealt with a challenge by Datafin, a company involved in a take-over bid, to a decision of the City Panel on Take-overs and Mergers. The Panel on Take-overs and Mergers (the Panel) is a self-regulating body that produced and manages the City Code on Take-overs and Mergers (the Code) governing the procedure to be followed in the take-over of listed public companies. The Panel has no direct statutory, prerogative or common law powers – no visible legal support – but is supported by a number of statutory provisions relating to the listing of companies on the Stock Exchange.

---

32 Ibid, p 1307.
33 Ibid, p 1308. In his judgment Fox LJ agreed with Lawton LJ's opinion that the authority of the stewards was derived wholly from contract and that the NGRC did not have rights or duties relating to members of the public as such: 'What the defendants do in relation to the control of greyhound racing may affect the public, or a section of it, but the defendants' powers in relation to the matters with which this case is concerned are contractual', p 1309.
34 [1987] 1 All ER 564.

Further, the Department of Trade and Industry has cited the existence of the Code as a reason why there is little statutory intervention in the area of take-overs. Sir John Donaldson MR stated:

R v City Panel on Take-overs and Mergers ex p Datafin

As an act of government it was decided that, in relation to take-overs, there should be a central self-regulatory body which would be supported and sustained by a periphery of statutory powers and penalties wherever non-statutory powers and penalties were insufficient or non-existent, or where EEC requirements called for statutory provisions. No one could have been in the least surprised if the panel had been instituted and operated under the direct authority of statute law, since it operates wholly in the public domain. Its jurisdiction extends throughout the United Kingdom.[35]

He went on to comment that the Panel was clearly performing an important public duty. Its decisions affected the rights of citizens, not all of whom had consented to being affected in this manner. The Panel's power was not only based upon moral persuasion and the assent of institutions and their members, but it was also provided with strength by the statutory powers exercised by the Department of Trade and Industry and the Bank of England. Donaldson MR continued:

I should be very disappointed if the courts could not recognise the realities of executive power and allowed their vision to be clouded by the subtlety and sometimes complexity of the way in which it can be exerted.[36]

Lloyd LJ endorsed and expanded upon this opinion, emphasising that the self-regulatory nature of the Panel did not make it any less appropriate for subjection to the scrutiny of judicial review.[37] He also commented that the source of the power was not the sole test in deciding upon a body's susceptibility to judicial review:

Of course the source of the power will often, perhaps usually, be decisive. If the source of the power is a statute, or subordinate legislation under a statute, then clearly the body in question will be subject to judicial review. If, at the other end of the scale, the source of power is contractual . . . then clearly [this is] not subject to judicial review. But in between these extremes there is an area in which it is helpful to look not just at the source of the power but at the nature of the power. If the body in question is exercising public law functions, or if the exercise of its functions have public law consequences, then that may . . . be sufficient to bring the body within the reach of judicial review . . . [t]he essential distinction . . . is between a domestic or private tribunal on the one hand and a body of persons who are under some public duty on the other.[38]

On its particular facts the application was rejected. However, the case is significant in that, despite not deriving its powers from statute or the exercise of the prerogative, the Panel was held to be a body susceptible to judicial review, because of its nature. This suggests three broad areas for consideration:

● whether a contractual relationship exists between the parties;
● whether the body challenged is one of a nature such that it is subject to judicial review; and

---

35 Ibid, p 574.
36 Ibid, p 577.
37 Ibid, p 582.
38 Ibid. Nicholls LJ concurred.

● whether the nature of the decision or act in question is of a nature, that is affecting the public at large, which is susceptible to judicial review.[39]

Datafin appeared to signal a shift away from a strictly source-based test of amenability to judicial review towards a more general, functional test where the source of power was only one of a number of factors to be considered. *Datafin* resulted in questions being posed relating to the nature of bodies considered susceptible to judicial review, once again raising the possibility that sports governing bodies would be subject to the process. A number of the subsequent cases involved challenges to decisions of such bodies.

Judicial review: the problem of contract and consensual submission

In R v *Football Association of Wales ex p Flint Town United Football Club*[40] the appellant club was a member of the Football Association of Wales (FAW), playing in the Welsh Amateur League. The club sought to leave that league to join another one, administered by the English Football Association. According to the FAW rules, by which the applicant was bound, the club required the consent of the FAW to play in a league administered by the English FA. The FAW refused permission and the applicant sought judicial review. In refusing the application at the leave stage,[41] the Divisional Court held that it was long established that certiorari (one of the prerogative writs available as a public law remedy) would not lie against private or domestic tribunals since their authority was derived solely from contract.[42] In *Flint Town* a contractual relationship existed between the parties, thus the court was bound by the decision in *Law*, and the remedy of certiorari could not lie against a domestic tribunal. *Datafin*, it appeared, had changed little where a contractual relationship existed between the parties.

In many cases sporting bodies possess a monopoly in their particular field. Those wishing to have significant involvement in association football or horse racing in England, for example, have little realistic choice but to submit themselves to the authority of the Football Association or the Jockey Club respectively. It can be questioned, therefore, whether it is right to disqualify such a relationship from the courts' supervisory jurisdiction of judicial review on the basis that it is viewed as being contractual. The rules making up the 'contract' are presented on a 'take it or leave it' or 'adhesionary' basis, with no opportunity for the negotiation of terms. Individuals have no choice but to accept the terms if they wish to be involved in the sport. Thus, to refuse to subject a body to judicial review on the basis that the relationship is based on consensual agreement is questionable. The adhesionary nature of the rules and regulations of sports governing bodies have, in fact, been recognised by the judiciary, albeit in the context of a private law action:

Enderby Town Football Club Ltd v The Football Association Ltd

> The rules of a body like [the Football Association] are often said to be like a contract. So they are in legal theory. But it is a fiction – a fiction created by lawyers to give the courts jurisdiction . . . Putting the fiction aside, the truth is that the rules are nothing more nor less than a legislative code – a set of regulations laid down by the governing body to be observed by all who are, or become, members of the association.[43]

The inherent risk in this approach is that those having a justifiable grievance may be denied redress. Further, the exercise of public power by those bodies that have clear links with the state is subjected

---

39 R v *Derbyshire County Council ex p Noble* [1990] ICR 808.
40 [1991] COD 44.
41 Before making a claim for judicial review an intending claimant must apply for leave to do so, stating the relief sought, the grounds upon which it is based, and provide an affidavit confirming the facts upon which the applicant is seeking to rely.
42 As established in *Law v National Greyhound Racing Club Ltd* [1983] 1 WLR 1302.
43 *Enderby Town FC Ltd v The Football Association Ltd* [1971] Ch 591, p 606, per Lord Denning MR.

to scrutiny not only through judicial review, but also through other means.[44] Decision-makers more easily identified with the exercise of public power because of their proximity to government are more likely to be made accountable through the democratic process or through other more specific grievance redress mechanisms, such as ombudsmen, which may be available to aggrieved individuals within the system of government. In contrast, sporting bodies which possess and utilise powers equivalent in effect to those exercised closer to government go relatively unscrutinised. Not only are they not accountable through the democratic process, but neither are there the internal governmental mechanisms by which they must justify their actions and decisions. This only serves to highlight the importance of effective judicial scrutiny of these bodies.

Judicial review: barriers beyond contract

Discrepancies in the application of the law post-*Datafin* are highlighted by the case of R v *Disciplinary Committee of the Jockey Club ex p Massingberd-Mundy*.[45] The applicant, Massingberd-Mundy, was a local steward appointed by the Jockey Club and was also on a list of stewards approved to act as chairman of stewards. He was chairman of stewards at a race meeting during which an incident took place that called for a stewards' inquiry. His conduct at that inquiry was criticised by the Jockey Club's Disciplinary Committee, which felt that he had taken too long to bring the inquiry to a conclusion. He was subsequently removed from the list of stewards approved to act as chairman. The applicant sought judicial review of the Jockey Club Disciplinary Committee's decision, by way of an order of certiorari.

The applicant argued that the decisions of bodies deriving their powers from statute or statutory instrument or from a Royal Charter are generally susceptible to judicial review. As the Jockey Club was reconstituted under a Royal Charter in 1970, the powers of the Jockey Club were now derived from its Charter, making it susceptible to judicial review. The applicant further suggested that the exercise of control over a large and important industry meant that the Disciplinary Committee of the Jockey Club was more than just a domestic tribunal. This 'special' position, it was argued, was underlined by the fact that the representatives of the horse racing industry on the Horse-Race Betting Levy Board were drawn exclusively from the Jockey Club.[46] The Jockey Club countered that it was a domestic body deriving its jurisdiction from contract and was not therefore susceptible to judicial review. Further, it argued, the fact of its incorporation by Royal Charter did not mean that its powers were derived from the prerogative any more than a public company's powers were derived from statute because of its incorporation under the Companies Act. Neill LJ decided that the Royal Charter was not the real source of the Club's power, it being more a sign of Royal 'approval', therefore it could not be properly regarded as deriving its power from prerogative. This suggests a paradoxical approach has developed where the source of power question is determined. *Flint Town*, outlined above, was decided in the post-*Datafin* era. There the court did not attempt to look beyond the obvious, being satisfied to accept the superficial view of the power of the FAW in terms of its source. However, in *Massingberd-Mundy* the Court was quite prepared to discount the Charter status of the Jockey Club in determining its susceptibility to review. This suggests judicial reluctance to subject sport's governing bodies to judicial review rather than the development of any systematic approach to the basis of review in such cases.

Neill LJ did extend his examination to the nature of the powers exercised in making the decision, going on to state that the character of the Charter and of the powers conferred upon the Club strongly suggested that in some aspects of its work it operated in the public domain, and that its functions were at least in part public or quasi-public functions.[47]

---

44 Mullan, D, 'Administrative law at the margins', in Taggart, M (ed), *The Province of Administrative Law* (1997), Oxford: Hart, p 137; Alder, J, 'Obsolescence and renewal: judicial review in the private sector', in Leyland, P and Woods, T (eds), *Administrative Law Facing the Future; Old Constraints and New Horizons* (1997), London: Blackstone, p 165.
45 [1993] 2 All ER 207.
46 Betting, Gaming and Lotteries Act 1963, s 24.
47 Ibid.

R v Disciplinary Committee of the Jockey Club ex p Massingberd-Mundy

Accordingly, if the matter were free from authority, I might have been disposed to conclude that some decisions, at any rate, of the Jockey Club were capable of being reviewed by judicial review.[48]

Nevertheless, despite the introduction of a broader test in *Datafin*, the courts demonstrated difficulty overcoming a tendency to base susceptibility to review on the basis of the body rather than the nature of the decision itself. Here the labelling of the Jockey Club as a 'domestic tribunal' meant the court felt unable to classify it as a body amenable to judicial review. Despite considering the nature of the decision, and accepting that certain decisions taken by the Jockey Club would be typically suitable for subjection to judicial review,[49] once again the nature of the body was decisive.

R v *Jockey Club ex p RAM Racecourses Ltd*[50] concerned a challenge to a Jockey Club decision not to allocate races to a new course following an internal report stating that 60 new fixtures ought to be allocated in 1990 and 1991 and that an unspecified number of fixtures ought to be made available to a new course. Copies of the report were distributed to existing racecourse owners and the Jockey Club announced that it would allocate an extra 30 fixtures in both 1990 and 1991. RAM Racecourses obtained a copy of the report, purchased a site and spent £100,000 on developing a new racecourse in anticipation of being allocated fifteen new fixtures in 1991. In June 1989 the claimant sent details of its development proposals to the Jockey Club, who replied stating that, notwithstanding the report, it had made no commitment as to the number of fixtures to be allocated to new racecourses. Shortly afterwards it was made clear by the Jockey Club that no fixtures would be allocated to the applicant's new racecourse in 1991 and that it would not indicate when such an allocation might be made. The claimant sought judicial review of the Jockey Club's decision, contending that the report had raised a legitimate expectation that the new racecourse would be granted a minimum of 15 fixtures for 1991.

On the substantive issue of whether the Jockey Club report had raised a legitimate expectation in the applicant that it would be awarded at least 15 fixtures in 1991, the applicant failed.[51] The judgment of Stuart-Smith LJ took a step back from the position in *Massingberd-Mundy*. He did not accept that the Jockey Club was affected by its Charter status:

R v Jockey Club ex p RAM Racecourses Ltd

[S]o far as its functions of issuing licences and controlling fixtures is concerned the Jockey Club is in no different a position from a practical point of view after the Charter than before.[52]

Stuart Smith LJ also affirmed the general principle that the majority of such cases would be entirely domestic in character, being based upon a contractual relationship between the parties.[53] Simon Brown J gave the most expansive judgment to date, assuming a more pragmatic stance. The nature of the power being exercised by the Jockey Club in discharging its functions of regulating race-courses and allocating fixtures was noted as being strikingly akin to the exercise of a statutory licensing power. Similarly, there was no difficulty in regarding that particular function as one

---

48 [1993] 2 All ER 207. Note that Neill LJ felt bound by the decision in *Law v NGRC* [1983] 1 WLR 1302, in as much as it rejected the expansion of the application for judicial review to the actions of domestic tribunals.

49 On the facts it was held that no public right was infringed.

50 [1993] 2 All ER 225.

51 The Divisional Court held that there had been no clear and unambiguous representation in the report that a new racecourse would receive 15 fixtures as of right in 1991. The Jockey Club had not made any direct representation to the applicant as the report had not been made available to it, therefore it was not within the class of persons entitled to rely on the report. Nor was it reasonable for the applicant to rely upon any representation in the report without approaching the Jockey Club directly to check whether its assumption was correct.

52 R v *Jockey Club ex p RAM Racecourses Ltd* [1993] 2 All ER 225, p 243.

53 Ibid, p 244.

belonging to a public law body, giving rise to public law consequences.[54] Simon Brown J noted the close affinity with the type of decision-making commonly accepted as reviewable by the courts and the inability to identify that particular exercise of power with that of an arbitrator or other domestic body, which would clearly be outside the court's supervisory jurisdiction.[55] In doing so Simon Brown J shifted towards the approach, outlined above, that the nature of the activity should be the focal point when deciding bodies' amenability to judicial review, not the label ascribed to the body carrying it out. Simon Brown J also disagreed with Stuart Smith LJ on the effect of the Jockey Club's Charter status. He accepted that it could not be a decisive consideration but stressed that it was not irrelevant when deciding upon the susceptibility of the Club to judicial review:

> It may indicate governmental (in the widest sense) recognition of the national importance of the Jockey Club's position, holding as it does monopolistic powers in this important field of public life.[56]

However, this approach still contrasts with the rigid approach taken where the basis of a body's powers is contractual. Simon Brown J failed to recognise the legislative nature of the rules of the Jockey Club in concluding that it made decisions which affected only those voluntarily and willingly subscribing to their rules and procedures, with an insufficient public interest to justify the application of judicial review. However, he did not see that as preventing the Club from being susceptible to review when operating in its occasional public law capacity, such as when exercising quasi-public licensing powers.[57]

Judicial review: the requirement of 'governmentality'

The necessity for a body to be interwoven with, or underpinned by, government for it to be susceptible to judicial review was highlighted in *Datafin* as well as in *Massingberd-Mundy* and *RAM Racecourses*, where the Jockey Club's Royal Charter was argued to represent governmental support for its activities. This question was dealt with in greater detail in *R v Football Association Ltd ex p Football League Ltd*,[58] concerning an attempt by the Football League to prevent the Football Association (FA) forming the FA Premier League. The FA is the governing body of association football in England. Part of its role is to sanction various competitions; the most significant of which was, at the time, the Football League. In 1991 the FA chose to form and co-ordinate a Premier League, making alterations to their rules in order to facilitate this. The Football League brought an application for judicial review of the FA's decisions to set up the Premier League and to make the required amendments to its rules. The Football League provided three arguments for the FA's susceptibility to judicial review. Firstly, it had a monopoly control over association football. Secondly, its rules, despite being contractual in form, were in effect a legislative code for the game. Finally, the FA regulated an important aspect of national life and, if it did not exist, the state would have to create a public body to perform its functions.

In the Divisional Court Rose J acknowledged the extension of the FA's powers beyond contract, suggesting this could characterise the FA as a body susceptible to judicial review, despite its private law constitution and accepting that its rules were effectively a legislative code.[59] Rose J went on to analyse the effect of the *Datafin* decision on the position of the FA, stating that prior to that case there was no argument for its susceptibility to judicial review. He accepted the effect of *Datafin* as extending

---

54 Ibid, p 247.
55 Ibid.
56 Ibid.
57 Ibid.
58 [1993] 2 All ER 833.
59 Ibid, p 841.

the scope of judicial review to a non-statutory body not derived from the exercise of prerogative. He interpreted the *ratio* of the decision in *Datafin* such that a body may be susceptible to judicial review when regulating an important aspect of national life, with the support of the state, in that, but for its existence, the state would create a public body to perform its functions.[60] Rose J questioned the judgment of Simon Brown J in *R v Jockey Club ex p RAM Racecourses*, suggesting the decision in *Law* to be a better guide in relation to those bodies deriving power, *prima facie*, from contract and stated that the *Datafin* decision in no way altered the law in this area.[61] His conclusion was that the FA was not a body susceptible to judicial review, stating that it was:

R v Football Association Ltd ex p Football League

. . . a clear and inescapable conclusion . . . that the FA is not a body susceptible to judicial review, either in general or, more particularly, at the instigation of the League, with whom it is contractually bound. Despite its virtually monopolistic powers and the importance of its decisions to many members of the public who are not contractually bound to it, it is, in my judgment, a domestic body whose powers arise from and duties exist in, private law only. I find no sign of underpinning directly or indirectly by any organ or agency of the state or any potential government interest, nor is there any evidence to suggest that if the FA did not exist that the state would intervene to create a body to perform its functions. On the contrary, the evidence of the commercial interest in the professional game is such as to suggest that if the FA did not exist that a far more likely intervener would be a television or similar company rooted in the entertainment business or a commercial company seeking advertising benefits such as presently provides sponsorship in one form or another.[62]

Again, the basis in private law is the prime consideration in deciding susceptibility to review, despite recognition of the potentially far-reaching and significant consequences of the FA's decisions. The key issues in this case are those of interweaving and underpinning, and substitution. The question of substitution, that is to say whether government would step in to fill a body's functions if it did not exist, is a highly speculative inquiry, and particularly vague. In establishing this test the courts have failed to lay down any detailed criteria against which particular bodies can be tested. The test relies upon the notion that public power and government powers are analogous. As noted in the judgment of Simon Brown J in *RAM Racecourses*, this is not the case. Powers akin to those wielded by government are utilised outside of the governmental sphere. While it is true that the majority of the FA's powers will be entirely within the realms of private law, this is not a compelling argument for the total exclusion of judicial review. It might be argued that in applying this test the courts fail to recognise the reality of 'mixed' administration,[63] where a private body performing private law functions can also operate in a public law capacity. The question of substitution can also be criticised as it is unlikely to be answered in the affirmative where government is in the process of actively downsizing,[64] as in the UK at the time of writing, delegating its functions and duties to the private sector. This may have the effect that private bodies, having powers analogous to those operated by sports governing bodies, but delegated directly from government, will be subjected to judicial review, whereas the bodies in the sporting sector will not. Despite the broad comparability in terms of the nature of power exercised, the same policy of de-centralisation which would make the first body amenable to judicial review could prevent sporting bodies from becoming susceptible.

---

60 Ibid, p 843.
61 Ibid, p 847.
62 [1993] 2 All ER 833, p 848.
63 Aronson, M, 'A public lawyer's response to privatisation and outsourcing', in Taggart, M (ed), *The Province of Administrative Law* (1997), Oxford: Hart, p 52.
64 Op. cit., fn 44 Mullan (1997), p 153.

Similar arguments relate to the interweaving and underpinning test. There is little evidence of *visible* governmental support for sporting bodies in the way in which there was for the Panel in *Datafin*. Though the FA is not supported by a statutory framework, this does not necessarily indicate the absence of government support, in its narrow sense, for the activities of the FA. The reactive, rather than proactive, nature of government may offer some clarification in this matter. Where a sport is generally seen as being well managed, there is unlikely to be any incentive for government to legislate for the sport's regulation.

Judicial review: the Court of Appeal in *Aga Khan*

The most important authority in this field is now *R v Jockey Club ex p Aga Khan*.[65] As an owner wishing to race horses in Great Britain, the Aga Khan was compelled to register with the Jockey Club, entering into a contractual agreement expressly submitting to the Rules of Racing and to the Club's disciplinary powers. After winning a race, a horse owned by the Aga Khan was found to have a substance prohibited by the Rules of Racing in its urine. Following an inquiry by the Disciplinary Committee of the Jockey Club, the horse was disqualified and the trainer fined. It was not proved that the applicant or the trainer had caused or arranged for the doping of the horse, nor that its performance had been in any way affected. The Aga Khan claimed that the decision was damaging to his status as a religious leader and to his reputation as an owner and breeder of racehorses. He also contended that the value of the horse for breeding purposes had been significantly reduced and applied for judicial review of the Disciplinary Committee's decision to disqualify the horse. He contended that the Jockey Club, despite being a private club in form, was susceptible to judicial review. As the body that regulated horse racing in Great Britain the Jockey Club, in making decisions of this kind, was exercising a public function in the *de facto* control of a major national industry. Further, the Jockey Club's decisions represented the exercise of powers public in character.

The opinions of the Court of Appeal are worthy of careful attention in that they are often divergent. All three judges accepted the source of power was inconclusive, but not irrelevant, in determining justiciability, and that the nature of the power exercised was important.[66] Sir Thomas Bingham MR and Hoffman LJ also recognised the position of the Jockey Club as having *de facto* control over an area of significant national activity.[67] Bingham MR stated that the powers exercised in this area were essentially of a public nature.[68] Hoffman LJ disagreed, believing the power to be entirely private in its nature.[69]

In respect of the governmental nature of the body, Bingham MR accepted that if the body ceased to exist, the government would be required to fulfil its functions.[70] Farquharson LJ, however, stated:

R v Jockey Club ex p Aga Khan

I do not detect in the material available to us, any grounds for supposing that, if the Jockey Club were dissolved, any governmental body would assume control of racing.[71]

In addition to recognising the public nature of its powers, and that it could satisfy the substitution test, Bingham MR accepted that the Club exercised effective monopoly power over a significant national activity. However, he also accepted the contention of the Jockey Club that the Club's origin,

---

65 [1993] 1 WLR 909.
66 Sir Thomas Bingham MR, pp 915–16; Farquharson LJ, p 927; and Hoffman LJ, p 931.
67 *R v Jockey Club ex p Aga Khan* [1993] 1 WLR 909, pp 916 and 932 respectively.
68 Ibid, p 916.
69 Ibid, p 932–33.
70 Ibid, p 916.
71 Ibid, p 930.

history, constitution and membership did not reflect that of a public body.[72] Bingham MR did not just demand that the powers exercised be governmental in nature, he also required that they be interwoven into a system of governmental control of the sport. As with previous cases he was unable to identify such a relationship between the regulation of racing and government. The apparent effect of this was that the powers exercised by the Club were public, but not governmental. Thus the Club was not susceptible to judicial review.[73] Bingham MR's final comment was that the Jockey Club's power was based on consensual agreement. This was the case in spite of the effective monopoly of the Club and the recognition in previous judgments of the legislative nature of such agreements.[74] The agreement established private law rights, which provided a basis for effective action in private law without need for resort to judicial review. Judicial review could not therefore be extended to encompass the Jockey Club.[75]

Judicial review: *Aga Khan* tested

The durability of the Court of Appeal decision in *Aga Khan* has since been tested in the case of R (o/a Mullins) v Jockey Club Appeal Board.[76] The claimant race horse trainer, Mullins, sought judicial review of a decision of the Jockey Club Appeal Board to disqualify his horse after it was found to have a prohibited substance in its bloodstream, effecting a breach of the rules of the Club. Mullins was initially refused permission to bring a claim for judicial review on the basis that it was established law that sports governing bodies were not amenable to such a claim. The case was permitted to move to deal with the issue of jurisdiction as a preliminary matter.

Mullins attempted to distinguish his case from that of *Aga Khan* on a number of grounds, but most notably by the material changes to the law brought about by amendments to the Civil Procedure Rules (CPR) and introduction of the Human Rights Act 1998 and subsequent case law.[77] The claimant argued that the changed definition of the claim for judicial review in CPR Part 54.1(2), as 'a claim to review the lawfulness of . . . a decision, action or failure to act in relation to the exercise of a public function', rendered the Jockey Club Appeal Board amenable to judicial review. The similarity of language between Part 54 CPR and section 6 of the Human Rights Act 1998, which conceives of 'quasi-public' bodies as being subject to the requirements of the Act in as much as they perform public functions, was emphasised. The impact of the Human Rights Act 1998 is discussed in greater detail later in this chapter and was, in this case, decided to be irrelevant as a matter of law as the decision of the Appeal Board did not amount to a public function. Stanley Burnton J found that the amenability to review of sports governing bodies had not altered since the Court of Appeal decision in *Aga Khan*; in particular the Jockey Club relied entirely on its contractual and property rights as a means to enforce the decisions of its disciplinary limbs. Further, in applying *Aga Khan* Stanley Burnton J concluded that the test to be applied in determining whether the Jockey Club was amenable to judicial review was whether its functions were governmental in nature.

R (on the Application of Mullins) v Appeal Board of the Jockey Club

The Jockey Club could not enforce its rules otherwise than by means of its contracts, or the exercise of its property rights. None of its rules had statutory force. A body which would

---

72 Ibid.

73 Ibid.

74 *Russell v Duke of Norfolk* [1949] 1 All ER 109, pp 113–14, per Tucker J; *Enderby Town FC Ltd v The Football Association Ltd* [1971] Ch 591, p 606, per Denning LJ.

75 R v *Jockey Club ex p Aga Khan* [1993] 1 WLR 909, p 924. Farquharson LJ followed this final statement. He also recognised the absence of realistic choice in the Jockey Club's contractual relationship but denied that this in any way undermined the consensual nature of the agreement. His suggestion was that this was necessary for the control and integrity of the sport concerned.

76 [2005] EWHC 2197 (Admin).

77 *Aston Cantlow and Wilmcote with Billesley Parochial Church Council v Wallbank* [2003] UKHL 37.

otherwise exercise only private functions could not assume public functions by its own action alone. Some governmental intervention was required. There had been none.[78]

The absolute nature of Stanley Burnton J's judgment is rather surprising, particularly given the judicial approach in previous cases admitting the possibility that certain functions of a sports governing body might be regarded as public in nature even if the characteristics of the body itself as being private in nature precluded judicial review. It seems likely that this approach was driven, to a degree at least, by the capacity of Mullins to bring a private law action in light of the decision in *Bradley v Jockey Club*[79] and the eventual consideration of Mullins' claim in a private law context (both discussed below).

Judicial review: conclusions

The tests applied in discerning justiciability can themselves be criticised in that they do not deal with the reality of the power exercised, concentrating instead upon the body exercising it. However, not only have the tests themselves been shown to be potentially flawed, but the manner in which the courts have applied them can also be criticised. This raises the question as to whether the way in which these tests have been applied has been influenced by other considerations. In *R v Football Association ex p Football League* Rose J suggested that there was a giant conceptual step to be taken before sports governing bodies could be considered as being susceptible to review:

R v Football Association ex p Football League

For my part, to apply to the governing body of football, on the basis that it is a public body, principles honed for the control of the abuse of power by government and its creatures, would involve what, in today's fashionable parlance would be called a quantum leap.[80]

Similarly in the *Aga Khan* case Hoffman LJ commented:

R v Jockey Club ex p Aga Khan

Power can be private as well as public. Private power may affect the public interest and the livelihood of many individuals. This does not mean the rules of public law should be available in law for curbing the excesses of private power . . . I do not think that one should try to patch up the remedies available against domestic bodies by pretending that they are organs of government.[81]

In this respect, rather than arguing that sporting bodies do not fit a particular model or test, the underlying approach has really been much more straightforward. The judicial view is simply that judicial review is a mechanism for the control of the exercise of public power by government and that, for all their legislative powers, governing bodies in sport are not part of this judicial view of government and are therefore beyond the scope of judicial review. This is supported by the judgment of Sir John Donaldson MR in *Datafin*, who referred to the control of *executive* rather than *public* power.[82] It is argued that the term *executive* used in relation to the nature of power, which will be subject to judicial review, implies a dual requirement that the power must be a *public* one exercised by *government*. If this twofold test is accepted, then this would make it very difficult to argue the case for the susceptibility to judicial review of sports governing bodies. Despite contending that it could

---

78 [2005] EWHC 2197 (Admin) at para H13.
79 [2004] EWHC Civ 2164 (QB); [2005] EWCA Civ 1056.
80 *R v Football Association ex p Football League* [1993] 2 All ER 833.
81 *R v Jockey Club ex p Aga Khan* [1993] 1 WLR 909, pp 932–33.
82 *R v Panel on Take-overs and Mergers ex p Datafin* [1987] 1 All ER 564, p 577.

be possible to view sporting bodies as being underpinned by or intertwined with government, it is not argued here that sporting bodies are *constituent parts* of government.

Whether or not this view is accepted, the case law in relation to the application for judicial review raises a number of important questions.[83] Is the judiciary predetermining the issue of susceptibility to review and then applying the law so as to meet the desired outcome? Have the courts simply decided that judicial review is a means of controlling power that is not only public, but also governmental in nature?

However, judicial review is only one part of a range of mechanisms for the control of the exercise of power, and the field of public law is not limited to judicial review: private law has absorbed principles from public law.[84] The question is whether the private law process can offer applicants sufficient protection in the light of the fact that judicial review will generally be unavailable.

Sports Governing Bodies: The Contractual Relationship

Throughout the judicial review case law, the importance of the contractual relationships by which sports governing bodies obtain their power is emphasised and cited in some instances as the primary ground upon which judicial review is refused. Thus, the extent to which contract can be utilised in rendering bodies accountable is important. Bodies controlling sport take on the form of either incorporated or unincorporated associations.[85] In the case of unincorporated associations, each of the association's members enters into a contractual relationship – the rules of the club – with each of the other members, as such associations are not recognised as having legal personality. Where an association is incorporated by becoming a limited company (or by obtaining a Royal Charter), each of the members contracts with the company and is subjected to its rules. Such rules are usually to be found in the company's memorandum and articles of association, constituting the contract by which members are bound.[86]

Contract: affirming jurisdiction

Perhaps in contrast to the position in relation to the claim for judicial review, the courts have developed a zeal for examining the contractual relationships between governing bodies and those subjected to their rules. The question of excluding the courts' jurisdiction by contract has been considered in a number of cases. *Baker v Jones*[87] examined the capacity of the Central Council of the British Amateur Weightlifters' Association (BAWLA), to pay out of BAWLA funds the legal costs of its members who had been sued in relation to their activities on the council. BAWLA rules purported to make decisions of the Central Council final, thus the defendants argued that the decision to meet the costs was final and impervious to challenge before the courts.

---

83 For a critical view of the application of judicial review to sports governing bodies see: Anderson, J, 'An Accident of History : Why the Decisions of Sports Governing Bodies are not Amenable to Judicial Review' (2006) 35(3) CLWR 173; Beloff, M, 'Watching out for the googly: judicial review in the world of sport' (2009) 14(2) JR; Pannick, D, 'Judicial review of sports bodies' (1997) 2(3) JR 150; Beloff, MJ and Kerr, T, 'Why *Aga Khan* was wrong' (1996) 1(1) JR 30. For a brief survey of the case law see: Bond, C, 'Sporting bodies and judicial review' (1993) 1 SATLJ 7.; Belloff, M, Kerr, T, and Demetriou, M, *Sports Law* (1999), Oxford: Hart, pp 227–28. By contrast it has also been suggested that the distinction between public and private process has become irrelevant, see Lewis, A and Taylor J (eds) *Sport: Law and Practice*, 2nd edn (2008), London: Tottel, pp 164–65.

84 Taggart, M, 'The province of administrative law determined?' in Taggart, M (ed), *The Province of Administrative Law* (1997), Oxford: Hart, p 2.

85 Beloff, MJ, 'Pitch, rink, pool . . . court? Judicial review in the sporting world' (1989) PL 96.

86 Kerr, T, 'Fortifying sport's governing bodies and clubs against legal challenge', paper presented at *Strategies for Sports: Developing Proactive Legal and Marketing Practices*, 4 December 1997, pp 2–3.

87 [1954] 2 All ER 553.

Lynskey J disagreed with the defendants' construction of the rules, stating that the rules constituted a contract and that public policy would prevent the ousting of the jurisdiction of the courts by such a contract. Thus the decisions of sports governing bodies regulated by contractual agreements would be subject to judicial scrutiny and the jurisdiction of the court could not be ousted in this way. In *Enderby Town v Football Association*[88] (discussed above and below) Lord Denning MR emphasised that such bodies would not be able to oust the jurisdiction of the courts by way of a contractual term.

Contract: the nature of the contractual nexus

The liberal approach to extending justiciability of sports governing bodies on the basis of contract was demonstrated in *Davis v Carew-Pole*.[89] The claimant, Davis, was a stable keeper required to appear before the National Hunt Committee (NHC) to answer an allegation that he had trained a horse for a steeplechase contrary to the rules of the NHC, as he was unlicensed. Davis attended the NHC inquiry, at which two other allegations concerning his unlicensed training of horses were considered, without him being given prior notice. At the inquiry Davis was declared to be a 'disqualified person' under the rules, thus depriving him of the ability to be involved in National Hunt racing at any level. Davis claimed a declaration that the decision of the NHC was *ultra vires* and void, and an injunction restraining the NHC from treating him as a disqualified person.

Pilcher J held that there *was* a contractual relationship between Davis and the NHC, despite the fact that Davis was unlicensed by the committee. The contractual nexus, Pilcher J said, arose when the claimant submitted to the jurisdiction of the committee in attending the inquiry.

Contract challenged: *Modahl v BAF*

The existence of a contract between the regulator and regulated was readily accepted over the following years and provided a basis for much of the litigation relating to sports governing bodies. The question of the existence or otherwise of a contract between governing bodies was not, however, uncontroversial, as emphasised by Lord Denning's description in *Enderby Town* of the existence of a contract as a legal fiction (see above). The nature of the relationship between athlete and sports federation as being contractual was a key point in the litigation between Diane Modahl and the British Athletic Federation (BAF).[90] Modahl was suspended from participating in athletics events by the BAF after she was found to have committed a doping offence by a BAF disciplinary committee after being tested at an athletics meeting in Lisbon. Modahl appealed to an independent appeal tribunal, which lifted the ban after hearing new evidence that the samples on which the suspension was based could have affected the reliability of the test. Modahl then brought an action for breach of contract, claiming damages for expenses and loss of income during the period of her suspension. This claim was on the basis that there had been a breach of an implied contractual term that the disciplinary committee would act fairly and without bias (as to the substance of which see below). At first instance it was held that there was no contract between the parties and that, in any case, the disciplinary committee had acted fairly and without bias. On appeal to the Court of Appeal there was extensive discussion of whether a contract existed between Modahl and the BAF. The claimant put forward three arguments in favour of finding the existence of a contract. The first was based upon Modahl's membership of Sale Harriers Athletic Club. The Club's rules and regulations specifically required Modahl to adhere to the rules of the BAF. Secondly, Modahl argued that her

---

88 [1971] Ch 591
89 [1956] 1 WLR 833.
90 *Modahl v British Athletic Federation (No 2)* [2002] 1 WLR 1192.

participation in events overseas meant that she submitted to the jurisdiction of the BAF. Rule 6(4)(a) of the BAF required participants in overseas competition to obtain the organisation's permission to do so. It was argued that the BAF had a disciplinary function which could only be sensibly dealt with in the context of a contract. Thirdly, it was argued that Modahl's invocation of her right to appear before a disciplinary panel and the exercise of her right of appeal created a contractual relationship as in the case of *Davis v Carew-Pole*. In response the BAF argued that it was not possible to identify any intention to create legal relations, sufficient certainty as to the terms, or any consideration. On appeal the claim was dismissed, but there was disagreement amongst the Court of Appeal as to the existence or otherwise of a contractual relationship. Both Latham and Mance LJJ found that overall it was appropriate to find the existence of a contract, though arriving at this conclusion by different routes:

Modahl v British Athletics Federation (No 2)

Per Latham LJ:

50. There is no doubt that over a period of many years the applicant accepted that if she entered meetings under the auspices of the respondent or of the IAAF, she would be subject to the relevant rules. Equally, it seems to me to be a proper inference that the respondent in its turn accepted the responsibility to administer those rules in relation to all subject to its jurisdiction who competed in those meetings. I see no difficulty, therefore, in identifying with certainty the basic obligations undertaken by both the athlete and the respondent. There is a benefit and a detriment to both. The benefit to the athlete is that he or she knows that every athlete competing will be subject to the same rules, and that to remain entitled to compete, both nationally and internationally, he or she must comply with those rules. The respondent accepted the burden of administering those rules, and the benefit of having recognised athletes compete both in national and international events. The latter benefit has become the more significant over the years as, from the documents we have, it is clear that the respondent obtained financial benefit in terms of sponsorship and media exposure for its events. I therefore see no difficulty in determining the consideration which each provides. Further, it seems to me to be clear that the athlete accepts the obligations under the rules whenever he or she enters a competition, or undergoes out of competition testing in order to be eligible to enter such competitions. The basic structure for a contract is, in my view, readily identifiable.

51. The remaining question is whether or not the parties can have had an intention to create a legal relationship. This seems to me to be the difficult part of the problem. It could be said that in the context of a sport, that involves imposing an inappropriate legal structure on what for many will be recreation. This could justify the conclusion that only in those cases in which an athlete is offered and accepts an express contractual obligation can it properly be said that there is a contract between him or her and a body such as the respondent. Further, an inevitable corollary of the existence of a contractual relationship is that both parties are bound by obligations, the breach of which are capable of giving rise to a claim for damages. It would follow that breaches by the athlete of his or her obligations would potentially give rise to a claim for damages on the part of a body such as the respondent. But that seems to me to beg, rather than answer, the problem. There are many contractual situations, the paradigm being employer and employee, where neither party may have applied their minds to or appreciated the consequence of the contractual obligations, namely that both parties are liable in damages for its breach, subject always to the proper construction of the relevant obligations under that contract.

52. In my judgment if a legally enforceable contract can be created, as seems to me is inevitable, where an athlete expressly agrees in an entry form to be bound by the relevant rules, I can see no escape from the conclusion that a contract can properly be implied when the circumstances make it clear that that is, in essence, what the athlete has promised. I consider for the reasons that I have already given, that the appellant, even on the facts that have been established in this case, undertook to be so bound, and the respondent in turn undertook the obligation to apply those rules. In my judgment, the contract extended in the present case to the meeting in Lisbon. Under the rules the appellant must have sought permission from the respondent to compete, and thereby accepted the offer to compete in the knowledge of the disciplinary consequences; and the respondent in giving permission obtained the benefit of her competing.

Per Mance LJ:

103. In the present case, although the language of the respondents' rules has the contractual aspects to which I have drawn attention, there is no conversation or document which can be identified as constituting an express agreement. Any contract must be implied from conduct, in the light of the rules. The rules, in my view, contain a framework of rights and duties of sufficient certainty to be given contractual effect, with regard to the athlete's entitlement and ability to compete. Consideration exists in the athlete's submission to the rules and to the respondents' jurisdiction, in the respondents' agreement to operate the rules and to permit the athlete to compete in accordance with them, and in both parties' agreement on the procedures for resolution of any disputes contained in the rules.

104. Neither the fact that the respondents only entered the scene in 1991 nor the fact that the rules may have changed from year to year affects this conclusion. One would expect athletes like the appellant to have been generally aware of such changes, so far as they affected them. The question is whether the conduct of the parties in operating the rules, as they existed from time to time, in relation to each other necessitates the implication of a contract.

105. In my judgment, the necessary implication of the appellant's conduct in joining a club, in competing at national and international level on the basis stated in the rules and in submitting herself to both in and out of competition doping tests, is that she became party to a contract with the respondents subject to the relevant terms of the rules. I have already identified three respects in which the rules appear to point towards a contractual analysis. I find unpersuasive the submission that an athlete had no personal right to enforce the obligations and standards of behaviour imposed expressly or impliedly on the respondents under their rules. The submission that no one can have intended this in a sporting context seems unrealistic in relation to the modern sporting scene, which, whatever the labels of amateurism, has aspects affecting substantially the career, livelihood and prosperity of participants. Further, since the existence of a contract falls to be assessed objectively, I do not think that it is illegitimate or circular to prefer an analysis which gives enforceable rights and remedies in respect of obligations which are terms expressed or implied in the rules, when compared with an analysis which provides no more than the colder comfort of declaratory or injunctive relief to restrain or annul any conduct by the national governing body which would constitute a restraint of trade. As at present advised, I would prefer to view the appellant's submission in 1994 to the jurisdiction of the respondents' Disciplinary Committee (and thereafter to the Independent Appeal Tribunal) as confirming the existence of a prior contract, although, if necessary, I would regard it as the final step bringing one into existence.

However, Jonathan Parker LJ was not convinced that a contractual relationship existed between the parties:

72. In any event, I am not persuaded that there was any contract between Mrs Modahl and the BAF. There is no written or oral contract, but [Modahl's Counsel] puts forward three possible bases for implying a contract containing an obligation of fairness on the part of the BAF in relation to the disciplinary process . . . I will consider each of these suggested bases in turn.

The 'club basis'

. . .

74. I agree with the judge that on the material before the court the 'club basis' for implying a contract between Mrs Modahl and the BAF cannot succeed. In the first place, the form which Mrs Modahl signed when applying for membership of Sale Harriers in 1977 has not been produced, nor is there any secondary evidence as to its terms. Secondly, the relevant disciplinary body in 1977 was the BAAB, and its rules have not been produced. Nor, for that matter, does the court know in what circumstances and on what terms the BAF succeeded the BAAB as the relevant disciplinary body. Thirdly, Mr Julius expressly disclaimed any argument based on agency.

75. In my judgment, the requisite evidential foundation for the implication of a contract between Mrs Modahl and the BAF via her membership of Sale Harriers has simply not been laid.

The 'participation basis'

76. . . . In the instant case . . . the Lisbon event was an EAA event, in respect of which the responsibility for doping control lay with the Portuguese Athletic Federation. The BAF exercised no control over the Lisbon event. The involvement of the BAF in the Lisbon event derives solely from its obligation under the rules of the IAAF to carry into effect its disciplinary procedures . . . In the instant case . . . there is no evidence as to the terms of the form (if any) which Mrs Modahl signed when applying to enter the Lisbon event, or, for that matter, to whom any such form was addressed. On such facts as are known, it seems that the application might have been addressed to the IAAF, to the EAA, or to the Portuguese Athletic Federation . . .

77. Further, on the material available it seems to me unlikely, to put it no higher, that in applying to participate in the Lisbon event Mrs Modahl intended to create legal relations between herself and the BAF; still less that the BAF had such an intention. As already noted, the BAF was obliged under the IAAF rules to operate its disciplinary process in respect of Mrs Modahl. The inference which I would draw is that in so doing the BAF was doing no more, and was intending to do no more, than fulfil that obligation.

78. I accordingly conclude that Mrs Modahl does not succeed in implying a contract on the 'participation basis'.

The 'submission basis'

79. If there is a sound basis for implying a contract between Mrs Modahl and the BAF in relation to its disciplinary process then in my judgment this must be it. To my mind, however, the 'submission basis' gives rise to significant difficulties both as to intention to create legal relations and as to consideration.

80. As to intention to create legal relations, it seems to me that the natural inference is that in submitting herself to the BAF's disciplinary process Mrs Modahl's intention was merely to seek to defend herself against the finding of a positive drugs test and to avoid the imposition of a mandatory ban which would have had the practical effect of preventing her competing at national or international level for the period of the ban. As for the BAF, I have already stated my view that the natural inference is that its intention was merely to fulfil its obligation to the IAAF.

81. In my judgment, it is also material to bear in mind in this connection that the absence of a contract does not, on the authority of *Nagle v. Fielden*, mean that Mrs Modahl is without a remedy should the sanction imposed as a result of the disciplinary process amount to an unreasonable restraint of trade. This is not, of course, a substitute for an action for damages for breach of contract, but it is a relevant feature of the context in which a contract is sought to be implied.

82. As to consideration, on the available evidential material I am unable to identify any benefit to the BAF capable of supporting the alleged contract, or for that matter any detriment to Mrs Modahl. As I see it, Mrs Modahl's interest in submitting to the BAF's disciplinary process was in maintaining her eligibility for national and international competition.

83. As Bingham LJ said in *Blackpool Aero Club v. Blackpool B.C.* at 1202, 'contracts are not lightly to be implied'. In my judgment the fact that the factual context may be consistent with the parties having made a contract does not suffice for this purpose, nor (by the same token) does the fact that the parties would have acted no differently had a contract been concluded. To my mind, that is simply the starting-point for the inquiry whether a contract is to be implied. Something more is required. I am, however, unable to find anything more in the instant case. I accordingly agree with the judge that the circumstances of the instant case, as they appear from the available evidential material, do not justify the implication of a contract between Mrs Modahl and the BAF.[91]

The importance of establishing a contractual relationship between participants and governing bodies is clear. It has already been noted in this chapter that the claim for judicial review has been ruled out by the courts as a means of calling sports governing bodies to account. This has been done primarily on the basis that such relationships have their foundation in contract and thus are not strictly 'public law' affairs. The risk is that if no contractual relationship is deemed to exist, and the courts persist with the view that governing bodies are not subject to the claim for judicial review, the potential is there for the appearance of a legal vacuum in which the individual may find themselves unable to effectively establish their rights and obligations in respect of governing bodies.[92]

Beyond contract: extending justiciability

However, it remained generally accepted that the use of contract, by way of 'legal fiction' if not on its strict interpretation, was the most appropriate means by which to regulate the activities of sports governing bodies. The willingness to extend justiciability of sporting bodies on the basis of contract is emphasised by two further cases.

Nagle v Feilden[93] involved a female, Florence Nagle, who challenged the Jockey Club's consistent refusal to issue her with a licence to train racehorses on the sole basis of her gender. The stewards automatically refused the grant of a trainer's licence to a woman. The claimant effectively trained racehorses; a licence to train was granted to her 'head lad' rather than to her. Nagle brought an action claiming a declaration that the practice of the stewards in refusing a trainer's licence to any woman was void as against public policy and an injunction ordering the stewards to grant her a licence. At first instance and on appeal the claimant's case was struck out on the ground that, as there was no contractual relationship between the two parties, the application disclosed no cause of action.

In the Court of Appeal the claimant argued that the Jockey Club and their stewards operated a monopoly in the control of horse racing on the flat in Great Britain, and that as such they were under a duty to all those involved in the sport to exercise their control reasonably and lawfully, in accordance with the Rules of Racing, and not to exercise the discretion vested in them by those rules capriciously. It was also maintained that the Jockey Club expressly and/or impliedly offered to prospective applicants that it would give consideration in accordance with the Rules of Racing to the bestowal of training licenses. The systematic refusal of women applicants on the basis of their sex, it was argued, constituted a breach of the duty owed as well as preventing females from earning a living in this area which was unlawful as being in restraint of trade and contrary to public policy.

---

91 Ibid.
92 On the indirect nature of contractual relationships between participants and governing bodies see Beloff, M, Kerr, T and Demetriou, M, *Sports Law* (1994) Oxford: Hart, pp 27–28.
93 [1966] 2 QB 633.

In the Court of Appeal Lord Denning MR decided that there was no contract between Nagle and the Jockey Club and thus ruled out the claimant's first argument, on the basis that the defendants had expressly declined to contract with the claimant.[94] However, Lord Denning MR was more receptive to the claimant's public policy argument, stressing the difference between the Jockey Club and social or other clubs. The Jockey Club was different as it was an operation administering a virtual monopoly in an important field of human activity and exercised significant power over individual livelihoods.[95] This had the effect that those wrongly rejected by the Jockey Club could have a remedy despite the absence of a contractual relationship.

An important point to stress in relation to this case is that no declaration was granted in favour of the claimant. The judgment in this case was that the claimant had an arguable case for claiming the relief sought on the ground that the practice of refusing a trainer's licence to a woman could be void as contrary to public policy, and thus the claimant's claim should not be struck out. The case may be analogous with the restraint of trade case law, discussed below, but nevertheless it is still useful in emphasising the extent to which the courts have gone in order to ensure accountability for governing bodies through the private law process.

There was a series of cases concerning the decision of the New Zealand Rugby Football Union (NZRFU) to send a touring team to the then apartheid state of South Africa, representing an extreme example of the broad manner in which the contracts by which sports are regulated will be interpreted. In *Finnigan v NZRFU (No 1)*,[115] a number of local level players sought a declaration claiming that, in sending a team to South Africa, the NZRFU were in breach of their contractual obligation to 'promote, foster and develop New Zealand rugby', as stated in their rules and regulations. The applicants in the case were members of a rugby club, which was a member of a local union, which in turn was a member of the national union. In the High Court the NZRFU was successful in striking out the action, on the ground that the claimants lacked standing as non-members of the NZRFU. The claimants appealed to the New Zealand Court of Appeal where the outcome was in stark contrast:

Finnigan v NZRFU (No 1)

Although not having contracts directly with the parent union, the claimants as local club members are linked to it by a chain of contracts . . . further the decision affects the New Zealand community as a whole, and so relations between the community and those specifically and legally associated with the sport . . . [and] may affect the international relations and standing of New Zealand.[96]

In allowing the appeal and according the claimants standing Cooke J commented:

While technically a private and voluntary sporting association, the NZRFU is, in relation to this decision, in a position of major national importance. Therefore we are not willing to apply to the question of standing the narrowest criteria that might apply, drawn from private law fields. In truth the case has some analogy with public law issues.[97]

The decision in this case, combined with that in *Nagle*, went some way to allaying fears that a gap may exist where a potential claimant could be denied redress through the courts by a combination of the rigid approach taken with regard to judicial review and a narrow construction of the nature of sport's governing bodies in private law proceedings.

---

94 Ibid, p 643.
95 Ibid, p 644.
96 *Finnigan v NZRFU (No 1)* [1985] 2 NZLR 159, p 179.
97 Ibid.

Clearly, these cases involved situations that were of unusually high public and political interest and to some extent could be regarded as anomalous. However, the lengths to which the courts went to create a cause of action for the claimants in these cases, and the breadth of the duties which they imposed upon the governing bodies, give cause to suggest that the contractual approach to regulating the activities of sporting bodies should not be too readily criticised for being overly narrow.

Beyond contract: a private law supervisory jurisdiction

The uncertainty surrounding the process by which rules and decisions of sports governing bodies can be scrutinised by a court now appears to have been resolved, following the case of *Bradley v Jockey Club*.[98] Graham Bradley was licensed by the Jockey Club as a jockey between 1982 and 1999. After retiring as a jockey he went into business as a bloodstock agent. During the course of a criminal trial in 2001, where he gave evidence as a witness, Bradley told the court that he had accepted money and presents in exchange for sensitive, privileged information about the horses he rode. As a result of this admission the Jockey Club contacted Bradley to inform him that it intended to carry out an investigation into these elements of his evidence and to invite him to submit to the Rules of Racing in order that he might be able to appeal against any penalty that might be imposed. Following a hearing conducted by the Disciplinary Committee of the Jockey Club, attended by Bradley and his counsel, Bradley was found to have breached the Rules of Racing and was thus disqualified for a period of eight years. The disqualification acted as an effective bar to conducting business as a bloodstock agent as it prohibited entry to any racecourse, employment with any stable and dealing in any capacity with a racehorse. Subsequent to this finding and penalty Bradley made an appeal to the Appeal Board of the Jockey Club on the basis of apparent bias, unfairness, errors in the application of the Rules of Racing, material new evidence, and the contention that the sanction imposed was disproportionate. The Appeal Board rejected the bulk of these claims, determining that there was ample evidence upon which a reasonable committee could have determined that there had been a breach of the Rules of Racing. The Board did, however, accept that the penalty imposed was too severe and replaced it with a period of five years' disqualification.

Following the conclusion of the Jockey Club's appeal processes Bradley issued proceedings in the High Court based on a claim of breach of contract and unlawful restraint of trade. The application of the substantive law is considered in a later section of this chapter; however, the chief significance of this case is in respect of the approach set out in relation to the accountability of sports governing bodies through the courts.

Bradley v Jockey Club

34. It is nevertheless common ground that, even in the absence of any contractual relationship, the decision of the Appeal Board is subject to the supervisory jurisdiction of the court in accordance with the principles stated in *Nagle v. Feilden* [1966] 2 QB 633. For all the doubts expressed about the jurisprudential basis of *Nagle v Feilden*, it has become an accepted part of the law and has perhaps assumed an even greater importance since the courts came to adopt a restrictive approach towards the application of judicial review to the decisions of sporting bodies . . .

35. . . . It is sufficient that even in the absence of contract the court has a settled jurisdiction to grant declarations and injunctions in respect of decisions of domestic tribunals that affect a person's right to work. That applies both to 'application' cases such as *Nagle v Feilden* itself and

---

98 [2004] EWHC Civ 2164 (QB); [2005] EWCA Civ 1056.

to 'expulsion' or 'forfeiture' cases in which a person is deprived of a status previously enjoyed, though in the latter category of case it is likely in practice that a contractual relationship will also have been established.

. . .

46. The importance of the court limiting itself to a supervisory role of the kind I have described is reinforced in the present case by the fact that the Appeal Board includes members who are knowledgeable about the racing industry and are better placed than the court to decide on the importance of the rules in question and the precise weight to be attached to breaches of those rules.[99]

His claim having been dismissed by the High Court, Bradley appealed to the Court of Appeal, unsuccessfully so, the judgment of Richards J being cited with approval. On the facts of *Bradley* it was determined that there was, in fact, a contract between the parties; however, the case is significant in that it formalises the position of sports governing bodies as susceptible to scrutiny by way of a private law supervisory jurisdiction. This being the case, concerns about a narrow interpretation of contractual relationships, as in the dissenting judgment of Jonathan Parker LJ in *Modahl*, become significantly less pressing.

The approach set out in *Bradley* has since been effected in subsequent cases. Having been rejected as a claim for judicial review the claimant in R (*on the Application of Mullins*) v *Appeal Board of the Jockey Club* was able to take advantage of the relaxation of the procedural exclusivity rule established in O'Reilly v Mackman. Claims that are found to be unsuitable to be considered through judicial review are now able to change track and be considered through private law processes. The facts of *Mullins v McFarlane*[100] are as set out previously. The judgment of Stanley Brunton J was that the court had unrestricted jurisdiction to grant declaratory relief in relation to the decisions of domestic disciplinary tribunals or private organisations governing sport. This, he decided, would not be limited to cases of an economic nature.

Mullins v McFarlane

[T]here is no jurisdictional (in the narrowest sense of the word) boundary to the power of the Court to grant declaratory relief in this context . . . The restrictions on the power are discretionary . . . the power to grant declaratory relief will not be excluded because, for example, the decision under challenge does not involve payment of a financial penalty.[101]

Contract and private law supervision: conclusions

In the contractual context, there can be demonstrated a general willingness on behalf of the courts to render sport's governing bodies accountable. In *Enderby Town*, Lord Denning MR emphasised that such bodies would not be able to oust the jurisdiction of the courts by way of a contractual term. Indeed the courts have been willing to stretch the contractual nexus extensively in order to ensure accountability on this basis. This may have given rise to the concern that the decisions in *Finnigan* and *Nagle* were somewhat anomalous and that affirmative action to control the actions of sporting bodies will only be taken where major public policy issues are at stake. However, the modern case law, developing the supervisory jurisdiction of the courts in private law, goes some significant way to ameliorating these concerns. That said, the extent of that jurisdiction is, it appears, limited to the

99 [2004] EWHC Civ 2164 (QB), per Richards J.
100 [2006] EWHC 986 (QB).
101 Ibid, per Stanley Brunton J at para 39. See also *Flaherty v National Greyhound Racing Club* [2005] EWCA Civ 1117; *Fallon v Horseracing Regulatory Authority* [2006] EWHC 2030 (QB); *McKeown v British Horseracing Authority* [2010] EWHC 508 (Admin).

decisions of domestic tribunals of sports governing bodies and does not, therefore, extend to scrutiny of the rules and regulations of the organisations themselves. The result of this may well be that, while an unjust *decision* affecting a claimant may be subject to judicial scrutiny, an unjust *rule* may remain impervious to review.

Economic Regulation: Restraint of Trade and Competition Law

Restraint of trade

This position is mitigated somewhat on considering the application of the restraint of trade doctrine, which serves to outlaw agreements in which powerful bargaining positions are abused. The function of the restraint of trade doctrine is to render partially or wholly void contracts or other agreements that are found to be unreasonably in restraint of trade. The doctrine in its current form evolved during the late nineteenth and early twentieth century when the courts began to pursue a general policy of enforcing the right of every man to work and to offer his services without restriction. The doctrine can be expressed very simply: a contract[102] in unreasonable restraint of trade is void. A restraining contract will be deemed valid, if it satisfies the three elements outlined by Lord Macnaghten.

Nordenfelt v Maxim Nordenfelt Guns and Ammunition Co Ltd

> The public have an interest in every person's carrying on his trade freely: so has the individual. All interference with individual liberty in action in trading, and all restraints in themselves, if there is nothing more, are contrary to public policy, and therefore void. That is the general rule. But there are exceptions; restraints of trade and interference with individual liberty of action may be justified by the special circumstances of a particular case. It is sufficient justification, and, indeed, it is the only justification, if the restriction is reasonable . . . reasonable that is, in the interests of the public, so framed and so guarded as to afford adequate protection to the party in whose favour it is imposed, while at the same time it is in no way injurious to the public.[103]

Thus in the absence of the following characteristics a restraining agreement will be considered in restraint of trade and be void:

- there must be an interest meriting protection;
- the restraint must be reasonable; and
- the restraint must not be contrary to the public interest.

The doctrine is based on the fluid concept of public policy in which it is important to emphasise the significant role of discretion. It is possible to highlight the general trends and development of the doctrine, but difficult to ascribe strict rules to it. Because of the doctrine's foundation on the general principles of public policy, cases characteristically involve the courts in performing a balancing act. In performing this function the courts seek to reconcile a competing range of subjective values.

---

102 It should be noted that the restraint of trade doctrine is not strictly limited only to contractual situations, a matter considered in more detail below.
103 [1894] AC 535, p 565.

In contrast with the growing pains experienced in the context of judicial review and contractual approaches the courts have had little difficulty in accepting that measures having an economic effect arising out of the regulation of sport are subject to scrutiny on this basis. In the sporting context the doctrine has been primarily utilised in three areas: challenges to employment and transfer systems; where a ban or suspension has been imposed; and where governing bodies purport to prevent a team or club from entering a competition.

Eastham v Newcastle United Football Club[104] first demonstrated the susceptibility of sport's governing bodies to attack on the basis of restraint of trade and the attitude of the courts towards such actions. It concerned a challenge to the rules of the English Football Association (FA) and Football League relating to the system of 'retain and transfer', governing the movement of players between clubs.[105]

George Eastham, the claimant, was a professional footballer who had come to the end of a contract under which he played for Newcastle United. The combination of the rules of the FA and League had the effect that, even though his contract had ended, Newcastle could still retain him. Despite the absence of a contract between himself and Newcastle, the claimant was prevented from moving to another club without Newcastle's consent. The claimant exhausted – unsuccessfully – all avenues of appeal open to him. Newcastle eventually capitulated to his demands for a transfer (to Arsenal) in an attempt to prevent proceedings from being brought. However, Eastham had spent three months out of professional football. He sought declarations against Newcastle United, the FA and the League that his agreement with the club, the rules of the FA and the regulations of the League relating to the 'retain and transfer' system were not binding upon him as being in unreasonable restraint of trade and in addition, or in the alternative, *ultra vires*.

Eastham argued that the retention system had the effect of impeding his ability to pursue further employment and make use of his abilities as a professional footballer after the termination of his contract. The FA and the League argued that the claimant was a stranger to their rules, not being a member of either and that, even if the rules were in restraint of trade, this would merely make them unenforceable; a stranger could not prevent the clubs continuing the practice on a voluntary basis. However, Wilberforce J disagreed:

> Is it open to an employee to bring an action for a declaration that the contract between the employers is in restraint of trade? To my mind it would seem unjust if this were not so. The employees are just as much affected and, indeed, aimed at by the employers' agreement as the employers themselves. Their liberty of action in seeking employment is threatened just as much as the liberty of the employers to give them employment, and their liberty to seek employment is considered by the law to be an important public interest.[106]

This contrasts with the law of judicial review, where the formalities of the relationship between the parties are highly significant. As has been noted in relation to private law challenges generally, there is a willingness to interpret the relationship broadly, to accept the reality of control by sporting bodies even in the absence of a contract between the parties.

Similarly in the case of *Pharmaceutical Society of Great Britain v Dickson*,[107] though not in a sporting context, even where a rule was not contained in a contract, in this case in a code, it could still be

---

104 [1963] 1 Ch 413.

105 Edward Grayson highlights some earlier cases where the doctrine might have been invoked. See 'The Ralph Banks road to Bosman via *Eastham, Greig v Insole* and beyond' (1996) 4(1) Sport and the Law Journal 19.

106 Ibid, p 443.

107 [1970] AC 403 (HL).

challenged on the basis of restraint of trade if, in effect, it was mandatory. This has been perceived as being particularly important,[108] implying that the doctrine could be applied to all restraints whatever their source. It also reinforces the suggestion that there may be non-proprietary interests that can be reasonably protected.

In *Gasser v Stinson*,[109] Sandra Gasser, a Swiss athlete given an automatic ban after having a prohibited substance found in a urine sample taken after she had finished third in the 1987 World Athletic Championships women's 1,500 metres, challenged the rules of the IAAF claiming that they were an unreasonable restraint of trade. The rules of the IAAF did not permit Gasser to try to establish her innocence, even in mitigation. It was argued that this was unreasonable and unjustifiable on the basis that a finding of guilt had the effect of imposing a mandatory suspensory penalty of fixed length. This had the effect that an athlete found guilty under the rules of the IAAF and being suspended accordingly could in fact be morally innocent, where they had not intentionally or knowingly taken a prohibited drug. It was argued that to treat those who were morally innocent in the same way as those who had knowingly cheated was unreasonable.

The IAAF attempted to argue that Gasser's status as an amateur athlete precluded her from bringing such an action. Scott J held that because the rules of the IAAF allowed athletes to obtain an income through sponsorship, and that income was directly related to participation in events governed by the IAAF, a suspension from competition could be justifiably regarded as being a restraint of trade. This is a notable extension to the doctrine; as will be noted each of the cases above has been closely related to the ability of the individual affected to trade. Here, the court, while not severing the economic link, extended the doctrine to cover a larger group than might otherwise have access to the courts.

This is not, however, without limitations. In *Chambers v British Olympic Association*[110] Dwain Chambers, a sprinter, sought to challenge the British Olympic Association (BOA) byelaw which prohibits those having been found to have committed a doping offence from selection for the British Olympic team ('Team GB'). Having won the 100-metre Olympic trials which, in principle, entitled him to be selected for Team GB for the 2008 Beijing Games, Chambers brought a claim for an interlocutory prohibitory order restraining the BOA from applying the byelaw. The case was heard a matter of days before the selection of the team was due and, in the view of MacKay J, was likely to, in effect, be determinative of the matter and, therefore, he would give more consideration to the merits than would ordinarily be the case. Most notably, MacKay J judged that it was unlikely that Chambers' case would be considered as a 'right to work' case and thus engage the restraint of trade doctrine. He was able to distinguish *Gasser* on the basis that the restraint applied only to Chambers' capacity to compete at the Olympic Games, indicating that even were it demonstrated that Chambers could obtain some indirect financial benefit from participation, this was at best speculative.

Competition law

The application of competition law to sports governing bodies is less well established in domestic law. The preponderance of competition law interaction with sports governing bodies has taken place in the context of European Union Law. The detail of this is discussed at length in the following chapter and so will not be considered at length here. It should also be noted that the applicable elements of competition law in the United Kingdom, Chapters I and II Competition Act 1998, are heavily modelled on those that operate at EU level under Articles 101 and 102 TFEU, the

---

108 Heydon, JD, *The Restraint of Trade Doctrine* (1971), London: Butterworths, p 74.
109 (1988) unreported, 15 June (QBD), though cf *Edwards v British Athletic Federation*.
110 [2008] EWHC 2028 (QB).

fundamental difference being the geographic area caught by each. Thus there is a high degree of convergence.[111]

There are a small number of instances of competition law being used in English courts as a means of challenging sports governing bodies. In *Hendry v World Professional Billiards and Snooker Association*[112] a group of professional snooker players brought an action against the governing body of the sport, the World Professional Billiards and Snooker Association (WPBSA), claiming that a rule of the organisation limiting participation in tournaments to those sanctioned by the WPBSA amounted to an abuse of a dominant position. The High Court had little difficulty in accepting that the WPBSA was caught by the provisions of the Competition Act 1998 as being regarded as an undertaking. Thus, under the terms of the law, such an undertaking could readily be regarded as being subject to competition scrutiny.

The players in *Hendry* were joined as a claimant by 110 Sports, a commercial entity seeking to exploit opportunities in professional snooker. This emphasises the extent to which competition law effectively broadens the potential pool of litigants who may be able to bring actions against sports governing bodies. While much of the case law set out above is concerned with the challenge of rules or decisions of sports governing bodies by those directly regulated, the application of competition in this field broadens the scope for potential challenge.[113]

Substantive Rights Against Sports Governing Bodies

It is now clear that there are a number of core principles that can be seen to lie against sports governing bodies. These are not always available in each cause of action set out above but can with a good degree of confidence be said to be available against these organisations in most circumstances, particularly in the context of professional sport.

Contract and private law supervision

The contractual and private law supervisory approach to the substantive application of the law to sports governing bodies is now seemingly well established. A number of core principles have developed that constrain sports governing bodies in the exercise of their powers. The nature of a court's role in supervising the activities of sports governing bodies was set out by Richards J in *Bradley v Jockey Club*:

Bradley v Jockey Club

37. That brings me to the nature of the court's supervisory jurisdiction over such a decision. The most important point, as it seems to me, is that it is *supervisory*. The function of the court is not to take the primary decision but to ensure that the primary decision-maker has operated within lawful limits. It is a review function, very similar to that of the court on judicial review. Indeed, given the difficulties that sometimes arise in drawing the precise boundary between the two, I would consider it surprising and unsatisfactory if a private law claim in relation to the decision of a domestic body required the court to adopt a materially different approach from a judicial review claim in relation to the decision of a public body. In each case the essential concern should be with the lawfulness of the decision taken: whether the procedure was fair, whether

---

111 See generally, Whish, R, *Competition Law*, 6th edn (2008), Oxford: OUP, Chapter 2.
112 [2002] ECC 8, see also *Wilander v Tobin (No.2)* [1997] 2 CMLR 346.
113 See also *Adidas-Salomon AG v Draper* [2006] EWHC 1318.

there was any error of law, whether any exercise of judgment or discretion fell within the limits open to the decision-maker, and so forth.[114]

Ultra vires

In the early case of *Baker v Jones* it was recognised that sports governing bodies may only act in conformity, not only with the specific rules contained within the body's regulatory framework but also within t he ambit of the general purpose of the organisation. In *Baker* the British Amateur Weightlifiting Association (BAWLA) was an unincorporated body, which had its primary object set out in rule 2 of its constitution, 'to promote weightlifting as a sport and weight training as a means of physical improvement'. The power to govern BAWLA was granted to the Central Council, including the power to act as the sole interpreter of the rules of BAWLA, and to act in any matter not dealt with by the rules.

As noted above, the claimant, Baker, was a member of BAWLA who objected to the legal costs, in respect of tort actions faced by members of the Central Council, being met from BAWLA funds. He sought a declaration, as against the officers of BAWLA and members of the Central Council, in that the payments made were unlawful, arguing that the rules did not give the Central Council the requisite authority.

On the facts in *Baker* Lynskey J accepted that there were no specific rules on the making of such payments and that the rules gave the council power to decide matters not covered by the rules. However, he also stated that this broad power should be utilised with the primary objects of BAWLA in mind. The council would be unable to use BAWLA funds for purposes outside of the objects. The defendants argued that those having their legal bills paid had been sued in their capacity as officers of BAWLA. Lynskey J was unable to construe the objects of the association, or a reasonably incidental purpose thereof, as extending to payment of the legal fees of its officers. The association was an unincorporated association with no legal personality and thus could not be liable for the tortious acts of its officers. Lynskey J ruled that there was no power under the rules for the council to authorise the payment of officers' legal fees and issued a declaration as requested by the claimant. This view is affirmed by the judgment of Pilcher J in *Davis v Carew Pole*:

Davis v Carew-Pole

If the powers of the quasi-judicial body are set out in a code of rules to which the party aggrieved is in the circumstances subject, the quasi-judicial body is also bound by its own rules and can only mete out punishment in strict accordance with such rules.[115]

Instances of 'simple' *ultra vires* should now be relatively rare; sports governing bodies are generally clearly mindful of the need to act within the limits of their jurisdiction.

Relevant considerations

It may, nonetheless, be possible for sports governing bodies to exceed their jurisdiction. In common with the approach adopted more generally in the context of judicial review, sports governing bodies will act unlawfully if they take into account factors that are irrelevant, or fail to consider relevant factors, when making decisions. This is an advance on the position set out above and has

---

114 [2004] EWHC Civ 2164 (QB).
115 [1956] 1 WLR 833, pp 837–38. See also *Aberavon & Port Talbot RFC v WRU Ltd* [2003] EWCA Civ 584; *Towcester Racecourse Ltd v Racecourse Association* [2002] EWHC 2141; *Meggeson v Burns* [1972] 1 Lloyd's Rep 223. Though cf the judgment of Jonathan Parker LJ (dissenting) in *Modahl v British Athletic Federation Ltd* [2002] 1 WLR 1192 at paras 70–88.

been developed in the recent case law. At first instance in *Bradley* the claimant sought to argue that in determining the penalty to be applied the Appeal Board of the Jockey Club had not taken account of relevant considerations. Whilst rejecting the claim Richards J did accept that it was incumbent upon the Appeal Board of the Jockey Club to take into account only relevant considerations in determining the penalty.

The position was developed more fully in the case of *Fallon v Horseracing Regulatory Authority*.[116] Kieron Fallon, one of the world's leading jockeys, was suspended by the Horseracing Regulatory Authority after criminal charges were laid against him for conspiracy to defraud bookmakers. Because of the decision to lay charges against Fallon, the Horseracing Regulatory Authority convened a special panel, before which Fallon was legally represented. The panel decided that Fallon was to be prohibited from riding in races in Great Britain until the criminal proceedings were resolved. Fallon appealed to an Appeal Board, which upheld the decision of the original panel. Fallon then brought proceedings in the High Court seeking to challenge the decision of the Appeal Board, first on the grounds that it had failed to take into account relevant considerations by refusing to hear Fallon's representations regarding the strength of the case against him and, second, by imposing a prohibition that was unjustified and disproportionate (as to which see below). Davis J concluded that it would have been inappropriate for the Appeal Board to consider the strength or otherwise of the case against Fallon, not least because the Appeal Board could not have all of the relevant information presented to it prior to the conclusion of criminal proceedings. In essence Fallon was seeking to refute part of the case against him and it was appropriate for the Appeal Board to take no account of this.

Proportionality

The test of proportionality has now emerged as a core principle in respect of the conduct of sports governing bodies. The position was set out in the judgment of Richards J in *Bradley v Jockey Club*, in a passage that has since been cited frequently:

Bradley v Jockey Club

43. [T]he issue in the present case . . . concerns the proportionality of the penalty imposed. To my mind, however, that underlines the importance of recognising that the court's role is supervisory rather than that of a primary decision-maker. The test of proportionality requires the striking of a balance between competing considerations. The application of the test in the context of penalty will not necessarily produce just one right answer: there is no single 'correct' decision. Different decision-makers may come up with different answers, all of them reached in an entirely proper application of the test. In the context of the European Convention on Human Rights it is recognised that, in determining whether an interference with fundamental rights is justified and, in particular, whether it is proportionate, the decision-maker has a discretionary area of judgment or margin of discretion. The decision is unlawful only if it falls outside the limits of that discretionary area of judgment. Another way of expressing it is that the decision is unlawful only if it falls outside the range of reasonable responses to the question of where a fair balance lies between the conflicting interests. The same essential approach must apply in a non-ECHR context such as the present. It is for the primary decision-maker to strike the balance in determining whether the penalty is proportionate. The court's role, in the exercise of its supervisory jurisdiction, is to determine whether the decision reached falls within the limits of the decision-maker's discretionary area of judgment. If it does, the penalty is lawful; if

---

116 [2006] EWHC 2030 (QB).

it does not, the penalty is unlawful. It is *not* the role of the court to stand in the shoes of the primary decision-maker, strike the balance for itself and determine on that basis what it considers the right penalty should be.[117]

In *Fallon*, outlined above, the court considered the proportionality of the Appeal Board's decision to suspend the jockey from racing pending the conclusion of criminal proceedings. Davis J observed:

Fallon v Horseracing Regulatory Authority

53. . . . Mr Pannick [Counsel for Fallon] . . . accepts that there is a generous margin of appreciation here. At the same time he submits, and I agree, that the court must not show unthinking servile obeisance to such a decision of an expert tribunal. If the court decides that a particular sanction is disproportionate and unjustified then it should not shrink from saying so.[118]

Fallon's claim was dismissed but ultimately Fallon was found not to be guilty of the criminal charges.

A further example of the application of the proportionality approach is highlighted by the case of *Chambers v BOA* (considered above). Here, in the context of a claim for interlocutory relief, MacKay J was insufficiently persuaded of the likelihood of Chambers' success in arguing that the contested BOA byelaw was disproportionate that he was unable to grant the relief sought.

Thus the position is that the courts will intervene on the ground of proportionality only where a decision-maker has taken a decision that falls out with the range of reasonable responses open to them. This maintains a margin of appreciation for the sports governing bodies, whilst reserving for the courts the capacity to ensure that they do not behave in an arbitrary or capricious fashion.

Evaluating the case law

The position has now been reached where, the nature of the jurisdiction having been settled in *Bradley*, the courts have begun to fully explore the nature of the relationship between legal and self-regulation in the sporting context. It is clear from the existing case law that great caution will be exercised where sports governing bodies are made the subject of a legal challenge. The adoption of a supervisory approach emphasises this point and indicates a strong tendency towards judicial deference to the expertise of governing bodies and significant regulatory autonomy. While the approach to be adopted in relation to decisions and other actions of sports governing bodies is emerging, it is unclear as to the extent, if at all, to which the courts will use their supervisory role in considering the validity of the rules and regulations themselves.

Restraint of trade and competition law

There is a strong link between the contractual and private law supervisory approaches adopted in respect of sports governing bodies and that found under the restraint of trade doctrine and under competition law. As in the context of proportionality, set out above, the doctrine requires the court to undertake a balancing exercise between the legitimate interests pursued and the restrictive measures imposed in that pursuit. This is best understood through examination of the key contexts in which the law in this respect has been applied to the activities of sports governing bodies. This is a more intensive standard of scrutiny, in that it requires that a sports governing body imposing a restraint justify its necessity in achieving legitimate goals.

---

117 [2004] EWHC Civ 2164 (QB).
118 [2006] EWHC 2030 (QB).

Transfer systems

The case of *Eastham*, noted above, demonstrates the approach of the courts in this balancing process. The claimant brought a challenge to the 'retain and transfer' system then operating in English professional football. The FA is the governing body of Association Football in England, and its rules are binding upon all players and member clubs. Any player wishing to play for a member club is obliged to lodge his registration for that club with the FA. The player may then only represent the club with which he has registered, and cannot play for any other. Players representing a club playing in the League were also required to register their affiliation with the League. Players were employed on twelve-month contracts, at the end of which they could be retained on a 'reasonable wage', determined by the FA, which had the capacity to refuse a club the right to retain a player if the wage offered was insufficient. Retained players were disqualified from playing for any other League club and there was no limit to the amount of time for which a player could be retained. A transfer to another club was possible upon a payment of a fee to the retaining club from the player's new club. Thus a player would be limited to seeking employment with clubs willing and able to meet the fee. A player unhappy with either the terms offered or transfer fee demanded by the retaining club, or who was unable to arrange a transfer, could make an appeal to the League's Management Committee in the hope of obtaining a 'free transfer', in which case the player could not be retained, nor a fee demanded. A transfer to a club outside of the League was, in any case, available to a retained player, on condition that FA rules were complied with. However, this was of little practical significance as opportunities for full-time professional players were largely limited to the League.

The first defendants, Newcastle United, argued that a contract in restraint of trade was not illegal; that without that system in place, the wealthier clubs would sign up all the best players. The global nature of the system, and thus approval of it by those best able to judge, was also cited by Newcastle as a justification of the retain and transfer system. The FA and the League maintained that the restraint imposed was no more than was necessary for the protection of the parties.

In considering whether there was a restraint, and if so whether it was justified, Wilberforce J chose to treat the retention and transfer provisions separately. In terms of the retention system Wilberforce J stated that to restrain players' liberty to utilise their skills in some other employment, after their employment with a particular club had ceased, would be considered as being contrary to public policy, were it not possible to demonstrate that the restraint was in the interests of both parties and in the public interest.[119] The practical effects of the retention provisions were considered by the judge, who noted that they were used by clubs as a tool to obtain a transfer fee for a player who, in reality, they did not wish to retain. Thus, as in this particular case, a situation could arise where players who are adamant that they will not re-sign with their club can be denied the opportunity to utilise their skills. Wilberforce J considered that placing such players on the retained list would 'substantially interfere with their right to seek other employment and – I emphasise this – does so at a time when they are not the employees of the retaining club. That seems to me to operate substantially in restraint of trade.'[120]

Wilberforce J then went on to evaluate the transfer system in isolation from the retention provisions. He considered that the transfer system alone imposed a less serious restraint upon the player than the retention system. Even though an out of contract player was still not free to seek employment as long as he remained on the transfer list – except where a club was willing to meet the fee set by his old club – the player had other courses of action open to him. A transfer-listed player could apply to the Football League Management Committee for a free transfer if he felt the fee to be excessive. He could also transfer to a club outside of the Football League without payment of a fee. Thus the imposition of the restraint was mitigated in two ways.

---

119 *Eastham v Newcastle United Football Club* [1963] 1 Ch 413, p 428.
120 Ibid, p 431.

When considering the question of the reasonableness of the restraints imposed by the system Wilberforce J did not deem the established justifications of protection of trade secrets and prevention of canvassing of customers as legitimate interests and also ruled out any suggestion that the employer could prevent the player from using skills acquired through employment with the club. Wilberforce J rejected the defendants' argument that without such a system in place the richer clubs would, when players became freely available at the end of each season, be in a position to accumulate the best players to the detriment of the public and the majority of the FA and League's member clubs. He suggested that richer clubs already tended to accumulate the better players and did not believe that this would be substantially affected by the abolition of the retention system. This was particularly so because it was open for clubs to award players longer-term contracts. Assertions that a player might be worse off under a long-term contract than under the retention system were dismissed by the judge, because of the unlimited time over which a player could be retained, and thus effectively restrained from employment. Wilberforce J also felt that factors such as family ties, loyalty to a club and a desire for first-team football would also stem the agglomeration of players by the wealthier teams. However, the fact that Wilberforce J felt that he was able to look beyond the traditional justifications for imposing post-termination restraints suggests that others might be considered to be reasonable in particular circumstances, stating, 'it would be wrong to pass straight on to the conclusion that no . . . interest . . . exists.'[121]

As regards the transfer system on its own, Wilberforce J saw that the transfer system alone may even have positive attributes, allowing money to circulate throughout the leagues, supporting the lowlier clubs, and to a certain extent facilitating the movement of players between teams. It was only as part of a package along with the retention system that the transfer system became objectionable. Wilberforce J concluded that the combination operated in unjustifiable restraint of trade, but refused to decide whether the transfer system an itself would also be regarded in this manner.

In deciding that the retention system was an unreasonable restraint of trade Wilberforce J demonstrated that the specialist abilities and knowledge of the governing body would not necessarily sway the courts:

Eastham v Newcastle United Football Club

The system is an employers' system, set up in an industry where the employers have succeeded in establishing a united monolithic front all over the world, and where it is clear that for the purpose of negotiation the employers are vastly more strongly organised than the employees. No doubt the employers all over the world consider the system a good system, but this does not prevent the court from considering whether it goes further than is reasonably necessary to protect their legitimate interests.[122]

On the question of *ultra vires* Wilberforce J decided that, although the rules formulating the retain and transfer system may not have been against the objects of the FA and League, 'it cannot be within the powers of associations such as these to commit their members to action which is against public policy'.[123] Thus the courts are able to examine the substance of a rule.

Disciplinary procedures

The application of restraint of trade law to the operations of sporting organisations has not been limited to measures concerning player transfers. It has also been applied in order to challenge the reasonableness of disciplinary measures.

---

121 Ibid, p 432.
122 *Eastham v Newcastle United Football Club* [1963] 1 Ch 413, p 438.
123 Ibid, p 440.

Greig v Insole[124] involved a challenge to the rules of the International Cricket Council (ICC) and the Test and County Cricket Board (TCCB). The ICC controlled the playing of international matches and the TCCB administered and controlled the playing of first-class county cricket in the UK. In May 1977 World Series Cricket (WSC), a company managed by the Australian entrepreneur Kerry Packer, announced that it had secretly signed up 34 of the world's foremost cricketers to play in a series of 'test matches' in Australia. In July 1977 the ICC altered its rules so that players taking part or making themselves available to play in a match previously disapproved of by the ICC, after 1 October 1977, would be disqualified from taking part in Test cricket without the express consent of the ICC. At the same time the ICC issued a resolution specifically disapproving of any match organised by WSC. The ICC also recommended that national governing bodies take similar action in respect of their domestic game. The TCCB then resolved to alter its rules so that any player who was subject to the Test-match ban would also be disqualified from taking part in first-class county cricket. Three cricketers – Tony Greig, Jon Snow and Mike Procter – all of whom had contracted with WSC to take part in the 'unofficial' tests, issued a writ seeking, against the TCCB and ICC, a declaration that the change of rules by the ICC and those proposed by the TCCB were *ultra vires* and in unlawful restraint of trade.

Slade J decided that both the ICC and TCCB had legitimate interests that they were entitled to protect for the purpose of the restraint of trade doctrine. The ICC argued that it was acting reasonably in introducing rules that would effectively protect it from the competition provided by WSC. Test match cricket provided a large proportion of the money through which the game at lower levels was financed. Thus, the ICC argued, it was acting reasonably in aiming to prevent players from taking part in a competition which could threaten the existence of Test match cricket, and result in cricket suffering at all levels. Slade J did accept that WSC posed at least a short-term threat, but that this was not particularly serious and indeed that the profile of cricket could be raised. However, the long-term threat, Slade J decided, could be adequately met by the imposition of a *prospective* ban on players playing in unsanctioned games. Though such bans would not necessarily be valid they could be more easily justified than the *retrospective* action taken in the case of these three players. Though Slade J recognised that the imposition of a retrospective ban may have broader advantages, he regarded it as being both a serious and unjust step. It would be to deprive a professional cricketer of the opportunity to be employed in a key area of his professional field. This further demonstrates the zealous application of the doctrine in respect of sporting bodies, in that the restraint need only affect a portion of the claimant's activities to fall within its scope. The justifications proffered by the ICC for the suspension of the players from Test match cricket were judged to be highly speculative and thus the ICC failed to justify its rule change. Thus the new rules of the ICC were held to be *ultra vires* and void as being in unreasonable restraint of trade.

The resolution of the TCCB to support the ICC bans at domestic level was regarded as being much more serious. Test cricket offered a limited opportunity to supplement a cricketer's income, but first-class cricket offered the only opportunity to earn a living by playing cricket. This was particularly relevant to players such as two of the claimants, Jon Snow and Mike Procter, who, by reason of age and South African nationality respectively, were effectively out of contention for selection for Test match cricket. Slade J also accepted that the length of their contracts with WSC combined with their ages would effectively mean that Snow and Procter would never play first-class cricket again were a ban imposed. Again Slade J felt that the public interest demanded that top players such as the claimants should be allowed to play the first-class game and that to remove them from it could prove injurious to the sport. The judge also considered that as WSC was more likely to be damaging to Australian domestic cricket, and the TCCB was concerned almost exclusively with

---

124 [1978] 1 WLR 302. Joined with *World Series Cricket v Insole*. World Series Cricket issued a writ seeking, in addition to the declaration of *ultra vires*, a declaration that the rules constituted an unlawful inducement to the cricketers to break their contracts.

cricket in the UK, that the TCCB had less justification in supporting the suspensions than the ICC. Accordingly the TCCB was held to be acting *ultra vires* and in unreasonable restraint of trade.[125]

In *Gasser v Stinson*,[126] the facts of which are set out above, Scott J agreed that the anti-doping rules acted so as to restrain an athlete but also found them to be 'reasonable'. He accepted the argument put forward by the IAAF that the difficulty of proving 'moral innocence' would lead to an opening of the floodgates and that attempts to thwart drug taking would become futile. Thus the blanket application of penalties for doping offences could be justified by the importance of the need to eliminate drug taking in sports.[127] This demonstrates the likely limits of the doctrine as a tool for calling governing bodies to account. It also suggests that the courts still choose to give significant weight to the values applied by governing bodies, particularly in relation to a *cause célèbre* such as the 'war against doping in sport'. This is despite the fact that a restraint on these grounds may not always be objectively justifiable.[128]

This is apparent in *Wilander v Tobin*[129] where two tennis professionals, Matts Wilander and Karel Novacek, unsuccessfully challenged a similar rule of the International Tennis Federation (ITF). Lord Woolf MR, giving the leading judgment of the Court of Appeal, noted the limits of the restraint of trade doctrine:

Wilander v Tobin

The history of these proceedings discloses that the claimants have taken point after point with a view to defeating domestic disciplinary proceedings which in relation to sporting activities should be as uncomplicated as possible. While the courts must be vigilant to protect the genuine rights of sportsmen in the position of the claimants, they must be equally vigilant in preventing the courts' procedures being used unjustifiably to render perfectly sensible and fair procedures inoperable.[130]

Participation in competition

The variety of situations in which the restraint of trade rules will be applied is demonstrated in two further cases that consider the restraint of trade rules as they apply to club membership of leagues and associations. In the case of *Newport AFC Ltd v The Football Association of Wales*,[131] three Welsh football clubs Newport, Caernarfon and Colwyn Bay, challenged a decision of the defendants, the Football Association of Wales (FAW) to pass a resolution preventing Welsh football clubs from playing in leagues making up part of the English pyramid system in order that a comparable Welsh competition could be established.[132] The three claimant clubs resigned their membership of the FAW and joined the English Football Association to facilitate their continued participation in the English pyramid competition. The FAW decision had potentially disastrous financial consequences for the claimant clubs and they sought an injunction against it. The award, by Jacob J, of an interlocutory injunction, is further evidence of the courts' willingness to utilise the restraint of trade doctrine as a mechanism by which to scrutinise the substance of sports governing bodies' activities, rather than merely the procedural or contractual elements, as highlighted above.

---

125 As regards WSC's case against the ICC and TCCB, Slade J agreed that there had been an unlawful inducement upon the players to break their contracts. See also *Hughes v Western Australian Cricket Association* [1986] 69 ALR 660.
126 (1988) unreported, 15 June (QBD).
127 Note though that the IAAF has reduced the length of its mandatory suspension from four to two years, as a result of restraint of trade legislation in Germany, Russia and Spain. German athletes made successful applications for reinstatement after two years of the ban (*The Independent*, 1 July 1997.) Also, in this particular instance a Swiss court refused to uphold the ban placed on Gasser by the national athletics body on the basis of her claim of 'moral innocence'.
128 See Chapter 8 in this book on the regulation of doping.
129 *The Times*, 8 April 1996; [1997] 2 Lloyd's LR 293. See also *Johnson v IAAF*, unreported, 25 July (Ontario Court (General Division)). Noted in C. Stoner 'Recent developments in doping control' (1997) 4(7) SLA&P, 1.
130 [1997] 2 Lloyd's LR 293, p 301. Millet and Potter LJJ concurred.
131 [1995] 2 All ER 87.
132 Resolution of the Football Association of Wales Ltd, 30 November 1991.

The most notable case in this respect is *Stevenage Borough FC Ltd v The Football League Ltd*.[133] In May 1996 Stevenage Borough finished top of the GM Vauxhall Conference (GMVC), a position which in principle entitled them to take the place in the Football League of the team finishing bottom of Division Three, Torquay United. However, Football League rules stipulated that this promotion would be dependent upon the winner of the GMVC satisfying certain admission criteria relating to ground capacity and safety, by December of that winning season. Stevenage failed to meet the League's deadline but would have met the requirements in time for the beginning of the new season. On this basis the Football League refused Stevenage entry.

Stevenage challenged the decision by the League to deny them promotion, on the grounds that the entry criteria were in unreasonable restraint of trade. They sought an injunction restraining the League from imposing the criteria for membership of the League so as to refuse entry to them.

In his judgment Carnwath J recognised that in normal circumstances the burden of demonstrating the reasonableness of the restraint would lie with the Football League, as it was the party seeking to impose it. Here, however, the restraint was a part of a regulatory system imposed by a body exercising control in the public interest, and therefore different considerations would arise. Carnwath J felt that the control exercised by the Football League could be attacked where it was 'arbitrary or capricious' or a 'pernicious monopoly'. In this case the Football League was operating in the public interest and so the onus was shifted upon the challenger to illustrate the unreasonableness of the rules.

Technically there was no legal relationship between the Football League and Stevenage when treated as strictly private bodies and therefore nothing unreasonable about the position adopted by the League. When viewed from this private aspect Stevenage were nothing more than an applicant for entry to the League – a company owned by its member clubs, each of whom were private trading organisations. From this point of view there was no need for the League to justify the restraint; it had no legal obligations binding upon it; neither were Stevenage prevented from conducting their business of playing football within the GMVC, or any other league willing to accept the club as a member. However, Carnwath J felt this was too simplistic a view to take and that a broader approach was apt. When considered more generally, the Football League could be seen to be operating as a part of the complicated system of control operating for the organisation of professional football, in the interests of participants and the general public. The fact of the Football League's operation in the public interest was seen as a reasonable basis upon which to extend the ambit of the restraint of trade doctrine. Stevenage had objected to the entry requirements on the basis that they would have had to complete ground improvements long before it was clear whether or not they would win the GMVC and be eligible for promotion. Secondly, the League also imposed financial requirements upon entrance to Division 3, which were not demanded of existing member clubs. Carnwath J agreed that these requirements would be open to attack on the grounds of restraint of trade. However, he had reservations as to whether the criteria could be regarded as arbitrary or capricious. He also felt that there was an important question of discretion to be decided, considering the question of delay and prejudice to third parties. Stevenage had argued that it would be unfair to expect them to begin legal proceedings until they had satisfied the first criteria for promotion to the League by winning the GMVC. Carnwath J accepted this was reasonable as from Stevenage's point of view, but that did not take account of the need to be fair to all others that would be affected. Stevenage had the opportunity to challenge the criteria at the beginning of the season. Even though this involved an element of commercial risk, in that Stevenage might not benefit from success in litigation, this did not make it unreasonable to expect them to do so. That route would have allowed the rules to be tested before the December deadline with time for the making of alternative arrangements. Carnwath J also felt that Torquay United's position was of particular

---

133 *The Times*, 1 August 1996.

relevance; relegation to the GMVC would be very significant for them, and to leave them uncertain as to their future so close to the beginning of the new season was unfair.

However, the judge did feel that the Football League's rules did require reconsideration, as failure to amend them would leave them open to challenge on restraint of trade grounds in the future. This highlights that even though an individual claimant may be unsuccessful in his action because of the overall situation, a judgment can still be effective in that rules are altered to be brought into line with the doctrine, as has now happened in this case. Carnwath J stated that the court would have jurisdiction in extreme cases to set aside rules such as these; however, the criteria had been accepted at the beginning of the season by Stevenage and all representative bodies, including the GMVC of which Stevenage was a member. Stevenage's delay in bringing proceedings to challenge the rules of the Football League resulted in the court refusing to grant relief.

On appeal the Court of Appeal held that the issue of a declaration was a discretionary remedy, thus the judge's refusal to grant such, despite finding that the League's rules could be in unreasonable restraint of trade, was justifiable. Carnwath J was adjudged to have been correct to withhold a declaration on the basis of the overall justice of the situation.[134] A similar view was adopted by MacKay J in *Chambers v BOA*, where he expressed the view that the delay in challenging the BOA byelaw would in itself have disposed him to exercise his discretion in favour of denying the relief sought.

Competition law: control of competitions

It is also the case that sports governing bodies will find themselves subject to scrutiny through the application of competition law. In *Hendry*, the facts of which are set out above, the WPBSA's near monopoly control over the operation of snooker tournaments had the result that the combined impact of a policy of refusing to sanction tournaments which competed with its own and a rule requiring players not to participate in unsanctioned tournaments was an abuse of a dominant position and thus unlawful. However, of note is that regulations pertaining to the wearing of logos by and sponsorship of players, controls over players' marketing activities and the WPBSA ranking system, were all regarded as reasonable regulatory measures.

Restraint of trade and competition: evaluating the case law

The restraint of trade route has clearly been the most fruitful for those seeking to call sport's governing bodies to account. Indeed, the doctrine has been applied more liberally in relation to sports governing bodies than has generally been the case. The doctrine itself is highly accessible, its invocation is not limited to those who are parties to the challenged agreement, and it can be utilised by a stranger to an agreement who is unreasonably restrained by its operation. The source of the restraint is not seen as being of particular significance; it is the effect that brings the doctrine into play. This has the result that the doctrine is not hindered by the procedural pitfalls found particularly in the context of judicial review. This is evident throughout the case law examined above.

The doctrine is primarily concerned with the effect of the challenged provision upon the ability to trade and less preoccupied with the 'specialist' position of sporting decision-makers. Sport's governing bodies cannot hide behind their rules in order to avoid scrutiny. The very content of those rules can be called into question and tested for reasonableness under the doctrine. This facilitates a more significant penetration of the regulatory sphere than previously encountered. The doctrine has been applied in such a manner that the operations of sports governing bodies are still protected, where their aims and objects are legitimate and reasonable. It has been accepted that the

---

134 (1997) Admin LR 109. See also *Hearn v Rugby Football Union* (2003) *The Times*, 15 September.

doctrine will not extend to all decisions taken by governing bodies, only those that affect the ability of others to trade. This has been expanded somewhat by the decisions in *Newport* and more notably *Stevenage* and *Chambers*, where the overall justice of the situation was taken into account. Competition law shares many of these characteristics and, in an era of growing commercialisation, it is likely that it will play a growing role.

Natural justice

One way in which private law has adopted public law principles is in relation to the rules of natural justice. These rules make up part of one of the heads of judicial review, procedural impropriety, outlined by Lord Diplock in *CCSU v Minister for the Civil Service*.[135] However, as suggested, the rules are applied not only in the context of judicial review actions but also those founded in private law – including the private law relationships of sports governing bodies. There are two main rules of natural justice: the rule against bias (*nemo judex in sua causa*) and the right to a fair hearing (*audi alteram partem*). The early case of *Russell v Duke of Norfolk*[136] concerned the withdrawal by the Jockey Club of the claimant's licence to train racehorses and subsequent disqualification from having an involvement in racing in any capacity. The licence was withdrawn at an inquiry held by the stewards of the Jockey Club and attended by Mr Russell, which arose after a horse trained by the claimant was found to have been doped, contrary to Jockey Club rules. The stewards of the Jockey Club acted under powers conferred upon them under the Club's rules, by which the claimant had agreed to be bound by making an application for a licence. The stewards on withdrawal of the licence intimated that it was withdrawn on the ground of misconduct, with the effect that he was effectively prevented from taking on any substantial role in the racing world. Because of the Jockey Club's practical monopoly over the holding of race meetings, this withdrawal effectively precluded the claimant from training racehorses.

Mr Russell brought an action arguing that his licence had been withdrawn, he had been found guilty of misconduct and had become a disqualified person without an inquiry being conducted in accordance with the demands of natural justice. At first instance the jury decided that the inquiry held by the stewards was fair.[137]

The majority in the Court of Appeal chose to reject Mr Russell's claim on the basis that the contract did not require a hearing to take place at all, so to require any hearing to be in accordance with the rules of natural justice would be perverse. Denning LJ submitted an alternative view. He suggested that in a situation where the conditions of the licence gave the Jockey Club absolute discretion as to its withdrawal that it would be sufficient that the Club act honestly and in good faith in making such a decision. However, where the withdrawal of a licence was coupled with disqualification (from involvement in racing in any form) this was much more serious. It had the effect of taking away a person's livelihood:

Russell v Duke of Norfolk

Common justice therefore requires that before any man be found guilty of an offence carrying such consequences, there should be an inquiry at which he has the opportunity of being heard ... It is very different from a mere dismissal of a servant or withdrawal of a licence, or even expulsion from a club.[138]

Denning LJ suggested such a disqualification could be contrary to public policy. He went on to note the position of the Jockey Club as having a 'monopoly in an important field of human activity. It has

---

135 [1985] AC 374.
136 [1949] 1 All ER 109.
137 [1948] 1 All ER 488.
138 [1949] 1 All ER 109, p 119.

great powers and corresponding responsibilities'.[139] On the facts Denning LJ held that the hearing that had taken place was in conformity with the principles of natural justice. Thus the claimant's appeal was dismissed. The judgment of Denning LJ represents an indication of the way in which the case law concerning natural justice, both generally and with specific relation to sport's governing bodies, was to develop.

The fair hearing rule exists now such that courts and tribunals with similar functions, as well as other bodies acting in a judicial capacity, will be subject to the demands of the fair hearing rule. In exceptional circumstances the rule requiring a fair hearing will be applied solely upon the basis of the substantial effect of a decision upon an individual's rights. The rule can require a variety of things from decision-makers, dependent upon the nature of the individual case. The rules may require prior notice of a decision, consultation and written representation, a duty to give adequate notice of a disciplinary charge, an oral hearing, the right to call and cross-examine witnesses, legal representation and a requirement to give reasons.

The *audi alteram partem* rule has been invoked most readily where the loss of a person's livelihood or reputation has been at stake, highlighting that the application of the rules will be highly dependent upon the individual circumstances of each case. There is an acknowledgement on behalf of the courts that it is not only statutory bodies that can affect rights and that statutory protection is not always sufficient: the approach favoured by Denning LJ in *Russell*. There it was recognised that the monopolistic nature of the Jockey Club combined with the significant effect that its decisions could have would be reason enough to subject it to the requirements of natural justice.

The right to a fair hearing and sporting bodies

Lord Denning MR followed his judgment in *Russell* and demonstrated that the principles of a fair hearing were applicable in relation to the actions of governing bodies of sport in *Enderby Town FC Ltd v The Football Association Ltd*.[140] The case concerned the ability of the FA to deny legal representation in the operation of its tribunals. The FA had control over association football, and the county associations affiliated to it. The claimants, Enderby Town, were fined and censured by their county association and made an appeal to the FA. They asserted the right to be represented by solicitor and counsel in their appeal hearing. The FA rejected this on the ground that their rule 38(b) excluded legal representation except where the chairman or secretary of the club being heard was a lawyer. The club sought an injunction restraining the FA from hearing the appeal without the club being legally represented. At first instance it was held that the provisions of the contract entered into between Enderby Town and their county association should be observed. Lord Denning MR highlighted the invalidity of any attempt to 'oust the jurisdiction of the court, unreasonably shut out a man from his work or lay down procedure contrary to natural justice'.[141] However, the club's argument that legal representation was essential in their appeal to the FA, because of the difficulty of the points of law involved, was rejected by Lord Denning MR. The club, he decided, were perfectly entitled to bring an action for a declaration on those points before the court. This would allow legal representation. In any case, it would be preferable that such intricate points of law should be decided by the courts rather than by a body such as the FA.[142] Significantly, once again, this highlights the balance that has to be struck by the courts between the demands of justice and the requirement that a governing body be given sufficient latitude to carry out its tasks efficiently.

---

139 Ibid.
140 [1971] Ch 591.
141 Ibid, p 606.
142 Ibid, p 605.

Enderby Town Football Club Ltd v The Football Association Ltd

In many cases it may be a good thing for the proceedings of a domestic tribunal to be conducted informally without legal representation. Justice can often be done, in them, better by a good layman than by a bad lawyer . . . But I must emphasise that the discretion must be properly exercised. The tribunal must not fetter its discretion by rigid bonds. A domestic tribunal is not at liberty to lay down an absolute rule.[143]

Lord Denning MR concluded that as long as a rule denying legal representation was merely directory and not imperative it would not be in breach of natural justice. He summarised:

The long and the short of it is that if the court sees that a domestic tribunal is proposing to proceed in a manner contrary to natural justice, it can intervene to stop it.[144]

This case serves to emphasise two key points. First, that the courts will use the combination of monopolistic control coupled with serious consequences for the individual to justify subjecting decisions to the demands of natural justice. However, secondly, there may be a tendency to avoid complicating sporting bodies' procedures too greatly.

The limits of the fair hearing rule

Throughout the early case law the recurrent theme was one of generally expansive judgments, aimed at protecting individuals from the capricious and arbitrary exercise of monopoly powers. *McInnes v Onslow-Fane*[145] dealt with the question of the requirement for governing bodies to inform an applicant of the case against him and to provide that applicant with the opportunity of a hearing. The case represents a slightly more conservative view of the courts' approach to the oversight of sports governing bodies. In 1976 the claimant, McInnes, applied to the British Boxing Board of Control (BBBC) for a licence to permit him to act as a boxing manager, coupled with a request that he might be given an oral hearing and prior notice of anything that might prevent him from obtaining the licence. The board refused his application without acquiescing to his additional requests. McInnes had previously held licenses to act as a promoter, a trainer and as a master of ceremonies; all of which were withdrawn in 1973. Between 1972 and 1975 McInnes had made five applications for a manager's licence, all of which were refused. The claimant sought a declaration against the British Boxing Board of Control that it had acted in breach of natural justice and/or unfairly in refusing his application for a boxers' manager's licence in that they failed to comply with his requests to be informed of the case against him, so as to allow him to reply prior to the consideration of his application, and that they failed to grant him an oral hearing. Additionally he sought a mandatory order that the BBBC should either grant him a manager's licence or, alternatively, that they inform him of the case against him and grant him an oral hearing.

Megarry VC questioned whether the situation was one in which the courts were entitled to intervene, emphasising the changes which had taken place in relation to the application of the rules of natural justice:

McInnes v Onslow-Fane

The question is not one that is governed by statute or contract, with questions of their true construction or the implication of terms; for there is no statute, and there is no contract

---

143 Ibid, per Denning MR, p 605.
144 Ibid, p 606. Fenton, Atkinson and Cairns LJJ concurred with Lord Denning MR's judgment and the claimant's appeal was dismissed.
145 [1978] 1 WLR 1520.

between the claimant and the board. Nevertheless, in recent years there has been a marked expansion of the ambit of the requirements of natural justice and fairness reaching beyond statute and contract.[146]

In conformity with the preceding case law Megarry VC held that the courts could intervene in order to enforce the requirements of natural justice before going on to question the nature of the particular decision and the requirements of natural justice in such circumstances. He distinguished between three types of situation: forfeiture cases, where a licence or membership is withdrawn; application cases, where an application for such a licence or membership is refused; and expectation cases, which are different from the application cases in that the applicant has some legitimate expectation from previous conduct that a licence will be granted.[147] The applicant had argued that the other licenses that he had held entitled him to have a legitimate expectation that his application for a manager's licence would succeed. Megarry VC rejected this; the claimant had had five previous applications for a manager's licence turned down and the other licenses were for different functions, thus there was no legitimate expectation that his application would succeed.[148]

Megarry VC also rejected the claimant's contention that the BBBC were under an obligation to provide reasons for their decision or an oral hearing. As the issue of a licence was not dependent upon particular criteria, the refusal did not place a slur upon the applicant's character. The judgment also highlighted that it is not just the status of the individual that is important in making decisions regarding licenses and other such matters; the needs of the particular sport as a whole also have to be taken into account by the regulator.[149] Megarry VC emphasised the need to keep bodies' procedures speedy and uncomplicated, with the result that they would be perfectly entitled to withhold reasons for any refusal of a licence that might allow a refused applicant access to the courts.[150] The situation in this respect has been somewhat altered by later case law.[151] While accepting the need for the individual to be protected against impropriety Megarry VC also recognised the need for this to be balanced against the requirement of the public interest, apparently accurately represented by the unfettered action of the BBBC. He did, nonetheless, make comment to the effect that the Board was under a duty to reach an honest conclusion, without bias and not in pursuance of a capricious policy.[152] In dismissing the application Megarry VC commented:

> I think that the courts must be slow to allow any implied obligation to be fair to be used as a means of bringing before the courts for review honest decisions of bodies exercising jurisdiction over sporting and other activities, which those bodies are far better fitted to judge than the courts. This is so even where those bodies are concerned with the means of livelihood of those who take part in those activities. The concepts of natural justice and the duty to be fair must not be allowed to discredit themselves by making unreasonable requirements and imposing undue burdens. Bodies such as the board, which promote a public interest by seeking to maintain high

---

146 Ibid, p 1528.
147 Ibid, p 1529.
148 Ibid, p 1531.
149 Ibid, p 1535.
150 Ibid, p 1536.
151 *R v Civil Service Appeal Board ex p Cunningham* [1991] 4 All ER 310, extended the position to one where a decision-maker should give outline reasons for its decision where procedural fairness demands, in that reasons will aid the individual to ascertain whether the decision was lawful and thus help an individual in any potential litigation. In *R v Home Secretary ex p Doody* [1993] 1 WLR 154, it was judged that reasons could be required where a decision has severe consequences, though in *R v Higher Education Funding Council ex p Institute of Dental Surgery* [1994] 1 WLR 242, it was decided that where a body was making a decision on 'expert' or technical reasons which a court would not be competent to assess, then reasons would not be required. This appears to conform to the 'trust to my expertise' approach to self-regulation. See also *R. (on the application of Hasan) v Secretary of State for Trade and Industry* [2008] EWCA Civ 1312.
152 *McInnes v Onslow-Fane* [1978] 1 WLR 1520, p 1533.

standards in a field of activity, which might otherwise become degraded and corrupt, ought not to be hampered in their work without good cause.[153]

This approach manifested itself in the case of *Calvin v Carr*,[154] which involved a challenge to the decision of the Australian Jockey Club (AJC) to disqualify an owner of a horse. Here once again, the need to avoid over-juridification in the decision-making processes of domestic bodies was highlighted:

Calvin v Carr

It is undesirable in many cases of domestic disputes, particularly in which an inquiry and appeal process has been established, to introduce too great a measure of formal judicialisation. While flagrant cases of injustice, including corruption or bias, must always be firmly dealt with by the courts, the tendency in their Lordships' opinion in matters of domestic disputes should be to leave these to be settled by the agreed methods without requiring the formalities of judicial process to be introduced.[155]

The modern law: *Jones v WRFU*

A recent indicator of the way in which the law has developed in this area is the case of *Jones v Welsh Rugby Football Union*,[156] which involved a challenge to the disciplinary procedures operated by the Welsh Rugby Football Union (WRFU).

Mark Jones played for Ebbw Vale Rugby Football Club. He was sent off the field of play for fighting during the club's game against Swansea in November 1996. Jones appeared before the Disciplinary Committee of the WRFU in order to offer explanation and comment on the referee's report. He was denied legal representation but, due to a severe speech impediment, he was allowed to be represented by an official of the Ebbw Vale club. The club representative was a QC, but his function was to speak in place of Jones rather than to act as his advocate. Standard WRFU procedure was followed, the player's representative commented on the referee's report, and the referee commented and was questioned by the Disciplinary Committee. However, the Committee refused Jones's request that his representative be given permission to comment on the video of the incident, in order that it might be demonstrated that Jones was acting in self-defence. The Committee also refused to allow Jones's representative to cross-examine the referee. The Committee viewed the video of the incident in private and again refused Jones or his representative the right to comment upon it. As a result of the hearing, the Disciplinary Committee decided that the referee had been correct in sending Jones off and imposed a 30-day suspension upon him. The constitution of the WRFU granted power in relation to disciplinary matters to the Committee. These rules had the effect of conferring upon the Committee complete discretion in relation to the manner and form of its hearings.

Jones and his club, Ebbw Vale, proceeding by way of writ, sought a declaration that the decision to suspend was invalid and an order obligating the WRFU to refrain from the imposition of the suspension until the completion of a new disciplinary process. Jones argued that any order should amend the disciplinary process in such a way as to allow him legal representation, to call and question witnesses and to compel the Committee to examine or review evidence in his presence, giving him the right to make submissions pertaining to it.

---

153 Ibid, p 1535.
154 [1980] AC 574.
155 Ibid, p 593. See also *Modahl v British Athletic Federation Ltd* [2002] 1 WLR 1192 per Latham LJ at para 67, Jonathan Parker LJ at para 87 and Mance LJ at para 116.
156 *The Times*, 6 March 1997, and *The Times*, 6 January 1998. See also Rose, N and Albertini, L, '*Jones v Welsh Rugby Union*: new law for the new era' (1997) 5(1) SATLJ 20.

Ebsworth J granted an interlocutory injunction preventing the imposition of a suspension prior to the final resolution of the issue.[157] In her judgment Ebsworth J agreed it was arguable that in refusing to vary its procedure, not on the basis of any rules but on the grounds of custom and practice, the Committee acted in a manner lacking in fairness. In this case Ebsworth J felt that it was arguable that the claimants had a right to defend themselves properly and effectively had been denied.

Following the interlocutory decision of Ebsworth J, the WRFU was keen that the matter should be resolved as speedily as possible. In response to the judgment the WRFU implemented changes to its rules, granting a player or his representative the right to question the referee and to call and cross-examine witnesses. The amendments also required video evidence to be viewed in the presence of all the parties and provided that the player's requests for legal representation should be treated on their merits, in conformity with the judgment of Lord Denning MR in *Enderby Town*.

The claimants then applied for an order restraining the WRFU from imposing any suspension related to the incident in the match against Swansea in November 1996 prior to the final resolution of the issue. Despite the argument of the WRFU that Ebsworth J's order was limited to the suspension imposed at the initial disciplinary hearing, Potts J granted the order requested by the claimants.[158]

The defendant appealed against both the decision of Ebsworth J and that of Potts J, and these appeals were heard in the Court of Appeal.[159] In his judgment Potter LJ recognised that the WRFU could well be successful in defending its actions if the case proceeded to trial. However, he refused its appeal against the decision of Ebsworth J on the basis that all that it was necessary for her to do when deciding upon the grant of an interlocutory injunction was to determine whether or not the claimants had an arguable case for relief. Potter LJ was willing to overturn the decision of Potts J, on the ground that in Potter LJ's view Ebsworth J's order related only to the first hearing: it was not apt to deal with any further hearing which could not be criticised on the ground of procedural unfairness.

The rule against bias

It is not only the rules relating to a fair hearing that are applied to sports governing bodies; they are also required to act in accordance with the rule against bias. The rule requires an adjudicator to be free from any interest in a case. This can be financial, which automatically disqualifies the adjudicator,[160] or where a 'fair-minded and informed observer, having considered the facts, would conclude that there was a real possibility that the tribunal was biased'.[161]

Morris, P and Little, G, 'Challenging sports bodies' determinations'

The rule is a distinct limb of natural justice and precludes a member of a disciplinary tribunal from sitting in any case where there is a reasonable likelihood or suspicion of bias; actual bias need not be established. In applying the rule stringently courts recognise its value as a tool in promoting confidence in the integrity of administrative justice. Factual circumstances in which the rule may be infringed are infinite, but there are particular instances of the rule in operation, which are particularly relevant to sports bodies' administrators when carrying out their role of designing and operating arrangements for the adjudication of disciplinary cases. First, the

---

157 *The Times*, 6 March 1997.
158 (1997) unreported, 17 November.
159 *The Times*, 6 January 1998.
160 *Dimes v Grand Junction Canal* (1852) 3 HLC 759.
161 *Porter v Magill* [2002] 2 AC 494 at para 103, per Lord Hope of Craighead.

disciplinary code should make provision for the rigid demarcation of 'prosecutorial' and 'adjudicating' functions. Any intermingling of these functions such as 'the prosecutor' participating or appearing to participate in the adjudication is likely to infringe the rule unless the essential and historic function of a sports official dictates such participation, one example being horse racing stewards who have long performed an 'evidence gathering' function as well as sitting in an adjudicating capacity during a disciplinary inquiry (*Hall v New South Wales Trotting Club* (1977) 1 NSWLR 378, 397, per Moloney JA). Secondly, in general a sports bodies' disciplinary code should strive to ensure, in the case of appeals, that an individual who sits (or is entitled to sit) in at the initial hearing does not also participate as an adjudicator during the appeal (*Hannan v Bradford Corporation* [1970] 1 WLR 937). The rationale for this prohibition is clearly articulated by Lord Widgery CJ, namely that 'when one is used to dealing with other people in a group or on a committee, there must be a built-in tendency to support the decision of that committee, even though one tries to fight against it' (at 946). Thirdly, it is perfectly proper for sports disciplinary tribunals to be composed exclusively or substantially of fellow sportsmen on the basis that the individual members of a profession or occupational group are ideally equipped to judge whether there has been a breach of the professional code of conduct and the gravity of it. This professional autonomy, however, is subject to the proviso that the architects of the disciplinary arrangements are 'careful in framing the constitution of the governing body, and of its disciplinary tribunal, to ensure that the task of presenting a complaint and the task of adjudicating upon it and, if it is proved, determining the appropriate sanction are in different hands' (*Re S, A Barrister* [1981] QB 670 at 683, per Vinelott J).

Perhaps the most pressing problem confronting sports' governing bodies in relation to the rule against bias is to resist the quite natural temptation to pack disciplinary tribunals with their own officials. Historically, governing bodies have succumbed to this temptation and the infamous *Don Revie* case (*The Times*, 14 December 1979) shows that it can contribute to a finding of bias by the courts.[162]

In *Revie* members of a Football Association disciplinary tribunal who had criticised Don Revie, the former England manager, before a hearing, were disqualified on the basis of a likelihood of bias. The tribunal's decision to impose a ten-year ban on Revie was subsequently revoked. In *Modahl* the Court of Appeal adopted a similar line of reasoning to that in *Calvin v Carr* in determining that overall the athlete had a fair hearing. Modahl's claim was that the five-man panel that had conducted her original disciplinary hearing and found her guilty of the doping offence had the appearance of bias. In particular, she was concerned that one member of the panel had voiced the view that all athletes are guilty of doping unless proven otherwise. The claim was dismissed at first instance[163] and this was endorsed by the Court of Appeal.

This position has since been affirmed by the Court of Appeal in *Flaherty v National Greyhound Racing Club Ltd*.[164] Here the appellant governing body successfully overturned a first instance decision that a stewards' inquiry concerning the doping of a greyhound had been defective, in that a member of the panel had demonstrated apparent bias and that the chief executive of the Club had retired with the panel.[165] In respect of the steward the Court of Appeal concluded that it was perfectly normal for a panel of this kind to be composed of members with expertise and views on the sport in question. That did not, however, amount to apparent bias. Further, the practice of the panel to retire with the Club's chief executive was criticised as being poor practice; however, given that the chief

---

162 Morris, P and Little, G, 'Challenging sports bodies' determinations' (1998) 17 Civ JQ 128, 139–40.
163 [2000] All ER (D) 2274.
164 [2005] EWCA 1117.
165 Cf *R v Sussex Justices ex p McCarthy* [1924] 1 KB 256.

executive was present in an administrative rather than prosecutorial capacity this did not in itself lead to the conclusion that there had been apparent bias. In particular, the inquisitorial rather than adversarial nature of the inquiry impacted upon this view. However, overall, it appears that the Court of Appeal was much swayed by the 'overwhelming' nature of the case against Flaherty and the arrival, overall, at a fair result.

Natural justice: evaluating the case law

The case law relating to natural justice demonstrates a general acceptance on the part of the courts of the need to subject sport's governing bodies to scrutiny. The monopoly positions held by many of these bodies have been acknowledged as being reason enough to supervise their activities. The broad range of values deemed worthy of protection by the rules of natural justice has meant that an extensive array of situations have been deemed to fall for consideration by the courts.[166]

However, though the courts have accepted the general susceptibility of the considerations of sports governing bodies to the rules of natural justice, the application of those maxims has been less vigorous. There seems to be concern that the courts should not inhibit the activities of such bodies to any great degree. While it may be desirable that sporting bodies should be reasonably free to conduct their affairs as they wish, their monopoly position demands that they should be prevented from acting unfairly. It is clear that those who are subject to the disciplinary procedures of sporting bodies should be prevented from hiding behind deficiencies in such procedures in order to avoid censure. The courts have tended to err on the side of administrative efficiency rather than individual justice.

However, cases such as *Jones* do demonstrate that the rules of natural justice can be extremely useful in helping sporting bodies to avoid acting unfairly. The speedy and comprehensive amendment of the WRFU's rules in that case demonstrated a desire on the part of sporting bodies to avoid having their decisions challenged in the courts.[167]

The usefulness of the natural justice rules as a method by which to call sport's governing bodies to account is further limited. The rules are largely restricted to procedural elements of governing bodies' activities, and thus have a limited capacity to penetrate bodies' regulatory sphere. The character of the natural justice rules combined with the manner of their application has the effect that, despite the courts' general willingness to subject these bodies to scrutiny, the usefulness of the rules in calling sport's governing bodies to account is marginal.

Sports governing bodies and the Human Rights Act 1998

One approach to remedying this shortfall comes in the form of the Human Rights Act 1998. The effect of the Human Rights Act 1998 is to give further effect to the provisions of the European Convention on Human Rights (1950) in the UK. This has been achieved primarily through the imposition of a new interpretative obligation upon domestic courts. They have a responsibility to interpret new and existing legislation as far as possible as being in accordance with the Human Rights Act 1998.[168] In addition to this courts and tribunals are required to take into account the jurisprudence of the Convention's Strasbourg institutions where relevant to proceedings before it.[169] The Act also compels public authorities to conduct themselves in a manner that is consistent with the principles set out in the Convention.[170] It seems possible that the Act will not only have an

---

166 See also McCutcheon, JP, 'Sports discipline, natural justice and strict liability' (1999) 28(1) Anglo-Am LR 37.
167 Note: the amendments were made not in response to a final judgment that had condemned the relevant rules, but as a reaction to proceedings for an interlocutory injunction where it was considered only that it was *arguable* that the rules were unfair.
168 HRA 1998, s 3, with provision for a declaration of incompatibility where this is impossible (s 4).
169 HRA 1998, s 2.
170 Ibid, s 6.

impact upon government in the narrowest sense, but that it will also impact upon the activities of self-regulating organisations such as those that govern sport.

Boyes, S, 'Regulating sport after the Human Rights Act 1998'

There appear to be two mechanisms by which the Convention rights incorporated by the Act are likely to impact upon the activities of sports governing bodies:

The first is what may be described as the 'horizontal effect' of the Act. The Act contains no explicit support for the extension of its provisions to the purely private relationships of private parties. However, whilst not creating a new and independent cause of action in these circumstances, it is possible that the provisions of the Act will exert an influence upon the courts as they interpret and develop pre-existing law. Despite statements made by the Lord Chancellor during the Bill's passage through Parliament that clearly signal that the enforcement of the rights as between private individuals is not the intention of the Act, there does appear to be an argument that the Act will, even must, impact upon purely private relationships. Section 6(3)(a) of the Act defines those public bodies that are compelled by section 6(1) to act in accordance with the rights laid down as including a 'court or tribunal'. When considered in combination with section 2 of the Act, requiring the courts to take into account the case law of the Strasbourg institutions, it is well arguable that this may have an impact upon purely private relationships. However, it is clear that the Act makes no provision for the creation of a new cause of action for potential litigants.

What is arguable is that where a cause of action already exists, the courts will necessarily be influenced in their decisions by the rights protected by the ECHR and expanded upon as case law has developed, on the basis of the obligations placed upon them as 'public authorities' under the Act. Thus where individuals are able to identify a cause of action against a sporting body they may well be able to argue that the Act should be taken into account where it is relevant to a case – in effect to 'attach' a Convention right to a pre-existing cause of action. This might impact upon the manner in which the courts interpret the contractual relationship between athlete and governing body or the way in which they choose to apply the restraint of trade doctrine.

The 'horizontal' impact of the Act has been the subject of fierce debate and is highly contentious. Even if the courts are influenced by the Convention in their regulation of private law relationships, the impact is likely to be a gradual one. A more likely and immediate effect is likely to be felt as a result of the classification of sports governing bodies as 'quasi-public authorities'.

Section 6 of the Act provides for the enforcement of the Convention's fundamental rights against what are described as 'public authorities'. Section 6(1) makes it unlawful for a 'public authority' to behave in a way contrary to a Convention right. This provision relates to bodies regarded as being 'pure' public authorities that are required to conform to the provisions of the Human Rights Act in respect of *all* of their activities. Sports governing bodies are unlikely to be classified in this way given that the courts have consistently refused to accept them as being public bodies for the purposes of the application for judicial review, and that this has been highlighted as being an indicator for the classification. Section 6(3)(b) of the Act obliges 'any person certain of whose functions are functions of a public nature' – 'quasi-public authorities' – to meet the requirements of the Act. However, this requirement is limited *only* to the public acts of those persons and thus has no bearing upon their private activities, smartly avoiding the problem of the public–private divide so often encountered in the field of public law . . .

During the Act's passage through Parliament, the Lord Chancellor suggested that bodies such as Railtrack would be of the type that would be encompassed by the 'quasi-public' classification. It would be acting as a public body, and thus susceptible to the provisions of the Act, in respect of its role as safety regulator. However, its role as an employer would be seen as a private law matter and thus would not be subject to the provisions of the Act. Of greater significance was the statement of the Home Secretary at the Committee stage of the Act's passage through Parliament, when he specifically drew attention to a sporting body as being of the type that he would expect to fall within the section 6(3)(b) 'quasi-public body' category:

> 'There will be occasions – it is the nature of British society – on which various institutions that are private in terms of their legal personality carry out public functions . . . I would suggest that it . . . includes the Jockey Club . . . The Jockey Club is a curious body: it is entirely private, but exercises public functions in some respects, and to those extents, but to no other, it would be regarded as falling within [this classification].'
>
> (*Hansard* HC, 20 May 1998, col 1018.)

This is likely to be of significance not only to the Jockey Club, but also to a range of other sports governing bodies.[171]

The introduction of the Human Rights Act 1998 in the United Kingdom, it appears, has the potential to have an impact upon both the manner and substance of sporting regulation. As yet there is little sports-specific case law related to the Act. However, it seems that the Act may impact in a growing number of areas. It has been suggested that these could include: Article 4 ECHR relating to forced or compulsory labour; Article 6 ECHR, the right to a fair and public hearing; Article 8 ECHR, the right to respect for privacy; and Article 10 ECHR, freedom of expression.[172]

The discussion above is necessarily speculative. It is notable that the Human Rights Act has not been utilised to any great degree in litigation pertaining to sports governing bodies as yet.[173] Even should the courts to decide not to interpret the Act in the manner suggested, an action before the European Court of Human Rights would be likely to be successful. An aggrieved athlete could bring a case against the United Kingdom on the basis of a failure on the part of domestic law to adequately protect a particular Convention right.

However, the judgment of Stanley Burnton J in R (o/a Mullins) v Appeal Board of the Jockey Club (discussed in detail above) has thrown into doubt the analysis of s 6(3)(b) set out above. In this case the claimant attempted to argue that the law in relation to judicial review had changed, such that the test to be applied in determining justiciability was analogous to that in s 6(3)(b). In rejecting this approach Stanley Brunton J also cast doubt upon the extent of the applicability of s 6(3)(b) to sports bodies. It was held that the Court of Appeal's decision in *Aga Khan* was authority for the view not only that the Jockey Club is not a 'core' public authority, either for the purposes of judicial review or section 6 Human Rights Act, but also for the proposition that the disciplinary functions exercised by the Appeal Board did not amount to a public function for the purposes of s 6(3)(b). The interpretation to be adopted was a narrow one: the function in question must be 'governmental' in nature to fall within the remit of the 'public function' classification. Given the restrictive approach applied to sports governing bodies in respect of judicial review more generally, this might seem to limit the opportunities for challenge under the Human Rights Act. However, the growing interaction between sports governing bodies and the state in respect of, amongst other

---

171 Boyes, S, 'Regulating sport after the Human Rights Act 1998' (2001) 151 NLJ 444–46. See also Stewart, W, Wallace, R and Dale-Risk, K, 'Sports Administration and Human Rights' (2000/2001) CIL 282.

172 Boyes, S, 'The regulation of sport and the impact of the Human Rights Act 1998' (2000) 6(4) EPL 517, 525–28. See also McArdle, D, 'Judicial Review, "Public Authorities" and Disciplinary Powers of Sporting Organisations' (1999) 30 Cambrian LR 31; Lewis, A and Taylor, J (eds) *Sport: Law and Practice* (2004), London: Butterworths, pp 231–58. See now on the point of the courts' obligation to conform with a Convention right in their role as public authority under s 6(1), *Re Attorney General's Reference (No.3 of 1999)*, [2009] UKHL 34; *Re S (A Child) (Identification: Restrictions on Publication)* [2004] UKHL 47.

173 Though cf *Rubython v Federation Internationale De L'Automobile* (unreported, 6 March 2003, QBD) for a brief discussion of the classification of sports governing bodies as 'public authorities' for the purposes of the Human Rights Act 1998.

things, anti-doping measures, development of elite athletes and the licensing and regulation of volunteers in sport[174] might suggest growing potential for challenge under this head. In any case the narrow approach adopted to section 6(3)(b) has attracted significant criticism, both from academics[175] and the Parliamentary Joint Committee on Human Rights.[176]

Despite this, and without engaging the courts to any great extent, the Human Rights Act appears to be having an impact upon the way in which sports governing bodies are carrying out their functions. There is little doubt that Article 6 ECHR has a significant impact on the rules of natural justice that are applied to sports governing bodies. The British Boxing Board of Control charged American boxer Mike Tyson after he continued to punch an opponent after a bout was stopped and subsequently aimed threatening and abusive language toward British heavyweight boxer Lennox Lewis. The Board restrained themselves to a mere censure of Tyson for the second offence after his representative at the disciplinary hearing warned that an action under the Human Rights Act 1998 would be likely to be successful. Geoffrey Robinson QC suggested that to punish Tyson for his outburst would be in breach of Art 10 of the European Convention on Human Rights, protected by the Act.[177] The previously neglected interface between human rights law and the administration of sport has been subject to academic scrutiny in this regard. In particular the compatibility of drug testing procedures has come to be considered in more detail.[178] In other areas, most obviously in relation to the protection of private and family life under Article 8 ECHR, the courts have been relatively proactive in evolving the law in the light of the introduction of the Human Rights Act 1998, though not as yet against sports governing bodies.[179] One leading instance of the application of the Act in relation to a sports governing body came in the case of *Jockey Club v Buffham*.[180] Here the High Court considered the obligation in s 12 of the Human Rights Act 1998 to take account of Article 10 ECHR (freedom of expression) when considering restricting freedom of the press. The case related to an attempt by the Jockey Club to restrain the BBC from broadcasting information by a former Director of Security for the Club, Roger Buffham. The information pertained to perceived problems with security in horse racing. The Jockey Club argued that Buffham was under a duty of confidence that also bound the BBC. In the event the Court found that the public interest in important information coming to light outweighed the interest in upholding confidentiality agreements. Though the Human Rights Act 1998 was not given as a primary reason for the outcome of the case, there is clear evidence of its influence in the balancing process.

The Act should be seen as contributing towards balance in the way that sports governing bodies are scrutinised under English law, and as a move towards subjecting their activities to greater public law scrutiny. While domestic courts have been reasonably keen to prevent these bodies escaping scrutiny, this appears to have been done primarily with the intention of protecting

---

174 Hedley-Dent, S and Wilde, K, 'Sporting rules and the Human Rights Act: current position' (2007) 5(6) WSLR 8.
175 Sunkin, M, 'Pushing forward the frontiers of human rights protection: the meaning of public authority under the Human Rights Act' (2004) PL 643; Quane, H, 'The Strasbourg jurisprudence and the meaning of a "public authority" under the Human Rights Act' (2006) PL 106.
176 Joint Committee on Human Rights, Seventh Report (2003–04 HL 39, HC 382).
177 'Human Rights Act Saves Tyson', *The Guardian*, 23 August 2000.
178 See Rigozzi, A, Kaufmann-Kohler, G and Malinverni, G, 'Doping and fundamental rights of athletes: Comments in the Wake of the World Anti-Doping Code' (2003) 3 ISLR 39; Soek, J 'The fundamental rights of athletes in doping trials' in O'Leary, J (ed) *Drugs and Doping in Sports: Socio-Legal Perspectives* (2001), London: Cavendish, p 57; Donnellan, L 'The Right to Privacy and Drug Testing: An Irish Perspective' (2002) 9(5) SLAP 11; Sithamparanathan, A and Himsworth, M, 'Are sporting bodies abusing human rights?' (2003) 11(3) SATLJ 138; Hiscox, W, 'Anti-doping policy after The Human Rights Act: Is mandatory blood testing compatible with Article 8 of the ECHR?' (2004) 12(2) SATLJ 12; Pendlebury, A and McGarry, J, 'Location, Location, Location: The Whereabouts Rule and the Right to Privacy' (2009) 40 Cambrian LR 63.
179 See generally, Phillipson, G, 'Transforming breach of confidence? Towards a common law right of privacy under the Human Rights Act' (2003) 66(5) MLR 726; *Campbell v MGN Ltd* [2004] 2 WLR 1232; *A v B* [2003] QB 195; *Theakston v MGN Ltd* [2002] EMLR 22; *Ashworth Hospital Authority v MGN Ltd* [2002] 1WLR 2033; *Venables v News Group Newspapers Ltd* [2001] 2 WLR 1038; *Mosely v News Group Newspapers Ltd* [2008] EWHC 1777 (QB); *Terry v Persons Unknown* [2010] EWHC 119 (QB).
180 [2003] QB 462.

economic rights. The introduction of the Human Rights Act 1998 offers a real possibility that parity between the protection of economic and fundamental rights may be achieved in the sporting field.

Alternatives to Litigation: Sports Governing Bodies and Alternate Dispute Resolution

The utilisation of alternate dispute resolution (ADR) processes, principally arbitration, has become commonplace in the resolution of disputes between sports governing bodies and those they regulate. Sports governing bodies frequently include in their rules and regulations an 'arbitration clause', compelling those falling within the jurisdiction of the body to refer any dispute to the arbitral process. Rule K of the Rules of the Football Association is an example of such:

Rule K, Rules of the Football Association

Agreement to Arbitration
1   (a) Subject to Rule K1(b), K1(c) and K1(d) below, any dispute or difference between any two or more Participants (which shall include, for the purposes of this section of the Rules, The Association) including but not limited to a dispute arising out of or in connection with (including any question regarding the existence or validity of):
    (i)   the Rules and regulations of The Association which are in force from time to time;
    (ii) the rules and regulations of an Affiliated Association or Competition which are in force from time to time;
    (iii) the statutes and regulations of FIFA and UEFA which are in force from time to time; or
    (iv) the Laws of the Game,

    shall be referred to and finally resolved by arbitration under these Rules.

Arbitration is often regarded as being preferable to litigation, in terms of speed, cost, adaptability and the ability to command high levels of expertise and consistency of outcome where cases are considered by a relatively small group of specialist arbitrators rather than case-by-case consideration by non-specialist judges.

Sports arbitration bodies

Though the arbitration process can be constituted independently by the parties to a dispute or by reference to a body's rules and regulations, there is increasing recourse to specialist sports arbitral bodies established for the sole purpose of resolving disputes arising in the sporting context. The resolution of disputes in this way is now well established at international level through the Court of Arbitration for Sport (CAS) and increasingly under the auspices of Sports Resolutions, the UK's sports dispute resolution body.

The Court of Arbitration for Sport

The CAS[181] is an international arbitration and mediation body, established for the purpose of resolving sports-related disputes. This extends not only to disputes between sports governing bodies and those they regulate, but to any sports-related dispute, regardless of the parties. The CAS

---

181 On the CAS, see generally Blackshaw, I, Siekmann, R, and Soek, J (eds), *The Court of Arbitration for Sport 1984–2004* (2006), The Hague: TMC Asser Press. On ADR in sport, see Blackshaw, I, *Sport, Mediation and Arbitration* (2009), The Hague: TMC Asser Press.

offers a set procedure to be followed in all cases of a particular type, established case law and a distinguished expert panel of arbitrators. It has its seat in Lausanne, Switzerland. Established in 1983, the CAS initially had a relatively small workload, but this has been significantly swollen during the late twentieth and early twenty-first centuries, principally due to the growth of arbitration clauses in sports governing bodies' rules, in itself due to the requirement under the Olympic Charter that '[a]ny dispute arising on the occasion of, or in connection with, the Olympic Games shall be submitted exclusively to the Court of Arbitration for Sport, in accordance with the Code of Sports-Related Arbitration'.[182]

The CAS statutes conceive of two types of cases being brought before it: ordinary arbitration proceedings, usually relating to contracts or civil disputes; and disputes brought about under the appeals arbitration proceedings. The appeals procedure is of particular note in the context of consideration of the position of sports governing bodies, as it contemplates the resolution of disputes concerning the decisions of federations, associations or other sports-related bodies where the rules of those bodies so provide. The CAS also has an Ad Hoc Division that offers speedy resolution of disputes occurring during major international sporting events such as the Olympic Games. In addition to resolving live disputes the CAS may also deliver non-binding advisory opinions where requested to do so at the request of the IOC, the International Federations, the National Olympic Committees, the World Anti-Doping Agency, the associations recognised by the IOC and the Olympic Games Organising Committees.

Sports Resolutions: sports arbitration in the UK

Sports Resolutions was originally set up as the Sports Dispute Resolution Panel (SDRP). It is an independent organisation established by the principal sports bodies representing athletes, governing bodies and sponsors to provide a specialist UK-wide dispute resolution service for sport. The SDRP began work in 1999 with initial funding from UK Sport and the support of the sports councils. In 2007 the organisation adopted the title 'Sports Resolutions' and embarked on a new mission to become the foremost body in the UK for sports dispute resolution. To this end Sports Resolutions offers similar services to the CAS, though the arbitration procedures are more narrowly cast than those of the CAS, being oriented toward disputes within sport, rather than the commercial environment surrounding it. However, in addition to the arbitration process, Sports Resolutions also offers sports governing bodies assistance in appointing tribunal members and the operation of panels under the control of the governing body itself.

Judicial responses to sports arbitration

Lord Denning's observation regarding domestic tribunals in Enderby Town FC v Football Association, that 'justice can often be done better in them by a good layman than by a bad lawyer',[183] is equally valid in the context of sports arbitration proceedings. In English law, under the Arbitration Act 1996, the capacity to challenge decisions of arbitral bodies is extremely limited, either to claims of want of jurisdiction or narrow grounds of irregularity in the arbitral process.[184] However, the context in which sports arbitration operates, with established arbitration clauses in rules and regulations and established and well-run arbitration processes, means that there is limited opportunity for aggrieved parties to the arbitration to bring their case before a court. Thus, in most instances, sports governing bodies are able to effectively shield themselves from litigation.

---

182 Olympic Charter (2010) Rule 59.
183 [1971] Ch 591 at 605.
184 Sections 67–69 Arbitration Act 1996.

Judicial approaches to the applicability of arbitration

Despite the limited opportunities for judicial intervention in the outcomes of arbitration procedures, there remains a role for the courts in the interpretation of arbitration clauses. Such a matter arose in the litigation between Petr Korda and the International Tennis Federation (ITF).[185] Korda was made the subject of disciplinary proceedings after being charged with a breach of the ITF's anti-doping rules by reason of testing positive for a prohibited substance. Such a breach would ordinarily result in the imposition of an automatic one-year ban from competition; however, the ITF Anti-Doping Appeals Committee found that exceptional circumstances pertained, meaning that the sanction would not be applied. The ITF made an appeal to the CAS on the basis that the Appeals Committee had applied the test of exceptional circumstances inappropriately. Korda contested the capacity of the ITF to make such an appeal to the CAS, arguing that the rules should be construed such that appeal to CAS was available to the ITF only on narrow procedural grounds and not in relation to the merits of the case. In particular he relied on section (L)8 of the Tennis Anti-Doping Programme, which stated, 'The Appeals Committee's decision shall be the full, final and complete disposition of the appeal and will be binding on all parties.'

At first instance Lightman J confirmed Korda's view that the general right of appeal set out in the Tennis Anti-Doping Programme must be read in conjunction with s (L)8 and confined the ITF to a limited right of appeal to CAS; this was partly informed by the need for anti-doping matters to be resolved speedily.

On appeal to the Court of Appeal, however, the first instance decision was overturned. The court did not accept that the right of appeal to the CAS was in any way limited by (L)8. Thus the ITF was able to proceed with its appeal to the CAS, which it eventually won.

In *Sankofa & Charlton Athletic v Football Association*[186] the High Court refused injunctive relief to a professional football player who had been sent off during a match. The sending off carried with it an automatic one-match suspension. Sankofa then sought to challenge the referee's decision before a Disciplinary Commission of the Football Association. However, his claim was rejected, found to be frivolous and as a result he was suspended for a further match. Sankofa then sought injunctive relief from the High Court, preventing the Football Association from effecting the suspension pending the commencement of arbitration proceedings under Rule K of the Rules of the Football Association, where Sankofa wished to argue that the Disciplinary Commission had acted in breach of Football Association rules. Simon J rejected the claim on the basis that there was no serious issue to be considered; the Disciplinary Commission was not required to give reasons and there was no indication that it had acted irrationally. It was held that a court could intervene in such circumstances, but that they would have to be exceptional.

In contrast the High Court did agree to injunctive relief in the case of *Sheffield United FC Ltd v West Ham Utd Football Club PLC*. This case related to the dispute surrounding the signing by West Ham United of the Argentina international forward Carlos Tevez, in breach of Premier League rules on the registration of players. Sheffield United contended that the breach of the rules by West Ham United had the result that Sheffield United had been relegated and West Ham United had not, as they would likely have done had Tevez not been signed in breach of the rules. Sheffield United brought arbitration proceedings against West Ham United in accordance with Rule K of the Football Association. The arbitrator issued a preliminary ruling that West Ham United were liable in damages for the loss suffered by Sheffield United with the final determination of damages to be determined subsequently. West Ham United then lodged an appeal with the CAS. Sheffield United sought interim relief from the High Court to prevent West Ham United proceeding with such an appeal. Teare J issued an injunction, deciding that Sheffield United had a very strong case that the effect of

185 *Korda v ITF* [1999] All ER (D) 84; [1999] All ER (D) 337, CA.
186 [2007] EWHC 78 (Comm).

the Football Association's rules, which provided for the award of the arbitral tribunal to be final and binding upon the parties, and the absence of a provision for an arbitral appeal, was that the award of the arbitral tribunal was final and binding on the parties. Unlike the position in *Korda* the Football Association's rules did not provide any right of appeal to the CAS.

Judicial responses to challenges to sports arbitration

A number of attempts to challenge the validity of sports arbitral proceedings have been made. Most notable in English law is the challenge by the football agent, Paul Stretford, to Rule K of the Football Association. Stretford was made the subject of disciplinary proceedings in respect of evidence provided during the course of criminal proceedings and his acquisition of the right to act as the agent for Wayne Rooney in 2002.[187]

Stretford sought, *inter alia*, to claim that Rule K did not form part of the contract between the Football Association and himself and that, if it did, Rule K was in conflict with Article 6 of the European Convention on Human Rights and with the principles of natural justice and was, therefore, null and void. Stretford's claim was rejected by the High Court and he appealed to the Court of Appeal. The Court of Appeal agreed with the trial judge that the terms of Rule K were not particularly onerous or unusual and that Mr Stretford was well aware of the rule. In any event, at all relevant times Mr Stretford was in possession of documentary material which included Rule K and its earlier versions, and if he did not know of its terms he could and should have done. Thus, the Court of Appeal ruled, an arbitration clause like Rule K, contained in the rules and regulations of a sports governing body, would not amount to an unlawful restriction on the right to a fair hearing.

The CAS has also experienced challenges to its authority. In 1992 a CAS panel made a decision issuing from disciplinary proceedings against Elmar Gundel.[188] Gundel was a German equestrian rider who was found to have effected an anti-doping offence. Gundel sought to challenge the validity of the CAS decision before the Swiss Federal Tribunal on the basis that the CAS did not meet the standards of impartiality and independence required of an arbitral tribunal.[189] The dispute arose because the CAS was directly funded by the International Olympic Committee and, in smaller amounts, by international sports federations and had arbitrators appointed to the panel by the International Equestrian Federation (FEI). The Swiss Federal Tribunal dismissed Gundel's claim, but noted that had a similar action been brought in respect of the International Olympic Committee, it would be likely to find that the CAS was not sufficiently independent, given the significant control the IOC had over it. The case resulted in the creation of an International Council of Arbitration for Sport (ICAS) to oversee the running and financing of the CAS, thus creating sufficient independence from the IOC.

The efficacy of these changes was evidenced before the Swiss Federal Tribunal where a skier sought to argue that the CAS was insufficiently independent from the IOC. The court determined that sufficient independence existed.[190]

Further, the durability of the CAS was evidenced in a case brought before the New South Wales Court of Appeal in Australia.[191] The dispute, concerning selection for the Australian judo team for the 2000 Sydney Olympic Games, led to a court challenge being brought on a point of law arising during the CAS proceedings. The Australian court declined to intervene in what it considered to be foreign arbitration proceedings, in light of the seat of CAS in Lausanne, Switzerland.

---

187 [2007] EWCA Civ 238; [2006] EWHC 479 (Ch).
188 CAS 92/63, *G v International Equestrian Federation* (FEI) (10 September 1992).
189 *Gundel v FEI* (1993) Swiss Federal Tribunal, 15 March.
190 *Lausutina v IOC and FIS.*, (2003) Swiss Federal Tribunal, 27 May.
191 *Raguz v Sullivan* (2000) 50 NSWLR 236.

CAS jurisprudence on sports governing bodies

As noted, the arbitration role of the CAS is not as a law-maker as such, but as a means by which disputes can be resolved under whichever legal system is applicable. So in many ways the CAS is an alternative to the courts in making that application. However, some clear trends can be found in the way that cases dealing with the accountability of sports governing bodies are handled in the CAS jurisprudence and these are important given its perceived function of creating a body of 'sports law'. Broadly speaking, CAS has ruled that sports decisions are subject to the same requirements under its jurisdiction as in English law. Notably, sports federations must act in accordance with their own rules and in accordance with the law,[192] without improper purpose and taking into account only relevant considerations[193] and in accordance with the principles of legitimate expectation.[194] There is also a requirement of proportionality where the fundamental interests of athletes are at stake.[195] Further, federations must also conduct any hearings in accordance with the rules of natural justice, providing a fair hearing[196] and a tribunal which is impartial and free of bias.[197] The CAS also has the capacity to scrutinise the validity of rules against both overarching sports regulations, such as the World Anti-Doping Code or the Olympic Charter,[198] and external legal principles including, notably, European Union competition law.[199] Thus the principles applied are very much comparable with those available in court.

The impact of sports arbitration on legal approaches to sports governing bodies

There is little doubt that sports arbitration has become a significant element in the regulation of sports governing bodies. In many respects, the adoption of arbitral procedures has acted as a significant exclusionary factor in the way in which courts will exercise their jurisdiction. So, while in theory, and in practice, the growth of sports arbitration has done much to offer new avenues of redress to sports participants and other affected parties, the effect has also been to further limit opportunities for litigants to bring their grievance before a court, the role of which is largely limited to intervening in cases of substantial injustice or significant procedural flaws. This effective ouster has been further strengthened by the internationalisation of sports arbitration, meaning that once a matter is with the CAS the capacity of the English courts to become involved is negligible.

Such an exclusion is not of necessity objectionable, particularly when the arbitration process offers much the same rights as those protected by the courts. However, when the arbitration clause is itself contained within a set of rules and regulations that are adhesionary in nature then it may be that it is questionable for the courts to apply the same approach to sports arbitration as is the case in ordinary commercial agreements.

Evaluation

With the exception of judicial review, the English courts have demonstrated a general readiness to subject the activities of sports governing bodies to scrutiny at the behest of those subject to their

---

192 CAS 2007/A/1363 *TTF Liebherr Ochsenhausen v ETTU*, award of 5 October 2007.
193 CAS 2008/A/1480 *Pistorius v IAAF*, award of 16 May 2008.
194 CAS 2008/O/1455 *Boxing Australia v AIBA*, award of 16 April 2008.
195 CAS 2005/A/830 *S v FINA*, award of 15 July 2005.
196 CAS 2008/A/1583 *Sport Lisboa e Benfica Futebol SAD v UEFA & FC Porto Futebol SAD & CAS 2008/A/1584 Vitória Sport Clube de Guimarães v UEFA & FC Porto Futebol SAD*, award of 15 July 2008.
197 CAS 2008/A/1549 *Luke Michael v Australian Canoeing*, award of 4 June 2008.
198 Advisory opinion CAS 2000/C/255 Comitato Olimpico Nazionale Italiano (CONI), 16 June 2000.
199 CAS 98/2000 *AEK Athens and Slavia Prague v UEFA* award of 20 August 1999.

rules.[200] However, this welcome general approach has been limited somewhat by a number of factors.

Firstly, there has been a general unwillingness in the context of the contractual, private law supervisory and natural justice cases to subject sports governing bodies to anything but the most limited scrutiny. Secondly, those approaches are somewhat limited in the influence they can have over the administration of sport, because of their very nature. Only in the restraint of trade approach has it been demonstrated that there is a general willingness to subject sport's governing bodies to the rules, with a vigorous application of those rules, and that the approach is capable of having anything other than the most superficial effect on the bodies. It is only in the most extreme situations, involving serious public policy considerations, that the natural justice, contractual and private law supervisory approaches have been shown to be similarly capable.

However, the restraint of trade doctrine is limited to those situations where the ability to trade freely is restricted and this will not extend to all situations. Judicial review might then be seen as a possible remedial tool in this respect. However, it is suggested that the courts have demonstrated a great deal of determination that they will not be moved from their present position in this respect. It may also be that the judicial review question is not just one that pertains to sports governing bodies and that litigants in such cases may well be the victims of a broader jurisdictional dispute.

In each of these instances there is a clear tension between the interventionist impulses of the courts in relation to matters concerning public policy and the desire to adopt a 'hands-off' approach where specialist, technical decisions arise. To date there appears to be broad satisfaction amongst the judiciary in reserving intervention for situations where major policy issues fall for consideration. This is particularly so where economic rights are at stake. Despite the extension of the economic relationship in *Gasser*, there appears to remain a key association between intervention and economic disadvantage. There appears to be little evidence, if any, of the courts stepping in to protect more fundamental rights. Even in relation to the rules of natural justice, the requirements appear to be greater as the (financial) stakes grow. The introduction of arbitral processes by sports governing bodies appears to have further distanced the courts from scrutiny of those bodies. The key questions then are the extent to which the courts will protect more fundamental non-economic rights – as none of the above mechanisms seems to hold significant promise in this regard – and the degree to which they are able to effectively supervise arbitration processes.

Key Points

- The regulation of sport's decision-makers has increasingly involved recourse to law, driven primarily by the increasing commercial interest in sport.
- It is important that sports decision-makers are subject to external scrutiny because of the important societal position they hold and the impact their rules and decisions may have on individuals.
- The English courts have adopted a liberal approach to providing access for those wishing to challenge sports decision-makers but employed a light-touch, supervisory approach in the application of the law, acknowledging the expert and specialist position of such bodies.
- In English law, sports governing bodies are not regarded as wholly public in nature and are not subject to judicial review.
- The basis of judicial scrutiny of sports decision-makers is either in contract or is public-policy based.

---

200 For a comparative perspective see Beloff, MJ and Kerr, T, 'Judicial control of sporting bodies: the Commonwealth jurisprudence' (1995) 3(1) SATLJ 5; Stewart, WJ, 'Judicial control of sporting bodies: Scotland' (1993) 3(3) SATLJ 45; McCutcheon, JP, 'Judicial control of sporting bodies: recent Irish experiences' (1995) 3(2) SATLJ 20.

- Sports bodies may not exceed their jurisdiction by acting *ultra vires*, in contravention of their own rules, must take into account only relevant considerations and must abide by the rules of natural justice.
- Only actions under restraint of trade and competition law have demonstrated significant success in challenging the substance of the rules of sports governing bodies.
- Arbitration is now the key means of challenging sports decisions.
- Arbitration clauses are now included in most sports governing bodies' rules and regulations and, in most cases, preclude access to the courts.
- Sports arbitration mechanisms, most notably through the agency of the Court of Arbitration for Sport, recognise and enforce the same broad principles of legality as in English law.

Key Sources

Anderson, J, 'An Accident of History: Why the Decisions of Sports Governing Bodies are not Amenable to Judicial Review' (2006), 35(3) CLWR 173.

Blackshaw, I, *Sport, Mediation and Arbitration* (2009), The Hague: TMC Asser Press.

Blackshaw, I, Siekmann, R, and Soek, J (eds), *The Court of Arbitration for Sport 1984–2004* (2006), The Hague: TMC Asser Press.

McCutcheon, JP, 'Sports discipline, natural justice and strict liability' (1999), 28(1) Anglo-Am LR 37.

Pendlebury, A and McGarry, J, 'Location, Location, Location: The Whereabouts Rule and the Right to Privacy' (2009), 40 Cambrian LR 63.

Chapter 4

Sport and the Law of the European Union

Chapter Contents

Introduction	146
Establishing the Relationship Between European Union Law and Sport	147
Bosman: The Application of European Union Law to Sport	151
The Applicability of EU Competition Law to Sport	176
The Application of EU Competition Law to Sport	181
Sports Broadcasting and EU Law	196
The Modern Era: The Path to Lisbon, the EU Reform Treaty and Beyond	199
Conclusions	205
Key Points	206
Key Sources	206

Introduction

The intersection of sport with European Union (EU) law is now one of the most important aspects of contemporary sports law. Since the seminal decision of the Court of Justice in the *Bosman*[1] case the EU has been at the vanguard of legal and regulatory interaction with sport.

Though *Bosman* may be regarded as the most prominent interaction between sport and the EU, there has been a much more complex relationship than the simple engagement of EU law through litigation before the Court of Justice. It is not only the Court that has been engaged; each of the major EU institutions has had a role to play in developing the relationship. The impact of this inter-relationship upon sport has been a significant re-modelling of aspects of the regulatory and commercial structures.

Because of the considerable impact that the EU has had upon sport within a relatively short time frame, its institutions have been compelled to give more detailed consideration of the nature of sport, and the extent to which regulatory and legal intervention are appropriate, than might be the case in the context of other jurisdictions. Similarly, this has had to be balanced against over-arching progress towards greater economic freedom and the existence of a single market across the Member States of the Union. It is also the case that the EU has been important in the development of the regulation of sport on a global scale, not just within the geographical boundaries of its jurisdiction.

In its earliest manifestation, the relationship centred upon the compatibility of sports regulations with EU measures concerning free movement of persons, in particular workers, but latterly the role of competition law has grown and become the primary mechanism by which EU law interfaces with sport.

It has been argued that the interaction of sport and the EU has undergone three phases of development: first, a phase of relative indifference, where the interaction between the EU and sport was limited and there was limited interest in EU intervention; second, a phase of litigation and conflict, where the autonomy of sport was severely tested by the application of EU law in a robust and direct fashion; and third, a phase of negotiation and relative co-operation between sports regulators and the EU institutions.[2]

It is arguable that the relationship has now entered a new fourth phase, characterised by the increasing predominance of a co-regulatory relationship between the EU institutions and sports regulators. This has come about principally because of the new direct competence in sport granted to the EU by virtue of Article 165 of the Treaty for the Functioning of the European Union (TFEU). This measure and its implications are considered in depth later in this chapter; however, it is clear that this has embedded a complementary, parallel regulatory role for the EU in the sporting context.

This chapter considers the development of the relationship between sport and the EU, from the earliest days of the European Economic Community (EEC), through to the impact of the direct competence in sport granted by the amendments made by the Lisbon Treaty.[3]

---

1   Case C-415/93 *Union Royale Belges des Sociétès de Football ASBL v Bosman* [1995] ECR I-4192.

2   Parrish, R, 'The path to a "sports policy" in the European Union' (1998) 2(1) SLB 10. See also, Foster, K, 'Can sport be regulated by Europe? An analysis of alternative models', in Caiger, A and Gardiner, S (eds), *Professional Sport in the EU: Regulation and Re-regulation* (2000), The Hague: TMC Asser Press, pp 44–45; Parrish, R 'The Birth of European Union Sports Law' (2003) 2(2) Ent L 20.

3   The relevant treaties have undergone significant changes in the period from their inception in the Treaty of Rome in 1957 to the present day. As a part of this development process both the names and numbering of the relevant treaties has changed. The Treaty of Rome was originally designated the European Economic Communities (EEC) Treaty, was amended to become the European Communities (EC) Treaty in 1992 and, finally, became the Treaty on the Functioning of the European Union (TFEU) following the entry into force of the amending Lisbon Treaty in 2009. The 1992 changes also saw the Treaty renumbered, as did the 2009 amendments. In addressing this in this chapter, when discussing issues in their historical context the denomination and numbering applicable at the relevant time is used, otherwise the present system is adopted. For ease of reference, the Treaty articles significant in this chapter have developed as follows: Article 48 EEC/EC, 39 EC, 45 TFEU; Article 59 EEC/EC, 49 EC, 56 TFEU; Article 85 EEC/EC, 81 EC, 101 TFEU; Article 86 EEC/EC, 82 EC, 102 TFEU.

Establishing the Relationship Between European Union Law and Sport

The European Union (then the European Economic Community) was not granted any specific competence in the field of sport at its inception by the Treaty of Rome in 1957. For the majority of the first two decades of its existence, this remained the case; there is little evidence of any relationship between sport and the EEC or, indeed, any desire on the part of the institutions for any significant involvement.

This should not be surprising as the EEC was, at that time, engaged in various formative processes of its own, establishing its character, remit and sphere of influence. Further, the EEC was, at the outset, a community of only six nations. The growth from six nations to the 27 that constitute the EU today has been a relatively recent phenomenon, having accelerated greatly in the last two decades, in particular since the break-up of the former Soviet bloc. Thus during the early period of development, the then EEC had significant in-house priorities and relatively limited jurisdictional capacity, obviating any impetus toward engagement with sport. This much was observed by Advocate-General Trabucchi in the early case of *Donà v Mantero*:

Case C-13/76 *Donà v Mantero*

Suppose that an officious bystander, at the time of the signing of the EEC Treaty, or, for that matter, at the time of the signing of the Treaty of Accession, had asked those round the table whether they intended that Articles 48 and 59 should preclude a requirement that, in a particular sport, a national team should consist only of nationals of the country it represented. Common sense dictates that the signatories, with their pens poised, would all have answered impatiently 'Of course not' – and perhaps have added that, in their view, the point was so obvious that it did not need to be stated.[4]

However, towards the close of this initial period the Court of Justice was called upon to consider the nature of the relationship between sports regulations and Community law.[5]

Sport is subject to Community law

Initial consideration of the applicability of Community law to sport arose in the context of a dispute concerning a rule change by the International Cycling Union (UCI) by which pacemakers and stayers competing as a team in the world championships were required to be of the same nationality. The plaintiffs in this case, Dutch nationals, offered their services for remuneration to act as pacemakers on motorcycles. Such services were provided under agreements with the cyclists, their associations or with sponsors. The plaintiffs argued that the nationality rule was incompatible with the EEC Treaty in that it prevented a pacemaker, being a national of one Member State, from offering his services to a stayer of another Member State. The case reached the Court of Justice by means of a preliminary reference under Article 177 EEC (now Article 267 TFEU).

Walrave & Koch v Union Cycliste Internacionale

The case of *Walrave*[6] posed four significant questions to be addressed by the Court of Justice: first, on what basis – if at all – did sport fall within the terms of the Treaty; second, were there any circumstances in which it would not apply; third, was Community law applicable to a non-public

---

4   [1976] ECR 1333 at 329.
5   See generally, Coopers and Lybrand, 'The Impact of European Union Activities on Sport' (1994–95) 17 Loy LA Intl & Comp LJ, 245.
6   Case C-36/74, [1974] ECR 1405.

regulatory body such as the UCI; and fourth, would Community law apply in the case of a sporting event taking place outside of the EEC, but having an impact within it?

The Court determined that sport would indeed fall within the scope of the Treaty, subject to limitations:

Case C-36/74 *Walrave and Koch v Union Cycliste Internationale*

[4] Having regard to the objectives of the Community, the practice of sport is subject to Community law only in so far as it constitutes an economic activity within the meaning of Article 2 of the Treaty.

[5] When such activity has the character of gainful employment or remunerated service it comes more particularly within the scope, according to the case, of Articles 48 to 51 or 59 to 66 of the Treaty.

[6] These provisions, which give effect to the general rule of Article 7 of the Treaty, prohibit any discrimination based on nationality in the performance of the activity to which they refer.

[7] In this respect the exact nature of the legal relationship under which such services are performed is of no importance since the rule of non-discrimination covers in identical terms all work or services.[7]

In the instant case, the parties placed particular emphasis on the question of the nature of the relationship between pacemaker and stayer as being one of employment or the provision of services. This was of particular importance at that time as the Treaty provision pertaining to freedom to provide services had not, at that point, been confirmed as being horizontally directly effective (i.e. capable of application by domestic courts as between private individuals). The Court was able to dispense with this issue, confirming that the freedom to provide services was a directly effective Treaty right.

Having established the applicability of Community law, the Court then went on to consider whether there were any circumstances in which the Treaty would not lie against sports rules, concluding:

[8] This prohibition, however, does not affect the composition of sports teams, in particular national teams, the formation of which is a question of purely sporting interest and as such has nothing to do with economic activity.

[9] This restriction on the scope of the provisions in question must, however, remain limited to its proper objective.

Thus the Court was prepared to accept that rules of a purely sporting, non-economic nature, such as those relating to the selection of national teams, were effectively outside the scope of the Treaty. This has proven to be an important and contentious principle.

Having set out the circumstances in which Community law could intervene in sport, the Court of Justice also dealt with the issue of whether such a challenge could lie against a non-state, private body such as an international sporting federation:

[14] The main question in respect of all the Articles referred to is whether the rules of an international sporting federation can be regarded as incompatible with the Treaty.

---

7 Ibid, at 332–33.

[15] It has been alleged that the prohibitions in these Articles refer only to restrictions which have their origin in acts of an authority and not to those resulting from legal acts of persons or associations who do not come under public law.

[16] Articles 7, 48 and 59 have in common the prohibition, in their respective spheres of application, of any discrimination on grounds of nationality.

[17] Prohibition of such discrimination does not only apply to the action of public authorities but extends likewise to rules of any other nature aimed at regulating in a collective manner gainful employment and the provision of services.

[18] The abolition as between Member States of obstacles to freedom of movement for persons and to freedom to provide services, which are fundamental objectives of the Community contained in Article 3 (c) of the Treaty, would be compromised if the abolition of barriers of national origin could be neutralised by obstacles resulting from the exercise of their legal autonomy by associations or organisations which do not come under public law.

[19] Since, moreover, working conditions in the various Member States are governed sometimes by means of provisions laid down by law or regulation and sometimes by agreements and other acts concluded or adopted by private persons, to limit the prohibitions in question to acts of a public authority would risk creating inequality in their application.

. . .

[21] It is established, moreover, that Article 48, relating to the abolition of any discrimination based on nationality as regards gainful employment, extends likewise to agreements and rules which do not emanate from public authorities.

[22] Article 7 (4) of Regulation 1612/68 in consequence provides that the prohibition on discrimination shall apply to agreements and any other collective regulations concerning employment.

[23] The activities referred to in Article 59 are not to be distinguished by their nature from those in Article 48, but only by the fact that they are performed outside the ties of a contract of employment.

[24] This single distinction cannot justify a more restrictive interpretation of the scope of the freedom to be ensured.

[25] It follows that the provisions of Articles 7, 48 and 59 of the Treaty may be taken into account by the national court in judging the validity or the effects of a provision inserted in the rules of a sporting organisation.

Thus the Court established that the rules of a sports federation could fall to be considered for compliance with Community law on the basis of the freedom of movement of workers or the freedom to provide services. In particular it was made clear that Community law would not tolerate any rule purporting to discriminate on the grounds of nationality.

Further, the 'reach' of Community law was set out, with the Court of Justice judging that a restrictive measure need not actually be enacted by a body operating within the Community's geographic boundaries, but need only take effect therein:

[28] By reason of the fact that it is imperative, the rule on non-discrimination applies in judging all legal relationships in so far as these relationships, by reason either of the place where they are entered into or of the place where they take effect, can be located within the territory of the Community.

Donà v Mantero

The position established in *Walrave* was quickly reaffirmed by the Court of Justice in *Donà v Mantero*. The case came to the Court of Justice by way of the preliminary reference mechanism, from an Italian court. Mantero, the defendant in the main action, was the chairman of an Italian professional football club who engaged Donà with a view to identifying overseas players willing to sign for Mantero's team. To this end Donà placed an advertisement in a Belgian sports newspaper. However, Mantero refused to either consider the offers engendered by the advertisement or to repay Donà for expenses incurred in the publication of the advertisement. Donà therefore brought an action for the recovery of the monies expended before an Italian court.

In defending the claim Mantero argued that Donà had acted precipitously. He supported this claim with evidence, citing the rules of the Italian Football Federation which limited participation in matches to players affiliated to the Federation. Affiliation was effectively limited to Italian nationals. Donà claimed that Mantero could not rely on these provisions as they were void as being contrary to Articles 7, 48 and 59 of the EEC Treaty.

In considering this question, the Court of Justice confirmed its earlier ruling in *Walrave*, reaffirming that Community law applied to sport only in as much as it constituted an economic activity – though it went so far as to set out that this included the activities of professional or semi-professional footballers. Similarly, it reiterated the exclusion of restrictions of sporting interest only from consideration under the Treaty. The Court did, however, note that any restrictions under these terms must remain limited to their sporting objective. While asserting the application of Articles 7, 48 and 59 of the EEC Treaty was mandatory in a case such as this, the Court left that application to the Italian court and did not venture a view as to whether the restrictions in question were compatible with the Treaty. Advocate-General Alberto Trabucchi did, however, consider this in his opinion, giving an indication that sporting rules with an economic element may, nonetheless, be regarded as valid under the terms of Community law:

Case C-13/76 *Donà v Mantero*

[T]here is, in my view, nothing to prevent considerations of purely sporting interest from justifying the imposition of some restriction on the signing of foreign players or at least on their participation in official championship matches so as to ensure that the winning team will be representative of the state of which it is the champion team. A condition of this kind seems all the more reasonable when it is borne in mind that the team which wins the national championship is often chosen to represent its own state in international competitions.[8]

The conclusions to be drawn from the two early cases was set out by Advocate General Lenz in his Opinion in *Bosman*:

Case C-415/93 *Union Royale Belge des Sociétés de Football Association v Bosman*

(1)   The rules of private sports associations are also subject to Community Law;
(2)   The field of sport is subject to Community law in so far as it constitutes an economic activity;
(3)   The activities of professional football players are in the nature of gainful employment and are therefore subject to Community law;
(4)   Either Article 48 or Article 59 [EC] applies to those activities, with no differences arising therefrom;

---

8   [1976] ECR 1333.

(5)   The Court allows certain exceptions to the prohibitions contained in those provisions. While in *Walrave* the question of the formation of teams in competitions is still excepted from the prohibition, in *Donà* the Court restricts the exception to the exclusion of foreign players from certain matches. In both judgments the exceptions are linked with non-economic grounds which relate exclusively to sport.[9]

Sport and Community law after *Walrave* and *Donà*

Having established the applicability of the free movement principles under the EEC Treaty to sport, it might have been expected that significant further developments would soon arise. However, in the two decades that followed the judgments there was very little effective activity by the Community institutions in respect of sport. The European Commission held a latent dissatisfaction regarding nationality limitations in football. The Commission had a running dialogue with the football authorities through the late 1970s and into the 1980s and ultimately made a 'gentlemen's agreement' with the governing body of European football – UEFA – implementing the '3+2' rule; limiting the number of foreign players that could be fielded by each team in any one match to three, plus two 'assimilated' players. This agreement has been labelled 'contradictory'.[10] It can perhaps be explained by a number of factors. First, the Commission and other Community institutions were, during that period, still preoccupied with the embedding and completion of the Single Market project; many of the key judicial and legislative developments which are now regarded as fundamental took place during this period – thus the appetite for intervention in sport may have been limited. Second, though membership of the Community grew over this period, in 1991 – the year in which the '3+2' agreement was made – there were only 12 Member States, in comparison to 27 at the time of writing, perhaps limiting the political leverage that the Commission had with UEFA. Third, though football was of great sporting significance, it remained of relatively small economic consequence; only through the 1990s, with the influx of huge sums of money from broadcasting rights and the subsequent commoditisation of the sport, did football become the economic heavyweight of today.

The relative lack of progress in ensuring football's compliance with the economic freedoms enshrined in Community law was noted by the European Parliament's Committee on Culture, Youth, Education and Media.[11] The Committee noted the extent to which professional sport, in particular professional football, was conducting its affairs in a fashion that was contrary to the free movement provisions of the Treaty. The report regarded the practices of sports federations as being intolerable abuses of free movement and competition provisions, calling for the Commission to investigate and intervene.

Bosman: The Application of European Union Law to Sport

The demands for action articulated by the European Parliament soon became redundant following the judgment of the Court of Justice in *Union Royale Belge des Sociétés de Football Association v Bosman*.

The background to the judgment in *Bosman*

Jean-Marc Bosman was a Belgian professional footballer with Belgian club RC Liège, with a contract running until 30 June 1990. In April 1990 RC Liège offered Bosman a contract for a further year but with a significant reduction in his basic wage to the minimum permitted under the statutes of

---

9   [1995] ECR I-4292, at para 125.
10 Parrish, R, *European Union Sports Law and Policy* (2003), Manchester: Manchester UP, p 92.
11 A3-0326/94/ Part A (27/4/94) Part B (29/4/94), 'Report on the European Community and Sport', Rapporteur: Mrs J Larive.

the Belgium Football Association (URBSFA). Bosman declined the offer and, in accordance with the rules, was made available for transfer with a fee fixed by a formula. No club sought to acquire Bosman's services in return for the fee but Bosman was eventually able to make an agreement with a French second division club, US Dunkerque. Dunkerque and RC Liège were able to conclude an agreement for Bosman's temporary transfer for one year, with an option for Dunkerque to make the transfer permanent on the payment of a set fee. Both agreements – between Bosman and Dunkerque and between RC Liège and Dunkerque – were contingent upon the grant of a clearance certificate by the URBSFA. In the event, because of doubts over the ability of Dunkerque to pay the requisite fee to RC Liège, there was a delay in requesting the clearance certificate. It was, therefore, not issued in time and both contracts lapsed. RC Liège had already, in any case, secured Bosman's suspension, in accordance with the relevant rules, preventing him from playing in the immediate future.

Judicial proceedings and procedural elements of admissibility

Following the failed move to Dunkerque, Bosman brought proceedings in the Tribunal de Prèmiere Instance in Liège against RC Liège and URBSFA for an interim order. The Belgian court made a reference to the Court of Justice for a preliminary ruling on matters of EU law raised by the case, but this element of the judgment was overturned by the Liège Court d'Appel and the reference was withdrawn.[12] An interim order was made which permitted Bosman to continue to play with a series of clubs in the lower divisions of France and Belgium pending the determination of the main proceedings brought by him. In those main proceedings Bosman sought damages from RC Liège for breach of contract and a ruling that the transfer system was unlawful. The URBSFA then intervened in the proceedings, seeking a declaration from the court that its transfer rules and the parallel rules operated by UEFA were lawful. Bosman then joined UEFA as a defendant and extended his action. Bosman sought a declaration that UEFA rules that permitted a transfer fee be demanded for a player who was no longer under contract, and those restricting access to competition on the basis of nationality, were null and void as being contrary to Articles 48, 85 and 86 of the EC Treaty (now Articles 45, 101 and 102 TFEU). The Tribunal de Prèmiere Instance upheld Bosman's claim for compensation against RC Liège and made a reference to the Court of Justice for a preliminary ruling in respect of the transfer system.[13] This reference was, however, withdrawn following the decision of the Liège Court d'Appel, concurring with the findings of the Tribunal de Prèmiere Instance and making a reference itself. It was on this basis that the case came before the Court of Justice, with the following questions to be examined:

Case C-415/93 *Union Royale Belges des Sociètès de Football ASBL v Bosman*

Are Articles 48, 85 and 86 of the Treaty of Rome . . . to be interpreted as

(i) prohibiting a football club from requiring and receiving payment of a sum of money upon the engagement of one of its players who has come to the end of his contract by a new employing club;

(ii) prohibiting the national and international sporting associations or federations from including in their respective regulations provisions restricting access of foreign players from the European Community to the competitions which they organise?[14]

---

12 Case C-340/90. Bosman had previously brought a direct action under Article 173 EEC (now Article 263 TFEU) seeking to have the Commission's agreement to the '3+2' rule annulled. This claim was rejected as the agreement was not a legally binding measure and could not, therefore, be challenged in this way. See Case C-117/91 *Bosman v Commission* [1991] ECR I-3353.

13 Case C-269/92.

14 [1995] ECR I-4192.

Before the Court of Justice UEFA argued that the case was inadmissible. In respect of the first question, it contended that Bosman's transfer to Dunkerque had failed because UEFA rules on transfers *had not* been applied. As regards the second it argued that this was purely hypothetical and had no bearing on the outcome of the case in question. The URBSFA went so far as to contend that the second element of the dispute was an artificial one engineered by pressure groups of professional players – a suggestion refuted by Bosman. Following on from an extensive analysis by Advocate-General Lenz, the Court of Justice determined that the question concerning the transfer rules was relevant as part of Bosman's claim involved imposing restrictions on the prospective application of those rules to him. It also concluded that the second question was admissible and not hypothetical, as the matter related to a request for declaratory relief which, while prospective, related to an admissible claim before a national court.

Proceedings before the Court of Justice

The parties to the action, in addition to a number of interventions, made numerous contentions relating to both the applicability and application of Community law in this case.

The applicability of Community free movement of persons law to professional football

Though it had previously been decided in *Donà* that the activities of professional and semi-professional footballers fell within the scope of economic activities caught by the Community law, both the Belgian federation and UEFA put forward arguments contending that, in fact, this was not the case.[15]

The Belgian federation advocated that only the largest football clubs in Europe could be considered as partaking in economic activity and that, outside of these clubs, any economic activity was trivial and, in many cases, did not involve clubs making a profit – a view supported by the German government. In addition UEFA asserted that the transfer rules could not be considered only within the narrow terms of Article 48 EEC, as the consequences of such consideration were likely to have much wider ramifications, impacting on the organisation of football as a whole. Further, it was contended that the transfer rules related only to the relationship between the clubs themselves and had no connection with the relationship between club and player. UEFA argued a number of wider points, propounding that Community law was not apt for application in the field of sport and that the principle of subsidiarity precluded the Court from engaging with these issues. The subsidiarity point was, again, supported by the German government, which drew parallels between sport and culture, noting the Treaty requirement that the Community respect the national and regional diversity of the cultures of the Member States, emphasising the autonomy enjoyed by sports federations under national law and concluding that the intervention by the Community should be limited to that which was strictly necessary.[16] UEFA also submitted that Bosman's situation was, in any case, a wholly internal matter with which the Court was barred from engaging as a matter of law.

A-G Lenz regarded many of these arguments as 'unconvincing'.[17] In its judgment the Court dismissed each in turn. First it reaffirmed the position established in *Donà*, that the activity of professional or semi-professional football constitutes an economic activity for the purposes of the Treaty irrespective of profitability.[18] Second, it dismissed the arguments relating to the

---

15 See generally paragraphs 126 to 131 of the Opinion of Advocate-General Lenz and paragraphs 69 to 91 of the judgment of the Court of Justice.
16 For consideration of sport as culture see Weatherill, S, 'Sport as Culture in EC Law' in *European Sports Law: Collected Papers* (2007), The Hague: TMC Asser Press.
17 At para 126.
18 At para 74.

business-to-business nature of the transfer rules, noting that the payment of a fee on a player moving from one club to another affected the opportunity for players to find employment and impacted upon its terms.[19] Third, the Court acknowledged the complex entwinement of the sporting and economic aspects of football and noted the potential for economic restrictions to be justified by sporting necessity. It held, however, that this could not be relied upon to provide a blanket exemption for the whole of the sport. It further determined that concerns about the consequences of a judgment, while relevant, could not preclude the application of the law – at most being a consideration in the temporal limitation of any judgment.[20] Fourth, the Court dismissed the arguments relating to culture on the basis that the context in which the reference had been framed concerned the rights protected under Article 48 EEC, a fundamental freedom, not the elements of the Treaty argued by the German government, and thus were not subject to the principle of subsidiarity.[21] On the broader question of subsidiarity and the autonomy of sports governing bodies, the Court recognised the principle but ruled that the regulations of sports federations could not effectively override the rights conferred by the Treaty as this would compromise the abolition of barriers to free movement demanded.[22] Fifth, the Court also dismissed arguments pertaining to the right to freedom of association under Article 11 of the European Convention on Human Rights. Finally the Court considered the extent to which Bosman's case could be considered a wholly internal matter and thus outside the scope of Community Law. It accepted that were this the case it would have no jurisdiction, but noted that the case arose out of the failure of Bosman's transfer between RC Liège and Dunkerque – clubs in Belgium and France respectively – and thus engaged Community law as relating to free movement between Member States. Thus the Court was satisfied that the questions referred could be addressed.

Having established that Community law could be applied to the questions referred by the Liège Court d'Appel, the detail of that application was then established. As before, the parties to the case made numerous submissions as to the nature and extent of application of Community law.

The application of Community free movement of persons law to professional football: nationality rules

In pertinent part, Article 48 EEC (now Article 45 TFEU) provided:[23]

Article 48 EEC

1. Freedom of movement for workers shall be secured within the Community by the end of the transitional period at the latest.

2. Such freedom of movement shall entail the abolition of any discrimination based on nationality between workers of the Member States as regards employment, remuneration and other conditions of work and employment

3. It shall entail the right, subject to limitations justified on grounds of public policy, public security or public health:
   (a) to accept offers of employment actually made;
   (b) to move freely within the territory of Member States for this purpose;
   (c) to stay in a Member State for the purpose of employment in accordance with the provisions governing the employment of nationals of that State laid down by law, regulation or administrative action;

---

19 At para 75.
20 At paras 76–77.
21 At para 78.
22 At paras 81–87.
23 In the current articulation of this freedom, Article 45 TFEU paragraph 1 provides, 'Freedom of movement for workers shall be secured within the Union.'

(d)   to remain in the territory of a Member State after having been employed in that State, subject to conditions which shall be embodied in implementing regulations to be drawn up by the Commission.

The view of A-G Lenz was that the restriction imposed on foreign players represented a 'classic case' of discrimination. The rules limited the number of players from other Member States able to be fielded by a club from another Member State in any given match. Thus, the Advocate-General reasoned, drawing on specific measures outlawing nationality quotas,[24] those players were at a disadvantage as regards access to employment as compared to home nationals. A-G Lenz rejected UEFA's contention that the rules did not breach Article 48 EEC, as they related to the number of players that could be fielded in any one game and not to the number of 'foreign' nationals that could be employed by that club as a whole. A club acting reasonably, he agreed with Bosman and the Commission, would be encouraged by the rules to employ only as many, or perhaps slightly more, 'foreign' nationals as were permitted in a match. Further, the rules were in breach of Article 48(3) EEC.

However, the Advocate-General did consider whether such rules could, nonetheless, be regarded as lawful. In doing so he alluded to the Court's previous decisions in *Walrave* and *Donà*, noting that the Court had identified an 'exception' permitting the exclusion of 'foreign' players in matches distinguished by specific character and context, so long as the restriction was limited to its proper objective. A-G Lenz acknowledged the views expressed by A-G Trabucchi in his Opinion in *Donà* (set out above), but took the view that these had not been effected by the Court's judgment in that case.

The Advocate-General went on to consider three further potential grounds for exception. First, the importance of nationality and identity were explored. It was argued that the restrictions were important to ensure that the fans of each team identified with its constituent players and that clubs went on to represent their nation in European club competitions. A-G Lenz dismissed this view; spectators, he said, were more interested in the success of their team than the nationality of the players and drew on a number of examples of foreign players popular with particular teams' fans. As regards the representative element of club teams, the Advocate-General was equally dismissive, pointing out that players from all over a country could represent a team of a particular locality and, in any case, most major European club teams already included foreign players and this was fatal to that argument. Second, it was argued that the restrictions were necessary to ensure a ready supply of players for each national team and that without this rule youth development would be stifled. This approach was similarly rebuffed; A-G Lenz saw no evidence to support the claim, conversely viewing the presence of a top foreign player as being of benefit to younger players developing their game. Further, the Advocate-General concluded that, though it was likely that a greater proportion of foreign players would be recruited by clubs, there was no obligation for them to do so and that it was unlikely that 'native' players would become the minority. Finally, the Advocate-General addressed the issue of competitive balance – it had been asserted that the abolition of the nationality rules would mean that the richest clubs would be able to secure the services of the best players and thus reduce competition between clubs. A-G Lenz admitted that the preservation of competitive balance was a legitimate objective, but that it could be achieved by less restrictive means. He also noted that no such provisions were in place at that time to prevent clubs from hoarding the best domestic players.

In its judgment the Court of Justice concurred with the opinion of the Advocate-General that the nationality restrictions constituted an obstacle to the freedom of movement for workers:

---

24 Article 4, paragraph 1 Regulation 1612/68; see also Case 167/73 *Commission v France* [1974] ECR 359.

Case C-415/93 *Union Royale Belges des Sociètès de Football ASBL v Bosman*

[117] Article 48(2) expressly provides that freedom of movement for workers entails the abolition of any discrimination based on nationality between workers of the Member States as regards employment, remuneration and conditions of work and employment.

[118] That provision has been implemented, in particular, by Article 4 of Regulation 1612/68 of the Council on freedom of movement for workers within the Community, under which provisions laid down by law, regulation or administrative action of the Member States which restrict by number or percentage the employment of foreign nationals in any undertaking, branch of activity or region, or at a national level, are not to apply to nationals of the other Member States.

[119] The same principle applies to clauses contained in the regulations of sporting associations which restrict the right of nationals of other Member States to take part, as professional players, in football matches.

[120] The fact that those clauses concern not the employment of such players, on which there is no restriction, but the extent to which their clubs may field them in official matches is irrelevant. In so far as participation in such matches is the essential purpose of a professional player's activity, a rule which restricts that participation obviously also restricts the chances of employment of the player concerned.

With regard to the claim for the rules as creating a link between club and country, the Court was similarly direct:

[131] First, a football club's links with the Member State in which it is established cannot be regarded as any more inherent in its sporting activity than its links with its locality, town, region or, in the case of the United Kingdom, the territory covered by each of the four associations. Even though national championships are played between clubs from different regions, towns or localities, there is no rule restricting the right of clubs to field players from other regions, towns or localities in such matches.

[132] In international competitions, moreover, participation is limited to clubs which have achieved certain results in competition in their respective countries, without any particular significance being attached to the nationalities of their players.

It also rejected claims that 'native' players would be displaced by incoming foreign players, noting that opportunities would also increase for those players in other Member States:

[133] Secondly, whilst national teams must be made up of players having the nationality of the relevant country, those players need not necessarily be registered to play for clubs in that country. Indeed, under the rules of the sporting associations, foreign players must be allowed by their clubs to play for their country's national team in certain matches.

[134] Furthermore, although freedom of movement for workers, by opening up the employment market in one Member State to nationals of the other Member States, has the effect of reducing workers' chances of finding employment within the Member State of which they are nationals, it also, by the same token, offers them new prospects of employment in other Member States. Such considerations obviously apply also to professional footballers.

The Court then approved the view of A-G Lenz in respect of competitive balance:

[135] Thirdly, although it has been argued that the nationality clauses prevent the richest clubs from engaging the best foreign players, those clauses are not sufficient to achieve the aim of maintaining a competitive balance, since there are no rules limiting the possibility for such clubs to recruit the best national players, thus undermining that balance to just the same extent.[25]

The application of Community free movement of persons law to professional football: transfer rules

As regards the compatibility of the transfer rules with Article 48 EEC, A-G Lenz emphasised that the provision did not only extend to overt discrimination but also to indirect discrimination and non-discriminatory restrictions on freedom of movement. Having undertaken an extensive review of the relevant case law, A-G Lenz concluded that restrictions on freedom of movement are compatible with Community law only if they are 'justified by compelling reasons of the general interest and comply with the principle of proportionality.'[26] He went on to explain the application of these principles in this case:

> **[209]** Even if one were to assume that the transfer rules were applied throughout the Community without distinction to transfers within a Member State and to transfers to another Member State, it would still be a fact that they restrict freedom of movement: contrary to what Article 48 requires, a professional football player cannot under those rules move freely to another Member State in order to work for another club there. Rather it is necessary in every case for the transfer fee due to be paid to his former club . . . There is thus a clear restriction here on the right to freedom of movement, which is caught by Article 48. That those rules also restrict the possibility of changing clubs freely within one and the same Member State can make no difference, on the view taken here.

> **[210]** The transfer rules directly restrict access to the employment market in other Member States. Therein they differ very significantly from other rules applicable without distinction which affect the exercise of an occupation. One example may suffice to make the difference clear. The question has just been raised again whether a professional league should for instance have 16, 18 or more clubs. It is perfectly plain that the number of clubs available affects a player's chances of finding employment with a club. The smaller the number of clubs, the more difficult it is likely to be as a rule to find employment. Nevertheless, provisions of that nature do not appear to me to raise doubts with respect to Article 48. They do not concern the possibility of access for foreign players as such, but the exercise of the occupation. The situation with respect to the rules on transfers is quite different: under the applicable rules a player can transfer abroad only if the new club (or the player himself) is in a position to pay the transfer fee demanded. If that is not the case, the player cannot move abroad. That is a direct restriction on access to the employment market. Since the transfer fee is demanded by the previous club and the hindrance to the transfer – even if it is also required by the rules of the international federations – thus originates in the sphere of the Member State of origin[.]

The Court of Justice shared the Advocate-General's assessment of the application of Article 48 EEC to transfer fees:

> **[95]** . . . nationals of Member States have in particular the right, which they derive directly from the Treaty, to leave their country of origin to enter the territory of another Member State and reside there in order there to pursue an economic activity.

---

25 [1995] ECR I-4192.
26 At para 190.

[96] Provisions which preclude or deter a national of a Member State from leaving his country of origin in order to exercise his right to freedom of movement therefore constitute an obstacle to that freedom even if they apply without regard to the nationality of the workers concerned.

[97] The Court has also stated, that even though the Treaty provisions relating to freedom of establishment are directed mainly to ensuring that foreign nationals and companies are treated in the host Member State in the same way as nationals of that State, they also prohibit the Member State of origin from hindering the establishment in another Member State of one of its nationals or of a company . . . The rights guaranteed by Article 52 et seq. of the Treaty would be rendered meaningless if the Member State of origin could prohibit undertakings from leaving in order to establish themselves in another Member State. The same considerations apply, in relation to Article 48 of the Treaty, with regard to rules which impede the freedom of movement of nationals of one Member State wishing to engage in gainful employment in another Member State.

[98] It is true that the transfer rules in issue in the main proceedings apply also to transfers of players between clubs belonging to different national associations within the same Member State and that similar rules govern transfers between clubs belonging to the same national association.

[99] However, as has been pointed out by Mr Bosman, by the Danish Government and by the Advocate General in paragraphs 209 and 210 of his Opinion, those rules are likely to restrict the freedom of movement of players who wish to pursue their activity in another Member State by preventing or deterring them from leaving the clubs to which they belong even after the expiry of their contracts of employment with those clubs.

[100] Since they provide that a professional footballer may not pursue his activity with a new club established in another Member State unless it has paid his former club a transfer fee agreed upon between the two clubs or determined in accordance with the regulations of the sporting associations, the said rules constitute an obstacle to freedom of movement for workers.

. . .

[103] It is sufficient to note that, although the rules in issue in the main proceedings apply also to transfers between clubs belonging to different national associations within the same Member State and are similar to those governing transfers between clubs belonging to the same national association, they still directly affect players' access to the employment market in other Member States and are thus capable of impeding freedom of movement for workers. They cannot, thus, be deemed comparable to the rules on selling arrangements for goods which in *Keck and Mithouard* were held to fall outside the ambit of Article 30 of the Treaty.

[104] Consequently, the transfer rules constitute an obstacle to freedom of movement for workers prohibited in principle by Article 48 of the Treaty. It could only be otherwise if those rules pursued a legitimate aim compatible with the Treaty and were justified by pressing reasons of public interest. But even if that were so, application of those rules would still have to be such as to ensure achievement of the aim in question and not go beyond what is necessary for that purpose.

In his opinion the Advocate-General had considered possible grounds of justification, acknowledging that it might be found not only in the non-economic reasons relating exclusively to sport noted in the earlier cases, but also in reasons of an economic nature capable of satisfying the requirement of being compelling in the general interest, and proportionate. In assessing the parties' submissions he was able to identify two major grounds in addition to a number of subsidiary points: the two major points of, first, the maintenance of financial and sporting equilibrium and, second, fees as compensation for the costs of training players, and subsidiary points relating to encouraging talent identification and development, guaranteeing the quality of football and promoting sporting activity and the sporting ethos, maintaining the worldwide stability of football of which the EEC was only a small part.

A-G Lenz accepted that the maintenance of balance between larger and smaller clubs and ensuring the financial stability of clubs amounted to a compelling reason in the public interest and therefore had the potential to justify the imposition of transfer fees if it could be demonstrated that they were a proportionate means of achieving those ends. The Advocate-General accepted the contention that transfer fees provided an important means by which the redistribution of wealth between clubs was effected and monies 'trickled down' to lower division clubs to maintain their financial viability, but opined that the transfer rules could not be justified on this basis because of the availability of other, less restrictive means of achieving the same objective. On the point of competitive balance, A-G Lenz did not accept that the transfer rules prevent the richest clubs from securing the services of the best players. Nor, in his view, was financial balance a necessary consequence of the rules; instead he agreed with the suggestion put forward on behalf of Bosman that either a wage-capping scheme or, more particularly, a systematic re-distribution of gate receipts and television monies between the clubs, would be more effective in achieving the goal, as well as being more reliable and consistent. The Court of Justice dealt with these points relatively briefly, referring to A-G Lenz's opinion and accepting the objective as legitimate but unable to reconcile this with the system of transfer fees:

> **[106]** In view of the considerable social importance of sporting activities and in particular football in the Community, the aims of maintaining a balance between clubs by preserving a certain degree of equality and uncertainty as to results and of encouraging the recruitment and training of young players must be accepted as legitimate.

> **[107]** As regards the first of those aims, Mr Bosman has rightly pointed out that the application of the transfer rules is not an adequate means of maintaining financial and competitive balance in the world of football. Those rules neither preclude the richest clubs from securing the services of the best players nor prevent the availability of financial resources from being a decisive factor in competitive sport, thus considerably altering the balance between clubs.

The approach of regarding transfer fees as compensation for the costs incurred in the training and development of a player was also dismissed by A-G Lenz on the basis that the amount paid for the transfer of an out of contract player varied dependent on a number of factors, none of which related directly to the costs of training and development. On the question of talent identification, A-G Lenz was unconvinced by the claim that transfer monies were necessary to fund this and the employment of staff – pointing to the redistribution question raised previously. The Court of Justice concurred:

> **[108]** As regards the second aim [of encouraging the recruitment and development of young players], it must be accepted that the prospect of receiving transfer, development or training fees is indeed likely to encourage football clubs to seek new talent and train young players.

> **[109]** However, because it is impossible to predict the sporting future of young players with any certainty and because only a limited number of such players go on to play professionally, those fees are by nature contingent and uncertain and are in any event unrelated to the actual cost borne by clubs of training both future professional players and those who will never play professionally. The prospect of receiving such fees cannot, therefore, be either a decisive factor in encouraging recruitment and training of young players or an adequate means of financing such activities, particularly in the case of smaller clubs.

[110] Furthermore, as the Advocate General has pointed out in paras 226 et seq. of his Opinion, the same aims can be achieved at least as efficiently by other means which do not impede freedom of movement for workers.

Neither Advocate-General nor Court of Justice perceived the challenges that would arise in football by the amendment of the transfer system as being insurmountable:

[111] It has also been argued that the transfer rules are necessary to safeguard the world organisation of football.

[112] However, the present proceedings concern application of those rules within the Community and not the relations between the national associations of the Member States and those of non-member countries. In any event, application of different rules to transfers between clubs belonging to national associations within the Community and to transfers between such clubs and those affiliated to the national associations of non-member countries is unlikely to pose any particular difficulties. As is clear from paragraphs [22] and [23] above, the rules which have so far governed transfers within the national associations of certain Member States are different from those which apply at the international level.

The decision of the Court of Justice

The Court of Justice thus ruled as follows:

1. Article 48 EEC precludes the application of rules laid down by sporting associations, under which a professional footballer who is a national of one Member State may not, on the expiry of his contract with a club, be employed by a club of another Member State unless the latter club has paid to the former club a transfer, training or development fee.

2. Article 48 EEC precludes the application of rules laid down by sporting associations under which, in matches in competitions which they organise, football clubs may field only a limited number of professional players who are nationals of other Member States.[27]

The Court declined to rule on the application of competition law, Articles 85 and 86 EEC, in the case, on the basis that it was not necessary to do so given the findings in respect of Article 48 EEC. A-G Lenz, however, did conclude that both the nationality clauses and transfer rules were in breach of Article 85 EEC.[28]

The impact of the *Bosman* case

Practical and regulatory impacts

As might be imagined, the impact of such a decision by the Court of Justice was profound. Despite the clarity of the ruling FIFA, football's world governing body, initially resisted the impact of it on the basis that a small part of its jurisdiction could not dictate rules to the majority. Prior to the delivery of the judgment FIFA issued a media release:

---

27 The Court also imposed a temporal limitation on the judgment excluding reliance upon it in claims relating to a fee in respect of transfer, training or development which had already been paid, or was still payable under an obligation arising before the date of the judgment.

28 See the discussion of competition law below.

FIFA Support for *Bosman* Case Policy

FIFA has been closely following the developments in the case of the Belgian player Jean-Marc Bosman and views with considerable concern the proposition that 18 of the 193 FIFA Member Associations might be obliged to disregard transfer regulations which are accepted and respected by all Member Associations worldwide.

In FIFA's view, it is clear that a small group of countries cannot be granted an exemption from sports regulations which are effective in all parts of the world and which operate successfully and efficiently and for the benefit of football at all levels.

FIFA feels that an international sports organisation simply cannot operate properly unless regulations are universally applied, and any other approach would lead to very serious problems. Such circumstances could even jeopardise the independent status of the 18 FIFA Member Associations concerned.[29]

This view was further reinforced following the judgment, with FIFA keen to emphasise the relatively small number of nations affected by the decision:

FIFA Reaction to *Bosman* Case Decision

FIFA has noted with disappointment the decision taken by the European Court of Justice regarding the case of Jean-Marc Bosman.

FIFA points out that the decision affects only 18 of the 193 national associations affiliated to the world body. The current transfer system is based upon the Statutes and Regulations which have been duly approved by all the FIFA member associations and has proved to be effective, and is therefore not cast into doubt by today's decision.

FIFA will study what adaptations UEFA may need to consider as far as the 18 affected European associations (of a total UEFA membership of 50) are concerned.[30]

Writing in the immediate aftermath of the ruling, Morris, Morrow and Spink saw the judgment as having relatively limited impact:

Morris, P, Morrow, S and Spink P, 'EC Law and Professional Football: *Bosman* and its Implications'

One point lost in the welter of publicity generated by Bosman is the severely restricted nature and consequent limited impact of the ruling, at least in relation to transfer fees. Such fees are only unlawful once the player is out of contract, and only then where the player is an EC (or EEA) national and is seeking a move to a club of another Member State or EEA State. So far as the English game is concerned, Bosman will probably not have an immediate substantial impact on transfer activity . . . In relation to the foreign players restrictions aspect of Bosman, UEFA has proved itself remarkably ignorant and obdurate. It initially refused to remove restrictions during European club competitions for the 1995–96 season on the basis that a change in competition regulations halfway through the competition was inappropriate and inconvenient. It eventually relented in the face of pressure from the European Commission.[31]

As indicated, the transfer fee element of the judgment was limited to cross-border transfers between Member States by EU nationals. The measure was only applied to domestic cases in England and

---

29 'FIFA Support for Bosman Case Policy', FIFA Media Release, 24 November 1995.
30 'FIFA Reaction to Bosman Case Decision', FIFA Media Release, 15 December 1995.
31 Morris, P, Morrow, S and Spink, P, 'EC Law and Professional Football: Bosman and its Implications' (1996) 59 MLR 893, 902.

other jurisdictions following substantial pressure from players' groups and the threat of litigation.[32] The right to move freely at the conclusion of a contract was extended to non-Member State nationals following a case lodged by a Hungarian professional, Tibor Balog.[33] Balog claimed that the continuing restriction of his capacity to move, despite being out of contract, was anti-competitive and amounted to a breach of Article 85 EC. His case reached the Court of Justice by way of a request for a preliminary reference from a Belgian court, but was withdrawn shortly before the Opinion of the Advocate-General was due to be given, with the rules being amended so as to extend to all professional players irrespective of nationality.

The *Bosman* judgment did, however, galvanise the previously largely inert Commission into action. The Commission was in receipt of a number of complaints about the anti-competitive nature of the football transfer system and launched an investigation. The result of the discussions between FIFA and the Commission resulted in a substantial amendment to the transfer regulations which came into force *globally* in 2001,[34] imposing new rules which, in summary, provided for the following:

- a system of training compensation should be in place to encourage and reward the training effort of clubs, in particular small clubs, for players aged 23 and under;
- creation of solidarity mechanisms that would redistribute a significant proportion of income to clubs involved in the training and education of a player, including amateur clubs;
- special provisions relating to young players;
- one transfer period per season, with a limited mid-season window and each player to be limited to one transfer per season;
- contracts to have a minimum of one year and maximum of five years' duration;
- contracts to be protected for a period of three years up to the age of 28 and for two years for older players, after which players may unilaterally breach their contract subject to compliance with regulations aimed at preventing abuse and in accordance with the payment of a fee calculated by objective factors;
- proportionate sporting sanctions to be applied to players, clubs or agents in the case of unilateral breaches of contract without just cause, in the protected period;
- creation of a FIFA Dispute Resolution Chamber (DRC) to deal quickly with disputes and allowing for the possibility of further appeal.[35]

The magnitude of the impact is emphasised by Parrish:

Parrish, R, 'Reconciling conflicting approaches to sport in the EU'

The impact of the ruling has been profound. The significant effect has been felt by sports organisations. The internal organisation of professional football has been dramatically re-shaped. International and domestic transfer regimes have been dismantled and nationality restrictions relaxed in all games except in the composition of national teams. Furthermore, the ruling has confirmed sport's linkage to the operation of the Single European Market whenever practised as an economic activity. Football is therefore not the only sport to be affected by the ruling. The second significant effect has been felt within the EU itself. In particular, the ruling sparked

---

32 Gardiner, S and Welch, R, 'The Contractual Dynamics of Team Stability Versus Player Mobility: Who Rules "The Beautiful Game"? (2007) 5(1) ESLJ (online); see also Weatherill, S, 'Discrimination on the Grounds of Nationality in Sport' and 'European Football Law' in *European Sports Law: Collected Papers* (2007), The Hague: TMC Asser Press. A more recent overview can be found in McHardy, D, 'Reconciling Soccer Authorities and European Union Institutions: Who is Best Placed to Administer Governance within the European Soccer Market?' (2008) 18 Seton Hall J Sports & Ent L, 105
33 Case C-264/98 *Tibor Balog v ASBL Royal Charleroi Sporting Club*, case withdrawn.
34 FIFA Regulations for the Status and Transfer of Players (2001).
35 See 'Commission closes investigations into FIFA regulations on international football transfers', IP/02/824, 5 June 2002.

renewed regulatory interest in sport from elements within the European Commission. This interest served to galvanise support from within other elements of the EU who wanted sport to be afforded a higher level of protection from EU legislation. In particular, the socio-cultural coalition wanted the EU to give the socio-cultural and integrationist qualities of sport a higher priority.[36]

The decision in *Bosman* and subsequent input into the detail of transfer regulations by the Commission have thus had a significant impact on the global regulation of sport and, despite FIFA's early protestations, there has been a significant re-regulation of football premised on the demands of EU law.[37] This much is emphasised in a case before the Court of Arbitration for Sport (CAS) brought by the Uruguayan club Peñarol.[38] Peñarol claimed a transfer fee for the transfer of Christian Rodriguez and Carlos Bueno to French club Paris St Gemain. The two players had their contracts unilaterally extended by Peñarol, in accordance with rules of the Uruguayan Football Federation, but contrary to FIFA transfer rules. Peñarol refused to issue a transfer certificate in the absence of payment of a fee. The DRC permitted the players to be registered by the French Football Federation without the payment of a fee or the production of a transfer certificate and the Uruguayan club appealed to the CAS, arguing that it was the domestic rules that ought to be applied and not FIFA's. In emphasising the need for the transfer rules to be universally applied the CAS found that the Uruguayan rules were not compatible and that the *FIFA Regulations for the Status and Transfer of Players* took precedence. This serves to demonstrate the significant extra-territorial impact of the application of EU law well outside its own jurisdiction.[39]

Policy and legal impacts

In addition to the renewed vigour of the Commission in sporting matters, the *Bosman* decision also provoked wider institutional responses. Notably, the European Parliament, having urged action in the 1994 Larive Report, undertook a significant about-face in the Pack Report, delivered in 1997, demanding restraint and a more holistic approach to sport in light of the 'notorious' judgment in *Bosman*:

The Pack Report

1. [The Committee] takes the view that, in the Treaty on which it is based and through its actions, the European Union must acknowledge the basic cultural, economic and social phenomenon that sport represents;

2. Calls on the current Intergovernmental Conference, to that end, to include at all events an explicit reference to sport in Article 128 of the Treaty;

3. Emphasizes that the European Union must recognize the specific nature of sport and the autonomy of the sports movement, it being understood that the economic activity generated by professional sport cannot be exempt from the provisions of Community law.[40]

---

36 Parrish, R, 'Reconciling conflicting approaches to sport in the EU', in Caiger, A and Gardiner, S (eds), *Professional Sport in the EU: Regulation and Re-regulation* (2000), The Hague: TMC Asser Press, pp 28–29.

37 See generally, Welch, R, 'Player Mobility, the FIFA Transfer Rules and Freedom of Movement' (2006) 4 (Nov) ISLR 83; McAuley, D, ' Windows, Caps, Footballs and the European Commission. Confused? You will be' (2003) 24(8) ECLR 394; McAuley, D, 'They Think it's All Over . . . it Might Just be Now: Unravelling the Ramifications for the European Football Transfer System Post-Bosman' (2002) 23(7) ECLR 331; McArdle, D, 'They're Playing R. Song. Football and the European Union after *Bosman*' (2000) 3(2) Football Studies 42; Hornsby, S, 'Sport in the EU: Has Self-Regulation a Future in Light of the Bosman Case' (1995) 1(5) INTTLR 181.

38 TAS 2005/A/983 & 984 *Club Atlético Peñarol v Carlos Heber Bueno Suarez, Cristian Gabriel Rodriguez Barrotti & Paris Saint-Germain*.

39 See generally on this point, Boyes, S, 'Law, Regulation and the Europeanisation of a Global Game' in Magee, J, Bairner, A and Tomlinson, A (eds), *The Bountiful Game? Football, Identities and Finance* (2005), London: Meyer & Meyer.

40 28 May 1997 A4-0197/97 Report on the role of the European Union in the field of sport Committee on Culture, Youth, Education and the Media. Rapporteur: Mrs Doris Pack.

The Member States did heed the report's call for action in the field of sport, but stopped short of a specific inclusion in the Treaty. Rather than including sport in the Treaty of Amsterdam, it addressed the issue by way of a non-binding declaration:

The 'Amsterdam' Declaration on sport

The Conference emphasises the social significance of sport, in particular its role in forging identity and bringing people together. The Conference therefore calls on the bodies of the European Union to listen to sports associations when important questions affecting sport are at issue. In this connection, special consideration should be given to the particular characteristics of amateur sport.

Following on from this declaration the Member States, acting as the European Council, invited the Commission to 'submit a report . . . with a view to safeguarding current sports structures and maintaining the social function of sport within the Community framework'.[41] In order to develop this report the Commission first issued a short working paper in which the sports policy of the Community was scoped and the complex nature of sport's economic and social functions noted.[42] This was followed by a consultation document – The European Model of Sport.[43] The consultation described the organisational model of sport in Europe as being a pyramid, with clubs at the base and then regional, national and European sports federations each progressively higher up. It also identified sport in Europe as being characterised by systems of promotion and relegation rather than the American model of closed leagues. Similarly the paper identified grassroots sport, sport as a focus of national identity and international competition as being particular features of European sport. It also highlighted football hooliganism as a challenge.

In identifying problems that might concern the Community the paper considered a number of issues: the role of governing bodies as being dominated by the large commercialised members of the federation and being drawn away from their role in respect of grass-roots sport; the monopolistic nature of federations and the lack of 'competition' for regulatory bodies; common ownership of multiple clubs participating in a competition, with the attendant risk of conflicts of interest; and financial stability and solidarity between sports clubs. The paper dedicated a chapter to broadcasting issues related to sport, focusing mainly on the competition law issues arising out of the sale of sports rights. In the final section the paper considered sport as a tool of social policy in respect of: education; social cohesion and combating racism; environment; public health; doping; and employment.

The result of the consultation was a report presented to the European Council meeting in Helsinki – the 'Helsinki Report on Sport'.[44] The report first highlighted the risks to sport brought about by increasing popularity, internationalisation and commercialisation: of the overloading of sporting calendars, which could lead to pressure on athletes to dope; the increase in lucrative events promoting a commercial approach, to the detriment of sport's core principles and social functions; the risk that large clubs and other sports operators focus on maximising their own economic benefit from sport, jeopardising the principle of financial solidarity and the principle of promotion and relegation; and the risk facing young athletes thrust into high-level competitive sport without proper preparation. The second theme noted by the Commission was the importance of sport in promoting education and social cohesion and it saw the improvement of this aspect as being a key issue for the Community and Member States. As a part of this role the central importance of co-operation in combating doping was given a high profile. Finally, the paper considered

---

41 Report from the Commission to the European Council with a view to safeguarding current sports structures and maintaining the social function of sport within the Community framework COM(1999) 644.

42 Commission Staff Working Paper, The Development and Prospects for Community Action in the Field of Sport (1998).

43 European Commission, The European Model of Sport: Consultation Document (1998).

44 See generally, Weatherill, S, 'The Helsinki Report on Sport' in European Sports Law: Collected Papers (2007), The Hague: TMC Asser Press.

the legal environment of sport, emphasising the high level of uncertainty that existed at that moment in time. The paper noted growing tensions between economic and sporting values and commented on the growing number of disputes arising and the increasing instance of litigation, in respect of: collective sale of television rights; mobility of sports professionals; taxation; Member State action on commercialisation; and the monopolistic nature of sports federations with the concomitant risk of unlawful economic restrictions. Moreover, in respect of the application of Community law to sport, the report gave some useful guidance:

The 'Helsinki' Report

4.2.1. The Community level

In terms of the economic activity that it generates, the sporting sector is subject to the rules of the EC Treaty, like the other sectors of the economy. The application of the Treaty's competition rules to the sporting sector must take account of the specific characteristics of sport, especially the interdependence between sporting activity and the economic activity that it generates, the principle of equal opportunities and the uncertainty of the results.

With a view to an improved definition of the legal environment, it is possible to give examples, without prejudice to the conclusions that the Commission could draw from the in-depth analysis of each case, of practices of sports organisations.

4.2.1.1. Practices which do not come under the competition rules

The regulations of sporting organisations drawing up rules without which a sport could not exist, or which are necessary for its organisation or for the organisation of competitions, might not be subject to the competition rules. The rules inherent to sport are, first and foremost, the 'rules of the game'. The aim of these rules is not to distort competition.

4.2.1.2. Practices that are, in principle, prohibited by the competition rules

These are restrictive practices in the economic activities generated by sport. They may concern, in particular, restrictions on parallel imports of sports products and the sale of entrance tickets to stadiums that discriminates between users who are resident in a particular Member State and those who live outside that Member State.

Sponsoring agreements that close a market by removing other suppliers for no objective reason are prohibited. The systems of international transfers based on arbitrarily calculated payments which bear no relation to training costs seem to have been prohibited, irrespective of the nationality of the player concerned.

Lastly, it is likely that there would be a ban on the practice of a sporting organization using its regulatory power to exclude from the market, for no objective reason, any economic operator which, even though it complies with the justified quality or safety standards, has not been able to obtain a document from this organisation certifying to the quality or safety of its products.

4.2.1.3. Practices likely to be exempted from the competition rules

● The *Bosman* judgment mentioned above recognised as legitimate the objectives designed to maintain a balance between clubs, while preserving a degree of equality of opportunity and the uncertainty of the result, and to encourage the recruitment and training of young players. Consequently, it is likely that agreements between professional clubs or decisions by their associations that are really designed to achieve these two objectives would be exempted. The same would be true of a system of transfers or standard contracts based on objectively calculated payments that are related to the costs of training, or of an exclusive right, limited in duration and scope, to broadcast sporting events. It goes without saying that the other provisions of the Treaty must also be complied with in this area, especially those that guarantee freedom of movement for professional sportsmen and women;

- it is likely that short-term sponsoring agreements based on an invitation to tender and with clear and non-discriminatory selection criteria would be authorised;
- any exemptions granted in the case of the joint sale of broadcasting rights must take account of the benefits for consumers and of the proportional nature of the restriction on competition in relation to the legitimate objective pursued. In this context, there is also a need to examine the extent to which a link can be established between the joint sale of rights and financial solidarity between professional and amateur sport, the objectives of the training of young sportsmen and women and those of promoting sporting activities among the population. However, with regard to the sale of exclusive rights to broadcast sporting events, it is likely that any exclusivity which, by its duration and/or scope, resulted in the closing of the market, would be prohibited.

It was further set out that national sporting authorities also needed to clarify the legal position of sport in order to facilitate and safeguard its social functions. Lastly in the legal context, the report stressed the need for greater transparency and precision in regulation by sports federations and called upon them to be more proactive in the promotion of sport across the spectrum of professional and amateur activity.

While it is significant that the Member States may be seen as reining in the Commission in its approach to the application of EU law to sports governing bodies, it must be equally significant that the Member States stopped short of legislating for a 'sporting exception' in order to make sport a special case. The message must be clear – EU law should be sympathetic to the particular needs of sport in its application; however, sport too must abide by the law as required. The overall impetus appears to be towards a position of co-operation, rather than the dogma that has so far characterised the approaches of both the Commission and the sporting federations with which it has dealt. This view is further supported by the adoption of the 'Nice Declaration on Sport', adopted by the European Council pursuant to the Helsinki Report on Sport:

European Council, 'The Nice Declaration on Sport'

1. The European Council has noted the report on sport submitted to it by the European Commission in Helsinki in December 1999 with a view to safeguarding current sports structures and maintaining the social function of sport within the European Union. Sporting organisations and the Member States have a primary responsibility in the conduct of sporting affairs. Even though not having any direct powers in this area, the Community must, in its action under the various Treaty provisions, take account of the social, educational and cultural functions inherent in sport and making it special, in order that the code of ethics and the solidarity essential to the preservation of its social role may be respected and nurtured.

2. The European Council hopes in particular that the cohesion and ties of solidarity binding the practice of sports at every level, fair competition and both the moral and material interests and the physical integrity of those involved in the practice of sport, especially minors, may be preserved.

Amateur sport and sport for all

3. Sport is a human activity resting on fundamental social, educational and cultural values. It is a factor making for integration, involvement in social life, tolerance, acceptance of differences and playing by the rules.

4. Sporting activity should be accessible to every man and woman, with due regard for individual aspirations and abilities, throughout the whole gamut of organised or individual competitive or recreational sports.

5. For the physically or mentally disabled, the practice of physical and sporting activities provides a particularly favourable opening for the development of individual talent, rehabilitation, social integration and solidarity and, as such, should be encouraged. In this connection, the European Council welcomes the valuable and exemplary contribution made by the Paralympic Games in Sydney.

6. The Member States encourage voluntary services in sport, by means of measures providing appropriate protection for and acknowledging the economic and social role of volunteers, with the support, where necessary, of the Community in the framework of its powers in this area.

Role of sports federations

7. The European Council stresses its support for the independence of sports organisations and their right to organise themselves through appropriate associative structures. It recognises that, with due regard for national and Community legislation and on the basis of a democratic and transparent method of operation, it is the task of sporting organisations to organise and promote their particular sports, particularly as regards the specifically sporting rules applicable and the make-up of national teams, in the way which they think best reflects their objectives.

8. It notes that sports federations have a central role in ensuring the essential solidarity between the various levels of sporting practice, from recreational to top-level sport, which co-exist there; they provide the possibility of access to sports for the public at large, human and financial support for amateur sports, promotion of equal access to every level of sporting activity for men and women alike, youth training, health protection and measures to combat doping, acts of violence and racist or xenophobic occurrences.

9. These social functions entail special responsibilities for federations and provide the basis for the recognition of their competence in organising competitions.

10. While taking account of developments in the world of sport, federations must continue to be the key feature of a form of organisation providing a guarantee of sporting cohesion and participatory democracy.

Preservation of sports training policies

11. Training policies for young sportsmen and -women are the life blood of sport, national teams and top-level involvement in sport and must be encouraged. Sports federations, where appropriate in tandem with the public authorities, are justified in taking the action needed to preserve the training capacity of clubs affiliated to them and to ensure the quality of such training, with due regard for national and Community legislation and practices.

Protection of young sportsmen and -women

12. The European Council underlines the benefits of sport for young people and urges the need for special heed to be paid, in particular by sporting organisations, to the education and vocational training of top young sportsmen and -women, in order that their vocational integration is not jeopardised because of their sporting careers, to their psychological balance and family ties and to their health, in particular the prevention of doping. It appreciates the contribution of associations and organisations which minister to these requirements in their training work and thus make a valuable contribution socially.

13. The European Council expresses concern about commercial transactions targeting minors in sport, including those from third countries, inasmuch as they do not comply with existing labour legislation or endanger the health and welfare of young sportsmen and -women. It calls on sporting organisations and the Member States to investigate and monitor such practices and, where necessary, to consider appropriate measures.

Economic context of sport and solidarity

14. In the view of the European Council, single ownership or financial control of more than one sports club entering the same competition in the same sport may jeopardise fair competition.

Where necessary, sports federations are encouraged to introduce arrangements for overseeing the management of clubs.

15. The sale of television broadcasting rights is one of the greatest sources of income today for certain sports. The European Council thinks that moves to encourage the mutualisation of part of the revenue from such sales, at the appropriate levels, are beneficial to the principle of solidarity between all levels and areas of sport.

Transfers

16. The European Council is keenly supportive of dialogue on the transfer system between the sports movement, in particular the football authorities, organisations representing professional sportsmen and women, the Community and the Member States, with due regard for the specific requirements of sport, subject to compliance with Community law.

17. The Community institutions and the Member States are requested to continue examining their policies, in compliance with the Treaty and in accordance with their respective powers, in the light of these general principles.[45]

This declaration is significant in that it begins to develop greater detail and gives a more clear indication of the areas in which legal and regulatory developments are likely to be focused. Indeed, this has proven to be an accurate forerunner of subsequent action in the field. As noted below, the declaration has been seen as a model to which to aspire in the most recent developments in this field.

Free movement principles and the Court of Justice after *Bosman*

Bosman's success in bringing European Union law to bear on professional sport encouraged other athletes and sports organisations to follow suit. Thus the Court of Justice delivered two judgments in the space of three days in April 2000 which further developed the jurisprudence of the Court having regard to the application of free movement principles to sport.

Deliège v Ligue Francophone de Judo et Disciplines Associees ASBL

In Deliège[46] – again brought on the basis of the free movement elements of the Treaty – the ECJ wrestled with the division between sporting and economic rules and regulations. Deliège had fallen into dispute with her federation and was not selected to participate in tournaments that would have allowed her the opportunity to qualify to participate in the Atlanta Olympic Games. Deliège argued that her performance and ability made her suitable for selection but that the federation had acted in bad faith because of her disputes with it. The federation maintained that decisions were taken on the basis of ability and taking account of Deliège's repeated infringement of disciplinary measures. Deliège therefore brought two separate actions in a Belgian court: first a claim against the Belgian judo federations seeking to mandate them to allow her participation in a competition in Paris; and second a claim against the same seeking a ruling that the method of selecting participants for international tournaments was unlawful as being in breach of Community Law. Thus the Tribunal de Première Instance in Namur made two separate references to the Court of Justice in the following terms:

> Whether or not rules requiring professional or semi-professional sportsmen or persons aspiring to such status to have been authorised or selected by their national federation in order

---

45 'Declaration on the specific characteristics of sport and its social function in Europe', Presidency Conclusions, Nice European Council Meeting, 7–9 December 2000; found at http://ec.europa.eu/sport/information-center/doc/timeline/doc244_en.pdf.
46 Cases C-51/96 and C-191/97, [2000] ECR I-2549.

to be able to compete in an international competition and laying down national entry quotas for similar competitions are contrary to the Treaty of Rome, in particular Articles 59 to 66 and Articles 85 and 86.

Whether or not it is contrary to the Treaty of Rome, in particular Articles 59, 85 and 86 of the Treaty, to require professional or semi-professional athletes or persons aspiring to professional or semi-professional activity to be authorised by their federation in order to be able to compete in an international competition which does not involve national teams competing against each other.

The Court of Justice was required to consider the preliminary matter of the applicability of Community law in the instant case. Deliège was essentially an amateur, though seeking to participate at the highest level, and the question arose as to whether she satisfied the well-established criterion that sport was only subject to scrutiny under Community law in as much as it constituted an economic activity. It was argued by the judo federations that as an amateur Deliège fell outwith the scope of the Treaty. Both Advocate-General Cosmas and the Court of Justice considered that Deliège did fall to be considered in the context of the Treaty's free movement provisions because she was able to adduce evidence that she obtained grants on the basis of results and this was also linked to sponsorship. Additionally, A-G Cosmas and the Court of Justice both saw that, while Deliège was not in receipt of direct payment for participation, the events in which she competed were commercial operations, attracting sponsorship and broadcasting monies, and that this too gave the situation an economic character and thus made it apt for consideration under Community law. This can be seen as a broadening of the scope of the applicability of the Treaty, beyond the obvious context of employed professional or semi-professional sports persons or those in receipt of direct payment in respect of their services. However, the Court of Justice was ready to concede that there would necessarily be restrictions on the numbers of participants in tournaments.

Cases C-51/96 and C191/97 *Deliège v Ligue Francophone de Judo et Disciplines Associées ASBL*

67. It naturally falls to the bodies concerned, such as organisers of tournaments, sports federations or professional athletes' associations, to lay down appropriate rules and to make their selections in accordance with them.

69. [A] rule requiring professional or semi-professional athletes or persons aspiring to take part in a professional or semi-professional activity to have been authorised or selected by their federation in order to be able to participate in a high-level international sports competition, which does not involve international teams competing against each other, does not in itself, as long as it derives from a need inherent in the organisation of such a competition, constitute a restriction on the freedom to provide services prohibited by Article 59 of the Treaty.[47]

In determining that such selection rules were not in contravention of Article 59 EC the Court of Justice gave specific mention to the Amsterdam Declaration on Sport, interestingly noting its consistency with the previous case law of the Court. What is particularly notable is the basis upon which the Court reached this determination. The Advocate-General held the view that Community law, and Article 59 EEC specifically, did not apply to the selection rules because they were inherent in the particular nature or context of the events. However, A-G Cosmas did offer an alternative possibility, noting that, as in *Bosman*, if the measures were not excluded from consideration they could, nonetheless, be justified as being an objective response to an overriding need in the public

---

47 [2002] ECR I-2549

interest. Indeed the Advocate-General took the view that were this to be applied in Deliège's case the result would also be in the federations' favour. As can be seen from the excerpt above, the Court shared A-G Cosmas' view that the inherent nature of the rules meant that it was not a restriction on the right to provide services to fall for consideration under the terms of Article 59 EEC. Thus the Court placed the rules in the same category as those highlighted in the previous case law relating to restrictions pertaining to national teams – what has become termed as the 'sporting exception'.[48] This distinction has become highly significant in subsequent case law.

Jyri Lehtonen & Castors Canada Dry Namur-Braine v Fédération Royale Belge des Sociétés de Basketball ASBL

Similarly in the case of *Lehtonen*,[49] again a case taken on the basis of free movement rules, a Finnish basketball player sought to challenge transfer rules imposed by the Belgian Basketball Federation, which prevented clubs from fielding players signed after a set deadline each season. Moreover, the date at which players coming from different geographic 'zones', defined by the International Basketball Federation (FIBA), differed so that the deadline for players from the European zone was approximately one month prior to that for players coming from outside of that zone. Lehtonen and his club Castors Namur-Braine brought an action before a court in Belgium after the Belgian federation penalised the club for fielding Lehtonen in two matches even though he had been registered after the relevant deadline. The Tribunal de Première Instance in Brussels thus referred a question of Community law to the Court of Justice:

> Are the rules of a sports federation which prohibit a club from playing a player in the competition for the first time if he has been engaged after a specified date contrary to the Treaty of Rome (in particular Articles 6, 48, 85 and 86) in the case of a professional player who is a national of a Member State of the European Union, notwithstanding the sporting reasons put forward by the federations to justify those rules, namely the need to prevent distortion of the competitions?

There was no suggestion that the case involved discrimination on the grounds of nationality as between nationals of Member States, and thus the question again was one of the application of Article 48 EC in respect of an obstacle to free movement of workers, as an effective ban on movement undoubtedly was. Advocate-General Alber was critical of the 'phased' nature of the deadlines, doubting any substantial link with any sporting justification such as comparability of results or competitive balance in the form exhibited in this case. In particular the phasing of deadlines contingent upon geographic origin was regarded as being wholly unjustified. However, A-G Alber did conclude:

Case C-176/96, Jyri Lehtonen & Castors Canada Dry Namur-Braine v Fédération Royale Belge des Sociétés de Basketball ASBL [2000] ECR I-2681

> Delayed transfer deadlines may be reasonable if they are not set arbitrarily. A transfer deadline may thus be justified on sporting grounds in the public interest if the deadline for sportsmen who have previously played for clubs in other Member States is chosen in such a way that comparability of the results of that competition is not affected by the transfers which take place before the deadline. . .

---

48 On the limited facts set out by the referring court, the Court of Justice was not able to assess the compatibility of the rules with competition law. On the point of sporting exception see Papaloukas, M, 'The Sporting Exemption Principle in the European Court of Justice's Case Law' (2009) 3-4 ISLJ 7.

49 Case C-176/96, [2000] ECR I-2681.

> A transfer period can therefore be justified on sporting grounds in the public interest only if the period is no shorter for players who previously played for clubs in other Member States than for players who previously played in third countries.[50]

Thus, transfer deadlines and transfer windows are not in themselves wholly objectionable, but may be justified if demonstrated as necessary to secure a legitimate sporting (or economic) objective.

It is implicit in the opinion delivered by A-G Alber that these transfer deadlines were not 'inherent' in the nature of the sporting activity and that it fell to be considered as to whether they were objectively justified by an overriding need in the public interest. They were similarly regarded by the Court of Justice, which noted the capacity for the scope of the Treaty to be restricted but did not engage in analysis of this point, simply stating the existence of an obstacle to the free movement of workers and the consequent pertinence of Article 48 EC to this case. The Court then considered the objective justification of the rules as a means of ensuring the regularity of competition:

53. On this point, it must be acknowledged that the setting of deadlines for transfers of players may meet the objective of ensuring the regularity of sporting competitions.

54. Late transfers might be liable to change substantially the sporting strength of one or other team in the course of the championship, thus calling into question the comparability of results between the teams taking part in that championship, and consequently the proper functioning of the championship as a whole.

55. The risk of that happening is especially clear in the case of a sporting competition which follows the rules of the Belgian first division national basketball championship. The teams taking part in the play-offs for the title or for relegation could benefit from late transfers to strengthen their squads for the final stage of the championship, or even for a single decisive match.

56. However, measures taken by sports federations with a view to ensuring the proper functioning of competitions may not go beyond what is necessary for achieving the aim pursued (see *Bosman*, paragraph 104).

57. In the main proceedings, it appears from the rules on transfer periods that players from a federation outside the European zone are subject to a deadline of 31 March rather than 28 February, which applies only to players from federations in the European zone, which includes the federations of the Member States.

58. At first sight, such a rule must be regarded as going beyond what is necessary to achieve the aim pursued. It does not appear from the material in the case-file that a transfer between 28 February and 31 March of a player from a federation in the European zone jeopardises the regularity of the championship more than a transfer in that period of a player from a federation not in that zone.

59. However, it is for the national court to ascertain the extent to which objective reasons, concerning only sport as such or relating to differences between the position of players from a federation in the European zone and that of players from a federation not in that zone, justify such different treatment.

60. In the light of all the foregoing, the answer to the national court's question, as reformulated, must be that Article 48 of the Treaty precludes the application of rules laid down in a Member

---

50 Ibid.

State by sporting associations which prohibit a basketball club from fielding players from other Member States in matches in the national championship, where they have been transferred after a specified date, if that date is earlier than the date which applies to transfers of players from certain non-member countries, unless objective reasons concerning only sport as such or relating to differences between the position of players from a federation in the European zone and that of players from a federation not in that zone justify such different treatment.[51]

The comparisons between *Lehtonen* and *Deliège* are striking. While both appear to validate restrictions aimed at legitimate sporting objectives[52] – the regularity and sustainability of competition respectively – this is achieved in different ways: in the case of *Deliège* by recognising the inherent sporting nature of the restrictions and exempting them from scrutiny under the Treaty; and in the case of *Lehtonen* by considering the measures under Article 48 EC and determining them to have the potential to be objectively justified. What, on the face of it, seem to be similar restrictions are treated rather differently, though the proximity of the issue in *Deliège* to matters of international teams first identified in *Walrave* may be regarded as the crucial factor. Nonetheless, the Court of Justice seems to have adopted a generous approach in restricting the scope of application of the Treaty in *Deliège*. More broadly, both cases made mention of the Amsterdam Declaration on Sport, and can be seen as representing, if not a softening, a more sympathetic approach, following to some extent the wishes of the Member States.

Broadening *Bosman*: *Kolpak* and *Simutenkov*

Beyond the application to different aspects of different sports within the EU, elements of the *Bosman* judgment have also had their geographical coverage extended by the Court of Justice in two cases concerning association agreements between the EU and third countries.

In *Deutscher Handballbund eV v Kolpak*[53] a Slovakian handball player, Maros Kolpak, had been employed as a professional handball player in the German Second Division. The Deutscher Handballbund (DHB) organises and regulates the national handball competitions and had issued Kolpak with a player's licence marked with an 'A'. This signified that Kolpak was considered a non-EU national, of whom clubs were limited to fielding two in any given match. Kolpak requested that the DHB remove the 'A' marking, and upon having his request refused he brought an action challenging the decision before a Regional Court in Dortmund. At first instance Kolpak was successful in his claim, but the DHB subsequently appealed to the *Oberlandsgericht*, which made a request for a preliminary reference to the Court of Justice. The issue for resolution by the Court was whether a Slovak national, once in lawful employment, enjoyed the right to non-discrimination on the basis of nationality as regards the terms of his employment. It was argued that this, extended to the treatment of Kolpak as a non-EU player for the purposes of limiting the number of foreign players, was contrary to the terms of the Association Agreement. The Court of Justice ruled, first that the Association agreement was capable of direct effect and could therefore be applied by the German court and, second, that the rules were in breach of the terms of the Association Agreement by placing Kolpak in a category whose participation, once in employment, was effectively limited.

The Court of Justice reached a similar decision in the later case of *Simutenkov v Ministerio de Educación y Cultura*.[54] In that case the same question arose in respect of a Russian professional footballer who played for Tenerife in the Spanish league. Simutenkov was classed as a non-Community national and

---

51 Both A-G Alber and the Court of Justice regarded the elements of the question relating to competition law as being inadmissible.
52 See Bell, A and Turner-Kerr, P, 'The Place of Sport Within the Rules of Community Law: Clarification from the ECJ? The Deliege and Lehtonen Cases' (2002) 23(5) ECLR 256, 260.
53 Case C-438/00, [2003] ECR I-4135.
54 Case C-265/03, [2005] ECR I-2579.

thus subject to limitations as to the number of such players that could be fielded in any one game. The issue was of a slightly different character than that in *Kolpak* as the instrument in question was a Partnership Agreement between the EU and Russia intended to further co-operation across wider Europe and with, unlike in *Kolpak*, no view to association or accession to the EU. Nonetheless, the provision of the relevant parts of the agreements were near identical and the Court of Justice took the view that the measure satisfied the conditions for direct effect and could thus be applied by the Spanish court. Further, and consistent with its ruling in *Kolpak*, the Court of Justice held that the Partnership Agreement with Russia must be construed such that it prohibited nationality-based discrimination against Russian nationals, once in employment, of the type imposed by the rules restricting numbers of non-EU nationals adopted by the Spanish Football Federation.

Taken in concert with the settlement made to end the *Balog* litigation, these cases broaden the ambit of elements of the *Bosman* principles: first, the capacity to leave one club and sign for another without the payment of a fee at the conclusion of a contractual term became applicable to all professional footballers – not just EU nationals; and second, players able to take advantage of the terms of an Association or Partnership agreement were able to benefit from the inapplicability of 'foreign-player' quotas to them, once employed. This does not mean that these players benefit from the full terms of the *Bosman* judgment; their capacity to move between Member States to seek and take up employment remains subject to relevant national law. Nonetheless, given the significant number and scope of these types of agreements they must be regarded as significant.[55]

Back to the future: training compensation and the return of quotas

In the more recent past the application of EU free movement provisions has led to consideration not simply of measures which might be considered obviously unlawful, but also to more detailed analysis of restrictive measures which may, nonetheless, be considered to be legitimate. This has arisen in a case before the Court of Justice and in the context of new regulations proposed by both FIFA and UEFA.

Quotas in professional football: '6+5' v home-grown players

Following the period of heavy re-regulation of rules relating to professional players, the football authorities have made attempts to re-establish mechanisms by which the eligibility of players to participate in matches is limited, contingent on their possessing particular characteristics. The most controversial of these has been the '6+5' rule proposed by FIFA, under the terms of which club sides would be required to field six players eligible to play for the national team of the association of which the club is based at the start of each match. The proposal was ultimately withdrawn following clear indications being given that such a measure would be considered to be directly discriminatory on the grounds of nationality and thus contrary to EU free movement provisions, Commissioners Figel and Špidla issuing a joint statement:

> We understand and sympathise with FIFA's – and others' – concerns to bring more balance to the game of football. We just differ about the means to achieve it. Our position is clear: FIFA's '6+5' Rule is based on direct discrimination on the grounds of nationality, and is thus

---

55 On which point see Branco-Martins, R, 'The *Kolpak* Case: *Bosman* Times Ten? Football fears the arrival of Bosman, Bosmanovic and Osman' in Gardiner, S, Parrish, R, and Siekmann, R (eds), *EU, Sport, Law and Policy: Regulation: Re-regulation and Representation* (2009), The Hague: TMC Asser Press; Boyes, S, 'The Bosman/Kolpak Effect: Has Sport Got it Wrong?' (2005) 13(2) SATLJ 33; Branco-Martins, R, 'The *Kolpak* case: Bosman times 10?' (2004) 1–2 ISLJ 26; van den Bogaert, S, 'And Another Uppercut from the European Court of Justice to Nationality Requirements in Sports Regulations' (2004) 29(2) EL Rev 267; Boyes, S, 'In the Shadow of Bosman: The Regulatory Penumbra of Sport in the EU' (2003) 12(2) Nott LJ 72; Boyes, S, 'Caught Behind or Following-On? Cricket, the European Union and the "Bosman Effect",' (2005) 3(1) ESLJ (online). For an earlier case determined in similar terms without reference to the Court of Justice see *Malaja v French Basketball Federation* (2000), Court Administrative d'Appel de Nancy, 3 February.

against one of the fundamental principles of EU law . . . [W]e in the European Commission remain open to discuss ways and means of bringing more balance to the game of football together with FIFA and other interested parties to find a solution that would be compatible with EU law.[56]

FIFA ultimately withdrew the proposal in the face of this clear opposition.[57]

However, an alternative proposal by UEFA met with less direct opposition and has been adopted for UEFA club competitions and by a number of European leagues. Under the terms of UEFA's 'Home-Grown Player' rule, clubs are limited to selecting their team from an 'A' squad of 25 players, plus an unlimited number of under-21 players having been at the club for at least two seasons – the 'B' squad. The 'A' squad must include a minimum of four players who satisfy the requirement of being 'association-trained' – that is having been registered with the club or another club in the same national association for a minimum of three seasons between the ages of 15 and 21 – and at least four 'club-trained' players – having been registered with the club under the same terms. The measure is intended to encourage clubs to develop and train young players – an objective regarded as legitimate under EU free movement law – and has been given a qualified welcome by the EU institutions. The principal objection to the rule under EU free movement provisions is that it indirectly discriminates in that it is more likely that 'home' nationals will be able to satisfy the 'home-grown' criteria and thus that it will impose an obstacle to the capacity of professional footballers who are nationals of other Member States to move between clubs in different Member States. Nonetheless, as an indirectly discriminatory measure the rule can be regarded as lawful if the restrictions are proportionate to the legitimate objective pursued.[58] For the present, at least, it is the case that the rules are regarded as meeting this requirement,[59] though the rule is likely to be subject to review in 2012.[60]

Compensation for the Training and Development of Young Players: *Lyon v Bernard*

Recent litigation has also required the Court of Justice to exercise more close scrutiny over the detail of compensation for the training and development of young players. Since *Bosman* it has remained possible for football clubs to obtain financial compensation for out of contract players up to the age of 24 years.[61] This compensation is paid in recognition of the financial outlay undertaken by the club(s) in developing the player. There is also a redistributive solidarity mechanism that ensures that clubs receive a share of any monies paid, recognising their role in developing the player from the age of 12.

In *Bernard*[62] the Court of Justice considered a rule of the French Professional Football Charter that required a youth player having been trained and developed by a particular club to either sign

56 Statement of 28 November 2008, http://ec.europa.eu/social/main.jsp?langId=en&catId=89&newsId=424&furtherNews=yes; see also INI/2007/2261 European Parliament non-legislative resolution, 8 May 2008; cf INEA, *Expert Opinion on the Compatibility of the '6+5 Rule' with European Community Law* (2008), Düsseldorf: INEA, available from http://inea-online.com/download/regel/gutachten_eng.pdf.

57 'Fifa scraps plans for "home-grown" player rule' (2010), BBC News, 10 June, http://news.bbc.co.uk/sport1/hi/football/8733164.stm.

58 For an excellent analysis of the legal issues pertaining to the rule see, Parrish, R and Miettinen, S, 'Nationality Discrimination in Community Law: An Assessment of UEFA Regulations governing Player Eligibility for European Club Competitions (The Home-Grown Player Rule)' (2007) 5 ESLJ (online); see also Freeburn, L, 'European Football's Home-Grown Players Rule and Nationality Discrimination under the European Community Treaty' (2009–10) 20 Marq Sports L Rev 177; McDermott, JJ, 'Direct v Indirect Discrimination in European Football: The Legal Differences Between UEFA's Homegrown Player Rule and FIFA's "6+5" proposal' (2009–10) 11 Tex Rev Ent & Sports L 267; Conzelmann, R, 'Models for the Promotion of Home Grown Players for the Promotion of National Teams' in Gardiner, S, Parrish, R and Siekmann, R (eds), *EU, Sport, Law and Policy: Regulation, Re-regulation and Representation* (2009), The Hague: TMC Asser Press; *Study on the Treatment of Non-Nationals in Individual Sports Competitions*, Commissioned by the European Commission, Directorate-General for Education and Culture (2010), http://ec.europa.eu/sport/library/doc/f_studies/study_equal_treatment_non_nationals_final_rpt%20_dec_2010.pdf.

59 See 'UEFA rule on "home-grown players": compatibility with the principle of free movement of persons' (2008) IP/08/807 28 May 2008; *Complementary study on training of young sportsmen/women in Europe*, http://ec.europa.eu/sport/pdf/doc272_en.pdf.

60 See later, Chapter 10, pp 485–96 for full discussion on playing quotas.

61 Article 20 and Annexe 4 *FIFA Regulations for the Status and Transfer of Players* (2010).

62 Case C-325/08 *Olympique Lyonnais SASP v Olivier Bernard and Newcastle United*.

his first professional contract with that club or be liable in damages should the player sign for another club side. The player in question – Olivier Bernard – having been trained by Lyon, chose to sign for Newcastle United. Lyon then brought proceedings claiming damages under the terms of the Charter. Lyon were successful at first instance, with the decision being reversed on appeal on the basis that the rule constituted a breach of EU free movement provisions, as being an impediment or disincentive to move between Member States. Lyon made a subsequent appeal and the Cour de Cassation sought clarification from the Court of Justice:

Case C-325/08 *Olympique Lyonnais SASP v Olivier Bernard and Newcastle United*

(1) Does the principle of the freedom of movement for workers laid down in Article 39 EC preclude a provision of national law pursuant to which a 'joueur espoir' who at the end of his training period signs a professional player's contract with a club of another Member State of the European Union may be ordered to pay damages?

(2) If so, does the need to encourage the recruitment and training of young professional players constitute a legitimate objective or an overriding reason in the general interest capable of justifying such a restriction?'[63]

Thus the Court of Justice was asked to assess the legitimacy of the compensation rule. Both Advocate-General Sharpston in her opinion and the Court in its judgment were satisfied that it is now well settled that measures discouraging free movement between Member States, such as the payment of compensation for training in this case, constitute an obstacle to free movement of workers and thus are, in principle, unlawful. However, both saw the objective of the development of young players as legitimate and that clubs may be disincentivised from training players where there was a danger that such investment would not be protected. Thus, the limitation imposed in this case had the potential to be considered justifiable. However, on the particular facts of this case, Lyon sought compensation based upon the annual salary that the player would have received under the terms of the contract offered to him. The Advocate-General and the Court both took the view that this was not legitimate. Instead, any compensation had to be based upon the actual costs incurred by the club in the training of the player. The level of compensation payable would depend upon whether it was to be paid by the player or his new club. The player could only be regarded as being liable for the costs incurred in respect of his particular training. The club, however, could legitimately be required to compensate the cost of producing one professional player, the Court recognising that though many young players may enter training and development of this kind only a few would be successful in securing a career as a professional footballer. Thus the new club could legitimately be required to meet the costs of training in the production of one player.

Bernard is an excellent example of the potential for sports regulators to operate effectively within the bounds of EU law while still meeting their objectives, and of the willingness of the Court to give effect to the legitimate justifications for the imposition of restrictions set out in the previous case law.

Conclusions: sport and the free movement of persons

The law relating to free movement of workers and the provision of services is particularly significant as being the effective gateway to sport for EU law. It is in the Court of Justice in these cases that the key principles that now govern the relationship between sport and the EU have emerged. These developments are important because, first, they establish the applicability of EU law to sports rules and regulations of an economic nature and, second, they found and extend the principles that are

---

63 Ibid, at para 16.

at the core of EU law's relationship with sport: discrimination based on nationality is unlawful, save in the narrow context of national teams; but legitimate sporting objectives are recognised by the law and proportionate restrictions which indirectly discriminate or impose an obstacle to free movement in pursuit of such will not be condemned.

The Applicability of EU Competition Law to Sport

Though the early work of the Court of Justice in the field of sport was related to the application of free movement of persons law, it is becoming increasingly clear that competition law has now become the most significant aspect of EU law germane to the sporting context. Competition law offers greater scope for potential litigants to challenge restrictive measures than the free movement provisions as it is not limited to the provision of services or employment situations and has the capacity to capture restrictions beyond those based on nationality or creating an obstacle to free-movement for individuals. Through *Bosman* and the cases which followed the Court of Justice did not take up the opportunity to consider the application of competition law to sport, because the question was considered either inadmissible (*Deliège, Lehtonen*) or immaterial in light of the application of free movement of persons provisions (*Bosman*). However, more recent judgments of the EU Courts and the activity of the Commission in this area highlight the immediate and growing importance of this area of law to sport.

The major components of EU competition law relevant to sport are Article 101 and Article 102 TFEU. These articles deal with anti-competitive, cartel-type agreements, and abuse of a dominant position in the relevant market respectively. It is noteworthy that the approach of the UK's Competition Act 1998 is almost identical, the principal difference being the geographic nature of the effect on competition; while the Competition Act 1998 is concerned with wholly internal matters, not impacting on trade between Member States, the EU measures are concerned only with matters that do have an impact in the internal market.[64]

The applicability of Article 101 TFEU to sport

Article 101 TFEU is broken into three parts: paragraph 1 sets out the conditions for a prohibition to arise; paragraph 2 renders agreements and similar falling within paragraph 1 as being void; but, paragraph 3 sets out the criteria by which paragraph 1 prohibitions may be exempted:

Article 101 TFEU

1. The following shall be prohibited as incompatible with the internal market: all agreements between undertakings, decisions by associations of undertakings and concerted practices which may affect trade between Member States and which have as their object or effect the prevention, restriction or distortion of competition within the internal market, and in particular those which:
    (a) directly or indirectly fix purchase or selling prices or any other trading conditions;
    (b) limit or control production, markets, technical development, or investment;
    (c) share markets or sources of supply;
    (d) apply dissimilar conditions to equivalent transactions with other trading parties, thereby placing them at a competitive disadvantage;

---

64 See generally, Weatherill, S, 'Sport under EC Competition and US Antitrust Law' in *European Sports Law: Collected Papers* (2007), The Hague: TMC Asser Press.

(e)   make the conclusion of contracts subject to acceptance by the other parties of supplementary obligations which, by their nature or according to commercial usage, have no connection with the subject of such contracts.

2.   Any agreements or decisions prohibited pursuant to this Article shall be automatically void.

3.   The provisions of paragraph 1 may, however, be declared inapplicable in the case of:
   ● any agreement or category of agreements between undertakings,
   ● any decision or category of decisions by associations of undertakings,
   ● any concerted practice or category of concerted practices,

which contributes to improving the production or distribution of goods or to promoting technical or economic progress, while allowing consumers a fair share of the resulting benefit, and which does not:
   (a)   impose on the undertakings concerned restrictions which are not indispensable to the attainment of these objectives;
   (b)   afford such undertakings the possibility of eliminating competition in respect of a substantial part of the products in question.

Undertakings and associations of undertakings in sport

In order to fall within the terms of Article 101 TFEU paragraph 1 the parties concerned must be considered as undertakings or an association of undertakings. The concept of 'undertaking' has been cast broadly by the Court of Justice to encompass any natural or legal person engaged in economic or commercial activity in the provision of goods or services. It is not necessary that such activities should be in pursuit of profit.[65] Thus in *Bosman* A-G Lenz was of the plain view that professional sports clubs fell within this meaning, irrespective of their size and even taking into account that they may operate on a not-for-profit basis. The Advocate-General was similarly unequivocal as regards the classification of individual football federations as being associations of undertakings for the purpose of Article 101(1) because of the membership by professional clubs – irrespective of the fact that they also included large numbers of amateur clubs. This view has been affirmed subsequently by the Court of First Instance in *Piau v Commission*.[66] Further, A-G Lenz considered that sports federations could also be considered to be single undertakings, dependent upon the activity being undertaken, and pointed out that the Commission had already treated FIFA as such in determining a competition issue related to the sale of tickets for the Italia '90 football World Cup tournament.[67] Thus the characterisation of a governing body for the purposes of competition law will not be wholly contingent on its particular characteristics, but also by reference to the nature of the activity that it is involved in.

Agreements between undertakings and decisions of associations of undertakings in sport

The classification of sports rules as an agreement between undertakings was also easily satisfied in the opinion of A-G Lenz in *Bosman* – it had been argued that the transfer rules were not an agreement as such, but that they merely represented the collective will of the clubs. A-G Lenz was unimpressed by this reasoning but took the view that, in any case, such an informal agreement would still fall to be considered under the terms of Article 85 EC (now Article 101 TFEU). This is consistent with the more general case law of the Court in this respect, which has seen the concept capture even the

---

65   Case C-41/90 *Höffner and Elser* [1993] I ECR 1979.
66   Case T-193/02, [2005] ECR II-209.
67   Commission Decision of 27 October 1992, Cases 33384 and 33378, *Distribution of Package Tours During the 1990 World Cup* [1992] OJ L326/31.

most informal of agreements which need not have any legally binding element.[68] Similarly, decisions of undertakings need not be binding and can encompass non-compulsory codes of conduct or recommendations by such organisations.[69] The overt nature of sports regulations and commercial agreements mean that it is relatively straightforward to reconcile them with the criteria relating to agreements or decisions of undertakings. Any rules and regulations are inevitably 'visible' and often in the public domain, and commercial agreements tend to be high profile by their very nature. As noted above, governing bodies have the capacity to act as a single undertaking or as an association of undertakings and thus whether their role is of an undertaking engaging in an agreement or as having the character of a decision will depend upon a number of factors. If the matter concerns a regulation or rule, the means by which that measure came into existence will be material. If it was the direct result of an agreement between the body and, for example, professional clubs, competition organisers and individual participants, that would be likely to be characterised as an agreement; whereas if the rule were promulgated by a sports federation under authority granted to it by its members, then this would likely fall into the category of a decision of association of undertakings. Because of the public and documentary nature of the arrangements, they are unlikely to require consideration under the catch-all category of 'concerted practice'.

Effect on trade between Member States

Whether an agreement between undertakings or a decision of an association, such measures must also satisfy the condition of having an effect on trade between Member States. Again this has been broadly cast by the Court, the test being that, 'on the basis of objective legal or factual criteria, [the measure] allows one to expect that it will exercise a direct or indirect, potential or actual effect on the flow of trade between member states.'[70] In *Bosman*, A-G Lenz had little difficulty perceiving this to be the case, particularly given that players already moved between Member States and had demonstrated a growing desire to continue to do so.

Object or effect the restriction of competition in sport

It is well established that these two elements – object and effect – are alternatives, not cumulative. Thus it is sufficient either to demonstrate that the object of the measure is the restriction of competition and is not necessary to evidence the effect or, if it is not possible to substantiate the objective, then an anti-competitive effect will be sufficient in itself.[71] Article 101 TFEU lists measures which are likely to be considered in this light, but this is not exhaustive. In *Bosman*, A-G Lenz saw that the foreign players rule restricted clubs from competing with each other by engaging players, supporting the Commission's view that this amounted to a sharing of a source of supply – listed under Article 101 TFEU. The Advocate-General took a similar view of the requirement that a fee be paid for a player whose contract had expired, again supporting the Commission in its view that the rules replaced the normal system of supply and demand with 'uniform machinery', preserving the competitive environment and limiting the capacity of clubs to acquire the services of players. Of further significance A-G Lenz observed that 'it is quite obvious that the restriction of competition is not only the effect of the rules in question, but was also intended by the clubs and associations'.[72] A-G Lenz was prepared to consider the 'rule of reason' approach put forward by UEFA – the argument that a measure cannot properly be regarded as anti-competitive where a restriction is imposed as a necessary means to facilitate competition in the first place. However, he remained unconvinced that the rules challenged were 'necessary and indispensable' as required.

---

68 See eg Case 41/69, *ACF Chemiefarma v Commission* [1970] ECR 661.
69 Case 32/78, *BMW Belgium v Commission* [1979] ECR 2435 cf Case C-74/04 P, *Commission v Volkswagen AG* [2006] ECR I-06585.
70 Case 56/65, *Société Technique Miniere v Maschinbau Ulm* [1966] ECR 235.
71 Ibid.
72 At para 262.

Exemptions under Article 101(3) TFEU

Should a measure meet the criteria set out in paragraph 1 of Article 101 TFEU, it is automatically void under the terms of paragraph 2. Nonetheless, measures may be made exempt from this if it can be demonstrated that the restrictions are objectively justified as creating beneficial outcomes. Exemptions are subject to the satisfaction of four conditions set out in Article 101(3) TFEU: first, that they effect some kind of improvement or progression; second, that the benefit should be shared by consumers in the broadest sense of the word; third, that the restriction is proportionate and limited to that indispensable for the achievement of the aim; and fourth, that it does not allow the possibility of limiting competition in a large part of the market. In his Opinion in *Bosman*, A-G Lenz did not dwell on the point, noting that exemptions could only be granted by the Commission; but whilst admitting that it was theoretically possible that the Commission could exempt the rules, the Advocate-General noted their incompatibility with free movement of workers provisions and argued that a uniform result would be desirable. The application of these to sport is, of course, highly contingent upon context and the application in different sporting aspects is considered in the round below.

The applicability of Article 102 TFEU to sport

As with Article 101 TFEU, Article 102 TFEU consists of three elements for a breach to be established: first, that an undertaking or group of undertakings has a dominant position within the Union or part of it; second, that the dominant position is abused; and third, that the abuse is capable of affecting trade between Member States.

Article 102 TFEU

Any abuse by one or more undertakings of a dominant position within the internal market or in a substantial part of it shall be prohibited as incompatible with the internal market in so far as it may affect trade between Member States.

Such abuse may, in particular, consist in:

(a) directly or indirectly imposing unfair purchase or selling prices or other unfair trading conditions;

(b) limiting production, markets or technical development to the prejudice of consumers;

(c) applying dissimilar conditions to equivalent transactions with other trading parties, thereby placing them at a competitive disadvantage;

(d) making the conclusion of contracts subject to acceptance by the other parties of supplementary obligations which, by their nature or according to commercial usage, have no connection with the subject of such contracts.

Dominant position

The classic exposition of the definition of dominant position comes from the Court of Justice judgment in *United Brands v Commission*:[73]

[A] position of economic strength enjoyed by an undertaking which enables it to prevent effective competition from being maintained in the relevant market by giving it the power to behave to an appreciable extent independently of its competitors, customers and ultimately of its consumers.

---

73 Case 27/76, [1978] ECR 207.

Central to the question of dominance is the concept of the relevant market. Market definition is a key factor in establishing whether or not an undertaking reaches the threshold. The more broadly it is defined, the more likely that an undertaking will be dominant. The methodology of market definition that has usually been adopted in EU competition law is demand-side substitutability – to what extent will consumers of the product in question accept a substitute? A good example of this in the sporting context is in the case of *Hendry v World Professional Billiards and Snooker Association*,[74] where a number of professional snooker players sought to challenge the legality of the Association's rule on the sanctioning of tournaments, the players' ranking system, logos and advertising, and players' promotional activities and media appearances. The players sought to argue that the WPBSA, as the sole regulator of professional snooker, was in a dominant position between professional snooker players and promoters of snooker tournaments. However, the relevant market might have been cast more widely, as a market in provision of ticketed sports events, a market in the provision of televised sport events or a market for sports events attracting sponsors and advertising. In the event Lloyd J found that the relevant market was relatively narrow as being that between professional snooker players and the promoters of snooker tournaments:

Hendry v World Professional Billiards and Snooker Association

The first criterion in deciding whether a particular suggested market is a relevant one for competition law purposes is as to demand substitutability: is there another product which is a close substitute in the eyes of purchasers for that which is the subject of the suggested market? As between snooker players and tournament promoters, there is clearly no substitute, as far as the players are concerned, for the services of promoters. As between broadcasters and promoters on the other hand, I am satisfied by the evidence that broadcasters do have close substitutes for snooker tournaments, namely other sporting events, even if I disregard, as not being a really close substitute, other entertainment material. It seems to me that the same is true of sponsors as well.[75]

It is noteworthy that the relevant market includes as a constituent part the geographic market as well as the product market. This means that in assessing dominance only the geographic area in which the conditions of competition are substantially similar is taken into account. In the sporting context this is likely to mean that few sports or events have a market that spreads across the whole of the EU, because they are not uniformly attractive to consumers. Thus the geographic market for Rugby Union within the EU may be limited to the UK, Ireland, France and Italy as being of little interest outside of that area. Similarly, the geographic market for Gaelic sports could be limited to the island of Ireland.

Once the market is established, the issue of dominance is assessed by reference to a variety of factors. Market share may be sufficient evidence of dominance in itself; a majority share could be a clear indication of dominance,[76] while a large, but minority, share in an otherwise fragmented market may indicate this also. In the context of sports governing bodies it may be relatively straightforward to establish dominance given the monopolistic nature of regulation of sport, but that also depends on how that monopoly is being exercised in a commercial context and whether it forms a barrier to entry. As well as market share the duration for which that share has been held, greater financial and technological resources than others in the market, vertical integration down the chain of production and the existence of barriers to entry such as high set-up costs or intellectual

---

74 [2002] ECC 8. See, generally, Veljanovski, C, 'Markets in Professional Sports: *Hendry v WPBSA* and the Importance of Functional Markets' (2002) 23(6) ECLR 273.
75 [2002] ECC 8, at para 88.
76 Case C-53/92 P, *Hilti v Commission* [1991] ECR I-667.

property rights can all indicate dominance. More contentiously, behaviour which appears to be abusive can in itself indicate dominance; the reasoning being that the undertaking would be unable to behave in this way if it were not in a dominant position. In *Hendry* Lloyd J applied the following analysis:

> WPBSA clearly has a high share in the market for the supply of players' services, whether as regards the number and significance of events or in terms of prize money. This of itself raises a presumption that the WPBSA has market power, and a dominant position in the relevant market. That conclusion may be shown to be wrong, for example if there are low barriers to entry. I can accept that WPBSA's existing contracts with broadcasters and sponsors do not amount to barriers to entry, and that the real problem [in respect of barriers to entry] is the WPBSA's regulatory role. I accept that in principle WPBSA is replaceable as regulator, though not quickly or easily . . . The question whether an undertaking has or has not got market power in relation to a particular identified market, or is in a dominant position in that market, is to be answered by looking at the entire context. Otherwise there is a risk of not seeing the wood for the trees. Given the special importance of the very high market share which WPBSA has, and in the light of the circumstances of the market overall . . . a conclusion that the WPBSA does not have market power nor a dominant position seems to me to defy common sense.[77]

Abuse of a dominant position

In common with Article 101 TFEU, Article 102 TFEU includes a non-exhaustive list outlining behaviour to be regarded as abusive where a dominant position exists; indeed there is a substantial overlap between the examples set out in both Articles. Thus the concept of abuse under Article 102 TFEU can be said to incorporate the concept of restriction of competition under Article 101.[78] However, abuse is not limited to this as it also extends to capture behaviour that is exploitative in nature; producing an advantage for the dominant undertaking at cost to the consumer, but without impacting on competition in, or the structure of, the market. Unlike Article 101 TFEU, Article 102 TFEU has no 'exemptions' element to it; instead the question of whether a measure adopted by a dominant undertaking is reasonable is wrapped up in the discussion of whether it constitutes an abuse. Thus the same sort of analysis as undertaken under paragraph 3 of Article 101 TFEU is applicable.

The Application of EU Competition Law to Sport

The application of EU competition law is best understood through an examination of the various cases that have arisen in the sporting context. These cases occur in a variety of different circumstances, but two broad categories can be drawn within which these fall. In the first category are cases where the restriction under consideration arises as a result of rules or regulations of the regulatory body or competition organiser which are closely linked to the performance of the sporting activity itself. Thus rules that impose restrictions or requirements in respect of the capacity of an athlete or a club to participate in competition, or the ability of an athlete to transfer between different clubs, and on clubs in relation to the release of players to participate in international competition, or in relation to the equipment that may be used in participating in the sport, may be considered as regulatory restrictions. There are some regulatory matters that overlap with more commercial considerations, such as the sanctioning by governing bodies of 'official' events; but

---

77 At para 98.
78 See Case C-250/92 *Gottrup Klim v DLG* [1994] ECR I-5461.

even thought these have some 'pure' commercial aspects, they remain within the regulatory category. In the second category are matters associated with the performance of a sport, but which are of a commercial rather than regulatory or sporting nature. Thus issues pertaining to sponsorship, endorsement, ticketing, merchandise and, most significantly, media rights will fall within this class.

EU competition law and sports regulation: the sporting exception revisited

Meca-Medina and Majcen v Commission in the Court of First Instance

The most significant competition case in respect of the regulatory functions of sports governing bodies is that of *Meca-Medina and Majcen v Commission*.[79] The case can perhaps be likened to *Bosman*, but in the context of competition law. Though the outcome of the case did not have the significant repercussions of *Bosman* it makes an important contribution to the development of the sports law jurisprudence in EU law because of the importance of the 'sporting exception'. In the narrower context of competition law it also offers a prime example of the issues encountered in weighing up the legality of restrictive regulations. The facts of the case were summarised by the Court of First Instance:

Case T-313/02, *Meca-Medina and Majcen v Commission*

7. The applicants are two professional athletes who compete in long-distance swimming, the aquatic equivalent of the marathon.

8. In an anti-doping test carried out on 31 January 1999 during the World Cup in that discipline at Salvador de Bahia (Brazil), where they had finished first and second respectively, the applicants tested positive for Nandrolone. The level found for Mr D. Meca-Medina was 9.7 ng/ml and that for Mr I. Majcen 3.9 ng/ml.

9. On 8 August 1999, FINA's Doping Panel suspended the applicants for a period of four years.

10. On the applicants' appeal, the CAS, by arbitration award of 29 February 2000, confirmed the suspension.

11. In January 2000, certain scientific experiments showed that Nandrolone's metabolites can be produced endogenously by the human body at a level which may exceed the accepted limit when certain foods, such as boar meat, have been consumed.

12. In view of that development, FINA and the applicants consented, by an arbitration agreement of 20 April 2000, to refer the case anew to the CAS for reconsideration.

13. By arbitration award of 23 May 2001, the CAS reduced the penalty to two years' suspension.

14. The applicants did not appeal against that award to the Swiss Federal Court.

15. By letter of 30 May 2001, the applicants filed a complaint with the Commission . . . alleging a breach of Article 81 EC and/or Article 82 EC.

16. In their complaint, the applicants challenged the compatibility of certain regulations adopted by the IOC and implemented by FINA and certain practices relating to doping control with the Community rules on competition and freedom to provide services. First of all, the fixing of the limit at 2 ng/ml is a concerted practice between the IOC and the 27 laboratories

---

79 Case T-313/02, *Meca-Medina and Majcen v Commission* [2004] ECR II-3291.

accredited by it. That limit is scientifically unfounded and can lead to the exclusion of innocent or merely negligent athletes. In the applicants' case, the excesses could have been the result of the consumption of a meal containing boar meat. Also, the IOC's adoption of a mechanism of strict liability and the establishment of tribunals responsible for the settlement of sports disputes by arbitration (the CAS and the ICAS) which are insufficiently independent of the IOC strengthens the anti-competitive nature of that limit.

17. According to that complaint, the application of those rules (hereinafter 'the anti-doping rules at issue') leads to the infringement of the athletes' economic freedoms, guaranteed *inter alia* by Article 49 EC and, from the point of view of competition law, to the infringement of the rights which the athletes can assert under Articles 81 EC and 82 EC.

18. By letter of 8 March 2002, the Commission informed the applicants . . . of the reasons for which it considered that the complaint should not be upheld.

19. By letter of 11 April 2002, the applicants sent the Commission their observations on the letter of 8 March 2002.

20. By decision of 1 August 2002 ('the disputed decision'), the Commission, after analysing the anti-doping rules at issue according to the assessment criteria of competition law and concluding that those rules did not fall foul of the prohibition under Articles 81 EC and 82 EC, rejected the applicants' complaint.[80]

Following the decision of the Commission not to uphold their complaint, Meca-Medina and Majcen sought annulment of the decision under Article 230 EC (now 263 TFEU) before the Court of First Instance (now the General Court). They did so on the grounds that the Commission had manifestly erred in fact and in law: in deciding that the International Olympic Committee was not an undertaking; in deciding that the restrictions imposed by the anti-doping rules was not a restriction of competition within the meaning of Article 81(1) EC (now Article 101(1) TFEU) as it was inherent in the organisation of sport and necessary and indispensable in achieving that objective; and in making the assessment that the complaint demonstrated no evidence upon which a breach of Article 49 EC (now Article 56 TFEU) could be based.

The Court of First Instance began by rehearsing the application of EU law to sport in cases considered in relation to the free movement of persons principles, set out above. The Court noted the approach adopted to 'purely sporting rules' and took the view that this should also be applied in respect of competition law on the basis that where there was no economic element, there could be no effect on competition. The Court characterised the anti-doping rules thus:

44. It is appropriate to point out that, while it is true that high-level sport has become, to a great extent, an economic activity, the campaign against doping does not pursue any economic objective. It is intended to preserve, first, the spirit of fair play, without which sport, be it amateur or professional, is no longer sport. That purely social objective is sufficient to justify the campaign against doping. Secondly, since doping products are not without their negative physiological effects, that campaign is intended to safeguard the health of athletes. Thus, the prohibition of doping, as a particular expression of the requirement of fair play, forms part of the cardinal rule of sport.

45. It must also be made clear that sport is essentially a gratuitous and not an economic act, even when the athlete performs it in the course of professional sport. In other words, the

---

80 Ibid.

prohibition of doping and anti-doping rules concern exclusively, even when the sporting action is performed by a professional, a non-economic aspect of that sporting action, which constitutes its very essence.

. . .

47. In view of the foregoing, it must be held that the prohibition of doping is based on purely sporting considerations and therefore has nothing to do with any economic consideration. That means, in the light of the case-law . . . that the rules to combat doping cannot, any more than the rules considered by the Court of Justice in *Walrave*, *Donà* and *Deliège*, come within the scope of the Treaty provisions on the economic freedoms and, in particular, of Articles 49 EC, 81 EC and 82 EC. The anti-doping rules are intimately linked to sport as such.

48. In the present case, the Court of First Instance considers that the same conclusion must apply as regards the anti-doping rules at issue.

The Court of First Instance considered that the anti-doping rules were aimed solely at achieving sporting, social and health-related objectives constituting the essence of sporting activity, even if performed in a professional context, and had nothing to do with economic considerations. The Court then went on to consider the implications of this finding in the case:

49. First, it is a fact established by the contents of the case-file that the anti-doping rules at issue have no discriminatory aim. In particular, the applicants have not in any way alleged – quite the contrary – that the limit mentioned in paragraph 3 above is applied selectively to certain athletes or categories of athletes to exclude them from competitions. If there were such discrimination, the restriction of the scope of the Treaty provisions on economic freedoms, accepted by the Court in respect of purely sporting rules (*Walrave*, paragraph 9), could not, it is clear, apply with regard to the rules concerned. That restriction would not be limited to its proper object, which is the preservation 'of the noble competition and other ideals of sport' (Opinion of Advocate General Cosmas in *Deliège*, paragraphs 50 and 74). Such rules would thus not escape the Treaty provisions on economic freedoms and those freedoms might thereby be infringed, which is a matter for the Commission to establish and penalise by way of proceedings pursuant to Articles 81 EC and 82 EC, if the rules in question entail failure to comply with competition rules.

50. Secondly, the Court of First Instance considers that the arguments by which the applicants attempt to challenge in two different respects the purely sporting nature of the anti-doping rules at issue cannot be accepted.

51. Third, the applicants submit that the anti-doping rules at issue infringe their economic freedoms because they have economic repercussions for them.

52. That argument, which is tantamount to a submission that rules cannot be purely sporting if they have economic repercussions, is at odds with the Court's case-law.

53. It is precisely because sporting rules have economic repercussions for professional sportsmen and sportswomen and because those rules are considered to be excessive by some of those professionals that the dispute arises and that the question is raised whether those rules are purely sporting in nature (like the rules which gave rise to *Walrave*, *Deliège* and *Donà*) or whether they cover the economic aspect of sporting activity (like the rules which gave rise to *Bosman*, *Lehtonen* and *Kolpak*).

54. Still as to the first aspect, the applicants argued, particularly at the hearing, that it is because of their allegedly excessive nature that the anti-doping rules at issue infringe the athletes' economic freedoms guaranteed by the Treaty. In other words, those rules, albeit non-discriminatory, have, because and in so far as they are excessive, become something other than anti-doping rules and, therefore, something other than purely sporting rules.

55. Those arguments cannot be accepted. It is common ground that the contested rules are, by their nature, anti-doping provisions. In particular, they have no discriminatory purpose. As a result, the allegedly excessive nature of those rules, were it to be established, would not result in them ceasing to be purely sporting rules, thereby making their lawfulness dependent on an assessment according to economic criteria under competition law, provided that they remain limited to their proper object, which is the campaign against doping and the safeguarding of the spirit of fair play. Furthermore, the applicants themselves accept the legitimacy of that objective.

56. Secondly, the applicants state, in their application, that the anti-doping rules at issue were not motivated solely by altruistic and health considerations, but also by the IOC's own economic considerations and, in particular, by its concern (in principle legitimate) not to see the economic potential of the Olympic Games diminished by scandals linked to doping. In so far as that allegation is intended to suggest that the contested anti-doping rules are not purely sporting rules, it must be rejected.

57. The fact that the IOC might possibly have had in mind when adopting the anti-doping rules at issue the concern, legitimate according to the applicants themselves, of safeguarding the economic potential of the Olympic Games is not sufficient to alter the purely sporting nature of those rules.

58. Moreover, even were it proved, *quod non*, that the IOC acted exclusively on the basis of its purely economic interests, there is every reason to believe that it fixed the limit at the level best supported by the scientific evidence. The IOC's economic interest is to have the most scientifically exact anti-doping regulations, in order both to ensure the highest level of sporting competition, and therefore of media interest, and to avoid the scandals which the systematic exclusion of innocent athletes can provoke.

59. It follows that the applicants' argument that fixing a limit which is allegedly too low serves the economic interests of the IOC is neither sustainable nor convincing and must be rejected.

60. As regards the disputed decision, the Court considers that the Commission's conclusion, that 'the rules and practices in question do not fall foul of the prohibition laid down in Articles 81 [EC] and 82 [EC]', is correct.

The decision of the Court of First Instance was the subject of academic criticism on the basis that the Court had failed to fully understand the previous case law in this area.[81] At the centre of this criticism was the difficulty the Court had in dealing with the distinction between sporting rules escaping the scrutiny of EU law and economic rules subject to it. This led the Court, according to Weatherill, 'into intellectually murky alleyways'.[82] Essentially the Court concluded that the anti-doping rules were outside the scope of the EC Treaty and thus competition law, on the basis that they were rules of a purely sporting nature and had nothing to do with economic activity. However, the Court's judgment itself has a tortured look to it and the approach has been challenged:

---

81 See Weatherill, S, 'Anti-doping Rules and EC Law' (2005) ECLR 416. See also, Weatherill, S, 'Anti-Doping Rules and EC Law' in *European Sports Law: Collected Papers* (2007), The Hague: TMC Asser Press.
82 Weatherill, S 'Anti-doping Revisited – The Demise of the Rule of ''Purely Sporting Interest''' (2006) ECLR 645 and in Weatherill, S, *European Sports Law: Collected Papers* (2007), The Hague: TMC Asser Press.

Weatherill, S, 'Anti-doping Rules and EC Law'

Perhaps there is a (small) category of purely sporting rules unassociated with economic activity, but regulations inherent in the organisation and proper conduct of sporting competition form a much larger category in which economic effect is commonly present . . . Anti-doping rules certainly have economic effects on those found to have contravened them. Attempts to present such rules as 'sporting' and not 'economic' are unhelpful. They are both. True, the notion that there is in principle a separation between sporting rules (which escape the scope of application of EC law) and rules of an economic nature (which do not) reflects the nature of the EC as an institution possessing a set of attributed competencies, of which sport [was] not one. But EC law has a broad functional reach because so few activities exert no economic impact. The CFI's attempt in *Meca-Medina* to roll back this general trend in the special case of sport, though doubtless a delight to sports federations, was constitutionally deeply unconvincing . . . What is really at stake is not a group of sporting rules and a separate group of economic rules, but rather a group of sporting rules which carry economic implications and which therefore fall for assessment, but not necessarily condemnation, under EC trade law.[83]

Meca-Medina and Majcen v Commission in the Court of Justice

In the event the decision of the Court of First Instance was appealed and the Court of Justice came to an altogether more satisfactory conclusion.[84] In deciding that the Court of First Instance had indeed erred in finding that the anti-doping rules fell outside the scope of the competition provisions of the Treaty the Court of Justice explained its reasoning and set out the approach to be adopted in respect of sport under EU law:

Case C-519/04 P, *Meca-Medina and Majcen v Commission*

27. [I]t is apparent that the mere fact that a rule is purely sporting in nature does not have the effect of removing from the scope of the Treaty the person engaging in the activity governed by that rule or the body which has laid it down.

28. If the sporting activity in question falls within the scope of the Treaty, the conditions for engaging in it are then subject to all the obligations which result from the various provisions of the Treaty. It follows that the rules which govern that activity must satisfy the requirements of those provisions, which, in particular, seek to ensure freedom of movement for workers, freedom of establishment, freedom to provide services, or competition.

29. Thus, where engagement in the sporting activity must be assessed in the light of the Treaty provisions relating to freedom of movement for workers or freedom to provide services, it will be necessary to determine whether the rules which govern that activity satisfy the requirements of Articles 39 EC and 49 EC, that is to say do not constitute restrictions prohibited by those articles (*Deliège*, paragraph 60).

30. Likewise, where engagement in the activity must be assessed in the light of the Treaty provisions relating to competition, it will be necessary to determine, given the specific requirements of Articles 81 EC and 82 EC, whether the rules which govern that activity emanate from an undertaking, whether the latter restricts competition or abuses its dominant position, and whether that restriction or that abuse affects trade between Member States.

---

83 Ibid, p 648.
84 Case C-519/04 P, *Meca-Medina and Majcen v Commission* [2006] ECR I-6991.

31. Therefore, even if those rules do not constitute restrictions on freedom of movement because they concern questions of purely sporting interest and, as such, have nothing to do with economic activity (*Walrave and Koch* and *Donà*), that fact means neither that the sporting activity in question necessarily falls outside the scope of Articles 81 EC and 82 EC nor that the rules do not satisfy the specific requirements of those articles.

32. However, in . . . the contested judgment, the Court of First Instance held that the fact that purely sporting rules may have nothing to do with economic activity, with the result that they do not fall within the scope of Articles 39 EC and 49 EC, means, also, that they have nothing to do with the economic relationships of competition, with the result that they also do not fall within the scope of Articles 81 EC and 82 EC.

33. In holding that rules could thus be excluded straightaway from the scope of those articles solely on the ground that they were regarded as purely sporting with regard to the application of Articles 39 EC and 49 EC, without any need to determine first whether the rules fulfilled the specific requirements of Articles 81 EC and 82 EC . . . the Court of First Instance made an error of law.[85]

In short the Court of Justice determined that a rule which is purely sporting in nature is not of necessity outside the scope of the Treaty and that where the rule does fall within the terms of the Treaty it must meet the specific terms of the measure concerned to be regarded as lawful. The Court also drew a distinction between the application of the free movement of persons provisions and competition law. The provisions relating to workers and the provision of services retain their capacity to treat sporting rules of non-economic purpose as falling outside their terms; this does not mean that they are also exempt from the application of competition law, should the conditions for its engagement be satisfied. This approach does offer some scope for dissonance between the application of the free movement principles and competition law which could lead to the uncomfortable situation of a sporting rule being condemned by one set of Treaty principles, whilst being regarded as permissible by another set. However, the Court of Justice, though allowing the appeal, chose to deliver judgment itself, rather than remitting the case back to the Court of First Instance. In doing so it gave a clear indication that, even though the route may be different, the outcomes in applying competition and other Treaty provisions would lead to consistent results or a 'convergence in outcome'.[86]

42. [T]he compatibility of rules with the Community rules on competition cannot be assessed in the abstract. Not every agreement between undertakings or every decision of an association of undertakings which restricts the freedom of action of the parties or of one of them necessarily falls within the prohibition laid down in Article 81(1) EC. For the purposes of application of that provision to a particular case, account must first of all be taken of the overall context in which the decision of the association of undertakings was taken or produces its effects and, more specifically, of its objectives. It has then to be considered whether the consequential effects restrictive of competition are inherent in the pursuit of those objectives and are proportionate to them.

43. As regards the overall context in which the rules at issue were adopted, the Commission could rightly take the view that the general objective of the rules was, as none of the parties disputes, to combat doping in order for competitive sport to be conducted fairly and that it included the need to safeguard equal chances for athletes, athletes' health, the integrity and objectivity of competitive sport and ethical values in sport.

---

85 Ibid.
86 Ibid at 649–50.

44. In addition, given that penalties are necessary to ensure enforcement of the doping ban, their effect on athletes' freedom of action must be considered to be, in principle, inherent itself in the anti-doping rules.

45. Therefore, even if the anti-doping rules at issue are to be regarded as a decision of an association of undertakings limiting the appellants' freedom of action, they do not, for all that, necessarily constitute a restriction of competition incompatible with the common market, within the meaning of Article 81 EC, since they are justified by a legitimate objective. Such a limitation is inherent in the organisation and proper conduct of competitive sport and its very purpose is to ensure healthy rivalry between athletes.

46. While the appellants do not dispute the truth of this objective, they nevertheless contend that the anti-doping rules at issue are also intended to protect the IOC's own economic interests and that it is in order to safeguard this objective that excessive rules, such as those contested in the present case, are adopted. The latter cannot therefore, in their submission, be regarded as inherent in the proper conduct of competitive sport and fall outside the prohibitions in Article 81 EC.

47. It must be acknowledged that the penal nature of the anti-doping rules at issue and the magnitude of the penalties applicable if they are breached are capable of producing adverse effects on competition because they could, if penalties were ultimately to prove unjustified, result in an athlete's unwarranted exclusion from sporting events, and thus in impairment of the conditions under which the activity at issue is engaged in. It follows that, in order not to be covered by the prohibition laid down in Article 81(1) EC, the restrictions thus imposed by those rules must be limited to what is necessary to ensure the proper conduct of competitive sport.

So, as far as restrictions of a regulatory character are concerned, the issue is one of the inherency and proportionality of the measure. Here the general objective of combating doping was seen as inherently necessary for the proper conduct of sport and the penalties as a necessary consequence of applying such a system. Thus the rules could be regarded as legitimate and falling without the conception of prohibited measures under Article 81(1) EC (now Article 101(1) TFEU). In addressing the appellants' claims that economic incentives underpinned the rules, the Court acknowledged the need for any restriction to remain within the bounds of that necessary for the proper conduct of sport. In applying this approach, the Court of Justice was able to make a comfortable judgment in favour of the validity of the rules on the basis that the sportsmen had failed to make out their case as to the proportionality of the relevant levels of Nandrolone.

EU competition law and sports regulation

While *Meca-Medina* is undoubtedly the most significant recent case in the context of EU law, because of its refinement of the 'sporting exception' principle, there are a number of further instances of significant applications of EU competition law in the regulatory context.

Sports regulation and competition: *Piau v Commission*

Laurent Piau, a football agent, made a complaint to the Commission in 1998 arguing that FIFA's rules on player agents were in contravention of Article 49 EC (now Article 56 TFEU) in as much as they prohibited players from engaging agents not licensed by FIFA. In addition it was alleged that the requirements imposed on those wishing to become licensed, including a deposit of an indemnity and the successful completion of an examination, were disproportionate restrictions. Following a further complaint, the Commission opened proceedings against FIFA on the grounds that the rules were in breach of Articles 81 and 82 EC (now Articles 101 & 102 TFEU). FIFA responded by making amendments to its regulations in 2000. As a result of these changes the Commission closed its proceedings on the basis that it considered that the rules satisfied Article 81(3) EC (now Article 56 TFEU).[87] In particular the new rules removed the requirement that an indemnity be deposited and replaced this with a rule requiring agents to take out insurance. The rules also required agents to pass an examination and to sign a code of conduct. As regards Article 82 EC, the Commission took the view that this was not engaged by FIFA as it did not hold a position in the market for provision of advice to players.

Piau subsequently brought an action for annulment of the Commission decision under Article 230 EC (now Article 263 TFEU). No consideration was given to the prospect of FIFA's rules being regarded as inherent in the organisation of football and thus, the Court of First Instance determined that the licence constituted a barrier to access, affected competition and must satisfy the conditions set out in Article 81(3) in order to be regarded as valid.[88] The Court identified the protection of players and clubs, by the raising of professional standards, as a legitimate objective and determined that the rules were appropriate for the attainment of the objectives. Further, the Court decided that the Commission erred in not applying Article 82 EC. The Court of First Instance held that the binding nature of the regulations and accompanying sanctions placed FIFA in a position of dominance:

Case T-193/02, *Piau v Commission*

115. It seems unrealistic to claim that FIFA, which is recognised as holding supervisory powers over the sport-related activity of football and connected economic activities, such as the activity of players' agents in the present case, does not hold a collective dominant position on the market for players' agents' services on the ground that is not an actor on that market.

116. The fact that FIFA is not itself an economic operator that buys players' agents' services on the market in question and that its involvement stems from rule-making activity, which it has assumed the power to exercise in respect of the economic activity of players' agents, is irrelevant as regards the application of Article 82 EC, since FIFA is the emanation of the national associations and the clubs, the actual buyers of the services of players' agents, and it therefore operates on this market through its members.

Despite acknowledging the dominant position of FIFA in the market, the Court of First Instance did not accept that its behaviour was abusive:

117. As regards abuse of the alleged dominant position, however, it follows from the above considerations regarding the amended regulations and the possible exemption under Article 81(3) EC that such an abuse has not been established. It has been found that those regulations did not impose quantitative restrictions on access to the occupation of players' agent that could be detrimental to competition, but qualitative restrictions that may be justified in the present circumstances. The abuses of the dominant position that, according to the applicant, stem from the regulations are not therefore established and his arguments in this regard must be rejected.[89]

---

87 Case COMP/37.124; see 'Commission closes investigations into FIFA rules on players' agents', IP/02/585 18/04/2002; Branco-Martins, R, 'The Laurent Piau Case of the ECJ on the Status of Players' Agents' in Gardiner, S, Parrish, R and Siekmann, R (eds), *EU, Sport, Law and Policy: Regulation: Re-regulation and Representation* (2009), The Hague: TMC Asser Press. See, generally, Szyszczak, E 'Competition and Sport' (2007) 32(1) EL RCev 95.
88 Case T-193/02, *Piau v Commission* [2005] ECR II-209; Case C-171/05, *Piau v Commission* [2006] ECR I-37.
89 [2005] ECR II-209.

Piau's application was dismissed and he made an appeal to the Court of Justice. The appeal against the judgment of the Court of First Instance was rejected by the Court of Justice, by Order, without a hearing taking place. Thus the rules as amended by FIFA following the Commission investigation stood as being lawful. It is of note that no real attempt was made to argue that an 'inherency' approach should be adopted here and so the measures were seen as being restrictive but either justifiable under the terms of Article 101(3) TFEU or not constituting abusive behaviour under Article 102 TFEU.

Sports regulation and competition: key cases

Various challenges have been made in the context of the regulation of sport. More often than not complaints to the Commission have been rejected as being related to the nature of sport itself. So, on the question of the requirement that football clubs participating in competition be required to be located within particular territories, the Commission has twice rejected complaints on the grounds that the restriction is anticompetitive.[90] The Commission's clear view on these restrictions was that they were inherent in the activity as making the clubs representative and facilitating the functioning of the competitions. The Commission has taken a similar view in relation to a UEFA rule prohibiting multiple ownership of football clubs.[91]

A more successful challenge was made in what has become known as the *Oulmers* case.[92] Abdelmajid Oulmers was a professional footballer with Belgian club Charleroi. In accordance with an obligation under FIFA rules, Oulmers was released by his club to play in an international friendly match. During international duties he suffered a serious injury and returned to his club unable to play for eight months. FIFA regulations required that club sides were responsible for insuring their players against any harm occurring while on international duty and that they would receive no other compensation should a player be injured. Charleroi brought an action against FIFA in the Belgian courts claiming breaches of Articles 81 and 82 EC. The G-14, an organisation incorporating the leading European club teams, had previously complained to the Commission about the rule and intervened in the case. The Belgian court made a preliminary reference to the Court of Justice, seeking clarification as to the application of competition law. Underlying the complaint was a frustration on the part of the club sides providing players for national teams, that they were not only expected to do so without payment for the players' services but also that they bore the risk of any injury that might befall their players while with their national teams. It also represented an opportunity for the clubs to obtain leverage in their quest for a greater voice for clubs in the management and regulation of football. FIFA ultimately settled the case before either an Opinion or judgment was delivered. The imposition of such restrictions was more than likely to fall foul of competition provisions as imposing an economic restriction upon the clubs without any realistic hope of demonstrating that the measures were either necessary or proportionate. Indeed, as a direct result of this case the G-14 agreed to disband and was absorbed into UEFA as the European Club Association, with a remit of protecting the interests of club sides. Further, it was agreed that clubs providing players for international matches would be entitled to receive payment for those players' services from revenues accrued in the playing of international matches. Following on from the discontinued litigation in *Balog* discussed above,[93] the case demonstrates the power of competition law to effectively challenge the regulatory authorities, certainly in respect of the freedoms of professional sportspersons and the capacity to regulate without thought for the consequences. The

---

90 Case COMP/36.851; see 'Limits to application of Treaty competition rules to sport: Commission gives clear signal', IP/99/965 09/12/1999.
91 Case COMP/37.806; see 'Commission closes investigation into UEFA rule on multiple ownership of football clubs', IP/02/942 27/06/2002; see also CAS 98/2000 *AEK Athens and Slavia Prague v UEFA.*
92 Case C-243/06 *SA Sporting Pays du Charleroi and G-14 Groupement des clubs de football européens v FIFA* OJ C 2121, 2 September, p 11.
93 See earlier p 173.

result of this case, without judgment even being delivered, is a serious concession of power by the football authorities and the need to remember that '[t]he lesson of *Bosman* is that the game can cope – but only if it responds imaginatively.'[94]

EU competition law reconciling regulatory and commercial functions

Motosykleistiki Omospondia Ellados Npid v Elliniko Dimosio (MOTOE)

The *Motoe* case[95] concerned the power of Elliniki Leshki Aftokinitoy kai Periigiseon (ELPA) as the nominated and representative body, under Greek legislation, of the International Motorcycling Federation (FIM), to authorise sporting competitions involving motorbikes and mopeds. Organisers of potential events had to submit a request for authorisation to a committee of ELPA providing details of the venue or route, the safety measures and wider conditions for the running of the event. The event could not clash with pre-arranged events. ELPA had the right of veto over all races within the territory of Greece as a result.

In addition, the organisers of events had to have their sponsors approved by the committee and participants could not be compelled to consent to advertising unless an agreement concluded by ELPA or its committee was in question. This gave rise to the issue that ELPA had a potential advantage in the organisation of such events where it acted in a commercial capacity, because of its regulatory monopoly over the sanction and oversight of such events.

Motosykleistiki Omospondia Ellados Npid (MOTOE) made an application for a licence, but after it had received no response after a number of months, MOTOE brought an action in the Greek courts challenging the implicit refusal of ELPA to issue authorisation. It did so on the basis that the combination of regulatory and commercial functions invested in ELPA gave it a monopoly position which it could abuse, contrary to EU competition provisions. The Greek court thus referred the questions as to:

Case C-49/07, Motosykleistiki Omospondia Ellados Npid v Elliniko Dimosio (MOTOE)

(1) Can Articles 82 EC and 86 EC be interpreted so as also to include within their scope the activity of a legal person which has the status of national representative of the [FIM] and engages in economic activity as described above by entering into sponsorship, advertising and insurance contracts, in the context of the organisation of motor sport events by it?

(2) Should the answer [to the first question] be in the affirmative, is Article 49 of [the Greek Road Traffic Code], which, in relation to issue by the competent national public authority (in the present case, the Ministry for Public Order) of permission to organise a motor-vehicle competition, gives the foregoing legal person the power to provide a concurring opinion as to the holding of the competition without that power being made subject to restrictions, obligations and review, compatible with those provisions of the Treaty?[96]

In answering the first question in the affirmative the Court of Justice highlighted that the exercise of public powers is not activity of an economic nature, which engaged the Treaty. However, the possession of such public powers did not, in itself, remove ELPA from the scope of competition law in as much as it was also engaged in economic activities.

In applying Article 82 EC the Court considered the relevant market applicable to the case. The Court determined that there were two distinct markets in which ELPA was operating, the first in the

---

94 Weatherill, S, 'A case that could transform international football' (2005), *Financial Times*, 12 September.
95 Case C-49/07, *Motosykleistiki Omospondia Ellados Npid v Elliniko Dimosio* (MOTOE) [2008] ECR I-4863.
96 Ibid.

organisation of motorcycle events and the second the commercial exploitation of those events in terms of sponsorship, advertising and insurance. Though the activities of ELPA were confined to the territory of Greece, the Court nonetheless allowed the possibility that this might be sufficient to constitute a substantial part of the Common Market necessary under the terms of Article 82 EC. As regards dominance in this context, the Court acknowledged that being granted special or exclusive powers which placed it in the position of determining the extent of other undertakings' access to the market could put an undertaking such as ELPA in a dominant position. However, the Court emphasised that Article 82 EC could not be infringed simply by the existence of a dominant undertaking; there was also the requirement that trade between Member States be affected. This was not precluded by the restriction of the regulatory power to one Member State; that could still have an effect by sealing off the domestic market or reinforcing the partition of markets along national boundaries. The Court concluded:

> **51.** A system of undistorted competition, such as that provided for by the Treaty, can be guaranteed only if equality of opportunity is secured as between the various economic operators. To entrust a legal person such as ELPA, which itself organises and commercially exploits motorcycling events, the task of giving the competent administration its consent to applications for authorisation to organise such events, is tantamount *de facto* to conferring upon it the power to designate the persons authorised to organise those events and to set the conditions in which those events are organised, thereby placing that entity at an obvious advantage over its competitors. Such a right may therefore lead the undertaking which possesses it to deny other operators access to the relevant market. That situation of unequal conditions of competition is also highlighted by the fact, confirmed at the hearing before the Court, that, when ELPA organises or participates in the organisation of motorcycling events, it is not required to obtain any consent in order that the competent administration grant it the required authorisation.

> **52.** Furthermore, such a rule, which gives a legal person such as ELPA the power to give consent to applications for authorisation to organise motorcycling events without that power being made subject by that rule to restrictions, obligations and review, could lead the legal person entrusted with giving that consent to distort competition by favouring events which it organises or those in whose organisation it participates.

This case came to the Court by way of a preliminary reference and, as such, the Court did not determine the outcome of the case, but provided answers to the questions posed by the domestic court in order that it could be resolved there. Nonetheless, what is plain from the judgment, although the Court was rather coy in outlining when abuse might arise, is that such bodies sharing regulatory and commercial functions must be subject to restrictions, obligations and review such that the power is not exercised in an abusive fashion.[97]

The *MOTOE* case is not the first instance of this type of situation to come under competition law scrutiny. In *FIA & Formula One* the Commission instigated proceedings against the governing body of world motor sport.[98] The Commission's investigation of the FIA regulations and commercial agreements pertaining to the FIA Formula One Championship arose after requests for clearance from European competition rules. The Commission objected to some rules on the basis that the FIA had

---

97 See, generally, Weatherill, S, 'Article 82 EC and Sporting "Conflict of Interest": the Judgment in *MOTOE*' (2009) 1–2 ISLJ 3; Miettinen, S, 'Policing the Boundaries between Regulation and Commercial Exploitation: Lessons from the *MOTOE* Case' (2008) 3–4 ISLJ 13 and in Gardiner, S, Parrish, R and Siekmann, R (eds) *EU, Sport, Law and Policy: Regulation, Re-regulation and Representation* (2009) The Hague: TMC Asser Press.

98 Case COMP/36.638; see 'Commission closes its investigation into Formula One and other four-wheel motor sports', IP/01/1523 Date: 30/10/2001. See earlier, pp 242–5 for discussion of subsequent debate about the need for effective governance in European sport.

abused its power by imposing restrictions on promoters, circuit owners, vehicle manufacturers and drivers that were unnecessary. The Commission acknowledged the need for sports regulators to manage the organisation of its sport, sporting rules and competitions, but noted that the significant economic activity associated with the sport meant that it was subject to the competition provisions of the Treaty. The FIA held discussions with the Commission and agreed to modify its rules to bring them into line with EU law. The FIA committed that: its role will be limited to that of a sports regulator, with no commercial conflicts of interest; its rules will not be used to prevent or impede new competitions unless justified on grounds related to the safe, fair or orderly conduct of motor sport; and it would strengthen both internal and external appeals processes. In order to facilitate this and to prevent conflicts of interest the FIA disposed of its rights in the FIA Formula One World Championship and agreed to permit the creation of similar races and series potentially in competition with Formula One. The rights were sold for a period of 100 years, at which point they will revert back to the FIA.

The severing of regulatory and commercial functions is not an inevitable consequence of the application of competition provisions, however. Advocate-General Kokott noted in MOTOE:

89. Certainly, not every exercise of the right of co-decision conferred on ELPA by Article 49 of the Road Traffic Code can automatically be regarded as abuse. If the behaviour of an undertaking in a dominant position can be objectively justified, it is not abuse. In fact, in a case such as this, there may be objective reasons why an association such as ELPA refuses to give its consent to the authorisation of a motorcycling event.

90. The existence of such an objective reason is particularly evident where, at a planned motorcycling event, the safety of the racers and spectators would not be guaranteed because the organiser did not take the appropriate precautions.

91. However, in addition to the purely technical safety requirements, there may be other objective reasons for refusing consent which relate to the particular characteristics of the sport. In a case such as this, it is worth bearing in mind the following considerations.

92. Firstly, it is in the interests of the sportspersons concerned, but also of the spectators and the public in general, that, for each sport, rules that are as uniform as possible apply and are observed so as to ensure that competitions are conducted in a regulated and fair manner. This applies not only to the frequently discussed anti-doping rules, but also to the ordinary rules of sport. If rules varied greatly from one organiser to another, it would be more difficult for sportspersons to participate in competitions and to compare their respective performances; the public's interest in and recognition of the sport in question might also suffer.

93. Consequently, the fact that an organisation such as ELPA makes the grant of its consent to the authorisation of a motorcycling event subject to compliance with certain internationally recognised rules cannot automatically be regarded as abuse. This is without prejudice, of course, to the substantive examination of each of those rules from the point of view of their compatibility with Community law, in particular its rules on competition.

94. Secondly, it is in the interests of the sportspersons participating in the event, but also of the spectators and the public in general, that the individual competitions in a particular sport are incorporated into an overarching framework so that, for example, a specific timetable can be followed. It may make sense to prevent clashes between competitions so that both sportspersons and spectators can participate in as many such events as possible.

95. Consequently, the fact that an organisation such as ELPA makes the grant of consent to the authorisation of a motorcycling event subject to the requirement that the event must not clash with other events that have already been planned and authorised cannot automatically be regarded as an abuse. However, it goes without saying in this regard that, when establishing a national Greek annual programme for motorcycling events, ELPA must not give preference to the events (co-)organised or marketed by it over those of other, independent organisers.

96. The pyramid structure that has developed in most sports helps to ensure that the special requirements of sport, such as uniform rules and a uniform timetable for competitions, are taken into account. An organisation such as ELPA, which is the official representative of the FIM in Greece, is part of that pyramid structure. Under its right of co-decision in the authorisation by a public body of motorcycling events, it may legitimately assert the interests of sport and, if necessary, refuse to give its consent. However, a refusal to grant consent becomes an abuse where it has no objective justification in the interests of sport, but is used arbitrarily to promote the organisation's own economic interests, to the detriment of other service providers that would like to organise, and above all market, motorcycling events on their own responsibility.

This is consistent with the approach of the High Court in *Hendry*, which had no objection to the possession of regulatory and commercial interests by one body, as long as that position was not utilised abusively.

EU competition law and commercial activities

Competition law has also been engaged in respect of sport's commercial activities. In this respect the engagement of law has been much less controversial, as the focus of legal regulation is more distant from the core activity of sport itself. Thus, in this aspect competition law has been applied in areas associated with sports events and activities but impacting directly upon sport or its immediate regulatory infrastructure. There are three prime examples of this in practice: first in respect of ticketing activities in relation to major sporting events; second, as regards commercial tie-ins, endorsements and sponsorships pertaining to sport and sporting events; and, third and most significantly, in respect of the commercial exploitation of broadcasting and other media rights for sports events. The issue of broadcasting is considered in a discrete section below, principally because this has engaged other aspects of EU law outside of the field of competition. However, the remaining elements are considered here.

Competition and ticketing for sports events

The first examination of ticketing for a major event arose in respect of the 1990 football World Cup. The complaint related to the ticket distribution system applied during the FIFA World Cup held in Italy in 1990.[99] A tour operator wishing to put together and sell package tours involving transport, accommodation and entrance tickets was frustrated in its efforts. The system of ticket distribution imposed outlawed the acquisition of match tickets for the purpose of putting together package tours save by one 'approved' operator. Further, attempts by the company to acquire tickets through other means were met with legal action brought by the 'official' package tour provider sanctioned by the organisers. As a result a complaint was made to the Commission that this arrangement amounted to anti-competitive practice under the terms of Article 85 EEC. The Commission held that the contract between the tournament organising committee and the official tour operator constituted an agreement for the purpose of Article 85(1) EEC, but also extended that agreement to cover FIFA and the Italian Football Federation (FIGC) as having strong representation and effective influence over the tournament committee, even though they were not signatories to the contract. The agreement was also adjudged to be anti-competitive as excluding other potential providers of

---

99 92/521/EEC: Commission Decision of 27 October 1992 relating to a proceeding under Article 85 of the EEC Treaty (IV/33.384 and IV/33.378 – 'Distribution of package tours during the 1990 World Cup').

package tours and could not be justified on the basis of safety considerations as a number of other package tour operators were able to meet the criteria set out. Notably, given the confinement of the breach to the period of the World Cup itself, the Commission chose not to impose a financial penalty.

A different issue arose in relation to the sale of tickets for the 1998 football World Cup in France.[100] In 1996 and 1997 the tournament organising committee sold more than half a million match tickets exclusively to purchasers able to provide an address in France. The Commission determined that these discriminatory sales arrangements amounted to an abuse of a dominant position in the market for the sale of entry tickets contrary to Article 82 EC. The Commission concluded that other practices, including advising the non-French consumers that tickets could be obtained only from national football federations and tour operators, exacerbated the discrimination against non-French residents seeking tickets for the competition. Following intervention from the Commission at the time, provisions were put in place to rectify the discrimination and widen the availability of tickets. Thus on conclusion of its investigation the Commission levied a symbolic €1,000 fine on the committee in light of its co-operation, but also reflecting that the arrangements might well have been viewed as legitimate in light of the law at that time. The Commission did, however, issue a warning that future abuse of this kind would be subject to the full force of the competition law provisions.[101]

The warning was certainly heeded in the organisation of ticketing for subsequent major events, with UEFA, amongst others, working with the Commission to ensure compliance.[102] Nonetheless, the Commission was required to intervene again in relation to the 2006 football World Cup in Germany.[103] Following discussions with the European Commission FIFA agreed to modify its arrangements for ticket payments. Initially tickets could only be purchased by means of a MasterCard or through a German bank account. Payment methods were expanded to allow purchasers to acquire tickets by making a domestic bank transfer in their local currency. In assessing the arrangements, the Commission considered whether there was reasonable access to tickets to consumers from across the EU.[104]

Competition law: sponsorship, endorsement and certification

Competition law also has a role to play in regulating the commercial tie-ins that sports events and regulatory bodies set up as a part of their activities. The Commission came to a formal conclusion about the contents of such a sponsorship contract for the first time in a case concerning the Danish Tennis Federation (DTF).[105] The issue concerned the issue of exclusive contracts to supply the 'official' tennis balls of the DTF. These rights were granted unilaterally by the DTF, with no objective selection criteria, and players in official DTF tournaments could only use balls sold by the official network in Denmark. Under the terms of the settlement with the Commission the DTF agreed an open procedure for calls for tender with objective conditions attached and allowed players to obtain their tennis balls from sources other than the official network. The DTF also agreed to stop using terms such as 'official ball' or 'official supplier'. The Commission was concerned that the rule limited free and fair competition by making one brand appear seemingly superior. Under the new procedure the selected balls are termed a 'sponsor of the DTF' with the term 'official' disappearing.

100 COMP/36.888.
101 See 'Commission takes action against the local organisers of the 1998 football World Cup finals competition in France', IP/99/541 20/07/1999.
102 COMP/37.424 UEFA Euro 2000; see 'Commission approves ticketing arrangements for Euro 2000', IP/00/591 08/06/2000; COMP/38.703 2004 Athens Olympic Games; see 'Commission clears ticketing arrangements for the Athens Olympic Games', IP/03/738 23/05/2003.
103 COMP/39.177 'Which?/DFB, MasterCard and FIFA (FIFA World Cup 2006 in Germany)'.
104 See 'Competition: Commission welcomes improved access to tickets for the 2006 World Cup', IP/05/519 02/05/2005.
105 COMP/33.055 and 35.759 Danish Tennis Federation; see 'The Commission conditionally approves sponsorship contracts between the Danish Tennis Federation and its tennis ball suppliers', IP/98/355 15/04/1998.

Decisions in this context can have a strong sporting element, however, and the specification of sporting goods for technical reasons has been considered as legitimate by the Commission in relation to FIFA's technical requirements for international-standard footballs.[106] The FIFA 'Denominations' programme set out technical criteria relating to the specifications of footballs mandatory in international matches and with the option for national associations to adopt this approach. The programme required those wishing to have their product recognised as meeting the standard to subject it to a certification procedure by an independent third party. After satisfying the criteria a product was eligible to be labelled as 'international match ball standard' at no cost. However, two further designations, 'FIFA Approved' and 'FIFA Inspected', including use of the FIFA logo, were available upon payment of a fee. The Commission investigation concluded that this did not limit access to the market as it was accessible without payment of a fee by simply satisfying the legitimate objective technical criteria established by FIFA. If a producer wished to obtain commercial benefit from use of FIFA's trademark, then it was legitimate for FIFA to charge a fee for this. Had a fee been payable on all three counts, then it is likely the Commission would have taken a more restrictive view of the rules. What is established in this case is the capacity of sports federations to apply genuine and objective technical criteria to the sporting goods certified for use in their sport. When, as in the DTF case, this becomes a purely commercial exercise, the sports federations must be careful to make sure that they do not stifle competition in granting 'official' status.

Competition law: conclusions

It is certainly clear that competition law offers a significant opportunity for would-be litigants to challenge, in particular, rules and regulations of sports bodies. Not least this is because the potential scope of competition law is apt to catch the type of relationships – either based on agreement or regulatory monopoly – that are prevalent in sport. Similarly, the global nature of sport means that it is likely to meet the requirements of impacting on trade between Member States and across a sufficiently substantial part of the single market to engage EU competition law. Further, the agreements and rules to be considered are, more often than not, in the public domain. Perhaps most importantly, those rules also tend to be restrictive in nature, placing limits on the number of participants or applying criteria to be satisfied before entry to a competition is permitted, for example. Thus they can usually be easily identified as the sort of measure which can be considered to be anti-competitive or abusive.

Despite the relative ease with which rules might be caught by competition law, it can also be seen that the Courts and the Commission have treated sport with some care and, by the clear application of principle, have offered a more stable environment in which sport can operate. So though the opportunities look great for challengers, the successes have been few and far between.

The case law also emphasises that sport is increasingly a commercial activity and that these activities can often be subject to competition law scrutiny precisely because the product is so desirable, which makes the relevant market much smaller and the likelihood of market distortion or abuse correspondingly so much greater.

Sports Broadcasting and EU Law

Though the *Bosman* litigation and its aftermath is the most prominent aspect of EU sports law, the relationship that EU law has with sports broadcasting is equally crucial.[107] Much of the finance that

---

106 Case COMP/35266 FIFA.
107 See, generally, Stewart, S, 'The Development of Sports Law in the European Union, Its Globalisation and the Competition Law Aspects of European Broadcasting Rights' (2009) 16 Sports Law J 183; Weatherill, S, 'The sale of rights to broadcasting events under EC Law' in *European Sports Law: Collected Papers* (2007), The Hague: TMC Asser Press.

has created the post-*Bosman* boom in football since the mid-1990s has come from the sale of the rights to broadcast live football matches. Competition law, and the Commission in particular, has been at the forefront of this relationship but other elements of the law of the single market have come into play, as have more socio-cultural-oriented approaches. Competition law has been focused mainly on the sale of broadcasting rights by sports bodies. Most recently the EU courts have been active in determining cases on cross-border transmissions and the listing of sports events.

Joint and exclusive selling of broadcasting rights

There are two main problems with selling broadcasting rights on a bloc, whole competition basis. First, where a league of sports clubs is concerned, the sale on a collective basis could be considered to be an anti-competitive practice under the terms of Article 101 TFEU; the teams, by pooling their rights, arguably reduce competition as between themselves for the sale of the rights. However, this collective selling has been seen as legitimate, given that clubs are not wholly competing with each other and are, in fact, combining their efforts to create a single product.[108] The second issue is that joint selling on an exclusive basis restricts competition as it reduces output and limits price competition. Where rights are sold exclusively to one broadcaster for an extended period of time this can entrench the position of that broadcaster and buttress their financial capacity to bid successfully for later rights. This reduces competition. In order to address this the Commission has acted in three instances in relation to the sale of rights to football competitions. The FA Premier League, the Bundesliga in Germany and the UEFA Champions' League have all had the sale of rights subjected to scrutiny by the Commission. The Commission approved the sale of rights to the UEFA Champions' League as being compatible with Article 101(3) TFEU on the basis that the rights were 'unbundled' and offered in different packages with any unsold rights reverting to the clubs.[109] UEFA also opened up the possibility of broadcast via internet, mobile phones and other new media, thus potentially widening the scope of competition. UEFA would also ensure that its rights were not sold for a continuous period of more than three years, thus permitting those broadcasters not securing the rights in one round of bidding to be excluded from the market for only a short time. Both the FA Premier League and Bundesliga made similar commitments to the Commission and these were made legally binding by decision.[110] Thus, in relation to sporting events, the sale of the broadcast rights on a collective basis is likely to be regarded as acceptable as long as the rights are unbundled and made available to more than one broadcaster, the bidding process is open and transparent, unused rights revert to the clubs to sell on and the opportunity to develop new media markets is encouraged.[111]

Broadcast blackouts

The Commission has approved UEFA Broadcasting Regulations that permit national football associations to restrict the broadcasting of football within their territories for a two-and-a-half-hour

108 See eg *Re an Agreement between the FA Premier League and BskyB* [2000] EMLR 78.

109 2003/778/EC: Commission Decision of 23 July 2003 relating to a proceeding pursuant to Article 81 of the EC Treaty and Article 53 of the EEA Agreement (COMP/C.2-37.398 – Joint selling of the commercial rights of the UEFA Champions League).

110 COMP/37.214 German Bundesliga; see 'Competition: German Football League commitments to liberalise joint selling of Bundesliga media rights made legally binding by Commission decision', IP/05/62 19/01/2005; COMP/38.173 The Football Association Premier League Limited; see 'Competition: Commission makes commitments from FA Premier League legally binding', IP/06/356 22/03/2006.

111 The collective purchase of rights may also infringe Article 101 TFEU. On two occasions the Commission approved arrangements for collective purchase of sports and other events by the European Broadcasting Union (EBU) only for the measures to be annulled by the Court. The activities of the EBU in this regard are now monitored by the Commission on an annual basis. See Case IV/32.150 – EBU/Eurovision System, OJ 1993 L 179, p. 23; Case IV/32.150 – Eurovision OJ 2000 L 151, p. 18; Case T-528/93 *Metropole télévision SA and Reti Televisive Italiane SpA and Gestevisión Telecinco SA and Antena 3 de Televisión v Commission* [1996] ECR II-649; T-185/00 *Métropole Télévision SA (M6) (T-185/00), Antena 3 de Televisión, SA (T-216/00), Gestevisión Telecinco, SA (T-299/00) and SIC – Sociedade Independente de Comunicação, SA (T-300/00) v Commission of the European Communities* [2002] ECR II-3805.

period on Saturdays or Sundays, corresponding to the main time at which domestic fixtures are played. So, for example, football cannot be broadcast in England between 2.45 pm and 5.15 pm on Saturdays.[112] This restricts the capacity of broadcasters to show games during this period, but the Commission took the view that the effect was not an appreciable limitation of competition and thus did not fall within Article 101(1) TFEU. The Commission was keen to stress that the decision 'reflects the Commission's respect of the specific characteristics of sport and of its cultural and social function in Europe in trying to play the role of an impartial referee between the different interests of broadcasters and football clubs'. An important part of this decision was that the Commission was content that the rule would not have a cross-border effect as broadcasting rights tend to be divided along national lines. However, in the light of what follows, the effectiveness of the blackout may be called into question.

Television without frontiers: cross-territorial broadcasting

Perhaps the most significant development in the context of EU law as it relates to sports broadcasting is in joined cases *Football Association Premier League Ltd & Others v QC Leisure & Others Karen Murphy v Media Protection Services Ltd*.[113] The cases arose out of two separate actions: a civil action by the FA Premier League (FAPL) and criminal proceedings brought against the landlady of a pub, Karen Murphy. The cases concern the use of imported decoder cards from Greece, which are sold on to pubs at a price below that charged by the UK broadcaster. These cards enable pubs in the UK to show the live broadcasts of Premier League football matches. In selling the rights to broadcast its matches the FAPL grants each broadcaster an exclusive right within the area in which they broadcast; typically this will be on the basis of national boundaries. Licenses also include a requirement that the broadcasters act in such a way as to stop their broadcasts being viewed outside that territory – usually by encryption of the signal. Subscribers of the broadcaster can receive and view the broadcast only by use of a decoder card, which the license also limits from being sold by the broadcaster outside its territory. In both cases the High Court has sought clarification from the Court of Justice as to the application of EU law. The validity of the territorial protection is vital to the outcome in both cases. The potential issue is that the rights effectively partition the internal market along national lines, which can be characterised as a serious restriction of the right to provide services protected by EU law.

At the time of writing Advocate-General Kokott had just delivered her Opinion. The Advocate General's view was that the partitioning of the market is objectionable as it is contrary to the concept of the single market and that there is nothing in the nature of the rights that justifies the imposition of any restriction.

If, as might reasonably be expected, this approach is adopted by the Court of Justice then this has significant potential to significantly alter the market for the broadcast of rights of this kind. If rights holders are unable to protect a number of territories then the only realistic means by which they will be able to market their rights is on an EU-wide basis. This will create a much larger single market for the rights rather than a larger number of discrete, fragmented markets. One significant impact of this could be that this reduces the overall financial yield from the sale of the rights in the EU.

Television without frontiers: listing

The UK has, for a number of years, had in place legislation to protect the ability of the public to access events of significant national interest.[114] The Broadcasting Act 1996 makes specific provision

---

112 COMP/37.576 UEFA Broadcasting Regulations.
113 Cases C-403/08 and C-429/08.
114 First found in the Television Act 1954.

for the 'listing' of events – meaning that they are events that enjoy a measure of protection from exclusive exploitation by a broadcast service which is unavailable to the vast majority of the population. Section 97 of the Broadcasting Act 1996 provides for the listing of 'sporting or other events of national interest'. This has the effect of placing restrictions upon the exclusive acquisition and exploitation of rights by broadcasters, particularly those reaching less than 95 per cent of the population. These restrictions are managed by the independent regulator Ofcom, which is required by the Broadcasting Act 1996 to maintain a code of practice giving guidance on the regulation of listed events.[115] Such measures are permitted under EU law under the terms of the Audiovisual Media Services Directive.[116] The Directive requires Member States to notify the Commission of any measures adopted for verification and notification to other Member States. The validity of the Commission's verification of the measures adopted by the UK and Belgium has been the subject of challenge before the General Court (previously the Court of First Instance) by FIFA and UEFA.[117] FIFA and UEFA sought to annul respectively the Commission's verification of the 'listing' of the FIFA World Cup finals tournament by Belgium and the UK and of the UEFA European Football Championships by the UK. The challenges were slightly different on each account, but focused principally around procedural errors, factual mistakes as to the societal importance of the events in the respective Member States and breaches of the rights of establishment and providing services and the fundamental human right to property. The General Court rejected all of the arguments proffered. In particular the Court rejected the view of UEFA and FIFA that the tournaments could be broken into 'prime' and other matches and instead treated the tournaments as whole events.

The Modern Era: The Path to Lisbon, the EU Reform Treaty and Beyond

As regards the relationship between sport and the EU the present era is undoubtedly best characterised as moving away from ad hoc conflict and litigation, to one of dialogue between the various stakeholders and measured policy-making. This should be seen as the fourth phase of development proposed by Parrish.

The Independent European Sports Review

The beginning of this phase is marked by the Independent European Sports Review.[118] The review was initiated under the UK Presidency of the EU in 2005, by the sports ministers of France, Germany, Italy, Spain and the UK in the aftermath of the collapse of the EU Constitutional Treaty. Article III-282 of the proposed treaty included a measure providing a competence for the EU in the field of sport. Though designated as a report on 'sport', it was commissioned in conjunction with UEFA and was principally focused upon football. The overall objective of the review was the implementation of the Nice Declaration, in particular determining how the EU institutions, Member States and the European and national football federations could best achieve this, and the provision of 'a more comprehensive and robust legal framework for sport in general and football in particular.'[119] The review considers three broad sporting themes: the specific nature of sport; the European

---

115 ITC OFCOM Code on Sports and other Listed or Designated Events, available from http://stakeholders.ofcom.org.uk/binaries/broadcast/other-codes/ofcom_code_on_sport.pdf.
116 Directive 2010/13/EU, Article 14, previously Article 3a of Council Directive 89/552/EEC.
117 Cases T-385/07, T-55/08 and T-68/08 FIFA and UEFA v Commission, judgments of 17 February 2011.
118 Arnaut, J-L, Independent European Sport Review (2006), available from www.independentsportsreview.com; see, generally, Garcia, B, 'The Independent European Sport Review: Half Full or Half Empty?' (2007) 4(3) ESLJ (online).
119 At paras 1.19–1.20.

sports model; and corporate governance models, before going on to consider the means by which proposals under these headings might be adopted.

The specific nature of sport

The review considers the issue of specificity as a means of determining those areas where the law should not intervene, and for this reason it is of particular significance here. The review organises the concept of specificity under three major headings, concerning regulation of: first, the regularity and functioning of competitions; second, the integrity of sport; and third, competitive balance.

Under the heading of 'the regularity and functioning of competitions' the review includes playing rules, structural aspects of competitions, sporting calendars, the composition of national teams and the territorial organisation of sport along national lines, and indicates that these are matters that must fall exclusively within the competence of governing bodies. The review also perceives the pyramid structure of European sport as immune from suit as well as stabilising measures such as transfer deadlines and the regulation of player transfers. Beyond the immediate, internal, specificities the review argues that measures encouraging attendance at matches and participation at amateur level, even though they may impose a restriction elsewhere, such as a broadcast blackout, remain in the best interests of sport. The realm of international competitions is characterised as one which should benefit from the status of specificity, with the major international tournaments being regarded as fundamental. In particular the rule requiring the release of international players by their club sides is highlighted as important to protect, in particular, smaller nations and the interest of the public in seeing the best possible tournament. The final element highlighted under the regularity heading is that there should be a wide margin of discretion permitted to sports governing bodies in dealing with cheating, in particular anti-doping measures.

The concept of integrity is also highly relevant to the legal context as it raises the issue of professional self-regulation in respect of club licensing and player agents' standards. Here the review is more equivocal regarding the exclusion of EU law, but still counsels monitoring and supervision.

Interestingly, competitive balance is treated separately from the regularity point. Here the review is emphatic in propounding that there is a necessity that sporting competition is protected and not left entirely to market forces. In particular the review promotes UEFA's 'home-grown' player rule and maximum squad size as appropriate measures for protecting this element. Financial redistribution through joint selling of broadcast and other media rights is highlighted as a useful redistribution mechanism and the review also advocates the principle of a system of redistribution based on penalties for excessive financial outlay.

Arnaut, J-L, *Independent European Sport Review*

In all these areas where we consider the specificity of sport, it is necessary, when applying the law, to take into account the legitimate autonomy or degree of discretion to be enjoyed by the sports governing body and also the particular features of sport that contribute to make it different from other forms of business.[120]

The European sports model

In considering the European sports model, the review adopts the pyramid concept accepted in previous policy discussions – the maintenance of open leagues with promotion and relegation highlighted as a key value as well as financial redistribution to the grass roots. Notably, the review emphasises the importance of accountability, transparency and separation of powers in the

---

120 Executive Summary, p 13.

governing bodies. In particular the review urges the engagement of a wide range of shareholders in democratising sports governing bodies. Of further note is the weight lent to sports-specific arbitration as a means of ensuring consistent decision-making.

Corporate governance issues

The review considers corporate governance in three contexts: the ownership and management of clubs; the governance of sports regulators; and issues of crime.

In respect of the clubs the review emphasises the need for there to be sound financial management and indicates that the UEFA club licensing system has a role to play, as well as the possible introduction of some form of limits on expenditure, whether by salary capping or similar means. The review also advocates the involvement of fans in club ownership and some method of ensuring that those in control of clubs are suitable persons. The review stresses the need for governing bodies to lead by example and for there to be ongoing improvements in democracy, transparency and professionalism by them. Finally, the review expresses concern at the role of crime in sport, in particular money laundering, the trafficking of young players, gambling and match fixing, and football hooliganism.

Implementation

The report draws the conclusion that the legal environment in which sport operates is not sufficiently stable to provide a basis for strong future development, noting that sport is generally subject to EU law, though at the time there was no Treaty basis. The chief focus is on the application of competition law, where the review calls for the adoption of two approaches: block exemptions consolidating previous decisions, such as in the case of central marketing of television rights; and guidelines which would set out, first, those matters considered outside of the scope of competition law and, second, those which engage the law but may be considered as justifiable. The review is a strong advocate of the use of specific guidelines as a tool in many areas in competition law and also extends this to being appropriate in the context of free movement of persons provisions.

Beyond such 'soft law' approaches, the review calls for EU directives on the protection of minors in sport; pan-European collective bargaining; the regulation of player agents; and matters relating to gambling. Perhaps most controversially the review advocates the establishment of a European Sports Agency to facilitate liaison between the various stakeholders and as a knowledge repository. The review is keen to stress that this would not be a threat to the autonomy of sports regulators.

Though not strictly an 'official' EU document, the Independent European Sports Review has nonetheless proven to be a clear indicator of subsequent developments within the EU institutions and not least in the White Paper on Sport.

The White Paper on Sport

In 2007 the Commission published its White Paper on Sport.[121] The White Paper adopted three broad areas for discussion relating to the social value of sport, the economic value of sport and the organisation of sport. It also proposed an action plan, named after the Olympic pioneer Pierre de Coubertin.

The social value of sport

In considering the societal role of sport the White Paper focuses on the issues of health and exercise, co-ordinating action in supporting anti-doping measures, developing the role of sport in education and training, promoting volunteering and citizenship, using sport as a tool for social inclusion and

---

121 COM(2007) 391 final.

integration, combating racism and violence, sharing European values with other parts of the world and supporting sustainable development.

The most closely legally oriented of these, the anti-doping measures, sees the White Paper propose the development of partnerships between Member State law enforcement agencies, the World Anti-Doping Agency (WADA) and Interpol, with the Commission to play a facilitating role. In connection with racism and violence the White Paper also promises that the Commission will promote co-operation between law enforcement agencies and consider the possibilities for legislation or soft-law measures aimed at preventing public disorder related to sports events.

The economic dimension of sport

The economic dimension contemplates the capacity of sport to contribute to economic growth. The White Paper proposes moving towards evidence-based policy on sport, in particular by seeking specific information and studies on its impact. It further proposes a study on the financing of grass-roots sport and consideration of reduced rates of VAT.

The organisation of sport

Focused on the question of good governance and the relationship between EU law and the regulatory autonomy of the sports governing bodies, the White Paper here centres on the issue of 'specificity':

European Commission, *The White Paper on Sport*

[S]port has certain specific characteristics, which are often referred to as the 'specificity of sport'. The specificity of European sport can be approached through two prisms:

- The specificity of sporting activities and of sporting rules, such as separate competitions for men and women, limitations on the number of participants in competitions, or the need to ensure uncertainty concerning outcomes and to preserve a competitive balance between clubs taking part in the same competitions;
- The specificity of the sport structure, including notably the autonomy and diversity of sport organisations, a pyramid structure of competitions from grassroots to elite level and organised solidarity mechanisms between the different levels and operators, the organisation of sport on a national basis, and the principle of a single federation per sport.[122]

Based on these principles, the White Paper acknowledges that there will be departures from the usual application of competition law. It does similarly in respect of the free movement provisions, while calling on the Member States and sports organisations to address issues of discrimination, noting the legitimacy of proportionate limitations in relation to the selection of national teams, the need to limit participants in a competition and the setting of transfer deadlines. It also overtly supports the football transfer system as a means of ensuring competitive balance.

Players' agents are highlighted as a particular problem and the Commission commits to undertaking a study considering the necessity for action at EU level.[123] Similarly, the protection of minors in sport is perceived as problematic and in need of co-ordination. The Commission acknowledges the value of the club licensing system as a means of achieving many legitimate objectives, but also counsels its proportionate use and expansion beyond European club competitions.

Corruption and money-laundering are also perceived to be a threat to sport and as having a particularly cross-border nature, thus the Commission commits to supporting the development of effective counter strategies.

---

122 At p 13.
123 See now, KEA-CDES-EOSE, *Study of Sports Agents in the European Union* (2009).

Finally, sports media issues are discussed, with the Commission committed to maintaining access to major events while accepting that rights may be sold on a collective basis, but emphasising the importance of redistribution and solidarity in legitimising the practice.

Implementation

The White Paper identifies three means by which this is to be implemented: structured dialogue, cooperation between Member States and social dialogue. The structured dialogue extends to a commitment to establish an EU Sports Forum – an annual meeting of all sports stakeholders; narrower discussions around particular themes; and giving the EU greater visibility at major sporting events. As to co-operation, the White Paper supported the informal ministerial meetings already taking place at that point.

Finally, the route of social dialogue is put forward as being a means by which employers and athletes could agree on employment relations and working conditions by means of codes of conduct or charters.

The Lisbon Treaty

Following the failure of the European Constitutional Treaty, the Member States concluded a less controversial amending Treaty at Lisbon.[124] The Lisbon Treaty – the European Reform Treaty – made numerous changes to the EU's treaty arrangements, in particular re-designating the EC Treaty as the Treaty on the Functioning of the European Union (TFEU). From the sports law perspective, the key element of the Lisbon Treaty is that, for the first time, it incorporates a specific Treaty-basis for sport. Article 165 TFEU, which contains the new competence states, in pertinent part:

1. ... The Union shall contribute to the promotion of European sporting issues, while taking account of the specific nature of sport, its structures based on voluntary activity and its social and educational function.

2. Union action shall be aimed at:. . .
   - developing the European dimension in sport, by promoting fairness and openness in sporting competitions and co-operation between bodies responsible for sports, and by protecting the physical and moral integrity of sportsmen and sportswomen, especially the youngest sportsmen and sportswomen.

3. The Union and the Member States shall foster co-operation with third countries and the competent international organisations in the field of education and sport, in particular the Council of Europe.

4. In order to contribute to the achievement of the objectives referred to in this Article:
   - the European Parliament and the Council, acting in accordance with the ordinary legislative procedure, after consulting the Economic and Social Committee and the Committee of the Regions, shall adopt incentive measures, excluding any harmonisation of the laws and regulations of the Member States
   - the Council, on a proposal from the Commission, shall adopt recommendations.

Exploring Article 165 TFEU

The key characteristic of Article 165 TFEU is that it provides only a 'soft-law' competence for the EU, meaning that only action of a complementary, co-ordinating or supporting nature can be

---

124 See, generally, Siekmann, R, 'Article III-282 of the Constitution for Europe and an EU Policy for Sport' (2004) 3-4 ISLJ 77.

implemented. Further, the measure is limited in its own terms to the promotion and fostering of co-operation (paragraphs 1 and 3). This means that legislative measures may not be adopted on the basis of Article 165 TFEU that seek to harmonise the actions of Member States (paragraph 4); though the capacity to do so still exists where sport falls under aspects of the Treaties which so provide. What the measure does is to give legal status to the idea that the specificity of sport is to be respected and its wider nature and functions. Whereas previously this has only been given voice in non-binding measures attached to the Treaties of Amsterdam and Nice, the appeal to specificity has added weight. Indeed, this was proven to be so in the first 'sports case' to be judged by the Court of Justice following the entry into force of the Lisbon Treaty in December 2009. In *Bernard* (considered above)[125] the Court made particular note of the entry into force of the provision, though this appeared to be merely ancillary to the decision in the case and did not impact substantially. Nevertheless, the existence of a Treaty article propounding this approach is likely to have some impact upon the Court when it is deciding matters, perhaps under the auspices of competition law; this has certainly been the case in the context of the Amsterdam Declaration, which was given specific mention by the Court in it judgments in both *Lehtonen* and *Deliège*.

Developing the European dimension in sport

The precise nature of the realisation of the objectives and powers set out in Article 165 TFEU has now been articulated in a Commission communication to other EU institutions.[126] The communication takes as its theme the expression 'European dimension in sport' set out in the Treaty, and frames the proposals for action in the context of the capacity of action at EU level to provide 'added value' by complementing Member States' activities where appropriate while having the capacity to bring particular benefits to bear in the context of transnational issues; similarly the role of facilitator of dialogue is emphasised.[127] Beyond this the paper is structured in the now well-established trio of the societal, economic and organisational elements of sport.

In the context of the societal role of sport the most significant element for consideration is the proposal to engage to a greater degree in the fight against doping through the drafting of a mandate for EU accession to the Council of Europe Anti-Doping Convention, the reinforcement of trafficking counter-measures and support for transnational anti-doping networks. The paper also proposes measures pertaining to: the development of guidelines on training, education and physical activity; safety and security arrangements at international sports event; accessibility to sports organisations and events for the disabled; and the promotion of women's access to leadership positions in sport.

On economic matters the communication has strong legal implications, with the Commission calling for: the establishment of mechanisms to secure adequate redistribution of revenues, financial solidarity and funding of grass-roots sport; a focus on dealing with intellectual property issues that may arise in the context of sports events; monitoring of state aid in sport; and sport as a tool of regional development and employability. The communication envisages each of the above as being premised on clear evidence and proposes the promotion of a network of universities to promote innovative means of securing detailed information.

The key focus from a legal perspective, however, is on matters concerned with the organisation of sport. The communication states at the outset that good governance is a precondition for the autonomy and self-regulation enjoyed by sport and the Commission sets out values of lawfulness, democracy, transparency, accountability and inclusiveness as being at the core. The communication does, nonetheless, reaffirm the significance of 'specificity' and that this should be taken into account

---

125 See earlier, pp 174–5.
126 Communication from the Commission to the European Parliament, the Council, The European Economic and Social Committee and the Committee of the Regions, *Developing the European Dimension in Sport* COM(2011) 12 final.
127 At p 3. See also *Council resolution on the EU structured dialogue on sport* (2010) 18 and 19 November.

when assessing sports' compliance with the requirements of EU law. As established by the case law in this area, the Commission confirms that any departure from these requirements must be in pursuit of a legitimate objective and that any restriction must be proportionate, but also acknowledges that the inherent sporting restrictions should be given particular weight. It undertakes to give specific guidance along particular themes regarding the application of the concept. This point is further expanded in respect of freedom of movement. Here the Commission outlines that direct nationality discrimination is incompatible with EU law, but acknowledges that indirect discrimination or hindrances to movement may be considered legitimate on the terms set out above.[128] The Commission has also undertaken to issue guidance in this respect and, interestingly, to review the home-grown players rule in 2012. Finally, this section proposes investigation of the regulation of player agents and to offer support for social dialogue in the sport and leisure sector.

Having undertaken an extensive impact assessment,[129] the Commission will propose a Communication defining a policy framework for co-operation in sport at EU level, including a new EU Agenda for sport with a view to a possible Sport Programme from 2014.

Conclusions

The development of European Union sports law since the mid-1990s has been extraordinary. Prior to the judgment in Bosman the interactions with sport were piecemeal and had little genuine impact. The rapid growth of the relationship was initially founded on privately initiated litigation based on free movement provisions, but was quickly fed by increased interest and intervention by, in particular, the Commission.

What has emerged is a relationship between the EU and sport that has become less confrontational and litigious with a pattern of dialogue, negotiation and parallel, complementary regulation beginning to materialise. There is growing acceptance by sports authorities of the inevitability, if not the desirability, of EU involvement in sport. Consequently a 'smarter' approach has emerged, with sports bodies increasingly acquiring a more sophisticated understanding of the approach of EU law and gaining an appreciation that many of their regulatory goals can still be met, albeit with a shift in approach. This is not to say that conflict does not continue to arise or will not do so in future – EU law, particularly competition law, is rightly perceived as offering a real opportunity to challenge the established orthodoxy in sport. Similarly, it is far from clear that the principles established in Bosman and the subsequent development of the law have been wholly absorbed across the spectrum of professional sport in the EU. The niceties of the free movement provisions, such as in Bernard, remain to be settled and the refusal to except sport from competition provisions in Meca-Medina means that it is likely that sport will be involved in frequent legal skirmishes in both contexts.

What is apparent is that, although the initial route into sport for the EU was through professional sport, EU policy in the area now conceives of sport much more broadly. The economic, organisational aspects of sport that attract scrutiny from the EU's single market rules remain an important part of the relationship and sport is unlikely to receive an 'exemption' from its application but, increasingly, the approach to sport has broadened to include a desire to underpin regulatory efforts aimed at resolving major sporting issues, such as anti-doping, and to encompass sport as a tool for the achievement of goals in other policy fields such as health and education. This

---

128 See also, Commission Staff Working Document, *Sport and Free Movement*, accompanying document to the Communication from the Commission to the European Parliament, the Council, The European Economic and Social Committee and the Committee of the Regions, *Developing the European Dimension in Sport* SEC(2011) 66 final.

129 Commission Staff Working Document, Impact Assessment, Accompanying document to the Communication from the Commission to the European Parliament, the Council, The European Economic and Social Committee and the Committee of the Regions, *Developing the European Dimension in Sport* SEC(2011) 66 final.

three-point approach is recognised and cemented by the advent of a specific, albeit soft, competence in Article 165 TFEU.

In just over a decade and a half the EU has been transformed from an organisation with little or no interest or impact in sport – save for two interesting but relatively trivial judgments of the Court of Justice and an ineffectual dialogue with the football authorities – into a key player in the regulation of sport, not just within its territories, but globally. A specific 'soft law' mandate in the field and a burgeoning policy portfolio will almost certainly lead to an even more prominent role for the EU in sport.

Key Points

- The involvement of the EU in sport has increased significantly over the last two decades;
- EU involvement was initially predicated upon and limited to the extent to which sport can be considered an economic activity;
- The judgment in *Bosman* had a profound effect upon the legal environment in which European and world football operates, significantly strengthening the position of professionals as regards movement between clubs and lowering restrictions to participation;
- EU law recognises that not all restrictions ought to be condemned as unlawful, but limits those deviations from this to measures that are objectively reasonable and proportionate;
- EU competition law is now at the forefront of the interface between sport and law;
- Competition law offers much greater potential to catch restrictive measures, above and beyond that provided under free movement of persons law;
- In its application, competition law has been used in a careful cautious way, again recognising the particular needs of sport;
- Sport has come under increasing scrutiny from competition law in respect of its commercial activities and not just its regulatory activities;
- Though there was no initial Treaty competence for sport, this has now been introduced by Article 165 TFEU;
- The EU now has a significantly wider remit in sport; not just that relating to economic regulation.

Key Sources

European Commission, Directorate General for Education and Culture, Sports Unit: http://ec.europa.eu/sport/index_en.htm.
Euractiv.com, Sports Section: http://www.euractiv.com/en/sports.
Parrish, R and Miettinen, S, *The Sporting Exception in European Union Law* (2008), The Hague: TMC Asser Press.
Study on the Equal Treatment of Non-Nationals in Individual Sports Competitions (2010) http://ec.europa.eu/sport/library/doc/f_studies/study_equal_treatment_non_nationals_final_rpt%20_dec_2010.pdf.
Van den Bogaert, S and Vermeersch, A, 'Sport and the EC Treaty: a tale of uneasy bedfellows?' (2006), EL Rev 821.

Part **2**

Legal Protection of the Commercial Integrity of Sport

5   Sport and Money: Accountability and
    Regulation   209

6   Sport, Match Fixing and Corruption   258

7   The Exploitation and Protection of
    Olympic Commercial Rights   302

Chapter 5

Sport and Money: Accountability and Regulation

Chapter Contents

Introduction	210
Professionalisation and the End of Amateurism	212
Commercialisation of Sport	219
The Economics of Sport	220
Characteristics of Sport Business	222
Commodification	225
Models of Regulation	227
Football Task Force	230
Effective Sports Governance	241
Competition and Broadcasting	245
Other Competition Law Intervention into UK Sport	254
Conclusion	257
Key Points	257
Key Sources	257

Introduction

Sport is a growing and significant global industry and represents more than 3 per cent of world trade.[1] And it is worth more than 1 per cent of the gross national product (GNP) of the European Union (EU).[2] In the EU alone, two million new jobs have been created directly or indirectly by the sports industry.[3] In the UK, consumer spend on sport in England was £17.384 billion in 2008.[4] The challenge that sports bodies and leagues face is increasingly how the commercial integrity of and financial investment in sport, from a range of stakeholders, can be protected and secured.

This phenomenal growth in the value of the sports industry is largely due to the increase in the broadcast coverage of sports events and the concomitant rise in the fees paid by broadcasters for the corresponding rights. An audience of 4.7 billion viewers or 70 per cent of the world's population watched Olympic broadcasts at least once during the Beijing Olympics in summer 2008.[5] Around one billion people watched some of the opening ceremony, the record television audience for a single event. Television and other media rights have soared in value.[6] Increased television coverage has also led to a spectacular rise in the value of sports sponsorship, by national and multinational companies wishing to associate themselves and their products and services with major national and international sports events, such as the Olympic Games and the FIFA World Cup. It has been estimated that the value of global sponsorship, $42.7bn in 2007, is predicted to rise to just under $60bn by 2012.[7] The worldwide recession since the end of 2008 seems to have had remarkably little negative impact.[8]

The increase in leisure time in the developed world has also played a significant part in the meteoric rise of the sports industry, with more people participating in and watching sport than ever before. This, in turn, has seen the rise of sportsmen and women as sports personalities with incomes – especially footballers in the age of £250,000 per week salaries – sponsorship and endorsement deals akin to the fabulous incomes of Hollywood 'stars'.[9] In fact, sport is now very much a part of the worldwide entertainment industry.[10]

All of this, combined with the development of the internet and other new forms of new media, including mobile phones, to deliver sports programming, content and information, means that the value of the sports industry is set to grow even further in the future – new media companies have used sport as very much the driving force in advertising new technologies. With all this new money and wealth around sport, winning is now everything – the privilege and satisfaction alone of taking part is obsolete. And, with the increasing use of performance-enhancing drugs by sportspersons, it seems to be a case of winning at all costs. For top sportspersons, winning means money and riches. So, in line with the old adage, where there is money to be fought over there are likely to be disputes, and it is not surprising that sports litigation is also on the increase.

---

1 European Commission, *The European Model of Sport* (1999).
2 Ibid.
3 Monti, M, excerpts of a speech given at a Commission-organised conference on sports, Brussels, 17 April 2000, http://europa.eu/rapid/pressReleasesAction.do?reference=SPEECH/00/152&format=HTML&aged=0&language=EN&guiLanguage=en.
4 'Sport makes heavyweight contribution to England's economy', www.sportengland.org/media_centre/press_releases/economic_value_of_sport.aspx.
5 Nielsen Report, http://blog.nielsen.com/nielsenwire/wp-content/uploads/2008/09/press_release3.pdf.
6 See later p 227 for figures.
7 Kolah, A, 'UK crowned number one in sports sponsorship market' (2008), *Marketing*, 18 June, www.marketingmagazine.co.uk/news/rss/817707/UK-crowned-number-one-sports-sponsorship-marke. If gate receipts and TV rights are added, the global value of sports marketing increases from $102.6bn in 2007 to an estimated $140.6bn by 2012.
8 'Recession fails to frighten sports sponsors', http://uk.reuters.com/article/idUKLNE64K00O20100521.
9 *Annual Report on Football Finance 2009*, Deloitte & Touche, August 2000; see http://www.deloitte.com/view/en_GB/uk/industries/sportsbusinessgroup/sports/football/index.htm.
10 See, for example, the sponsorship of the new Union of European Basketball League, the SuproLeague, formed in July 2000 and sponsored by the Spanish telecommunications giant, Telephonica; see *Soccer Investor Weekly*, 19 September 2000.

This chapter will provide a theoretical basis for the law's intervention and regulation of sport within this context of greater commercialisation. This will be carried out in three connected ways. The first section explores the process of professionalisation and 'growing pains' when there is a transformation from an amateur to a professionalised sport, which invariably involves fragmentation, leading to litigation and many legally related problems. The changes in the late 1970s in cricket and the mid-1990s in rugby will be explored. The particular characteristics of 'sports business' will be examined and it will be seen that the financial dynamics in sport are often idiosyncratic.[11]

The second section will consider alternative regulatory regimes concerning sport. British sporting organisations are of course varied in size and form. They range from the small sports club, invariably one that is, in the eyes of the law, an 'unincorporated association', its members contractually bound together towards compliance with the rules of the association. There are tens of thousands of them around the country. At the other end of the spectrum are the National Governing Bodies (NGBs) in sport, which are likely to be 'incorporated' as limited liability companies. These sporting organisations have traditionally been seen as autonomous and private 'self-regulating' bodies. The question that is increasingly asked is, within this overtly commercialised sporting world, can these bodies be trusted to continue to be the 'custodians' of their sport and essentially be self-policing? Periodic financial scandals and allegations of corruption have made this question more pressing.[12] Within the overtly commercialised world of elite professional sport, there is the danger that sport's requirement of 'uncertainty as to outcome' and a degree of equality between clubs and individual athletes to be able to participate in 'real competition' – the essence of sport – is increasingly compromised. Essentially the argument can be summarised that, if law is the regular form of regulation for market relations and if sport is now essentially commercialised, it needs to be subject to similar regulation.

The two opposing models that will be considered are, on the one hand, the continuation of self-regulation or, on the other, external regulation of some sort. This latter model can clearly be of a variable degree. The debate concerning the ability of the law to intervene into these 'private' and 'autonomous bodies' to challenge decisions and procedures through judicial review has been examined in Chapter 3. An important distinction can be made between sports regulation and governance. Although they are intertwined, regulation concerns outside supervision of some type, while governance concerns the procedures and issues of power within the organisation or body itself.

To illustrate the issue of sports regulation, it is football that will primarily be examined. Calls for external regulation have been partly premised on the observation that effective governance of football by the authorities has failed. Not only is football culturally the primary British national sport; it has also been impacted upon by the changes in the surrounding commercial dynamics more than any other sport. On a general level the sports industry has distinct and unusual commercial characteristics that need to be carefully understood in terms of regulation. The 1999 report, *Commercial Issues*, produced by the Football Task Force, will be used to illustrate alternative regulatory regimes as they might apply to football.

The third section will be a consequential discussion of the issues concerning sports governance – that is, the internal running of a sport from the national governing body (NGB) through regional and county bodies to the individual sports club. This creates a pyramid structure with the NGB at the apex. Above this structure are of course European and international sports federations. In the recent past there has been an increasing belief that the sports governance in the UK has been substandard. The qualities of effective corporate governance, comparable to that needed in NGBs and international sports federations (ISFs), will be considered.

---

11 See later, pp 222–3.
12 See Chapter 6 for a further examination of these issues.

The fourth and last section will focus on the impact of competition law on the sports industry, including the role that television and other forms of media have had on contemporary sport. Media companies and their ever-developing new technologies are very much the driving force in changes in the contemporary sports world.[13] Perhaps the best example is the effect that BSkyB television has had in the UK. The business model it employed to grow its business was based primarily on availability of first-run movies and live Premiership football. It has brought enormous amounts of 'new money' into the game.

Professionalisation and the End of Amateurism

In the UK, some sport has been commercialised and professionalised for many years. For example, professional football clubs have been run, sometimes badly, as commercial entities since the late 1880s. Nonetheless, large areas of sport have been essentially amateur or have masqueraded under this guise in terms of 'shamateurism'; athletics and rugby are two such sports. However, commercialisation around sport in recent years, for example with the vast increases in sponsorship, marketing and merchandising operations, has led to modern sport becoming a huge business.[14] Television, and increasingly other technologies, have helped change its financial contours.[15]

Edward Grayson has clearly indicated that professionalism can be seen as diametrically opposed to the inherent values of Corinthianism.[16] The attraction of the values of amateur Corinthianism and the ruination of contemporary sport due to professionalisation continues to be powerful.[17] Professionalism in sports, however, has clearly brought many positive characteristics as well as these perceived negatives. In rugby union, for example, in 1995 Will Carling, the then England captain, famously characterised the members of the Rugby Union Football Committee (RFU) as '57 old farts', crystallising the legacy of the past in sports administration and governance. A few months later, around the World Cup in South Africa, rugby union became a professional game. This was partly due to the facade of shamateurism, but also the significant changes going on in the rival code rugby league, where in Australia a battle between the media tycoons Rupert Murdoch and Kerry Packer was being fought for control of the game:

'Shamateurism's end: taking the money and running'

The timing could not have been more ironic: on the very weekend rugby league was celebrating its centenary, rugby union announced it too was now a professional game. Rugby league was launched 100 years ago tomorrow by 21 union clubs, which wanted to pay their players for taking time off from work to play, but failed to persuade other union clubs to go along. It led to the two separate rugby codes – one openly professional and the other where payments were not supposed to be made. Slowly but inexorably, union's amateur status has become a sham. First came expenses, then came lucrative PR jobs with big companies, and then full blown product endorsement (so long as there was no direct mention of the individual player's links with rugby). Other countries went much further than the home nations. France began paying some of its top players in the thirties. But it was television – and the large audiences generated by the 1987 and

---

13 Whannel, G, *Fields in Vision: Television Sport and Cultural Transformation* (1992), London: Routledge, pp 1–2.
14 See, for example, 'United put finishing touches to £300 m kit deal', *The Guardian*, 4 November 2000 – a 13-year deal concerning the playing kit has been agreed between Manchester United and Nike worth £302.9 million – the most lucrative tie-up in sporting history.
15 The value of the current deal (for three seasons from 2010 for 138 games per season) is worth £1.782bn, an average of £4.3m per game; see Spink, P and Morris, P, 'The TV rights in professional football', in Caiger, A and Gardiner, S (eds), *Professional Sport in the European Union: Regulation and Re-regulation* (2000), The Hague: Asser.
16 See earlier, pp 70–3.
17 *Inside Sport*: 'Is Professionalism Killing Sport?' BBC TV, 27 September, 2010.

1991 World Cups – that tolled the final amateur bell. Rugby has become a multi-million pound business. Just before the start of this year's world cup, Murdoch's News Corporation struck a £360 million deal with the rugby unions of Australia, New Zealand and South Africa.

It was the fear of Murdoch – or his rival Kerry Packer – grabbing control of the sport that finally forced the International Rugby Union Board to move this weekend. Some rugby union officials were expressing regret yesterday. They should not have been. The new system will end the hypocrisy of the old. It will allow a few – and it will only be a few – top players to a share in the game's growing riches. They deserve that. The main core of the sport – just as in tennis, golf, even soccer – will remain amateur. Remember, even within rugby league, the vast majority of players have another job as well as playing rugby. Our own sports reporters put the number of union players who are likely to receive direct payments at between 60 and 100. Even within this group, few are likely to be full-time rugby players. The risks are too great – both from injury and loss of form. Big policemen and massive army officers are still likely to be found in the pack. Although payments can be made at any level, few clubs are likely to be in a position to offer them. Even the most successful club, Bath, holds fewer than 10,000. Compare that to United's 40,000 plus.[18]

This change in the status of the game[19] has brought obvious changes: sports agents;[20] a professional players' union;[21] and significantly increased television revenues. However, there were those who lamented the end of the amateur ethos.[22]

Similar changes have occurred in athletics:

Downes, S and Mackay, D, *Running Scared: How Athletics Lost Its Innocence*

Athens was also the venue in 1982 for the greatest revolution in a century of modern athletics. There were no races run, no jumps leaped nor implements thrown: the revolution took place in a conference hall, where the IAAF took the first tentative steps towards allowing athletics to go professional.

The process had begun at the IAAF's conference in Moscow prior to the 1980 Olympics. There, the Federation established a nine-man working group on 'eligibility' – in other words, to examine the amateur status of athletes.

During the 1960s and 1970s amateurism, although increasingly regarded as an anachronism in the modern sporting world – cricket had abandoned its 'Gentlemen and Players' distinction, and the Wimbledon tennis championships had gone open – had still been strictly applied by the International Olympic Committee, first under the autocratic leadership of the American, Avery Brundage, and then under the Irish peer, Lord Killanin. The Games were still the most important event in any amateur sportsman's career, so no athlete could risk being banned for receiving money. But with Michael Killanin set to retire as IOC president in July 1980, the ground was laid for a moderniser to succeed him. The Spaniard Juan Antonio Samaranch duly became the IOC's first full-time president. Fittingly, he was to preside over a period which made it increasingly possible for Olympic competitors to become full-time, professional athletes.

The mood at the IAAF's congress in Moscow had reflected this turning point in world sport. When the IAAF working party on eligibility delivered its report to the governing council when it met in Cairo the following March, its findings were hardly a surprise. The tone of the report was

---

18 'Shamateurism's end: taking the money and running', *The Guardian*, 28 August 1995.
19 'Small change for most Rugby Union players', *The Guardian*, 28 August 1995, p 3; for a full history see Collins, T, *A Social History of English Rugby Union* (2009), London : Routledge.
20 'The future starts here: Rugby sports agents', *The Observer*, 31 December 1995, p 26.
21 'Moon is the man as sun sets on amateurism', *The Guardian*, 20 December 1995, p 21.
22 'Rugby Union: top club official quits over "ethos" ', *The Guardian*, 1 September 1995, p 23.

categorical: the very future of the IAAF was in the balance. The shamateur game was up, according to the working party. 'The year 1980 has brought to a head the fact that the future of the IAAF and its members is at stake,' the report began. 'It is felt that at international level, athletics is a semi-professional (in the widest sense) sport already, with many leading athletes in top countries training for at least 30 hours per week. The Group aims, however, to make a clear distinction between a professional sport and athletics, which, by its very nature, can never become this. It is recognised that there is dissatisfaction among the elite athletes and meeting organisers with the present rules on eligibility, and in different countries, violations of the rules occur, which causes accusations of hypocrisy to be levelled against the whole sport of athletics.'

Conscious of the need to prevent an amateur–professional schism in the sport, but also subjected to political pressures from the eastern bloc nations – who wanted the status quo maintained, so that their State-funded athletes would maintain their apparent advantage over part-time western athletes – the working party proposed a set of rule changes which would openly allow payments to athletes, through a system of prize-money and trust funds. The recommendations, though, were only a majority view of the working party.

The proposed new eligibility rules were debated heatedly when put before the IAAF Conference held just before the European Championships in Athens in September 1982. The reactionaries on the working party, who wanted to avoid change, seemed to have swung opinion among the IAAF Congress – the sport's 'parliamentary' body, made up of representatives of every national member federation, with the authority to make or change the sport's rules.

Compromise was offered. Although the working party had favoured prize-money over appearance fees ('an athlete receiving money merely because he is a champion is felt to be an unfair and unworthy system for the sport. Appearance money inevitably takes the stimulus away from competition, just as it may be argued that prize money gives added stimulus'), it was the latter, appearance money scheme which had attracted more support. Yet even moves towards this new system of appearance payments seemed to have stalled until a rousing address by a member of the British delegation. The man who turned the day in favour of appearance fees was Andy Norman.

Before breakfast, sensing that the mood of the Congress might reject all proposals for athletes' payments at that afternoon's debate, Norman had banged on the door of the hotel bedroom of the *Guardian* reporter, John Rodda. After a typically journalistic late night, Rodda was feeling a little fragile when he was awoken by the knock on the door from the policeman, but he was persuaded nonetheless to help Norman by writing what Rodda later described as 'a blatantly provocative speech' in favour of change.

Standing in front of all the IAAF's power brokers at the Athens conference, and with Rodda's speech to guide him, Norman warned that if the national governing bodies continued to pretend that under-the-counter payments were not happening, then what they all feared most – a breakaway, professional circuit – might happen. Norman 'knew what the athletes wanted', Rodda recalled, 'and how it was obtainable'.

'Rule 17 – Athlete's Funds', the new payment rule, went through by 367 votes to 16 . . . the tide had turned professionalism's way.[23]

Although the enormous amount of amateur sporting activity, often in the form of recreational activity, must never be forgotten in these discussions, virtually all of elite modern sport is essentially professional.[24] The general commercialisation and commodification of sport has been shown to be

---

23 Downes, S and Mackay, D, *Running Scared: How Athletics Lost Its Innocence* (1996), Edinburgh: Mainstream, pp 100–02.
24 See Strenk, A, 'Amateurism: the myth and the reality', in Segrave, JP and Chu, D, *The Olympic Games in Transition* (1988), Champaign, IL: Human Kinetics, pp 307–21; Holt, R, 'Amateurism and its interpretation: the social origins of British sport' (1992) 5(4) *Innovation* 19.

influential in this process.[25] The law is never far behind in these circumstances, and the commercial origins of much legal intervention in sport are clear to see.

A good deal of elite sport is played on the world stage. The quadrennial Olympic Games and football World Cup are clear examples. The two processes of globalisation – where social activities and processes are increasingly ceasing to be explained purely in national terms – and professionalisation of sport can be seen as advancing hand in hand. Changes in cricket at the end of the 1970s and subsequently will be discussed to illustrate these developments.

Cricket wars: the Packer legacy

The development of World Series Cricket, sponsored by Kerry Packer, as a challenge to established Test cricket in Australia had major implications and consequences for world cricket. The mid-1970s cricket world was ideally placed for commercial exploitation. Although there was a semi-professional game in Australia and a professional game in England, wages were very low compared with other similar sports and the television rights were cheap. In Australia the top players who played Test cricket were continually in dispute over pay. Kerry Packer, who owned a series of commercial TV stations in Australia, was under pressure to increase audiences and televised sport was seen as a cheap way to achieve this. He had successfully obtained exclusive rights to golf; he saw cricket as an even more attractive product in terms of the ability to fit in commercial breaks.

Television rights had been presented to the non-commercial channel Australian Broadcasting Corporation (ABC) since the 1950s ritually, on a non-exclusive basis with local commercial TV bids then being made. This process had kept down the price paid for rights. Packer wanted to buy exclusive rights to Test cricket. Even though in 1976 he was prepared to pay over six times the price that ABC had agreed with the Australian Cricket Board, he failed in his bid. Effectively closed out of established cricket, he decided to develop a rival international cricket competition and began to sign up established Australian test cricketers such as Ian Chappell and to approach established international stars from England, the West Indies, Pakistan and India, and talented South African players excluded from international cricket because of sporting bans induced by apartheid. Instrumental in the recruitment of a number of these players was Tony Greig, then the England Test captain. One legal issue that needed to be reconciled was first what name could be used: the term 'Supertest' was viewed as sufficiently distinct. Also:

Haigh, G, *Cricket War: The Inside Story of Packer's World Series Cricket*

> Benaud worried, though, that the Laws of Cricket themselves might have a legal character. The MCC did hold their copyright. It would be important to play a form of stand alone rules 'based on' the Laws to avoid further legal troubles.[26]

The vast majority of the world's best players were signed up and 'Packer's Circus', as the press described it, was launched in May 1977. The plan met a lot of resistance from the cricket establishment and although there were attempts at a compromise between the Packer organisation and the International Cricket Conference (now Council) (ICC), the international governing body, the issue of exclusive rights to Tests in Australia proved insurmountable. This led over two months later to:

> Reports . . . of an International Cricket Conference ultimatum issued the previous evening at Lord's: WSC players should be barred from all first-class and Test Cricket if they did not shred their contracts before 1 October 1977. Though the Test and County Cricket Board's Doug Insole

---

25 See later p 219.
26 Haigh, G, *Cricket War: the Inside Story of Packer's World Series Cricket* (1993), Melbourne: Text Publishing Company, p 82.

and Donald Carr had received Queen's Counsel advice that enforcement would be legally diffi-cult, the counties were passionate. Glamorgan's Ossie Wheatley went into the TCCB minute book expressing the view: 'Our duty is to drive this wedge of uncertainty into the player's mind.' Insole echoed: 'War situation. We must make sure this thing does not get off the ground.'[27]

The World Series Cricket (WSC) matches that were to be played during the winter of 1977–78 in Australia were then scheduled to be played at the same time as the Test series between Australia and the West Indies. The contracted players would not be available for Test selection whatever the moves of the ICC. The view was that:

> The ICC's self-appointing as cricket's sole promoter could not go unchallenged and barring signatories from first-class cricket appeared an unenforceable restraint of trade ... CPH (Packer's Consolidated Press Holdings), it was decided, would back Greig, Snow and Proctor in a High Court challenge to the ICC.[28]

The High Court in London became the focus of attention that October:

> WSC, Greig, Proctor and Snow were litigants; the defendants were the Test and County Cricket Board and chairman Doug Insole – the ICC had no legal personality. A barrage of lawyers and twenty-one star witnesses were gathered to impress Justice Sir Christopher Slade.
>   The sole absentee was Sir Donald Bradman. Ray Steele arrived in his stead. 'He was such a shrewd little bugger, of course,' Steele chuckles. Nobody relished the fiery court wicket with hostile Queen's Counsels from both ends: WSC's Robert Alexander downwind, the ICC's Michael Kempster coming uphill but making Greig flinch as testimony began. Ross Edwards was struck at how detested Greig had become. 'Jeez, he was like Lord Haw-Haw,' says Edwards. 'He was very bad meat.'
>   'For some reason, I felt like a criminal,' Greig recalled. 'Especially when I was first attacked by the opposition counsel. My initial impulse was to tell all our opposition to go jump in the lake . . . It became like a battle, with the opposition trying to pull me apart and Alexander protecting me.'[29]

The decision was in favour of the players. The ICC's only solace came in Justice Slade's observations that cricket administrators were a thoroughly decent breed, who 'believed that they acted in the best interests of cricket'. The judge could also understand the sense of betrayal at Greig's recruiting role, but retaliation had 'strained the bounds of loyalty'. In fact, they should have foreseen events:

> The very size of profits made from cricket matches involving star players must for some years have carried the risk that a private promoter would appear on the scene and seek to make money by promoting cricket matches involving world class cricketers.[30]

Greig v Insole

> The question for decision has been whether the particular steps which the ICC and TCCB took to combat what they regarded as the threat from world series cricket were legally justified. The long investigation has satisfied me that the positive demonstrable benefits that might be achieved by introducing the ICC and TCCB bans and applying them to players who had already committed themselves to contracts with WSC were at best somewhat speculative. On the other

---

27 Ibid, p 114.
28 Ibid, p 85.
29 Ibid, p 101.
30 Ibid, p 120.

hand there were, as has been mentioned, a number of demonstrable disadvantages if the bans were to be applied in this way. They would preclude the players concerned from entry into the important fields of professional livelihood. This would subject them to the hardships and injustice of essentially retrospective legislation. They would deprive the public of any opportunity of seeing the players concerned playing in conventional cricket, either at test or at English county level, for at least a number of years. By so depriving the public, they would carry with them an appreciable risk of diminishing both public enthusiasm for conventional cricket and the receipts to be derived from it. Furthermore the defendants by imposing the bans, in the form which they took and with the intentions which prompted them, acted without adequate regard to the fact that World Series Cricket had contractual rights with the players concerned, which were entitled to the protection of the law. The defendants acted in good faith and in what they considered to be the best interests of cricket. That, however, is not enough to justify in law the course which they have taken. In the result, I find for the plaintiffs in both actions.[31]

The legal costs of the ICC amounted to nearly £200,000. World Series Cricket was played over a period of about 18 months, mainly in Australia but also in the West Indies. A mixture of 'Supertests' and one-day internationals led to many innovations such as improved televising and day–night games that have become a norm of the modern game. Detractors point to the increased gamesmanship in the form of 'sledging' and intimidatory fast bowling stimulated by WSC. What is not in doubt is that this period of history led to the financial contours of the game changing at the elite levels of cricket. Additionally, as an example of a breakaway league, WSC introduced many innovations including one-day internationals and matches under floodlights. It is an example of how development in one country triggered change in that sport on the world stage: the globalisation of sport.[32]

Whereas this challenge to the existing hegemony in world cricket came from Australia, a more recent challenge has come from the Indian sub-continent, which can be seen as the economic powerhouse of world cricket.

Greenfield, S and Osborn, G 'Regulating sport: finding a role for the law?'

The fundamental issue is a financial one; the professional game played between counties (the national level in England and Wales) is uneconomic as it fails to draw any significant level of spectator support. The revenue from test match cricket, which is played at a limited number of venues, subsidizes the professional game and efforts have been made to make cricket more attractive. A variety of one-day competitions have been introduced. The latest version, Twenty20, started in 2003 and was a much-shortened version of the game with both innings (20 'overs', or 120 deliveries long) completed in three hours. The aim was to attract a new audience and offer a new experience that concentrated on continuous action. The Laws were adjusted to increase the action and excitement. It proved to be an unqualified success and was subsequently adopted by other countries and led to a World Cup in South Africa in 2007, won by India, who beat Pakistan in the final. The Twenty20 World Cup in England in 2009 was similarly a massive success, with devoted and passionate crowds making it a real spectacle.

Ticket sales were very encouraging, reflecting the enduring popularity of cricket despite the global economic situation. There was a 96 per cent take-up of tickets for this event and certainly the atmosphere created by those large crowds formed part of why it was so successful. Outside of these international country-led events, it was clear that the format could be massively exploited and the market was not slow in realizing the opportunity. First off was the Indian Cricket League (ICL) a private initiative that was not sanctioned by the Board of Control for Cricket in India. Similarly

---

31 *Greig v Insole* [1978] 1 WLR 302, per Slade LJ, pp 364–65.
32 Also see McFarline, P, *A Game Divided* (1977), Richmond: Marlin Books.

to its predecessor, the 'rebel' WSC, the impetus for the formation came from a broadcaster, Zee Telefilms, who had been unable to obtain access to the national side's television rights. Interestingly Tony Greig, one of the leading WSC 'rebels', was also involved. This brought the organizers into direct conflict with the Indian Board and consequently other national Governing Bodies. The ICL had attracted a number of overseas players from the major cricket-playing nations, including the former West Indian captain Brian Lara and his Pakistani counterpart Inzaman–ul-Haq. A number of English players also joined, including internationals Darren Maddy and Vikram Solanki, who had been in England's Twenty20 World Cup squad. The nature of the domestic contractual arrangements meant that County players who were not contracted during the winter would be free to join the ICL; however, those English internationals in receipt of a central contract would be prohibited. Despite the fact that the players were free agents the ECB sought to actively discourage ICL participation on the grounds that the ICL competition was unauthorized.

The challenge to the IPL and ICL players could be focused on the same model as was adopted in *Greig*, effectively trying to stop players from joining the IPL or ICL using their contracts as the vehicle to do this. This would be based around the exclusivity elements of the contracts the players had signed with the ECB, if centrally contracted, or with the counties themselves otherwise. Any attempt by the ECB to tackle this retrospectively is fraught with difficulties, largely because of the precedent of *Greig*. In terms of a prospective ban, that is to say blocking county registrations of those that have played in the ICL and IPL, again this too very likely falls foul of the restraint of trade argument. In addition, given that Mascarenhas was given permission to miss the first weeks of the domestic season to play in the IPL, it is unlikely that an attempt to ban other players will work on the basis of such a restraint being justifiable. Given that, the ICL have said they will support any international players wanting to bring an action against the ECB if the ECB were to reject registration applications for the domestic game.[33]

The Indian Cricket League (ICL) was disbanded in 2009. As a Media company-sponsored breakaway league it did not have any formal authorisation from the Board of Control for Cricket in India (BCCI) or the International Cricket Council. It ceased to be a finically viable endeavour after the Indian Premier League (IPL), officially sanctioned by the BCCI, was created. However, there were attempts to penalise players who were contracted to the ICL and county teams in England playing such players. Three players, Justin Kemp (Kent), Andrew Hall and Johannes van der Wath (both Northamptonshire), were initially refused registration by the ECB under Regulation 2.1(b) of the ECB's 2008 Regulations Governing the Qualification and Registration of Cricketers, after they took part in the ICL.[34] They won their appeal to an ECB appeal tribunal with solicitor, Andrew Fitch-Holland, who represented Hall, stating that the ban was 'unlawful, unreasonable, capricious and discriminatory'.[35] Additionally, county teams who fielded ICL players have been denied participation in the Champions League, the Twenty20 competition involving winners from T20 national competitions from the international playing countries. This ban has not been challenged.[36]

The IPL has become a great financial success as probably the most overtly commercialised cricket competition to date. It has also been recognised by the ICC and accommodated within the calendar of world cricket, although it occurs at the same time as first-class club cricket in a number of countries and potentially international cricket fixtures. It is also a reflection of the power of the Indian cricketing authorities, with any idea to penalise players for participating in the IPL by clubs or other national cricketing governing bodies inconceivable.[37]

---

33 Greenfield, S and Osborn, G, 'Regulating sport: finding a role for the law?' (2010) 13(2) Sport in Society 367–79.
34 'ICL-county situation as clear as mud', cricinfo, 13 March 2008, www.espncricinfo.com/england/content/story/342292.html.
35 Ibid.
36 'Kent lose Champions League place', BBC News 1 August 2008, http://news.bbc.co.uk/sport1/hi/cricket/7534952.stm.
37 Mehdevy, E, 'Player Contracts: New cricket leagues: contract challenges' (2009) 7(1) WSLR .

Commercialisation of Sport

The argument has already been made that the commercial orientation of contemporary sport is not a new phenomenon. However, the vast amounts of money currently found in sport make it one of the most commercially powerful forms of business. The extract below shows that players and athletes have become members of the super-rich. This is primarily due to their earning power as vehicles for advertising, not the salaries from actual performing.

'Forbes Celebrity 100–2010'

[Tiger] Woods, who is struggling to find his old dominating form on the course and is having to adjust to living without his wife and children after taking a battering from the media over his no-longer secret life of illicit liaisons, is listed as having earned $105 million, as having a TV/Radio ranking of 7th, a press ranking of 6th, a web ranking of 35th and a social ranking of 34th. At 5th (in the top 100 celebrities) Woods is well clear of the next of the 17 sports men and women on the Top 100 list and the 10 among the top 50. The 2nd, 3rd and 4th highest ranked sportsmen behind Woods are all US basketball stars – Kobe Bryant ($48), Michael Jordan ($55m) and LeBron James ($43m) – with tennis ace Roger Federer ($43m) next at 5th and boxer Floyd Mayweather ($65m) the 6th highest placed sportsmen.

Only two football (soccer) players, England's David Beckham (36th among the world celebrities and 7th among the athletes) and Portugal's Cristiano Ronaldo (48th and 9th) made the top 100 this year, ironically at a time when the World Cup is dominating the sporting headlines around the world. A second golfer, Phil Mickelson, also made the top 50 in 45th place while the highest ranked baseball player, Alex Rodriguez, just squeezed in in 49th place. Other sports persons who made the top 100 are basketball's Shaquille O'Neal (52nd), boxer Manny Pacquiao (55th), tennis star Serena Williams (61st), baseballer Derek Jeter (64th), cyclist Lance Armstrong (65th), Russian tennis player Maria Sharapova (81st), and women's NASCAR race driver Danica Patrick (96th).[38]

It may have been generally accepted in the past that although sport was a form of business, sporting success should traditionally outweigh financial profit as the primary aim. However, in the UK the pursuit of money has increasingly come to represent the aim of sport.[39] Sport has become an ideal medium for sponsorship and advertising, mainly due to the vast exposure on television. This has led to a debate concerning the extent to which sport is in control of sponsors and television companies. Ethical issues have been raised concerning particular types of advertising; for example, whether there should be prohibitions on alcohol and tobacco advertising.[40]

Gardiner, S, 'Alcohol-related sponsorship of sport'

Alcohol companies continue to be major sponsors of sport. In football, Liverpool has had a long relationship with Carling lager. In Rugby Union, Heineken has also had a lengthy relationship with the European Club competition. There is also evidence that sponsorship from the alcohol industry has partly replaced tobacco advertising banned under the European Union tobacco sponsorship ban. Last year, Formula 1 racing team McLaren signed a multi-million pound

---

38 See www.forbes.com.
39 See Hofmann, D and Greenberg, MJ, Sport$biz (1989), Champaign, IL: Leisure Press, p xi, where this has been the primary aim for many years for the professional leagues.
40 In the US, for example, these types of sport-related advertising are heavily regulated. In the UK, tobacco advertising is formally prohibited; alcohol sponsorship is partially restricted and otherwise left to self-regulation, see Lewis, A and Taylor, J, (eds) *Sport: Law and Practice*, 2nd edn (2008), Haywards Heath: Tottel Publishing, pp 1268–70.

sponsorship deal with whisky manufacturer Johnnie Walker. Not surprisingly the McLaren team's global deal was immediately condemned by alcohol-concern groups who feared the move would herald the start of alcohol replacing tobacco advertising as a major source of revenue for the sport.

There is a real danger of alcohol sponsorship of sport linking alcohol consumption with sporting prowess, fitness and success. This can be particularly an issue for the young, who see a sporting brand whether it be a league or team closely aligned with an alcohol brand. For the alcohol companies, children and young people constitute an important target group because they represent the market of tomorrow, the drinkers of the future. Creating brand allegiance among children and young people is an investment the industry is sure to cash in on. The temptation to advertise alcohol to youngsters is too strong to resist.

Can the alcohol industry be left to exercise responsible self-regulation or is there an argument for external intervention? Together with European Union provisions, the Tobacco Advertising and Promotion Act 2002 comprehensively banned the advertising and promotion of tobacco products, including the use of brand sharing and sponsorship of cultural and sport events. Is there an argument for similar provisions concerning alcohol-related advertising or can the drinks and sports industry be trusted to responsibly self-regulate?[41]

It is interesting to see how some sports in Britain became commercialised in the early years of being in an organised form, and others did not. Wray Vamplew notes how at the end of the nineteenth century, some sports such as football became fully commercialised and others, such as cricket, decided not to go down that path. Indeed, he shows how the cricket establishment positively resisted commercial opportunities.[42] Although football has been run as a business since the birth of the professional game, it has rarely been seen as a serious way to make money. The investors have often been local businesspeople uninterested in a return on their money. There will be a specific focus on the business of football below. Before that a general examination of the business dynamics in sports will inform the debate about alternative mechanisms of regulation.

The Economics of Sport

A major issue is how sports are to be structured and financed in the professional world of team sports. There are various economic models that can be applied to the structure of sport. One useful model distinguishes between 'win maximisation' – where the main goal is sporting success, with profits being reasonably unimportant – and 'profit maximisation' – where generating of profits is the main aim. The former model reflects the traditional view of team sports in Europe, where even in football most professional clubs make a loss in the long run. The latter model characterises American team sport.[43]

Similarly, a comparison can be drawn between European sport and North American sport in terms of the regulatory models. In a recent debate, the leading sports economist Stefan Szymanski argues that European sports is based on a model of 'sporting capitalism' (or if focussing on football, a more specific 'football capitalism')[44] and the maintenance of a free market. Alternatively, William Gallard of UEFA supports a move to a model reflecting a significantly more interventionist position, what he terms 'sporting socialism' (or again being more specific to a sport, 'football socialism'),

41 Gardiner, S, 'Alcohol-related sponsorship of sport' (2006) 14(2) SATLJ.
42 Vamplew, W, *Pay Up and Play the Game* (1989), Cambridge: CUP.
43 See Gratton, C and Taylor, P, *Economics of Sport and Recreation* (2001), London: Spon; Sandy, R, Sloane, P and Rosentraub, M, *The Economics of Sport: An International Perspective* (2004), London: Palgrave.
44 'The Reassuring Stability of Football Capitalism', http://coventryuniversity.podbean.com/2009/06/10/the-reassuring-stability-of-football-capitalism-stefan-szymanski.

the system that exists for professional sport in North America. In European football (soccer), the market has been a dominant regulatory mechanism; in North American football (the National Football League) a range of interventionist mechanisms have been developed to provide financial stability.

This includes stability in terms of regulation of the labour market.[45] In the early days of all the main American sports, a player reservation system of 'reserve clauses' gave clubs exclusive rights over the services of each player registered to them. The player was only free if the rights were traded to another club. This process was similar to the transfer system in a number of European sports. As a mechanism for even distribution of player talent between teams, it seems that the reserve clause or transfer system is not very effective.[46] In American sport, free agency for players at the end of their contracts was supported with the case of *Flood v Kuhn*[47] in major league baseball. Additionally the draft system operates in the US professional leagues and in other leagues around the world, where new, young playing talent is distributed amongst the teams, with those that do poorly in the previous season usually getting to choose first in the post-season draft to encourage parity.

Some professional leagues in the United States, such as the National Football League (NFL) and the National Baseball League, have accepted a system of revenue sharing between clubs in order to help guarantee a reasonable degree of competition and uncertainty of outcome. This involves the collective selling of team merchandising and notably the collective selling of TV rights. In the NFL, the gate receipts are split 60/40 between the home and away teams and broadcasting rights are almost equally divided.

Another attempt to improve the competitive balance in US sports leagues is the salary cap. This is a league-wide maximum on team payrolls, but not on individual salaries. It has been suggested that a salary cap is the most effective way to bring about competitive balance in a league.[48] With the same overall money spent by each team on their players, all teams have roughly the same strength. Enforcement problems exist, though: the large teams have to stay below the cap, while the small teams have a problem affording it and may need subsidising. The National Basketball Association (NBA) has perhaps been the most successful professional league and has seen enormous growth over the last twenty years. The salary cap that has operated reflects the growth in the revenue capacity of the NBA: it was set at $3.6 million in the 1984–85 season, rose to $23 million in the 1995–96 season and is set at $58.044 million for the 2010–11 season – the highest in NBA history. It can decrease though: for the 2002–03 season, the figure dropped from $42.5 million to $40.27 million – the first drop since the salary cap system was adopted. Built upon stars such as 'Magic' Johnson and Michael Jordan, the NBA has been a great business success.[49]

Within European sport there is a search for appropriate regulatory mechanisms that provide this 'competitive balance', without necessarily adopting American-designed approaches.[50] There is a strong case for the development of hybrid mechanisms – for example, greater revenue sharing, which has happened in an ad hoc basis in the past in English football – that acknowledge the deep-rooted traditions and characteristics of European sport.[51]

---

45 For further information, see Gray, J, 'Regulation of sports leagues, teams, athletes and agents in the United States' in Caiger, A and Gardiner, S (eds), *Professional Sport in the European Union: Regulation and Re-regulation* (2000), The Hague: Asser.
46 See Cooke, A, *The Economics of Leisure and Sport* (1994), London: Routledge; El-Hodri, M and Quirck, J, 'An economic model of a professional sport league' (1971), *Journal of Political Economy*; Cairns, J, Njennet, S and Sloane, P, 'The economics of professional team sports: a survey of theory and evidence' (1986), 8(2) *Journal of Economic Studies*.
47 *Flood v Kuhn* 407 US 258 (1972).
48 Quirk, J and Fort, RD, *Pay Dirt: The Business of Professional Team Sports* (1992), Ewing, NJ: Princeton UP. Also see Farrell, R, 'Salary caps and restraint of trade' (1997) 5(1) SATLJ 53.
49 See Greenberg, MJ, 'The NBA – a model for success' (1995) 3 SATLJ 9; 'The NBA needs to do some Globetrotting', *Business Week*, 19 July 1999.
50 On the use of salary caps in UK Sport, see Bitel, N, 'Salary Caps: Lawful, Workable and Imminent' (2004) 12(1) SATLJ 132.
51 See Nafziger, J, 'A comparison of the European and North American models of sports organization' in Gardiner, S, Parrish, R and Siekmann, R (eds.) *EU, Sport, Law and Policy: Regulation, Re-regulation and Representation* (2009) The Hague: Asser Press Series.

**Késenne, S, 'Player market regulation and competitive balance in a
win maximizing scenario'**

If European sports clubs are indeed non-profit organisations as distinct from the American
clubs, the results of economic research show that there is a case for some regulation of the
sector by the league authorities in order to guarantee a more balanced competition. However,
the transfer system turns out to be totally ineffective in that respect. If the salary cap seems to
be effective in the profit maximizing US world of professional sports, it raises some doubts in
the non-profit European sports sector. If one conclusion from our research can be drawn for
European professional team sports, this conclusion will be that revenue sharing between
teams in a league is the best way to guarantee a more balanced competition without running
into the ethical and legal problems of the transfer market.[52]

Characteristics of Sport Business

There are important distinctive and unusual characteristics of the sports industry. They are illustrated below by examples from professional football:

Cut-throat competition is limited

Sporting clubs are mutually dependent on each other's well-being. Although cartels operate in
many industries (and are often regulated through the law) and there may be some notion of mutual
interest in each other's business strength, sporting entities are actually economically dependent. In
sport there is a critical need for sporting competition and 'uncertainty of outcome'. Each team
needs another team or opponent to play, and there is a need for some sort of level playing field as
without it, sport loses its unpredictability and dies. Dominance by one team or a small number of
teams in a league can adversely affect the whole 'product'. This has been identified as a potential
problem in the English Premier League, where a number of 'leagues within a league' have been
identified, with Manchester United, Chelsea and Arsenal being almost permanent members of a top
four, almost in a league of their own. The traditional 'corporatism' in professional football, evidenced
by the sharing of gate receipts and television rights deals, has increasingly dissipated over the last
twenty or so years. Clubs often see their 'individual interests' as paramount over those of other
clubs in a league.

The search for talent

Sports businesses are able to subsidise a number of losses in their quest for the 'blockbuster'. As
with the wider entertainment industry, the Hollywood film companies are a good example; a
number of losses can be sustained by the periodic big hit and accompanying financial reward. In
club football, the ultimate prize is qualification for the European Champions League: the realistic
aim of only a relatively small number of Premier League clubs – for the others it is simply to avoid
relegation. This dynamic of the sports business world leads to business practices that would be seen
as irrational in regular industries.

The aim of winning

Traditionally European clubs have primarily aimed to win competitions and not make money – this
move from a primarily 'win-maximisation' model to a 'profit-maximisation' model has been noted
above. The increasing tendency for football clubs to seek plc status has created tensions that control

---

52 Késenne, S, 'Player market regulation and competitive balance in a win maximizing scenario', in Jeanrenaud, C and Késenne, S
    (eds), *Competition Policy in Professional Sports: Europe after the Bosman Case* (1999), Antwerp: Standard Editions, p 121.

decision making in clubs, for example on the purchases of new players and the move to improve stadiums. Who is the main constituency to be consulted – the shareholders or the fans?

Who is the sports consumer?

There is confusion as to who are the ultimate consumers: paying spectators or TV viewers. The demands of TV – 'he who controls the purse strings calls the tune' – have led to concerns over whose interest is paramount, the primary spectator consumer, or the secondary TV consumer. It seems that the voice of the spectator fan and the notion of 'fan equity' – the social and cultural rights football fans have in the game – have increasingly been marginalised and ignored.[53]

Who owns sport?

Ownership of the sport or the game has been an increasingly important issue. Although there are shareholders in sporting companies and teams, it is more appropriate to talk of a range of stakeholders: sports administrators, team owners, players, the commercial interests of sponsors and TV companies, and fans (fan equity) all having some interest. In addition, sports administrators, and even team owners, are also best understood as temporary custodians with a responsibility towards the stakeholders.[54]

National element to sport

Team games have historically been primarily limited to competition within national boundaries. However, with the developments of 'Europeanisation' on the one hand – the emergence of European Leagues[55] and European teams[56] – and 'globalisation' on the other – with wider international competition between club teams[57] – this parochialism has been challenged. Within Europe there is also the proposed development of regional competitions; for example, the so-called Atlantic League.[58] Additionally, international competition between national teams has, of course, a long history. Some of the greatest rivalries include football between England and Scotland, and the 'fight' for 'The Ashes' between England and Australia in cricket. However, there are increasing tensions becoming visible; for example, the 'country versus club battle' in football for the services of a player, and the introduction of 'central contracts' paid by the national association in addition to the club contract. A connected debate has surrounded the justification for quotas that restrict the number of 'foreign' players who can play for clubs in domestic leagues, due to the adverse effect that the lack of opportunities for indigenous players might have on the quality and performance of the national team.[59]

Idiosyncratic labour market

The working life of most professional athletes is reasonably limited. As already stated, there is a continual search for talent – specific rules of supply and demand apply. This results in managers and coaches in football and other sports such as ice hockey looking widely for potential players. This has led to

53 A good example of 'fan equity' and the power relations between clubs and supporters is the fight that some Newcastle United season ticket holders had when their seats were moved due to ground improvements; see *Duffy and Others v Newcastle United Football Club*, The Times, 7 July 2000; (2000) 3(5) Sports Law Bulletin 6. Note the significant value provided by the emotional investment of fans argued in the report by Salomon Brothers, 'UK Football Clubs: valuable assets?' (1997), Global Equity Research: Leisure, November, London: Salomon Brothers.

54 This list may not be exhaustive, it was reported that player agent, Mel Stein has argued that player agents are stakeholders of professional football in England; quote from Parliamentary Select committee hearings on football governance, see later p 249.

55 Eg the FIBA SuproLeague in basketball, which started in 2000.

56 Eg the European Ryder Cup team in golf.

57 In rugby league, annual games are played between English and Australian clubs.

58 See Caiger, A and Gardiner, S (eds), *Professional Sport in the EU: Regulation and Re-regulation* (2000), The Hague: Asser, p 7 for a discussion on the proposed league of leading clubs from small national football markets, such as Scottish clubs Glasgow Rangers and Celtic, Dutch clubs Ajax and PSV and Portuguese clubs Sporting Lisbon and Porto.

59 See later, p 492.

complex patterns of player migration.[60] The use of fixed-term contracts is normal and in football, the search for contract stability within the post-*Bosman* years has led to distinct contractual dynamics.

Ken Foster, who has written extensively on the legal regulation of sport, presents alternative models of the Sports Market to assist in determining appropriate regulatory regimes.

Foster, K, 'How can sport be regulated?'

Models of Sports Market

1 The Pure Market Model

This model treats sport purely as a business. Money comes before sporting success and unregulated economic competition occurs. The prevailing ideology is 'competition is the best regulator'. Governing bodies of sport have broad functions but mainly provide a loose regulatory framework in which profit maximisation occurs. The public interest is ignored and fans have limited power to resist their exploitation. There is a network of contracts between economic units with an individualistic ideology. The normal form of regulation is through the market and the predominant legal instrument is the contract.

2 The Defective Market Model

The limitations of the pure market model are manifest. The major one is that free markets tend to eliminate the weakest economic units. Sport cannot tolerate this market logic for too long, for good sporting competitions need near equal teams or players. Monopoly of success is bad for sport; unpredictable outcomes are a key value. Governing bodies of sport, and the competitions they licence, are often monopoly controllers of sport. They can use this power to restore the sporting balance by reallocating resources. The main legal method of regulation in a defective market is competition policy. If the market fails, competition law can be used to counterbalance the tendency to monopoly, or to correct an abuse of a dominant position.

3 The Consumer Welfare Model

This model addresses the other main limitation of the pure market model. Different interests may be linked through contracts but there can be very unequal economic power and bargaining power between contracting parties. The fan has weak market power against the football club. Players historically had limited economic power against their clubs. Players and clubs may need protecting against sporting federations who can take decisions over them with major economic consequences. The legal form of regulation is protective legislation to protect the weaker party, or to allow a greater protection of the wider public interest.

4 The Natural Monopoly Model

One of the arguments to support statutorily backed regulation is that the regulated industry is a natural monopoly and therefore market competition is absent. A natural monopoly is said to be characterised by a single seller, a unique product and barriers to easy entry to the market. Sport, it is claimed, has these characteristics. It therefore needs a regulatory structure that assumes it is a private monopoly that is likely to ignore the public interest. Competition law is an inappropriate mechanism of regulation because the market cannot be freed if there is a natural monopoly. An alternative regulatory strategy is needed.

5 The Socio-Cultural Model

This model argues that sporting values are dominant and that profit is ancillary. It also stresses the social and cultural significance of sport. It rejects all the assumptions behind the free market model. The importance of autonomy for sport is emphasised. The form of governance

---

60 Lanfranchi, P and Taylor, M, *Moving with the Ball: The Migration of Professional Footballers* (2001), Oxford: Berg.

has historically been the private club, for example the Jockey Club. Clubs are ideally not-for-profit organisations with limited scope for maximising profits. Fans are seen as stakeholders in 'their' clubs. The difficult question to answer is what form of regulation best suits this model. The private club, with amateur voluntary administrators, has been one solution with consensus regulation in the 'best interests of the sport'. But commercialism can and has undermined this voluntarism and autonomy. Nevertheless, the sporting judgment of governing bodies needs to be protected from commercial interests to preserve the best features of this model. The preferred regulatory strategy may be 'supervised self-government'. This allows governing bodies to be autonomous and to regulate the sport without external interference in sporting matters. But this sporting autonomy must be matched by an internal constitutionalism, due process and good governance. This has links with the concept of 'enforced' or 'mandated' self-regulation. It shares with the pure market model a preference for 'non-intervention' but for diametrically opposed reasons. The pure market model argues for *laissez-faire* minimum interference to protect commercial interests. The socio-cultural model argues for autonomous self-government with 'constitutional' safeguards to protect sporting values.[61]

These models can be represented in a table:

Model	Values	Form of regulation	Governing bodies
Pure Market	profit/private interest (shareholders)	contract/intellectual property	maximise commercial opportunities
Defective Market	equal sporting competition (teams and players)	competition law	reallocate
Consumer Welfare	fans and viewers	protective legislation	widen democracy and accountability
Natural Monopoly	public interest	independent regulator	overcome rival organisations
Socio-cultural (traditional)	private club	immunity/voluntarism	preserve sporting values
Socio-cultural (modern)	fairness, internal constitutionism and rule of law	supervised self government	preserve sporting values with due process

This typology of the sports market suggests that the development of effective regulatory mechanisms is problematic – the sports industry or market is a complex one with availability of alternative regulatory regimes. Foster indicates that there are many interests to balance and potential ways to attempt to achieve this. In English football there are many tensions concerning power: between the football authorities, potential external regulators, shareholders of clubs, the increasingly powerful top players and, importantly, the fans.

Commodification

This creeping commercialisation that has been outlined in football is mirrored in other sports to varying degrees and has brought incremental changes to sport. The financial base of sport has

---

61 Foster, K, 'How can sport be regulated?', in Greenfield, S and Osborn, G (eds), *Law and Sport in Contemporary Society* (2000), London: Frank Cass, pp 268–70.

become increasingly dependent on sponsorship and marketing activities. Sports clubs have become a brand and have a corporate identity as distinctive as Disney or McDonalds. In world sport, none is more powerful than Manchester United. Built on a combination of tragedy and glory, the club saw staggering growth in the 1990s. In 1996 it was valued at £429.85 million; in 1998, it was valued at £623 million by BSkyB in their aborted takeover;[62] in March 2000 it reached a value in excess of £1.02 billion.[63] In 2009, the value peaked at £1.15 billion.[64] This includes revenue of around £280 million from merchandising such as the sales of replica shirts. However, this unprecedented sporting business success over the last two decades may be heading for an uncertain future, especially in the context of spiralling player salary costs:

> With more sponsorship and television money flooding in this year and next, the immediate future looks bright enough. But businesses which can't control their costs are inherently fragile. And football may still be more of a religion than a business.[65]

Sport is developing as an integral part of the leisure industry, as a 'brand' and 'product' that can be consumed in recognisable and discrete entities. As such it is increasingly indistinguishable from other sectors of the entertainment business.

The process of the commodification of sport as an extension of the process of commercialisation is important to explain. The theory has developed within the discipline of 'Marxism' and can be seen as originating in the work of the Italian political writer, Antonio Gramsci.[66] He developed the concept of hegemony, that is, the achievement of consent or agreement to dominant ideology (values and ideas) in society. Those groups who have most social, economic and political power in any particular society create these ideas. The argument is that 'the masses' (the public) largely agree to and accept these ideas and values even though they are not in their best interests, because they are transmitted and reinforced by the many different institutions in society, such as education and the media.

The concept of hegemony has been identified with the commodification of culture, commodity fetishism and the creation of 'false needs'. Writers such as Marcuse,[67] Horkheimer and Adorno,[68] aligned with the Frankfurt School of Political Thought, indicate how individuals are seduced into compliance in capitalist society by the attraction of superficial commodities, especially entertainment. Sport falls neatly into this theoretical analysis. Modern sport is used to make money through attracting spectators, selling satellite subscriptions and increasingly by selling sports merchandise. We as sports fans seem to be reasonably happy to accept this.

Through this process of commodification of increasing areas of social life such as sport, the argument is that the masses increasingly become compliant and in agreement with capitalism. However, it has been acknowledged that an absolute notion of hegemony is never attained, with cultural resistance or counter-hegemonic strategies coming from sub-cultures expressing antipathy towards these dominant views.[69] Perhaps some of the football fans' pressure groups and activities such as fanzines are good examples of this:

---

62 See p 228 for more on this.
63 'Man Utd pass £1bn', BBC News, 8 March 2000, http://news.bbc.co.uk/1/hi/business/670227.stm.
64 The figure for 2010 was £1.04 billlion, see www.forbes.com/lists/2010/34/soccer-10_Manchester-United_340001.html.
65 'It's a funny old game', The Economist, 10 February 2001.
66 See Gramsci, A, The Prison Notebooks (1971), London: Lawrence & Wishart.
67 Marcuse, H, One-Dimensional Man (1968), London: Abacus.
68 Horkheimer, M and Adorno, T, The Dialectic of Enlightenment (1973), London: Allen Lane.
69 The creation of new teams by fan groups disillusioned with developments of the club, e.g. AFC Wimbledon following the relocation of Wimbledon FC to Milton Keynes and re-naming as MK Dons; and FC United, created in response to the ownership of Manchester United by the Glazer Brothers. Additionally the wearing of green and yellow scarves (the colours of Newton Heath FC, which was the original name for Manchester United) at matches is an alternative strategy.

Strinati, D, *An Introduction to Theories of Popular Culture*

The cultivation of false needs is bound up with the role of the culture industry. The Frankfurt School sees the culture industry ensuring the creation and satisfaction of false needs, and the suppression of true needs. It is so effective in doing this that the working class is no longer likely to pose a threat to the stability and continuity of capitalism.[70]

The Frankfurt School has developed a neo-Marxist analysis seeing culture and, in this context, sport promoted as a 'product'; to be consumed to help pacify the populace and achieve consent to the existing social order. This of course is in opposition to theoretical perspectives that see sport as a natural human activity. It is clearly true that the modern form of elite sport is 'packaged' and increasingly primarily consumed via technologies such as television and the internet. This has led to complaints that the nature of modern sport has changed for the worse.

Certainly TV companies have had enormous impact upon how and when particular sports are played.[71] The argument is that no longer is sport something to admire in terms of its many virtues; sport is sullied by commercial priorities, gamesmanship and a 'winner takes all' mentality. There may be some revisionism in terms of the way that sport in the past is viewed, as exemplified by Grayson's 'Corinthian values', a false nostalgia of a perfect past where 'playing the game' was the sole aim. In fact, the historical evidence suggests that sport has been subject to these unsportsman-like characteristics throughout its history.[72]

Models of Regulation

The alternative forms of regulation that might be applied to sport have been presented earlier. There is a 'turf war' in terms of the right to govern: international and national governing bodies and sports administrators or the government through agencies, lawyers and the courts. In Britain there has been increasing concern about the ineffectiveness of sports administrators in the modern commercialised world of sport. Conversely there has been a view from sports administrators that 'legal intervention disrupts the good administration of sport'.[73]

The business of football

In Britain, football has seen the strongest calls for external regulation. It is important to evaluate the financial position of English football. The game in England became a professional sport in 1885, but for much of the subsequent period it could not be considered financially successful. Clubs on the whole have relied on wealthy benefactors to subside their activities. In the 1970s and 1980s, new income streams from sponsorship and merchandising started to be exploited. However, the financial contours changed with the creation of the Premier League, a breakaway league from the existing four divisions of the Football League at the start of the 1992–93 season. This coincided with exclusive live television rights to Premier League matches being purchased in 1992 by Sky TV (now BSkyB) in a deal that ran for five seasons for 60 games per season and was worth £190m, an average of £633,000 per game. Each subsequent deal has seen the value of the rights rise significantly and has been responsible for bringing significant amounts of new money into the sport. The value of

70 Strinati, D, *An Introduction to Theories of Popular Culture* (1993), London: Routledge, p 63.
71 Premier League football matches are played on Sundays and Mondays together with the traditional Saturday afternoon. The US network NBC, who paid over £1,000 million for the TV rights to the Sydney 2000 and Salt Lake 2001, time-delayed all the coverage from Sydney 2000; see Moss, T, 'OK, the cameras are ready, start the race,' *The Guardian*, 11 September 2000.
72 See Gardiner, S and Felix, A, 'Juridification of the football field: Strategies for giving law the elbow' (1995) 5(2) MSLJ 189.
73 Op. cit., fn 61, Foster (2000).

the current deal (for three seasons from 2010 for 138 games per season (23 of which will be shown on ESPN) is £1.782bn, an average of £4.3m per game. BSkyB has very successfully grown its business, mainly based on a business model of paying substantial amounts of money for these excusive live Premier League rights. Although the value of the contracts has risen, due to intervention on competition law grounds, the length of contacts has decreased and the rights have been grouped into six packages, of which a maximum of five can be obtained by any one purchaser. The partnership between the Premier League and BSkyB has been mutually beneficial in financial terms and has brought a significant amount of new money into English football, albeit very disproportionally to the benefit of the Premier League.

The other major development has been the decision by the European Court of Justice (ECJ) in *Bosman*,[74] which has had a seismic impact not only on the contractual dynamics of UK and European professional football, but also on the global game. The impact of *Bosman* continues to be felt, for example with the changes to the transfer system in football,[75] in the context of what is now Art 45 of the Treaty on the Functioning of the European Union (TFEU) and freedom of movement provisions. The likelihood of a successful challenge under European law was one that had been noted for quite a period of time – it was perhaps only a question of when someone would bring a discrimination case to court.[76] Contrary to the arguments raised by the Opinion of Advocate-General Lenz,[77] the ECJ largely ignored the position relating to Arts 101 and 102 TFEU concerning controls on anti-competitive practices. The impact that the competition rules have had on sport has occurred in other areas.[78]

The nature of investment in English professional football clubs has changed during this recent period. With large amounts of new money coming into sport from the selling of TV and other media rights, sponsorship and merchandising, a different type of investor has been attracted to invest in the major clubs. In the 1990s, a number of clubs, including Manchester United and Tottenham Hotspur, became Public Limited Companies listed on the Stock Exchange and alternatives such as the Alternative Investment Market (AIM), the junior stock market for small and growing companies. Media companies including BSkyB and ITV purchased significant shares in a number of the top clubs.[79] In 1998 a £623m takeover bid by BSkyB for Manchester United was turned down by Secretary of State for Trade and Industry, Stephen Byers, on the recommendation of the Monopolies and Mergers Commission (MMC). The MMC was asked by the Office of Fair Trading to investigate the merger. Their report was unequivocal in its opposition to the merger. There were five main areas of concern:

- the merger would be anti-competitive in the pay TV market because it would give BSkyB an unfair advantage in the negotiation of Premier League and other TV rights;
- the already dominant position of BSkyB and the market power of Manchester United would exacerbate such an advantage;
- any advantage that BSkyB might gain could not be overcome by the imposition of 'Chinese walls' (barriers to the flow of information such as between subsidiary and parent boards), non-exclusive deals or even exclusion from the rights negotiations;
- the merger would also damage the quality of British football by increasing the 'wealth gap' between richer and poorer clubs through a greater retention of TV revenue by the most popular clubs;

---

74 Case C-415/93 *Union Royale Belge des Socéitiés de Football ASBL v Bosman* [1995] ECR I-4921; [1996] 1 CMLR 645, para 237.
75 A detailed analysis of *Bosman* is found in Chapter 9.
76 See the arguments pre-*Bosman* in Weatherill, S, 'Discrimination on grounds of nationality in sport', in *Yearbook of European Law 1989* (1990), Oxford: Clarendon, p 55 and Miller, F and Redhead, S, 'Do markets make footballers free?', in Bale, J and Maguire, J (eds), *The Global Sports Arena: Athletic Talent Migration in an Interdependent World* (1994), London: Frank Cass.
77 See earlier pp 151–63.
78 See later pp 245–57.
79 See 'Football club dealings' (1999) 2(6) SLB 6.

● the merger would give BSkyB additional influence over Premier League decisions which would be against the long-term interests of the game.[80]

Not only was there considerable political and media condemnation of the possible takeover,[81] but Manchester United fan groups were vociferous in their opposition. Manchester United obviously still remains a prize asset, however, and in 2005, American businessman Malcolm Glazer gained a controlling interest. Over the last few years, a number of foreign investors, such as Roman Abramovich at Chelsea and Thaksin Shinawatra, and subsequently Sheikh Mansour, at Manchester City, have gained controlling interests in other Premier League sides. However, as evidenced wih Portsmouth FC's move into administration in 2010,[82] all is not well in the Premier League.[83]

A major issue in British Football is that the gap between the rich elite clubs and the smallest clubs in the lower professional leagues has widened. *Bosman* has contributed to the increasing of this division. There could well be a terminal threat to the lower division professional or semi-professional clubs. The accountants Deloitte have provided an annual review of English football finances since 1993. They provide a yearly 'snapshot' of the changing financial contours of the game – particularly illuminating in view of the dramatic changes over the last decade.[84]

Boon, G, '1996 football survey'

The financing of clubs in the lower divisions is clearly a cause for concern. With escalating wage bills and less money filtering down from the top clubs, some difficult decisions will have to be taken if professional football in England is to remain in its present form. The transfer market has historically been the saviour of many clubs, not only the smaller ones, and if this source of funding diminishes then an alternative mechanism of distributing monies to the lower divisions' clubs, perhaps through a redistribution of TV income, will have to be found to save clubs from either going part-time or out of business completely.[85]

The financial picture in 2010 for the vast majority of the 92 professional football clubs in England is not very rosy.[86]

Deloitte, 'Annual Review of Football Finance 2010'

Overall, The Football League is now spending 86% of its revenues on total wages, with only an £82m surplus of revenue over wages to manage the rest of the business, fund operating costs, and consider transfer budgets, which is a huge, and ultimately unsustainable, financial challenge.[87]

An ongoing debate has focused the impact that the transfer system has had on the movement of money between the clubs in the different leagues. It is argued that the transfer system has acted in the past as 'a powerful mechanism for redistributing wealth'.[88] This redistributive effect of the transfer

---

80 British Sky Broadcasting Group Plc and Manchester United Plc: A report on the proposed merger CM 3045 9 April 1999, available at www.competition-commission.org.uk.

81 Brown, A and Walsh, A, *Not For Sale: Manchester United, Murdoch and the Defeat of BskyB* (1999), Edinburgh: Mainstream.

82 'Pompey become first top-flight club in administration', BBC News, 26 February 2010 http://news.bbc.co.uk/sport1/hi/football/teams/p/portsmouth/8538457.stm.

83 Vast wages at the heart of Premier League's £3.5bn mountain of debt, *The Guardian*, 23 February 2010, www.guardian.co.uk/sport/david-conn-inside-sport-blog/2010/feb/23/premier-league-debt-wages-uefa.

84 Copies can be obtained at www.deloitte.com/view/en_GB/uk/industries/sportsbusinessgroup.

85 Boon, G, '1996 Football survey' (1996) 4(2) SATLJ 46.

86 See recent financial crises for Leeds United, Crystal Palace and Portsmouth FC among others.

87 'Annual Review of Football Finance 2010', www.deloitte.com/view/en_GB/uk/industries/sportsbusinessgroup/sports/football/0a4be867d38f8210VgnVCM200000bb42f00aRCRD.htm

88 Lee, M, 'A game of two halves: putting the boot in' (1995) *New Statesman and Society* 27.

system is, however, one that has been contested. What is clear is that new money, vast amounts of it, has entered English professional football in recent years from the sale of TV and other media rights and the expansion in sponsorship and marketing opportunities. However, it seems that the top clubs, in particular Manchester United, and the top players have been the main beneficiaries. With clubs there are clearly the 'haves' and the 'have-nots'. As far as players are concerned, there are the super-rich, the merely comfortable and an increasingly growing number who, although reasonably paid, face greater uncertainty when it comes to contract renewal as clubs cut the size of playing squads.

It is clear that the early corporatism of professional clubs in England, in the sense of all clubs being mutually reliant on each other, is a thing of the past. There may be alliances between groups of clubs but these are shifting ones and tend to be based around particular single issues. But, as generally with sport, and unlike most other businesses, football clubs have a mutual interest in each other's business health. Each club plays each other. In team sport the product to be marketed is the game itself. Therefore no single team can sell the product itself. A team needs to play another in a league or cup. There is a need for competition and although this may be keen on the field, the clubs are dependent on each other to a much greater extent than is the case in other businesses.

The next part of the chapter will consider the debate that has unfolded as to whether English football needs external regulation to put its house in order. In addition the various regulatory mechanisms that have been implemented within football, both in England and more widely in Europe, will be examined.

Football Task Force

In July 1997, soon after coming into power, the Labour Government appointed a Task Force comprising different interest groups in football. In 1996, while in opposition, the Labour Party had produced a *Charter for Football*. Therein a Football Task Force was promised that would *inter alia* consider the restructuring of the Football Association, investigate links between football and television, consider the treatment of fans and the financing of football and look at the future development of the game. The subsequent remit of the Task Force changed somewhat and was divided into seven areas of work, including issues of racism and participation by ethnic minorities,[89] improving access to disabled spectators[90] and the responsibility that players have as role models in the community.[91] The other areas had a financial context:

- encourage greater supporter involvement in the running of clubs;
- encourage ticketing and pricing policies that are geared up to reflect the needs of all on an equitable basis, including for cup and international matches;
- encourage merchandising policies that reflect the needs of supporters as well as commercial considerations;
- reconcile the potential conflict between the legitimate needs of shareholders, players and supporters where clubs are floated on the Stock Exchange.[92]

The consideration of these issues led to the fourth and main report entitled *Commercial Issues* – how football should best be governed in the future and how the interests of the governing bodies, clubs and supporters might be reconciled. In fact there were two conflicting reports: one representing the perceptions of football fan groups sitting on the Task Force – the 'Majority Report'; the other from

---

89 Football Task Force, *Eliminating Racism* (1998), London.
90 Football Task Force, *Improving Disabled Access* (1998), London.
91 Football Task Force, *Investing in the Community* (1999), London.
92 Football Task Force, *Commercial Issues* (1999), London, p 1, para 1.3.

the football establishment, the FA and the Premier and Football Leagues sitting on the Task Force – the 'Minority Report'.

Football has of course been the focus of government regulation in recent years, where football's ability to self-regulate the game has been adjudged to have failed. The Hillsborough Disaster in 1989 led to the Taylor Report[93] in 1990 and the subsequent legislative framework concerning safety at football matches and football hooliganism. The perception that football needed to be regulated as a business was, however, a new development:

Summary of Main Proposals in Commercial Issues Report (1999)

Report One – The Majority Report: The Fans' View
Summary of Recommendations:

Regulation

A Football Audit Commission
The Task Force proposes that a Football Audit Commission be established, properly resourced, as a permanent standing body with terms of reference to include the following:

- the FAC will seek to achieve a greater accountability of clubs to a range of stakeholders, including supporters and shareholders;
- ensure the implementation of Task Force recommendations;
- specify objectives and reporting requirements on football clubs and authorities to cover financial management, involvement of supporters, development of new models of ownership, redistribution of income within the game, management of partnerships and resources, customer satisfaction and impact on society;
- set performance targets and monitor compliance;
- deal with non-compliance through sanctions if necessary;
- the FAC should be composed of members from a range of backgrounds appointed by the Secretary of State, under Nolan rules, and chosen for their expertise, experience, appropriate skills and commitment to and interest in football;
- the FAC will, where necessary, oversee the appointment of auditors for all football clubs and require them to publish a range of performance indicators relating to the social and economic impact of football clubs, customer satisfaction, and relationships with supporters and other stakeholders;
- the FAC will use this information to produce an annual report on commercial issues, highlighting areas where targets are not being met, and describing compliance with the Code of Practice;

A Football 'Ombudsfan':

- the Task Force recommends the establishment of an 'Ombudsfan' who investigates individual complaints and reports to the FAC;
- he/she would be appointed by the FAC in consultation with the Minister, football authorities and fans' groups;
- the Ombudsfan would have powers to requisition evidence and call on the FAC to impose sanctions/solutions;
- this person would be a credible independent individual;
- the Ombudsfan will operate within clear terms of reference and guidelines and have the power to fine clubs in clear cases of maladministration.

---

93 Taylor LJ, *The Hillsborough Stadium Disaster: Final Report* (1990), London: HMSO; see Chapter 12 for a further discussion.

Financial Compliance Unit:

- the Football Task Force supports the FA's proposals to establish a financial compliance unit;
- to introduce a 'fit and proper persons' requirement for persons wishing to own a substantial number of shares in a football club;
- the Task Force would expect the compliance unit to review club business plans on an annual basis;
- this Unit would also be subject to review by the FAC.

Code of Practice:

- a prerequisite of more effective regulation of football is the development of a coherent, constitutionally entrenched and detailed Code of Practice for the game, on and off the field;
- this code should be drawn up by the FAC in consultation with the governing bodies, clubs and supporters;
- the Code of Practice will set out minimum standards to be met by their clubs in their treatment of supporter-customers and all clubs should be expected to reach them;
- the FAC's Code of Practice should take as its starting point all of the appropriate recommendations contained in the four reports of the Task Force;
- the FAC will keep this code under review and in consultation with the game will develop new rules to reflect changing circumstances.

Ticketing Policies
The Football Audit Commission should:

- receive reports from all clubs annually on how they have widened access to fans who would otherwise have been excluded;
- encourage and ensure compliance on best practice amongst clubs on issues of ticketing policy, aiming to encourage accessibility to all supporters;
- review regularly all matters relating to the treatment of away fans.

All clubs should:

- stretch the range of prices offered, so that fans paying the highest prices are effectively cross subsidising those who pay new, lower prices;
- for the lower priced tickets, increase prices annually by no more than the rate of inflation in the Retail Price Index;
- reduce prices for restricted view seats and those at the very front or to the sides of major goal end areas;
- offer better access for fans who have difficulty paying current prices by being more flexible and imaginative in the marketing of less popular matches;
- extend concessionary tickets to embrace a wider section of the population particularly those who have felt excluded from football;
- under-16s and those in full-time education should be offered half-price tickets for all competitive matches covering at least 10 per cent of ground capacity (both home and away);
- offer payment for season ticket by instalment, over the six months from June to December. Clubs should not charge interest that is higher than base rate;
- limit the number of season tickets they sell in order to encourage home support from those who cannot afford to buy a season ticket;
- increase the proportion of tickets available for away fans wherever possible;

- at the beginning of each season be required to provide the FAC with details of their pricing policies. At the end of the season each should also report on how they have offered better access to fans who might otherwise have been excluded from matches because of price.

Clubs should not:

- charge away fans higher prices than home fans for the same facilities;
- restrict ticket sales to club members;
- offer tickets for away matches, including for European competition, on condition that supporters have to purchase travel from the club.

Merchandising

All football clubs and the FA so far as these measures are relevant to the sale of England kits, should:

- ensure that each strip has a minimum life-span of two full seasons;
- consult supporters on the design of new kits and take care to ensure it is in keeping with club traditions;
- carry a 'sell-by' date in the collar of the shirt indicating when the shirt will be replaced;
- adhere to the assurances given to the Director General of Fair Trading on retail price maintenance;
- the FAC should work with all clubs to encourage best practice on merchandising issues.

Supporter Involvement in the Running of Clubs

The FAC should promote best practice amongst clubs in consulting and working with supporters' groups.

- Supporters' associations should be encouraged as far as possible to be represented at national level with a single voice.

All clubs should:

- establish democratic forums through which all fans can be involved in decision-making;
- recognise and encourage as a collective body supporter trusts and supporter shareholder associations; this could involve promoting a representative from a trust, group or shareholders' association on to the board in a director or observer capacity;
- as far as practical provide appropriate financial and administrative support to the supporter bodies and the proper functioning of their elected representatives' duties;
- consult supporters on major decisions being taken by the club, such as ground relocation, stock market flotation, major sale of shares or changes in pricing policy;
- provide an opportunity, at least once a year, for a supporters' representative to discuss their concerns at boardroom level;
- where no other mechanism for supporter liaison exists, work with a supporter liaison committee.

The football authorities should:

- continue to provide a forum for regular consultation with supporters' representatives on the major issues facing the game;
- provide sufficient funding for the proper running and effective functioning of a national supporter representative body.

Reconciling Conflict in Football Club plcs

- Where a club is intending to float on the Stock Exchange or other public market in shares, or sell a majority of its shares, or perform any act substantially affecting its constitution or its football stadium, it must satisfy the FAC that it is intending to do so in the best long-term interests of the club and all sections of its supporters and of the game of football itself.

- A minimum of twenty-five per cent of shares in any club intending to take up a public listing must be offered to season ticket holders, subject to Stock Market rulings.
- All floated clubs and all clubs with more than 5,000 season ticket holders should produce a public statement of intent and should organise twice-yearly meetings at which matters of club policy and structure can be debated.
- The club shall where possible consult supporters about all aspects of flotation.

The Government should:

- ensure that all clubs should be subject to the Department for Trade and Industry's referral criteria for take-overs;
- encourage communities, through local councils, to take an equity stake in their club.

The FAC should:

- ensure that all floated clubs adhere to football's new Code of Practice;
- investigate means of encouraging democratic supporter representation at floated clubs through the collectivisation of supporters' shareholdings; this should include advising supporter-shareholders, including current shareholders, how to hold their shares in a collective or mutual trust form;
- hold a legal charge over the ground of every club so that they cannot be sold without the consent of the FAC;
- in consultation with club-companies and supporters, develop detailed rules designed to reconcile the potential conflict between the needs of shareholders and supporters. These rules, to govern member club companies, including floated companies, would be designed to preserve the long-term interests and survival of the companies as football clubs, working to the broad principle of balancing commercial requirements with responsibilities to promoting the aims of football and the Football Association.

Report Two – The Minority Report: The Football Authorities

The Football Association, the FA Premier League and the Football League have completed their own report after considering the majority report. Their recommendations can certainly be characterised as very much less radical and essentially about keeping the status quo. Their shared view is that football needs to be understood as a leading international industry with significant revenue and cost demands, a sporting business in a modern leisure market. The report focuses on a number of issues:

Ticketing:

- whilst supporting the promotion of good practice concerning ticket pricing and distribution, there is an acceptance that each club is an individual business and should be able to make its own 'sensible and balanced decisions on the right ticket policy';
- the report emphasises the role of concessionary tickets and the need to 'stretch' the range of ticket prices. The main emphasis is on the availability and distribution of tickets rather than restrictions on pricing.

Merchandising:

- the report notes that purchase of a range of products is not an essential part of watching football and they dismiss calls for 'sell-by-dates' on replica kits;
- they do however acknowledge that all clubs 'should have a published, well-communicated kit cycle policy' particularly on any proposed changes.

Clubs and their supporters:

- clubs should consult their fans as stakeholders on a regular basis, through forums, questionnaires and focus groups and through the publication of current policy on major issues in an easily digested format;
- clubs should take steps wherever possible to promote supporter and community liaison. To that end each club should be encouraged to produce a customer charter that would cover the following: what can the customer reasonably expect from the club; how will this service be delivered; how can a customer feed back to the club; and what recourse do they have.

Financial compliance:

- although it is stressed that the financial affairs of each club remain with that club, the FA proposes to create a financial compliance team that would review annual returns from clubs and monitor financial health, help clubs to set up their own business processes.

Regulation:

- the football authorities note that in their view 'English football is not an under-governed sport';
- they state that there are an interlocking set of rules, regulations and codes of conduct which across the three bodies have recently been subject to amongst other things, modernisation, consistency, improved independent scrutiny and promoted best practice;
- the football authorities state that they 'do not believe that the overall well-being of the game will be helped by new layers of regulation or bureaucracy';
- the view is that especially in the global market that many football clubs exist in, the creation of an additional set of rules is not appropriate;
- however, the football authorities acknowledge they need to 'actively demonstrate their commitment to the good governance of the game'. They see improved self-regulation and more obvious public accountability as necessary aims;
- this aim they see as being achieved by the creation of an Independent Scrutiny Panel. Carrying out a function not dissimilar to the British Standards Institution, it would not sit permanently but carry out work from time to time and produce an audit report every two years. It would provide an independent assessment of the quality of regulation, best practice and governance, evaluation of compliance and non-compliance and recommendations for improving performance.[94]

The Majority Report that represented the fan groups' perspective supported a radical interventionist approach, with support for the creation of a permanent standing body, the Football Audit Commission (FAC), and the establishment of a new consumers' voice for football, the 'Ombudsfan'. Supporters' groups would have formal involvement in the FAC. In addition, where a club intended to float on the Stock Exchange, the long-term interests of the club ought to be considered.

The Minority Report from the football authorities' perspective was significantly more conservative. It argued that increased regulation was not needed for what is 'not an under-governed sport'. They recommended that the emphasis should be on self-regulation, but found merit in supporting an advisory body, the Independent Scrutiny Panel (ISP), to provide assessment of the quality of regulation, best practice and governance found within individual clubs. This body would merely provide advice and have no powers to intervene.

Adam Brown was a member of the Task Force and was a co-author of the Majority Report.

---

94 'Football Task Force: commercial issues' (2000) 3(1) SLB 1.

Brown, A, 'In my opinion: the Football Task Force Final report'

The Government's Football Task Force concluded its business in December with a split Final Report on commercial issues. Having published three unanimous reports on racism, disabled access and football in the community, it was the controversial areas of regulation, ticket policies, supporter representation, merchandising and 'floated' clubs which were always going to test the body most.

This is not to say that the project has been a failure: far from it. The Task Force represents the biggest consultation exercise with English football ever undertaken – we saw 73 fans' groups and 30 clubs amongst others as well as commissioning key research. The Task Force has also seen, for the first time, all elements of the game sitting around the same table. The Government is already committed to alter laws on racist chanting; to improve disabled facilities; and to create a dedicated unit to help fans form shareholding trusts (instrumental in the salvation of a number of clubs in the lower leagues). The Premier League has also promised to reinvest 5% of its TV revenue from the next television deal, reportedly worth some £1 billion, in the grass roots.

However, the Final Report now presents a dilemma for the Government's Sports Minister, Kate Hoey. The minority report, representing the football establishment, advocates an Independent Scrutiny Panel for football, of 3–5 people sitting for just four weeks a year to assess the performance of the FA, as well as a token Code of Conduct. The majority report, representing fans' organisations and independent members, has called for a much more thorough Football Audit Commission, and a series of robust recommendations on the key areas of tickets, representation and commercial activities.

I have supported the latter because it promises that the performance of football authorities and clubs will be thoroughly examined by an independent body which will also include a fans' champion in the form of a football 'Ombudsfan' to investigate individual complaints. We have recommended that firm measures are needed to ensure that the top level of football does not price supporters out of attending and to make sure fans' interests are represented at all levels. Whilst some recommendations are shared by both sides – such as the need for clubs to 'stretch' prices, lowering the 'bottom end', some changes to merchandising policies and for some independent regulation – there is a gulf between the perceptions of the game. One sees it as a business which should be able to operate virtually unfettered; the other recognises football's importance in local communities and the lifeblood of the game that is the loyalty of ordinary supporters.

For 'our side', which includes the Chair and Vice Chair, the football establishment were simply not able to move far enough to satisfy both what we and the thousands of fans who made testimony to us wanted to see: namely, effective independent auditing of football's relationship to its community, protection for its customers and measures to try and balance some of the inequities in modern football. A limit on price increases, meaningful representation of fans at club and national level and checks on the effects of clubs floating, as well as calls for better redistribution of wealth in football to the lower leagues, were all key planks of our report. These went too far for the football establishment and top clubs and the Government, who established the Task Force to get a better deal for fans, must now choose.

11 full members of the Task Force (out of 17), including Chair, Vice Chair, all fans groups and all independent members, together with Pamela Taylor (of Water UK) from the Working Group, have written to Kate Hoey asking her to meet us and them to implement the majority report. This is backed by unanimous support from the All Party Football Group of MPs, and an Early Day Motion to which nearly 100 MPs have put their names. However, word is that Number 10 is reluctant to pick a fight with the football authorities and public pressure needs to be maximised in the coming weeks, with a fans' lobby of Parliament due on March 2nd. Watch this space.[95]

---

95 Brown, A, 'In my opinion: the Football Task Force final report' (2000) 3(1) SLB 2.

The two Reports, although sharing some areas of commonality, seem far apart, particularly on the issues of governance and accountability. The highly interventionist FAC favoured by the Majority Report is a very different form of regulation from that of the ISP favoured by the Minority Report. The FAC would essentially see the existence of two bodies overseeing English football: the FA controlling the playing side of the game, including supervising rule changes and enforcing disciplinary matters, and the FAC controlling financial and commercial issues concerning the individual professional clubs.

The ISP was supported in the Minority Report with the view that:

> . . . in our view English football is not an under-governed sport[96] . . . English football does not need an additional set of imposed rules which prohibit and restrict the ability of clubs to make their own footballing and commercial decisions, particularly given the globalisation of the market place within which they are operating.[97]

The Independent Football Commission

In October 2000, plans were announced for the creation of an Independent Football Commission – a regulatory body very much in the form of the ISP supported by the Minority Report. The football authorities seem to have heavily influenced the development of what would be an essentially 'soft touch' independent monitoring body. As Brown comments:

Brown, A, 'The Football Task Force and regulation'

The division of the Task Force was also one of philosophical disagreement about what football is and should be – a business first or foremost, or a sport with too much cultural and social importance for it to be left to market forces. Given other developments, such as the increasing influence of media corporations in the ownership and future directions of the game, the decision of the government on which report to support is even more crucial.[98]

The IFC came into being in March 2002.

Independent Football Commission, 'Terms of Reference'

1. To review and report on the promotion by the FA, The FA Premier League and The Football League ('the governing bodies') of best practice in commercial and financial matters within professional football, particularly with regard to customer service. In particular to review and report on:

- the establishment of a code of best practice, customer charters and customer relations units by each of the governing bodies, and by individual clubs
- the governing bodies' establishment of a complaints resolution hierarchy based on the Code of Best Practice, with the Independent Football Commission as the final step in that hierarchy: and
- the establishment of a Financial Advisory Unit by the Football Association which will review and monitor aspects of clubs' financial performances and promote best practice.

---

96 'Football's response to the Football Task Force', Football Task Force, *Commercial Issues* (1999), London, para 125.
97 Ibid, para 128.
98 Brown, A, 'The Football Task Force and regulation', in Greenfield, S and Osborn, G (eds), *Law and Sport in Contemporary Society* (2000), London: Frank Cass, pp 268–70.

The IFC is to have particular regard to:

- ticket prices
- accessibility to matches
- merchandise; and
- supporter and other stakeholder involvement.

2. To review the rules and regulations of the governing bodies relating to financial and business matters within their competitions, and the Code of Best Practice, and to recommend changes where appropriate.

3. To review and report on the adoption and/or promotion (as appropriate) by the governing bodies of the customer service related in the recommendation in the Football Task Force Reports 1–3.

4. To publish their findings by way of an annual public report.

The IFC was met with a largely cynical view as to its likely effectiveness.[99] A major perceived problem is that it is fully funded by the football authorities and therefore open to charges that it is not truly independent. It has produced two Annual Reports, focusing on such issues as the financial crisis at club level, governance in the game and racism. The IFC has indicated that as a body it is pretty impotent in its ability to engage with the pressing financial and socio-cultural problems in English football.[100] In the early part of the last decade financial problems continued. The collapse of ITV Digital in 2002 severely damaged the financial dynamics in the Football League clubs.[101] The FA continues to be seen as one of the worst examples of sports governance.[102] The conduct of professional players, a significant number highly paid, continues to be under scrutiny.[103]

The arguments for effective external regulation are strong. In May 2004, the IFC published a 'Report on Self Regulation',[104] a document partly reviewing its role and partly suggesting proposals on alternative structures that could be employed beyond its initial two-year terms of reference. These alternatives are:

1.   discontinue the IFC;
2.   do nothing;
3.   extend the IFC terms of reference and increase its funding;
4.   a radically revised role and structure for the IFC;
5.   immediate revolution; or
6.   statutory regulation.

The IFC believed that it had a 'lack of power, inadequate resources, restrictive terms of reference and limited access to information'. In evaluating the options presented, the first five options would have perpetuated self-regulation; options 2 to 5 would continue to see the IFC having a role; option 6

---

99 'The IFC's flawed potential', 13 March 2002, BBC Sport, http://news.bbc.co.uk/sport1/hi/football/1870875.stm; Chaudhary, V, 'Soccer watchdog "has no bite" ', *The Guardian*, 14 March 2002.

100 Bower, B, *Broken Dreams: Vanity, Greed and the Souring of British Football* (2003), London: Simon & Schuster.

101 'ITV Digital: Where did it all go wrong?', 30 April 2002, http://news.bbc.co.uk/1/hi/business/1897316.stm; also see information on the failed attempt by the Football League to seek damages against Carlton and Granada TV: 'League loses football cash battle', BBC News, 1 August, 2002, http://news.bbc.co.uk/1/hi/business/2165700.stm; see *Carlton Communications Plc (2) Granada Media Plc v Football League* [2002] EWHC 1650 (Comm), LTL 1/8/2002 (unreported elsewhere).

102 'Minister wants FA to face review', BBC News, 24 October 2004, http://news.bbc.co.uk/sport1/hi/football/3948715.stm.

103 On the criminal trial of Leeds United players Lee Bowyer and Jonathan Woodgate for assault, see Redhead, S, 'Leeds United on Trial' (2002) 1(3) Entertainment Law 98–106.

104 Independent Football Commission, 'Report on Self Regulation' (2004), www.theifc.co.uk/publications/documents/SelfRegulationReport.pdf.

would lead to direct government intervention through legal provisions and an end to self-regulation. Option 4 is the one favoured by the IFC. The IFC believed that keeping the status quo was not a realistic option. The FA is a particular target, whose dual role of a regulatory function of the English game and a representative function within the international game is seen as problematic. The IFC saw the FA as not being wholly independent, with many inadequacies including tensions around the national team and club interests, the handling of commercial interests, lack of accountability and a lack of codes of practice.

Essentially the IFC argued that English football must demonstrate more clearly that it has the ability and will to regulate itself, and that it must be prepared to shoulder the responsibilities that go with self-regulation. The IFC put the ball in the court of the football authorities to see if they are prepared to cede more power to a body such as the IFC so as to have more of a risk than essentially just passive scrutiny. However, the football authorities have not been prepared to accede any more power to an external body. And as often happens, essentially the same body continues but with a new name – the Independent Football Ombudsman was created in 2008.[105]

The Burns Report

The English FA has been seen as out of touch with the realities of modern sport. There have been concerns voiced about the unwieldy nature of the FA's management structure. It has certainly not been seen as a good exemplar of effective sports governance. Government has brought pressure on the FA to modernise its structure and improve its internal governance. The FA structural review by Lord Burns was the response and was published in 2005, proposing radical changes in the structure and operation of the FA.[106] The focus was on modernising the internal structure to make the organisation more in step with the corporate world in which they increasingly operate. Lord Burns concentrated on how to make the FA a more efficient and dynamic entity by streamlining its organisational structures. The recommendations included different management structures for the professional game on the one hand and the recreational game on the other, an independent chairman and a more authoritative compliance unit. The difficulty is that these recommendations are just that, and lack the force of legislation or court judgments. The implementation within the FA has been a protracted and difficult process and even then, the review has not been implemented as originally envisaged by Lord Burns.

Pressure for reform has also come from other quarters, particularly on the FA and the Premier League. In Parliamentary Reports in 2004 and 2008 ('English Football and its Governance'),[107] the All Party Football Group has suggested a range of reforms that are needed in the context of the financial realities of English football. One of the key proposals that has been acted upon by both the Premier League and the Football League is the application of a 'Fit and Proper Test' for owners and directors of professional clubs.

Bond, D, 'FA playing a high-risk game'

One idea being discussed, however, is to appoint a commission headed by a political grandee who could examine the way the whole game is run – not just the FA but the Premier League and Football League – and, if necessary, look at introducing an independent regulator. This is not a new idea. Far from it. Every new government threatens football with the spectre of a regulator or watchdog similar to those that exist to police the media and the utilities. Nothing ever changes.[108]

---

105 See www.theifo.co.uk.
106 www.thefa.com/TheFA/WhoWeAre/NewsAndFeatures/2005/ReviewConclusions.
107 www.allpartyfootball.com.
108 'FA playing a high-risk game' David Bond's Blog, 19August 2010, http://www.bbc.co.uk/blogs/davidbond/2010/08/ fa_playing_a_high-risk_game.html.

Measures to promote financial probity

A number of initiatives have been developed to help provide financial stability within the UK and more widely around European football and to engage with the phenomenon of 'Financial Doping',[109] where huge amounts of money are injected into a club to buy success. In English football, both the Premier League and Football League have introduced point deduction penalties for clubs who become insolvent.[110] This is designed as a punitive deterrent which it is hoped will promote good financial husbandry of clubs. However, insolvency has become a reasonably frequent occurrence in the Football League,[111] and occurred in the Premier League for the first time with Portsmouth FC in 2010.[112] One issue of controversy has been the application of the 'football creditors rule', which prioritises football creditors, such as other clubs, over non-football creditors including the Inland Revenue and general commercial suppliers such as catering companies.[113]

At a European level, UEFA introduced club licensing in the 2004/5 season and issued a second version for the 2008/9 season and beyond, focusing on issues such as sporting matters, infrastructure, legal compliance, and, vitally, financial affairs. More recently, in 2009, UEFA introduced a set of 'Financial Fair Play' regulations requiring clubs to, 'over a period of time, balance their books, or break even . . . Clubs will not be allowed to repeatedly spend more than their self-generated revenues'; and they must 'honour their commitments at all times'.[114] It is not only football that has adopted a licence-based approach to eligibility to participate in competitions and promote effective financial governance. Rugby league's Super League competition moved from the traditional promotion and relegation model to a licensed club league structure in 2009.[115]

Reflecting continuing concerns, the government's Culture, Media and Sport Select Committee sessions on football governance took place in spring 2011.[116] It is important to note, however, that not all academic analysis of the state of football finances presents a gloomy picture. One of the leading UK sports economists, Stefan Szymanski, argues that what he terms 'football capitalism',[117] that is the maintenance of a free market in English football, has served the sport well and brought a remarkable degree of stability.

The key issue that sports bodies need to appreciate is that to restrict the argument that there is a need for external regulation as a challenge to self-regulation is to develop effective governance. Some of the mechanisms that will help achieve this have been identified above and a more general discussion will be the focus of the next section.

---

109 See Banks, S, 'Financial "doping" ' (2009) 144 *Accountancy* 97–99.
110 See Hennigan, J, 'Credit Crunch: Options for clubs facing insolvency' (2009) 7(2) WSLR.
111 *Re Football Association Rule K Arbitration Leeds United 2007 Ltd v The Football League Ltd* Arbitration Tribunal 1 May 2008 [2008] BCC 701; more recently, see 'Plymouth Argyle go into administration', BBC News, 4 March 2011, http://news.bbc.co.uk/sport1/hi/football/teams/p/plymouth_argyle/9414349.stm.
112 'Portsmouth go into administration', *The Guardian*, 26 February 2010, www.guardian.co.uk/football/2010/feb/26/portsmouth-premierleague; Portsmouth City Football Club Ltd (In Administration) Report to Creditors pursuant to Paragraph 49 of B1 of the Insolvency Act 1986', http://i.telegraph.co.uk/telegraph/multimedia/archive/01621/Portsmouth_Report_1621382a.pdf.
113 Watkins, T, 'Insolvency/Tax: Football insolvency and the "football creditors" rule' (2010) 10(8) WSLR.
114 Findlay, R, 'Finances: Regulating club financial expenditure to avoid debt' (2010) 10(2) WSLR; also see Burnett, R, Totman, M and Young, V, 'UEFA's Financial Fair Play Regulations: analysis' (2010) 8(12) WSLR, 14–16.
115 Ibid, Findlay (2010).
116 'Football governance "weaker than any other sport" ', BBC Today programme, 8 February, 2011, http://news.bbc.co.uk/today/hi/today/newsid_9390000/9390736.stm; see transcripts at www.publications.parliament.uk/pa/cm201012/cmselect/cmcumeds/792/79202.htm.
117 'The Reassuring Stability of Football Capitalism', http://coventryuniversity.podbean.com/2009/06/10/the-reassuring-stability-of-football-capitalism-stefan-szymanski.

Effective Sports Governance

The move to professionalisation in rugby union during the mid-1990s was accompanied by Will Carling's description of the English Rugby Union Committee as '57 old farts running Rugby Union'.[118]

In athletics similar disharmony has reigned:

Downes, S and Mackay, D, *Running Scared: How Athletics Lost Its Innocence*

Until 1990, British athletics was organised by 16 different governing bodies in a confusing miasma of administration, full of duplication, as well as conflicting and contradicting interests. The AAA (Amateur Athletic Association), the oldest athletics body in the world, which still governed the affairs of men's athletics in clubs throughout England, was the richest and most powerful and was not alone in its reluctance to cede its independence and authority to a new group. But after 30 years of debate, wrangling, consultation reports and more discussion, the sport finally, if somewhat reluctantly, came together under the umbrella of a single federation, the BAF (British Athletics Federation), in 1991.[119]

BAF went into administration largely due to the action by Diane Modahl.[120] It has since been resurrected as UK Athletics. Often disputes within the administrative structure of sports have been between competing governing bodies or internal power struggles, or between governing bodies and players' associations as to the right to administer. There has been an awareness of a need to improve the standards of organisational governance and also a need for the operation of NGBs to comply with the external norms dictated by the law.

The traditional ethos of sports administrators has been built on a base of amateurism and voluntary contributions, with individuals rising through the ranks of the particular sport, driven primarily by their love of the sport. In recent years this has started to be replaced by individuals brought in from outside the sport with particular professional skills. The organisation of English cricket has gone through changes, with the Test and County Cricket Board becoming the England and Wales Cricket Board in 1997. Major criticisms have been voiced over the years as to the lack of vision for the future of the game. The appointment of Lord MacLaurin, ex-chairman of the Tesco supermarket chain, was designed to inject new ideas and a more rational plan for the future of cricket. The Chief Executive of the FA from 1999 until 2002 was Adam Crozier, whose background was in advertising. Since 2002, the FA has had five CEOs. In comparision, the big American professional leagues have been very much about continuity: David Stern, the Commissioner of the National Basketball Association, has been in post since 1994 (and not surprisingly is extremely well remunerated with a reported income of over US$70 million per year).

Stern is a lawyer by training and there has been support for the involvement of more lawyers in top positions in NGBs. What do lawyers have to offer to improve sports administration? In the United States, lawyers have been actively involved in running and regulating sport for some time.[121] The big four professional team sports in the USA – American football, basketball, baseball and ice hockey – all have lawyers as commissioners or presidents of their respective national associations.[122]

---

118 'Amateur status "not accurate" ', *The Guardian*, 17 March 1995, p 21 and 'Commentary: time to tackle the thorny question of "shamateurs" ' *The Guardian*, 17 March 1995, p 24.
119 Op cit, fn 23, Downes and Mackay (1996), pp 29–30.
120 See later, Chapter 8, p 364.
121 Judge Landis was commissioner of baseball from 1920–44; Clarence Campbell, a lawyer, was the National Hockey League President from 1946–77. See Kaplan, J, 'The most fun they've ever had: lawyers in the world of pro sports' (1992) 78 American Bar Association Journal 56; and Shulruff, L, 'The football lawyers' (1985) 71 American Bar Association Journal 45.
122 See 'Student note' (1990) 67 Denver University Law Review 110.

Lawyers clearly have qualities to offer: rational thinking, objectivity, foresight and development of preventive methods.[123] British sport may be learning from the United States. A number of sports administrators have a legal background, an acknowledgment that legal expertise has a role to play in sports administration.[124]

Characteristics of Sports Governance

What has been increasingly apparent is that there has been a need to develop more effective mechanisms of governance within sports NGBs. This is partly due to the need to achieve compliance with the external legal norms; that is, to operate within the law. It is also about balancing all the interests that were discussed in chapters 1 and 2.[125]

So what are the qualities of effective sports governance? Sport has looked to the world of corporate governance for guidance. In 1992, the *Cadbury Report* was published, providing the values and standards required of corporate behaviour.[126] A Code of Best Practice was directed at the Boards of Directors of all listed companies in the UK:

Cadbury Report, 'Code principles'

3.2. The principles on which the Code is based are those of openness, integrity and accountability. They go together. Openness on the part of companies, within the limits set by their competitive position, is the basis for the confidence which needs to exist between business and all those who have a stake in its success. An open approach to the disclosure of information contributes to the efficient working of the market economy, prompts boards to take effective action and allows shareholders and others to scrutinise companies more thoroughly.

3.3. Integrity means both straightforward dealing and completeness. What is required of financial reporting is that it should be honest and that it should present a balanced picture of the state of the company's affairs. The integrity of reports depends on the integrity of those who prepare and present them.

Boards of directors are accountable to their shareholders and both have to play their part in making that accountability effective. Boards of directors need to do so through the quality of the information which they provide to shareholders, and shareholders through their willingness to exercise their responsibilities as owners.

The arguments for adhering to the Code are twofold. First, a clear understanding of responsibilities and an open approach to the way in which they have been discharged will assist boards of directors in framing and winning support for their strategies. It will also assist the efficient operation of capital markets and increase confidence in boards, auditors and financial reporting and hence the general level of confidence in business.[127]

Are these values of openness, integrity and accountability the only relevant values of effective governance? Are they as appropriate to sports governing bodies as to general business? Perhaps it is

---

123 Common qualities discussed by lawyers generally and recounted in a series of interviews with leading sports lawyers in Britain in 1994 by the author. Generally, on lawyers' qualities and values, see Cotterrell, R, *The Sociology of Law: An Introduction*, 3rd edn (2003), London: Butterworths.

124 See 'Why every FC will soon need its own QC', *The Guardian*, 1 March 1997, p 20.

125 See earlier diagram of competing models of the sports market, p 225.

126 *Report of the Committee on the Financial Aspects of Corporate Governance* (1999), London: Gee.

127 Ibid, paras 3.2–3.5.

not an exhaustive list.[128] Other terms can be substituted for these listed – values such as transparency are closely linked to openness. Transparency is partly about openness, but also allows outsiders to see, for example in sport, how disciplinary procedures operate and how decisions are made. It is also about the need for effective communication of key information in a form and way that is meaningful to target audiences. Can greater democracy be added? With companies, this is constructed in terms of the rights of the shareholders vis à vis the directors of a company. Some sporting bodies and clubs may have shareholders, but it is more accurate to talk of 'stakeholders' in sport, including owners, administrators, fans, media and commercial interests. What say should these constituent groups have in the future direction of a sports body?

The value of compliance with external legal norms of sport could be added. With the tradition of self-regulation permeating sport, this is something that sport has had difficulty in engaging with. Lastly, the requirement that organisations should act with 'social responsibility' has developed in recent years and this increasingly should apply also to sporting bodies.[129]

These values and goals are commendable, but an issue is always how they are 'policed' and how compliance is to be guaranteed. In addition, how should these values be applied to the sports world – how different are specific sporting to general organisations?

The EU and Sports Governance

In recent years sport governance has fallen into disrepute primarily because of the involvement of sports federations not only in the rules of the game but also in wide-ranging commercial activities. Because of the monopolistic position of virtually all sports federations, this distinction, which appeared so clear in the past when governing sport for the 'good of the game', has become blurred by commercial activities.

There have been increasing demands that sports NGBs are more responsive and democratic, together with other sports organisations lower in the pyramid structure. In Europe, the increasing pressure from the European Commission for NBGs and ISFs to comply with EU law and notably the competition law regime, together with the scandals that have enveloped the IOC, have put the spotlight on sports governance. Directorate General IV (DG IV: competency for competition issues) of the EU Commission and the European Court of Justice have on several occasions drawn attention to this dichotomy (rules for the governance of the game on the one hand and rules that have a commercial impact on the other). Cases such as *Deliège*[130] and *Lehtonen*[131] are examples but *Meca Medina*[132] has obfuscated this division.[133]

The European Competition Commission has on several occasions indicated that where the rules of sports federations have an economic or commercial dimension, they will attract the attention of European law; particularly the four basic freedoms, namely free movement of persons, of services, of goods and of the rights of establishment, as well as the competition rules pertaining to cartels and abuse of dominant positions. The majority of sport federations find themselves in a monopolistic position by virtue of the way in which their sport is organised. It is in this context that in March 2001, the First European Conference on the Governance of Sport was held.[134]

---

128 Note that there have been many more reports on corporate governance since the Cadbury Report, e.g. OECD – Principles of good practice (2004), see www.oecd.org/dataoecd/32/18/31557724.pdf.
129 See (2003) 6(3) SLB 2 – this will include environmental concerns.
130 Cases C-51/96 and C-191/97 *Deliège v Liège Ligue Francophone de Judo*, judgment of 11 April 2000.
131 Case C-176/96 *Lehtonen & Castors Canada Dry Namur-Braine v FRBSB* (Belgian Basketball Federation), judgment of 13 April 2000.
132 Case C-519/04 P, *Meca-Medina and Majcen v Commission* [2006] ECR I-6991.
133 See Chapter 4, p 182.
134 *The Rules of the Game*, 'Europe's first conference on the Governance of Sport', was jointly organised by the FIA, the European Olympic Committee and lawyers, Herbert Smith. For more information, see www.fia.com/public/fia_structure/resources/governance_sport.pdf; Caiger, A and Gardiner, S, 'The rules of the game: Europe's first conference on the governance of sport' (2001) 4(2) SLB 1, and *SportBusiness*, April 2001, p 26.

The intention of the conference was to encourage a debate as to how it may be possible to separate out the rules of the game of a non-economic nature from those that have an economic dimension. This dichotomy is clearly more important in the large federations than in the case of small ones, where economic activity is insignificant and would probably fall within the *de minimus* rules of European law and be ignored.

An important example of the problems of dichotomy can be illustrated by the negotiations between the *Fédération Internationale de L'Automobile* (FIA) and DG IV. There had been many years of tension between the Competition Commission and Formula One racing; of particular concern was the close relationship between the FIA and Formula One Administration, the company that markets the rights to Formula One racing. In June 1999, the EU Commission made formal objections to this relationship. The agreement announced in January 2001 lays down that the FIA will concentrate on managing the rules of the governance of the FIA whilst licensing their commercial rights for one hundred years to Bernie Ecclestone's 'F1 Races'.[135]

Commission ended its monitoring of FIA/Formula One compliance with 2001 settlement

The Commission is satisfied that the conflict of interests identified in the FIA regulations and the restrictions that had been put on circuit owners, F1 teams and TV broadcasters have been ended. This assessment comes after a period of monitoring compliance of the settlement reached in October 2001 with international motor racing body FIA and the Formula One companies. FIA's role is now limited to that of a sports regulator. Circuit owners can, if they wish, organise rival championships and car manufacturers will in the future be able to participate in races other than those organised by the Formula One company. Television contracts have also been significantly shortened, which allows broadcasters to bid for coverage of this popular sport at regular intervals.[136]

The 'corporate experience' provides valuable lessons for the development of higher and more consistent standards of governance in sport. The key governance principles developed for companies are also highly relevant to sports and sports' governing bodies. Two extracts from the papers given at the conference are particularly useful:

Gaved, M, 'Corporate governance today and its relevance to sport'

2. Differences between sports and companies

However, when reviewing the development of improved standards of governance in corporations, it is also important to recognise that there are a number of fundamental differences between sports organisations and companies. In general, these differences should make it easier to develop a general governance framework for sports and codes for individual sports. The three most important differences are:

(1) Members of sports organisations do not 'own' their sports in the way that shareholders own companies. Shares can be purchased and sold but membership of sports organisations generally cannot. The ownership of shares and companies is essentially a legal construct, whilst most sports organisations are associations of people with a common interest in:
    a)   the broad development and funding of their sports;
    b)   training and participation;

---

135 See earlier, pp 192–3.
136 IP/03/1491, 31 October 2003 – see http://europa.eu/rapid/pressReleasesAction.do?reference=IP/03/1491&format=HTML& aged=0&language=EN&guiLanguage=en.

c)   competitions and events; and

d)   the setting and application of rules.

Shareholders and companies have interests in common but these are seldom as broad in their scope.

(2)   Members of sports organisations are also real people who typically belong to only one organisation. In contrast, most shares are owned by competing financial institutions who normally own shares in many – or sometimes hundreds – of companies. Historically, this diversification has made it difficult for shareholders to coordinate their common interests. The creation of common and widely supported codes of governance has made it considerably easier.

(3)   Boards and shareholders are strongly focused on the commercial activities and perform-ance of companies. Where companies have activities which are not aligned to the inter-ests of shareholders, governance processes may have an important role to play. Whilst many sports now have a commercial element – and in some cases this has grown dramat-ically over the last few years – in Europe commercial activities are not sports' funda-mental reason for existing.[137]

The President of the IOC also took part in the conference.

Rogge, J, 'Governance in sport: a challenge for the future'

As demonstrated earlier, governments or public authorities are linking the recognition of the role of sports governing bodies to the way they operate. The issue of governance and the *contend* sports bodies are ready to give to it are essential for the future relations between sports, its stakeholders and public authorities.

Governance is about clarification between the 'rules of the games' and the economic and commercial dimension related to the management of a sport. Because sport is based on ethics and fair competition, the governance of sport should fulfil the highest standards in terms of transparency, democracy and accountability.[138]

How best can bodies such as the EU Commission ensure sports governing bodies (NGBs and ISF) take seriously the need to seek greater compliance with external legal norms? Is it always possible to distinguish between sporting rules concerning governance of the game and those concerning the commercial dynamics of sport? What mechanism can best monitor continued compliance with these values of effective sports governance?

Competition and Broadcasting

The last section of this chapter will focus on the regulation of TV, which has such a significant impact upon contemporary elite professional sport. The details of the current domestic Premier League TV deal have been detailed above.[139] Additionally, the selling of media rights internationally for £1.4 billion over three years means annual revenue of around £2.2 billion. Similarly, from 2009/10, Football League clubs have benefited from new three-year broadcasting deals with the BBC and BSkyB worth £264m. Overseas rights have increased by 300 per cent to £24m over the

---

137 Gaved, M, 'Corporate governance today and its relevance to sport', *The Rules of the Game* (2001).
138 Rogge, J, 'Governance in sport: a challenge for the future', *The Rules of the Game* (2001).
139 See earlier, p 228.

same period, highlighting the attractiveness of all levels of English football to the global market. When combined with the increased parachute payments and enhanced solidarity package from the Premier League, Championship revenues will be around £470m per annum. However, in the recent challenging economic environment, the value of the TV rights agreement for the Football League for seasons 2011/12 to 2013/14 has decreased by around 23 million per season.[140]

There are two key issues that have emerged. Firstly, what are the anti-competitive issues around the collective selling of rights, which have led to competition law intervention? Secondly, there are a number of sporting events which are protected as so-called 'Listed Events' and are thus not able to be purchased on the 'open market'.

Property rights in televising sports events

Under English Law, there are no legally recognised broadcasting or other propriety rights in a sporting event.[141] This is provided by Latham, CJ in the following Australian case:

Victoria Park Racing and Recreation Grounds Co. Ltd v Taylor and Others

Latham CJ: It has been argued that by the expenditure of money the plaintiff has created a spectacle and that it therefore has what is described as a quasi-property in the spectacle which the law will protect. What it really means is that there is some principle (apart from contract or confidential relationship) which prevents people in some circumstances from opening their eyes and seeing something and describing what they see. The court has not been referred to any authority in English law which supports the general contention that if a person chooses to reorganise an entertainment or to do anything else which other persons are able to see he has a right to obtain from a court an order that they shall not describe to anybody what they see . . . the mere fact that damage results to a plaintiff from such a description cannot be relied upon as a cause of action . . . I find difficulty in attaching any precise meaning to the phrase 'property in a spectacle' . . . A 'spectacle' cannot be 'owned' in any ordinary sense of that word.[142]

The investment and value in sports events needs to be protected with other legal mechanisms. Primarily this will be through contractual relationships, where the rights will be created and protected under the contract. In the modern broadcasting environment around sport, the rights of the broadcaster will be protected by complex contractual and licensing arrangements. It also needs to be recognised that with the use of technologies such as mobile phones and digital cameras, individuals can film and transmit moving pictures of a sports event they are attending. Official broadcasters can seek protection by event organisers restricting entry with certain equipment, ticketing conditions making filming unlawful and applying civil and possibly criminal provisions for infringement under any specific copyright law.[143]

There are a few competition issues relevant in broadcasting of sporting events. In order to create a product it must be decided what is to be sold and bought. If one considers English football as an example one observes that TV rights to matches have been sold collectively. This is also true in other European markets, such as Germany and the Netherlands, while in Italy and Spain selling individually has been the norm although there is a move towards collective selling.[144] In the US

---

140 'Sky Sports and Football League agree £195m deal', BBC News, 4 April 2011, www.bbc.co.uk/news/business-12965536.
141 Note the position is different in US law, where a broadcasting right has been recognised; see *Pittsburgh Athletic Co. et al v KQV Broadcasting Co* (1937) 24 F Supp 490.
142 *Victoria Park Racing and Recreation Grounds Co. Ltd v Taylor and Others* (1937) 58 CLR 479.
143 Se op. cit., fn 40, Lewis and Taylor (2008).
144 Apa, E and Pecoraro, Y, 'Italy: Legislation: a return to collective sale of sport TV rights' (2008) 6(1) WSLR.

professional leagues, collective selling has been the norm and has gained exemption from the intervention of anti-trust law by reason of the Sports Broadcasting Act 1961.[145]

The broadcasting world can be divided into three different markets: free-to-air TV viewing, subscription-based pay-TV and pay-per-view TV. It is the emergence of subscription-based pay-TV, most notably in the guise of BSkyB, that has changed the dynamics between sport and television. Sport has made a major contribution to the growth of satellite and digital technology. Traditionally it has been the view of buyers and sellers of broadcasting rights that in order for the product to have value it can only be sold once, to a principal buyer, who may then decide to license certain rights in respect of the 'property' bought. In the current technological world, several products may be created from a specific event, which may be sold to a variety of buyers.

Several different products can be created out of the football Premiership competition:

- Live broadcasts in the UK – the contract usually specifies how many matches may be broadcast. The broadcaster may be able to license another European or international broadcaster to show a selection of matches live abroad;
- Delayed broadcasts of matches – of less commercial value than live broadcasts;
- Match highlights;
- Pay per view on cable and satellite;
- The new media, which includes mobile phones and the internet.

However, as noted above it is clearly BSkyB that has dominated as the buyer of these rights. The trick, from a competition point of view, is how to achieve an adequate balance between revenue and seeing to it that the output of sports events is not unduly restricted by collective agreements to sell broadcasting rights, and also how to give each medium adequate and fair access to broadcast sporting events, especially in football – the global sport – where these issues arise most readily.

Collective selling of TV rights

The first BSkyB deal with the Premier League, which ran for five years from the 1992–93 season, was reviewed under the (now repealed) Restrictive Trade Practices Act 1976 (RTPA) when applied by the Restrictive Trade Practices Court (RTCP).[146] This judgment rewards careful reading as it is a most detailed description of football and broadcasting. The Director General of Fair Trading objected to the restrictive nature of the Premier League (PL) and the BSkyB agreement. The PL granted BSkyB the exclusive rights to broadcast only 60 live matches of the league. The court found the agreement to be restrictive of competition but to be generally in the public interest.

Green, N, 'Collective selling of sports television rights'

The Judgment

Collectivity:

The Court was convinced by the point that the 'product' sold by the PL was the league championship as a whole and not just individual games; 'if a club were to withdraw from the PL for whatever reason it could not produce the derived product it helped produce as a member of the PL cartel'. The Court thus accepted the argument that each of the clubs in a league contributes to the creation of a single product – the championship – being a product that no one club could individually produce.

---

145 See Halgreen, L *European Sports Law* (2004), Copenhagen: Forlaget Thomson, for a good guide to comparisons between sports broadcasting in Europe and North America.

146 *Re FA Premier League Ltd.* Agreement Relating to the Supply of Services Facilitating the Broadcast of Premier League Football Matches (Restrictive Practices Court, 28 July 1999).

Collective Selling and Individual Selling of Television Rights:

A central tenet of the argument of the DGFT was that whilst collective selling is per se unobjection-able, clubs should be able to sell the unallocated rights themselves individually. The Court described this argument as 'fundamentally flawed' and 'facile'. As the Court concluded, it would be intolerable to find that both the PL and an individual club were attempting to sell the same television rights. No broadcaster would be willing to deal with either of them or, if he was willing, would pay one vendor a different price for the rights that might be sold by the other vendor to a different purchaser.

The Court also expressed the view that the right of the home club to veto who entered its ground to make a broadcast was not an answer to the question: who owned the right to sell the match, whether it was the home team, the visiting team or both. The court considered that a concurrence of two teams was required.

Competition Between Broadcasters: Exclusivity

The Court heard a great deal of technical, commercial and economic evidence about the broadcasting market. It concluded that competition was largely determined by the need to differentiate programming and that the ability to differentiate programmes was a key driver for Pay-TV subscriptions and hence a key means by which Pay-TV operators entered the broadcasting market and expanded, once in.

Exclusivity was a critical device to facilitate differentiation. Other facts in broadcasting competition included: terms of the agreements conferring exclusivity; the popularity of the sports competition; the timing of the programme and whether it is a repeat event week in week out, or an irregular event; quality of coverage; and the existence of a single seller.

The Court concluded that the fact that BSkyB had entered the market, and had done exceptionally well in the market, had had the effect of 'sharpening' competition not dimming it.

Legal Conclusions

The Court concluded that the restrictions . . . benefits outweigh the disadvantages.[147]

The UK Competition Act of 1998 came into force in 2000, replacing the RTPA. Although the Court found the broadcasting agreement restrictive the agreement nevertheless passed through one of the 'gateways' that would make it permissible. The RTPA was rather formalistic; now the Competition Act is in line with the EC competition rules, this case may no longer constitute reliable law.[148] What is interesting, however, is that the RTPC applied the rule of reason, in essence, and approved of collective selling and a rather broad-based notion of exclusivity.

In the UK two sets of competition rules apply in parallel. Anti-competitive behaviour which may affect trade within the UK is specifically prohibited by Chapters I and II of the Competition Act 1998 and the Enterprise Act 2002. Where the effect of anti-competitive behaviour extends beyond the UK to other EU Member States, it is prohibited by Articles 101 and 102 TFEU. UK and EU competition law prohibits two main types of anti-competitive activity: anti-competitive agreements (under the Chapter I and Article 101 prohibitions); and abuse of dominant market position (under the Chapter II/Article 102 prohibitions).

Both domestic and European competition law is essentially modelled on United States law and notably the Sherman Act 1890. The Act's original intention was to promote consumer welfare and to protect US citizens against the power of 'big business'. Restraints on consumer welfare which

---

147 Green, N, 'Collective selling of sports television rights' (2000) ISLJ 4–6. For a full discussion of the issues raised in the BSkyB/PL case see Spink, P and Morris, P, 'The battle for TV rights in professional football', in Caiger and Gardiner (2000); Caiger, A, 'BSkyB/BBC TV deal upheld' (1999) 2(5) SLB 4.

148 Also note that the attempted merger between BSkyB and Manchester United was decided before the Competition Act 1998; see Toms, N, 'Ownership and control of sports clubs; the Manchester United Football Club "Buy-Out" ', in Greenfield, S and Osborn, G (eds), *Law and Sport in Contemporary Society* (2000), London: Frank Cass; Brown, A and Walsh, A, *Not for Sale: Manchester United, Murdoch and the Defeat of BSkyB* (1999), Edinburgh: Mainstream.

are 'illegal per se', such as price fixing, are outlawed. Other potential restraints will be subject to the aforementioned 'rule of reason' test by scrutiny of the market in question and weighing of anti-competitive and pro-competitive impacts.

The Subsequent PL/BSkyB agreements have come under the regulatory gaze in that the agreement is a vertical cartel. Since the 1992 deal, which was for five years, BSkyB has consistently secured exclusive broadcasting deals for live matches with the Premier League, simply by outbidding all competition on a regular basis. No other broadcaster has been able to match BSkyB's superior spending power. As a result, BSkyB attracted the investigative interest of both the Office of Fair Trading under the CA 1998, and the European Commission. In 2001, BSkyB paid around £1.2 billion for 66 live matches per season for three seasons. However, in response to pressure from the European Commission the PL divided up its broadcasting rights into a number of packages, to attract more competition to the auction. However, for the next three-year deal running from 2004, BSkyB again secured exclusive rights to all live PL matches. The EU Competition Commission investigated and the commitments signed by the PL and the Commission dictated that no single auction bidder could win all six marketed packages. The aim was to ensure that greater access to PL matches was available to more than one broadcaster in the United Kingdom. In 2007, a second pay-TV broadcaster, Setanta, won rights to matches in two of six packages to show 46 matches per season. Setanta, however, only won rights to one of the packages – that is, 23 matches per season – for the deal starting in 2010. Due to overextending its purchase of sports rights and failing to earn enough subscribers, it went into receivership in 2009. ESPN, a Disney-owned company, now has these rights.

The Competition Commission has wanted to see greater competition in the market for the live rights to see them made more affordable for consumers. The belief was that BSkyB had made excessive profits from the commercialisation of their exclusive rights though the selling of subscriptions and maximisation of advertising revenues and that there was an indication that they were abusing a dominant position. BSkyB's counter-argument was that if any broadcaster was able to bid for any of the PL packages, this indicated that it was a competitive environment. What is clear is that the competition authorities have seen themselves able to intervene on issues of exclusivity and the length of the contracts. It seems that total exclusivity will be outlawed if it can be shown to inflate the value of sports rights to the detriment of the consumer, and a length of more than three years will be problematic. However, BSkyB continues to have a pre-eminent role in the subscription TV market for sport.

BSkyB also faces other legal issues. More recently, Ofcom, the independent regulator and competition authority for the UK communications industries, has intervened under the Communications Act 2003 to examine the wholesale market that BSkyB operates with its selling of its matches to rival digital platforms, notably Virgin Media and BT Vision. In summer 2010, an interim agreement was reached between Ofcom and BSkyB providing a fixed wholesale price for the Sky sports channels to all potential retailing digital platform buyers, old and new. This decision is likely to be appealed to the Competition Appeal tribunal and possibly on to the Court of Appeal.[149] Additionally there are a range of issues such as interception of satellite signals and the use of unauthorised decoder equipment that have been subject to litigation. Similarly, internet transmission of broadcasts of sports events raises many issues of protection of the commercial integrity of rights holders.[150]

Restrictions on selling of sports events

In the EU there is recognition of sports' cultural aspect and there has been concern that commercialisation may preclude public access. The Commission has adopted the 'Television Without

---

149 See Hornby, S, 'Broadcasting: BSkyB appeals Ofcom "price setting" for sports content' (2010) 8(6) WSLR.
150 See Harrington, D, 'Piracy: Sports broadcasting: waking up to online piracy' (2004) 4(2) WSLR, and Anderson, J, 'The curious case of the Portsmouth publican: challenging the territorial exclusivity of TV rights in European professional sport' (2011) 3 ISLR 53–60; 'Premier League games can be shown on foreign decoders', 4 October 2011, www.bbc.co.uk/news/business-15162241.

Frontiers Directive', in terms of which each Member State may select the sporting events that are culturally significant to the people of that Member State. Since the 2007 revision, it has been renamed the 'Audio Media Services Directive.' Wachmeister explained the justification for this directive thus:

Wachmeister, AM, 'Competition Newsletter'

I. Priority for free-access television for the coverage of major sports events

1. There are advantages for viewers if important sports rights are broadcast by free-access television, so that consumers are not obliged to make additional payments for decoders, receiving equipment or cable subscription to view such events, in particular, those in which their compatriot sports men and women take part in international events.

2. More generally, concern has arisen, with the growth and development of pay-TV, that viewers are being denied free access to important national events because large subscription broadcasters have been buying up those rights to develop their own services. It is said that some sporting events are of such national or heritage importance, that they reflect common identity and value, so that broad free access should be given to them. The complaints are from 'public interest' or 'national heritage' concern, rather than on competition grounds, and a regulatory approach would be necessary to achieve the desired result.

3. Competition law is not the right instrument for achieving cultural or regulatory aims. As confirmed by the Eurovision judgment, competition rules are neutral with respect to different types of broadcasting and in principle, do not provide a legal base for favouring one category of broadcaster over others.

4. Further to an amendment by the European Parliament, the directive modifying directive 89/552/EEC ('television without frontiers') includes a new Article 3A. The purpose of this Article is explained in recital 18, which reads as follows:

> 'Whereas it is essential that Member States should be able to take measures to protect the right to information and to ensure wide access by the public to television coverage of national or non-national events of major importance for society, such as the Olympic Games, the football World Cup and the European football Championship; whereas to this end Member States retain the right to take measures compatible with Community law aimed at regulating the exercise by broadcasters under their jurisdiction of exclusive broadcasting rights to such events'.

5. Article 3A paragraph 3 stipulates, moreover, that Member States shall ensure that broadcasters under their jurisdiction do not exercise the exclusive rights purchased by those broadcasters in such a way that a substantial proportion of the public in another Member State is deprived of the possibility of following events, which are designated by that other Member State, on free television. According to information supplied to the Commission by national delegations to the Contact Committee set up by the Directive, a large majority of Member States intend to notify their measures taken under Article 3A paragraph 1 in the course of 1998. All Member States have indicated timetables for transposition of Article 3A paragraph 3 by the deadline required by the Directive, i.e. 30 December 1998.

6. The procedure laid down in Article 3A paragraph 2 requires the Member States to notify their measures and the Commission to verify their compatibility with Community law within a period of three months. The Commission must seek the opinion of the Committee established by the Directive. Measures taken by Member States in order to guarantee the availability of coverage of certain events must be in accordance inter alia with Article 90 of the Treaty.[151]

In the UK, Ofcom is the body that ensures that the listed events procedure works. Existing listed events rules, which were updated by the Broadcasting Act 1996, require that sport's 'crown jewels' must be shown either fully live on free-to-air, terrestrial television channels which at least 95 per cent of viewers can receive (the BBC, ITV or C4), or in highlights form by one of those broadcasters.

The Category A list of events which must be screened live by one of those three broadcasters includes: the Olympic Games; the FIFA World Cup Finals Tournament; the FA Cup Final; the Scottish FA Cup Final (in Scotland); the Grand National; the Derby; the Wimbledon Tennis Finals; the European Football Championship Finals Tournament; the Rugby League Challenge Cup Final; and the Rugby World Cup Final.

The Category B list of events that those broadcasters must be allowed to show highlights of includes: Test cricket matches played in England; non-finals play in the Wimbledon Tournament; all other matches in the Rugby World Cup finals tournament; Six Nations Rugby Tournament matches involving home countries; the Commonwealth Games; the World Athletics Championship; the Cricket World Cup – the final, semi-finals, and matches involving home nations' teams; the Ryder Cup; and the Open Golf Championship. This intervention into the market can lead to a decrease in the value of the rights.

In July 2001, The House of Lords delivered a ruling in R v Independent Television Commission ex p TVDanmark 1 Ltd[152] concerning the sale of sports TV rights. The case arose out of a dispute between the ITC (the forerunner of Ofcom) and TVDanmark 1. This Danish satellite cable service, based in London, broadcast Denmark's five away World Cup qualifying games even though they are listed events in Denmark. The ITC challenged this arrangement. The Court of Appeal had earlier held that, although 'the object of Art 3(a) is maximum coverage, it is not an object to be achieved at any cost'. Other factors have to be borne in mind, 'such as the need to sustain competition, and to prevent public service broadcasters becoming over dominant as well as the need to have regard to ordinary commercial realities'. Therefore, the Court of Appeal held that TVDanmark's holding the rights rather than the free-to-air broadcaster was lawful.

Overruling this decision, the House of Lords held that the Art 3(a) protection for certain designated events 'was not qualified by considerations of competition, [or] market economics'. The right of the public to have access to listed events is paramount.[153]

Where the major sports events such as the Olympic Games and World Cup are at stake Europeans have been guaranteed free-to-air coverage. The European Broadcasting Union has co-ordinated broadcasts of significant sporting events to the citizens of Europe. However, for the first time the rights to the World Cup Finals in South Korea and Japan in 2002 were purchased by a private company, the German Kirsch Group. The company subsequently went into liquidation, after attempting to sub-license the rights and realised less income than was anticipated. At a European level, recent attempts to challenge the listing provisions before the General Court have failed.[154]

The UK's classification of Listed Events was examined in 2009 by an expert Committee appointed by the Secretary of State for Culture, Media and Sport.[155] The Committee proposed changes to the classification but any change will not happen until 2013 at the earliest.[156]

---

151 Wachmeister, AM, 'Competition Newsletter', June 1998.
152 [2000] 1 WLR 1604.
153 See 'Listed sports events are protected against the TV rights market' (2001) 4(4) SLB 1.
154 See Cases T-385/07, T-55/08 and T-68/08 FIFA and UEFA v Commission, judgments of 17 February 2011.
155 Review of Free-to-air Listed Events, http://webarchive.nationalarchives.gov.uk/+/http:/www.culture.gov.uk/images/consultations/independentpanelreport-to-SoS-Free-to-air-Nov2009.pdf.
156 http://www.parliament.uk/briefingpapers/commons/lib/research/briefings/snha-00802.pdf.

Barr-Smith, A, 'Listed Events: "He's got 'em on the list and they'll none of 'em be missed" '

Current review

The current review of the UK listed events regime, initiated by the Department of Culture Media and Sport (DCMS) in December 2008, was undoubtedly long overdue. The most recent review before the current one was chaired by Lord Gordon of Strathblane who reported in 1998. His principal innovations were the introduction of transparent and published criteria for selecting an event for listing and the division of the list into Groups A and B. Both innovations were welcomed by rights holders and accepted by the decision-maker, the Secretary of State. The list approved by the Secretary of State and currently in force includes 10 Group A events and 9 Group B events. These cover both individual 'stand-alone' events (e.g. the Grand National, the FA Cup Final), and entire tournaments/championships or at least a series of matches within a tournament (e.g. the World Cup football finals, the men's and women's finals at the Wimbledon tennis championships).

This time around, to assist in its deliberations, the DCMS appointed an 'independent' Advisory Panel (the Panel) chaired by the former executive director of the Football Association and broadcasting consultant, David Davies, and comprising luminaries from the worlds of sport, broadcasting and academia.

The consultation period administered by the Panel ran from 8 April 2009 until 20 July 2009 during which it received responses from a wide range of sporting, media and other affected organisations. The Panel held hearings at which many of those organisations were given the opportunity to present their views orally and also attended sessions convened at the Scottish Parliament and Welsh Assembly and by the All Party Media and Sports Group at Westminster.

The Panel's findings were set out in a report dated 11 November 2009 (Davies Report), which triggered a welter of comment and further debate. The Panel did not commission any independent expert to carry out a detailed analysis as to the economic impact on the rights holders concerned of any proposed changes to the list.

Report of Davies Panel

In sum, the Davies Report concluded:

The principle of listing, which the Panel described by reference to the wording of the Directive in terms of the protection of events for a TV audience of 'major importance to society', remained relevant. Notwithstanding evidence of changes to the media landscape and viewer consumption patterns (e.g. the move away from the TV as the means by which to watch/follow sporting action), the Panel believed the public *understood instinctively and supported the concept*.

The criteria previously established by Lord Gordon to determine those events which should be considered for listing by the Secretary of State should be simplified, in particular by removing the existing requirement that an event should 'unite the nation' and be a 'shared point on the national calendar' (which the Panel felt to be too aspirational). An existing requirement that an event had a 'history' of being broadcast live on a FTA basis was also seen by the Panel as unnecessary given the need to keep the list relevant and up to date.

In framing their recommendations as to the future constituents of the list, the Panel should not (or could not) include aspects of the criteria which required political judgments, most notably as to the economic impact on a particular sport of being included in the list – this being a matter for consideration by the Secretary of State.

The Group B list of events should be abolished: highlights/delayed coverage were an insufficient substitute for the live event and, with the proliferation of channels and increase in broadcast capacity through 'red button' coverage, scheduling issues which had previously been used to justify events being placed on the Group B (as opposed to Group A) list were no longer relevant.

Various changes were needed to the Group A list of events in its current format with the removal (de-listing) of certain events (e.g. Winter Olympics) and addition (e.g. Home Ashes Test

Match cricket series between England and Australia) or re-classification (6 Nations Rugby Matches to be listed only in respect of coverage in Wales of matches involving the national team in that tournament).

The Secretary of State issued a consultation document on 7 December 2009 in which he stated he was 'minded' to accept the recommendations put forward by the Panel and which granted interested parties an opportunity to present their views. Responses to that consultation were due by 19 March 2010. The Secretary of State had hoped to be in a position to announce his findings prior to the dissolution of Parliament, but the process was subsequently put on hold pending the outcome of the general election.

The incoming coalition now faces a difficult decision whether or not to take this Review forward, or to await the outcome of digital switchover.

Achieving a balance

In particular, it will be necessary for the new Secretary of State to justify his conclusions as being properly in the public interest, particularly when balanced against the obvious impact which listing an event has on the finances of the sports rights holder concerned and the knock-on effects on broadcasters and the wider broadcasting market.

In the *TV Danmark case*, the House of Lords (Lord Hoffman giving the lead judgment) held that the Television Without Frontiers Directive imposed a 'clear' obligation on Member States to protect designated events for the benefit of the viewing public. Moreover, that obligation was not to be qualified by *'considerations of competition, free market economics, sanctity of contract and so forth'*. However, their Lordships also recognised that the Commission had to approve any national measures as being compatible with European law such that:

> *'the balance between the interests of sports organisers and pay-TV broadcasters in maintaining a free market and the perceived interest of the citizen in being able to watch important sporting events has already been struck . . .'*

This balancing act was, apparently, not properly considered by the Panel as a consequence of its refusal to consider the financial impact which any listing proposals would have on the sports rights holders concerned. To redress this obvious gap in the analysis, the Secretary of State in his consultation on the Davies Report specifically asked those affected by the proposals to put in detailed evidence as to financial impact, albeit there has been no confirmation as to whether consultees will have an opportunity to review the Secretary of State's own economic impact assessment.

Lawyers will be interested how the Secretary of State will deal with arguments put forward by several of the sports affected by the proposals in the Davies Report that, irrespective of whether their events meet the requirement of being of 'major importance for society', the proposals put forward by the Panel are disproportionate and therefore contravene EU law. Whereas the Panel looked at the evolving media landscape and concluded that, for the foreseeable future, most people's first choice of how to view sporting events would be via their TV sets, it is not easy to reconcile a system which reduces choice with an environment in which the consumer increasingly wishes to be able to decide precisely when and how to access content.

Correspondingly, there is a question as to whether listing is necessary to ensure any public interest is properly protected. Sports governing bodies (who tend also to be the owners of the rights affected by listing, or at least to exercise some control over the exploitation of those rights) need to have regard, in the exercise of their duties, to a wide range of considerations. Generating sufficient income is, of course, one such consideration, but balanced against this will be the needs to seek quality of coverage and widespread exposure for their sport. For these same reasons, rights holders will generally ensure that, when tendering their broadcast rights, they are under no obligation to accept the highest monetary offer made for any broadcast rights package.

Assuming a sports rights holder complies with its obligation under the competition law rules to conduct open and non-discriminatory tender processes, the removal of the listing legislation would not prevent any broadcaster from participating. In particular no FTA broadcaster would be excluded from acquiring rights to an event which they properly considered to be of particular relevance to their audience and/or the public. Presumably, it is for these reasons that the overwhelming majority of EU Member States have exercised their discretion not to put in place any listing measures.

Once the Secretary of State has navigated his way through these issues, he will also need to look in further detail at arguments put forward by rights holders to events of more than a few hours' duration as to whether a blanket decision to list the entire event (and protect its coverage on FTA television) can be justified. For example, an Ashes Test cricket series comprises up to 175 hours of sporting action across a two-month period, much of which takes place during the working day. Can every minute of that series properly be regarded as being of such public importance that it needs to be protected for live FTA coverage? The Gordon Committee did not think so and recommended that Test Match cricket occupy its current berth as a Group B event. The Panel's response to this conundrum appeared to be that there was sufficient merit in an entire series being guaranteed for FTA coverage and that concerns as to scheduling availability on FTA channels were no longer relevant given that digital switchover (and the opening up of more spectrum capacity) was likely to lead to a proliferation of qualifying FTA channels on which to broadcast. The Panel largely ignored the question whether coverage on a non-destination channel, which viewers have to trawl down their EPG to find (e.g. ITV4), could be regarded as protecting the public interest of access to an event.

These same points cut across the main arguments in the UEFA and FIFA appeals being heard in the European courts; both organisations contend that listing the entire European Championship/World Cup finals tournaments in the UK (and Belgium) cannot be proportionate when so doing includes games either not involving the national team and/or of insufficient public interest.[157]

The status quo seems set to continue with the government indicating no changes are to be made until 2013 at the earliest.

Other Competition Law Intervention into UK Sport

Under the UK Competition Act of 1998, the Office of Fair Trading (OFT), which has been in place for many years, continues to be the investigative body concerning all forms of anti-competitive behaviour, including cartels and the abuse of market power under the Competition Act. When an infringement is found, the OFT has the power to apply appropriate penalties in accordance with published guidance and in the light of developments in UK and EC case law. The OFT will refer to the Competition Commission (CC) mergers believed to result in a substantial lessening of competition in a UK market.

The Competition Enforcement (CE) Division of the OFT plays a key role:

- enforcing EC and United Kingdom competition laws including Articles 101 and 102 of the TFEU and the Competition Act 1998;
- stopping cartels and other damaging anti-competitive agreements;
- stopping any abuse of a dominant market position;

---

157 Barr-Smith, A, 'Listed Events: "He's got 'em on the list and they'll none of 'em be missed" ' (2009) 17(2) SATLJ 5.

- promoting a strong competitive culture across a wide range of markets;
- informing business, through a widespread education programme, about changes in legislation;
- working with the European Commission and national competition authorities of other EU Member States on Article 101 and 102 TFEU cases.

Since the enactment of the Competition Act, two major issues have fallen under the investigative gaze of the OFT. The first has involved the suspicion of a vertical cartel between football replica shirt manufacturers, sports apparel retailers and a number of clubs. The OFT commenced informal investigation of the sector in the late 1990s. In 2002 they announced that they were instituting an investigation of a number of companies including Umbro, JJB Sports and Manchester United, who they alleged had entered into a number of agreements to fix the price of football kits manufactured and supplied by Umbro, infringing Chapter 1 of the Competition Act 1998.[158] The investigation established price fixing and refusal to supply shirts to retailer who wanted to sell at a discount.

In August 2003, the OFT, after concluding its investigation, levied fines against a number of businesses including JJB Sports (£8.373m), Umbro (£6.641m), Manchester United (£1.652m) and the FA (£198,000). The OFT may impose a penalty of up to 10 per cent of UK turnover for a maximum of three years for infringement of the Competition Act 1998. In autumn 2004, the Competition Appeal Tribunal (CAT) dismissed the appeals brought by Allsports Ltd and JJB Sports plc.[159]

The second major investigation by the OFT concerned the governance of horse racing in the UK. In 2001, a competition inquiry into the British Horseracing Board's (BHB) supply of pre-race data to internet betting sites was launched. This followed a complaint from bookmaker William Hill that BHB was abusing a dominant position as the sole provider of race and runner data on UK horse racing. The bookmaker alleged that this enabled BHB to set excessive and discriminatory pricing and restrictive licensing terms.[160] In April 2003, the OFT reported on this and wider issues of governance.[161]

Gardiner, S, 'The Competition of Horse Racing'

The Office of Fair Trading (OFT) has told the bodies that run British horse racing that it believes some of their rules infringe competition regulations. The OFT has made its preliminary view that certain Orders and racing rules are anti-competitive because they:

- limit the freedom of racecourses to organise their racing, in particular by fixing how often and at what times they stage races and the type of racing they stage;
- fix the amounts that racecourses must offer owners to enter their horses in a race; [and]
- monopolise the supply of race and runners data to bookmakers by foreclosing competition from alternative suppliers.

The OFT is requiring the British Horseracing Board (BHB) and the Jockey Club to end these apparent infringements of the ACT and to increase the freedom of race courses operating under this regulatory regime to compete and open up the market for potential competition in the supply of race and runners data.

The OFT has recognised that there are non-commercial sporting rules, such as specifying the earliest age at which horses can run and how jockeys are allowed to use their whips, that are unlikely to affect competition and are outside of its ambit. These are essentially sporting

---

158 'Football kit "price fixing" inquiry', BBC News, 16 May, 2002, http://news.bbc.co.uk/1/hi/business/1990969.stm.
159 JJB Sports plc v OFT [2004] CAT 17; judgment at http://www.catribunal.com/238-586/1022-1-1-03-JJB-Sports-PLC.html.
160 See Chapter 7, p. 325.
161 'The British Horseracing Board and The Jockey Club: a Summary of the OFT's case' April (2003) OFT 654, http://www.oft.gov.uk/OFTwork/publications/publication-categories/reports/competition-policy/oft654.

rules. This reflects the approach adopted by the European commission in cases such as *Deliège* and the agreement reached with the FIA and Formula One Racing in 2001.

However, the rules identified are considered by the OFT to have 'significant economic and commercial consequences' and are not compatible with Chapter 1 prohibition, which under the Competition Act 1998 provides indications of what are uncompetitive practices which prevent, restrict or distort competition. The OFT may exempt an agreement from the Chapter 1 prohibition if it is seen as contributing to the improvement of production or distribution or promotes technical or economic progress while allowing consumers a fair share of the resulting benefit. These two provisions assume that the agreement does not firstly contain any restrictions that are not indispensable to the attainment of those objectives or secondly allow the undertakings concerned substantially to eliminate competition.

The OFT state that consumers want 'orderly and trustworthy racing'. The Orders and Rules are viewed by the OFT as 'going beyond what is indispensable to ensure a viable, orderly and trusted British racing industry'.

Not surprisingly the response to this report from the racing authorities has been defensive. In an initial response, BHB chief executive Greg Nichols said the OFT had 'fundamentally misunderstood how and why British racing operates as it does [and there would be] a comprehensive and robust response'. [162]

The OFT investigation focused on a number of agreements, including the Orders and Rules of Racing. These competition concerns arose from the high level of central control exerted by the BHB over how and when racecourses could offer horse racing and over the way BHB could exploit horse racing commercially through its control over racing data. The OFT was concerned that these agreements had the overall effect of restricting competition between racecourses, by preventing them from altering their racing in response to consumer demand, and prevented the emergence of alternative providers of racing data. After a period of consideration, the BHB responded with its view of future governance of racing.[163]

BHB, 'The Modernisation of British Racing'

The Report recommends seven key changes to the structure of the sport:

(i)   the separation of the governance and commercial functions of the British Horseracing Board (BHB);
(ii)   the restructuring of the BHB Board;
(iii) changes to the management of racing's commercial interests;
(iv)   changes to the method of allocation and distribution of data income;
(v)   the establishment of a prize money agreement between racecourses and the recipients of prize money (owners, trainers, jockeys and stable staff);
(vi)   the introduction of greater competition between racecourses for fixtures;
(vii) the modernisation of the Orders & Rules of Racing.[164]

This plan was provisionally accepted by the OFT in June 2004. It reflects the developing criteria and framework for appropriate sports governance with a clear position on the desirability of the separation between the governance of the 'rules of the game' and the exploitation of the commercial interests in a given sport.

---

162 Gardiner, S, 'The Competition of Horse Racing' (2003) 6(2) SLB 1.
163 See BHB, 'The Modernisation of British Racing' (2004, June): www.britishhorseracing.com/images/inside_horseracing/ media/The_Modernisation_of_British%20Racing.pdf.
164 Ibid, p 4.

Conclusion

This chapter has considered the complex issue of when and how sports bodies should be subject to external regulation. The reasons for this have been discussed along with the development of effective governance, which is key to limiting exposure to the aforementioned external regulation. As enormous amounts of money have poured into sport with the significant growth of the sports industry, managing and protecting the commercial integrity of sport has become a central role for sports administrators. The next chapter will focus on the connected issues of how sports related financial corruption can best be engaged with.

Key Points

- Commercialisation around sport in recent years, for example with the vast increases in sponsorship, marketing and merchandising operations, has led to modern sport being a huge business.
- There are various economic models that can be applied to the structure of sport. One useful model distinguishes between 'win maximisation', where the main goal is sporting success with profits being reasonably unimportant, and 'profit maximisation', where generating of profits is the main aim.
- There are important distinctive and unusual characteristics of the sports industry, which need to be understood.
- Various different forms of external regulation are available where sports bodies are seen as not 'managing' the competing values of maximising the commercial interest and ensuring the proper development of the rules of the game.
- Effective sports governance has been seen as a key development for sports bodies to limit their exposure to the risks of external regulation.
- English football has been subject to ongoing concerns about the lack of effective governance.
- In the selling of TV rights of sports events, anti-competitive issues have been identified around the collective selling of rights, exclusivity and length of contracts.
- There are a number of sporting events which are protected as so-called 'listed events' and are not able to be purchased on the 'open market'.
- The UK competition authorities have intervened in a number of sports industries including that of horse racing.
- Upholding the commercial integrity of sports bodies and events has become a central role for sports administrators.

Key Sources

Football Task Force, *Commercial Issues* (1999), London: DCMS.

Foster, K, 'How can sport be regulated', in Greenfield, S and Osborn, G (eds), *Law and Sport in Contemporary Society* (2000), London: Frank Cass, pp 268–70.

Haigh, G, *Cricket War: the Inside Story of Packer's World Series Cricket* (1993), Melbourne: Text Publishing Company.

Independent Football Commission, 'Report on Self Regulation' (2004), www.theifc.co.uk/publications/documents/SelfRegulationReport.pdf.

The Rules of the Game, 'Europe's first conference on the Governance of Sport' (2001), www.fia.com/public/fia_structure/resources/governance_sport.pdf.

Chapter 6

Sport, Match Fixing and Corruption

Chapter Contents

Introduction   259

Football: Bungs and Brown Paper Bags   259

Regulation of Sports Agents   265

Ethics and Hosting of Major Sports Events   270

Match Fixing in Sport   272

Gambling and Sport   290

Developments in Fighting Match Fixing and
    Sports-related Gambling   297

Conclusion   301

Key Points   301

Key Sources   301

Introduction

Where there are significant amounts of money, sin and greed are not far behind. As elite sport has become increasingly professionalised, the increased money in sport leads to more opportunities for fraudulent and corrupt activities. This chapter will examine the variety of ways in which this can happen. A recurring issue is how best these nefarious activities can be challenged and attempts made to eradicate their occurrence and alter the behaviour of participants in both the playing and administration of sport. Governance is once again the crucial issue. How can the values and characteristics discussed in earlier Chapters be developed to help ensure financial probity within sport?

This chapter is divided into five parts. The first section will focus on how allegations of general financial corruption and impropriety have been 'managed' by sporting national Governing Bodies (NGBs) and there will be a specific focus on English football. The second section will focus on a connected issue, which has been increasingly highlighted, concerning the regulation of players' agents, especially in the context of their role in player transfers – financial transactions that often involve huge amounts of money. The third section will focus on how the International Olympic Committee (IOC) and international sporting federation (ISFs) have engaged with corruption concerning issues such as the tendering process for major tournaments. In recent times the focus has been on the world of football and FIFA with the awarding of future World Cup competitions to Russia and Qatar.

The fourth and main section of the Chapter will focus on the phenomenon of match and so-called 'spot' fixing (where a particular event is manipulated by participants), which has been highlighted in a range of sports in recent years. An examination of some specific sports including international cricket and tennis will be carried out to see how these sports and the relevant ISFs have engaged with the problem to reinforce integrity within that sport.

Lastly, the fifth section will examine the relationship between the sports and gambling industries. Horse racing is, of course, a sport whose *raison d'être* is as a forum for gambling to legally take place. Merrill Lynch projects that the turnover for the online sports gambling industry will top $100 billion by 2015.[1] Throughout the chapter, the enduring theme is how best the integrity of sport can be supported within the context of the overtly commercialised sport world and related industries.

Football: Bungs and Brown Paper Bags

Irregular financial dealings have long been seen as part of professional football. The 'bung' became part of public parlance in the 1990s. These payments, not declared for tax purposes and made to facilitate or sweeten particular transactions, have been common in sport.[2] They have been very much in the tradition of 'doing business'. It is football, the most commercialised of British sports, that has the most infamous history as far as questionable financial payments are concerned.[3] There are historical examples that date back to the early days of the professional game. Call them what you will – bungs, sweeteners or plainly illegal payments – they have been made to ensure deals are concluded. The illegality derives from the fact that they are secretive and not disclosed for tax purposes. A major question is whether they are illegal just as far as the internal rules of football are concerned or whether they are also illegal in relation to the law.

The development of the professional game was in fact first initiated by 'illegal payments' to players by Preston North End in 1884. The payments were contrary to the rules of the Football

---

1 'Match Fixing in Sport on the Rise', *The Sport Review*, 6 November 2009, http://www.thesportreview.com/tsr/2009/11/match-fixing-sport.

2 Downes, S and Mackay, D, *Running Scared: How Athletics Lost Its Innocence* (1996), Edinburgh: Mainstream, pp 16–17.

3 See Burrell, I and Palmer, R, 'Taxman blows whistle on football's fiddles', *The Sunday Times*, 6 June 1993, p 7.

Association at the time, but as the scale of payments by other clubs in the north of England increased, this led to professional football primarily developing in the north of England. In 1919, Leeds City was expelled from Division Two for illegal payments to players. Leeds United was formed to replace them. Until the 1960s and the introduction of a minimum wage for professional footballers, largely achieved by the campaign of Jimmy Hill of the Professional Footballers' Association (PFA), the wages were reasonable in terms of average wages, but in no way comparable with wages of foot-ballers today. In the context of the insecurity, risk of injury and short-term nature of the job, the scope for additional backhand payments was obvious.

There are more recent examples of tax-free (*ex-gratia*) payments, often involving collusion between clubs. In the early 1990s, the Swindon Town chairman was given a prison sentence after he was found guilty of conspiracy to defraud the Inland Revenue. It was discovered that a number of other clubs had colluded with Swindon concerning transfers between the clubs. The other clubs agreed that as part of the transfer Swindon would pay thousands of pounds direct to the player. To disguise the payment, the selling club agreed to act as a conduit for the money by describing it as a signing-off fee, which they were paying their player. This payment would be disguised as a lump sum payment terminating the services of the player. To facilitate this, the funds (from Swindon) would be routed through the club that was selling the player.

The position of taxation in sport has always been problematic. There are many opportunities for tax evasion. In addition there have been continued claims that sport should not be subject to the formal application of taxation, especially VAT, in the same way as other businesses.[4] There has been a concerted campaign for non-profit-making suppliers of sports services to be zero rated for VAT purposes.[5] As Baldwin argues:

> Despite expressing vigorous support for sport and exhorting us all to participate in what is good for us, successive governments for the last 25 years have done little to alleviate the significant tax burden that the tax regime places on sport. The Sports Council estimates that for every £1 contributed by Central Government to sport, it returns £5 in tax to the Exchequer – not a bad return![6]

The bigger clubs use more sophisticated methods to avoid paying tax, such as offshore tax havens. Agents invariably play a significant part in any transaction. The one modern incident that has led to financial dealings coming under the gaze of the law is that involving Tottenham Hotspur.

Williams, R, *Football Babylon*

> June 1992 saw a routine check of Tottenham Hotspur's PAYE files by the Inland Revenue which revealed serious financial irregularities – a can of worms had been opened. As the taxmen probed deeper into the club's affairs, more and more irregularities were uncovered and a full-scale Inland Revenue investigation began. Spurs commissioned city accountants Touche Ross to do a thorough review of the club's affairs. The irregularities under Irving Scholar's regime were numerous and scandalous. Amongst the revelations uncovered were *ex-gratia* payments to players that would result in considerable back tax liabilities for Spurs. Belgian Nico Claesen had been given a secret payment of £42,000 when he joined Spurs in 1986 which had not included the statutory PAYE deductions. Icelandic international Gudni Bergsson also benefited from a payment which was, like Claesen's, made via his former club. Irving Scholar authorised both payments.

---

4   See Grayson, E, *Sport and the Law*, 4th edn (1999), London: Butterworths.
5   Connor, G, 'A review of recent UK developments in taxation relating to sport' (2001) 4(1) SLB 11.
6   Baldwin, R, 'Taxation of sport' (1996) 4(3) SATLJ 95.

Paul Gascoigne's and Chris Waddle's pension papers were backdated by two years and loans to both players used to buy houses around London were illegal. Scholar also gave a secret undertaking to both players, guaranteeing them *ex-gratia* payments of up to £120,000 after they had left Spurs. A letter from Scholar to Gascoigne's agent Mel Stein promised to pay the player '£70,000 net of all UK taxes, up to a maximum of £120,000 gross'. The implications of such payments were, in the words of Touche Ross, 'like having a gun held to the club's head'. The special inquiry at Tottenham began on 17 July 1992. A few months later, in November, the Inland Revenue demanded a payment of £500,000, with the promise of more to come.

The transfers of Chris Waddle to Marseille and Paul Gascoigne to Lazio both involved payments to the football agent Dennis Roach who, as *The Sunday People* reported, was being paid by both sides in the deals which was in total breach of FIFA, UEFA and FA regulations. Scholar brought Roach into the equation and, even after Italian fixer Gino Santin was detailed to finalise Gascoigne's Lazio transfer, he received a pay-off payment of £27,500. However, this was not the end of the line for Roach, who continued to receive money. A Spurs document stated: 'It would appear that Mr Roach has been on the payroll of the club, unknown to Mr Solomon and Mr Berry, having been paid £64,400 in the year ending 31 May 1991. It would also appear that Lazio may also be paying Mr Roach in connection with the Gascoigne sale. This is forbidden both under Football League and FIFA regulations.'

Most damaging of all were the irregular payments made over three transfers: the £250,000 transfer of Mitchell Thomas from Luton to Spurs in 1986; the £425,000 signing of Paul Allen from West Ham in 1985 and the £387,500 transfer of Chris Fairclough from Nottingham Forest in 1987. Thomas had been given a £25,000 loan when he joined Spurs but papers forwarded to the Football League Tribunal at the time of transfer omitted to mention it. Thomas also received a letter stating that, in effect, the money was never going to have to be repaid. The loan was made three weeks before he actually became a Spurs player. Allen and Fairclough also received loans before joining Spurs – £55,000 and £25,000 respectively – and neither payment was disclosed to the Transfer Tribunal.

When Irving Scholar left Spurs the club was in big trouble. Terry Venables desperately searched for a business partner to save the club from financial ruin and certain closure. His knight in shining armour (or so he thought) was Amstrad boss Alan Sugar, a man with a bruising business reputation. It was not long before Sugar became concerned about the goings on at Spurs, the result of a combination of rumours and Inland Revenue facts. The relationship between Venables and Sugar became increasingly uneasy. Venables was dismissed by Sugar in a blaze of publicity and in 1993 the two men slugged it out in the High Court as Venables took legal action against his former partner. The legal proceedings were the usual claim and counterclaim, including evidence suggesting that some managers accept cash bungs as part and parcel of transfer deals. Alan Sugar knew that Tottenham's troubles with the Inland Revenue were to be laid directly at Scholar's door, yet Venables felt that Sugar consistently tried to portray him as the bad guy. As manager of the team under Scholar, Venables was employed by Tottenham Hotspurs FC, a subsidiary of Tottenham Hotspurs PLC and each organisation had its own independent board of directors. The FA examined the evidence and cleared Venables of any wrongdoing. They must have been satisfied because, two years later, they appointed him England coach.[7]

An FA Commission of Inquiry ruled Tottenham Hotspur were guilty of 'avoidance and evasion of fees' concerning transfers. They were fined £600,000, had 12 points deducted from the next season's FA Carling Premiership total and were barred from the 1994–95 FA Cup. The subsequent

7   Williams, R, *Football Babylon* (1996), London: Virgin, p 139.

three-man FA Appeals Board cut the 12-point deduction to six. The ban on the club's participation in the 1994–95 FA Cup remained and the fine was increased from £600,000 to £1.5 million.[8] Tottenham then considered taking the FA to the High Court but agreed to go to arbitration in keeping with the guidelines of FIFA, the sport's world governing body. The independent arbiters made a confidential decision but decreed that the FA acted outside its jurisdiction.[9] Subsequently the FA ruled that Tottenham still had to pay the £1.5 million fine imposed for financial irregularities but it was confirmed that the FA Cup ban and six-point deduction from their FA Carling Premiership total had been annulled.[10] It was the end of that particular saga.

The 'Bungs' Inquiry I

Certainly 'the bung' has become part of football parlance. Allegations were made in the High Court in a case between Terry Venables and Alan Sugar surrounding the transfer of Teddy Sheringham from Nottingham Forest to Tottenham Hotspur, concerning allegations of illegal payments made to Venables and the Nottingham Forest manager, Brian Clough. This court action was the culmination of a drawn-out feud between Venables and Sugar and ongoing allegations as to the fitness of Venables' acting in financial dealings.[11] Some bemoaned this as another example of the malaise of football and sport in general. Questions were raised in parliament, primarily by the Labour MP Kate Hoey.[12] Many people in football said that this was all part of the culture and tradition. In another court case involving Terry Venables, the former Scottish international Frank McLintock, whose First Wave Agency acted in the Sheringham transfer, was paid £50,000 in cash on an invoice that did not mention his help in transfers. Justifying the payment, he said at the trial that:

> This is used by a number of clubs to get out of what they consider to be the antiquated laws of the Football Association. Some agents call it merchandising and have done no work of that kind whatsoever, but we have at least done some genuine work, which we can prove.[13]

The bung allegations led to an FA investigation carried out by an inquiry team consisting of the Premier League chief executive Rick Parry, Robert Reid QC and ex-player Steve Coppell. After more than three and a half years of investigation, their report was published in September 1997.[14] The main 'prosecution' made under FA rules was against the then Arsenal manager, George Graham. The investigation of Graham followed disclosures made in *The Mail on Sunday* and an investigation by the Inland Revenue was convened to look into the whereabouts of £50,000, which had allegedly gone missing from the £2.1 million transfer of Teddy Sheringham from Clough's Nottingham Forest to Tottenham in 1992. But here the inquiry immediately met the problem that would plague it again and again: an allegation followed by a denial – and few powers to get to the truth. Over the following months, more and more allegations were referred to the inquiry. Three years, 60 witnesses, tens of thousands of pages of evidence and over £1 million later, few individuals were the subject of any FA proceedings. As far as the alleged £50,000 bung in the Sheringham transfer was concerned, the Report concluded, 'We are satisfied that cash payments were made from the £50,000 to members of staff at (Nottingham) Forest'.[15] A cash culture was exposed as existing at Forest, with members of the management and coaching team regularly receiving money-filled brown envelopes after transfers.

---

8 'Tottenham save six points but pay £1.5 m', *The Times*, 7 July 1994, p 44.
9 'Arbiters give Tottenham new hope of cup reprieve', *The Times*, 26 November 1994, p 48.
10 'FA upholds Spurs' £1.5 m fine', *The Times*, 14 December 1994, p 42.
11 See Harris, H and Curry, S, *Venables: The Inside Story* (1994), London: Headline, for further details; and *Panorama*, 'The Manager', BBC TV, 16 September 1993.
12 'Why I'm so angry: bungs are tainting the game I love', *The Observer*, 5 November 1995, p 10.
13 'Soccer: clubs often dodge FA rules – McLintock,' *The Guardian* 13 December 1995, p 22.
14 The Bungs Report, *The FA Premier League Inquiry into Transfers* (1997), London: FA Premier League.
15 See 'Bung-busters prepare to act on "cult of dishonesty" ', *The Daily Telegraph*, 20 September 1997, p 28.

Graham received a national and international ban lasting for one year.[16] The police and the Serious Fraud Office (SFO) continued to be interested in some of the events investigated but no further action arose. The Premier League acted in a multi-agency approach with the police, the SFO, the Inland Revenue and overseas fraud police.[17] Graham quickly returned to the world of football at the end of his ban.[18] Ronnie Fenton, the assistant manager at Nottingham Forest at the time of the allegations, and chief scout, Steve Burtenshaw, were charged with misconduct. Due to his ill health, no further action was taken against Brian Clough.

So was the inquiry, as some would suggest, merely a cosmetic exercise? The report is over 1,000 pages in length. It certainly exposed the lack of financial probity within English football. What seems to be clear is that many of the dealings investigated cannot really be characterised as any form of villainy. It does seem to be a part of football culture, albeit a part that needs to be challenged and exposed. The report also looked at the transfers of all foreigners to England between 1992 and 1994 – around 35 cases – and the increasing influence that agents were having on financial transactions.

The 'Bungs' Inquiry II

In March 2006, the Premier League initiated a second inquiry into bungs in football. Lord Stevens, the ex-Metropolitan Police Commissioner, was appointed to head a team of investigators. A team of forensic accountants examined 362 transfers which took place between 1 January 2004 and 31 January 2006. This investigation was in response to a number of allegations made by high-profile individuals. The Luton Town manager, Mike Newell, said he had been offered bungs a number of times. He commented: 'I think it's become a culture in football and it's almost accepted and brushed under the carpet.'[19] Sven-Goran Eriksson, at the time England coach, claimed three unnamed Premiership clubs were riddled with corruption.[20] The Premier League stated the report was commissioned simply to find out where money in football transfers went – to clubs, players or agents – and if there were illicit payments to managers. In September 2006, a BBC TV *Panorama* programme was aired entitled 'Football's Dirty Secrets'. Undercover filming purported to show a number of agents claiming that some mangers routinely accepted bungs during transfer deals.[21]

In October 2006, an interim report which focused on over 350 transfers involving Premier League Clubs that took place between January 2004 and January 2006 was presented. Lord Stevens declared 323 transfers as being clean but indicated that he would seek to use Football Association rules to force agents to open their bank accounts as investigations continued into the remaining 39 transfers, most of which were domestic transfers.

A total of 39 recommendations were made in the interim report, including:

- the creation of a body to handle the audit of transfers, instead of the Football Association;
- a culture of rule compliance to be developed within football;
- relatives acting as agents should not be paid in deals;
- the Professional Footballers' Association should not act as agents.

---

16 'FA hands Graham one-year ban', *The Times*, 14 July 1995, p 40; 'Ban Graham for life, says UEFA Chief' *The Guardian*, 4 March 1995.
17 See 'Souness in new "bung" inquiry', *The Guardian*, 6 March 1995.
18 'The resurrection of brother George', *The Observer*, 7 April 1996; and 'Soccer: Leeds forget past and pin faith on Graham', *The Guardian*, 11 September 1996, p 20.
19 'Newell has evidence of bung offer', BBC News, 13 January 2006, http://news.bbc.co.uk/sport1/hi/football/teams/l/luton_town/4608688.stm.
20 See 'New allegations in Eriksson saga', BBC News, 21 January 2006, http://news.bbc.co.uk/sport1/hi/football/internationals/4636032.stm.
21 Programme can be accessed at http://news.bbc.co.uk/1/hi/programmes/panorama/5363702.stm.

The first three of these are welcome indications that the Report may bring about meaningful change and reflect principles of good governance. However, the fourth seems to be odd. The PFA has shown itself able to provide a sound agency service for a number of its members, free from the motivation of making money. As PFA chief executive Gordon Taylor commented:

> I find it totally incongruous and bizarre that instead of concentrating on transfer dealings he chose to single out the PFA, without even having the courtesy to contact us, and tell us what we should and shouldn't do . . . anyone with any knowledge of football would know we are fully transparent in what we do . . . put it this way: if it was just the PFA acting as agents for players, there would be no suspicions of any backhanders at all.[22]

In response to the interim report and earlier concerns, the FA has already imposed some initial reforms. There is now a regulatory structure over player agents operated by the FA. Clubs will also now not be able to pay agents directly – instead payment will be deducted from a player's salary. Together with the internal governance changes accepted by the FA in response to the Burns Report, the FA is likely to be more responsive in engaging with financial impropriety.[23]

The final report was published in early 2007. Transfers involving five Premiership clubs – Chelsea, Newcastle, Bolton, Middlesbrough and Portsmouth – were named, primarily concerning the activities of 15 agents and third parties involved in some 17 transfers. Lord Stevens' report specifically lists concerns about two managers.[24] Subsequently, the City of London Police have carried out an investigation involving a number of the managers and agents named in the report, although no criminal charges have been brought.[25]

If the first bungs inquiry can be adjudged to have been a window-dressing exercise that failed to engage with the reality of the problem and produced one symbolic prosecution, how confident should one be that the second will be more effective?

Evaluation of inquiry

A number of points can be made. This investigation seems to have had greater independence than its predecessor, taking a lead from the International Cricket Council's investigation into match fixing. The FA compliance unit has been given more resources and greater powers. The Football Association has approved new regulations concerning agents following a meeting of the FA Council during summer 2006 (see below). The *Panorama* programme has added weight to the feeling that there is a real problem of financial probity in football. The football authorities have acknowledged that they need to act at this time in terms of the exercise of effective good governance so that their self-regulation can continue to be the dominant form of regulation. This dynamic is increasingly determined by growing political calls for more external regulation of professional football in particular and professional sport generally (see the Independent European Sports Review).[26]

However, a more cynical view might be that this Report has again, as in the 1990s, resulted in action against a relatively small number of scapegoats without really changing the pervasive culture of English football. Sporting organisations are extremely closed institutions and football has shown itself very resolute at resisting meaningful inspection and change. There are grounds for optimism that, whatever the result of the ongoing bungs inquiry, positive change is occurring. There is

---

22 'Bung inquiry targets 39 transfers', BBC News, 2 October 2006, http://news.bbc.co.uk/sport1/hi/football/eng_prem/5398006.stm.
23 Can be found at http://www.thefa.com/TheFA/WhoWeAre/NewsAndFeatures/2005/ReviewConclusions.
24 'Stevens names and shames 17 transfers in bungs inquiry', *The Guardian*, 15 June 2007 www.guardian.co.uk/football/2007/jun/15/newsstory.boltonwanderers.
25 'Football corruption dossier handed over to prosecutors', *The Guardian*, 13 July 2008, www.guardian.co.uk/uk/2008/jul/13/ukcrime.premierleague1.
26 See Chapter 4 at p 199.

increasing awareness within the football world that the characteristics of effective sports govern-ance need compliance with the legal and ethical requirements of financial probity.

Over the last twenty years, significantly large amounts of 'new monies' have come into the English game from the much increased value of TV rights and the exploitation of other commercial rights, and as such it is now a big business. What is required is adoption of and adherence to appro-priate corporate codes of conduct that commit clubs to a strict anti-corruption policy. On the international stage, the ICC can be seen as a good exemplar of a body that has taken financial corruption, in that case match fixing, seriously. An emphasis on robust investigation monitoring and a new punitive disciplinary code, together with prevention evidenced by protection for whistle-blowers and education of players and officials, have upheld the integrity of international cricket. On the national stage, the changes in the organisational structure and interventionist powers in horse racing have again improved the integrity of that sport. English football needs to show that it has the same resolve to aspire to the highest standards of ethical behaviour.

Regulation of Sports Agents

The bung saga has been influential in calls for a greater regulatory framework for football agents. FIFA first introduced regulations in 1994.[27] Players' agents have been active in sport for a significant period of time. They are the 'fixers' for their clients and are invariably the contact for anyone wanting to do business with their client. For the client they are there to provide advice on and to negotiate contracts and commercial endorsements, etc. There are a number of large agencies, such as the SFX group with Jon Holmes prominent in the UK and the International Management Group established by the late Mark McCormack. There are a number of lawyers who act as agents. There are issues of conflict of interest that can arise, but lawyers have the professional code of ethics as guidance. Players' associations as forms of trade unions increasingly have an active role in representing players as their agents. The Professional Footballers' Association (PFA), formed at the end of the nineteenth century, represents the vast majority of professional footballers in England. Newer bodies have recently been formed in boxing, rugby and athletics. A greater form of collective representation of professional sportsmen and women, often representing their interests on an individual as well as collective level, is developing, perhaps in response to the greater commercialisation of modern sport.

In comparison with the United States, sport agency is not highly regulated in Europe. It is an example of an unregulated area of private entrepreneurial activity. It has attracted a variety of indi-viduals into the industry, some of whose business practices and ethical stances are questionable. A developing issue has been what regulatory framework is appropriate: for example, if there should be increased licensing, registration or certification.

Agents act in many sports – but it is in those that are most professionalised and commercialised that agents have most impact. Since the professionalisation of rugby union in the mid-1990s, agents have become more common. But transfers in rugby are reasonably rare. In cricket, the England and Wales Cricket Board has indicated that it wants individuals acting as agents to register with it and to agree to abide by its regulations. Concern has grown over some agents who know little about professional cricket and come primarily from a football background.

FIFA regulations

Since 2002, FIFA have required national football governing bodies to effectively have their own regulatory framework 'using the FIFA regulations as guidelines for incorporating the principles set

---

27 See Miller, F, 'Not every agent is a bad guy' (1996) 4 SATLJ 36, for details of old regulations and how they have been incorporated within English national footballing regulations.

out therein, whilst taking national and international legislation into account.'[28] Initially the FA incorporated the FIFA rules into its own regulations, as is still the case in a number of other European countries. After a period of consultation and some delay, the FA introduced its own regulations in 2007.[29] They are claimed to be more proscriptive than the FIFA regulations and have key provisions of a ban on dual representation (an agent can only represent one party); payment to a player's agent must be made by that player; players' agents cannot own any interest in registration rights of players; all agents, whether UK based or based overseas, must register with the FA before representing players working in England.[30] Although there were extensive claims that the regulations would be challenged through litigation, this has not transpired. However, in 2009 FIFA indicated that it was to end its current regulations on players' agents at some point in the near future, claiming that only around 30 per cent of international transfers involve licensed agents.[31] It is an admission that it has lost this regulatory battle and is now looking at mechanisms such as the 'Transfer Matching System', which requires both clubs in a player's transfer to enter verified details of the payments and parties involved online. This accountability is responding to claims that transfers can be used to launder monies gained through criminal activity as all individuals involved in a transfer will be formally recorded.

How the FA will respond to the withdrawal of FIFA from this regulatory role remains to be seen. After investment of considerable resources to develop their own extensive regulations, it is likely that they will be reluctant to make any swift changes.

There is clearly a problem with unlicensed agents. There are more than 500 FIFA agents in the world, but there are many more that work without licenses. In addition, the many unregistered agents who operate in the business are only after the highest possible commissions.

Bower, T, *Broken Dreams: Vanity, Greed and the Souring of British Football*

Lured by easy money, the number of football agents in England had proliferated. In 1995, agents had been legalized but were required to be registered by FIFA . . . by 2002 there were 179 licensed agents in England, compared to 92 in Germany, 88 in France and 54 in Italy. Hundreds of others fluttered around as unofficial agents. Sharp dealers, operating from mobile telephones, encouraged players to initiate a transfer by feigning unhappiness or illness, with the assurance that the agent's fees would usually be paid by the clubs, not the players.[32]

Whether the business dynamics of agents in football, or sports more generally, amount to any legal wrongdoing is questionable but certainly there are highly unethical practices.[33] In addition, there have been increasing concerns about the links that exist between clubs and certain agents and agency firms leading to potential conflicts of interest.[34]

In America many States have regulatory legislation concerning sports agents:

28 Lewis, A and Taylor, J (eds) *Sport: Law And Practice* (2009), Haywards Heath: Tottel Publishing, p 671.
29 For the most recent version of the regulations, revised in July 2009, see http://www.thefa.com/TheFA/RulesandRegulations/NewsAndFeatures/2009/AgentRegulations09.
30 For a full analysis, see Ellen, L, 'Critique of the Regulation of Football Agents' (2007) 15(3) SATLJ.
31 'Fifa to give up regulating player agents', *The Guardian*, 12 November 2009, www.guardian.co.uk/football/2009/nov/12/fifa-agents-regulation.
32 Bower, T, *Broken Dreams:Vanity, Greed and the Souring of British Football* (2003), London: Pocket Books, p 252.
33 'FIFA to probe Kewell deal', BBC News, 15 July 2003, http://news.bbc.co.uk/sport1/hi/football/teams/l/liverpool/3068093.stm.
34 See, for example, 'United cut Ferguson agency link', BBC News, 25 May 2004, http://news.bbc.co.uk/1/hi/england/manchester/3746565.stm; and *Fergie and Son*, BBC 3, 27 May 2004; after the airing of this programme concerning transfer dealings between Manchester United and Elite Sports agency run by manager Sir Alex Ferguson's son Jason, Alex Ferguson vowed never to give interviews to BBC reporters.

Gray, J, 'Agent Regulation in the United States'

With the advent of multi-million-dollar American professional athlete salaries, problems have occurred regarding the handling and investment of these significant sums of money. Some athletes have encountered financial problems because their agents were dishonest or unscrupulous. Others have experienced problems because they do not possess the requisite business or negotiation skills necessary to protect their personal and business financial interests from their advisors and other business partners. Over the last twenty years, American athletes have lost their sports-related fortunes while investing in highly speculative business ventures such as gas, oil, music groups and restaurants. In an attempt to protect professional athletes from financial ruin and from unscrupulous agents and advisors, a number of regulatory schemes in the United States have been developed and implemented.

State Athlete Agent Registration Laws

Over the last ten years, American states that have big-time college football and men's basketball passed athlete agent registration laws. The states which passed athlete agent registration laws include: Alabama, Arkansas, California, Florida, Georgia, Indiana, Iowa, Kentucky, Louisiana, Maryland, Michigan, Minnesota, Mississippi, Nevada, North Carolina, Ohio, Oklahoma, Pennsylvania, Tennessee, and Texas. The authority of states to enact athlete agent registration laws exists through the states' 'police power'. In the past, the states have used this police power to regulate the professional conduct of lawyers and doctors. Typically, these laws require a player agent to complete a state athlete agent registration application, pay a registration fee, file a surety bond, obtain state approval of agent/athlete contract forms, establish a maximum agent fee, and prohibit inducing college athletes with prospective professional careers which result in making these athletes ineligible for National Collegiate Athletic Association competition.

Athlete Labor Union Regulation of Agents

Likewise, professional athletes who are represented by a union have established an agent certification and regulation program. The player union's authority to regulate agents is found in the National Labor Relations Act ('NLRA'). The NLRA provides the player unions with the authority to ensure that they certify every agent before the agent can negotiate an employment contract with any unionized team. Under the NLRA, the player unions have the power to be the exclusive representative for all employees in such unit. (See 29 USC §159(a)–(e) (1982).) As the exclusive representative of players, the union can then delegate individual contract negotiations to certified player agents.

The exclusive use of union certified player agents is addressed in the league's collective bargaining agreements. For example, the NFL collective bargaining agreement under Article VI states that both the owners and players recognize that the union regulates the conduct of all agents who negotiate contracts for players with NFL teams. Under no circumstances can a non-certified agent negotiate an employment player contract with a team. If this rule is violated, the NFL shall impose a $10,000 fine on a club who negotiates a player contract with a non-certified agent.

In general, the requirement for union certification of player agents includes the completion of an application which requests information regarding an agent's education, professional and employment background. In order to maintain certification, the payment of an annual union fee is required along with annual attendance at a union-sponsored continuing education seminar addressing player contract negotiations and collective bargaining interpretations made by leagues, unions, and arbitrators.

Prohibited agent activities include: the offering of money in order to induce an athlete to become a client of an agent, providing false information on the union's agent certification form, and charging in excess of the union's established contract negotiation fees. All disputes between athletes and agents are required to be settled by the arbitration system, as established by the unions.

National Collegiate Athletic Association Regulation of Agents

The rules governing athletic eligibility for most college and university athletes in the United States are implemented and enforced by the National Collegiate Athletic Association ('NCAA'). Further, the NCAA has the responsibility to maintain the ideals of amateurism as well as uphold the integrity of intercollegiate sports. On the other hand, most agents recruit athletes who participate in NCAA sponsored sports. As a result, a tension and uneasiness occurs between the NCAA, the college athlete and an agent during the transition of the athlete from an amateur to a professional career.

In order for a college athlete to retain his eligibility, he must remain an amateur athlete as defined by the NCAA. If an active athlete is found to be represented by an agent or an athlete has received any financial compensation from a prospective agent, the NCAA will declare that athlete ineligible from any future competition. Eligibility is important for prospective professional athletes because college competition prepares them for a potential professional sports career. Once an athlete loses NCAA eligibility, the prospects for a professional career are dim. Further, the NCAA can impose significant economic sanctions against their member schools when an ineligible athlete competes during a game.

While NCAA has the power to impose penalties over its member schools and their individual athletes, the NCAA does not possess any mechanism to control the recruiting actions of agents. As a result, agents can act with impunity relative to NCAA rules so long as agent NCAA rule violations are not codified and enforced in the state athlete agent registration laws or the player union agent certification program.

Conclusion

There is an old adage that 'Money is the root of all evil'. Truer words were never spoken in the context of large sums of money, unscrupulous player agents and unsophisticated professional athletes. The three agent regulation schemes currently used have met with mixed results. For example, paltry government enforcement and investigatory budgets limit the effectiveness of state athlete agent registration laws. This problem is worsened by the public perception that professional athletes are viewed as pampered, spoiled and immature and that limited public resources should be expended on crime prevention, adequate housing and job creation instead.

In comparison, player union agent certification programs can directly punish a player agent for misconduct by limiting his ability to negotiate player employment contract within unionized American sports leagues. However, those athletes without the benefit of a unionized league, such as golfers, tennis players and figure skaters, are left to their own resources in dealing with player agents.[35]

Should the UK introduce regulatory legislation similar to that in the United States? Where is the balance to be struck in allowing a highly entrepreneurial activity to flourish, but protecting the vulnerable from exploitation? The debate in English football has revolved around a view that the regulation of agents is too onerous and essentially unworkable and fails to understand the reality of

---

35 Gray, J, 'Agent regulation in the United States' (2000) 3(6) SLB 9; also see Focus, special section on 'Sports agents and agency' (1992) 16(2) Journal of Sport and Social Issues, especially Roberts, G, 'Agents and agency: a sport's lawyer's view'; Cohen, G, 'Ethics and representation of professional athletes' (1993) 4(1) MSLJ; Arkell, T, 'Agent interference with college athletics: what agents can and cannot do and what Institutions should do in response', and Shulman, J, 'The NHL joins in: an update on sports agents regulation in professional team sports' (1997) 4(1) TSLJ; Champion, Jr, W, 'Attorneys qua sports agents: an ethical conundrum', and Stiglitz, J, 'A modest proposal: agent deregulation', both in (1997) 7(2) MSLJ. Also note the film, *Jerry Maguire*, starring Tom Cruise, about the US sports agent of same name.

the business they are involved in.[36] The opposite view is that agents' actions are often not in the interests of football. Few managers have been prepared to criticise the activities of agents for fear that individuals might decide not to deal with that particular club.[37]

There have been few disciplinary actions against agents for contravention of the player agent regulations. Such action has sometimes arisen out of a high-profile incident, such as the Ashley Cole tapping-up affair,[38] where Cole's agent Jonathan Barnett was banned for 12 months and had a fine imposed.

Farrow, S, 'Agent Regulations: Football Agents Regulations: application to relatives'

In 2006, Safi Rubie was briefly suspended for failing to provide information on his company Up 'n' Up Management Limited, his professional indemnity insurance and his annual declaration form (which all licensed agents are required to submit) to the FA. On paying a £600 fine and providing the required information, his suspension was lifted. Ian Elliott received a warning after failing to supply to the FA his representation contract with Sunderland's Grant Leadbitter.

In September 2008, Faisal Kashmiri, agent for the Crystal Palace midfielder Nick Carle, had his licence suspended for the January 2009 transfer window and was fined £25,000 for a breach of section C of the Regulations governing Dual Representation and Conflicts of Interest. Agents are prohibited from acting for two different clubs in two consecutive transactions involving the same player and clubs are not allowed to use the services of the agent in such circumstances. Crystal Palace were also fined £25,000.

Perhaps the most infamous case against a football agent arose from Paul Stretfords signing of Wayne Rooney to his agency Proactive Sports Management Limited in July 2002, even though Rooney was under contract with Pro-Form Sports Management Limited. Stretford was charged for breaches of the FIFA Players' Agents Regulations (with the Regulations not yet in force) in 2005, but responded by challenging the FA's right to compulsory internal arbitration for disciplinary proceedings as a contravention of the Human Rights Act. He lost at both the High Court (in March 2006) and the Court of Appeal (in March 2007) and his attempts to take his case to an arbitration tribunal prior to the FA's disciplinary hearing were also rejected. Stretford's disciplinary hearing finally took place in 2008, and in July he was found guilty of seven of the nine charges against him, fined £300,000 and suspended from all activity as a football agent for 18 months. This decision was upheld on appeal.[39]

One important issue that the Stretford case has raised is the agents' relationship with young players, classified legally as minors.[40] The ruling emphasised that such athletes must be given a genuine opportunity to obtain independent legal advice on the terms of the agreement they are being invited to sign. As Sweeney and Castor state, 'It is not sufficient to include a term in the contract stating that all parties have been advised if they have not – particularly when a party is wholly unsophisticated in legal and commercial matters.'[41]

Of course, football is not the only sport that has developed regulatory frameworks concerning the activities of agents. In boxing, the player's agent is known as his manager, who must be licensed

---

36 Stein, M, 'Opinion: The case for the agents' (2007) 5(5) WSLR.
37 'Game remains in state of denial', The Independent, 15 January 2006, www.independent.co.uk/sport/football/news-and-comment/game-remains-in-state-of-denial-523101.html.
38 See later page 416.
39 Farrow, S, 'Agent Regulations: Football Agents Regulations: application to relatives' (2009) 7(1) WSLR, which also highlights the application of FA regulations concerning controls on relatives acting as 'agents' for sportsmen.
40 Duthie, M and Arbuthnot, L, 'Representing Minors: Agents: breaches of representation agreements' (2007) 5(2) WSLR.
41 Sweeney, C and Castro, G, 'Player Contracts: Player representation: Proactive v Wayne Rooney' (2010) 8(9) WSLR.

by the British Boxing Board of Control (BBBC).[42] Both codes of rugby in the UK require player agents to be registered with the respective national governing body.

Ethics and Hosting of Major Sports Events

Major international sports federations such as the Fédération Internationale de Football Association (FIFA)[43] and the International Olympic Committee (IOC)[44] have become increasingly monitored as to their actions.

The selection process for host cities of major sports events has particularly been under scrutiny, especially the process for choosing the host of the summer and winter Olympics. However, it was not until 1998 and the successful bid by Salt Lake City for the Winter Olympics that the full situation was exposed. Andrew Jennings comments:

Jennings, A, *The Great Olympic Swindle: When the World Wanted Its Games Back*

There was no problem until people outside the Olympic family found out, and that wrecked Christmas 1998, the world's press united in disgust at the notion that bribery should taint the near sacred Olympics, and the family set about defending what credibility it had left . . . he [President Samaranch] personally selected five trusty IOC members to investigate their peers . . . there was bad behaviour, they said, and the hosts were the culprits. Those people were so insistent, and persistent, and well, so darned friendly down in Utah that some vulnerable members thought that those lovely gifts were about personal friendship, nothing to do with the business of getting the games. A few Olympic heads rolled.[45]

It was clear, however, that radical actions were necessary in order to uphold the integrity of the IOC.

Boyes, S, 'International Olympic Committee corruption and bribery scandal'

The International Olympic Committee has been embarrassed by a swathe of allegations of corruption and bribery amongst its ranks, stemming from the selection of Salt Lake City as the venue for the 2002 Winter Olympic Games. The accusations have led to the discovery by an IOC ad hoc inquiry of inducements totalling over US$500,000, presented to a significant number of IOC members by Salt Lake City during the bidding process. IOC rules state that members may not accept gifts above the value of $150 from cities bidding to host the Games. The inducements took the form of all expenses paid holidays for members and their families, support for the accommodation, employment and education of relatives of IOC members as well as other lavish gifts. The findings of the ad hoc inquiry implicated twenty-two IOC members, six of whom have been expelled: Lamine Keita (Mali); Agustin Arroyo (Ecuador); Jean-Claude Ganga (Congo); Zein El Abdin Abdel Gadir (Sudan); Sergio Santander (Chile); and Seiuli Paul Wallwork (Samoa). Four others resigned over the affair prior to the meeting: Pirjo Haggman (Finland); Bashir Mohamed Attarabulsi (Libya); David Sibandze (Swaziland); and Charles Mukora (Kenya).

---

42 For more see Anderson, C, 'Player Agents: Conflict between promoters and agents in boxing' (2009) 7(6) WSLR.
43 For a discussion of the role of IOC, see Jennings, A, *The New Lords of the Rings* (1996), London: Pocket Books and *The Great Olympic Swindle: When the World Wanted Its Games Back* (2000), London: Simon & Schuster; Tomlinson, A and Whannel, G (eds), *Five Ring Circus: Money, Power and Politics at the Olympic Games* (1984), London: Pluto; and Hill, C, *Olympic Politics* (1992), Manchester: Manchester UP.
44 For a discussion of the role of FIFA, see Yallop, D, *How They Stole the Game* (1999), London: Poetic Products; Duke, V, and Crolley, L, *Football Nationality and the State* (1996), Harlow: Longman; Sugden, J and Tomlinson, A, *FIFA and the Contest for World Football* (1998), London: Polity; and 'Who rules the people's game? FIFA versus UEFA in the struggle for control of world football', in Brown, A (ed), *Fanatics! Power, Identity and Fandom in Football* (1998), London: Routledge; Jennings, A. *Foul! The Secret World of FIFA: Bribes, Vote Rigging and Ticket Scandals* (2006), London: HarperSport.
45 Op. cit., fn 43, Jennings (2000), p 2.

Nine IOC members were warned and three exonerated. The decisions were taken at an extra-ordinary meeting of the IOC on the 17 and 18 March 1999.

It is becoming increasingly apparent that the Salt Lake City affair is not an isolated incident. The Japanese Olympic Committee has revealed that IOC members broke the rules of the bidding process in the run up to the selection of Nagano for the 1998 Winter Games. Sydney, the venue for the 2000 Summer Games, has also found itself embroiled in the controversy. The Australian Olympic Committee revealed that it had offered funding for training and other sports-related purposes to eleven African nations, dependent upon Sydney securing the 2000 Games. The Australian Olympic Committee have denied that these offers were intended as bribes, high-lighting the distinction between inducements paid to individuals and funding aimed at supporting sport in developing countries. The Australian Olympic Committee voluntarily proffered the infor-mation in order to distance itself from the scandal, but it now seems significant that Sydney won the right to stage the 2000 Games by only two votes. It has also been reported that Sydney frequently breached IOC guidelines in their treatment of visiting IOC members, presenting them with gifts and hospitality. However, this is not thought to be similar in scale or seriousness to the bribery and corruption in the Salt Lake City affair. However, a report into Sydney highlighted that, in any case, the guidelines governing the activities of cities bidding for the Games were vague and ambiguous, and that the IOC had demonstrated little interest in policing them.

The row has brought to a head increasing concerns over the capacity of the IOC President, Juan Antonio Samaranch, to meet the demands of the position. There have been widespread calls for Samaranch's resignation. Despite this Samaranch received an almost unanimous vote of confidence from the IOC at the extraordinary meeting in March. It was suggested Samaranch was facing more internal opposition in his attempts to reform the process by which Olympic venues are selected. Host cities are currently selected by a full vote of the IOC's members. The change involves a 'filter' process whereby bids are screened by a committee which reduces the field to two competing cities. The full membership of the IOC will then decide which of the two should be successful. The filter committee consists of sixteen representatives of the IOC membership, athletes, the International Winter Sports Federation, the Association of National Olympic Committees, the IOC President and the Chairman of the Evaluation Committee. It appears that, despite the can of worms opened by the Salt Lake City affair, many of the IOC's members are reluctant to give up their voting rights. However, the IOC membership did vote unanimously for a proposal to ban members from visiting cities in the 2006 bidding process.

The affair has brought into question wider concerns relating to the transparency and accountability of what is perhaps the world's most influential and important sporting organiza-tion, with widespread calls for the IOC to take the appropriate steps to restore its blemished credibility. The IOC has also come under pressure from its corporate sponsors to restore its image. To this end the IOC Executive Committee has proposed the establishment of an 'Ethics Commission', consisting of both IOC and non-IOC representatives. This Commission would have the role of ensuring the integrity of the IOC and maintaining the basic principles of 'fair play'. It would also have the role of establishing a code of ethics, enforcing that code and considering and proposing further reforms within the IOC. The IOC has also recently published its financial accounts for the first time in many years in an attempt to demonstrate greater transparency.[46]

The Ethics Commission produced a wide-ranging code of ethics in 1999.[47] Do such codes have a meaningful impact upon the dominant cultures in organisations such as the IOC? Are there

---

46 Boyes, S, 'International Olympic Committee corruption and bribery scandal' (1999) 2(2) SLB 14.
47 The current Olympic Code of Ethics can be found at www.olympic.org/Documents/Reports/EN/Code-Ethique-2009-WebEN.pdf.

effective mechanisms in place to make sports bodies such as the IOC properly accountable for their actions?[48] How about international sports federations?

Football's world governing body FIFA has been subject to allegations over a period of time concerning corrupt activities.[49] In 2010, allegations were made about FIFA members accepting monies in return for voting a particular way on the hosting of the 2018 and 2022 World Cups.[50] Additionally a BBC TV *Panorama* programme made allegations of financial mismanagement against individual FIFA members taking part in the voting process.[51] The IOC, FIFA and a large number of other ISFs are located in Switzerland and, in addition to enjoying a range of financial benefits which that country provides, under Swiss law not-for-profit bodies cannot be pursued through anti-corruption laws, which apply only to commercial organisations. In the wake of the World Cup bidding controversy, it appears such a policy of legal immunity is going to be reviewed.[52]

Match Fixing in Sport

There have been incidents of match fixing in sport over many years. One of the most notorious was the fixing of the 1919 baseball World Series. In English football, although this was certainly not the first instance, the scandal involving Peter Swan, David Layne and Tony Kay in 1964 led to prison sentences.[53] Fast forward to the 1990s and criminal prosecutions based on allegations of match fixing were brought against Premier League goalkeepers, Bruce Grobbelaar and Hans Segers and the footballer, John Fashanu.[54] At their first trial, the prosecution allegations were that Grobbelaar, whilst playing for Liverpool FC, and Segers for Wimbledon FC, let in goals to try to achieve certain results and thereby fix matches in Premier League games during the 1993–94 season.

In addition it was alleged that there was a conspiracy involving Fashanu acting as a middle-man in the payment of sums to the two goalkeepers for a Malaysian businessman, Heng Suan Lim. At their first trial, lasting 34 days, the jury could not reach a verdict.[55] At their second trial, with the prosecution only relying on the conspiracy to defraud charges, the four were acquitted. It has been estimated that the two trials cost more than £10 million.[56] Rather than relying on the vagaries of criminal prosecutions and trials, the football authorities have introduced investigative and improved disciplinary mechanisms concerning match-fixing allegations. For example, in 2008, five Accrington Stanley players received eight-month bans for placing bets on opponents Bury in a League Two match.[57]

Football has faced similar problems in other countries. A twenty-six-year-old German football referee, Robert Hoyzer was sentenced in 2005 to two years and five months in prison and banned

---

48 See 'Buying the Games', *Panorama*, BBC TV, 4 August 2004.

49 See Jennings, A, *Foul! The Secret World of FIFA: Bribes, Vote Rigging and Ticket Scandals* (2006), London: HarperSport.

50 'Fifa widens World Cup bidding inquiry', BBC News, 18 October 2010, http://news.bbc.co.uk/sport1/hi/football/9103645. stm.

51 'FIFA's Dirty Secrets', BBC *Panorama*, 29 November 2010, http://news.bbc.co.uk/panorama/hi/default.stm.

52 'Swiss authorities to look into Fifa cash for World Cup votes scandal', *The Guardian*, 25 November 2010, www.guardian.co.uk/football/2010/nov/25/swiss-investigate-fifa-world-cup.

53 See Tongue, S, 'Bribery and corruption: English football's biggest ever match fixing scandal', *Total Sport*, March 1997, p 52.

54 Also note conviction of the former president of Olympic de Marseille, Bernard Tapie, for match fixing, 'Tapie just a scapegoat for Paris', *The Guardian*, 16 May 1995, p 22.

55 See Gardiner *et al*, *Sports Law*, 2nd edn (2001), pp 359–62, for further analysis.

56 See *Grobbelaar v News Group Newspapers Ltd* [2002] 4 All ER 732 – in November 1994 *The Sun* newspaper published a series of very prominent articles charging Grobbelaar with corruption. He promptly issued writs claiming damages for libel. After some delay caused by the intervening criminal prosecution of the appellant and others, these libel proceedings came before Gray J and a jury. The jury found in favour of the appellant and awarded him compensatory damages of £85,000. On the newspaper's appeal against this decision the Court of Appeal (Simon Brown, Thorpe and Jonathan Parker LJJ) set it aside as perverse in November 1994. The House of Lords allowed an appeal against the Court of Appeal but awarded Grobbelaar nominal damages of only £1.

57 'FA rejects appeals from banned Accrington Stanley and Bury players', *The Guardian*, 1 October 2009, www.guardian.co.uk/football/2009/oct/01/fa-rejects-appeals-accrington-stanley.

for life by the German Football Association for his role in match fixing after having been found to have accepted payment from a Croatian syndicate to influence the outcomes of six matches. In 2006, the Italian football authorities punished a number of Serie A clubs for collusion and match fixing. Additionally, in 2009 UEFA announced that 40 Champions League and UEFA Cup fixtures were to be investigated. The fixtures involved predominantly eastern European teams in early qualifying rounds.[58]

This spectre of match fixing has been identified along with drug use in sport as a major threat to the integrity of sport and in need of rigorous scrutiny and control. But football is not the only game to have allegations raised as far as match fixing is concerned. The truth is that all sports are vulnerable to corruption. Horse and greyhound racing, two sports whose *raison d'être* is to provide a forum for gambling, periodically are particularly subject to such scandals.[59] There have been allegations in sports as diverse as boxing[60] and snooker.[61] The common theme is sports where gambling and betting are common. More recently, international cricket and tennis have also come under the spotlight of allegations concerning match fixing. This section will focus on cricket, horse racing and tennis.

The opportunities for gambling around sporting events in the UK have become generally easier and accessible, culturally more acceptable and certainly more sophisticated in the products that are available such as spread betting and online betting exchanges, which facilitate person-to-person betting with no traditional bookmaker taking a profit and also allowing the gambler to be the bookmaker and 'lay' bets. In this form of betting, not only the bet itself but also the size of the stake won or lost are determined by events during the sports event. For example, in a cricket match, a bookmaker may make a forecast on the number of runs scored in an over and gamblers bet on whether that prediction is too high or low. Their winnings or losses will correspond with the difference between the runs actually scored and the bookmaker's forecast. This form of gambling, also known as 'spot-fixing' or 'spot-betting', has increased, and is a type of gambling on markets that are effectively 'games within games'. Although there are different cultural and jurisdictional controls on gambling in countries around the world, these are increasingly difficult to enforce due to the technological nature of gambling, primarily via the internet.

It's just not cricket

There have been many concerns over a number of years that match fixing is prevalent in international professional cricket. Cricket is an ideal vehicle for all types of betting. You do not have to persuade all eleven players to throw a match to make illicit money from cricket. The rise of spread betting makes it much easier for corrupt players, gamblers or bookmakers to 'make a killing' on a match. In 'traditional' fixed-odds betting, a punter can usually put money only on which team will win the game, or who will be top batsman. But spread betting allows you to bet on much smaller events as discussed above. The admissions in 2000 by the ex-South African Captain Hansie Cronje, of his involvement in match forecasting and the charges of his involvement in match fixing have validated those concerns.

During the 1980s and 1990s there were sporadic rumours concerning irregularities in international matches, usually focused on one-day internationals. These matches have dramatically grown in frequency over the last 20 years. Many of these allegations, although not all, surround

---

58 'Uefa name clubs in match-fixing investigation', BBC News, 25 November 2009, http://news.bbc.co.uk/sport2/hi/football/europe/8379251.stm.
59 See 'Racing' and 'New arrests In Hong Kong race fixing scandal' (1998) 1(6) SLB; 'Sports corruption: floodlight failures and betting scandal' (1999) 3(1) SLB 3.
60 See 'ABA concerned about referee cash allegation', *The Daily Telegraph*, 3 December 1996.
61 See 'Scan: bunged out', *The Guardian*, 28 April 1995, p 4, concerning a match between Jimmy White and Peter Francisco, prompted by what were officiously described as 'irregular betting patterns'.

games involving Pakistan and India. Allegations often involve the payment of sums of money to players to provide information or to perform badly and impact upon the result. One-day matches provide many betting opportunities. In recent years they have all been televised and shown around the world on subscription channels. Tournaments in places such as Singapore and Sharjah have become regular events. Gambling is almost universally prohibited in countries such as Malaysia, India, Pakistan and Sri Lanka. There is, however, huge underground betting activity and cricket has become a very attractive product. It is estimated that up to many millions of pounds can be bet on just a single one-day international.[62]

In domestic English cricket allegations have also been made. Don Topley, the ex-Essex player, claimed that there had been collusion between Essex and Lancashire in two matches in 1991. In the Sunday League match a win for Lancashire helped their aspirations to win the League that year. A day later, in a County Championship match, Lancashire made a generous declaration that led to an Essex victory, which greatly assisted Essex in winning the County Championship that season by 13 points. Topley claimed that there had been collusion in advance to fix these results. The allegations were investigated, but no further action was taken.[63]

The English cricket team has also been involved in suspect matches. In 2000, the Fifth Test of the South African tour was affected by rain for the first four days. An agreement was made between the captains to forfeit each team's first innings at the start of the final day's play. England won the match by two wickets in a dramatic finale. This was the first time in 122 years of Test cricket that each side had forfeited its first innings. Subsequently it has arisen that the South African Captain, Hansie Cronje, was approached by a bookmaker with the suggestion of achieving a result in this way. In August 1999, the ex-England all-rounder Chris Lewis was allegedly approached by an Indian sports promoter to influence a number of teammates to perform poorly in the rest of the Test series in return for £300,000. Lewis has also made allegations that three well-known England international cricketers had been involved in match fixing. Again a subsequent investigation failed to provide any evidence to support further action.[64]

The story unfolds

There is a complex chronology of how the match fixing revelations have unfolded.[65] The following are the main events. From the mid-1990s onwards investigations had taken place in Pakistan, India and Australia concerning allegations of match fixing. A number of international players have reported being approached by bookmakers seeking information on issues such as pitch conditions, team selection and current form of players. During the Singer World Series of one-day internationals in Sri Lanka in September 1994, it has subsequently transpired that Australian players Mark Waugh and Shane Warne accepted money from an Indian bookmaker, known to them as 'John'. Information was provided on a match between Pakistan and Australia in Colombo. In the subsequent Test series in Pakistan in October 1994, Warne and Tim May subsequently claimed that the Pakistani Captain, Salim Malik, approached them offering money if they bowled badly. A subsequent inquiry reported that a Lahore bookmaker had paid a total of US $100,000 to Malik and leg spinner Mushtaq Ahmed to ensure that Australia won a further one-day international later in October 1994. In the match, the Pakistanis, batting second, collapsed dramatically when victory seemed to be easily within their grasp.

---

62 Anti-Corruption Unit, *Report on Corruption in International Cricket* (2001), London: ACU – a figure of US$150 million has been estimated but in games between certain teams, e.g. India and Pakistan, it is likely to be many times more.
63 Ibid.
64 Ibid.
65 For some background, see www.espncricinfo.com/infocus/content/story/infocus.html?subject=4.

Warne, Waugh and May waited a number of months before they reported what had happened in Sri Lanka and Pakistan. In February 1995, after an internal report by the Australian Cricket Board (ACB),[66] Waugh was fined a sum of Aus$10,000 and Warne, Aus$8,000, concerning their involvement. The International Cricket Council (ICC) agreed at the time to the ACB's request to keep the details of the players' actions and penalties confidential.

In March 1995, Malik was sacked as Pakistani captain and, although initially suspended from all first-class cricket, was reinstated pending a Pakistani Cricket Board (PCB) investigation. The inquiry headed by Justice Fakhruddin Ebrahim concluded, in October 1995, that Malik had no case to answer and stated that the allegations made by Waugh, Warne and May were concocted. In April 1997, the Pakistani international Aamer Sohail was banned from international cricket by a PCB disciplinary committee for allegations he had made against teammates concerning match fixing. It seems that in the world of cricket, whistleblowing has not been encouraged.

In recognition of the mounting allegations surrounding betting and match fixing, in July 1995 the ICC added a clause to its Code of Conduct that specifically outlaws players and administrators' direct or indirect involvement in betting, gambling or any form of unofficial speculation on the outcome of any cricket match.

In June 1997, the Indian magazine *Outlook* published revelations made by former Indian international Manoj Prabhakar concerning match fixing and Indian players. The Board of Control for Cricket in India (BCCI) asked the former Chief Justice of India, Mr YV Chandrachud, to conduct a wide-ranging inquiry. In November 1997 he concluded his investigation, and, although his views were not publicly released for a further two and a half years, he stated that although there is a great deal of cricket-related betting occurring in India, he failed to find that any Indian player or official has been involved in betting activities.[67]

In August 1998, a further PCB-appointed panel headed by Justice Ejaz Yousuf investigated match fixing and concluded that the conduct of Malik, Wasim Akram and Ijaz Ahmed had been suspicious. It recommended a further detailed investigation take place. A new government-initiated Commission of Inquiry headed by Lahore High Court Judge, Malik Mohammad Qayyum, was instituted and started its investigation. In October 1998, Mark Taylor, the Australian captain, and Mark Waugh gave evidence to the inquiry.

In December 1998, the ACB admitted it secretly fined Waugh and Warne in 1995. It stated that both players agreed that they 'were stupid and naive' but denied they gave information concerning team line-ups or tactics. The ACB convened an independent inquiry into any other possible involvement of players headed by former Chairman of the Queensland Criminal Justice Commission, Rob O'Regan. In February 1999, the O'Regan Inquiry pronounced no evidence of Australian players' involvement in the practice of match fixing and reported that players had always played to their optimum potential. The report was critical of the ACB's handling of the Waugh/Warne affair. In October 1999, the Qayyum Inquiry was concluded and the findings handed to the Pakistani Government.

The Hansie Cronje affair

In April 2000 the lid was blown off the whole issue of cricket match fixing. On 7 April, the Indian police claimed they had evidence that four South African cricket players, including the then captain, Hansie Cronje, had taken money for match fixing during their series against India in March 2000. In the course of a separate investigation, they had intercepted mobile phone calls between Cronje and an Indian bookmaker, Sanjay Chalwa. Criminal charges were laid down against Cronje,

---

66 ACB Executive Report (February 1995).
67 See Magazine, P, *Not Quite Cricket* (2000), London: Penguin.

Herschelle Gibbs, Pieter Strydom and Nicky Bojé. Cronje initially denied the allegations. However, on 11 April he admitted that he had not been 'entirely honest' in his earlier denials, and that he had taken nearly US$15,000 from bookmakers for 'providing information and forecasting'. The United Cricket Board of South Africa (UCBSA) together with the South African Government set up the King Commission to carry out an investigation.

The ICC in its May 2000 meeting at Lord's announced the introduction of new regulations and potential bans concerning players found guilty of being involved in match fixing. The bans ranged from five years to life for a range of actions including gambling or entering into any other form of financial speculation on any match or event and being a party to contriving or attempting to contrive the result of any match.

Justice Qayyum conducted the inquiry from September 1998 to October 1999 and about 70 players, officials and alleged bookies testified. In late May 2000 the Qayyum Report was finally published.[68] The commission's finding was that there was no planned betting and match fixing as a whole by the players of the Pakistan cricket team. However, doubts of varying intensity were cast on the integrity of some members of the team in their individual capacities. Judge Qayyum said the censured players should be kept under observation. Its main recommendations were a life ban on former captain Salim Malik and a fine of US$6,000 for former captain Wasim Akram. Akram was given the benefit of the doubt. The report states: 'He cannot be said to be above suspicion. It is, therefore, recommended that he be censured and be kept under strict vigilance.' On Malik, Judge Qayyum said:

> In the light of evidence to support allegations made by Shane Warne and Mark Waugh, the commission recommends that a life ban be imposed on Salim Malik and he be not allowed to play cricket at any level . . . He should not be allowed to even associate himself with any cricketing affairs as he may be able to influence the new generation.

In addition to the ICC Code of Conduct Commission, in late June 2000, former Commissioner of the Metropolitan Police, Sir Paul Condon (now Lord Condon), became the head of the International Cricket Council's new anti-corruption unit, with a brief to investigate match-fixing allegations worldwide. It published an Interim Report in May 2001.[69]

The King Commission

In the wake of the allegations against the South African players and Cronje's admissions, the King Commission of Inquiry into match fixing and related matters completed its first session of hearings in Cape Town on 26 June 2000. An interim report was submitted in August 2000 to the South African Sports Minister Ngconde Balfour and South African President Thabo Mbeki. In December 2000 a second interim report was submitted and a final report was published in July 2001.

The first three weeks of the hearings were notable for Cronje's admissions that he had been talking to bookmakers or people involved in match fixing since 1995. Cronje said that he had repeatedly lied to cover his tracks, and then went on to detail a five-year flirtation with bookmakers that yielded tens of thousands of dollars. He admitted to inducing Herschelle Gibbs and Henry Williams to help him throw a match and to approaching several other players. He denied, however, that he had ever thrown a match. Cronje said in his testimony that he had decided to sever all his ties with the game, pre-empting what was certain to have been a life ban imposed on him by the authorities. The cases of Gibbs and Williams are more problematic, as both claimed in mitigation that they failed to follow through on their arrangements with Cronje.

---

68 The report can be found at http://static.espncricinfo.com/db/NATIONAL/PAK/NEWS/qayyumreport/qayyum_report.html.
69 See below, p 278.

Another important witness was the UCBSA managing director Ali Bacher, who implicated Pakistan, Bangladesh and India in World Cup matches that were fixed in 1999 and who also accused Pakistan umpire Javed Akhtar of being on the payroll of a bookmaker. How much the UCBSA knew of match fixing prior to April 2000 remains a moot point, with particular reference to the 1996 team meeting in Bombay at which an offer to throw a game was debated in some detail. Although Bacher admitted that Cronje briefly referred to the offer, he denied having believed it to be serious and also denied reading a newspaper report about the offer in 1998.

Disciplinary hearings were held for all four players. Cronje received a life ban for all playing and related activities in September 2000. He failed to pre-empt a life ban being imposed on him by the authorities in his challenge of the ban in the South African High Court.

Le Roux, R, 'The Cronje Affair'

His legal team argued that his life ban was unconstitutional since he was not given an opportunity to state his case and that the ban constituted an unreasonable restraint of trade. They argued that the constitutional right to fair administrative action also applied to private bodies . . . [At] the time of the UCBSA's imposing of the life ban, its contract with Cronje had already been terminated. The court did not accept that the ban was in effect disciplinary and punitive, but held that the UCBSA was merely relying upon its constitutional rights of non-association. The court also held that banning Cronje from activities of the UCSBA was not an unreasonable restraint of trade. He may, for instance coach, sponsor or promote cricket in schools not affiliated to the UCBSA. Prior to the decision it was generally expected that the court would extend the constitutional right to fair administrative action (such as the right to be heard), applicable to public bodies, to private bodies such as the UCBSA. The court unequivocally stated that the UCBSA is a private body and in the absence of a binding contractual term, it was under no legal obligation to give Cronje an opportunity to be heard before the resolution to ban him for life was passed. The public and private law divide therefore continues to exist in respect of South African sports bodies.[70]

Gibbs, Williams and Strydom all received a six-month ban from international cricket.[71] After the failure of his legal action, Cronje indicated he would disclose 'the truth' in a future book. He was initially granted immunity from criminal prosecution in South Africa on condition he told the whole truth about his involvement in the affair. In June 2001 that was withdrawn.[72] Cronje died in a plane crash in June 2002.[73] Conspiracy theories were rife that his death was linked to the match-fixing scandal. In a report by South Africa's Civil Aviation Authority, it was subsequently held that human error and bad weather were the cause of the crash.[74]

The Indian CBI Report

In July 2000, in the wake of the Indian police investigation, a series of nationwide tax raids on the homes and offices of top Indian cricketers, officials and bookmakers uncovered alleged direct evidence of match fixing. In November 2000, the Indian Central Bureau of Investigation presented

---

70 Le Roux, R, 'The Cronje Affair' (2002) 2 The International Sports Law Journal 11.
71 Gibbs refused to tour India with the South African team in 2004 as the Indian police authorities indicated they would want to carry on investigations regarding match-fixing allegations if he was in the country; see 'Gibbs set to skip India long-term', BBC Sport, 22 November 2004, http://news.bbc.co.uk/sport1/hi/cricket/other_international/south_africa/4032433.stm.
72 'Cronje immunity deal off', BBC Sport, 21 June 2001, http://news.bbc.co.uk/sport1/hi/in_depth/2000/corruption_in_cricket/1412993.stm; also see Gouws, D, '. . . And Nothing But the Truth?' (2000), Cape Town: Zebra.
73 'Thousands mourn Cronje', BBC Sport, 5 June 2002, http://news.bbc.co.uk/sport1/hi/cricket/2024311.stm.
74 For further discussion of the Cronjé affair, see Alfred, L, Lifting the Covers: the Inside Story of South African Cricket (2001), Claremont: Sperahead; Oosthuizen, A and Tinkler, G, The Banjo Players: Cricket's Match Fixing Scandal (2001), Hout Bay: Riverside.

a report concerning match-fixing allegations in Indian cricket.[75] It named a number of Indian cricketers, most notably Mohammad Azharuddin, and also a number of former international team captains including Alec Stewart, Brian Lara and Martin Crowe. This was based on allegations made by another Indian bookmaker, Mukesh Kumar Gupta. There have been attempts to get him to repeat the allegations under oath, but he refused to do this by a given deadline. Azharuddin was given a life ban by the BCCI in December 2001.

A number of investigations have taken place in Test-playing countries in the light of these allegations:

Australia

The CBI Report named Mark Waugh and Dean Jones. The Australian Cricket Board appointed Greg Melick, a barrister, to investigate. Melick submitted an interim report to the Australian Cricket Board in early August 2001. Melick said that, based on his findings, Waugh had 'no case to answer' in relation to the allegations.[76]

England

The ECB asked the ACU to investigate the allegations relating to Alec Stewart. An interview took place in June 2001 and he was cleared in an announcement by Gerard Elias QC, the chairman of the ECB's Discipline Standing Committee.

New Zealand

The New Zealand Cricket Board appointed a Commission of Inquiry headed by Sir Ian Barker, a former High Court judge, to examine allegations against Martin Crowe. Crowe was exonerated of charges in late July 2001.[77]

Sri Lanka

The Board of Control for Cricket in Sri Lanka appointed Desmond Fernando, President's Counsel, as their Special Investigator. Arjuna Ranatunga and Aravinda de Silva, who were named in the CBI Report, were cleared of involvement in mid-July 2001.

Pakistan

The Pakistan Cricket Board had already taken robust action against a number of players, as a result of the Commission of Inquiry by Mr Justice Qayyum, and felt that no residual action arose from the CBI Report for them. Salim Malik was given a life ban.

The West Indies

Brian Lara was implicated in the CBI Report and Elliott Mottley QC was appointed by the West Indian Cricket Board to investigate the allegations. He was cleared of the allegations in November 2002.[78]

Cricket Match Fixing: The Anti-Corruption Report

In April 2001 the ACU produced its Report on Corruption in International Cricket. The Report is far-ranging and represents a consolidation of the other worldwide investigations. The Report's author Lord Condon stated:

---

75 The report can be found at http://static.espncricinfo.com/db/NATIONAL/IND/NEWS/CBI-REPORT.html.
76 The report can be found at http://im.rediff.com/cricket/2001/aug/07mark1.htm.
77 A summary of the report can be found at http://www.espncricinfo.com/newzealand/content/story/102143.html.
78 'West Indies Board clears Lara of match-fixing charge', *One India Cricket*, 12 November 2002, http://cricket.oneindia.in/news/2002/11/12/lara_matchfixing.html.

Anti-Corruption Unit, *Report on Corruption in International Cricket*

4. This report will make disturbing reading for all those who love and follow the game of cricket. It describes at least twenty years of corruption linked to betting on international cricket matches. Corrupt practices and deliberate under-performance have permeated all aspects of the game.

5. I am confident that recent measures, including the creation and work of the ACU, have stopped much of this corrupt activity. I also believe, however, that corruption continues to happen and the potential for a resurgence of corruption in cricket remains a real threat.

6. International cricket is at a critical point of development. If the ICC continues as a loose and fragile alliance it is unlikely to succeed as a governing body. It must become a modern, regulatory body with the power to lead and direct international cricket. All the constituent cricket boards, in the member countries, must show equal determination to deal with the ongoing challenge of corruption.[79]

Section 1 concerns the role and work of the Anti-Corruption Unit. It details the relationship between cricket match fixing and organised crime.

11. Within days of taking up this new appointment, it became clear to me that many people within cricket had significant information about corruption within the game. However, the prevailing culture was not helpful. As a result of the interviews carried out by my unit I realised the allegations in the public domain were only the tip of the iceberg. Many people had not reported attempts to corrupt them or suspicions about other people they believed to be corrupt.

. . .

15. The most disturbing aspect of the tolerance of corruption is the fear that some people have expressed to me about their own personal safety or the safety of their families. I have spoken to people who have been threatened and others who have alleged a murder and a kidnapping linked to cricket corruption. In order to respond to these anxieties I have interviewed some people away from their normal lifestyles.[80]

It reported on the findings from the self-declaration forms sent to international players (including former players still playing first-class cricket), team officials, umpires, referees, curators (groundsmen) and certain senior employees and administrators of national boards. This policy had been initiated at the ICC meeting in May 2000.

ICC, 'Players' Declaration Form'

This is a copy of the Players' Declaration form issued to all international cricketers by the ICC. Similar forms have been issued to all cricket administrators, team officials, coaching staff and groundsmen/curators. Completed Declarations are lodged with the ICC Anti-Corruption Unit for recording and analysis.

CONFIDENTIAL – PLAYERS TO BE WRITTEN ON THE HEADED NOTEPAPER OF THE BOARD OF EACH MEMBER COUNTRY

Form of Declaration

---

79 Op. cit., fn 62, Anti-Corruption Unit (2001), paras 4–6.
80 Ibid, paras 11 and 15.

This form applies to every international player, to whom the ICC Code of Conduct applies, involved in the playing of the game of cricket and is to be treated as a supplement to any contract with your Board.

This form requires you to declare in the interest of protecting the good name of cricket, whether you have been approached to be involved in cricket corruption in any form.

1. Have you taken part in, or been approached to take part in, any arrangement with any other person involved in the playing or administration of the game of cricket which might involve corruption in any form? YES/NO

2. Have you for personal reward or for some other person's benefit agreed, or been approached, in advance of or during a match to act in deliberate breach of the Laws of Cricket, the ICC Standard Playing Conditions, the ICC Code of Conduct or contrary to the spirit of the game of cricket? YES/NO

3. Have you for personal reward or for some other person's benefit agreed, or been approached, to give information concerning the weather, the ground, team selection, the toss or the outcome of any match or any event in the course of a match other than to a newspaper or broadcaster and disclosed in advance to your Board? YES/NO

4. Have you ever for personal reward or for some other person's benefit, deliberately played, or agreed to play or been approached to play, below your normal standard, or encouraged any other person to play below his normal standard, in order to contrive an event during the course of a match? YES/NO

5. Have you for personal reward or for some other person's benefit been involved, or approached, in any attempt to pervert the normal outcome of a match? YES/NO

Where an answer of yes is given full details should be provided to Head of the Anti-Corruption Unit of ICC.

I hereby declare that I will not be involved in the future in any of the conduct described above and I will immediately inform the Chief Executive of my Board either directly or through the Team Manager and/or the Head of the Anti-Corruption Unit of ICC if I receive any approach to be involved in any such conduct.

NOTE – IF YOU KNOWINGLY ANSWER ANY OF THESE QUESTIONS INCORRECTLY OR IF YOU FAIL TO TELL THE HEAD OF THE ANTI-CORRUPTION UNIT OF ICC OF ANY CHANGE TO YOUR ANSWERS, YOU WILL BE LIABLE TO BE DISCIPLINED BY YOUR BOARD AND HEAVY PENALTIES MAY APPLY. I HEREBY DECLARE THAT THE ANSWERS I HAVE GIVEN TO THE ABOVE QUESTIONS ARE TRUE AND NOT MISLEADING . . .

The ACU Report presented the following data from the forms:

55. Some 911 completed declarations have been received by the Anti-Corruption Unit and of these 21 indicated a yes or positive answer about involvement or knowledge of corruption. The unit as a result of previous contact, reports and investigations, already knew 10 of these positive responses. The remaining 11 positive responses were scrutinized and 6 do not require follow-up action. The remaining 5 positive responses are being investigated.[81]

However, the ACU have argued that this approach was methodologically flawed. There were concerns voiced by players over confidentiality of the forms after they had been completed. In

---

81 Ibid, para 55.

addition, this approach of self-incrimination is likely to have low levels of success in identifying perpetrators. What is the advantage of admitting wrongdoing, especially in the context of the bans being implemented? The ACU advised that this approach should not be repeated.

Section 2 of the ACU Report concerns the 'analysis of corruption in cricket'.

The Seeds of Corruption

64. It has been suggested to me that the seeds of corruption in cricket were sown in the 1970s when county and club games in domestic tournaments, in England and other countries were allegedly fixed by teams to secure points and league positions. Players were not bribed with money but relied on mutual interest. If a match was of vital importance to one team and not to the other then an accommodation would be reached between the teams as to who would win. Similar arrangements would be made to secure bowling and batting points, if applicable. The movement of players around the world gave players from a number of countries experience of these 'friendly' fixed matches. As a result, in a number of matches the ethic of winning or losing on merit was replaced by a pragmatic arrangement to divide the points and/or agree in advance who would win.

. . .

74. My unit has received allegations from a number of different sources of the following being pre-arranged or fixed in order to allow a betting coup to take place.

- The outcome of the toss at the beginning of a match.
- The end from which the fielding captain will elect to bowl.
- A set number of wides, or no balls occurring in a designated over.
- Players being placed in unfamiliar fielding positions.
- Individual batsmen scoring fewer runs than their opposite numbers who batted first.
- Batsmen being out at a specific point in their innings.
- The total runs at which a batting captain will declare.
- The timing of a declaration.
- The total runs scored in a particular innings and particularly the total in the first innings of a One Day International.

Why Has Corruption Developed in Cricket?

79. I have taken every opportunity to allow people involved in cricket to explain to me why they think corruption established such a strong foothold. Whilst the explanations and excuses have varied in emphasis they embrace some or all of the following:

- International cricketers are paid less than top soccer players, golfers, tennis players or formula one drivers and are therefore more vulnerable to corrupt approaches.
- During the last World Cup and other major events the cricketers received a low single-figure percentage of the proceeds from the event and resent the distribution of profits elsewhere.
- Cricketers have little say or stake in the running of the sport and limited recognition of their representative bodies, where they exist.
- Cricketers have relatively short and uncertain playing careers, often without contracts and some seek to supplement their official earnings with money from corrupt practices.
- Some administrators either turn a blind eye or are themselves involved in malpractice.
- Cricketers play a high number of One Day Internationals and nothing is really at stake in terms of national pride or selection in some of these matches.
- Cricketers can take money from potential corruptors in return for innocuous information and yet refuse to fix matches.

- Whistle blowing and informing on malpractice was ignored or penalised rather than encouraged.
- There was no structure in place to receive allegations about corruption.
- Cricketers were coerced into malpractice because of threats to them and their families.
- It was just too easy . . .

90. The spectre of a more sinister regime of fear and coercion has been raised to explain some aspects of cricket corruption. The Central Bureau of Investigation (CBI) in India has an investigation underway into the links between organised crime and cricket. My unit has met people who have made allegations about threats to their life as a result of exposing cricket corruption and I have met a number of people who were, in my opinion, genuinely frightened of the consequences if it became known they were cooperating with the Anti-Corruption Unit.

. . .

98. I believe the blatant cases and excesses of cricket corruption have been stopped. I know from the work of the ACU that most of the preliminary approaches to players, umpires, groundsmen and others, to sound out their willingness to be drawn into corruption, have stopped. What is left is a small core of players and others who continue to manipulate the results of matches or occurrences within matches for betting purposes. They may be doing so out of greed, arrogance or because they are not being allowed to cease. Some may fear their previous corruption will be exposed if they try to stop and some may fear threats of violence if they stop. It will take some time before those who have developed a corrupt lifestyle within cricket have sufficient fear of exposure and punishment to stop.[82]

The final section 3 of the ACU Report is comprised of 'Recommendations to the ICC'. There is an emphasis on the education of players. A number of practical steps are suggested such as controlling the use of mobile phones by players during matches and limiting access to players. A clear indication in the report concerns the need for significantly improved governance. The ICC must be more open, transparent and accountable:

> . . . the ICC has tried to address 'conflict of interest' issues for those who serve on the Executive Board of the ICC. The matter has not been resolved satisfactorily and needs to be revisited.[83]

There has been controversy over the role that the ex-president of the ICC, Jagmohan Dalmiya, has had in the award of TV rights. This is another clear example of the conflict that sports governing bodies have in governance over commercial issues and sporting rules.[84] The former needs to clearly comply with external regulatory norms. The latter need to be competently regulated by the ICC. The report suggests that players and ex-players should have a 'more productive relationship with the ICC'.[85] The ICC Code of Conduct Commission has responded to the ACU Report.

ICC Code of Conduct Commission, 'Report of Official Inquiry'

A panel of the Code of Conduct Commission of the International Cricket Council (ICC) has been invited by the President of ICC to review the report of the Anti-Corruption Unit (ACU) of the ICC presented by Sir Paul Condon QPM, Director of the ACU, and report thereon to the Executive Board of ICC.

---

82 Ibid, paras 64, 74, 79, 90 and 98.
83 Ibid, para 135.
84 See earlier, p 242.
85 Op. cit., fn 62, Anti-Corruption Unit Report (2001), para 120.

The Panel members are Lord Griffiths, Chairman, Mr Richie Benaud, Sir Oliver Popplewell, Chief Justice Nasim Shah and Sir Denys Williams.

Before meeting to discuss the report we had each read the report. We met for a full day to discuss the report on Tuesday 15th May and continued our discussions on Wednesday 16th May. During the first day we met with Sir Paul Condon and had the opportunity to question him on various aspects of the report and on the investigations of the ACU both past and ongoing. We are very grateful to Sir Paul for the assistance we received from him. Obviously we can not reveal in this report all the information he gave us as much of it was of a confidential nature which if revealed would prejudice ongoing investigations by the ACU and by the other National Boards that have instituted enquiries into alleged corruption or are about to institute such enquiries.

This is an excellent but most disturbing report. It traces the insidious growth of the corruption of international cricketers by the illegal betting industry in the 1980s and 1990s after televised cricket had stimulated an enormous increase in illegal gambling on cricket matches. At first the authorities took little action and when it came to the attention of ICC they mistakenly decided it better to hush the matter up rather than bring it into the public domain; at that time they thought they were dealing with isolated incidents rather than a growing cancer. But now the public realises the grave extent of the problem and the damage that has been done to the game. Vigorous action has been taken by some of the National Boards to bring retribution to those who have been guilty of corrupt practices in the past. The Pakistan Cricket Board has banned Salim Malik and Ata-ur-Rehman for life, stripped Wasim Akram of the captaincy and also imposed fines on other players. The Board of Control for Cricket in India has banned the Indian cricket captain Mohammad Azharuddin and Ajay Sharma for life and has imposed 5 year bans on Manoj Prabhakar, Ajay Jadeja and on the team physiotherapist Dr Ali Irani. The United Cricket Board of South Africa has imposed a life ban on Hansie Cronje and six months' bans and fines on Gibbs and Williams.

Inquiries are proceeding by the National Boards in Sri Lanka, Australia, New Zealand and the West Indies and we understand a further inquiry will also be undertaken by Pakistan. These may result in the exposure and punishment of other players, umpires or administrators for past corrupt behaviour. But it can at least be said that three of the principal villains have been removed from the game.

However, what we find particularly worrying is that, despite the public disgrace of the banned players, Sir Paul believes that certain persons are still continuing this corrupt association with illegal gambling in cricket. When these persons read Sir Paul's report and realise the effort and resources that are now being devoted to exposing them and others tempted to follow their example and the retribution that will follow exposure, we hope they will think hard before continuing their corrupt activities; particularly now that so much money is coming into international cricket from television that it should be possible for international cricketers to be much more highly rewarded.

The report convinces us that however much we may regret the past and in some cases the difficulties of proving past corruptions, it is upon the present and the future we must concentrate and that every practical measure must be taken to break the links between cricketers and unlawful gambling and return to a game where every player gives of his best.

The report contains 24 recommendations. We recommend that ICC should adopt them all, although we realise that some may be easier to implement than others. We will comment briefly on some of the recommendations.

Education and Awareness

There are five recommendations under this head and we endorse them all.

Recommendation 4 refers to encouraging the reporting of improper approaches. Nobody likes the idea of having to tell tales about his colleagues but stern measures are necessary to stamp out corruption and we repeat the advice we have already given in an earlier report that there should be an obligation on a player to report any corrupt approach to another player of which he becomes aware. We cannot find any such obligation in November 2000 Code of Conduct. If it is meant to be achieved by incorporating Appendix A of the ICC Code of Conduct Commission Terms of Reference into paragraph C of the Code of Conduct paragraphs 9 and 10 we doubt if this achieved the object and it is in any event a very clumsy way to set out an important if unpalatable obligation. We suggest a redraft of the Code of Conduct without resorting to the Terms of Reference of the Code of Conduct Commission.

In addition to this recommendation we suggest that match referees should be instructed to report to ICC any suspicious or unusual characteristics in the conduct of the game as for example very slow batting when a run race was obviously required to win the match, reckless batting when wickets were at a premium, bowling excessive numbers of wides and no balls, or a very large number of lbw decisions against one side; this is not an exhaustive list but illustrative of matters that may give rise to suspicion.

Security and Control

There are four recommendations under this head. These recommendations are aimed at preventing contact between players and bookmakers or gamblers. They are of the utmost importance in breaking the links between cricketers and unlawful gamblers.

For the future, an essential ingredient of the ICC's structure should be that the Security Unit be provided with funds, offices and whatever else might be necessary to prevent and detect corruption.

The ICC must accept that a proper percentage of the money, which they have, coming in from television rights and all other sources, has to be put into the prevention of corruption and match fixing.

Every national authority should take immediate steps to ensure the security of their players' dressing rooms at home or on tour. It is difficult to envisage hotel security ever being totally adequate and, in any case, players need space for relaxation and quiet. Draconian measures such as totally banning mobile phones may be difficult to enforce. However, there should be written into the players' contracts in every country, that players will be prepared to make available to the ICC's Security Unit, printouts of any mobile phones of which they have use.

These security measures will require the players to surrender some degree of privacy and freedom of action, and in our view they must be looked at together with recommendation number 10. The security measures require the full co-operation of the players themselves and we emphatically support recommendation number 10 which urges ICC to bring the players themselves through their representative body into greater involvement in the administration of the game so that they can share the responsibility for the health of the game and take a real part in the solution of its problems.

Prevention and Investigation of Corruption

For the immediately foreseeable future the ACU in its present form must continue to operate as envisaged in recommendations 16 and 17. Once security managers have been appointed by ICC and the National Boards, further thought will have to be given to the structure of the ACU and the scope of its operations as foreshadowed in recommendation 19.

The Future of ICC

It has become apparent that the present structure of ICC is inadequate to run international cricket and to manage the vast sums of money it now receives from television rights and other sources. It is essential that the ICC, within the next 12 months, be geared to provide the best possible infrastructure for control, finance and, in the case of matches under its control, corruption. There is no point in lamenting that this has not been the case in past years; it is a matter of getting it right now and for the future. To this end the recommendations in this report for the future of ICC must be tackled as a matter of urgency.

It is time for all countries, which after all make up the ICC, to ensure that cricket as a game again becomes paramount, and that in the fight against corruption and match fixing, national pride and embarrassment come a poor second.[86]

What are the legal implications?

Bans that the ICC has put into place are likely to be enforceable. All professional players' contracts will usually include an express term that a player should play to the best of his ability and not bring the game into disrepute. If not, a court will readily imply such a term.[87] An employer can also sue a player for any damages that might flow from any such breach. However, the length of ban may be susceptible to legal challenge. There are restraint of trade issues. Playing bans as a consequence of positive drugs tests have been successfully challenged in some national courts. Consequently, in 1997, the International Association of Athletics Federations (IAAF) reduced mandatory bans from four years to two. A second positive doping offence is, however, met with a life ban. Is there a distinction between the enforceability of bans between those who are found guilty of doping on the one hand and match fixing on the other? Should a ban cover all activities in cricket or just playing?

There are some privacy issues for players. Do the suggestions in the ACU Report concerning restriction of movement and the use of mobile phones infringe privacy rights? In the second King Commission Interim Report published in December 2000, wider powers were suggested including random lie detector tests for players, room and luggage searches and the right of the UCBSA to monitor all players' phone calls and email messages. Additionally it was proposed that only mobile phones issued to players by the UCBSA should be allowed and possession of an unauthorised mobile telephone should be a punishable offence.[88] Are such powers for an employer and/or governing body legitimate?

In addition to any civil law measures, a player could be subject to criminal liability. Cronje was charged in India with criminal conspiracy, fraud and cheating. Proof can be a problem, however. The prosecutions of Grobbelaar and Segers failed when expert evidence from top ex-goalkeepers such as World Cup 1966 England keeper, Gordon Banks, supported the view that there was no evidence that the goalkeepers threw the game. In addition, there will always be problems over admissibility of evidence; for example, bookmaker Gupta's allegations, which have been the basis of the CBI Report claims, have not been repeated on oath and therefore could not be used in a court of law.

There may be arguments for imposing formal liability on governing bodies. It is not only the ICC that needs to take much more responsibility. The national cricket boards around the world need to review their procedures and be more responsible for the actions of players within their supervision. The move to all Test-playing countries centrally contracting with their players seems a positive move to develop an appropriate relationship of accountability on the players' part and responsibility on the part of the governing body.

The ACU (now known as the Anti-Corruption and Security Unit – ACSU) and ICC have put into place an extensive regulatory framework and continue to be vigilant.[89] At the time of the 2003

86 ICC Code of Conduct Commission, 'Report of Official Inquiry', see http://icc-cricket.yahoo.net/anti_corruption/condon-report.php.
87 See later, Chapter 9.
88 King Commission. See www.info.gov.za/view/DownloadFileAction?id=70293.
89 See interview with then Head of Security at ACSU in Gardiner, S and Naidoo, U, 'Against Corruption in Cricket' (2007) 15(3) SATLJ, 21–30.

World Cup in South Africa, Lord Condon indicated he believed that match fixing had been eradicated. Such claims appear to have been premature. Sporadic allegations by players continue to be made not so much on fixing of matches but of players facilitating events in matches that have significant amounts of money laid on them, for example the score after 15 overs of an innings. In summer 2004, the Ebrahim Report was published, which recommends a five-year ban for former Kenyan captain Maurice Odumbe after a hearing on charges that he had received money, benefits or other rewards that could bring him or the game of cricket into disrepute.[90] After passing on team information to a bookmaker during a one-day series in India in January 2007, West Indies batsman Marlon Samuels was given a two-year ban imposed by the ICC.

More recently, the Metropolitan Police investigated three Pakistani players over alleged behaviour during the fourth Test with England in August 2010. This followed a *News of the World* newspaper investigation where it was claimed that, in exchange for £150,000, a middleman gave the paper details of the three no-balls which players later bowled at the predicted times. The allegation was that three Pakistani players, Mohammad Amir, Salman Butt and Mohammad Asif, were secretly paid to deliberately bowl them in order to allow gambling syndicates to make money from betting on them. The players were also charged under Article 2 of the ICC Anti-Corruption Code for Players and Player Support Personnel.[91] After disciplinary hearings in February 2011, Butt received a 10-year ban, five suspended, Asif seven years – two suspended – and Amir five years.[92] There is a right of appeal to CAS. Additionally, the three players have been charged with conspiracy to obtain and accept corrupt payments and also conspiracy to cheat.[93]

There have been incidents in English domestic cricket too. It was reported that Essex player Mervyn Westfield had been charged with conspiracy to defraud connected to allegations concerning a one-day 40-over match between Durham and Essex in September 2009, by allowing the scoring of a certain number of runs off his bowling.[94]

Horse racing – the sport of kings

Horse racing has never been a stranger to allegations of financial corruption. The growth of racing in numerous countries is inextricably linked to the regulatory regimes of gambling which have allowed on-course and off-course gambling. This has been shown to be a worldwide phenomenon, with periodic reports and investigations concerning allegations of corruption.

Such a scandal has enveloped racing n the UK over the last few years. In November 2002, the former national hunt jockey, Graham Bradley was banned for eight years (reduced on appeal to five years) for corruption offences, following quickly on the heels of the screening in October 2002 of a BBC *Panorama* programme on horse racing, which claimed that the sport was 'institutionally corrupt'.[95] Allegations were made that links existed between criminal gangs and leading jockeys and trainers and that betting was used as a way of laundering drug-related money.

The programme revolved round Roger Buffham, the Jockey Club's former head of security, who acting as a 'whistleblower' made allegations against various individuals; jockeys, trainers and outside criminals. He also alleged a lack of action on the part of the Jockey Club to address the issues he had raised. The Jockey Club is the guardian of racing's rules, and it was formed by a band

---

90 'Maurice Odumbe banned for five years', www.espncricinfo.com/ci/content/story/135253.html.
91 Current details can be found at http://static.icc-cricket.yahoo.net/ugc/documents/DOC_C26C9D9E63C44CBA392505B49890B5AF_1285831667097_391.pdf.
92 'ICC bans Salman Butt, Mohammad Asif & Mohammad Amir', BBC Sport, 5 February, 2011, http://news.bbc.co.uk/sport1/hi/cricket/other_international/pakistan/9388422.stm.
93 See later p 000 for further analysis on the offence of cheating under the Gambling Act 2005.
94 'Mervyn Westfield appears at Old Bailey on cricket fixing charge', *The Guardian*, 28 October 2010, www.guardian.co.uk/sport/2010/oct/28/mervyn-westfield-betting-allegation.
95 See 'The Corruption of Racing', *Panorama*, BBC TV, 6 October 2002.

of enthusiasts in the Star and Garter pub in Pall Mall in 1751. Initially its 'Rules of Racing' applied only to Newmarket but they soon gained wide acceptance. Within a few years it was the sole authority in British racing, and retained its regulatory powers after the formation of the British Horseracing Board in June 1993.

Before the *Panorama* programme aired, the Jockey Club had sought an injunction in the High Court to ban Buffham from providing the BBC with what was alleged to be 'confidential incriminating information'.[96] Refusing to award the injunction, Mr Justice Gray ruled that it was in the public interest for this information to be disclosed, even though Buffham had signed a confidentiality agreement on leaving his employment, and had been given a 'golden handshake' of £50,000. The judge held that the 'public interest' in disclosing this information outweighed the Jockey Club's right of privacy because it revealed '. . . the existence, or apparent existence, of wide-scale corruption in racing'. And this was of 'legitimate concern to a large section of the public who either participate in racing or follow it, or who bet on the results of races'. The view of the court was that the right to privacy protected by Article 8 of the European Convention on Human Rights is not an absolute one. It is subject to the needs of a democratic society to know certain things in the interests of, among others, morals, the prevention of crime and the protection of the rights and freedoms of others.[97]

The Jockey Club itself is no stranger to controversy or the courts. It has long been active in defending its right to regulate the affairs of the racing world without any outside interference. This is also of course true of many other sports governing bodies that jealously guard their right to self-regulation.

In July 2003, a Security Review Group, jointly carried out with the British Horseracing Board, focused on the identification of the nature of the threats to the integrity of horse racing in Great Britain, assessing the breadth and depth of such threats and considering how best the Security Department of the Jockey Club should be structured and organised to deal with the threats to racing's integrity. A number of recommendations ensued.[98]

In addition to a major overhaul of its security operation, one proposal that was seen as controversial by jockeys was a ban on the use of mobile phones on a racecourse during racing from about half an hour before the first race. A number of jockeys raised the argument that such a move could be a denial of rights of privacy and a possible restraint of trade.[99] In addition, trainers are not able to bet on any horse on betting exchanges. The Jockey Club has also assumed responsibility for weighing-room security, and has installed improved closed-circuit TV systems in the stables at Britain's 59 racecourses.

Bradley appealed to the High Court in 2004 against the disqualification from racing. He challenged the imposition of the penalty, contending that it was disproportionate and unlawful. It was further argued that a proportionate penalty would have been measured in weeks or months rather than years. In reviewing the role of the Appeals Board decision in reducing the initial eight-year disqualification to one of five years, there were no findings that Bradley did not receive a fair hearing, suffered procedural unfairness or that the decision was perverse. The main contention was that the penalty imposed was disproportionate.

Bradley v The Jockey Club

Per Richards J: In my judgment the Board was fully entitled to conclude, as the final result of its balancing exercise, that a period of five years' disqualification was a proportionate penalty.

---

96 *The Jockey Club v Buffham & BBC* [2002] EWHC 1866.
97 For more on the case, see earlier Chapter 3, p 137.
98 Also see 2008 report, The British Horseracing Authority and Integrity in Horseracing: An Independent Review, www.britishhorseracing.com/images/inside_horseracing/media/Neville_Review_Exec_Summ_Recomm_May_08.pdf.
99 'Phone row could end in court', BBC Sport, 14 September 2003, http://news.bbc.co.uk/sport1/hi/other_sports/horse_racing/3104616.stm.

Such a conclusion was within the limits of the discretionary area of judgment open to the Board in the application of the test of proportionality; it was within the range of reasonable responses to the question of where a fair balance lies between the conflicting interests. In my judgment there is no basis for the court, in the exercise of its supervisory jurisdiction, to hold that the Board acted unlawfully in imposing that penalty.[100]

This decision provides the Jockey Club with significant means to penalise those found to have been involved in corrupt practices. However, again it will depend on how effectively the problem is policed and investigated in the first place.[101]

A separate and long-term police investigation into the extent of involvement of jockeys, trainers and others connected to the racing industry has led to prosecutions against a number of jockeys including the champion jockey Kieren Fallon.[102] Fallon was charged with conspiracy to defraud account holders of a betting company and people who had placed bets with bookmakers by dishonestly agreeing not to permit horses he rode to run on their merits, in that riding practices would be used that would interfere with the horses' running and affect the result of the races, and laying those horses to lose on exchanges provided by the betting company. Fallon was suspended from horse racing by the British Horseracing Board pending the completion of the criminal case and failed in an attempt to seek a declaration that such a suspension was unlawful.[103] At his trial he was acquitted along with other two jockeys. The case identified again the problem of securing convictions in such circumstances and the vagaries of expert evidence. The prosecution's main expert witness at the trial was Australian racing steward Ray Murrihy, who found fault with the jockeys in 13 of the 27 races, but also admitted he knew little about the rules and culture of British racing. The judge, Mr Justice Forbes, was reported as commenting, 'It is abundantly clear that his evidence fell far, far short of establishing a prima facie breach of UK racing rules . . . I have reached the conclusion that even if it was appropriate to admit Mr Murrihy's expert opinion . . . very little value can be attached to it.'[104]

International tennis

Over the last few years it has become evident that international tennis has a problem with potential match fixing. This came to public attention in 2007, when betting exchange, Betfair, voided all bets placed on a match involving then world number five Nikolay Davydenko. Davydenko was a heavy pre-match favourite against his 87th-ranked opponent Martin Vassallo Arguello but retired due to injury when trailing in the third set. Despite winning the first set 6-2 the Russian's odds lengthened dramatically. The volume of money wagered on the market and the size of individual bets placed suggested a number of people were certain Davydenko would lose. The bulk of the winnings were traced to three accounts in Russia. One punter had wagered $590,000 dollars on the underdog

---

100 (2004) EWHC 2164. See SLJR (2004) 12(2) SATLJ 105. This case seems to clarify the ambiguity of decision in *Colgan v Kennel Club* (2001, unreported) in indicating that the court is not entitled to put itself in the position of the tribunal in sentencing. A decision on length, for example, of sentence may be wrong, but the court may only interfere with the decision when the tribunal stepped outside its discretionary area of judgment; also see Stoner, C, 'A question of proportionality: the determination of fines and sanctions in disciplinary matters' (2003) 10(4) SLA&P 1.

101 On wider issues of governance in racing see Chapter 5, p 255 and OFT investigation into horse racing and the role of the British Horseracing Board and The Jockey Club; also see 'OFT reaches provisional agreement with BHB over reform of British horseracing', press release 94/04, 10 June 2004, http://www.oft.gov.uk/news-and-updates/press/2004/94-04; 'BHB and OFT Reach Agreement on How Racing Should be Modernised', June 2004, http://www.britishhorseracing.com/inside_horseracing/about/press/view.asp?item=001818; and Vamplew, W, 'Reduced Horse Power: The Jockey Club and the Regulation of British Horseracing' (2003) 2(3) Entertainment Law 94.

102 'Fallon slams fixing claims', BBC Sport, 3 September 2004, http://news.bbc.co.uk/sport1/hi/other_sports/horse_racing/3619876.stm.

103 *Fallon v Horseracing Regulatory Authority* (2006) 103(37) LSG 33.

104 'Jockeys acquitted of race-fixing', BBC News, 7 December 2007, http://news.bbc.co.uk/1/hi/uk/7105207.stm.

before the match while another had bet $368,000 on Vassallo Arguello when he was a set down. The Association of Tennis Professionals (ATP) launched an official investigation, but Davydenko was eventually cleared.

The ATP and ultimately the International Tennis Federation (ITF) became aware of a significant problem within its sport. In 2008, a report was commissioned to be written by two ex-police officers, Ben Gunn and Jeff Rees (who had previously worked at the ICC's Anti-Corruption and Security Unit) entitled 'Environmental Review Of Integrity In Professional Tennis'.[105] The report is far-ranging in its scope and focuses on a number of investigations carried out by the ITF, evaluates the risks that tennis has as far as potential match fixing and proposes future actions.

In a separate report commissioned for the CCPR (now the Sport and Recreation Alliance) it was claimed that 'tennis meets many of the criteria for a sport at risk of betting-related corruption. Contests are one-on-one, so events are easier to fix and the amount available for bribes can be spent on just one individual; pay-offs to fixes can be high because large wagers can be accommodated in a highly liquid market; and betting exchanges provide novel ways of manipulating a match for gain even without necessarily losing it'.[106]

The tennis integrity report highlights the practice of 'tanking' or underperforming in games.

Environmental Review of Integrity in Professional Tennis

2.38. However, one activity identified as a threat to the integrity of the sport is 'tanking'. This term covers a range of behavior which, at the lower end, is regarded almost as 'part of the game' and at the higher level is a definite threat to the integrity of tennis.

2.39. 'Tanking' is a word to approach with caution as it means different things to different people. During the consultation phase we found that players and officials alike used the term to describe different degrees of activity and other stakeholders, including media representatives, were equally imprecise.

2.40. Essentially, 'tanking' involves a player not giving 'best efforts' in a match. However, the reasons for doing so are wide and various, ranging from motivational/tactical issues to action motivated by corruption . . .

This continuum is identified as ranging from 'player is tired, wants out; player does not want to aggravate an injury; player starts with good intentions but loses heart; player tactically cedes point/game/set', through to 'player prefers to reserve his/her best efforts for a more lucrative tournament elsewhere', and on to 'opponents agree outcome in advance for mutually beneficial reasons, e.g. ranking points in exchange for share of prize money' and, at its most extreme and corrupt, when the 'player deliberately loses a match to facilitate corrupt betting activity'. Interestingly the report finds that the general view among both players and officials was that tanking in its mildest form was '"all part of the game" even though all recognized that failing to provide "best efforts" is a breach of the rules'. This is another example of the notion of a playing culture that clearly is outside the rules but can be seen as normative behavior.

The ITF and other tennis organisations have adopted similar policies to those of cricket and horse racing that have been discussed above so as to secure the working environment of sports participants and limit opportunities for criminals to have contact. In addition, the disciplinary

---

105 Gunn, B and Rees, J, 'Environmental Review of Integrity In Professional Tennis', May 2008, www.itftennis.com/shared/medialibrary/pdf/original/IO_32705_original.PDF.

106 'Risks To The Integrity Of Sport From Betting Corruption', University of Salford, February 2008, http://www.epma-conference.net/Download/22012009/SalfordREPORT_Feb08.pdf; also see Transparency International (Czech Republic), 'Why Sport is not Immune to Corruption' (2008), www.coe.int/t/dg4/epas/Source/Ressources/EPAS_INFO_Bures_en.pdf.

structures have been reformed.[107] And also, again along with other sports federations, an emphasis has been placed on player education, particularly with younger players starting their careers, on issues such as the inappropriateness of tanking.[108] This education has also come from some interesting sources.[109]

Gambling and Sport

Gambling has been indentured as being at the root of match fixing. The ethics of sports athletes gambling on games and events they participate in have also been increasingly addressed. The days when international cricketers could openly bet against their team winning, as Dennis Lillee and Rod Marsh did in the famous 1981 Headingley Test Match between England and Australia (at massive odds of 500 to 1), are long gone. Sports governing bodies are required to have specific rules prohibiting players from betting on matches to protect the integrity of the game, and which provide for effective investigation and policing of such actions. The regulatory approach to gambling in the UK is now considered.

Gambling and sport have almost been inseparable and gambling has been subject to considerable regulation by the state. Gambling has close links with the general commercialisation of sport and with corrupt practices in sport. An extended extract on gambling follows, again looking at its historical context, with an aim to understanding its vast significance within modern sport:

Mason, T, *Sport in Britain*

Gambling has always been a part of the modern sporting world, although the public response to it has varied from one period to another. Gambling was endemic in eighteenth-century Britain, but before 1850 a puritanical reaction had begun, aimed particularly at working-class betting. The greatest achievement of the anti-gambling lobby was probably the Street Betting Act 1906, but it remained a powerful and influential opponent certainly up until the second Royal Commission on the subject in 1949. Since then gambling on sport has been increasingly raided by governments to provide income for the state and has also played a crucial role in the financing of the major sports of football and horse racing.

Betting had always been a part of rural sports, both those involving animals, such as cock fighting and bear baiting, and those involving contests between men. Pedestrianism, for example, probably began in the seventeenth and eighteenth centuries, when aristocrats and gentry promoted races between their footmen. These men had been used as message carriers between town house and country residence, although this function lapsed as roads improved and coaches became speedier and more reliable. Their masters often gambled heavily on the results of such races. Sometimes the young master ran himself. Pedestrianism, like prize-fighting, seems to have enjoyed a fashionable period from about 1790–1810. It could almost be characterised as the jogging of the early nineteenth century. Its most famous gentlemanly practitioner was Captain Barclay, a Scottish landowner whose real name was Robert Barclay Allardice. He was prepared to bet 1,000 guineas in 1801 that he would walk 90 miles in 21 and a half hours. He failed twice and lost his money each time. But on 10 November 1801 he did it, for a stake of 5,000 guineas.

---

107 'Alessio Di Mauro says 9-month ban for betting on tennis is too severe', *USA Today*, 11 November 2007, www.usatoday.com/sports/tennis/2007-11-11-226904025_x.htm.

108 'Walter Palmer Opinion: Education: something we can all bet on' (2010) 8(7) WSLR.

109 'Ex-Mob Boss discusses Match Fixing at Coventry Cathedral', Play the Game Conference June 2009, www.youtube.com/watch?v=BfMFuzuTOK4.

Betting on horses was also commonplace, often taking the form of individual challenges between members of the landed classes. In the eighteenth century it was the usual practice to ride your own horse, but the employment of a professional jockey became increasingly common. Betting added another dimension of excitement to the uncertainty of sport itself and it was excitement, which the leisured rural classes were especially seeking, particularly in a country-side whose range of more conventional pursuits soon began to pall in the eyes of the young, married, leisured, pleasure-seeking males.

Cricket was another rural pastime that the landed bucks found attractive. By the begin-ning of the eighteenth century newspaper advertisements told of forthcoming matches 'between 11 gentlemen of a west part of the county of Kent, against as many of Chatham, for 11 guineas a man'. With money at stake it was important to reduce the chances of disagreement by drawing up a body of rules and regulations by which both sides would abide. In this way gambling made its contribution to the development of the laws of cricket. In fact, in the code of 1774 it was specifically mentioned:

> If the Notches of one player are laid against another, the Bet depends on both Innings, unless otherwise specified. If one Party beats the other in one Innings, the Notches in the first Innings shall determine the Bet. But if the other Party goes in a Second Time then the Bet must be determined by the numbers on the score.

Football was, of course, a very attractive proposition both to bookmakers and punters. Before 1900 some newspapers had offered prizes for forecasting the correct scores as well as the results of a small number of matches and early in the twentieth century a system of betting on football coupons at fixed odds had developed in the north of England. It has been suggested that the early pools might have been partly emulating the pigeon pools by which a prize fund was collected for a particular pigeon race, with each competitor subscribing. The owner of the winning bird collected.

Newspapers began publishing their own pools coupons (until the courts declared the practice illegal in 1928) and individual bookmakers offered a variety of betting opportunities. By the end of the 1920s, the football pools, and particularly Littlewoods, under the entrepreneurial guidance of the Moores brothers, had begun to thrive. The pool for one week in 1929–30 reached £19,000. By the mid-1930s the firm was sponsoring programmes on Radio Luxembourg which broadcast the results of matches on Saturdays and Sundays. The football coupon asked backers to forecast the results of a given number of matches from a long list or a selected short list. The latter was given attractive names like 'family four' and 'easy six', 'three draws' or 'four aways'. In January 1935 the penny points was introduced and soon became the favourite pool with the largest dividends, consisting of fourteen matches chosen for their special degree of difficulty. The eight draw treble chance replaced it as the most popular pool after 1945. By 1935 estimates put the number of punters at between five and seven million and it was 10 million by the time war broke out. In 1934 those companies founding the Pools Promoters' Association had a turn-over of about £8 million, which had increased by 1938 to £22 million, of which the promoters retained a little over 20 per cent. This is not the place to animadvert on the place of the pools in British society.

By the mid-nineteenth century, therefore, betting and sport were firmly established as the closest of associates. But the middle-class evangelicalism of the new urban industrial Britain was already beginning to take steps against what was increasingly characterised as a social evil. Gambling was typical of a corrupt aristocracy and it served them right if it led to the sale of their estates and the impoverishment of ancient families. But when the poor were led to emulate those who should have set a better example then something had to be done. By 1850 the state was being pressurised into doing it. The arguments used by the opponents of working-class betting remained more or less unchanged for the next 100 years. Betting by the poor led to debt, which led to crime. Even where crime was avoided, deterioration of character was not, especially among the young and women. Spending sums on betting which could not be afforded weakened the material basis of family life, thereby making a major contribution to poverty. Finally, gambling undermined proper attitudes to work. As *The Times* so succinctly put it in the 1890s, it 'eats the heart out of honest labour. It produces an impression that life is governed by chance and not by laws'. These arguments carried most days until the Royal Commission of 1949–51.

The anti-gamblers' first legislative success was an Act of 1853 to suppress betting houses and betting shops, which had been springing up in many places, very often inside public houses. In future, bookmakers operating from such places, exhibiting lists or in any way informing the public that they were prepared to take bets were liable to a fine of £100 and a six-month prison sentence. The Bill went through both Houses without a debate. Betting shops may have found difficulty in surviving: betting itself moved outside to the streets and places of employment. The expansion of horse racing in particular, with, after 1870, the electric telegraph and a cheap press providing tips and results, provoked the opposition to organise itself, which eventually resulted in the formation of the National Anti-Gambling League. It was in its heyday in the two decades or so before 1914. Sociologists such as BS Rowntree, the economist JA Hobson and radical politicians like J Ramsay MacDonald contributed to its publications. They saw the working-class gambler exploited by the bookmaker and those upper-class sportsmen who supported him. After failing with the law the League turned to Parliament with the clear aim of eradicating street betting. It was this off-course variety which was responsible for the bulk of working-class gambling. A House of Lords Select Committee first examined the matter in 1901–02. In 1906 came the legislation.

The Street Betting Act of 1906 has gained some notoriety as an example of class-biased legislation. It was not aimed at all off-course betting. A person who could afford an account with a bookmaker who knew his financial circumstances well enough to allow him to bet on credit did not have a problem. This ruled out many working men and women. It was ready-money betting of the sort they went in for that was to be prosecuted. In future it was to be an offence for any person to frequent or loiter in a street or public place on behalf of himself or any other person for the purpose of bookmaking or betting or wagering or agreeing to bet or wager or paying or receiving or settling bets.

It is unlikely that the Act did much to diminish the amount of betting. It did of course enhance the excitement of it all, especially at those times and in those places where local magistrates decided that the full rigour of the law must be enforced. Moreover it placed the police in an increasingly difficult position trying to enforce a law for which there was little popular support. Allegations that they frequently looked the other way or had an agreement with local bookmakers to prosecute a runner from each of them in turn were commonplace. By 1929 the police were very critical of both the law and their role in enforcing it and said so before the Royal Commission which was examining the police service in that year. It took the liberal-ising impact of the Second World War and the relatively buoyant economic circumstances which eventually succeeded it to bring about a more relaxed attitude to gambling. This was also facil-itated by the Royal Commission of 1949–51 having relatively sophisticated economic and statis-tical apparatus which enabled it to show that personal expenditure on gambling was only about 1 per cent of total personal expenditure, that gambling was then absorbing only about 0.5 per cent of the total resources of the country and that it was by then rare for it to be a cause of poverty in individual households. They still regarded gambling as a fairly low-level activity and were not impressed by the amount of intellectual effort some enthusiasts brought to it. But they were in favour of the provision of legal facilities for betting off the course and the licensed betting shop reappeared in 1960, 107 years after it had first been made illegal. Six years later the government's betting duty reappeared too.

Gambling's relationship with sport has been significant in two other respects: as a motive for malpractice and corruption and as a source of finance for sporting activities. The latter is closely connected to the growth of football pools, of which more in a moment. Not all sports lend themselves to result fixing with equal facility. The team games should, in theory, prove the most difficult, because there are so many more players who would have to be 'squared' if an agreed result was to be secured. In the early nineteenth century the relatively small number of professionals could exert a disproportionate influence on some cricket matches and they were occasionally bribed or removed from the game by false reports of sickness in the family. One professional was banned from Lord's in 1817 for allegedly 'selling' the match between England and Nottingham. The gradual assumption of authority by the MCC and the county clubs, the improvement in the material rewards of the average professional cricketer and the increasing opportunities to bet on other sports – notably horse racing and, after 1926, grey-hound racing – probably killed off gambling on cricket by cricketers. Today the Test and County Cricket Board (TCCB) has a regulation forbidding players to gamble on matches in which they take part. It was thought to be overly cynical even by late twentieth-century standards when Dennis Lillee and Rodney Marsh won £5,000 and £2,500 respectively by betting against their own team, Australia, in the Leeds Test of 1981. By then, of course, betting by spectators could be encouraged because it brought in revenue. Ladbrokes had been allowed to pitch their tent at Lord's since 1973.

Football has occasionally been shaken by allegations that matches have been thrown, usually in the context of championship, promotion or relegation struggles. Attempts to fix the results of matches in order to bring off betting coups appear to have been very rare but in 1964, 10 players received prison sentences for their part in a so-called betting ring. Three of the players were prominent English internationals and they were banned from football playing and management for life. Two, Peter Swan and David Layne, were later re-instated on appeal but by then were too old to take up where they had left off. Certainly the FA and the Football League were anxious to keep betting and football apart. When coupon betting first appeared in the north of England, before 1914, the FA Council threatened to suspend permanently any player or official who could be proved to have taken part in it. In 1913 they failed, but in 1920 succeeded in getting Parliament to push through a Bill forbidding ready-money betting on football matches.

Football itself had not profited from the growth of pools. But it seems clear that early in 1935 discussions were taking place between the League's Management Committee and repre-sentatives of the Pools Promoters' Association about the possibility of the pools making a payment to the League for the use of their fixtures. But the public attitude of many of the leaders of League football was that the pools constituted a menace to the game and should be suppressed either by the action of the football authorities or by state intervention via an Act of Parliament. The negotiations broke down, perhaps because the pools promoters did not wish to pay what was being asked so long as there was some doubt about whether the fixtures were copyright. All-out war was declared and an attempt made to damage the pools by secretly changing the fixtures on two consecutive Saturdays at the end of February and the beginning of March 1936. Unfortunately for the Football League, dissention in the ranks led to the plans being leaked and the scheme sank. They had no better luck with a Private Members' Bill to abolish the pools, which was easily defeated in the Commons in the same year. Moreover, the League felt it did not need tainted money from the pools, whose promoters therefore kept their hands in their pockets. They did not take them out again until 1959 (although they offered to, briefly, at the end of the war).

It is hard to escape the feeling that not only football but sport in Britain missed a real financial opportunity, although it is clear that it would have required government help to have realised it. In the 1930s the private firms running British football pools set up offices and agencies in several European countries. In Sweden, for example, where betting on pools was illegal, around 200,000 people were completing coupons every week, the stake money swelling the profits of Littlewoods and Vernons among others. The Swedish government acted to stop it in 1934 by establishing the Swedish Betting Corporation to run a state-owned pool. Switzerland and Finland soon followed and by 1950 similar state-run pools had begun in Norway, Spain, Italy, West Germany, Denmark and Austria. Later Poland, Czechoslovakia, Belgium and Holland adopted similar schemes. After administration and prize money had been found, much of what remained was channelled into the support not merely of football but of sport and physical recreation in general. For example £8 million had been so raised by the Swedish government over a three-year period at the end of the 1930s. There were three moments when a similar scheme might have been set up in this country.

The first was early in the Second World War when it was clear that some rationalisation of existing commercial institutions in a range of fields would have to take place. The Secretary of the Football Association, Stanley Rous, together with Sir Arthur Elvin, who ran Wembley Stadium, proposed the creation of an independent pools company, half of whose profits would go to football. Nothing came of it. Instead the government agreed to an amalgamation of the existing companies for the duration. It was known as Unity Pools.

Rous returned to the problem with even more radical proposals in 1943. Reconstruction was in the air and he had been finding out about Sweden in particular. Rous proposed that appropriate government departments should be approached with the suggestion that part of the proceeds from the pools should go into a centrally administered fund, out of which would come money for sports grounds, gymnasia, recreation rooms and sports centres. Again nothing came of it.

The subject was raised for a third time during the sitting of the Royal Commission on Betting Lotteries and Gaming 1949–51. The English, Scottish and Welsh Football Associations all supported the idea of a non-profit-making football pool under government control. But the Commission disagreed, partly because they felt a considerable body of public opinion would not like it, partly because of practical difficulties and partly because of the loss of revenue to the government. If there had been a moment for such radical change, it must have been during those reforming years of the third Labour government. By 1951, its legs were very shaky indeed. Moreover it had been the Labour government that had instituted a 10 per cent tax on the pools in 1947 and increased it to 30 per cent in 1949. Football, of course, could always do its own deal with the pools and in the summer of 1959 it did. In the previous October the Football League had issued a writ against Littlewoods claiming that the League fixtures for the following season were its copyright. In May 1959 a judge agreed. By July an agreement had been signed, to last for 10 years, by which the Pools Promoters' Association was to pay the Football League and the Scottish League a royalty of 0.5 per cent on total stake money, which would not be less than £245,000 a year. There have been several subsequent agreements, the latest a 12-year one signed in December 1984 which ensures the Football League £5 million per year. This, though, is but a small proportion of the income of the pools companies, three of whom – Littlewoods, Vernons and Zetters – paid the government £220 million in tax in 1984–95 but still made a profit of £17 million.

The treatment of football was different to that of horse racing. The government did not introduce a tax on gambling on horse racing until 1966. In 1985 it was still being levied at only 8 per cent. As we saw above, the tax on pools betting came much earlier and was much higher: 42 per cent in 1985. When betting shops were legalised the government established a Horserace Betting Levy Board, allegedly to compensate racecourses for the fall in attendance that would ensue. Its role was to assess and collect a levy from bookmakers and the Tote and use the money for the benefit of racing. According to the leading authority on the subject, the Levy Board saved racing in this country. Perhaps there should be a Football Betting Levy Board. It is not clear why there has not been. British sport has had to get on terms with gambling in the twentieth century; it seems that the terms could have been better.[110]

Betting on sport is growing in popularity, with many new forms such as spread betting.[111] Specialist companies now operate to give advice and odds.[112] The current law on betting is to be found in the Betting, Gaming and Lotteries Act 1963, which, despite its title, no longer deals with gaming and lotteries. Betting is not defined by statute, but is generally regarded as entering into a contract by which each party undertakes to forfeit to the other money or money's worth if an issue, in doubt at the time of the contract, is determined in accordance with that other party's forecast. Unlike a lottery, a bet may involve skill or judgement. No person may act as a bookmaker without the authority of a permit issued by the licensing justices. The essential test applied by the licensing justices in considering an application is whether or not the applicant is a fit and proper person. A bookmaker operating from a betting office requires a licence for the premises issued by the licensing justices. From 1 September 1997 the duration of betting permits and licences has been extended from one to three years. A licence may be refused on the grounds that there are already sufficient licensed betting offices in the locality to meet the demand for betting. No person under 18 years may be admitted to a betting office.

The regulatory framework of the British betting industry was liberalised during the first half of the 1990s. The advertising of individual betting offices and their facilities was originally prohibited under the 1963 Act but since 1997 the ban has been relaxed to allow advertisements in material form, for example in newspapers and journals and on posters, and in 2007 the ban on television advertising was also lifted.[113]

The principles of gambling legislation in the UK

The government set up a Gambling Review Body in 1999 under the chairmanship of Sir Alan Budd.[114] A wide-ranging review of the legislation on gambling in Britain, it submitted its report in June 2001. New legislation was introduced in autumn 2004 to liberalise the regulatory framework in the UK. It has three main objectives:

- gambling remains crime-free;
- players know what to expect and are not exploited; and
- there is protection for children and vulnerable people.

A continued worry in horse racing has been the relationship between gambling and organised crime:

The Jockey Club, 'Submission to the Gambling Review Body'

The Jockey Club is concerned about the vulnerability of horseracing to criminal behaviour and other undesirable activity as a consequence of betting, and the submission to the Gambling Review Body makes the case for greater regulation of betting and changes to the criminal law so as to maintain the public's confidence in the integrity of the sport. Principal concerns stem

---

110 Mason, T, *Sport in Britain* (1998), London: Faber & Faber, pp 59–68.
111 'Bookies bet on a football bonanza' *The Observer*, 7 January 1996, p 6.
112 See Hunter, W, *Football Fortunes: Results, Forecasting, Gambling and Computing* (1996), Harpenden: Oldcastle; 'A good bet', *Fair Game*, Channel 4, 22 May 1995.
113 Derbyshire, D, 'Betting shops and casinos will be free to advertise on TV', *Daily Telegraph*, 18 July 2006, http://www.telegraph.co.uk/news/uknews/1524178/Betting-shops-and-casinos-will-be-free-to-advertise-on-TV.html.
114 *Gambling Review Report* (2001), London: The Stationery Office, http://www.publications.parliament.uk/pa/cm200102/cmselect/cmcumeds/827/827.pdf.

from the fact that, by comparison with other forms of gaming and gambling, the business of bookmaking (including spread betting) is under-regulated and lacks the necessary measures to deter corruption and thus renders racing vulnerable to malpractice.

There is evidence that betting and racing are being used for money laundering purposes. The police have indicated that there is some corruption within racing by criminals and that illegal betting, to the detriment of both government and racing revenues, is being carried out on a large scale.[115]

Sports-related gambling has exploited new technologies with internet betting exchanges having proliferated together with the opportunities provided by interactive services via digital television. A number of betting exchanges have signed contractual agreements with specific sports bodies designed to provide more effective monitoring of betting irregularities and transfer of information.

Gardiner, S and Gray, J, 'Can sport control its betting habit?'

Since the dawn of sport, gambling has been its constant companion. Ancient drawings on primitive cave walls show that gambling has existed for thousands of years. During modern times, sports betting is the most popular form of gambling worldwide, with Internet-related gambling generating over $3 billion in annual revenues in 2002.

Gambling and sports creates an 'unholy alliance'. Gambling has enhanced sport's popularity, particularly on television whereby bettors are more interested in the point spread, not the outcome of a contest. While sports leagues welcome the popularity that gambling provides, they must guard against match fixing, point shaving, and bribery of athletes and referees because the public appeal of sport also rests on the integrity of the contest.

Computers, technologies, and the Internet have facilitated a sophisticated and popular way to gamble on sports events known as 'betting exchanges'. In essence, betting exchanges allows people to swap bets. For instance, one can serve as a 'bookmaker', offering odds to other Internet users concerning a sports competition or event. Betting exchanges have created a fundamental change in gambling because now anyone with a credit card can make money from either a horse, a player, or a team by offering odds on the website and then keeping the stakes when people fail to beat the odds. However, there is a realistic fear that people who have privileged or 'insider' information – knowing for certain that a horse, a player, or a team is going to lose – are offering odds on betting exchanges and then maximising their revenues on unsuspecting gambling customers.

In the United Kingdom, the market leader is Betfair.com. This web site claims to be 'the world's largest online betting company' with an estimated turnover of £50 million per week. Betfair simply serves as a broker, matching people who want to bet with people prepared to offer odds and bringing them together on its website. Betfair makes its money by charging a commission to those who win their bets.

Horseracing is a major attraction for Internet betting exchange gambling. Recently in the United Kingdom, as a result of horseracing betting exchange abuses, there has been a succession of inquiries by the Jockey Club into suspicious betting practices around horse races. Similarly, it has been reported that the Association of Tennis Professionals ('ATP') has discovered that bets of up to £80,000 were being placed on individual matches and that there had been irregular betting patterns around matches involving players not ranked in the top 100. It is alleged that tennis players have been able to profit from insider information concerning their matches.

Betfair has responded to these concerns by signing a 'Memorandum of Understanding' with several sport governing bodies. This has included the Jockey Club and ATP, whose security

---

115 Find the submission at http://www.britishhorseracing.com/resources/about/press/regulationDetail.asp?item=084110.

departments will have access to individual identities and betting records of Betfair gamblers when a race or match produces unusual betting patterns or competition results.

Betfair points out that by developing internal policing relationships with relevant sport governing bodies, sports corruption will be deterred because electronic transactional records will help investigators catch any wrongdoers, and, therefore create 'safe' Internet gambling sites. The downside is that if an exclusive commission is paid to sport governing bodies when they recommend that gamblers deal with 'official' or 'approved' betting exchanges a conflict of interest is created where a sports contest's integrity is sacrificed in order to maximise sports-related gambling revenues.

As with the regulation of gambling generally, there are a number of differing regulatory regimes ranging from prohibition, on the one hand, through to very liberal licensing. Since 2001, for example, in the United Kingdom, an extensive consultation process has taken place that generally supports a more liberal regime. Further, in April 2003, the Department for Culture, Media and Sport produced a position paper, 'The Future Regulation of Remote Gambling' (see www.dcms.gov.uk). The stated objective is to have 'effective regulation [that will] see Britain become a world leader in the field of on-line gambling'.

In contrast, the United States has passed federal anti-gambling legislation. This includes the Professional and Amateur Sports Protection Act of 1992 (28 USC §3702) that prohibits the expansion of state-sanctioned, authorized, or licensed gambling on amateur and professional sporting events in the United States. Similarly, the Comprehensive Internet Gambling Prohibition Act of 2002 (s 3006) was proposed to prohibit all Internet gambling.

Striking a balance between sports competition and Internet gambling is a tricky proposition. The early indication is that Internet betting exchanges are creating opportunities for lucrative 'remote gambling' while resulting in gambling anonymity that may ultimately endanger the integrity of sports competition.[116]

The match-fixing scandal in cricket shows that there is a need for an effective regulatory framework concerning gambling and sport. In some countries around the world, gambling is essentially prohibited. It of course flourishes as an 'illegal undergound activity'. It is prohibited in some areas and regulated in others through strong and enforceable government legislation. In the United States, there are many instances of specific sports gambling legislation to govern the behaviour of people within and outside sports. In a third grouping of countries a liberal regulatory framework exists. In Britain, over the last few years an increasingly liberal approach has been adopted as far as permissible gambling activities are concerned together with the establishment of a unified regulatory body in the form of the Gambling Commission.[117]

At a time when the administration of sport has become more complex than ever before, and vast amounts of new money are flowing into sport, it is essential that more effective regulatory frameworks are developed in the sporting world to counter the impact of gambling on particular sports and players. It is also vital that there is effective policing of these new regulatory frameworks.

Developments in Fighting Match Fixing and Sports-related Gambling

A number of specific measures have been introduced and proposed to engage with illegal gambling and match fixing.

---

116 Gardiner, S and Gray, J, 'Can sport control its betting habit?' (2004) 89 Sport Business International 55.
117 See MacDonald, J, 'The Gambling Commission's Role defending Sport's integrity' (2010) 8(12) WSLR 2.

Memoranda of understanding

The fight against match fixing has involved ISFs and NGBs developing networks with governments, police forces, betting exchanges, gambling boards, other sports and all other relevant entities. Over the last few years, sports bodies have signed a number of agreements with betting companies and internet betting exchanges, including industry leader, Betfair, in the UK. Information which they supply can assist in identifying unusual betting activities and patterns, which may be cause for concern. Betfair has signed a 'Memorandum of Understanding' with several sport governing bodies in addition to the ICC. This has included the Jockey Club and the Association of Tennis Professionals (ATP), whose security departments will have access to individual identities and betting records of Betfair gamblers when a race or match produces unusual betting patterns or competition results. Betfair points out that by developing internal policing relationships with relevant sport governing bodies, sports corruption will be deterred because electronic transactional records will help investigators catch any wrongdoers, and therefore create 'safe' Internet gambling sites. The downside is that if an exclusive commission is paid to sport governing bodies when they recommend that gamblers deal with 'official' or 'approved' betting exchanges, a conflict of interest can be created where sports contest integrity is sacrificed in order to maximise sports-related gambling revenues.

As these Memoranda of Understanding play a pivotal role in the investigation of corruption in sport, it is inevitable that at some point in time they will by scrutinised by a criminal or civil court, whether in the UK or abroad. Under many jurisdictions there may be privacy issues relating to exchange of data. For example, in the UK, the Data Protection Act 1998 provides the regulatory framework over the transfer of data (for example unusual patterns of betting on a particular match including information on who made certain bets) that would be provided by Betfair to a sports governing body such as the ICC. Currently, the transfer works on the basis that 'the data subject has given his explicit consent to the processing of the personal data'. The legal arguments behind this approach are strong, resting on the fact that Betfair's website terms and conditions extract explicit consent for the transfer. However, it may be that what is essentially a private form of regulation involving commercial bodies, such as bookmakers and sports bodies, requires a new and clear statutory gateway to be created to permit these data transfers. Such a gateway would make lawful the transfer of personal data from any organisations concerned with gambling to any licensed organisation concerned with the investigation of corruption in sport. This may be an appropriate development, especially in reinforcing the reliability of this data as formal evidence, particularly where there is increased criminalisation in the area (see below).[118]

Increased criminalisation

Past prosecutions, discussed above in this chapter, have generally involved the common law offence of conspiracy to defraud and have resulted in acquittals. A new development has been the introduction of a new offence of 'cheating' while gambling under the Gambling Act 2005.[119] A person commits a crime if he or she 'cheats at gambling' or 'does anything for the purpose of enabling or assisting another person to cheat at gambling' and, on conviction, he or she may receive up to a two-year custodial sentence. In the context of sport, section 42 introduced a specific offence to punish those who do anything to enable another to cheat at gambling; this would include underperforming in sport.

Gambling Act 2005 Section 42: Cheating

1. A person commits an offence if he: (a) cheats at gambling, or (b) does anything for the purpose of enabling or assisting another person to cheat at gambling.

---

118 Room, S, 'Corruption: The use of personal data when investigating corruption' (2005) 3(1) WSLR.
119 See op. cit, fn 117, MacDonald (2010); and White, N, 'Great Britain's new gambling regime' (2005) SLA&P (Aug) 15–16.

2. For the purposes of subsection (1) it is immaterial whether a person who cheats: (a) improves his chances of winning anything, or (b) wins anything.

3. Without prejudice to the generality of subsection (1) cheating at gambling may, in particular, consist of actual or attempted deception or interference in connection with: (a) the process by which gambling is conducted, or (b) a real or virtual game, race or other event or process to which gambling relates.

The word 'cheating' under the Act is not defined but has its normal, everyday meaning. The offence is committed by both cheating directly or by doing something for the purpose of assisting or enabling another person to cheat. Lord Condon felt that the introduction of this legislation was a major step for the ICC, although the ICC had sought tougher penalties to help protect the integrity of sport. He stated: 'I am of the view that legislation and, therefore, regulation of betting on sport provides a more effective framework for dealing with the total criminalisation of the activity. If betting is effectively regulated by governments then effective penalties can be introduced to deal with corruption.'[120]

In comparison, in South Africa similar provisions of sports-specific criminalisation can be found in the Prevention and Combating of Corrupt Activities Act [No. 12 of 2004]. Whether criminalisation is the answer is a moot point. It may of course merely have a symbolic value, backing up other quasi and non-legal measures. However, at the time of writing in early 2011, there have been no sports-related prosecutions under GA s.42, although the three Pakistani cricketers involved with match fixing during the Test match between England and Pakistan in August 2010 have been charged with conspiracy to cheat.[121] One incident, where a prosecution might have been brought if the sportsman had actually put into effect a plan he was alleged to have been implicated in, was where the *News of the World* made recordings of snooker player, John Higgins, allegedly accepting bribes from a 'Russian businessman', who was actually an undercover journalist, to throw single frames in four future unspecified events for a sum of £261,000. It has been argued that if there might have been grounds for a prosecution under s 42, Higgins would have possibly had a defence of duress.[122]

Another legislative development has been the broadening of the scope of the Fraud Act 2006 to criminalise conduct amounting to match fixing which had not been previously caught by the Theft Acts of 1968 and 1978. A person is guilty of match fixing under section 2 if he dishonestly makes a false representation and intends – by making the false representation – to make a gain for himself or another, or to cause loss to another or to expose another to a risk of loss. Provisions in the Gambling Act also criminalise the misuse of inside information.[123]

Sports Betting Integrity Unit

In 2009, the government commissioned a report to be compiled by a committee of sports betting experts under the chair of Rick Parry, former Chief Executive of Liverpool FC, entitled 'Report of the Sports Betting Integrity Panel'.[124] The report's key proposal was the setting up of a Sports Betting Intelligence Unit (SBIU) within the Gambling Commission. Other proposals include:

- sports governing bodies will be required to improve education programmes, run with the help of sports governing bodies and players' associations, to warn players against illicit gambling;

---

120 Lord Condon in ICC Annual Report for 2004–2005, http://icc-cricket.yahoo.net/publications/annual_report.php.
121 See earlier p 286.
122 Findley, R, 'Corruption: Agreeing to match fixing under duress: analysis' (2010) 8(6) 2010 WSLR.
123 See Burger, R and Dodsworth, W, 'Horse whisperers' (2007) NLJ 157(7284) 1102–03.
124 'Report of the Sports Betting Integrity Panel' (2009), http://webarchive.nationalarchives.gov.uk/+/http://www.culture.gov.uk/images/publications/reports_sports_betting_integrity_panel.pdf.

- advice, assistance and counseling to those sportspeople who have identified themselves as having problems with gambling;
- a 'dedicated whistleblowing line' should be established;
- a new code of conduct on sports betting integrity for all sports governing bodies to adhere to;
- the setting up of a Sports Betting Group, made up of individuals from the world of sport, that will assess sports' compliance with the code of conduct;
- every sport to have a system for capturing intelligence and reporting regularly to the SBIU;
- a review of the definition of 'cheating' in the Gambling Act 2005 to see if it needs greater clarity.

The terms of reference for the SBIU are:

- The SBIU will produce intelligence products to inform investigative decision making on the prosecution or disruption of criminal offences (e.g. cheating) or regulatory action under the Gambling Act. Where relevant and appropriate, these intelligence products may be made available to third parties to assist disciplinary action. The intelligence products will also inform strategic analysis on Sports Betting Integrity issues.
- The SBIU will focus upon collecting and analysing information and intelligence relating to potentially criminal activity in respect of sports betting, where that activity:
  - relates to a sporting event that occurred in Great Britain, and/or
  - involves parties based within Great Britain, and/or
  - occurred with a Gambling Commission licensed operator.
- The SBIU will undertake targeted monitoring of betting on specific events and by specific individuals. It will not undertake general, pre-emptive monitoring of betting markets or sporting events. This remains the role of betting operators and sports governing bodies respectively.[125]

The SBIU will act as the Commission's gateway for sports betting intelligence matters by establishing national and international channels of communication for the receipt and dissemination of information and intelligence with relevant partners. Further clarification of the role of the SBIU and the Gambling Commission was published in December 2010.[126]

World Anti-Corruption Agency

A proposal that has been centrally discussed within the regulatory debate and for which there has been growing support is the creation of an equivalent body to the World Anti-Doping Agency (WADA) to engage in a similar way with the financial corruption of sport.[127] Such a body, it is argued, would be able to adopt a more coherent and wide-ranging approach to this problem and, as with WADA, would be able to be part of a multi-agency approach together with law enforcement bodies such as Interpol. There would also be the opportunity to pool resources and allow the type of forensic investigation that is required to unravel the financial complexities inherent in corrupt financial dealings. Such a body, if it came to fruition, would clearly be able to adopt the good exemplars which have been developed within specific sports such as international cricket and tennis to fight corruption and match fixing. However, unlike WADA, which was very much a creation of the IOC, it is hard to see where the specific political impetus will come from. In addition, is it realistic

---

125 For more information, see www.gamblingcommission.gov.uk.
126 'The Gambling Commission's betting integrity decision making framework' (2010), www.gamblingcommission.gov.uk/pdf/Betting%20integrity%20decision%20making%20framework%20-%20December%202010.pdf.
127 See 'European betting agencies call for independent global sports anti-corruption agency', playthegame.org, 22 September 2009, www.playthegame.org/news/detailed/european-betting-agencies-call-for-independent-global-sports-anti-corruption-agency-4525.html; and 'Sport minister to lead corruption fight', swissinfo.ch, 23 November 2010, www.swissinfo.ch/eng/politics/internal_affairs/Sport_minister_to_lead_corruption_fight.html?cid=28858632.

that such a body could adequately respond to money laundering and other activities of criminal gangs? Similarly, as with a central evaluation of WADA, such a move runs the risk of primarily adopting a self-regulatory approach to this issue. It is probably true that law enforcement bodies must have the central role in this regard.

Conclusion

What this chapter has shown is that elite sport is subject to immense commercial and financial pressures. The spirit of sport as an activity in its own terms, and not merely as a form of entertainment, is in some danger in the face of these pressures. There are interesting interactions between sports-created regulatory mechanisms and the law's involvement in engaging with issues such as match fixing. There are clearly some important governance issues in sport that need to be addressed to improve its financial probity and protect the integrity that is seen as central to sporting endeavour.

Key Points

- Financial irregularities have been endemic in professional football as evidenced by the two 'bungs inquiries'.
- The emphasis on resolving this problem has been through more effective self-regulation within football.
- Player agents have been implicated in being involved in these irregular activities and consequentially have been subject to a variety of regulatory frameworks.
- In England, only a small number of player agents have been subject to disciplinary action.
- Major sports organisations such as the IOC and FIFA have been subject to significant pressure to develop clear principles of ethics in areas such as the bidding process for potential host cities of major events.
- Match fixing and spot fixing have been identified as a major challenge to the integrity of a number of professional sports.
- International cricket has been at the forefront of developing structures to identify and eliminate match fixing.
- A range of sports such as cricket, horse racing and tennis have developed extensive educational programmes for participants on issues such as match fixing.
- The regulation of the sports-related gambling industry has come under scrutiny especially with regard to the use of new technologies such as the internet.
- Among a number of developments to fight financial corruption in sport, there have been calls for a new 'World Anti-Corruption Agency'.

Key Sources

Gunn, B and Rees, J, 'Environmental Review of Integrity in Professional Tennis' (2008), London: International Tennis Federation, www.itftennis.com/shared/medialibrary/pdf/original/IO_32705_original.PDF.

Hill, D, *The Fix: Soccer and Organized Crime* (2010), London: McClelland & Stewart.

Jennings, A, *The Great Olympic Scandal: When the World Wanted its Games Back* (2000), London: Simon & Schuster.

Jennings, A, *Foul! The Secret World of FIFA: Bribes, Vote Rigging and Ticket Scandals* (2006), London: HarperSport.

'Report of the Sports Betting Integrity Panel' 2009, http://webarchive.nationalarchives.gov.u/+/http://www.culture.gov.uk/images/publications/reports_sports_betting_integrity_panel.pdf.

Chapter 7

The Exploitation and Protection of Olympic Commercial Rights

Chapter Contents

Introduction	303
Sponsorship	304
Licensing	310
Ticketing	312
Intellectual Property Rights	318
Ambush Marketing	329
Looking into the Future	355
Conclusions	357
Key Points	359
Key Sources	360

Introduction

This chapter will examine the complex myriad of commercial rights which the Olympic movement owns. It will firstly look at Olympic marketing in detail and discuss why it is important to the Olympic movement. Secondly, the main problems that threaten the financial achievements of Olympic marketing will be identified, in particular trademark infringement and ambush marketing. Some of the solutions to these problems, both legal and non-legal, will be considered. Throughout the chapter, specific reference will be made to the forthcoming London 2012 Olympics. It should be stated at the outset that the chapter is written from the perspective of the event owners who seek to protect the commercial integrity of their sporting events. A practical approach is taken to the subject in this text. Other texts highlight a more legal approach and where appropriate these will be identified to assist the reader with further studies on this topic.

What are commercial rights?

In English common law which is applied in most Commonwealth countries there are no rights in an event itself. The actual spectacle of an event is not protected by any property rights. The event owner therefore has to use other methods to protect its ownership. Firstly, by controlling access – we examine ticketing below – and secondly by protecting and carefully monitoring intellectual property rights.

The principal case, which established this, is an Australian case, *Victoria Park Racing and Recreation Grounds Co. Ltd v Taylor and others*.[1] In the US case law has established that there is a property right in a sports event itself; see *International News Service v Associated Press*[2] and *Pittsburgh Athletic Co v KVQ Broadcasting Company*.[3]

The principal rights which an event owner can exploit are:

- trade marks
- copyright
- patents
- designs
- naming rights
- individual rights
- new media rights
- social networking
- mobile/internet streaming
- video gaming rights
- database rights/statistics rights.

Commercial rights exist for all sports events, not just the Olympics. Sport has become a multi-billion-dollar business by industriously looking at ways to exploit its properties while at the same time avidly protecting those rights. Companies recognise the value of sports events and have turned to them to sell their products or services. The Olympics is no different from any other sports event in this regard. For the Olympics this is also not a new phenomenon as commercial entities have always played a part in the modern Games. Certain sponsors have been involved for decades. Coca-Cola, for instance, has had a marketing association with the Games since 1928 (the sponsorship in 1928 involved delivering 1,000 cases of Coca-Cola to the Olympics in Amsterdam) and Kodak first became involved in 1896.

---

1   *Victoria Park Racing and Recreation Grounds Co. Ltd v Taylor and others* (1937) 58 CLR 479 as discussed in Lewis, A and Taylor, J, *Sport: Law and Practice*, 2nd edn (2009), Haywards Heath: Tottel Publishing, Chapter G15. For further analysis in this book, see earlier Chapter 5, p 246.
2   *International News Service v Associated Press* 248 US215, 63 L Ed 211, 39, SCt 68 (1918).
3   *Pittsburgh Athletic Co v KVQ Broadcasting Company* 24 F Supp 490 (WD Pa 1938).

Olympic commercial rights model

Staging an Olympic Games is a complex operation. There are multiple stakeholders, multiple sports (and then various disciplines within those sports), multiple venues and often multiple jurisdictions and districts. However, essentially the model is that the Olympic Games are owned in their entirety by the International Olympic Committee (IOC). Cities bid to host the summer and winter Games. The successful bid city goes on to enter into a very detailed Host City Contract with the IOC and forms a separate entity called an Olympic Games Organising Committee (OCOG) which handles all the arrangements for the Games in that city.[4] All logos, mascots, documents, policies and procedures developed by an OCOG revert back to the IOC.

The Olympic movement generates revenue through six major programmes:

1. Broadcast
2. The TOP global sponsorship programme
3. The IOC official supplier and licensing programme
4. The OCOG's domestic sponsorship programme
5. Ticketing
6. The OCOG's domestic licensing programme.

For each Olympic Games there will be several programmes in operation simultaneously: the IOC's marketing programme, the OCOG marketing programme and the National Olympic Committee (NOC) of the Host country marketing programme. If we take a wider view we see that each NOC of the participating countries also runs marketing programmes and seeks sponsors for their team and their individual athletes. Given the multiple stakeholders involved it is very important that each party knows what their rights are and that they do not sell a right that they are not capable of delivering.

For instance, in accordance with the Olympic Charter clean venue provisions, national sponsors of participating teams are not allowed to have exposure on the athlete uniforms and equipment; this includes the warm-up kit and the official uniform for the Opening Ceremony parade of athletes.

It is worth noting that while the Paralympics are hosted in the same city shortly after both the summer and winter Olympic Games, the commercial rights which relate to the Paralympics are separate. A company will usually sign up to be a domestic sponsor of both Olympics and Paralympics with the OCOG but in relation to international commercial rights these are owned by the International Paralympic Committee, not the IOC. For instance, in London, the supermarket Sainsbury's has signed up to be a sponsor of the Paralympics only.

The confines of this chapter do not permit a discussion around all of the commercial rights. The issues relating to broadcasting have been explored in Chapter 4. The focus will therefore be mainly on sponsorship, licensing, ticketing, ambush marketing and brand protection.

Sponsorship

Olympic marketing revenue: the past four quadrenniums

The following table provides details of the total revenue generated from each major programme during the past four Olympic quadrenniums. All figures in the chart have been rounded to the nearest US$1 million. (NB This does not include the Host National Olympic Committee's domestic commercial programme revenues.)

---

4   For a more detailed examination of the Olympic Movement and London 2012 see op. cit., fn 1, Lewis and Taylor (2009), Chapter H1.

Source	1993–1996 Lillehammer and Atlanta	1997–2000 Nagano and Sydney	2001–2004 Salt Lake and Athens	2005–2008 Torino and Beijing
Broadcast	US$1,251,000,000	US$1,845,000,000	US$2,232,000,000	US$2,570,000,000
TOP programme	US$279,000,000	US$579,000,000	US$663,000,000	US$866,000,000
Domestic sponsorship	US$534,000,000	US$655,000,000	US$796,000,000	US$1,555,000,000
Ticketing	US$451,000,000	US$625,000,000	US$411,000,000	US$274,000,000
Licensing	US$115,000,000	US$66,000,000	US$87,000,000	US$185,000,000
Totals	US$2,630,000,000	US$3,770,000,000	US$4,189,000,000	US$5,450,000,000

Source: IOC Figures from Olympic Marketing Fact File 2010

The strength of the Olympic brand ensures that the returns for the commercial association with the Games are higher than any for other sporting event.

Gyehyun Kwon, Samsung Head of Sports Marketing and Vice President Global Marketing Operations

Sponsoring the Olympic Games not only plays an important role in elevating Samsung's brand recognition, but also demonstrates our commitment to corporate citizenship and global friend-ship. Olympic sponsorship has enabled Samsung to enhance its brand equity by associating our brand with the values of the Olympic Games. We have also created stronger emotional bonds with global sports fans by leveraging their passion and devotion for the Games.[5]

Almost every product or service that touches our lives is branded. The IOC defines a brand as 'a message either visual or verbal or both that (a) communicates the identity and image of a product or service and (b) conveys a set of expectations of and associations with a product or services. A brand may take the form of a word, a mark, a symbol, a design, a term or a combination of these.'[6]

In many cases the value of a brand cannot be quantified into a monetary figure but it may be true to say that in modern commercial terms the value of a brand can be the most precious asset that a company has. Consumers are drawn to brands as they trigger all sorts of psychological connections such as quality, value, status, goodwill, nostalgia and tradition.

In 1998 the IOC initiated a research project to develop a marketing plan.

Olympic Marketing Matters

The 1998 research further illustrated a strong differentiation in the public's mind about the Olympic brand/image as compared to other brands. The research concluded that the Olympic Games were held in higher esteem than the world's leading commercial brands and other top global sport properties/brands because of the value-based core of the Olympic brand/image. The research also found that the Olympics were held in equal esteem as such humanitarian brands as the Red Cross and UNICEF.[7]

---

5   Gyehyun Kwon, Samsung Head of Sports Marketing and Vice President Global Marketing Operations, (2009), *Olympic Review*.
6   See *IOC Handbook – Ambush Prevention and Clean Venue Guidelines*.
7   *Olympic Marketing Matters* (1999), 15 June, http://multimedia.olympic.org/pdf/en_report_277.pdf.

This remains unchanged today despite the Salt Lake 2002 voting corruption scandal.[8] Concurrent with each Olympic Summer and Winter Games, the IOC conducts global Olympic brand research to understand the thoughts and perceptions of people around the world, to discover what drives consumer interest in the Olympic Games and to study the attributes that differentiate the Olympic Games from all other sporting and cultural events.

The Games rank as one of the highest in appeal and awareness among major sports and entertainment events. Research conducted in 2006 demonstrated that:

- Global consumer awareness of the Olympic Winter Games increased from 87 per cent in 2004 to 94 per cent in 2006.
- Almost half of all research respondents stated: 'Some of my most memorable TV moments involve the Olympic Winter Games.'

The following elements were identified:

- The Olympic Games are special because they happen only once in a while: 77%.
- Performance of Olympic athletes encourages children to participate in sport: 75%.
- The Olympic Games are more than just a sports event: 73%.
- The Olympic Games provide a good role model for children: 73%.
- The Olympic Games are as much about taking part as they are about winning: 70%.
- There is no better achievement in sport than winning an Olympic gold medal: 69%.
- No event brings the world together quite like the Olympic Games: 67%.
- The Olympic Games are the pinnacle of all sports events: 65%.
- The Olympic Games have something for everyone: 65%.[9]

The Olympic brand still triggers powerful notions and images: humanity, contributions to world peace, the transcendence of national boundaries, goodwill, inspiration and friendship. The drama and excitement of top-level international sporting competition combined with all the factors above leads to the creation of one of the most powerful brands of all time. It is, therefore, no surprise that having a commercial association with the Games is a tremendous marketing tool and one which is highly coveted by corporate entities worldwide.

Meenaghan, T, 'Ambush marketing a threat to corporate sponsorship'

As a sponsorship property, the Olympic Games can fulfill a variety of corporate objectives, they provide access to the Olympic logo of interlocking rings, which research suggests is the world's most recognised symbol. Sponsors can achieve brand awareness through access to a unique global audience whilst simultaneously conferring on associated sponsor brands a range of highly beneficial images. Recent research in the United States, United Kingdom, and Spain showed that people considered Olympic sponsors to be modern, innovative and leaders in their fields while socially responsive and dedicated to excellence . . . In a sponsorship arrangement, there is an intended transfer of Olympic brand values to the sponsoring brand.[10]

---

8 'Olympic bribes scandal, *The Guardian*, http://www.guardian.co.uk/Olympic_scandal. For further details about this corruption see Pound, D, *Inside the Olympics: A behind the scenes look at the politics and the scandals and the glory of the games* (2004), Toronto: John Wiley & Sons; and Jennings, A, *The Great Olympic Swindle* (2000), London: Simon and Schuster.

9 During the Torino 2006 Olympic Winter Games, the IOC conducted research in 12 countries. Statements about the attributes of the Olympic brand included in this section of the Torino 2006 Marketing Report are derived from the results of that research project.

10 (1996) 3(1) *Sloan Management Review*.

In terms of sponsorship the 1984 Los Angeles Games was a turning point for the Olympic movement. Los Angeles (LA) was the only city to bid to host the 1984 Summer Games and this gave the City of LA and the OCOG a certain amount of power. They were able to make the Games a commercial operation by implementing a marketing strategy which allowed, for the first time, the Games to be financially independent from the City. LA taxpayers refused to pay for the Games themselves although they did end up paying for the infrastructure, such as roads and city amenities. The City of LA and the OCOG had to turn to private business enterprise in order to raise funds to stage the Games. Their marketing programme was so successful that the Games not only broke even but actually made a profit. They were the first Olympic Games to be funded solely from marketing revenue.[11]

Distribution of funds

According to the IOC official publications over 90 per cent of Olympic marketing revenue is distributed to organisations throughout the Olympic movement, in order to support the staging of the Olympic Games and to promote the worldwide development of sport. The IOC retains under 10 per cent of Olympic marketing revenue for the operational and administrative costs of governing the Olympic movement.[12]

The Olympic Partners worldwide sponsorship programme (TOP) is administered by the IOC and benefits 205 National Olympic Committees, Olympic teams from around the world and the Organising Committees for the Olympic Games. All participants in TOP have provided financial, product and service support to the staging of the Games. TOP companies are awarded exclusive worldwide marketing rights in their designated product category for a period of four years. This is the highest level of sponsorship and offers the most benefits and exposure at Games time. It was created a year after the LA Games and has gone from strength to strength as the table below shows. Prior to the creation of the TOP programme broadcast companies had a financial stronghold over the Olympic movement. Funds and support from TOP have enabled the IOC to break the broadcast companies' stronghold.

TOP programme evolution

Quadrennium Games	Partners	NOCs	Revenue
1985–1988 Calgary / Seoul	9	159	US$96 million
1989–1992 Albertville / Barcelona	12	169	US$172 million
1993–1996 Lillehammer / Atlanta	10	197	US$279 million
1997–2000 Nagano / Sydney	11	199	US$579 million
2001–2004 Salt Lake City / Athens	11	202	US$663 million
2005–2008 Torino / Beijing	12	205	US$866 million
2009–2012 Vancouver/ London	9	205	Figure not yet released.

Source: IOC figures from Olympic Marketing Fact File 2010

In June 2010 the TOP Programme marked its 25th Anniversary. Gerhard Heiberg, Chairman of the IOC Marketing Commission, stated that the programme had evolved and adapted with the times,

---

11 For a more detailed analysis of the commercialisation of the Olympics and the history of Olympic marketing see Payne, M, *Olympic Turnaround: How the Olympic Games Stepped Back from the Brink of Extinction to Become the World's Best Known Brand – and a Multi Billion Dollar Global Franchise* (2005), London: Business Press.

12 According to Olympic website: http://www.olympic.org/ioc-financing-revenue-sources-distribution.

building long-term partnerships with some of the world's leading companies, and he strongly believed that the TOP programme would continue to grow and develop.[13]

In July 2010, despite the economic downturn, the IOC announced that it had secured two new TOP sponsors, Procter & Gamble and the Dow Chemical Company.[14] Procter & Gamble's decision followed its sponsorship of the USA Team for the Vancouver 2010 Olympics. Apparently that sponsorship generated favourable ratings, greater market share and nearly $100 million in incremental sales.[15]

The OCOG and the NOCs are not permitted to sell sponsorships which conflict with the TOP sponsors' product category so for instance they cannot contract with MasterCard because Visa is the official card of the Olympics.

Domestic sponsors

These companies enter into contracts with the OCOG and the NOC where the Games are being held. The OCOG and NOC co-ordinate and operate a single marketing programme in the country hosting the Games. Domestic sponsors commit financial, technological, product and service support integral to funding each Olympics and Paralympics and the Olympic teams.

For example, BMW is the official Automotive Partner of the London 2012 Games. The company will supply around 4,000 vehicles to transport the 'Games family' during the Olympic and Paralympic Games – including athletes, technical officials, the media, international sports federations and the IOC personnel. BT (British Telecom) is the Official Communications Services Partner and a Sustainability Partner for London 2012, providing £80 million in terms of cash and value in kind to furnish all Olympic and Paralympic Venues with telecommunications equipment and services.

What benefits does a sponsor receive?

The main benefits to an Olympic sponsor include:

- Use of OCOG trade marks and designations for the purposes of advertising and marketing;
- product/service exclusivity;
- hospitality;
- preferred option to purchase TV advertising and billboards;
- preferred option to purchase sponsoring of other events (test events, cultural Olympiad exhibitions, celebration sites, etc.);
- sponsor workshops;
- sponsor recognition and acknowledgements;
- protection of sponsorship rights.

In July 2010 the London Organising Committee of the Olympic and Paralympic Games (LOCOG) announced it had raised over £600 million against a target for domestic sponsorships sales of US $1.1 billion (£700 million).[16]

---

13 'IOC marks 25th Anniversary of the TOP Programme', IOC Media Release June 2010. http://www.olympic.org/media?q=top+2 5th+anniversary&chkcat=111&articlenewsgroup=-1&articleid=92572&searchpageipp=10&search page=1.

14 'The Dow Chemical Company joins the TOP programme', – IOC Media Release July 2010. http://www.olympic.org/media?q=d ow+chemical&chkcat=111&articlenewsgroup=-1&articleid=94356&searchpageipp=10&search page=1

15 *Olympic Review* (2010) 76, July, August, September.

16 Bloomberg reported 23 July 2010.

Jagodic, T, 'Sponsorship agreement as a formal legal instrument of modern sport'

The TOP and NOC/OCOG contracts are based on the value of the Olympic Rings. The image of the Olympic rings as a world famous trade mark makes the essence of the contract in a way which looks as if it were a licensing agreement. A closer look at the structure of the TOP contract proves the thesis of making a distinction between the sponsorship agreement and an ordinary licensing agreement. The basic difference lies in the way the object of the contract is used. As a licensee is trying to use the trademark itself, the sponsor is trying to connect the trade mark with his own name, brand or product. It is very common that sponsors use the Olympic rings together with their own brand names and logos (a composite logo) trying to raise the image and value of their own brand.[17]

This is an interesting point, as the development and use of composite logos is something which the IOC monitors very carefully. All its contracts ensure that final approval of these composite logos rests with the IOC or the OCOG. Similarly the contract also controls the development and use of an official designation such as 'Official/Partner/Sponsor/Supplier of the 2002 Olympic Winter Games' or for instance, for McDonalds, 'Official Restaurant of the 2002 Olympic Winter Games'.

Sponsorship contracts

Several sports law texts give a very detailed outline of what a sponsorship agreement should contain and some even give a sample agreement for consideration.[18] This analysis focuses on a few issues which are increasingly relevant. What is vital is that sponsorship contracts need to be very carefully drafted to ensure there is no ambiguity and confusion later on, especially during the event. This is especially important in relation to exclusivity.

Becker, D, *The Essential Legal Guide to Events*

It is essential in this case to define the brand sector carefully. Do beverages include alcoholic beverages and fruit juices, for instance? Will a beer sponsor want exclusivity in cereal malt beverages only (such as lager, bitter, pilsners, ales, stouts and cider) or will it want to include hard alcohol such as vodka, gin and rum?

Precise contract drafting will be required. Typically the event organizer will want the product or brand sector definition to be as narrow as possible, so as to potentially exclude the opportunity of attracting other similar sponsors (the All England Tennis Championships at Wimbledon, for example, has split the drinks category into a number of distinct categories, concluding separate deals with manufacturers of mineral waters, cordials, wines and champagne). On the other hand, a sponsor will want the definition to be as broad as possible, so as to exclude the possibility of a similar sponsor being secured.[19]

The BBC reported in June 2010 that the UK competition enforcer the Office of Fair Trading was investigating whether the exclusivity afforded to TOP Sponsor Visa, whereby they would be the only card accepted at Olympic Venues and for the purchase of Olympic tickets, was unfair to consumers.[20]

One other aspect of note, especially in relation to the Olympics, is the use of 'value in kind'. Most Olympic sponsorship contracts offer as consideration not just cash but also merchandise or

---

17 Jagodic, T, 'Sponsorship agreement as a formal legal instrument of modern sport' (2007) 7(1) ISLR.
18 See Becker, D, *The Essential Legal Guide to Events* (2006), David Becker Pub.; op. cit., fn 1, Lewis and Taylor (2009), Chapter G5.98; and Verow, R, Lawrence, C and McCormick, P, *Sport, Business and the Law* (1999), London: Jordan.
19 Op. cit., fn 18, Becker (2006).
20 'Olympics 2012: Fans must use Visa for tickets', BBC News, 24 June 2010, http://www.bbc.co.uk/news/10394970.

services up to the value of a fixed amount. The clauses need to be very clear so as to specify exactly what the 'value in kind' will entail, how the value of the merchandise or services will be quantified, when it will be supplied, and who pays for delivery and/or incidental expenses; for instance, if Xerox is supplying photocopiers, who pays for the maintenance and service of the machines? Also what happens to any products or services which have not been utilised at the end of the contract term? For example, the mobile phone provider will supply handsets for all staff and key volunteers and at the end of the event these will have to be returned.

Another vital component of agreements are so-called 'morality clauses': so as to ensure commercial integrity and to protect the event brand and goodwill a right of termination is inserted to cover circumstances whereby the sponsor conducts itself in a way which will damage the image of the event.[21] These clauses have become more important when drafting athlete sponsorship agreements. For instance, Tiger Woods' $30 million per year contract with Nike could have been terminated by the sponsor following the recent public scandal involving his multiple marital infidelities.

Domestic suppliers/providers

These are companies that contract with the OCOG and/or NOC to provide specific goods and services necessary for the staging of the Games. For instance, for London 2012 United Parcel Service (UPS) is the Lead Logistics Supporter. Most OCOGs do not grant suppliers the right to use the Olympic trademarks, as LOCOG explains:

London 2012 'No Marketing Rights Protocol for suppliers, consultants and contractors'

Businesses supplying goods and services to the London 2012 Organising Committee, the ODA and other organisations involved in the delivery of the Games ('Suppliers'), will benefit from the experience and kudos gained from undertaking work in relation to, and/or providing goods and services for, the Games. However, Suppliers do not pay to receive the benefits of being an official marketing partner of the Games; indeed, they are paid full value for the supply of their goods and services.

As such, unless they become an official marketing partner of the London 2012 Organising Committee or are one of the International Olympic Committee's worldwide partners, suppliers cannot benefit in other ways – for example, beyond making certain factual statements about the work they are being paid to undertake, they cannot use the Protected Marks or promote themselves as associated with the Games.[22]

Sponsorships can also be entered into by the NOCs and by the individual athletes. As discussed below, the athletes who compete in the Olympics are required to sign an entry form/contract which confirms they will comply with the Olympic Charter and its strict byelaws. The Olympic regulations prevent the athlete's personal sponsors from receiving any exposure during the time of the Olympics. Although some athletes do try to circumvent this[23] and carry out a form of ambush marketing, the majority of athletes do comply with the Olympic Charter and regulations.

Licensing

Licensing or merchandising is essentially where an event owner grants a manufacturer a licence to use the event trademarks on its products and then sell them in return for a fee – a royalty from the

---

21 See 'Sponsorship Contracts: Stanford case: clauses giving bodies right to terminate' (2009) 7 (3) ISLR.

22 London 2012, 'No Marketing Rights Protocol for suppliers, consultants and contractors', http://www.london2012.com/publications/no-marketing-rights-protocol-for-suppliers-consultants-a.php.

23 See p 348 below.

sales of the products. Licensing is another important method of raising commercial revenue from sports events. Sports fans have a desire to be associated with their team and their sporting heroes and visibly demonstrate their support. Official licensed merchandise of the National Basketball Association and National Hockey League in North America sells in vast quantities and all UK Premier League football teams generate huge amounts of revenue each year from sales of replica kit and other merchandise.

According to the US-based business publisher, Forbes, Manchester United remains the most valuable sporting club in the world. Valued at $1.8 billion it is not just the richest soccer team but also the biggest property in all of sports. It has a worldwide core fan base of 139 million. A deal was struck with Nike to pay the club $470 million over 13 years plus a 50 per cent share of profits on specific merchandise through to 2015. The club also signed a new shirt sponsorship with insurance company Aon worth $34 million annually over four years, which was 50 per cent more than its previous deal with AIG.[24]

As discussed above, the Olympic brand and values have an elevated status so the Olympic fan's desire is to associate with the event more than with the actual athletes. Olympic branded merchandise ranges from the obvious – T-shirts, hats, sweatshirts, mugs, key rings, cuddly toys, postcards, playing cards, notepads, pens and pencils – to the less obvious – bed linen, towels, shower curtains, coins, stamps, video games, jigsaws and radios. Essentially anything that is manufactured and sold is capable of being branded; however, the Olympics are mindful of the need to ensure that the quality of all official merchandise is of a high standard so that fans have a lasting good memory of the 'greatest sporting event ever'.

Licensees enter into a contract with the OCOG and/or the NOC. Only official licensees are authorised to manufacture and sell products relating to that Olympic Games which use the official trademarks of the OCOG, the NOC and the IOC. This contract also has to be well drafted to ensure that commercial protections are in place for the event owners. For instance, the event owner may limit the territory in which the licensee is granted rights to manufacture and sell their products so as to maximise the range of merchandise available globally. The event owner will also need to carefully consider the term of the agreement and what happens to official licensed merchandise once an event is over. The contract will need to specify all these details.

Sydney 2000 licensing was a huge success, with merchandise available as early as 1997. More than 3,000 products were licensed and these were sold in over 2,000 retail outlets across Australia. Total retail sales amounted to $490 million. Total revenue raised was $52 million.[25]

At the Vancouver Winter Games, the Olympic Superstore was one of the Olympic city's biggest attractions, with more than 15,000 people per day visiting the store to purchase official apparel and souvenirs. The store had 32 different licensees with a wide assortment of products from a 59-cent postcard to a $7,500 (CAD) canoe. The Vancouver Olympic Committee (VANOC) factored retail sales of official merchandise into its $1.7 billion (CAD) budget and was confident it would meet its target of $54 million (CAD) in sales.[26]

One of the unique aspects relating to the Olympics is the licensing and trading of official pins or badges. Olympic pins have become such collectibles that Coca-Cola mounts a huge pin trading exhibition at the time of each Olympic Games. Even these lapel pins have to be official and each OCOG has to monitor trade in illegal pins, i.e. those pins which use the trademarks without authority.

As discussed above, the licensing contract will set out commercial protections for the event owner but it will also need to set out very clearly the protections that the event owner can afford to prevent counterfeit merchandise from being sold. The success of each licensing/official merchandise

---

24 21 July 2010, http://www.forbes.com/business/sportsmoney.
25 IOC figures from *Olympic Marketing Matters* (2001) 18 (May), http://www.olympic.org/Documents/Reports/EN/en_report_274.
   pdf.
26 Source – Reuters 18 February 2010.

programme lies in the ability to afford these protections and this is discussed later under trademark infringement.

Most OCOGs also establish an education campaign so that the public understands why it is wrong to buy cheaper unofficial merchandise.

Vancouver 2010

By purchasing only official Vancouver 2010 merchandise, customers are supporting the Vancouver 2010 Olympic and Paralympic Winter Games and the Canadian Olympic and Paralympic Teams.

To ensure their money is going directly to the Games and athletes, consumers should note that all official Vancouver 2010 merchandise is:

- Produced using strict quality assurance standards;
- Made of quality materials and is manufactured to last;
- Produced according to a high level of ethical sourcing and social responsibility;
- Created to support the visual identity of Vancouver 2010 and the core values upon which the Olympic and Paralympic Movements are based.

Consumers are encouraged to look for the unique hologram affixed to each item of official Vancouver 2010 merchandise. A symbol of the product's authenticity, these holograms feature Vancouver 2010 emblems along with several layers of security and have been designed to prevent unauthorized copying, protect consumers and assist customs officers.

As with sponsorship contracts, licensing/merchandising agreements have to carefully define product category:

Becker, D, *The Essential Legal Guide to Events*

The rights will normally be granted for a particular category of products that are to be manufactured by the merchandiser. The range of the products will need to be discussed by the parties and defined carefully in the contract. The event organizer may wish to license the rights in a certain product category (e.g. clothing) to one merchandiser and the rights in another product category (e.g. pendants) to another merchandiser.[27]

Ticketing

As illustrated above, ticketing makes a significant contribution to the overall revenue generated by each Olympics. A major problem for all Olympics has been the re-selling of tickets, which is known as 'ticket touting' in Britain and 'ticket scalping' in North America.

In Vancouver the OCOG filed a lawsuit against 'Roadtrips', a travel agent in Winnipeg, over re-selling 2010 Olympic tickets at higher than the purchased value. Besides being in breach of the ticketing licence agreement, this also affected the exclusivity of the official ticket agents, Tickets. com and Jet Set Sports. The case was settled out of court but the problem still remained in that other companies were open to do the same because ticket scalping was not illegal in the province of British Columbia. The action of selling the tickets on city streets without a vending licence was illegal but there was nothing to prevent re-sale in stores and over the internet.

The Vancouver Organising Committee (VANOC) decided to set up its own re-sale ticket system. The system enabled ticket holders to simply sign into their existing Vancouver 2010 ticketing

---

27 Op. cit., fn 18, Becker (2006).

account and then click the 'sell my tickets' option for the seats they wanted to sell. Ticket holders could set their own selling price and buyers could browse for available tickets in the same location as other tickets sold at the official VANOC website. This system helped to ensure that there were full venues at Games time and also guaranteed that all tickets re-sold through this official channel were valid.

In most jurisdictions ticket touting or ticket re-selling is not illegal. In 2006 the UK introduced new legislation which made ticket touting of football tickets illegal. The following article was written just before the provisions came into force.

Duthie, M and Giles, C 'Anti-ticket touting: the campaign continues'

Changes to the law
The existing legislation (section 166 of the Criminal Justice and Public Order Act 1994, the CJPOA) has become increasingly outdated. Its focus is on isolated touts loitering outside football stadia on a Saturday afternoon, whereas modern touts are more sophisticated, and it is on the internet where the bulk of unauthorised sales are made. The Violent Crime Reduction Act 2006 (the 2006 Act) received Royal Assent on 8 November 2006. It covers a variety of subjects, including drinking banning orders, sales of alcohol to children, new firearms offences, new provisions on sexual offences and ASBOs. And in amongst all that are some critical improvements to the anti-ticket touting provisions in section 166 of the CJPOA, which are due to come into force during the first half of 2007.

Section 166 of the CJPOA applies to most professional football matches played in England and Wales. It currently makes it an offence, in relation to such matches, for an unauthorised person to 'sell, or offer or expose for sale, a ticket . . . in any public place or place to which the public has access or, in the course of trade or business, in any other place'. It has been the subject of some debate whether this provision would catch unauthorised sales made on the internet, since that depends on whether the internet is a 'public place' or (for commercial sales) 'any other place'. And aside from that issue, the existing formulation arguably allows touts to give away tickets when bundled with another purchase ('a baseball cap for £100 with a free City v United ticket thrown in').

Under the 2006 Act, section 166 will be amended so that the offence covers not just selling, offering for sale and exposing for sale but also (i) making a ticket available for sale by another; (ii) advertising that a ticket is available for purchase; (iii) giving/offering a ticket to a person who agrees to pay for some other goods or services; and (iv) otherwise disposing of a ticket. There is no requirement that the sale, offer, exposure etc need occur in a 'public place' or 'any other place', which means there can be no argument that internet sales are not covered.

That will make it clear that the selling party will be caught by the new legislation. But if the sale is made via an auction site like eBay, what about the host website – will they be caught as well? The short answer is yes, so long as they know what's going on. The new section 166A essentially provides that in those circumstances online information service providers (including eBay) will not commit an offence unless (a) they know that tickets are being sold illegally at the time the tickets are advertised or, (b) they become aware that tickets are being sold illegally but do not take immediate steps to remove the advertisements. Importantly, there will be no general duty for service providers to monitor for illegal tickets; the onus will be on the ticket issuer to notify the service providers of each infringement.

Criminal prosecutions
The new legislation will mean that the police and the Crown Prosecution Service ought to be in a stronger position to crack down on touting. And it is not just the CPS that has the powers to bring criminal prosecutions. Local authorities may authorise their respective Trading Standards services to bring enforcement proceedings against ticket touts under section 166 of the CJPOA.

(This is in addition to the duty on such Trading Standards services to enforce consumer protection legislation against ticket touts, including where there has been a failure to inform customers of the face value of tickets and the location of seats).

So, when the new legislation comes into force, an internet tout is more likely to be successfully prosecuted under section 166. But there has been no change to the penalty tariff applicable under section 166, and so the maximum fine remains at £5,000 (and fines have typically been as low as £500). That on its own might not be a sufficient deterrent for some of the sophisticated online operations (tickets for the Chelsea v Manchester United match in April 2007 are already being advertised by touts at prices in excess of £350 each). But if there were ways to get at the touts' profits, that might make the touts more circumspect about what they do. One such way would be for the CPS to seek confiscation orders under the Proceeds of Crime Act 2002 (POCA), which would require convicted touts to pay an amount equal to the benefit they had made from the illegal sales. Another way would be for the appropriate ticket issuers (the clubs, event organisers or governing bodies) to bring civil claims against the touts and seek awards of damages. The relevant causes of action include breach of contract, inducement to breach, conversion, passing off, breach of statutory duty and threatened trespass.

An international approach

The passing of the new legislation is a considerable success for FIFA, UEFA, the FA and the FA Premier League who together lobbied hard to convince the government that the statute needed amending. And due to similar pressure from the Olympic movement, virtually identical provisions to those contained in the 2006 Act have already been enacted for the London 2012 Olympics.

And this latest strengthening of the football anti-ticket touting provisions comes relatively soon after the list of matches (to which the legislation is applied) was significantly extended. Previously, the CJPOA applied only to matches in which an English or Welsh side were actually competing, whereas since the passing of the Football Spectators (Prescription) (Amendment) Order 2006, it now covers all matches in a FIFA or UEFA tournament in which an English or Welsh side is competing (so it will cover the FIFA World Cup Final, even if England get knocked out in the quarter-finals).

Lord Pendry, the peer and former Sports Minister, described the new anti-ticket touting regime in the UK as *'the most stringent laws against ticket touting anywhere in the world'*. That might well be the case, and we should be rightly proud. But touts now operate in a global market, and where they are based out of the jurisdiction, the ability of the English criminal and civil courts to restrain their activity is compromised. Efforts need to be made to get all countries to adopt similar legislation so that there can be no hiding places.[28]

The provisions in the UK have also been extended to protect tickets for the London 2012 Olympic Games and the Glasgow 2014 Commonwealth Games. The article below discusses this and also examines a problem with fraudulent tickets for the Beijing 2008 Olympics.

Acreman, L, 'Tackling ticket touting in sport with criminal legislation'

In September 2008, the Serious Fraud Office launched an investigation into ticket agencies suspected of online ticket fraud for failing to supply tickets to consumers for the Beijing Olympics, amongst other events, last summer . . .

Following its September 2008 investigations, the SFO and the Metropolitan Police Service arrested five people connected to Xclusive Tickets Limited, an online ticket agent, and its

---

28 Duthie, M and Giles, C, 'Anti-Ticket Touting: The Campaign Continues' (2006) http://www.twobirds.com/English/News/Articles/Pages/Anti-ticket_touting_campaign_continues.aspx.

related companies ('Xclusive'). According to the SFO press release, Xclusive purported to sell tickets to the 2008 Olympic Games in Beijing but tickets were not received by those that had paid for them. This apparently unprecedented action by the SFO has sparked interest among sports governing bodies, many of which have tried for many years to combat ticket touting, often with relatively little support from the authorities.

Anti-ticket touting measures taken by the police have traditionally focused on individuals selling, or offering for sale, tickets outside football grounds. But the internet has changed the modus operandi of touts. Increasingly, without being authorised by the event organiser, companies like Xclusive are being set up to sell tickets to sporting events online. By their nature these companies have a much wider customer base than any stadium-based tout; but they pose the same issues for event organisers. If such companies are not authorised to sell tickets to events, the event organisers cannot regulate the sale of tickets, which can compromise both the organiser's commercial interests and any practices put in place to safeguard spectators. Unauthorised ticket sales can also result in fans being ripped off when tickets never materialise, as demonstrated by the allegations against Xclusive. Now the criminal justice authorities are beginning to catch up with the new breed of touts.

Criminal liability

. . . In years past, the application of criminal law against touts was limited, confined to football and reliant on the CJPOA. Now there are a greater number of resources that can be used against touts. We take a look at the Fraud Act 2006 and POCA 2002, on which the SFO based its investigations into Xclusive, and briefly London's legislative answer to avoiding the ticket touting problems suffered at the Beijing Olympics.

London Olympic Games and Paralympic Games Act 2006 ('LOPGA')

Like football, the London Olympics and the Glasgow Commonwealth Games will also benefit from specific legislation criminalising ticket touting. While the focus here is on LOPGA, it should be borne in mind that the CJPOA and GCGA contain very similar anti-ticket touting provisions.

An offence under s.31 LOPGA is committed each time a tout (amongst other things):

1. is not authorised in writing by the London Organising Committee for the Olympic Games ('LOCOG') to sell tickets to an event at the London Olympics;
2. offers for sale and/or sells a ticket to that event; and
3. undertakes (2) in the course of business or in a public place.

Under s.31 (6), a tout, if found guilty, is liable to a fine not exceeding the maximum for level 5 (£5,000) on summary conviction only.

LOCOG has also announced a crackdown on ticket touting activities through LOCOG's ticketing policy, due for publication in 2010, prior to any ticket sales. The policy is expected to incorporate physical restrictions on the transfer of tickets, to work in tandem with the criminal sanctions outlined here.

From the description of the offences, it is clear that the provisions of the CJPOA/LOPGA/GCGA only apply to tickets to football matches/London Olympic and Commonwealth events, thereby leaving a vast number of sporting events untouched. Since the Olympics and Commonwealth Games are not subject to the same public safety concerns as football matches, the presence of dedicated anti-ticket touting legislation for these events indicates an awareness of the broader concerns surrounding touting, namely the commercial gains made by touts at the expense of real fans and the commercial interests of event organisers. This being the case, there is a strong argument for introducing similar dedicated legislation for all sporting events.

In the meantime, all other sport event organisers have had to rely on civil remedies when enforcing their ticket terms and conditions to prevent ticket touting. Recently, the Metropolitan Police Service has begun to bring charges against ticket touts under the Fraud Act 2006 and the

Proceeds of Crime Act 2002, indicating that some anti-ticket touting measures could be universally applied within the sporting community.

Fraud Act 2006 ('Fraud Act')

The Fraud Act, which came into force on 15 January 2007, repealed the deception offences under the Theft Act 1968. In its place, the Fraud Act introduced a number of dishonesty offences. Of the offences contained within the Fraud Act, fraud by false representation under s.2 of the Fraud Act is the most clearly applicable to ticket touting. A tout will be guilty of fraud by false representation if the tout dishonestly makes a representation that he is authorised/legally able to sell the tickets, knowing that the representation is or might be false, with a view to making a financial gain and/or exposing the buyer to the risk of a loss.

Under the Fraud Act regime, it is immaterial whether anyone actually purchases tickets from the tout or whether any gain or loss is made. The tout will be guilty of a s.2 offence as soon as the criteria above are satisfied. Under s.1 (3) of the Fraud Act, if a tout is found guilty of fraud by false representation, he is liable to 12 months' imprisonment and/or a fine on summary conviction. If the matter proceeds to trial, the sentence could be increased to a maximum of 10 years and/or a fine. These sanctions are much stiffer than those under the CJPOA/LOPGA/GCGA, making the threat of conviction under the Fraud Act much more of a deterrent to touting.

The SFO is able to investigate Xclusive for alleged Fraud Act offences because ss.2 (4) and (5) of the Fraud Act bring within the remit of the offence representations made via the internet. The Fraud Act can therefore be used against both individual touts making face to face ticket sales, and ticket agencies selling tickets online.

However, the Fraud Act is not intended to exclusively deal with ticket touting. As a result, ticket touting does not fit as comfortably within the framework of the Fraud Act as it does under the provisions of the CJPOA/LOPGA/GCGA. The evidential requirements of the Fraud Act increase the burden of proof on those seeking to convict ticket touts. For example, under s.2 of the Fraud Act, there is no fraud by false representation unless/until it is shown that the tout was dishonest in their actions. The explanatory note to the Fraud Act sets out what is required to successfully prove dishonesty. Essentially, the usual two-stage test for dishonesty will apply, which requires not only an objective determination of what is dishonest but also proof that the tout was aware that his conduct would be thought of as such. By comparison, the wording of s.166 CJPOA/s.31 LOPGA do not require proof of any knowledge on the part of the tout. As a result, it may be easier to secure a conviction under the CJPOA/LOPGA/GCGA than the Fraud Act (or POCA, see below).

Further, s.2 (2) requires proof that the tout knew that the statements he made about the tickets were 'untrue or misleading'. However, this element may not be as problematic as it appears since the key ticket terms and conditions are usually written on the physical ticket itself (regardless of whether or not the terms and conditions have been incorporated into the transaction in which the tout acquired the ticket). If these terms include reference to unauthorised ticket sales rendering the ticket invalid then, arguably, the tout can be said to have known that any representation that the ticket is valid (whether express or implied) was untrue or misleading.

Proceeds of Crime Act 2002 ('POCA')

Money laundering offences under POCA are applicable to any crime. Therefore, if the tout is liable under the Fraud Act or the CJPOA/LOPGA/GCGA then they may also be charged with money laundering offences under POCA. Of the money laundering offences listed in POCA, 'acquisition, use and possession of criminal property' is the most obviously applicable to ticket touting. A tout will commit a s.329 offence if he:

- in any way deals with the profits from the illegal sale of tickets; and
- knows or suspects that the profits were gained through criminal conduct.

'Criminal property' in the context of ticket touting will be the money gained by the tout from selling the ticket(s). The tout may also contravene s.328 of POCA if he is involved in an organised form of ticket touting, such as a company specifically set up to sell tickets to sporting events. Under s.334 POCA, if a tout is found guilty of money laundering, he is liable to up to 14 years' imprisonment and/or an unlimited fine on indictment; or up to 6 months' imprisonment and/or a fine to the statutory maximum of £5,000 on summary conviction.

While an offence under POCA requires a criminal act to have been committed one incidence of ticket touting may give rise to separate offences under the Fraud Act, the CJPOA/LOPGA/GCGA and POCA. However, the CPS suggests that where the proceeds gained by ticket touting are minimal and have only been enjoyed by the tout, rather than (for example) used to fund further criminal activity, an application under POCA for confiscation of the actual proceeds gained may be preferable to the additional evidential burden of prosecuting the tout under POCA. This suggestion would appear to cover individual touts who do not generate a significant income from touting, but, for wider networks of touts, particularly where the criminality extends beyond 'mere' ticket touting, a confiscation order alone may be inappropriate. Additionally, under POCA a confiscation order can only be obtained when the ticket tout is tried at a Crown court. A confiscation order will not be available for s.166 CJPOA/s.31 LOPGA/s.17 GCGA offences where conviction is summary only.

Conclusion

Other than football, the Olympics and Commonwealth Games, sporting events are not the subject of dedicated anti-ticket touting legislation. But a greater interest in curbing touts' activities, coupled with a willingness to use general legislation, has meant the fight against touts is intensifying. Due to the evidential burden of proof and the need for a conviction on indictment in order to use the full force of the Fraud Act and POCA, touting activity may need to be sufficiently serious for prosecutors to be willing to invest in prosecuting it. Despite these drawbacks, the investigations into Xclusive indicate that a tougher stance is being taken against ticket touts across all sports. For organisers of all sporting events, this should be a welcome development. Cracking down on touting in sports generally means not only can the organiser better control attendance at its event but also that real fans should not be disappointed by ticket touts.[29]

Ticket agreements

The other aspect of ticketing is the ticket licence agreement, which establishes the terms and conditions of entry into a sports event. This is also very relevant in relation to controlling ambush marketing inside the venue. This is discussed later in this chapter.[30]

The ticket agreement for all sports events will have clauses inserted to confirm what the cancellation and returns policy is. This is important in all events but especially in relation to sports, where the weather can mean that there is no event to watch. There will also always be a disclaimer relating to safety at the venue. In some cases this disclaimer is very wide:

Athens 2004 Olympic Conditions of Ticket Sales and Terms of Admission

You release ATHOC, the IOC/IPC, the Hellenic Olympic/Paralympic Committee (including the Directors, Officers, Employees, Consultants, Contractors, Agents and Volunteers) from any

---

29 Acreman, L, 'Tackling ticket touting in sport with criminal legislation' (2009) 7(2) WSLR. For a discussion about Glasgow 2014 ticket touting see Schmidt, J and Boag-Thomson, J, 'Scotland: Commonwealth Games Bill: ticket touting and advertising' (2008) 6(2) IASL.

30 See later p 349.

liability for any damage, loss, liability or injury you may suffer in relation to your attendance at a venue howsoever caused including due to any negligence or other act or omission of ATHOC.

In most jurisdictions a disclaimer this wide would not be upheld in court, particularly in relation to injuries caused by negligence. In the UK the Unfair Contract Terms Act 1977 s 2(1) provides that a person cannot exclude or restrict liability for death or personal injury resulting from negligence.[31]

The ticket agreement also provides detailed information on what is prohibited and/or restricted inside the venue. Again the list is quite lengthy:

Athens 2004 Olympic Conditions of Ticket Sales and Terms of Admission

The following items may not be brought into the venues: weapons, explosives, chemical or detonation devices, tear gas, smoke bombs . . . fireworks, firecrackers, poles, bats and any objects in general that may cause bodily harm . . . motorbikes, bicycles, rollerskates, skateboards . . . broadcasting equipment of any broadcasting company without broadcast rights, flags of non participating countries, flags of participating countries which are larger than 2m × 1m, alcoholic drinks, banners larger than 1m × 1m . . . horns, laser devices and other items which may be bothersome . . . commercial items with obvious logos of competitive companies to sponsors . . . pirate Athens 2004 products . . . unauthorised publications . . . glass bottles, canteens, thermos flasks, coolers, ice cube trays, water, beverages and generally any material which Security may have characterised as dangerous or inappropriate. In addition food is not allowed . . .

The following actions are not allowed at venues: smoking, gambling, unauthorised collection of money (for charity or other goals), coordinated group promotion or advertising efforts (such as a group of spectators in adjacent seats with a letter or symbol on each shirt that together form an advertising, political or religious activity or protest), ambush marketing activities, political or religious activities and protests, the sale of goods by unauthorised individuals (street traders) . . . unauthorised ticket sales, unauthorised transmission and/or recording through mobile phones or other recording devices . . . flash photography, dangerous, indecent or intrusive behaviour . . . entry attempt to areas requiring accreditation, soliciting for money . . . (for example by playing music) . . . involvement in activities that may deter spectators from watching events or involvement in any activity deemed dangerous or inappropriate by ATHOC.

Finally the ticket agreement confirms that the ticket holder may be ejected from the venue if the ticket terms and conditions are not adhered to.[32]

Intellectual Property Rights

The production and sale of officially licensed merchandise has become an important part of the Olympic marketing programmes. The figures above illustrate this. The success of Olympic licensing is two-fold. Firstly, the unique nature of the event and its huge international media exposure has widened fan interest. The Olympics is universal in nature, and merchandise becomes a piece of sporting memorabilia which can be highly collectible. Secondly, the intellectual property laws protecting the Olympic symbols, logos and insignia are strengthened by special domestic legislation. This makes it easier to take action against counterfeiters and those who infringe Olympic trade marks.

---

31 See Chapter 11, p 508.
32 For further ticket conditions see op. cit., fn 1, Lewis and Taylor (2009), 'Match day control and exploitation', p 1147.

Special protection for the Olympic rings

The Olympic brand is exalted to such a level that it demands special legislation and co-operation between nations. For example, in September 1981 the IOC and the World Intellectual Property Organisation (WIPO) created the Nairobi Treaty on the Protection of the Olympic Symbol especially for the purpose of protecting the Olympic Mark. Under the Treaty all parties shall be obliged 'to refuse or to invalidate the registration as a mark and to prohibit by appropriate measures the use, as a mark or other sign, for commercial purposes, of any sign consisting of or containing the Olympic symbol, as defined in the Charter of the IOC, except with the authorisation of the IOC'. As at July 2010 47 countries had become a party to the treaty.[33]

The treaty does not offer protection in relation to trade mark enforcement so individual marks, such as the Salt Lake Organizing Committee (SLOC) Games mark, still have to be registered in accordance with trademark legislation. Each NOC is given the duty of protecting the brand in their own country. In most cases, this involves passing special legislation.

The UK decided to enact its own legislation to protect the Olympic and Paralympic symbols, mottos and various words. The Olympic Symbols etc. (Protection) Act 1995 specifically gives the British Olympic Association the right to exploit the IOC trademarks and sets out the protection afforded to those trademarks. This Act was amended in 2006 (when London won the bid to host the 2012 Olympics) by the London Olympic Games and Paralympic Games Act 2006. The main aspects of the amendments relate to the creation of a new protection against unauthorised Olympic association. This is discussed later in the chapter under Ambush Marketing.[34] In relation to Olympic trademarks the 2006 Act extended protections to the symbols specifically designed for the 2012 Olympic and Paralympics and also gave LOCOG the right to use the marks and to take action to protect against unlawful infringement of the marks.

The trademarks protected under the current legislation include:

- the Olympic five-ring symbol (or anything similar);
- the words Olympic(s), Olympiad(s), Olympian(s) (and similar words such as 'Olympix');
- the motto 'Citius, Altius, Fortius' and its English equivalent, 'Faster, Higher, Stronger';
- the Paralympic symbol;
- the London 2012 Olympic and Paralympic symbols.

Trade marks

In the UK other sporting bodies do not have special legislation and instead rely on the law relating to trade marks, and if a mark is not registered but is a 'common law' mark then they have to rely on the doctrine of the tort of 'passing off'. The Trade Marks Act 1994 is the legislation in the UK which defines what can be registered as a trade mark and sets out the procedure for registration.[35] A trade mark is defined as:

Section 1 (1) of the Trade Marks Act 1994 (as amended)

Any sign capable of being represented geographically which is capable of distinguishing goods or services of one undertaking from those of other undertakings. A trademark may, in particular, consist of words (including personal names) designs, letters, numerals or the shape of the goods or their packaging.[36]

---

33 http://www.wipo.int/treaties/en/ip/nairobi/trtdocs_wo018.html.
34 Below, p 337.
35 The Act was amended so as to implement and comply with European Law – EU Directive No 89/104 makes provision for trade mark law for all EU Member States.
36 Part 1, Section 1 (1) of the Trade Marks Act 1994 (as amended).

As long as the requirement of distinctiveness is satisfied it is possible to register team names and logos. For example, in 2002 the Rugby Football Union sought to prevent the manufacture and sale of shirts bearing a red rose, which they had registered as a trademark, for the England rugby team, in 1996. They also claimed it was passing off. The court held that the use of the rose itself was not a breach of trademark and that the red rose was more of a national emblem so the action for passing off also failed.[37] Attempts to register 'World Cup' have also failed.[38]

In 2002 Tottenham Hotspur Football Club successfully managed to register the name 'Tottenham' as it successfully argued that the word had come to be associated with the football club rather than the geographical area of London. However, in 2007 when LOCOG applied to register the number '2012' in the UK the Intellectual Property Office made it clear that the number was not distinctive enough to be a trademark and LOCOG later withdrew the application.

Tort of 'passing off'

A specific sports-based case law has developed in the UK and this clarifies what can be registered, what amounts to an infringement of the rights of the registered owner of the mark and how passing off can be used in a sporting context. There are very few Olympic cases in the UK so it is worth looking instead at some of the other sports cases.

The tort of passing off has been developed through case law[39] but very briefly it can be established if:

- the claimant's goods or services have acquired a goodwill or reputation in the market and are known by some distinguishing feature; and
- there is a misrepresentation by the defendant (whether or not intentional) leading or likely to lead the public to believe that goods or services offered by the defendant are goods or services of the claimant; and
- the claimant has suffered, or is likely to suffer, damage as a result of the erroneous belief engendered by the defendant's misrepresentation.

In *Trebor Bassett Ltd v The Football Association (FA) Ltd*, Trebor, a confectionery manufacturer, produced football cards (sold with their sweets) showing photographs of the England football team in their playing kit which carried the 'three lions' logo, a trademark of the FA. The FA brought an action for trademark infringement. However, the application was struck out as the use of the 'three lions' logo was incidental and there was no association with the FA trademark itself.[40]

In *BBC v TalkSport*, the BBC was the official broadcaster in the UK for the Euro 2000 football tournament. TalkSport, a British radio station, was not a member of the European Broadcasting Union and was therefore denied access to the stadiums. TalkSport commentators sat in front of a television set and described to their radio listeners what they saw on the screen. The BBC sued for passing off, claiming that TalkSport was representing, by the use of sound effects, that its commentary came from inside the stadiums. The claim was rejected as it was not established that the BBC had acquired goodwill in the broadcast and the BBC had not demonstrated that it had suffered damage.[41] However, TalkSport was required to formally inform listeners that they were not the 'Official Broadcaster' for the tournament.

---

37 *RFU and Nike v Cotton Traders Ltd* [2002] EWHC 467 (Ch). Also note that Liverpool Football Club was unable to register the Liver Bird as a Trademark; see McCahearty, M, 'Trademarks: Liverpool FC withdraws its "Liver Bird" application' (2008) 6(1) IASL.
38 See op. cit., fn 1, Lewis and Taylor (2009), Chapter G1.114.
39 See *Reckitt & Colman Products Ltd v Borden Inc* [1990] RPC 341; *Erven Warnink BV v J Townend & Sons (Hull) Ltd* [1979] AC 731.
40 [1997] FSR 211 Ch D.
41 (2001) Fleet Street Reports 53.

In *Irvine v TalkSport*,[42] Eddie Irvine, a Formula One racing driver, sued TalkSport for passing off. The radio station had edited a photograph of Irvine holding a mobile phone by removing the phone and instead superimposing a radio bearing the TalkSport name. It was held that this was a form of 'passing off' as Irvine was misrepresented as endorsing the radio station. Irvine was initially awarded damages of only £2,000 having sought £50,000. On appeal this was raised to £25,000 as the court stated that it should be realistic and reflect the amount that Irvine would have received if he had endorsed TalkSport.[43]

It is interesting to note that as the sports market becomes more advanced, the types of marks which are being protected are expanding beyond just the name and logo. For instance, Damon Hill, the Formula One racing driver, registered an image of his eyes looking out from his helmet as a trademark. Australian Olympian Ian Thorpe has registered his nickname 'Thorpedo'.[44] Whilst not a trademark case, in 2004, David Bedford, a former long-distance runner from the 1970s, complained to Ofcom that a television advertisement for the directory enquiries number 118 118 had used his image without permission and created a caricature of him. The complaint was upheld as Ofcom believed the athlete's running kit and style were distinctive enough that the agreed advert did refer to him.[45]

The case of *Arsenal Football Club Plc v Reed* also considered both trademark infringement and passing off. The defendant, Mr Reed, had been selling Arsenal memorabilia and souvenirs from a stall at the entrance to the Arsenal stadium for over thirty years. His stall displayed a notice indicating that the products sold by him were not official products from Arsenal Football Club. The club had registered the words 'Arsenal' and 'Arsenal Gunners' and logos depicting the Arsenal crest and the Arsenal cannon. Arsenal sued for trademark infringement and for passing off. In the first instance, the court rejected the passing off action because of the use of the disclaimer notice and because no evidence had been presented of confusion. In relation to the trademark infringement the defendant denied that he had used the registered trademarks and claimed that the products were merely a badge of support, loyalty and allegiance.

The case was referred to the European Court of Justice for a ruling on this aspect of the case. The ruling specified that it was irrelevant whether the use was a badge of loyalty, the test was whether use of the sign was likely to affect or jeopardise the guarantee of origin, which was considered an essential function of the trade mark. Put another way, the sale of Mr Reed's merchandise meant that goods not coming from Arsenal, but bearing the registered trade marks, were in circulation. That affected the ability of the trade marks to guarantee the origin of the goods.

The case was remitted back to the High Court. The judge found that the ECJ had exceeded its authority and had made findings of fact. He felt compelled to rely on the evidence presented at the original trial and found in favour of the defendant. The football club appealed to the Court of Appeal, who re-examined the ECJ ruling and found that the use by Mr Reed did amount to a trade mark infringement. Additional evidence was presented which showed that there were instances of confusion, albeit few, and that some consumers, seeing identical signs to Arsenal's registered marks, had complained to the club.[46]

US trade mark law

The US sports industry is quite different from that in the UK and Europe and it is therefore interesting to have some information, for comparative purposes, on US trade mark legislation and case

---

42 Compare to the much earlier case of *Tolley v Fry*, [1931] AC 333, where the athlete successfully sued for defamation.
43 *Irvine & Ors v TalkSport Ltd* [2002] 1 WLR 2355.
44 *Torpedoes Sportwear Pty Ltd v Thorpedo Enterprises Pty Ltd* [2003] FCA 901 Australia (27 August 2003).
45 'Runner wins 118 118 image rights battle', *The Guardian*, 27 January 2004, http://www.guardian.co.uk/media/2004/jan/27/newmedia.advertising; 'Outcome of appeal by The Number (UK) Ltd regarding complaint by David Bedford', Ofcom, 27 January 2004, http://stakeholders.ofcom.org.uk/enforcement/advertising-complaints-bulletins/appeal-the-number-david-bedford.
46 *Arsenal Football Club Plc v Reed* [2001] RPC 922 and [2002] EWHC 2695 (Ch) and [2003] ECWA Civ 696.

law. The Federal Trademark Act of 1946, commonly known as 'The Lanham Act', is the federal statute in the US which governs the law in relation to registration of trade marks. It defines a trade mark as 'any word, name, symbol or device, or any combination thereof used by a person, or which a person has bona fide intention to use in commerce to identify and distinguish his or her goods, including a unique product, from those manufactured or sold by others and to indicate the source of goods, even if that source is unknown.'[47]

The Act also sets out the remedies and enforcement procedures against infringements by third parties. Anyone who, without the consent of the registrant, counterfeits a trade mark or a service mark for the purposes of causing confusion, mistake or deception regarding the origin, sponsorship or approval of the mark, shall be liable in a civil action by the mark registrant.

To establish a trade mark infringement under s 114 of the Act five criteria must be met:

- There must be a reproduction, counterfeit copy or colourable imitation of a mark;
- The reproduction must occur without the consent of the registrant;
- The reproduction must be used in commerce;
- The use must be in connection with the sale, offering for sale, distribution or advertising of goods or services;
- The use of the reproduction must be likely to cause confusion or to cause mistake or to deceive.

Damages can only be recovered if it can be established that the acts have been committed with knowledge that such imitation is intended to be used to cause confusion or to cause mistake or to deceive.

The USA has started to develop case law particularly on trade mark infringement involving professional sports teams and leagues and their logos.[48] The case law has reiterated that the 'likely to cause confusion' element is an essential factor. A case will be successful if the public believes the goods are endorsed by the professional sports club or league. In order to establish this, the plaintiff has to produce survey evidence of what the public perception is.[49]

In addition to the existing trade mark legislation, the USA also has unique legislation which protects the Olympic symbols and designations. The Olympic and Amateur Sports Act 1978,[50] also known as the Ted Stevens Act, gives the United States Olympic Committee (USOC) exclusive domestic jurisdiction over Olympic related marks, such as the five-ring symbol, and terminology, such as the words Olympic and Olympiad and the motto 'Citius, Altius, Fortius'.

The USOC has the exclusive right to license use of these marks and they have the power to pursue civil action against unauthorised commercial use of any protected trade mark, symbol, insignia or emblem. Exceptions permitted by the Act are:

- Grandfather rights – if the use commenced before 21 September 1950 then it may continue for the same purpose, i.e. for the same goods or services.
- Olympic Mountains – if the use refers to this district in the State of Washington and it is clear that it does not refer to the USOC or any Olympic activity and the use is contained to that area or any use outside the area is not substantial then it is permitted.

---

47 15 USC § 1051–1127 (1946).
48 See *Dallas Cowboys Cheerleaders Inc v Pussycat Cinema Ltd* [1979] 604 F. 2d 200, 204–05 (2nd Cir 1979); *National Football League Properties Inc v Wichita Falls Sportswear Inc* [1982] 532 F. Supp. 651 (WD Wash 1982); *National Football League Properties Inc v New Jersey Giants Inc* [1986] 637 F Supp 507 (DNJ 1986) and *Boston Athletic Association v Sullivan*, 867 F. 2d 22 (1st Cir 1989).
49 See Greenburg, M and Gray, J *Sports Law Practice* (1998), New York: Lexis Law, and Berry, R and Wong, G, *Law and Business of the Sports Industries: Common Issues in Amateur and Professional Sports* (1998) New York: Praeger Publishers, for further analysis of these and other US trade mark cases.
50 36 USC Sec 220501.

The Act grants special provision and protections in Section 380 which are broader than trademark rights. In the case of counterfeit use of the Olympic marks or terminology, all that needs to be established is that such use was not authorised by the USOC. In the case of a simulation of a protected mark or slogan the USOC does not need to prove that the alleged infringer's use creates a likelihood of confusion. The wording of the statute refers to 'tending to cause confusion', and this lesser burden of proof makes it easier for the USOC to successfully prevent unauthorised use of Olympic marks and designations. This can be illustrated by the case law.

For example, in the case of *San Francisco Arts and Athletics Inc (SFAA) v USOC*,[51] the SFAA were promoting the Gay Olympic Games. USOC brought action in the Federal District Court, where they were granted judgment and a permanent injunction. The Court of Appeal upheld this and so did the US Supreme Court. The US Supreme Court held that:

San Francisco Arts and Athletics Inc (SFAA) v USOC

The protection offered to the USOC's use of the Olympic words and symbols differs from the normal trademark protection in two respects: the USOC need not prove that a contested use is likely to cause confusion and an unauthorised user of the word does not have available the normal statutory defences . . . Congress could reasonably conclude that most commercial uses of the Olympic words and symbols are likely to be confusing. It also could determine that unauthorised uses, even if not confusing, nevertheless may harm the USOC by lessening the distinctiveness and thus the commercial value of the Marks.[52]

Another interesting element of US sport-specific trade mark case law has been the long-standing case brought by a group of American Indians to prevent the use of the NFL team trade mark 'Washington Redskins' on the basis that the term 'Redskins' is derogatory, offensive and disparaging to American Indians. The case commenced in 1992 in the district courts and progressed slowly until it was concluded in the federal court that the American Indians had waited too long to bring the action, the original trade mark having been registered in 1967. In November 2009 the US Supreme Court declined to hear the case.[53]

Patents and designs

The intellectual property rights to protect patents and designs are somewhat less important in a sports event context. Patents are, simply put, the way to protect inventions and innovations and designs are the way to protect a design, aesthetic shape or configuration. These rights can be relevant if the event owner is also manufacturing items such as sporting equipment.

An interesting example concerns the recent re-design of cricket bats. In 2004 Kookaburra Bats introduced a new bat with a colourful fibreglass sheet glued on to the back of the bat. The bat was ruled to be in contravention of the Laws of Cricket and has since been withdrawn. In 2006 Newbery patented and issued a new cricket bat with a carbon-fibre-enhanced handle. The bat was also ruled to be in contravention of the Laws of Cricket. The Marylebone Cricket Club (MCC), which owns the Laws, amended them in October 2008 so as to maintain the traditional construction and

51 *San Francisco Arts and Athletics Inc (SFAA) v USOC* 483 US 522 107 S. ct.2971, 97 L Ed 2d 427 (US 1987).
52 Ibid. Op. cit., fn 49, Berry and Wong (2008) p 671, 'Trademark Law and the Olympics'.
53 See Cummings, A and Harper, S, 'Wide Right: Why the NCCA's policy on American Indian mascot issue misses the mark' (2009), University of Maryland Law Journal of Race, Religion, Gender and Class, 135; Behrendt, K, 'Cancellation of the Washington Redskins' Federal Trademark Registrations: Should Sports Team Names, Mascots and Logos Contain Native American Symbolism?' (2000) 10 Seton Hall J Sport L 389; Brock, L, 'A New Approach to an Old Problem: Could California's Proposed Ban on "Redskins" Mascots in Public Schools Have Withstood a Constitutional Challenge?' (2005) 12 Sports Law J 71; Brown, K, 'Native American Team Names and Mascots: Disparaging and Insensitive or Just a Part of the Game?' (2002) 9 Sports Law J 115.

performance of cricket bats and to restrict the introduction of potentially performance-enhancing materials.[54]

In 2008 another new bat, the Mongoose MMi3, was launched specifically with Twenty20 cricket in mind. The revolutionary design, with a shorter blade and a longer handle, enables the batsman to hit the ball faster, harder and further. After some detailed discussions with the MCC, finally, in 2010, the bat was declared to be in compliance with the Laws of Cricket and it is now being used by cricketers all around the world. The Mongoose bat is protected by a range of intellectual property registrations including an International Patent, a UK Patent, European Community Design protection and a UK Trade Mark.

Another interesting aspect is whether or not an athlete's 'sports move' or specific 'sports technique' can be protected. In the UK it is unlikely, but in the USA there are more possibilities if patentability requirements of utility, novelty and non-obviousness can be established.[55]

Copyright

Copyright is an area which is of huge importance to sports and sports events particularly because copyright exists in all the broadcasts, sound recordings, filming, commentary, highlights packages, etc. Also, with the growth of the internet, all content on websites would be subject to copyright protection. So too would all the numerous documents produced by an OCOG which are essential to run such a huge international event, such as venue operations manuals, logistics manuals, spectator guides and volunteer handbooks.

In the UK, copyright protections are governed by the Copyright Designs and Patents Act 1988 (as amended). The law can protect:

- literary works, including novels, instruction manuals, computer programs, song lyrics, newspaper articles and some types of databases;
- dramatic works, including dance or mime;
- musical works;
- artistic works, including paintings, engravings, photographs, sculptures, collages, architecture, technical drawings, diagrams, maps and logos;
- recordings of a work, including sound and film;
- broadcasts of a work.

For an Olympic Games, as well as the broadcast and documents mentioned above, the theme songs and music used in the opening and closing ceremony would also be subject to copyright protection by the OCOG. The IOC also has copyright protection in the Olympic Hymn (anthem) which was first performed at the 1896 Athens Olympic Games opening ceremony.[56]

The scope of copyright rights can be varied by contractual arrangement. For example, if an OCOG commissions a graphic artist to design a specific event logo, that artist would automatically own the copyright in that logo. So the contract commissioning the work would specify that the design artist would assign his/her copyright in the logo to both the OCOG and the IOC. The IOC/OCOG would then grant a licence to enable parties to copy and utilise the copyrighted material. The terms of the licence would clearly state the rights and obligations of both licensor and licensee and,

---

54 See 'Changes to the Law concerning Cricket Bats: A guide for Manufacturers', http://www.lords.org/data/files/changes-to-the-law-concerning-cricket-bats-manufactures-10184.pdf.
55 See Smith, J, 'It's Your Move – No it's Not!: The Application of Patent Law to Sports Moves' (2000) U Colo L Rev 1051, and Kieff, F, Kramer, R and Kunstadt, R 'It's your turn but is my move: Intellectual Property Protection for Sports "Moves" ' (2009) 25 Santa Clara Computer & High Tech LJ 765.
56 For further reading on intellectual property law see Bentley, L and Sherman, B, *Intellectual Property Law* 3rd edn (2009), Oxford: OUP and Cornish, W, *Intellectual Property: Patents, Copyrights, Trademarks and Allied Rights*, 7th edn (2010), London: Sweet and Maxwell.

in the case of the contracts relating to the Olympics, would also contain specific clauses to ensure that the licensee would not act in a manner which would adversely affect or impair the Olympic marketing rights.[57]

Database rights

Intellectual property protection for a database is a new right which has been established and discussed a great deal in the last decade in a sporting context. A database is defined as a collection of data or other material that is arranged in such a way that the items are individually accessible. In the UK, for copyright protection to apply, the database must have originality in the selection or arrangement of the contents, and for a database right to apply, there must have been a substantial investment in obtaining, verifying or presenting the database contents.

There is no registration for database right – it is an automatic right like copyright and commences as soon as the material that can be protected exists in a recorded form. In the UK a database right lasts for 15 years from when it was made but, if it is published during this time, then the term is 15 years from publication.

In the case *William Hill and the British Horseracing Board*,[58] the claimant bookmakers tested this new area of intellectual property law.

Stephens, K, 'British Horseracing Board (BHB) v. William Hill (WH): The race is never lost, till won'

In the *BHB v. WH* case, Laddie J held that BHB's database was protected by database rights. The database comprised a huge number of records relating to horseracing, including the names of horses, owners, trainers, jockeys, as well as the fixture lists. He also held that WH's use of the fixture lists on its Internet betting site was an infringement of those database rights.

WH appealed. The Court of Appeal, whilst referring various questions to the ECJ, appeared broadly supportive of the position taken by Laddie J. Advocate General Stix-Hack also gave an opinion in BHB's favour. However, and much to my surprise, the ECJ did not follow the AG's opinion, instead giving a judgment very much in favour of WH.

Database rights defined

The Directive defines a database for both the purposes of database protection and copyright protection as: a collection of independent works, data or other materials arranged in a systematic or methodical way and individually accessible by electronic or other means.

The ECJ stated that a database should be defined very broadly. Thus, any collection of independent works is covered, provided that each work can be separately retrieved. Consequently, not only will those things which are normally thought of as databases qualify, including contact lists, telephone directories and compilations of copyright works such as collections of poems, but also websites, newspapers, magazines and training manuals.

Database rights exist where: there has been qualitatively and/or quantitatively a substantial investment in either the obtaining, verification or presentation of the contents.

In a key part of its judgment, the ECJ held that the investment has to be in the obtaining, verification or presentation of the contents of the database. This is to be distinguished from the investment in the data itself which cannot be taken into account when considering whether the investment has been substantial.

The ECJ provided the following definitions: 'obtaining' – seeking out and collecting the data in the database; 'verification' – ensuring the reliability of the information contained in the database

---

57 See above section on licensing, p 310.
58 *British Horseracing Board & the Jockey Club v William Hill Organisation Ltd* [2001] EWHC 517 and ECJ Case C-203/02 [2004] ECR I-10415.

and monitoring its accuracy; and 'presentation' – the arrangement of the data in the database. The requirement for 'quantitative' investment refers to quantifiable resources, whereas 'qualitative' investment refers to efforts which could not be quantified such as intellectual effort or energy.

Infringement occurs where there has been: extraction and/or re-utilization of the whole or of a substantial part, evaluated qualitatively and/or quantitatively, of the contents of that database . . .

(a) 'extraction' – the permanent or temporary transfer of all or a substantial part of the contents of a database to another medium by any means or in any form;

(b) 're-utilization' – any form of making available to the public all or a substantial part of the contents of a database by the distribution of copies, by renting, by on-line or other forms of transmission. The first sale of a copy of a database within the Community by the right holder or with his consent shall exhaust the right to control resale of that copy within the Community.

The ECJ held that, on the question of whether a part of a database is quantitatively or qualitatively substantial, reference has to be made to the investment in that database and the prejudice caused to that investment by the infringement. Thus, there will be infringement where the volume of data taken by the infringer is substantial when compared to the total volume of the contents of the database, i.e. it is quantitatively substantial. Further, a quantitatively negligible part of the database which requires significant human, technical or financial investment may amount to a 'substantial part evaluated qualitatively' when compared to the scale of investment in the obtaining, verifying and presenting of the contents of the database.

Both 'extraction' and 're-utilisation' have wide meanings, referring to any unauthorised act of appropriation or distribution. Neither term implies that the infringer has to have direct access to the database concerned. Third parties can consult a published database, but the maker's rights are not exhausted by such publication. As a consequence, the contents of the database can be protected even if the infringer obtains the data from an intermediate source such as a newspaper or the Internet.

Infringement also occurs where there has been: the repeated and systematic extraction and/or re-utilisation of insubstantial parts of the contents of the database implying acts which conflict with a normal exploitation of that database or which unreasonably prejudice the legitimate interests of the maker of the database shall not be permitted.

The ECJ held that infringement only occurs if the cumulative effect of the extraction or re-utilisation leads to the reconstitution of the database as a whole or a substantial part of it and thereby seriously prejudices the investment made by the database maker.

Applying the definitions in the *BHB v. WH* case

The ECJ found that the resources deployed by BHB in the selection of the horses admitted to run in each race related to the creation of the data and not the database. In other words, the investment was not independent of the resources spent on creating the database, despite the fact that the process of entering a horse in a race requires a significant number of checks as to the identity of the person making the entry, the horse, its owner and the jockey. Since such investment was not of the right sort, no account could be taken of it when considering whether database rights existed in the database.

Further, the ECJ found that WH had not taken a quantitative or qualitative substantial part of the database, despite the fact that the data were vital to the organisation of horse races, because no account could be taken of the intrinsic value of the data. As a consequence of its findings that the investment made by BHB in such data was not of the right sort for the purposes of whether database rights existed, the ECJ stated that the same data could not comprise, in qualitative terms, a substantial part of the database.

The ECJ also found that there was 'no possibility' that through their actions of putting information relating to each day's races on the Internet, WH might reconstitute the whole or a substantial part of BHB's database.

As a consequence, the ECJ clearly signalled that, in its view, database rights did not exist in the BHB database. In any event, WH did not infringe those rights by taking either a substantial part or insubstantial parts.

. . . and in the Fixtures Marketing cases

These three cases were referred to the ECJ from Sweden, Finland and Greece. Fixtures Marketing is backed by the Football Association and others and handles the exploitation of the football fixtures lists for the Premier League, the Football League and the Scottish Football League. Before the start of each season, the fixtures lists are drawn up. The fixtures lists are set out both chronologically and by reference to each team participating in the relevant league. In both Sweden and Finland, Fixtures Marketing objected to the defendant's use of the data in the fixtures lists in pools betting. In Greece, the defendant used the data on its Internet site.

The ECJ held, following the broad definition it had given to databases, that the football fixtures lists qualified as databases. The date of the matches, the time and identity of the teams were all independent data. The fact that lots were drawn to decide which teams played each other was irrelevant.

However, the ECJ was of the view that finding and collecting the data which makes up football fixture lists does not require any particular effort on the part of the professional leagues as those activities are indivisibly linked to their responsibility to create those data. Further, no particular effort is required in monitoring the accuracy of the data and that its presentation is too closely linked to the data's creation to be taken into account. Therefore, the ECJ found that there was no independent investment in the database over and above that put into creating the data. In other words, it accepted the argument that the database was merely a spin-off of the work done in putting together the fixtures lists.

In the light of its findings, the ECJ held that further questions related to infringement did not need a reply.

Consequences for BHB

The case will be returned to the Court of Appeal which will have to consider how to apply the judgment of ECJ. Unusually for the ECJ, it applied its construction of the Directive to the facts in the case. Those finding contrast with statements made by the Court of Appeal and Laddie J. In particular, the Courts found that BHB had expended considerable costs, of the order of £4 million per annum, in the development and maintenance of the database, a significant and painstaking process which involved approximately 80 employees.

The Court of Appeal would be entitled to disregard any conclusion reached by the ECJ, in so far as it was based upon a factual background inconsistent with its judgment. No doubt this will be the subject of the parties' submissions before the Court of Appeal, as it was in *Arsenal Football Club v Reed*. In that case the Court of Appeal held that the conclusions of the ECJ were not inconsistent with the findings of fact and Laddie J. should have followed the ruling of the ECJ. The outcome of the Court of Appeal's decision is awaited with interest.

If the Court of Appeal follows the ECJ's findings, it will have a significant impact on horseracing in the UK. At present, a large proportion of funding for the horseracing industry is derived from a payment to the Levy Board made by the betting industry on a statutory basis which is then distributed back into racing. Following a Competition Act inquiry by the Office of Fair Trading ('OFT'), which was published a few days after the AG's opinions, BHB announced that, as part of a package to modernise British horseracing, it would be replacing the levy by a licence fee. The fee would be payable by all betting companies before they could make use of racecard information, such as runners and riders, derived from BHB's database. The current plan is for the Levy Board to close on 30 September 2006. The ECJ's judgment therefore threatens to jeopardise the whole of BHB's modernisation plans for the horseracing industry.

. . . and for Fixtures Marketing

The cases will now be returned to their national courts. Fixtures Marketing is unlikely to prevail, given that the ECJ clearly held that establishing the dates, times and the team pairings did not attest to substantial investment which could justify database right protection in the football fixtures lists, despite the fact that £11.5 million per annum is spent on the upkeep of the fixtures lists.

The ECJ's judgment came at a difficult time in negotiations for the 2004–5 UK season between the Newspaper Publishers Association, who negotiate on behalf of all newspaper publishers, and Football DataCo, the company charged with exploiting the fixtures lists on behalf of the football leagues in the UK. Football DataCo was reportedly seeking restrictions on use of pictures from Premier League and Football League matches, and licences for use of league match data in newspapers' fantasy football league competitions. I have since found one report stating that these negotiations have been concluded, and that 'Fleet Street seems to have won'.

Wider implications

The effect of the ECJ's judgments is to rein in database rights, particularly in relation to what is protected. The requirement for investment to be in the creation of the database, as opposed to the data, is a significant hurdle for database owners to overcome.

Distinguishing between monies spent on collecting data and monies spent on creating data will be very difficult for some companies, such as BHB, which create both the data and the database. They may therefore fail to prove that they have a protectable database. Companies which do not create the data, merely collect them, as in telephone directories, will not have such a problem. Companies in the first category should, therefore, consider whether they need to restructure their organisation so that the functional aspects of creating the data and creating the database are kept separate and are separately budgeted.

Another difficulty arising out of the ECJ's judgments is how to effectively protect large databases. The ECJ held that no infringement will occur unless the investment in the whole database is prejudiced. As BHB found, small, but intrinsically valuable pieces of data, will not be protected. One solution may be to chop a large database into a number of smaller databases, making it easier to prove that there has been a substantial taking of the whole, or a number of insubstantial takings which cumulatively amount to a substantial part of the whole.

The ECJ's judgments may also cause concern regarding the potential to create monopolies in raw data where those data come from a single source. The point can be clearly demonstrated using the facts in the Fixtures Marketing cases. The data on the pools coupons comes from various sources including daily newspapers, teletext and the football teams themselves. But all this data will have been sourced indirectly from the Fixtures Marketing database at one stage or another. Following the ECJ's judgments, it will be no defence to say that the information was sourced from publicly available information. However, the effect of this is very much watered down by the other aspects of the ECJ's judgment.

One effect of the ECJ's judgments will be to turn attention again to whether a database can be protected by copyright. The database right differs materially from copyright in both duration, 15 years, and scope. (It should be noted that the ECJ did not refer to the existence of a rolling right in dynamic databases. But the definition given to the word 'substantial' will in any event curtail, and in most cases extinguish, the possibility of such a right existing.)

For copyright protection to apply to a database, the database has to be the author's own intellectual creation. This is a significant qualitative hurdle: sheer 'sweat of the brow' will not do. Nevertheless, claimants may be able to rely on copyright in those databases in which the investment has not been substantial, but the resulting database could not have been created by many others and therefore qualifies as the author's own intellectual creation. Such situations are likely to be few.

To conclude, the effects of the ECJ's judgments will be significant for two major reasons. Firstly, securing database right protection will be more difficult since investment has to be of the right sort. Secondly, the ECJ's narrow construction given to the infringement provisions will mean that proving infringement will be more difficult unless there has been wholesale copying from the database.[59]

The more recent case involving database protection for football fixtures was considered by the English Courts twice in 2010. The High Court ruled in the case of *Football Dataco Limited v Brittens Pools and Yahoo!*[60] that football fixture lists may be protected by a form of UK copyright, database copyright. However, other forms of protection, notably the EU-wide database right, were held not to apply to the fixture lists in question. The Court of Appeal referred specific questions to the European Court of Justice (ECJ) asking whether the High Court was correct to find that database copyright exists under the Database Directive for English and Scottish football fixture lists.[61] At the time of writing the ECJ case has not yet been heard.[62]

In the USA two cases have considered the rights to sports scores: *NBA v Motorola, Inc*[63] and *Morris Communications v PGA Tour.*[64] The *Motorola* court determined that real-time sports scores are mere facts that no one can own, while the *PGA Tour* court suggested that a compilation of scores constitutes property that the company who created the compilation may legally protect.[65]

Ambush Marketing

What do we mean when we use the term 'ambush marketing'?

Meenaghan, T, 'Ambush marketing a threat to corporate sponsorship'

By purchasing sponsorship, a sponsor seeks to attract the attention that an event generates to its own product. In a typical sponsorship arrangement, a sponsor purchases the sponsorship property rights and does further promotion to draw attention to itself. In ambush marketing another company, often a competitor, intrudes, thereby deflecting attention to itself and away from the sponsor. The term was initially coined to describe the activities of a company that associated itself with an event without paying the requisite fee to the event owner.'[66]

LOCOG, *Business – What you need to know: Brand protection*

Also known as parasitic or guerrilla marketing, ambush marketing describes a business's attempts to attach itself to a major sports event without paying sponsorship fees. As a result,

---

59 Stephens, K, 'British Horseracing Board (BHB) v.William Hill (WH): The race is never lost, till won' (2005) January, Institute of Trade Mark Attorneys Review, also see White, N, 'The Database Right and The Spin Off Theory' (2005) 3/4 ISL J; Duthie, M, 'Database Rights – The Form Guide', (2001) 8(2) SLA&P; and op. cit., fn 1, Lewis and Taylor (2009), Chapter G1 6 B. The relevant 'fixture marketing cases' are Fixtures Marketing Ltd v Oy Veikkaus AB (C-46/02); Fixtures Marketing Ltd. Svenska Spel AB (C-338/02); Fixtures Marketing Ltd v Organismos Prognostikon Agonon Podosfairou (C-444/02).

60 [2010] EWHC 841 (Ch) April 2010 [2010] WLR (D) 104.

61 [2010] EWCA Civ 1380 December 2010.

62 See Fitzpatrick, N, 'Sporting Data: Rights in sporting data after Football Dataco v Stan James' (2010) 18 (6) WSLR; Wentworth, M, 'Database Directive offers protection for fixture lists' (2010) 8(4) WSLR.

63 NBA v Motorola, Inc, 105 F. 3d 841, 2d Cir. 1997

64 Morris Communications Corp v PGA Tour, Inc, 235 F. Supp. 2d 1269, 1274 (MD Fla 2002) and 364 F.3d 1288 Eleventh Circuit Court of Appeals 2004.

65 See Freeman, A, 'Morris Communications v PGA Tour: Battle over the Rights to Real-Time Sports Scores' (2005) 20(3) Berkeley Technology Law Journal.

66 Meenaghan, T. 'Ambush marketing – a threat to corporate sponsorship' (1996) 38(1) Sloan Management Review 103–13.

the business gains the benefits of being associated with the goodwill and public excitement around the event for free. This damages the investment of genuine sponsors, and risks the organiser's ability to fund the event.[67]

Of course, with such a wide definition all incidents of counterfeiting, trademark infringement and cybersquatting would fall into the category of ambush marketing as well.

Why do companies ambush?

- The official marketing programme is too expensive.
- The official marketing programme is limited in the number of sponsors it can have.
- The official marketing programme may already have a long-standing relationship with their competitor; for example, Coca-Cola's link with the Olympics since 1938 means that Pepsi Cola has no opportunity to become an official sponsor.
- Their product may be prohibited from the official marketing programme; tobacco products, for instance, are not allowed to advertise with the Olympics.
- They may just view it as creative marketing. It makes good business sense to get the exposure without paying for it.

Let us consider the last point here. Is it just smart business practice to ambush your competitor or is it unethical? Of course, the answer depends on whom you are addressing the question to. Event owners and official marketing partners who have a stake in the outcome argue that, yes, it is unethical. It threatens the integrity and financial viability of the event. What if everyone was to participate in ambush marketing? There would be confusion in the marketplace as to who the official sponsors are. Sponsors would lose their exclusive marketing rights and commercial association with the event. The value of sponsorship would diminish to such a level that companies would not be willing to pay for an official association with the event and, worse yet, they may drop out and join the ranks of the ambushers. As we have seen above, the Olympic movement is dependent upon marketing revenue and without it the Games and sports worldwide would suffer. In the opinion of event owners and official sponsors, ambush or parasitic marketing threatens the whole structure of sports sponsorship:

Heiberg, Gerhard (IOC Executive Board member)

The IOC and its partners in the Olympic Movement take the threat of ambush marketing very seriously . . . Ultimately, companies which try to create the false impression that they are an official partner of the Olympic Games, or create a false association with the Olympic Games, are cheating Olympic athletes . . . It is important that the public is made aware of these organizations and how they are depriving the Olympic Games and sport development around the world of essential support.[68]

Non-sponsoring companies and ambush marketers argue that it is just good business practice. They are exercising their right to free speech. They use economic justification to serve their own interests. They argue that they owe it to their shareholders to use sports events to their commercial advantage. It is just creative and clever advertising used to sell their products or services. For them it is just part of the normal cut and thrust of business, and ethics do not come into it. Many also adopt the view that if the ambush is legal, the law doesn't care so why should they?

---

67 LOCOG publication, *Business – What you need to know: Brand protection*, http://www.london2012.com/documents/brand-guidelines/guidelines-for-business-use.pdf.
68 Heiberg, G, an IOC Executive Board Member who chairs its Marketing Commission, as reported on USOC website and Reuters, http://www.reuters.com/article/2010/02/12/olympics-marketing-idUSLDE61A2ZG20100212.

Schmitz JK, 'Ambush Marketing: The Off-Field Competition at the Olympic Games'

People think ambush marketing hurts the Olympics? Good. Who cares? Are the Olympics going to disappear from the planet? I don't think so. This isn't religion or virginity here, it's business. Marketing is a form of warfare, and the ambush is a hell of a weapon.[69]

Which brings us to the question: so what is the legal position relating to ambush marketing?

In the UK, ambush marketing can be countered by bringing an action for trade mark infringement, but it is difficult to establish that ambush marketing is such an infringement. The plaintiff has to show likelihood of confusion and that they have suffered relevant damage as a result of the defendant's activities. If there is no registered trade mark the tort of passing off has to be used and this is difficult to establish.[70]

In the USA a lawsuit against an ambush marketer trying to benefit commercially from the Olympic Games, without authority, could be based on several legal provisions: the Lanham Act and the common law. As discussed above, the Lanham Act is the principal federal statute which protects against trade mark infringement. The key factor in establishing a successful claim under this legislation is to show that there is a likelihood of confusion. In the case of ambush marketing, is the public confused as to source of goods, sponsorship of the event, characteristics and/or quality of the goods.

Bean, L, 'Ambush Marketing: Sports sponsorship and the Lanham Act'

Section 43(a) of the Lanham Act combines these two goals by providing a civil cause of action for use of a mark if it is likely to cause confusion, mistake or deception as to the affiliation or association of that entity with another. As such, section 43(a) may prohibit competition from an entity that falsely develops an association with the trademark, thereby deceiving and diminishing the owner's market. It is within this arena of trademark protection, the protection of business interests, that the courts and trademark owners seek to prevent ambush marketing.[71]

Bean's article continues by outlining the courts' response to such claims, the plaintiff's burden of proof and some of the common defences adopted by defendants. These include the following:

- use of disclaimers;[72]
- laches, where the defendant states the plaintiff unreasonably delayed filing the action;
- First Amendment rights: in the US these grant freedom of speech which includes commercial speech, as long as such speech is not false, deceptive, disparaging or misleading;
- antitrust provisions which prevent interference with legitimate free competition;
- challenges to survey evidence which is produced by the plaintiff to show the public's likelihood of confusion.

It is impossible to consider, in this chapter, all aspects of the common law provisions of unfair competition in the USA, particularly as they vary depending on the individual states. However, the equivalent action in the USA to the tort of passing off, misappropriation, where one business alleges another has damaged its goodwill or reputation through the use of false representation of products or services, should be considered.

---

69 Schmitz, J, 'Ambush Marketing: The Off-Field Competition at the Olympic Games' (2005) NW J Tech & Intell Prop 203, http://www.law.northwestern.edu/journals/njtip/v3/n2/6/.

70 See *Trebor Bassett v FA Ltd* and *Arsenal Football Club plc v Matthew Reed* discussed under trade mark infringement above, pp 320–1.

71 Bean, L, 'Ambush Marketing: Sports sponsorship and the Lanham Act' (2005) Boston University Law Review.

72 The use of disclaimers is discussed at length in the case of *Home Box Office Inc v Showtime the Movie Channel*, 56 USLW 2336 4 USPQ 2D Nov 3 (1987).

In the case of *NFL v Governor of Delaware*,[73] the district court held that the State of Delaware's football lottery did not constitute a misappropriation of league property even though the lottery was based on NFL games. In the later case of *Boston Athletic Association v Mark Sullivan*,[74] the court agreed that the defendant was trying to cash in on the plaintiff's goodwill by creating the false impression that their T-shirt business was in some way approved or endorsed by the plaintiff. The plaintiff organised the Boston Marathon and had registered marks related to that event. The defendant's T-shirts infringed those marks. To date there have been no cases brought by the United States Olympic Committee which focus on ambush marketing; all cases have concentrated on trade mark infringement. It therefore remains to be seen how a court in the USA would react to an allegation of consumer confusion over Olympic sponsorship.

The only specific court case to directly address ambush marketing is the Canadian case of *NHL v Pepsi Cola*.[75] Pepsi ambushed the official NHL sponsor, Coke, by running promotional advertisements at the time of the 1990 Stanley Cup ice hockey play-off games. Using a concept similar to that used in the Governor of Delaware case, Pepsi did not use NHL trade marks or names but instead used the names of the cities the teams were from. They also used disclaimers in their advertisements. The Supreme Court of British Columbia dismissed the action as there had been no trade mark infringement and the defendant's actions did not constitute a direct interference with the due performance of the NHL's contractual relationship with Coke. Hangtags were placed over the Pepsi bottles. They contained the rules of the competition and a disclaimer, which stated, 'Diet Pepsi $4,000,000 Pro Hockey Playoff Pool is neither associated with nor sponsored by the NHL or any of its member teams or affiliates.' This was also printed on promotional material and appeared on the bottom of the screen in television advertisements. The court believed that the disclaimers used were sufficient to communicate to the consumers that there was no official affiliation with the NHL, hence there was no likelihood of confusion.

Following the *NHL v Pepsi* case further court actions, unsurprisingly, have not been forthcoming. However, it would be helpful for the courts in the US to conclusively address the issue of ambush marketing. As Bean writes:

Bean, L, 'Ambush Marketing: Sports sponsorship and the Lanham Act'

. . . corporate sponsors and trademark owners are seriously concerned about unfair competition in the realm of sporting events sponsorships. In order to create a strong deterrent against future ambush marketing, courts must explicitly specify their intentions to protect sports sponsorship contracts through contract law, common law, and federal trademark law. Courts' acknowledgement that they will use section 43(a) not only to protect consumer confusion, but also to protect the investments of trademark owners, will set a clear precedent for future litigation. If such a deterrent exists, non-sponsor competitors may think twice before implementing certain advertising and promotional campaigns, and the number of future sporting events or lucrative sponsorship contracts will flourish rather than diminish.[76]

Just by looking at these three cases we can see that, although each case will be taken on its own merits, bringing a successful misappropriation claim is difficult. More recently in the US, the problem of ambush marketing via tattoo advertising was considered in the article below:

---

73 *National Football League v Governor of Delaware et al* 195 USPQ Aug 11 (1977).
74 *Boston Athletic Association v Mark Sullivan* (1989) 867 F 2d 22 1st Cir.
75 *National Hockey League v Pepsi Cola Canada Ltd* 2 BCLR 3rd 3 1995 Feb 17 (1995).
76 Op. cit., fn 71, Bean (2005).

Vukelj, J, 'Post No Bills: Can the NBA Prohibit its Players from Wearing Tattoo Advertisements?'

Tattoo advertising can best be compared to what is known as ambush marketing . . . the tattoo advertiser could defend on the grounds that there is no likelihood of confusion between its mark and that of the NBA. There is no law against aggressive marketing, and no precedent exists for holding a marketer liable for this type of activity. As one commentator has stated, 'The difficulty [for sporting event organizers] with ambush marketing is that the law is on the side of the ambushers. Purely defined, ambush marketing does not involve counterfeiting or the illegal use of trademarks, tradenames or symbols.' It could be argued that ambush marketing – in whatever form it is carried out – is in fact good for consumers. It informs them of more available products and services, and denies the granting of an advertising monopoly in a forum that should be open to more than one advertiser. Rather than confusing the consumer, it can expose the consumer to a greater number of products. The tattoo advertisement is not replacing or displacing an official sponsor's ad. Rather, it is merely adding to the swirl of marketing that already exists in professional sports.[77]

Another interesting consideration is the problem of ambush marketing in the digital age:

Reid, F, 'Combating traditional and "New Age" ambush marketing'

The rapid development of new media technology has provided rights owners with new plat-forms to generate new revenue streams. These include the internet and the provision of 'e-commerce' activities; the introduction of Wireless Application Protocol (WAP) technology and the provision of 'm-commerce' services, all of which are driven by content. To attract subscribers to a new media service or traffic to a website, sports content is seen as vital, and used with and without the authorisation of the rights owner. Unofficial event websites spring up seeking to benefit indirectly from the goodwill generated by an event. Companies or entrepre-neurs register 'domain names' similar to, or, in some cases, the same as the name of an event or sponsored property. Given the number of sports websites and the opportunities available on the Internet to reproduce material and information, rights owners must be especially vigilant of these 'new age' ambushers.

Whilst the Internet provides opportunities for rights holders to exploit new revenue streams it also provides opportunities for ambushers. There are numerous types and princi-pally they concern the registration of 'domain names' and the setting up of unofficial websites.

Event websites are an important additional revenue source for events rights holders. They provide information on fixtures, results and statistics, further opportunities for sponsorships and offer other e-commerce activities, such as ticketing, merchandising and prizes/promotions.

There is little that a rights holder can do against unofficial sites unless they contain regis-tered marks belonging to the event or contain copyright material such as fixtures and sports data owned by the rights holder. If a site has the same design, look and feel of an official site then copyright protection may also be available.

A major problem for rights holders on the Internet has been a practice referred to as 'cyber squatting' in relation to domain name registration. The domain name system (DNS) serves the central function of facilitating users' ability to navigate the Internet. It does so with the aid of two components: the domain name and its corresponding Internet Protocol (IP) number.

---

77 Vukelj, J, 'Post No Bills: Can the NBA Prohibit its Players from Wearing Tattoo Advertisements?' (2005) 15 Fordham Intell Prop Media & Ent LJ, 507.

A domain name is the human-friendly address of a computer, usually in a form easy to remember or identify, such as www.wimbledon.com. Domain names are, effectively, addresses used to call up a location, such as a web page, on the Internet. There is nothing in traditional trade mark law to prevent a business from using the same mark as that belonging to someone else, but using it for dissimilar goods or services, as long as it is not likely to cause confusion. Given there can only be one worldcup.com this raises serious problems for the rights holder if he is not first to register the domain name.

If the rights holder wishes to challenge the registration of the domain name and have that name transferred, a dispute resolution procedure is available under the World Intellectual Property Organisation (WIPO). In order to succeed, the complaint must include, and seek to prove, all of the following information:

(i)   the manner in which the domain name(s) is/are identical or confusingly similar to a trademark or service mark in which the complainant has rights; and

(ii) why the respondent (domain name holder) should be considered as having no rights or legitimate interests in respect of the domain name(s) that is/are the subject of the complaint; and

(iii) why the domain name(s) should be considered as having been registered and being used in bad faith.

By way of illustration, the domain names worldcup.org and worldcup-tv.com were registered by a company called Metplus Communicate. A complaint was initiated by the Fédération Internationale de Football Association (FIFA) and ISL World-wide (FIFA's agents) to obtain a transfer of the domain name back to FIFA, the rights owner. In accordance with the criteria required, it was successfully argued that:

(i)   the subject domain name was almost identical (and, therefore, confusingly similar) to its registered service mark, 'worldcup' (the class of good and services for which this mark was registered did not matter);

(ii) the respondent did not have any rights or legitimate interests in the domain name. (There had been an earlier settlement between the parties, arising out of the Respondent's use of the domain name worldcup.fr as part of which the Respondent agreed that it did not have any rights in the phrase 'worldcup');

(iii) the respondent registered and used the subject domain name in bad faith, because it knew at the time of registration that the Claimant owned the service mark 'worldcup'.

The domain names were subsequently transferred back to FIFA.

Sites are also appearing under the name [x]sucks.com and whilst the principal purpose of these sites is a protest vehicle, the effect is that traffic is attracted on the back of the official site as with 'typo squatting'. Complaints against these types of domain name registrations need to prove that the domain name is 'confusingly similar'. The difficulty lies in establishing 'bad faith'. For instance, had the registered owner of worldcup.org been using the site for a legitimate purpose, then it would have been extremely difficult for FIFA to establish bad faith.

Keyword systems are technological systems permitting terms (keywords) to be resolved to a Uniform Resource Locators (URL) or an e-mail address. They assist Internet users to carry out searches for a particular site or sites that contain the information they require. For instance, in order to benefit from the goodwill generated by the FIFA World Cup, some website owners may use the words 'football' and 'worldcup' as meta tags for attracting traffic to the site. Trademark infringement, if available, would be the appropriate remedy.

The principal lesson to be learned from these illustrations is that the Internet provides new opportunities for rights holders but provides endless opportunities for ambushers. The initiation of careful vigilance and policing methods are prerequisites and should be backed up by utilising the dispute resolution procedures available.

Conclusions

Given the growth of sports marketing and the value of rights now sold, practices such as ambush marketing are viewed very seriously by rights owners.

Ambush marketing – traditional and 'new age' – will never be eradicated and, in some respects, it is arguable that it should be permitted since sponsors would have unfair monopolistic rights over their competitors. A fair balance must be maintained, although the current remedies available in England and Wales do not provide rights owners with adequate protection. In the United States, such marketing practices can violate the Lanham Act (typically, Section 43(a)) if, for example, they convey the false message that a company is an official sponsor when, in fact, it is not.[78]

More recent social media developments such as YouTube, Facebook, blogs, MySpace and smartphone applications, give ambush marketers even more potential and extra vigilance is required to ensure that event owner rights are not infringed.

Ambush marketing and the Olympics

Whilst legal protection against ambush marketing is limited in most jurisdictions, the Olympics is unique in that not only does it have the special legislation discussed above, which protects its intellectual property, but it is also now firmly included in the bid documents for those cities who wish to host an Olympics that if they win the bid they must introduce additional special legislation and local ordinances to enable maximum protection for the Olympic properties and the official Olympic partners.

This special legislation was first introduced in Australia, in New South Wales. The intention was to create precautionary measures to ensure smooth operation of the event and to protect the Olympic brand and image during the Sydney 2000 Olympic Games. The Olympic Arrangements Act 2000 was passed by the New South Wales government to modify existing legislation and to empower a specially convened authority, the Olympic Co-ordination Authority (OCA), to curtail unapproved commercial activities throughout the city of Sydney and other key areas specifically at the time of the Games. In relation to ambush marketing the following preventative steps were covered in the Act:

- the prohibition of certain advertising on buildings and structures;
- the prohibition of certain aerial advertising if visible from the Olympic or Paralympic venues or live sites;
- greater control over airspace above outdoor Olympic/Parlaympic venues and the Olympic/ Paralympic Athlete Village;
- the prevention of sale and distribution of tickets to the events without the approval of OCA;
- the creation of a new offence for selling or distributing articles without OCA approval during the Games period in public places within 3km of an Olympic/Paralympic venue, live site or major transport area such as park and ride. In certain instances items could be seized and forfeit to the Crown.[79]

In the run-up to Athens 2004, similar measures were introduced under Paragraph 7 of the second article of the law N.2833/2000 (Fek A 150), which specifically prohibited during the period from 15 July 2004 to 30 September 2004 the placing or hanging up of advertisements:

---

78 Reid, F, 'Combating traditional and "New Age" ambush marketing' (2001) 4(4) SLB 10; also see White, N, Couchman, N and Harrington, D, 'Ambush Marketing: Major Sporting Events and the Limits of the Law' (2004) 11 (3) SLA&P 1.

79 See Roper Drimie, M, 'Sydney 2000 Olympic Games – Worst Game Ever for Ambush Marketers' (2001) ELR for further details.

- at the Olympic and Paralympic venues (including the Olympic Village);
- along the Olympic and Paralympic official routes;
- at places where Olympic and Paralympic events are to be held (e.g. Cultural Olympiad and Celebration sites);
- at places where other Olympic and Paralympic activities will take place (e.g. training facilities);
- along the Olympic and Paralympic main road networks.

As well as prohibiting advertising in these specific venues and roads, further regulations were introduced to also cover the surrounding area and roads up to the depth of one building block for locations within the Athens Olympic city plan or 200 metres for those outside the city plan. Where the location or venue was not surrounded by a road, to determine a building block then the surrounding zone began from the venue perimeter fence. Of course the laws excluded some 2,000 outdoor advertising spaces which the OCOG had purchased for official sponsors.

The regulations also prohibited any advertising by any means on painted vehicles, buses, trains, the underground/metro and taxis during the designated period. The measures in Greece were very ambitious and policing them was a costly exercise. Imagine in London if advertising on all private taxis were prohibited for a 10-week period.[80]

In Canada the Olympic and Paralympic Act 2007 c25 was passed in preparation for the Vancouver 2010 Olympic Winter Games. Section 4(1) provides:

(Canadian) Olympic and Paralympic Act 2007 s 4(1)

No person shall by use of trademark or other mark: promote or otherwise direct public attention to their business, wares or services in a manner that misleads or is likely to mislead the public into believing that a) the person's business, wares or services are approved, authorised or endorsed by an organising committee, the Canadian Olympic Committee or the Canadian Paralympic Committee; or a business association exists between the person's business and the Olympic Games, the Paralympic Games, an organising committee, the Canadian Olympic Committee or the Canadian Paralympic Committee.

Section 4(2) provided that a court should take into account any use of expressions contained in Schedule 3 when determining whether or not the actions were illegal. The Expressions were all generic such as Games, 2010, 21st, 10th, Medals, Winter, Gold, Silver, Bronze, Sponsor, Vancouver and Whistler.

Unfortunately the legislation was not good enough to prevent an ambush by Scotiabank. Although the official banking sponsor was Royal Bank of Canada, Scotiabank unveiled a photo and story-submitting contest called 'Show Your Colours', which used images of fans in red and white cheering a sporting event. Canadian ice hockey Olympic champion Cassie Campbell was featured in a red and white sports kit in the adverts and promotions, which also used the Canadian national symbol, the maple leaf. Whilst the campaign sought to invoke national pride and an association with the forthcoming Winter Olympics was implied, it did not contravene Section 4(1) and did not use any of the prohibited phrases in Schedule 3. Scotiabank came to an agreement with the Vancouver Organising Committee but the damage had already been done and there was confusion in the marketplace as to who the official banking sponsor was.[81]

In London, as well as the Olympic Symbols etc. (Protection) Act 1995, further protection is afforded under the London Olympic Games and Paralympic Games Act 2006. The following article explains the provisions in the legislation.

---

80 From the author's personal knowledge and experience as she volunteered in the Athens 2004 Brand Protection team.
81 From the author's personal knowledge and experience as she volunteered in the Vancouver 2010 Commercial Rights team.

Lowen, D, 'The London Olympic Games and Paralympic Games Act 2006'

On 30 March 2006, the somewhat controversial London Olympic Games and Paralympic Games Act 2006 gained Royal Assent. The swift introduction of the London Olympics Bill (the 'Bill') following the 2012 Olympic Games being awarded to London in July of last year was an indication of the importance of the Bill to all those involved with the Olympic movement and the London Games.

However, the Bill's speedy introduction was followed equally rapidly by somewhat provocative media reports on the application of the Bill's provisions. Fuelled partly by these reports, but also as a result of genuine concerns held by the advertising industry, the Bill faced significant opposition despite its importance to the viability of the 2012 Olympic Games. Opponents of some of the Bill's provisions looked on in horror as reports surfaced of organisations such as Basingstoke 2012, which was set up to promote Basingstoke as a site for an Olympic training team, changing its name to 'Basingstoke 2011 plus one' to avoid contravening the rules. Many of the Bill's opponents have now been appeased by the amendments made prior to the Bill's passage into law.

The provisions of the Act are crucial to enable the London Organising Committee for the Olympic Games ('LOCOG') to fight ambush marketing practices which undermine the event's sponsorship programme and also to control advertising, street trading, the sale of tickets and transport around the event. Furthermore, provisions of the sort contained in the Act were to be expected in light of the similar legislation adopted for the Sydney 2000 and Athens 2004 Games and the requirements of the International Olympic Committee.

The relevant legal framework before 30 March 2006
In the absence of any specific law against ambush marketing in the UK, the Olympic Symbol etc. (Protection) Act 1995 (the 'OSPA') has, for the last decade, provided the British Olympic Association with an important weapon in its fight to protect sponsorship revenues. The OSPA created an 'Olympic association right', a quasi-trade mark right, and protected the five-ring Olympic symbol, the Olympic motto and the protected words such as Olympics, Olympiad, etc. However, it does not specifically prevent ambush marketing. Indeed, in the absence of any general law against unfair commercial practices, organisers of sports events in the UK have struggled to combat ambush marketing and have been forced to look to a number of established legal doctrines to protect their events and commercial programmes. These have ranged from copyright and trade mark law, through to relying on contractual provisions on tickets and close co-ordination with local Trading Standards Departments. However, practical experience of relying on such legal tools demonstrates that there are limits to their usefulness and, arguably, the existing legal framework before 30 March 2006 in the UK was inadequate to protect the commercial rights to an event the size of the Olympics.

The New Law
The London Olympic Association Right
The most debated provision is Schedule 4 of the Act, which introduces the 'London Olympics Association Right' ('LOAR'). This confers on the LOCOG the exclusive right to authorise persons to use and exploit any visual or verbal representation (of any kind) which is likely to create, in the public mind, an association between the London Olympics and goods or services (or a person who provides goods or services).

The Act sets out a number of words such as 'games', 'Two Thousand and Twelve', '2012' and 'twenty twelve' which must not be used in combination with any of 'gold', 'silver', 'bronze', 'London', 'medals', 'sponsor' or 'summer' in an unauthorised manner which is likely to suggest to the public that there is an association with the London Olympics. There is provision for the list of words to be extended, subject to consultation (see below), and the right is therefore potentially very wide in scope. The Act authorises LOCOG to grant exclusive rights to official sponsors and commercial partners to associate themselves with the Games.

It will be down to the Courts to rule on whether the new intellectual property right, the LOAR, has been infringed by the use of the combinations of words referred to above. Paragraph 3(1) states that, '[f]or the purpose of considering whether a person has infringed the [LOAR] a court may, in particular, take account of his use of a combination of expressions of a kind [noted above].'

A person may therefore be held to infringe the LOAR by making any kind of unauthorised representation in a manner likely to suggest to the public that there is an association (whether through a contractual or commercial relationship or corporate connection) between the London Olympics and that person or the goods or services of that person.

Advertising, Street Trading and Transport

The Act also empowers the Secretary of State to make regulations (subject to consultation as explained below) controlling advertising and street trading in the 'vicinity' of Olympic venues, and an 'Olympic Transport Plan' to enable LOCOG to fulfil its obligations under its host city contract with the IOC. Unless authorisation has been granted, trading restrictions may apply to activities in public places and on private land to which the public has access. However, the restrictions will not apply to trading in buildings (other than car parks).

Secondary legislation in the run-up to 2012 will set out restrictions relating to advertising and street trading and will therefore reflect any changes in IOC policy or the Olympic venues between now and the games.

Ticket Touting

The previous UK law concerning ticket touting would have been insufficient to prevent the proliferation of the black market sale of tickets during the London Olympics. The Act introduces a direct prohibition on the unauthorised sale of Olympic tickets in a public place by an un-authorised person or in the course of business. 'Sale' is defined widely and includes offering to sell a ticket, exposing a ticket for sale, advertising the availability of a ticket for purchase and offering or giving a person a ticket in return for goods or services.

The DCMS Factsheet and Opposition to the Bill

On 31 August 2005 the Department of Culture, Media and Sport (the 'DCMS') released a factsheet in response to the criticism of the restrictions on the use of Olympic words to 'counter some of these myths'.

The factsheet explained that the purpose of the LOAR is to prevent instances of unfair association with the Games, not the mere use of words such as 'games' and 'London'. The factsheet also explained that 'It will have to be decided on a case by case basis whether infringement has occurred' and consequently whether, using a common sense approach, civil proceedings will be brought.

Despite circulation of the factsheet, there was still significant opposition to certain of the Bill's provisions, in particular the LOAR and the provisions relating to its infringement. The Advertising Association (a federation of trade bodies and organisations representing the advertising and promotional marketing industries) claimed that IOC requirements would be satisfied by the appropriate enforcement of existing UK law and that the additional protection set out in the Bill limited genuine freedom of commercial expression. Furthermore, it asserted that the LOAR as proposed was not proportionate or equitable, and that it would introduce unreasonable protection for official sponsors and organisers to the detriment of all other businesses.

So what has changed in the Act?

The automatic presumption of infringement

The most fierce opposition to the Bill concerned the proposal for a presumption of infringement when the prescribed words are used in combination. Furthermore, under the Bill as originally drafted the burden of proof rested with the person using the words to show that no association with the London Olympics would be likely to be created in the public mind. After considerable discussion and months of pressure from the House of Lords and the advertising industry, the Government agreed to amend the proposed restrictions that had been branded by Lord Glentoran as a 'draconian constraint'. As a result, the Act provides that the Courts will take into account the use of combinations of the specified words in their assessment of whether the LOAR has been infringed. In essence, the amendment changes the effect of paragraph 3(1) of Schedule 4 from being one in which the use of protected words and expressions in certain combinations would constitute an automatic presumption of infringement, to an indication of a possible infringement of Schedule 4.

However, it is likely that the Courts will still frown upon any commercial entity attempting to take advantage of the publicity surrounding the Games for its own ends, in particular where it uses any of the designated words or symbols in any confusing or associative way to imply some sort of connection.

Nonetheless, the removal of the automatic presumption that the law has been broken has appeased the advertising industry. Though arguing that the restrictions have come into force too far in advance of the Games, Andrew Brown (the director general of the Advertising Association) has stated that 'These changes to the Bill go a long way towards addressing the concerns expressed about its provisions by the AA and the Institute of Practitioners in Advertising as well as the wider advertising and media business since July 2005.'

Other amendments

Two other notable amendments in the Act also concern the provisions of Schedule 4. First, the Act places a duty on the Government to consult with the advertising industry before adding, removing or varying the list of protected words and expressions. In particular, the Secretary of State must consult 'one or more persons who have relevant responsibility for regulating the advertising industry', 'one or more persons who represent the interests of the advertising industry' and 'such other persons as [s]he thinks appropriate'. The value and impact of this consultation will no doubt be watched closely by the advertising industry.

Secondly, the journalistic reporting defence has been modified. The Act now includes a defence when using the designated phrases in publishing or broadcasting a report of a sporting or other event forming part of, or information about, the London Olympics. Furthermore, the defence extends to the inclusion of the designated phrases in an advertisement for any such publication or broadcast. However, this provision cannot be relied upon in respect of advertising material which is published or broadcast at the same time as, or in connection with, a report or information. This qualification is intended to prevent 'wraparound advertising', for example the publication of a sponsored supplement. Incidental inclusion of designated phrases in literary, dramatic or artistic works or a sound recording, film or broadcast will also not infringe the LOAR.

In relation to the provisions concerning the control of advertising and street trading in the 'vicinity' of Olympic venues, the Act places a duty on the Government to consult with the industry before introducing restrictions on the physical location of advertising around Olympic venues. In particular, as with the making of regulations extending the list of designated words, amongst those that the Secretary of State is required to consult are 'one or more persons who appear to the Secretary of State to represent interests within the advertising industry which are likely to be affected by the regulations'.

Conclusion

Of all the major sports events, the Olympics is perhaps most vulnerable to (and therefore in most need of protection from) ambush marketing. This is a direct consequence of the fact that the Olympic Games are a clean event – there is no sponsor branding in the stadia or on competitors' clothing. Despite this fairly unique characteristic, the substantial revenue generated by an extensive sponsorship programme built around the Games ensures the economic well-being, and indeed viability, of the event and many of the international sports federations whose events comprise the Games. Thus, official sponsors need a greater degree of protection in order to make their substantial investment in financing the Games worthwhile.

The coming into force of the Act in its revised form evidences the degree of success achieved by the lobbyists in watering down the legislation to remove the presumption of infringement of the LOAR and ease fears that media coverage could trigger proceedings. Nonetheless, businesses should be cautious when referring to the Olympics in any advertising or promotional material from now until 2012. The Act provides strong, and it is submitted crucial, protection against such practices.[82]

Ambush marketing and other major sports events

In South Africa special legislation has been introduced which can apply to all events. In November 2002, one of sport's biggest global brand wars came to South Africa's parliament with legislators voting to shield Pepsi Cola from ambush by its major rival Coca-Cola during the ICC Cricket World Cup 2003.

The then Trade and Industry Minister, Alec Erwin, told legislators the Merchandise Marks Amendment Bill was vital to protect South Africa's small but growing position in the world sports and entertainment market. Behind his concern was fear of a repeat of the 1996 Cricket World Cup row in the Indian sub-continent, where Pepsi contracted key players to carry its brand during an event officially sponsored by Coca-Cola, and flew a branded airship above stadiums. Legislators voted overwhelmingly to give the minister the right to grant the ICC Cricket World Cup and other events of similar size protection against ambush marketing from companies not registered as official sponsors of the event. It was this same legislation which was used during the FIFA World Cup 2010.

South African law already prohibited attempts to pose as an official sponsor of an event, but the amendment introduced in 2002 criminalised any misuse of an event logo to promote a product not listed as an official sponsor.

The law also prohibits rival advertising in the vicinity of a stadium and advertisements referring to an event even without the implication or suggestion of sponsorship:

South Africa Trade Practices Act No 76 of 1976

. . . No person shall –

(a) publish or display any advertisement which is false or misleading in material respects or cause such advertisement to be published or displayed; or

(b) in connection with the sale or leasing of goods or the rendering or providing any service directly or indirectly make any statement or communication or give any description or indication which is false or misleading in material respects in respect of the nature, properties, advantages or uses of such goods or service or in respect of the manner in, conditions on or prices at which such goods may be purchased, leased or otherwise acquired, or such service is rendered or provided.

(c) in connection with a sponsored event, make, publish or display any false or misleading statement, communication or advertisement which represents, implies or suggests a contractual or other connection or association between that person and the event, or the person sponsoring the event, or cause such statement, communication or advertisement to be made, published or displayed.

Offences and penalties: Any person who contravenes or fails to comply with any provision of this Act shall be guilty of an offence and shall be liable upon conviction –

---

82 Lowen, D, Couchmans LLP, http://www.couchmansllp.com/documents/news_press/London%20Olympics%20Act.pdf. See Alexandrakis, V, 'The Fight against ambush marketing and London 2012: How has this phenomenon been dealt with by the UK Legislation and what is the role of the EU Legislation' (2009), 8(1–2) ISLR.

(a)   in the case of a first conviction, to a fine or to imprisonment for a period not exceeding two
       years or to both a fine and such imprisonment;

(b)   in the case of a second or subsequent conviction, to a fine or to imprisonment for a period
       not exceeding five years or to both a fine and such imprisonment.[83]

Following this examination of the law in a variety of jurisdictions, ambush techniques can
be broadly broken up into those that are unlawful and those that are lawful. For the Olympic
movement they can be summarised as follows:

Unlawful ambush techniques

- Commercial use of rights, benefits and privileges without authorisation.
- Clear attempt to associate with the Olympic Games or Paralympic Games and benefit from the
  goodwill of the Games without a license.
- Unauthorised commercial use of copyrighted photographs, illustrations, film or satellite feed.
- Use of words, symbols or pictorials confusingly similar to Olympic or Paralympic marks.
- Use of words, symbols or pictorials covered under the legislation.
- The production of print publications or television features about the Olympics by non-rights
  holders for commercial gain, beyond that which is considered appropriate for news and edito-
  rial coverage.
- Producing, selling and distributing counterfeit merchandise.
- Sampling or selling competitive products in Olympic and Paralympics venues owned or leased
  by OCOG.
- False, misleading or deceptive advertising practices.
- Unfair trade practices.
- Registering website domain names using famous marks in bad faith with intent to profit.
- Warehousing domain names with the intent to profit.
- Using protected marks in metatags.
- Using protected marks in trade names.
- Downloading copyrighted satellite feed of the official Olympic broadcast and transmitting it
  via the internet without proper authorisation.
- Unauthorised use of athlete appearances, images or likenesses for advertising purposes during
  the Olympic Games in conflict with athlete agreements and Rule 49 of the Olympic Charter.
  (Rule 49 prevents athletes from acting as journalists/media commentators during the
  Olympics.)

Lawful ambush techniques

- Displaying banners and billboards outside the perimeter of Olympic venues.
- Displaying or selling products and services through vendors located nearby.
- Running adverts and promotions in which visuals are used that relate to Olympic sporting
  events, without making any direct reference. For example, congratulatory advertisements: the
  confectionery company, Mars, was one of the official sponsors of the England Football team,
  which participated in the FIFA World Cup Finals but Nestlé released an advert for KitKat which
  just simply said 'Fingers Crossed'. The implication regarding the forthcoming football event
  was very subtle and while Mars complained no legal action was forthcoming.
- Featuring former Olympians in adverts, as in the Scotiabank ambush of Royal Bank of Canada
  prior to the Vancouver 2010 Winter Olympics.

---

83 Summary of South Africa Trade Practices Act No 76 of 1976 as amended by Merchandise Marks Amendment Act 2002; also see
    Cornelius, S, 'South African Measures to Combat Ambush Marketing in Sport' (2003) (1) ISLJ 38.

- Sponsorship of athletes' teams, National Governing Bodies, Olympic training facilities and other sub-categories.
- Third-party tie-ins and promotions.
- Advertising gifts and donations made to the Olympics and related sub-categories.
- Engaging in promotions coinciding with the Olympics, which incorporate the use of validly purchased licensed merchandise and travel awards, which can be legitimately described within the context of advertising and promotions.
- Purchasing uncommitted commercial time on the Olympic host broadcaster or domestic broadcaster.
- Referencing the location of the Olympics in print and internet adverts without direct infringement.
- Incorporating news and political commentary into public relations campaigns and news releases.
- Describing factual information only in promotions
- Running advertising comparative to Olympic marketing partners.

So, considering all the above factors, at the current moment legal action may not be the best solution for the following reasons:

- Companies become more sophisticated in their advertising strategies and are aware of loopholes in intellectual property laws.
- If the ambush only occurs at the time of the event then litigation is expensive and time-consuming. Even to get injunctive relief takes several days, by which time the damage has already been done as the ambusher has achieved the exposure desired.
- As we have seen, the courts may not be willing to support the event owners, particularly if the ambusher has used adequate disclaimers and there is no element of public confusion.
- Event owners run a risk that a decision in favour of the ambusher will make future ambushers bolder. They will be fuelled to go on and develop even more creative and damaging advertising strategies.
- The ambusher may have a legal defence. The USA has defences of permitted comparative advertising and constitutional rights granted by the First Amendment to free speech, which includes commercial free speech provided such speech is not false, deceptive, disparaging or misleading.
- Adverse publicity regarding the ambush and subsequent court action only draws further attention to the ambushing company and adds fuel to the ambush.

At the time of writing the FIFA World Cup Finals are taking place in South Africa. Unfortunately an ambush which occurred at the same event in 2006 was repeated. In 2006 a rival brewery company to the official beer sponsor handed out to Dutch fans orange lederhosen; these garments were branded with the logo of the company. When fans showed up to the matches they were asked to remove the articles and this led to the bizarre spectacle of fans being forced to watch the match in their underwear. This spectacle achieved the objective of drawing attention to the rival beer as the incident was widely reported.

In 2010 the same brewery company handed out orange mini dresses to Dutch female fans.[84] The dresses were apparently unbranded but 36 women were removed from the stadium and two of them were later charged under the 2010 FIFA World Cup South Africa Special Measures Act (2006) and the Merchandise Marks Amendment Act (2002). The offence, which had been purposely

---

84 'Advertising: Ambush marketing: FIFA's rights protection programme' (2010) 8(8) ISLR.

amended for FIFA, was based on 'unauthorised use of a trade mark at a protected event' and 'entry into a designated area while in possession of a prohibited commercial object'. The case against the women was later dropped but the damage had already been done. The fiasco only succeeded in drawing worldwide attention to the ambush. The rival company achieved approximately US$106,000 worth of free editorial coverage in local print and broadcast news alone, thanks to its ambush marketing campaign. FIFA's heavy-handed approach has also damaged the goodwill of the event, particularly for Dutch fans.[85] The women concerned all denied knowing about the ambush and said they were merely wearing a fashionable dress in their national team colours.

When questioned about FIFA's stance on ambush marketing, Jerome Valcke, FIFA's General Secretary said:

Valcke, Jerome – *Sportcal* Magazine

You have to protect the World Cup. If you don't protect it, you put in danger the whole (soccer) pyramid. At least 50 per cent of our member associations rely on us for financial support. If the World Cup is in danger, all our systems are in danger . . . maybe it was different 20 years ago. People weren't so aware of the commercial position. Today when you make an agreement (with a sponsor) it is likely to be a 300-page document. They need and want to be fully protected. They want to be exclusive.[86]

In 2010 the FIFA World Cup generated US$1.2 billion, comprised of sponsorship $1 billion (domestic sponsors $195 million); hospitality $110 million and licensing $80 million.[87] With the bulk of the income coming from global sponsors it is not surprising that FIFA takes a tough stance on ambush marketing and puts extensive protections in place. However, the question is whether the response to the incident with the Dutch fans was too draconian.

Brand protection

Naming and shaming

In 1992 the IOC launched a campaign to position ambush marketing as unethical rather than clever marketing. One of the first cases of ambush that they decided to approach in this way was that of American Express's ambush of Visa at the 1992 Barcelona Games. This was not well received:

'Foolishness at the IOC'

The IOC and its various offspring continue to harass marketers who aren't official sponsors for what the IOC calls ambush marketing, i.e. when companies act to protect their market shares against the boasting of official Olympic sponsors. The goofiest attack is against American Express for its refusal to sit quietly while Olympic sponsor Visa fills the airwaves with announcements that 'the Olympics don't take American Express'. Visa's credit card is the exclusive card of official Olympic events, but AmEx cards are widely accepted at hotels, restaurants and other places in and around Barcelona. And American Express rightfully made that point strongly in response to Visa's ads, which implied they weren't. That's an ambush like Custer's return fire was an ambush.[88]

85 '"Orange dress" campaign worked', *Times Live*, 29 June 2010, http://www.timeslive.co.za/business/article524593.ece/Orange-dress-campaign-worked.
86 'FIFA: we'll re-think ticketing for the 2014 World Cup' (2010), 19 *Sportcal Magazine*.
87 Ibid.
88 'Foolishness at the IOC' (1992), *Advertising Age*, 3 August.

McKelvey writes about how the IOC anti-ambush strategies were put into practice at the Atlanta 1996 Games. Atlanta Centennial Olympic Properties (ACOP) (Atlanta's equivalent of Olympic Properties of the United States (OPUS), a joint marketing venture that generated support for the staging of the 2002 Olympic Winter Games and the USOC) went so far as to state:

McKelvey SM, 'Atlanta 96: Olympic Countdown to Ambush Armageddon'

Ambush marketing is unethical, dangerous, and illegitimate resulting in negative impact on legitimate corporate sponsors who are investing in the Olympic Games and the US Olympic Team . . . ambush marketing is theft, supporting a company engaged in ambush marketing takes funds away from America's athletes and the Olympic Games.[89]

Atlanta took the strong line that ambush marketing is unethical and theft. The Salt Lake Organizing Committee (SLOC) and the USOC developed a more subtle campaign for the 2002 Winter Olympics. SLOC released an advertisement which referred to 'unprincipled or misinformed marketers', whereas the USOC advertisement referred to 'marketers who unscrupulously or unknowingly portray themselves as official sponsors'.

McKelvey also points out that campaigns to expose, identify or publicly embarrass those guilty of ambush tactics may backfire as the public perceives the Olympics as a million-dollar business enterprise and thus the 'name and shame' campaign is viewed as inappropriate and strong-armed.

A further problem with name and shame is that claims of unethical practice may be slanderous, although the truth will always stand as an absolute defence.

McKelvey, SM, 'Atlanta 96: Olympic Countdown to Ambush Armageddon'

Would a company engaged in ambush marketing have a legitimate slander claim against the Olympic organisation if the latter were to stage a press conference accusing the company of illegitimate activity that was not in fact illegal?[90]

Commercial bodies such as the International Chamber of Commerce (ICC) and the European Sponsorship Association (ESA) seek to promote good practice. The ICC's Code of Advertising and Marketing Practice specifically references ambushing of sponsored properties as follows:

The Consolidated ICC Code of Advertising and Marketing Communication Practice Article B4

No party should seek to give the impression that it is a sponsor of any event or of media coverage of an event, whether sponsored or not, if it is not in fact an official sponsor of the property or of media coverage.[91]

ESA has produced a very detailed position statement specifically on ambush marketing, which agrees that there should be legislation in place to protect the rights of official sponsors. However, ESA does not believe that ambush marketing should be a criminal matter and also advocates using non-legal measures to combat ambush marketing and to foster an environment where ambush marketing is seen by the public and by non-sponsors as unattractive (and where appropriate, unpatriotic and/or dishonourable).[92]

---

89 See McKelvey, SM, 'Atlanta 96: Olympic Countdown to Ambush Armageddon' (1994) Seton Hall Journal of Sport Law, 397.
90 Ibid.
91 The Consolidated ICC Code of Advertising and Marketing Communication Practice Article B4, available at http://www.iccwbo.org.
92 Full Position Statement can be found at http://www.sponsorship.org/content/esaPressDetail.asp?id=816.

Clean venue

Venue advertising was allowed for the first and only time in 1924 during the Paris Olympic Games. Ever since then the Olympics have been staged in accordance with the Olympic Charter. Rule 51 of this Charter sets out the clean venue policies of the IOC. Essentially, in order to protect the integrity of the Games and highlight the performance of the athletes, Olympic competition is presented in an environment free from commercial, political, racial or religious messaging. Essentially the clean venue policy aims to:

- preserve the integrity and image of the Olympic Games;
- maintain an environment that is focused on sport competition and prevent over-commercialisation;
- ensure the Olympic Games spectacle remains true to the philosophy of Olympism and to the Olympic spirit;
- ensure that the core presentation of the Olympic Games is not tarnished by ancillary messages of any kind;
- enhance the value of Olympic association;
- protect the exclusive marketing rights of official Olympic Partners.

For the Olympics the enforcement of a clean venue policy is also very much about protecting against ambush marketing. FIFA and the Olympics have now developed the sports event further by introducing the notion of an event 'look'. Essentially the event owner uses their own logos and house colours to decorate the city where the event is being held and this theme of colours and logos runs throughout. The look should be applied consistently to merchandise, programmes, banners, venues, etc. so that all are using the same colours and logos. Where it is a very large event then 'look' banners and decorations can be manufactured to be sold to host cities so that they can replicate the atmosphere immediately around the venue across the whole of their city.

From an ambush marketing perspective the benefit of the look in and around the venue is that it offers additional protection to the official event sponsors. If the venue and the host city are erecting look banners and signage then this means there will be no space for competitors to erect their banners and signage. The Olympic movement also uses the look to promote and thank the official event sponsors, so some banners would have the event sponsors' names on them. From a purely aesthetic point of view the look is integral to creating a carnival atmosphere at the event and it also leaves a clear and lasting impression in the minds of the spectators of the event owner's colours and logos.

The IOC clean venue policy ensures that they control the presentation and identification of the event to a worldwide audience, hence no advertising or commercial identification of any kind, even by an official games sponsor, is permitted unless it has been expressly approved by the OCOG and the IOC. The Olympic Charter is not a legally binding document in itself but the IOC ensures compliance with the Charter and especially the clean venue policy by writing this into all their contracts.[93] From a legal perspective, this is what is interesting about the clean venue policy: how the IOC and the OCOG use contract to enforce the concept and image of the Games and thus ensure maximum protection for the Olympic brand.

Olympic zones

The IOC has also developed zones which determine the application of the clean venue rule. Let us consider these zones and some of the crucial contracts which protect them.

---

93 'Comment: The legal basis of the Olympic Charter' (2007) 15(11) ISLR.

Zone 1: The competition area, spectator area, and other areas that can be seen by television cameras or seated spectators

No advertising of any kind is allowed in this zone, other than limited identification of the manufacturers of sporting equipment, technical equipment, personal equipment and uniforms. Several key contracts ensure this.

Firstly, for existing venues a lease agreement is signed to grant the OCOG exclusive use of that venue for the Olympics. So, for example, the O_2 Arena in London has been renamed the North Greenwich Arena and it will host Artistic Gymnastics, Trampoline Gymnastics and the Basketball finals during the Olympic Games and then, a few weeks later, Wheelchair Basketball during the Paralympic Games. The venue contract is extensive and in relation specifically to the clean venue requirements covers the application of Rule 51 of the Olympic Charter. All commercial signage and displays will be covered during the exclusive use period. All contractors, agents and licensees of the venue are also bound to co-operate with this provision. The OCOG is given the ultimate authority to cover or remove all signage and erect 'Look of the Games' installations. The venue is also prohibited from entering into any conflicting agreements for the exclusive use period and that includes displaying banners, billboards or other signage off site, away from where the events will actually take place. Agreements will have been reached with every venue that will be used during the event.

In relation to the athletes, they all sign an entry form/contract confirming that they will comply with the Olympic Charter, in particular Rule 49 and Rule 51. Rule 51 states that no competitor, coach, trainer or official may allow his person, name, picture or sports performance to be used for advertising during the games. Rule 49 prevents athletes from acting as journalists or in any other media capacity and Rule 51 restricts the commercial identification permitted on the clothing and equipment of athletes, coaches, trainers and officials.

Of course this does not protect against former Olympians ambushing the event or summer Olympics athletes ambushing the winter Olympics. Just prior to the Vancouver 2010 Olympics sandwich chain Subway launched an advertisement using 14-time gold medal winner Michael Phelps. Phelps swims right through the wall of an indoor pool and smashes through the building, leaving streams of concrete in his wake as he strokes across the street. As he passes a nearby Subway restaurant, the ad states, 'Phelps fuels up . . . so he can get to where the action is this winter.' A map flashes, appearing to chart the swimmer's route, and the destination is Vancouver.

Olympic Charter, 'Full Text of Rule 51 and its Bye-law'

1. The IOC Executive Board determines the principles and conditions under which any form of advertising or other publicity may be authorised.

2. No form of advertising or other publicity shall be allowed in and above the stadia, venues and other competition areas which are considered as part of the Olympic sites. Commercial installations and advertising signs shall not be allowed in the stadia, venues or other sports grounds.

3. No kind of demonstration or political, religious or racial propaganda is permitted in any Olympic sites, venues or other areas.

Bye-law

1. No form of publicity or propaganda, commercial or otherwise, may appear on persons, on sportswear, accessories or, more generally, on any article of clothing or equipment whatsoever worn or used by the athletes or other participants in the Olympic Games, except for the identification – as defined below – of the manufacturer of the article or equipment concerned, provided that such identification shall not be marked conspicuously for advertising purposes.

1.1. The identification of the manufacturer shall not appear more than once per item of clothing and equipment.

1.2. Equipment: any manufacturer's identification that is greater than 10% of the surface area of the equipment up to a maximum of 60 cm^2 that is exposed during competition shall be deemed to be marked conspicuously.

1.3. Headgear (e.g. hats, helmets, sunglasses, goggles) and gloves: any manufacturer's identification over 6 cm^2 shall be deemed to be marked conspicuously.

1.4. Clothing (e.g. T-shirts, shorts, sweat tops and sweat pants): any manufacturer's identification which is greater than 20 cm^2 shall be deemed to be marked conspicuously.

1.5 Shoes: it is acceptable that there appear the normal distinctive design pattern of the manufacturer. The manufacturer's name and/or logo may also appear, up to a maximum of 6 cm^2, either as part of the normal distinctive design pattern or independent of the normal distinctive design pattern.

1.6. In case of special rules adopted by an International Sports Federation, exceptions to the rules mentioned above may be approved by the IOC Executive Board. Any violation of the provisions of the present clause may result in disqualification or withdrawal of the accreditation of the person concerned. The decisions of the IOC Executive Board regarding this matter shall be final.

The numbers worn by competitors may not display publicity of any kind and must bear the Olympic emblem of the OCOG.

2. To be valid, all contracts of the OCOG containing any element whatsoever of advertising, including the right or licence to use the emblem or the mascot of the Olympic Games, must be in conformity with the Olympic Charter and must comply with the instruction given by the IOC Executive Board. The same shall apply to contracts relating to the timing equipment, the scoreboards, and to the injection of any identification signal in television programmes. Breaches of these regulations come under the authority of the IOC Executive Board.

3. Any mascot created for the Olympic Games shall be considered to be an Olympic emblem, the design of which must be submitted by the OCOG to the IOC Executive Board for its approval. Such mascot may not be used for commercial purposes in the country of an NOC without the latter's prior written approval.

4. The OCOG shall ensure the protection of the property of the emblem and the mascot of the Olympic Games for the benefit of the IOC, both nationally and internationally. However, the OCOG alone and, after the OCOG has been wound up, the NOC of the host country, may exploit such emblem and mascot, as well as other marks, designs, badges, posters, objects and documents connected with the Olympic Games during their preparation, during their holding and during a period terminating not later than the end of the calendar year during which such Olympic Games are held. Upon the expiry of this period, all rights in or relating to such emblem, mascot and other marks, designs, badges, posters, objects and documents shall thereafter belong entirely to the IOC. The OCOG and/or the NOC, as the case may be and to the extent necessary, shall act as trustees (in a fiduciary capacity) for the sole benefit of the IOC in this respect.

5. The provisions of this Bye-law also apply, mutatis mutandis, to all contracts signed by the organising committee of a Session or an Olympic Congress.

6. The uniforms of the competitors and of all persons holding an official position may include the flag or Olympic emblem of their NOC or, with the consent of the OCOG, the OCOG Olympic emblem. The IF officials may wear the uniform and the emblem of their federations.

7. The identification on all technical gear, installations and other apparatus, which are neither worn nor used by athletes or other participants at the Olympic Games, including timing equipment and scoreboards, may on no account be larger than 1/10th of the height of the equipment, installation or apparatus in question, and shall not be greater than 10 centimetres high.

8. The word 'identification' means the normal display of the name, designation, trademark, logo or any other distinctive sign of the manufacturer of the item, appearing not more than once per item.

9. The OCOG, all participants and all other persons accredited at the Olympic Games and all other persons or parties concerned shall comply with the manuals, guides, or guidelines, and all other instructions of the IOC Executive Board, in respect of all matters subject to Rule 51 and this Bye-law.[94]

Further protection against commercial marks on equipment is determined by the World Federation of the Sporting Goods Industry (WFSGI), which signed an agreement in 1997 with the IOC to determine guidelines for marketing and advertising practices. This states that members of WFSGI shall not use any Olympic marks without express consent. Also all WFSGI members will comply with the Olympic Charter and in particular Rule 51 and its byelaws. For each Olympics, guidelines regarding authorised manufacturer identifications are written and distributed to all WFSGI members beforehand to ensure compliance.

Rule 51 prevents the ambush tactic of athletes advertising during the three weeks of the competition but it does not prevent advertisements which appear prior to and after the event. For example, in Sydney the airline Qantas ambushed the official airline sponsor Ansett by using high-profile Australian athletes, such as runner Cathy Freeman and swimmer Susie O'Neill, in billboard advertisements throughout Australia. Following negotiations between the companies and the Sydney Organising Committee (SOCOG), a confidential settlement was reached and the billboards were taken down shortly before the period of the Games so Rule 51 was not breached.

A classic example of a breach of Rule 51 in Zone 1 arose in Barcelona in 1992 when Michael Jordan and the USA Dream Team won the Gold Medal in Men's Basketball. Nike, which was not an official sponsor, privately sponsored Jordan and many of his teammates. Reebok had the exclusive right to provide uniforms for all US Olympians. Reebok were briefed about the Rule 51, Clean Venue issues and ensured that their uniforms complied with this. Jordan had been paid millions to wear Nike clothing in public. In defiance of Reebok and his NOC he showed up at the medal ceremony wearing Nike clothing which contained their commercial branding. Officials were faced with two main conflicts. Firstly they were bound by Rule 51 of the Olympic Charter, and this was a direct contravention of that policy. Secondly, they were bound in contract to offer exclusivity to Reebok. Allowing Nike worldwide commercial exposure as Jordan was awarded the medal would have been a breach of contract. After considerable agonising, officials managed to persuade Jordan and his teammates to drape USA flags over their competing logos, thus saving the day.[95] Similarly, at the 1996 Olympics in Atlanta, British athlete Linford Christie attended a press conference wearing Puma-branded contact lenses, despite Reebok being the official clothing partner of the games.

---

94 Olympic Charter in force as from 11 February 2010. Available from the IOC Website: http://www.olympic.org/Documents/Olympic%20Charter/Charter_en_2010.pdf.
95 Note that Rule 51 does not apply to the Paralympics.

An example of a recent ambush in Zone 1 was when Li Ning a famous Chinese gymnast and Olympian was chosen by the Beijing OCOG to light the Olympic cauldron at the opening ceremony. The problem was that Li Ning had also founded a very popular sportswear company which is branded 'Li Ning' and which is very prominent in the Asian markets. Adidas was the official sponsor but had to stand by and watch its biggest Chinese competitor steal one of the biggest moments of the Games. Adidas could not challenge the selection of Li Ning to light the cauldron because he was a national sports legend. Li Ning's role in the opening ceremony gave him a huge amount of global exposure and many Chinese consumers will have believed he was wearing his own sportswear, whereas he was actually wearing the official Adidas uniform.

Another vital contract required in Zone 1 is the ticket licence agreement which has been discussed above. This is sent to all ticket holders and it allows the event owner to impose a code of conduct on the spectator.[96] This code of conduct specifically prohibits the spectator from conducting political, racial, religious or commercial activity inside the venue. Any spectator attempting to gain television exposure for any of these causes can be removed from the venue and denied re-admission.

Finally, but probably most importantly, the Olympic Broadcast Agreements require that the sports transmission be kept clear of any commercial messages besides the normal advertising breaks. The terms of the contracts vary but can be summarised as follows:

IOC Handbook, 'Ambush prevention and clean venue guidelines'

There must be no overlay of any commercial message or logo during coverage of Olympic sporting action, ceremonies or commentary.

There may be certain opening and closing broadcast credits for an Olympic programme – but if the advertiser is not an Olympic partner, there must be clear separation from any form of Olympic imagery.

Olympic marketing partners have exclusive rights to in-studio presence.

The only acceptable on-screen credits are those connected to the official timing and data information/results service provider of the Olympic Games.[97]

Zone 2: corridor area, concourses, spectator amenities, other public areas within venue, and back of house areas

No advertising of any kind is permitted in this zone, other than some controlled commercial identification by official sponsors and suppliers who are providing a service in that area, and only as approved in writing. In order to achieve this each sponsor, supplier, donor or contractor who is providing a service in Zone 2 has a very specific clause inserted into their contract. This clause explains Rule 51, how it will affect their operations and how they may apply for exceptions to the rule. In this way expectations are managed from the beginning of the commercial relationship. By virtue of the venue agreement, existing signage inside the venue is either removed or covered and is replaced with generic 'Look of the Games' signage. This includes all food and beverage signage. In a venue such as the O_2 arena this cover-up operation is substantial and can take days; consider that every sign for the toilets, exit signs, as well as food and beverage signs will need to be replaced with the 'Olympic Look' signs.

Zone 3: ancillary areas such spectator plaza areas, the venue perimeter, operations and other compounds, and official car parks

No advertising or commercial identification is allowed in this zone, other than through controlled recognition or presence programmes for office marketing partners, and this must be approved in

96 See above, p 318 for an extract of the ATHOC ticket conditions.
97 IOC Handbook – 'Ambush prevention and clean venue guidelines'.

advance by the OCOG. Many of the areas in Zone 3 are leased space, for example 'Park and Ride' lots. When drafting these leases the OCOG legal team ensures that Rule 51 is effective from the moment that OCOG gains exclusive use of that space until the end of the contract term.

The OCOG also negotiates with major transport authorities, both government and private entities, to limit signage on the exterior and interior of the buses and trams. Or in the alternative, if there is to be advertising, then the OCOG tries to ensure that the official marketing partners are offered the right of first refusal to purchase such advertising space. As discussed above, Athens took the added step of preventing advertising on taxis in the city during the Games.

Zone 4: airspace, roads, buildings overlooking venues, and other areas

The OCOG works with the venue, local authorities and others to exert as much control as possible over advertising in this level. The host city contract ensures that outdoor commercial activities such as billboards, banners, hoardings and street vendors are controlled by the OCOG at the time of the Games. It is beyond the scope of this chapter to discuss or analyse the over-commercialisation of sports and of the Olympic Games in particular. The IOC is aware of the problems that occur when there is over-commercialisation as this was first experienced at the Atlanta Games in 1996.

The prevention of over-commercialisation is achieved through the host city agreement. Learning from Atlanta, the IOC strengthened this agreement. Starting with Athens 2004 a comprehensive IOC outdoor signage policy came into operation. Every city that wishes to bid to host an Olympic Games in the future has to agree to:

- protect the fundamental marketing principles;
- guarantee all venues are clean;
- provide the strongest possible protection for the exclusivity of all the Olympic Partners;
- take steps to maximise the promotion of the Olympic brand in the host city;
- prevent uncontrolled commercialism and the problems faced with the city of Atlanta in 1996.

If a bid is successful the city is required to:

- enter into a single marketing programme;
- obtain rights to purchase all outdoor advertising throughout the city and at main transportation access points;
- review with government the steps necessary to improve protection of the Olympic marks and rights.

Innovations from Salt Lake City

In order to achieve a themed celebratory decor throughout the city, for the Salt Lake 2002 Olympics and Paralympics, the 'Look of the Games' department developed a 'Cityscape' programme. Previous Olympic Games and sports events had taught that buildings could be the perfect medium for ambush marketing. Erecting a neon sign, or any large sign on a building, in the camera view, could be an effective way of gaining some commercial exposure. Another successful tactic was the draping of banners, flags and colours from the tops of buildings.

The Salt Lake Organising Committee (SLOC) was well aware of these tactics and was particularly concerned about the camera views from the downtown venues. Consequently they developed and put into operation an extensive initiative, the Cityscape Programme, to prevent ambush and create a lasting impression of the Salt Lake 2002 Games. The programme required the SLOC legal department to negotiate with building owners in the downtown area. For a relatively nominal monetary consideration, these owners entered into contracts with SLOC. The contracts allowed SLOC to wrap their entire walls and in some case the whole building with a Games picture during the period of the event. The main incentive for these building owners was to participate in the Olympics but it also promoted the notion of being a good community citizen. The programme was aesthetically pleasing, the alternative being a fairly bland, grey city skyline.

SLOC lawyers also negotiated with building owners who did not wish to have their building wrapped with a SLOC design. In these instances a forbearance agreement was entered into. This stated that the building owners agreed that they would not lease the space of their building to any other advertiser.

In addition agreements were reached with certain other building owners in the downtown area, who were displaying signage which competed with SLOC's official marketing partners, to ensure that their neon signs would be switched off during Games time. The terms of these agreements are confidential.

Creating the Cityscape programme involved hours of complex negotiations and contract drafting. It is a good example of how contract can be used in Zone 4, in advance of the event, to prevent ambush marketing during the event. Through contract SLOC preserved the image and colours of the Olympics and prevented ambush. The Salt Lake City skyline saw the 'Look of the Games' graphics and colours as opposed to an American Express banner or a Nike billboard.

Another very interesting innovation was the creation of another venue. The 2002 Winter Games had two key venues in the heart of Salt Lake City: the Salt Lake Ice Center (SLIC), which was the venue for figure skating and short-track speed skating, and the Olympic Medals Plaza (OMP), which hosted nightly medals ceremonies and celebratory concerts. SLIC had a total capacity of 15,500; OMP had a total capacity of 20,222. Both venues were operative for 16 days continuously. The OCOG recognised that as the two venues were right next to each other this area of the city would be a hive of activity. All this was a concern for clean venue and brand protection. In accordance with local ordinances, SLOC successfully negotiated for and obtained from the city authorities of Salt Lake City a special use permit. This permit entitled SLOC to close the streets surrounding SLIC and OMP. Those streets then become a third venue, Salt Lake Olympic Square (SLOS). SLOS had a fenced-in perimeter and entry to the venue was controlled by SLOC. It was free to the public and no ticket was required. SLOS was built into a fun venue with an Olympic superstore, sponsor showcases, such as Coca-Cola pin trading, a celebration stage and a video board showing Olympic competition and the medals ceremonies. The venue had over 50,000 visitors each day that it was in operation. Having gained exclusive use of the streets for the entire period of the Games, the probability of ambush marketing arising in this crucial downtown area was lessened.[98]

Given the size and scale of the Olympics, each event usually covers several districts within the Host City. For instance, in London five London boroughs will be involved: Greenwich, Hackney, Newham, Tower Hamlets and Waltham Forest. Local communities in each of these boroughs will be hosting Olympic celebrations and parties. Each of these city celebration sites is a potential ambush marketing risk. In order to approach this risk proactively the OCOG develops close working relationships with community leaders and city authorities. They work to achieve the long-term objectives of extending the 'Look of the Games' into the venue communities while preserving marketing partners' rights and preventing over-commercialisation.

Each venue city has local ordinances and byelaws that govern street vending, signage, distribution of handbills, promotional give-aways and parking. These ordinances may vary according to each district but once mastered they can be used effectively to prevent certain forms of ambush marketing. Working in partnership with local authorities, local ordinances can become an additional weapon to head off ambush marketers. This is another area where advance planning and groundwork will pay off at Games time.

---

98 Information is based on the author's personal knowledge and experience as she worked for the SLOC Brand Protection department. Also see Naidoo, U, 'Salt Lake City Brand Protection Programme – Ambush Marketing and Its Repercussions' (2001) 4 SLB 13.

Henderson, P, 'Hosting: City of Vancouver Olympic regulatory framework'

Regulatory framework

In 2007, the City began a process to review its regulatory framework both to meet its specific obligations under the Multi-Party Agreement, but also to ensure that the City's regulatory framework would support the Games more broadly.

Commencing in June of 2008, a total of seven reports were submitted to Vancouver City Council to develop the City's Games-time regulatory framework.

More than 10 City by-laws were amended as part of the 2010 Winter Games By-law in support of the Games. All changes – with the exception of changes to the Fire By-law – were temporary. Individual provisions had specific durations based on the minimum identified requirement.

Building By-law

Vancouver Building By-law provisions are intended for permanent buildings. To simplify permitting of temporary buildings during the Games, the 2010 Winter Games By-law created technical requirements specific to temporary buildings and developed a permitting process to streamline the permit application process.

The 2010 Winter Games By-law building requirements apply to tents and other similar structures. The provisions modify technical requirements to account for operational character-istics of temporary buildings. As an example, the 2010 Winter Games By-law provisions relax the snow load rating for tents subject to the tents being heated to ensure that snow does not accumulate.

The 2010 Winter Games By-law allows temporary building developers to use third party consultants to perform plan review and building inspection tasks. The City responsibilities are administrative only, improving plan processing speed.

City Land Regulation By-law

The City Land Regulation applies to City property that is not street or park. Both of the City of Vancouver LiveCity celebration sites, LiveCity Yaletown and LiveCity Downtown were developed on City Land. The amendments to the City Land Regulation created rules for the LiveCity sites allowing security measures to be put in place.

Examples of the LiveCity rules include prohibitions on:

- creating a disturbance on the sites;
- bringing weapons or alcohol onto the sites;
- selling or advertising on the sites without the City's authorization.

One challenge for the City was communicating that 2010 Winter Games By-law advertising provisions applied only to commercial advertising material and would not restrict freedom of political expression or free speech. The December 2009 version of the 2010 Winter By-laws explicitly differentiates between commercial advertising material and non-commercial material, such as anti-Olympic literature or signs.

Graffiti By-law

Under the Graffiti By-law, there is a requirement to provide 10 days' notification to the property owner prior to the City removing graffiti.

In the fall of 2009, the Municipal Enabling and Validating Act (No. 3) British Columbia allowed for the cities of Richmond, Vancouver, and Whistler to temporarily enter onto real property to remove graffiti without notice. If graffiti is removed without notice, the municipality would bear the cost of the removal rather than charging the cost back to the property owner, as is the normal process. The municipality bearing the cost the graffiti removal is reasonable given that the owner is not provided time to remove the graffiti, and the owner was not respon-sible for the graffiti.

Licence By-law

The 2010 Winter Games By-law modified the licences for restaurants and bars such that liquor service hours that are normally allowable on weekends were allowable seven days per week during the Games. Restaurants were allowed liquor service until 1:00am and some bars allowed liquor service until 3:00am.

Liquor service hours for temporary licences are dictated by the Province of B.C. in consultation with the City. City Council directed staff to support temporary liquor service no later than 2:00am seven days per week.

Noise Control By-law

Changes to the Noise Control By-law facilitated Games operations, recognized increased activities throughout the City and set planning frameworks for a range of temporary Games-time activities.

The changes allowed for 24-hour operations for VANOC Venues, City sites and Robson Square (a Province of British Columbia celebration site in downtown Vancouver) and other sites impacted by road closures. Activities that would typically be prohibited at night include waste pick-up, installation or removal of temporary facilities, maintenance, repairs and deliveries.

Other activities were permitted more broadly than just at VANOC venues, City sites and Robson Square, including expansion of garbage collection hours and overnight deliveries to minimize truck traffic in the downtown core.

The definition of day-time for noise generation purposes was extended to recognize additional activities throughout the City.

The by-law permitted broadcast production 24 hours per day.

Sign By-law

Under the 2010 Winter Games By-law, a number of relaxations were put in place:

- To streamline approvals, the relaxation eliminated the requirement for permits for VANOC venues, City sites and Robson Square;
- Permits were also not required for projection public art with no commercial content;
- Signs celebrating the Games were allowed on a similar basis as murals, permits were required and only limited commercial content was permitted;
- Celebratory signs of less than 10% of a building face were permitted from June 2008 to 31 December 2010;
- Celebratory signs more than 10% of a building face were permitted from 1 October 2009 to 31 March 2010;
- Commercial content was permitted on the signs up to 10% of the total area of the sign or 20 square metres, whichever is smaller;
- Only first party or VANOC partner commercial content was permitted on the signs; and
- VANOC marks were permitted as part of the celebratory content, but only if the party erecting the sign was authorized to use the VANOC marks.

Street Distribution of Publications By-law

The 2010 Winter Games By-law allows celebratory images to be placed on news boxes on City streets.

Street and Traffic By-law

The 2010 Winter Games By-law amended the Street and Traffic By-law to close streets to motor vehicles in the vicinity of VANOC venues for public safety or operational reasons. The amendments also closed streets to be used as pedestrian corridors in downtown Vancouver, and prohibited the operation of any vehicle – including bicycles – in Olympic Lanes.

The 2010 Winter Games By-law created new temporary truck routes and permitted VANOC vehicles and public transit buses to temporarily operate on streets not designated as truck routes.

To minimize litter and congestion associated with commercial advertising activities, the 2010 Winter Games By-law restricted distribution or display of commercial advertising on specific streets in Vancouver. These were the streets in the immediate vicinity of venues, the pedestrian corridors and along Olympic Lanes. These restrictions did not apply to newspapers and non-commercial materials.

The 2010 Winter Games By-law prohibited automatic changeable messaging on vehicles on City streets, and prohibited the use of vehicles solely or primarily for the purpose of advertising.

To minimize congestion, the 2010 Winter Games By-law prohibited street performing on streets in the immediate vicinity of VANOC venues, City sites and Robson Square, and created new areas for street performing without a permit in the downtown away from those sites.

The 2010 Winter Games By-law created rules for special events taking place in the downtown core on the pedestrian corridors. The rules also applied to businesses adjacent to the pedestrian corridors that expanded their business activities onto the streets within the corridors. The rules balanced the desire to animate the pedestrian corridors while minimizing commercial advertising.

Ticket Offences By-law

The 2010 Winter Games By-law created a series of new Municipal Ticket Information (MTI) Offences for the Games. The goal of the MTI expansion was to provide additional tools for by-law compliance officers to ensure by-law compliance. By-laws with new MTI offences included:

- Fire By-law
- Single Room Accommodation By-law
- Street and Traffic By-law
- Street Vending By-law
- Vehicles for Hire By-law.

The 2010 Winter Games By-law also expanded the powers of by-law compliance officers to allow them to enforce a broader suite of by-laws to maximize response efficiency in the event of by-law violations.

Vehicle for Hire By-law

Taxi and limousine licensing is jointly regulated by the Province of British Columbia through the Passenger Transportation Board (PTB) and individual municipalities. The PTB determines the number of taxis and limousines allowed to operate in each municipality while municipalities regulate driver permits, vehicle age and condition and meter accuracy.

Given the expected increased demand for vehicles for hire, the PTB relaxed rules for taxis and limousines to increase the numbers of taxis in Vancouver during the Games. The City changed the Vehicle for Hire By-law to facilitate these changes. The changes allowed for existing companies to add additional vehicles and for non-Vancouver companies to pick up fares in Vancouver.

The 2010 Winter Games By-law changed Pedicab routing requirements to ensure that Pedicab operations did not conflict with vehicle traffic, particularly on Olympic Lanes. Rickshaws were temporarily permitted on pedestrian corridors in limited numbers with limited commercial advertising.

Zoning and Development By-law

The Zoning and Development By-law prohibits the rental of most housing types for periods less than 30 days to minimize neighbourhood disruption.

To assist in providing temporary housing for visitors during the Games, the 2010 Winter Games By-law allowed for the short-term rental of dwelling units during the Games. To rent during the Games, owners required a $106 licence and in addition, the dwelling unit could not have been occupied by a tenant or boarder or lodger after 1 June 2009. The City's goal was to ensure that temporary Games-time accommodation did not displace existing tenants.

The 2010 Winter Games By-law also allowed the Director of Planning to permit Games-time uses of property for Games purposes that might not be included in the allowed uses under the property zoning.

CD-1 By-Law 9733

The 2010 Winter Games By-law allowed temporary parking and ancillary uses on a site in south east Vancouver known as East Fraser Lands. The site was historically a lumber mill, and is scheduled for residential redevelopment. The 2010 Winter Games By-law changes allowed the site to be used as a bus depot for the VANOC bus fleet.

Fines

Historically, the maximum fine permitted under the Vancouver Charter was $2,000. One of the Vancouver Charter changes made by the Province was to allow maximum fines of $10,000, consistent with maximum fines in other municipalities. Under the 2010 Winter Games By-law, all violations of the by-law could be levied a maximum fine of $10,000. The Fire By-law was changed to permanently allow $10,000 fines. Maximum by-law fines are specified in the by-law, but the specific infraction fine is determined by the court.[99]

Working in co-operation with local and national tourism bureaux and local and national chambers of commerce the OCOG can ensure that the area of Olympic competition is protected from obvious ambushes. For example, at Barcelona 1992 American Express ambushed Visa by becoming the official sponsor of the Spanish tourist board.

Each OCOG develops its own strategy for brand protection and clean venue provision, learning from and building on previous OCOG experiences. Over the years this experience has enabled the Olympics to almost perfect its anti-ambush strategies.

Looking into the Future

After London the next Summer Olympic Games will be in the Brazilian city of Rio de Janeiro. It is worth briefly considering here what provisions have already been promised and put in place for that Olympics.

Rio 2016 Candidature File

Rio 2016 is committed to the Olympic image, the Olympic brand and all associated intellectual property, in close partnership with the IOC and, for the Paralympic brand the IPC.

Rio 2016 will develop the strongest possible program, including all legal and other related measures, to prevent any form of ambush marketing and thereby guarantee the exclusive rights of the sponsors and the integrity of the Olympic brand. This program is already underpinned by existing City Legislation.

The Brazilian Olympic Committee gained valuable experience in developing a comprehensive anti-ambush programme for the 2007 Pan American Games and Para Pan American Games. The integrated activation by Rio 2007, public authorities and the agency and media sectors ensured there were no serious incidents of ambush marketing during the event.

All outside advertising is licensed by the City of Rio and it has ensured that all licences will expire in time for the Olympics and Paralympics in 2016. Any which will not expire will have a carve-out clause inserted to allow the OCOG complete control.

---

99 Henderson, P, 'Hosting: City of Vancouver Olympic regulatory framework: part 1' (2010) 8(6) WSLR.

New laws were introduced for the 2007 Pan American Games and these will be adapted for use during both the FIFA World Cup in 2014 and the Olympics and Paralympics in 2016.

The Olympic Acts provide special protection for the Olympic intellectual property. General intellectual property protection is provided by the 1988 Federal Constitution and the following legislation:

- Decree 75.572 validating the Paris Convention for the Protection of Intellectual Property 1975 Decree
- 1.355 validating the International Agreements on Trade Related Aspects on Intellectual Property Rights 1994
- Industrial Property Law 1996 which gives specific protection against ambush marketing.
- Counterfeit Law 2003
- Pele Law 1998
- Decree 90.129 validating the Nairobi Treaty which provides worldwide protection of the Olympic symbol.[100]

Brazil: Industrial Property Law, 14/05/1996, No. 9.279[101]

Article 124 of the Industrial Property Law prohibits companies which are not official sponsors, providers or supporters from registering any brand, symbol or item which could be easily confused with the official partners and symbols.

Article 195 provides quite extensive protections:

A crime of unfair competition is perpetrated by anyone who:

I.   publishes, by any means, false statements, to the detriment of a competitor, for the purpose of obtaining some advantage;

II.   provides or divulges false information about the competitor in order to obtain an advantage;

III.   employs fraudulent means to divert the customers of another person to his or another party's advantage;

IV.   uses another person's advertising phrase or sign, or imitates it, in order to create confusion among the products or establishments;

V.   uses, improperly, another person's trade name, title of establishment, or insignia, or sells, displays, offers for sale, or has in stock a product bearing these references;

VI.   substitutes his own name or firm name on another person's product in place of that person's name or firm name, without his consent;

VII.   attributes to himself, for advertising purposes, a reward or distinction that he has not received;

VIII.   sells, displays or offers for sale, in another person's container or wrapper, an adulterated or counterfeited product, or uses that container or wrapper to negotiate a product of the same type, although not adulterated or counterfeited, provided the act does not constitute a more serious crime;

IX.   gives or promises money or some other benefit to an employee of a competitor so that said employee, by neglecting his job duties, provides him an advantage;

X.   receives money or some other benefit, or accepts a promise of payment or reward, to provide an advantage to the employer's competitor, by neglecting his duties as an employee;

XI.   divulges, exploits, or utilizes, without authorization, confidential knowledge, information or data that could be used in industry, commerce or rendering of services,

---

100 'Nairobi Treaty on the Protection of the Olympic Symbol 1981', http://www.wipo.int/treaties/en/ip/nairobi/trtdocs_wo018.html.
101 http://www.wipo.int/wipolex/en/details.jsp?id=515.

other than that which is of public knowledge or that would be evident to a technician versed in the subject, to which he gained access by means of a contractual or employment relationship, even after the termination of the contract;

XII.   divulges, exploits or utilizes, without authorization, the kind of knowledge or information to which the previous Item refers, when obtained by illicit means or when access was gained through fraud; or

XIII. sells, displays or offers for sale a product declaring that it is object of a patent that has been filed or granted, or of an industrial design that has been registered, when it has not, or mentioning it in an advertisement or a commercial paper as being filed or patented, or registered, when it has not;

XIV.   divulges, exploits, or utilizes, without authorization, results of tests or other undisclosed data whose preparation involves considerable effort and that were submitted to government agencies as a condition for obtaining approval to commercialize products.

Penalty – imprisonment, for 3 (three) months to 1 (one) year, or a fine.

Obviously Rio 2016 will have in place a brand protection team and will put in place a vigorous programme. The organising committee has also promised to introduce new legislation if necessary, particularly in relation to emerging technologies and new media posing additional intellectual property challenges.

Conclusions

It is clear from this chapter that sports event owners, especially the Olympics, will go to extensive lengths to protect their commercial properties. In the case of the Olympics this has meant pushing for greater legislative protection in all jurisdictions for their trade marks and expecting host cities to enact far-reaching additional protective legislation and additional measures, such as city byelaws, in order to prevent against ambush marketing and afford maximum protection to the official sponsors of the event.

It is also clear that this ferocious protection of rights shows no signs of abatement in the near future, and indeed in the case of the Olympics and FIFA may even be seen to be overzealous. As mentioned above, the chapter is written from the perspective of an event owner but it is worth noting that opposing arguments exist which claim such measures to be draconian and out of control.

The following article challenges the legal enforceability of the anti-ambush marketing provisions as they relate to non-commercial entities:

Mouritz, A, 'Challenging the Legal Enforceability of the Vancouver 2010 Olympic Games Anti-ambush Marketing Provisions'

'[S]chools should not host "Mini Olympics" or "2012 Days", or use the Games' Marks in school literature'
When I read this statement on LOCOG's website, various things came to mind, including terms such as 'madness', 'nitpicking' and 'so much for the Olympic Spirit . . .'

VANOC's intentions are not bad. To the contrary, VANOC is trying to safeguard justified interests of the main sponsors who are in fact making the Vancouver 2010 Olympic Games possible. VANOC surely wants to go after the 'big fish' because those certain big ambush marketers jeopardize VANOC's current sponsor contracts as well as sponsor contracts for future Olympic Games.

However, if VANOC is truly only interested in such big fish, then it would only be logical for VANOC to also make this clear in the Bill. Currently the text of the Bill is, pursuant to an expression from my country, a 'cure for an elephant'.

The down side of the overly broad wording is not just that it is too restrictive towards individuals and clubs who have good intentions, i.e. who are making supportive or otherwise noncommercial use of the Olympics' intellectual property rights. There is also really no advantage to outlawing such non-commercial use. If VANOC pursues such 'infringers', then, apart from potential public ridicule and mockery, it is likely to lose many of such legal battles. If, however, VANOC chooses not to pursue, then it may set precedents and this may well prevent VANOC being able to undertake future actions in similar cases.

The key issue here is the apparent lack of focus and clarity. A distinction needs to be made between friend and foe. After all, will VANOC really go after schools, fans, etc?! So far the Bill and VANOC have not been successful in conveying the right message. It should be made clear to the public that the aim is to prevent and combat the real 'commercial parasites' truly posing a genuine threat. In this respect I strongly suggest VANOC to 'puts its money where its mouth is', i.e. to make it clear to the public that pure non-commercial use of the Olympics' intellectual property rights is, in principle, allowed.[102]

The Civil Liberties Association in Canada issued proceedings against the City of Vancouver for the draconian anti-ambush marketing byelaws described above. The case was only withdrawn when the Bye-law was re-worded so as to protect the right to freedom of expression and peaceful assembly. VANOC released the following media statement:

Robinson, L, 'The Vancouver Olympics; a critical retrospect'

A balance of interests: freedom of expression in public spaces, athletes competing at their best and spectator enjoyment at the 2010 Games

The Vancouver Organizing Committee for the 2010 Olympic and Paralympic Winter Games (VANOC) is working closely with its partners to provide a reasonable balance of interests at the 2010 Winter Games including freedom of expression in public spaces; the protection of Olympic marks and Games sponsors against commercial infringement and ambush marketing; and venues where athletes can compete at their very best before spectators who can fully enjoy the events.

The following outlines VANOC's position and intentions on freedom of expression in public areas, commercial rights management and the terms and conditions of attendance at Games venues, which are entirely consistent with international sporting event norms:

I.   Respect for Freedom of Expression in Balance with the Celebration of Sport
- VANOC and its partners respect every citizen's right to freedom of expression as protected by Canadian law.
- VANOC also recognizes the need to find the balance for all; including respecting and protecting the rights of athletes, spectators and sponsors, as agreed to when Canada won the right to host the 2010 Winter Games.[103]

In the Gay Olympics case[104] one of the Judges was in dissent:

Justice Brennan referred to the insufficient 'balance between the governmental interest and the magnitude of the speech restriction' to justify the USOC's trademark monopoly. For

---

102 Mouritz, A, 'Challenging the Legal Enforceability of the Vancouver 2010 Olympic Games anti ambush marketing provisions' (2009) 16(1) SATLJ.
103 http://www.playthegame.org/news/detailed/the-vancouver-olympics-a-critical-retrospect-4964.html
104 *International Olympic Committee et al. v San Francisco Arts and Athletics et al.* (1982) 219 USPQ (BNA) 982; (1982) *US Dist and San Francisco Arts and Athletics Inc et al v USOC et al*, 483 US 522 (1987).

Brennan J., section 380 directly advanced federal government interests by allowing the USOC to raise money to support various Olympic endeavours. As such, constitutional guarantees of free speech and equal protection could not be contravened. Many USOC functions involved Congressional sanction through legislation, which in turn defined the organisation as a state instrumentality. Congress thus enabled the USOC to be 'endowed . . . with traditional governmental powers' to perform its essential functions on behalf of the IOC throughout the US . . . Brennan J expressed concern over the regulation of a term 'with a deep history in the English language and Western culture'. The trail of USOC litigation highlighted how the legislative control of language could be viewed as a 'guise for banning the expression of unpopular views'. To restrict or privatise the use of terms with a universal linguistic meaning could ridiculously dilute popular speech, with the greatest effect 'on those groups that may benefit most' from their connotations . . . Brennan J had no hesitation in declaring the USOC's language monopoly 'substantially overbroad' (*SFAA et al v. USOC et al*, 1987, p. 562). The 'extraordinary range of non-commercial speech' protected by the Amateur Sports Act was in effect a blanket prohibition qualified only by the USOC's enforcement discretion. With no express requirement to prove actual public confusion, 'unfettered' discretionary enforcement powers, and a substantial level of 'Government interest', the reforms appeared to enhance the USOC's revenue raising power at the expense of the right to dissent.[105]

As has been discussed above, in some jurisdictions, ambush marketing amounts to a criminal offence. Commercial bodies such as the ESA oppose this criminalisation and advocate using alternative methods to promote a culture whereby ambush marketing is seen by the public as abhorrent. Also as mentioned earlier, in the UK it is currently being investigated whether provisions to insist that all Olympic tickets are purchased only with Visa cards because that is the official TOP sponsor breach fair trading provisions.

Public watchdogs and the judiciary in all jurisdictions will have to continue to monitor the development of anti-ambush marketing strategies and legislation to ensure that they do not infringe on the rights of others. However, given the commercial returns involved in hosting an event such as the Olympics or the FIFA World Cup it is clear that governments and cities are willing to do their utmost and push the boundaries to the absolute limit in order to win the right to host such prestigious events. It is also clear from the case law that courts are reluctant to find against the event owners, especially in relation to the Olympics.

Key Points

- The Olympics are the pinnacle of all sports events. The brand is so strong it has its own UN Treaty and unique global legislation to afford it maximum trademark protection.
- The Olympic sponsorship model is complex, involving multiple stakeholders and multiple jurisdictions, but it works well through carefully drafted contracts.
- The sale of Olympic branded merchandise also generates considerable income for the Olympic movement and the OCOG will be required to protect against counterfeiting and enact a public education campaign to ensure the public buy official merchandise.
- In many jurisdictions ticket touting is not illegal, thereby allowing the tout to make profit on the re-sale. The model used by VANOC is one which was successful. For London 2012 and Glasgow 2014 ticket touting will be illegal.
- Database protection is a new intellectual property right which is still evolving.

---

105 Symons, C and Warren, I, 'David v Goliath: The Gay Games, the Olympics, and the Ownership of Language' (2006) ESLJ.

- Ambush marketing is not illegal but actions can be brought in passing off/misappropriation (in USA) or under relevant trademark law. Case law in both the UK and USA illustrates that such actions rarely succeed.
- Since the Sydney 2000 Olympics sophisticated, specific-event-encompassing domestic legislation and local city ordinances have been enacted by each host city to protect against ambush marketing.
- A highly efficient clean venue programme protects the Olympics against ambush marketing and protects and promotes the Olympic brand.
- The imposition of criminal sanctions and a heavy-handed approach against ambush marketing serves to add to a 'greedy event owner' public perception. Alternative non-legal solutions should be explored.
- Prevention and public education is the only way that event owners can achieve a balance between being heavy-handed and protecting their own commercial integrity.

Key Sources

Blackshaw, I and Siekmann, R, *Sports Image Rights in Europe* (2005) The Hague: TMC Asser Press.

Fabien, S, (ed.) *Sports Sponsorship and the Law: Expert Legal Opinion on Sponsorship Contract Issues* (2010), management report published and distributed by International Marketing Reports Ltd.

IOC Website: http://www.olympic.org/documents-reports-studies-publications.

Lewis, A and Taylor, J, *Sport Law and Practice* (2009) Haywards Heath: Tottel Publishing, parts G and H.

Payne, M, *Olympic Turnaround: How the Olympic Games Stepped Back from the Brink of Extinction to Become the World's Best Known Brand – and a Multi Billion Dollar Global Franchise* (2005), London: Business Press.

Part 3

Legal Issues in the Sports Workplace

8	The Regulation of Doping in Sport	363
9	Sport and Contracts of Employment	393
10	Sports Participants and the Law of Discrimination	460
11	Safety and Participants in Sport	498
12	Sports Venues and the Law	543

Chapter 8

The Regulation of Doping in Sport

Chapter Contents

Introduction	364
Anti-Doping Institutions	369
The World Anti-Doping Code	371
The Future	390
Key Points	391
Key Sources	392

Introduction

Doping is cheating[1] in the sense that it is a breach of the rules of sport. So is a handball or a dive in football, a deliberate knock-on or collapsing a scrum in rugby or deliberately taking the ground of another horse during a race. Sports regulations provide sanctions against all these different types of cheating. Most forms of cheating are punished as part of the game, race or tournament although some may result in some post-competition sanctions such as a fine. The reality of elite sporting competition is that cheating in one form or another is relatively commonplace; however, none carry the stigma nor result in such punitive and emotive reaction as doping cheats. The philosophy behind the extraordinary treatment of doping cheats is difficult to comprehend. It cannot be due to the premeditated nature of doping, as positive doping tests result in sanctions even if no culpability can be attached to the athlete in question. Nor can it be because drug taking is viewed by many as contrary to the very essence of sport, for surely any form of deliberate cheating challenges the essence of sport. For whatever reason, doping, more than any other type of sports cheating, has transcended sport and entered the public domain. The public consciousness of anti-doping has been raised in part because of the stringent sanctions attached to such a breach and because the loss of a lucrative career often forces the hand of the sanctioned athlete to utilise appeal mechanisms built in to the regulations of sports governing bodies and, if unsuccessful, to seek recourse from the courts. So, not all forms of cheating in sport are considered equal. This, allied to the fact that not all forms of cheating are unlawful, means that anti-doping and the law enjoy a complex and special relationship.[2]

The object of this chapter is to analyse both the law and the regulation of anti-doping. A study of sports regulations might be considered extraneous in a book on sports law but, whether it is considered conceptually as a process of juridification or as an example of legal pluralism, the interaction between law and regulation has become so interwoven that the significance to the actor of this distinction is practically irrelevant. Equally, as lawyers are actively involved in both the process of law and in regulation, such a distinction might be considered more accurately as the difference between hard and soft law. Although doping in humans is used almost exclusively to enhance performance, the doping of racehorses, greyhounds and other animals is often a destructive technique aimed at adversely affecting performance. This chapter concentrates on the doping of humans, but most of the issues raised are equally applicable to the doping of animals.[3]

Anti-doping regulation is predicated on two important legal principles. Firstly, the relationship between sportsmen and women and their governing bodies is a contractual one, the terms of which include, inter alia, the doping regulations of that particular sport. Diane Modahl's action against the British Athletics Federation Ltd (BAF – the predecessor of UK Athletics) was based on the breach of an implied contractual term that her hearing following a positive doping test would be fair and objective. The Court of Appeal discovered that Modahl, like all athletes, was affiliated to a club which, in turn, was affiliated to the BAF (who conducted the hearing), which was affiliated to the International Amateur Athletics Federation (IAAF) which drafted the rules of competition.

Modahl v British Athletics Federation Ltd

Lord Justice Latham: A court should not merely assume a contract to exist, but must consider all the surrounding circumstances to determine whether or not the contract can properly be implied. We are handicapped in the present case by a lack of basic factual material. Although

---

1 Green S. 'Cheating' (2004) 23(2) Law & Phil., 135–187; Beloff, M. 'Fair play – is there still room for the Corinthian spirit in sport?' (2009) 3 ISLR 34–44.
2 Ruijsenaars P et al, 'Manifesto: "stop the doping inquisition!" ' (2007) 3/4 ISLJ, 84–85.
3 Flaherty v National Greyhound Racing Club Ltd [2005] EWCA Civ 1117; Blakely, A, 'A new era for anti-doping in equestrian sports (2010) 8(5) WSLR, 12–14.

the court has been provided with the rules of the IAAF and the respondent, the court has not seen any document setting out the constitution of either organisation, although we have been given a general description of both. We have not seen any documents which indicate whether or not any individual athlete on entering any relevant competition, signs any document by which he or she agrees to be bound by either set of rules; and in particular we have not been shown any documents in relation to the applicant's entry for the meeting at Lisbon. It may or may not be, therefore, that, contained in such documents was the sort of wording which enabled Lightman J to conclude that Mr Korda became contractually bound by the ITF Rules when entering the All England Lawn Tennis Championships. It is clear from documents that we have seen that the successor body to the respondent envisages that individual contracts may be entered into by athletes which could contain such express provisions. This suggests to me that there is nothing inherently improbable about the concept of a contractual obligation being entered into by an individual athlete which would create a contractual relationship between the athlete and the respondent. The question therefore is whether or not on the material which we do have, it is proper to infer such a contract.[4]

Latham LJ and Manse LJ agreed there was a contractual relationship. Jonathan Parker LJ disagreed. The view of Jonathan Parker LJ followed a line of argument promulgated by Lord Denning who, in cases such as *Nagle v Feilden*[5] and *Lee v The Showman's Guild of Great Britain*[6] expressed his concern that the identification of a contractual nexus in such situations was little more than a fiction.

The second important legal principle is that anti-doping regulation, as represented by the World Anti-Doping Code, is considered by the law to be a proportional response to doping in sport. This was established in the European Court of Justice decision in *Meca-Medina v Commission of the European Communities*.[7] David Meca-Medina was one of two swimmers who tested positive for nandrolone and were subsequently banned from competition. The swimmers challenged the proportionality of the anti-doping rules before the ECJ. They argued that the nandrolone limit had no scientific legitimacy and, in their case, raised nandrolone levels were as a result of the consumption of boar meat. The European Court of First Instance agreed with the European Commission that the anti-doping rule fell outside the scope of European competition law. The ECJ disagreed and gave an important judgment which helps to establish the sphere of legal influence and also whether the anti-doping regulations contained within the World Anti-Doping Agency Code (the Code) are a proportional response to the perceived problem.

Meca-Medina v Commission of the European Communities

22. It is to be remembered that, having regard to the objectives of the Community, sport is subject to Community law in so far as it constitutes an economic activity within the meaning of Art.2 EC.

23. Thus, where a sporting activity takes the form of gainful employment or the provision of services for remuneration, which is true of the activities of semi-professional or professional sportsmen, it falls, more specifically, within the scope of Arts 39 EC et seq., or Arts 49 EC et seq.

24. These Community provisions on freedom of movement for persons and freedom to provide services not only apply to the action of public authorities but extend also to rules of any other nature aimed at regulating gainful employment and the provision of services in a collective.

---

4   2001 WL 1135166.
5   [1966] 2 QB 633.
6   [1952] 2 QB 329.
7   (C-519/04 P) [2006] ECR I-6991; [2006] 5 CMLR 18.

25. The Court has, however, held that the prohibitions enacted by those provisions of the Treaty do not affect rules concerning questions which are of purely sporting interest and, as such, have nothing to do with economic activity.

26. With regard to the difficulty of severing the economic aspects from the sporting aspects of a sport, the court has held that the provisions of Community law concerning freedom of movement for persons and freedom to provide services do not preclude rules or practices justified on non-economic grounds which relate to the particular nature and context of certain sporting events. It has stressed, however, that such a restriction on the scope of the provisions in question must remain limited to its proper objective. It cannot, therefore, be relied upon to exclude the whole of a sporting activity from the scope of the Treaty.

27. In light of all of these considerations, it is apparent that the mere fact that a rule is purely sporting in nature does not have the effect of removing from the scope of the Treaty the person engaging in the activity governed by that rule or the body which has laid it down.

28. If the sporting activity in question falls within the scope of the Treaty, the conditions for engaging in it are then subject to all the obligations which result from the various provisions of the Treaty. It follows that the rules which govern that activity must satisfy the requirements of those provisions, which, in particular, seek to ensure freedom of movement for workers, freedom of establishment, freedom to provide services, or competition.

29. Thus, where engagement in the sporting activity must be assessed in the light of the Treaty provisions relating to freedom of movement for workers or freedom to provide services, it will be necessary to determine whether the rules which govern that activity satisfy the requirements of Arts 39 and 49 EC, that is to say do not constitute restrictions prohibited by those articles.

30. Likewise, where engagement in the activity must be assessed in the light of the Treaty provisions relating to competition, it will be necessary to determine, given the specific requirements of Arts 81 and 82 EC, whether the rules which govern that activity emanate from an undertaking, whether the latter restricts competition or abuses its dominant position, and whether that restriction or that abuse affects trade between Member States.

31. Therefore, even if those rules do not constitute restrictions on freedom of movement because they concern questions of purely sporting interest and, as such, have nothing to do with economic activity that fact means neither that the sporting activity in question necessarily falls outside the scope of Arts 81 and 82 EC nor that the rules do not satisfy the specific requirements of those articles.

32. However, in para. [42] of the contested judgment, the Court of First Instance held that the fact that purely sporting rules may have nothing to do with economic activity, with the result that they do not fall within the scope of Arts 39 and 49 EC, means, also, that they have nothing to do with the economic relationships of competition, with the result that they also do not fall within the scope of Arts 81 and 82 EC.

33. In holding that rules could thus be excluded straightaway from the scope of those articles solely on the ground that they were regarded as purely sporting with regard to the application of Arts 39 and 49 EC, without any need to determine first whether the rules fulfilled the specific requirements of Arts 81 and 82 EC, as set out in para. [30] of the present judgment, the Court of First Instance made an error of law.

34. Accordingly, the appellants are justified in asserting that, in para. [68] of the contested judgment, the Court of First Instance erred in dismissing their application on the ground that the anti-doping rules at issue were subject to neither Art.49 EC nor competition law.

It is now clear that an examination of the legitimacy of anti-doping regulations falls within the ambit of the law. This does not mean, however, that doping regulations are in breach of the law for, as the ECJ continued,

43. As regards the overall context in which the rules at issue were adopted, the Commission could rightly take the view that the general objective of the rules was, as none of the parties disputes, to combat doping in order for competitive sport to be conducted fairly and that it included the need to safeguard equal chances for athletes, athletes' health, the integrity and objectivity of competitive sport and ethical values in sport.

44. In addition, given that penalties are necessary to ensure enforcement of the doping ban, their effect on athletes' freedom of action must be considered to be, in principle, inherent itself in the anti-doping rules.

45. Therefore, even if the anti-doping rules at issue are to be regarded as a decision of an association of undertakings limiting the appellants' freedom of action, they do not, for all that, necessarily constitute a restriction of competition incompatible with the Common Market, within the meaning of Art. 81 EC, since they are justified by a legitimate objective. Such a limitation is inherent in the organisation and proper conduct of competitive sport and its very purpose is to ensure healthy rivalry between athletes.

46. While the appellants do not dispute the truth of this objective, they nevertheless contend that the anti-doping rules at issue are also intended to protect the IOC's own economic interests and that it is in order to safeguard this objective that excessive rules, such as those contested in the present case, are adopted. The latter cannot therefore, in their submission, be regarded as inherent in the proper conduct of competitive sport and fall outside the prohibitions in Art. 81 EC.

47. It must be acknowledged that the penal nature of the anti-doping rules at issue and the magnitude of the penalties applicable if they are breached are capable of producing adverse effects on competition because they could, if penalties were ultimately to prove unjustified, result in an athlete's unwarranted exclusion from sporting events, and thus in impairment of the conditions under which the activity at issue is engaged in. It follows that, in order not to be covered by the prohibition laid down in Art. 81(1) EC, the restrictions thus imposed by those rules must be limited to what is necessary to ensure the proper conduct of competitive sport.

48. Rules of that kind could indeed prove excessive by virtue of, first, the conditions laid down for establishing the dividing line between circumstances which amount to doping in respect of which penalties may be imposed and those which do not, and second, the severity of those penalties.

49. Here, that dividing line is determined in the anti-doping rules at issue by the threshold of 2 ng/ml of urine above which the presence of Nandrolone in an athlete's body constitutes doping. The appellants contest that rule, asserting that the threshold adopted is set at an excessively low level which is not founded on any scientifically safe criterion.

50. However, the appellants fail to establish that the Commission made a manifest error of assessment in finding that rule to be justified.

51. It is common ground that Nandrolone is an anabolic substance the presence of which in athletes' bodies is liable to improve their performance and compromise the fairness of the sporting events in which they participate. The ban on that substance is accordingly in principle justified in light of the objective of anti-doping rules.

52. It is also common ground that that substance may be produced endogenously and that, in order to take account of this phenomenon, sporting bodies, including the IOC by means of the anti-doping rules at issue, have accepted that doping is considered to have occurred only where the substance is present in an amount exceeding a certain threshold. It is therefore only if, having regard to scientific knowledge as it stood when the anti-doping rules at issue were adopted or even when they were applied to punish the appellants, in 1999, the threshold is set at such a low level that it should be regarded as not taking sufficient account of this phenomenon that those rules should be regarded as not justified in light of the objective which they were intended to achieve.

53. It is apparent from the documents before the court that at the material time the average endogenous production observed in all studies then published was 20 times lower than 2ng/ml of urine and that the maximum endogenous production value observed was nearly a third lower. While the appellants contend that, from 1993, the IOC could not have been unaware of the risk reported by an expert that merely consuming a limited quantity of boar meat could cause entirely innocent athletes to exceed the threshold in question, it is not in any event established that at the material time this risk had been confirmed by the majority of the scientific community. Moreover, the results of the studies and the experiments carried out on this point subsequent to the decision at issue have no bearing in any event on the legality of that decision.

54. In those circumstances, and as the appellants do not specify at what level the threshold in question should have been set at the material time, it does not appear that the restrictions which that threshold imposes on professional sportsmen go beyond what is necessary in order to ensure that sporting events take place and function properly.

55. Since the appellants have, moreover, not pleaded that the penalties which were applicable and were imposed in the present case are excessive, it has not been established that the anti-doping rules at issue are disproportionate.

56. Accordingly, the second plea must be dismissed.[8]

So, although anti-doping regulations fall within the ambit of the law as an economic activity, they did not, on the facts, breach principles of proportionality under EU law. It would be fair to state, therefore, that those sporting bodies that draft anti-doping regulation that is broadly in conformity with the Code will not be susceptible to legal challenge. The Code allows for deviation in certain articles and it is here that governing bodies must beware if they deviate to any significant degree by making their regulations more stringent.[9]

Weatherill, S, 'Anti-doping revisited – the demise of the rule of "purely sporting interest"?'

Meca-Medina and Majcen seems to have brought to an end the practical value to sports bodies of arguing that their rules are of 'purely sporting interest'. This will be true only in trivial circumstances where one could scarcely imagine litigation being pursued. Instead the emphasis will be on whether rules, carrying economic impact, produce consequential restrictive effects which are inherent in the pursuit of their objectives. If so, but only if so, they escape prohibition under Art. 81(1). The same point, delivered in slightly different vocabulary and in relation to Art. 39 not Art. 81, is found in *ECLR 657, the Court's judgment in *Bosman*, which accepts as

---

8   C-519/04 P) [2006] ECR I-6991.
9   Subiotto, R, 'The adoption and enforcement of anti-doping rules should not be subject to European competition law' (2010) 31(8) ECLR 323–30; Pijetlovic, K, 'Paragraph 31 of C-519/04 Meca-Medina reversed' (2009) 1/2 ISLJ 137–38; Subiotto, R,'How a lack of analytical rigour has resulted in an overbroad application of EC competition law in the sports sector' (2009) 2 ISLR 21–29; Manville, A, 'European court vs sports organisations – who will win the antitrust competition?' (2008) 3/4 ISLJ 19–26; Szyszczak, E, 'Competition and sport' (2007) 32(1) ELRev. 95–110; Baily, D, 'Taking the governance of sport out of court' (2007) SLA&P 5–6.

'legitimate' the perceived sports specific anxiety to maintain a balance between clubs by preserving a certain degree of equality and uncertainty as to results and to encourage the recruitment and training of young players. And in *Deliege*, an Art. 49 case, the Court accepted that selection rules limited the number of participants in a tournament, but were 'inherent' in the event's organisation. Such rules are not beyond the reach of the Treaty, but they are not incompatible with its requirements. But, as *Meca-Medina* itself shows, there remains scope for sport to protect its right to assert internal expertise in taking decisions that have both sporting and economic implications. The ECJ has collapsed the idea that there are purely sporting practices unaffected by EC law despite their economic effect, but it has not refused to accept that sport is special. Its message to governing bodies – explain how![10]

A good example of a governing body imposing conditions above and beyond the Code is the lifetime Olympic Games ban imposed by the International Olympic Committee on anyone banned for a doping offence. The legality of this measure was challenged by Dwain Chambers following his return from a two-year doping ban in 2007.[11] In the High Court Mackay J refused an injunction preventing the British Olympic Committee from excluding Chambers on the grounds that, on balance, justice was better served by maintaining the status quo.[12] It must be remembered, however, that this was an application for injunctive relief and decisive factors in this application, such as the status quo and the last-minute nature of the application, would not be so crucial at a full trial. There remains the possibility then that the four-year IOC ban might be challenged successfully on the grounds of restraint of trade or a breach of natural justice under the court's inherent jurisdiction.[13]

Anti-Doping Institutions

It is significant in gauging governmental response to anti-doping to note the conventions of UNESCO and the Council of Europe.[14] These supra-national governmental organisations reflect international political views even if those views are not necessarily manifested in national laws. The UNESCO International Convention Against Doping in Sport[15] states that its purpose 'within the framework of the strategy and programme of activities of UNESCO in the area of physical education and sport, is to promote the prevention of and the fight against doping in sport, with a view to its elimination'.[16] The convention is interesting because it adopts, overtly, the World Anti-Doping Agency (WADA) Code while asserting the primacy of the Convention where there is conflict.[17] Such conflict is inevitable as the Convention stands, referring as it does to the repealed 2003 Code. It also emphasises how little distinction there is between law and regulation. Article 3 of the convention confirms that state parties agree to:

---

10 Weatherill, S, 'Anti-doping revisited – the demise of the rule of "purely sporting interest"?' (2006) 27(12) ECLR 645–57.
11 Blackshaw, I, 'Dwain Chambers loses his High Court challenge to overturn his lifetime '(2008) 3/4 ISLJ 155; Dovey, D, 'Challenging decisions of sports governing bodies revisited: the impact of Dwain Chambers v British Olympic Association' (2009) SLA&P (Dec) 13–16.
12 *Chambers v British Olympic Association* [2008] EWHC 2028 (QB) (QBD).
13 *Bradley v Jockey Club* [2004] EWHC 2164 (QB); *Nagle v Fielden* [1966] 2 QB 633; *McInnes v Onslow-Fane* [1978] 1 WLR 1520; *R (on the application of Mullins) v Jockey Club Appeal Board (No.1)* [2005] EWHC 2197 (Admin); *Times*, October 24, 2005 (QBD (Admin)); *R. v Disciplinary Committee of the Jockey Club Ex p. Aga Khan* [1993] 1 WLR 909 (CA (Civ Div)); *Law v National Greyhound Racing Club* [1983] 1 WLR 1302 (CA (Civ Div)); *Wilander and Another v Tobin and Another* [1997] 2 CMLR 346.
14 See also the Helsinki Report on Sport, which refers specifically to the role of the EU in global anti-doping strategy. See Weatherill, S, 'The Helsinki Report on Sport' (2000) 25(3) EL Rev, 282–92.
15 Paris, 19 October 2005.
16 Article 1.
17 Article 2.

Article 3, UNESCO International Convention Against Doping in Sport

(a) adopt appropriate measures at the national a state parties and international levels which are consistent with the principles of the Code;

(b) encourage all forms of international cooperation aimed at protecting athletes and ethics in sport and at sharing the results of research;

(c) foster international cooperation between States Parties and leading organizations in the fight against doping in sport, in particular with the World Anti-DopingAgency.

The Council of Europe Convention defines its terms independently of WADA and other sports bodies. Like the UNESCO Convention it is a statement of political intent requiring that 'The Parties, with a view to the reduction and eventual elimination of doping in sport, undertake, within the limits of their respective constitutional provisions, to take the steps necessary to apply the provisions of this Convention.' Both conventions are indicative of a willingness on the part of politicians to engage in an anti-doping dialogue at state level and may be a precursor of a trend towards greater criminalisation of doping cheats.

The International Olympic Committee (IOC) is at the apex of world sports organisations and 'fights' a 'war' against dopers. The unyielding position, and rhetoric, adopted by the IOC and the governing bodies is based on the premise that doping is wrong. In 1999 the IOC restated its stance in a press release:

> The International Olympic Committee (IOC) wishes to reiterate its total commitment to the fight against doping, with the aim of protecting athletes' health and preserving fair play in sport. Any declarations which go against these principles are both wrong and misplaced.[18]

Although the IOC has long held these principles sacred, its influence over governing bodies was ineffective. The history of doping regulation in sport is littered with examples of governing bodies failing to draft their doping codes competently. Little thought was given to the compatibility of doping rules between sports. Also, governing bodies seemed unaware of how previous doping rules of their own sport interacted with new provisions. The danger was that a successful legal challenge could not only call into question the reliability of the testing procedure and encourage other athletes to initiate court action, but could also prove disastrously expensive for the domestic federation.[19] What was required was an effective international standard that could transcend such problems as athlete mobility because 'the problems of undertaking testing among an elite group of athletes who were increasingly mobile and who were likely to be in their native country, and therefore accessible by their national doping control officers, for only part of each year. Indeed there was a growing number of athletes who spent most of their elite career outside their home country. For example, world-class Australian road cyclists spent most, if not all, of their time in Europe where the major events and teams were located. Much the same could be said for the increasing number of South American and African track and field athletes who followed the American and European calendar of competitions. Such a high level of athlete mobility required a set of anti-doping regulations that would prevent athletes exploiting the loopholes and inconsistencies found in the anti-doping regulations of various countries and domestic affiliates of international federations'.[20]

As Michael Beloff QC, an arbitrator at the Court of Arbitration for Sport explained:

---

18 Lausanne, 8 July 1999.
19 Houlihan, B, 'The World Anti-Doping Agency: prospects for success', in O'Leary, J (ed), *Drugs and Doping in Sport* (2000), London: Cavendish Publishing, p 128.
20 Ibid.

Beloff, M, 'Drugs, laws and Versapaks'

. . . in my experience, rules of domestic or international federations tend to resemble the archi-tecture of an ancient building: a wing added here; a loft there; a buttress elsewhere, without adequate consideration of whether the additional parts affect adversely the symmetry of the whole.[21]

As a result of this, sport has harmonised the doping regulations of the various national and inter-national governing bodies. In the vanguard of this movement is the World Anti-Doping Agency (WADA). The rise of WADA can be seen as a response to the inadequacies of earlier regimes and a realisation that successful anti-doping policies come at a price. From a jurisprudential perspective WADA might be viewed as one of many quasi-judicial global administrators; 'the extent that they develop a law-like quality, they do so after-the-fact, consequential upon the administrative tasks in which they are engaged. They develop substantive rules of conduct, and also procedural rules for decision-making and decision-accounting, but they lack any constitutive co-ordinates to underpin these substantive and procedural rules. In other words, they are non-autochthonous – unrooted in any state or other stable site of public authority or even at the contested boundaries between different sites of public authority, and instead generate such authority as they have purely out of the regulatory purposes that they pursue and practices that they develop.'[22]

In order that doping and other sport-related disputes, as they arise, can be contained within the sporting world, the Court of Arbitration for Sport (CAS) was conceived in 1981. A full analysis of the CAS and its jurisprudence can be found in Chapter 4. It is interesting to note at this point, however, that doping cases make up a significant proportion of the CAS caseload and doping cases have influenced significantly the development of the jurisprudence of the CAS.[23] It is arguable, however, that the role of the CAS in anti-doping has been marginalised by the develop-ment of the World Anti-Doping Code. As it will be seen below, the uniform application of a single code throughout sport leaves the CAS with little residual discretion to influence doping policy.[24]

At a national level responsibility for implementing anti-doping measures falls on anti-doping agencies. These are commonly state-related bodies. In the UK, UK Anti-Doping (UKAD) delivers information and education programmes as well as testing across a range of sports. UKAD exerts considerable influence, as lottery funding is predicated on compliance with testing and whereabouts requirements.

The World Anti-Doping Code

The World Anti-Doping Code was first adopted in 2003 and became effective in 2004. The current, revised World Anti-Doping Code became effective as of 1 January 2009. Article 23.1.1 states: 'The following entities shall be Signatories accepting the Code: WADA, The International Olympic Committee, International Federations, The International Paralympic Committee, National Olympic Committees, National Paralympic Committees, Major Event Organisations, and National Anti-Doping Organisations. These entities shall accept the Code by signing a declaration of acceptance upon approval by each of their respective governing bodies.' Such is the influence exerted by WADA

---

21 Beloff, M, 'Drugs, laws and Versapaks', in O'Leary, J (ed), *Drugs and Doping in Sport* (2000), London: Cavendish, p 40.
22 Walker, N, 'Out of place and out of time: law's fading co-ordinates' (2010) 14(1) Edin LR 13–46; Casini, L, 'Global hybrid public-private bodies: the World Anti-Doping Agency (WADA)' (2009) 6(2) IOLR 421–46.
23 'CAS Doping Jurisprudence: What Can We Learn?' (2006) 1(Feb) ISLR 4–22; Tarasti, L, 'The Athlete's Liability for Doping' (2005) 43 Bulletin of the International Council of Sport Science and Physical Education.
24 McClaren, R, 'CAS doping jurisprudence: what can we learn?' (2006) Feb 1 ISLR 4–22.

and the IOC that participation by a sport at international level is virtually impossible unless that governing body is a signatory to the Code.[25]

The Code consists of a set of model regulations that aims to ensure consistency in the application of anti doping regulation.[26] In its introduction it explains that 'The Code does not, however, replace or eliminate the need for comprehensive anti-doping rules adopted by each Anti-Doping Organisation.[27] While some provisions of the Code must be incorporated without substantive change by each Anti-Doping Organisation in its own anti-doping rules, other provisions of the Code establish mandatory guiding principles that allow flexibility in the formulation of rules by each Anti-Doping Organisation or establish requirements that must be followed by each Anti-Doping Organisation but need not be repeated in its own anti-doping rules.' Article 23.2.2 clarifies which sections of the code must be incorporated 'without substantive change' into the regulations of the governing bodies. They include Art 1 (definition of doping), Art 2 (anti-doping rule violations), Art 3 (proof of doing) and Art 4.2.2 (specified substances). The 2009 Code differs from the 2003 Code in many respects, including a broadening of the proof of doping counterbalanced in part by a wider range of complex sanctions which are applied according to the degree of culpability of the athlete.[28]

One of the major obstacles for any body intent on implementing a rule for the whole world is that it must encompass a diverse range of religious, legal and social perspectives. The imposition at a global level of blood testing, for example, would meet with resistance on the grounds of religion and might prove counter-productive for 'where resistance to the global regime has arisen at a local level, whether as a result of cultural, social or legal disparities, this has had the effect of creating a situation of imbalance, where athletes are either subject to much stricter controls or effectively allowed to act irrespective of the rules "imposed" by the global regulator'.[29]

The fundamental rationale of the Code is:

World Anti-Doping Code: Preamble

. . . to preserve what is intrinsically valuable about sport. This intrinsic value is often referred to as 'the spirit of sport'; it is the essence of Olympism; it is how we play true. The spirit of sport is the celebration of the human spirit, body and mind, and is characterized by the following values:

- Ethics, fair play and honesty
- Health
- Excellence in performance
- Character and education
- Fun and joy
- Teamwork
- Dedication and commitment
- Respect for rules and laws
- Respect for self and other participants
- Courage
- Community and solidarity.

Doping is fundamentally contrary to the spirit of sport.

---

25 For an interesting examination or non-compliance see CAS opinion CAS 2005/C/976 & 986, FIFA & WADA.
26 The notion of one-size-fits-all is by no means universally popular. See Bailey, D, 'The specificity of sport' (2009) SLA&P (Dec) 5–9; Farrow, S, 'Team sports' issues with the WADA Code' (2009) 7(6) WSLR 14–16.
27 Charlish P. 'Cricket pair "not out" in doping row' (2007) 4 ISLR 57–66.
28 Teitler, S and Ram, H, 'Analysing the New World Anti-Doping Code: A Different Perspective' (2008) 1/2 ISLJ 42–49; Tarasti, L, 'Some juridical question marks in the revised World Anti-Doping Code' (2008) 2/3 ISLR 17–23; Marshall, J and Hale, A, 'Will the new WADA Code plug all the gaps? Will there be by-catch?' (2008) 1/2 ISLJ 37–42.
29 Boyes, S, 'The International Olympic Committee, transnational doping policy and globalisation', in O'Leary, J (ed), *Drugs and Doping in Sport* (2000), London: Cavendish Publishing, p 178.

Anti-doping rule violations

The definition of a doping offence under Article 1 is the violation of an anti-doping rule contained in Article 2. They are: the presence of a prohibited substance or its metabolites in an athlete's sample;[30] use or attempted use by an athlete of a prohibited substance or a prohibited method;[31] refusing or failing without compelling justification to sample collection;[32] violation of applicable requirements regarding athlete availability for out-of-competition testing;[33] tampering or attempted tampering with any part of doping control;[34] possession of prohibited substances or prohibited methods;[35] trafficking or attempted trafficking in any prohibited substance or prohibited method;[36] and administration or attempted administration to any athlete of any prohibited method or prohibited substance.[37]

Out-of-competition testing is an important element of anti-doping policy as doping substances and methods used in training may not be detectable at an event.

World Anti-Doping Code, Article 2.4

Violation of applicable requirements regarding Athlete availability for Out-of-Competition Testing, including failure to file required whereabouts information and missed tests which are declared based on rules which comply with the International Standard for Testing. Any combination of three missed tests and/or filing failures within an eighteen-month period as determined by Anti-Doping Organizations with jurisdiction over the Athlete shall constitute an anti-doping rule violation.

Christine Ohuruogu missed three out-of-competition tests and was suspended for 12 months by a UK Athletics disciplinary committee. The impact of the suspension was greater still as another consequence was a lifetime Olympic ban. Her appeal was upheld on the basis of 'significant mitigating circumstances'. It was held that it was irrelevant that Ohuruogu had no intention to engage in doping activities or that no notice was given of the test (indeed the Committee upheld that the surprise element is an important weapon against dopers). They did, however, concede that there was insufficient training and instruction available to athletes at the time (now rectified by the UK Anti-Doping Advice Card 2010[38]). The Committee, conscious of opening the floodgates, did add that with improved education for athletes, such a ground of appeal would be likely to fail in future. Strong and logical arguments are put forward for the necessity of such a regime, but important issues remain around the validity of a draconian out-of-competition testing regime, not least the right to privacy and a family life. With all due respect to sports' anti-doping aspirations, these rights, enshrined in the European Convention on Human Rights, are of rather greater importance. It remains the task of sports regulators to ensure that out-of-competition test regulations exhibit due deference to such principles.[39]

The WADA Code operates a system of strict liability. This means a positive test is sufficient in itself to establish liability. The governing body would not have to show that the competitor or

---

30 Art 2.1.
31 Art 2.2.
32 Art 2.3.
33 Art 2.4.
34 Art 2.5.
35 Art 2.6.
36 Art 2.7.
37 Art 2.8.
38 To be found at the time of publishing at http://www.ukad.org.uk/documents/advice-card-2011/.
39 Editorial BOA Appeals Panel: Christine Ohuruogu v BOA (2008), 2/3 ISLR SLR113. See also Soek, J, 'The athlete's right to respect for his private life and his home' (2008) 3/4 ISLJ, 3–13; Horvath, P and Lording, P, 'WADA's International Standard for Testing: privacy issues' (2009) 7(2) WSLR 14–16; Nicholson, G, 'Anti-doping and the World Anti-Doping Code: does one size fit all and is the whereabouts system fair, reasonable and efficient?' (2009) SLA&P (Apr) 8–11.

another person transmitted into the competitor's body a banned substance with the *aim* of achieving an increase in performance, nor that the substance did actually increase performance. The concept of *mens rea* or 'guilty mind' is well known to criminal lawyers. Although there is a considerable difference between doping proceedings and criminal trials, some lawyers have suggested that the strict liability provisions of many sports governing bodies are fundamentally unjust. Strict liability in doping regulations allows a governing body to ban an athlete without showing that the athlete intended to take the substance. Despite the obvious concerns over a rule of this nature, both the CAS and the English High Court have held that a strict liability rule is lawful, bearing in mind that it may be the only way to effectively police the doping problem.

A rule that a positive test leads to an automatic ban is attractive in its clarity and simplicity but denies what many of us would view as the fundamental right of an opportunity to show a lack of fault, knowledge or intent. In practice this means that even if an athlete could prove that the consumption of the drug was accidental or a result of malice on the part of another, he or she would still be in breach. Strict liability may appear to be a draconian provision. The reason for it is a fear that rules requiring proof of intent would be impossible to implement: it is feared that athletes would find little difficulty in producing someone prepared to take responsibility and vouch for the athlete's innocence.

Quigley v UIT

It is true that a strict liability test is likely in some sense to be unfair in an individual case, such as that of Q, where the Athlete may have taken medication as the result of mislabeling or faulty advice for which he or she is not responsible – particularly in the circumstances of sudden illness in a foreign country. But it is also in some sense 'unfair' for an Athlete to get food poisoning on the eve of an important competition. Yet in neither case will the rules of the competition be altered to undo the unfairness. Just as the competition will not be postponed to await the Athlete's recovery, so the prohibition of banned substances will not be lifted in recognition of its accidental absorption. The vicissitudes of competition, like those of life generally, may create many types of unfairness, whether by accident or the negligence of unaccountable Persons, which the law cannot repair.

Furthermore, it appears to be a laudable policy objective not to repair an accidental unfairness to an individual by creating an intentional unfairness to the whole body of other competitors. This is what would happen if banned performance-enhancing substances were tolerated when absorbed inadvertently. Moreover, it is likely that even intentional abuse would in many cases escape sanction for lack of proof of guilty intent. And it is certain that a requirement of intent would invite costly litigation that may well cripple federations – particularly those run on modest budgets – in their fight against doping.[40]

This logic was upheld by the English High Court:

Gasser v Stinson and Another, LexisNexis 15 June 1988

Scott J: Mr Blackburne submitted with great force that a rule which did not permit an athlete even to try to establish his or her innocence, either in resisting conviction or in mitigation of sentence was unreasonable and unjustifiable. But the consequences if the absolute nature of the offence was removed or if the length of the sentence became discretionary and not mandatory must be considered.

Suppose an athlete gives evidence that he or she did not take the drug knowingly and that it must therefore be inferred that the drug was digested unknowingly. How is the IAAF to deal

---

40 CAS 94/129.

with such an explanation? How can credibility be tested? Suppose a third party, perhaps a member of the athlete's team of coaches, perhaps a medical adviser, perhaps a malicious prankster, gives evidence that he or she administered the drug to the athlete and that the athlete had no knowledge that this was being done. How is the credibility of the third party's evidence to be tested? The pressure for success in international athletics, as well as domestic athletics and the national pride and prestige which has become part of international athletics has to be borne in mind. Will the credibility of the athlete or the third party vary depending on the nation to which he or she belongs? If a competitor or third party from nation A is believed, what will be the position when similar evidence is given by a competitor or third party from nation B? The lengths to which some people will go in order to achieve the appearance of success for their nation's athletes in athletics competitions is in point. The long jump in last year's World Championship illustrates the point. Cynicism, sadly, abounds. Mr Holt in his evidence, said that in his view, if a defence of moral innocence were open, the floodgates would be opened and the IAAF's attempts to prevent drug-taking by athletes would be rendered futile. He had, in my opinion, reason for that fear.

Mr Blackburne submits that it is not justifiable that the morally innocent may have to suffer in order to ensure that the guilty do not escape. But that is not a submission that is invariably acceptable. The criminal law in this country (and in, I would think, all others) has various absolute offences and various mandatory sentences. For my part I am not persuaded that the IAAF's absolute offence and mandatory sentence applicable to an athlete who is found to have dope in his or her urine is unreasonable.[41]

Scott J is correct when he states that there are a number of examples of English criminal sanctions that are strict in their liability.[42] The Misuse of Drugs Act 1971, however, the criminal provision that most closely parallels the WADA Code, does not impose strict liability. Section 28(2) states that 'in any proceedings for an offence to which this section applies it shall be a defence for the accused to prove that he neither knew of nor suspected nor had reason to suspect the existence of some fact alleged by the prosecution which it is necessary for the prosecution to prove if he is to be convicted of the offence charged'. WADA defends the strict liability policy by insisting that the code, as a whole, strikes an appropriate balance between the needs of anti-doping and the fair treatment of athletes.

Article 2.1.1 Explanatory notes

For purposes of anti-doping rule violations involving the presence of a Prohibited Substance (or its Metabolites or Markers), the Code adopts the rule of strict liability which was found in the Olympic Movement Anti-Doping Code ('OMADC') and the vast majority of pre-Code anti-doping rules. Under the strict liability principle, an Athlete is responsible, and an anti-doping rule violation occurs, whenever a Prohibited Substance is found in an Athlete's Sample. The violation occurs whether or not the Athlete intentionally or unintentionally used a Prohibited Substance or was negligent or otherwise at fault. If the positive Sample came from an In-Competition test, then the results of that Competition are automatically invalidated (Article 9 (Automatic Disqualification of Individual Results)). However, the Athlete then has the possibility to avoid or reduce sanctions if the Athlete can demonstrate that he or she was not at fault or significant fault (Article 10.5 (Elimination or Reduction of Period of Ineligibility Based on Exceptional Circumstances)) or in certain circumstances did not intend to enhance his or her

---

41 Lexisnexis, 15 June 1988.
42 Such an example is s 58(2) of the Medicines Act 1968, which provides that no person shall sell by retail specified medicinal products except in accordance with a prescription given by a medical practitioner.

sport performance (Article 10.4 (Elimination or Reduction of the Period of Ineligibility for Specified Substances under Specific Circumstances)). The strict liability rule for the finding of a Prohibited Substance in an Athlete's Sample, with a possibility that sanctions may be modified based on specified criteria, provides a reasonable balance between effective anti-doping enforcement for the benefit of all 'clean' Athletes and fairness in the exceptional circumstance where a Prohibited Substance entered an Athlete's system through No Fault or Negligence or No Significant Fault or Negligence on the Athlete's part. It is important to emphasize that while the determination of whether the anti-doping rule violation has occurred is based on strict liability, the imposition of a fixed period of Ineligibility is not automatic. The strict liability principle set forth in the Code has been consistently upheld in the decisions of CAS.

However much the code, in its entirety, attempts to strike a fair balance, it is inevitable that unusual circumstances will emerge periodically that highlight a degree of injustice. Tennis player Greg Rusedski tested positive for nandrolone that, it was established, derived from supplements given to him by his governing body, the Association of Tennis Professionals (ATP).

Charlish, P, 'Tennis – When Strict Liability is Not So Strict'

Based on the applicable principle of strict liability, once illegal substances have been found in a urine sample, then the individual should be found guilty, however the illegal substances got into the person's body in the first place. The World Anti-Doping Agency in the wake of the Rusedski decision expressed its concern. David Howman, WADA Director-General, stated:

> 'We have been concerned about all of these nandrolone cases in tennis in two aspects; one because there is the erosion of strict liability (the regulation by which competitors are always responsible for what they consume) and also because of the large number of nandrolone findings in tennis.'

There can be no justification for this erosion of the principle of strict liability. It is pointless having such a standard available if at the first sight of an unjust outcome, the principle is disregarded. The decision to completely exonerate Greg Rusedski is without doubt a humane decision, which will be welcomed by his legion of fans. It seemed to be based on the principle that it would have been unfair of the ATP to ban Rusedski for taking, in good faith, substances provided by the ATP. In more legal terms, the stated reason was based on the principle of estoppel, which:

> 'prevents a person from adopting a position inconsistent with an earlier position if it results in injury to someone else.'

However, what this decision has done is add an unnecessary layer of uncertainty to an already difficult area. There must be clarity when dealing with this issue, and the principle of strict liability brought such clarity. The decision of the tribunal, in disregarding the principle of strict liability, and erring on the side of morality and justice rather than clarity and certainty may well have been a satisfactory result for Greg Rusedski, but it is one which individuals such as Dwain Chambers will look upon with a certain amount of anger. Tennis has, by this verdict, left itself open to charges of incompetence at best or cover-up and corruption at worst. It is a course of action that they may come to regret.[43]

---

43 Charlish, P, 'Tennis – When Strict Liability is Not So Strict' (2004) 3 ISLR (Aug) 65–68; Taylor, J, 'The strict liability test in tennis after Rusedski' (2004) 2(3) WSLR 3–7; Blackshaw, I, 'Why Strict Liability is Essential in Policing Doping' (2006) 4(11) WSLR, 4–5; Ruskin, B, Leader, J and Sarinsky, M, 'NFL defends anti-doping policy against state employment law challenge' (2009) SLA&P (Aug) 7–9.

If it is accepted that elite sporting competition is predicated on natural inequality then the distinction between fair and unfair competition is further confused by provisions within doping regulations that allow for exceptional use of substances, which would otherwise give rise to a doping offence, on medical grounds. An obvious example of this is the use of inhalers to assist asthma sufferers. This has potential consequences for the relationship between athlete and doctor.[44]

Article 4.4: Therapeutic Use

WADA has adopted an *International Standard* for the process of granting therapeutic use exemptions. Each International Federation shall ensure, for *International-Level Athletes* or any other *Athlete* who is entered in an *International Event*, that a process is in place whereby *Athletes* with documented medical conditions requiring the *Use* of a *Prohibited Substance* or a *Prohibited Method* may request a therapeutic use exemption. Athletes who have been identified as included in their International Federation's registered testing pool may only obtain therapeutic use exemptions in accordance with the rules of their International Federation. Each International Federation shall publish a list of those International Events for which a therapeutic use exemption from the International Federation is required. Each National Anti-Doping Organization shall ensure, for all Athletes within its jurisdiction that have not been included in an International Federation Registered Testing Pool, that a process is in place whereby Athletes with documented medical conditions requiring the Use of a Prohibited Substance or a Prohibited Method may request a therapeutic use exemption. Such requests shall be evaluated in accordance with the International Standard for Therapeutic Use Exemptions . . . Presence of a Prohibited Substance or its Metabolites or Markers (Article 2.1), Use or Attempted Use of a Prohibited Substance or a Prohibited Method (Article 2.2), Possession of Prohibited Substances and Prohibited Methods (Article 2.6) or Administration or Attempted Administration of a Prohibited Substance or Prohibited Method (Article 2.8) consistent with the provisions of an applicable therapeutic use exemption issued pursuant to the International Standard for Therapeutic Use Exemptions shall not be considered an anti-doping rule violation.[45]

Proof of doping

The standards of proof in establishing a doping infraction are prescribed in Article 3 of the WADA Code.

Article 3.1: Burdens and standards of proof

The Anti-Doping Organization shall have the burden of establishing that an anti-doping rule violation has occurred. The standard of proof shall be whether the Anti-Doping Organization has established an anti-doping rule violation to the comfortable satisfaction of the hearing panel bearing in mind the seriousness of the allegation which is made. This standard of proof in all cases is greater than a mere balance of probability but less than proof beyond a reasonable doubt. Where the Code places the burden of proof upon the Athlete or other Person alleged to have committed an anti-doping rule violation to rebut a presumption or establish specified facts or circumstances, the standard of proof shall be by a balance of probability, except as provided in Articles 10.4 and 10.6 where the Athlete must satisfy a higher burden of proof.

---

44 James, M, and Gillett, M, 'Therapeutic use exemptions and third party medical practitioners' (2009) SLA&P (Oct) 12–14.
45 See Hamilton, B, 'Inhaled beta agonists: ergogenic, dangerous and against the spirit of sport: fact or fallacy?' (2004) 12(2) Sport and the Law Journal 4.

This Article needs to be read in conjunction with Art 3.2.1, which establishes a rebuttable presumption that the accredited laboratory conducted the analysis correctly. The effect is that once a positive finding has been made by the laboratory, the athlete faces an uphill task to disprove the allegations. The idea that the standard of proof is pitched somewhere between balance of probability and reasonable doubt might seem like a reasonable position in that the standard on governing bodies is higher than that required in a civil case but lower than the criminal standard of proof. In practice, however, this definition may prove difficult to apply: does the balance lie exactly in the middle of the two standards? How, in practical terms, is this concept to be elucidated?

In addition to what are commonly known as 'analytical findings', the code also establishes important non-analytical methods by which a doping violation might be established.[46] Irrebuttable proof of doping may be 'established by a decision of a court or professional disciplinary tribunal of competent jurisdiction'[47] and an adverse inference may be drawn from 'the Athlete's or other Person's refusal, after a request made in a reasonable time in advance of the hearing, to appear at the hearing (either in person or telephonically as directed by the hearing panel) and to answer questions from the hearing panel or the Anti-Doping Organization asserting the anti-doping rule violation'.[48] Non-analytical methods move away from a scientifically verifiable standard. This would allow use of such evidence that emerged from a 2002 US Federal Government investigation following the BALCO revelations.[49]

Fair hearings

Athletes' procedural safeguards are based on Art 8 of the WADA Anti-Doping code, which deals with the right to a fair hearing.

Article 8: Right to a Fair Hearing

Each Anti-Doping Organization with responsibility for results management shall provide a hearing process for any person who is asserted to have committed an anti-doping rule violation. Such hearing process shall address whether an anti-doping rule violation was committed and, if so, the appropriate Consequences. The hearing process shall respect the following principles:

- a timely hearing;
- a fair and impartial hearing panel;
- the right to be represented by counsel at the Person's own expense;
- the right to be informed in a fair and timely manner of the asserted anti-doping rule violation;
- the right to respond to the asserted anti-doping rule violation and resulting Consequences;
- the right of each party to present evidence, including the right to call and question witnesses (subject to the hearing panel's discretion to accept testimony by telephone or written submission);
- the Person's right to an interpreter at the hearing, with the hearing panel to determine the identity, and responsibility for the cost, of the interpreter; and
- a timely, written, reasoned decision, specifically including an explanation of the reason(s) for any period of Ineligibility.

---

46 Roberts, H, 'BALCO and beyond: the changing landscape in the fight against doping in Sport' (2007) SLA&P (Aug) 1–7.
47 Art 3.2.3.
48 Art 3.2.4.; Morgan, M, 'Doping: sample collection – failure to submit to doping control' (2009) 7(11) WSLR.
49 The Bay Area Laboratory Cooperative (BALCO) was behind the biggest drugs scandal in sports history, implicating, amongst others, athletes Tim Montgomery, Marion Jones, Dwain Chambers and baseball stars Barry Bonds and Jason Giambi.

Diane Modahl's hearing into the test results was heard before a panel under the auspices of the British Athletic Federation. Rather than adopting an inquisitorial style which may appear the most appropriate for such a tribunal hearing, the style was adversarial, with the BAF both judge and prosecutor. Modahl's defence attempted to establish reasonable doubt as to the credibility of the test procedure and result. By this time it had been established that the test had lain unrefrigerated for two days in the Lisbon heat. This would have accounted for the changes in pH. It was also argued that taking testosterone would have produced a reaction in the liver causing the production of metabolites. No metabolites were discovered in the sample. To explain the high testosterone level, the defence called an expert medical witness who explored the theoretical possibility that bacteria could have caused the corrupted sample to produce testosterone. The panel took two hours to reach a unanimous verdict that a doping offence had been committed. The panel was unconvinced that the theoretical arguments altered the balance of probability. A four-year ban was imposed.

Diane Modahl's appeal against her ban was heard by an independent appeal panel. The same evidence was put forward. By this time, however, the defence could show that the bacterial transformation theory could be replicated under laboratory conditions. On this ground the panel held that the drug-taking allegations could no longer be sustained on the balance of probabilities. The finding was overturned and the ban quashed. Modahl brought an action against the BAF claiming that the hearing panel of Sir Arthur Gold, Dr Lucking and Mr Guy were biased against her. At first instance Douglas Brown J found no actual or apparent bias on the part of the three. Modahl appealed:

Modahl v British Athletics Federation Ltd

Lord Justice Latham:

It seems to me that in cases such as this, where an apparently sensible appeal structure has been put in place, the court is entitled to approach the matter on the basis that the parties should have agreed to accept what in the end is a fair decision. As Lord Wilberforce said, this does not mean that the fact that there has been an appeal will necessarily have produced a just result. The test which is appropriate, is to ask whether, having regard to the course of the proceedings, there has been a fair result. As Lord Wilberforce indicated, there may be circumstances in which by reason of corruption or bias or such other deficiency, the end result cannot be described as fair. The question in every case is the extent to which the deficiency alleged has produced overall unfairness.

The case for the appellant depends upon her being able to establish bias sufficient to produce such unfairness. As I have said, she challenges the findings of Douglas Brown J which exonerated Dr Lucking, Mr Guy and Sir Arthur Gold of both bias and apparent bias. I cannot see any justification for concluding that the judge was wrong to acquit Mr Guy and Sir Arthur Gold of both actual and apparent bias. There was wholly insufficient evidence to justify those allegations. Nor do I consider that the appellant can challenge the conclusion of the judge that Dr Lucking was not in fact biased. There was ample material from the witnesses who were members of the Disciplinary Committee to justify that conclusion. Equally, there was nothing about the decision itself which could in any way suggest it was infected by bias. The judge rightly concluded, in my view, that there was no real prospect of any different decision being reached on the material before the Disciplinary Committee, by any other Committee, however constituted. The appellant is, however, on stronger ground in arguing that the judge was wrong to hold that Dr Lucking was not infected by apparent bias. This concept has to be approached with some caution in a contractual context. It is essentially a precautionary concept intended to exclude the risk of bias, hence the definition in domestic law enunciated by Lord Goff in *R v Gough* [1993] AC 646E. At page 668C, he expressed the test in the following well-known words:

'In my opinion, if, in the circumstances of the case (as ascertained by the court), it appears that there was a real likelihood, in the sense of a real possibility, of bias on the part of a justice or other member of an inferior tribunal, justice requires that the decision should not be allowed to stand.'

It is clear that Lord Goff envisaged that the court should examine all the facts whether they be known or unknown to anyone considering the matter at the time of the original hearing. As Sir Thomas Bingham MR (as he then was) said in *R v Inner West London Coroner ex parte Dallaglio* [1994] 4 All ER 139 at page 162g:

> 'the famous aphorism of Lord Hewitt CJ in *R v Sussex Justices ex parte McCarthy* [1924] 1 KB 256 at 259 . . . "justice . . . should manifestly and undoubtedly be seen to be done" it is no longer, it seems, good law, save of course in the case where the appearance of bias is such as to show a real danger of bias.'

This approach has been modified, it seems to me, in relation to decisions of public bodies by the effect of the Human Rights Act 1998, as explained in the judgment of the Master of the Rolls in *Director General of Fair Trading v the Proprietary Association of Great Britain and the Proprietary Articles Trade Association* given on the 21st December 2000. The court there concluded that the provisions of Article 6 entitling a person to a fair public hearing by an independent and impartial tribunal in the determination of his civil rights and obligations required a modest adjustment to the test in *Gough*. In paragraph 86 of the judgment the Master of the Rolls said:

> 'When the Strasbourg jurisprudence is taken into account, we believe that a modest adjustment of the test in *Gough* is called for, which makes it plain that it is, in effect, no different from the test applied to most of the Commonwealth and in Scotland. The court must first ascertain all the circumstances which have a bearing on the suggestion that the judge was biased. It must then ask whether those circumstances would lead a fair minded and informed observer to conclude that there was a real possibility, or a danger, the two being the same, that the tribunal was biased.'

It is clear that this test, whichever way it is formulated, is intended to obviate both the appearance of unfairness, and the risk of unfairness. As far as the appearance of fairness is concerned, that is an essential ingredient of public justice in order to ensure a respect for the administration of justice, and is clearly an appropriate concept also for the supervision of public bodies. It may also be an appropriate tool in certain circumstances for the supervision of domestic bodies. For example a court may well consider it appropriate to interfere by way of injunction to prevent a particular person or persons from hearing disciplinary proceedings where a real danger of bias could be established on the basis that it might produce a real risk of unfairness.

But it does not seem to me to be appropriate to apply this test after the event to the determination of the question of whether or not there has been a breach of contract giving rise to a claim for damages. One returns at that stage to ask the question posed in *Calvin v Carr* (supra). The court's task is to determine whether or not, on the evidence, there has been a fair result. In a case such as the present, where the danger of bias can be evaluated and excluded, I consider that taken together with a wholly untainted appellate process, a fair result has been achieved. Any apparent bias on the part of Dr Lucking did not amount to a breach of the obligation on the disciplining body to provide a fair hearing overall.

If I am wrong in approaching the matter on this basis, I am prepared to accept that Dr Lucking was tainted by apparent bias. An informed person, that is a person knowing, as the judge found, that Dr Lucking had in 1991, albeit in the heat of the moment, asserted that athletes were guilty unless they were able to prove that they were innocent of doping, would consider that there was a risk that he might, albeit unconsciously, be affected by that attitude. His comments after the decision by the Independent Appeal Panel could not have allayed any such concern, so that, in my view, it would be likely that such a person would conclude that there had been a real risk of bias absent any further inquiry into the way the hearing was in fact conducted. If, contrary to my preferred view, this, of itself, produced unfairness amounting to a breach of contract, the judge's findings of fact however conclusively establish that that breach caused no loss. Whatever Dr Lucking's state of mind, the evidence of the other three members of the Committee who gave evidence satisfied the judge that they were not in any way infected by Dr Lucking, and came to a wholly independent judgment on the evidence which was fully justified by the material before them. The judge was correct, as I have already indicated, in concluding that the only basis for the decision of the Independent Appeal Panel in the appellant's favour was the new material giving support for what had previously merely been assertion as to the possibility that bacterial contamination could affect the testosterone reading.

But for the reasons I have already given, I consider that the appeal should be dismissed.[50]

It is interesting to note that the approach of the Court of Appeal is similar to that taken by the Court of Arbitration for Sport, which relies on the notion that 'all's well that ends well'. What should be considered is the impact of the hearing, the time between the hearing and appeal, and the impact on the athlete's career. In many instances the Code does attempt to provide the athlete with rights akin to those one might expect in a national court of law. However, this cannot be guaranteed, as:

> The athlete facing doping charges is in many cases unable to invoke the rules of procedural fairness, unlike his fellow citizens in proceedings before governmental bodies, if the regulations of the IF in force in his particular branch of sport do not provide these.[51]

Banned substances

In order for a governing body to regulate doping in sport it is necessary that it is able to identify accurately those substances which are not permitted. The WADA banned list is exhaustive, giving not only a list of substances outlawed but also their metabolites (further substances present as a result of the body converting banned substances) and other 'related' substances. In most cases this prevents the athlete's representatives from distinguishing the substances discovered from those specified in the schedules.

Many drugs which feature on the WADA banned list also appear in Schedule 2 of the Misuse of Drugs Act 1971. The MDA 1971 is the principal legislation criminalising the consumption of drugs in Britain and contains a list of various prohibited drugs. There are substances banned under the Code, however, the consumption of which does not amount to a criminal offence[52] and it is clear that the list of banned substances and techniques goes far beyond the scope of UK criminal provisions. The fact that many substances on the banned list are able to be used lawfully by athletes under national laws causes an obvious, irreconcilable tension.

The WADA Anti-Doping Code gives criteria for a substance's inclusion on the list. Although some may favour an attempt to justify logically why certain substances are on the list, others will see Art 4 as an attempt to justify the unjustifiable. After all, the preferred response to finding oneself in a hole is to stop digging. Inclusion on the banned list is dependent on satisfying two of the three categories for inclusion.

---

50 2001 WL 1135166.
51 Soek, J, 'The fundamental rights of athletes in doping trials', in O'Leary, J (ed), *Drugs and Doping in Sport* (2000), London: Cavendish Publishing, p 73.
52 Steroids, for example.

Article 4.3: Criteria for Including Substances and Methods on the Prohibited List

WADA shall consider the following criteria in deciding whether to include a substance or method on the Prohibited List.

4.3.1 A substance or method shall be considered for inclusion on the Prohibited List if WADA determines that the substance or method meets any two of the following three criteria:

> **4.3.1.1** Medical or other scientific evidence, pharmacological effect or experience that the substance or method, alone or in combination with other substances or methods, has the potential to enhance or enhances sport performance;

> **4.3.1.2** Medical or other scientific evidence, pharmacological effect or experience that the Use of the substance or method represents an actual or potential health risk to the Athlete;

> **4.3.1.3** WADA's determination that the Use of the substance or method violates the spirit of sport described in the Introduction to the Code.

4.3.2 A substance or method shall also be included on the Prohibited List if WADA determines there is medical or other scientific evidence, pharmacological effect or experience that the substance or method has the potential to mask the Use of other Prohibited Substances or Prohibited Methods.

It is very difficult to define the 'spirit of sport'; a concept that seems inherently subjective. Some cynics may conclude that its violation encompasses any unacceptable conduct not caught by the other two categories. On the basis of Art 4.3, it is unlikely that the CAS will be of assistance in clarifying its boundaries. Such nebulous phrases do little to enhance the credibility of the code. On the other hand, the concepts of unfair advantage and risk to health are well rehearsed.

Enhancing sport performance

On a philosophical level it is argued that taking drugs will give the taker an advantage over a competitor who has not taken drugs and therefore constitutes cheating.[53] Therefore, there are two grounds on which the prohibition of performance-enhancing drugs may be justified. First, they give some athletes an unfair advantage over other athletes.[54] Secondly, they give the athlete an unfair advantage over the sport. Governing bodies run the risk that the image and validity of their sport would be undermined by a belief that their sport was conducted on an uneven playing field; this knowledge would lead to a damaging loss in popularity. Following the drugs revelations surrounding Ben Johnson, the Canadian sprinter, a governmental inquiry chaired by Mr Justice Charles Dubin concluded:

de Pencier, J, 'Law and athlete drug testing in Canada'

The use of banned performance-enhancing drugs is cheating, which is the antithesis of sport. The widespread use of such drugs has threatened the essential integrity of sport and is destructive of its very objectives. It also erodes the ethical and moral values of athletes who use them, endangering their mental and physical welfare while demoralising the entire sport community.[55]

---

53 Simon, RL, *Fair Play: Sports, Values and Society* (1991), Boulder: Westview Press, Chapter 4.
54 Gardner, R, 'On performance-enhancing substances and the unfair advantage argument' (1989) XVI Journal of the Philosophy of Sport 59; Brown, WM, 'Drugs, ethics and sport' (1980) VII Journal of the Philosophy of Sport 15; Brown, WM, 'Fraleigh performance enhancing drugs in sport' (1985) XI Journal of the Philosophy of Sport 23; Brown, WM, 'Comments on Simon and Fraleigh' (1984) XI Journal of the Philosophy of Sport, 14.
55 De Pencier, J, 'Law and athlete drug testing in Canada' (1992) 4(2) MSLJ, 259.

While we may concur with these sentiments, eradicating all the unfair advantages that one participant may have over another may not only be impossible but also undesirable. Competitive sport is all about one athlete being better than another and therefore it is beneficial to have physiological and psychological differences between the participants.[56]

There are many advantages inherent in, for example, the nationality of an athlete. The skier raised in Austria or Switzerland has an advantage over one raised in Belgium; the runner living at altitude over the runner at sea level; the height advantage of the average American basketball player over the average Asian player; or the technological, training and dietary advantages of the rich nation over the impoverished third world county. All of these factors are advantages and may be considered unfair in terms of sporting equality. The argument that the above examples are natural advantages compared to the artificial advantage of drug taking is countered in the following extract:

Gardner, R, 'On performance-enhancing substances and the unfair advantage argument'

In the first case we do not object to differences in the endurance capabilities of athletes resulting from increased haemoglobin count, provided that increase is the result of high-altitude training. In the second case, we do not object to discrepancies in the size of skeletal muscles, providing that size results from genetic endowment or training (eg weight lifting). In each case, we are not objecting to the advantage but to the way in which the advantage is gained. So what is it about blood doping or human growth hormone that somehow distinguishes these methods of securing an advantage and seems to render their effects unacceptable? The obvious difference is the advantages gained by blood boosting and HGH are achieved through the use of a (supplemented) substance. However, if the basis of our objection is to be that using a substance is an unacceptable means to gaining an advantage, then the inconsistencies are more than apparent.

There are many legal substances used by athletes in their attempt to gain an advantage over competitors, for example, amino acids, protein powders, vitamin and mineral supplements (sometimes injected), caffeine (legally limited to 12 micrograms per millilitre of urine, about seven cups of coffee), glucose polymer drinks and injections of ATP (a naturally produced chemical involved in muscle contraction). The list could go on and on. Clearly we do not object to gaining an advantage through the use of a substance; it is only particular substances to which we are opposed. This being the case, it seems that some form of definitive criteria would have to be established in order to differentiate between permissible and prohibited substances. Yet, such criteria do not seem to exist.[57]

An alternative argument is that, rather than cheating fellow competitors, the drug taker is cheating 'the sport' itself. Clearly the essence of a sport would be compromised by certain breaches of the rules. It would be totally unacceptable for Usain Bolt to be beaten in an Olympic 100 metres final by a competitor riding a horse or for Tiger Woods to lose the Masters to a player with a radio-controlled golf ball. As Gardner has asked, 'would allowing unrestricted use of steroids in the 100 metres be somewhat like providing the participants with motorcycles?'[58]

There are two problems with an affirmative answer. First, not all tactical or technical deviations from the norm are prohibited. Indeed there is a lack of uniformity in the equipment used in many sports (boots, racquets, bats, etc.). Secondly, the question presumes that performance-enhancing drugs are an extrinsic aid unrelated to the skills and physical condition of the athlete. However, as

---

56 Oscar Pistorius, a disabled runner bidding to run against able-bodied athletes with the aid of prosthetic legs, raised interesting issues of inclusivity and performance enhancement. Wolbring, G, 'Oscar Pistorius and the future nature of Olympic, Paralympic and other sports' (2008) 5(1), SCRIPT-ed Internet.
57 Op. cit., fn 54, Gardner (1989), p 59.
58 Ibid.

their name would suggest, these drugs enhance performance, that is, they allow the athlete to reach their full potential; and so parallels with motorcyclists are difficult to sustain.

Can a competitor truly claim victory if it is achieved with the assistance of drugs? Victory is inextricably linked to rules. It is questionable whether the drug-taking athlete has competed in the first place. Successful athletes are afforded a unique place in society. Sporting heroes are society's heroes. By heralding the success of a drugs-assisted athlete we are in danger of undermining society itself.[59]

Perhaps the most acceptable reason for prohibiting performance-enhancing drugs is that otherwise sporting competition fails to be a test of persons:

Simon, R, 'Good competition and drug-enhanced performance'

Where athletic competition is concerned, if all we are interested in is better and better performance, we could design robots to run the 100 yards in three seconds or hit a golf ball 500 yards when necessary. But it isn't just enhanced performance that we are after. In addition, we want athletic performance to be a test of persons. It is not only raw ability we are testing for; it is what people do with their ability that counts at least as much. In competition itself, each competitor is reacting to the choices, strategies and valued abilities of the other, which in turn are affected by past decisions and commitments. Arguably, athletic competition is a paradigm example of an area in which each individual competitor respects the other competitors as persons. That is, each reacts to the intelligent choices and valued characteristics of the other. These characteristics include motivation, courage, intelligence and what might be called the metachoice of which talents and capacities are to assume priority over others for a given stage of the individual's life.

However, if outcomes are significantly affected not by such features but instead by the capacity of the body to benefit physiologically from drugs, athletes are no longer reacting to each other as persons but rather become more like competing bodies. It becomes more and more appropriate to see the opposition as things to be overcome – as mere means to be overcome in the name of victory – rather than persons posing valuable challenges. So, insofar as the requirement that we respect each other as persons is ethically fundamental, the prevailing paradigm does enjoy a privileged perspective from the moral point of view.[60]

Health risk to the athlete

There is no doubt that doping can damage your health.[61] To some sporting participants the side effects of these drugs outweigh the advantages of taking them. At the highest level, however, the competitive instincts of many participants may blind them to the dangers.

Goldman, B and Klatz, R, *Death in the Locker Room*

The desire to win is so great that people sometimes lose the concept of right and wrong due to being single-minded driven individuals. Sometimes it is very difficult to view life as a whole, as sports goals for the obsessed individual are the only true tangible goal. It can totally dominate your life and effectively shut out any vision of the world beyond. Mental perceptions of right and wrong may become misty and clouded and your attempts at experiencing the ethics and fun of sport are so nebulous, that it is hardly worth mentioning, let alone planning for in your mind. In some athletes' minds, the present is a set of stair steps of relatively minor competitions leading up to the moment when they have the opportunity to be the best in their designated sport.

---

59 Ibid, p 68.
60 Simon, RL, 'Good competition and drug-enhanced performance' (1994) XI JPS, 13.
61 Although what is debatable is the quantities needed to do so.

There is great uncertainty in their minds about life-beyond-victory and that is one of your toughest challenges as an athlete. To be a good sports champion and leader you must not only compete successfully but also have an overview of your true life goals.

An example of this mindset was the results of a poll performed by Gabe Mirkin MD, author of *The Sports Medicine Book*. He is a devoted runner and in the early 1980s polled more than a hundred top runners and asked them this question: 'If I could give you a pill that would make you an Olympic champion and also kill you in a year would you take it?' Mirkin reported that more than half the athletes he asked responded that yes, they would take the pill. I was stunned by Mirkin's survey and wondered whether this indicated the willingness to die was universal among athletes; perhaps it was idiosyncratic to runners.

I performed a series of polls on athletes in the mid and late 1980s, those in combative and power sports such as weightlifting, track and field competitors, discus throwers, shot putters, jumpers, football players, etc. I found these competitors were just as crazy as runners.

I asked 198 top world-class athletes a question similar to Mirkin's: 'If I had a magic drug that was so fantastic that if you took it once you would win every competition you would enter, from the Olympic decathlon to the Mr Universe, for the next five years but it had one minor drawback, it would kill you five years after you took it, would you still take the drug?' Of those asked, 103 (52%) said yes, that winning was so attractive, they would not only be prepared to achieve it by taking a pill (in other words through an outlawed, unfair method that is, in effect, cheating) but they would give their lives to do it.[62]

How justified are governing bodies in taking a paternalist approach to protect the welfare of sporting participants?[63] Traditional paternalist jurisprudence would argue that such an approach is only valid if the effect of the prohibition is to protect those unable to make an informed and rational judgement for themselves or to prevent harm to others. An obvious example of the former would be a ban on the taking of performance-enhancing drugs by children and junior athletes, yet the extension of the ban beyond this point is more difficult to justify. If the governing bodies genuinely wished to protect the health of sportsmen and women, would they not introduce a provision which forbade a competitor competing while injured? Women's gymnastics would also need to be reviewed bearing in mind the incidence of arthritis and other diseases of the joints suffered by competitors in later life. There are also a number of contact sports which, by the nature of the activity, are likely to cause injury. No doubt the governing bodies of sport would argue that the risks of injury in certain sports are well known and that competitors are in some way consenting to the possibility of harm. The difficulty with this argument is that it could apply equally to doping.

It can be argued that drugs are not taken freely. Athletes are coerced into taking them by a belief that without them they would have little chance of sporting success.[64] However, there are many training regimes which athletes can and do reject on the basis that they may cause long-term physiological damage: if injury is the mischief, it is difficult to understand why drug taking should be treated differently. On what basis then can society be justified in favouring the prohibition of performance-enhancing drugs when intervention in an athlete's life can amount to a greater wrong than the risk of illness voluntarily accepted?

---

62 Goldman, B and Klatz, R, *Death in the Locker Room 2* (1992), Chicago: Elite Sports Medicine Publications Inc, p 23.
63 Simon, RL, 'Good competition and drug-enhanced performance' (1984) XI JPS 6; Brown, WM, 'Paternalism, drugs and the nature of sports' (1984) XI JPS 14; Lavin, M, 'Sports and drugs: are the current bans justified?' (1987) XIV JPS 34; and Fairchild, D, 'Sport abjection: steroids and the uglification of the athlete' (1987) XIV JPS 74.
64 Thomas, CE, *Sport in a Philosophic Context* (1983), Philidelphia: Lea & Febiger; Wertheimer, A, *Coercion* (1989), Princeton: Princeton UP.

Brown, WM, 'Paternalism, drugs and the nature of sport'

Often, too, we stress human factors such as determination, fortitude and co-operativeness over risk taking and technology. But in other cases such as skiing, mountain climbing, hang gliding risk and technology dominate. We believe in the capacity of sports to promote health and fitness but many originate in the practice of war and routinely involve stress and injury, sometimes death. We fashion rules and continually modify them to reduce hazards and minimise serious injury but few would seek to do so entirely. Perhaps we are tempted to require in athletes only what is natural. But our sports have evolved with our technology and our best athletes are often unnaturally, statistically, endowed with abilities and other characteristics far beyond the norm. It seems artificial indeed to draw the line at drugs when so much of today's training techniques, equipment, food, medical care, even the origin of the sport themselves, are the product of our technological culture. Nevertheless, something more may be said for the claim that sports reflect a broader set of values. In discussing the justification of paternalism in coaching the young, I have stressed the formation of the values of honesty, fairness and autonomy, values central to my conception of personhood. But they are not the only ones that might be stressed. Obedience, regimentation, service to others or sacrifice might have been proposed. These, too, in the proper context, might also be developed together with the skills of athletics. The values, perhaps even a conception of what is good for human life, are associated with sports, not because of their nature but due to the way we choose to play them. We can indeed forbid the use of drugs in athletics in general, just as we do in the case of children. But ironically, in adopting such a paternalistic stance of insisting that we know better than the athletes themselves how to achieve some more general good which they myopically ignore, we must deny them the very attributes we claim to value: self-reliance, personal achievement and autonomy.[65]

As the BALCO Enquiry has shown, no matter how comprehensive the list of banned substances there is always the danger that the chemist will be one step ahead, altering the chemical structure of compounds so as to distinguish the drug from those encompassed by the regulations. An alternative to the ever-increasing list system would be to look generally for abnormalities in samples. This proposition, although clearly attractive in many ways, is fundamentally flawed. An athlete could argue that it becomes impossible to act within the rules of the governing body if it is unclear exactly what those rules are until they are broken. While it is accepted that the introduction of such a system would enable WADA to ensnare the 'cheats', it may be at the expense of many innocent athletes.

Equally, the list contains some substances that would appear to have nothing but a negative effect on sporting performance – the so-called 'recreational drugs' typify this anomaly. For example, former Bath and England Rugby Union prop, Matt Stevens, received a two-year ban from the game in 2009 for testing positive for a substance alleged to be cocaine.

Welch, R, 'A snort and a puff: recreational drugs and discipline in professional sport'

A clear line of demarcation should be drawn between drugs which are considered performance enhancing and those which should more properly be considered as recreational. Whilst there are clearly problems both practical and philosophical in banning sports participants for taking the former, it is contended that consumption of the latter should cease to be the concern of regulatory bodies. Such bodies did not come into existence to act as moral watchdogs, and it is clearly debatable whether, today, such bodies are in touch with public opinion and thus the opinion of many of those who pay money to view particular sports. . . . It is also the case that

---

65 Brown, WM, 'Paternalism, drugs and the nature of sport' (1994) XI JPS 22.

regulatory bodies, along it seems with politicians, ignore the increasingly widespread view, particularly amongst those who reached adulthood in the 1960s or during the decades since, that some or all drugs should be legalised or at least their possession decriminalised.[66]

Sanctions

Under Article 9 of the Code, a doping violation detected at a specific sport event results in the disqualification of the athlete from that event. However:

Article 10.1.1

If the Athlete establishes that he or she bears No Fault or Negligence for the violation, the Athlete's individual results in the other Competitions shall not be disqualified unless the Athlete's results in Competitions other than the Competition in which the anti-doping rule violation occurred were likely to have been affected by the Athlete's anti-doping rule violation.

Article 10 deals with sanctions above and beyond the immediate event disqualification. The regulations covering sanctions represent the most complex part of the WADA Code as they attempt to deal with a number of variables distinguishing between teams and individuals and among different types of doping infractions and the various degrees of culpability. The 2009 Code has built greater flexibility into the system of sanctions, the compromise for which is an even greater degree of complexity.

Article 10.2: Ineligibility for Presence, Use or Attempted Use, or Possession of Prohibited Substances and Prohibited Methods

The period of Ineligibility imposed for a violation of Article 2.1 (Presence of Prohibited Substance or its Metabolites or Markers), Article 2.2 (Use or Attempted Use of Prohibited Substance or Prohibited Method) or Article 2.6 (Possession of Prohibited Substances and Prohibited Methods) shall be as follows, unless the conditions for eliminating or reducing the period of Ineligibility, as provided in Articles 10.4 and 10.5, or the conditions for increasing the period of Ineligibility, as provided in Article 10.6, are met:

First violation: Two (2) years Ineligibility.

Article 10.3: Ineligibility for Other Anti-Doping Rule Violations

The period of Ineligibility for anti-doping rule violations other than as provided in Article 10.2 shall be as follows:

10.3.1 For violations of Article 2.3 (Refusing or Failing to Submit to Sample Collection) or Article 2.5 (Tampering with Doping Control), the Ineligibility period shall be two (2) years unless the conditions provided in Article 10.5, or the conditions provided in Article 10.6, are met.

10.3.2 For violations of Articles 2.7 (Trafficking or Attempted Trafficking) or 2.8 (Administration or Attempted Administration of Prohibited Substance or Prohibited Method), the period of Ineligibility imposed shall be a minimum of four (4) years up to lifetime Ineligibility unless the conditions provided in Article 10.5 are met. An anti-doping rule violation involving a Minor shall be considered a particularly serious violation and, if committed by Athlete Support Personnel

---

66 Welch, R, 'A snort and a puff: recreational drugs and discipline in professional sport', in O'Leary, J (ed), *Drugs and Doping in Sport* (2000), London: Cavendish Publishing, p 88; Horvath, P, 'Recreational Drugs and the WADA Code' (2008) 6(3) WSLR 14–16.

for violations other than Specified Substances referenced in Article 4.2.2, shall result in lifetime Ineligibility for Athlete Support Personnel. In addition, significant violations of Articles 2.7 or 2.8 which may also violate non-sporting laws and regulations, shall be reported to the competent administrative, professional or judicial authorities.

10.3.3 For violations of Article 2.4 (Whereabouts Filing Failures and/or Missed Tests), the period of Ineligibility shall be at a minimum one (1) year and at a maximum two (2) years based on the Athlete's degree of fault.

The Code allows athletes to argue mitigation in respect of the above sanctions depending on the degree of culpability. Sanctions can be reviewed on a variety of grounds: that a specified substance gave the athlete no advantage;[67] where there was no fault or negligence on the part of the athlete, such as when an athlete's drinks bottle is contaminated by a rival competitor;[68] or when there is no significant fault on the part of the athlete.[69] The Code states specifically that the use of mislabelled or contaminated substances, the administration of banned substances by the athlete's trainer or doctor without the athlete's knowledge, or sabotage by one of the athlete's circle of associates (including the athlete's spouse) may not be invoked under Art 10.5.1. It is less clear whether these explanations will find favour under Art 10.5.2 as being a good explanation for departing from the expected standard of behaviour.

Article 10.5.3 introduces a whistle-blowing mitigation:

Article 10.5.3: Substantial Assistance in Discovering or Establishing Anti-Doping Rule Violations

An Anti-Doping Organization with results management responsibility for an anti-doping rule violation may, prior to a final appellate decision under Article 13 or the expiration of the time to appeal, suspend a part of the period of Ineligibility imposed in an individual case where the Athlete or other Person has provided Substantial Assistance to an Anti-Doping Organization, criminal authority or professional disciplinary body which results in the Anti-Doping Organization discovering or establishing an anti-doping rule violation by another Person or which results in a criminal or disciplinary body discovering or establishing a criminal offense or the breach of professional rules by another Person. After a final appellate decision under Article 13 or the expiration of time to appeal, an Anti-Doping Organization may only suspend a part of the otherwise applicable period of Ineligibility with the approval of WADA and the applicable International Federation. The extent to which the otherwise applicable period of Ineligibility may be suspended shall be based on the seriousness of the anti-doping rule violation committed by the Athlete or other Person and the significance of the Substantial Assistance provided by the Athlete or other Person to the effort to eliminate doping in sport. No more than three-quarters of the otherwise applicable period of Ineligibility may be suspended. If the otherwise applicable period of Ineligibility is a lifetime, the non-suspended period under this section must be no less than eight (8) years. If the Anti-Doping Organization suspends any part of the otherwise applicable period of Ineligibility under this Article, the Anti-Doping Organization shall promptly provide a written justification for its decision to each Anti-Doping Organization having a right to appeal the decision. If the Anti-Doping Organization subsequently reinstates any part of the suspended period of Ineligibility because the Athlete or other Person has failed to provide the Substantial Assistance which was anticipated, the Athlete or other Person may appeal the reinstatement pursuant to Article 13.2.

---

67 Art 10.4.
68 Art 10.5.1.
69 Art 10.5.2.

Article 10.5.4 rewards co-operation:

Article 10.5.4: Admission of an Anti-Doping Rule Violation in the Absence of Other Evidence

Where an Athlete or other Person voluntarily admits the commission of an anti-doping rule violation before having received notice of a Sample collection which could establish an anti-doping rule violation (or, in the case of an anti-doping rule violation other than Article 2.1, before receiving first notice of the admitted violation pursuant to Article 7) and that admission is the only reliable evidence of the violation at the time of admission, then the period of Ineligibility may be reduced, but not below one-half of the period of Ineligibility otherwise applicable.

The sanctions above are also subject to increase on the grounds of aggravating circumstances.[70] Overall, the system of sanction reflects more intelligently the range of circumstances that anti-doping institutions might face and gives those institutions greater flexibility in matching the appropriate violation with the appropriate sanction. WADA should be applauded for this development. Any system of regulation, however, must be clear and understandable in order that athletes and other parties might abide by it. The complexity in circumstances where there might be more than one offence either concurrently or consecutively or more than one head of mitigation is frightening. WADA deals with these scenarios with accompanying notes and tables but, no matter how erudite, they illustrate the difficulties in drafting law or regulations that are both just and simple.[71]

The sanctions described above are drafted with the intention of ensuring a consistency of duration. They are not, however, drafted to provide a consistency of sanction. A two-year ban for athletes in some sports where the sporting career is short, gymnastics for example, is akin to a life ban. In other sports noted for the longevity of a competitor's career, equestrianism for example, the sanction merely interrupts a career. This is particularly so in individual competition where there is nothing to prevent the competitor from practising and refining their skills while banned.

Article 10.10.1: Prohibition Against Participation

During Ineligibility no Athlete or other Person who has been declared Ineligible may, during the period of Ineligibility, participate in any capacity in a Competition or activity (other than authorized anti-doping education or rehabilitation programs) authorized or organized by any Signatory, Signatory's member organization, or a club or other member organization of a Signatory's member organization, or in Competitions authorized or organized by any professional league or any international- or national-level Event organization. An Athlete or other Person subject to a period of Ineligibility longer than four (4) years may, after completing four (4) years of the period of Ineligibility, participate in local sport events in a sport other than the sport in which the Athlete or other Person committed the anti-doping rule violation, but only so long as the local sport event is not at a level that could otherwise qualify such Athlete or other Person directly or indirectly to compete in (or accumulate points toward) a national championship or International Event.

The word 'activity' makes it clear that, as well as being banned from competing in competitions in that particular sport, the ban extends to other involvement such as coaching, and to other sports.[72] It is interesting to note that the 2009 Code acknowledges that to deprive an athlete banned for

---

70 Art 10.6.
71 Celli, A, Valloni, L and Pentsov, D, 'Sanctions for anti-doping rule violations in the revised version of the World Anti-Doping Code' (2008) 3/4 ISLJ 36–42.
72 As long as that other sport is a signatory to the Code.

more than four years from undertaking another organised sport for recreational purpose is draconian beyond the point of necessity. Article 11.2 deals with team sanctions:

> If more than two members of a team in a Team Sport are found to have committed an anti-doping rule violation during an Event Period, the ruling body of the Event shall impose an appropriate sanction on the team (e.g., loss of points, Disqualification from a Competition or Event, or other sanction) in addition to any Consequences imposed upon the individual Athletes committing the anti-doping rule violation.

The Future

It is clear from *Meca-Medina v Commission of the European Communities* that the law is prepared to play an active part in adjudicating on the lawfulness of anti-doping regulations. It is also clear, however, that the WADA Code has been given the green light by the courts. Legal challenges by athletes on the basis of the Code's substantive provisions are therefore unlikely to succeed. Challenges will remain possible if the body or bodies charged with giving effect to the Code fail to do so. These will be broadly procedural.

Rigozzi, A, Kaufmann-Kohler, G and Malinverni, G, 'Doping and fundamental rights of athletes: comments in the wake of the adoption of the World Anti-Doping Code'

> WADA's effort might be seen by some as the latest attempt of the sports world to immunise sports from state control. The situation is more complex, however. The adoption of a Code, which complies with the fundamental rights of athletes, was only made possible thanks to a broad consultation of all stakeholders. Indeed, as a result of such consultation, the concerns about fundamental rights were duly taken into account in the course of the drafting process. This represents a major step forward as opposed to an approach that ignores fundamental rights requirements and, thus, leaves the enforcement of such rights to the courts. In that situation, the only rights protected are those of the individual athlete who has access to a court willing to interfere in sports matters and who can afford legal proceedings. By contrast, all the athletes will benefit from the fundamental rights protection incorporated into the Code.[73]

It is difficult to understand why it appears that only 'fundamental rights' are at issue. Why shouldn't a broader raft of rights, such as the right to be treated reasonably, fairly and equitably, be considered? The above authors claim that the Code is not designed to immunise against the intervention of law but then justify the Code only in terms of identifiable legal rights. Certainly, in its preamble WADA does not attempt to promote the Code as a document protecting athletes' rights. Indeed, the only 'fundamental right' that the Code acknowledges athletes deserve is to 'participate in doping-free sport' and thus promote health, fairness and equality for 'Athletes worldwide'.

Nevertheless, on balance, the 2009 Code is an improvement on the 2003 model, although there may be some interesting legal issues surrounding the imposition of a sanctions regime the complexity of which is daunting. Athletes may still seek legal redress as a matter of principle because an athlete who tests positive but is shown to be entirely without fault has still committed a doping violation (no fault does not vindicate the athlete – it merely goes to the severity of sanction). In any anti-doping code there will always be a degree of irreconcilability between the rights of athletes to compete freely and the rights of sport to regulate competition. The 2009 Code makes a much better attempt at balancing these tensions than the Code of 2003.

---

73 (2003), 3 ISLR (Aug) 39–67.

Anti-doping is far from a settled legal landscape, however. New unresolved legal issues will emerge to ensure anti-doping remains a vibrant and interesting legal area. Some of these issues revolve around the ambit of anti-doping regulation; others relate to the increasing political influence over anti-doping matters. There is still some ambiguity about the culpability of trainers, doctors and other support staff and the degree to which the Code is lawfully binding on their activities.[74] There may well be further judicial activity surrounding the termination of a contract of employment following a positive test and the quantum of damages owed by the athlete to the employer as a consequence. The CAS confirmed Chelsea Football Club's right to claim compensation from Adrian Mutu, who was dismissed by the club following a positive test for cocaine in 2004.[75] There are also interesting legal issues surrounding privacy,[76] free speech and a right to a home life. Given the nature of out-of competition testing, which requires athletes to notify the relevant doping control of their whereabouts, there are legal questions as to whether the Code complies with the right to privacy in the European Convention on Human Rights 1950 Art 8.[77] There might also be judicial activity relating to the retrospective impact of revelations of doping impropriety by retired athletes such as in autobiographies.[78] Such is the negative public profile of athletes involved in doping that such an allegation is likely to lower them in the eyes of right-thinking people. Actions for defamation may well result on a more regular bases as athletes attempt to defend their reputation (and indeed their future commercial prospects) in the face of media allegations reported on the basis of public interest.[79] Such an action was brought successfully by Lance Armstrong in the Court of Appeal against The Times newspaper following allegations that Armstrong had used doping substances.[80]

Perhaps the most significant anticipated development, however, is the continued politicisation of doping activities. Symbolised by the Helsinki Report on Sport, one might expect greater political engagement with anti-doping which will result in calls for greater criminalisation of doping. The result to date is that many nations have enacted laws which specifically criminalise doping in sport.[81] There are obvious difficulties in reconciling the WADA code with principles of criminal law at a national level, not least the differing standards and burdens of proof and the notion of criminalising activities carried out in sport which would not necessarily be criminal in a non-sporting context. Nevertheless, the movement has already resulted in the increased involvement in anti-doping of international policing bodies such as Interpol and cross-border co-operation on anti-doping. This development, which on the face of it might seem to enhance the harmonisation of anti-doping policies, might prove to be divisive in the long term as countries with more liberal drug laws resist the establishment of global anti-doping crimes.

Key Points

- Anti-doping duties and obligations are contractual in nature.
- As an economic activity, professional sport is subject to review by the courts.

74 Finlay, A, 'Trainers, negligence and anti-doping rules' (2010) 8(1) WSLR 6–7; O'Leary, J and Wood, R, 'Doping, doctors and athletes: the evolving legal paradigm' (2006) 3/4 ISLJ 62–66.

75 Mutu v Chelsea Football Club Ltd (unreported) 31 July 2009 (CAS) (2009) 4, ISLR 138–58.

76 Verroken, M, 'WADA's international standard for the protection of privacy' (2008) 5(6) DPL&P, 9–11.

77 Horvath, P and Lording, P, 'WADA's international standard for testing: privacy issues' (2009) 7(2) WSLR 14–16; Soek, J, 'The athlete's right to respect for his private life and his home' (2008) 3/4 ISLJ 3–13; Nicholson, G, 'Anti-doping and the World Anti-Doping Code: does one size fit all and is the whereabouts system fair, reasonable and efficient?'; (2009) SLA&P (Apr) 8–11.

78 Grove, S and Parks, J, 'Sanctioning ex-athletes for autobiographical revelations' (2010) 8(1) WSLR 4–5.

79 See Reynolds v Times Newspapers Ltd [2001] 2 AC 127; Chapman v Lord Ellesmere and Others [1932] 2 K.B. 431; Cooke, J, 'Doping and free speech' (2007), 5(2) E&SLJ.

80 Lance Armstrong v Times Newspapers Ltd, David Walsh, Alan English [2005] EWCA Civ 1007.

81 See for example Halgreen, L, 'The Danish Elite Sports Act' (2005), 3 ISLR (Aug) 74–75; Hufschmid, D and Giesser, T, 'Switzerland: Stricter rules against doping abuse in Swiss legislation project' (2010) 1 ISLR, 25–27; Ndlovu, P, 'Anti-doping law in South Africa – the challenges of the World Anti-Doping Code' (2006) 1/2 ISLJ 60–63.

- Anti-doping disputes constitute a significant proportion of the work of the Court of Arbitration for Sport.
- The European Court of Justice has held that the World Anti-Doping Code 2009 is a proportional response to doping.
- The Code is a document prescribing minimum standards of anti-doping regulation.
- The World Anti-Doping Code applies to nearly all sports and its adoption is a pre-requisite for Olympic competition.
- The World Anti-Doping Code is drafted on the basis of strict liability. This means that a doping violation can be committed without fault or knowledge.
- The complex system of sanctions attempts to balance the strictness of liability by imposing sanctions based on culpability.
- Future legal challenges are more likely to revolve around issues of human rights and the scope of the code.
- There is growing political involvement in anti-doping and a move toward more extensive criminal sanctions.

Key Sources

Houlihan, B, *Dying to Win; Doping in sport and the development of anti-doping policy* (1999) Strasbourg: Council of Europe Publishing.

Mottram, DR, *Drugs in Sport* (2003), London: Routledge.

O'Leary, J, (ed), *Drugs and Doping in Sport* (2000), London: Cavendish.

Reeb, M, *Digests of CAS Awards 1986–1998*, Berne, Staempfli Editions SA, 1998–2000; New York: Aspen Publishers, 2001–2003.

Waddington, I, *Sport, Health and Drugs* (2000), London: Spon.

Chapter 9

Sport and Contracts of Employment

Chapter Contents

Introduction	394
Who is an Employee?	394
Formation and Terms of a Contract of Employment	397
Performance of the Contract	402
Judicially Implied Terms	404
Restraint of Trade	409
Termination of Contracts of Employment in Sport	418
Remedies for Wrongful Dismissal	423
Unfair Dismissal	426
Procedural Fairness	435
The *Bosman* Case and the Transfer System	441
Conclusions	457
Key Points	458
Key Sources	459

Introduction

Participants in sport fall into three main categories: a) amateurs; b) self-employed professionals; c) employed professionals. It is this last category that this and the following chapter concentrate on. Professional sportsmen and sportswomen and those who coach and manage them, who are regarded in law as employees, will find themselves subject to and protected by the ordinary law of employment in both its common law and statutory forms. The major source of statutory employment rights is the Employment Rights Act 1996 (ERA) (previously the Employment Protection (Consolidation) Act 1978). This chapter will examine the formation, performance and termination of the contract of employment, and will analyse the interaction between the core legal principles and the relationship between clubs and their employees in the world of sport. Detailed attention will be paid to legal rules that connect with or generate the specific regulation of professional sport.

Who is an Employee?

In order to ascertain which sports participants are covered by the law of employment it is necessary to understand the legal tests for defining an employee. This question is essential in the contexts of: a) statutory employment protection rights; b) contractual rights and duties; c) health and safety; d) vicarious liability. Surprisingly perhaps there is no useful statutory definition of an employee; s 230 of the ERA 1996 merely defines an employee as a person who has entered into or works under a contract of employment. Thus it is case law arising out of disputes concerning these practical issues that provides us with the tests to help resolve specific problems. The 'control test' was the traditional common law means for ascertaining whether a person engaged in work was an employee. A person was controlled by an employer if that person was told not only what to do but also how to do it. Arguments that skills possessed by individual sportsmen took them beyond the control of clubs who paid them were quickly discounted.

Walker v Crystal Palace Football Club

Cozens-Hardy MR: It has been argued before us . . . that there is a certain difference between an ordinary workman and a man who contracts to exhibit and employ his skill where the employer would have no right to dictate to him in the exercise of that skill; eg the club in this case would have no right to dictate to him how he should play football. I am unable to follow that. He is bound according to the express terms of his contract to obey all general directions of the club, and I think in any particular game in which he was engaged he would also be bound to obey the particular instructions of the captain or whoever it might be who was the delegate of the authority of the club for the purpose of giving those instructions. In my judgment it cannot be that a man is taken out of the operation of the Act simply because in doing a particular kind of work which he is employed to do, and in doing which he obeys general instructions, he also exercises his own judgment uncontrolled by anybody.[1]

It is interesting to note the emphasis given to the authority of the team captain as the 'delegate of the authority of the club'. Is the notion of captain as 'foreman' consistent with the status and attitudes of the modern professional footballer? On the other hand, there is no doubt that the footballer who exercises too much individual initiative, contrary to instructions during training, is likely to find himself dropped from the first team.

---

1   [1910] 1 KB 87 CA, at p 92.

Similarly, cricketers are to be considered employees. Clause 5(a) of the Contract For Professional Cricketers requires the cricketer to '. . . obey all the lawful and reasonable directions of the captain or deputy captain . . .'.[2]

Any problems for modern professional sport which might have been posed by relying on decisions at the start of the century have been pre-empted, as the control test in itself has long been regarded as inadequate. The modern emphasis is much more on whether an individual who provides a service is or is not working on his or her own account. This is determined not by a single test but by taking into account and weighing up a number of different factors.[3] It is clear from the decision in *Walker* that whilst control may be a significant factor in a given situation, an individual will still not be an employee if she or he bears the risk of loss. Compare professional footballers or cricketers with sports participants who are not considered in law to be employees – such as professional boxers or snooker or tennis players. These individuals, albeit under the guidance or even control of an agent or manager and subject to the rules of the sport, negotiate their own entry into matches and the consequent payment they receive.[4]

The method by which tax is paid is a relevant but by no means decisive factor.[5] It is clear from case law that club managers will generally be considered employees even if they were to be treated as self-employed for tax purposes. On the other hand, the decision in *Massey* might be applied to those who occupy special positions such as Director of Football, as exemplified in past years by Kenny Dalglish at Blackburn FC or Terry Venables at Portsmouth FC. Both of these clearly possessed the bargaining power to enter into 'genuine agreements' concerning their employment status and indeed what precisely their roles at the clubs involved. This was especially true with Terry Venables, who did not regard himself as under contract to Portsmouth and went on to buy the club for £1 (although his ownership of the club was subsequently disputed when Venables and Portsmouth parted company in 1998).

An interesting development in the context of employee status and sport is provided by the case of *Singh*.[6] One of the issues dealt with by the employment tribunal in the case is whether referees can be considered employees of the Football League and/or the Football Association and are thus, for example, eligible to claim unfair dismissal. In line with the authorities, established above, the tribunal placed no emphasis on the fact that referees are normally taxed as self-employed (though S had completed his tax returns as an employee). Similarly, the tribunal emphasised that there is no single test for determining the issue. Rather, a tribunal must 'stand back and consider all aspects of the relationship between the applicant and the particular respondent with no single factor being decisive or determinative but seeking to appropriate weight to all relevant factors'. Thus the tribunal placed little emphasis on facts such as the requirement on referees to wear particular dress or on a referee's lack of entitlement to sick pay or holidays.

Recent case law, approved by the House of Lords in *Carmichael v National Power* [1998] ICR 1167, has placed much emphasis on the need for mutuality of obligations as part of the irreducible minimum required for the presence of a contract of employment. Thus in *Carmichael* guides 'employed' by National Power were held by the HL not to be employees on the basis that there was no obligation to offer them work and nor was there any obligation on the part of guides to accept

---

2   This standard contract of employment for professional cricketers was originally negotiated between the Test and County Cricket Board (TCCB), acting on behalf of County Cricket Clubs, and the Cricketers' Association, acting on behalf of professional cricketers. See further below, at p 399.

3   This 'multiple' approach is exemplified by the judgment of Mackenna J in *Ready Mixed Concrete (South East) Ltd v Minister of Pensions and National Insurance* [1968] 2 QB 497 QBD.

4   However, this position might not be so clear cut if a more flexible approach is taken to determining who is an employee. By way of comparison see Engelbrecht, G and Schinke, M, 'The social status of the sporting profession' (1996) 4(2) SATLJ 16–19. In particular, consider the argument that in German law a competition organiser or a sponsor could be considered an employer.

5   Cf *Massey v Crown Life Insurance Co* [1978] ICR 509 CA with *Young and Woods Ltd v West* [1980] IRLR 201 CA.

6   *Singh v The Football Association Ltd, The Football League Ltd & Others* (2001) ET Case Number 5203593/99.

any work that was offered. Similarly, referees are able to refuse to officiate a match on grounds of personal inconvenience. The tribunal, however, found there to be mutuality of obligations on the basis that there was an expectation that referees on the list would be offered work and they in turn were subject to the League's disciplinary control.

Thus as matters stand – that is, unless in a relevant future case the Employment Appeals Tribunal (EAT) or a higher court takes the contrary view – referees must now be perceived as employees of the Football League (and where appropriate presumably the Premier League), and therefore as fully in possession of statutory employment protection rights. However, the case also established that referees are not employees of the Football Association as the FA is only intermittently concerned with decisions over the refereeing of games – namely the FA Cup and FA Trophy matches. The irregularity and casual nature of the relationship between the FA and referees thus 'strongly militates against the existence of a contract of employment'.

The above judicial tests are also illustrated by an EAT decision[7] that a bar manager whose contract described him as self-employed was nevertheless an employee as the terms of his contract revealed that he could not be considered 'his own boss'. This case also serves as a reminder that generally sports employers will employ 'ordinary' employees as well as sportsmen and women. It should also be noted that s 23 of the Employment Relations Act 1999 empowers the Secretary of State to extend the protection conferred by statutory rights to other groups of workers, such as casual and agency workers, who may not be regarded as employees. (To date these powers have not been exercised.) The Working Time Regulations 1998 and Part-time Workers Regulations 2000 provide examples of rights given to workers as well as to employees.[8]

Agents

Of major importance in today's world of sport is the role and position of agents/managers engaged by individual sportsmen and women. A professional boxer in formal terms employs a manager despite in general being the subordinate party. The manager will enter into a contract of agency which will normally permit him to enter into similar contracts of his choice, and in reality will control the boxers who employ him. The boxer is in an analogous contractual position to professional musicians who to secure fame are dependent on securing a recording contract, but technically are in the position of principal in the agency relationship. Such professionals are excluded from employment protection rights, but receive some protection from the common law doctrine of restraint of trade.[9]

Similarly, the professional footballer who has an agent is the principal in that relationship. The essential difference between the boxer and footballer is that the latter is an employee of his club, and is more genuinely employing an agent's services to assist in negotiations with the employer. The boxer, on the other hand, like the aspiring rock band, is dependent on the 'agent' for work and thus remuneration. Compare the boxer with, as examples, professional golfers, tennis players and snooker players, who generally more clearly possess the economic independence to be regarded as self-employed professionals. In so far as they employ agents they may be genuinely regarded as principals in what are essentially commercial relationships.

Individual sports participants who employ agents are bound by any contract entered into by the agent deemed to be within the scope of the latter's express and usual authority. The concept of usual authority covers any contract which it is reasonable for the third party to assume the agent to possess the authority to make in light of the norms of the commercial situation and other relevant factors. Usual authority may thus be wider than express authority. Therefore, for example, could a

7   *Withers v Flackwell Heath Football Supporters Club* [1981] IRLR 307.
8   SI 1998/1833 and SI 2000/1551.
9   See below, pp 409–11.

boxer ever object to a contract made by his manager to fight a particular boxer or to fight at a particular venue?

Football agents are different from agents in general, be it in the sporting or wider worlds, as they do not possess the authority to make contracts on behalf of their individual footballer clients. Indeed, it is expressly stipulated in clause 14(b) of the Premier League and Football League Contract that 'clubs and players shall arrange all contracts of service and transfers of registrations to any other Football Club between themselves.'

Rather, the role of the agent is to advise their clients and negotiate on their behalf. Moreover, the standard contracts used by clubs in the Premier and Football Leagues require the player to specify the name of any agent who has been involved in negotiations prior to the contract being signed. As football agents are outside of the normal common law definitions it has never been clear the extent to which they are subject to duties such as not making a secret profit or creating conflicts of interests. In recent times, this has constituted the background to concerns about football corruption, and the role played by some agents in the murky world of bungs and the like.[10]

The Football Agent Regulations 2007, which came into effect on 1 September 2007, are designed to resolve this problem. In particular, agents must be registered in order to secure a licence to act as an agent in professional football, and their role in contract negotiations must be clear, as must any family relationship they have with a player or club officials. Most importantly, they are prohibited from generating a potential conflict of interest by acting on behalf of both the player and the club he is negotiating with. Breach of the Regulations may result in a three-year ban.

Formation and Terms of a Contract of Employment

In accordance with common law principle a contract of employment may, but need not, be in writing. In practice contracts entered into by sportsmen and sportswomen, irrespective of their employment status, will be in writing. Therefore, it can be noted in passing that sports participants, in so far as they are considered employees, are entitled to specified information in writing – ss 1–3 of the ERA 1996. This includes all the major contractual terms, the identity of any relevant collective agreements and copies of disciplinary rules and procedures.[11]

The ordinary rules of offer and acceptance apply to contracts of employment in the same way that they do to any other type of contract. However, in practice it is not that uncommon for an employment contract to be entered into informally through oral agreement, and the full contract is only later put into written form. The following two cases illustrate the problems this process can cause.

In *Stransky v Bristol Rugby Ltd*[12] the club's Director of Rugby was authorised to approach Joel Stransky, a former international player, to discuss his possible employment as a backs coach. Following these negotiations Stransky met the club's chief executive in a restaurant in Bath in April. The terms of the contract were discussed and agreed to over the meal. Stransky returned to his home in Leicester and informed his wife that he had a new job and thus they would be looking for

---

10 For example the 'tapping up' of Ashley Cole by Chelsea, the well-publicised allegations by Luton Town manager, Mike Newell and the *Panorama* television programme that followed. For an assessment of the Regulations see De Marco, N., 'The New Football Agents Regulations', paper given to the CLT Professional Training Conference 'Sports Law The 2006 Update' on 29 November 2006. Although the Regulations may be effective in contributing to the fight against corruption, it is interesting to note that De Marco presents arguments to the effect that they be susceptible to legal challenge on the basis of the doctrine of restraint of trade; see below pp 409–11.

11 It is interesting to note that in *Singh*, op. cit., fn 6, the tribunal did not accept that it was significant, in determining whether Singh was an employee, that referees were not provided with a written statement of their terms and conditions of employment. (Indeed it would be rather ironic if employers who fail to comply with a statutory duty owed to employees could use that failure to establish the lack of an employment relationship.)

12 11/12/2002 QBD (Eady J), unreported.

a new home in the Bath/Bristol area. In the months after this meal, to the knowledge of the chief executive, preliminary steps were taken to secure a work permit for Stransky and he was introduced to the players. The chief executive was also asked to draw up the written contract for Stransky and his response indicated that he was intending to do so. In June, Stransky discovered that the club had decided not to employ him. In court the chief executive stated that he did not recall meeting Stransky for a meal, let alone offering him employment. On the basis of the evidence this statement was rejected and the court concluded that a contract had been entered into during the meal in April. Thus the club was in repudiatory breach in refusing to employ Stransky for the agreed period.

In *White v Bristol Rugby Club*[13] White, a professional rugby player, signed a three-year contract to move from his previous club to Bristol RC. The contract expressly stipulated that it was subject to an 'entire agreement' clause, so that no oral representations made in the course of negotiations applied in respect of its express terms and conditions. White subsequently decided not to join Bristol and asserted that he had been told during pre-contract negotiations that he could opt out of the contract on repayment of the advance. The High Court held that the 'entire agreement' clause prevented White from relying on an oral opt-out term.

Apprentices and scholars

Minors do not normally possess contractual capacity. This is, however, not a problem in sport, as a contract of employment or analogous contract for services is deemed to be for the minor's benefit.[14] It matters not that the contract contains particular terms which the minor regards as detrimental, providing that the contract taken as a whole is to the minor's benefit.[15]

Where they exist, contracts of apprenticeship put apprentices in a special position. The contract must be in writing, and the contract cannot be terminated during its currency other than by reason of grave misconduct on the part of the apprentice. Note the apprentice may accrue statutory employment rights, including the right not to be unfairly dismissed. However, ironically but nevertheless the norm in employment law, a dismissal may be fair even though it constitutes a breach of contract.[16] On the other hand, contrary to the normal principles of contract law, apprentices dismissed in breach of contract can receive damages for loss of future prospects as well as immediate financial loss.[17] Thus employers are ill-advised prematurely to terminate an apprentice's contract .

Unless the contract of apprenticeship expressly permits dismissal for reason of redundancy such a dismissal will be in breach of contract. This will not be so if an employer can establish a complete closure of the workplace or a fundamental change in the nature of the business.[18] Short of, for example, an employing club going into liquidation, it is hard to conceive how these exceptions could apply in sport. However, it is clear that on expiry of the contract the apprentice cannot argue that he has been made redundant.[19]

Contracts of apprenticeships were important in professional football but they, along with youth trainees engaged by a club under a statutory training scheme, have been replaced with a

---

13 [2002] IRLR 204. For further comment on this case see Blackshaw (2002), 5(1) SLB, p 3.
14 For example, *Roberts v Grey* [1913] 1 KB 520, in which damages were awarded against a minor who broke a contract to accompany a professional snooker player on a world tour in order to receive training and develop experience.
15 See *Doyle v White City Stadium Ltd* [1935] 1 KB 520, in which a minor boxer was bound by rules permitting suspension and a fine for hitting his opponent below the belt. Indeed the court held that the rules were just as much for his protection as for the protection of his opponents. Cf *De Francesco v Barnum* [1890] 45 Ch 430, in which a minor was released from her contract as a professional dancer where she was contracted to work only for the defendant, whilst he was under no duty to find her engagements, and her remuneration was deemed inadequate.
16 See *Finch v Betabake (Anglia) Ltd* [1977] IRLR 470.
17 *Dunk v George Waller & Son Ltd* [1970] 2 All ER 630.
18 *Wallace v CA Roofing Services Ltd* [1996] IRLR 435.
19 *North East Coast Shiprepairers v Secretary of State for Employment* [1978] IRLR 149.

system of scholars linked to clubs' academies and centres of excellence. Contracts entered into by scholars are expressly stipulated not to be contracts of employment and thus scholars are generally excluded from the protection conferred by statutory employment rights. However, they are covered by health and safety legislation and the Equality Act 2010, which prohibits various forms of discrimination (see the following chapter). The Premier and Football Leagues also have special regulations for the protection of children. Any player under the age of 17 can only be registered as a scholar.

Collective bargaining

Trade unions and the world of industrial relations are not immediately associated in people's minds with the world of sport. (At least, this is so in Britain. In the USA, by way of contrast, professional sport is a heavily unionised sector of the economy.) However, the Professional Footballers' Association (PFA) is affiliated to the British Trade Union Congress (the major national trade union confederation) and cricketers also have their own trade union, the Professional Cricketers' Association. The role of both of these organisations, as is the case with any trade union, is to represent the individual and collective interests of their members.

Trade unions are most significant in the workplace when they are recognised by employers for the purposes of collective bargaining. The objective of collective bargaining is for trade unions to reach collective agreements with employers. In Britain such agreements are *presumed*, both at common law and under statute law, not to be legally binding on the respective parties, and thus normally do not have the status of contracts.[20] However, part or all of the content of a collective agreement can be incorporated into the individual contracts of employment of the employees on whose behalf the union was negotiating. (Note that this will normally be all relevant employees, not just those who happen to belong to the union.) A collective agreement so incorporated is, of course, legally enforceable between the individual employee and the employer.

The standard contract for professional cricketers is a major example of this process. The contract is derived from a collective agreement which was originally negotiated between the Professional Cricketers' Association and the Test and County Cricket Board. This contract is not legally binding on either of the organisations which negotiated it, but it is binding as an individual contract on any club which adopts it with respect to its individual players. Note that both collective agreements and individual contracts derived from them can survive even if one of the parties, in formal terms, ceases to exist. Thus cricketers' contracts are not substantially affected by the fact that the TCCB was replaced by the England and Wales Cricket Board in 1997.

Another major role of trade unions is to represent individual members who have a grievance with or are being disciplined by the employer. Both professional footballers and professional cricketers have the contractual right to union representation at individual hearings.[21] Footballers may be represented by the PFA before a Compensation Committee (or transfer tribunal).[22]

The PFA has a higher public profile than the Professional Cricketers' Association, and like many trade unions also engages in active campaigning on behalf of its members. One of its most important and relatively successful campaigns in recent years has been 'Let's Kick Racism Out of Football'.[23] The PFA can also perform a similar role to that played by agents in advising a player over contract negotiations with a club.

If collective bargaining is not associated with the world of sport then this is even more the case with strikes. In 1996, however, the PFA balloted its members employed by clubs in the Football

---

20 See *Ford v AUEW* [1969] 2 QB 303, and s 179 of the Trade Union and Labour Relations (Consolidation) Act 1992.
21 Sections 10–15 of the Employment Relations Act 1999 give all workers the statutory right to be represented at formal disciplinary and grievance hearings. If the worker so chooses the representative may be a trade union officer.
22 See below, p 413.
23 See Chapter 10 on discrimination, p 413.

League on strike action. This would have involved the collective withdrawal of labour with respect to games to be broadcast live on television. The cause of the dispute was the decision by the Football League to terminate a 30-year agreement under which the PFA receives 10 per cent of the income from television. This money is used by the PFA for the welfare of its members – particularly those who are forced by injury prematurely to end their careers. Strike action was ultimately averted as the dispute was resolved by agreement between the League and the PFA. However, the dispute was not permanently resolved as the PFA conducted and won a second strike ballot on this issue in the winter of 2001. The following extract considers the issues involved.

Welch R, 'Greedy footballers, trade disputes and the right to strike'

The early months of 2002 have witnessed the return of media headlines concerned with a rise in industrial conflict as rail workers, postal workers and teachers vote to take industrial action. Running in parallel to these developments was Tony Blair's much publicised speech denouncing those who are 'wreckers' of the public services. Despite his protestations to the contrary, many public sector trade unionists and some trade union leaders took this to be a reference to themselves. It is perhaps ironic that this concern over a return to industrial militancy was prefaced not in traditional industrial sectors but in the world of professional football.

In the latter months of 2001 the front as well as the back pages of the press were generally highly critical of the decision by footballers to take strike action, from December 1, at any game where a TV camera was present. Moreover, the Premier and Football Leagues came very close to seeking an injunction to prevent the strike from taking place. Thus professional footballers found themselves in a position very familiar to more traditional trade unionists. Firstly, a ballot for industrial action held in accordance with statutory requirements produces a large majority for strike action (in this case the ballot produced an unprecedented 99% majority in favour). Secondly, an employer and media onslaught is launched on 'greedy trade unionists for holding the public to ransom'. Thirdly, employers issue a threat to resort to use of legal action to prevent the strike from taking place. The purposes of this article are twofold. Firstly, to explain why litigation by the Football Leagues may have succeeded. Secondly, to discuss whether the proposed footballers' strike illustrates, albeit in an untypical context, that the law prevents industrial action which can be considered, at least in moral terms, to be legitimate.

The cause of the dispute was the breakdown in negotiations over the distribution of money secured from television companies. Under a fifty-year-old arrangement, the Professional Footballers Association (PFA) has received a share of the money earned from the televising of matches in return for players giving up individual appearance fees. This money is used by the PFA to provide hardship funds for players who are in financial difficulties or need to retrain for a new career having retired from the game. Such funds are particularly important for players in the lower leagues who are on comparable salaries with other members of the labour force; especially for players who are forced out of the game through physical injuries with long-term debilitating consequences.

Therefore, whichever side you are on (and I am not attempting to hide my sympathies with the players) it is important to clarify that players in the Premier League and First Division were not contemplating strike action to secure more money or benefits for themselves. To put it in an admittedly subjective manner such players were motivated by concern for their less fortunate colleagues and were prepared to take strike action in solidarity with them. (The view of the employers, on the other hand, was that these players could demonstrate their concern by increasing their individual subscriptions to the PFA as a source of increased revenue for the hardship fund.) The dispute was resolved though a last-minute compromise but it is useful to examine what the legal outcome may have been had litigation taken place.

Since the end of the last century a tort first developed in *Lumley v Gye* (1853) 2 E & B 216 has been applied to the organisation of industrial action. Thus any trade union or trade unionist who persuades or calls on employees to take strike or most other types of industrial action is committing the tort of directly inducing those employees to act in breach of their contracts of employment. To this day this remains the position at common law. Thus the organisation of virtually any form of industrial action is unlawful in the sense that it is tortious and can be restrained by a court injunction. There is not and never has been any right to strike in the UK. However, since the Trade Disputes Act 1906 there has been statutory immunity from the above mentioned tortious liability providing the industrial action is in 'contemplation or furtherance of a trade dispute'. (It should be noted that since 1984 industrial action must also be sanctioned by a valid secret ballot if it is to attract statutory immunity. However, this was not an issue in the proposed players' strike for the reasons identified above.)

Under the original Trade Disputes Act and its successor, the Trade Union & Labour Relations Act 1974, a dispute could be regarded as a trade dispute provided it was *connected* to terms and conditions of employment even though it had a wider dimension such as a trade union campaign. Moreover, a dispute could be between employees and any employer. Thus in a case, *NWL Ltd v Woods* [1979] ICR 867, which has direct relevance to this discussion, the Law Lords held that the boycotting of a ship flying a 'flag of convenience' could be regarded as action taken in furtherance of a trade dispute and was thus lawful. The workers who took this action were not employed by the shipowner and nor did they benefit directly from it. The action was taken in support of the (ongoing) campaign by the relevant union, the International Transport workers Federation (ITWF), to improve the pay and conditions of crews recruited from third world countries.

However, in a case decided in 1982, *Universe Tankships Inc of Monrovia v ITWF* [1982] ICR 262, the Law Lords modified this conclusion where the taking of such action was resolved by the shipowner paying money into the Seafarers' International Welfare Fund. A majority of the Law Lords held that the payment of this money was not connected to the employment conditions of the crew or anyone at all. Rather the payment should be viewed as analogous to a political party or a revolutionary 'guerrilla group'. Having identified the absence of a trade dispute, the Law Lords were then able to apply the contractual doctrine of duress to grant restitution to the shipowner of the money paid into the welfare fund. Essentially the Law Lords concluded that money secured through industrial action, which was not in furtherance of a trade dispute, was money secured by duress. The decision also raises the possibility that such action could constitute the tort of duress. This development in tortious liability has yet to occur but it should be noted that statutory immunity for such liability does not and never has existed.

The parallels between *Universe Tankships* and the proposed PFA strike are obvious. Moreover, the definition of a trade dispute today is different to the 1974 definition that was the subject of the Law Lords' decision. As a result of amendments introduced by the Employment Act 1982 a dispute must be wholly or mainly related to terms and conditions of employment as against merely connected to such issues and must be between employees and their own employer. The House of Lords' decision in the subsequent case of *Dimskal Shipping v ITWF* [1992] IRLR 78 vividly illustrated that these amendments render action of the sort organised by the ITWF unlawful. In this case the industrial action was taken in a Swedish port and was lawful under Swedish law. However, the agreement to pay money into the welfare fund was governed by the English law of contract. Under the post-1982 definition of a trade dispute it was clear that statutory immunity was not available as the dispute was seen as a dispute between the union and the shipping company rather than between the latter and its employees. Thus, as in *Universe Tankships*, the remedy of restitution was granted to the shipowner.

In the context of the PFA dispute, on the basis of the balance of convenience test contained in *American Cyanamid v Ethicon* [1975] AC 396 . . . there would have been a strong chance that any club seeking an interlocutory injunction would have been successful. With respect to the future it should also be commented that, in the absence of a lawful trade dispute, a TV company could also seek an injunction. This is because such strikes constitute tortious interference with the commercial contract between the clubs and TV companies through the unlawful means of inducing the players to act in breach of their employment contracts.

It must be emphasised that it remains uncertain that the proposed strike was unlawful as the PFA may have succeeded in arguing that the distribution of TV money was wholly or mainly related to the terms and conditions of the employment contracts between players and their own clubs. However, I suspect this argument would have failed and, in my view, the whole incident illustrates why the current legal regulation of industrial action is unduly restrictive. For me, the likes of a very rich man such as David Beckham taking strike action on behalf of players for clubs such as Hartlepool and Macclesfield is worthy of praise not castigation. Equally, in the wider trade union world the taking of solidarity or as it is now known secondary action is a manifestation of the noblest form of trade unionism. It is also arguably the case that the taking of such action is a right protected by international law. Have our professional footballers provided the world of employee relations with a very good example of why, as is the case elsewhere in Western Europe, workers in the UK should be granted positive rights to strike?[24]

In line with the legal positions in and industrial relations systems of most Member States, the EU attaches rather more significance to consultation and negotiation with trade unions as social partners than has been the norm in Britain over the past few decades. Indeed the EC Treaty provides for the making of EU social law through agreement between European employers' associations and the European Trade Union Confederation (ETUC). In this context it should be noted that the players' representative organisation FIFPro, with the support of the European Commission and the ETUC, is engaged in the social dialogue procedures contained in the EC Treaty with the ultimate objective of securing a European Collective Agreement for professional football.[25]

Performance of the Contract

Express terms

The interplay between the standard terms in a sports professional's contract and general employment law is of central importance. This is particularly the case with the rights and duties of the contracting parties. As is generally the case with written employment contracts, many of the respective rights and duties of the parties derive from express contractual terms. For example, on the club's part there are normally express obligations to provide medical treatment and to continue to pay a player's basic wages during periods when he is injured or otherwise incapacitated. (Note for employees in general such rights may not be in their contracts, and there are no equivalent statutory duties imposed on employers.) Contracts could also contain provisions regulating marketing and sponsorship deals. Clearly, the personal terms agreed to by a player when he signs for a club will constitute part of the express terms of the contract.

On the player's part there are duties to behave in a professional manner and to abide by the rules of the game. Consider the practical implications and consequences of the following.

---

24 Welch R, 'Greedy footballers, trade disputes and the right to strike' (2002) 5(2) SLB 14–15. Also see *The Guardian*, 15 October 1996 for a report on the possible legal implications of the original proposed strike.
25 FIFPro Press Releases of April 4 and November 19 2003, see www.fifpronet.com. Also see Branco-Martins, R, 'European sport's first collective labour agreement EFFC', Asser Instituut, 2003. The relevant provisions are now to be found in Articles 154 and 155 of the Treaty on the Functioning of the European Union.

The Premier League & Football League Contract

Clause 2. The Player agrees to play to the best of his ability in all football matches in which he is selected to play for the Club and to attend at any reasonable place for the purpose of training . . .

Clause 5. The Player agrees to observe the Rules of the Club at all times. The Club and the Player shall observe and be subject to the Rules and Regulations of the Football Association and the Football League. In the case of conflict such Rules and Regulations shall take precedence over this Agreement and the Rules of the Club.

Clause 7 . . . The Player shall at all times have due regard for the necessity of his maintaining a high standard of physical fitness and agrees not to indulge in any sport, activity or practice that might endanger such fitness . . .

Clause 13 . . . The Player may, save as otherwise mutually agreed and subject to the overriding obligation not to bring the game of Association Football into disrepute, contribute to the public media in a responsible manner. The Player, whenever circumstances permit, shall give to the Club reasonable notice of his intention to make such contributions to the public media in order to allow representations to be made to him on behalf of the Club if it so desires.

Clause 14(a). The Player shall not induce or attempt to induce any other player employed or registered by the Club, or by any other Football League Club, to leave that employment to cease to be so registered for any reason whatsoever.

Similar provisions to the above can be found in the standard Contract For Professional Cricketers and in the England and Wales Cricket Board's (formerly the TCCB) Rules and Regulations. Of particular interest, in both football and cricket, is the catch-all offence of 'bringing the sport into disrepute'.

Relate the above terms to the following much-publicised incidents that have occurred over the past 20 or so years: the ban on Ian Botham after being convicted for the possession of cannabis; the alcoholism of Tony Adams and Paul Merson and the latter's addiction to cocaine and gambling; the short ban imposed on Chris Armstrong for smoking cannabis; the dismissal of Craig Whittington for the same offence; the dismissal of Roger Stanislaus for using cocaine; the termination of the cricketer Ed Giddins' contract for the same offence; the decisions by Chelsea FC and Manchester United FC not to impose club penalties on Dennis Wise and Eric Cantona after their respective convictions for assault; the fine imposed by the TCCB (and its subsequent lifting) on Ray Illingworth for publicising his version of the dispute with Devon Malcolm, after the latter was dropped from the England test team during the 1995 tour of South Africa.[26]

The convictions of Jonathan Woodgate and Lee Bowyer for acts of violence outside a Leeds nightclub did not result in negative consequences for either player's career. In the case of Woodgate it did not affect his selection for the national team, and this situation was effectively replicated in October 2010 with respect to the then Newcastle player, Andy Carroll. Similarly, allegations of sexual misconduct against a number of players during the 2003–04 season did not result in any

---

26 Further ramifications of the latter were evidenced by the criticisms of staff and students at Leeds Metropolitan University of the decision to award an honorary degree to Ray Illingworth. See *The Guardian*, 13 May 1997 and the *Higher Education Guardian*, 27 May 1997. With respect to dismissals for the use of drugs see below at pp 443–4; *The Guardian Sport 96*, 1 November 1996; *The Express*, 27 November 1996. In an article entitled 'Cocaine, the lurking danger', *The Guardian*, 26 November 1994, Christopher Elliott analyses the relationship between drug taking and the demands imposed on and lifestyles expected of the modern professional footballer. Also see *The Guardian*, 31 January 1996 ('Positive drug tests up by 15 per cent') for an analysis of the extent of drug taking in sport. Adrian Mutu was the most high-profile footballer professional footballer to hit the headlines for proving positive in a drug test for cocaine – see *The Guardian*, 19 October 2004. However, his consequent dismissal by Chelsea, after being suspended for seven months by the FA, has not had long-term repercussions for his career, as he subsequently signed a five-year contract with Juventus – see *The Guardian*, 13 January 2005. This saga provides yet another example of different attitudes by different clubs to what arguably should not be seen as an issue for regulatory bodies such as the FA, though inevitably it is always likely to be an issue between an employer, including professional clubs, and its employees.

disciplinary action at club level (though it must be emphasised that none of the allegations were proven). Many people had some sympathy with Rio Ferdinand, when he was suspended for forgetting to attend a drug test, but it did not interfere with his career at club or international levels once his period of suspension had been served. The most prolonged dispute has resulted from Chelsea's sacking of Adrian Mutu for taking cocaine. This was followed by an award of compensation of 17 million euros plus costs by the Court of Arbitration for Sport (CAS) to Chelsea FC. At the time of writing this award has been suspended by the Swiss High Court.[27]

Clubs appear to have extremely wide discretion in these matters either towards lenience or towards harshness. This can be related to the range of reasonable responses test in unfair dismissal law.[28] Providing a player is not cheating, should not his private behaviour be his own affair? With respect to 'whistle-blowing', are we as the paying public (not to mention loyal and often longsuffering supporters) not entitled to be told what is happening behind the scenes? Although recently there appears to be a shift in football culture, there certainly seems to have been a different attitude taken towards drugs as against alcohol. The former may involve commission of a criminal offence, but is it as damaging, let alone more damaging, to a player's fitness, than the 'refuelling'[29] for which some professional footballers have been renowned? Drug-taking would also appear to be viewed more seriously than acts of violence on or off the field of play.

With respect to clause 14(a) in the Football League Contract, it is a tort for any individual to induce another to act in breach of contract (as explained below pp 425–6). A cynic might observe that in football the major culprits are the clubs themselves with respect both to players and managers. This is, however, a context where commodification plays a rather more important role in practice than juridification, given that private out-of-court settlements are the norm.[30]

Judicially Implied Terms

Judges are more prepared to imply terms in contracts of employment than is the case with contracts in general. The orthodox 'business efficacy' and 'officious bystander' tests are not without relevance, but judges recognise that certain rights and duties arise naturally from the relationship between employers and their employees, and will identify and imply contractual terms accordingly.

---

27 CAS 2008/A/1644 *Adrian Mutu v Chelsea Football Club Limited* and FIFpro press release, 7 October 2009.
28 See below, pp 431–5.
29 This was the term used regarding Paul Gascoigne's drinking habits at a time in the mid-1990s when there was still very much a drinking culture in English football. This culture has dissipated over the last decade but a player getting drunk is still viewed differently to a player taking recreational drugs.
30 See below for further discussion of this tort. A recent example of the issue concerns Chelsea FC, which was temporarily subjected to a transfer ban by FIFA, for the illegal recruitment of the teenage forward Gaël Kakuta from Lens. The ban was overturned by agreement between parties during a formal appeal hearing by CAS, www.tas-cas.org/d2wfiles/document/3947/5048/0/2010.02.04%20PR%20Eng%20_Final_.pdf

The issue of player 'poaching' became an issue of public concern in the light of alleged 'poaching' when Mike Walker left Norwich to become the manager at Everton. For further controversy surrounding Mike Walker (after his return to Norwich), and an analysis of the legal issues concerning 'poaching', players' contracts and the transfer system, see Nash, M, 'The legality of poaching: footballers' contracts revisited' (1997), 5(1) SATLJ 49–52. Also see Nash, M, 'Playing offside: footballers' contracts' (1992), New Law Journal, 1 July and 'Players and their promises: footballers' contracts' (1993), *Solicitors Gazette*, 15 October. This issue concerns managers as well as players, see *The Times*, 6 November 1993 for a report of threatened legal action by West Bromwich Albion after the club's manager, Ossie Ardiles, was appointed by Tottenham Hotspur to replace Terry Venables. Also see *The Guardian*, 4 July 1995 for an article by Lawrence Donegan, 'New kicks on the block', on the poaching of young players and a dispute between Arsenal and Manchester United over an England schoolboy international, Matthew Wicks. For an analysis of the availability of equitable relief to prevent a player from acting in breach of contract through moving to another club, and a comparison with North American law, see McCutcheon, P, 'Negative enforcement of employment contracts in the sports industries' (1997) 17(1) Legal Studies, 65–100. An important example of litigation around these issues was the long-running dispute between Middlesbrough FC and Liverpool FC over the transfer of Christian Ziege to Liverpool in the summer of 2000. A confidential out-of-court settlement resolved this matter – see *The Guardian*, 13 March 2004 – but some of the legal issues underlying this dispute will be discussed below at pp 425–6.

Judicially implied duties of the employer

The duty to provide work

Traditionally this duty applied only to those who were paid on a commission or piecework basis, or an exceptional category of employee who needed to work in order to establish and enhance a professional reputation, for example, an actor or a singer. For other employees, irrespective of their status, the following dictum applied:

> It is true that the contract of employment does not necessarily, or perhaps normally, oblige the master to provide the servant with work. Provided I pay my cook her wages regularly, she cannot complain if I choose to take any or all of my meals out.[31]

An alternative view was put forward by Lord Denning.[32]

> In these days an employer, when employing a skilled man, is bound to provide him with work. By which I mean that the man should be given the opportunity of doing his work when it is available and he is ready and willing to do it. A skilled man takes a pride in his work. He does not do it merely to earn money. He does it so as to make his contribution to the well-being of all. He does it so as to keep himself busy, and not idle. To use his skill, and to improve it.

Could (should) sports professionals be included in the traditional exceptional category of employees who need to work in order to develop a reputation? Lord Denning's reasoning may be of limited value as it was used to grant an injunction restraining a dismissal in the politically controversial context of the closed shop, under which employers agreed with a trade union to dismiss any employee who failed to join or decided to leave that union. Nevertheless, it seems more compatible with modern perspectives on the employment relationship than in the days where all employees were considered servants.[33] (Note that the 'servant' Collier was employed as a sub-editor of a newspaper.) If Lord Denning's view is to be followed it must surely cover professional footballers and the like. If this is the case, to what extent is there a right to be selected for a competitive game, if only for a reserve team? Or will a club be fulfilling its duty in requiring a player to attend training sessions?

The most important recent developments with respect to a duty to provide work have come about through cases concerning the imposition of 'garden leave' by employers. Essentially, this is where employees are required to work out long notice periods before they are able to resign, but are instructed not to come to work. Typically this will be to prevent employees from continuing to access confidential information and/or have dealings with the organisation's customers. It has been held that in the absence of an express term permitting 'garden leave' the imposition of it constitutes a breach of the duty to provide work.[34] Such express terms will not be enforceable if they are deemed to be in restraint of trade. However, they will be enforced providing the employer has legitimate interests to protect and the clause is otherwise reasonable; for example, its duration is not longer than necessary to protect the employer's interests.[35]

The case of *Crystal Palace FC Ltd v Bruce*[36] revealed that 'garden leave' clauses may be found in the employment contracts of some football managers. At the time of the case Steve Bruce was the

---

31 Per Asquith J in *Collier v Sunday Referee Publishing Co Ltd* [1940] 2 KB 647, 650.

32 *Langston v AUEW* [1974] ICR 180, 190.

33 Lord Denning's view has received subsequent approval by way of *obiter dicta* in subsequent cases. See *Breach v Epsylon Industries Ltd* [1976] IRLR 180 EAT.

34 *Provident Financial Group plc v Hayward* [1989] ICR 160 CA.

35 For the leading case law on garden leave and restraint of trade see *Credit Suisse & Asset Management Ltd v Armstrong* [1996] IRLR 450 & *FSS Travel & Leisure Systems v Johnson* [1998] IRLR 382. For further discussion on the doctrine of restraint of trade, see below pp 409–11.

36 (2002) QBD (unreported). For further comment on this case and the granting of interlocutory injunctions see Welch, R (2002) 5(2) SLB, pp 3–4. It is not known whether 'garden leave' clauses are typically to be found in managers' contracts but it has been reported that Barnet intended to enforce garden leave against Martin Allen when he walked out of the club to manage Brentford. However, the dispute was settled by an out-of-court settlement between the two clubs. See *The Independent*, 30 March 2004.

manager of Crystal Palace. Bruce wished to leave the club to become the manager of Birmingham City FC. Crystal Palace sought an injunction to enforce a 'garden leave' clause to prevent him from doing this. Burton J decided that Crystal Palace might well have legitimate interests to protect as it and Birmingham were both in the First Division and indeed were both rivals for a play-off position at the end of the 2001/02 season. Steve Bruce's departure to manage Birmingham would thus have been duly detrimental to Palace's prospects for the rest of the season. Moreover, the departure of a manager to another club not infrequently results in other members of the coaching and playing staff joining him shortly thereafter. The court granted an interlocutory injunction for a short period (around two months) to restrain Bruce from leaving Crystal Palace in breach of contract.

The duty to take reasonable care with respect to the health, safety and welfare of the employee

All employers are subject to this common law duty as well as various statutory duties imposed by legislation and the requirements of EC law. Such duties will normally be more than met by professional clubs, given that their employees will be perceived as valuable investments. (There is nothing more infuriating to the club – and the supporters – than learning that a valued player has received a serious injury during training). Contrary to the norm in employment law, it is the player's corresponding duty to the employer that is potentially of more practical significance.

The duty to maintain mutual trust and confidence

This duty is an example of the dynamism of judicial creativity in implying new terms into employment contracts. The duty was identified during the 1970s – particularly in order to expand the circumstances where a resignation by an employee could be construed as a dismissal.

The classic statement of the duty is provided by Browne-Wilkinson J.

Woods v W/M Car Services

. . . it is clearly established that there is implied in a contract of employment a term that the employers will not, without reasonable and proper cause, conduct themselves in a manner calculated or likely to destroy or seriously damage the relationship of confidence and trust between employer and employee . . . To constitute a breach of this implied term it is not necessary to show the employer intended any repudiation of the contract: the tribunal's function is to look at the employer's conduct as a whole and determine whether it is such that its effect, judged reasonably and sensibly, is such that the employee cannot be expected to put up with it . . .[37]

Many of the decided cases in which employers have been found to be in breach of this duty have revolved around the issues of verbal and physical abuse and harassment. Given the oft-quoted statement (tautology) that professional football is a man's game, to what extent can the individual player be expected to tolerate swearing, barracking, public criticism (humiliation) and practical jokes from manager, team captain and teammates? Generally, this could be considered part of the necessary 'locker room' culture to build and maintain team solidarity and spirit. However, in law, established workplace culture can still be found unlawful – particularly in the context of behaviour that constitutes racial or sexual harassment.[38] In football, being required to accept a verbal 'bashing' may be one thing. It would be altogether different if, for example, a public dressing-down was tainted with racist language or innuendo.

Could a refusal to select a player for the first team ever constitute a breach of this duty (and/ or the duty to provide work)? This could assume importance where a player is not being picked in

---

37 [1981] ICR 666 EAT, at pp 670–71.
38 See Chapter 10 pp 477–83.

order to punish that player, for example, for expressing a legitimate disagreement with a manager rather than for sporting or disciplinary reasons. In the context of a player seeking a transfer it could be counter-productive to leave a player to 'rot in the reserves' if this is adopted as a tactic to pressurise a player into staying with a club. If such a practice constitutes destruction of mutual trust and confidence on the club's part it would enable a player to claim he had been constructively dismissed and thus was now free to negotiate a new contract with any club of his choosing.[39]

As confirmed by the House of Lords in *Malik v BCCI*[40] this overriding duty can take a variety of forms, from failing to treat employees with respect to adversely affecting an employee's reputation through operating a business in a dishonest and corrupt manner. Breach of this duty can give rise to an action for damages as well as enabling an employee to claim wrongful and unfair dismissal.[41]

Judicially implied duties of the employee

The duty of obedience

An employee must obey all lawful and reasonable instructions of the employer. An instruction is reasonable if it is compatible with the job the employee is employed to do and is not excessive in terms of the demands imposed on the individual. It is clear that the duty can extend to personal factors such as appearance and dress, and to behaviour in the employee's own time.

In light of the clauses in the Football League Contract quoted above, consider what types of instructions can be issued to professional footballers beyond attending training sessions and reporting on match days; for example with respect to diet, family life and standards of personal behaviour. Under the Cricketers' Contract, cricketers owe an express duty not to 'engage in any activity or pursuit which is or may be prejudicial to the Club . . .' – clause 6(e).

The duty to take reasonable care

Given the financial consequences to a club if a player injures himself, a teammate or, in certain circumstances, an opponent, and the high salaries that some sports professionals may command, it is at least conceivable that a club (or its insurance company) could require a player to indemnify it for such loss where it is the consequence of reckless conduct or negligence on the player's part. This might be especially so if the player concerned is no longer with the club, and therefore the effect on the player's morale would not be an issue for the plaintiff.

The employer's right to an indemnity was upheld by the House of Lords in *Lister v Romford Ice and Cold Storage Co Ltd*.[42] The decision has attracted much criticism because of the implications for good employee relations, and has been subjected to some judicial restriction.[43] However, in a 'non-industrial' context such as sport, contemporary judges might feel more inclined to apply the reasoning in *Lister* that an employee who breaks a contractual obligation of care, and thereby causes damage to the employer, is accordingly liable to compensate the employer, or perhaps more likely the club's insurance company.[44] The potential importance of *Lister* is now particularly

---

39 Under the new transfer regulations adopted by FIFA (see below pp 451–4), players are permitted to terminate their contracts if they have 'sporting just cause'. A wilful refusal to select a player for first-team matches is very likely to fall into this category even if it does not amount to a repudiatory breach of contract on the part of the employing club.

40 [1997] IRLR 462.

41 The fact that breach of this term can result in the awarding of a large sum of damages is illustrated by *Horkulak v Cantor Fitzgerald International* [2003] EWHC 1918 where an employee, who had been the victim of bullying, was awarded just under £1,000,000 in damages. The employee was employed as a broker and thus, like many professional sports participants, was employed in a world where very high salaries are enjoyed.

42 [1957] ALL ER 125.

43 See, for example, the Court of Appeal's decision in *Morris v Ford Motor Co* [1973] QB 792 which restricts the possibility of subrogation, ie an insurance company substituting itself as the plaintiff to recover the money that it has paid to the insured.

44 Note that in *Morris* the majority of the Court of Appeal refused to accept Lord Denning's argument that an insurer should never be able to benefit from subrogation in an employment context.

significant in the light of high-profile cases of litigation arising from fouls committed on the field of play.[45]

The duty of fidelity – exclusivity

Employees are under an obligation not to use or disclose confidential information obtained in the course of employment without the employer's consent. In other circumstances, however, there is no general obligation not to engage in 'moonlighting'. Employers who wish to secure the exclusive services of their employees will need to incorporate appropriate clauses into contracts of employment.

Clause 7 of the Football League Contract (above) prevents players from participating in their sport, or any other form of sporting activity, without the club's previous consent. Professional cricketers are subject to a wider restriction.

The Contract for Professional Cricketers

Clause 5(c) . . . The Cricketer will . . . not without the prior consent in writing of the Club accept other employment or on his own account carry on any business calling or profession. Such consent will not be withheld where in the reasonable opinion of the Club the proper performance by the Cricketer of his obligations under this Agreement is not affected and where the interests of the club are not harmed.[46]

The duty of fidelity – maintaining confidentiality

Duties relating to confidential information are important in the context of 'whistle-blowing'. The scope of the implied duty of fidelity can be amplified by express terms in the contract, as in cl 13 of the Football League Contract (above). The concept of public interest may be invoked to justify a disclosure which would be otherwise a breach of contract.

Initial Services Ltd v Putterill

Lord Denning . . . disclosure must, I should think, be to one who has a proper interest to receive the information. Thus it would be proper to disclose a crime to the police; or a breach of the Restrictive Trade Practices Act to the Registrar. There may be cases where the misdeed is of such a character that the public interest may demand, or at least excuse, publication on a broader field, even to the press . . .[47]

The Public Disclosure Act 1998 also protected employees from dismissal or being subjected to any other detriment if they disclose information relating to, for example, criminal behaviour on the part of an employer. The statutory provisions, now contained in ss 43c-h ERA 1996, override any contractual terms requiring employees to maintain confidentiality.

However, employers are still able to use employment contracts to a significant extent to conceal information which it can be argued the public have a legitimate interest in receiving. For example, the Act would make no difference to keeping confidential the details of the much-publicised row between Devon Malcolm and Ray Illingworth, even though the disclosure of such information could be seen as a matter of public interest. There is nothing in law that requires the public to be told why a player has been selected or dropped from a national team. Moreover, even where

---

45 See further, Chapter 11 on sports field violence.

46 On the other hand, cricketers had the contractual right to play international cricket if selected – cl 5(d). Indeed, today, as a result of the central contracts system, a player under contract to play for the England Test team may only play for his club with the permission of the ECB. Cf the position of footballers, where a club may decide not to release a player whom the England manager has indicated he would like to select.

47 [1968] 1 QB 396 CA, at p 406.

disclosure is permitted it will generally only be protected if it is made to the proper authorities rather than the media. For example, if a player or an agent or a manager discovered financial irregularities within a club, publication should be limited to bodies such as the Football Association/ Football League or the England and Wales Cricket Board, and therefore might not necessarily enter the public domain.[48]

The Premier League Rules require players and agents to maintain confidentiality with respect to the personal terms in the player's employment contract. It was breach of this rule that led to the litigation between Middlesbrough FC and Liverpool FC over Christian Ziege.[49]

Confidentiality (Clause 16)

A contract between a Club and a Player shall be treated as being private and confidential and its contents shall not be disclosed or divulged either directly or indirectly to any Person whatsoever by either party thereto except:

24.1 with the prior written agreement of both parties; or

24.2 as may be required by any statutory, regulatory, governmental or quasi-governmental authorities or (where appropriate) any recognised stock exchange or as otherwise required by law or pursuant to these Rules, or

24.3 in the case of the Player, to his duly appointed Agent and professional advisers including the Professional Footballers' Association; or

24.4 in the case of the Club, to its duly appointed Agent and its professional advisers or to such of its Officials or Auditors to whom such disclosure is strictly necessary for the purpose of their duties and then only to the extent so necessary.

Restraint of Trade

The duty of fidelity applies whilst the contract subsists but ceases to apply on its termination except to information which comes within the category of a trade secret. Nevertheless, contract law permits express terms which affect an individual's freedom to work for whom he pleases once an employment contract has come to an end. Such clauses are *prima facie* in restraint of trade and thus void. However, a restraint is permitted if an employer has a legitimate interest to protect and the clause is reasonable in that it is no wider than necessary, with respect to its scope, duration and area of geographical operation, to protect the employer.

An example of a reasonable restraint is provided by a term in the contract between Kevin Keegan and Newcastle United FC. Keegan resigned as manger in September 2008 and subsequently successfully claimed constructive wrongful dismissal (see below, p 422). However, one of the issues that the Premier League Managers' Arbitration Tribunal had to consider was whether Newcastle could enforce a term in Keegan's contract, which prohibited him from working in any capacity for any other Premier League Club for a period of six months if his contract was terminated by the club. The tribunal found that the term was wide enough to cover constructive as well as actual dismissal, and that it was reasonable and thus enforceable. It was only for six months, and did not prevent Keegan from working for clubs outside the Premier League, or for any other club in another country or at international level. The tribunal agreed with Newcastle's argument that it was reasonable to prevent Keegan from working in any capacity for another Premiership club, as putting his detailed knowledge of Newcastle's players and their contracts at the disposal of a rival

---

48 However, rights to disclose information to the media may well have been extended as a result of the Human Rights Act 1998 and the incorporation of Art 10 of the European Convention on Human Rights into UK law. The actual legal position remains to be clarified through case law.

49 See above, fn 30.

Premiership club would have given the latter an unfair advantage. The tribunal also noted that during the operation of the restraint it was permissible for Keegan to negotiate a contract with another Premiership club; the restraint merely prevented the contract from commencing until the six-month period had expired.

One application of the doctrine of restraint of trade is to protect a contracting party who is a vulnerable position vis-à-vis the other contracting party. This is of potential importance to sports professionals, as they often begin their careers when young. They are thus in a similar position to entertainers such as pop/rock musicians in that in order to get a foot on the rung of the ladder of success they may sign a contract without fully understanding the practical implications of what they are agreeing to. Indeed, even if they do fully understand what the contract provides they may feel they have no option but to sign if their careers are to progress.[50] However, where a sports professional employs an agent, then, providing the contract of agency is in itself fair and reasonable,[51] this should ensure the doctrine is of no relevance as it will be the agent's legal duty to ensure that contracts negotiated on behalf of the client are in the latter's interests.

The doctrine is of particular significance in professional football in light of the transfer rules laid down by the Premier and Football Leagues. These rules used to apply to all professional players whose contracts with their clubs had come to an end. The position under the English law of contract was (is) that these rules are valid and thus enforceable.

Eastham v Newcastle United FC

The transfer and retain system as it operated at the time was challenged by the footballer George Eastham as constituting an unlawful restraint of trade. Under the system, on termination of a contract a club could decide to put a player on the retain list. As a consequence the player so retained could not play for any club in any country which was a member of FIFA. If the club refused to place him on the transfer list he had no choice but to accept the offer of a new contract from the club if he wished to work as a professional footballer. These regulations were declared in restraint of trade. However, the rules enabling a club to require a transfer fee were upheld.

Wilberforce J: The transfer system has been stigmatised by the plaintiff's counsel as a relic from the Middle Ages, involving the buying and selling of human beings as chattels; and, indeed, to anyone not hardened to acceptance of the practice it would seem incongruous to the spirit of a national sport. One must not forget that the consent of a player to the transfer is necessary, but, on the other hand, the player has little security since he cannot get a long-term contract and, while he is on the transfer list awaiting an offer, his feelings and anxieties as to who his next employer is to be may not be very pleasant.[52]

Despite this, Wilberforce J was prepared to uphold the transfer system taken alone as, although there was an element of restraint, a player could apply to have a transfer fee reduced or eliminated

---

50 For an analysis of the operation of the implications of the doctrine of restraint of trade for boxers' contracts, see Greenfield, S and Osborn, G, 'A gauntlet for the glove: the challenge to English boxing contracts' (1995) 6(1) Marquette Sports Law Journal 153–71. Of particular concern is the situation where a young boxer signs a contract under which the same person is 'employed' by the boxer to manage him and promote his fights.

51 See *Proactive Sports Management Limited v (1) Wayne Rooney (2) Coleen Rooney (formerly McLoughlin) (3) Stoneygate 48 Limited (4) Speed 9849 Limited* [2010] EWHC 1807 (QB) where the contract of agency, entered into by Wayne Rooney when he was aged 16, was declared invalid as a restraint of trade. This contract had a duration of eight years and entitled Proactive to 20 per cent of monies earned by Rooney under sponsorship and marketing contacts. For a full analysis see Sweeney, C and Castro, G, (2010) 8(9) WSLR.

52 [1963] 3 All ER 139 Ch D, 145. Although it was decided that it was unlawful for clubs to retain players who were out of contract, it was this landmark case that decided that the transfer system, on its own, did not constitute a restraint of trade and was thus legal.

and could play professional football for a non-League club. The transfer system was protecting a legitimate interest as:

> . . . within the League it provides a means by which the poorer clubs can, on occasions, obtain money, enabling them to stay in existence and improve their facilities; and, rather more generally . . . it provides a means by which clubs can part with a good player in a manner which will enable them to secure a replacement. One player cannot easily be exchanged for another; the transferee club may not – indeed by the nature of things probably will not – have a player to offer in exchange: by giving cash, the transferor club is able to look all around the League for a replacement. Given the need to circulate players, money is necessarily a more efficient medium of exchange than barter, and the system helps both money and players to circulate. Looked at in this way the system might be said to be in the interests of players themselves.[53]

There has been no indication on the part of the English courts in the years since *Eastham* that there has been any rethinking of the reasoning of Wilberforce J. However, as a result of changes that were introduced, in the wake of the *Bosman* ruling (see below, pp 442–7), at the start of the 1998/99 season, players who are aged 24 or over and who are out of contract are completely free to negotiate a new contract with any club.

For players who are under 24 and out of contract the position remains as follows. When a player's contract comes to an end he is not unconditionally free to negotiate a contract with a different club unless (and this is relatively unlikely with younger players who have successfully embarked on a professional career) he is given a free transfer. In this case he is literally a free agent who can move to a new club on whatever terms he (or his agent) can negotiate. Alternatively, and the more likely position in practice, the club can retain him as a registered player by offering a new contract on terms no less advantageous than the expired contract. The player is 'free' to negotiate a move to another club but this is subject to the clubs agreeing a transfer fee. If a fee cannot be agreed between the two clubs the issue may be referred to the Professional Football Compensation Committee, whose decision on the value of the transfer fee is final. In practice, a player's desire to move may be frustrated if other clubs are not prepared to pay the required or prescribed transfer fee. Moreover, a player may submit to pressure to sign a new contract with a club to regain some security of employment.

The details of the rules are set out as follows.

FA Code of Practice and Notes on Contract Retain and Transfer Rules

The Player's contract will run for a stated period. During that time the Club and Player have binding obligations to each other. These can be ended by agreement, so it is possible for the Club to suggest to the Player that he might like to consider joining another Club, and the Player can indicate to the Club that he would like to leave. Agreement of both sides is essential. No one is entitled in law to induce either a Club or Player to break a contract; such action is tortuous and could lead to an action for damages.

The aim of the current rules is to enable a Player to leave a Club freely at the end of his contract, but to recognise that the Club is entitled to compensation from the Club he joins, provided that this does not seriously hamper the Player's moving. It is implicit in the rules that the happy Club and Player should be able to continue their relationship smoothly. Contracts of any length are possible and a contract can be re-negotiated so that it runs for a further or a longer period.

---

53 [1963] 3 All ER 139, 149.

If, however, Player and Club decide to part at the end of a contract then the Player is free to look for another Club. He may do this even though his Club has made him a fresh offer. In three instances there will be no compensation payable:

(a) the Club has announced that he is free to move without fee,
(b) the Club has made no offer to him,
(c) the Club's offer is less favourable than his previous terms.

To calculate the position under (c) it is necessary to look at the most favourable year of the contract that has expired and to calculate the financial value and the bonus structure (the actual amount of bonus paid will of course depend upon appearances and results and is variable). If the previous contract contains a signing-on fee, paid in annual parts, the last part will be added unless the contract made clear that it was paid on a 'once only' basis. Players wishing to claim a Free Transfer on the basis that their offer of re-engagement is less favourable must make written application to The FA Premier League or The Football League (dependent on which League the Club is in membership) with a copy to their Club, by 30th June otherwise the Club's compensation rights will be retained. If there is a dispute over whether or not the terms are as favourable, the matter will be determined by the Board of the appropriate League and, on appeal, by The Football League Appeals Committee. A Player granted a Free Transfer is entitled to receive from his Club as severance payment his basic wage for a period of one month from the expiry date of his contract or until he signs for another Club, whichever period is the shorter, provided that where a Player signs for a Club within the month at a reduced basic wage then his old Club shall make up the shortfall in basic wage for the remainder of the month.

There is a timetable for the various stages that must be followed:

(i) Third Saturday in May
This will usually be immediately after the end of the season. The Club must have made its offer by that date. Practice varies but it should be noted that some Clubs make a 'starting offer' at the old rates and negotiate, others decide what they regard as the contract they wish to make at the outset. It is important that during the period set aside for negotiation the Club officials (usually manager and secretary but often a director) and the Player are available. In special cases, eg where Clubs have outstanding fixtures affecting promotion or relegation, the notification may be delayed until no later than four days after the Club's last such fixture.

(ii) Period for consideration
The Player has at least a month (the offer may be sent early) to decide whether to accept the contract, to discuss it with the Club and to let the Club know his decision. Rules and Regulations provide that the Player must at the end of the period give the Club his decision. A list of these Players refusing offers (or free to move without compensation) will be circulated by the League concerned. It is in the interests of a Player who receives an offer of re-engagement with which he is dissatisfied to inform the Club in writing and in person in order to give the Club the opportunity to make a revised offer

(iii) Offer refused
If the Player turns down the offer he can approach other Clubs and they can talk to him. His Club too can ask other Clubs if they are interested in signing the Player.

As a matter of courtesy, Clubs intending to negotiate with Players who have not accepted offers of re-engagement, should give notice of approach to the Player's existing Club. It is essential that both Club and Player keep each other informed where serious enquiries are made or interest shown. It is not only courteous, it is essential for the proper working of the scheme. Copies of all firm offers made for a Player should be notified to The FA Premier League and/or The Football League as appropriate. A Player who has refused his Club's offer of re-engagement may notify The FA Premier League or The Football League and The Professional Footballers' Association of his refusal and his name will be circulated to all Clubs.

The Club may leave its offer open so that the Player may, after talking to other Clubs, decide to stay. On the other hand it is entitled to withdraw that offer (without losing the right to compensation) if it feels it must do so to finalise its squad of Players for the new season.

A Player is free to train with another Club during this period, even though his transfer has not been fully agreed or the compensation fee settled and paid.

(iv) Compensation Fee

The compensation fee is a matter between the Clubs and only affects the Player if it makes his transfer difficult or unlikely. The Clubs themselves will discuss and settle the fee. If no fee has been settled, then after 30th June the Clubs, or the Player to whom terms have been condition-ally offered may appeal to The Football League Appeals Committee to determine the fee. The Player must have either signed for his new Club, or agreed terms subject to the fee being satis-factory.

(v) 30th June

All contracts apart from Monthly Contracts are dated to run out on this date. If the Player has not been transferred by this date the Club holding his registration may propose various action [*sic*]:

(a) the Club may enter into a 'conditional' contract with the Player. A 'conditional' contract allows a Player to continue playing for a Club until such time as another Club wishes to sign him in which case he must be released even if the two Clubs cannot agree on a compensation fee. A conditional contract should take the form of a normal contract with the Player's remuneration and incentives being subject to mutual agreement. The following clause should also be included to safeguard the Player's rights: 'This agreement is signed with the proviso that, should another Club wish to acquire the Player's registra-tion, the registration will be transferred for a fee determined in accordance with the provi-sions of The FA Premier League Rules and The Football League Regulations';

(b) the Club may continue to pay the Player the basic wage payable under the contract which shall have expired in which case the Player is not eligible to play for the Club nor is he subject to the regulations or discipline of the Club. A Club taking up this option is, by continuing to pay the Player, retaining its rights to a compensation fee. This need not go on indefinitely and on or after the first day of the season, the Club may apply to The Football League Appeals Committee to cease paying the basic wage, at the same time retaining its right to a compensation fee if it feels that circumstances warrant such action, for example, if the Player has, without good reason, refused offers of employment with another Club;

(c) where a Club is desirous of playing a Player who is 'in dispute' yet does not wish to enter into a conditional contract, it may agree in writing with the Player that he should continue to play for the Club on a week to week basis under the financial terms of his last contract until such time as either the weekly agreement is terminated by either party or another Club is prepared to sign the Player. Copies of all weekly agreements must be forwarded to the League in which the Club is a Member and The Football Association and it is recom-mended that they take the following form: 'The Player agrees to continue playing for the Club on a week to week basis under the financial terms of his last contract unless the Club incentive schedule paid in accordance with that contract has been changed in which case the Player will receive the revised incentives, and to be subject to Club Regulations and discipline and to the Rules and Regulations of The Football Association and The FA Premier

League/The Football League. The Player agrees to give the Club at least seven days' notice of his intention to terminate this agreement. It is understood that the notice need not apply where a Player chooses to join another Club in which case the agreement will terminate forthwith.' It would seem to be in the interests of all parties for the Player to continue playing for a Club as it gives other Clubs who may be interested in signing him a chance to assess him in a match situation;

(d) the Club may cease paying the Player in which case he becomes a free agent.

A Player who is paid under either option (b) or option (c) is entitled to fourteen days' notice of the cancellation of his registration.

So that the Player is able to understand the options open to him he is advised, if in any difficulty, to contact his PFA representative or The PFA Office.

It should be noted that equivalent rules and procedures are contained in Section M of the Premier League Rules. Further restrictions on the ability of players under contract to negotiate moves to other clubs are imposed by the transfer window system, and rules which prevent players or their agents approaching other clubs or being approached by clubs during the currency of their contracts. The following extracts from the Premier League's rules are replicated in the rules of the Football League.

Section M

Transfers of Players' Registrations

Transfer Windows

1. **'Transfer Windows'** means the 2 periods in a year during which, subject to Rule M 5, a Club may apply for the New Registration of a player or to have the registration of a player transferred to it.

2. The first Transfer Window in any year shall commence at midnight on the last day of the Season and shall end at 5.00 pm on 31st August next.

3. The second Transfer Window in any year shall commence at midnight on 31st December and shall end at 5.00 pm on 31st January next.

4. A Club making an application during the second Transfer Window must satisfy the Board that it is made for strictly sport related reasons or in exceptional circumstances.

5. Outside a Transfer Window the Board in its absolute discretion may:
    5.1. refuse an application; or
    5.2. grant an application and, if thought fit, impose conditions by which the Club making the application and the player shall be bound.

6. Except in the case of a Temporary Transfer, the transfer of a player's registration shall not be permitted more than once in the same Season. It can be commented that the introduction of transfer windows, whilst in accordance with the new FIFA rules for international transfers, remains controversial and is certainly not universally liked either by clubs or their supporters.[54]

---

54 See 'Window gets the thumbs down from the pros', *The Guardian*, 1 February 2003. This certainly was the experience of Portsmouth FC in its first season in the Premiership (2003–04), where the manager, Harry Redknapp, frequently claimed that the club's fortunes on the field of play were unduly hampered by injuries in circumstances where new players could not be brought in.

Section K

Players' Contracts

Approaches to Players

1. A Club shall be at Liberty at any time to make an approach to a Player with a view to negotiating a contract with such a Player:

    1.1. if he is an Out of Contract Player, or,

    1.2. in the case of a Contract Player, with the prior written consent of the Club (or club) to which he is contracted.

2. A Club shall be at Liberty after the third Saturday in May in any year and before the 1st July next following to make such an approach to a Contract Player:

    2.1. who will become an Out of Contract Player on that 1st July; and

    2.2. who has received no offer from his Club under Rule M.17.2 or

    2.3. who has received but has declined such offer.

3. Any Club which by itself, by any of its Officials, by any of its Players, by its Agent, by any other Person on its behalf or by any other means whatsoever makes an approach either directly or indirectly to a Contract Player except as permitted by either Rule K.1.2 or Rule K.2 shall be in breach of these Rules and may be dealt with under the provisions of Section R.

Rule K5 prohibits players or their agents making similar approaches to clubs without the permission of the player's current club. Arguably, these rules and/or transfer windows can be challenged under the doctrine of restraint of trade and/or the freedom of movement provisions of EU law.

Welch R. 'Player Mobility, The FIFA Transfer Rules & Freedom of Movement'

Ironically, given that they operate to constrain player mobility, the only aspect of the FIFA rules that has been adopted in the UK's domestic leagues (in line with UEFA's requirements) is the introduction of transfer windows. Thus transfers may now only take place in the close season and during the months of August and January. It is the case that transfer windows exist in other sports and were accepted as valid for basketball by the ECJ in its ruling in *Lehtonen*.[55] However, the fact that transfer windows have been objectively justified as having sporting benefits connected with team stability and 'regularity' of sporting competition in one sport does not automatically mean that this must also be the case in all other sports.

Indeed, it can be argued that the transfer windows, as they operate in European football, would fail the test of proportionality in that they are too restrictive. The suspicion is that that they essentially favour the larger richer clubs who can afford to assemble large squads and spend significant sums on transfers in a concentrated period of time. FIFPro has issued a statement that supports the view that that transfer windows in the UK constitute an invalid restraint of trade.[56] Although the Premier League has essentially accepted their legitimacy, the Football League has led an orchestrated campaign against them. It has argued: 'League clubs have traditionally relied on the flexibility to buy, sell or loan players whenever needed for either football or financial reasons. If this freedom is restricted clubs' financial health will suffer.'[57]

55 Case C-176/96 *Jyri Lehtonen & Castors Canada Dry Namur-Braine v Fédération Royale Belge des Sociétés de Basketball ASBL.*

56 This view is based on advice provided by Paul Golding QC – see FIFPro press statement, 'International transfer windows could fail if challenged nationally', 21 December 2004.

57 Football League Press Release, 'Statement by Chairman Sir Brian Mawhinney', 23 September 2004.

Tapping-Up

One aspect of the UK rules on players' contracts that have recently attracted criticism are the rules preventing a player from talking to another club without the consent of his current club. As is well documented, Ashley Cole and Chelsea FC were fined by the FA for breach of Rule K5, which prevents clubs making an illegal approach to ('tapping-up') a player. Whilst it is the case that this specific incident has not resulted in litigation,[58] the validity of the rule is still open to challenge and thus litigation in the future cannot be ruled out. The essential question is what makes footballers different to other employees, including those on fixed term contracts, who may seek to negotiate with a prospective employer either on entering into an employment contract with that employer on the expiry of the current contract or with a view to the buying out of that contract. In short, it may be argued that Rule K5 constitutes an illegal restraint of trade. Additionally, it could be argued that the rule is an unjustifiable constraint on a player's freedom of movement under Article 39. The latter contention is reinforced by the fact other leagues in Europe do not have an equivalent to Rule K5.[59]

It should be taken into account that Rule K5 also constitutes a term in a player's contract, and, in counterposition to the above, it can be argued that other mechanisms to prevent valuable employees from acting in breach of contract, such as the use of garden-leave provisions and post-employment restraints, have been upheld as valid by the courts. Moreover, players enjoy significantly high salaries and untypical security of employment during the currency of their contracts. Footballers are paid handsomely even when injured or when not selected. In short, players are major business assets and thus clubs have a proprietary interest in holding them to their contracts. Overall, there is an analogy between the operation of the Rule and using contractual mechanisms to protect other proprietary interests such as trade secrets and goodwill. With respect to proportionality, the FAPL has argued that the Rule is necessary for competitive integrity, contractual stability, team stability and competitive balance.[60]

However, the arbitrary nature of the Rule does seem invidious. As the Rule stands, no distinction is made between a player whose contract has several years to run and a player who is in the last year of his contract and is free to move on expiry of that contract. The latter needs to ascertain his prospects both with his current club and prospective new clubs as far as the signing of a new contract is concerned. It is hard to see how preventing a player from doing this can be anything other than an unreasonable restraint or disproportionate restriction on his freedom of movement.

Conclusions

. . . The transfer window can be seen as a symbol of wider tensions between the interests of the elite top European clubs and football clubs in general (including arguably the majority of clubs in the English Premiership). Transfer windows serve the interests of the rich and inhibit the manoeuvrability of the poor. The introduction of transfer windows was not part of the changes that the European Commission was seeking. It remains to be seen whether they will be subject to any legal challenge, and, if so, whether they will meet the criteria of proportionality. In any case, it is contended that transfer windows should be abolished (smashed) as they do not provide any general sporting benefits to the majority of clubs, players or fans.

---

58 The Court of Arbitration for Sport (CAS) has declined on jurisdictional grounds to review the 'Cole Case', but a player in the future may still challenge the rule in an English court by invoking the doctrine of restraint of trade and/or EU law.
59 Indeed, legal advice provided to FIFPro by its lawyer Wil van Megen suggests that the rule is contrary to EU law – see FIFPro press statement 'Fines in "Tapping Up" Case may be contrary to European law', 7 June 2005.
60 See Shear, G and Green, A, 'Footballers and Fixed Term Contracts' (2005) 13(2) SATLJ 16. For further discussion also see Goldberg, M and Pentol, S, 'Football "Tapping Up" Rules – Anachronism or Necessity?' (2005) 13(1) SATLJ 15.

With respect to Rule K5 there is some basis for believing that any legal challenge to the Rule could succeed. Arguably, the Rule should be scrapped on the basis that it is not part of the general European system for regulating players' contracts . . .[61]

Similar rules apply in English rugby league. For example, the Rugby Football League decided to suspend Paul Cooke, after its Operational Rules Tribunal found that the player had broken its rules by approaching Hull Kingston Rovers while still under contract to local rivals Hull FC. Whilst the same argument set out above applies with respect to restraint of trade, it is less likely that a rugby league player could succeed in challenging the rules under EU law. This is because it would be difficult to establish that the English RFL has a dominant position in the European market and/or its rules affect trade between Member States contrary to Article 102 TFEU.[62]

As stated above, the 'older' professional, who is out of contract, is able to enter into negotiations with any clubs which express interest in signing him. This includes, of course, negotiations with his current club, and a player who is still wanted by his club is in a strong bargaining position to re-negotiate personal terms including a salary increase and loyalty bonuses. Clubs also have a financial incentive to allow a player to move prior to the expiry of his contract in order still to be able to secure a transfer fee.

The way that even older players may be able to play the transfer system to their advantage is set out below in the extract from Garry Nelson's autobiography. Arguably, the downside, from such a player's perspective, to absolute freedom of contract is that once he is out of contract his position is now the same as any other type of employee employed under a fixed-term contract that has expired. In short, the immediate future might be unemployment, as the player may be free to move but without a club to move to. As a lesser evil, the player may find employment with a new club, but on inferior personal terms to those that he previously enjoyed. There is, however, the possibility, if a fixed-term contract is not renewed, of being able to claim unfair dismissal or a statutory redundancy payment.[63] With respect to the latter, the player's contract may contain provision for a rather more generous severance payment in the event of the contract not being renewed.

Nelson, G, *Left Foot Forward*

Transfer tribunals were the logical and inevitable consequence of the PFA gaining 'freedom of contract' rights for players. Their coming into being arose from the need for an independent body to reconcile the 'legal rights' of the parties – existing employer club, employee player, would-be employer club – involved in negotiations/dispute as an existing contract comes to its end. A player's current club have two options. They can dispense with a player – i.e. give him a 'free' – or retain him. Crucially, to retain him they must offer him a new contract that is at least as favourable as the one just ending. This does create problems for Boards. With players who are doing the business well enough to justify the original outlay on them and justify their first-team selection, the club will not want the contract to expire. Every attempt will usually be made to offer a new one that is sufficiently attractive for the player to want to sign. But he (and certainly, where applicable, his agent!) will appreciate that he is negotiating from a position of strength. What he now considers 'attractive' may be a considerable escalation on his previous terms.

But the player may not be such an obvious asset. He may be getting long in the tooth, no longer performing at his former level. This may not weaken his bargaining position as much as might appear at first glance. Initially, he may have been signed for a large transfer fee plus a

---

61 Welch, R., 'Player Mobility, The FIFA Transfer Rules and Freedom of Movement' (2006) International Sports Law Review 83.
62 For further analysis, see Sandlant, D, and Silkin, L, 'Player Contracts: Paul Cooke: RFL Tribunal findings and European Law' (2007) 5(12) WSLR.
63 See below, p 427.

huge signing-on fee and very substantial wages. The common sense move now may be to sell him. But in order to be able to command a transfer fee (as opposed to giving him the free and writing off all their past investment), the club must have him on their books. That's to say, they must renew his contract on at least the same terms. Knowing a good thing when he sees it, the player is almost certain to re-sign at once. The club are now paying the same high level of monies as before to a player they don't really want but whom, if they want to balance their books at all, they need to sell at the same top end of the market they bought him in.

'Freedom of contract' has made it possible for players to let their contracts expire and yet put themselves in an enhanced bargaining position. Consistently good form should clearly earn appropriate reward – no problem, you would think. But in many cases clubs offer even on-song players the legal limit they are obliged to – the same terms the players are already on. The Board's hope in such instances is that, not attracting any interest from other clubs, the player will be forced to re-sign on the old terms. But if there is outside interest and the player has more than one option, the club's gamble is more than likely to misfire. The player has leverage. He can wait to see what is the best offer on the table; even play both ends against the middle. If, finally, a player refuses to re-sign with his existing club and signs for another, a transfer fee still has to be agreed between the two clubs. If they don't agree – and usually they don't – by now there's likely to be a lot of acrimony flying about and the transfer tribunal enters the equation. It will arbitrate and decide the fee.[64]

Termination of Contracts of Employment in Sport

Sporting contracts can be lawfully terminated in exactly the same way as any other type of contract, that is, by mutual agreement, performance or expiry. However, there are special rules, primarily as a result of statutory rights of unfair dismissal that apply to all contracts of employment including those entered into by professional sports participants.

Common law termination

Any employment contract can be terminated without cause if due notice is given. This can be the case with fixed-term contracts although the normal expectation is that such contracts will end on the date of their expiry. Non-renewal does not constitute a dismissal. In the case of football, it is on expiry of a player's contract that the transfer system as outlined above applies (that is, providing the player is under the age of 24 at the date of the contract's expiry).

A summary dismissal, where no notice or inadequate notice is given or a fixed-term contract is terminated prior to its date of expiry, is prima facie a breach of contract and thus a wrongful dismissal by the employer unless the employee is guilty of gross misconduct. For this to be the case the employee must be in breach of a term – express or implied – which is at the root of the contract (or have repudiated the contract in its entirety). From a contractual perspective the dismissal is simply the employer communicating to the employee that the latter's breach has discharged the employer from his obligations under the contract, and the employer has consequently elected to regard the contract as terminated.

Disobedience of a lawful and reasonable instruction by the employer may constitute gross misconduct. On the other hand, it may be that an employee's disobedience, though misconduct, is

---

64 This extract, from Nelson, G, *Left Foot Forward* (1995), London: Headline, pp 261–63, provides a useful insight into the view the professional footballer takes of the transfer system. Garry Nelson played for a number of Football League teams including Plymouth Argyle, Southend United and Charlton Athletic between 1979 and 1997. His book focuses on his time with Charlton when Alan Curbishley was his manager. After Nelson's retirement from the professional game in 1997 he became Commercial Executive of the PFA.

not sufficiently serious to constitute a repudiatory breach. It is clear that there is no standard test for ascertaining whether misconduct is gross. The circumstances of the case must be taken into account in determining whether or not the employee has committed a repudiatory breach of contract. Only if this is the case is the employer justified in treating the contract as at an end.[65]

Examine the clauses in footballers' and cricketers' contracts (see above, pp 403–4). In what circumstances could sports professionals be regarded as repudiating their employment contracts? Roger Stanislaus and Adrian Mutu were clearly regarded by Leyton Orient and Chelsea respectively as being guilty of gross misconduct once they had been found guilty by the FA of having tested positive for cocaine.

Contracts of employment can also be terminated by means other than dismissal (or resignation). For example, contracts may be terminated by mutual agreement or through frustration. Consider the position of cricketer Ed Giddins after he tested positive for cocaine, and the argument by Sussex CCC that the cancellation of his registration by the Test and County Cricket Board automatically terminated his contract. Case law has established that the courts will not permit a dismissal to be disguised as termination of the contract through mutual agreement.[66]

Clause 2(c) of the Cricketers' Contract states that '. . . this Agreement will terminate immediately if the Board cancels or terminates the registration of the Cricketer by the Club'. Do these decisions render this clause unenforceable? If so, then surely Ed Giddins was dismissed by Sussex CCC as, in reality, the decision not to continue to employ him was taken unilaterally by the club and thus, in law, constituted a dismissal.

Players and athletes may also receive bans for breaching a sport's disciplinary rules. Can such a ban frustrate the contract? If so, then the contract is deemed to be terminated through operation of law and the player is consequently not the victim of a dismissal. A term of imprisonment can frustrate a contract of employment. Should a ban for a lengthy period be considered analogous on the basis that it is qualitatively different to a ban for several matches? On the other hand, a short ban must be considered a normal occupational hazard.

For the manager of a professional football club instant dismissal is certainly par for the course. It is rarely based on allegations of gross misconduct. Indeed it is often the result of pressure from fans, who – sometimes rightly and no doubt sometimes wrongly – hold the manager to blame if their team's performances are below expectations. The function of contract law here is essentially to provide a legal framework within which an out-of-court settlement can be negotiated; an action for wrongful dismissal is thereby precluded.[67]

However, the following case both shows how the concept of wrongful dismissal can relate to football managers and discusses the interplay between contractual duties imposed on both employers and employees through the judicially implied terms previously discussed in this chapter (see above, pp 403–4).

Macari v Celtic Football and Athletic Co Ltd

Luigi (aka Lou) Macari was appointed manager of Celtic in October 1993. In March 1994 the club was taken over by a consortium headed by Fergus McCann. The latter made it clear from the outset that he did not want Macari as manager and excluded him from meetings of the Board

---

65 For contrasting cases on gross misconduct, see *Laws v London Chronicle Ltd* [1959] 2 All ER 285 CA; *Wilson v Racher* [1974] IRLR 114 CA; *Pepper v Webb* [1969] 2 All ER 216. Taken together these cases demonstrate just how difficult it is to predict in advance whether employee misconduct will constitute gross misconduct.

66 See *Tracey v Zest Equipment Co* [1982] IRLR 268; and, in particular, the Court of Appeal decision in *Igbo v Johnson Matthey* [1986] IRLR 215.

67 The 'merry go-round' of managers sacked from one club but then moving to another, generating speculation as to which manager is next due for the 'sack' (or indeed first to lose his job in the early weeks of a season), has become part of the staple diet of football punditry both in newspapers and on television. For further discussion of the legal framework see McCahearty, M, 'Employment: Lawful Termination of Football Manager Contracts' (2007) 5(11) WSLR.

(which, under the previous regime, Macari had attended). In June 1994 Macari was summarily dismissed for wilful acts of disobedience. In particular, a failure to comply with a residence requirement to live in or near to Glasgow (Macari had previously been the manager of Stoke City FC and his family home remained in Stoke), and his consequent frequent absences from Celtic Park. The Court of Session accepted that the club's treatment of Macari amounted to destruction of mutual trust and confidence. However, the Court rejected his claim for wrongful dismissal as it did not accept that the club's breach of contract justified Macari's wilful failure to obey the reasonable instructions of his employer.

Lord President: . . . The defenders' breach of the trust and confidence term was a material breach of contract on their part which the pursuer would have been entitled to accept by leaving his employment and suing them for damages. In fact he did not do so: he remained and drew his salary under his contract but failed to comply with the instructions given to him by the managing director. Of course, as the defenders pointed out, the pursuer did not refuse to obey these instructions because he had lost trust or confidence in the defenders. Rather, he deliberately chose not to comply with them, believing that he knew best what was involved in managing a football club and being determined to do it in his own way. In itself that point would not assist the defenders: whatever his reasons, the pursuer would not have been in breach of contract if any breach of the implied term by the defenders meant that they were not entitled to insist on him complying with their instructions.

As his counsel acknowledged, if sound, the argument for the pursuer would have potentially far-reaching consequences. If it were the case that a breach of the implied term of trust and confidence meant that an employee was entitled to ignore his employer's instructions, then it would mean, for instance, that he could continue working and draw his salary but refuse to obey instructions relating to matters of health and safety. The true position seems to me to be that, if an employee is faced with a breach of the trust and confidence term by his employer but chooses to continue to work and draw his salary, he must do the work in accordance with the terms of his contract. That in turn means that, as regards his work, he must obey any lawful and legitimate instructions which his employer gives him. It is in return for such work in conformity with the contract that the employer is obliged to pay the employee his salary under the contract.

On the other hand, in no relevant sense can it be said that an employee's obligation to do his work in accordance with the lawful and legitimate instructions of his employer is, in the words of Lord Jauncey, 'the counterpart of' his employer's obligation under the implied term. I note en passant that similarly, on the approach of Lord Maclaren in *Sivright*, the employee's right is not 'conditional with respect to' that obligation of his employer. Nor does the employee undertake to work in accordance with his employer's instructions 'in exchange for' his employer's performance of his obligation under the implied term (to apply the test in '*ESE Financial Services*'). So, where the employee chooses to continue to work under the contract, his employer's breach of the implied term does not entitle the employee to disregard the employer's lawful and legitimate instructions as to his work. In the present case the pursuer continued to work as manager of the club and to draw the salary for that work. The defenders' managing director gave him instructions about residence, attendance and reporting, all of which were lawful and legitimate and related to his work under the contract. For the reasons which I have given, the pursuer was obliged to comply with those instructions and his persistent failures to do so were not only breaches but material breaches of his contract with the defenders.

In any event, the pursuer had an obligation under a specific term of his contract, rather than by virtue of any instruction, to reside within 45 miles of George Square. When asked what obligation the defenders had breached which was the counter part of this obligation, counsel for the pursuer could refer only to the general implied obligation of trust and confidence. But there is nothing in the residence obligation which relates to that implied obligation, or makes it the counter part of that obligation. Therefore any breach of the implied term would not disable the defenders from insisting that the pursuer should comply with the residence clause.

For all these reasons in June 1994 the pursuer was in material breach of contract by reason of his failure to comply with the residence clause, by reason of his failure to comply with the instruction to attend more regularly at Celtic Park and by reason of his failure to comply with his undertaking to report to Mr McCann on a weekly basis. Referring to the undated fax sent in reply to Mr McCann's letter of 10 June, the Lord Ordinary describes the situation in the strongest possible terms: 'It seems to me that by the defiant, contumacious terms of that letter and of his subsequent telephone conversation, the pursuer was indicating that he was not intending to be bound by the directions of his employer and was opposing his lawful authority. I consider that the circumstances were then such, having regard also to his flouting of specific directions in particular in respect of residence, attendance at Celtic Park and the provision of weekly reports, as to entitle the employer to consider his employee's conduct was indicative of an intention not to fulfil his obligations under the contract and as an intimation of a repudiation of it, justifying his dismissal.'

Not surprisingly, counsel for the pursuer accepted that, if the general law of contract applied, in that situation the defenders were entitled to dismiss the pursuer. Analysing the matter more formally, under the general law they would be entitled to accept the pursuer's material or repudiatory breach with the result that they would thereafter be released from their obligations to the pursuer under the agreement with him.[68]

This decision clarifies that, despite the overriding nature of the duty on the employer to maintain mutual trust and confidence, if the employee affirms a breach of his employment contract by continuing to work under it then he must continue to obey any instructions given by the employer which are in themselves reasonable. The case also illustrates that, providing any contractual procedures are adhered to, the failure to follow normal disciplinary procedures[69] will not be decisive in an action for wrongful dismissal. If, in court, the employer can establish that the employee did commit a repudiatory breach of contract then the dismissal cannot be wrongful as the employer was entitled to choose to treat the contract as at an end.

Constructive dismissal

An employee may formally resign or leave employment in circumstances that constitute constructive wrongful dismissal. Such a dismissal has exactly the same legal consequences as an actual wrongful dismissal, and thus the employee will be entitled to damages. However, where the employee terminates the contract this only constitutes constructive dismissal where it is the employee's response to a repudiatory breach by the employer. Unreasonable conduct by the employer will not in itself convert a resignation into a constructive dismissal.[70]

Although unreasonable behaviour by an employer cannot turn a resignation into a constructive dismissal, it must be remembered that a breach of the duty to maintain mutual trust and confidence will constitute the requisite repudiatory breach of contract. As discussed above (pp 406–7), this could include a refusal to select a player where this is motivated by reasons other than merit; for example to pressurise a player to agree to go on to or to leave the transfer list. From the Court of

68 Court of Session, Case 0/309/6/98.
69 For example, the disciplinary procedures as set out in the ACAS Code of Practice. However, a failure to follow the ACAS procedures will normally result in damages being increased by up to 25 per cent in the event of a successful wrongful dismissal claim before an employment tribunal (but not a court) – see below, pp 435–8.
70 See Lord Denning's judgment in *Western Excavating Ltd v Sharp* [1978] ICR 221 CA, in which he clarified that the 'contract test' is the only test that can be used to determine whether a resignation by an employee can in law constitute a constructive dismissal.

Session's findings it seems that Lou Macari could have resigned and claimed constructive dismissal on this basis. Had he done so then his action for damages would have succeeded.

Destruction of mutual trust and confidence clearly includes any form of unlawful discrimination on grounds of race, sex, sexual orientation or religious belief.[71] This includes subjecting an employee to harassment or abuse. A particular problem for sport (and also for other occupations such as the police) is the tradition of 'locker-room' behaviour where players are subjected to levels of banter and practical jokes that would probably not be tolerated in more typical forms of employment. It is very likely that a club will be in breach of contract if such behaviour gets out of hand and the club does not discipline the culprits. Abuse of a player by a team captain, coach or manager constitutes a similar problem area. Certainly, there will be a breach of contract if 'banter' and the like crosses the line with bullying and the club fails to protect the player who is the victim in such circumstances.

It may also be the case that a club is in breach of an express term in a contract. Where such a breach is repudiatory then again this can provide the basis for a constructive dismissal. This argument was at the heart of Kevin Keegan's successful claim against Newcastle United FC.[72] The background to the case is the introduction into the English game over the past decade of a continental-style management structure where the team manager operates alongside a director of football. Obviously this can create tensions where the lines of responsibility are not clear and/or not kept to.

At Newcastle, Kevin Keegan was the manager and Dennis Wise was the director of football. The tribunal found that it had been expressly agreed with Keegan that he was to have the final say regarding the recruitment of players, and that his contract should be interpreted accordingly. Subsequently, Newcastle entered into a loan agreement for the Uruguayan international, Ignacio Gonzalez, on the recommendation of Dennis Wise, but contrary to the wishes of Kevin Keegan. The latter made several attempts to resolve the ensuing conflict with the Newcastle board before deciding he had no option other than to resign. The tribunal found that there had been a fundamental breach of Keegan's contract and thus he had been constructively and wrongfully dismissed.

As can be seen from the Macari case (above, pp 419–22), delay in resigning can constitute affirmation of the employer's breach and the right to claim constructive dismissal is consequently extinguished. However, it is well established in case law that a series of events culminating in one event which can be regarded as constituting the final straw can justify a decision to resign.[73] The tribunal found that Keegan's attempts to ascertain whether the dispute could be amicably resolved did not constitute affirmation, and that the final straw was provided by a letter to Keegan stating the Board did not accept that he had a right to the final say over the recruitment of Gonzalez.

Similar facts led to a claim for constructive wrongful dismissal by Alan Curbishley against West Ham in 2009. Contrary to a term in Curbishley's contract, West Ham sold Anton Ferdinand and George McCartney to Sunderland against his wishes. In finding that Curbishley had been constructively and wrongfully dismissed, the Managers' Arbitration Tribunal viewed the Keegan case as a direct precedent.[74]

---

71 See following chapter for full discussion.
72 See 'Managers Contracts: Constructive Dismissal: Kevin Keegan v Newcastle FC' (2009) 7(12) WSLR. Access http://www. premierleague.com/page/Headlines/0,,12306~1815495,00.html for a link to the actual ruling of the Premier League Manager's Arbitration Tribunal.
73 Lewis v Motorworld Garages Ltd [1986] 1CR 157, CA; Omilaju v Waltham forest LBC [2005] ICR 481, CA.
74 For a summary of the ruling see http://www.premierleague.com/page/Headlines/0,,12306~1845645,00.html. Also see Guardian Sport, 4 November 2009.

Remedies for Wrongful Dismissal

The normal remedy for a wrongful dismissal – that is, a dismissal in breach of contract – is damages for actual financial loss suffered. In the case of fixed-term contracts, which are the norm in professional sport, this will, subject to the normal duty of mitigation, be loss of earnings for the period of time that the contract had left to run. Therefore, in professional sport there is an obvious potential for the awarding of high levels of damages. However, for the reasons given above, in the circumstances where actions for wrongful dismissal would be most likely to occur, clubs typically seek to ensure the issue is dealt with by agreement.

Now that behaviour by professional sports participants – both on and off the field of play – has become an issue of national interest or concern it is perhaps only a matter of time before a player who has been dismissed summarily brings an action for wrongful dismissal. However, as was the case with Ed Giddins (who was signed to play for Warwickshire once he had served his ban), the issue might be effectively resolved by a rival club employing the player who has been dismissed. If nothing else, this shows that clubs, who may regard themselves as occupying the moral high ground, are upholding their own standards rather than standards observed within the sport as a whole.[75]

Injunctions

It is a fundamental legal principle that courts will not compel performance of a contract of employment or any contract which involves the provision of personal services. Ever since the actress Bette Davis sought to break her contract with her film studio,[76] it has been clear that this principle applies to the entertainment industry. On the other hand, injunctions will not be granted where their effect is in practice to compel performance of a contract.[77] Thus it may be very difficult to secure injunctions in the context of sport[78] unless the sports participant is in a position to earn an equally remunerative living by other means, such as acting or television work, for the duration of his contract.

Modern case law suggests a very strong reluctance on the part of judges to follow the decision in *Warner Bros*. In *Warren v Mendy*[79] the Court of Appeal refused an injunction to restrain the defendant from inducing boxer Nigel Benn to break his contract with his manager by participating in a match arranged by the defendant. The court held that it was unrealistic to conclude that a boxer could choose between his sport and alternative employment. This case was cited and followed by the High Court in *Subaru Tecnica International Inc v Burns & Others*.[80] The court refused an injunction which would have prevented Richard Burns, the 2001 World Rally Champion, from breaking his contract with Subaru by driving for Peugeot.

On the other hand, an injunction was granted for a short period to enforce garden leave provisions in Steve Bruce's contract with Crystal Palace.[81] This does suggest that there may be circumstances in which the courts will accept that sports employers have legitimate interests to protect, and that these interests can only be protected effectively by court injunctions.

It should be noted that in *Warren v Mendy* the injunction was sought not against Nigel Benn but against another promoter seeking to induce Benn to act in breach of contract. Thus the action was

---

75 See *The Guardian*, 1 November 1996 for a discussion of the Ed Giddins affair and the fact that, once Sussex terminated his contract, he was approached by ten of the other seventeen first-class counties. The report also suggests that it was the general view of his fellow professionals that, in sporting terms, he had done nothing wrong.

76 *Warner Brothers Pictures Incorporated v Nelson* [1937] KB 209.

77 *Page One Records Ltd v Britton* [1968] 1 WLR 157.

78 [1989] ICR 525. Note US courts are much readier to prevent professional sports participants from 'jumping contracts'. See McCutcheon, P, 'Negative enforcement of employment contracts in the sports industries' (1997) 17 Legal Studies 65.

79 [1989] 1 WLR 853.

80 (2001) Ch D (unreported).

81 See above, pp 405–6.

based on the tort of direct inducement to act in breach of contract as established in *Lumley v Gye*.[82] The elements of the tort require the claimant to establish the following conditions:

- that the defendant persuaded or procured or induced the breach of contract;
- that the defendant when so acting knew of the existence of that contract;
- that the defendant intended to persuade, procure or induce a breach of that contract;
- that the claimant had suffered more than nominal damage; and
- that the claimant could rebut any defence of justification put forward by the defendant.[83]

With respect to football, this tort is of potential significance where one club induces a player to break his contract with his current club. Even if it can be argued that Art 39 permits a player to jump contracts[84] it seems unlikely that, arguments over freedom of movement notwithstanding, a court would accept that EU law has overridden this long-established tort. Indeed, the FIFA transfer rules regulating international transfers (see below, pp 451–4) are of significance in this regard. The rules impose the sport's sanctions where a player is induced by another club to move to it in breach of the player's contract with his existing club. Essentially, the player may be prevented from playing for the new club for up to 12 months.

With respect to sport in general, it could be argued by way of analogy to the sanctions contained in the FIFA rules that a court should grant an injunction for a period in that sport, which would equate as a competitive period to a football season, on the basis that there are legitimate sporting interests to protect. This is particularly the case where a sports participant has been induced to act in breach of contract as it can be argued that he (or she) is only being specifically restrained from working for the party who has committed the tort. The injunction would not in itself prevent the individual sportsman (or sportswoman) from still walking out and seeking employment else-where – particularly where the player has good reason to believe a number of clubs, promoters or sponsors are interested in his services if he becomes a free agent.[85]

It should be noted that it is also possible for employees to secure injunctions to prevent their employers from acting in breach of contract. This has been particularly the case where injunctions have also been sought to restrain dismissals in breach of disciplinary procedures contained in the employment contract. In *Dietman v Brent LBC*[86] the High Court confirmed that an injunction could be so granted if:

- the claimant acts quickly as otherwise the employee will be deemed to have accepted the termination of the contract;
- mutual trust and confidence have not been destroyed;
- damages are inadequate; this might be the case if the dismissed employee could show that were he allowed to plead his case at a hearing the employer might decide against dismissal.

Both professional footballers and cricketers have contractual rights of appeal against dismissal to the appropriate authorities. A player could seek an injunction where these procedures are not followed,

---

82 [1853] 2 E&B 216.
83 These elements of the tort were most recently confirmed in *Timeplan Education Group Ltd v NUT* [1997] IRLR 457.
84 See Caiger, A and O'Leary, J, 'The end of the affair: the "*Anelka Doctrine*" – the problem of contract stability in English professional football', in Caiger, A and Gardiner, S (eds), *Professional Sport in the EU: Regulation and Re-regulation* (2000), The Hague: Asser Press, pp 197–216.
85 There does seem to be some discrepancy between the reluctance of the courts to hold entertainers to their contracts, as exemplified by *Warren v Mendy* despite the latter having committed a tort, and a greater readiness to enforce lengthy garden leave clauses or post-employment restraints to protect an employer's interests in protecting their trade secrets or clientele. Generally, such clauses will be upheld providing they are reasonable as to their duration and area of geographical and/or commercial application.
86 [1987] IRLR 259.

but it might be the case in sport that the necessary mutual trust and confidence will have been destroyed. If this were so, an injunction would be refused.[87]

Damages

The calculation of the compensation to which a club should be entitled presents another difficulty in circumstances where a player acts or is induced to act in breach of contract. The underlying principle in contract law for calculating damages is that the claimant should be awarded a sum of money which would put him in the same financial position that he would have enjoyed had the contract been properly performed. In some circumstances – for example where a player jumps contracts – the amount of damages that may be awarded may be smaller than anticipated.[88] It is possible for a clause to be inserted into a player's contract that specifies the amount of compensation to be paid in the event of the player breaking that contract. However, if the stipulated sum is excessive a court will regard it as a penalty and the clause will be declared void. It will then be for the court by reference to normal principles to determine the amount of damages to be awarded. The equivalent position applies where the specified sum is substantially lower than the actual financial loss that the injured party is likely to incur.

Some indication as to how the courts may calculate damages is provided by the decision of the Court of Appeal in the action for breach of contract brought by Middlesbrough FC against Liverpool as a result of their signing of Christian Ziege.[89] This case revolves around the legal principles upon which damages will be calculated for breach of the contract entered into between all football clubs in the Premiership whereby they agree to abide by the rules of the Football Association Premier League (FAPL). The relevant rules were at the time of the case contained in section J of the FAPL's Rules.

Rule J.1.2 prohibited a club from approaching a player under contract without the prior permission of his club. Rule J.5 prohibited a player under contract from approaching another club with a view to negotiating a contract without the prior consent of his club. Rule J.22 provided that a contract between a player and his club is confidential and thus disclosure of its contents to any other person is a breach of contract.

A Commission of Inquiry appointed by the FAPL found that both Liverpool FC and the player Christian Ziege were in breach of these rules and thus Liverpool had acted in breach of contract. The specific cause of the complaint was that the personal terms between Middlesbrough FC and Ziege contained a clause under which Middlesbrough agreed that if any other club offered at least £5.5 million for Ziege Middlesbrough would permit him to discuss personal terms with that club and, if these were agreed, would permit him to transfer to that club. Through relying on this term in his contract Ziege was able to secure his release from Middlesbrough whilst still under contract with the club and become a Liverpool player. The Court of Appeal agreed with the Commission of Inquiry that there must have been a breach of Ziege's contractual duty not to disclose confidential terms of his employment contract with Middlesbrough. This was because in the normal way of things Liverpool's transfer bid would have been either below or above £5.5 million rather than the specific sum required to trigger the clause in Ziege's contract under which Middlesbrough was bound to release him.

---

87 Furthermore, in *Boyo v Lambeth LBC* [1995] IRLR 50 the Court of Appeal indicated support for a more restrictive view that a dismissal, even in breach of contract-based procedures, automatically terminates the contract of employment. Were this position to have been endorsed by the House of Lords, then even as a theoretical possibility injunctions would cease to be available, and the only remedy would be damages for wrongful dismissal. However, in the case of cricketers' and footballers' contracts this might include the length of time the player would still have been employed if the dismissal had not occurred until after contractual procedures had been followed. In this case even if a player was guilty of gross misconduct he would be entitled to some compensation on the basis that his dismissal was procedurally wrongful.

88 See op. cit., fn 84, Caiger and O' Leary (2000), pp 209–11. They argue that damages would include neither the loss of a transfer fee nor the cost of replacing a player.

89 *Middlesbrough Football & Athletic Co v Liverpool Football & Athletic Grounds plc* [2002] EWCA Civ 1929.

On the basis of this breach of contract, Middlesbrough argued it was entitled to be granted damages from Liverpool as a result of the financial loss suffered by it. This loss was either (a) the loss of a chance to sell Ziege at a higher sum, or (b) the loss of a chance to have enjoyed a financially more successful season (2000/01) had Ziege remained a Middlesbrough player. In the High Court, Astill J dismissed Middlesbrough's claim with respect to (a) as effectively Middlesbrough had given up any right to negotiate a transfer fee providing £5.5 million was offered. The judge dismissed Middlesbrough's claim with respect to (b) on the grounds that it 'was wholly speculative'.

The Court of Appeal upheld Middlesbrough's appeal as while it could not be said that at full trial Middlesbrough would succeed in either of their claims for damages, neither could the claims be struck out because there was no real prospect of establishing any entitlement to damages. The Court's decision thus illustrates the old contractual rule that a court cannot refuse to award damages on the basis that quantification of loss is difficult to establish because loss is based on events that may or may not have occurred. In the view of the Court of Appeal it was feasible that Liverpool may have offered more than £5.5 million if the club had not known about the confidential clause in Ziege's contract. Similarly, Middlesbrough may have had a more successful season had there not been a 'business interruption' to his staying with the club.[90]

The Kevin Keegan case (see above p 422) also demonstrates this issue. One of the clauses in his contract specified that, should he be entitled to compensation from Newcastle, he would receive £2 million. Keegan argued that his actual loss was greater than this amount, and that the clause constituted a penalty which should be set aside. The arbitration tribunal found that it was impossible accurately to pre-estimate any loss. For example, following his constructive dismissal, Kevin Keegan could have almost immediately entered into a contract with a new club, or could have remained unemployed for a significant period of time. The sum of £2 million reflected his salary over a six-month period (the duration of the restraint in his contract, see above p 409) plus a cushion of £500,000 were he unable to obtain employment once this period had expired. In the circumstances, the clause constituted a valid attempt to provide for liquidated damages and could not be regarded as a penalty.

Unfair Dismissal

The right not to be unfairly dismissed is a statutory right which has been in existence since 1971. The right was contained in the Employment Protection (Consolidation) Act 1978 (EPCA). This has been replaced by the Employment Rights Act 1996 (ERA) which came into force in August 1996.[91] Employees' rights are based on statutory principles which operate independently of and often in contradiction to the principles of contract law – although it is more than possible that a summary dismissal will be both wrongful and unfair. Claims for unfair dismissal must be presented to employment tribunals (formerly called industrial tribunals) no later than three months from the effective date of termination of the contract of employment – normally the date on which the dismissal took effect.

---

90 Similarly, in *Stransky* (see above, pp 397–8) the court rejected the argument that Stransky was entitled only to nominal damages as there was no guarantee that he would have secured a work permit and thus been in a position to take up employment with the club. Consequently, Stransky was entitled to damages for loss of earnings for the period of the contract. The case of *Murphy v Southend United Football Club* (1999, unreported) also provides a useful example of how damages may be calculated in a sporting context. Murphy, who was the manager of Southend United, left the club in breach of contract. He successfully sued for money that the club owed him as a result of the sale of Stan Collymore to Nottingham Forest. However, in accordance with a term in his contract the equivalent of six months' salary was deducted from his damages to reflect the club's loss through Murphy's premature termination of his contract. For further discussion of this case see (1999) 2(3) SLB 3.

91 Thus a number of important cases are based on provisions of the EPCA. However, as the ERA merely further consolidates the law, the cases remain authoritative interpretations of the statutory rights.

Employment tribunals have jurisdiction over a number of areas of employment law which are governed by statute law – particularly the rights contained in the ERA and in the area of discrimination law (see following chapter). They also have jurisdiction to hear claims of wrongful dismissal where the amount of damages being claimed is no more than £25,000. Tribunals have a distinctive composition. The chair (who can now be called an employment judge) of the tribunal must be legally qualified and will often be a practising solicitor or barrister. The other two members will be lay persons with either an employer or trade union background. Any individual has the right of audience before an employment tribunal, and therefore employees are often represented by officials of trade unions or appropriate professional associations. Although costs can be awarded against the losing party it is normal for the parties to bear their own costs. As is the case with most types of tribunals, legal aid is not available.

An appeal from a tribunal is permitted on points of law only. The appeal will be heard by the Employment Appeals Tribunal (EAT). The composition of the EAT is similar to that of an employment tribunal, although the Chair will be a High Court judge. Legal aid is available in proceedings before the EAT. Further appeals lie to the Court of Appeal and the Supreme Court. Decisions of the EAT (and relevant decisions of the Court of Appeal and the Supreme Court) are often reported in the specialist Industrial Cases Reports (ICR) and the Industrial Relations Law Reports (IRLR).

For the large majority of employees, claiming unfair dismissal is more advantageous than claiming wrongful dismissal as, typically, damages for the latter are restricted to net pay for an employee's notice period. This is also the case for many sports participants, including footballers in the lower leagues.[92] However, for the highly paid 'star' player and managers in the higher leagues wrongful dismissal will often be the preferred claim, as compensation for unfair dismissal is subject to a statutory cap (see below, p 441), although compromise agreements to secure out-of-tribunal settlements are not subject to this cap. There are occasions where even the highly paid professional will have no option other than to claim unfair dismissal. This includes where a club has gone into administration, as a player (or manager) will be an ordinary creditor as far as any court award of damages is concerned. Most importantly, dismissal will not always be in breach of contract – particularly where, as is common, a player has been employed under a fixed-term contract and that contract has expired.

The Chris Schofield case provides a good example of the latter. On expiry of his contract at the end of the 2004 season, leg-spinner Schofield was released by Lancashire. The reason for this was revealed by coach Mike Watkinson's remark to Schofield that he had 'perhaps not reached his full potential'. In claiming unfair dismissal, Schofield argued that he should have been informed at an earlier date of the decision to dispense with his services. The club's failure to do this had adversely affected his chance of finding a new club for the following season. The employment tribunal agreed, and found that the club had acted unreasonably and thus unfairly in the way it decided not to renew Schofield's contract.[93]

Continuity of employment

Only employees with one year's continuous employment can claim unfair dismissal. Such continuity can be acquired by a series of fixed-term contracts. Where an employee has been made redundant s/he must have two years' continuity of employment to be eligible to claim a statutory

---

92 See Harris, N, 'Pitch Battle', *The Guardian*, Work, 8 August 2009, for an analysis of professional footballers on short contracts earning salaries equivalent to those in other professions. In 2006, the average basic pay of footballers in Leagues One and Two was £67,850 and £49,600 respectively. The typical wage in the Scottish First Division and the English Conference League was between £20,000 and £30,000 a year.

93 See 'Schofield wins case for unfair dismissal', http://www.espncricinfo.com/england/content/story/207245.html.

redundancy payment. Unfortunately, redundancy situations are no longer uncommon in professional sport as redundancy dismissals, particularly of non-playing staff, will inevitably occur where a club is put into administration.

A cricketer may be employed on a season-by-season basis. Does such a break in employment break continuity so that a player is never able to secure statutory rights? Under s 212 of the ERA, weeks during which the employee has no contract of employment still count if the employee's absence from work is because of a 'temporary cessation of work'. Should the close season period be considered a 'temporary cessation' so that a cricketer employed on a seasonal basis can in the due course of time establish continuity through a succession of fixed-term contracts?

Ford v Warwickshire CC

A part-time college lecturer was made redundant after ten years' employment. She was not employed during the summer period between academic years. The Law Lords held that this period constituted a temporary cessation and thus she secured statutory rights.

Lord Diplock: ... the length of successive fixed term contracts on which part-time lecturers are employed and the intervals between them vary considerably with the particular course that the part-time lecturer is engaged to teach; so it by no means follows that a similar concession would be made or would be appropriate in each of their cases. It also follows from what I have said that successive periods of seasonal employment of other kinds under fixed term contracts, such as employment in agriculture during harvest-time or in hotel work during the summer season, will only qualify as continuous employment if the length of the period between two successive seasonal contracts is so short in comparison with the length of the season during which the employee is employed as properly to be regarded by the industrial tribunal as no more than a temporary cessation of work in the sense that I have indicated.[94]

This 'mathematical' approach might operate against a cricketer given the length of the out-of-season period (generally mid-September to mid-March). However, the Law Lords have also espoused what has been described as the 'broad brush' approach where the whole history of the employment has to be taken into account.[95] Through applying the latter, it could be argued that a cricketer who has been with a county for a number of years has established continuity despite the lengthy breaks between seasons. Certainly, it would seem unjust if a player who had stayed loyal to a particular club was to discover that, in the event of dismissal during a season, and thus during the currency of his contract, he had no statutory rights through a lack of continuous employment.

This issue was considered in the case of *Singh* (2001).[96] One of referee Singh's claims against the Football League was that he was unfairly dismissed. A barrier to this claim succeeding could have been that he was not employed by the League outside of the football season (which runs from August to May). However, the tribunal found Singh did have the necessary continuity of employment. The tribunal decided that the close season period could be considered a 'temporary cessation', which under s 212(3) of the ERA did not constitute a break in continuity. This conclusion was reached on the basis of the fact that during the close season there was an ongoing relationship between the League and its listed referees.

It seems likely that there is similar continuity of employment between cricketers and their clubs, despite the longer close season period. The problem of continuity does not arise, of course, where (as is the norm for professional footballers) a cricketer is employed for a period of years.

---

94 [1983] ICR 273 HL, 286.
95 *Fitzgerald v Hall, Russell & Co Ltd* [1970] AC 984.
96 See above, p 395.

Here, the contract continues during the out-of-season period and thus there is no break in the continuity of employment.

It should be noted that the Fixed Term Employees (Prevention of Less Favourable Treatment) Regulations 2002, which were introduced to implement the EU's Directive on Fixed Term Work, apply to the use of fixed-term contracts in sport.[97] The purpose of the Directive is to prohibit the differential treatment of workers on fixed-term contracts in comparison with employees on 'indefinite' contracts. In this context, the Regulations will not impact on players' contracts, as typically they are all 'fixed term employees'. However, the Regulations may also convert fixed-term contracts into ordinary indefinite contracts (terminable by notice) once a contract or series of contracts has lasted four years. This will not apply if the employer can justify the continued use of fixed-term contracts. It is presumed that, should this issue ever arise, such justification will be available to clubs for sporting and commercial reasons.

Claiming unfair dismissal

Section 95(1) of the Employment Rights Act 1996

For the purposes of this Part an employee is dismissed by his employer if . . .

(a) the contract under which he is employed is terminated by the employer (whether with or without notice),

(b) he is employed under a contract for a fixed term and that term expires without being renewed under the same contract, or

(c) the employee terminates the contract under which he is employed (with or without notice) in circumstances in which he is entitled to terminate it without notice by reason of the employer's conduct.

A dismissal with notice, and thus in accordance with the contract, may still be unfair. Similarly non-renewal of a fixed-term contract, which is of no legal consequence at common law, may constitute an unfair dismissal (as demonstrated by the Chris Schofield case, see above).

Grievance procedures and constructive dismissal

In *Goold Ltd v McConnell* [1995] IRLR 516 the EAT held that failure by the employer to provide a grievance procedure also constituted a repudiatory breach. As a result of the Employment Act 2002 (Dispute Resolution) Regulations 2004 employers were effectively required to have written grievance (and disciplinary) procedures. However, this is no longer the case as these statutory procedures were abolished with effect from April 2009. Consequently, the decision in *Goold* is once again of practical importance.

The primary purpose of grievance procedures is to encourage employers and employees to resolve problems internally rather than regarding tribunal claims as a first course of action. Thus in general terms employees who have a grievance should not resign in order to claim constructive dismissal until the employer has been given an opportunity to provide appropriate redress through internal procedures. Failure to do this may result in any compensatory award for unfair dismissal (or damages if the claim is for constructive wrongful dismissal) being reduced by up to 25 per cent (s.207A Trade Union & Labour Relations (Consolidation) Act 1992). Similarly, if an employer does not have an adequate grievance procedure, or refuses to allow an employee to invoke it properly, any compensatory award (or damages) may be increased by up to 25 per cent.

---

97 Council Directive 1999/70/EC.

The Advisory Conciliation and Arbitration Service (ACAS) Code of Practice sets out the basis for model grievance procedures. Essentially, procedures should require an employee to set out the grievance in writing, and the employer should arrange for a formal hearing without unreasonable delay after the grievance is received. The employee has a statutory right to be accompanied at this hearing by a trade union official or colleague. If the employee is unsatisfied with the outcome of this hearing then the procedure should provide for a final right of appeal. Any failure by an employee to follow a grievance procedure will only result in a reduction in compensation where a tribunal claim is made. The ACAS Code has no relevance to actions for constructive wrongful dismissal which are brought to the ordinary civil courts.[98]

The grievance procedure contained in clause 19 of the standard Footballer's Contract should meet the ACAS criteria. Having raised the issue informally with the manager, the player can raise a grievance in writing with the Club Secretary. There is a right of appeal to the appropriate League board with a final right of appeal to the Football League Appeals Committee. Players have the right to be accompanied by a representative from the PFA.

The meaning of unfair dismissal

Section 98 of the Employment Rights Act 1996

(1) In determining for the purposes of this Part whether the dismissal of an employee is fair or unfair, it is for the employer to show –
  (a) the reason (or, if more than one, the principal reason) for the dismissal, and
  (b) that it is either a reason falling within subsection (2) or some other substantial reason of a kind such as to justify the dismissal of an employee holding the position which the employee held.

(2) A reason falls within this subsection if it –
  (a) relates to the capability or qualifications of the employee for performing work of the kind which he was employed by the employer to do,
  (b) relates to the conduct of the employee,
  (c) is that the employee was redundant, or
  (d) is that the employee could not continue to work in the position which he held without contravention (either on his part or on that of his employer) of a duty or restriction imposed by or under an enactment.

(3) In subsection (2)(a) –
  (a) 'capability', in relation to an employee, means his capability assessed by reference to skill, aptitude, health or any other physical or mental quality, and
  (b) 'qualifications', in relation to an employee, means any degree, diploma or other academic, technical or professional qualification relevant to the position which he held.

(4) Where the employer has fulfilled the requirements of subsection (1), the determination of the question whether the dismissal is fair or unfair (having regard to the reason shown by the employer) –
  (a) depends on whether in the circumstances (including the size and administrative resources of the employer's undertaking) the employer acted reasonably or un-reasonably in treating it as a sufficient reason for dismissing the employee, and
  (b) shall be determined in accordance with equity and the substantial merits of the case.

---

98 The current ACAS Code of Practice on Disciplinary and Grievance Procedures came into force on 6 April 2009, and can be accessed from www.acas.org.uk/drr.

Under s 98(1) the burden of proof is on the employer to show the reason (or the principal reason) for the dismissal. If the employer cannot satisfy the tribunal that the reason was one or more of the above then the dismissal must be unfair. The case of *Singh*[99] illustrates this, as the tribunal found that his dismissal was the product of unlawful race discrimination, and therefore the Football League was unable under s 98 of the ERA to prove the dismissal was for a potentially fair reason.

The only other possibility, in accordance with s 98(1)(b), is that the employee was dismissed for 'some other substantial reason of a kind such as to justify the dismissal of an employee holding the position which the employee held.' As explained above, footballers whose contracts expire after they have reached the age of 24 must be allowed to move to a new club if they so wish. Conversely, once the transfer rules no longer apply, there is no mechanism to encourage a club to retain on its books a player it no longer wants. It remains to be seen whether an unfair dismissal claim will be brought by a player who does not want to be released by a club. Such a claim would certainly be possible in law. The tribunal would then have to be satisfied that the club was acting reasonably in reaching a decision that it no longer wanted a player's services and thus the dismissal was fair by reference to 'some other substantial reason'. This position, of course, applies to any other type of professional sports participant who is employed under a fixed-term contract, or series of fixed-term contacts, lasting for more than one year (see, for example, the Chris Schofield case, above, p 427).

In the main, it is the categories of incapability and misconduct which are clearly the most important in sport. Such dismissals will still be unfair if an employment tribunal does not consider that the employer acted reasonably in deciding to dismiss. The decision as to the fairness of the dismissal is for the tribunal to make. The burden of proof is neutral. However, as a point of law, it is of primary importance that a tribunal does not substitute its views for that of the reasonable employer. Employers may operate within a range of reasonable responses. Only if a dismissal is outside of this range will it be unfair.

British Leyland (UK) Ltd v Swift

Lord Denning MR: The correct test is: was it reasonable for the employer to dismiss him? If no reasonable employer would have dismissed him, then the dismissal was unfair. But if a reasonable employer might reasonably have dismissed him, then the dismissal was fair. It must be remembered that in all these cases there is a band of reasonableness within which one employer might reasonably take one view; another quite reasonably take a different view . . . if it was quite reasonable to dismiss him, then the dismissal must be upheld as fair: even though some other employers may not have dismissed him.[100]

Iceland Frozen Foods Ltd v Jones

Browne-Wilkinson P: . . . (1) the starting point must be the words [of the section] themselves; (2) in applying the section an Industrial Tribunal must consider the reasonableness of the employer's conduct, not simply whether they (the members of the Industrial Tribunal) consider the dismissal to be fair; (3) in judging the reasonableness of the employer's conduct an Industrial Tribunal must not substitute its decision as to what was the right course to adopt for that of the employer; (4) in many (though not all) cases there is a band of reasonable responses to the employee's conduct within which one employer might reasonably take one view and another quite reasonably take another; (5) the function of the Industrial Tribunal, as an industrial jury, is to determine whether in the particular circumstances of each case the decision to dismiss the employee fell within the band of reasonable responses which a reasonable

---

99 See earlier p 395, and following chapter pp 467–8.
100 [1981] IRLR 91 CA, at p 93.

employer might have adopted. If the dismissal falls within the band the dismissal is fair; if the dismissal falls outside the band it is unfair.[101]

It is clear that a dismissal may be reasonable, even if a particular tribunal regards it as harsh, if it can be shown that other employers, particularly those in the same line of business, would regard dismissal as an appropriate penalty. This test has been subjected to much academic criticism and has also received judicial criticism by the EAT. However, it is clear from subsequent decisions by the Court of Appeal that the test is still the correct law.[102] Therefore, it is clear that the test can now only be overruled by the Law Lords or through legislation. However, given that clubs, like most employers, vary in their responses to acts of misconduct by their employees, it is useful to take note of the reasons given by the EAT for the test to be disregarded.

Haddon v Van Den Burgh Foods

Morison J: . . . First the question for the tribunal is the reasonableness of the decision to dismiss in the circumstances of the particular case having regard to equity and the substantial merits. Because the tribunal are applying an objective test, that is, a test of reasonableness, it is not sufficient for them simply to say 'well, we would not have dismissed in those circumstances'. They must recognise that, however improbable, their own personal views may not accord with the reasonableness. Just asking 'what would I have done' is not enough. However, it is neither reasonable nor realistic to expect the objective question to be asked and answered without the members of the tribunal having first asked 'what would we have done'. And provided that they do not stop there, we see nothing wrong with that approach.

The mantra 'the tribunal must not substitute their own decision for that of the employer', is simply another way of saying that the tribunal must apply the reasonableness test by going somewhat further than simply asking what they themselves would have done. It is likely, however, that what the tribunal themselves would have done will often coincide with their judgment as to what a reasonable employer would have done. The tribunal is, after all, composed of people who are chosen to sit as an industrial jury applying their own good sense of judgment. The task of the tribunal is to pronounce judgment on the reasonableness of the employers' actions and whenever they uphold an employee's complaint they are in effect 'substituting their own judgment for that of the employer'. Providing they apply the test of reasonableness, it is their duty both to determine their own judgment and to substitute it where appropriate.

The second point simply recognises that there may be cases where a decision not to dismiss would be reasonable and a decision to dismiss would also be reasonable. This point is based upon logic. Because course A would have been reasonable, it does not follow that every other course is unreasonable. In other words, in some marginal cases, the tribunal might well consider that a dismissal by the particular employer was reasonable even though another reasonable employer might not have dismissed. The mantra 'the band or range of reasonable responses' is not helpful because it has led tribunals into applying what amounts to a perversity test, which, as is clear from *Iceland* itself, was not its purpose. The moment that one talks of a 'range' or 'band' of reasonable responses one is conjuring up the possibility of extreme views at either end of the band or range. In reality, it is most unlikely in an unfair dismissal case involving misconduct that the tribunal will need to concern itself with the question whether the deployment of each of the weapons in the employers' disciplinary armoury would have been reasonable. Dismissal is the ultimate sanction. There is, in reality, no range or band to be

---

101 [1982] IRLR 439 EAT, at p 442.
102 In *Post Office v Foley* and *HSBC Bank plc v Madden* [2000] IRLR 827 the Court of Appeal confirmed the range of reasonable responses test and ruled that it is binding on the EAT.

considered, only whether the employer acted reasonably in invoking that sanction. Further, the band has become a band or group of employers, with an extreme end. There is a danger of Tribunals testing the fairness of the dismissal by reference to the extreme.

In our view the approach taken in *Gilham* is to be followed. The statute is clear and unambiguous. The two points referred to above are no more than obvious statements which flow from the natural and ordinary meaning of the words of the subsection. In other words, we respectfully suggest that tribunals now return to the task in hand, which is to apply the section without embellishment, and without using mantras so favoured by the lawyers in this field.

Mr Freer suggested to us that the tribunals, and the courts in particular, had difficulty in coming to terms with this piece of social legislation which changed the balance of power between employer and employee [the master/servant relationship]. Employers are no longer free to dismiss with impunity those whom they judge to be worthy of dismissal. As Lord Justice Roskill observed, the right to dismiss is tempered by the right of the individual not to be unfairly dismissed and the balance between the two is to be struck by the industrial jury.

We believe this balance will be best achieved by the industrial jury, the Employment Tribunals, applying the statute as it stands, no more and no less.

There is some anecdotal evidence with which we were presented which suggests that 'conduct' is the most frequent reason in contested Employment Tribunals unfair dismissal cases and that employees lost more than 50 per cent of them, but that where they did succeed it was almost always because of the procedure being found faulty. Mr Freer points out, we think with justification, that a combination of the judicial embellishments upon the statute has led tribunals to adopt a perversity test of reasonableness and to depress the chances of success for applicants.[103]

The case of *Beck v Lincoln City FC*[104] provides an example of a dismissal which would probably be regarded as fair even on the basis of the more flexible approach advocated in *Haddon*. The case echoes that of *Macari* (see above) in that Beck was dismissed for taking an unauthorised leave of absence to go on holiday. However, initially, Beck made misleading statements about the reasons for his absence, claiming first bereavement and then a breakdown in the relationship with his girlfriend. Beck had previously received two written warnings for other forms of misconduct. The tribunal decided that Beck's dismissal was reasonable and fair in light of his breach of contract, subsequent prevarications and misleading statements with respect to the reason for his absence and previous record.

The continuing fundamental importance of the range of reasonable responses test means that the essential questions remain a) who constitutes the reasonable employer, and b) what stance will this elusive person take in response to misconduct etc. on the part of an employee? The answers are no clearer in sport than in any other field of employment. In recent times the quite different reactions of football clubs to the use of drugs by their players – particularly those deemed recreational in nature and consumed in a social not sporting context – is a good example of the problem.[105]

---

103 [1999] ICR 1150 EAT.

104 IT Case No 2600760/98 (unreported) – see (1998) 1(6) SLB, p 6 for further comment on this case.

105 See above, pp 403–4. Contrast the dismissals of Craig Whittington (Huddersfield) and Roger Stanislaus (Leyton Orient) with the lenient decision by Barnsley FC to take no further action with respect to Dean Jones, who was banned for three months by the FA for taking an amphetamine-based substance. Of particular interest, with respect to possible inconsistency of treatment, was the decision by Charlton Athletic FC to dismiss Jamie Stuart after he had tested positive for marijuana and cocaine. Previously, the club had retained the services of Chris Armstrong and Lee Bowyer when, whilst Charlton players, they had received short bans from the FA after testing positive for cannabis. See Welch, R, 'A snort and a puff: recreational drugs and discipline in professional sport', in O'Leary, J (ed), *Drugs and Doping in Sport* (2000), London: Cavendish, pp 75–90, for a discussion of these issues and the view that clubs should not dismiss players for taking recreational, as against performance-enhancing, drugs unless such decisions are taken on fitness grounds. If the latter is the case then clubs should not differentiate between illegal drugs and legal intoxicants such as alcohol.

It is interesting to note that FIFPro has argued that players should not be banned for the use of cannabis in the course of their private lives on the basis that use of the drug impairs rather than enhances a footballer's performance.[106] Were cannabis to be removed from the list of prohibited substances this would render disciplinary action purely an internal issue between a player and his club.

Recently the issue of drug use has also surfaced in rugby union. At the start of 2009, the England and Bath prop, Matt Stevens, was suspended for two years following his positive drug test for cocaine in December 2008, in breach of the WADA Code. In May and June 2009, four Bath players, Justin Harrison, Michael Lipman, Alex Crockett and Andrew Higgins, left the club amid accusations that they had refused to submit to internal drugs tests.[107] It can be argued that if clubs are to punish their players for using drugs, and wish to introduce their own drug testing regimes, it is in their interests to ensure that the taking of specified drugs is explicitly identified as a breach of contract and that players are contractually obliged to submit to drug testing. Failure to do this could lead to dismissal being found to be wrongful and unfair and also raises the issue of human rights in the context of Article 8 of the European Convention on Human Rights which protects the right of privacy. On the other hand, where there are appropriate clauses in players' contracts, and clubs are consistent in the way they discipline and/or dismiss offenders, they are likely to be acting within the range of reasonable responses and any dismissal will then be fair.

Incapability constitutes an alternative basis (to misconduct) for dismissing a player who has become addicted to drugs, be they legal or illegal. It is again important in this respect that there are clauses in players' contracts requiring them to maintain appropriate standards of fitness, form and health.

To date clubs have shown what could be viewed as remarkable tolerance of players convicted for violent offences on, off or adjacent to the field of play. Does this mean that the dismissal of a player in the future for such an offence should be regarded as beyond the range of reasonable responses and thus unfair? It is perhaps significant that all the names that immediately spring to mind are 'star' footballers from leading sides in the Premier League. Could a player employed by a Torquay United or a Crewe Alexandra anticipate such a lenient response in similar circumstances – particularly if his absence through suspension and/or imprisonment had significant repercussions for the fortunes and/or finances of the club concerned? Would the reasonable club adopt a policy of the greater the 'star' the greater the latitude that will be given?[108] Is violent conduct by a player more or less acceptable in other professional sports such as rugby or cricket?

Professional sports participants are obviously particularly prone to absence through physical injury, which may be long term in nature. Again there are clauses in their contracts dealing with the rights of clubs and players respectively in this situation. The Cricketers' Contract expressly permits a club to dismiss a player who, having been injured in the previous season, is still unfit for play at the start of the new season – clause 8. Given the presence of such a contractual term it is likely, although by no means in all circumstances definite, that such a dismissal would be considered within the range of reasonable responses and thus fair.

A long-term and certainly a permanent injury may terminate the contract through frustration, in which case, as there is no dismissal, the player has no statutory rights which can be pursued (unless the disability discrimination provisions in the Equality Act 2010 can be invoked; see

---

106 See FIFPro press release, 7 October 2009.
107 See further, Farrow, S, 'Doping: Drug testing under club employment contracts' (2009) 7(8) WSLR.
108 Mark Bosnich provides an example of one 'star' footballer who did have his contract terminated in January 2003 by Chelsea FC, having tested positive for cocaine. However, Bosnich was not at this time the club's first-choice goalkeeper, and there was some speculation of continued Premiership interest in him; for example, on the part of Charlton Athletic FC – see *Sunday Mirror Sport*, 25 July 2004. Nevertheless, Chelsea's dismissal of Adrian Mutu does demonstrate evidence of consistency of treatment as far as that particular club is concerned, and this would enable tribunals to regard future dismissals by Chelsea for drug offences as being within the range of reasonable responses.

following chapter). Note that clause 10 of the Football League Contract gives players contractual rights to termination through notice in the event of permanent injury.

The cases of *Post Office v Liddiard* and *Doherty v Consignia*[109] illustrate the application of the range of responses test in a rather different sporting context, this being football fans accused of acts of football hooliganism. The general lesson from these cases is that acts that are wholly carried out in an employee's private life can be the basis of a fair dismissal if they adversely impact on an employer's commercial reputation, even though an employee's competence is not affected. However, employers must act consistently, should take the employee's previous work into account and should not over rely on evidence from external sources such as newspaper reports.

Procedural Fairness

A reasonable employer will develop and comply with proper disciplinary procedures. Model procedures are provided by the Advisory Conciliation and Arbitration Service (ACAS).[110]

The salient features of this Code are that:

- Employers should raise and deal with issues promptly and should not unreasonably delay meetings, decisions or confirmations of those decisions.
- Employers should act consistently.
- Employers should carry out any necessary investigations to establish the facts of the case.
- Employers should inform employees of the basis of the problem and give them an opportunity to put their case in response before any decisions are made.
- Employers should allow employees to be accompanied at any formal disciplinary or grievance meeting.
- Employers should allow an employee to appeal against any formal decision made.

The following disciplinary procedures are standard in professional football and should be regarded as compatible with the ACAS Code.

FA Code of Practice and Notes on Footballers' Contracts

A Player is governed by four principal sets of rules, which will be found to overlap to a large extent – The Football Association and The FA Premier League Rules or The Football League Regulations, the Club rules and the provisions of the contract (Clause 5). Obviously whilst playing, a Player is subject to the Laws of the Game (Clause 4). The Club will provide the Player with an up-to-date copy of all the Rules and Regulations, the Club rules and the provisions of the contract (Clause 5). The Player must also be given a copy of any insurance policy conditions affecting him that he needs to be aware of.

These rules are underpinned by a system of discipline. Each Club may operate its own system, although The FA Premier League, The Football League and Professional Footballers' Association have drawn up a disciplinary schedule containing recommended guidelines for Clubs to follow. It is essential that the method adopted is both consistent and fair. If rules are laid down they must be followed. The Player must always be made clear as to what is being

---

109 *Post Office v Liddiard* CA Tuckey LJ, Latham LJ, Arden LJ 7 June 2001 (unreported); *T Doherty v Consignia plc & M Doherty v Consignia plc* (2001) Case Number 2204805/00; (2001) Case Number 2205635/00.

110 See above, fn 98.

alleged and he must be given a proper opportunity to state his case. Some Clubs have found that discipline on minor matters can be enforced with the help of a Club Committee including Players and Officials. Representations on behalf of a Player by his PFA representative should always be considered. Rarely will matters need to go further than the dressing room level. It is important to keep records.

The contract, however, lays down a formal system of discipline and punishment, with a system of appeals. Offences are divided into two categories:

Serious (Clause 16) or persistent misconduct: serious or persistent breach of the rules of the club or terms of the contract (which incorporates Football Association and FA Premier League Rules and the Football League Regulations). If the Player is found to be guilty then his contract may be terminated by 14 days' notice being given. The Club must set out its reasons in writing and notify the Player.

Less Serious (Clause 18) misconduct: breach of training or disciplinary rules or lawful instructions, breach of the provisions of the contract (which incorporates Football Association and FA Premier League Rules and the Football League Regulations). The player may be suspended, with or without pay, for up to 14 days or fined up to 14 days' basic wages. The Club must set out its reasons in writing and notify the Player.

A Club may, if it so wishes, treat conduct that might be classed as serious under Clause 16 as a lesser transgression under Clause 18 so as to impose a lesser penalty. Each action by a Club under Clauses 16 and 18 carries with it the right of appeal and the penalties are suspended until the appeal procedure is exhausted. A fine may be paid directly by the Player or may be stopped from his wages. If this procedure is used then the sum deducted in any week should not be greater than half the Player's basic wage (Clause 18). Under this procedure, for example, a two-week fine (the maximum) would be deducted over four weeks.

The appeals procedure has two stages once the matter progresses beyond the level of the Club (Clause 16):

To The FA Premier League or The Football League Board.

By either Club or Player, depending of course on the outcome of the first appeal, to The Football League Appeals Committee.

In each case the appeal must be lodged within seven days of the formal notification of the previous decision. The Football League Appeals Committee has to hear a case within 14 days of its receipt.

The Football League Appeals Committee consists of an independent chairman and one member nominated by each of The Professional Footballers' Association and the Institute of Football Management and Administration together with a Football League and/or a FA Premier League representative for cases involving their member Clubs. It meets usually in London and Manchester or elsewhere convenient to the Club and Player.

In all appeals the Player will be able to obtain advice and representation from the PFA (Clause 20) if he so desires.[111]

Procedural fairness and disciplinary investigations

One of the central aspects of the ACAS Code is that a reasonable employer will form an appropriate view of the facts before reaching a decision to dismiss. The conducting of a reasonable investigation

---

111 FA Notes on Contract, pp 4–5.

by the employer should be, therefore, a prerequisite to both the convening of a formal hearing and the reaching of a decision by the employer. As a general rule, failure to conduct an investigation, or one that in the circumstances will be considered adequate by a reasonable employer, will render a dismissal unfair. The cases involving the Doherty Brothers are a good illustration of this.[112]

British Home Stores v Burchell

Arnold J: First of all, there must be established by the employer the fact of that belief; that the employer did believe it. Secondly, that the employer had in his mind reasonable grounds upon which to sustain that belief. And thirdly, we think, that the employer, at the stage at which he formed that belief on those grounds, at any rate at the final stage at which he formed that belief on those grounds, had carried out as much investigation into the matter as was reasonable in all the circumstances of the case. It is the employer who manages to discharge the onus of demonstrating those three matters, we think, who must not be examined further. It is not relevant, as we think, that the tribunal would themselves have shared that view in those circumstances.[113]

It is clear from Burchell[114] that if an employer satisfies this three-staged approach his view of the facts must be accepted by an employment tribunal. A tribunal cannot substitute its view of the facts for that of the reasonable employer. It does not follow, however, that an employer who fails to conduct an investigation must have acted unreasonably, and therefore that a dismissal, not preceded by an investigation, must be unfair. For example, an employee is caught removing the employer's property from the workplace and is dismissed summarily 'on the spot'. The failure to conduct a formal investigation will be of no legal significance if the employee is guilty, even though the employer has not sought to establish the facts.

If an appropriate investigation does establish that it is reasonable to view an employee as guilty of misconduct a dismissal will stand as fair even if, by the time of the tribunal hearing, the employee's innocence has been established. For example, a drugs test proves positive. By the time of the tribunal hearing new medical evidence, not available to an employer at the time of dismissal, reveals that the test was in some way flawed. In professional sport it will often be the sports regulatory bodies which carry out investigations and hold hearings prior to imposing a penalty on a participant. This is very much the case with respect to a positive drugs test, or to a player who has committed a serious offence on the field of play. The governing bodies in professional team sports such as cricket, both codes of rugby and football provide for detailed disciplinary procedures for players charged with on-field or off-field offences.[115] Generally, clubs will be acting reasonably if they rely on the evidential findings of disciplinary committees established by regulatory bodies.

Irrespective of whether a club could justify not conducting its own investigation, it should still permit a player to attend a formal hearing convened by the club and to exercise a further right of appeal. This is because it is only through such formal hearings that a player will have the opportunity to argue that factors such as past loyalty to the club or personal problems should be taken into account. Moreover, as explained above, consistency of treatment is another relevant factor to be considered within the context of the range of reasonable responses. Thus clubs which in the past have taken a lenient or liberal view of the use of drugs by their players (such as Arsenal in the case of recreational drugs) might find it harder to justify, as fair, decisions to dismiss other players – at

---

112 See above, p 435.
113 [1980] ICR 303 EAT, 304.
114 It should be noted that the Court of Appeal approved this approach in *Foley and Madden*, op. cit., fn 102.
115 The FA's disciplinary procedures can be accessed from http://www.thefa.com/TheFA/Disciplinary – other sports operate very similar procedures.

least for first-time offences. Where a club is conducting its own drug testing investigation then it is important that it is exercising a contractual right to do so (see above p 000).

Legal status of the ACAS Code

It is important to appreciate that, in the final analysis, the ACAS Code sets out guidelines not binding legal rules. Therefore, as held by the House of Lords in *Polkey v AE Dayton Services Ltd*,[116] a failure to follow the Code does not automatically render a dismissal unfair. However, a dismissal will normally be procedurally unfair unless an employer could show that in the circumstances of the case adhering to the Code could be considered by the reasonable employer to be futile or useless. As is the case with the grievance procedures in the ACAS Code, a failure to adhere to disciplinary procedures that are in accordance with the Code will result in up to a 25 per cent increase or reduction in any compensation awarded for unfair or wrongful dismissal.

Moreover, dismissals will normally be procedurally unfair where employers fail to follow their own procedures – particularly, as is often the case in sport, where such procedures have contractual force.[117] It is also important to remember that where disciplinary procedures are incorporated into players' contracts a failure to observe them will constitute wrongful dismissal and may entitle the player to claim damages or even secure an injunction to restrain the dismissal.[118]

A claim for unfair dismissal, brought by footballer Dennis Wise (subsequently player-manager of Millwall and director of football of Newcastle United), illustrates the importance of ensuring internal procedures are in accordance with the ACAS Code. The decision is based on the principle that even where rights of appeal are exercised a dismissal will still be unfair if the decision to dismiss is based on initial procedural irregularities.

Wise v Filbert Realisations Respondent (Formerly Leicester City Football Club) (In Administration)

In July 2002, during a pre-season training club tour of Finland Dennis Wise was involved in an incident with a team-mate, Callum Davidson. As a result of a blow or blows in the face administered by Wise, Davidson sustained a fractured cheekbone with bruising and swelling around the right eye. Initially, the club manager fined Wise two weeks' wages and sent him home. However, the club decided to take disciplinary proceedings. On 22 July Wise was suspended pending an investigation into allegations of serious misconduct. A disciplinary hearing took place before the club chairman, Mr George, on 26 July. That hearing was conducted in a way which the employment tribunal found to be procedurally unfair in a number of respects. The club decided to dismiss Wise with 14 days' notice on 1 August, as provided for in clause 16 of his contract of employment.

Wise's contract provided for a two-stage appeal process detailed above. Wise exercised his right of appeal to the Football League Disciplinary Committee (FDC). The panel decided to conduct a full rehearing. Oral evidence was given by Wise, who pleaded self-defence and Davidson and Matt Elliott, the club captain, were also called. The panel preferred the evidence of Davidson and Elliott, rejecting the plea of self-defence advanced by Wise. They found as fact that Wise had gone into Davidson's room looking for trouble and had struck him twice, causing the injuries earlier mentioned. Even applying the criminal standard of proof, the panel was satisfied that Wise had committed an assault occasioning Actual Bodily Harm. On these findings, the panel found that Wise was guilty of serious misconduct under clause 16 of the

---

116 [1988] ICR 142.
117 See *Stoker v Lancashire CC* [1992] IRLR 75.
118 See above, pp 424–5.

contract. Having done so, the panel proceeded to find that the sanction of dismissal was disproportionate and substituted a penalty of two weeks' loss of gross wages.

The Club appealed to the Football League Appeals Committee (FLAC) against the FDC
decision. The main point of appeal was that, having found serious misconduct, the FDC had no
power to say that dismissal was disproportionate, and in any event, FDC was wrong because
dismissal was the appropriate penalty. The appeal came before a FLAC panel on 18 September
2002. FLAC agreed with the Club that, having found serious misconduct, the FDC was clearly
wrong to substitute a two-weeks' wages fine for dismissal. They took into account the various
factual findings made by FDC as to the assault itself and upheld the original dismissal.

The EAT upheld the appeal by Wise by applying the principle that in order to cure initial
procedural failings the appeal process must be by way of rehearing and not review of the initial
decision.

Clark J: In the present case the first instance decision at Club level was procedurally
flawed. The FDC appeal was by way of rehearing and was conducted fairly; it was capable of
curing the earlier procedural deficiencies. However, and this in our view is the crux of the
appeal, the FDC hearing did not result in a decision which upheld the original dismissal decision; had it done so, we are satisfied, the Tribunal's decision would be unimpeachable; that
hearing resulted in the dismissal being overturned. It was the subsequent FLAC hearing, itself,
we accept, taking the form of a review of the FDC decision and not a rehearing, which reinstated
the original Club decision to dismiss.

. . . In these circumstances . . . the Respondent cannot rely, either on the FDC rehearing
which imposed a sanction short of dismissal, nor the FLAC decision, which followed a review,
to cure the procedural irregularities at the initial hearing . . . fairness requires not only that the
sanction falls within the range of reasonable responses, but also the procedure by which that
sanction was reached. It is on this latter requirement that the Respondent falls down. The
dismissal is unfair.

. . . It follows that the Tribunal fell into error in their approach . . . They were not entitled to
amalgamate the two levels of appeal and take the final sanction of dismissal at the review stage
(FLAC) where the panel rehearing the case (FDC), after hearing the witnesses, found not only
that the Appellant was guilty of serious misconduct, but that such misconduct did not merit
dismissal.[119]

It is clear from the ACAS Code that in many circumstances penalties short of dismissal should be
imposed in the event of first-time offences and/or offences short of gross misconduct. By virtue of
contract law and s 13(1) ERA[120] an employee should not be suspended without pay and/or fined
unless this is permitted by an express term in the contract of employment. Clause 18 of the Football
League Contract and cl 13(a) of the Cricketers' Contract incorporate the necessary provisions.
Indeed the use of such penalties is much more common in professional sport than in many other
fields of employment.

Strictly speaking the procedures contained in the ACAS Code need not be followed where an
employer decides on a penalty short of dismissal. However, a dismissal based on a series of offences
by an employee will be unsafe if in the earlier stages proper procedures were not followed. Thus
there should be an investigation and the holding of a formal hearing each and every time an
employee is disciplined. Moreover, in the cases of cricket and football, players have contractual
rights of appeal against the imposition of suspensions and fines. Note further that under the ACAS
Code a disciplinary decision should not stay permanently on an employee's record. The norm is that
it should be removed if the employee 'keeps a clean sheet' for one year.

---

119 EAT/0660/03 9 February 2004.
120 Formerly s 1(1) of the Wages Act 1986.

Remedies for unfair dismissal

Reinstatement and re-engagement

Sections 114 and 115 of the ERA provide for tribunal orders of reinstatement and re-engagement. The difference between the two is that a reinstated employee returns to the job he or she was doing prior to dismissal, whereas re-engagement requires the complainant to be engaged in comparable employment. This could be with an associated employer. A reinstated employee must receive arrears of pay and the full restoration of rights, including seniority and pension rights. The tribunal sets out the terms on which an employee must be re-engaged.

In practice it is relatively rare for either remedy to be awarded. However, with respect to the Doherty brothers[121] both tribunals took the view that they should be reinstated as had the employer acted reasonably on the basis of the evidence available, and consistently with respect to how the brothers' colleagues were treated, neither would have been dismissed. Moreover, the tribunals took into account that there was strong support for the reinstatement of both amongst the workforce, and the relevant managers had either changed or could be expected to respond professionally by accepting that the decisions to dismiss had been mistaken. Therefore, the issue of trust and confidence was not a barrier to the practicality of reinstatement. In professional sport, arguably, the crucial issue is whether trust and confidence still exists with respect to managers, coaches and teammates rather than between the dismissed player and club officials.

Orders may be refused on the basis that it is not just and equitable to require an employer to take back an employee who has contributed to the dismissal through misconduct or incapability, or on the basis that it would not be reasonably practicable for the employer to comply. Moreover, employers are not obliged to comply with either of these orders. Failure to do so will entitle the employee to basic and compensatory awards plus an additional award of between 26 and 52 statutory weeks' pay. A tribunal order notwithstanding, in most cases a club would be able to afford to compensate a player whom it did not wish to take back.

Basic award

Under s 119 of the ERA this is calculated by reference to age, actual completed years of employment and a statutory week's pay. The latter reflects gross pay but is subject to a statutory maximum. In 2011 this was £400 – well below the actual weekly wage of many salary earners, let alone professional sportsmen. Only the last 20 years of employment can be credited, although such a length of employment will be uncommon in professional sport. Alan Knight, the Portsmouth goalkeeper (known as 'The Legend' to the Portsmouth 'faithful'), along with Paul Scholes and Ryan Giggs are some of the few players in these recent (more mercenary!) times who have come anywhere near this period of service with a single club.

Three scales apply: half a week's pay for every year completed aged under 22; one week's pay for every year completed aged 22 to 40; one and a half weeks' pay for every year completed aged 41 or more. With some obvious exceptions, such as Graham Gooch, who was still playing for Essex CCC when he was in his early forties, the highest scale will rarely be of relevance in sport.

A statutory redundancy payment is calculated in the same way as the basic award, although redundancy is not normally an issue for sports participants. However, in recent years a number of football clubs have come perilously close to insolvency, and employees not on the playing staff have been made redundant. Moreover, were a club ever to fold, all its employees, including players, would have their entitlements to statutory payments calculated on the above basis. Players would also be redundant if a club reduced the number of players it employed, for example to reduce the

---

121 See above, p 435.

wage bill, as against not renewing a player's contract because it wished to replace him with a different player.[122]

Compensatory award

Section 123(1) of the ERA specifies: 'the amount of the compensatory award shall be such amount as the tribunal considers just and equitable in all the circumstances having regard to the loss sustained by the complainant in consequence of the dismissal in so far as that loss is attributable to action taken by the employer.'

Section 123(4) applies the common law rule of mitigation. The function of the compensatory award is thus to compensate the dismissed employee for the actual financial loss suffered, and has the equivalent purpose to damages for breach of contract. However, unlike damages, loss of future earnings and pension rights can be taken into account, that is, to cover the period after due notice or a fixed-term contract has expired. There is a statutory ceiling, and in 2011 this ceiling was £68,400. This upper limit is still far below the salary of many professional footballers. However, the levels of compensation may make claiming unfair dismissal more of an attractive option (in comparison with wrongful dismissal) to players in the lower divisions, or indeed to participants in less well-paid sports such as cricket and rugby. If a player is dismissed with due notice, or is faced with the non-renewal of a fixed-term contract then, of course, a claim for unfair dismissal is the only legal course of action open to him.

Both basic and compensatory awards can be reduced as the tribunal considers just and equitable by reference to the contributory conduct of the dismissed employee. Such a deduction from the compensatory award should be made from the actual loss the individual incurs. Only after such deduction should the reduction to the statutory maximum figure take place. Moreover, under s 123(1) it is permissible to reduce the compensatory awards to nil where this can be considered by a tribunal to be just and equitable. A tribunal might decide to do this, in line with the decision in *Polkey*, where misconduct discovered after the dismissal retrospectively justifies it. Such a dismissal may be technically unfair but the employee may not receive any compensation whatsoever. In the Dennis Wise case[123] the EAT noted that such *Polkey* reductions might be appropriate, but it was remitted to the tribunal to decide, on the basis of the evidence before it, what the extent of any such deductions should be.

The *Bosman* Case and the Transfer System

In football the central issue regarding the termination of a footballer's contract is the transfer system. As a result of the decision in *Eastham* (see above), it was the case that in Britain even an out-of-contract player could be prevented from moving to another club unless that club agreed to pay a transfer fee for him. This position was replicated in the rules of other national associations, but a major reform to this system was required as a result of the preliminary ruling given by the European Court of Justice (ECJ) in *Bosman*.

---

122 It is likely that a number of out-of-contract players were so redundant at the end of the 2001/02 season when a significant reduction in television income and the collapse of ITV Digital created severe financial problems for a number of clubs – particularly in the lower leagues. The loss of income to the Nationwide League clubs was in the region of £178 million – see Lacey, D, 'January sales were more about beggars than choosers', *Guardian Sport*, 1 February 2003.

123 See above, pp 438–9.

The *Bosman* case

The European Court's ruling in this case is based on its interpretation of what is now Article 45 of the Treaty on the Functioning of the European Union (TFEU),[124] which provides for the right of EC nationals to work and reside in any Member State on equal terms with the nationals of that State. This Article is directly applicable and thus enforceable by national courts and tribunals. The Article takes precedence over any conflicting national laws. Under Article 267 of the TFEU, at the request of either party, or at its own discretion, a national court may decide to request a preliminary ruling from the European Court of Justice on the meaning of Article 45 (or any other EC law). The European Court is not deciding the case on appeal but is answering the questions put to it by the national court. This court will then decide the case by applying the interpretation of the Article contained in the European Court's ruling, and any relevant national law which does not conflict with it, to the facts of the case. The opinion of an Advocate General to the European Court is highly influential, but not binding, on any ruling (or decision) that the Court gives.

This case came about because Bosman, a Belgian national, was placed on the transfer list by his club, RFC Liège, once he refused to accept a new contract at a lower wage. Bosman wished to move to a French club, USL Dunkerque, but RFC Liège ultimately refused to process the transfer as it doubted USL Dunkerque's ability to pay the agreed fee. Subsequently, the Belgian Football Association and UEFA became parties to the case as both bodies argued that their respective rules requiring transfer fees were lawful. The Cour d'Appel, Liège requested a preliminary ruling from the European Court. One question put to the European Court was whether what is now Article 45 TFEU is to be interpreted as:

> . . . prohibiting a football club from requiring and receiving payment of a sum of money upon the engagement of one of its players who has come to the end of his contract by a new employing club.

The Opinion of Advocate General Lenz was in the affirmative on the basis that:

> . . . the transfer rules directly restrict access to the employment market in other Member States . . . under the applicable rules a player can transfer abroad only if the new club (or the player himself) is in a position to pay the transfer fee demanded. If that is not the case, the player *cannot* move abroad. That is a *direct* restriction on access to the employment market.[125]

In reaching his conclusion the Advocate General considered and rejected, inter alia, the need to protect smaller clubs and providing compensation to clubs for training players as constituting grounds for justifying the retention of the transfer system. In so far as these objectives were legitimate they did not meet the requirement of proportionality as they could be achieved through a redistribution of income from larger to smaller clubs. In short, any legitimate interests could be achieved by means other than a transfer system impeding rights of freedom of movement.

---

124 At the time of the ruling this was Article 48 of the EC Treaty, which was subsequently renumbered as Article 39 by the Treaty of Amsterdam. Similarly, Article 85 became Art 81 and Art 86 became Art 82; these are now Arts 101 and 102 TFEU respectively. The author's commentary refers to the current articles of the TFEU.

125 Paragraph 210 of the Opinion of Advocate General Lenz. This reasoning was adopted by the European Court in its preliminary ruling. The Advocate General also argued that the transfer system was contrary to what is now Art 101 TFEU, which prohibits anti-competitive practices within the EC. However, this position did not form part of the European Court's ruling. For an analysis of this dimension of Bosman, and further discussion of restraint of trade, see Morris, PE, Morrow, S and Spink, PM, 'EC law and professional football: Bosman and its implications' (1996) 59 Modern Law Review 893–902; Caiger, A and O'Leary, J, 'The end of the affair: the '*Anelka Doctrine*' – the problem of contract stability in English professional football', pp 197–216, in Caiger, A and Gardiner, S (eds), *Professional Sport in the EU: Regulation and Re-regulation* (2000) The Hague: Asser Press.

ASBL Union Royale Belge des Societes de Football Association & others
v Jean-Marc Bosman

A number of points have been put forward as justification of the transfer rules. The most significant of them is in my opinion the assertion that the rules on transfers are necessary in order to preserve a certain financial and sporting balance between clubs. It is argued that the purpose of those rules is to ensure the survival of smaller clubs. At the hearing before the Court of Justice URBSFA expressly submitted in this connection that the transfer fees paid guaranteed the survival of the amateur clubs.

That argument amounts to an assertion that the system of transfer rules is necessary to ensure the organisation of football as such. If no transfer fees were payable when players moved, the wealthy clubs would easily secure themselves the best players, while the smaller clubs and amateur clubs would get into financial difficulties and possibly even have to cease their activities. There would thus be a danger of the rich clubs always becoming even richer and the less well-off even poorer.

If that assertion was correct, then in my opinion it could indeed be assumed that the transfer rules were compatible with Article 48 . . .

As regards the professional clubs . . . the interested associations have produced little convincing, specific material to support their argument. In my estimation the report on English football by Touche Ross, submitted by UEFA and already mentioned above, has the greatest significance for the examination required here. In England there is of course a four-level professional league divided up into – from top to bottom – the Premier League and the First, Second and Third Divisions. From the figures given in that report it can be seen that in the period used as a basis the clubs in the Premier League spent a total of about £18.5 million net (that is, after deducting income from transfer fees received by them) on new players. After deducting that sum from total receipts, the clubs were still left with a total profit of £11.5 million. The clubs in the First Division, by contrast, made a surplus on transfer deals of a good £9.3 million, those in the Second Division a surplus of just £2.4 million and those in the Third Division a surplus of around £1.6 million. It is noteworthy in addition that for the latter three divisions there was in each case a loss on ordinary trading which was more than covered by the income from transfers.

Those figures are an impressive demonstration of what an important role the lower divisions play as a reservoir of talent for the top division. They also show that income from transfers represents an important item in the balance sheets of the lower division clubs. If the transfer rules were to be regarded as unlawful and those payments thus ceased, one would expect those clubs to encounter serious difficulties.

I thus entirely agree with the view, once more put forward clearly by URBSFA and UEFA at the hearing before the Court, that it is of fundamental importance to share income out between the clubs in a reasonable manner. However, I am nevertheless of the opinion that the transfer rules in their current form cannot be justified by that consideration. It is doubtful even whether the transfer rules are capable of fulfilling the objective stated by the associations. In any event, however, there are other means of attaining that objective which have less effect, or even no effect at all, on freedom of movement.

With reference to the question of the suitability of those rules for achieving the desired objective, it must first be observed that the rules currently in force probably very often force the smaller professional clubs to sell players in order to ensure their survival by means of the transfer income thereby obtained. Since the players transferred to the bigger clubs are as a rule the best players of the smaller professional clubs, those clubs are thereby weakened from a sporting point of view. It is admittedly true that as a result of the income from transfers those clubs are placed in a position themselves to engage new players, in so far as their general financial situation permits. As has been seen, however, the transfer fees are generally calcu-lated on the basis of the players' earnings. Since the bigger clubs usually pay higher wages, the smaller clubs will probably hardly ever be in a position themselves to acquire good players from those clubs. In that respect the rules on transfers thus strengthen even further the imbalance which exists in any class between wealthy and less wealthy clubs. The Commission and Mr Bosman correctly drew attention to that consequence.

Mr Bosman has also submitted with some justification that the rules on transfers do not prevent the rich clubs from engaging the best players, so that they are only suitable to a limited extent for preserving the sporting equilibrium. The obligation to expend a sometimes substan-tial sum of money for a new player is indeed no great obstacle for a wealthy club or a club with a wealthy patron. That is emphatically shown by the examples of AC Milan and Blackburn Rovers.

The financial balance between the clubs is moreover also not necessarily strengthened by the rules on transfers. If a club engages players from clubs in other Member States or non-member countries, the funds required for the purchases flow abroad without the other clubs in the same league as the club in question benefiting therefrom.

Above all, however, it is plain that there are alternatives to the transfer rules with which the objectives pursued by those rules can be attained. Basically there are two different possi-bilities, both of which have also been mentioned by Mr Bosman. Firstly, it would be possible to determine by a collective wage agreement specified limits for the salaries to be paid to the players by the clubs. That possibility was described in more detail by Mr Bosman in his obser-vations. He observed, however, that that possibility is not as effective as the alternative, which I am about to discuss. In view of what I am about to say, it is thus not necessary for me to say any more on this possibility. Secondly, it would be conceivable to distribute the clubs' receipts among the clubs. Specifically, that means that part of the income obtained by a club from the sale of tickets for its home matches is distributed to the other clubs. Similarly, the income received for awarding the rights to transmit matches on television, for instance, could be divided up between all the clubs.

. . . It can scarcely be doubted that such a redistribution of income appears sensible and legitimate from an economic point of view. UEFA itself has rightly observed that football is characterised by the mutual economic dependence of the clubs. Football is played by two teams meeting each other and testing their strength against each other. Each club thus needs the other one in order to be successful. For that reason each club has an interest in the health of the other clubs. The clubs in a professional league thus do not have the aim of excluding their competitors from the market. Therein lies – as both UEFA and Mr Bosman have rightly stated – a significant difference from the competitive relationship between undertakings in other markets. It is likewise correct that the economic success of a league depends not least on the existence of a certain balance between its clubs. If the league is dominated by one overmighty club, experience shows that lack of interest will spread.

If every club had to rely on financing its playing operations exclusively by the income it received from the sale of tickets, radio and television contracts and other sources (such as advertising, members' subscriptions or donations from private sponsors), the balance between the clubs would very soon be endangered. Big clubs like FC Bayern Munchen or FC Barcelona have a particular power of attraction which finds expression in high attendance figures. Those clubs thereby also become of great interest for television broadcasters and the advertising sector. The large income resulting from that permits those clubs to engage the best players and thereby reinforce their (sporting and economic) success even more. For the smaller clubs precisely the converse would happen. The lack of attractiveness of a team leads to correspondingly lower income, which in turn reduces the possibilities of strengthening the team.

Mr Bosman has admittedly pointed out that there are those who consider that the necessary balance results as it were automatically, since by reason of the facts described above no club can be interested in achieving an overwhelming superiority in its league. Experience shows, however, that club managements do not always calculate in that way, but may at times allow themselves to be led by considerations other than purely sporting or economic ones. It therefore is indeed necessary, in my opinion, to ensure by means of specific measures that a certain balance is preserved between the clubs. One possibility is the system of transfer payments currently in force. Another possibility is the redistribution of a proportion of income.

Mr Bosman submitted a number of economic studies which show that distribution of income represents a suitable means of promoting the desired balance. The concrete form given to such a system will of course depend on the circumstances of the league in question and on other considerations. In particular it is surely clear that such a redistribution can be sensible and appropriate only if it is restricted to a fairly small part of income: if half the receipts, for instance, or even more was distributed to other clubs, the incentive for the clubs in question to perform well would probably be reduced too much.

Neither URBSFA nor UEFA disputed that that solution is a realistic possibility which makes it possible to promote a sporting and financial balance between clubs. If I am not very much mistaken, they did not even attempt to rebut the arguments put forward by Mr Bosman in this connection.

It seems to me that that is not a matter of chance. The associations too can scarcely dispute that that possibility is an appropriate and reasonable alternative. The best evidence for that is the circumstance that corresponding models are already in use in professional football today. In the German cup competition, for example, the two clubs involved each to my knowledge receive half of the receipts remaining after deduction of the share due to the DFB. The income from awarding the rights of television and radio broadcasts of matches is distributed by the DFB among the clubs according to a specified formula. The position is presumably much the same in the associations of the other Member States.

A redistribution of income also takes place at UEFA level. Under Article 18 of the UEFA statutes (1990 edition), UEFA is entitled to a share of the receipts from the competitions it organises and from certain international matches. A good example is the UEFA Cup rules for the 1992/93 season, which have been produced to the Court by URBSFA. Under those rules UEFA receives for each match a share of 4% of gross receipts from the sale of tickets and 10% of receipts from the sale of the radio and television rights. For the two legs of the final UEFA's share is increased to as much as 10% and 25% respectively.

While that system serves to cover the expenditure of UEFA and thus only indirectly – by means of corresponding grants by UEFA to certain associations or clubs – leads to a redistribution of income, the case is different with the 'UEFA Champions League'. That competition, which took the place of the earlier European Champions' Cup, was introduced by UEFA in 1992. A UEFA document produced to the Court by Mr Bosman provides information on the purpose and organisation of that competition. The objective is stated to be the promotion of the interests of football. It is specifically noted that the profit is not only to be for the benefit of the clubs taking part, but all the associations are to receive a share of it.

A balance of the 1992/93 season makes that clear. According to that, the eight clubs which took part in the competition each kept the receipts from the sale of tickets for their home matches. In addition to that, the competition produced an income of 70 million Swiss francs from the marketing of television and advertising rights. That amount was divided up as follows. The participating clubs received SFR 38 million (54%). A further SFR 12 million (18%) was distributed to all the clubs which had been eliminated in the first two rounds of the three UEFA competitions for club teams. SFR 5.8 million (8%) was distributed between the 42 member associations of UEFA. The remaining SFR 14 million (20%) went to UEFA, to be invested for the benefit of football, in particular for the promotion of youth and women's football.

The example of the Champions League in particular clearly demonstrates, in my opinion, that the clubs and associations concerned have acknowledged and accepted in principle the possibility of promoting their own interests and those of football in general by redistributing a proportion of income. I therefore see no unsurmountable obstacles to prevent that method also being introduced at national level or at the level of the relevant association. By designing the system in an appropriate way it would be possible to avoid the incentive to perform well being reduced excessively and the smaller clubs becoming the rich clubs' boarders. I cannot see any negative effects on the individual clubs' self-esteem. Even if there were such effects, they would be purely of a psychological nature and thus not such as to justify a continued restriction on freedom of movement resulting from the transfer system.

Finally, it must be observed that a redistribution of a part of income appears substantially more suitable for attaining the desired purpose than the current system of transfer fees. It permits the clubs concerned to budget on a considerably more reliable basis. If a club can reckon with a certain basic amount which it will receive in any case, then solidarity between clubs is better served than by the possibility of receiving a large sum of money for one of the club's own players. As Mr Bosman has rightly submitted, the discovery of a gifted player who can be transferred to a big club for good money is very often largely a matter of chance. Yet the prosperity of football depends not only on the welfare of such a club, but also on all the other small clubs being able to survive. That, however, is not guaranteed by the present rules on transfers.

In so far as the rules on transfers pursue the objective of ensuring the economic and sporting equilibrium of the clubs, there is thus at least one alternative by means of which that objective can be pursued just as well and which does not adversely affect players' freedom of movement. The transfer rules are thus not indispensable for attaining that objective, and thus do not comply with the principle of proportionality.

The second important argument on which the associations concerned base their opinion that the transfer system is lawful consists in the assertion that the transfer fees are merely compensation for the costs incurred in the training and development of a player. The Italian and French Governments have also adopted that argument. It is of course closely connected with the first argument, which I have just discussed.

However often that view has been repeated in the course of these proceedings, it still remains unconvincing.

The transfer fees cannot be regarded as compensation for possible costs of training, if only for the simple reason that their amount is linked not to those costs but to the player's earnings. Nor can it seriously be argued that a player, for example, who is transferred for a fee of one million ECU caused his previous club to incur training costs amounting to that vast sum. A good demonstration that the argument put forward by the associations is untenable can be found in the DFB transfer rule, described above, for the transfer of an amateur player to a professional club. As we have seen, under that rule a first division club had to pay a transfer fee of DM 100,000, whereas a second division club had to pay only DM 45,000 for the same player. That shows that the amount of the transfer fee quite evidently is not orientated to the costs of training.

A second argument against regarding transfer fees as a reimbursement of the training costs which have been incurred is the fact that such fees – and in many cases extraordinarily large sums – are demanded even when experienced professional players change clubs. Here there can no longer be any question of 'training' and reimbursement of the expense of such training. Nor does it make any difference that in such cases it is often 'compensation for development' (not compensation for training) which is spoken of. Any reasonable club will certainly provide its players with all the development necessary. But that is expenditure which is in the club's own interest and which the player recompenses with his performance. It is not evident why such a club should be entitled to claim a transfer fee on that basis. The regulations of the French and Spanish associations have, quite rightly in my opinion, drawn the conclusion that – at least after a specified moment in time – no transfer fees can be demanded any more.

. . . That does not mean, however, that a demand for a transfer fee for a player would, following the view I have put forward, have to be regarded as unlawful in every case. The argument that a club should be compensated for the training work it has done, and that the big, rich clubs should not be enabled to enjoy the fruits of that work without making any contribution of their own, does indeed in my opinion have some weight. For that reason it might be considered whether appropriate transfer rules for professional footballers might not be acceptable . . .

Such rules would in my opinion have to comply with two requirements. First, the transfer fee would actually have to be limited to the amount expended by the previous club (or previous clubs) for the player's training. Second, a transfer fee would come into question only in the case of a first change of clubs where the previous club had trained the player. Analogous to the transfer rules in force in France, that transfer fee would in addition have to be reduced proportionately for every year the player had spent with that club after being trained, since during that period the training club will have had an opportunity to benefit from its investment in the player.[126]

The transfer rules at issue in the present case do not meet those requirements, or at best meet them in part . . .[127]

It is interesting to reflect with the benefit of hindsight on the fact that many of the initial responses to the *Bosman* ruling concentrated on the extent to which it would still be 'business as usual'. There was a strong argument that the ruling would not affect the transfer system then operating within the Premier, Football and Scottish Leagues. It was assumed by almost everyone (including this writer) that *Bosman* had no implications for players who wished to secure transfers whilst still under contract.[128] On the other hand, while the actual legal position has not been and in practice never may be clarified, there were arguments that *Bosman* did impact on transfers within Member States and thus the changes voluntarily introduced in Britain were necessary to avoid the threat of legal challenge.

Gardiner, S and Welch, R, 'The winds of change in professional football: the impact of the *Bosman* ruling'

It must be emphasised that in adopting the reasoning of Advocate General Lenz the European Court did not rule that a transfer system operating within the territory of a single Member State violates Article 48. Indeed, The European Court stated:

---

126 The new FIFA rules concerning the calculation of compensation for the training of younger players would appear to conform to these principles; see below, p 451.

127 [1996] 1 CMLR 645 (Case C-415/93). The ECJ's ruling was delivered on 15 December 1995. For an immediate reaction to the ruling see press reports of 16 and 17 December 1995. On the personal fate of Jean-Marc Bosman and a survey of responses across the EC to the ruling, see *The Independent On Sunday*, 18 February 1996. For the definitive academic analysis of *Bosman*, see Blanpain, R and Inston, R, *The Bosman Case: The End of the Transfer System?* (1996), London: Sweet & Maxwell; Leuven: Peeters.

128 See, for example, the contribution by Robert Reid to the 'FA Premier League Seminar' on the *Bosman* case, 8 January 1996, organised in conjunction with the British Association for Sport and Law. Indeed, the overall view of the speakers at the seminar was that the *Bosman* case could not have arisen in Britain as it would not have been permissible to retain a player on a lower wage. Moreover, the ruling did not explicitly cover the situation where a player wishes to move to another club within the same country. Thus, it was argued, the Premier and Football Leagues should not be panicked into making changes to the current transfer fee system.

'... the provisions of the Treaty concerning the free movement of workers, and particularly Article 48, cannot be applied to situations which are wholly internal to a Member State, in other words where there is no factor connecting them to any of the situations envisaged by Community law.'[129]

The ruling only expressly covers transfer systems that require a transfer fee to be paid before an out of contract player is able to move to a club in a different Member State. Nevertheless, as will be detailed below, voluntary reform to the UK transfer system has recently occurred in the wake of the *Bosman* ruling. However, it has been argued that the ruling had no direct impact on this transfer system as it stood where an out of contract player was seeking to move to another club within the UK. It is useful to identify arguments which, if correct, would contradict this perspective.

One possibility is provided by human rights law. This equates freedom of movement with freedom of choice as it requires states to permit nationals to move freely within their own country as well as recognising their rights to leave and return to it.[130] Arguably, this freedom is effectively being denied to an out of contract player if he is forced to move abroad if this is the only way in which he can evade the transfer system. On this point it is interesting that various rulings by the European Court interpreting Article 85 have made it clear that anti-competitive practices within a Member State can adversely affect trade in other Member States. If Article 85 can apply to a course of conduct in one Member State why should this also not be the case with Article 48? In short, it could be argued that a transfer system operating within a Member State is not 'wholly internal' to that state if it restricts the operation of Article 48 as far as that Member State's own nationals are concerned.[131]

Another argument supporting the proposition that the UK transfer system was in violation of Article 48 is derived from the concept of indirect discrimination. In the context of employment Article 48 prohibits discrimination against nationals of Member States on grounds of their nationality. Whilst this would normally be understood as protecting individuals who are nationals of other Member States from discrimination, arguably, there is no logical reason why this should not also protect nationals of the Member State concerned. Under *Bosman* it is clear that an English club could not prevent an English player (just like any other player possessing EU nationality), on the termination of his contract, from moving to another club within the EU. However, it is likely that many English players would prefer to move to another club within the UK rather than one in another Member State.

EC law prohibiting sex discrimination in employment[132] stipulates that an employer who imposes a requirement that adversely affects a greater number of employees of one sex as against the other has committed an act of indirect sex discrimination. This discrimination is unlawful unless it can be justified by reference to objective business or organisational interests and these are not outweighed by the impact of the discrimination.[133]

Applying this approach to the above situation it could be argued that it is indirect discrimination, contrary to Article 48, for a club effectively to require an out of contract player to move to a club in another Member State if he is seeking to exercise the right to freedom of movement conferred by Article 48. The reason being that this might have a deterrent effect on British

---

129 Paragraph 89 of the European Court's Ruling.
130 These rights were first proclaimed by Art 13 of the United Nations Universal Declaration of Human Rights in 1948 and are enshrined in Art 12 of the International Covenant on Civil and Political Rights 1966. The rights were incorporated into the European Convention on Human Rights by Arts 2 and 3 of the Fourth Protocol which was adopted by the signatory governments in 1963.
131 Cases illustrating how practices by undertakings within a single Member State can adversely affect interstate trade contrary to Art 81 include *Re German Ceramic Tiles Discount Agreement* [1971] CMLR D6 and *Brasserie de Haecht v Wilkin and Wilkin* [1968] CMLR 26.
132 The Equal Treatment Directive (76/207/EC) and Art 141 (formerly Art 119) of the EC Treaty which prohibits sex discrimination in the context of pay.
133 These principles were laid down by the European Court in *Bilka-Kaufhaus GmbH v Weber von Hartz* [1987] ICR 110.

players, as against players of other nationalities, who for family and/or other reasons might regard it as detrimental to work outside of the UK and thus feel they have no practical option other than to accept that any transfer will be subject to a transfer fee being agreed. If the requirement that a transfer fee be paid before an out of contract British player could move to another UK club was found to constitute indirect discrimination then this would be unlawful unless it could be justified objectively.

It is, however, possible that the transfer system in the UK met the criteria for justifying indirect discrimination as the specifics of this transfer system were different to the Belgian system challenged by *Bosman*. Firstly, a British club lost the right to retain the registration of an out of contract player unless it offered him the same or a higher salary to that he was receiving under his former contract. Secondly (as referred to above), if the player was offered a contract by another club, but the amount of the transfer fee could not be agreed by the two clubs concerned, the player was entitled to have the amount of the fee determined by an independent transfer tribunal. Bosman had no recourse to such a tribunal, and, in any case, if UK rules had applied RFC Liège would have lost the right to retain him as the immediate cause of Bosman's dispute with the club was the imposition of a wage cut as part of the new contractual terms offered to him.

Indeed, for these reasons it has been argued that had a similar case to *Bosman* arisen in this country it would have been found that the principle of proportionality required by Article 48 would have been satisfied, and the UK system would not have been found to have been in violation of EC law.[134] If this is correct then logically, even it was possible to argue that the transfer system indirectly discriminated against British players, the same reasoning could have been used to justify such discrimination.[135]

The Bosman ruling did not and does not directly apply to players recruited from outside of the EU and EEA. Players from, as examples, European States outside of the EU, the Americas, most African countries, Asia and Australia are not protected by Art 45 TFEU. As a matter of historical record it should be noted that FIFA decided with effect from 1 April 1997 to change its rules to permit any player to move to other clubs within the EU on free transfers once their contracts expire.[136] Thus a British club still had to pay a transfer fee to import a player from, for example, a Brazilian club. However, if it retained that player until his contract expired a transfer fee could not be claimed unless that player negotiated a move to a club outside of the EU.

The significance of the 1997 FIFA decision has been dwarfed by the overhaul of the international transfer system agreed by the Executive Committee of FIFA on 5 July 2001, as further amended in 2005. Before examining the new system it is valuable to consider the other main contention that has emerged in the wake of Bosman (and again it is a contention that has not been resolved by judicial decision); that is, the view that EU law requires some recognition that a club must release a player's registration where a player breaks his existing contract of employment in order to sign a new contract with a new club.

If it is correct to restrict Bosman to players who are out of contract[137] then, while the transfer rules as they currently operate in Britain continue to apply, it is possible for clubs to introduce new contractual devices to maximise the possibility of securing a transfer fee for a player who wants to leave the club, or is no longer wanted by it. One possibility is to use 'long' fixed-term contracts. Another is to introduce lengthy notice periods with 'garden leave' provisions. However, the latter

---

134 See Sir John Wood's contribution to the FA Premier League Seminar on the *Bosman* Case (London: Middle Temple Hall) 8 January 1996, p 6.
135 (1998) 3(4) Contemporary Issues in Law 289–312.
136 See *The Guardian*, 27 March 1997.
137 Paragraph 246 of the Opinion of Advocate General Lenz, does seem quite explicit on this point.

may offend the duty to provide work. Both devices are subject to the doctrine of restraint of trade.[138] This is particularly the case for the younger player, although arguably not where the contract is negotiated by an agent who genuinely has his client's best interests at heart (see above pp 396–7).

However, these arguments become academic if players are entitled to break their contracts, providing compensation is paid to the employing club. If both the transfer rules and contract law are overridden by EU law, i.e. by Articles 45 and/or 102 of the TFEU, then national associations will have no option other than to adopt the transfer rules agreed to by FIFA. This is particularly so given that the European Commission has, at least informally, approved these rules as being compatible with EU law.[139] However, as discussed below, it should be understood that even these rules could be challenged on the basis that any form of transfer system offends EU law.

The initial background to the introduction of the FIFA rules was the announcement by Nicolas Anelka in the summer of 1999 that he no longer wanted to honour his contract to play for Arsenal FC. Anelka wished to leave the UK and play for the Italian club, Lazio. At the time of this announcement Anelka had another four years of his contract to run. The problem for Anelka was that Arsenal was not prepared to release him from his contractual obligations, and Lazio was not prepared to pay the sizeable transfer fee that Arsenal required.

This situation generated legal debate (initiated by Jean-Louis Dupont, the Belgian lawyer who advised Bosman) that to prevent a player from terminating his employment contract, as the transfer system does, is as much a restraint on a player's freedom of movement as where a player is prevented from moving to another club on the expiry of his contract. The argument on behalf of Anelka was that he should have the right to break his contract providing he was prepared to pay compensation to Arsenal by reference to the normal contractual principles for calculating damages.

Interestingly, estimations of the actual amount of compensation to which Arsenal would have been entitled varied from around £5 million to a figure nearer the £22 million transfer fee that Arsenal required. The position with respect to Anelka was ultimately resolved when Arsenal accepted a transfer bid submitted by Real Madrid. However, the incident cast doubt on the original assumption, in the aftermath of *Bosman*, that Art 39 only applied to out-of-contract players.

The legal situation was further complicated by a complaint to the Commission by the Italian club Perugia. The basis of the club's complaint was that it wished to recruit an Italian player, Massimo Lombardo, from the Swiss club, Zurich Grasshoppers. Although Lombardo was at the end of his contract with Grasshoppers, *Bosman* did not directly apply to his situation, as Switzerland is not covered by EC law. In December 1998 the Commission ruled that the then existing transfer system in its entirety, not just on expiry of a player's contract, violated EC competition law. This resulted in FIFA coming under considerable pressure to formulate proposals for reform, although the Commission had also emphasised it was not seeking the complete abolition of the transfer system as it recognises the 'specificity of sport'.[140]

---

138 See Gardiner, S and Welch, R, 'The Winds of Change in Professional Football: The Impact of the Bosman Ruling' (1998) 3(4) Contemporary Issues in Law 289, 297–302.

139 See Commission press release of 5 March 2001 on the outcome of discussions between the Commission and FIFA/UEFA on FIFA Regulations on international football transfers. Also see the statement by Mario Monti, the Competition Commissioner, of 11 June 2003 stating that the Commission had closed its investigation into the validity of the new rules. FIFPro, on the other hand, has stated that in its view there may still be issues to resolve – see press release of 13 June 2003 – www.fifpro.org. Revised rules were adopted by FIFA in October 2003 and came into force on 1 July 2005. However, the salient features of the rules remain the same.

140 For a general discussion of the issues see Caiger, A and O'Leary, J (1999) 2(5) SLB 2; Tsatsas, N, 'Anelka's costly walk-out case has a hole in it', *The Guardian*, 23 July 1999. On applicability of Art 39, see *The Helsinki Report on Sport*, European Commission (COM(1999)644 – C5-0088/2000) and the Opinion to the European Parliament of the Committee on Legal Affairs and the Internal Market (A5-0208/2000). For an account of the 'Lombardo case' see 'Sports focus: the end of transfer fees', *The Observer*, 3 September 2000. For reference to the Commission's views on the compatibility of the transfer system with EC law see the speech of Commission Member Viviane Reding to the European Parliament on 7 September 2000 (Speech/00/290).

It is not absolutely clear that the FIFA rules conform with EC law, as, to date, the ECJ has never been called upon to rule on this issue, and litigation challenging the rules could still occur in the future. For example, Andrew Caiger and John O'Leary have provided a particularly intriguing argument supporting the contention that *Bosman* applies to players denied a mid-contract transfer.[141] They argue that any player who unilaterally breaks his contract should be considered to be out of contract. Thus, in line with *Bosman*, the employing club has no option other than to release his registration. The club's only remedy is to seek damages for breach of contract. Caiger and O'Leary also stress that to permit professional footballers to act in this way is simply to allow them to act as any other employee under any other contract of employment is able to do.

These arguments are certainly cogent. However, as discussed above, there are mechanisms that can be used by an employer to restrain an employee from acting in breach of contract, or from working for a competitor on termination of an existing contract. Thus it is not always the case that an employee is always free to walk away from a job by unilaterally breaking the contract of employment. It is also debatable whether a player who terminates a contract through committing a unilateral breach can be regarded as being 'out of contract' in the sense that that concept was used in *Bosman*. The general tenor of the ruling was that an 'out of contract' player is a player whose contract has run its course and thus expired.

It remains to be seen whether the correct legal position will ever be clarified by a ruling from the ECJ. For the time being, the position is at least now clear for players who enter into new contracts in accordance with the FIFA Regulations for the Status and Transfer of Players. These first came into force on 1 September 2001, and an amended version has applied from 1 July 2005. It must be emphasised that the FIFA rules apply only to international transfers where a player has negotiated a move to a club in a different national association.[142]

The salient features of the FIFA Regulations are as follows.

- The rules only apply to international transfers between national associations.
- International transfers of players under the age of 18 are restricted to protect the families and the education of the player concerned.
- Clubs will be able to receive compensation for players under the age of 23 who move during the currency or at the end of their contracts.
- This compensation will no longer be in the form of a negotiated transfer fee but calculated according to agreed criteria set out in an Annex 4 to the Rules. These criteria generally reflect the principles set out by Advocate General Lenz in *Bosman* for compensating clubs for training players.[143] The amount to be paid should be between all clubs which contributed to the training of the player in question, starting from the age of 12.
- Contracts should be for a minimum of one season and a maximum of five years.
- There will be one transfer period per season, and a further limited mid-season window, with a limit of one transfer per player per season.
- In the case of a contract signed up to the 28th birthday of a player, there is a protected period of three seasons. A unilateral breach during this period will give rise to rights to compensation and the application of sports sanctions restricting a player's ability to play immediately for his new club.

---

141 Op. cit., fn 84, Caiger and O'Leary (2000).
142 A complete version of the rules is contained in the FA Handbook – these can be accessed from http://www.thefa.com/TheFA/ RulesandRegulations/FARegulations. For discussion of the background to the introduction of the new rules see McAuley, D, 'They think it's all over . . . It might just be now: unravelling the ramifications for the European football transfer system post-Bosman' (2002) 23(7) European Competition Law Review 331–40. For an interdisciplinary analysis see Morris, P and Spink, P, 'The new transfer fee system in professional soccer: an interdisciplinary study' (2000/1), 5(4) Contemporary Issues in Law 253–81. Also see MacDonald, M, 'Transfers, contracts and personhood – an anthropological perspective' (2003) ISL Review, 3–10 for an analysis of the relationship between transfer markets and the legal status of players as employees.
143 See para 239, above p 447.

- In the case of a contract signed after a player's 28th birthday, the above will apply but the protected period will only be for the first two seasons of the contract.
- Players may be prevented from playing for another club for up to one year if that club, or others such as the player's agent, has induced the player to act in breach of his contract.
- Players will be permitted to terminate contracts if they have due or a 'sporting just' cause. The meaning of sporting just cause is not defined and there is clearly scope for different interpretations at the level of national courts. However, for the purposes of international transfers only, Article 15 of the FIFA rules stipulates that sporting just cause includes failure to involve an 'established Professional' in less than 10 per cent of a club's official matches.
- A club intending to conclude a contract with a Professional must inform his current club in writing before entering into negotiations with that Professional. A Professional shall only be free to conclude a contract with another club if his contract with his present club has expired or will expire within six months. Any breach of this provision shall be subject to appropriate sanctions.

Under Article 17 of the FIFA rules, once the protected period has expired, a player is able to terminate his contract in order to join a new club provided compensation is paid to his current club. This compensation should be at least equal to the remaining value of the player's contract plus any transfer fee that the club paid for the player (the value of this fee decreases over the period of time that that the contract has lasted). It should be noted that even when the protected period has expired, or the player wishes to terminate for sporting just cause, he may not terminate his contract during a season. Indeed, a player only has 15 days after the last official match of the season to notify his club that he has decided to terminate his contract with it.

If there is a unilateral breach without just cause during the protected period his club will again be entitled to claim compensation, but sporting sanctions will also be applied against the player. Under Article 23, a player is prevented from participating in any official football match, except for the club to which he was contracted, for an effective period of four months as from the beginning of the next season. This period can be extended to a maximum period of six months in cases of aggravating circumstances, such as failure to give notice or recurrent breach.

If a club has induced a player to act in breach of contract the ban may continue until the expiry of the second transfer window following the date the breach of contract was committed. However, any such ban cannot last for longer than 12 months. Where appropriate, sporting sanctions may also be imposed against the player's agent and the club inducing the breach. Sanctions against the latter may include fines, bans on participating in the transfer market, deduction of points and exclusion from competitions.

Potentially then, the current FIFA transfer rules enhance player mobility by enabling a player over the age of 23 unilaterally to terminate his existing contract to move to another club once the appropriate protected period has expired. Even greater mobility is provided by the ability of a player to terminate a contract for sporting just cause even though his club has not committed any breach of contract. In short, what can be perceived as the right to contract-jump is expressly recognised by the FIFA transfer rules.

However, the complexities involved in implementing this right are demonstrated by the findings of FIFA's Dispute Resolution Chamber (DRC) in the *Webster* case. Andy Webster terminated his contract with the Scottish football club, Hearts FC at the end of the 2005–06 season and then agreed to move to Wigan FC. Hearts successfully argued that Article 17 did not apply, even though the protected period of Webster's contract had expired, as he had failed to give the requisite 15 days' notice. In fact, Webster gave notice within 15 days of the Scottish Cup Final, which he argued by custom and practice constituted the last match of the Scottish season. The DRC disagreed but, on the basis that this constituted a minor breach of the rules, only banned him from the first two matches of the following season.

With respect to compensation, the DRC rejected Hearts' claim of £5 million and awarded the club £625,000. This figure was arrived at by reference to the residual value of Webster's contract with Hearts which, because his salary in the first year of his contract with Wigan was also taken into account, was then multiplied with a 1.5 coefficient (this being the permitted maximum). The basis for awarding this lower amount of compensation has recently been approved by the Court of Arbitration for Sport (CAS).[144]

The *Webster* case has been hailed as the 'new Bosman' in so far as it confirms the right of a player to change clubs irrespective of whether his current club is prepared to release him from his contract. However, the case also demonstrates the narrow nature of the freedom of movement provided by Article 17 in that it limits the window of opportunity for contract termination to 15 days. This is particularly problematic given prohibitions on under-contract players from talking to or being approached by other clubs. It is only in the final six months of a contract that FIFA rules permit players to negotiate a contract with a new club, and again this is only the case where the player is seeking to move to a club in a different national association. By way of contrast, in Britain, players can only approach clubs in domestic leagues after their contracts have expired.

The way in which the ability of a player unilaterally to terminate his contract can in practice be substantially restricted is particularly illustrated by the decision of the CAS in *Matuzalem*.[145] The CAS granted compensation of EUR 11,258,934 plus interest and this sum was effectively a penalty imposed on the player for his conduct in breaching his contract. In English law, by way of contrast and as explained above, damages for breach of contract must be based on the actual financial loss of the injured contracting party and cannot reflect the reasons why the breach was committed. Arguably, therefore, if a decision similar to *Matuzalem* was to be challenged before the British courts this level of compensation would be reduced.[146]

The FIFA rules permit players to terminate their contracts where they have due cause or a 'sporting just cause'. Clearly, the former position is in accordance with English contract law if a club is in repudiatory breach and thus the player is able to establish constructive dismissal. However, there is no automatic correlation between the notion of a 'sporting just cause' and a club acting in breach of contract. Failure to secure selection for first-team matches on a long-term basis may constitute an example of 'sporting just cause'. However, it is difficult to establish any breach of contract by a club in this respect providing selection decisions are in good faith; for example, the player's position is filled by another player genuinely perceived to be in better form and/or better suited to the tactics that the team coach has decided to deploy.

It is of interest to note that the Premiership and Football League rules have yet to embrace the principle, let alone the detail, of contract termination for sporting just cause. If this situation persists, this, in itself, could provide the basis for future litigation between a player and his club.

Conversely, it remains to be seen whether clubs will be prepared to forego any contractual rights and remedies where a player, for sporting reasons, is deemed entitled to terminate his contract and have his registration transferred to a new club. It similarly remains to be seen whether

---

144 CAS 2007/A/1298/1299/1300 *Wigan Athletic FC/Heart of Midlothian/Webster*.

145 CAS 2008/A/1519-1520 *Matuzalem/Shaktar Donetsk/Real Zaragoza/FIFA*.

146 *Matuzalem* has subsequently been followed by the CAS in CAS 2009/A/1880 *Essam El-Hadaray v FIFA & Al-Ahly Sporting Club*. In its commentary on the *El-Hadaray* case, see FIFPro press release 23 June 2010: FIFPro has criticised the *Matuzalem* ruling on the basis that it operates as a significant restraint on a player's ability to move to a new club once the protected period of his contract has expired, and this contradicts the enhanced mobility which it was intended should be given to players under Article 17 of the FIFA Regulations. Thus, in FIFPro's view, the only basis for compensation should be the residual value of a player's contract. However, the approach in *Matuzalem* has also been applied by the CAS in a case involving Stephen Appiah, although, here, the approach worked in the player's favour as no damages were awarded on the basis that the club had not suffered any financial loss – see Limbert, P, 'Player Contracts: Appiah: compensation not due for breach of contract' (2010) 8(8) WSLR. As a result of injury, Appiah was unable to play for his club, Fenerbahce, for the remainder of his contract. The CAS refused to award Fenerbahce any compensation on the basis that it had suffered no financial loss, and this was despite the fact that Appiah's breach was within the protected period of his contract.

clubs will refrain from litigation once a contract ceases to be protected after the third year of its duration (or after the second year in the case of a player who was aged 28 or over at the date the contract was entered into). In these circumstances the inclusion of negative restraint clauses and the arguments over whether, on the basis of them, injunctions can be secured to prevent a player playing for a new club remain of practical importance in football, as well as in other professional sports (see above, pp 423–4).

Though the EU Commission approved the FIFA rules it is by no means certain that they will withstand a legal challenge before the ECJ. It has been argued that any form of transfer system should be regarded as offending EU Law. Even if this is not the case there are aspects of the Regulations which are arguably unduly restrictive as evidenced by the *Webster* and *Matuzalem* cases.

Gardiner, S. And Welch, R', 'The Contractual Dynamics of Team Stability Versus Player Mobility: Who Rules "The Beautiful Game"?'

It is clear that professional sport in general will have to ensure that it complies with the provisions of EU law in areas such as freedom of movement and competition law, and the complexities involved in determining when EU law will be applicable are vividly demonstrated by the ECJ's ruling in Case C519/04P *Meca-Medina v Commission of the European Communities* [2006] 5 CMLR 18. The case itself concerned swimmers who were banned after testing positive for the banned drug Nandrolone. Whilst the ECJ upheld the Commission's decision that this ban did not violate EU competition law, it also rejected the reasoning of the European Court of First Instance that EU law had no jurisdiction over purely sporting rules relating to questions of purely sporting interest, which, as such, have nothing to do with economic activity.

The ECJ ruled that this was an error of law as 'the mere fact that a rule is purely sporting in nature does not have the effect of removing from the scope of the Treaty the person engaging in the activity governed by that rule or the body which has laid it down. If the sporting activity in question falls within the scope of the Treaty, the conditions for engaging in it are then subject to all the obligations which result from the various provisions of the Treaty' (paragraphs 27 and 28).

As Infantino (2006)[147] has argued, this opens the 'Pandora's box' of what constitutes a condition for engaging in sporting activity. There are many rules, which might be perceived as purely sporting rules in that they are designed to ensure fair play, which can also be regarded as constituting a condition for participating in a sport. The fears of judicial decision may in themselves be sufficient to induce sports authorities to reach a settlement to pre-empt or terminate litigation. The *Anelka* [see above], *Balog* and *Oulmers* cases provide important examples of litigation withdrawn for this reason.[148]

The essential problem is that long-established rules drawn up by sports regulatory bodies are now permanently subject to the vagaries of litigation. This generates uncertainly with respect both to the validity of particular rules and to whether any legal challenge to such rules will take place. In the context of stability and certainty it is arguably desirable that sports rules are given the sanctity of legal rules. This problem is encapsulated by debates over the legality

---

147 Infantino, G, 'Meca-Medina: a Step Backwards for the European Sports Model and the Specificity of Sport?' (2006) Sports Law Administration & Practice (Oct) 1.

148 In *Balog*, the ECJ had been asked to rule on whether applying transfer rules to out-of-contract players offended EU competition law and, if so, whether the protection of EU law extended to nationals of countries with third-party status. As had also been so with the *Anelka* case, this could have resulted in the transfer system being declared contrary to EU law. Indeed, *Balog* proceeded as far as being the subject of an Advocate General's Opinion before it was withdrawn. In *Oulmers*, litigation was initiated in the Belgian courts to test the validity of FIFA's rules concerning the obligatory release of players from clubs to national teams for international games. Although this resulted in a request for a preliminary ruling from the ECJ, the parties ultimately preferred to reach their own voluntary settlement which resulted in the disbanding of G14 and the establishment of a more complex management structure within European football involving UEFA and the newly created European Club Association (ECA).

of transfer systems under EU law and how legal intervention should best occur. One possibility, based on the model of EU social law, is to adopt a system of reflexive law which could be based on a modified version of the FIFA transfer rules.

Who rules? – the future

The transfer system is not in itself a legal construct given that its central regulatory mechanism is to enable clubs to restrain player mobility by retaining their registrations. However, the whole edifice of the transfer system is dependent on law insofar as it can be constrained, or indeed dismantled, by jurisprudential developments – in particular future rulings or decisions of the ECJ. Indeed, it may still be the case that the FIFA transfer rules will be challenged on the basis of Article 39 or EU competition law. Whilst there is no indication that such arguments will succeed, the ECJ is yet to rule on these issues, and there is never any guarantee that the Court will agree with the Commission's interpretation of what EU law requires or permits.

Ultimately, the determining factor will be whether the revised FIFA transfer system meets the requirement of proportionality. Arguably this is the case, given the circumstances in which a player is permitted to leave a club through unilaterally terminating his current contract in circumstances where the club will have no option other than to release that player's registration. However, it is acknowledged that there is some validity to the argument that any form of transfer system reduces players to mere chattels and thus can be regarded as offending the freedoms that lie at the core of EU law.

Whilst it cannot be guaranteed that the FIFA transfer rules are compatible with EU law, the *imminent* destruction of the transfer system by legal means appears improbable given that both the European Commission and FIFPro have approved the current FIFA transfer rules. Indeed, arguably, the maintenance of some form of transfer system has been reinforced and validated by the fact the FIFA rules have been accepted by FIFPro. Moreover, there is the potential for future modifications to be secured through collective bargaining rather than the product of judicial interventions (Branco-Martins, 2003).[149] Thus, for better or for worse, from a legal perspective it can be predicted that the transfer system in some form or another is here to stay for the foreseeable future. If the transfer system goes, this is more likely to be the result of economic rather than juridical factors . . .

. . . In his analysis of the application of regulatory theory to the employment relation, Collins (2000)[150] argues that external regulation is necessary where deregulated market mechanisms generate injustices and/or imbalances and private law fails to provide appropriate correctives. By analogy, it can be argued that self-regulation in professional football has distorted the market through a transfer system that both restrains players' freedom of movement and inflates transfer fees for players under contract who wish to move clubs. The application of the doctrine of restraint of trade, the availability of private law remedies such as injunctions and potential regulation by EU law are all characterised by juridical uncertainty.

Once justified, legal regulation can obviously take the form of detailed substantive rules. However, reflexive law provides an alternative to this approach . . . The advantage of reflexive law is that it enables a set of principles to be provided, that must be adhered to as a minimum, but permits delegation of detailed implementation to relevant bodies be they (as examples) national legislators or governing bodies of particular sports. A system of reflexive law can provide a compromise between ensuring that particular standards are complied with and respecting the autonomy of those concerned with operating a particular system or activity and

---

149 Branco-Martins, R, 'European Sport's First Collective Labour Agreement EFFC' (2003) ISLJ 1.
150 Collins, H, 'Justification and Techniques of Legal Regulation of the Employment Relation', in Collins, H, Davies, P and Rideout, R (eds) (2000), *The Legal Regulation of the Employment Relation*, London: Kluwer.

who understand the specificities involved. This presents a symbiotic relationship between normative rules within and without the particular activity in question . . .

Thus, as Wynn[151] (in Collins, 2000) has argued, reflexive law can be seen as the most appropriate form of legal regulation in any context where the relevant system or relationship is resistant to external intervention. Reflexive law can both reflect the norms of that system and impose modifications to those norms that can be enforced by legal means. This perspective seems to encapsulate the situation in football given the ongoing but intermittent tensions between self-regulation and external regulation.

It is contended that the best basis for resolving these tensions is by moving to a system of reflexive law using the method of EU social law as a paradigm. The advantage of EU social law is that it requires the involvement of the relevant social partners. Under Article 138 of the EC Treaty, the European Commission must engage in dialogue with the social partners as to the content of any proposed Directive. Moreover, Article 139 permits the relevant social partners to conclude their own collective agreements, which, if the social partners so request, may then be given legal force through an EC Directive . . . The advantage of these processes is obvious, as those directly affected by legal regulation become central to the formulation of the specific rules to be adopted. The role of law is reduced to acting as a mechanism for ensuring that agreed minimum standards are complied with.

As stated above, there is the possibility that a collective agreement regulating football could be entered into in the future. Arguably, this constitutes the ideal method of abolition or reform of the transfer system. However, if the conclusion of such an agreement were to prove impossible, at least in the shorter term, an EU Directive, laying down binding principles but leaving detailed implementation to footballing authorities, could provide the way forward. In our view such a Directive could take the FIFA transfer rules as its starting point.

This is not to suggest that the FIFA rules should be adopted in their entirety. Indeed, one possible basis for reform would be to abolish the registration system and permit clubs to use contractual mechanisms such as post-employment restraints or garden-leave clauses to impose some element of contract stability. This would have the advantage of ending a system where players are treated as assets and bought and sold by clubs accordingly. However, if the registration system were to go, it is clear from the above discussion that the circumstances in which UK courts should grant injunctions to enforce such clauses would have to be put on a statutory basis rather than left to judicial discretion. The FIFA rules permitting contract-jumping, but also limiting the circumstances in which it is permitted through the concept of a contract's protected period, could provide the basis for determining when statutory injunctions should be granted.

Similarly, the concept of contract termination for sporting just cause, as contained in the FIFA rules, should be incorporated into any Directive. Post-employment restraints and 'garden leave' clauses would thus cease to be enforceable not only in circumstances in which a player could terminate his contract for due cause, but also in contexts in which for sporting reasons a player should be permitted to leave his current club. The latter could be defined as including circumstances in which a player (whilst fit) has not been selected for *x* number of first team games, and where a player is informed, or has good reason to believe, that he is no longer wanted by his current club.

As argued by Gardiner and Welch (1998),[152] there will be circumstances in which the way in which a player is treated by his club constitutes destruction of mutual trust and confidence, and

---

151 Wynn, M, 'European Social Dialogue: Harmonisation or New Diversity', in Collins, H, Davies, P and Rideout, R (eds) (2000), *The Legal Regulation of the Employment Relation*, London: Kluwer.

152 Gardiner, S and Welch, R, 'The Winds of Change in Professional Football: The Impact of the Bosman Ruling' (1998) 3(4) Contemporary Issues in Law 289, 302–03.

thus that player can argue that he has been constructively dismissed and immediately terminate his contract for just cause. However, simply informing a player that the club would be prepared to release him at the right price is unlikely in itself to constitute any breach of contract, let alone one which is repudiatory in nature. Nevertheless, it can be argued that this should justify unilateral termination by the player on the basis of sporting just cause.

It is important to understand that, whilst such contractual mechanisms might replace the formal transfer system and thus the notion of a formal transfer fee, it would not end what in effect is the buying and selling of players. This is because, for both sporting and financial reasons, many players under contract will wish to move to another club, or will be happy to do so if the right deal, including an appropriate signing-on fee, can be struck. In such circumstances players, let alone clubs, will not want the complications that litigation tends to involve. In practice, therefore, whether a player can move will often be down to whether the new club is prepared to buy out the existing contract. As argued above, the sum of money involved may or may not reflect the compensation a court might award for breach of contract, as the actual sum may be more linked to commercial and sporting considerations than to formal legal principles. In short, the buying out of a player's contract would be a transfer fee by any other name. Such arrangements already take place with respect to managers and coaches; they would simply be more frequent with respect to players.

The main drawback with the above approach is that litigation becomes the ultimate enforcement mechanism. This will often be costly, and in all probability will continue to contain an element of uncertainty. The alternative would be to leave the registration system intact whilst providing for appropriate rights to contract-jump on the basis of the FIFA rules. This would end the transfer system as it currently operates in the UK's domestic leagues, and would introduce the concept of contract termination for sporting due cause into the domestic system.

One possible variation to the current FIFA rules would be, on the expiry of a contract's protected period or where the contract is terminated for sporting just cause, to permit contract-jumping *during* a season if a player has negotiated a move to a club which is in a different league, and which is thus not in competition with his current club. The normal rules relating to such a player being cup-tied could continue to apply as far as cup competitions are concerned. Such a change should also reduce the complexities involved in the implementation of Article 17, as demonstrated by the '*Webster* case' [see above].

It is true that this would leave intact a transfer system, which some will continue to find objectionable. However, as we have sought to demonstrate, unless players are given an absolute right to terminate their contracts unilaterally, any legal mechanism to secure some degree of contract stability will result in some form of transfer system, albeit an informal one, if players under contract are to be able to move to other clubs.

Moreover, it is important to take account of the fact that contract stability is not only the concern of clubs as employers. It is at least equally the concern of those large numbers of people who are normally forgotten in debates on the issues with which this article has been concerned. These people are the loyal football fans who almost from cradle to grave invest in their clubs at great personal expense – both financial and emotional – and who deserve some guarantee that *their* star players cannot simply walk out of *their* club at will because they have received a better offer elsewhere.

Conclusions

The ongoing issues concerning the dynamics of contractual relations reflect tensions concerning the right to govern in football. It would seem that some accord has been reached between the football authorities (in the form of UEFA and FIFA) and external regulators (such as the European Commission and the ECJ), though this could yet be challenged by the outcome of the *'Oulmers'* litigation – particularly in the light of the *Meca-Medina* ruling. Indeed, as has been argued above, it cannot be concluded that the existing consensus as represented by the FIFA transfer rules will definitely be able to withstand legal challenge. It is suggested that sports bodies, at least at an international level, have taken legal compliance seriously and have indicated that they are prepared to develop effective internal governance. In turn, the external regulators have provided some delineation in the sand as to the limits of their intervention. The threat to this world of re-regulated sports bodies comes primarily from commercial interests who are motivated by self-interest and financial greed rather than 'the good of the game'. Perhaps it is the time for the regulators to support the sports bodies in this regard. Surely, the optimum way in which this can be done is by encouraging a systematic basis for regulation throughout Europe based on the method of reflexive law rather than relying on the vagaries of individual litigation?

It is contended that the essential principles underlying such regulation, either through collective agreement or EU legislation, should be:

- Provision within all European Associations for unilateral termination of a contract by a player after the expiry of a protected period, or for 'sporting just cause'.
- Permitting players to approach other clubs in any European Association in the latter stages of their contracts, or towards the end of a contract's protected period.
- The abolition (or extensive liberalisation of transfer windows) – both within and between European Associations.[153]

Key Points

- Only sports participants who have employee status enjoy statutory employment protection rights such as unfair dismissal rights. Players, coaches and managers employed by clubs in professional team sports are employees.
- Only sports participants who have employee status will be protected by a contractual duty imposed on the employing club to maintain mutual trust and confidence.
- Breach of this implied contractual duty, as illustrated by Kevin Keegan's claim against Newcastle United FC, will enable managers and players to secure compensation for constructive wrongful and/or unfair dismissal.
- A player with one year's service can claim unfair dismissal if dismissed during the currency of the contract, or, as illustrated by the Chris Schofield case, the contract is not renewed on its expiry.
- As held in the *Eastham* case, the transfer system is not a restraint of trade under English law.
- Sporting rules prohibiting players under contract from talking to other clubs could be a restraint of trade and/or a restriction of freedom of movement in violation of Article 45 TFEU.
- As a result of the *Bosman* ruling, out-of-contract players over the age of 24 have an absolute right to move to another club, and a transfer fee cannot be required.
- Under the FIFA international transfer rules, a player under contract can move to another club in a different country at the end of a season if the protected period of his contract has expired, provided due compensation is paid to his club.
- Under the FIFA transfer rules, a player can move to another club in a different country at the end of a season, on the grounds of sporting just cause, provided due compensation is paid to his club.

---

153 Gardiner, S and Welch, R, 'The Contractual Dynamics of Team Stability Versus Player Mobility: Who Rules "The Beautiful Game"?' (2007) 5(1) ESLJ.

● Issues such as the legality of the transfer system could best be resolved by collective agreement, or an EU directive, based on a system of reflexive law.

Key Sources

Blanpain, R and Inston, R, *The Bosman Case The End of the Transfer System?* (1996), London: Sweet & Maxwell; Leuven: Peeters.

Gardiner, S and Welch, R, 'The Contractual Dynamics of Team Stability Versus Player Mobility: Who Rules "The Beautiful Game"?' (2007), 5(1) Entertainment and Sports Law Journal.

McCutcheon, P, 'Negative Enforcement of Employment Contracts in the Sports Industries' (1997), 17(1) Legal Studies 65–100.

Opinion of Advocate General Lenz in *ASBL Union Royale Belge des Societes de Football Association & others v Jean-Marc Bosman* [1996] 1 CMLR 645 (Case C-415/93).

Welch, R, 'Player Mobility, the FIFA Transfer Rules and Freedom of Movement' (2006), International Sports Law Review 83.

Chapter 10

Sports Participants and the Law of Discrimination

Chapter Contents

Introduction	461
Unlawful Discrimination	465
Unlawful Harassment	477
Discrimination and European Law	483
Key Points	496
Key Sources	497

Introduction

In 2010 the Equality Act came into effect and this Act replaced the old system of discrimination law where each form of unlawful discrimination was regulated by legislation specific to it. Section 4 of the Equality Act identifies the characteristics protected by the Act as:

- age;
- disability;
- gender reassignment;
- marriage and civil partnership;
- pregnancy and maternity;
- race;
- religion or belief;
- sex;
- sexual orientation.

The world of sport remains a highly segregated one – particularly between men and women and those who are fully able and disabled. With respect to the latter, events such as the Paralympics and the London Marathon notwithstanding, professional sport is predominantly and inevitably restricted to the fully abled – indeed generally to the super fit. Therefore, disability discrimination will not be fully discussed as part of this chapter, although its provisions do of course apply to those employed by clubs in a variety of positions not concerned with sports participation.[1] However, the extent to which reasonable adjustments should be made to enable disabled persons to participate in a sport will be examined below.

Similarly, ageism will not be fully examined. Typically, in society, the victims of ageism are youth and the middle-aged to elderly. In professional sport there is for obvious reasons a fundamental interest in spotting and nurturing young talent, and, as referred to in the previous chapter, sports have regulations and contracts in place designed to protect young persons. Again, for obvious reasons, those entering early middle age will not normally be able to maintain the levels of personal fitness required to continue as professionals in team sports such as cricket, football and rugby. The statutory provisions relating to age have no exceptions now that the default retirement age of 65 has been abolished. However, what would otherwise normally constitute age discrimination where an individual is compelled to retire below this age can be objectively justified (see below pp 470–1) and thus lawful. Normally, such justification will be available to professional clubs. Age, of course, is not a significant factor in being employed as a manager or coach. It remains to be seen whether match officials will be able to challenge compulsory retirement. For example, professional football referees must currently retire at the age of 48.[2]

Inroads have been made in the context of race as more and more professional sportsmen (but not women) come from the Afro-Caribbean and Asian communities. However, there is more than a nagging suspicion that racism remains an issue in sport, albeit for different sports in different ways – the lack of professional footballers of Asian origin being a clear example. It is disturbing that the article below, which was published in 1994, would still be accurate if published for the first time today.

---

1 For possible potential implications of the Act for sports participants with specific disabilities, such as heart complaints or diabetes, see Bitel, N and Bloohn, J, 'Fair play for disabled people in sport' (1997) 5(1) SATLJ 8–11.

2 The nature of professional sport means that compulsory retirement is not the issue that it is in most sectors of employment. However, it was generally thought that Jeff Winter was not 'over the moon' at being forced to retire from professional football refereeing at 48. Similarly, there was speculation that Pierlugi Collina, regarded at the time by many as the best football referee in the world, might officiate in the Premiership as a result of being too old at the age of 45 to continue to referee international matches – see *The Daily Mail*, 29 January 2004.

Chaudhary, V, 'Asians can play football, too'

Why is there no Indian or Pakistani John Barnes playing the professional game? When the Premier League season kicks off on Saturday, there will not be a single professional footballer of Asian origin on the field around the country. While Afro-Caribbean players continue to make their mark in the highest echelons of the game, both at a domestic and international level, Asian players have remained largely invisible. Black players make up almost 20 per cent of the 2,000 professionals currently playing in the Premier and Football Leagues. But the prospect of an Asian John Barnes remains as distant as England winning the World Cup.

There are currently around 60 Asian footballers playing in semi-professional high-level amateur teams and six professional apprentices of Asian origin. But that's about it. Just why there is a dearth of Asian professionals is an enigma. If racism is endemic within football, why do black players do so well?

A project due to begin at the end of August will examine how and why Asians are being overlooked by the football industry. The project is backed by the Sports Council and the Commission for Racial Equality. Raj Patel, aged 35, and Jas Bains, aged 31, the project directors, were both keen amateur footballers in the Midlands and gained first-hand experience of how Asian footballers are marginalised. Bains says: 'Scouts never watch the Asian teams play, and Asian players are hardly ever asked for trials. When I was playing, old stereotypes, like Asians aren't big enough and can't physically compete, were always mentioned. It's just nonsense.'

. . . Both men believe it is not simply a matter of racism. The problem, they claim, lies between stereotyping of Asian players at all levels of the game and a reticence towards professional sport by older members of the Asian community. Unlike the black communities in Britain and America, sport has never been seen as a path to improving social status. Asian parents have, traditionally, coaxed their children towards commerce or professions like law or medicine.

. . . However, they maintain that the crux of the problem lies in the attitude of coaches, managers and scouts. One young Asian footballer, who had trials at Chelsea, says: 'From the moment I got on the pitch I didn't stand a chance. I got abused by other players and was played out of position by the coach. Maybe I didn't have the talent to make it, but how do I know when I was never given fair treatment?'

Sally Westwood, a senior lecturer at Leicester University and a member of the research advisory group for the project, spent several weeks studying a mixed Asian–Afro-Caribbean football team in 1991. She says: 'The stereotyping of Asian players is linked with the way South Asians are seen as culturally more different. White society sees them as "not like us", whereas Afro-Caribbeans are seen as conforming more to North European values.' She found that while some black players in the team were offered trials with Leicester City, Asian players of similar ability were overlooked.

Patel and Bains are confident that the football industry will eventually recognise the wealth of talent in the Asian community. After all, they maintain, it's less than 10 years since 12 English first division managers said – in an article by the *Sunday Times*'s Rob Hughes – they would not sign a black player because 'they lack bottle, are no good in the mud and have no stamina'. Back in 1975 not a single black player represented England at any level and there were fewer than 20 black professionals.

'We are not asking for special treatment, just a chance for our youngsters to be given a fair chance,' says Bains . . .[3]

---

3   Vivek Chaudhary, 'Asians can play football, too' *The Guardian*, 17 August 1994. It is a matter of concern that this piece is as pertinent today as when it was first written ten years ago.

The problem of racism is of course partly, but only partly, derived from the attitudes of sections of the paying public. That issue is beyond the scope of this chapter.[4] The concern here is for the more covert forms of racism and other forms of discrimination that may exist at the level of the sports club as an employer. Moreover, the institutions and structures of sport are such that the law as it stands can play only a limited role in regulating and eroding discriminatory attitudes and practices. This section is thus as much about the limits of the law as the protection it provides. This is particularly the case with the huge gulf in status which exists between men and women participants in sports such as football, rugby, cricket and indeed, albeit to a lesser extent, in tennis and golf. Again, although women's professional football can today be viewed on satellite and cable sports channels, times have not fundamentally changed since the article below was published in 1997.

Williams, J, 'Support for all?'

According to FIFA, 20 million women play organised football worldwide. In Scandinavia, where views about women as athletes, and almost anything else, are at least post-Jurassic, football is the most popular sport for females. Most local clubs cater for both male and female teams and foreign stars such as the USA's Michelle Akers are brought over to join semi-professional ranks. No surprise, then, that Norway won the recent women's World Cup in Sweden and that they and Denmark are as tough as they come in international competition. England? Well, you reap what you sow; in Sweden we were simply outclassed by, no avoiding it now, the Germans.

. . . And what, generally of the women's game today? Well, things looked ready for major take off as far back as 1989. Then, Channel 4, looking for cheap and 'exotic' alternatives to mainstream sport, showed the Women's FA Cup Final. This was pre-Sky, of course, and fans, 2.5 million of them, a record for sport on C4, gobbled it up . . .

Now? Well, serious TV coverage has pretty much disappeared. *Serie A* arrived on C4. The BBC, desperate for soccer action, disgracefully provided the barest highlights of the recent women's World Cup and always around midnight. On Sky you can watch Northern Ireland v Scotland schoolboys live to your heart's content, but no female coverage. Why is at least some female coverage not part of the new TV deal? . . . Without media coverage, serious sponsorship for the women's game is pretty much out of the question.

Whilst some clubs, like Southampton, have taken female teams on board, here again progress is slow and uneven. Only Arsenal offer female players a full-time paid coach/manager and a real level of integration into the male club. Not surprisingly, the Arsenal women have produced recent successes, and media coverage, to match this commitment. A few others – Wimbledon, Millwall, Wolves – have shown a real interest in the women's game and cash and staff support to match . . .

But, at best, even large professional clubs still tend to offer a kit, use of some gym space and the occasional mention in the matchday magazine in the hope that some women will keep out of their hair and provide the club with some good PR. And, off the WFCs troop to the park or local leisure complex to perform in front of 60 to 100 diehard fans and family members who can manage to track down the kick-off time. The 'blue riband' Women's FA Cup Final still struggles for a prestige venue (recently, Crewe, Watford, Oxford, Tranmere, Millwall) while, recently, the German women's final took place immediately before the men's equivalent in the Olympic Stadium, Berlin. Ho hum.

This all provides for real equivocation about the development of the top level of the women's game here. Is the FA devoting enough resources to the women's game? Are we really improving and what, exactly, is the plan? . . .

---

4 The 'Kick It Out' (originally 'Let's Kick Racism Out of Football') campaign, established by the Commission for Racial Equality in conjunction with the Professional Footballers' Association, is primarily concerned with combating racism amongst football supporters. For an account of the Campaign, see 'Kicking racism out of football' (1995) 84(4) Labour Research. Also see pp 477–83.

. . . The PFA's Community programme has done some great work in promoting football for girls over the past few years and in starting up female teams in connection with professional clubs. We have female players who could inspire the next generation. Kerry Davies and Hope Powell of Croydon and their former team mates Brenda Sempare, Doncaster captain Gillian Coulthard, and the charismatic Marianne Spacey of Arsenal have all served the women's game here with verve and distinction. We need them, and others, *working* in English football as coaches. Is anybody listening? You do *want* to beat the Germans, don't you?[5]

The issue of sports bodies discriminating against women participating in a sport was at the heart of the case of *Sagen v Vancouver Organizing Committee for the 2010 Olympic and Paralympic Winter Games*, in which a group of 15 highly ranked female ski jumpers from five countries brought a claim against the Vancouver Organizing Committee for the 2010 Winter Games (VANOC), contending that a female ski jumping event should be included in the Games, just as it is for men. Their argument, which was rejected by the court, was that because VANOC planned, organised, financed and staged the ski jumping events for men, failure to offer an equal event for women was an infringement of women's equality rights as protected under Section 15(1) of the Canadian Charter of Rights and Freedoms.[6]

Arguably, sexism in professional sport will continue until male athletes' attitudes to women in general change. The feminist journalist Beatrix Campbell has commented that, although racism may have successfully been challenged in the world of professional football, sexism is still rife and unchecked. This is shown by the private behaviour of footballers, and the relaxed attitudes of club managements to such behaviour. In the words of Campbell:

Campbell, B., 'Time to kick sexism out of football'

But for all the sound and fury, footballers' misogyny is apparently sanctioned. When footballers sexually exploit women, go to lap dancing clubs, buy sex or 'harvest' local girls to line them up for shagging parties, it still doesn't count, somehow, as sexism . . .

Sexism may not yet be recognised for what it is, but something about masculine attitudes to morality is shifting on the terraces. Men taking their kids to the game don't want them to hear the c-word any more than they want to hear the n-word.

But if there is a critique of sordid, cheating, whoring sexism, then it isn't coming from the places with the institutional power to do something about it: club management.[7]

Hidden attitudes to women in football on the part of leading figures within the game were revealed by recorded off-camera comments by Sky commentators, Richard Keys and Andy Gray in January 2011. They questioned the ability of a female assistant referee understand the offside rule. In fact, Sian Massey, the assistant referee concerned, was subsequently to get a key offside decision right in the game between Wolverhampton Wanderers and Liverpool to allow a goal by the Liverpool striker, Fernando Torres. They also criticised Wendy Toms, who in the late 1990s was the first female assistant referee in the Premier League, as well as making a sarcastic comment about Karren Brady, the deputy chair of West Ham.[8]

---

5 Williams, J, 'Support for all?', *When Saturday Comes* (1997), 121 (March), 32–33. Since the publication of this article there has been some greater interest displayed by the media in women's football – particularly on dedicated sports television channels. However, there is still a long way to go before women's football will have anywhere near the same status as the established professional game.

6 [2009] BCSC 942 (Sup Ct (BC). For a comprehensive discussion of this case and the background to it see Patel, S, 'Gender Issues: Women's Ski Jumping and Olympic programme inclusion' (2009) 18(7) WSLR.

7 Campbell, B, 'Time to kick sexism out of football', *The Guardian*, 6 September 2010.

8 See Booth, R, 'Sky's top football team in sexist rant against official', *The Guardian*, 24 January 2011. The incident is reminiscent of the off-camera remark by Ron Atkinson about the black player, Marcel Desailly – see below, fn 52.

The fact that sports bodies formally take issues of discrimination seriously (even if they do not always do so in practice) is illustrated by the FA's Equality policy.

FA Equality Policy

The FA is responsible for setting standards and values to apply throughout football at every level. Football belongs to, and should be enjoyed by, anyone who wants to participate in it. The aim of this policy is to ensure that everyone is treated fairly and with respect and that The FA is equally accessible to them all.

The FA's commitment is to confront and eliminate discrimination whether by reason of gender, sexual orientation, marital status, race, nationality, ethnic origin, colour, religion or belief, ability or disability and to encourage equal opportunities.

This policy is fully supported by the Board of The FA and the Director of Football Governance and Regulation is responsible for the implementation of this policy.

The FA, in all its activities, will not discriminate, or in any way treat anyone less favourably, on grounds of gender, sexual orientation, marital status, race, nationality, ethnic origin, colour, religion or belief, ability or disability.

The FA will ensure that it treats people fairly and with respect and that it provide access and opportunities for all members of the community to take part in, and enjoy, its activities.

The FA will not tolerate harassment, bullying, abuse or victimisation of an individual, which for the purposes of this policy and the actions and sanction applicable is regarded as discrimination. This includes sexual or racially based harassment or other discriminatory behaviour, whether physical or verbal. The FA will work to ensure that such behaviour is met with appropriate action in whatever context it occurs.

The FA is committed to the development of a programme of ongoing training and awareness-raising events and activities in order to promote the eradication of discrimination within football.

The FA is committed to a policy of equal treatment of all members and requires all members to abide and adhere to this policy and the requirements of the following (but not limited to) equalities legislation – Equality Act 2006, Race Relations Act 1976, Sex Discrimination Act 1975 and Disability Discrimination Act 1995 as well as various amendments to these acts.

The FA commits itself to the immediate investigation of any claims, when it is brought to their attention, of discrimination on the above grounds and where such is found to be the case, a requirement that the practice stop and sanctions be imposed as appropriate.

Unlawful Discrimination

In terms of understanding the legal framework for combating discrimination it is necessary to understand that in the contexts of sex, race, sexual orientation and religion or belief discrimination may be direct or indirect. For the sake of clarity these different forms of discrimination will be discussed with reference to gender and race, and cases, decided under the Sex Discrimination Act 1975 (SDA) and Race Relations Act 1976 (RRA), which remain of relevance in interpreting the Equality Act 2010 (EA), will be discussed.

Under s 13 of the EA an employer discriminates on grounds of sex if it treats a woman differently to a man or vice versa. Under s 9 race includes colour, nationality and national or ethnic origins. The meaning of ethnic origins has been determined by the House of Lords.

Mandla v Dowell Lee

Lord Fraser: . . . It is not suggested that Sikhs are a group defined by reference to colour, race, nationality or national origins. In none of these respects are they distinguishable from many other groups, especially those living, like most Sikhs, in the Punjab. The argument turns entirely upon whether they are a group defined by 'ethnic origins' . . .

For a group to constitute an ethnic group in the sense of the Act of 1976, it must, in my opinion, regard itself, and be regarded by others, as a distinct community by virtue of certain characteristics. Some of these characteristics are essential; others are not essential but one or more of them will commonly be found and will help to distinguish the group from the surrounding community. The conditions which appear to me to be essential are these: (1) a long shared history, of which the group is conscious as distinguishing it from other groups, and the memory of which it keeps alive; (2) a cultural tradition of its own, including family and social customs and manners, often but not necessarily associated with religious observance. In addition to those two essential characteristics the following characteristics are, in my opinion, relevant; (3) either a common geographical origin, or descent from a small number of common ancestors; (4) a common language, not necessarily peculiar to the group; (5) a common literature peculiar to the group; (6) a common religion different from that of neighbouring groups or from the general community surrounding it; (7) being a minority or being an oppressed or a dominant group within a larger community, for example a conquered people (say, the inhabitants of England shortly after the Norman conquest) and their conquerors might both be ethnic groups.[9]

Section 10 of the EA prohibits discrimination by reference to a person's religious or philosophical belief (this includes a lack of religious belief). This form of discrimination is primarily relevant to sport in the context of race, as discrimination overtly manifested by reference to religion can be motivated by racism. This has always been the case with anti-Semitism – for example, the blood libel against the Jews. In football, the hostility between Glasgow Rangers and Celtic, in modern times at least, has much more to do with difference in national origins than with theological differences. Currently, Islamophobia constitutes the most disturbing phenomenon of racism expressed through religious metaphors. Islamophobia is most virulently promoted by the English Defence League (EDL), and this is important to sport because of the overt relationship between the EDL and many 'firms' of football hooligans (see below, p 478). World religions such as Islam, and indeed Christianity, cross national and racial boundaries, and will thus be outside the scope of s 9 EA, but adherents to these religions will be protected by s 10. It is also possible for discrimination to occur in sport purely by reference to a person's religion.[10] It should be noted that s 14 EA recognises the problem of combined discrimination, that is, where a person is discriminated against on more than one of the protected grounds; for example on grounds of both race and religion.[11]

The scope of unlawful discrimination in employment covers arrangements for recruiting employees; refusal of employment; the terms on which employment is offered; opportunities for promotion or training; access to benefits, facilities or services; dismissal; subjection to any detriment. Unlike the Employment Rights Act, protection is not restricted to 'employees' but covers employment under a contract 'personally to execute any work or labour' – s 83(1) EA. This extension of the meaning of 'employment' is of obvious importance in sport, as it covers any competition or sponsorship deal that involves a sportsman or sportswoman entering into a contract to

---

9 [1983] ICR 385 HL, at p 390. Applying the above test the Law Lords decided that Sikhs were an ethnic as against simply a religious group. Similarly: Jews (*Seide v Gillette Industries* [1980] IRLR 427); Gypsies (*CRE v Dutton* [1989] QB 783); and the Welsh have an ethnic status different to that of the wider Afro-Caribbean community (*Dawkins v Department of the Environment* [1993] IRLR 284). However, Rastafarians are protected by s 10 EA, which covers discrimination by reference to a person's religion or beliefs.

10 For example, the rules in amateur boxing have recently been changed so that Sikhs are no longer exempt from the requirement for fighters to be clean – see Cottrell, S, 'Boxing: Freedom of Religion and Rules on Safety' (2010) 8(20) WSLR. This problem has arisen in ordinary employment law where hygiene regulations have prevented Sikhs from being employed in food production – see *Panesar v Nestlé* [1980] ICR 144.

11 At the time of writing, the provision had not been brought into force.

perform – be it in a match or a marketing activity. The legislation also prohibits discrimination by qualifying bodies that can confer authorisation or qualification for engagement in a particular trade. This covers sporting authorities that are empowered to restrict participation in professional sport to those to whom a licence has been granted by the authority concerned. This is illustrated by the successful case brought by the boxer, Jane Couch (see below, pp 472–3).

The essential difference with respect to most forms of discrimination is between direct and indirect discrimination.

Direct discrimination

Section 13(1) of the Equality Act 2010

A person (A) discriminates against another (B) if, because of a protected characteristic, A treats B less favourably than A treats or would treat others.

In *James v Eastleigh Borough Council*[12] the House of Lords decided that Mr James was directly discriminated against when he was charged a higher price than his wife for admission to a swimming pool. The sole reason for the differential treatment was that the concessionary cheaper price was for pensioners only. Although Mr and Mrs James were both aged 61 she was a pensioner and he was not. Clearly, there was no discriminatory intent and motive on the part of the Council. Nevertheless, but for the fact that Mr James was a man he would have been treated the same as his wife.

As a result of the 'but for' test direct discrimination is in theory easier to establish as it is not necessary to establish an intention to discriminate and direct discrimination cannot be justified. However, there is a very real practical difficulty with regard to proof. As a result of an EC Directive[13] the burden of proof formally shifts to the employer where the evidence enables the tribunal to draw inferences of discrimination. Where this is the case, the tribunal must find discrimination proven if the employer is not able to provide an adequate explanation of his decisions or actions by reference to non-discriminatory factors.

However, the employer might be able to show that the decision not to appoint the applicant was taken for grounds that are not discriminatory, such as the applicant's perceived personality. Indeed, it is the fact that subjective value-judgements are so inherently connected to employers' decisions over matters such as recruitment and promotion that makes a direct discrimination claim so hard to win. Even where there is evidence of discrimination, as a result of what the employer writes or says, a claim is not guaranteed of success.

In *Saunders v Richmond Borough Council*[14] the applicant, a former women's golf champion, was rejected for the post of professional golf coach. Despite questions such as: 'So you'd be blazing a trail, would you? Do you think men respond as well to a woman golf professional as to a man?; If all this is true, you are obviously a lady of great experience, but don't you think this type of job is rather unglamorous?', she was not able to prove sex discrimination. Possibly the tribunal was influenced by the fact that the interviewer was a woman. Nevertheless, the reasoning is that there are cases when it is appropriate or at least permissible to inquire into whether a person's gender, or race/ethnic grouping, may affect their suitability for a particular job.

The case of *Singh*[15] provides an example of how direct race discrimination may succeed as a result of a tribunal drawing inferences of discrimination. The basis of Mr Singh's complaint was that he was withdrawn from the Football League's 'National List' of referees at the end of the 1998/99

---

12 [1990] ICR 554.
13 To implement EC Directive 97/900 the Sex Discrimination (Indirect Discrimination and Burden of Proof) Regulations 2001 No 2660 inserted a new s 63A into the SDA. This formal shift in the burden of proof now applies to all areas of discrimination law under s 135 EA.
14 [1977] IRLR 362.
15 See previous Chapter p 395.

season and thus ceased to be eligible to referee professional football matches. At this time he was the only person of Asian ethnic origin on the List. The reason given for the decision not to re-appoint him was that there had been a marked deterioration in his position on the merit list over the previous three years. Singh denied that there had been any such deterioration in his performance and successfully claimed direct race discrimination under s 1 of the RRA against the Football League.

Part of Singh's argument was that there is a subculture in professional football that generates institutionalised (and often unconscious) racism. The tribunal decided that it was unable to take judicial notice of the submission that a racially biased and stereotyped perception of Asians existed in high circles in football. Nevertheless, it was able to accept that there was evidence that individual respondents in this particular case were influenced by a stereotypical assumption that the applicant could never be a top-performing referee by virtue of his ethnic origin. Relevant evidence here included a comment by one of the individual respondents, who was Secretary of the National Review Board[16] established to ensure consistency of refereeing, that 'We don't want people like him [Mr Singh] in the PL [Premier League]'. This comment was viewed as a race-specific statement by the tribunal and, as such, formed part of the evidence that led to the tribunal deciding that there had been a sustained 'whispering campaign' against Singh from which the inference of racism could be drawn. Consequently, though Singh was unable to prove that his ethnic origin was the specific reason for his removal from the National List, the tribunal was able to accept his complaint of direct race discrimination on the basis that a hypothetical white referee, with the same perform-ance record as Singh, would not have been so treated.

A similar result was reached in the case of the rugby player Paul Sterling against Leeds Rhinos Rugby League Club. Sterling was 36 years old and towards the end of his career. In early 2000, the team's coach decided that he had six players from whom to choose two for the wing position where Sterling played, that the applicant was sixth in order of preference and that he would not be picked that season. Stirling brought a claim for direct race discrimination, and the tribunal decided that it was proper to draw an inference that the principal reason for the decision not to allow the applicant the chance to compete for a place in the first team was the applicant's racial origin. The tribunal noted that the team coach had indicated that Afro-Caribbean players were not as well suited to playing rugby league in Australia. Moreover, at the tribunal hearing the coach had stated that 'those boys' played basketball and other sports and the tribunal members interpreted this as re-inforcing evidence of racial bias. It is worth noting that the club was liable despite the fact that it had a policy entitled 'Tackle it' against racism and had incorporated equal opportunities clauses into employment contracts. Thus, this case also illustrates that it is not sufficient to adopt paper policies: clubs must ensure that such policies are implemented in practice.[17]

The definition of direct discrimination in the EA is drafted so as, other than in the context of discrimination related to marriage or civil partnership, to include associative and perceptive discrimination. In the context of disability discrimination, for example, this would protect an athlete who was also a carer for a disabled child if he or she was subjected to discriminatory treat-ment because of the child's disability. Similarly, an athlete who is subjected to discrimination because he or she is perceived to be gay or a transsexual will succeed in a claim even though the perception is inaccurate.

---

16 The National Review Board was also one of the respondents in the case as it is this body that decides which referees should be added to or removed from the National List. It was thus liable under s 12 of the RRA. This section regulates bodies that can confer authorisation or qualification. It is interesting to note that another part of the evidence from which the tribunal inferred racism was that officials of the NRB denied there was any racism in football beyond racist abuse from the terraces. This was despite the fact that the FA's 'Kick It Out' campaign recognises the under-representation of certain ethnic groups in the game. Thus the tribunal refused to believe that individual respondents were 'colour blind' when it came to decisions concerning the refereeing of matches.

17 See Case 1802453/00, *Sterling v Leeds Rugby League Club and Others* (2000) (ET) as discussed in (2000) 4(2) Sports Law Bulletin 3.

Indirect discrimination

The statutory definition of indirect discrimination is contained in s 19 of the Act.

Section 19 Equality Act 2010

(1) A person (A) discriminates against another (B) if A applies to B a provision, criterion or practice which is discriminatory in relation to a relevant protected characteristic of B's.

(2) For the purposes of subsection (1), a provision, criterion or practice is discriminatory in relation to a relevant protected characteristic of B's if—

(a) A applies, or would apply, it to persons with whom B does not share the characteristic,

(b) it puts, or would put, persons with whom B shares the characteristic at a particular disadvantage when compared with persons with whom B does not share it,

(c) it puts, or would put, B at that disadvantage, and

(d) A cannot show it to be a proportionate means of achieving a legitimate aim.

The case of *Holmes v Home Office* provides a good illustration of the concept of indirect discrimination. Holmes exercised her right to statutory maternity leave but decided not to exercise her statutory right to return on a full-time basis. Rather, she requested that she be permitted to return to her job on a part-time basis and this request was denied. This constituted indirect sex discrimination as the way in which child care typically operates in this society means that the number of working mothers who can satisfy a requirement to work full-time is substantially fewer than the number of working fathers who can do so. The Home Office was unable to justify this refusal to allow Holmes to work part-time and she won her claim of unlawful indirect sex discrimination.

It is clear that any policy or practice of an employer can form the basis of an indirect discrimination claim. Almost certainly, restrictive interpretations under the old legislation, which stated that failure to meet an employer's criteria must constitute an 'absolute bar' to appointment etc., have ceased to be applicable.[18]

Much difficulty has surrounded the 'pool of comparison' a tribunal should use in determining whether indirect discrimination has occurred. The approach to be followed (in sex discrimination cases) was set out by the Court of Appeal in *Jones v University of Manchester*.[19]

First, the relevant totals are all women (WT) and all men (MT) who would qualify were it not for the requirement or condition complained of. It is then necessary to calculate in percentage terms what proportion of women in their group (WY) do comply in comparison to the number of men in their group who do so (MY). This is achieved by dividing WT into WY and MT into MY and converting the figures into percentages.

For example:

WT = 50, WY = 25; MT = 50, MY = 45
WY is 50% of WT and MY is 90% of MT

This reveals that as a percentage the proportion of the former (WY) is considerably smaller then the proportion of the latter (MY). On this basis there is indirect discrimination. There was no doubt that a similar method was to be used in all cases of alleged indirect discrimination.

---

18 See *Perera v Civil Service Commission* [1983] ICR 428. However, this approach was rejected by the EAT in *Falkirk Council v Whyte* [1997] IRLR 560. In the EAT's view if particular criteria were in practice 'decisive factors' in a selection process then they should be regarded as constituting a 'requirement or condition' within the meaning of the old s 1(1)(b) of the Sex Discrimination Act.

19 [1993] IRLR 218.

Whilst this approach conformed with the words of the old s 1(1)(b) of the Sex Discrimination Act, it did permit the possibility of allowing requirements to be imposed which might have a discriminatory impact against women. For example, Jones argued that an age requirement discriminated against women, as women mature students tend to graduate at an older age than their male counterparts. The court took the view that the pool of comparison was all graduates with relevant experience. Mature students were merely a sub-group within this pool, not a pool of comparison in their own right.

It remains to be clarified whether the current definitions of indirect discrimination will require a more flexible and less restrictive approach to be taken. However, it is likely that the position adopted by the Court of Appeal in *London Underground v Edwards*[20] represents the approach to be taken under the EA. Edwards was employed by London Underground as a train driver. The workforce was predominantly male and Edwards was the only single mother. As such she was unable to work a new shift system introduced by London Underground. The Court refused to regard the workforce as the appropriate pool of comparison and found that she had been indirectly discriminated against on the basis that the majority of single parents are mothers.

Even where indirect discrimination is so established the employer may be able to justify it. The test for justification is derived from EC law as propounded by the European Court of Justice in *Bilka-Kaufhaus Gmbh v Weber von Hartz*.[21] The employer must establish:

- that there is an objective economic or operational need for the discriminatory practice; and
- the discriminatory effects are no greater than necessary to secure the employer's objectives.

The requirement of proportionality means that even where an employer can establish genuine commercial objectives the discrimination will not be justified if the objectives can be secured by other non-discriminatory means, or if the discriminatory policy etc. produces merely marginal advantages. Thus, in the *Edwards* case, although the new system did enhance efficiency London Underground failed in its plea of justification as it disproportionately impacted on Edwards, who was forced to give up her job. The efficiency gains secured by the new shift system would not have been undermined if London Underground had exempted Edwards from it and allowed her to continue to work her established hours.

Indirect discrimination in employment occurs typically with respect to issues such as job-sharing, part-time working[22] and forms of dress and appearance. These sorts of issues are not likely to occur in the context of sport — at least as far as participants are concerned.[23] However, the issue of indirect discrimination does potentially arise in the very important context of UEFA's Home Grown Players rule (see below pp 492–6).

Residence requirements may also give rise to unlawful indirect discrimination, but the potential problems in determining this can be illustrated by this hypothetical situation. A sports club decides that it would prefer to select its players from those born and/or who have lived in the locality for most of their lives. The club announces that 'outsiders', however, will be considered. X is a member of a particular ethnic group and has only lived in the locality for six months. Under the definition of indirect discrimination X should be able to establish that the issues of birth and residence constitute 'criteria' for selection, and therefore should succeed in establishing this element of indirect (race) discrimination.

---

20 [1998] IRLR 364.
21 [1987] ICR 110.
22 It should be noted that the EU Part-time Work Directive (97/81/EC) requires Member States to introduce legal rules prohibiting discrimination against part-time workers (not just employees). In the UK the Directive has been implemented by The Part-time Workers (Prevention of Less Favourable Treatment) Regulations SI 2000/1551. This enables part-time workers to compare their terms and conditions of employment, including pay, with full-time colleagues, including those of the same sex. The Regulations do not, however, entitle full-time workers to move to part-time contracts or to job-share.
23 Though see op. cit., fn 10, Cottrell (2010).

However, X may still have a problem in identifying the correct pool of comparison. For example, different ethnic groupings, including his own, live in the area in similar numbers. Thus it would not be possible for X to show statistically that the residence requirement indirectly discriminated against the ethnic group to which he belongs. Nevertheless, the majority actually selected by the club come from one particular ethnic group. Members of the group to which X belongs are eligible for selection, but choose not to apply.

The hidden, even unconscious, reason, why X is not selected is his membership of a particular ethnic group, as there is a perception that members of that group are not interested in and/or lack ability or the perceived necessary temperament for that particular sport. In reality, X is being discriminated against as a result of belonging to that group whilst having a minority interest in the sport concerned. The over formalistic approach demonstrated by *Jones* precludes this form of cultural racism from being exposed. Nor is it definite that the more flexible approach demonstrated by *Edwards* will apply, as, geographically, it can be argued the appropriate pool of comparison in this instance is regional rather than national.

Even if X could establish indirect discrimination there would still be the possibility of justification. For example, what if the club says that it is part of the local community and wants to contribute to tackling local unemployment; or it can show that local people are less likely to move and therefore will be potentially more loyal to the club?

Could not the above add up to a policy which in crude terms is actually saying members of this ethnic group need not apply? X could, of course, argue that he has been the victim of direct discrimination, but how can this be proved if he is no more but no less talented than those actually selected?

Even if X could establish direct discrimination there is a further statutory 'sting in the tail'. This is because s 195 of the Equality Act re-enacts what was s 39 of the Race Relations Act 1976.

Section 195 of the Equality Act 2010

(5) A person who does anything to which subsection (6) applies does not contravene this Act only because of the nationality or place of birth of another or because of the length of time the other has been resident in a particular area or place.

(6) This subsection applies to—
   (a) selecting one or more persons to represent a country, place or area or a related association, in a sport or game or other activity of a competitive nature;
   (b) doing anything in pursuance of the rules of a competition so far as relating to eligibility to compete in a sport or game or other such activity.[24]

If X is a woman, it is necessary to consider the situation where a club might impose factors based on physical strength and stamina, rather than on, or in addition to, nationality or residence. While it might be easier to establish indirect discrimination in this context, it could be predicted that justification would be similarly easier for clubs to plead, given the perceptions that still exist that most men are stronger than most women. Scope for re-evaluating these arguably bigoted perceptions are unlikely given the sports exemption contained in s 195.

---

24 This section has not generated any case law and its scope could be restricted by the interpretation of 'represent'. As noted by Osborn and Greenfield: 'Clubs and leagues do not represent as opposed to cover geographical areas.' They nevertheless conclude: 'Overall s 39 permits a very wide measure of discrimination that appears difficult to rationalise.' Osborn, G and Greenfield, S, 'Gentlemen, players and the 6' 9" West Indian fast bowler' (1995) 2(3) Working Papers in Law and Popular Culture, (Manchester Metropolitan University) 28.

Section 195 of the Equality Act 2010

(1) A person does not contravene this Act, so far as relating to sex, only by doing anything in relation to the participation of another as a competitor in a gender-affected activity . . .

(3) A gender-affected activity is a sport, game or other activity of a competitive nature in circumstances in which the physical strength, stamina or physique of average persons of one sex would put them at a disadvantage compared to average persons of the other sex as competitors in events involving the activity.[25]

This overt manifestation of sexist prejudice, of course, ignores the fact that professional sports participants are by definition not average men and women. With specialist weight training and coaching, women in sport can match the strength and stamina of many, albeit not all, men. Moreover, all of us can think of, for example, top-class professional footballers whose brilliant ball skills may not be matched with a 'Charles Atlas' physique. Should an Act intended to eliminate sex discrimination legitimise the sexist assumptions long ago questioned in popular culture by the likes of the film *Gregory's Girl* and the British television series *The Manageress*?

For the time being, sport remains segregated on a gender basis – particularly where it is played as a professional game. Moreover, media interest and thus national/international prestige and the 'big' money remains focused on the game as played by men. Desegregation might not be appropriate in all sports – that is, those where physical strength is at the core of the sport – but should not women at least be given the option to compete on equal terms where skill with hands and/or feet is the essence of the game concerned?

If traditional attitudes persist as far as players and thus managers are concerned, inroads have at least been made when it comes to referees and officials.

Petty v British Judo Association

Petty argued unlawful discrimination when the British Judo Association refused to permit her to referee an All-England's men's contest. The association pleaded s 44 of the Sex Discrimination Act on the basis that a woman would not have the strength to separate two male combatants.

Browne-Wilkinson J stated: It is common ground that judo is a sport in which men and women ought not to compete one with the other. Section 44 saves from being unlawful 'any act related to the participation of a person as a competitor in that activity,' ie judo . . . we cannot see how provisions as to referees relate to the 'participation' of the competitors in the contest . . . We think the words should be given their obvious meaning and not extended so as to cover any discrimination other than provisions designed to regulate who is to take part in the contest as a competitor. Any other construction would lead to great uncertainty: for example, would the section be extended to discrimination against the lady in the box office at a football ground? . . .[26]

Today, of course, in football the 'lady' may be found not only in the box office but on the pitch as a match official. We still await the day when the 'lady' will also be present as a member of a mixed-sex professional club side.

It has been clarified that what is now s 195(3) cannot be invoked as a defence where the relevant sports participants are of the same gender. In *Couch v British Board of Boxing Control*[27] it was held that the decision of the Board to withhold a licence to box professionally from Jane Couch, the

---

25 This effectively re-enacts s 44 of the Sex Discrimination Act 1975.
26 [1981] ICR 660 EAT, at pp 665–66.
27 Unreported, Case No 2304231/97. For further discussion of this case see Felix, A, 'The "Fleetwood Assassin" strikes a blow for female boxing' (1998) 1(3) SLB 1, 6 and the 'In my Opinion' Column by Ferris, E, Vice-President of The Olympians in the same edition of SLB 2.

women's world welterweight champion, constituted unlawful sex discrimination. The decision of the Board was criticised for being based on 'gender-based stereotypes and assumptions', and s 44 of the Sex Discrimination Act was of no assistance to the Board in circumstances in which Couch was seeking a licence to participate in professional boxing bouts with other women. The section only applied where women were seeking to compete with men.[28]

Section 195(4) of the EA contains a new provision relating to children participating in sport. This requires consideration as to whether it is appropriate to take into account a child's age and state of development in determining whether a sport or game is gender-affected. This suggests that differences in strength and physical stamina may not be so pronounced in child, as against adult, competitors and therefore children should be permitted to compete on an equal basis irrespective of gender.

The other defence to direct discrimination in the Sex Discrimination Act related to gender as 'a genuine occupational qualification.' Section 7 made an exception 'where the job needs to be held by a man to preserve decency or privacy because . . . the holder of the job is likely to do his work in circumstances where men might reasonably object to the presence of a woman because they are in a state of undress or are using sanitary facilities.' Changes required by EU law, and which are now contained in Schedule 9 of the EA, permit pleading what is now the occupational requirement defence where this is a proportionate means of achieving a legitimate aim. Whilst, in the context of gender, preserving privacy and decency will remain a legitimate aim this defence should fail on the grounds of proportionality. Without doubt, dressing room team talks and locker room culture are integral aspects of professional sport, but one hopes, indeed assumes, that if the barriers erected by s 195(3) are ever overcome, the occupational requirement defence will not be permitted to act as the final bastion of a male preserve. It should not be beyond the wit or resources of professional clubs to provide the separate facilities to be found in any gymnasium or swimming pool, whilst allowing players of both genders to mix once appropriately enrobed in the team kit.

Both the SDA and RRA inherently prohibited positive discrimination. This remains the case under the EA. Therefore, it would be unlawful, for example, for a football club to recruit a player for the specific reason that he was a member of the Asian British community. However, positive action is permitted by the legislation and has indeed been increasingly encouraged by EU law.[29] Thus it would be permissible for a club deliberately to seek to increase the number of players it employs from ethnic groups under-represented in the sport or club concerned. This could be done by, as examples, targeting schools containing high numbers of members of the relevant ethnic groups, or advertising in languages spoken by and/or in media popular with members of under-represented groups. The club may emphasise that it welcomes applicants from the ethnic group(s) concerned. However, specific decisions to recruit one individual as against another must be made on objective criteria and not be motivated by a desire to engage in positive discrimination.[30]

The main remedies available under the Acts are declarations and compensation. The latter covers actual financial loss and is not subject to any statutory maximum figure.[31] Moreover, compensation can include an element of aggravated damages where injury to feelings is caused by a deliberate intention to discriminate.

---

28 See Bennett v Football Association (1978) unreported CA Transcript 591; also see discussion of case and s 44 of the SDA in McArdle, D, From Boot Money to Bosman: Football, Society and the Law (2000), London: Cavendish.

29 In Badeck v Hessischer Ministerpräsident [2000] IRLR 432 the ECJ ruled that positive action is not contrary to EU law unless it requires women to be afforded automatic and unconditional preference over men (or vice versa). Council Directive 2000/78/EC of 27 November 2000 encourages Member States to take positive steps to compensate for disadvantages produced by past forms of discrimination.

30 Section 159 EA does permit employers to take ethnic, gender-based etc under-representation into account in recruitment where candidates are as qualified as each other, although quota systems remain unlawful. However, at the time of writing, it was uncertain whether these provisions will be brought into effect.

31 Cf the ERA 1996 and remedies for unfair dismissal; see previous chapter, pp 440–1.

Sexuality

Until December 2003, discrimination against gays and lesbians in sport was not directly prohibited. Indeed, in the past, in appropriate circumstances it was even permitted. As established in *Saunders*[32] it may have been within the range of reasonable responses for clubs to dismiss gay players. A dismissal could have been regarded as reasonable and thus fair if the presence of an openly gay player was causing tensions within the team and/or hostility from the paying public. The latter point is of particular significance when it is remembered that in *Saunders* emphasis was placed on the attitudes of parents. By analogy, gay professional players coaching young children or simply existing as role models could be perceived by parents as a potential source of corruption. That this confusion between gay sexuality and paedophilia is based on a misconception, which can best be described as superstitious bigotry, was not for a tribunal to find once it was clear that the reasonable employing club may have acted to preserve its reputation and paying support. Today, it is unlawful for an employer to succumb to homophobia on the part of sections of its workforce or third parties such as its customers.

Over the last decade attitudes to people who are gay, lesbian or bisexual have substantially changed, and homophobia is no longer as common as it was. Nevertheless, it still exists and arguably, at least in its softer forms such as 'jokes', is still regarded as more acceptable than racism. If this is so in wider society, then it is likely that this is even more the case in the particularly macho world of professional sport. Thus, the fact that the law now prohibits discrimination on grounds of sexuality is significant to clubs as employers.

The trigger for a historic change in the law rendering discrimination on grounds of sexual orientation to be unlawful was the decision of the European Court of Human Rights in *Lustig-Prean and Beckett v the United Kingdom*.[33] In this case the ECHR ruled that it was contrary to Art 8 of the European Convention on Human Rights, which protects rights to a private life, to discharge individuals from the Royal Navy on the sole ground that they were homosexuals. The wide-sweeping consequences of this decision were immediately clear as the European Court rejected arguments from the Ministry of Defence that the presence of homosexuals in the armed forces 'can cause offence, polarise relationships, induce ill-discipline and, as a consequence, damage morale and unit effectiveness', and therefore any discrimination could be justified by the interests of national security.

As a result of this decision it has become impossible for any clubs to argue that discrimination against a gay player is justified by reference to the reaction of his teammates or the club's supporters. However, the impact of the decision in *Lustig-Prean* was significantly reduced by the fact that the Human Rights Act only permits rights guaranteed by the European Convention to be enforced directly against public bodies. Moreover, discrimination against an employee on the basis of his or her sexuality could be considered unlawful either under the Sex Discrimination Act[34] or under the Equal Treatment Directive.[35]

The original legal basis for the current law was contained in Art 13 of the Treaty of Amsterdam. This empowered the Council of Ministers by unanimous agreement to approve legislation drafted by the Commission to prohibit a variety of forms of discrimination. Such legislation was adopted in the form of the Framework Directive,[36] which prohibits discrimination on grounds of religion

---

32 *Saunders v Scottish National Camps Association* [1981] IRLR 174.
33 [1999] IRLR 734.
34 *Smith v Gardner Merchant Ltd* [1998] IRLR 510. In *Macdonald v Ministry of Defence; Pearce v Governing Body of Mayfield Secondary School* [2003] ICR 937 it was accepted, before the House of Lords, by the employees that, despite s 6 of the HRA, the SDA can still not be interpreted as covering sexuality as well as gender. The Law Lords held that there is no direct sex discrimination where employers treat male and female homosexual employees in the same way.
35 In *Grant v South-West Trains Ltd* [1998] ICR 449 it was ruled by the ECJ that EU law prohibiting sex discrimination did not cover discrimination by an employer on grounds of an employee's sexual orientation.
36 Council Directive 2000/78/ EC of 27 November 2000 establishing a general framework for equal treatment in employment and occupation.

or belief, sexual orientation, disability and age and which came into force in December 2003 (although Member States had until 2006 to introduce measures on age and disability).

With respect to sexual orientation the provisions of the Directive were implemented by statutory instrument.[37] The Equality Act re-enacts the relevant provisions. Under s 12(1) 'sexual orientation' means a sexual orientation towards –

(a)   persons of the same sex;

(b)   persons of the opposite sex; or

(c)   persons of the same sex and of the opposite sex.

In addition to the rights and remedies provided by the Act, it should be noted that any dismissal on grounds of unlawful discrimination would be an unfair dismissal under the Employment Rights Act. A player who resigns in response to being subjected to homophobia at the workplace will succeed in a claim for constructive and wrongful and/or unfair dismissal (see previous chapter). However, action taken against a player for sexual misconduct will not be covered by the Act and a dismissal on such grounds may well be considered within the range of reasonable responses and thus fair.[38]

The problem of homophobia in sport was most tragically demonstrated by the suicide of the footballer, Justin Fashanu, who came out as gay in 1990. (Fashanu was even publicly rejected by his brother John, who was also a professional footballer.) However, whilst there has been no case law concerning sport, there are signs that attitudes are changing for the better. This is exemplified by the general positive responses to the Welsh rugby union international, Gareth Thomas, when he came out. In football, the then captain of Sheffield Wednesday, Darren Purse, gave an interview demonstrating his sympathy for gay footballers, although this interview also reveals just how difficult it still is for a gay professional footballer to reveal his sexuality.[39]

Transsexuals

That the stigma attached to homosexuality is also attached to transsexuality is shown by the problems encountered by the professional tennis player Dr Renée Richards who prior to a sex change operation had been Dr Richard Raskind.[40] However, in *P v S and Cornwall County Council*[41] the ECJ ruled that dismissal of an employee was contrary to the Equal Treatment Directive where the reason for the dismissal was that the employee proposed to undergo gender reassignment surgery. The EAT's view had been that such discrimination is not by reason of gender providing male and female transsexuals are treated in the same way. The ECJ's view was the sex discrimination arises from 'comparison with persons of the sex to which he or she was deemed to belong before undergoing gender reassignment.' Alternatively such discrimination constitutes 'failure to respect the dignity and freedom to which he or she is entitled, and which the Court has a duty to safeguard'.

The SDA was amended to cover discrimination against transsexuals, and the law is now contained in s 7 of the EA. A transsexual is defined by s 7(1) as a person who has started, is undergoing or has undergone a process (or part of a process) of gender reassignment by changing physiological or other attributes of sex. Under the SDA, gender reassignment was primarily seen as a medical process under which the individual would be under medical supervision culminating in gender

37   The Employment Equality (Sexual Orientation) Regulations 2003, SI 2003/1661 came into force on 1 December 2003.

38   See *X v Y* Court of Appeal [2004] EWCA Civ 662.

39   See Doward, J, 'Gay activists praise rugby star Gareth Thomas's decision to come out', *The Guardian*, 19 December 2009; McRae, D, 'Darren Purse: "There can't be anything worse than living a lie"', *The Guardian*, 25 September 2010. Also see Williams, R, 'How one gay footballer could change the world', *The Guardian*, 14 December 2010.

40   See Grayson, E, *Sport and the Law* (1994), London: Butterworths, pp 240–41.

41   [1996] ICR 795.

reassignment surgery. On the basis of the above definition this is no longer the case. It is sufficient that a man decides to live as a woman or vice versa, although it should be noted that the legislation still excludes transvestism (for example, where a man as a man regularly engages in cross-dressing).

However, medical considerations cannot be completely discarded as there are persons who are intersexual, rather than transsexual, who fall between the definitions of men and women and have not embarked on any process of gender reassignment. In sport, the primary example of a person who can be considered intersexual is Caster Semenya, an 18-year-old South African athlete who won the women's 800m gold medal in the 2009 World Championship for athletics in Berlin. There has been much media discussion as to whether she has the physiological constitution of a man and thus should be banned from competing in her sport as a woman.[42]

It could be argued that an intersexual could be perceived to be transsexual and thus protected by s 7. However, even if this is the case there is another hurdle to be overcome in the context of sport. Section 195 (see above) permits discrimination in sport where it is gender-related activity. This expressly covers participation in sport by a transsexual, and thus does permit a person perceived to be a male transsexual to be prohibited from participating in any sport in which the physical strength, physique or stamina of the average man puts a man at a competitive advantage with respect to the average women. This clearly covers most team sports and athletics events.[43] British law, as it stands, is not adequate to deal with the types of issues raised by the Semenya case, but, as Ioannidis argues, the matter is best resolved by sporting bodies adopting an approach which has a clear legal foundation in international human rights law.

A specific problem for transsexuals in sport could occur in the context of changing rooms. As a result of a case decided by the Court of Appeal,[44] it appears that an employer will not be committing unlawful discrimination in providing separate toilet facilities for pre-operative transsexuals. It would seem logical to apply this decision to the provision of separate changing rooms, shower facilities and the like, despite the offence to a person's dignity that might be caused. If anything this problem is likely to be enhanced by the fact that a transsexual person no longer has to undergo gender reassignment surgery, and therefore may be permanently subject to such arrangements.

As a result of a decision of the European Court of Human Rights,[45] and as implemented by the Gender Recognition Act 2004, a post-operative transsexual is entitled to have his or her new sex fully recognised through a change in that person's birth certificate. Thus it would seem that should a sports professional change sex and continue to participate in the sport in his or her new gender, other participants of that sex would not be able to object to sharing changing rooms with that person on the grounds that he was once a man, or vice versa.

As is the case with gay and lesbian sports participants, the most likely form of discrimination against transsexuals in sport is likely to be in the form of harassment. It was held in *Chessington World of Adventures v Reed*[46] that employers will incur direct or vicarious liability if they fail to protect transsexual employees from harassment by co-workers. The EA contains comprehensive new provisions on harassment (see below, pp 479–81).

Disability and professional sport

Section 6 of the EA defines disability as having a physical or mental impairment which has a substantial and long-term effect on a person's ability to carry out normal day-to-day activities.

---

42 For a discussion of the legal and medical issues involved see Ioannidis, G, 'Gender Testing: The Caster Semenya case: gender verification in sport' (2009) 7(10) WSLR.
43 Note this provision replaces s 19 of the Gender Recognition Act 2004 which has been repealed by the EA.
44 *Croft v Royal Mail Group Plc* (CA) [2003] IRLR 592.
45 *Goodwin v UK* [2002] IRLR 664.
46 [1998] ICR 97.

Moreover, certain progressive conditions, such as cancer, HIV infection[47] or multiple sclerosis, are considered as disabilities from the point of diagnosis without the need to demonstrate a current effect on a person's ability to carry out an activity.

Section 15 prohibits discrimination against a disabled person if a) that person is treated different because of something arising in consequence of the disability; and (b) the different treatment cannot be justified as a proportionate means of achieving a legitimate aim. Moreover, under s 20, an employer, qualification body etc. is subject to a duty to make reasonable adjustments, and will be liable if it fails to do so unless this can be justified.

'Reasonable adjustments' include: altering the physical state of the premises; providing the provision of special equipment to enable a disabled person to work despite the disability; permitting a disabled person to have a different working pattern; or to provide auxiliary aids. At first sight it is not obvious how this could apply to professional sports participants. However, technological developments have to be taken into account in this context.

For example, under equivalent provisions in US law, the Supreme Court held that the golfer, Casey Martin, had been discriminated against because of the refusal to allow him to use a golf cart to compete on the United States professional tour.[48] Martin suffers from a degenerative circulatory disorder, Klippel-Trenaunay-Weber Syndrome, a progressive disease that obstructs the flow of blood to his heart. As a result he is unable to walk around a golf course, and thus is unable to play golf, unless he is allowed to use a cart. The Supreme Court held that permitting Martin to use a cart constituted what would be regarded as a reasonable adjustment under British law. The refusal to allow him to do this could not be justified on the basis that it gave him a competitive advantage over other golfers because he did not suffer from the fatigue inevitably incurred through walking around a professional golf course over the duration of a match.[49]

Developments in prosthetic limb technology has also raised the issue as to whether refusing an athlete fitted with such limbs to participate in a sport constitutes unlawful discrimination, or is justified because it gives that person a competitive advantage. This problem is illustrated by the decision of the International Olympics Committee (IOC) that Oscar Pistorius, a South African sprinter, was ineligible to participate in the 2008 Beijing Olympic Games. Pistorius was born without fibula bones and consequently had both legs amputated below the knee before his first birthday. He is only able to sprint by using a pair of prosthetic limbs attached to his legs. In the view of the IOC, springs in these limbs gave Pistorius an undue competitive advantage over other sprinters.[50] Were it to be decided in the future, under the EA, that such a decision constitutes an unjustifiable failure to make a reasonable adjustment, then sports bodies in general would need to review their rules to ensure they were not discriminatory.

Unlawful Harassment

The gender segregated nature of professional sport means that the problem of racist rather than sexist behaviour is of greater significance. However, this may not always be the case, and harassment of women employees who are not sports participants also needs to be considered as a possibility. Homophobic abuse can also rear its ugly head in a sports context.[51] Moreover, given its ideological

---

47 For a consideration of the need both to protect HIV positive sports participants and other participants on the field of play see, Wolohan, JT, 'An ethical and legal dilemma: participation in sport by HIV infected athletes' (1997) 7(2) MSLJ 373–97.

48 See PGA Tour, Inc. v. Martin (Martin III), 532 US 661 (2001).

49 See additional discussion on case, Chapter 3, pp 67–8.

50 For a full consideration of these issues see Charlish, P and Riley, S, 'Should Oscar Run?' (2008) 18 Fordham Intell Prop Media & Ent LJ 929–57, and additional discussion on case, Chapter 3, pp 68–9.

51 A recent and well-publicised instance of homophobic abuse by spectators involved abuse by some Tottenham Hotspur fans aimed at Sol Campbell at Fratton Park in a game with Portsmouth in September 2008. For consideration of the general problem of homophobic bullying at the workplace, see Cahalane, C, 'Is it safe to come out yet?', The Guardian, 13 November 2010.

roots in Islamophobia, the emergence of the English Defence League (EDL) during the course of 2010 also requires the issue of religious harassment to be taken into account. The link between the EDL and football hooligan 'firms' is overt, as demonstrated by the websites and Facebook pages that supporters of a significant number of British (not just English) clubs have set up to promote their 'EDL Divisions'. Whatever the protestations of the EDL their activities are also rooted in racism, and it is this form of harassment that has been the most common in the world of professional sport.

The display of racist attitudes by white players to black teammates, at least in football, is thankfully becoming a thing of the past. Similarly, there has been in recent years a significant reduction in racist chanting at most football grounds, although individual racists still appear uninhibited in racially abusing individuals. The most likely context in professional sport in which black players will be subject to racist abuse is on the field of play by members of the opposing team. However, it would be wrong to conclude that racism within all clubs in all sports has disappeared.

This latter problem is demonstrated by the Bobby Gould incident and a case concerning the player-manager, Kevin Ratcliffe. The former concerned the decision of striker Nathan Blake to refuse to play for Wales after the manager, Bobby Gould, had made racist statements about opponents in the dressing room. This incident was particularly revealing as initially Gould was not even capable of understanding that he had voiced racist sentiments, or, at least, why this should upset one of his own players.[52]

Arguably even more disturbing is the case of *Hussaney v Chester City FC and Kevin Ratcliffe*.[53] Hussaney was an apprentice at Chester and had played for the youth and reserves team. On one occasion, when he was due to play for the Chester City Reserves against Oldham Athletic Reserves, he was called a 'black cunt' by the first-team manager, Kevin Ratcliffe, who was also due to play for the reserves. Hussaney had put the wrong-sized studs into Ratcliffe's football boots. Hussaney made a formal complaint to the club. Shortly after this incident, Hussaney was informed he would not be offered a professional contract. The club agreed that Ratcliffe made the alleged racial abuse, but denied it amounted to racial discrimination. Ratcliffe made some attempts to provide an apology to Hussaney. The tribunal held that the abusive language amounted to discrimination by both Ratcliffe and the club on grounds of race and made a compensatory award of £2,500 for injury to feelings.

This case illustrates how, as is the case with any employer, a professional club will be directly liable for acts of racist abuse on the part of those in managerial positions. The case also highlights the difficulties of establishing whether decisions are racially motivated, albeit unconsciously. Hussaney brought a second claim against Chester FC stating that he had been victimised contrary to the Act for bringing the claim against Ratcliffe. The victimisation consisted of the decision by the club not to offer him a professional contract. The tribunal rejected this claim as it found that the decision was made 'purely on footballing grounds'. In January 2001, the EAT upheld Hussaney's appeal on the basis that the tribunal had provided insufficient reasons as to why it had reached the conclusion that there was no unlawful unconscious motivation. The tribunal had over-relied on the club's view that Ratcliffe had simply used his experience as an assessor of footballing skill in recommending that Hussaney not be offered a contract.[54]

In its advice to professional footballers on players' employment contracts the Football Association (FA) specifies that racial harassment is a disciplinary offence. This is defined as including 'physical abuse, offensive language or jokes, offensive graffiti or posters and enforced isolation on

---

52 As reported in *The Guardian*, 2 April 1997; also see Mitchell, K, 'Gould has the gift of the gaffe', *The Observer*, 6 April 1997. Another example of how influential people in sport find it difficult to distinguish between racist language and racism is provided by the incident where former manager turned television summariser, Ron Atkinson, believing himself to be off-air, described the Chelsea defender, Marcel Desailly, as a 'fucking lazy, thick nigger'. See Edoba, M, editor of *New Nation, The Observer*, 25 April 2004 for a response to this by a leading member of the black community.
53 Unreported, IT Case No 2102426\97.
54 See (2001) 4(3) SLB 5 for case note.

the grounds of an individual's colour, race, ethnic or national origin or nationality'.[55] Moreover, as a result of EC law, the Race Relations Act was amended in 2003 to include a statutory definition of racial harassment.[56] It is also of relevance to note that there were similar definitions in the Sexual Orientation and Religion or Belief Regulations 2003 to render abuse etc. unlawful where it concerned an individual's sexuality or religion (or lack of one). The Equality Act (EA) 2010 replaces these statutory provisions and now prohibits harassment with respect to number of specified protected characteristics including race, sexual orientation and religious belief.

Under these provisions a person (A) harasses another (B) if he engages in unwanted conduct related to a relevant protected characteristic, and the conduct has the purpose or effect of:

a)   violating B's dignity, or

b)   creating an intimidating, hostile, degrading, humiliating or offensive environment for B.

In deciding whether conduct has the above effect each of the following must be taken into account:

a)   the perception of B;

b)   the other circumstances of the case;

c)   whether it was reasonable for the conduct to have that effect.

On the basis of the above definition, and in light of the incidents/cases referred to in this chapter, it is now the case that any racist abuse perceived by the victim to be 'degrading' or 'offensive' will constitute racial harassment, contrary to the Act, even if this was not the actual purpose or intention of the perpetrator.

Judicial perceptions of what types of comments or behaviour constitute harassment have a somewhat chequered history. For example, in the case of De Souza[57] it was held that a racist comment may be no more than an insult and this is not sufficient to constitute an act of harassment. On the basis of the above definition it is anticipated that, finally, De Souza can now be regarded as bad law, as this view of the law could have very serious consequences for how racist abuse in sport is perceived.

Potentially it could reinforce (not uncommon) arguments that insulting a player by referring to his skin colour is no more significant than referring to his size, weight or hair colour, particularly when such comments are made 'in jest' or in the heat of competition. It is contended that the realities of racism in Britain are such that it is qualitatively different to be called, for example, 'a black bastard' as against being called one from a region of the country such as Yorkshire or even a different country such as Denmark. In the latter context it is true that the player's different nationality is referred to, but Danes in Britain do not have the collective memory and ongoing legacy of centuries of oppression, rooted in the slave trade and the spread of Empire, that remains the experience of the Afro-Caribbean and Asian communities. Racism in sport is as much derived from this history as it is in any other area of society.[58]

---

55   See p 12 of The FA Code of Practice and Notes on Contract.

56   See Directive 2000/43 implementing the principle of equal treatment between persons irrespective of racial or ethnic origin and Directive 2000/78 establishing a general framework for equal treatment in employment and occupation.

57   De Souza v Automobile Association [1986] IRLR 103. In this case the claimant overheard a colleague refer to her as 'the wog' but the Court of Appeal regarded this as insult rather than harassment.

58   For an analysis of racism in football see Greenfield, S and Osborn, G, 'When the whites go marching in? Racism and resistance in English football' (1996) 6(2) MSLJ 315–35. For comparative analysis and an examination of the experiences of black athletes in the USA, see Williams, P, 'Performing in a racially hostile environment' (1996) 6(2) MSLJ 287–314. For a discussion of the role of racism in undermining the interest in cricket in the British Afro-Caribbean Community and the decline in the West Indian test team see Steen R, 'Calypso Collapso', Observer Sport, 25 July 2004. Of particular interest is the long shadow cast by the public criticism of Devon Malcolm by Ray Illingworth in 1995 – see Chapter 9 fn 26. It was also at the start of the 1995 season that Wisden Cricket Monthly published an attack on black cricketers by Robert Henderson for not being 'unequivocal Englishmen'.

The provisions in the former Race Relations Act contained a major gap in the law as a result of the decision of the House of Lords in *MacDonald v AG for Scotland* (2004) in the context of sexual harassment. The Law Lords stated that harassment is only unlawful sex discrimination where an employee is treated differently by reference to her or his own gender. This view of the law applied equally to the statutory definition in the RRA and would prevent a harassment claim if, for example, a white or Asian player was offended by racist abuse directly aimed at players of African or Afro-Caribbean origins (or vice versa). The new definition overrules *MacDonald* as the words 'on the grounds of' have been replaced with the words 'related to'. Thus, today, if a white player followed Nathan Blake's example (see above, p 478) in objecting to racism directed at an opponent he would be able to bring a personal claim under the Equality Act.

Vicarious liability

It has long been clear that a sustained campaign of verbal and/or physical racist harassment designed to force a player to leave a club would have constituted an unlawful harassment under the RRA. The *Hussaney* case notwithstanding, if such behaviour was to occur in a club then, as in any other field of employment, it is more likely to come from teammates than the club management. A club is potentially liable in such a situation by virtue of the imposition of statutory vicarious liability. Under s 32 of the RRA, anything done by a person in the course of her/his employment was to be treated for the purposes of the Act as done by her/his employer as well as by her/him, whether or not it was done with the employer's knowledge or approval.

Under s 32(3) an employer was able to avoid vicarious liability if disciplinary codes prohibited acts of racial harassment, the rules were properly communicated to employees and complaints of harassment were investigated and otherwise properly acted upon. With respect to all forms of unlawful harassment, the imposition of vicarious liability and the statutory defence to it have been re-enacted by ss 40 and 109 of the EA respectively. Thus, clubs which recognise the importance of tackling racism, homophobia etc. within the club, and display a practical commitment to doing so, are likely to receive the protection of this statutory defence.

The effectiveness of providing for statutory vicarious liability was potentially and seriously undermined by the heavily criticised decision of the EAT in the case of *Jones v Tower Boot Co*. In this case the applicant was subjected, at the workplace, to a series of brutal acts. It was clear that the employees responsible were motivated by racism. It was decided that the company could not be vicariously liable on the basis that the employees could not be regarded as acting within the course of their employment.

This reasoning required the conclusion that the more extreme the acts of racism (or sexism), the easier it becomes for an employer who takes no action nevertheless to evade liability. These criticisms were taken on board by the Court of Appeal in reversing the EAT decision.[59] Waite LJ clarified that it was wrong to apply the (then) common law approach to vicarious liability to the Race Relations and Sex Discrimination Acts, as the purpose of the Acts is to make employers vicariously liable where in a work context they fail to protect employees from racist or sexist behaviour. Since this decision it has been clear that only the pro-active employer who takes reasonable steps to stamp out harassment will escape vicarious liability.

Under the former legislation it was also held that the scope of an employer's vicarious liability potentially includes behaviour when employees are 'socialising' with one another as part of work-place culture. This was decided in a case concerning a police party in a pub.[60] This case has implications for professional clubs as sport, like the police force, is a form of employment where club

---

59 See [1997] IRLR 168. The EAT decision is reported in [1995] IRLR 529.
60 *Chief Constable of the Lincolnshire Police v Stubbs & Others* [1999] ICR 547.

culture and team bonding may require or at least put pressure on players to participate in post-training or post-match social activities.

Another important gap in the law, which again resulted from the House of Lords decision in MacDonald, was that clubs could not be liable for third-party harassment. In reaching this decision the Law Lords overruled the decision in Burton v DeVere Hotels Ltd (1996), which held that an employer will be directly liable if its degree of control over a situation is such that it can take steps to protect employees from third-party racist abuse and fails to do so.[61] As the law stood, the employer could only be liable for third-party harassment where the failure to protect the employee was itself racially motivated. The factor of control was no longer in itself sufficient to establish employer liability.

Under ss 40(2) and 40(3) of the Equality Act, it is once again possible to make the employer legally liable for third-party harassment. The employer will be liable where the employer fails to take such steps as would be reasonably practicable to protect the employee from third-party harassment. However, this will only be the case where the employer knows the employee has been subjected to third-party harassment on at least two other occasions, although it does not matter that the acts of harassment were carried out by different persons.

It is also the case, as decided by the House of Lords in Majrowski v Guy's and St Thomas's NHS Trust (2006), that under s 3 of the Protection from Harassment Act 1997 (PHA) an employer will be vicariously liable for an employee who harasses another, be that other a colleague or any other person. In the context of this legislation the employer's knowledge is not necessary to establish liability. The victim can sue the relevant employer for damages providing, in accordance with s 1 of the Act, there is 'a course of conduct' constituting harassment (which does not have to be linked to, for example, race) in that (again) it has occurred on at least two previous occasions. The perpetrators of such harassment can also be sued for damages and made subject to a court injunction to prevent the harassment from being repeated.

Whilst the above statutory provisions apply to clubs as employers in the same way as they do to any other type of employer, it can be argued that the provisions are not completely adequate to deal with racist or other forms of harassment as these can occur in the world of sport.

Gardiner, S and Welch, R, 'Football, Racism and the Limits of "Colour Blind" Law: Revisited'

In professional sport the issue of third party racist abuse is most likely to arise during a match. Such abuse will either come from spectators or members of the opposing team. Clubs, of course, have less control once their players are on the field of play. However, with respect to racist chanting or racist abuse of individual players by spectators it seems that, in the light of the new provisions under the EA, a club could incur liability if there is a failure to implement efficient stewarding operations to clamp down on such behaviour. This is also the case with respect to chants involving homophobia or Islamophobia. Under the PHA, a player could take matters into her/his own hands by seeking a court injunction providing it is possible to identify individual culprits from CCTV and the like. This would be in addition to any other measures that have been taken such as the granting of a football banning order.

However, the provisions on harassment contained in the PHA and the EA were not drafted with the world of professional sport in mind,[62] and it is a case of applying the law in a sporting context to the extent that it makes sense to do so. This creates a serious practical problem for football, or for any other professional team sport, in that on the field of play any racist abuse is more likely to come from an opponent than a team-mate.[63] Moreover, the motive behind such

---

61 In this case the hotel management failed to protect black staff from racist 'jokes' by Bernard Manning by, for example, withdrawing them from the function during Manning's speech.

62 In the case of the PHA the legislation was not even devised for the world of employment in general – it was designed to deal with the problem of stalking.

63 Where a player does racially abuse a teammate during a match, then if the latter complains the employing club can and should respond to this in the same way that it should respond to any allegation of racial harassment that occurs at the workplace.

abuse may not even be hard-core racism so much as a cynical and calculated act of 'gamesman-ship' to wind up an opposing player to put her/him off his game, and/or provoke her/him into committing a foul or offence which results in the victim of racism, rather than its perpetrator, being sent off.

The law does not and cannot adequately deal with this situation. The only effective measure a club could take to protect its player would be to substitute her/him, and this would be self-defeating from the perspectives of both player and club, and indeed would be tantamount to giving in to racism.[64] Rather this issue demonstrates a major gap in the RRA and now the EA, as the legislation does not require employers to take disciplinary action against employees who engage in racist behaviour towards individuals outside of the employing organisation. There is the possibility of liability under the PHA if one player racially abuses an opponent more than once during a match. Moreover, it would be preferable to develop the law so that even a single act of racist (or homophobic etc.) abuse could constitute a new tort (civil wrong) of racial harassment so that the opposing player's club could then be rendered legally responsible for any racist behaviour by one or more of its players during a match.

However, even if the law was changed in this way, on-pitch racism demonstrates the limits of the law in combating racism in professional sport, as a legal claim would only be heard long after the relevant game had finished and the 'punishment' would only be an award of financial compensation that most clubs would find relatively affordable. Thus, the law can neither provide an immediate solution to, nor meaningful penalty for, racism on the field of play. This is a context where regulatory action on the part of a sport's governing bodies has the potential to be much more effective. The Football Task Force has proposed making racism a red card offence and incorporating anti-racist clauses into players' and managers' contracts (see Gardiner and Welch, 1998).[65] These measures should be implemented as they would operate in a two-pronged and mutually reinforcing manner. First, referees will be obliged to send off players who are guilty of racism during the course of a game. Second, clubs can regard such players as having acted in beach of their employment contracts and can take disciplinary action against them accordingly.

The fact that the player committing the offence has been sent off and consequently damaged her/his team's prospects of success will, hopefully, encourage her/his club to subject her/him to disciplinary proceedings. A further consequence is likely to be a growing consensus against on-pitch racism as clubs will begin to demand that referees are consistent in treating racism as constituting a red card offence. Anti-racist clauses in managers' contracts will also deter the more cynical manager (should she/he exist) from encouraging her/his players to engage in racist 'gamesmanship'. These measures would be very significantly reinforced by current proposals to deduct points from clubs that fail to take effective action to combat racist abuse.[66]

. . . Both authors of this chapter have had the misfortune of seeing their clubs relegated as a result of points deductions resulting from financial mismanagement on the part of those who have run their clubs (Leeds United and Portsmouth). In such cases supporters are punished for behaviour for which they have no responsibility and are unable to exercise any control. Preventing racist abuse 'on the terraces' is, however, something which supporters can contribute to. If a club going into administration can lead to a club being relegated then it can be argued that this is an appropriate punishment for clubs and its supporters who, on a regular

---

64 This would be similarly the case if a club decided to substitute a player or even not to select a player for a game where racism from sections of the crowd was taking place or had been anticipated prior to the start of the match.

65 Gardiner, S and Welch, R, 'Anti-racist clauses in footballers' contracts' (1998) 4(2) Sports Law Bulletin 1.

66 See The Times, 5 May 2009. These proposals are recommended by a FA Working Party, chaired by John Mann, a Labour MP and Leeds United supporter.

basis, engage in or permit racist, Islamophobic or homophobic chanting in their grounds, or indeed do so as away supporters in the grounds of other clubs. In the final analysis, it will be action taken by footballing authorities that will have a far greater impact than can be the case with legal measures – particularly given the immediate and potentially longer term financial consequences for a club where the loss of a key player and/or points results in relegation. Damages or fines can be paid: relegation may even send a club out of business.[67]

Overall, it can be concluded that changes to the law that strengthen the regulation of harassment are to be welcomed, but it needs to be appreciated that the law is not a completely effective instrument for protecting sports participants from acts of unlawful harassment. However, overt racism within football clubs at least appears to be very much on the wane. The reasons for this are probably the large numbers of black and overseas players playing professional football (fans racially abusing a black player on the opposing team will also adversely affect their 'own' black players) and the relative success of the 'Kick It Out' campaign. If there are problems within clubs in other professional sports then it is perhaps what has happened in football, rather than relying on the law, that shows the way forward.

Moreover, even within football it would be wrong to conclude that racism on the part of both fans and players has ceased to be a problem. Similarly, the insidious attitudes on which more overt racism is actually based have still to be eradicated. Indeed, while most football fans now seem to be inhibited from loudly voicing racist sentiments there are not the same inhibitions with respect to, as examples, homophobic and Islamophobic abuse. It is also likely that racism often remains the motivation for engaging in these supposedly 'more acceptable' forms of harassment.

Discrimination and European Law

Pregnancy and maternity rights

Article 2 of the Equal Treatment Directive[68] provides: 'the principle of equal treatment shall mean that there shall be no discrimination whatsoever on grounds of sex either directly or indirectly by reference in particular to marital or family status.' In accordance with the norms of EU law the Directive is only directly enforceable within the UK by state employees. Nevertheless, through the preliminary ruling process, the ECJ has delivered a number of significant rulings conferring protection on women which, at the time of the rulings, may not have been provided for by national legislation.

In the landmark rulings of *Dekker v VJV Centrum* and *Hertz v Aldi Marked*[69] the ECJ ruled that refusal of employment to or dismissal of women on grounds of pregnancy is contrary to the Directive. It was initially unclear whether it was unlawful to refuse employment to a pregnant woman under a temporary contract where she would be unable to fulfil all or most of that contract. This could have been relevant in sport with respect to the Wimbledon fortnight or the Olympic Games. Similarly, it could have been of relevance where a woman would not have been available for selection by a club for a large part of a current season. That such arguments are not available to employers, clubs or sporting bodies is clarified by the ECJ ruling in *Brandt-Nielson*.[70] This ruling states that refusal of employment to a woman because she is pregnant will be unlawful in all circumstances, irrespective of the economic consequences for the employer etc.

---

67 Gardiner, S and Welch, R, 'Football, Racism and the Limits of "Colour Blind" Law: Revisited', in Burdsey D. (ed.) *Race, Ethnicity and Football* (2011), Abingdon: Routledge, pp 222–36.

68 Council Directive 76/207/EC.

69 [1991] IRLR 27, 131.

70 The *Tele Danmark* (Brandt-Nielson) Case [2001] IRLR 853.

It is very important to understand that these rulings were delivered in the context of European discrimination law, and, consequently, protection is not restricted to pregnant women or mothers who meet the legal tests for having employee status. Thus, typically, women in sport generally will be protected as, even if they are not employees, they have entered into contracts to provide personal services.

The current law is to be found in s 18 EA and applies to a woman who is subjected to un-favourable treatment during the protected period in relation to her pregnancy (associative discrimi-nation is not covered by this provision). The protected period begins at the start of a woman's pregnancy and continues until the end of the period of her compulsory maternity leave. For women who are not employees this is two weeks after the end of her pregnancy. For women who are employees this will be for the statutory maternity period of 52 weeks. Under s 99 of the ERA 1996 a woman who is an employee and is dismissed by reason of her pregnancy will automatically succeed in a claim of unfair dismissal (see previous chapter, pp 426–7).[71]

Statutory rights providing for paternity leave and parental leave are only available to employees. The Paternity and Adoption Leave Regulations 2002[72] permit fathers, with 26 weeks' continuous employment, to take 26 weeks' paid paternity leave to care for a newborn child or support its mother. As a result of the EC Parental Leave Directive[73] parents – that is, fathers as well as mothers – with one year's service are entitled to 13 weeks' unpaid leave to care for a child under the age of five.[74] It is unlawful to subject an employee to any detriment for exercising these rights, and any dismissal will be automatically unfair. These rights should be appreciated by professional clubs who employ fathers and parents either as players or in a variety of managerial or administrative capaci-ties. This is important protection in the world of professional team sports, as fathers have these rights to time off irrespective of the implications their absences will have for the fortunes of their clubs.[75] Match officials will normally be considered employees (see previous chapter), and thus women who are employed as referees and the like will also enjoy these rights.

Although there has not been a sports-specific case in the English courts, it is clear that the law gives significant rights to professional sportswomen in the context of pregnancy and maternity. In Australia, case law has suggested restricting participation of a pregnant player will be unlawful.[76]

Equal pay

Article 157 of the TFEU,[77] as amplified by the Equal Pay Directive,[78] provides for the right of equal pay for work of equal value. In the UK this right was implemented by the Equal Pay Act 1970 and is now contained in ss 64 to 70 of the EA. As is generally the case with the provisions of the EA, an applicant need not be an employee, but may be any individual who has entered into a contract to perform work. As a directly applicable treaty provision, Art 157 can be relied upon as the basis of a

71 Ironically perhaps, a woman who has rights under the ERA and the Regulations might prefer to bring a claim under the SDA. This is because compensation is not subject to any statutory maximum limit. For highly paid professionals, therefore, a claim under the SDA will incorporate compensation for loss of any career opportunities. In all likelihood this will be far greater than the basic and compensatory awards available under the ERA.

72 SI 2002/2788. The initial period of two weeks was extended by the Additional Paternity Leave Regulations SI 2010/1055 to the current period of 26 weeks. Pay is subject to a statutory maximum, which at the time of writing in 2011, was £128.73 a week, or 90 per cent of normal weekly earnings if lower.

73 Directive 96/34.

74 This is extended to 18 weeks in the case of a disabled child until that child's 18th birthday.

75 See Farrow, F, 'Paternal Leave: Sportsmen and family leave rights in the UK' (2008) 6(5) WSLR for the adverse reaction by some club managers and ex-players to footballers exercising their rights to paternity and parental leave.

76 See Gardner v National Netball League [2001] FMCA 50 (18 July 2001) (www.austlii.edu.au). Also see Taylor, S, 'In My Opinion – Netball Australia' (2001) 4(4) SLB 2.

77 Formerly Art 141 of the EC Treaty.

78 Council Directive 75/117/EC.

claim in an industrial tribunal. Claims can thus be brought under EC law or the EA or both. In recent years, in particular, this area of law has been driven by rulings of the ECJ.

However, one of the problems with the law as a mechanism for achieving equal pay for women is that both Art 157 and the Equal Pay Act require the applicant to identify a male comparator. In the segregated context of professional sport with different competitions and different teams for men and women this is generally a non-starter. This has long been an issue in, for example, professional tennis, where women players generally earn less than their male counterparts.[79]

Moreover, performance-related pay and salary structures determined by market forces are legitimate grounds for pay differentials, even where the equal pay laws are applicable. In sport, these factors often render pay differentials the norm between members of the same team. For example, the pay that an individual footballer earns will be very much linked to the transfer and/or signing-on fee that a club is prepared to pay to secure his services. This is similarly the case where a club wishes to persuade a player to re-sign for it on expiry of his contract. In the event of a mixed-sex team ever being fielded, these factors would make it extremely difficult for a female member of the team to compare successfully, in terms of a legal challenge, the pay she received with that of a male teammate earning a higher salary.

The equal pay laws do, of course, protect women employed by clubs as administrators, public relations officers and the like. Moreover, they apply to paid match officials. However, for the sports participant, with whom this chapter is primarily concerned, equal pay law will generally remain of abstract relevance until and if mixed sport in terms of gender becomes a reality.

Freedom of movement provisions – Article 45 TFEU

The main impact of EU law on professional sport has clearly been the ECJ's ruling in *Bosman*. One of Bosman's complaints was that UEFA's '3+2' rule violated Art 48. This rule restricted the number of foreign players whose names could be included on a team-sheet in a UEFA competition to three. An additional two players could be included if they had played in a country for five years uninterruptedly, including three years in junior teams.

Bosman's argument was that this restricts the freedom of movement of players who are EC nationals as clubs with their 'full quota of foreign players' are likely to restrict new contracts to indigenous players. The ECJ agreed with the Opinion of Advocate General Lenz that this offends the rule that all EC nationals must be treated on an equal basis.

Arguments seeking to justify the '3+2' rule were considered and rejected by Advocate General Lenz. It is valuable to examine in depth the reasons why the ECJ regarded the '3+2' rule to be unjustifiable, given the introduction of UEFA's Home Grown Players' rule and FIFA's proposal for nationality quotas in the form of its '6+5' rule.

URBSFA v Jean-Marc Bosman

A number of further considerations have been advanced as justification for the rules on foreign players, and these must now be examined. Three groups of arguments can essentially be distinguished. First, it is emphasised that the national aspect plays an important part in

---

79 Equal prize money is awarded at the Australian and US Open Championships, but for many years this was not the case at the French Open Championships or Wimbledon. For example, at Wimbledon 2004 Roger Federer, the Men's Singles Champion, won £602,500 in contrast with Maria Sharapova's prize money of £560,000. In 2006, Roger Federer received £30,000 more than Amelie Mauresmo in the singles events at Wimbledon. For an interview with Billie Jean King on, *inter alia*, the issue of prize money, see *Observer Sport*, 6 July 2003. Also see 'Equal pay champion attacks "sexist" Wimbledon', *The Times*, 27 June 2002 for criticisms by several players and DTI Secretary and Minister for Women, Patricia Hewitt. Since 2006, the winners of the French Open Championships have received the same prize money, and equal match fees were introduced at Wimbledon in 2007. For comment on these changes see Guinan, G,' Equal prize money at the Wimbledon tennis championships is of no advantage to the equal pay lobby', *Personnel Today*, 13 March 2007.

football; the identification of the spectators with the various teams is guaranteed only if those teams consist, at least as regards a majority of the players, of nationals of the relevant Member State; moreover, the teams which are successful in the national leagues represent their country in international competitions. Second, it is argued that the rules are necessary to ensure that enough players are available for the relevant national team; without the rules on foreigners, the development of young players would be affected. Third and finally, it is asserted that the rules on foreigners serve the purpose of ensuring a certain balance between the clubs, since otherwise the big clubs would be able to attract the best players.

The arguments in the first group would appear to latch on to the Court's observation in *Dona* that matches from which foreign players can be excluded must have a special character and context. In this connection the representative of the German Government spoke with particular emphasis at the hearing before the Court. He asserted that the 'national character of the performance' characterised first division professional football. A glance at the reality of football today shows that that does not correspond to the fact. The vast majority of clubs in the top divisions in the Member States play foreign players. In the German Bundesliga, for example, I am not aware of any club which does without foreign players altogether. If one considers the most successful European clubs of recent years, it becomes clear that nearly all of them have several foreign players in their ranks. In many cases it is precisely the foreign players who have characterised the team in question – one need only recall the AC Milan team in the early 1990s, whose pillars included the Dutch players Gullit, Rijkaard and Van Basten. There may indeed be certain differences from country to country with respect to the playing style or the mentality of players. That has, however, by no means prevented foreign players playing in the national leagues.

Even if the 'national aspect' had the significance which many people attribute to it, however, it could not justify the rules on foreign players. The right to freedom of movement and the prohibition of discrimination against nationals of other Member States are among the fundamental principles of the Community order. The rules on foreign players breach those principles in such a blatant and serious manner that any reference to national interests which cannot be based on Article 48(3) must be regarded as inadmissible as against those principles.

As to the identification of spectators with the teams, there is also no need for extensive discussion to show the weakness of that argument. As the Commission and Mr Bosman have rightly stated, the great majority of a club's supporters are much more interested in the success of their club than in the composition of the team. Nor does the participation of foreign players prevent a team's supporters from identifying with the team. Quite on the contrary, it is not uncommon for those players to attract the admiration and affection of football fans to a special degree. One of the most popular players ever to play for TSV l860 Munchen was undoubtedly Petar Radenkovic from what was then Yugoslavia. The English international Kevin Keegan was for many years a favourite of the fans at Hamburger SV. The popularity of Eric Cantona at Manchester United and of Jurgen Klinsmann at his former club Tottenham Hotspur is well known.

The inconsistency of those who put forward that view is moreover apparent if one considers an argument advanced by URBSFA in this context. It is argued that since the clubs often bear the name of a town, the spectators should be able to see players of the same nationality in the team in question. However, if a club adopts a name which contains the name of a place, it could at most be expected or demanded that that club's players should come from the place in question. Yet it is a well-known fact that in the case of Bayern Munchen, for instance, only a few of the players come from Bavaria (let alone Munich). If nationals who come from other parts of the relevant State are accepted without question, one cannot see why that should not also be the case for nationals of other Member States.

Finally, it should be observed that the success and playing style of a team are largely determined by the manager. The Court has already held, however, that football trainers enjoy the right to freedom of movement under Article 48. It did not even consider that those persons might perhaps be subject to restrictions other than those expressly permitted by Article 48. In practice frequent use is in fact made of that right. The best-known example is probably FC Barcelona, which has had a Dutch manager for a long time. Hamburger SV achieved its greatest success with an Austrian manager, and Bayern Munchen has had a whole series of foreign managers in recent decades. A country's national team is not always managed by a national of that country either. Thus the manager of the Irish national team, for example, is an Englishman. That emphasises that a 'national' characterisation of football, in the sense that players and managers must be nationals of the country in which the club in question is based, hardly comes into question.

It is further argued that the clubs which are successful in the national leagues represent the Member State in question in the European competitions and must therefore consist of at least a majority of nationals of that State; and that the 'German champions', for example, can thus emerge only from a competition between club teams for which 'at least a minimum number of German players play'. That argument too fails to convince. Firstly, the proponents of that view are unable to explain why precisely the rules currently applied are necessary to ensure that. If what mattered was that a team should consist predominantly of nationals of the State concerned, with eleven players in a team it would suffice generally to allow up to five foreign players. And if only a 'minimum number' of players had to possess the nationality of the State concerned, even more foreign players would have to be allowed. Moreover, it should be observed that the concept of 'German champion' can be interpreted without difficulty in a different way from that sought by the proponents of that view. There is no reason why that term cannot be taken as designating the club which has finished in first place following the matches played in Germany.

The argument fails to convince, however, for another reason too. In Germany, for example, the rules on foreign players do not apply to amateur teams. Some of those teams take part in the cup competition organized by the DFB. It is thus theoretically possible for an amateur team consisting of 11 foreign players to win the DFB cup and thus qualify to enter the European Cup-Winners' Cup. That this is not a purely hypothetical case is shown by the example of the Hertha BSC Berlin amateurs who reached the German cup final in 1993. The weakness of the argument becomes even more apparent if one considers that an association such as Scotland has no rules on foreign players and the other British associations have special rules for their mutual relations. It can thus perfectly well happen that clubs from those associations use a large number of players from other Member States in the leagues and competitions organised by their associations, but are forced to limit the number of such players when they take part in UEFA competitions. I cannot see how in such a case the abovementioned argument could be used to justify professional footballers from the European Community being forbidden to take part in the European Cup competitions.

The arguments in the second group are not convincing either. Nothing has demonstrated that the development of young players in a Member State would be adversely affected if the rule on foreign players were dropped. Only a few top teams set store on promoting their own young players as, for instance, Ajax Amsterdam do. Most talented players, by contrast, make their way upwards via small clubs to which those rules do not apply. Moreover, there is much to support the opinion that the participation of top foreign players promotes the development of football. Early contact with foreign stars 'can only be of advantage to a young player'.

It is admittedly correct that the number of jobs available to native players decreases, the more foreign players are engaged by and play for the clubs. That is, however, a consequence which the right to freedom of movement necessarily entails. Moreover, there is little to suggest that abolition of the rules on foreign players might lead to players possessing the nationality of the relevant State becoming a small minority in a league. The removal of the rules on foreign players would not oblige clubs to engage (more) foreigners, but would give them the possibility of doing so if they thought that promised success.

The argument that the rules on foreign players are needed to ensure that enough players develop for the national team is also unconvincing. Even if that consideration were to be regarded as legitimate in the light of the Court's judgments in *Walrave* and *Dona*, it could not justify the rules on foreigners. As I have already mentioned, it is unlikely that the influx of foreign players would be so great that native players would no longer get a chance. It is also significant here that the success or failure of the national team also has an effect on the interest in the club matches of the country in question. Winning the World Cup, for instance, generally brings about increased interest of spectators in national league matches as well. It is therefore in a country's clubs' very own interests to contribute to the success of the national team by developing suitable players and making them available. The prestige which those players acquire in the national team also benefits the clubs as such. Moreover, the example of Scotland may be noted, where the lack of rules on foreign players has plainly not led to a shortage of players for the national team.

Moreover, the national teams of the Member States of the Community nowadays very often include players who carry on their profession abroad, without that causing particular disadvantages. It suffices that the players have to be released for the national team's matches, as is also provided for in the current rules of the associations. The best example is perhaps the Danish national team which won the European Championship in 1992. In the German national team which became world champions in 1990 there were several players who played in foreign leagues. It is therefore not evident that the rules on foreigners are necessary in order to ensure the strength of the national team.

Third and finally, it is argued that the rules on foreign players serve to preserve the balance between clubs. In the opinion of URBSFA, the big clubs would otherwise be able to secure the services of the best players from the entire Community and thereby increase further the economic and sporting distance between them and the other clubs. The interest thus given expression is – as I shall explain later – a legitimate one. Like Mr Bosman, however, I am of the opinion that there are other means of attaining that objective without affecting the right of freedom of movement. Moreover, the rules are in any case only to a very limited extent appropriate to ensure a balance between the clubs. The richest clubs are still in a position to afford the best – and thus as a rule the most expensive – foreign stars. At the same time, such clubs have the opportunity to engage the best native players, without any comparable rule setting them limits.[80]

This limb of *Bosman* has generated far-reaching effects in the years since the ruling was delivered. Clubs in European competitions now have a wide number of nationalities to select a team from. There is an obvious interface here with the ongoing relaxation of transfer rules as required first by the *Bosman* ruling and subsequently by the European Commission. Indeed the only real restrictions will be derived from a Member State's immigration rules. For example, European footballers, who are not nationals of EU Member States, and players from outside Europe are still required to be in possession of a work permit if they are to play for a club in the Premier and Football Leagues. Similarly, the regulations of national sporting associations may still impose quotas on the fielding of foreign players.

Welch, R, 'Swamping the British game?: Foreign footballers and the new work permit regulations'

Almost from the date the European Court of Justice gave its historic ruling in the *Bosman* case on 15 December 1995 there has been concern over the number of foreign players playing professional football in the football leagues in England and Scotland. The impact of *Bosman* on

---

80 [1996] 1 CMLR (Case C-415/93).

this situation is partly the result of the greater mobility that the ruling has given to footballers at the end of their employment contracts. However, it is the second limb of the ruling that has had rather more significance for the increased recruitment of non-British players by domestic clubs. This is because *Bosman* essentially permits clubs to field as many non-British players in any given team as they wish providing those players are nationals of other Member States of the EU and EEA (Liechtenstein, Iceland and Norway). Moreover, freedom of movement, as required by Article 39 of the EC Treaty (formerly Article 48), prohibits Member States from applying their normal immigration rules to players from these countries.

However, of course, EU law does not extend to players from the many high-ranking footballing countries around the globe, and, in the here and now at least, does not apply to European countries outside the EU/EEA. Thus players from these countries may only enter the UK to play for a British club if they have been granted a work permit. The rules concerning work permits were amended by the Government in July 1999 prior to the start of the current season. These changes were immediately criticised for constituting a tightening rather than relaxation of the rules. Thus Gordon Taylor, on behalf of the PFA, stated that the changes 'will open the way for cheap, foreign imports' and Frank Clark, on behalf of the League Managers' Association, also expressed concern about 'the number of foreign players currently in the British game' (see *The Guardian*, Saturday 3 July 1999). This article will outline the changes that have been made and seek to evaluate arguments for and against the work permit system.

Anyone seeking a work permit in the UK must meet criteria which are issued by the Department for Education and Employment. (The scheme is administered by the DEE's Overseas Labour Service under the Immigration Acts 1971, 1988.) Thus work permit rules apply to all areas of employment including professional sports. There are, for example, rules relating to cricket, ice hockey and rugby that are analogous to the rules governing football.

Prior to July 1999, a foreign footballer would not generally have been eligible for a work permit unless he was an international player who had played for his country's 'A' team for approximately 75 per cent of competitive matches in the previous two seasons. He was also required to be one of the six highest earners for the British club concerned. The work permit only applied to a single season unless an extension was granted on the basis that the player had proven himself to be a regular player for the club, and was thus making a significant contribution to the British game. Under the new regulations the wage requirement has gone and work permits apply to the whole of the player's contract. The requirement to be an international player is retained, and the FIFA ranking of the player's national side will now be taken into account. In *R v Secretary of State for Education and Employment ex parte Portsmouth Football Club* [1988] COD 142 it was held that the 75 per cent test must not be applied too rigidly, as, for example, a player having missed international matches through injury should be taken into account. The new rules permit the requisite flexibility through provision of an appeals committee to consider an application where the player does not meet the criteria, but a club has provided evidence that he is of the highest calibre.

In announcing the changes (then) Minister of Sport, Tony Banks, stated: 'The criteria strike a sensible balance between allowing clubs to recruit the best available international talent and the need to provide opportunities for home grown young players.' The Employment and Equal Opportunities Minister, Margaret Hodge, described the new system as 'straightforward, open and transparent', which would 'ensure a faster and fairer application process' (see DEE press release 307/99).

Since *Bosman* there has been a 1,800 per cent increase in foreign players in the Premiership (see *The Guardian*, 18 July 1999). As predicted by Gordon Taylor ('The World Cup, foreign players and work permits' (1998), 5(4) Sports Law Administration & Practice), the 1998 World cup finals has also contributed to this development. However, whether the new rules really represent a relaxation which will generate an even greater number of 'foreign imports' remains debatable. Certainly, the consequences of taking into account the FIFA ranking of a player's national side still need to be fully evaluated. The fact that a permit can now last for the period of a player's contract will make the prospect of playing in the UK more attractive to the overseas player, but then it seems fair and just that if a player is offered and accepts a contract his job security should not be jeopardised by the possibility that a work permit will not be renewed at the end of a given season.

It is contended that the problem with the debate over whether work permit rules should be tightened or relaxed, or as an alternative whether a system of quotas should be introduced, is that it obscures the question as to whether such systems are desirable in the first place. Much attention has been focused on whether the increase in foreigners in the Premiership is deleterious to the international prospects of the English team. The essence of the argument is that fewer Englishmen are able to play club football at the highest level and are forced to ply their trade in the lower divisions. Thus they do not develop the skills required at international level. However, casual observation appears to indicate that a significant number of foreign players currently in the Premiership, probably the majority, come from EU/EEA countries (not to mention other countries in the UK) and thus do not require work permits in the first place.

. . . Moreover, there is an assumption that arguably the most important group in football, the paying public, collectively prioritise the success of the English team over the success of the club they support week in and week out, and pay good money to watch in all weathers. Speaking for myself, but believing myself to be a typical football fan, it is definitely a case of club over country. Equally, for many football fans (especially for those of us who support lower division clubs) it a pleasure to be able to watch the likes of Emmanuel Petit, David Ginola and Gianfranco Zola on a regular basis rather than occasionally during international tournaments.

A political and philosophical objection to work permit rules and quota systems is that they are derived from immigration controls which it is contended – sporting issues aside – are objectively racist. This is so whether we are reflecting on the racist speeches of the likes of Enoch Powell, the infamous 'swamping' comments of Margaret Thatcher which contributed to her winning the 1979 general election or the current controversy over the numbers of asylum seekers 'flooding' into the UK. Moreover, the world of football is not yet totally free from the racism and xenophobic nationalism which has been associated with the game in recent decades. Irrespective of what is intended (and no one can doubt the commitment of the PFA to combating racism in football) any statements which increase perceptions of foreigners as a problem tend to fan the flames of racism and, in turn, may give credibility to the English 'nationalist' posing as a genuine football fan.

Surely, one of the (few) beneficial consequences of globalisation should be, alongside the already free movement of capital, the free movement of labour throughout the globe. Would this present an insuperable problem for football and other professional sports? I think not. In any case, the best solution to reducing the number of foreigners that clubs are recruiting, as indeed Gordon Taylor has identified, is for clubs to redevelop their youth academies to develop cheap home-grown and, indeed, local talent. Much as I love to watch him, give me Pompey's own Stevie Claridge over Ginola any day![81]

The work permit rules discussed in the above extract are still essentially in force. However, it should be noted that they now operate within the context of the points system as introduced by the last Labour government. Under this system a player's country must be at or above 70th place in the official FIFA World Rankings when averaged over the two years preceding the date of the application for a work permit. The permit can last for three years providing the player can demonstrate

---

81 Welch, R, 'Swamping the British game?: Foreign footballers and the new work permit regulations' (2000) 3(2) SLB 6–7.

sufficient competence in the English language. If this is not the case then the club must apply for a work permit on an annual basis. Applications can be made for work permits to be renewed on their expiry. However, if a player moves to a new club whilst under or at the end of his contract a new application for a permit must be made.[82]

In the immediate aftermath of *Bosman* the only clear conclusion that could be drawn was that a sports professional, who was an EU national and out of contract, had the right under what is now Art 45 TFEU to move to another Member State to play for a new club. However, further player mobility was generated by the ECJ ruling in *Kolpak*.[83] The facts of *Kolpak* are straightforward. Kolpak was a Slovakian goalkeeper for the German Handball club, TSV Ostringen eV Handball. According to the rules of the DHB, the German Handball Federation clubs were prohibited from fielding more than two non-EU nationals. The ECJ was asked to give a preliminary ruling on whether, under Art 38 of the Europe Agreement between Slovakia and the EU, Slovakian workers were entitled to general equality of treatment with nationals of the relevant Member State.

Applying its reasoning in *Bosman*, the ECJ ruled that nationals of third countries who were parties to Europe Agreements were entitled to be treated in the same way as national players for the purposes of a sport's rules. In short, they could not be considered ineligible for team selection because there was already the specified quota of non-EU nationals selected for the game. Subsequently, in *Simutenkov*,[84] a case involving a Russian national playing professional football in Spain, the ECJ ruled that he was protected by a non-discriminatory provision contained in an agreement on partnership and co-operation signed between the EU and the Russian Federation in 1994.

Essentially, nationals of a number of countries, which have entered into agreements with the EU containing non-discrimination clauses which can be interpreted as taking direct effect, must be treated on an equal basis with nationals of the Member State in which they have secured employment. Thus quota restrictions on 'foreign players' do not apply to them as such restrictions constitute 'working conditions' for the purposes of non-discrimination clauses in relevant agreements. Not all agreements between individual countries and the EU will contain such provisions, but, in addition to football, the *Kolpak* case has had an effect on sports such as both codes of rugby and cricket; games which *Bosman* has only minimally impacted upon as they are not widely played professionally in Europe.

The 'Cotonou Agreement' between the EU and the African, Caribbean and Pacific Group of States (ACP) concerning the objectives of sustainable development and poverty reduction has had a significant impact. For example, a number of players have been signed by rugby league sides from countries such as Fiji, Tonga and Samoa. In rugby union and cricket, a significant number of South Africans have taken advantage of the ruling to play for professional clubs in England. In English county cricket, in comparison to say Australian players, South African cricketers can no longer be subject to rules which restrict the number of overseas players that can play for a county to one in any given season. As a response to a concern that many county teams are fielding a significant number of players not eligible to play for the England national team, the governing body for cricket, the England and Wales Cricket Board (ECB), has linked the central payments made to counties to the number of English qualified players who represent the county. This in effect means that every game a 'Kolpak' player plays instead of an English qualified player, a county receives over £1,000 less from the ECB.[85]

---

82 The full details of the system can be accessed from the FA website at http://www.thefa.com/TheFA/RulesandRegulations/ FARegulations. For further discussion, see Osborne, A., 'UK: Immigration laws: implications for sport' (2009) 7(4) WSLR.
83 Case C-438/00 *Deutscher Handballbund eV v Maros Kolpak* [2003] ECR I-4135.
84 Case C-265/03 *Igor Simutenkov v Abogado del Estado, Real Federacion Espanola de Futbol and Ministerio Fiscal* [2005] ECR I-2579.
85 For more, see Boyes, S, 'Caught behind or following-on? Cricket, the European Union and the "Bosman effect"', (2005) 3(1) ESLJ, http://www2.warwick.ac.uk/fac/soc/law/elj/eslj/. Note that a stricter interpretation by the EU Commission of the Cotonou Agreement has lead to narrower work permit criteria based on the need for past international record of recipients; see 'ECB wins overseas player battle', BBC Sport, 26 October, 2009, http://news.bbc.co.uk/sport1/hi/cricket/counties/8325975. stm. Also see Farrow, F, 'Cotonou: Commission clarifies permitted player restrictions' (2008) 6(8) WSLR for clarification that the Cotonou Agreement does not alter the requirement for overseas cricketers to secure a work permit to play for an English club. However, if they are nationals of associate countries then, if they secure work permits, quota restrictions will not apply to them.

Prior to the ruling in *Kolpak*, there had been some speculation that the ECJ was going to extend Art 45 TFEU to nationals of associate countries. Such radical change was not given effect and Art 45 remains inapplicable to such nationals. Thus, they have no rights to enter a Member State to take up employment, or to move from Member State to Member State in order to do so.[86] A transfer to a club in another Member State will still be subject to that country's immigration rules. National laws requiring work permits, on the expiry of a non-national's contract, still apply to nationals of countries with associate status. Moreover, a number of the European countries, to which *Kolpak* applied, are now EU Member States and their nationals will be protected fully by Art 45.

Nationality quotas: the debate continues

In the aftermath of *Bosman* and *Kolpak* it was generally assumed that any form of quota for team selection did not apply other than to players from outside of the EU where they were nationals of countries with no relationship with it. The Home Grown Players Rule introduced by UEFA and the 6+5 rule proposed by FIFA have proven this assumption to be wrong.

The latter, which was agreed at the FIFA Congress in May 2008, essentially provides that at the beginning of each match, each club must field at least six players who are eligible to play for the national team of the country of the club. However, there are no restrictions proposed on the number of non-eligible players under contract with the club (although restrictions on size of squads that may be permitted in individual leagues will have to be taken into account).[87] This restriction applies to the starting line-up of the team, and coaches will be able to modify the ratio of national players in the team with up to three permitted substitutions, all of whom can be non-eligible players.

At the time of writing this proposal has reportedly been deferred.[88] Although FIFA itself had argued that the rule was not contrary to *Bosman* and thus to EU law, there was a widespread belief that the rule, based as it was on nationality, constituted direct discrimination. As held by the ECJ in *Commission v Italy*,[89] direct discrimination cannot be justified and can be saved only by reference to one of the express derogations in Art 39(3) of the Treaty on grounds of public policy, public security or public health or through secondary legislation. It is difficult to see how the 6+5 rule, any more than the original 3+2 rule, could permit derogation under any of these headings and therefore it should be ruled as inherently unlawful.

Even if the 6+5 rule is not directly discriminatory, but can correctly be seen as indirect discrimination, it is unlikely that it could be successfully justified. The arguments put forward in favour of justification are essentially the same as those put forward by UEFA to justify the home grown players rule, but, as discussed below, it is by no means certain that this rule is in accordance with EU law, as it could fail on the basis of proportionality. If this view is correct then justification of the patently more discriminatory FIFA rule must surely be impossible.[90]

The UEFA rule was first proposed in 2005. The rule requires clubs participating in the Champions League and the UEFA Cup to have a minimum number of home grown players, that is,

86 See Boyes, S, 'In the Shadow of Bosman: The Regulatory Penumbra of Sport in the EU' (2003) 12(2) Nottingham Law Journal 72; Hendrickx, F, 'The European Non-EU Player and the Kolpak Case' (2003) ISLJ 12; Van den Bogaert, S, 'And Another Uppercut from the European Court of Justice to Nationality Requirements in Sports Regulations' (2004) 29(2) European Law Review 267.

87 The English Premier League has been criticised over the squad sizes operated by many clubs, eg it is reported that in the 2008–09 season, Liverpool FC had a first team squad of 62 players; see 'Uefa slam "ridiculous" Big Four squad sizes', *The Guardian*, 29 March 2009, www.guardian.co.uk/football/2009/mar/29/uefa-liverpool-squad-sizes-premier-league.

88 See 'Team sports and IOC to work on way of protecting national teams' (2010) 8(7) WSLR for a statement from FIFA that it has not abandoned the 6+5 proposal. Rather it is seeking to work with other international team sports federations and the IOC to see how such a proposal could be introduced in a number of sports.

89 Case C-283/99 *Commission v Italy* [2001] ECR I-4363.

90 For a critique of why FIFA and UEFA regard the reintroduction of nationality quotas to be necessary and why neither rule can be justified under EU law see Gardiner, S and Welch, R, 'Bosman – There and Back Again: the Legitimacy of Playing Quotas under European Union Sports Policy' (2011) 17(6) *European Law Journal* 828–49. For a view that the 6+5 Rule is compatible with EU law see Battis, U, 'Player Contracts: FIFA's "6+5" proposal: compatibility with EU law' (2009) 7(3) WSLR.

players who, regardless of their nationality, have been trained by their club or by another club in the same national association for at least three years between the ages of 15 and 21. This was set at four players in a maximum squad of 25 in the first season of application, 2006–07. This rose to eight out of the maximum squad of 25 players in the 2008–09 season.[91]

The perceived legitimacy of this policy has led to a number of domestic leagues introducing similar restrictions to their playing squads. In England, the Football League introduced restrictions, which started in the 2009–10 season, which require four players in a matchday squad to have been registered by a domestic club for three years before their 21st birthday.[92] In fact, for most Football League clubs this will merely be reflecting the status quo that has existed for many years, with clubs already complying with this requirement. The Premier League has adopted similar rules with effect from season 2010–11.[93]

Any policy or rule that is intrinsically liable to affect migrant workers more than national workers and thus impede access to the labour market and freedom of movement constitutes indirect discrimination. It is clear that UEFA's rule falls into this category but, as such, will be lawful if it can be justified. Justification of the UEFA rule requires it to be established that the rule does further the objective needs of football and meets the criterion of proportionality. For this to be the case the objectives secured by rule must not be outweighed by the discriminatory impact of it and there must be no other means by which these objectives can be met just as effectively.

With respect to potential justification, it is important to take into account that the rule has received a positive response from a number of quarters. Like the European Commission and FIFPro, the European Parliament has been supportive and 'expresses its clear support for the UEFA measures to encourage the education of young players by requiring a minimum number of home-grown players in a professional club's squad and by placing a limit on the size of the squads . . . [it] believes that such incentive measures are proportionate and calls on professional clubs to strictly implement this rule'.[94]

The Arnaut Report, published in 2006, contended that the measure would: encourage training programmes in order to promote, develop, nurture and educate new talents; promote the local nature of clubs, so fans identify more with their team; maintain competitive balance by reducing the importance of money; reduce the tendency towards 'hoarding' of players; and widen the pool of talent within an association eligible to represent the national team.[95]

However, even if the rule is seen as justifiable in political and footballing contexts, it still has to satisfy the legal requirement of proportionality, and, arguably, the above purported justifications fail to take into account that there are alternative ways of securing the legitimate interests of professional football.[96]

As made clear by Advocate General Lenz in *Bosman*, redistribution of income provides the most effective and fairest way of ensuring that the vast sums of money secured by large clubs are shared with their smaller brethren.[97] This both increases the potential for competitive balance and provides income for the development and enhancement of youth academies and the establishment of

---

91 UEFA, Regulations of the UEFA Champions League 2008/2009, www.uefa.com/multimediafiles/download/regulations/uefa/others/70/22/60/702260_download.pdf.

92 'Clubs vote for "home-grown" rule', BBC Sport, 18 December 2008, http://news.bbc.co.uk/sport1/hi/football/7789808.stm.

93 Conn, D, 'Homegrown doesn't mean English but rule will help', *The Guardian*, 2 September 2010. Premier League squads may be up to 25 senior players and must include no more than 17 players who are not home grown. A player is home grown if he has spent three seasons with any English or Welsh club. However, there are no restrictions on the number of players in a squad below the age of 21.

94 European Parliament, Resolution on the Future of Professional Football in Europe, 29 March 2007, at p 34.

95 Independent European Sport Review, http://www.independentfootballreview.com/doc/Full_Report_EN.pdf, p 115.

96 An underlying issue is the extent to which, if at all, sport should be exempt from the norms of EU law. For a discussion of this, see Weatherill, S, 'Anti-doping Revisited – the Demise of the Rule of "Purely Sporting Interest"?' (2006) 27(12) European Competition Law Review 645.

97 *Bosman*, at para 233.

national scouting networks. Rather than preventing clubs from fielding foreign players is it not much better to encourage the provision of the requisite financial and physical resources for the identification and development of young local talent?

It may be the case at present for it to be commercially more attractive to attract youth talent from other clubs who are classified as 'home grown' rather than investing in potentially costly infrastructure. Indeed, in the context of post-*Bosman* transfer systems, academies are increasingly seen as not commercially viable. This is because once a player has reached the age of 23 or 24 and is out of contract, free agency applies with no right to a transfer fee or compensation from the former employing club.[98] This is despite the money that club may have invested in training that player in his youth. However, in this regard it could be possible for clubs to enter into a collective agreement with one another to reserve a share of the income from broadcasting rights and the like for clubs that agree to invest in youth academies. Such an agreement would also meet the aspirations of football fans who, typically, enjoy seeing their club field a mixture of international stars and players with local connections and thus a genuine commitment to the club.

Other possibilities that may constitute a more proportionate response to solve the perceived problems in football include salary caps, though these have rejected by FIFPro and operate artificially to restrict the income that professional players can earn. FIFPro has suggested as an alternative that there be a cap on transfer fees. Arguably, this is the best solution as it will contribute to the restoration of competitive balance and prevent the richer clubs gazumping attempts by smaller clubs to sign star players. Admittedly, it will reduce the signing-on fee that such players will earn but this is preferable to a permanent restriction on their incomes.

The weakest argument for the UEFA rule, and indeed FIFA's 6+5 rule, is the view that it will increase the number of players eligible for national teams by increasing the pool of national talent. The best clubs will always recruit the best national players and there should always be sufficient numbers of these to provide the squads for international competitions. As Advocate General Lenz observed, the fortunes of the Scottish team are hardly affected by the fact that their best players often choose to play in the English Premier League. Indeed, as he also commented, the importing of foreign internationals into a domestic league has a tendency to improve the skills of domestic players rather than have a negative impact on their development.[99]

Miettinen and Parrish have argued that the UEFA rules may offend EU law in that they cannot be justified by reference to normal principles 'on the grounds that they are disproportionate, unfit for the purposes they are relied upon or pursue economic as well as legitimate and justifiable non-economic objectives.'

Miettinen, S, and Parrish, R, 'Nationality Discrimination in Community Law: An Assessment of UEFA Regulations Governing Player Eligibility for European Club Competitions (The Home-Grown Player Rule)'

In the White Paper on Sport the European Commission argued that '[r]ules requiring that teams include a certain quota of locally trained players could be accepted as being compatible with the Treaty provisions on free movement of persons if they do not lead to any direct discrimination based on nationality and if possible indirect discrimination effects resulting from them can be justified as being proportionate to a legitimate objective pursued' (Commission of the European Communities 2007, p 6).[100] The home-grown player rule seeks to achieve similar

---

98 It should be noted that, in Case C325/08 *Olympique Lyonnais SASP v Olivier Bernard and Newcastle United*, a reference for a preliminary ruling under Article 234 EC from the Cour de Cassation in *Olympique Lyonnais SASP v Olivier Bernard and Newcastle United FC*, Judgment of the Court dated 16 March 201, the ECJ impliedly approved the FIFA transfer rules as they require compensation to be based on the cost of a training a young player not the loss that the transferring club sustains. See Carr, A, 'Player Contracts: Training compensation: ECJ ruling in the Olivier Bernard case' (2010) 8(4) WSLR.

99 *Bosman*, at paras 145 and 146.

100 Commission of the European Communities, 'White Paper in Sport' (2007), COM (2007) 391 final.

aims as the *Bosman* 3+2 rule. However, it is legally distinguishable in that although the objective is an attempt to link attributes of residence and players' club affiliations, the method employed does not constitute direct nationality discrimination but indirect discrimination which arises from requirements which more nationals than non-nationals are likely to fulfil. Since it is indirectly but not directly discriminatory, categories of objective justification beyond the limited Treaty grounds may be available. It does not fall within the ambit of the 'sporting exception' which in the light of modern case law appears restricted to nationality rules in national team sports. Whilst UEFA may make a case for the 'inherency' of the rule, it should be noted that those cases in which the 'inherent' nature of the rule precluded a restriction under either free movement or competition law were all limited to rules that were indistinctly applicable and non-discriminatory in both law and fact. This is not the case with the home-grown players rule, which favours nationals over non-nationals. Consequently, the rule will be tested against the strength and proportionality of the objective justifications presented by UEFA . . .

With its adoption of the home-grown players rule, UEFA has reintroduced regulations that closely correspond to nationality requirements which the EC Treaty expressly prohibits and which the Court of Justice struck down in *Bosman* for that reason. If its arguments are based on a sporting exception that is much broader than that afforded to 'purely sporting' rules, they are questionable following the Court's clarification in *Meca-Medina*. In line with its historical case law, if the rule has even the slightest economic effect, a sporting rule other than a nationality restriction in the context of competitions organised exclusively on that basis cannot be considered *a priori* exempt but must be justified. Nationality rules have been found 'purely sporting' only in the context of competitions between ostensibly non-commercial national teams, a limitation that is reinforced by the ruling of the European Court of Justice in *Meca-Medina*. Since the home-grown player rule is capable of economic effects, where the competition is not structured around nationality, it is difficult to accept that the very fundamental Treaty objections to nationality discrimination in the context of commercial activity could be justified in the manner proposed by UEFA.

UEFA's introduction of the rule has been justified with reference to considerations which in *Bosman* did not serve to justify the 3+2 rule. Unlike the 3+2 rule and FIFA's proposed 6+5 rule, which constitute direct nationality discrimination, the notion of home-grown players is structured by reference to residence and other requirements which appear to indirectly favour nationals of the home state and thereby constitute indirect discrimination. The legal significance of this is that whatever doubts one might harbour regarding the justifiability of directly discriminatory rules, it is clear that indirectly discriminatory rules are in principle capable of objective justification beyond the limited Treaty grounds. Although the Court has had some time to enunciate a single, coherent framework to tackle the notion of discrimination across the fundamental freedoms, it has opted not to do so (Davies 2003, pp 93–115).[101] The reluctance of the Court to expressly treat overt discrimination on the basis of nationality and residence requirements as analogous is not entirely satisfactory, particularly where a residence requirement is a nationality provision in all but name and is intended to segment markets according to national boundaries. The rationale for requiring 'home-grown players' as per UEFA's regulations is to enable markets in commercial sport to maintain a geographic character and reinforce partitions within the Community by discriminating against Community workers. Had the rules contained express nationality clauses, they would be justifiable with reference only to the limited Treaty grounds, none of which would include those objective justifications currently relied on by UEFA.

UEFA's justifications may be attacked on the grounds that they are disproportionate, unfit for the purposes they are relied upon or pursue economic as well as legitimate and justifiable

---

101 Davies, G, *Nationality Discrimination in the European Internal Market* (2003), Dordrecht: Kluwer Law International.

non-economic objectives. In this connection, rules designed to preserve competitive balance in football, encourage youth development and protect national teams are legitimate objectives which the EU should permit as defences to the adoption of restrictions on free movement in sport. The issue rests on whether UEFA's home-grown player rule amounts to an appropriate and proportionate means of achieving these objectives and whether it genuinely seeks to achieve these rather than prohibited economic aims. Some of the analysis presented above suggests that the two proposed regimes are neither fit for purpose nor proportionate. The issue for UEFA is much wider. The cumulative effect of ECJ jurisprudence in this field amounts to an effective prohibition on the use of nationality restrictions in sport. The erosion of the nationality principle is altering the European model of sport and this raises serious regulatory and financial questions for UEFA. Furthermore, at issue in the *Charleroi* case is not only the principle of obligatory player release clauses, but wider considerations of stakeholder participation and financial rebalancing. For UEFA, these issues, coupled with the inability to maintain a partitioned European market, threatens to disturb the vertical channels of regulatory authority which have historically underpinned the European model.[102]

Key Points

- Under The Equality Act 2010 (EA), it is unlawful for a club or a sport's governing body to discriminate against players or athletes by reason of protected characteristics such as gender, pregnancy, being a transgendered person, race, religion, sexual orientation or disability.
- Discrimination will be direct if a person is treated less favourably by reference to one (or more) of the above characteristics.
- Discrimination will be indirect if polices, practices and the like put persons who share one of the above characteristics at a disadvantage in comparison with persons who do not share that characteristic.
- Under s 195 EA, discrimination in sport is lawful where a nationality or residence requirement is imposed as a condition for selecting a person to represent a country, place or area.
- Similarly, under s 195, discrimination in sport is lawful where it is a gender-related activity in circumstances in which the physical strength, stamina or physique of average persons of one sex would put them at a disadvantage compared to average persons of the other sex as competitors in events involving the activity.
- Clubs will be directly or vicariously liable if a player is subjected to harassment by reason of one of the above protected characteristics, and the club fails to take such steps as would be reasonably practicable to protect the player from such harassment.
- As a result of the *Bosman* ruling, it is unlawful to impose nationality restrictions on clubs' team selections where these adversely affect recruiting or fielding players from other EU member states.
- As a result of the *Kolpak* ruling, it is unlawful to impose quota restrictions on the selection of foreign players where these adversely impact on players from countries which have associate status with the EU.
- Despite the sporting reasons which have been advanced, FIFA's proposal for a '6+5' rule probably constitutes unlawful direct discrimination under EU law.
- UEFA's Home Grown Players rule probably constitutes indirect discrimination, and could be ruled unlawful under EU law unless it can be justified as a proportionate means of achieving the sporting objectives which have been advanced in support of it.

---

102 Miettinen, S and Parrish, R., 'Nationality Discrimination in Community Law: An Assessment of UEFA Regulations Governing Player Eligibility for European Club Competitions (The Home-Grown Player Rule)' (2007) 5(2) ESLJ.

Key Sources

Burdsey, D (ed), *Race, Ethnicity and Football* (2011), London: Routledge.

Charlish, P and Riley, S, 'Should Oscar Run?' (2008), 18 *Fordham Intell Prop Media & Ent LJ*, 929–57.

Gardiner, S and Welch, R, 'Bosman – There and Back Again: the Legitimacy of Playing Quotas under European Union Sports Policy' (2011), 17(6) *European Law Journal* 828–49.

Miettinen, S, and Parrish, R, 'Nationality Discrimination in Community Law: An Assessment of UEFA Regulations Governing Player Eligibility for European Club Competitions (The Home-Grown Player Rule)' (2007), 5(2) *Entertainment and Sports Law Journal*.

Opinion of Advocate General Lenz in *ASBL Union Royale Belge des Societes de Football Association & others v Jean-Marc Bosman* [1996] 1 CMLR 645 (Case C-415/93).

Chapter 11

Safety and Participants in Sport

Chapter Contents

Introduction	499
What Is Sports Violence?	500
Civil Law Liability for Sports Participant Violence	500
Potential Defendants	503
Criminal Liability for Sports Participant Violence	515
Prosecutorial Discretion – the Solution?	520
Risk Management and Extreme Sports	526
Child Protection: Sports Coaches and Child Athletes	533
Conclusion	540
Key Points	541
Key Sources	542

Introduction

The creation of a safe working environment for those who participate in sport is important for the well-being and integrity of sport. However, this does not mean that sport should be sanitised and overtly controlled with respect to its physicality. Physical endeavour and vigour are essential elements of most sports. As Di Nicola and Mendeloff state: 'Much of sport's appeal comes from its unrestrained qualities, the delight of its unpredictability, the exploitation of human error, and the thrill of its sheer physicalness.'[1]

This chapter will focus on one of the major issues involved in the burgeoning development of sports law in Britain during the last two decades, namely the degree to which the law should get involved in regulating behaviour on the sports field. The debate has revolved around the opposing contentions that 'the law does not stop at the touchline'[2] on the one hand and that the laws' intervention is highly problematic on the other.[3] The debate has moved on to attempt to prescribe when and where the law should regulate violent and unacceptable play with a recognition that due to the competitive nature of contact sports, especially team sports where physical interaction is pervasive, some test needs to be developed to systemise the law's intervention. Recent cases in the United Kingdom in both criminal and civil law have seen legal regulation used in substitution for the internal mechanisms of the relevant sporting supervisory bodies.[4]

The first part of the chapter will focus on the use of the civil law as a remedy to obtain compensation for injuries that have suspended or ended careers. This is a recent development in professional sport that seems to be becoming more attractive to injured players.[5] The second part of the chapter will focus on the criminal law, which, however, has a longer history of intervention. It has been recognised since the late nineteenth century that sports participants who use intentional or reckless force, which is likely to cause bodily injury to another, will be acting illegally.[6] The third part of the chapter will focus on how boxing and other inherently dangerous sporting activities should be regulated and the opposing moral positions concerning the state's right to be paternalistic and controlling and the libertarian rights of individuals to take part in dangerous activities.

The fourth and last part of the chapter will examine the crucial issue of child protection in sport. The issue of the treatment of children in sport mirrors increasing awareness of the rights of children generally in society.[7] Although the focus is on participation in sport, there is evidence of considerable exploitation of children within the wider sports industry.[8] Sport provides many positive opportunities for young people to participate individually, or more commonly in groups. This is generally at a recreational 'play' level; however, increasingly young people are taking part in highly competitive and sometimes elite-level sport. The image of parents shouting at their children and haranguing the officials has become a not uncommon one in school and Sunday morning football: even at this level winning is all.[9] In sports such as tennis, swimming and gymnastics the age of participants at elite level has become ever younger.

---

1   Di Nicola, R and Mendeloff, S, 'Controlling Violence in Professional Sport: Rules Reform and the Federal Professional Sports Violence Commission' (1983) 21 Dusquesne Law Review 845.
2   Grayson, E, 'On the field of play' (1971) NLJ 413 and, with Bond, C, 'Making foul play a crime' (1993) SJ 693.
3   Gardiner, S, 'The Law and the Sportsfield' (1994) Crim LR 513.
4   General analysis can be found in Andoh, B, Parsons, S, Jones, P and Watts, B, 'Personal injuries in professional football: legal aspects' (2010) International Sports Law Review; also see Fafinski, S, 'Consent and the Rules of the Game: The Interplay of Civil and Criminal Liability for Sporting Injuries' (2005) Journal of Criminal Law 414.
5   Perhaps the most significant case in recent years has been *Condon v Basi* [1985] 2 All ER 453, which held that a duty of care is owed by one sports participant against another.
6   R v *Bradshaw* (1878) 14 Cox Crim. Cases 83 and R v *Moore* (1898) 14 TLR 229.
7   See the Children Act 1989.
8   *A Sporting Chance* (1997), Christian Aid, p 217, concerning exploitation of children in India, some, as young as 10, stitching footballs for about 10 pence a ball. Pieri, M, 'Labour standards in the manufacture of sporting goods: a tarnished trophy?' (1999) 2(2) SLB 10; see One World Trust report at http://www.oneworldtrust.org/publications/cat_view/64-publications-by-project/65-global-accountability-report.
9   See 'Soccer brawl father is told to pay £750', *The Daily Telegraph*, 15 February 1997.

What Is Sports Violence?

The issue of determining liability in sports participation as with all areas of social life reflects changing values concerning the degree of physical interaction between participants and what behaviour might be constructed as 'violence'. The term violence has no specific definition in English law; it is largely a social construction. In the sporting domain it is created not only by mainstream social norms but sporting norms too. A great deal of academic inquiry has focused on the phenomenon of sports violence, particularly highlighting its patriarchal nature.[10]

Many research reports could be cited. In a Canadian study by Michael Smith,[11] sports violence is divided into four types:

1. 'brutal body contact' – that is part of sports participation;
2. 'borderline violence' – assaults which, although prohibited by the formal rules, are essentially the province of referees, umpires etc;
3. 'quasi-criminal violence' – which violates not only the rules of the sport but also the informal playing culture;
4. 'criminal violence' – serious and obviously outside the boundaries of sport.

Of course sporting codes use terms such as 'violent conduct' in their playing and disciplinary rules.[12] In the legal literature, terms such as 'participator violence' have been used. More pejorative terms have been used by the courts, such as stating that sport is not a 'licence for thuggery'.[13] The reality is that different sports involve the use of variable degrees of force and physicality between individuals. Conduct in a number of sports is inexorably a form of violence.[14] Smith's taxonomy above highlights this truism. At a time of considerable consternation about levels of 'violence' in society generally, it is important to remember how 'violence' on the sports field is understood in the debate about what role the law has in regulating its manifestation.[15]

Civil Law Liability for Sports Participant Violence

Over the last few years, civil liability is the branch of the law that has become most used concerning on-field injuries. Sports participants have increasingly resorted to pursuing civil law actions to seek financial compensation for loss caused through injury, in both professional and amateur sport. This has involved actions against other players,[16] the referee,[17] medical personnel,[18] sports clubs and sports governing bodies.[19] It has been argued: 'Tort law is the best way to deter violent conduct

---

10 Note there is an extensive sociological literature concerning the understanding of violence in sport; see eg Young, K, 'Violence, Risk, and Liability in Male Sports Culture' (1993) Sociology of Sport Journal 373–96; Parry, J, 'Violence and Aggression in Contemporary Sport' in Parry, J and McNamee, M (eds) *Ethics and Sport* (2001), London: Routledge; and Kerr, J, *Rethinking Aggression in Sport* (2005), London: Routledge.
11 Smith, MD, *Violence and Sport* (1983), London: Butterworths.
12 For example the Fédération Internationale de Football Association (FIFA) Laws of the Game, Law 12 includes punishment of sending off for 'Violent Conduct'; the International Rugby Board (IRB) Laws of the Game, Law 10 uses the term 'Dangerous Play and Misconduct'.
13 R v Hardy [1994] *The Guardian*, 27 July 1994.
14 Note George Orwell's belief that 'Serious sport has nothing to do with fair play. It is bound up with hatred, jealousy, boastfulness, disregard of all rules and sadistic pleasure in witnessing violence. In other words, it is war minus the shooting', *Shooting an Elephant*, 'The Sporting Spirit' (1950).
15 For more on the construction of 'sports violence', see Gardiner, S, 'Tackling from Behind: Interventions on the Playing Field', in Greenfield, A and Osborn, G, *Law and Sport in Contemporary Society* (2000), London: Frank Cass.
16 Elliot v Saunders (1994) unreported. See Felix, A and Gardiner, S, 'Drama in Court 14: Elliot v Saunders' (1994) 2(2) SATLJ; *Watson & Bradford City FC v Gray & Huddersfield Town FC* unreported (1998), see 1(6) SLB.
17 Successful actions in the last few years include *Smoldon v Whiteworth & Nolan* (*The Times*, 18 December 1996).
18 Brady v Sunderland Football club (1998), unreported case, see SLB, vol 1, no 5, 1998, p 4.
19 *Watson v British Boxing Board of Control* (1999), *The Law Times*, 24 September 1999, see 2(6) SLB.

among athletes and provide them an adequate remedy for their injuries. Tort law imposes financial liability on the athlete . . . and this will hit him where it hurts most – in his pocket.'[20] Civil actions available for injuries suffered during the course of a game are either trespass to the person, or more specifically a battery, or alternatively negligence. It is the latter action that is in practice invariably pursued by claimants due to the need with trespass to the person to establish intent on the part of the defendant.[21]

Trespass to the person

Intent is a specific state of mind to prove and evidentially this can be difficult to establish.[22] Additionally, very few sports participants are likely to admit that they intended to injure an opponent. The infamous admission of the ex-Manchester United player, Roy Keane, that he had intended to foul the Manchester City player, Alf-Inge Haaland, in the newspaper serialisation of his autobiography is a notable exception. Even though Haaland's playing career was ended by the ensuing injury, he did not pursue any civil action. It would appear that he would have been able to succeed under trespass to the person.[23]

James, M, 'The Trouble with Roy Keane'

Keane's apparent confession would also appear to give rise to an action for trespass to the person, specifically battery, against him. A civil battery requires only that the defendant intended to make contact with the claimant, *Collins v. Wilcock* [1984] 1 WLR 1172. There is no additional requirement that the defendant foresees or intends to cause the claimant any harm. Thus, the elements of battery appear complete. As would be the case if there was to be a prosecution, consent negates a claim of trespass to the person and raises the same discussions as above in respect of a criminal assault: was the challenge an integral part of the playing of the game and was it within the playing culture of football? Normally such a challenge would be considered to be on the borderline of what is considered to be acceptable conduct, as is demonstrated by the sending off and the subsequent playing ban. However, such actions for battery are extremely rare.

The main reason for this was raised in the case of *Elliott v Saunders and Liverpool Football Club*, 10 June 1994 unreported HC judgment. Elliott began his action by pleading both battery and negligence in respect of a career-ending challenge involving Saunders where the two players had gone for the ball at the same time. During the early part of the trial, it was agreed by the parties that the claim for battery should be dropped, not for any lack of evidence, but because it would mean that if successful, Liverpool's insurance would not pay out. Their employer's liability insurance covered only negligent conduct of employees such as Saunders, not their deliberate acts. Thus, despite its seeming appropriateness, it is extremely unlikely that an action in trespass to the person would be pursued by either Haaland or Manchester City FC.[24]

Negligence

Reflecting the wider trends involving the development of liability based on negligence, the tripartite 'neighbourhood' test as established in *Donoghue v Stevenson*[25] has been applied to potential liability

---

20 Jahn, G,' Civil Liability: an Alternative to Violence in Sporting Events' (1994) 15 Ohio University Law Review 243.
21 *Letang v Cooper* [1964] 2 All ER 929.
22 However, see case of *Rogers v Bugden & Canterbury-Bankstown* (1993) ATR 81-246, concerning Australian rugby league.
23 See James, M, 'The trouble with Roy Keane' (2002) Entertainment Law 1(3), 72–92.
24 James, M, 'The Trouble with Roy Keane' (2002) 1(3) Entertainment Law 72–92.
25 *Donoghue v Stevenson* [1932] AC 562.

on the sports field.[26] The traditional test for negligence has been based on the following: i) a duty of care is owed to those who it is reasonably foreseeable to be affected by the act; ii) breach of that duty in that the defendant has failed to take reasonable care; and iii) the claimant suffering damages which are not too remote from the defendant's act.

In *Caparo Industries v Dickman*,[27] this test was restated as being: i) is damage reasonably foreseeable; ii) is there sufficient proximity between the parties; and iii) is it fair, just and reasonable to impose the duty? This development had provided greater precision in determining whether liability should be imposed in particular circumstances. The establishment of negligence can be problematic in many circumstances. In sport, this includes its inherent physicality and the multifarious nature of rules, and these factors contribute to the context within which the test of the reasonableness of actions is determined.

Duty of care

In *Condon v Basi*, where one footballer was held liable in negligence for breaking the leg of an opponent in a tackle, it was confirmed by the Court of Appeal that a sports participant owes a duty of care to an opponent to take reasonable care in all circumstances. Two specific issues were discussed. Firstly, the application of consent of the claimant (or more formally the issue of *volenti non fit injuria*) will not be treated formally as a defence but one of the circumstances considered in determining the issue of whether the defendant has acted with reasonable care. Secondly, the role of 'the rules of the game' was considered and it was acknowledged that to incur liability the defendant's actions would be outside the playing rules of the sport. Clearly, however, actions that involve foul play and are outside the rules of the sport may not necessarily amount to negligence: there is no duty of care never to commit a foul or infringe a rule. In the Australian case of *Rootes v Shelton*,[28] a water skier sued the driver of his boat who caused him to collide with another boat in the course of a water skiing display. Barwick CJ said that the extent of a duty 'must necessarily depend in each case upon its own circumstances . . . the rules of the sport or game may constitute one of those circumstances, but, in my opinion, they are neither definitive of the existence nor of the extent of the duty'.[29]

The extent to which actions are beyond the playing rules and additionally beyond the playing culture of that specific sport so as to be negligent will be dependent on the sport being played. In horse racing, for example, there will be 'no liability for errors of judgement, oversights or lapses of which any participant might be guilty in the context of a fast-moving contest. Something more serious is required.'[30]

Standard of care

A major issue has been determining the relevant standard of care that must be exercised so that a defendant who falls below it renders himself or herself liable to an action in negligence. In English law, generally, the position is that the standard is that which is reasonable in all the circumstances. Such a test allows all particular factual circumstances to be considered. However, it has also been argued that ordinary negligence standards cannot be applied in the sporting context. In *Wooldridge v Sumner*,[31] it was stated that the appropriate standard should be reckless disregard, a test that has been adopted in certain states in America.[32] The facts were that a horse competing in a show bolted from the arena and into two spectators. One of them, a photographer, was injured. Diplock LJ stated:

---

26 *Condon v Basi* [1985] 2 All ER 453.
27 *Caparo Industries v Dickman* [1990] 2 AC 605.
28 *Rootes v Shelton* [1968] ALR 33.
29 Ibid.
30 *Caldwell v Maguire and Fitzgerald* [2001)] PIQR 45.
31 [1963] 2 QB 43.
32 See *Nabozny v Barnhill*, 334 NE 2d 258 (Ill App Ct 1975), see Narol, M, 'Sports Torts: Emerging Standards of Care' (1990) *Trial* (Jun) 20. Also see *Lestini v West Bend Mutual Insurance Co.*, 176 Wis 2d 901, 501 NW 2d 28 (1993).

Wooldridge v Sumner

... a person attending a game or competition takes the risk of any damage caused to him by any act of a participant done in the course of and for the purposes of the game or competition notwithstanding that such act may involve an error of judgement or a lapse of skill, unless the participant's conduct is such as to evince a reckless disregard of the spectators' safety.[33]

However, subsequent cases have indicated that there is no formal requirement to establish reckless disregard in sporting cases, but evidence of such reckless conduct may be required to establish negligent conduct in the complexity of sporting action. In *Caldwell v Maguire and Fitzgerald*,[34] the defendants were alleged to have been negligent in their riding during a two-mile novice hurdle race, when career-ending injury was caused to another jockey who was unseated due to the defendants' pulling in front of other riders to keep an inside 'racing line'. Under the racing rules the defendants were found guilty of 'careless riding' in disciplinary action by the Jockey Club. On appeal, Woolf LCJ extracted five propositions as guidance for determining the standard of care, and thus whether there had on the facts been a breach of the duty:

Caldwell v Maguire and Fitzgerald

1) Each contestant in a lawful sporting contest owes a duty of care to each and all other contestants.

2) That duty is to exercise in the course of the contest all care that is objectively reasonable in the prevailing circumstances for the avoidance of infliction of injury to such fellow contestants.

3) The prevailing circumstances are ... its rules, conventions and customs, and the standards of skills and judgements reasonably to be expected of that of a contestant.

4) The threshold of liability is in practice inevitably high; the breach of a duty will not flow from proof of no more than an error of judgment ... or momentary lapse in skill ... when subject to the stresses of a race. Such are no more than incidents inherent in the nature of the sport.

5) In practice it may therefore be difficult to prove any such breach of duty absent proof or conduct that in point of fact amounts to reckless disregard for the fellow contestant's safety ...'[35]

The view of the Court of Appeal was therefore that the ordinary standards of negligence must be established in all the circumstances of the cases, albeit in reality evidence that may amount to reckless disregard may be required to establish liability.

Potential Defendants

An important development in negligence liability in sport has concerned which potential defendants can possibly be liable. This has been based on the normal principles of the law of negligence with the application of the neighbourhood principle and who might owe the claimant a duty of care and concepts such as vicarious liability. This has had important policy implications for sport as the scope of potential liability has extended.

---

33 [1963] 2 QB 23, para 68.
34 *Caldwell v Maguire and Fitzgerald* [2001] PIQR 45.
35 Ibid.

Playing participants

The most common cause of actions has been injuries caused by one sports participant against another. Two sports in which cases have occurred in both amateur and professional fields over the last few years have been football and rugby union. A case such as *Elliott v Saunders & Liverpool FC*,[36] where Dean Saunders from Liverpool FC was sued for a tackle on Paul Elliott from Chelsea FC which resulted in the severance of his cruciate ligaments in the process, illustrates the vagaries of the law of negligence and the evidential problems involved in establishing liability. Elliot failed in his action.

Elliott v Saunders & Liverpool FC (1994) QB transcript 10 June 1994

'. . . an intentional foul or mistake, or an error of judgement may be enough to give rise to liability on the part of the defendant, but whether or not it does so depends on the facts and circumstances of each individual case'. He also stated that he 'did not agree with the *obiter dictum* from *Condon v Basi* in that there might be a higher standard of care required of a player in say, the Premier League. The standard of care required in each case was the same' (per Drake J).[37]

After hearing expert evidence and viewing video footage of the incident, the court accepted Saunders' evidence that he had raised his feet at the last moment of the tackle in an instinctive attempt to avoid probable injury to himself. Drake J held there was no evidence to demonstrate that Saunders had been guilty of 'dangerous and reckless play'.[38] The case also highlighted the fact that the standard of care required is the same irrespective of the level of the game that is being played.

In comparison, the claimant was successful in *McCord v Swansea City AFC*,[39] a case against John Cornforth, who challenged Brian McCord for a loose ball and broke his opponent's leg, an injury which was career-ending. Kennedy J ruled that the tackle, in which Carnforth slid on one leg with his right foot over the ball as the pair went for a fifty-fifty ball, was 'an error which was inconsistent with his taking reasonable care towards his opponent'. It was judged to be an intentional foul and the defendant was liable. McCord was awarded around £250,000 in damages.

Liability has been, similarly, something of a lottery in other sports which are essentially non-contact. For example, in golf a number of cases have concerned wayward balls causing injuries. In *Clark v Welch*, a ball hit by the defendant was diverted after hitting the toe of another player and injured the claimant. It was held that there was no liability as such a risk was inherent in the game. In comparison, in *Pearson v Lightning*,[40] the defendant was playing on the eighth hole of a golf course which ran parallel, but in the opposite direction, to the ninth hole upon which the claimant and two others were playing. The holes were separated by about fifteen metres of light rough which contained some bushes and trees. The defendant, whose ball was lying in the rough between the fairways closer to the ninth hole than the eighth, decided to play a difficult shot over the top of an area of bushes. However, the shot failed to clear the bushes and was deflected, hitting Pearson who was ninety yards away, causing an injury to his eye and knocking him to the ground. Although the defendant had shouted 'fore', Pearson had not heard him. It was held, dismissing the appeal, that the shot, which the defendant had played, had clearly been a difficult one and the likelihood of deflection from the bush towards the ninth fairway was

36 *Elliott v Saunders & Liverpool FC* (1994) QB transcript 10 June 1994.
37 Ibid.
38 Drake J stated that video evidence that was adduced in the Court was considered by the judge to be of limited use and two-dimensional; see Gardiner, S and Felix, A, 'Elliot v Saunders: Drama in Court 14' (1994) 2(2) SATLJ 1.
39 *McCord v Swansea City AFC* [1996] QBD.
40 *Pearson v Lightning* [1998] 95(20) LSG.

foreseeable. A duty of care was thus established and Lightning had been in breach of it. As his ball had been lying closer to the fairway on which Pearson was playing, Lightning should have called to him before playing his shot out of courtesy and in order to alert Pearson to the risk. Although the risk of causing injury was small, it was sufficient to render the defendant liable. It was stated that proof of negligence in 'any case concerning golf courses injuries must depend on its particular facts'.[41]

Employers: vicarious liability

The normal principles of vicarious liability have been applied in the sports arena where an employment relationship exists.[42] An employer is liable for the actions of his/her employee if performed during the course of employment. The two stages to establishing vicarious liability are: the person who committed the tort was an employee of the defendant; and the tort was committed during the course of employment. An act is within the course of employment if it is within the scope of activities included or incidental to the job, and the employer will also be liable for authorised acts performed in an unauthorised manner. However, the employer is not liable for acts caused by an employee going on a 'frolic of his own'.[43] In a number of the cases discussed above, including *McCord*, it is almost axiomatic that where the defendant is an employee, his or her employer will be co-joined as a defendant.[44]

In *Watson and Bradford City Football Club v Gray and Huddersfield Town FC*, there was a successful claim in negligence by Watson, a professional footballer, against Gray and his employing club, Huddersfield Town, under the principle of vicarious liability. The tackle was described as being 'very dangerous, appalling, diabolical and quite unacceptable'. Additionally there was an action by a second claimant, Gray's employer, Bradford City FC against Watson for the tort of unlawful interference with the employment contract between Gray and Bradford. This claim was unsuccessful, as this tort requires an 'intentional' unlawful act; although the tackle had been described as above, on the facts, it could not be seen as an intentional act. However, clearly, if the successful action by Watson had been for the tort of trespass, intention would have been established.

In *Gravil v Carroll and Redruth Rugby Football Club*,[45] Gravil, a Halifax prop forward, was punched in the face by Carroll, who was Redruth's second-row forward. Gravil suffered a 'blow out fracture' to his right eye socket and as a consequence he had to undergo reconstructive surgery. Gravil brought a personal injury claim against Redruth Rugby Club, claiming it was vicariously liable for the actions of its player. Reversing the decision at first instance that no vicarious liability could be established in this case, the Court of Appeal held that it was indeed just to hold Redruth vicariously liable for Carroll's action. The Court felt that the critical question was the nature of the employment and the assault. There was an obvious nexus between the punch and Carroll's employment and this decision raised some interesting issues.

Summerhayes, J, 'Injury Liability: Off-the-ball player attacks: club liability'

Sir Anthony Clarke MR made it clear in his judgment that in holding the Club liable, he was only prepared to do so where a player was employed under a contract of employment. Of course in

41 Per Sir Christopher Slade, also see *Lewis v Blackpool Golf Club* 1993 SLT (Sh Ct) 43; also see liability in other non-contact sports in uni-hockey, *Leatherland v Edwards* (unreported, 28 November 1998) (QBD) and skiing, *Gilsenan v Gunning* (1982) 137 DLR (9sd) 252.
42 See *Lister and Others v Hesley Hall* [2001] UKHL 22, [2001] 2 WLR 1311.
43 *Ruddiman v Smith* [1889] 60 LT 708.
44 Additionally there are examples of cases where the action has been directly against the employing club of sportsmen where the vicarious liability test was clearly fulfilled, see *Pitcher v Huddersfield Town Football Club* [2001[QBD 5953 and *Gaynor v Blackpool* [2002] CLY 3280.
45 *Gravil v Carroll and Redruth Rugby Football Club* [2008] EWCA Civ 689.

Mr Carroll's case, this was made altogether easier because he had a written contract of employment; but, in exploring the limits of the judgment, what we do not know is how far Courts will be prepared to go in upholding the vicarious liability of Clubs for the acts (or omissions) of their players where they do not have a written contract of employment. As was commented on at paragraph 10 of the judgment: 'We agree with the trial judge that until then [the introduction of contracts of employment] no question of vicarious liability on the part of such clubs could have arisen'.

Does this mean, in all probability, that absent a written contract the courts will not entertain a claim? If that is right, then surely all this will lead to is sporting clubs being advised to dispense with written contracts of employment (but presumably still offering fees and/or players' expenses) so as to avoid the likelihood of then being found vicariously liable for the acts of their players. In this day and age, with the panoply of employment legislation, that hardly seems likely.

In the case of Mr Carroll it was accepted that the only reason for the development of contracts of employment (in the area of semi-professional rugby) was to bind players to their clubs and stop them moving around to other clubs. Surely at the lower divisions this is less likely to happen and the main motivation is playing for the love of the game.

If this is the route that clubs choose to go down, then surely it throws open the likelihood that the courts will be asked to consider the case law and statutory definition of employee. This is an area of law that is replete with cases where the distinction between a contract of service and a contract for services is often easier to spot than it is to explain the difference between the two.[15]

Where does this leave the Sunday league player who simply plays for the love of the game and receives no fees or expenses? In all probability the clubs will not be caught by vicarious liability, but again because of the fact-specific nature of this area of law it would be wrong to rule out liability altogether.

What about the situation where clubs arrange for a player to go on loan? Who then is the employer?[46]

Match officials

In Smoldon v Whitworth & Nolan,[47] liability for causing personal injury was established against an official in a contact team sport. During the course of a game of rugby being played between two teams at Colts level, Ben Smoldon, who was the hooker for one of the teams, suffered a broken neck when a scrum collapsed. Proceedings were issued against one of the opposing players, Whitworth, and the match referee, Nolan. The action against the first defendant, Whitworth, failed since no one player could be identified as being singularly responsible for the critical collapse. The case against Nolan was successful at first instance in the High Court and was subsequently the subject of an unsuccessful appeal. The significance of the case lies in the fact that it was the first time in the jurisprudence of major rugby playing nations that such liability had been established in court.

A clear limitation was placed on liability along the lines of the 'floodgates principle'. The judge went so far as to say that it could not be stressed 'too strongly' that the decision was based upon special considerations, namely: the particular facts of the case; the vital fact that this was a Colts game; the law of rugby as modified for Colts; and the laws and customs of rugby in the 1991/92 season. It was held that it was 'fair, just and reasonable' to impose a duty on the referee and that the duty of referees was to exercise that degree of care for the safety of players, which is appropriate in

---

46 Summerhayes, J, ' Injury Liability: Off-the-ball player attacks: club liability' (2008) 6(7) WSLR.
47 Smoldon v Whitworth & Nolan (The Times, 18 December 1996). See Felix, A and Lee, T, 'Sports Injuries: Smoldon v Whitworth & Nolan: The Liability of Officials (part 1)' (1998) 1(2) SLB and 'Sports Injuries: Smoldon v Whitworth & Nolan: The Liability of Officials (part 2)' (1998) 1(3) SLB.

the circumstances. The Judge felt it appropriate to accept the test of a higher degree of foreseeability stipulated in the Lord Chancellor's speech in *Smith v Littlewoods*.[48] Thus, in determining liability, it was necessary to take account of the special considerations that applied in the context of Colts matches, in particular the duty to enforce the 'crouch – touch – pause – engage' phased sequence (CTPE) that had earlier been introduced for the formation of the scrum in Colts matches.

At the appeal, the defendant accepted that a duty of care was owed. However, it was argued that the appropriate standard of care was not merely that which was reasonable in all the circumstances, but a need to show a reckless disregard for the safety of the person injured. This was the degree of duty of care for both players and officials. The defendant had relied on the argument that for liability to arise, the damage must be a highly foreseeable consequence and not merely a possibility. The Lord Chief Justice, however, ruled the standard test should be applied, the circumstances of the incident in the game being crucial.

Subsequently in *Vowles v Evans and the Welsh Rugby Union and Others*,[49] the referee in an adult rugby match was held liable for injuries, sustained to a player due to repeated set scrums, which left him paralysed. Counsel for the defendant claimed that as a matter of policy or decision, a referee does not owe a duty to take reasonable care with respect to the safety of adults playing in a rugby match. *Smoldon* was distinguishable because that case concerned the existence of a duty of care in the context of a Colts game. It was submitted that whether it was fair, just and reasonable to impose a duty upon a referee would depend upon a number of factors, including the interests of rugby as a game and the overall public interest. He stressed that such an imposition would discourage participation in rugby.

However, it was held that the referee was in breach of his duty to take reasonable care for the safety of the front row forwards in failing to order non-contested scrums. A front row forward was injured and there was no suitable replacement. However, an inexperienced teammate agreed to play the position and contested scrums continued to take place, but with most of them collapsing.

The referee should have acted differently with this inexperienced replacement in the scrum. According to Law 3 (5), 'Any team must include suitably trained/experienced players'; and Law 3(12) states that 'In the event of a front row forward being ordered off or injured or both, the referee, in the interests of safety, will confer with the captain of his team . . . When there is no other front row forward available . . . then the game will continue with non-contestable scrummages'.

The judge applied the evidential test of liability from that of *Smoldon* in that a full account should be taken of the circumstances of the game and that due to the fast-moving and vigorous contest, the threshold of liability would be high and not easily crossed. The claimant succeeded on liability against the first defendant and liability was accepted by the Welsh Rugby Union (WRU) under vicarious liability. The judge further did not consider it logical to draw a distinction between amateur and professional rugby.

In *Mountford v Newlands School and Another*,[50] a fifteen-year-old played over age in an under 15s match. He caused the injury of a broken elbow during a lawful tackle. The victim successfully sued the referee (and sports master) who had selected the fifteen-year-old and the school through vicarious liability, arguing that age-eligibility rules designed to manage potential injury to smaller and less physically mature players had been ignored. As Mehdevy states, 'Whilst this case relates to rugby union, there is a clear lesson to be learnt here. It is imperative that officials and organisers of youth sport matches are fully aware of the rules and take steps to ensure compliance with eligibility requirements. Advice should be taken where it is planned that an individual should "play down" and a suitable risk assessment undertaken.'[51]

---

48 [1987] 1 AC 241.

49 *Vowles v Evans and the Welsh Rugby Union and Others* [2002] EWHC 2612.

50 *Mountford v Newlands School and Another* [2007] EWCA Civ 21.

51 Mehdevy, E, 'School Sport: Court of Appeal: school liable for fielding ineligible player' (2007) 5(6) WSLR.

The cases of *Smoldon* and *Vowles* led to major concerns that volunteer referees would be increasingly reluctant to expose themselves to potential liability. However, an increased use of insurance to manage this risk does not seem to have caused a major decrease in numbers of volunteers.

Sports governing bodies

The death of luger Nodar Kumaritashvili during training at the Vancouver 2010 Winter Olympics raised the difficult question of who, if anyone, is liable when an athlete dies at a competition. The event organiser could be a potential defendant as a result of the duty to provide a safe facility under the Occupiers Liability Act 1957. But what liability might governing bodies have? What liability might the IOC have in Olympic competition?

Grimberg, H, 'Injury Liability: Liability for death or permanent injury: analysis'

The Olympic Charter provides that National Olympic Committees must insure their sportsmen in respect of death or injury, and there is an agreement that athletes must sign exempting the International Olympic Committee (IOC) from liability in respect of their death. Neither of these measures can, in themselves, shield the IOC from liability. It is the policy of English law that individuals should be able to claim for injury from tortfeasors even when they are insured, as to prevent such claims would deter people from taking out insurance policies. The judges have so far held that the law should promote such virtuous behaviour. Also, contracts which seek to exclude negligence liability for death are void, and cannot be relied on to demonstrate that a party either agreed to or was aware of a particular risk (Unfair Contract Terms Act 1977).[52]

Of course in terms of civil liability anyone can potentially be liable as long as they owe a legally recognisable duty of care to the aggrieved party. It is often a very pragmatic decision – sue the party that has the deepest pockets. The case of *Watson v BBBC*[53] saw British boxer Michael Watson win his case for compensation against the sport's governing body, the British Boxing Board of Control (BBBC), after he suffered irreparable brain damage in a punishing super-middleweight world title fight in 1991 against world champion and fellow Briton, Chris Eubank. He collapsed in the ring at the end of the fight and later underwent emergency surgery to remove a blood clot from his brain. He was left paralysed down his left side and has never worked again after losing half his brain function.

Mr Justice Kennedy ruled that the BBBC owed Watson a duty of care to provide medical staff in attendance on the night with the 'training and equipment to resuscitate a fighter in his condition.' He regarded the BBBC and its medical advisors as being rather complacent as they had not instituted what he called the 'medical protocol' concerning the need for early resuscitation of those with serious head injuries that had been accepted in medical circles since the 1970s and had not 'looked outside their own personal expertise'. They had failed to be 'prospective in their thinking and seek competent advice as to how a recognised danger could best be combated'. In making the safety arrangements for a professional boxing contest held under its aegis, the defendant owed a duty of care to a participant in that contest, and it was in breach of this duty by failing to ensure that adequate resuscitation equipment and medical assistance was available at ringside in the event of the claimant suffering a serious head injury in the course of the bout. *Watson* is considered to be the first case in which a regulatory body has been held liable for the negligent failure to regulate.

The following case extract is instructive:

---

52 Grimberg, H, 'Injury Liability: Liability for death or permanent injury: analysis' (2010) WSLR.
53 *Watson v British Boxing Board of Control* (1999), The Law Times 24 September 1999; [2001] 2 WLR 1256.

Watson v British Boxing Board of Control

Although the BBBC did not create the initial danger to the boxers, only those who were licensed by the Board and followed its rules, particularly its safety rules, could hold a bout. The BBBC is a body with specialised knowledge in matters of safety and this knowledge is relied on by those involved in the sport, including the boxers. It is therefore under a duty to ensure that its rules provide a safe system by which injuries incurred as the result of a fight can be properly treated.

Further, the Board advises promoters on issues of safety and lays down requirements for them to follow if they wish to promote a bout. As this advice is relied on by the boxers for their own safety, there is sufficient proximity between the Board and the boxers for a duty to arise in respect of the insufficiency of the guidelines regarding post-bout medical treatment.

The duty was breached by the Board failing to provide adequate guidelines on what medical personnel and equipment should be present at a bout. The guidelines that were available were not in line with current medical procedures and practice. The most important time to begin treatment of a brain haemorrhage is in the minutes immediately following the initial injury. The longer the delay, the greater the likelihood that the injuries suffered would be exacerbated by the swelling damaging the brain. The ringside treatment should therefore be much quicker and in effect be able to begin preparing the injured fighter for surgery. If it had been, then it is likely that the claimant's injuries would have been significantly reduced. As serious brain injury is a foreseeable though infrequent outcome of a boxing bout, there should be in place guidelines that reflect this risk and ensure that a boxer's health is protected as far as is possible.

Thus, by reason of its position as the governing body of the sport and that an important part of that role was to produce safety guidelines for bouts, the Board owed a duty of care to the claimant. That duty was breached by the inadequacy of the guidelines and this caused foreseeable harm by exacerbating a serious brain injury incurred during the course of the bout.[54]

Watson has been a paraplegic since the bout. However, his recovery has been a great example of the strength of the human spirit in the face of adversity. He can now walk unaided and completed the London Marathon in 2003 over a number of days.

Post-*Watson*, there was significant concern on the part of governing bodies and international federations of potential liability for safety of participants within a particular sport. This was tested in *Wattleworth v Goodwood Road Racing Company Ltd, Royal Automobile Club Motor Sports Association Ltd and Federation Internationale De L'Automobile*,[55] where the claimant brought an action on behalf of herself and as administratrix of her husband's estate, alleging that certain safety barriers in place at the Goodwood motor racing circuit were not adequate, and as a result her husband was killed when he crashed into them. The actions were against the first defendant under the Occupier's Liability Act 1957 s 2, for breaching its duty to provide a safe place to race motor vehicles, and against the second and third defendants for their failure to carry out sufficient or adequate inspections of the Goodwood circuit, thereby breaching their duty of care towards users of the race track. From around 1991, Goodwood Road Racing Company (GRRC) began to develop and renovate the Goodwood circuit to bring it up to the standards required to host International Racing Calendar vintage car races. At all times, they consulted with Royal Automobile Club Motor Sports Association (MSA) technical and safety managers and, when necessary, the Federation Internationale De L'Automobile's (FIA) Circuits and Safety Commissions. The role of the MSA and FIA, for the purposes of this case, can be summarised as being to produce safety specifications for motor racing tracks, to conduct

---

54 Ibid at paras 79–83.
55 *Wattleworth v Goodwood Road Racing Company Ltd, Royal Automobile Club Motor Sports Association Ltd and Federation Internationale De L'Automobile*
[2004] EWHC 140.

inspections and make recommendations about safety issues and to issue licences to tracks that reach the appropriate level of safety for the relevant categories of race.

It was held that the liability of the MSA, using a similar formulation to that used by the Court of Appeal in *Watson*, was based on a sufficiently proximate relationship on which to base a duty of care. Thus, where A (MSA) advises B (GRRC) as to action to be taken which will directly and foreseeably affect the safety of C (the deceased), then a situation of sufficient proximity exists to found a duty of care on the part of A towards C. As the MSA's inspectors were aware that their advice would be used in respect of events licensed by the MSA and those that were not licensed, the imposition of a duty of care on the MSA was fair, just and reasonable in the circumstances. The crash site had been identified as a low-risk site, which was backed up by the very few accidents that had occurred there, but the risk was still a foreseeable one. However, the recommendations on the choice of crash barrier made by the MSA inspectors were reasonably made after proper consideration. They were made for good cause and were ones that an inspector skilled in motor racing circuit safety matters would reasonably and properly make and approve. Therefore, the duty of care imposed on the MSA was not breached by the advice of its inspectors.

As far as liability of the FIA was concerned, the court held that at the time of the accident, Goodwood held only an MSA licence. Further, the FIA's structure ensured that the primary responsibility for safety and track licensing lay with the national body, the MSA, and the FIA licensed only specific events. Thus, the relative lack of proximity between GRRC and the FIA ensured that no duty of care could be imposed upon the FIA. For these reasons, all claims were dismissed by the court. The form of the duty imposed on a governing body will vary dramatically from sport to sport. In *Watson*, the BBBC failed to provide the necessary post-match care, through guidelines to its promoters, to a boxer who had suffered a brain injury. This type of injury is a foreseeable result of boxing and it is further foreseeable that if it is not treated quickly the injuries will be exacerbated. In *Wattleworth*, the duty of the governing/licensing body, the MSA, was to ensure that motor racing tracks were reasonably safe for drivers and spectators. This duty was discharged by its inspectors having acted reasonably by carrying out the series of inspections. Although the reasoning for declining to impose a duty of care on the FIA is not convincing, if a duty had been imposed, it too would not have been breached in this case.

A useful comparison can be made between the cases above and *Agar v Hyde*,[56] where the High Court of Australia dealt with a novel claim brought by two rugby union players who, as adult teenagers, had broken their necks in separate incidents and suffered quadriplegia while playing the position of 'hooker' in interclub competition. Both had suffered their injuries when the two sides of the scrum engaged. Their claim was against a range of defendants including the International Rugby Board (IRB), the ISF of rugby union, alleging that it owed them a duty of care in negligence to amend the rules to remove unnecessary risks. This is equivalent to claiming that there is a responsibility to deal with design defects on the part of a manufacturer.[57]

Opie, H, 'Australian Medico-Legal Issues in Sport: the View from the Grandstand'

The High Court unanimously rejected the claim. A number of reasons were given, but for present purposes it is sufficient to note that the Court considered that a person's voluntary participation in a sport would defeat any claim where the injury was caused by an inherent risk of participation. The Court appears to have believed that the plaintiffs knew what they were doing when they participated and they had to take the consequences, no matter how unfortunate. To reinforce the point, Justice Callinan described the sport of rugby union as 'notoriously a dangerous game.'

---

56 *Agar v Hyde* (2000) 201 CLR.
57 For more analysis of these cases see Lines, K, 'Thinking outside the box (-ing ring): the implications for sports governing bodies following *Watson*' (2007) ISLR.

While the Court's reasoning is consistent with the established approach in relation to responsibility for inherent risks, it did not explore the meaning of that expression. Had it done so the result may have been different. The incidents occurred in August 1986 and August 1987, before the introduction in 1988 of the crouch-touch-pause-engage ('CTPE') sequence for scrum formation that was intended to reduce the incidence of injuries of the kind suffered by the plaintiffs. In the years preceding the injuries suffered by the plaintiffs, there had been a growing number of reports and expressions of concern in the medical and scientific literature about the occurrence of spinal cord injury in rugby union, especially to players in the front row of scrums. There was debate about the mechanism of injury and the best measure for reducing the number of cases. The CTPE rule was the outcome.

Sport governing bodies routinely review their sport's rules to assess, *inter alia*, issues of safety. Some sports have standing committees of scientific and coaching experts for this purpose. Rule changes are often the result and may bring changes in the inherent risks of participation. In comparison to the decision in *Watson*, the High Court has in effect held that this is a moral, not a legal, responsibility of sport governing bodies. However, it is difficult to argue that people such as the plaintiffs are in any real position to assess these emerging risks. They place their trust in the hands of those who govern the sport to be watchful and responsive to emerging scientific knowledge of the risks of participation and what can be done about them. Again central here are the medical experts.

This case seems to run counter to the general expansionary development of the tort of negligence over the past seventy years. Society tolerates avoidable injury less and less. Its cost in human and financial terms is too great. The trend has been to require those in positions of power and knowledge to be proactive. Not to impose some legal responsibility permits a sport's governing body to ignore emerging medical and scientific evidence of systematic injury and to cocoon the sport's rules within the traditions of bygone eras. Where the risk is one known or understood only by a few because it is in the realm of emerging medical knowledge, it is undesirable for the sport governing body that has access to that knowledge to have no legal obligation to even consider rule changes as a protective measure.[58]

Liability for injuries caused on international duty

A connected issue concerning damages has also occurred in team sports where players have been injured in international games. This has been a major issue within the wider tensions of control and player release for international matches that has been characterised as the 'club v country' debate. In cricket, the players who are regular internationals are centrally contracted by the ECB. In rugby union in England, an agreement is in place between the RFU and professional clubs regarding release of players for a certain number of club matches during competitions such as the Six Nations. In football, clubs are required to release players selected for international matches under FIFA regulations. The so-called *Oulmers* case, discussed in detail elsewhere,[59] highlighted the problem when players contracted to clubs are injured in international matches (in this incident the player Abdelmajid Oulmers was injured while playing for Morocco) when the clubs have little or no control over matters such as the type of medical treatment provided. The settlement reached in the litigation between FIFA, the G14 group of clubs and Oulmers' club Charleroi, included payments from national football associations to clubs essentially for the players' services during these periods of participation in international matches. However, no specific agreement was reached concerning compensation for injuries received during these periods.[60]

---

58 See Opie, H, 'Australian Medico-Legal Issues in Sport: the View from the Grandstand' (2002) MSLR.
59 See pp 190–1.
60 Ibid.

A number of national associations including the FA have extensive insurance cover to compensate clubs for injured players, but many national associations around the world seem to have deficient or no cover.[61] The international striker Michael Owen was unable to play for Newcastle United for a period of more than one whole season when he was seriously injured playing for England.[62] Newcastle threatened legal action against FIFA, who reached a settlement reported to be between six and seven million pounds.[63] In addition to payments from the FA under its insurance policy, it was reported that Newcastle received around £10 million in compensation from FIFA and the FA. FIFA now operates a compensation fund for injuries sustained in the World Cup Finals.

Sports medical practitioners

A connected issue is the role that medical experts have in advising sports governing bodies. *Watson* and *Agar* not only indicate the potential liability for governing bodies in providing a safe environment for sports participation, they also illustrate the role that sports medical practitioners have in advising governing bodies and sports clubs of medically related risks. The quality of this advice can expose them to potential liability. Additionally, sports doctors and physiotherapists have become subject to actions in negligence directly from individual sportsmen and clubs.

Of course, it is well known that general medical practitioners have become subject to medical negligence actions. As the potential cost of medical negligence liability has increased, it is clear that there are a number of judicial and legal developments in tort law that have had the effect of slowing the expansion of liability in negligence. In the UK, the *Bolam* test has limited the liability of doctors generally to 'professional standards of care that conform to medical practice'.[64] For comparison, in Australia, following the Ipp Report on the Review of the Law of Negligence in 2002,[65] individual states have implemented new law. For example, in Queensland, the Civil Liability Act 2003 has modified the standard of care as it applies to professionals. Section 22 states that professionals can avoid liability if it is established 'that they acted in a manner that was widely accepted in Australia by peer professional opinion as competent professional practice'.

However, the legal position in the UK and Australia can be usefully compared to the US as far as sports medical practitioners are concerned. It has generally been accepted that sports medical practitioners have a legal duty to conform to the standards of care corresponding to their actual specialty training, in this case sports medicine. The traditional test has been one of 'good medical practice',[66] i.e. what is commonly done in the physician's specialism is the measure by which the physician's conduct is measured. However, these recent cases suggest that a more progressive and arguably preventative standard has emerged, namely that of 'accepted practice'.[67] This equates with determining what the medical practitioner *should* have done in the circumstances. As Mitten states: 'Physicians have a legal obligation to keep abreast of new developments and advances in sports medicine, and they may be liable for using outdated treatment methods that no longer have a sound medical basis or that do not currently constitute appropriate care.'[68]

The medical care and welfare of sports athletes is in the hands of a number of medical professionals. The two most prominent are the sports physiotherapists and sports doctors. Professionals who practise in this area do not always have specific training in this specialism. It is still common

61 Limbert, P, 'Injury Liability: Players injured on national duty: issues and suggestions' (2010) 8(5) WSLR.
62 Limbert, P, 'Injury Compensation: Compensating clubs for players injured during international duty' (2007) 5(3) WSLR.
63 'Newcastle claim victory over £10m Owen pay-out', *The Guardian*, 26 June 2007, www.guardian.co.uk/football/2007/jun/26/newsstory.sport8.
64 *Bolam v Frien Hospital Management Committee* [1957] 1 WLR 582.
65 Can be found at http://revofneg.treasury.gov.au/content/review2.asp.
66 See Mitten, M, 'Emerging Legal Issues in Sports Medicine: A Synthesis, Summary and Analysis' (2002) St John's Law Review 76(5).
67 See *Nowatske v Osterloh* (1996) 534 NW 2d 256.
68 Op. cit., fn 66, Mitten (2002).

for doctors in many professional sports to be appointed not so much in terms of what they know and possess by way of sports-specific experience and qualifications, but who they know, for example a friend of a retiring sports club doctor. However, a number of professional groupings are appearing. It would have been expected that with the increase in volume and scope of litigation for sports-related injury that these medical professionals would have been subject to legal actions on an increasing basis. This would certainly reflect the trend in levels of litigation in health care generally in the UK and similar countries. However, in the UK there have been few sports medical cases. Why might this be? As Hayden Opie opines: 'Speculation upon the reasons for this remarkable state of affairs might prove interesting. Perhaps the standards of care are very high. Is there something in the culture of sport or in the personal relationship that medical professionals have with athletes – especially at the elite level – which militates against litigation?'[69]

In *Brady v Sunderland Football Club* (1998), an action against Sunderland Town FC by a player was based on a claim that an injury was negligently diagnosed and treated by the club's physiotherapist.[70] Although the action failed, it clearly indicated that the qualifications, experience and working practices of such staff are issues of importance. One research report in UK professional soccer suggested that club physiotherapists, for example, act differently dependent on whether they have predominantly originated from a sports background – ex-players who have subsequently qualified in the area – or alternatively come from a medical background and have then moved into the sports world.[71] The former tended to make decisions with little consultation; the latter tended to seek second opinions from other practitioners. Indeed it was found that many physiotherapists had limited relevant qualifications and were often ex-players.

In *West Bromwich Albion Football Club Ltd v El-Safty*,[72] it was held that the surgeon owed no duty of care in tort in respect of any foreseeable economic loss to the club resulting from the negligent treatment of one of its players. In team sports professional players are major assets to clubs, and it has become apparent that greater care needs to be exhibited. Although there have been a number of problems in terms of characterising cumulative injuries in sport as industrial diseases,[73] there is significant evidence emerging of the long-term harm that can arise from certain types of play and/ or medical treatment.[74]

Additionally, sports medical practitioners can be liable for agreeing to competition and training of players in extreme environmental conditions such as high heat and high levels of pollution.[75] In 2004 multiple defendants were sued by the victim's estate for around for US$100 million. It was contended that Korey Stringer, an NFL All-Pro offensive lineman, did not receive proper medical care when he collapsed during the 2001 football training camp season. The 335-pound (24-stone) lineman died of heat stroke one day after his collapse. The facts were that Stringer had repeatedly suffered from heat illness as a result of his participation in the Minnesota Vikings' pre-season summer camps in 1998, 2000 and again on 30 July 2001. The temperature during this training session was over 40° Celsius with extreme humidity. In May 2003, the Estate of Korey Stringer, along with his widow, reached a settlement for an undisclosed sum with the Minnesota Vikings' training camp physician, Dr David Knowles, and his Mankato Clinic, both of whom were independent contractors

69 Opie, H, 'Australian Medico-Legal Issues in Sport: the View from the Grandstand' (2002) MSLR.
70 *Brady v Sunderland Football Club* (1998), unreported case, see (1998) 1(5) SLB 4.
71 Waddington, I, Roderick, M and Parker, G, *Managing Injuries in Professional Football: A Study of the Roles of the Club Doctor and Physiotherapist* (1999), Centre for Research into Sport and Society, University of Leicester.
72 *West Bromwich Albion Football Club Ltd v El-Safty*, Court of Appeal (Civil Division) [2007] PIQR 7; see 'Legal position of independent orthopaedic surgeon' (2007), 6 PI Comp, Feb, 6.
73 See the unsuccessful attempts by Billy McPhail, the ex-Glasgow Celtic player, to claim industrial disability for medical conditions including pre-senile dementia which he argues were caused by persistent heading of old-style leather footballs during the 1950s; see (1998) 1(4) SLB; also see on relationship with heading footballs and injury, Schwartz, RC, 'Heading the Ball in Soccer: What's the Risk of Brain Injury?' (1998) 26(11) *The Physician And Sportsmedicine*.
74 The long-term disabling consequences of pain-killing cortisone injections, for example, have been acknowledged; see *Daily Mail*, 14 February 2000.
75 For more analysis, see Gardiner, S, 'Sports Participation in Extreme Environmental Conditions' (2007) 15(3) SATLJ.

for the team. In January 2009, Stringer's widow's suit against the NFL was settled, with the only disclosed term of the settlement being that the NFL will support efforts to create a heat illness prevention programme.[76]

Coaches

It is clear that on application of the neighbourhood principle, coaches and other supervisors owe a duty to take reasonable care of those whom they are engaging with. Where this involves case of children, the concept of being 'in loco parentis' will apply and the duty will be more defined. In Britain there is surprisingly little case law directly involving coaches.[77] In *Van Open v Clerk to the Bedford Trustees*, it was suggested that there was potential liability on the part of an individual who failed to instruct a schoolboy as to how to tackle properly in rugby, although on the facts the action failed. In *Gannon v Rotherham Metropolitan Borough Council*, a claimant schoolboy who broke his neck successfully sued a PE teacher who had failed to provide adequate instruction on diving into a swimming pool. In *Fowles v Bedfordshire County Council*,[78] it was ruled that coaches may be liable for the self-imposed injuries of another if they have (or should have) assumed some responsibility for giving advice which it is reasonable for the latter to rely on. In this case, the defendant was liable for a twenty-one-year old's injuries for failing both to give an express prohibition against practising somersaults without a supervisor present and for failing to stress the importance of placing safety mats in the correct position.

A major question is what liability might coaches incur when their charges participate in voluntarily undertaken 'over exercise' and subsequently are injured. In *Davenport v Farrow*,[79] a young athlete's internationally renowned coach was not liable to him for vertebral stress fractures. The claimant's case was that Farrow negligently aggravated his condition by pushing him to train harder. However, he failed because on the evidence he had probably sustained the injury before he engaged the coach. The claim failed without the court considering what the duties of the coach were.[80]

Defences

Volenti non fit injuria (voluntary assumption of risk)

As described above, in a range of cases including *Wooldridge* and *Smoldon*, this concept is somewhat superfluous in that if there is evidence of negligence, this will be beyond the rules of the game and playing culture and therefore the line will have been crossed where there can be a claim of assumption of risk to defeat the claimant's action.

Contributory negligence

Under the Law Reform (Contributory Negligence) Act 1945, a successful claimant can have their damages award reduced by the percentage which the court believes the individual has contributed to the overall negligence, for example where a sports player has contributed to his or her own injury, perhaps through engaging in horseplay.[81]

---

76 Note that in Australia, there is an official Extreme Heat policy operated by Sports Medicine Australia, where temperature highs are set which where exceeded should lead to sports events and training programmes being stopped or postponed; see www.sma.org.au.

77 See Gardiner, J, 'Should Coaches Take Care?' (1993) NLJ, 1598, concerning potential liability of sports coaches; and Greenfield, S and Osborn, G, 'Aesthetics, Injury and Liability in Cricket' (1997) 13 Professional Negligence 9, concerning potential liability of groundsmen.

78 *Fowles v Bedfordshire County Council* [1995] ELR 51.

79 *Davenport v Farrow* [2010] EWHC 550 (QB).

80 Grimberg, H, 'Injury Liability: Liability for death or permanent injury: analysis' (2010) 8(5) WSLR.

81 *Grinstead v Lywood* [2002] EWHC 1743 (QB), where an owner of a speedway track sought the defence of contributory negligence from the claimant stewards.

Damages

The normal role of damages is to compensate the injured claimant victim for the losses caused by the defendant to put him or her in the position as though the tort had not been committed. In the context of negligence, of course, it is necessary to establish that the damage suffered is not too remote from the defendant's breach of duty.[82] The quantum or measure of damages can be high with professional sports players. In Collett v Smith,[83] the claimant, who was then eighteen years old, was playing for Manchester United reserves in a match against Middlebrough FC reserves. In the course of the game, the first defendant tackled him. The tackle was high and 'over the ball' and, as a consequence, the claimant suffered fractures of the tibia and fibula of his right leg.

The witnesses all spoke highly of the claimant's technical skills on the field, together with his speed, agility, stamina and energy. He worked hard on the pitch and was a consistent team player. In addition to these attributes, the witnesses referred to four particular strengths possessed by the claimant:

Collett v Smith

i) He was a dominantly left-footed player, although he was able to use both feet effectively. Left-footed players are a rarity in the professional game, particularly at international level. Left-footed players are especially well suited to playing left midfield, which was the claimant's favoured position. I was told that a good left-footed player has a scarcity value that makes him particularly attractive to football clubs.

ii) The claimant had the ability to combine an attacking game at left midfield with a defensive game. Sir Alex (Ferguson) told me that players rarely possess this ability. Indeed, he said that he had seen only one or two players in his lifetime who had it.

iii) The claimant was an intelligent young man with a keen interest in and good understanding of the game. Mr McClair described him as a 'student of football'. He said that one of the claimant's great strengths was his speed of thought and knowledge of the game.

iv) His character and attitude were ideally suited to a career in football. They were described by Sir Alex as 'A Class' and 'magnificent' and the evidence of the other lay witnesses echoed this. He was self-disciplined, focused and professional, both on and off the pitch. His work ethic was described by one witness as 'phenomenal'. He demonstrated commitment and determination to improve his game. He was regarded as a model for other young players to emulate.[84]

Collett was awarded £4.3 million. The implications of the decision are that in such circumstances, because of the potential level of damages, it may well be worthwhile for a player whose career has ended to bring an action in court rather than accept a settlement with the other party's insurance company. In addition, it is a warning that professional players and clubs should make sure that their insurance policies will cover this potential level of damages.[85]

Criminal Liability for Sports Participant Violence

The second part of this chapter will focus on the application of the criminal law to participator violence. Historically, English common law during its centuries of development has been relatively liberal in the construction of consensual force between individuals. The use of violence to others short

---

82 Overseas Tankship (UK) Ltd v Morts Dock and Engineering Co Ltd or The Wagon Mound (No 1) [1961] UKPC 1.
83 Collett v Smith [2008] EWHC 1962 (QB); ISLR. 2008, 4, SLR 125–45.
84 Ibid.
85 Farrow, S, 'Injury Compensation: Collett v Smith: compensation for future earnings' (2008) 6(9) WSLR.

of permanent maiming has been justified in the past.[86] In the late eighteenth century, there were contrary views as to the effect of consensual use of force in sporting situations. Hale argued that death occurring in a mutually consensual activity such as wrestling would result in liability for manslaughter because the participants in such a sport intend to harm each other.[87] Conversely, Foster stated that two individuals who 'engage by mutual consent' in such activities have no intention to harm one another, and therefore there could be no liability for manslaughter on the death of the other participant.[88] During the nineteenth century, concern over activities such as prize fighting and duelling leading to death led to some regulation by the criminal law. Two nineteenth-century cases (R v Bradshaw and R v Moore), indicated that players who used intentional or reckless force likely to cause bodily harm to another would be acting illegally.[89] Neither of the cases specifically considered the issue of what effect the victim's consent to involvement in the game would have on the defendant's liability. However, there was an inference that if the defendant was playing within the rules and practices of the sport, the player would not be acting in a manner likely to cause bodily harm. As stated in Bradshaw:

R v Bradshaw

If a man is playing according to the rules and practices of the game and not going beyond it, it may be reasonable to infer that he is not actuated by any malicious motive or intention, and that he is not acting in a manner which he knows will be likely to be productive of death or injury.[90]

During the twentieth century there were spasmodic prosecutions, but these have increased in frequency over the last 25 years or so. Indeed recently in football, the President of FIFA, Sepp Blatter, called for criminal prosecutions to be brought against those who commit dangerous tackles.[91] These prosecutions can be classified in terms of the offence individuals are charged with, but the following taxonomy, based on the geographical setting of the incident, is more instructive. Three can be identified.

Environs of the sports field

Fights and brawls that occur adjacent to the sports field, for example in the players' tunnel or at the side of the pitch, have led to convictions for assault offences. In Kamara,[92] a professional footballer was convicted under s 20 Offences Against the Persons Act 1861 (OAPA) for punching and breaking the jaw of an opponent after the final whistle for a match had been blown. In Cantona,[93] the infamous flying kung-fu kick by Eric Cantona targeted at an opposition fan, inflicted after the defendant had been sent off for an on-field foul, led to conviction for common assault.[94] In these incidents, the claim by both of the defendants was that their actions were in response to racist provocation. Also similar to both incidents was that their occurrence was outside of the pitch, beyond the playing rules of the game and the supervision of the referee and that they were arguably not sporting incidents. Consent will not operate here. Both Kamara and Cantona were, however, 'charged' with wider disciplinary offences by the English Football Association (FA).

---

86 Hawkins, W, *A Treatise of the Pleas of the Crown*, 8th edn (1824), London, vol 1. Also see Stephen, JF, *A Digest of the Criminal Law*, 5th edn (1894), London: Macmillan.
87 Hale, M, *History of Pleas of the Crown* (1778), London.
88 M. Foster, *Crown Cases and Crown Law* 260 (1763), Dublin: Sarah Cotter.
89 R v Bradshaw (1878) 14 Cox CC 83 above (football player killed when charged by one opponent with a protruding knee); R v Moore (1898) 14 TLR 229 (football player killed when violent push from behind caused his head to strike another player's knee).
90 (1878) 14 Cox CC 83, at 85.
91 See 'Jail players who commit dangerous tackles' (2008) ISLJ.
92 R v Kamara (1988) Times, 15 April.
93 R v Cantona (1995) Times, 25 March.
94 See Gardiner, S, 'The Law and Hate Speech: "Ooh Aah Cantona": Demonisation of "the Other" ' in Brown, A (ed), *Fanatics* (1998), London: Routledge.

Off-the-ball incidents

Incidents on the sports field but off the ball and away from the play have led to many convictions in team sport for assault and public order offences. There have been a significantly higher number of prosecutions in amateur rugby and football compared to the professional game, which seems to be partly determined by a greater likelihood that offences are reported to the police and that the Crown Prosecution Service will decide to prosecute.[95] In addition, the internal sporting disciplinary procedures at regional level are not enforced as effectively as is the case in the professional game, which has a national enforcement procedure.[96] More high-profile cases in professional football have occurred than in both the codes of rugby union and league,[97] probably explained by the higher levels of 'violent conduct' in off-the-ball fights that are accepted in rugby.[98]

In football, *Ferguson v Normand* involved the conviction, under s 18 OAPA, and imprisonment of striker Duncan Ferguson for an off-the-ball head butt against John McStay during a match between Glasgow Rangers and Raith Rovers.[99] Individuals have also been convicted for public order offences including *Butcher v Jessop*[100] when, during the Glasgow derby, a number of Rangers and Celtic players were charged with breach of the peace following a goalmouth 'scrum'. Two players were convicted, one was found not guilty and another had his case 'not proven'. The heavily publicised but relatively minor skirmish between Newcastle players Lee Bowyer and Kieron Dyer in April 2005 is a more recent example, with Bowyer charged under the wide s 4 Public Order Act offence of Fear and Provocation of Violence.[101] Additionally, police have cautioned professional players for swearing and other anti-social behaviour, by intervening during the actual course of a game.[102]

On-the-ball incidents

Events with very close proximity to the point of play can be termed 'on-the-ball' incidents. The prosecution in *Blissett* is an exemplar of the problem of demarcation of the criminal law's involvement. The Brentford footballer, Gary Blissett, was charged with causing grievous bodily harm under s 18 of the Offences against the Person Act 1861 to the former Torquay United player, John Uzzell.[103] Up to that point in time most prosecutions had been for the lesser offence of assault occasioning actual bodily harm under s 47. Blissett was involved in a flying collision when both he and

---

95 In rugby union reported cases primarily concerning appeals against sentence, include *R v Billinghurst* [1978] Crim LR 553; *R v Gingell* (1980) 2 Cr App R (S) 198, who was convicted of inflicting grievous bodily harm when his assault during a rugby match led to a fractured cheekbone, jaw and nose. Sentence of six months reduced to two on appeal. In *R v Johnson* (1986) 8 Cr App R (S) 343 the defendant was convicted under s 18 OAPA for biting off part of an opposing player's ear during a rugby match and received a six-month sentence. Also see *R v Bishop* (1986 unreported); *R v Lloyd* (1989) 11 Cr.App.R (s.) 36; *R v Chapman* (1989) 11 Cr App R (S) 93, *R v Calton* (1998) unreported, see (1998) 1(5) SLB, 3. In football convictions include *R v Birkin* [1988] Crim LR; *R v Shervill* (1989) 11 Cr App R (S) 284; *R v Lincoln* (1990) 12 Cr App R (S) 250; *R v Davies* [1991] Crim LR 70, *R v McHugh* (1998) unreported: see 2(4) SLB, 2, *R v Moss* (1999) unreported (see (1999) 2(4) SLB 2.

96 See www.thefa.com/TheFA/Disciplinary.

97 See *R v Stein* (1983) unreported, where Mark Stein of Stoke City was convicted of assault occasioning actual bodily harm for injury caused to Jim Gannon of Stockport County.

98 But see *R v Mills* (2005) unreported; see 'Doncaster winger is guilty of GBH', BBC Sport, 14 November 2005, http://news.bbc.co.uk/sport1/hi/rugby_league/national_league/4436716.stm.

99 *Ferguson v Normand* [1995] SCCR 770; also see the conviction of Scott McMillan for assault after chasing an opponent and head-butting him during a Scottish rugby match in an example of a clear act of retaliation (*The Times*, May 1994).

100 *Butcher v Jessop* 1989 SLT 593; also see conviction of Charlie George, in 1990, for behaving in a way that was likely to cause a breach of the peace during a match.

101 See 'Pitch fight lands Bowyer in court', BBC News, 8 June 2005, http://news.bbc.co.uk/1/hi/england/tyne/4073598.stm.

102 Also see *R v Diouf* (2005) unreported – El Hadji Diouf, the Senegalese international footballer, was convicted for disorderly conduct, s 5 Public Order Act 1986, after an 11-year-old Middlesbrough fan alleged he was hit by liquid the Bolton player had expelled from his mouth: 'Diouf fined over spitting water', BBC News, 16 November 2005, http://news.bbc.co.uk/1/hi/england/tees/4442640.stm. The case highlighted that on conviction, it would have been possible to impose a Football Banning Order under the Football (Disorder) Act 2000 which by restricting his attendance at designated football matches could have restricted his ability to play for his employer club.

103 *R v Blissett* (1992) *Independent*, 4 December; also see Gardiner, S, 'Not Playing the Game – Is it a Crime?' (1993) SJ 628; also see response by Grayson, E (1993) SJ.

Uzzell were challenging to get possession of the ball. Uzzell suffered a fractured eye socket and cheek-bone, and subsequently retired from football. The referee saw the incident and Blissett was sent off. Blissett said at his trial that what had occurred was an accident, as the two players had jumped for a fifty-fifty ball. He had tried to avoid colliding with Uzzell when he realised he was not going to win the ball. Acting as an expert witness, Graham Kelly, then the FA's chief executive, caused some controversy when he said it was an 'ordinary aerial challenge', which he would see 200 times a week if he attended four matches. He considered that this type of play was one that occurred regularly and of a type that participants implicitly consent to. Blissett was acquitted. No clear guidance was provided as to how the law of consent should be applied to sports participation incidents or how it might be possible to determine where the line of demarcation should be drawn for the criminal law's involvement.

The Court of Appeal case of *Barnes* highlights this issue again.[104] The incident in question occurred during an amateur match in the Thanet local league between Minster FC and Punch and Judy FC. With twenty minutes to go, Minster were two goals ahead. At the time of the alleged offence, the victim, who was playing for Minster, guided the ball towards the corner flag as a means of using up time. Barnes attempted to tackle him and in doing so committed a foul. Minster were awarded a free kick. The referee, Mr Lawrence, who had over 30 years' experience, interjected in a heated exchange of words between the two and told them both 'to grow up'. Ten minutes later the victim was in a shooting position around seven yards in front of the goal. He scored, but just after he had kicked the ball, Barnes tackled him from behind, making contact with his right ankle. Barnes was reported to have said words to the effect of 'have that'. The victim was seriously injured, with damage to his ankle and right fibula. The referee sent Barnes off the field for violent conduct. The foul, resultant injury and sending off are not particularly infrequent occurrences and would usually be dealt with within football's disciplinary procedures.

However, a prosecution ensued and at the trial the referee considered that, in making the tackle, Barnes 'had gone in with two feet'. Barnes' contention was that he had made a legitimate 'sliding tackle'. In his summing up the Judge stressed that although the consequential serious injury was not in dispute, the characterisation of the tackle was, however, open to doubt. The Judge indicated that the prosecution had to prove that what happened was 'not done by way of legitimate sport' and that 'what was done was a deliberate act'. By doing so he focused on both the necessary elements of *actus reus* and *mens rea*. No specific mention was made by the Judge on the issue of consent; although the prosecution argued that the phrase 'legitimate sport' used by the Judge obviously embraced the issue of consent. Barnes was convicted of a s 20 OAPA offence, which he appealed.

The Court of Appeal found that although the jury had asked for clarification of what was legitimate sport, they were 'not given any examples of conduct' that might have amounted to it. No attempt was made to determine clearly whether what was happening in the game at the time of the incident was legitimate or not. The Court concluded that 'the summing-up was inadequate' and the conviction therefore unsafe. Lord Woolf attempted to articulate what he believed was the narrow area where there might be criminal liability:

R v Barnes

The starting point is the fact that most organised sports have their own disciplinary procedures for enforcing their particular rules and standards of conduct . . . in addition to a criminal prosecution there is the possibility of an injured player obtaining damages at a civil action from another player . . . a criminal prosecution should be reserved for those situations where the conduct is *sufficiently grave* to be properly categorised as criminal [emphasis added].[105]

---

104 R v *Barnes* [2004] EWCA Crim 3246.
105 Ibid.

The Court of Appeal stated that the test for determining 'the gravity' of the incident was an objective one. The criteria 'likely to be relevant in determining whether the defendant's actions go beyond the threshold' were:

- the type of the sport;
- the level at which it is played,
- the nature of the act;
- the degree of force used;
- the extent of the risk of injury;
- the state of mind of the defendant.

This was very much the application of guidance that has been laid down in R v Brown[106] and further amplified by the Law Commission in their post-Brown consultation. Brown provided the opportunity to review the problematic of the law generally on the law of assaults and consent and in specific circumstances such as sadomasochistic sexual activity and sporting activity. What was accepted as settled law was that participants in 'properly conducted games and sport' could as an exception to the general position, legally consent to injury beyond actual bodily harm.[107]

Construction of consent

The Law Commission has had two attempts at formulating how consent should be constructed generally in the criminal law and in specific circumstances.[108] As far as sport is concerned, what has transpired is a clear articulation of an overtly objective test as to where the line of demarcation is drawn between that consequential injury which can be consented to and that which cannot and could therefore be subject to criminal liability. In the first Consultation Paper in 1993, the Law Commission argued that any perceived subjective construction of consent should be replaced by an objective test.[109] The Paper suggested that it was artificial to talk of participants (subjectively) consenting to risk of injury, as opposed to consenting to take part in the game.[110]

The approach in a number of Canadian cases to the legal regulation of violence in ice hockey matches, which were reviewed in Brown, was used by the Commission to support this move to an objective construction of consent. It should be noted that ice hockey in North America is a widely played sport both recreationally, at a number of amateur levels, and professionally. It is one of the four major professional sports and in Canada is clearly the national game. Its popularity is based on its fast-moving and highly competitive dynamic. It can be classified as a semi-contact sport but one that involves significant body-checking and contact with the stick. Fights, which can sometimes be quite brutal, between players 'off-the-puck' are not uncommon in games and are viewed by some as part of the game's appeal, but by others as an example of unacceptable conduct. As Horrow argues, 'in no other sport are the risks to health subordinated to victory and accepted as an inherent part of the game'.[111]

---

106 R v Brown [1994] 1 AC 212. See Bibbings, L and Alldridge, P, 'Sexual Expression, Body Alteration and the Defence of Consent' (1993) Journal of Law and Society 356 and Weait, M, 'Fleshing it Out', in Bently, L and Flynn, L (eds), Law and the Senses (1996), London: Pluto Press.
107 Attorney General's Reference (No 6 of 1908) (1981) QB 715.
108 'Consent and Offences Against the Person' (1994) LCCP 134, London: HMSO. For a general analysis see Ormerod, D, 'Consent and Offences Against the Person' (1994) 57 MLR 931.
109 'Consent and Offences Against the Person' (1994), LCCP 134, London: HMSO. For a general analysis see op. cit., fn 108, Ormerod (1994).
110 Op. cit., fn 109, LCCP 134, para 41.3.
111 Horrow, R, Sports Violence: the Interaction between Private Law making and the Criminal Law (1980), Arlington, VA: Carrollton Press. Also see Whitson, D and Gruneau, R, Hockey Night in Canada: Sports, Identities, and Cultural Politics (1993) Toronto: Garamond Press.

This objective test was first articulated in the case of *Cey*[112] and has been supported in later cases.[113] This case concerned an assault in an amateur match where the accused used his hockey stick to push the victim into the boards surrounding the rink. The objective criteria constructed were:

- the conditions under which the game in question is played;
- the nature of the act which forms the charge;
- the extent of the force employed;
- the degree of the risk of injury;
- the state of mind of the accused.[114]

The criteria discussed in *Barnes* are clearly based on these. Gerwing JA for the majority in *Cey* considered that the trial judge had been wrong in giving a direction only on the issue of whether the accused had intended to cause serious injury and to thereby exceed the standards by which the game of hockey should be played. She stated that the subjective state of mind of the accused is only one factor, and in fact 'not particularly significant',[115] in determining whether actions fall within the scope of activity to which the victim implicitly consents. She considered the objective criteria discussed should be used to determine whether the actions of the accused were so 'violent and inherently dangerous as to be excluded from the implied consent'.[116]

Prosecutorial Discretion – the Solution?

The second area of discussion on the role of the criminal law and sports injuries focuses on how discretion is exercised in deciding when to prosecute in sports violence incidents. In June 2005, the Crown Prosecution Service (CPS) held a conference entitled 'Crime in Sport', focusing on the criminal liability of a range of issues including corruption and match fixing, football hooliganism and on-field violent incidents including racial abuse. It was the regulation of on-field violence that was highlighted during the conference, with the CPS indicating that it was to review its policy concerning when and where prosecutions are brought, particularly in team contact sports.[117] Nazir Afzal, the Sector Director for the CPS in London West argued: 'The growing feeling among the public is that players are getting away with crime – that footballers in particular escape punishment by criminal justice – and that is wrong . . . It is unlawful to assault or racially abuse someone on the street and we prosecute for that. But when it comes to events on the pitch, we don't get involved, usually because there is no complaint and no police investigation.'[118]

The CPS had recognised that its existing policy towards violence on the pitch was ad hoc and there was no clarity or consistency in prosecutions, together with little guidance for the police. This is in comparison with disorderly conduct by spectators and supporters in and around matches, where in addition to a range of public order offences – and in the case of football its own specific legislation – clear prosecution guidelines have been developed. This specific focus on the sports field seems to be predicated on the belief that there needs to be firmer action concerning violent and abusive behaviour in the light of public concerns that players escape public prosecution for their actions. As with the discussion of the substantive law, the major issue in the exercise of

---

112 R v *Cey* (1989) 48 CCC (3d) 480.
113 These were followed in R v *Ciccarelli* (1989) 54 CCC (3d) 121, R v *Leclerc* (1991) 67 CCC (3d) *and* R v *Jobidon* (1991) 2S. SCR 714.
114 R v *Cey* (1989) fn 108 above at pp 490–91.
115 Ibid at p 481.
116 Ibid at p. 481.
117 For a review of some of the presentations see Barker, S, 'Is there a Case for more Criminal Justice Involvement in Sporting Incidents' (2005) 13(2) SATLJ 13.
118 See CPS London website at http://www.cps.gov.uk/london.

prosecutorial discretion is determining where the line is to be drawn as to the type of conduct that will be prosecuted.

During the autumn of 2005, the CPS, in collaboration with the Association of Chief Police Officers (ACPO), produced some draft guidelines charting the respective responsibilities of the police and the CPS.[119] The main stated principle is that 'any conduct on the field of play which breaches the criminal law cannot be tolerated and, as with any criminal behaviour in any other walk of life, will be investigated and prosecuted whenever it is appropriate to do so.'[120]

The Guidelines highlight that the police have discretion in how to deal with any incident, including talking to an individual and/or issuing an informal caution. It will be for them to decide 'which allegations of criminal behaviour are investigated'. Once they decide on a potential offence, the CPS applies the standard two-tier test in deciding whether to bring a prosecution, and this can create difficulties in sporting situations.

First, sufficient evidence needs to be adduced to provide a realistic prospect of conviction. This means establishing that the evidence that can be used is reliable and that a jury or a bench of magistrates, properly directed in accordance with the law, will be more likely than not to convict the defendant of the charge alleged. The Guidelines seem to lean heavily on the Objective Criteria stated by the Lord Chief Justice in *Barnes*. These Guidelines provide essentially an indication of the qualitative nature of the available evidence and whether the threshold that demarcates the criminal from the non-criminal has been reached.[121] Perhaps of equal importance, but not discussed in the prosecutorial Guidelines, are more practical and quantitative issues concerning the availability of evidence. As noted earlier most prosecutions occur in amateur football and rugby.

In professional team sport, the specific sporting culture and the prevalent 'code of silence' means injured parties are unlikely to make a complaint and other participants are unlikely to give incriminating evidence as witnesses. This clearly strikes at the 'reliability of the evidence'. Of course, unlike amateur sport, most professional sport is now video recorded for television transmission so pictorial evidence is invariably available for on-the-ball incidents and sometimes for those which are off the ball. However, this has been criticised as it can often provide a two-dimensional image that is far from conclusive.[122]

Second, if the case does pass the evidential test, the CPS must then decide whether a prosecution is needed in the public interest. The CPS Draft Guidelines list the following criteria:

- the nature of the conduct in the context of the sport under consideration;
- what was the degree of pre-meditation;
- did the offender seek to ensure that match officials were unsighted when the offence was committed;
- who the conduct was directed at, e.g. other participants, match officials, spectators;
- what was the impact on those other people and their subsequent behaviour, e.g. did the incident lead to further violence or disorder on the field of play or by spectators;
- previous incidents of a similar nature;
- any action taken by the match officials or the governing bodies in relation to the incident.

It is important to note that these draft guidelines have not been formalised in terms of a specific CPS policy. It seems, however, that the guidelines above will help decide when and where a prosecution

---

119 Draft – Crown Prosecution Service and ACPO, 'Guidance to Prosecutors and Police Officers – Crime in Sport' (2005); see http://www.cps.gov.uk/news/press_releases/archived_press_releases.

120 Ibid, p 1.

121 These were discussed above on pages 519 and 520.

122 In the civil action between two professional footballers in *Elliot v Saunders* (1994) unreported, video evidence that was adduced in the Court was considered by the judge to be of limited use and two-dimensional; see Gardiner, S and Felix, A, 'Elliot v Saunders: Drama in Court 14' (1994) 2(2) SATLJ 1.

will be initiated, along of course with both the evidential and public interest tests. It is useful to apply these guidelines to the prosecutions against Bowyer for his off-the-ball incident and in *Barnes* for the on-the-ball incident.

Application of CPS Guidelines to the *Bowyer* case

The Bowyer–Dyer incident, although legally a common assault, was, in the context of contemporary football, little more than a scuffle or, using the vernacular, 'handbags' with no or only minor resulting harm. This can be usefully compared to the context of the daily occurrence of many similar incidents, and indeed significantly more serious ones, in British high streets that are not prosecuted. There was clear visual evidence to support a prosecution of Bowyer as the protagonist. Dyer's involvement was primarily in defending himself. How would this incident pass the public interest test? It was clearly a fight off the ball and away from play. There did not seem to be obvious premeditation although the individuals seemed to have had words beforehand. The position of the match referee seems to have been irrelevant in the sense that no deception was achieved. The fight was between players of the same team, which is a reasonably rare event compared with the more frequent and similar tussles between opponents in football and rugby. The crowd may well have been bemused by the incident and there was no indication of an adverse crowd reaction.[123] Bowyer has no real reputation for violent conduct on the football field but has some notoriety from other non-football incidents.[124] The referee sent both players off and subsequent disciplinary action was taken. So why the prosecution? As Barnes argues: 'One could certainly take the view that pursuing a criminal action against Bowyer is at least partly a result of political expediency.'[125]

The fact that this was a 'fight' between two high-profile footballers, and indeed teammates, before more than 50,000 spectators and subsequently millions on TV may provide support for making an example of the perpetrator. But this incident in terms of the physical force used occurs regularly in a range of sports including football, rugby and ice hockey throughout the country. It is not obvious how the public interest was served in albeit what was a minor criminal prosecution. The distinction between, on the one hand, on-the-ball incidents, and, on the other, off-the-ball incidents outside the play and the playing rules could give better guidance on where the public interest test might be satisfied. This would target 'violent conduct' that is clearly not within the particular game. The determination of whether the prosecution is in the public interest, however, is a balance between factors for and against prosecution. As the CPS states: 'a prosecution will usually take place, however, unless there are public interest factors tending against prosecution which clearly outweigh those tending in favour'.

In *Bowyer*, it can be argued that even though the incident was clearly off the ball and outside the playing rules and culture, a prosecution was still not warranted in light of the guidelines.[126] The Chief Crown Prosecutor for Northumbria, Nicola Reasbeck, saw it differently:

Reasbeck, N, 'Lee Bowyer pleads guilty to public order offence'

The criminal law doesn't cease to operate once you cross the touchline of a sports field . . . neither does being disciplined by an employer or a sport governing body make an athlete immune to the law . . . when we reviewed the case, we considered charges of assault as well as

---

123 See Gardiner, S and Felix, A, 'Juridification of the Football Field: Strategies for Giving Law the Elbow' (1995) 5(2) MSLJ 189.

124 See his acquittal for s 20 OAPA 1861 concerning allegations that he was involved in a fight with a student in Leeds City Centre in 2000, but note his settling of a civil action by the victim, 'Bowyer payout for attack victim', BBC News, 29 November 2005, http://news.bbc.co.uk/1/hi/england/4482622.stm.

125 Barnes, M, 'Discipline: Crime and Punishment on the Sports Field' (2005) 3(9) WSLR 3.

126 The Bowyer incident occurred in April 2005 with his court appearance delayed until 14 November 2005. It was reported that Bowyer had sought judicial review of the decision to prosecute. This was refused by Mr Justice Bean in September 2005, when he described the application as 'without foundation'. An Appeal failed at a hearing in the High Court in January 2005.

public order act offences and decided that the most appropriate charge was an offence under Section 4. In making that decision we had to be sure that both the evidential test and the public interest test were met.[127]

Application of CPS Guidelines to the *Barnes* case

Applying the Prosecution Guidelines to *Barnes* and the more problematic issues of on-the-ball incidents, the tackle from behind, although outside the playing rules, is one that occurs frequently in matches at all playing levels, often leading to a determination of foul play by the referee. There was evidence of premeditation on Barnes' part to commit the foul. It was committed after earlier altercations between the two players. Where the incident is during the play the referee is always likely to see it. The conduct was directed at the victim – he was an opponent, of course. It is likely that this incident created significant disquiet on the part of the teammates of the victim. This is a common reaction and reflects the adrenalin-induced excitement and the culture found in team sports. There had been previous incidents in the match and Barnes was sent off for violent conduct. There was no evidence submitted of any history of violent conduct on Barnes' part in his past career. It is not obvious, in applying these criteria, that there was any outstanding case for bringing a prosecution. If there were, then potentially similar prosecutions could arise for analogous circumstances every weekend around the country. Prosecutions continue to occur but not to any widespread degree, although in a small number of incidents they have led to custodial sentences.[128]

Scottish guidelines

This is not, of course, the first time that the prosecution authorities in the UK have considered their policy in relation to conduct on the sports field. In Scotland in the mid-1990s there was an increase in the number of prosecutions brought by the Glasgow Region Procurator Fiscal, including the high-profile case involving Duncan Ferguson.[129] In response to these sports participation criminal prosecutions, the Lord Advocate drew up guidelines for bringing such prosecutions in Scotland. These proposed that prosecutions should only occur in instances where the violence used was 'well beyond' that which would be expected to occur in normal play in any particular sport.[130] This rather general test was criticised in a number of ways. The guidance 'simply reminds the police of their powers rather than defining how and when those powers should be used'.[131] Concern was also voiced that if the threshold of criminal law intervention was for violence well beyond the normal, this was too high a standard that would lead to a dearth of criminal cases.[132]

However, it may well be that the Lord Advocate's Instructions are an appropriate formulation. Prosecutions continue to occur in Scotland and the evidence is that the threshold test provides effective guidance for general on-field incidents and particularly the rare occasions when an on-the-ball incident might be prosecuted. They share with the recent draft guidelines for England and Wales an emphasis on police officers exercising discretion over which avenue of action to take as an alternative to involving the prosecution authorities. This high threshold works in putting sports

---

127 'Lee Bowyer pleads guilty to public order offence', 5 July 2006, http://www.cps.gov.uk/news/press_releases/143_06/index.html

128 'Footballer Mark Ward jailed for vicious tackle', *Gazettelive*, 20 May 2009, www.gazettelive.co.uk/news/teesside-news/2009/05/20/footballer-mark-ward-jailed-for-vicious-tackle-84229-23670434; and 'Footballer first to be jailed for on-field tackle', *The Telegraph*, 4 March 2010, www.telegraph.co.uk/news/uknews/crime/7369009/Footballer-first-to-be-jailed-for-on-field-tackle.html.

129 *Ferguson v Normand* [1995] fn 96 above.

130 See Lord Advocate's Instructions to the Chief Constables in Scotland under s 12 Criminal Procedure (Scotland) Act 1995.

131 James, M and Gardiner, S, 'Touchlines and Guidelines: The Lord Advocate's Response to Sportfield Violence' (1997) Crim LR 41.

132 Miller, S, 'Criminal Law and Sport in Scotland' (1996) 4(2) SATLJ 40.

governing bodies on notice that criminal action is a possibility in limited circumstances and encourages the existence of robust and proportionate disciplinary powers.

The reality of sport is that it has some degree of physicality. Team sports can be characterised as heavy contact sports, such as rugby; medium contact sports, such as football and ice hockey; or light contact sports, such as basketball and netball. They all share rules and playing cultures that help demarcate what is legitimate or illegitimate. Where the physical contact is illegitimate it is often characterised in rather simplistic terms as sports violence or thuggery. There is variation between different sports as to what is accepted beyond the rules. Significant physical contact takes place. Mistimed tackles in football occur regularly. In rugby, some tackling and rucking can seem brutal. Further, outside the rules but in the playing culture, minor fisticuffs during particular parts of the play in both rugby union and league are familiar events. In ice hockey, skirmishes between players are acknowledged as a routine part of many matches.[133]

Many spectators expect these, and with the body protection used by players the chance of injury is minor. The difference between these events happening in the street or other public place on the one hand and the sport arenas on the other is that sportsmen are subject to complex regulation by a network of normative rules including playing rules, disciplinary rules and codes of conduct. These sporting incidents are the subject of disciplinary action by clubs and governing bodies rather than prosecuted in the courts. The media-generated 'moral panic' over incidents such as that involving Bowyer and Dyer in football needs to be put into context. These incidents happen periodically but are not endemic within that particular sport. Where they occur they are generally policed well by the relevant sporting body. Sports governing bodies have been criticised over administering deficient disciplinary measures, but increasingly reconstituting these procedures has made disciplinary tribunals more effective.[134] For example, Bowyer was banned for seven matches and fined £30,000 by the FA in addition to the club fine of around £200,000. Both codes of rugby have their own examples of foul play that again are subject to increasingly effective disciplinary procedures.[135]

The search for principle – social utility and disutility

The position of both the courts and the CPS is clearly based on pragmatism. One principle that can be discerned has been based on a notion that once injury reaches a certain level of objective behaviour so as to be deemed beyond consent, it should be prohibited on public policy grounds. The burden of proof seems to be on the accused to justify his or her behaviour. Sport has a higher profile in the mind of the public, with more media coverage of professional sport than ever with incidents of alleged violence replayed endlessly. At a time when any violence in society is a matter of condemnation, the specific characteristics of sport seem to have been distorted. The positive reasons for participating in sport of physical endeavour, benefits to health and competitive rivalry have been superseded by this urge to prohibit. Within this current climate it has become more

---

133 A criminal prosecution may of course be more valid for such an off-the-puck incident. In 2004, Todd Bertuzzi of the Vancouver Canucks punched Steve Moore of the Colorado Avalanche, knocking Moore unconscious, and then drove Moore head-first into the ice. Moore sustained two chipped vertebrae, concussion, and facial lacerations. Bertuzzi was charged by police, and given a conditional discharge after pleading guilty to assault causing bodily harm. His 20-game suspension resulted in a loss of $500,000 in pay and the Canucks were fined $250,000: see 'Bertuzzi denies charge', BBC Sport, 26 August 2004, http://news.bbc.co.uk/sport1/hi/other_sports/us_sport/3603396.stm. Also see Swiss criminal case *Bundesgericht (Kevin Miller)* (6B 298/2007) (unreported, 24 October 2007): Gasser, C and Schweizer, E, 'Case Comment Switzerland: ice hockey/criminal law' (2008) ISLR.

134 The effectiveness of such in-house procedures is always going to be contested as either being too lenient or too harsh by different constituencies but they are procedures that are demonstrably compliant with rules of proper procedure and natural justice and judicially reviewable.

135 The Wales Rugby International Gavin Henson was banned for seven weeks for elbowing an opponent, see 'Henson's ban reduced after appeal', BBC Sport, 10 January 2006, http://news.bbc.co.uk/sport1/hi/rugby_union/european/4557890.stm.

difficult to justify the 'social utility' of allowing unfettered physical sporting activity to take place. An alternative construction of liability, which might be usefully employed, is one based on the burden of proof being on the prosecution to justify prohibition and is forcibly argued by Kell in his support for a 'social disutility' model.[136] Arguing in the context of his concerns relating to the *Brown* ruling, he provides two main arguments for supporting this alternative approach:

1. It is better suited to a modern democratic society which places significant value on individual autonomy – the question that needs to be answered by the prosecution is 'What justifies the intervention?'
2. The model may actually provide a better explanation to the exceptions to the general rule to consent, including sport, than the social utility model.

Kell finds that the ruling of the majority in *Brown* applied concepts of paternalism and legal moralism in their attempts to justify why these sadomasochistic activities should be prohibited. It is the minority judgement of Lord Mustill which is held up by Kell as advocating a social disutility model, and indeed he considers that it 'points the proper way forward'[137] for a more coherent jurisprudential development of consent in the future.

So how might this social disutility approach be applied to sport? Firstly, what justification is there for the intervention of the criminal law onto the sports field? A response often made is that acts of violence should be acted upon in the same way whether they occur on the sports field, the street or in the home. This of course fails to recognise the physicality and specific dynamics of sport, and, as argued above, sport is a heavily rule-bound social activity. As with domestic violence, the most effective and lasting regulation and remedy for the victim has arguably not been through the criminal law but the injunctive civil relief limiting access by the perpetrator.

Secondly, can the social disutility model support sport being an exception to legal intervention? It is clearly recognised that many sports could not take place if sport was not an exception. But with the line of demarcation difficult to draw, this model may provide guidance. It is perhaps useful to consider levels of injury that might be caused. Statistics that indicate increases in levels of injury can be misleading. Higher levels of fitness and physical endeavour in professional sport contribute to more frequent but less serious injuries than in the past.[138] There is no indication that amateur sport is any different. It might also be argued that violence on the field causes crowd violence or subsequent disorder between violent fans. However, there is no reliable evidence to support this assertion. Indeed, in Britain, in football and both codes of rugby, the game is relatively sanitised in comparison to 20 or 30 years ago with rule changes, the introduction of formal codes of conduct and more rigorous officiating leading to safer and less violent play.

This social disutility model may help provide a clear role for sport to engage with incidents of sports violence within its own normative rule structure, which has been shown to be increasingly robust. As with all the issues on the penumbra of the law of assaults where consent remains problematic, it is not a good use of scarce resources for prosecution authorities to be contemplating criminal actions. This is particularly apposite when there is a view (albeit one contested on the basis of competing statistical measures) that violence generally in society is on the increase. Can it be argued that contemporary debates over a perceived need to engage with anti-social behaviour have seeped on to the sports field?

---

136 Kell, D, 'Social Disutility and Consent' (1994) OJLS 121.
137 Ibid, p 123.
138 See, eg, Wilson, B, Quarrie, K Milburn, P and Chalmers, D, 'The Nature and Circumstances of Tackle Injuries in Rugby Union' (1998) 2(2) Journal of Science and Medicine in Sport 153.

Risk Management and Extreme Sports

The maintenance of a safe sporting environment has been high on the agenda of the sports governing bodies that oversee sporting codes which involve an inherently dangerous activity.[139] This form of risk management has partly been caused by an increasing awareness of the need to provide a safe working environment for participants that has been created by the consequences of serious incidents such as the threat of legal liability, increased insurance premiums and the response by the variety of stakeholders in sport including fans, media companies and sponsors. Many examples can be used to illustrate this – driver safety has been improved immeasurably in motor racing; the wearing of helmets in cricket is compulsory. In some instances this has led to particular sporting activities such as pole vaulting not taking place in schools. Responding to the threat of legal liability so as to minimise its risk is an effective element of risk management. This approach has also involved education programmes for players emphasising the need to play the game in an ethical manner.[140]

Should boxing be banned?

For supporters of boxing, the sport is about bravery and determination in the face of extreme physical danger. Boxing is seen as 'the noble art', the epitome of man's instinct to fight, a fine way of teaching self-discipline.[141] The history of sport discussed in Chapter 1 suggests that boxing can be seen as a continuum of the need for man to be able to fight to survive.

Opponents say that a civilised society should not tolerate organised brutality, however brave and heroic it might appear.[142] Professional boxing, in contrast to the highly regulated amateur game, is banned in Sweden, Norway and Iceland.[143] Such boxing is seen as far too violent and barbaric.[144] Boxing, compared with other sports, is distinguished by a clear goal of the infliction of physical injury upon the opponent:

R v Brown

Lord Mustill: for money, not recreation or personal improvement, each boxer tries to hurt the opponent more than he is hurt himself, and aims to end the contest prematurely by inflicting a brain injury serious enough to make the opponent unconscious, or temporarily by impairing his central nervous system through a blow to the midriff, or cutting his skin to a degree which would ordinarily be well within the scope of s 20 (Offences Against the Persons Act 1861). The boxers display skill, strength and courage, but nobody pretends that they do good to themselves or others. The onlookers derive entertainment, but none of the physical and moral benefits, which have been seen as the fruits of engagement in many sports.[145]

In Brown it was concluded that although there was some legal authority to support the legality of 'sparring', essentially a training regime connected to boxing, the law is silent on its general legality.

---

139 Griggs, L, 'Dangerous recreational activities – stay at home and be safe!' (2010) ISLR 9.

140 Also note the more general campaign by Graham Allen MP suggesting there is a correlation between the inappropriate behaviour by footballers on the pitch, including referee baiting and diving, and increases in anti-social behaviour in society at large: The Observer, 15 April 2006.

141 For a wide examination of boxing, see Sugden, J, Boxing and Society: An International Analysis (1996), Manchester: Manchester UP.

142 'Boxing – ban it?' Panorama, BBC Television, 25 October 1995; and 'Boxing on the ropes', BBC Sport, 18 December 2000, http://news.bbc.co.uk/sport1/hi/other_sports/1076244.stm.

143 Note also call for ban in Australia: see 'Another boxing ban call', BBC Sport, 28 April 2001, http://news.bbc.co.uk/sport1/hi/boxing/1301909.stm.

144 Though note the problem of defining violence and sports violence: see Gardiner, S, 'Tackling from behind: interventions on the playing field', in Greenfield, S and Osborn, G (eds), Law and Sport in Contemporary Society (2000), London: Frank Cass, pp 91–115.

145 [1994] 1 AC 212, p 265.

As Anderson states, 'the courts hold boxing to be legal, or in any event, that any change in that status is primarily a matter for the legislature'.[146] The legitimacy of boxing as currently organised has been increasingly questioned. Greater safety and regulation are seen as a necessary development by almost everyone, especially in the professional game. The following extracts will assist the evaluation of competing perspectives on the legitimacy of boxing:

Sutcliffe, S, 'The Noble Art?'

James Murray's death last year polarised opinion about the future of boxing. A disciplined forum for innate aggression or unreformable barbarism inviting brain damage and worse?

Dr Helen Grant is one of a handful of specialists who have looked inside the skull of a dead boxer. An expert on diseases of the nervous system, in 1986 she examined Steve Watt, who collapsed and went into a coma after being stopped in the tenth round of a Southern area title fight. 'He died, as Bradley Stone did last year, and Michael Watson and Gerald McClellan nearly died, of an acute bleed from a severed vein which led to rapid accumulation of blood squashing the brain stem down against the base of the skull. Although he was treated in hospital for a couple of days, it was clear that he had been brain dead in the ambulance.'

But the fatal injury was not all Grant saw when she examined Watt's brain. 'There were about 20 lesions in his brain from that fight and hundreds of scars from old lesions. Each one was about the size of a cherry. Such lesions heal after about six weeks. But the scars represent lost brain cells. In addition, the septum dividing the two ventricles (main cavities) was torn away; that was also old damage. Steve Watt was 29. He had been boxing for 10 years, I think. In my opinion, he was on the slippery slope to punch-drunk syndrome. The only logical place to hold a boxing match is in the operating theatre of a neurosurgical hospital,' she concludes. 'But major traumas are not the main point. It is the long-term diminution of the man's ability that is awful. If you take part in boxing for long, a great deal of your grey matter bites the dust, that is what it amounts to. I say that with every respect for boxers. I think they are the bravest people in the world.'

In 1982, prompted by concern over the hazards of *dementia pugilistica* and recurring ring fatalities, the British Medical Association (BMA), representing 80 per cent of doctors, called for the abolition of boxing, professional and amateur. Their argument was that any punch to the head causes the soft tissue of the brain to 'swirl' in what by some evolutionary aberration is the skull's 'inhospitable environment' of internal bumps and ragged edges: damage is therefore inevitable and cumulative even where not traumatic. Ever since, the BMA has been an energetic and persuasively credible focus for the campaign against the sport in the UK. So began the latest phase of the boxing debate, a sporadic war of words in which a new volley is fired after every tragedy – most recently when James Murray died on 17 October last year [1995]. But the entrenched battle lines never move. They cannot. As presented, it is a for or against issue. To box or not to box.

Both combatants summon up science to state their case. The BMA is keen on the Haslar report which 'finds evidence of brain impairment among amateur boxers in the armed forces'. Boxing counters with the Butler report which found 'no evidence of cumulative effect'. Then both sides will quote the Johns Hopkins University Stewart Study of 'central nervous system function in US amateur boxers', the biggest research project ever undertaken on the sport. It notes an association between a large number of bouts and diminished performance in selected cognitive domains', as the BMA points out. Yet it also says that 'none of the changes we have observed to date, however, are clinically significant' – delighting the International Amateur

---

146 Anderson, J, *The Legality of Boxing: A Punch Drunk Love?* (2007), Abingdon: Birkbeck Law Press provides a comprehensive legal and regulatory analysis of boxing; also see Gunn, M and Ormerod, D, 'The Legality of Boxing' (1995) 15 Legal Studies 181.

Boxing Association so much that they published the whole report in a booklet of encouraging medical evidence 'to offensively counteract the permanent and unfounded attacks on Olympic style boxing'.

To the layman watching this ultimately pathetic ping-pong of tentative conclusions and prudent reservations, it soon becomes plain that the scientific jury is still out. Then a further cogent thought occurs: while both sides are keen to establish a hard-fact justification for their enthusiasms, that is not the heart of the debate at all. Nobody significant on the pro-boxing side denies the risk of brain damage. They would dispute only matters of quantity and degree. What really counts for both sides is their own gut feelings about common sense, decency and civilised behaviour.

BMA spokeswoman Dr Fleur Fisher insists that the anti-boxing campaign is scientific, not moral or emotional, yet she moves on to say 'it is difficult for doctors to see trauma inflicted on that most exquisite computer, the brain, and not take action. It would be unethical for us not to speak up. It is bizarre that it is utterly ungentlemanly to hit a man in the balls and OK to hit him in the brain. I see Nigel Benn fighting, psyched up, I think 'Ooh' (cry of pain and frustration), you recognise the bravery, the determination but, in that McClellan fight, you see his head bouncing around, you are in agony watching it, thinking what the cost could be. After the Murray tragedy I watched the boxing world go through mourning in a state of denial, still trying to say it's a wonderful sport.'

Nicky Piper, chair of the Professional Boxers Association (PBA), the fighters' trade union, does say 'it is a wonderful sport. It is the oldest of all sports. It is man's instinct to want to fight and it is far better done in a civilised form with rules and controls. It comes down to knowing the risks, freedom of choice, making your own decision'. 'Boxing really does teach discipline,' adds Dr Adrian Whiteson, chief medical officer of the British Boxing Board of Control and chair of the World Boxing Council's medical commission. 'Diet, not smoking, very little drink, certainly no drugs, getting up early in the morning to do your roadwork, training, sparring. To do all this properly adds up to being true to yourself. Then it gives people from underprivileged areas – I know it sounds trite – a chance to better themselves.'

If British boxing is to survive through the twenty-first century, it will have to bind itself together better than ever and, paradoxically, the sport's foot soldiers – the boxers – are going to have to lead the way. In one important detail government help is needed. For the 'official' sport to prosper, professional and amateur, and secure the safety standards developed at such cost, unlicensed boxing with its unsupervised and dangerous conditions must be made illegal.[147]

Boxing can be subject to Elias's 'civilising process' as discussed in Chapter 1. Perhaps the increased safety provisions in recent years are an extension of a continuing regulatory approach to boxing that has been going on since the mid-nineteenth century when prize fighting (pugilism), where the winner took all, was a popular 'sport'. The facets of such a regulatory approach are outlined below:

Sheard, K, 'Aspects of boxing in the western "civilising process" '

There is little doubt that the pugilists of the eighteenth and nineteenth centuries would have difficulty recognising the boxing of today as being the same activity as the prize-fighting of their own time. In the intervening period the rules governing the sport have become increasingly complex, the bureaucratic organisations controlling it have become more powerful, and the law of the land has become more intrusive, more protective, than ever before. The violence of

---

147 Sutcliffe, P, 'The Noble Art?', *Total Sport*, February 1996, pp 92–94.

boxing has been controlled and contained. Prize-fighting, like fox hunting, can be said to have gone through a 'sportisation' process as it metamorphosed into boxing.

Using the framework developed by Dunning . . . the modern sport of boxing can be said to have become more 'civilised' by a number of interrelated processes which include the following:

(1) Boxing in the early period of its development – ie from approximately the mid-seventeenth to the early decades of the nineteenth century – was by present standards an extremely violent, brutal and bloody activity. However, this aspect of the sport has since become increasingly regulated by a complex set of formal written rules. These rules not only define and control the sorts of violence which are permitted, but also outlaw violence in certain forms. The type of violent blow permitted and the areas of the body allowed to be attacked have been carefully delineated. Thus in the early stages of the sport's development it was possible to use a variety of what we would now call 'wrestling' holds to subdue an opponent. For example, the 'cross-buttock' throw, in which the opponent could be thrown over one's hip to the ground, was allowed. This could then be followed by a leap upon the fallen adversary, smashing one's knees into his exposed ribcage. Eyes could be gouged, hair pulled, and the testicles attacked. The natures of the punch, and the shape of the fist, have also been more carefully defined. The 'target' must be hit with the knuckle part of the hand. Hitting with an open glove – 'slapping' – is not allowed, possibly because it once permitted one's opponent to be injured by the lacing of the glove. 'Straight finger' blows to the eyes are also banned.

(2) The rules also allow for penalties to be imposed upon boxers who infringe these rules. For example, points may be lost by boxers who hit 'below the belt', use the head illegally, or who receive constant warnings for holding and hitting. As early as 1838, under the London Prize Ring Rules, if a fighter went down deliberately without being hit or thrown – thus allowing him to rest for a while or corruptly 'throw' the fight – he could be disqualified and thus prevented from gaining any pecuniary or other advantage from the ploy. Under modern conditions champions who refuse to defend their titles within a specified time period, or who turn up to defend their titles overweight, may have the titles taken from them.

(3) Weight divisions have been introduced in an attempt to equalise conditions for all boxers. In the early days of the prize-ring, there were no weight divisions and men fought each other irrespective of poundage. It was not until the 1880s, after the widespread adoption of the Queensberry Rules of 1865, that a real effort was made to standardise weight divisions both in Britain and the United States. This innovation, of course, allowed boxing skill to have a greater impact upon the outcome of a contest than extra poundage or extra reach.

(4) Boxing has also been civilised by having restrictions placed upon the length of contests and the length of 'rounds'. These restrictions differ according to the experience of the boxers and the nature of the contest, for example whether or not a fight is for a title or whether it is an amateur or a professional fight. Most professional championship contests in Britain now follow the lead given by the European Boxing Union and are fought over 12 rounds. In America until relatively recently the stipulated 'distance' was 15 rounds. And before this – in both the US and Britain – the usual distance was twenty rounds of three minutes each. By contrast, prior to the 1860s, a round ended with a fall, and fights would be fought to a finish or until one of the fighters could not continue for any reason. In Britain, the largest number of rounds to be fought under this system was the 276 fought between Jack Jones and Patsy Tunney, in Cheshire in 1825.

(5) Physical protection has been introduced to protect boxers from the permitted and accidental violence they can inflict upon each other. For example, padded gloves, gum shields, head guards and groin protectors have all been introduced over the years. Gloves are

claimed to have been first introduced in 1747, by Jack Broughton, an ex-prize-fighter, early 'entrepreneur' and boxing tutor, and supposed originator of the first code of written rules governing the 'sport' of boxing.[148]

The British Medical Association has been a particularly vociferous campaigner for the abolition of boxing. Their arguments are primarily on medical grounds, not only as far as the risk of traumatic tragedy is concerned, but also in terms of the cumulative damage that almost inevitably occurs during a prolonged boxing career.[149] The danger that banning boxing will drive it underground is also a fear that is often raised: the spectre of an increase in prize fighting could be the consequence.[150] However, unlicensed boxing or prize fighting still occurs.[151] In addition, there is also a hybrid of unregulated boxing and martial arts, variously called 'Extreme, Ultimate or Total Fighting', that first emerged in a number of US states, and has been commercially promoted in the UK. It is a form of fighting where two bare-knuckled combatants are pitted against each other in a ring until only one is left standing. There are no rounds, no time-outs and no holds barred – just a lot of punching, kicking, choking, nose pinching, ear yanking and groin kneeing. Only eye gouging and biting are forbidden.[152]

Sheard, K, 'Aspects of boxing in the western "civilising process" '

Donnelly's belief that, if banned, boxing as we now know it would be driven underground is valid. Indeed, such a ban would probably have all sorts of unintended and unanticipated consequences. Boxers fighting under such circumstances might be at greater risk than they are at present. Donnelly's claim that 'the sport may, under present social conditions, be defensible' might also be concurred with. However, it is doubtful whether the 'dominant class' or 'culture' is deterred from legislative action by a fear that death or serious injury might befall a few working-class young men. The debate, as Donnelly implicitly recognises, is primarily about the morality of boxing and the 'bad example' which it sets, and not the pain and suffering it causes. If boxing were to be made illegal and pushed behind the scenes as prize-fighting was in the nineteenth century – and even if it continued to exist in a subterranean way – this would indeed be a reflection of greater 'civilisation' as the term is used here.[153]

The debates concerning the legitimacy of boxing will no doubt continue, especially in the aftermath of periodic tragedies in the ring. Will there be a tragedy too far at some time in the future? Now women are able to apply for licences and box, would the death or serious injury of a female boxer lead to a ban?[154] A paternalistic approach based on the protection of fighters is often advanced. Although it is argued that the incidents of catastrophic and traumatic injuries such as blood clots are less common, and medical treatment has meant that the consequences are less severe, there is growing evidence of the cumulative nature of repetitive injuries to the head that can lead to

---

148 Sheard, K, 'Aspects of boxing in the western "civilising process" ' (1997) 32(1) IRSS 35, 36.

149 For the BMA's current position see www.bma.org.uk/health_promotion_ethics/sports_exercise/boxing.jsp, and links to the Report from 2001, and the *Boxing Debate* (1993), London: BMA. Also see Constantoyannis, C and Partheni, M, 'Fatal Head Injury from Boxing: a Case Report from Greece' (2004) 38 British Journal of Sports Med 78–79.

150 See Parpworth, N, 'Boxing and prize fighting: the indistinguishable distinguished?' (1994) 2(1) SATLJ, 5; Jones, R, 'Deviant sports career: towards a sociology of unlicensed boxing' (1997) 21(1) Journal of Sport and Social Issues, 37–52; op. cit., fn 148, Sheard (1997); 'Raw scrap from boxing's underbelly', *The Guardian*, 23 May 1997, p 6; 'How bare-knuckled savagery became a noble art', *The Times*, 30 June 1997.

151 Darling, A, 'You cannot beat a good right hander', *Total Sport*, August 1997.

152 Mitchell, K, 'Mortal combat', *Observer Sport Monthly*, April 2001; Hall, S, 'Opposition grows to new sport of total fighting', *The Guardian*, 28 February 2000.

153 Op. cit., fn 148, Sheard (1997), p 54. Also see Donnelly, P, 'On boxing: notes on the past, present and future of a sport in transition' (1989) 7(4) *Current Psychology: Research and Reviews* 331.

154 Felix, A, 'The "Fleetwood Assassin" strikes a blow for female boxing' (1998) 1(3) SLB 1.

degenerative brain conditions and possibly Parkinson's Disease.[155] Medical assistance at ringside and improved medical techniques have assisted in dealing with traumatic injuries, but the litigation that has arisen from the Michael Watson tragedy against the British Boxing Board of Control has put the responsibility on governing bodies to provide the most up-to-date medical support. In terms of risk management, this has sent a clear warning to governing bodies in other sports.[156]

'Safety measures in boxing'

In 2001, the BBBC introduced new safety measures:

For championship fights:

(1)   Initial and secondary weight checks

For boxers:

(2)   Training diaries
(3)   Random weight checks
(4)   Late arrival for official weigh-in will constitute a breach of the regulations
(5)   Compulsory courses for trainers and seconds with particular respect to weight reduction, diet and nutrition
(6)   The investigation of an amendment to permit the taking of isotonic drinks between rounds to combat dehydration.[157]

Dangerous sports

There are some involved in boxing who argue that when compared with sports such as mountaineering and rock-climbing, the risks of boxing are minimal.[158] Boxing can usefully be compared with the equestrian sport of three-day eventing, another sport that has suffered a number of fatalities to riders (in addition to their horses) in recent years.

Latta, V, 'Report on the Eventing International Safety Committee Recommendations'

Following five fatalities in eventing in as many months in Britain last year [in the first half of 2000, there were a further five deaths – one in each of Britain, Switzerland and the USA, and two in Australia], the International Safety Committee was formed jointly by the Fédération Equestre Internationale (FEI) and the British Horse Trials Association (BHTA), the body responsible for administration of eventing in Britain. Its task was to review the findings from the fatalities, consider any areas of commonality and put forward recommendations to the FEI (as the world governing body) for making the sport safer. Although a large number of events come under national, rather than international control, the Committee expressed the hope that national federations adopt the recommendations as 'a positive step in the development of the

---

155 Claims have been made that Muhammad Ali's illness is linked to punishing fights he was involved in towards the end of his career. In Britain, there have been attempts to prove links between heading footballs, especially in the 1950s and 1960s when old-style leather balls were used that would soak up water and become extremely heavy, and medical conditions such as pre-senile dementia. If such a link can be proven, an individual could be eligible for Industrial Disability Benefit; see 'Industrial disability (Billy McPhail)' (1998) 1(4) and (1999) 2(3) SLB, 3 and 'Heading the ball killed striker', *The Guardian*, 12 November 2002, where South Staffordshire coroner Andrew Haigh recorded a verdict of 'death by industrial disease' on the former West Bromwich Albion striker Jeff Astle.

156 For a further analysis of this case see p 508.

157 See 'Safety measures in boxing' (2001) 4(2) SLB 7.

158 Statistics discussed in a Parliamentary debate on a Private Members' Bill in 1991 stated that between 1969 and 1980 in Britain, compared with two deaths in professional boxing, there were 93 in mountaineering and rock climbing, *Hansard*, 4 December 1991, col 293.

sport'. The establishment by the FEI of a system for overall monitoring was considered necessary and could be established under the rules of membership.

The main objective of the Committee was to try and minimise the risk of horses falling and
thereby to reduce the chances of riders being seriously injured. The majority of fatalities have
been as a result of horses falling on the riders; some fatalities, however, have occurred as a
result of horses crushing the riders against an obstacle. One of the recommendations was that
a statistical database be established and maintained by the FEI for collation of information
about accidents and to monitor safety provisions. In this way earlier recognition of common
features in accidents could be detected. Mandatory rider passports were suggested. This would
include details of three-day event results (qualifying events for progression through the international levels), medical information regarding falls and any disciplinary measures. Such a
system would alert organisers and officials to riders who had been recently injured, those disciplined for actions likely to give rise to problems and it would enable qualifications to be verified.

The Committee considered courses to have become too technical and the suggestion was
for a limitation on the 'intensity of effort'. The recommendation was made to reduce the
distance of the roads and tracks phase and add another compulsory break at three-day events,
also to reduce speeds where conditions warrant and at one-day events. These proposals are
designed to ensure horses are fresher for the cross-country phase, thus reducing the likelihood of falls from tiredness. While falls can result with tired horses, they can result where
horses are too fresh – particularly as they are generally ridden faster!

Fence construction was noted as important in helping minimise the risk of horses falling.
While there has been discussion regarding 'deformable' fences, it was considered much more
research is needed before such fences are introduced. This would include studies on their
impact on the rules. Olympic and World Champion Blyth Tait broke his leg last year in a fall
where his horse crushed him against a fence. Had the rail collapsed with the impact, Blyth
believes his horse would have fallen on him.

Looking at the recommendations, many are sensible suggestions for constant monitoring
and keeping abreast of changes in the sport and to ensure the sport is kept as safe as possible.
It has to be remembered though that riding half a ton of animal with a mind of its own, involves
risk. When you introduce undulating terrain, speed and obstacles into the equation, the risks
increase . . . Increased effort has been put into making courses safer and more inviting since
the three horse fatalities at Badminton in 1992. Maybe those changes have resulted in a reduced
consciousness of the risks. What has to be kept in mind is that a healthy respect for the fences
is necessary to keep riders alert to the risks involved.

Different combinations of factors have been involved in each of the recent deaths in
England. There is no common denominator of fence type, level of competition, conditions, and
speed or experience of either horse or rider. In each case mistakes have been made by either
horse or rider or in the communication between the two. Such incidents always bring greater
awareness of the risks, particularly when involving someone you know. Unfortunately the
nature of the sport makes those risks unavoidable.

In the final analysis, it is a risk sport. While all parties must work towards ensuring the sport
is as safe as possible, riders must take ultimate responsibility for their actions. Changes will from
time to time be necessary but hopefully they will not alter the character of the sport completely.[159]

There have been no concerted calls for the banning of three-day eventing. A risk management
approach has been adopted to attempt to minimise the risk and learn more about the causes.[160] The

---

159 Latta, V, 'Report on the Eventing International Safety Committee Recommendations' (2000) 3(4) SLB 4.
160 See Singer, E, Saxby, F and French, N, 'A Retrospective Case Control Study of Horse Falls in the Sport of Horse Trials and Three
Day Eventing' (2003), 35(2) *Equine Veterinary Journal* 139–45.

number of fatalities has dropped.[161] In some sports such as marathon running, environmental factors such as extreme heat, as discussed above, can be an issue that needs to be managed through policies concerning issues such as proper re-hydration.[162]

There is now a plethora of 'adventure' and 'extreme' sports with continued inherent risks.[163] For example, new legislation came into force in 1996, namely the Activity Centres (Young Persons' Safety) Act 1995, which requires those individuals or companies that run adventure holiday centres to be licensed. This was in the wake of the 'Lyme Bay Tragedy', when four schoolchildren were drowned while taking part in sea canoeing in the English Channel as part of a supervised activity day.[164]

Child Protection: Sports Coaches and Child Athletes

The final section of this chapter will focus on regulatory issues around providing a safe participatory experience for children in sport. The issue of the treatment of children in sport mirrors increasing awareness of the rights of children generally in society.[165] Although the focus is on participation in sport, there is evidence of considerable exploitation of children within the wider sports industry.[166] Sport provides many positive opportunities for young people to participate individually or more commonly in groups. This is generally at a recreational 'play' level; however, increasingly young people are taking part in highly competitive and sometimes elite-level sport. The image of parents shouting at their children and haranguing the officials has become common in school and Sunday morning football: even at this level winning is all.[167] In sports such as tennis, swimming and gymnastics the age of participants at elite level has become ever younger.

Awareness of the existence and extent of sexual and physical abuse of children has appeared fairly recently in sport as it has generally in society,[168] with the realisation that more effective protection from exploitation of children in sport is required.[169] This exploitation ranges from clear acts of sexual and physical abuse at one extreme to oppressive encouragement at the other. Clear acts of abuse are almost inevitably going to be contrary to the criminal law. Oppressive encouragement is much more problematic to regulate. However, detection of all forms of exploitation in sport is difficult.

The main area of concern has been with the relationship between coaches and child athletes. In Britain over the last few years, there have been a number of criminal trials of sports coaches. The most notable has been the conviction of the swimming coach Paul Hickson, who was the British team coach at the 1988 Olympics in Seoul. He was sentenced to 17 years after he was found guilty of two rapes, 11 indecent assaults and two other serious sexual offences. He was cleared of two other indecent assaults. Hickson had denied all charges, saying he was the victim of teenage girls'

---

161 But note 'Silent tribute for UK rider', BBC Sport, 5 September 2004, http://news.bbc.co.uk/sport1/hi/other_sports/3628324. stm.
162 'Race defends safety preparations', BBC Sport, 19 September 2005, http://news.bbc.co.uk/sport1/hi/athletics/4260858.stm.
163 See Gardiner, S et al, Sports Law, 1st edn (1998), London: Cavendish Publishing, pp 131–35, and the regulation of certain types of adventure holidays by the Activity Centres (Young Person's Safety) Act 1995, as a response to the Lyme Bay canoe tragedy. Also see Grant, D, 'Is the activity tourism industry paying enough for safety?' (1999) 2(1) SLB 11; and Hartley, H, Sports, Physical Recreation and the Law (2009), London: Routledge, pp 200–08.
164 A subsequent prosecution in corporate manslaughter against the company running the adventure centre was the first successful conviction under English law, see R v Kite, R v Stoddart, R v OLL Ltd, Unreported, 9 December 1994, Winchester Crown Court.
165 See the Children Act 1989.
166 A Sporting Chance (1997), Christian Aid, p 217, concerning exploitation of children in India, some as young as 10, stitching footballs for about 10 pence a ball. Pieri, M, 'Labour standards in the manufacture of sporting goods: a tarnished trophy?' (1999) 2(2) SLB, 10; see One World Trust report at http://www.oneworldtrust.org/publications/cat_view/64-publications-by-project/65-global-accountability-report.
167 See 'Soccer brawl father is told to pay £750' The Daily Telegraph, 15 February 1997.
168 See Report of the Inquiry into Child Abuse in Cleveland 1987, Cm 412 (1988), London: HMSO.
169 Research at Huddersfield University suggests that 52% of children know heir abuser through community based organisations such as swimming clubs; see 'Child abuse in sport' (2001) 4(2) SLB 7.

fantasies. One of his victims, who was 13 when he first molested her, was reported as saying 'he was evil, a monster':

'Olympic coach jailed for rapes', *The Times*, 28 September 1995

The woman, an undergraduate, was angry that the Amateur Swimming Association seems to have failed to investigate complaints by three senior swimmers in 1986 about Hickson's behaviour towards women. The Association said yesterday that there had been no allegations of criminality, but it would re-examine the way it protects athletes. The woman said: 'Investigations should have been made because some people were aware that something was not quite right.' The woman cannot bring herself to utter the name of Hickson, who fondled her and forced her to perform oral sex. 'I was so young', she said, 'and I just felt that what he was doing was something I had to endure, something that was necessary. I trusted in everything that he told me.'[170]

The case of Hickson came to light almost accidentally when an off-duty policeman at a party overheard some teenage girls recounting allegations against Hickson. He had been reprimanded in 1987 by his employer, the University of Wales at Swansea, for telling a woman to strip for a 'naked fitness' test, and then undressing himself. He subsequently moved to the public school Millfield as swimming coach.

One real problem is that often allegations are greeted with disbelief from those associated with the individuals in question. Victims often believe that they are the only ones involved and only find out later that other fellow athletes were subject to similar treatment. The sports coach–child athlete relationship is one where the coach has immense power and influence over the child and it is difficult for the child to raise the alarm. Celia Brackenridge has produced a significant body of work concerning the causes of abuse in sport, particularly against women, and she shows how abusive coaches take care and time to 'groom' their athletes so that they will submit to their advances.[171] Child sport, as with other activities involving working with children, attracts those with a propensity to paedophilia. What has arisen is a rightful awareness of the reality of this problem, but also confusion and uncertainty; issues such as how to deal with false allegations, as with the suicide of Cliff Temple, the athletics correspondent of *The Sunday Times*, after false allegations of sexual harassment,[172] and the problem of how to develop good practice for sports coaches when working with child athletes so that both parties are not inhibited from working effectively together. Hickson's case has subsequently led to many more prosecutions and heightened awareness.[173] There continues to be a clash of cultures that construct particular incidents in different ways. The then Chelsea FC coach Graham Rix's consensual underage sex with a 15-year-old girl is an example.[174] Should Rix and Hickson's acts be similarly defined? What is clear is that more effective mechanisms need to be put in place in sport to protect children from exploitation and abuse.

---

170 'Olympic coach jailed for rapes', *The Times*, 28 September 1995, p 1. See also 'Swimmer blew whistle on Hickson nine years ago', *The Times*, 28 September 1995, p 5; 'The great betrayal' *The Sunday Times*, 1 October 1995, p 14.
171 See Brackenridge, C, 'He owned me basically . . .: women's experience of sexual abuse in sport' (1997) 32(2) IRSS; 'Sexual harassment and sexual abuse in sport', in Clarke, G and Humberstone, B (eds), *Researching Women and Sport* (1997), London: Macmillan; 'In my opinion' (1999) 2(2) SLB 2; *Spoilsports: Understanding and Preventing Sexual Exploitation in Sport* (2001), London: Routledge; *Child Welfare in Football* (with Pitchford, A, Russell, K and Nutt, G) (2006), London: Routledge.
172 See Downes, S and Mackay, D, *Running Scared* (1996), Edinburgh: Mainstream.
173 See the cases of Cecil Mallon, a gym coach jailed for indecent assault; and David Low, an athletics coach given 18 months' probation for sending obscene questionnaires to young girls. Also see TV programmes, 'Bad sports', *On the Line*, BBC2, 26 January 1994 (on sexual misconduct in US sport); *On the Line*, BBC2, 25 August 1993 (on sexual harassment and sexual abuse in UK sport); and *Diverse Reports*, Channel 4, 23 January 1997 (on sexual abuse in English football).
174 See Nelson, M, *The Stronger Women Get, the More Men Love Football: Sexism and the Culture of Sport* (1996), New York: The Women's Press.

Defining abuse

Clear proven allegations of sexual and physical abuse can be subject to the general criminal and civil law. What is more problematic is how oppression, short of abuse of child athletes, should be defined and regulated.[175] Of course, as has already been noted, brutality is sanctioned in sports, whose nineteenth-century origins lie in 'militarism and muscular Christianity, the Chariots Of Fire ethos: a Bible under one arm and a ball under the other . . . Sport promotes and protects bad behaviour, because it is not politically responsible. The coaches' word is law, they dominate players' every waking moment – it is not about empowerment or democracy. It is like a cult.'[176]

A number of graphic accounts have been made of the treatment of children, to which girls especially are subject. In gymnastics, there has been growing concern about the pressures on girls to conform to a certain body size and weight seen as most likely to lead to success. There is evidence that puberty is artificially delayed and its effects minimised.[177]

Joan Ryan's Little Girls in Pretty Boxes provides a moving account of elite female gymnasts and ice skaters who, every four years, captivate millions by their seemingly effortless skill and grace at the Olympic Games. However, she provides a very different image of the frail, tiny figures performing feats of co-ordination and power and exposes the suffering and sacrifice they have endured, and the hundreds who did not make it, broken in their early teens by the demands of their sport. Unerringly, Ryan, one of America's leading sports journalists, presents a catalogue of what she describes as 'legal, even celebrated child abuse', in which girls starve themselves (her research shows that 60 per cent of college gymnasts in the US suffer from eating disorders) and risk osteoporosis, curvature of the spine, and untold psychological damage, at the behest of brutal, self-promoting coaches, and parents driven by misguided sentiment. With respect to coaches' impropriety, Ryan focuses on the Romanian Bela Karolyi, who spotted Nadia Comaneci as a six-year-old and groomed her to Olympic stardom. His coaching approach:

Ryan, J, *Little Girls in Pretty Boxes*

. . . was based on militaristic control. His gymnasts lived in dormitories at the gym in Romania, trained seven to eight hours a day, fit in a few hours of school and ate only what Karolyi fed them. There was no talk or fooling around inside the gym. The only proper response to Karolyi's instructions was a nod. He trained them like boxers, like little men, introducing rigorous conditioning and strengthening exercises to their workouts, transforming their bodies into muscled machinery. Karolyi insisted on small young girls for his team, not only for their pliability and resilience but for the little doll look he believed enchanted the spectators and swayed the judges.[178]

After his defection to the United States, Ryan produces evidence of continued physical and emotional exploitation by Karolyi:

He rushed the gymnasts back in the gym sooner than doctors recommended, rationalising that the doctors were simply concerned with (legal) liability . . . Kristie Phillips, for instance, trained for three years with a fractured wrist because Karolyi did not feel it was serious enough to warrant full rest. Nearly ten years later the wrist barely bends . . . Similarly before the 1991 World Championships a Karolyi doctor diagnosed Kim Zmeskal's wrist injury pain as a sprain, leading Karolyi to suggest on national television that the injury was more in Zmeskal's head

175 'Chelsea to stand by jailed Rix', The Guardian, 27 March 1999.
176 Brackenridge, C, quoted in Campbell, B, 'Why the coast is clear', The Guardian, 7 November 1996, p 4.
177 See 'Hungry For Success', Fair Game, Channel 4, 10 June 1996.
178 Ryan, J, Little Girls in Pretty Boxes (1995), New York: Warner, pp 198–99.

than in her wrist. It turned out that Zmeskal's problem was a fracture of the distal radius, or growth plate – a common injury amongst elite gymnasts but one with which Karolyi's doctor was apparently unfamiliar.[179]

Injuries had no place in Karolyi's carefully designed formula for producing a star every four years. He built his program around the girl with the most talent. 'Your top athlete is a very strange creature', Karolyi explains. 'Of course, I never studied psychology, but through these years these little guys have taught me. We paid our dues on our mistakes, praising our little guys and cheering and clapping and showing our enthusiasm and baying them. And those are the ones who turn around and show disappreciation, ignorance and even arrogance. They take advantage of your sincere urge to show your appreciation. Give them everything in the world and ensure you're getting a big, big, big, big slap. She is the first to turn her back.'

So Karolyi constructed a training environment that kept his star athlete questioning her worth. In selecting five other gymnasts to train with her, he carefully chose each to play a specific role. Perhaps the most tortuous position was that of the secondary star: like the under-study in a play, the girl was just talented enough to present a threat to the star's status. Nadia had Teodora Ungureanu, Dianne Durham had Mary Lou Retton, Kristie Phillips had Phoebe Mills, and Kim Zmeskal had Betty Okino. The four remaining gymnasts were the 'crowd', as Karolyi called them, chosen as much for their personality traits as their talents. One girl from the 'crowd' was always chosen as his pet. She might be the least talented, but she possessed the qualities he wanted to reinforce in his star: hard work, discipline and stoicism. Karolyi would praise her lavishly and hold her up as an example, angering the more talented gymnasts who resented his favouritism. Anger, Karolyi knew, was a powerful motivator.[180]

Development of an effective child protection policy

In the United States, many strategies to expose and eradicate exploitation of child athletes have been developed including criminal and civil law remedies, organisational awareness and pro-active development of plans, specific codes of conduct, screening potential coaches, etc.[181] In Britain, the issue of developing greater awareness and recognition of child abuse and promotion of good practices for working with children has also become a priority. In response to the Hickson case, the Amateur Swimming Association has been at the forefront of confronting child abuse in sport.

Gray, A, 'Swimming and child protection: the story so far'

Ensuring the safety of young persons to enjoy sport must surely be the highest priority of any sports governing body. The sport of swimming has over the last eighteen months been endeavouring to understand the problems of child abuse in all its various forms and to implement strategies to deal with the problems. It must be appreciated that child abuse is a problem in our society and sport is not immune. Recent highly publicised cases involving 'caring' services have illustrated that there exist many opportunities within society for those who would prey on our young children to gain the necessary intimate access to children. Amateur sport inevitably relies upon the efforts of thousands of volunteers who give so much in support of the development of children in sport. Herein lies the opportunity for that small minority of people who would harm our children to gain the necessary opportunities to abuse these children.

---

179 Ibid, p 209.
180 Ibid, p 211.
181 Fried, GB, 'Unsportsmanlike contact: strategies for reducing sexual assaults in youth sports' (1996) 6(3) Journal of Legal Aspects of Sport 155.

The starting point for the sport of swimming was the trial of Paul Hickson, Olympic Swimming Coach. Convicted September 1995 on two counts of rape and eleven indecent assaults. Sentenced to seventeen years' imprisonment. This happened in the first few months of David Sparkes' period of office as Chief Executive of the Amateur Swimming Association. Whilst the sport had been considering child protection issues prior to the Hickson trial what the case brought clearly into focus was the following:

- Recognition of the fact that the sport of swimming was a sport of some 300,000 members of whom approximately 90 per cent were under 16 years of age.
- The sport's governing body needed to act swiftly and decisively to restore the confidence of the membership, its parents and the public at large.
- To deal with these various problems of child abuse there was the need for the Association to develop short and medium term strategies.

Steps which were taken by the sport in the light of Hickson

1. The sport entered into a wide consultation process including the Home Office, Sports Council and other agencies with expertise in the area of child protection. As a result of this process there were produced clear procedures for recognising and acting upon suspicions of child abuse. It is considered that there are two problem areas, which are not entirely distinct:

    - Physical and sexual abuse of children.
    - Emotional abuse (eg threatening and taunting of children) which may manifest itself in teaching and coaching and which are clearly unacceptable practices.

    The Association sought to produce guidelines which were embodied in the publication 'Child Protection Procedures in Swimming'. The principles enshrined in the procedures are:

    - The child's welfare is paramount.
    - All children whatever their age, culture, disability, gender, language, racial origin, religious belief and/or sexual identity have the right to protection from abuse.
    - All suspicions and allegations of abuse will be taken seriously; and responded to swiftly and appropriately.

    The procedures offer guidance in the recognition of child abuse and how to respond if abuse is suspected or alleged. The NSPCC in particular provided great assistance to the Association in the formulation of this document, which was published in June 1996 and circulated to all affiliated clubs and organisations. It was recognised that clear and concise procedures for dealing with child abuse cases were necessary due to the perception that clubs had a tendency to react in panic to allegations, e.g. ignoring the problem hoping it would go away/suspending the children.

    The Guidelines also recognise and establish procedures for dealing with complaints of 'poor practice' in coaching or teaching.

2. Emergency powers were given to the Chief Executive by the sports governing body, the ASA Committee, to allow:

    - Temporary suspension of suspected child abusers who were the subject of a police investigation.
    - The withdrawal of teaching and coaching certificates of convicted offenders – thereby effectively excluding them from the sport.

    The above represents the 'rapid response' phase of the Association's developing child protection procedures. But ASA knew that it needed to do more to follow through this process.

The medium term

1. The Association set about establishing a child protection database upon which would be included details of all individuals with access to young swimmers. It was considered a necessary starting point to find out who is involved in our sport at this level. A standard form questionnaire was produced which asked questions of previous criminal records and whether the individual was known to Social Services. It also sought consent of the individual for the undertaking of police checks anticipating the amendments now contained in the Police Act. Whilst in some quarters initially there were reservations with regard to the efficacy of a self-certification process the message from the experts was that paedophiles do not like lists and monitoring and their natural response to such vigilance and scrutiny will be to move on.

2. Working in conjunction with bodies representing teachers and coaches the Association produced a Code of Ethics (unacceptable coaching practices). The purpose of the Code was principally to endeavour to instil good coaching practice amongst coaches/teachers by highlighting the unacceptable practices. Many of the practices may fall within the definition of emotional abuse as explained in the Child Protection Procedures. However, it was considered of vital importance that coaches/teachers would 'buy into' this new development and accordingly there was wide consultation with bodies representing the interests of coaches and teachers.

3. To reinforce the Code from an educational perspective. It has been included as a syllabus item on all higher level teaching and coaching certificates.

4. The Association has substantially reviewed its domestic disciplinary Tribunals with effect from 1 April 1997 in the following respects:

    -   Chairmen of Tribunals now have greater flexibility in the procedures they adopt for particular Tribunals to allow informal mediation in particular cases and for a Tribunal hearing to be held in a manner sensitive to cater for the needs of young children witnesses.
    -   Chairmen may co-opt onto Tribunal panels specialists with expertise in the area of child protection (e.g. senior police officers in child protection units and employees of other agencies).

    As with many sports the Association has detailed disciplinary rules with procedures for persons within the jurisdiction of the sport to be subject to disrepute charges in the event that, for instance, they bring the sport into disrepute. It has to be recognised that not all allegations of child abuse will result in a police charge and conviction but whether or not the police proceed (and they may not due to evidential or other difficulties) there is still the possibility of the child's family wishing to take action under the laws of the sport. Indeed due to the difficulties that may prevent a criminal prosecution proceeding it still may be appropriate for action to be taken within the sport – the Chief Executive is charged with the responsibility of considering the bringing of proceedings for alleged breaches of the Code of Ethics.

5. Having established clear procedures there is a need to ensure that there has been a general raising of awareness and acceptance on the ground. For that reason working very closely with the NSPCC the Association produced a series of road shows which very much presented the procedures to the clubs at a local level through a series of seminars and question and answer sessions.

    The purpose of this was to:

    -   Explain the procedures and their practical effect.
    -   Identify persons within clubs at a local level who have the necessary skills to offer guidance and advice.
    -   To ascertain further training needs, particularly of these individuals.

6. The Association has been in contact with Mr Tony Butler. the Chief Constable of Gloucestershire and a leading representative of the ACPO (Association of Chief Police Officers) Child Protection Group. Mr Butler has agreed to circulate the Guidelines produced to the 43 individual police forces. The purpose of this is to raise awareness of the steps that the sport of swimming is trying to make and at the same time we are looking for feedback on our procedures in order to see if there are ways in which things can be done better.

Recent initiatives

1. We have established a standing Child Protection Working Group to monitor the practical operation of our procedures and to formulate and develop new strategies. The group includes representatives from all ASA affiliated district associations and the NSPCC.

   We have established a 'hot line' known as Swimline (telephone number 0808 100 4001) manned by members of the Working group who are skilled counsellors and who will provide telephone assistance in the following areas:

   - To children and parents of children who have suffered child abuse (the intention is to complement Childline and other agencies by giving sport specific advice e.g. advice in relation to coaching practices and where this strays into the area of emotional abuse).
   - To coaches and teachers (individuals who are concerned as to how they should be acting).

   Anyone telephoning Swimline has the option of being automatically transferred to the NSPCC Childline for emergency assistance.

Conclusion: longer term strategies

1. The response of participants in the sport generally to the significant developments, which have taken place over the last three years, has been overwhelmingly supportive.
2. The Association believes that the amendments to legislation contained in the Police Act with regard to criminal record checks together with the proposed new ban on convicted offenders working with children are very positive moves which will help sport in its efforts to combat this problem of child abuse.

   As is stated in the Foreword to our Procedures document. undoubtedly some individuals will actively seek employment or voluntary work with children in order to abuse their position. Any steps that make this attempt more difficult have the support of the ASA. Our paramount aim is the welfare of our younger members.
3. But there is a need for coordination strategies within sport (indeed society) as a whole. One fear of the Association is that it will be successful but only at the expense of driving paedophiles from the sport of swimming into other sports which have similar disciplines or to which there is similar methodology in coaching and teaching.
4. To avoid this scenario that ASA believes that a co-ordinated approach is needed across all sports and that this should be regarded as a priority issue by the Home Office, CCPR, UK and Home Countries Sports Councils. However, recognising that there will necessarily need to be further consideration of the funding ramifications of this as an interim measure there needs to be greater information sharing between governing bodies which in turn depends upon their taking appropriate steps to ensure that they have in place the necessary Data Protection Act licenses to enable them to be free to disseminate information to other governing bodies regarding suspected offenders. The Association has in place a licence enabling it to accept as a 'source' and to make 'disclosures' to other sporting

bodies having as one of their areas of concern the protection of the welfare of young children in their sport. The Association is always willing to sit down with other sporting bodies to share experiences in this area.[182]

Conclusion

Other sports have been praised for developing coherent child protection policies. Bodies such as the Child Protection in Sport Unit (partly run by the National Society for the Prevention of Cruelty to Children – NSPCC) and Sports Coach UK (formerly the National Coaching Foundation) have produced considerable literature in this area.[183]

> **Brackenridge, C,** *Spoilsports: Understanding and Preventing Sexual Exploitation in Sport*
>
> Codes of Practice constitute an important part of an overall policy infrastructure that can guarantee safe and enjoyable sporting experiences. They set out expectations and help to delimit the boundaries between ethical and unethical practices . . . However, they are also limited in that they provide only one view of ethical practice – a contractual one – that might militate against the notion of individual virtue and responsibility in sport . . . a code of practice should be seen as only *one*, limited step towards the prevention or eradication of sexual exploitation . . . sports managers therefore need to acknowledge the limitations of codes: without a comprehensive implementation strategy, they are often meaningless in practice.[184]

More effective vetting and screening of applicants to coaching positions needs to be implemented. The Criminal Records Bureau is empowered under the Police Act 1997 to allow 'organisations in the public, private and voluntary sectors to make safer recruitment decisions by identifying candidates who may be unsuitable for certain work, especially that involve children or vulnerable adults'.[185] This is a requirement for both employees and volunteers working for children in sport.[186] However, it is estimated that only a small percentage of those with a propensity to abuse children have a criminal record. Brackenridge believes that:

> What is certain is that the clamour for some form of official checking will continue in voluntary sport because of the widespread, mistaken belief that criminal checks will somehow, in themselves, purify sport of the dangers of sexual exploitation.[187]

Some people have called for a register of convicted paedophiles who have been, or who have attempted to be, involved in sport to be initiated, similar to the Sex Offenders Register.[188] Conversely, plans to require volunteers to be vetted, who give lifts to children to and from sports events on a regular basis, were criticised and dropped.[189]

There clearly is a problem of balance here. Young athletes need support and encouragement in their endeavours. In sport, all the emotions from elation to despair can be experienced. Coaches

---

182 Gray, A, 'Swimming and child protection: the story so far' (1999) 2(2) SLB 8; also see Myers, J and Barrett, B, 'In at the Deep End' (2002), NSPCC.
183 See http://www.nspcc.org.uk/inform/cpsu/cpsu_wda57648.html and http://www.sportscoachuk.org.
184 Op. cit., fn 171, Brackenridge (2001), p 189.
185 http://www.homeoffice.gov.uk/agencies-public-bodies/crb/about-crb
186 Williams, Y, 'Child protection in sport' (2000) 8(1) Sport and the Law Journal 8; Williams, Y, 'Government sponsored Professional Sports Coaches and the Need for Protection' (2003) 2(1) Entertainment Law 55.
187 Op cit, fn 171, Brackenridge (2001), p 189.
188 See the general provisions for regulation of convicted paedophiles in the Sex Offenders Act 1997.
189 'NSPCC criticises volunteer checks', BBC News, 19 September 2009, http://news.bbc.co.uk/1/hi/uk/8253099.stm

need to be able to show encouragement, sometimes in a physical way: a hug of joy or a shoulder to cry on. In some sports, for example gymnastics, physical contact is needed between coach and child to assist in certain techniques.

Oppressive encouragement and abuse in all its forms needs to be exposed and effectively eradicated. What is of importance is that a safe working environment for child athletes needs to be guaranteed. This is of course clearly an international problem.[190] In football, a problem involving child abuse has been identified with the trafficking of young players from developing countries, particularly Africa, largely carried out by unlicensed agents and outside regulatory frameworks.[191] As things stand, FIFA has estimated that there are around half a million transfers of minors in football per year.[192] This is movement of young people on a very significant scale. FIFA has recently modified its transfer regulations so that young players under 18 can now move to a club in a different region or country as long as the family relocates to it for non-football reasons, such as a parent changing jobs.[193] There is evidence that, in the past, parents have in fact been provided with 'manufactured' jobs by clubs in the local area.[194] The new regulation does, however, require a sub-committee of the FIFA Players' Status Committee to vet all transfers of minors,[195] but it can be anticipated that new circumventions of the system will be devised.[196]

The law has a role to play in the whole area of abuse and exploitation of children in sport, but this will need to be alongside other regulatory mechanisms such as codes of ethical practice. All parties need to be better informed of the distinction between acceptable and unacceptable behaviour.

Key Points

- Much of sport is highly physical and involves a degree of contact between participants – what conduct might be termed 'violence' is determined by a range of issues and is a socially constructed concept.
- The civil law remedy of negligence has been employed increasingly by injured players suing for compensation.
- The standard of care is that the ordinary standards of negligence must be established in all the circumstances of the cases, albeit in reality evidence that may amount to reckless disregard may be required to establish liability.
- The range of potential, defendants has increased to include opposing participants, employers, sports coaches and sports governing bodies.
- Criminal liability has been less common than civil liability but players have been prosecuted periodically in both amateur and professional sport.
- A crucial issue in determining criminal liability is what the victim is consenting to, and the courts have developed a set of objective criteria to aid a jury in determining this issue.

---

190 See 'Protecting children from violence in sport. A review with a focus on industrialized countries', (2010), UNICEF, www.unicef-irc.org/publications/pdf/violence_in_sport.pdf.

191 Note a recent CAS case concerning the upholding of FIFA Players' Status Committee judgment against the Danish FA and FC for registering minor players from Nigeria 06.03.2009 – Final Award – CAS 2008/A/1485 FC Midtjylland v. FIFA; also see Backe Madsen, L and Johansson, JM, *Den Forsvunne Diamanten (The Lost Diamond)* (2008): Oslo: Tiden Norsk Forlag.

192 'Fifa cracks down on child transfers', *The Guardian*, 5 September 2009, www.guardian.co.uk/football/2009/sep/05/uefa-fifa-child-footballer-transfers.

193 See 'FIFA Regulations on the Status and Transfer of Players, Article 19', www.fifa.com/mm/document/affederation/administration/66/98/97/regulationsstatusandtransfer%5fen%5f1210.pdf.

194 'Chelsea facing legal threat over signing boy of 11', *The Guardian*, 5 September 2009, www.guardian.co.uk/football/2009/sep/05/chelsea-legal-threat-alleged-player-poaching. Chelsea FC were under a FIFA-imposed transfer ban over the illegal recruitment of the teenage forward Gaël Kakuta from Lens, overturned by agreement between the parties before a formal appeal hearing by CAS, www.tas-cas.org/d2wfiles/document/3947/5048/0/2010.02.04%20PR%20Eng%20_Final_.pdf.

195 'FIFA tighten minor player transfer regulations', 8 December 2008, http://www.africansoccerunion.com/index.php?option=com_content&view=article&id=95151:fifa-tighten-minor-player-transfer-regulations&catid=481&Itemid=200117.

196 Anderson, C, 'Player Contracts: New FIFA Regulations on the transfer of minors' (2009) 7(11) WSLR.

- In addition to the substantive criminal law, the issues involved in prosecutorial discretion are vital.
- Risk mananagment policies and assessments have has become vital in promoting safety in sport.
- There are periodic calls for boxing to be banned on medical grounds.
- Ensuring a safe environment for participation for children in sport has become a primary concern.

Key Sources

Anderson, J, *The Legality Of Boxing: A Punch Drunk Love?* (2007) Abingdon: Birkbeck Law Press.

Fafinski, S, 'Consent And The Rules Of The Game: The Interplay Of Civil And Criminal Liability For Sporting Injuries' (2005), The Journal Of Criminal Law 414.

Griffith-Jones, D, 'Civil Liability Arising Out of Participation in Sport', in Lewis, A and Taylor, J (eds), *Sport: Law And Practice* (2009), Haywards Heath: Tottel Publishing.

Smith, MD, *Violence and Sport* (1983), London: Butterworths.

UNICEF, *Protecting Children From Violence In Sport: a Review with a Focus on Industrialized Countries* (2010), www.Unicef-irc.org/publications/pdf/violence_in_sport.pdf.

Chapter 12

Sports Venues and the Law

Chapter Contents

Introduction	544
Parliamentary Enquiries	544
Stadium Liability Issues	552
Spectators	564
Crowd Management	567
Football Hooliganism	574
Spectator Racism in Sport	579
Key Points	589
Key Sources	589

Introduction

Most major sports clubs or competitions are defined to a degree by their venues. In many instances these venues are purpose-built sports stadiums[1] but the nature of the venue will, by necessity, vary according to the character of the sport in question.[2] This chapter focuses on a range of legal issues connected with sports venues. Spectator injuries[3] are, rightly, an important element of this discussion but they are just one consideration in a complex interaction involving owners, players, spectators,[4] police and local residents. As will be seen, issues of law even extend to those spectators watching an event from the comfort of their own homes.[5] In order to acquire an overview of the various legal considerations involved in facility management, reference should also be made to the relevant intellectual property issues raised elsewhere in this book.[6] This chapter is divided into three sections: parliamentary enquiries; stadium issues and hooliganism. This division is, to a degree, arbitrary, as the issues and themes are intertwined. The reader will be able to make many other connections between the various materials presented.

Parliamentary Enquiries

It is almost certain that venue-related disputes or injuries arise in the UK on a daily basis. Parliament does not intervene specifically in the vast majority of these incidents because the ordinary principles of law which guide and regulate citizens' behaviour deal with these issues through the normal dispute resolution mechanisms such as the courts or insurance. Parliament, however has, on occasion, intervened where the incident breaches a threshold of seriousness; where the nature of the issue crosses over from a matter of private concern to public concern. Often, Parliamentary action involves an enquiry followed by a report including recommendations for the avoidance of future occurrences. Parliament then decides how, if at all, to implement its recommendations. An example of this occurred following the incident at Sheffield Wednesday's Hillsborough stadium during an FA Cup semi-final between Liverpool and Nottingham Forest on 15 April 1989, as a result of which 96 lives were lost. The Hillsborough disaster is discussed in more detail later. It is pertinent at this stage to cite the words of Lord Justice Taylor, whose opening words in his final report read:

The Hillsborough Stadium Disaster Final Report (Taylor Report)

It is a depressing and chastening fact that mine is the ninth official report covering crowd safety at football grounds. After eight previous reports and three editions of the Green Guide, it seems astounding that 96 people could die from overcrowding before the very eyes of those controlling the event.[7]

This comment is one in a long line of indictments of our ability to ensure the safety of the public at sporting events. It is perhaps more chilling when considered alongside the comment of

---

1   Pugh-Smith, J, *Environmental Impact Assessments: The Continuing Jurisprudence* (2002) JPL (Nov) 1316–24; *R (on the application of Catt) v Brighton and Hove CC* [2006] EWHC 1337 (Admin); Lightner Maisashvili R, and Smith, N, 'Naming Rights: Stadia naming rights, key considerations' (2006) WSLR 4(2) 14–16; Gerlinger, M, 'Stadiums for FIFA World Cup Germany 2006 and European law on state aid: a case of infrastructure measures?' (2003) ISLJ 1 9–12.
2   For example the America's Cup or the World Rally Championship.
3   For example *McDyer v The Celtic Football and Athletic Co Ltd* [2000] SC 379.
4   Weatherill, S, 'Fining the Organisers of the 1998 Football World Cup' (2000) ECLR 21(6) 275–82.
5   *Alcock v Chief Constable of South Yorkshire* [1991] 4 All ER 907.
6   See Chapter 7.
7   *The Hillsborough Stadium Disaster Final Report* (Taylor Report) (1990) London: HMSO, Cm 962, p 4.

Mr Justice Popplewell, the author of the eighth report[8] in 1986, that 'almost all the matters into which I have been asked to inquire and almost all the solutions I have proposed have been previously considered in detail by many distinguished inquiries over a period of 60 years'.[9]

The first government report into ways of controlling and ensuring the safety of spectators, the Shortt Report,[10] was commissioned following concerns over crowd control highlighted by the massive overcrowding of Wembley Stadium for the 1923 FA Cup Final. It was the first time the stadium had hosted the final. However, it would be wrong to assume that this was the first occasion that safety at sports stadiums had been called into question. Indeed, there is considerable evidence of stadium inadequacies prior to 1923. Stands had collapsed causing injury at the Cheltenham National Hunt Festival in 1866,[11] Ewood Park in Blackburn in 1896[12] and at Ibrox in Glasgow in 1902, where 26 people were killed at a Scotland v England international.

The Shortt Report of 1924 highlighted a lack of apportionment of responsibility between the police and the ground authority. It suggested that responsibility should lie in the hands of a single, competent officer. It also recommended the increased use of stewards. Issues such as police responsibilities and adequate stewarding would again come under the microscope following Hillsborough. The report also observed:

The Shortt Report

We have been somewhat surprised to find that in many cases little or no precaution has been taken against the risk of fire in stands. We do not suppose that either the risk or the consequences of fire would be so serious in an open stand as in a closed building but we consider it most important that adequate arrangements should be made to deal with any outbreak which might occur.[13]

The tragic consequences of inadequate fire precautions became apparent following the Bradford City fire disaster in 1985, where the Main South Parade Stand was razed to the ground in nine minutes leaving 56 people dead.

If these issues could be identified in 1923 then why were adequate measures not taken in the intervening years to prevent the later disasters? One reason which is particularly pertinent to the Shortt Report is the unwillingness to view the events as a matter of governmental responsibility. The report concluded 'anaemically':[14] 'We are assured that these governing bodies are only too anxious to secure that their sport is carried on under conditions which will promote the public safety and we feel at this stage it is safe to leave the matter to them.'[15]

A good example of Parliament's inability or disinclination to act was the response to the Moelwyn Hughes Report of 1946.[16] The report followed the disaster at Bolton Wanderers' ground in that year. Here a crowd of 85,000, far exceeding anything experienced or expected, had crammed into Burnden Park. Two barriers collapsed resulting in the death of 33 people. The Moelwyn Hughes Report recommended mechanical means of counting those entering the ground, scientific calculations of maximum attendances and inspections of enclosures. The report concluded:

---

8 The Popplewell Final Report: Final Report of the Committee of Inquiry into Crowd Safety and Control at Sports Grounds (1986) London: HMSO, Cm 9710.
9 Ibid, para 10.
10 The Short Report, Report of the Departmental Committee on Crowds (1924), London: HMSO, Cm 2088.
11 Francis v Cockrell (1870) 5 QB 501.
12 Brown v Lewis (1896) 12 TLR 455.
13 Op. cit., fn 10, The Shortt Report, para 40.
14 The description given by The Moelwyn Hughes Report (1946), London: HMSO, Cm 6846.
15 Op, cit,, fn 10, The Shortt Report, para 47.
16 Enquiry into the Disaster at Bolton Wanderers (1946), London: HMSO, Cm 6846.

The Moelwyn Hughes Report

No ground of any considerable size should be opened to the public until it has been licensed by, I suggest as an appropriate licensing authority, the local authority. The issue of the licence would depend upon satisfying the authority as to the construction and equipment of the ground, its compliance with regulations and the proposed maximum figures of admission to the different parts.[17]

The issues raised by the Hughes Report in 1946 were finally addressed by the Safety of Sports Grounds Act 1975 following another disaster at Ibrox. The recommendations of the Moelwyn Hughes Report were not implemented. The reasons for this are unclear but cost cannot be ignored as a factor. As the report concluded, 'Compliance with the recommendations of this report will cost money. They will involve grounds in a loss of gate money. The insurance for greater safety for the public demands a premium'.[18]

It may seem cynical to suggest that safety measures should be balanced against cost but it is a fact of life that the legal standard of reasonableness often involves such reasoning. For example, the Green Guide, which prescribes safety standards for football grounds, remains advisory, it is said, because of the disparate nature of our football grounds, but this could also be in part due to the costs of enforcing safety specifications. In the same vein the Sporting Events (Control of Alcohol) Act 1985 attempts to stop the consumption of alcohol on trains and buses going to a match and also prevents consumption whilst watching the match but allows consumption at pubs and bars in and around the ground. The only logic for this is that the restrictions on the drinking habits of supporters are being balanced against the interests of local business.

Sporting Events (Control of Alcohol etc) Act 1985

1.   *Offences in connection with alcohol on coaches and trains*
     (1)   This section applies to a vehicle which –
           (a)   is a public service vehicle or railway passenger vehicle; and
           (b)   is being used for the principal purpose of carrying passengers for the whole or part of a journey to or from a designated sporting event.
     (2)   A person who knowingly causes or permits intoxicating liquor to be carried on a vehicle to which this section applies is guilty of an offence –
           (a)   if the vehicle is a public service vehicle and he is the operator of the vehicle or the servant or agent of the operator; or
           (b)   if the vehicle is a hired vehicle and he is the person to whom it is hired or the servant or agent of that person.
     (3)   A person who has intoxicating liquor in his possession while on a vehicle to which this section applies is guilty of an offence.
     (4)   A person who is drunk on a vehicle to which this section applies is guilty of an offence.
2.   *Offences in connection with alcohol, containers, etc. at sports grounds*
     (1)   A person who has intoxicating liquor or an article to which this section applies in his possession –
           (a)   at any time during the period of a designated sporting event when he is in any area of a designated sports ground from which the event may be directly viewed; or

---

17 Ibid, p 11.
18 Ibid, p 12.

(b) while entering or trying to enter a designated sports ground at any time during the period or a designated sporting event at that ground, is guilty of an offence.

(2) A person who is drunk in a designated sports ground at any time during the period of a designated sporting event at that ground or is drunk while entering or trying to enter such a ground at any time during the period of a designated sporting event at that ground is guilty of an offence.

(3) This section applies to any article capable of causing injury to a person struck by it, being –

(a) a bottle, can or other portable container (including such an article when crushed or broken) which –

(i) is for holding any drink; and

(ii) is of a kind which, when empty, is normally discarded or returned to or left to be recovered by, the supplier; or

(b) part of an article falling within paragraph (a) above.

Section 1 applies not only to the person in possession of the alcohol but also to the person who permits the alcohol to be carried on a public service vehicle. Section 1(2)(a) makes it clear that the offence will be committed by coach operators or the railway authorities and their staff. Although being drunk at the ground,[19] taking alcohol to the ground[20] and being in possession of alcohol while viewing the match are all offences,[21] it is not an offence to drink alcohol before entering the ground nor to drink at the club's bars. It could be argued that the consumption of alcohol at a public house near the ground is a more effective measure of a person's intoxication than his mere possession of alcohol. Clearly the measures are aimed at preserving the individual right to moderate consumption of alcohol as well as protecting the business interests of public houses and restaurants but it is uncertain as to how effective the provisions can be. Effective enforcement of these measures at a Premier League football match where there may be in excess of 30,000 people is impossible. The Act makes no attempt to define 'drunk', unlike the road traffic provisions relating to drinking and driving, and so even extremely intoxicated but discreet supporters should evade detection. The only time that drunkenness is likely to be observed is if the spectator's behaviour is such as to draw the attention of the police. At this stage it is likely that other offences such as public order offences would have been committed, thus negating the need for the Act. The main benefit of the Act may be to enable the police to filter out a small percentage of the most visibly or audibly drunk prior to admission.

Another important factor is the complexity of the issues involved. As the Lang Report 1969 commented, 'The working party was dealing with a subject which has been discussed almost *ad nauseam* during recent years. Not unexpectedly the working party has not found a single simple solution for a problem which is often due to a combination of factors.'[22] The Lang Report was commissioned to look into what was considered to be an increasing problem at football grounds: that of crowd behaviour. Subsequent major disasters such as Bradford and Hillsborough have highlighted that whilst hooliganism remains a worrying social condition it is in most instances a distinct problem from that of stadium safety.[23]

---

19 Sporting Events (Control of Alcohol etc) s 2(2).

20 Ibid, s 2(1)(b).

21 Ibid, s 2(1)(a).

22 *The Lang Report, Crowd Behaviour at Football Matches: Report of the Working Party* (1969), London: HMSO, p 3.

23 The Heysel Stadium disaster of May 1985 is an unusual example of where the issues of crowd management and crowd disturbances were both integral factors.

The Wheatley Report 1971 was commissioned following the disaster at Ibrox Park where inadequate stairways and handrails caused the death of 66 spectators.[24] The report is of great significance as it was the first of the reports to directly spawn an Act of Parliament, the Safety of Sports Grounds Act 1975. In his report Lord Wheatley was conscious of both the history of recommendations such as his and the economic arguments against imposing stringent safety conditions. He dismissed such misgivings emphatically:

The Wheatley Report

I recognise that a decision to introduce a licensing system for grounds along the lines I have recommended may cause anxiety to some football clubs and football administrators. As I see it, their misgivings are associated with a fear that such stringent conditions may be attached to the granting of a licence, that many clubs may not be able to afford the cost and some may have to go out of business . . . My answer to that is this. My task is to consider the problem of crowd safety at the grounds. Clubs which charge the public for admission have a duty to see that their grounds are reasonably safe for spectators. That is a primary consideration. It is accordingly necessary that some standards should be imposed and observed. This has been recognised by the football authorities themselves . . . I have canvassed all the alternatives that have been proposed or which I personally thought were reasonable to consider and the one I decided was best to meet the situation in the interest of the public is a licensing system by a local authority. There is nothing new in this proposal. It has been mooted for almost 50 years. It can come as no surprise to the football world and in the light of happenings over the years the demand for an independent appraisal and determination of the safety of grounds becomes almost irresistible. I certainly cannot resist it.[25]

Other reports such as the Harrington Report,[26] The McElhone Report,[27] which looked at *inter alia* the consumption of alcohol, and the Department of the Environment Working Group 1984, which was commissioned following violence by football supporters in Luxembourg in 1983 and France in 1984, all focused on what was perceived to be an increase in football crowd violence. None of these reports resulted directly in legislation. Popplewell J's Report published in the aftermath of the Bradford City fire disaster concluded:

The Popplewell Report

A study of all these reports (and there are numerous reports and discussion papers by other bodies) shows that the following are measures which have been frequently recommended: closed circuit television; membership cards; segregation; more seating at football grounds; encouragement of supporters' clubs; a ban on alcohol; involvement of the clubs with the community and heavier penalties. I too shall argue for these and related measures . . . It is to be hoped they will be more vigorously pursued by the appropriate bodies than in the past.[28]

Whilst the Popplewell Report is often perceived as being an inquiry into the Bradford fire disaster, its terms of reference were in fact wider. On the same day as the Bradford fire, one supporter was killed and another 200 were injured in violent clashes at Birmingham City's home ground,

---

24 *The Wheatley Report* (1971), London: HMSO, Cm 4952.
25 Ibid, paras 66 and 67.
26 *The Harrington Report, Soccer Hooliganism: A Preliminary Report* (1968), Bristol: John Wright and Sons Ltd.
27 *The McElhone Report, Report of the Working Group on Football Crowd Behaviour*, Scottish Education Department, HMSO 1977.
28 Op. cit., fn 8, *Popplewell Final Report* (1986), para 16.

St Andrew's, with rival supporters of Leeds United. During this period football violence was a high-profile issue. Popplewell J was asked to inquire into both these events.

This tendency to amalgamate issues of crowd management and crowd disturbances sets a dangerous precedent. The incident at the Heysel Stadium, Brussels, before the 1985 European Cup Final between Liverpool and Juventus, where 39 supporters were killed was also considered by Popplewell J. The incident represents a rare occurrence where fighting spectators (crowd disturbance) caused a concentration of people, causing a wall to collapse (crowd management). Bradford and subsequently Hillsborough were disasters caused by an inability to house large numbers of people in safety and crowd disturbance played little if any part. One of the most significant developments following Hillsborough was the government's ill-fated attempt to introduce a membership system: a means of curbing crowd disturbances. Measures aimed at curbing crowd violence such as controlling the consumption of alcohol, increasing police powers of arrest and courts' powers to punish, are very different from the measures needed to manage large numbers of spectators in an enclosed space. This calls for good stadium design, adequate safety margins and good stewardship.

Lord Justice Taylor was appointed to conduct the inquiry into the Hillsborough disaster. He inter alia was particularly critical of the layout and capacity of the Leppings Lane end of the stadium (the stand allocated to Liverpool supporters). Following the crushing that had occurred at the earlier 1981 semi-final, additional fencing was erected which, in effect, segregated the terrace into three sections. Pens three and four formed the central section. Within the central section modifications were made to the layout with a number of barriers being removed. Although extensive modifications had been made, compensatory safety measures had not. Access to the central section could still be made through any of the turnstiles for the terrace. Therefore, although the turnstiles had been computerised, the system could give no information as to the number of supporters in any particular section.

Under s 1 of the Safety at Sports Grounds Act 1975 as amended by the Fire Safety and Safety of Places of Sport Act 1987, Hillsborough had been designated as a stadium requiring a safety certificate in 1979. Section 2(2)(a) of the 1975 Act as originally enacted[29] stated that the safety certificate 'shall specify the maximum number of spectators to be admitted to the stadium'. However, s 2(2)(b) stated merely that a safety certificate 'may specify the maximum number to be admitted to different parts of it'. The certificate for Hillsborough did not contain maximum numbers for the pens at the Leppings Lane end and although evidence showed that engineers were aware that the alterations to the terrace would impact on spectator numbers no alterations were made to the certificate.

Although s 2(2) had been repealed by s 19 of the Fire Safety and Safety of Places of Sports Act 1987, it was still effective because s 19 gave power to the Secretary of State to lay down terms and conditions for the granting of a certificate and, as no order had been made, the Home Office had recommended that certificates continue to be granted in accordance with the repealed section. According to s 2(2) of the 1975 Act, terms and conditions would include those relating to 'the number, strength and situation of any crush barriers'[30] and although it was not a mandatory requirement under the Act to specify capacity of the particular sections of the terrace there was a breach of the provisions in not amending the certificate to reflect the lowering of overall capacity.

Another weakness of the provisions became evident when the Inquiry considered how the local authority exercised their supervisory duties under the Act. The Officer Working Party, formed to comply with the regulations, was informal with no chair or record of decisions. The report

---

29 Before it was amended by s 19 of the Fire Safety and Safety of Places of Sport Act 1987.
30 Safety at Sports Grounds Act 1975, s 2(2)(c)(iii).

commented that 'the attention given to this important licensing function was woefully inadequate'.[31] This illustrates the valuable point that the best intentions of Parliament can be thwarted by inadequate application.

On the issue of crowd control, Lord Justice Taylor concurred with Justice Popplewell's earlier report that 'it cannot be too strongly emphasised that it is upon the club or the occupier of the ground who is putting on the function, that the primary or continuing obligation rests'.[32] This causes certain problems. *Harris v Sheffield United Football Club*[33] suggests that the money paid to police is for more than normal policing duties. On the assumption that both stewards and police will be present, how might their functions, in fact, be divided? Justice Popplewell acknowledged the reality of the police's *de facto* control but this does not resolve the problem of legal responsibility. In the interim report Taylor LJ concluded:

The Hillsborough Stadium Disaster (Interim Report)

There remains, however, the question of whether there are some grounds or parts of grounds where the club may need to rely on the police (whom they pay to attend) to control the filling of pens and monitoring them for overcrowding. In other words, whilst the duty in law to insure safety rests upon the club, they may need and by arrangement be entitled, to employ the police as their agents in certain circumstances.[34]

This appears to be a non-delegable duty to spectators, the running of which may be delegated to the police. This would mean that an injured spectator's recourse in law would be with the club but would not resolve the legal position regarding the police's legal obligation to the club. Taylor LJ's solution was a Written Statement of Intent:

The Hillsborough Stadium Disaster (Final Report)

I therefore repeat my recommendation that there should be a written document setting out the respective functions of club and police for crowd safety and control 'and in particular for the filling of each self-contained pen or other terraced area and the monitoring of spectators in each such pen or area to avoid overcrowding'. The aim should be for the club through its stewards to perform all those functions of controlling spectators of which they are capable having regard to the quality of the stewards, the layout of the ground and the nature of the match. Where they are not able to discharge any such function the police should perform it. As the proportion of seating at grounds increases, control by stewards should become the norm.

In making interim recommendation four,[35] I used the phrase 'written agreement'. This led to anxiety that what was required was a binding legal contract which would deprive the police of any flexibility in response to circumstances of the day. My intention was not to shackle either party by a binding contract; it was simply to have a document setting out how the functions were to be divided so that no misunderstanding would arise whereby one party thought that the other had undertaken some duty or vice versa. I am content that the document be referred to simply as a 'statement of intent', so it can be subject to alteration without breach of contract should circumstances so demand.[36]

---

31 *The Hillsborough Stadium Disaster* (Interim Report) 1989 Cm765 para 158.
32 Op. cit. fn 8 para 4.13.
33 [1988] QB 77
34 Op. cit. fn 28 para165.
35 *The Hillsborough Stadium Disaster* (Final Report) (Taylor Report) (1990), London: HMSO, Cm 962, p 57.
36 Ibid, paras 213 and 214.

There are legal implications for such a document. There is clearly a contract between the club and the police and, according to *Harris*, this can be for the provision of a crowd control function. It is possible that a Statement of Intent could be used to evidence terms as to the extent of the police's contractual obligation.

In *Chief Constable of Greater Manchester v Wigan Athletic AFC Ltd*,[37] the police had increased its presence at match days when the football club had gained promotion to the Premier League. At no time had the club agreed to the increase in policing and, therefore, it had objected to the higher payments for special policing services demanded by the police pursuant to s 25 of the Police Act 1996. The Court of Appeal by a majority, overturning the decision at first instance,[38] held that in the face of the express rejection by the club of the need for extra policing, it could not be implied that the extra policing had been requested by the club.[39]

Lord Justice Taylor's most important recommendation, that of all-seater football stadiums,[40] has ensured, arguably, that there has not only been a reduction in football hooliganism but, most importantly, there has been no repetition of the Hillsborough disaster.

The Hillsborough Stadium Disaster (Final Report)

It is obvious that sitting for the duration of the match is more comfortable than standing. It is also safer. When a spectator is seated he has his own small piece of territory in which he can feel reasonably secure. He will not be in close physical contact with those around him. He will not be jostled or moved about by swaying or surging. Small, infirm or elderly men and women as well as young children are not buffeted, smothered or un-sighted by large and more robust people, as on the terraces. The seated spectator is not subject to pressure of numbers behind, nor around, him during the match. He will not be painfully bent double over a crush barrier. Those monitoring numbers will know exactly how many there are without having to count them in, or assess the density by visual impression. There will still, of course, be scope for crowd pressure on standing whilst entering and, especially, when leaving but involuntary and uncontrolled crowd movements occasioned by incidents at the game are effectively eliminated.[41]

The effect of all-seater stadiums has also reduced the importance of ground capacity at football matches, but other sporting grounds are not so well protected. The enactment of the Fire Safety and Safety of Places of Sport Act 1987 is to be applauded for its attempt to broaden the scope of the safety legislation to cover all sports grounds. However, as has been seen, this was achieved at the expense of the original s 2 of the Safety of Sports Grounds Act 1975 which enshrined in statute the need for safety certificates to identify ground capacity and the option of stating stand or pen capacity. Section 27 of the Fire Safety and Safety of Places of Sport Act 1987, which deals with the contents of safety certificates for stands at undesignated matches, states: 'A safety certificate for a regulated stand shall contain such terms and conditions as the local authority consider necessary or expedient to secure reasonable safety.' The local authority can call upon the latest edition of the Green Guide but the Taylor Report advised against incorporating its provisions into statute. The Taylor Report highlighted the cursory adherence to the legislation by the local authority when that legislation merely gives a discretion rather than instruction. It is difficult to see, outside of football, any direct improvement in safety legislation.

---

37 (2008) SLJR 3
38 [2007] EWHC 3095 (Ch).
39 See also *Reading Festival Ltd v West Yorkshire Police Authority* [2006] EWCA Civ 524, [2006] 1 WLR 2005 and *Bookmakers Afternoon Greyhound Services Ltd v Wilf Gilbert (Staffordshire) Ltd* [1994] FSR. 723 Ch D.
40 Ibid, p 12.
41 Ibid, para 62.

The legislation spawned as a direct consequence of the Taylor Report was aimed not at the causes of the Hillsborough disaster but more at the problems of crowd disturbances. The restrictions on spectators travelling overseas under Part 3 of the Football Spectators Act 1989 and the provision contained within the Football (Offences) Act 1991 continued the trend of previous reports into stadium disasters of combining provisions relating to crowd management and crowd disturbance. Anyone with an understanding of the history of stadium disasters in Britain will appreciate the dangers of dealing with crowd disturbances to the detriment of crowd management.

Over the years, Parliament, through various reports, has considered the causes of death and serious injury at sports stadiums and latterly has responded to those reports with legislation. The reality, however, as Taylor LJ stated in his report, is that 'There is no panacea which will achieve total safety and cure all problems of behaviour and crowd control . . .'[42] On 11 April 2001 at a football match between Kaizer Chiefs and Orlando Pirates at Ellis Park Stadium, Johannesburg, 43 people died and many more were injured in South Africa's worst football disaster. The Commission, chaired by Mr Justice Ngoepe, heard that the deaths and injuries occurred as a result of crushing when too many spectators were crammed into the ground. The circumstances were frighteningly similar to those encountered at Hillsborough. The Commission recommended the adoption of legislation broadly similar to the English law.[43] Without suggesting that safety in the UK and South Africa was ignored prior to the respective disasters, it is unfortunate that it takes major losses of lives to galvanise authorities into taking appropriate measures. The similarities between the disasters suggest that legislation is necessary to ensure that the enthusiasm and excitement of sports spectators is channelled safely. This is easier said than done, however, and the problem with most legislative measures is that they impose a financial burden on clubs and stadium owners.

Stadium Liability Issues

Occupiers and owners

The first recorded example of stadium occupiers being held liable for a defective stand was *Francis v Cockrell*,[44] where part of a stand collapsed at the Cheltenham National Hunt Festival. The court upheld a claim for damages against the occupiers even though it was builders with whom the occupiers had contracted to build the stand who were negligent. The courts held that a contract existed between the spectator and the occupier with an implied term ensuring a reasonable standard of safety. Today a cause of action would most likely lie in negligence, occupiers' liability or under one of the sports-specific Acts which have proliferated in recent years.

Occupiers of stadiums and sporting clubs quickly became aware of their potential liability for stadium defects. Football clubs and bodies which initially existed in legal form as unincorporated associations soon became incorporated as limited companies. In *Brown v Lewis*[45] the court held that members of the club committee were individually liable for £25 damages following the collapse of a stand at Blackburn Rovers Football Club. By this time the benefits of incorporation were widely known. Incorporation brings into being an entirely separate legal entity, which means that liability in most cases will be limited to the club and its resources, the membership being protected by the 'veil of incorporation'.[46] It was not long before most sporting clubs took advantage of this. More

---

42 Ibid, para 61.
43 *Commission of Inquiry into the Ellis Park Stadium Soccer Disaster Of 11 April 2001* Report at http://www.info.gov.za/otherdocs/2002/ finalellispark.pdf. See also the *Activity Centres (Yong Persons' Safety) Act 1996* introduced following the Lyme Bay canoeing tragedy.
44 (1870) LR 5 QB 501.
45 (1896) 12 TLR 455.
46 *Salomon v Salomon & Co Ltd* [1897] AC 22 HL.

recently, sporting clubs, like other commercial enterprises, have sought to exploit the benefits of limited liability by hiving off areas of business into separate subsidiary companies under the general umbrella of a holding or parent company. This has the effect of divorcing the liability of smaller economic units from the whole. The primary motive for this exercise is clearly not to avoid liability for injured spectators; however, it must form part of a greater design to ensure clubs' solvency. To this end sporting clubs may often not own their own ground. Although from a legal perspective the ground will be owned by a different person, that person will often be another company with some of the same directors and shareholders as the club itself. An attempt was made by Lord Denning[47] to start a trend of considering groups of companies as a whole but this movement has fallen from favour in recent years.[48] This does not mean that other companies in a group will not be liable, as the courts have construed the Occupiers' Liability Acts so that it is possible for there to be multiple occupancy of premises:[49]

Occupiers' Liability Act 1957, s 2

(1) An occupier of premises owes the same duty, the 'common duty of care', to all his visitors, except in so far as he is free and does extend, restrict, modify or exclude his duty to any visitor or visitors by agreement or otherwise.

(2) The common duty of care is a duty to take such care as in all the circumstances of the case is reasonable to see that the visitor will be reasonably safe in using the premises for the purposes for which he is invited or permitted by the occupier to be there.

(3) The circumstances relevant for the present purpose include the degree of care and of want of care, which would ordinarily be looked for in such a visitor, so that (for example) in proper cases –

    (a) an occupier must be prepared for children to be less careful than adults; and

    (b) an occupier must expect that a person, in the exercise of his calling, will appreciate and guard against any special risks ordinarily incident to it, so far as the occupier leaves him free to do so.

(4) In determining whether the occupier of the premises has discharged the common duty of care to a visitor, regard is to be had to all the circumstances, so that (for example) –

    (a) where damage is caused to a visitor by a danger of which he had been warned by the occupier, the warning is not to be treated without more as absolving the occupier of liability, unless in all the circumstances it was enough to enable the visitor to be reasonably safe; and

    (b) where damage is caused to a visitor by a danger caused by the faulty execution of any work of construction, maintenance or repair by an independent contractor employed by the occupier, the occupier is not to be treated without more as answerable for the danger if in all the circumstances he had acted reasonably in entrusting the work to an independent contractor and had taken such steps (if any) as he reasonably ought in order to satisfy himself that the contractor was competent and that the work had been properly done.

(5) The common duty of care does not impose on an occupier any obligation to a visitor in respect of risks willingly accepted as his by the visitor (the question whether a risk was so accepted to be decided on the same principles as in other cases in which one person owes a duty of care to another).

---

47 *DHN Food Distributors Ltd v Tower Hamlets LBC* [1976] 1 WLR 852.
48 *Woolfson v Strathclyde Regional Council* [1978] SLT 159; *Adams v Cape Industries Plc* [1990] 2 WLR 657.
49 *Wheat v Lacon* [1966] 1 All ER 582.

The 1957 Act lays down in statutory form the standard of duty required of all sporting clubs inviting spectators on to their premises. The standard is similar to that for common law negligence.[50] The occupier must also take into account that child supporters may be owed a higher duty than adults.

Following *White v Blackmore*[51] it appeared that s 2(1) allowed occupiers to avoid liability by warning notices. In that case the deceased was a competitor at a 'jalopy' meeting. Having competed in one race he watched another. In that race a car ran into a safety rope which, because it had been staked negligently, pulled at a rope segregating spectators, causing the deceased to be catapulted into the air, sustaining injuries from which he died. The Court of Appeal held that warning notices placed at the entrance to the venue stating that the organisers would not be liable for accidents to spectators however caused had effectively excluded liability.

The Unfair Contract Terms Act 1977, which applies to business liability only, appears to have closed this loophole. Section 2(1) of the Act prevents the exclusion or restriction of liability by contractual term or notice for death or personal injury resulting from negligence. Section 2(2) extends this by stating that liability for other loss or damage caused by negligence can only be excluded or restricted where reasonable.

It is important to note that the duty is only owed to a visitor who is 'using the premises for the purposes for which he is invited or permitted to be there'.[52] Injury sustained through standing on a faulty seat which subsequently collapses or whilst running on the field of play to celebrate victory may transform the visitor into a trespasser for 'when you invite a person into your house to use the staircase, you do not invite him to slide down the banisters'.[53]

Trespassers such as these or spectators who have gained entry to a sporting event unlawfully are considered to be owed a lesser duty than lawful visitors. Trespassers are governed by the Occupiers' Liability Act 1984.[54] However, the 1984 Act is unlikely to have an important impact in the sporting context as s 3(a) states that the duty is only owed where the occupier 'is aware of the danger or has reasonable grounds to believe it exists'.

Local authorities

The Safety of Sports Grounds Act 1975 introduced a system of licensing of major sports grounds by local authorities. Section 1(1) of the Act as amended allows the Secretary of State to designate as a sports ground requiring a certificate any sports ground which in his opinion has accommodation for more than 5,000 spectators at football matches and 10,000 spectators at other sports. The certificate is appropriate for a number of activities during an indefinite period or individual occasion.[55] Section 2 explains that 'a safety certificate shall contain such terms and conditions as the local authority consider necessary or expedient to secure reasonable safety at the sports ground when it is in use for a specified activity or activities and the terms and conditions may be such as to involve alterations or additions to the sports ground'. If the local authority believes that the ground or parts of the ground are a serious risk to spectator safety then they are empowered under s 10 to prohibit or restrict admission and direct the holder of the licence as to the steps that must be taken before the order will be lifted.

---

50 For example see *Hall v Holker Estate Company Ltd* [2008] EWCA Civ 1422.
51 [1972] 2 QB 651.
52 Section 2(2).
53 *The Carlgarth* [1927] P 93, 110, per Scrutton LJ. See also *Ratcliff v McConnell and Others* [1999] 1 WLR 670 and *Poppleton v Trustees of the Portsmouth Youth Activities Centre* [2008] EWCA Civ 646.
54 See *Tomlinson v Congleton Borough Council* [2003] UKHL 47 where the claimant failed in his action after sustaining serious injury diving into a shallow lake. The defendant council had satisfied their duty to a trespasser with warnings by signs and patrolling officials prohibiting use of the lake.
55 Section 1(3).

At the time of writing the local authority's licensing duties in relation to designated football matches are overseen by the Football Licensing Authority (FLA) although the government has announced that from 2012 it will be replaced by a new body. The duties and powers of the FLA are contained in the Football Spectators Act 1989. The Secretary of State's criteria for labelling designated football matches is unclear but will be no less stringent than under the provisions of the 1975 Act. The Football Licensing Authority has the power to grant licences[56] as well as 'keeping under review the discharge by local authorities of their function under the Safety of Sports Grounds Act 1975'.[57] This supervisory role was recommended by Lord Justice Taylor following his critical analysis of the local authority's performance of its functions under the 1975 Act.

A licensing system also operates for those sports grounds that are undesignated but provide covered accommodation in stands for 500 or more spectators. This system is provided for by the Fire Safety and Safety of Places of Sport Act 1987. Again the system is operated by the relevant local authority, which has the power to issue a certificate for a regulated stand containing 'such terms and conditions as the local authority considers necessary'.[58]

Whilst the Acts put in place a structure for the certification of sports grounds they are couched in general terms and do not specify minimum safety measures. Reference therefore must be made to the Green Guide, the provisions of which form the basis of local authority enforcement of a safety standard and could be adopted by the courts as the benchmark for safety standards. The Green Guide provides such details as the capacity of stands, evacuation procedures and fire safety as well as general conditions and maintenance.

Neighbours

Legal issues relating to sporting venues are not limited to the stadium itself. One would need only to speak to residents living near to major sporting venues to appreciate that whilst the sporting action may be contained, legal issues, like spectators, tend to spill over and affect the surrounding environment. Legal protection for those outside the stadium is important for two reasons.

Firstly, because in order to arrive at and depart from the stadium, spectators need to pass through residential areas. Large numbers of fans need to be managed in such a way as to avoid encroaching on the safety and peaceful enjoyment of the property of local residents.

Secondly, because what goes on inside the stadium directly impacts on those outside. For example, sixes in cricket could clear the ground and could cause injury to property and persons and it is not beyond the realms of possibility that a passer-by could be killed. This problem is even more evident at the village green level, where cricket grounds are often situated next to the highway or adjoining property where there is little or no protection.

A less tangible concern, but one which may impact on a greater number of local residents, is the level of noise emanating from the stadium.[59] This noise may be particularly acute if the stadium in question hosts motor or speedboat racing, for example, although these events tend to be held in less built-up areas.

In tort, claims against the stadium owners may prove problematic since, generally speaking, owners are not responsible for the actions of spectators outside the stadium. In *AG v Corke*[60] the defendant was held responsible under the principle in *Rylands v Fletcher*[61] for the nuisance created off his land by travellers staying on the land. The principle in *Rylands v Fletcher* is a variation on the tort

---

56 Section 10.
57 Section 13(1).
58 Section 27(1).
59 See *Stretch v Romford Football Club* (1971) 115 Sol J, 641.
60 [1933] Ch 89.
61 (1886) LR 3 HL 330; [1861–73] All ER Rep 1.

of nuisance as it imposes strict liability for foreseeable damage caused by the escape from the defendant's land of things accumulated or brought there by the defendant which amounts to a non-natural use of the land.[62] Had this principle continued to be applied to human beings it may have proved to be a means by which local residents could have sought redress from stadium owners. Subsequent decisions suggest, however, that the rule is not applicable in these circumstances.[63]

The law relating to damage outside the stadium caused by the activities inside the stadium has resulted in many of the most famous sporting legal cases. It is a possibility in many sports that a ball may be hit out of the stadium: in football a defender's desperate clearance from an onrushing forward; in rugby a kick into touch to move play up-field. Incidents of these types of projectiles causing harm are rare. Much more likely, although not exclusively, is the potential damage from a golf ball[64] or a cricket ball.[65] Not only is a cricket ball hard but, by awarding six runs for a shot which clears the boundary, the game encourages big hits and potential danger. Any liability for such an occurrence is likely to be based on the torts of negligence and nuisance.

Negligence can be defined as the breach of a duty to take care, owed by the defendant, which causes harm to the claimant.[66]. Private nuisance occurs where the use by the defendants of their land results in unreasonable interference with the claimant's enjoyment of their land. As nuisance requires the plaintiff to have an interest in land it follows that this tort can only be invoked by those with an interest in land in the vicinity of the stadium[67] whereas a claim in negligence can be made by property owners or unfortunate passers-by.

In *Bolton v Stone and Others*[68] a visiting cricketer struck a six which had cleared the boundary, 75 feet from the wicket, and a 17-foot fence and had travelled a further 100 yards before striking the plaintiff who was standing on the highway. The cricket ground had been used for 90 years and evidence from the last 30 revealed only six incidents of escaped balls with no damage having been caused by any. The House of Lords allowed the appeal on the basis that the likelihood of injury occurring was so slight that a reasonable man would be justified in ignoring it:

Bolton v Stone [1951] 1 All ER 1078

Lord Reid: This case, therefore, raises sharply the question what is the nature and extent of the duty of a person who promotes on his land operations which may cause damage to persons on an adjoining highway. Is it that he must not carry out or permit an operation which he knows or ought to know clearly can cause such damage, however improbable that result may be or is it that he is only bound to take into account the possibility of such damage if such damage is a likely or probable consequence of what he does or permits or if the risk of damage is such that a reasonable man, careful of the safety of his neighbour, would regard that risk as material? I do not know of any case where this question has had to be decided or even where it has been fully discussed. Of course there are many cases in which somewhat similar questions have arisen but, generally speaking, if injury to another person from the defendants' acts is reason-ably foreseeable the chance that injury will result is substantial and it does not matter in which way the duty is stated. In such cases I do not think that much assistance is to be got from

---

62 *Cambridge Water v Eastern Counties Leather Plc* [1994] 1 All ER 53; *Read v J Lyons* [1947] AC 156.
63 *Smith v Scott* [1973] Ch 314; *Matheson v Northcote College Board of Governors* [1975] 2 NZLR 106.
64 In *Castle v St Augustines Links Ltd and Another* (1922) 38 TLR 615, a taxi driver was successful in an action for nuisance (although today this would most probably be brought under the tort of negligence) against a golf club, when a golfer's wayward tee shot from the 13th tee smashed through the window of the plaintiff's taxi resulting in the loss of an eye. Williamson, DS, 'Some legal aspects of golf' (1995) 3(1) Sport and the Law Journal.
65 For example, see (1996) 39 *Legal Times* 24.
66 *Donoghue v Stevenson* [1932] AC 562; *Peabody Donation Fund v Parkinson* [1985] AC 210; *Smith v Littlewoods Organisation* [1987] AC 241; *Caparo Industries v Dickman* [1990] 1 All ER 568.
67 *Hunter and Others v Canary Wharf Ltd; Hunter and Others v London Docklands Development Corporation* [1997] NLJ 634.
68 [1951] 1 All ER 1078.

analysing the language which a judge has used. More assistance is to be got from cases where judges have clearly chosen their language with care in setting out a principle but even so, statements of the law must be read in light of the facts of the particular case. Nevertheless, making all allowances for this, I do find at least a tendency to base duty rather on the likelihood of damage to others than on its foreseeability alone . . .

. . . Counsel for the respondent in the present case had to put his case so high as to say that, at least as soon as one ball had been driven into the road in the ordinary course of a match, the appellants could and should have realised that that might happen again and that, if it did, someone might be injured and that that was enough to put on the appellants a duty to take steps to prevent such an occurrence. If the true test is foreseeability alone I think that must be so. Once a ball has been driven on to a road without there being anything extraordinary to account for the fact, there is clearly a risk that another will follow and if it does there is clearly a chance, small though it may be, that somebody may be injured. On the theory that it is foreseeability alone that matters it would be irrelevant to consider how often a ball might be expected to land in the road and it would not matter whether the road was the busiest street or the quietest country lane. The only difference between these cases is in the degree of risk. It would take a good deal to make me believe that the law has departed so far from the standards which guide ordinary careful people in ordinary life. In the crowded conditions of modern life even the most careful person cannot avoid creating some risks and accepting others. What a man must not do and what I think a careful man tries not to do, is to create a risk which is substantial. Of course, there are numerous cases where special circumstances require that a higher standard shall be observed and where that is recognised by the law but I do not think that this case comes within any such special category.

The fact that the ball had left the ground previously, and the chances of it doing so again had been guarded against to some extent by the fencing, shows that the decision was not based on foreseeability alone. The House of Lords was able to look at the history of cricket balls leaving the ground and concluded that there were some foreseeable risks that it was possible to ignore.

It is interesting to note that Miss Stone's action was taken against those responsible for the ground and not the batsman. It will be no defence in this type of situation for those in control of the ground to shift responsibility on to the players. The onus remains with those who control the cricket ground or driving range to take action should the occurrence of balls leaving the ground reach an unacceptable level. The difficulty will be to set such a level.

The law is clear that the level of duty owed by sportsmen will be that of the reasonable sportsman with the level of skill and knowledge of the defendant. It is in this way that we can require a higher level of skill from doctors and other professionals.[69] Clearly then we cannot expect a child to have the knowledge and experience of a reasonable adult.[70] It is possible that a professional sportsman may be liable in circumstances where a child who hits a ball from a playground cage may not. The potential liability of the owners of the stadium will depend on their assessment of the likelihood of risk, taking into account the age and skill of the participants.

In *Hilder v Associated Portland Cement Manufacturers Ltd*[71] the defendant landowners allowed children to play on their land situated adjacent to a highway. During a game of football the ball was kicked over a small fence on to the highway. The husband of the plaintiff was killed as a result of avoiding the ball:

---

69 *Whitehouse v Jordan* [1981] 1 All ER 267 HL; *Phillips v Whiteley Ltd* [1938] 1 All ER 566; *Roe v Ministry of Health* [1954] 2 QB 661; *Nettleship v Weston* [1971] 3 All ER 581.
70 *McHale v Watson* (1966) 115 CLR 199.
71 [1961] 1 WLR 1434.

Hilder v Associated Portland Cement Manufacturers Ltd [1961] 1 WLR 1434

Ashworth J: In my judgment, a reasonable man would come to the conclusion that there was a risk of damage to persons using the road and that risk was not so small that he could safely disregard it. While it is true that a football itself is unlikely to damage a person or vehicle on the road in the way that might occur with a cricket ball or a golf ball, I think that the sudden appearance of a football in front of a cyclist or motor-cyclist is quite likely to cause him to fall or to swerve into the path of another vehicle and in either event sustain serious injury . . . Accordingly, I find that the defendants failed to take reasonable care in all the circumstances and that this failure unhappily caused the death of the deceased. The claim in negligence therefore succeeds.[72]

It can be seen that it is often difficult to predict when liability will be imposed: *Bolton* and *Hilder* are difficult to distinguish. No reference is made in *Hilder* to the frequency with which the football left the field. It may well be that the reasonable man, with the knowledge that it is one of the objectives of the game of cricket to hit the ball off the playing field, may conclude that *Bolton* posed a greater risk than *Hilder*. The next extract is from *Overseas Tankship (UK) Ltd v Miller SS Co Pty*,[73] commonly known as *The Wagon Mound (No 2)*. This is not a sport case but is the leading case in this area, where Lord Reid made it clear that just because likelihood is remote does not mean that one has carte blanche to ignore it:

Overseas Tankship (UK) Ltd Miller SS Co Pty

Lord Reid: It does not follow that, no matter what the circumstances may be, it is justifiable to neglect a risk of such a small magnitude. A reasonable man would only neglect such a risk if he had some valid reason for doing so, e.g. that it would involve considerable expense to eliminate the risk. He would weigh the risk against the difficulty of eliminating it. If the activity which caused the injury to Miss Stone had been an unlawful activity there can be little doubt but that *Bolton v Stone* would have been decided differently. In their Lordships' judgment *Bolton v Stone* did not alter the general principle that a person must be regarded as negligent if he does not take steps to eliminate a risk which he knows or ought to know is a real risk and not a mere possibility which would never influence the mind of a reasonable man. What that decision did was to recognise and give effect to the qualification that it is justifiable not to take steps to eliminate a real risk if it is small and if the circumstances are such that a reasonable man, careful of the safety of his neighbour, would think it right to neglect it.[74]

It would seem that foreseeability and likelihood are part of a larger equation. Whereas the ground owner may be justified in ignoring a foreseeable risk of a rare occurrence if the outcome would cause limited damage, he may not be at liberty to ignore the same risk if the possible outcome is more serious. Does the law adequately protect the likes of Miss Stone? It is important to note that, in *Bolton*, Lord Reid was of the opinion that the cost of remedial measures should not be taken into account when considering the standard of duty owed by the ground owners; however, in *The Wagon Mound (No 2)* he appeared to conclude that the cost of prevention was a factor to be considered. It would be judicious for stadium owners to take all low-cost safety precautions.

In the above cases liability centred on the tort of negligence; however, as the courts have stated, the likelihood of someone being injured is remote. Most wayward tee shots or six-hits will injure

---

72 Ibid, p 1438.
73 Privy Council [1966] 2 All ER 709.
74 Ibid, p 718.

no one. However, for people dwelling beside stadiums and grounds the fear of damage to person and property can undermine the enjoyment of that property. In *Miller v Jackson*[75] the defendant cricket club had played cricket on a small ground for many years. A small housing estate was built on land abutting the cricket field so that, despite there being a boundary fence, some balls were bound to be hit into the houses or their gardens. The plaintiffs sued in nuisance and negligence in respect of cricket balls being hit into their garden:

Miller v Jackson

Geoffrey Lane LJ: . . . have the plaintiffs established that the defendants are guilty of nuisance or negligence as alleged? The evidence . . . makes it clear that the risk of injury to property at least was both foreseeable and foreseen. It is obvious that such injury is going to take place so long as cricket is being played on this field . . . It is true that the risk must be balanced against the measures which are necessary to eliminate it and against what the defendants can do to prevent accidents from happening . . . In the present case, so far from being one incident of an unprecedented nature about which complaint is being made, this is a series of incidents or perhaps a continuing failure to prevent incidents from happening, coupled with the certainty that they are going to happen again. The risk of injury to person and property is so great that on each occasion when a ball comes over the fence and causes damage to the plaintiffs, the defendants are guilty of negligence.

In circumstances such as these it is very difficult and probably unnecessary, except as an interesting intellectual exercise, to define the frontiers between negligence and nuisance: see Lord Wilberforce in *Goldman v Hargrave*.

Was there here a use by the defendants of their land involving an unreasonable interference with the plaintiffs' enjoyment of their land? There is here in effect no dispute that there has been and is likely to be in the future an interference with the plaintiffs' enjoyment of No 20 Brackenridge. The only question is whether it is unreasonable. It is a truism to say that this is a matter of degree. What that means is this. A balance has to be maintained between on the one hand the rights of the individual to enjoy his house and garden without the threat of damage and on the other hand the rights of the public in general or a neighbour to engage in lawful pastimes. Difficult questions may sometimes arise when the defendants' activities are offensive to the senses, for example, by way of noise. Where, as here, the damage or potential damage is physical the answer is more simple. There is, subject to what appears hereafter, no excuse I can see which exonerates the defendants from liability in nuisance for what they have done or from what they threaten to do. It is true that no one has yet been physically injured. That is probably due to a great extent to the fact that the householders in Brackenridge desert their gardens while cricket is in progress. The danger of injury is obvious and is not slight enough to be disregarded. There is here a real risk of serious injury.

There is, however, one obviously strong point in the defendants' favour. They or their predecessors have been playing cricket on this ground (and no doubt hitting sixes out of it) for 70 years or so. Can someone, by building a house on the edge of the field in circumstances where it must have been obvious that balls might be hit over the fence, effectively stop cricket being played? Precedent apart, justice would seem to demand that the plaintiffs should be left to make the most of the site they have elected to occupy with all its obvious advantages and all its equally obvious disadvantages. It is pleasant to have an open space over which to look from your bedroom and sitting room windows, so far as it is possible to see over the concrete wall. Why should you complain of the obvious disadvantages which arise from the particular purpose

---

75 [1977] 3 All ER 338 CA.

to which the open space is being put? Put briefly, can the defendants take advantage of the fact that the plaintiffs have put themselves in such a position by coming to occupy a house on the edge of a small cricket field, with the result that what was not a nuisance in the past now becomes a nuisance? If the matter were *res integra*, I confess I should be inclined to find for the defendants. It does not seem just that a long-established activity – in itself innocuous – should be brought to an end because someone chooses to build a house nearby and so turn an innocent pastime into an actionable nuisance. Unfortunately, however, the question is not open. In *Sturges v Bridgman* this very problem arose . . . That decision involved the assumption, which so far as one can discover has never been questioned, that it is no answer to a claim in nuisance for the defendant to show that the plaintiff brought the trouble on his own head by building or coming to live in a house so close to the defendant's premises that he would inevitably be affected by the defendant's activities, where no one had been affected previously: see also *Bliss v Hall*. It may be that this rule works injustice; it may be that one would decide the matter differently in the absence of authority. But we are bound by the decision in *Sturges v Bridgman*; it is not for this court as I see it to alter a rule which stood for so long.

Lord Denning MR: (dissenting): In support of the case, the plaintiffs rely on the dictum of Lord Reid in *Bolton v Stone*: 'If cricket cannot be played on a ground without creating a substantial risk, then it should not be played there at all.' I would agree with that saying if the houses or road were there first and the cricket ground came there second. We would not allow the garden of Lincoln's Inn to be turned into a cricket ground. It would be too dangerous for windows and people. But I would not agree with Lord Reid's dictum when the cricket ground has been there for 70 years and the houses are newly built at the very edge of it. I recognise that the cricket club are under a duty to use all reasonable care consistent with the playing of the game of cricket but I do not think the cricket club can be expected to give up the game of cricket altogether. After all they have their rights in their cricket ground. They have spent money, labour and love in the making of it: and they have the right to play upon it as they have done for 70 years. Is this all to be rendered useless to them by the thoughtless and selfish act of an estate developer in building right up to the edge of it? Can the developer or a purchaser of the house say to the cricket club: 'Stop playing. Clear out.' I do not think so . . .

. . . I would, therefore, adopt this test. Is the use by the cricket club of this ground for playing cricket a reasonable use of it? To my mind it is a most reasonable use. Just consider the circumstances. For over 70 years the game of cricket has been played on this ground to the great benefit of the community as a whole and to the injury of none. No one could suggest that it was a nuisance to the neighbouring owners simply because an enthusiastic batsman occasionally hit a ball out of the ground for six to the approval of the admiring onlookers. Then I would ask: does it suddenly become a nuisance because one of the neighbours chooses to build a house on the very edge of the ground in such a position that it may well be struck by the ball on the rare occasion when there is a hit for six? To my mind the answer is plainly No. The building of the house does not convert the playing of cricket into a nuisance when it was not so before. If and in so far as any damage is caused to the house or anyone in it, it is because of the position in which it was built. Suppose that the house had not been built by a developer but by a private owner. He would be in much the same position as the farmer who previously put his cows in the field. He could not complain if a batsman hit a six out of the ground and by a million to one chance it struck a cow or even the farmer himself. He would be in no better position than a spectator at Lord's or the Oval or at a motor rally. At any rate, even if he could claim damages for the loss of the cow or the injury, he could not get an injunction to stop the cricket. If the private owner could not get an injunction, neither should a developer or a purchaser from him . . .

. . . In this case it is our task to balance the right of the cricket club to continue playing cricket on their cricket ground as against the right of the householder not to be interfered with.

On taking the balance, I would give priority to the right of the cricket club to continue playing cricket on the ground, as they have done for the last 70 years. It takes precedence over the right of the newcomer to sit in his garden undisturbed. After all, he bought the house four years ago in mid-summer when the cricket season was at its height. He might have guessed that there was a risk that a hit for six might possibly land on his property. If he finds that he does not like it, he ought, when cricket is played, to sit on the other side of the house or in the front garden or go out: or take advantage of the offers the club have made to him of fitting unbreakable glass and so forth. Or if he does not like that, he ought to sell his house and move elsewhere. I expect there are many who would gladly buy it in order to be near the cricket field and open space. At any rate he ought not to be allowed to stop cricket being played on this ground.

This case is new. It should be approached on principles applicable to modern conditions. There is a contest here between the interest of the public at large; and the interest of a private individual. The public interest lies in protecting the environment by preserving our playing fields in the face of mounting development and by enabling our youth to enjoy all the benefits of outdoor games, such as cricket and football. The private interest lies in securing the privacy of his home and garden without intrusion or interference by anyone. In deciding between these two conflicting interests, it must be remembered that it is not a question of damages. If by a million to one chance a cricket ball does go out of the ground and cause damage, the cricket club will pay. There is no difficulty on that score. No, it is a question of an injunction. And in our law you will find it repeatedly affirmed that an injunction is a discretionary remedy. In a new situation like this, we have to think afresh as to how discretion should be exercised. On the one hand, Mrs Miller is a very sensitive lady who has worked herself up into such a state that she exclaimed to the judge: 'I just want to be allowed to live in peace ... have I got to wait until someone is killed before anything can be done?' If she feels like that about it, it is quite plain that, for peace in the future, one or other has to move. Either the cricket club has to move: but goodness knows where. I do not suppose for a moment there is any field in Lintz to which they could move. Or Mrs Miller must move elsewhere. As between their conflicting interests, I am of opinion that the public interest should prevail over the private interest. The cricket club should not be driven out. In my opinion the right exercise of discretion is to refuse an injunction; and, of course, to refuse damages in lieu of an injunction. Likewise as to the claim for past damages. The club were entitled to use this ground for cricket in the accustomed way. It was not a nuisance, nor was it negligent of them so to run it, nor was the batsman negligent when he hit the ball for six. All were doing simply what they were entitled to do. So if the club had put it to the test, I would have dismissed the claim for damages also. But as the club very fairly say that they are willing to pay for any damage, I am content that there should be an award of £400 to cover any past or future damage. I would allow the appeal, accordingly.[76]

The judgments given by the Court of Appeal have tended to muddy these waters rather than clear them.[77] The two issues at stake were whether there was liability in negligence or nuisance by the cricket club in allowing balls to be struck regularly into neighbouring gardens, and if there was liability, what would be an appropriate remedy? On the second issue the appellant sought an injunction: a discretionary remedy to prevent recurrence of the tortious act. They had been offered compensation by the club, which was also prepared to undertake preventative measures such as the installation of safety glass. A fence had already been erected and expert advice had suggested weather conditions would make a higher fence unviable. However, damages would be

---

76 Ibid, p 342.
77 See Parpworth, N, 'Lord Denning and the "Other Cricket Ball Case" ' (1994) 2(2) Sport and the Law Journal 4 and 'A further cricket ball case: *Lacey v Parker and Bingle*' (1994) 2(3) Sport and the Law Journal 9.

unsatisfactory in these circumstances. What the appellant wanted was an end to the nuisance of cricket balls landing in her garden.

Geoffrey Lane and Cumming-Bruce LJJ thought that there was liability on the part of the cricket club; Lord Denning MR thought not. Geoffrey Lane LJ was prepared to grant an injunction – Lord Denning MR and Cumming-Bruce LJ were not. The public interest, thought Geoffrey Lane LJ, could not be put before the rights of individuals to quiet enjoyment of their land. Lord Denning, on the other hand, thought that the public interest was such a vital consideration that it made the playing of cricket and the inevitable six-hits into neighbouring gardens a reasonable activity that did not therefore attract liability in the first place. Cumming-Bruce LJ did not invoke the public interest to deny liability but considered it a factor in his refusal to grant an injunction. Geoffrey Lane LJ, whilst sympathetic toward the respondents' argument that the club had existed long before the housing estate was built, felt bound by precedent to disregard this consideration whereas the fact that the appellant had come to the nuisance appeared to be an important factor in Lord Denning MR's denial of liability. Cumming-Bruce LJ, appearing to take a middle line, felt that coming to the nuisance was an important factor in refusing the injunction.

Some of the issues that had concerned the Court of Appeal in *Miller* resurfaced in a different guise in *Kennaway v Thompson*.[78] Here the plaintiff lived in a house next to a lake on which there were water sports. The club had begun racing on the lake some ten years before the plaintiff built and occupied her house adjoining the lake. She had always lived in the vicinity and had inherited the land from her father. Over the years immediately prior to and after this the use of the lake and the noise level increased considerably. In the Court of Appeal the defendants, a motor boat racing club, accepted that some of their activities caused a nuisance. The judge had awarded damages but refused an injunction. The Court of Appeal granted an injunction and applied the principle in *Shelfer v City of London Electric Lighting Co*:[79]

Kennaway v Thompson

Lawton LJ: Our task has been to decide on a form of order which will protect the plaintiff from the noise which the judge found to be intolerable but which will not stop the club from organising activities about which she cannot reasonably complain.

When she decided to build a house alongside Mallam Water she knew that some motor boat racing and water skiing was done on the club's water and she thought that the noise which such activities created was tolerable. She cannot now complain about that kind of noise provided it does not increase in volume by reason of any increase in activities. The intolerable noise is mostly caused by the large boats; it is these which attract the public interest.

Now nearly all of us living in these islands have to put up with a certain amount of annoyance from our neighbours. Those living in towns may be irritated by their neighbours' noisy radios or incompetent playing of musical instruments; and they in turn may be inconvenienced by the noise caused by our guests slamming car doors and chattering after a late party. Even in the country the lowing of a sick cow or the early morning crowing of a farmyard cock may interfere with sleep and comfort. Intervention by injunction is only justified when the irritating noise causes inconvenience beyond what other occupiers in the neighbourhood can be expected to bear. The question is whether the neighbour is using his property reasonably, having regard to the fact that he has a neighbour. The neighbour who is complaining must remember, too, that the other man can use his property in a reasonable way and there must be a measure of 'give and take, live and let live'.

---

78 [1981] QB 88 CA.
79 [1895] 1 Ch 287.

Understandably the plaintiff finds intolerable the kind of noise which she has had to suffer for such long periods in the past; but if she knew that she would only have to put up with such noise on a few occasions between the end of March and the beginning of November each year and she also knew when those occasions were likely to occur, she could make arrangements to be out of her house at the material times. We can see no reason, however, why she should have to absent herself from her house for many days so as to enable the club members and others to make noises which are a nuisance. We consider it probable that those who are interested in motor boat racing are attracted by the international and national events, which tend to have the larger and noisier boats. Justice will be done, we think, if the club is allowed to have, each racing season, one international event extending over three days, the first day being given over to practice and the second and third to racing, In addition there can be two national events, each of two days but separated from the international event and from each other by at least four weeks. Finally there can be three club events, each of one day, separated from the international and national events and each other by three weeks. Any international or national event not held can be replaced by a club event of one day. No boats creating a noise of more than 75 decibels are to be used on the club's water at any time other than when there are events as specified in this judgment. If events are held at weekends, as they probably will be, six weekends, covering a total of ten days, will be available for motor boat racing on the club's water. Water skiing, if too many boats are used, can cause a nuisance by noise. The club is not to allow more than six motor boats to be used for water skiing at any one time. An injunction will be granted to restrain motor boat racing, water skiing and the use of boats creating a noise of more than 75 decibels on the club's water save to the extent and in the circumstances indicated.[80]

As Lawton LJ stated, actions of this kind depend to a degree on the reasonableness of the activities undertaken: it is a matter of give and take. The facts of *Kennaway* lend themselves more readily to a give and take solution than *Miller*. In *Kennaway* the club admitted that the extra activity of recent years amounted to a nuisance, so liability was less of an issue than the appropriate remedy. The plaintiff had, in a sense, come to the nuisance for although she had lived in the area all her life, the land beside the lake on which she now lived had been inherited from her father approximately ten years after the club had commenced activities on the lake. The court was able to reach a compromise solution therefore by granting the injunction to limit activities above and beyond that which the plaintiff was deemed to have accepted as normal when coming to the lake. This logic would not have been easy to apply in *Miller*. It would not have been possible to grant an injunction limiting the number of sixes every season. It could be argued that the courts have reached a level on consistency by granting an injunction only where the level of activity extends beyond what the claimant is deemed to have accepted in coming to the nuisance.

In *Tetley v Chitty*[81] the local authority had granted permission to a go-karting club to use land in a residential housing area. McNeill J held that the noise generated by go-karting activities was an ordinary and natural consequence of the operation of go-karts on the council's land. In the same way as it would be difficult to play cricket without hitting sixes it would be difficult to run a go-karting club without noise. The difference, however, would lie in the frequency of the nuisance. McNeill J granted an injunction against the local authority's allowing use of the land for the purpose which gave rise to a nuisance, effectively terminating the activity in that area.[82]

It is important to note that the local authority, as landlord, was liable for allowing the nuisance committed by its tenants. McNeill J cited the headnote from *White v Jameson*,[83] which states: 'Where

---

80 [1981] QB 88 CA, at p 332.
81 [1986] 1 All ER 663.
82 Also note *Stretch v Romford FC* (1971) 115 Sol Jo 7461.
83 (1874) LR 18 Eq 303.

the occupier of lands grants a licence to another to do certain acts on the land and the licensee in doing them commits a nuisance, the occupier may be made a defendant to the suit to restrain the nuisance.' The owners of sporting stadiums will not avoid liability merely because they are not legally the party controlling the sporting function.

Spectators

Legal issues involving spectators are likely to fall into one of three categories. The first but least frequent occurrence would be an injury caused by the overspill of occurrences taking place on the pitch. The second is an injury caused by the stadium itself. This would cover both defective premises and faulty safety procedures. The third category is injuries inflicted by other spectators.

One need only consider the clamour for tickets at major sporting events to appreciate that two of the most important reasons for attending certain sporting functions are the intensity and importance of the competition. This is particularly so of top-level professional sport, where the participants are performing to the maximum of their endeavours. Such extremes of performance, if misjudged, can result in balls, pucks, cars and even the participants themselves coming into contact with spectators.

An early case that examined the issue of liability was *Hall v Brooklands Auto Racing Club*.[84] Brooklands owned a two-mile oval racing track which held regular races. Spectators paid to gain access to the track and were provided with stands from which they could view. The racetrack itself was partitioned from the spectators by railings and spectators preferred to stand just outside the railings rather than sit in the stands. During one long-distance race two of the competing cars touched, causing one of them to be catapulted into the railings. Two spectators were killed and many others injured. The Court of Appeal allowed an appeal against the findings of a special jury at first instance that the club had failed to provide adequate safety facilities:

Hall v Brooklands Auto Racing Club

Greer LJ: In my judgment both parties must have intended that the person paying for his licence to see a cricket match or a race, takes upon himself the risk of unlikely and improbable accidents, provided that there has not been on the part of the occupier a failure to take reasonable precautions. I do not think it can be said that the content of the contract made with every person who takes a ticket is different. I think it must be the same and it must be judged by what any reasonable member of the public must have intended should be the term of the contract. The person concerned is sometimes described as 'the man in the street' or 'the man in the Clapham omnibus' . . . Such a man taking a ticket to see a cricket match at Lord's would know quite well that he was not going to be encased in a steel frame which would protect him from the one in a million chance of a cricket ball dropping on his head. In the same way, the same man taking a ticket to see the Derby would know quite well that there would be no provision to prevent a horse which got out of hand from getting amongst the spectators and would quite understand that he himself was bearing the risk of such a possible but improbable accident happening to himself. In my opinion, in the same way such a man taking a ticket to see motor races would know quite well that no barrier would be provided which would be sufficient to protect him in the possible but highly improbable event of a car charging the barrier and getting through to the spectators.[85]

---

84 [1933] 1 KB 205.
85 Ibid, p 223.

It is interesting to note that the cause of action in this instance was breach of contract with the club in breach of an implied term to ensure that the spectators were safe. Greer LJ held that there was an implied term whereby the plaintiff agreed to take the risk of this kind of accident occurring.[86] Today such an action would be brought in negligence (an area of law that has developed considerably since 1933) or under the Occupiers' Liability Act 1957, rather than in contract.

The principle enunciated in *Hall v Brooklands Auto Racing Club* was applied in *Murray and Another v Harringay Arena Ltd*.[87] There a six-year-old spectator was injured by a puck hit out of the playing area during an ice hockey match. The Court of Appeal held that the defendants, by installing nets at both ends of the rink only, had satisfied their duty in that the limited netting was in conformity with other ice hockey rinks. The child's injury, as a result of something incidental to the game, was held to be a risk the spectator accepted. Again this case was decided on contractual grounds with the two competing implied terms, first that it was implied into the contract that the occupier would take reasonable precautions to ensure safety and secondly that there was an implied term whereby the visitor would accept all risks beyond what was reasonable for the occupier to protect against. Singleton LJ commented: 'It may strike one as a little hard that this should apply in the case of a six-year-old boy'[88] but considered it right that the implied term should be consistently applied. This works with contractual matters but gives rise to difficulties in negligence, where the courts are more inclined to allocate culpability by contributory negligence rather than to deny any recovery on the grounds that the plaintiff had accepted the risk. This is an important legal distinction. The concept of contributory negligence allows the court to find liability and apportion culpability. However, if the plaintiff has accepted the risk, the concept of *volenti non fit injuria*, then there is no liability and the defendant escapes entirely.

This issue was clarified in *Wooldridge v Sumner*[89] where the plaintiff, an official photographer, was injured at a horse show when a horse being galloped around the arena went out of control, plunged through a bordered area and struck him. The facts differed materially from the above cases in two ways. First, the plaintiff was not a paying spectator, which meant that the issue could not be resolved in terms of implied contractual terms. Secondly, it was acknowledged that no fault could be attributed to the occupiers of the arena and so the action was brought against the owners of the horse through the negligence of their servant, the rider.

One of the issues raised by the defendants was *volenti*: that the plaintiff had volunteered to accept the inherent risk of injury. This would seem to be compatible with the earlier plaintiff's implied contractual term to assume the risk. However, *volenti* is a defence to negligence and implies that a *prima facie* case of negligence has been established. Under the old contractual actions, liability had always been denied on the basis that there had not been a breach of contract by the defendant in the first place. One of the problems facing the court was whether liability was to be denied on the basis that there was no *prima facie* negligence or whether there was *prima facie* negligence but with the successful defence of *volenti*. Sellers LJ considered the plaintiff's claim that the horse had been ridden too fast:

Wooldridge v Sumner

Sellers LJ: In my opinion 'too fast' in these circumstances would only be an error of judgment of a highly competent rider all out to succeed. It is no doubt a misfortune for a skilled batsman to be bowled or caught in a supreme effort to hit a six. It is also a misfortune if, on the other hand, he succeeds in hitting a six and the ball hits someone over the boundary. The

---

86 Ibid, p 224.
87 [1951] 2 KB 529.
88 Ibid, p 536.
89 [1963] 2 QB 43.

three-quarter who dives at speed over the line for a try at Twickenham or on occasions at Wembley or the opponent who dives into a tackle to prevent a try may and sometimes does roll over and come into heavy contact with the surrounding barrier, sometimes to his own hurt and to the possible injury of an adjacent spectator. No court or jury would, I think, condemn such endeavour as negligent.[90]

On the issue of *volenti* he continued:

In my opinion a competitor or player cannot in the normal case at least of competition or game rely on the maxim *volenti non fit injuria* in answer to a spectator's claim, for there is no liability unless there is negligence and the spectator comes to witness skill and with the expectation that it will be exercised. But provided the competition or game is being performed within the rules and the requirement of the sport and by a person of adequate skill and competence the spectator does not expect his safety to be regarded by the participant.[91]

It would appear that *volenti* is unlikely ever to feature in sports spectator injury cases as legal issues would revolve around the establishment of negligence rather than defences to negligence. The spectator struck by a puck, ball or car, as long as it was done as an accepted part of the game, is subject to a lower standard of duty owed by the plaintiff and will have impliedly accepted that lower standard.

At the other end of the spectrum, incidents where spectators are injured as a result of deliberate actions outside of the rules of the game will be subject to both the criminal and civil law. The infamous incident of Eric Cantona kicking a spectator, following his dismissal during Manchester United's FA Cup match against Crystal Palace FC at Selhurst Park in 1995, resulted in a criminal conviction for assault.[92]

It is in between these two extremes that the law is a little less clear. When will the actions of the participant fall below this lower standard of duty?

Wooldridge v Sumner

Sellers LJ: If the conduct is deliberately intended to injure someone whose presence is known or is reckless and in disregard of all safety of others so that it is a departure from the standards which might reasonably be expected in anyone pursuing the competition or game, then the performer might well be held liable for any injury his act might cause. There would, I think, be a difference, for instance, in assessing blame which is actionable between an injury caused by a tennis ball hit or a racket accidentally thrown in the course of play into the spectators at Wimbledon and a ball hit or a racket thrown into the stands in temper or annoyance when play was not in progress.[93]

The majority view of the Court of Appeal in *Wooldridge* was that there would be no breach of duty if the defendant had taken 'reasonable care in all the circumstances'.[94]

It might appear that there would be no remedy even to a spectator who deliberately positions himself in such a place in a cricket ground that only a totally mis-hit six could cause him harm because, as Diplock LJ stated in *Wooldridge*, 'the duty which [the participant] owes is a duty of care,

---

90 Ibid, p 53.
91 Ibid, p 56.
92 Gardiner, S, ' "Ooh Ah Cantona": racism as hate speech' (1996) 23 CMJ 23.
93 [1963] 2 QB 43, at 57.
94 Note also *Caldwell v Maguire* [2001] All ER (D) 363 with disapproval of 'reckless disregard' test.

not a duty of skill'.[95] He continued, 'It may well be that a participant in a game or competition would be guilty of negligence to a spectator if he took part in it when he knew or ought to have known that his lack of skill was such that even if he exerted to the utmost he was likely to cause injury to a spectator watching him.' It would seem that the injudiciously located spectator struck by a mis-hit six from an England international would be unsuccessful in his action but the same spectator struck by a similarly mis-hit six from an incompetent cricketer, unable to do any better, may well be successful.

Sellers LJ's notion of actions within the rules of the game also causes problems. Singleton LJ in *Murray* spoke of the breach of ice hockey rules of a participant who deliberately hits the puck out of the rink when pressed and the two-minute penalty it invoked but did not seem to consider it negligent.

Crowd Management

The issues of crowd management and crowd disturbances have been responsible for more debate, media coverage, parliamentary time and official reports than any other stadium safety issue. Indeed, an analysis of official reports has shown a concerning trend to amalgamate these issues when, in fact, they are quite separate sporting problems. It is ironic that the introduction of all-seater stadiums, arguably the most important factor in reducing crowd disturbances in recent years, was recommended by the Taylor Report into the Hillsborough Disaster where hooliganism was not a major issue.

Although it has often been said that crowd control is the responsibility of the clubs and their stewards, it has equally been acknowledged that, in many instances, the police do assume *de facto* control as part of their policing duties. This debate as to the role of the police in crowd management formed an important part of the Taylor Report considered later. In *Harris v Sheffield United Football Club*[96] the club argued that by fulfilling their policing duties the police were doing no more than was required of them under their public duty and the club were not liable to pay for 'special police services' under s 15(1) of the Police Act 1964. In the High Court, Boreham J considered the extent of the police's duty:

Harris v Sheffield United Football Club

Boreham J: . . . the police were not discharging their own duty to the public; they were in fact discharging the club's duties to the spectators whom the club invited to the ground. The club chose to invite large numbers to their private premises; it was the club's duty to provide for their safety, health and comfort. They could have employed a security firm as banks and others have to do to protect their interests; they chose to request the police to perform those duties knowing that the police expected payment . . . the police within the ground provided services which it was not within the scope of their public duty to perform. For instance, they assisted in crowd management and in the enforcement of such ground regulations as refused entry to those who tried to enter without paying or prohibited spectators encroaching on parts of the ground which their entry fee did not entitle them to enter. It may be . . . that the maintenance of law and order was the predominant aim but there were other services performed.[97]

---

95 Op. cit., fn 93, *Wooldridge v Sumner*.
96 [1987] 2 All ER 838.
97 Unreported: QBD 26 March 1986.

The Court of Appeal did not examine this issue to the extent of Boreham J but in rejecting the club's arguments Neill LJ did say:

> The club has responsibilities which are owed not only to its employees and the spectators who attend but also to the football authorities to take all reasonable steps to ensure that the game takes place in conditions which do not occasion danger to any person or property. The attendance of the police is necessary to assist the club in the fulfilment of this duty.[98]

Participants

Whilst intra-spectator violence has become a familiar if unacceptable sight at many large sporting occasions, spectator violence towards players is relatively rare. Being within touching distance of sporting heroes remains an intimacy that many other nations have relinquished. It is precisely in order to protect this intimacy at sports events that laws have been introduced to outlaw racist chanting, the throwing of missiles, running on to the playing area and being drunk at certain sporting occasions. What is most likely to change the relationship between player and spectator would be successful legal action brought by players against the owners of sporting venues. The more frequent the attacks on players the more likely that courts will be prepared to conclude that stadium owners are negligent by ignoring a foreseeable risk to players' safety.

Player safety is recognised by the sports governing bodies as highly important and these sports have developed standard protective clothing and other safety measures to ensure that players remain safe. Injuries caused by faults in the stadium or playing area, because they are much rarer, attract less attention. In professional rugby union, the lower parts of rugby posts are padded but often collisions with the stadium are considered to be a risk the players must accept. With top sportsmen's careers being increasingly well paid but brief, players may feel more inclined to pursue claims for injuries of this nature more energetically. There is no legal reason why a player should not bring an action against the ground-owner, club or governing body for injuries sustained as a result of a frozen pitch or a slippery surface.

The Occupiers' Liability Act 1957 places such a duty on the occupiers of premises to all visitors. This would cover all participants irrespective of whether they were 'home' or 'away' players. The limitations of these provisions were exposed in *Sims v Leigh Rugby Club*.[99] The plaintiff was a winger for Oldham Football Club and was involved in an 'away' rugby league match against Leigh. In attempting to score a try, the plaintiff was bundled over the touchline which, he alleged, resulted in his colliding with a concrete wall more than seven feet from the touchline. The plaintiff sustained a broken leg and brought an action against the 'home' club for a breach of their duty under the Occupiers' Liability Act 1957. Wrangham J in the High Court rejected the plaintiff's claim because, on the balance of probabilities, the injuries were sustained as a result of the tackle rather than the collision with the wall. Comments made *obiter* should be of great interest to all stadium occupiers and the standard of duty required of them under the Act:

Sims v Leigh Rugby Club

Wrangham J: Now what did the defendant actually do? The answer to that is, it provided a playing field which complied in all respects so far as the evidence goes with the requirements of the governing body of the game. The governing body of the game is the Rugby Football League and that league directs through a council which consists of representatives of each club. They have made (I do not know when) bylaws which govern the layout of the playing fields

---

98 [1987] 2 All ER 838, 847.
99 [1969] 2 All ER 923.

which clubs are to provide for the games they play. One of those rules is that there shall be a distance of not less than seven feet from the outside of the touch line to the ringside. This concrete post was seven feet three inches from the touch line. Therefore it complied with the bylaw of the governing body of the game. Nevertheless, it is said that the defendant, which I suspect operates through a committee, ought to have been wiser than the governing body of this game and ought to have said to itself: 'although the governing body consider the barrier between the playing pitch and the spectator's area may be as near the touch line as seven feet, we think it ought to be much further off and therefore we will set our barrier not at seven feet but much further away.' And it is said that the defendant ought to have assumed this greater wisdom although it had not got one jot or one tittle of evidence to support its opinion, because it is common ground that a serious accident arising from the too great proximity of the barrier to the touch line has not been known at all. No one has been able to assist me with evidence of a single case arising from a barrier being too close to the touch line. It is true that on quite a number of occasions players have stopped themselves at the barrier; they have run into the barrier in that sense and only just stopped themselves at it, perhaps even had to hurdle the barrier because they were running so fast that they could not stop themselves in time. But no one has suggested that, apart from this unfortunate accident, a single accident has been caused in this way. So that it amounts to this, that it is said that the defendant was unreasonable because it did not set up its opinion against that of the governing body of the sport, although such evidence as there was entirely supported the view of the governing body of the sport. I think that is wholly unreasonable criticism to make of the defendant.[100]

Even if his Lordship had been convinced of the breach of duty, the plaintiff would still have fallen at the final hurdle:

The matter perhaps does not quite stop there, for by s 2(5) of the Occupiers' Liability Act 1957 it is provided that a duty of care does not impose on an occupier any obligation to a visitor in respect of risk willingly accepted by the visitor. Now, it is not in dispute, of course, that anyone who accepts employment as a professional footballer by a club playing under the rules of the Rugby Football League willingly accepts the risk of playing football, risks which are by no means small because it is a game involving great physical effort by one side and the other. It seems to me that a footballer does not merely accept the risks imposed by contract with the players on the other side. He willingly accepts all the risks of playing a game on such a playing field as complies with the bylaws laid down by the governing body of the game. I am sure that footballers who go to the Leigh ground, go to that ground willingly accepting the risks that arise from playing the game under the rules of the league, on a ground approved by the league.[101]

Thus it would appear that liability revolves around compliance with the rules of the governing body of the sport. In the unlikely event that the court considers the standards of the governing body to be inadequate, the participant will still be held to have accepted the risks inherent in the stadium. The conclusion reached by the judge, that accidents involving collisions with partitions, walls or advertising hoardings are extremely rare, is nonsensical.[102] Keen observers of cricket, rugby union, rugby league, football, boxing or basketball will be all too familiar with the image of participants crashing into hoardings etc. after leaving the arena of play. It is suggested that Wrangham J's approach of considering injuries in rugby league is too narrow. Racing driver Ayrton Senna's death

---

100 [1969] 2 All ER 923, pp 926–27.
101 Ibid, p 927.
102 See the contradictory comments of Sellers LJ in *Wooldridge v Sumner* [1963] 2 QB 43, 53.

when he crashed into a tyre wall at the 1994 San Marino Grand Prix at Imola serves to highlight the importance of boundary walls and fences and the danger to sportsmen should they prove inadequate. Although injuries of this kind may be rare, they are nevertheless frequent enough to put occupiers on notice that injuries are more than an unlikely eventuality.

The judgment assumes that standards set by governing bodies are adequate. In this instance, seven feet may well have been a reasonable distance, but to assume as much is an abdication of the responsibilities of the court. Equally, the judgment is of little use to the providers of recreational sporting facilities whose standards would not be governed by sporting bodies. In order for the law to be comprehensive, courts would need to start with the rebuttable presumption that, confronted with an injured participant, safety measures were inadequate.

Even if the plaintiff managed to overcome this hurdle he would still be faced with the view that, in continuing with his participation, he had accepted the risks of playing in an arena in conformity with the rules of the governing body. This is not broad enough to encompass the problems encountered by the recreational sportsman who is entitled to assume that adequate measures have been taken to ensure his safety.

On a professional sporting level, the judgment fails to take into account the sportsman as employee. Faced with an ultimatum of play or dismissal many professional sportsmen, reluctantly, may decide to continue. The courts have often acknowledged this imbalance of power in the contracting relationship between employer and employee and, it is submitted, the judge was wrong in the circumstances to conclude that the plaintiff had 'willingly' accepted the risk.

A potential source of liability in instances such as *Sims*, but which was not raised in that case, is the employer's statutory duty under the Health and Safety at Work Act 1974:

Health and Safety at Work Act 1974

2. *General duties of employers to their employees*
   (1) It shall be the duty of every employer to ensure, so far as it is reasonably practicable, the health, safety and welfare at work of all his employees.
   (2) Without prejudice to the generality of an employer's duty under the preceding subsection, the matters to which the duty extends include in particular –
      (a) the provision and maintenance of plant and systems of work that are, so far as is reasonably practicable, safe and without risks to health;
      (b) the provision and maintenance of a working environment for his employees that is, so far as is reasonably practicable, safe, without risks to health and adequate as regards facilities and arrangements for their welfare at work.
3. *General duties of employers and self-employed to persons other than their employees*
   (1) It shall be the duty of every employer to conduct his undertaking in such a way as to ensure, so far as is reasonably practicable, that persons not in his employment who may be affected thereby are not thereby exposed to risks to their health and safety.

Section 2 covers 'home' players while s 3 covers visiting players. Section 2 would also cover home players in actions against their own employers for a failure to provide a safe system of work; although the stadium would not be under the control of the visiting employer, his duty towards his employees is non-delegable. While he may delegate the operation of the system of work he cannot avoid liability should that system prove inadequate.[103]

When a participant is injured their well-being can depend in part on the skill and availability of medical treatment at the stadium. An injured participant who is poorly treated prior to removal

---

103 *McDermid v Nash Dredging Ltd* [1987] AC 906.

to hospital may suffer prolonged rehabilitation, an end to their career, permanent disability or even death. The legal implications of these scenarios are critical. Outside of the sporting context, negligence claims against medical staff tend to hinge on the issue of causation rather than whether they owed a duty; that is, did the lack of emergency treatment or the poor quality of treatment cause the injuries sustained?

In *Hotson v East Berkshire AHA*,[104] Hotson, aged 13, fell from a tree and suffered an acute traumatic fracture of the left femoral epiphysis. He was not correctly treated for five days and suffered avascular necrosis, involving disability of the hip joint and the virtual certainty of osteoarthritis. The health authority admitted negligence. The trial judge assessed at 75 per cent the chance the avascular necrosis would have developed from the fall anyway, and awarded damages based on the loss of a 25 per cent chance of full recovery. The House of Lords allowed the Authority's appeal stating that, on the balance of probabilities, the treatment had not caused the disability. It is clear, therefore, that poor or non-existent medical treatment does not give rise to an action in itself. It is necessary to establish not only a causal link between the treatment or lack of it, and the resulting injury or disability, but that the treatment was a material contributory cause.

The governing body

The issue of the medical provision provided at a facility to an injured participant arose in the case of *Watson v British Boxing Board of Control*.[105] Michael Watson, a professional boxer, sustained head injuries during a WBO world super-middleweight title fight against Chris Eubank. The fight was regulated by the British Boxing Board of Control (BBBC), the sole body controlling professional boxing in the United Kingdom. Watson received medical attention from doctors present at the fight as required by the board and was then taken to hospital where, some half an hour after the end of the fight, he was given resuscitation treatment. He was later transferred to a neurosurgical unit where he underwent surgery. By that time he had suffered permanent brain damage. Watson brought an action in negligence against the BBBC on the basis that the board had failed in its duty both to see that all reasonable steps were taken to ensure that he received immediate and effective medical treatment should he sustain injury in the fight, and by failing to require immediate resuscitation at the ringside which would have prevented him from sustaining permanent brain damage. Lord Phillips MR concluded that the standard of reasonable care required that there should be a resuscitation facility at the ringside, and in failing to require the provision of such a facility the board was in breach of its duty of care to the claimant. His Lordship further concluded that if ringside resuscitation had been available the outcome for the claimant would probably have been significantly better, which was sufficient to establish causation.

It should be noted that this is a decision based very much on its facts and it should not be considered by other governing bodies as what his Lordship described as the 'thin end of the wedge'. Governing bodies, event organisers and facility managers need to assess their duties and responsibilities on an individual basis, adopting the criteria prescribed in the *Watson* case.[106]

The police

The civil actions taken by victims against the police as a result of the Hillsborough disaster gave rise to important legal issues that have had repercussions extending far beyond the context of sport. It was one thing to establish that the police were negligent in their actions but entirely another to

---

104 *Hotson v East Berkshire AHA* [1987] 3 WLR 232.
105 *Watson v British Boxing Board of Control* [2001] QB 1134 CA – for fuller discussion, see Chapter 11 p 000.
106 But note *Wattleworth v Goodwood* [2004] EWHC 140 (QB).

establish that they owed a duty to the 'indirect' victims, that is, those who did not suffer physically as a result of the alleged negligence.

Usually psychiatric injury can only be claimed successfully as an adjunct to physical injury. There are two reasons for this. Firstly, there is the difficulty in substantiating a claim for psychiatric injury. The courts are concerned over the possibility of false claims. Secondly, there was the 'flood-gates' argument: the courts feared that anyone witnessing injury could potentially claim. The importance of this risk has been overemphasised. The courts have always found ways of limiting the scope of such claims with tests of foreseeability and proximity. Their caution is probably attribut-able to a fear of indeterminate liability, that is, where it is not known how many claimants may exist, rather than a fear of a multitude of good claims.

The approach of the courts for secondary victims – those who suffer no physical harm – has been circumspect. Usually, claims will be entertained only from applicants within a close familial proximity to the primary victims:[107] more distant relatives and friends are considered by the courts to have the 'reasonable phlegm'[108] to overcome such a vicissitude. It is a general principle of negli-gence that the injury must have been foreseeable by the defendant.[109] It has been successfully argued that although liability toward the primary victim has been established, liability cannot be extended to secondary victims because such an eventuality could not have been foreseen as a conse-quence of the tortfeasor's action.

Other ways of restricting claims have been to limit them to those who have personally witnessed the shocking scene rather than those told second hand.[110] The requirement that the secondary victim should suffer injury at approximately the same time as the injury to the primary victim has been relaxed following *McLoughlin v O'Brian*.[111] In that case, the plaintiff was informed of a road accident involving her husband and children approximately one hour after the incident. At the hospital, she was told that one child was dead and she saw the other injured members of her family. The House of Lords, relaxing the definition of proximity in time, gave judgment in favour of the plaintiff. Although she had not witnessed the accident, she had come to it in the immediate aftermath and this was sufficient to establish a claim.

Following the Hillsborough disaster, claims were brought by a number of plaintiffs. By the time the cases reached the House of Lords, that number had been reduced to ten. They represented a range of familial relationships. Two were at the ground whilst others saw the horror unfold on television or listened to it on radio. All the appeals failed.

Alcock v Chief Constable of the South Yorkshire Police

Lord Keith: It was argued for the appellants in the present case that reasonable foreseeability of the risk of injury to them in the particular form of psychiatric illness was all that was required to bring home liability to the respondent. In the ordinary sense of direct physical injury suffered in an accident at work or elsewhere, reasonable foreseeability of the risk is indeed the only risk that need be applied to determine liability. But injury by psychiatric illness is more subtle . . . In the present type of case it is a secondary sort of injury brought about by the infliction of physical injury or the risk of physical injury, upon another person. That can affect those closely connected with that person in various ways. One way is by subjecting a close relative to the stress and strain of caring for the injured person over a prolonged period but psychiatric illness due to such stress and strain has not so far been treated as founding a claim in damages. So I am of

---

107 *Page v Smith* [1995] 1 WLR 644.
108 *Alcock v Chief Constable South Yorkshire* [1991] 4 All ER 907. Reported sub nom *Jones v Wright* [1991] 1 All ER 353 per Hidden J, 839c.
109 *The Wagon Mound (No 2)* [1967] 1 AC 617.
110 *Hambrook v Stokes Bros* [1925] 1 KB 141.
111 [1983] AC 410.

the opinion that in addition to reasonable foreseeability liability for injury in the particular form of psychiatric illness must depend in addition upon a prerequisite relationship of proximity between the claimant and the party said to owe the duty.[112]

Their Lordships went on to explain that there were two elements to the concept of proximity: proximity of love and affection and then spatial proximity:

Lord Keith: As regards the class of persons to whom a duty may be owed to take reasonable care to avoid inflicting psychiatric illness through nervous shock sustained by reason of physical injury or peril to another, I think it sufficient that reasonable foreseeability should be the guide. I would not seek to limit the class by reference to particular relationships such as husband and wife or parent and child. The kinds of relationships which may involve close ties of love and affection are numerous and it is the existence of such ties which lead to mental disturbance when the loved one suffers a catastrophe. They may be present in family relationship or those of close friendship and may be stronger in the case of engaged couples than in that of persons who have been married to each other for many years. It is common knowledge that such ties exist and reasonably foreseeable that those bound by them may in certain circumstances be at real risk of psychiatric illness if the loved one is injured or put in peril. The closeness of the tie would, however, require to be proved by the plaintiff, though no doubt being capable of being presumed in appropriate cases.[113]

On the issue of spatial proximity, Lord Ackner explained:

Lord Ackner: It is accepted that the proximity to the accident must be close both in time and space. Direct and immediate sight or hearing of the accident is not required. It is reasonably foreseeable that injury by shock can be caused to the plaintiff, not only through the sight and hearing of the event but of its immediate aftermath. Only two of the plaintiffs before us were at the ground. However, it is clear from McLoughlin's case that there may be liability where subsequent identification can be regarded as part of the 'immediate aftermath' of the accident. Mr Alcock identified his brother-in-law in a bad condition in the mortuary at about midnight, that is some eight hours after the accident. This was the earliest of the identification cases. Even if this identification could be described as part of the 'aftermath', it could not in my judgment be described as part of the immediate aftermath. McLoughlin's case was described by Lord Wilberforce as being upon the margin of what the process of logical progression of case to case would allow. Mrs McLoughlin had arrived at the hospital within an hour or so after the accident. Accordingly, in the post-accident identification cases before your Lordships there was not sufficient proximity in time and space to the accident.[114]

Finally the court addressed the issue of those friends and relatives who witnessed the disaster on television. Lord Ackner was of the opinion that it was indeed possible to suffer psychiatric illness as a result of viewing pictures on the television and therefore there was a possibility of recovering damages for that shock. However, the Chief Constable would have been aware of the television restriction on showing pictures of individual suffering and 'although the television pictures certainly gave rise to feelings of the deepest anxiety and distress, in the circumstances of this case there were no such pictures'.[115]

---

112 [1991] 1 WLR 814, at 913.
113 Ibid, 914.
114 Ibid, 921.
115 Ibid, 921.

Whilst many of the claimants[116] satisfied one of the elements of a successful claim none could satisfy them all. The case can be criticised for setting arbitrary and artificial limits on who can claim. However, the repercussions of extending the boundaries of liability are enormous and in an area such as nervous shock objective judgments will always have to be made to limit the claims.

Football Hooliganism

Sports events attract large numbers of spectators who wish to see the attraction live 'in the flesh' rather than through the variety of media available. For the sports events organisers, these spectators also represent a significant income stream. The vast majority of these crowds and meetings of people are well ordered. However, incidents of disorder do occur in all sports and the question is how it should be addressed. Of course the most chronic manifestation has been with football hooliganism, which has often been termed the 'English disease', and this section provides some of the historical and policy background to its current and specific legal regulation.[117] There are more general legal provisions to control any potential disorder at sports events. Ticketing terms and conditions can be used to restrict what can be legitimate behaviour whilst the individual ticket holders are within a specified area. Unacceptable behaviour and infringements of these stated conditions would facilitate ejection.[118] There are also many legal grounds, already discussed earlier in the chapter, on which the event organisers could be liable for injuries caused to spectators who get caught up in disorder at a sports events.[119]

As discussed in Chapter 1, folk games akin to modern football have been played for many centuries. Often, in terms of the participants, they were highly physical and bloody. But there are few indications that there was physical disorder in the 'crowds' that watched up until the period when the game became codified during the second half of the nineteenth century. The historical and sociological aetiology of what is contemporarily understood as football hooliganism is uncertain. Football hooliganism is often portrayed as a modern phenomenon, which developed in the 1970s. In reality it is likely that crowds within the era of organised football from the end of the nineteenth century have often been the locus for disorder. It has been suggested that over 4,000 incidents of what one might term 'football hooliganism' (rather than just individual fights) occurred in the 20 years before the First World War.[120] This has not been limited to English football.[121] In 1909, goalposts were torn down and over 100 people were injured in a pitched battle between fans and police after the Scottish Cup Final in Glasgow. Similarly, Kuper provides many examples of crowd disorder at professional games in both the Netherlands and Germany during the Second World War.[122] Further afield, many examples of hooligan activity can be found historically in a number of South American countries.[123] Although only subject to specific state scrutiny in the UK over the last 30 years or so, it has existed as a social phenomenon for much longer.

However, in the discourse of the media, the modern era of football hooliganism is often viewed as starting in 1961, when a major riot occurred after an equalising goal during a Sunderland

---

116 Including the rescuers; see *White and Others v Chief Constable of South Yorkshire Police & Others* [1999] 1 All ER 1.
117 For excellent accounts of these issues, see McArdle, D, *From Boot Money to Bosman: Football, Society and the Law* (2000), London: Cavendish Publishing; and Greenfield, S and Osborn, G, *Regulating Football: Commodification, Consumption and the Law* (2001), London: Pluto Press.
118 Hudson, K and Findlay, R, 'Event Management: Legal Issues around Ejecting Spectators from Sport Events' (2010) 8(8) WSLR.
119 Riley, E, 'Fan Behaviour: Sporting organisations' liability for spectator behaviour' (2009) 7(1) WSLR.
120 Dunning, E, Murphy, P, Williams, J and Maguire, J, 'Football Hooliganism in Britain Before the First World War' (1984) 19 IRSS 215.
121 Op. cit., fn 117, McArdle (2000), p 64.
122 Kuper, S, *Ajax, the Dutch, the War: Football in Europe During the Second World War* (2003), London: Orion.
123 Archetti, EP, 'Death and violence in Argentinean football', in Giulianotti, R, Bonney R, and Hepworth, M, *Football, Violence and Social Identity* (1994), London: Routledge.

versus Tottenham game in 1961. 'That the hooligans were seen on television, *The Guardian* later said, 'provided . . . encouragement to others.'[124]

There is an extensive body of sociological literature concerning the study of football hooliganism.[124] Marxist analysis competes with functionalist analysis in attempting to explain its existence.[125] The work of Norbert Elias and his figurational analysis informed some of the early academic research, much of it carried out at Leicester University. Subsequently a good deal of research has come from wider perspectives, including anthropological studies based on participant observation.[126] Popular culture has also provided many accounts, often from the professional 'reformed' hooligan.[127] But why football hooliganism exists as a social phenomenon remains contested.

Not only has hooliganism been recognised as a national 'problem' within the English game, but fans travelling to see the England national side have also been involved in numerous incidents. Complex issues of nationalism and national identity are being played out in football fandom, of course, within the more general contemporary political and social momentum towards a more formalised integrationist Europe and additionally the decline of the former British Empire.

Legal responses

What is contested and unclear as far as football hooliganism is concerned, is what social policy and legal responses should be made on both a national and European level. In England, significant amounts of legislation have been enacted, often in response to particular incidents that have led to significant media coverage. Two such incidents in 1985 televised matches at the grounds of Chelsea FC and Luton Town are of import. Both games involved spectators encroaching on to the playing area and mass fights ensuing between opposing groups.[128] Also in that year, a government inquiry leading to the Popplewell Report took place after the fire at the Bradford City ground, which led to the death of 54 people. The recommendations were also based on an analysis of the tragedy at the Heysel Stadium in Brussels at the UEFA Cup Final. This tragedy led to a number of recommendations concerning safety on the one hand and the consideration of a membership scheme for all football spectators on the other. Although enabling legislation was introduced in the form of the Football Spectators Act 1989, a compulsory membership scheme was never introduced.

The other pivotal event, of course, was the Hillsborough Stadium disaster. Although it is now recognised that this was caused primarily by safety defects and failures of policing, it was initially portrayed as being the latest manifestation of hooligan activity. In the Taylor Report[129] discussed above, similarly to the earlier Popplewell Report, recommendations were divided into ones concerning safety at stadiums (looked at earlier) and further specific football-related legislative provisions that led to the amending of the Football Spectators Act 1989, then passing through

---

124 See for example Armstrong, G and Harris, R, 'Football Hooligans: Theory and Evidence' (1991) 39(3) *Sociological Review* 427; Williams, J, Dunning, E and Murphy, P, *Hooligans Abroad: The Behaviour of English fans at Continental Matches*, 2nd edn (1989), London: Routledge; Dunning, E, Murphy, P and Waddington, I, 'Anthropological versus sociological approaches to the study of soccer hooliganism: some critical notes' (1991) 39(3) *Sociological Review* 459; Taylor, I, 'On the sports violence question: soccer hooliganism revisited', in Hargreaves, J (ed), *Sport, Culture and Ideology* (1981), London: Routledge; Marsh, P, Rosser, E and Harre, R, *The Rules of Disorder* (1978), London: Routledge; and Hobbs, D and Robins, D, 'The boy done good: football violence, changes and continuities' (1991), 39(3) *Sociological Review* 551.

125 See earlier discussion of the application of these sociological theories to sport generally, Chapter 3, pp 125–30.

126 For example, see Armstrong, G, *Football Hooligans: Knowing the Score* (1998), London: Berg.

127 See Buford, B, *Amongst The Thugs* (1993), New York: Vintage; Brimson, D, *Capital Punishment: London's Violent Football Following* (1997), London: Headline; Brimson, D, *The Crew* (2000), London: Headline.

128 Until the 1990s and the creation of all-seater stadia in the higher professional leagues, the most ardent younger fans often stood on a terrace behind one goal and the away supporters behind the other goal. The aim of invading the pitch and 'taking an end' was prized.

129 *The Hillsborough Stadium Disaster (Final Report)* ('Taylor' Report) (1990), London: HMSO, Cm 962 – see pp 542–43.

Parliament, and the enacting of the Football (Offences) Act 1991, which criminalised entry on to the playing area, throwing missiles and racist chanting. Arguably, significant amounts of legislation have been passed without any real analysis of the causes of football hooliganism.

Greenfield, S and Osborn, G, *Regulating Football: Commodification, Consumption and the Law*

Two distinct strands to the issue can be detected during the Conservative administrations that enacted the legislation from 1985 to 1994. First it was seen as football's problem, as something to be controlled by the sport's governing bodies. Second, if it couldn't be dealt with in this manner it would be treated as a public-order problem and subject to firm policing. There was no attempt to understand how and, more important, why, outbreaks of hooliganism occurred; the symptoms would merely be tackled in an authoritarian manner.[130]

As discussed earlier, such measures can be seen as 'panic law'.[131] The subsequent Football (Offences and Disorder) Act 1999, Football Disorder Act 2000 and the Violent Crime Reduction Act 2006 have amended and strengthened many of the provisions in the earlier 1989 and 1991 Acts.[132] In addition, the normal Public Order Act offences apply together with sports-specific alcohol legislation introduced in the 1980s.[133] Adding to this the measures introduced by the Criminal Justice and Public Order Act 1994,[134] which criminalised the practice of ticket touting, what is now in place is an extensive legislative framework. Many people see the current legislative framework in the UK as having 'criminalised' the ordinary football fan.[135]

The location of hooliganism has shifted over a period of time. Whereas it 'traditionally' took place in or near to stadiums, it has relocated away from the highly regulated environment of modern football grounds to other points where rival supporters can meet. However, football stadia portray a powerful cultural identity.

McArdle, D, *From Boot Money to Bosman: Football, Society and the Law*

Many of the most illuminating recent discussions of hooliganism have been predicated upon John Bale's exploration of the significance of space as a social and cultural construct. For Bale, space provides an outlet for the personal and collective expression of social agency, and for the imposition and exercise of power. For a football club's supporters, the football ground is the space that provides this outlet, and this is the case for the most sedate supporters as much as it is for those with a propensity for hooligan activity.[136]

. . .

For the real football hooligans, the spatial significance of the ground has been transformed by segregation. Prior to the erection of the fences, the ground had been the only forum in which rivalries were played out. In the years after segregation, hooligan confrontations increasingly occurred in train stations and, to a lesser extent, in pubs and towns, city centres and the streets surrounding them.[137]

---

130 Op. cit., fn. 117, Greenfield and Osborn (2001), p 6.
131 See earlier, Chapter 2, pp 74–6.
132 See p 577.
133 See p 546.
134 See earlier discussion, Chapter 7, 312 and R (*on the application of Brown*) v *Inner London Crown Court* (2003) concerning provision of banning order on conviction for ticket touting, LTL 15/12/2003 (unreported elsewhere).
135 For a review of the legislative framework, see Home Office Guidance on Football-Related Legislation, HC 34/2000.
136 Op. cit., fn 117, McArdle (2000), p 62; see also Bale, J, 'Playing at Home', in Williams, J and Wagg, S (eds), *British Football and Social Change* (1994), Leicester: Leicester University Press.
137 Op. cit., fn 117, McArdle (2000), p 69.

The policing of matches by the police and club stewards, together with the widespread use of CCTV,[138] would suggest that the various legal prohibitions concerning football fandom would be rigorously enforced. So what are the rates of arrest and prosecution under these various offences? Although there is national co-ordination in the 'fight' against football hooliganism, it might be suspected that the local policy and actual practice of policing these offences will be an important factor in determining these rates.[139] Each year the Home Office produces an analysis of the past football season's figures:

Football Offences Season 2009–2010 – Statistical Highlights

- Total attendance in excess of 39 million at regulated football matches (37 million in England and Wales). The total number of arrests represents less than 0.01 per cent of all spectators.
- During the 2009–10 season the total number of people arrested in connection with all international and domestic football matches involving teams from England and Wales was 3,391. This represents a decrease of 10 per cent, or 395 arrests. The downwards trend in football-related arrests is continuing, but there is no complacency. This covers all arrests designated in law under Schedule 1 of the Football Spectators Act 1989 (as amended) reported by police to the Football Banning Orders Authority. This includes football-specific offences (e.g. throwing missiles in a stadium, pitch encroachment) and a wide range of generic criminal offences committed in connection with a football match. This is any arrest at any place within a period of 24 hours either side of a match.
- During the season an average of 1.05 arrests were made per match (inside and outside of stadia).
- No arrests at 70 per cent of all matches. Two arrests or less were made at 85 per cent of matches.
- 47 per cent of all matches were police free – continuing to free up police resources to deal with local police and community priorities.
- More than 90,000 English and Welsh club fans travelled to Champions League and Europa League matches outside of England and Wales. These 42 matches resulted in just 12 arrests.
- No football-related arrests of England or Wales supporters at overseas matches, including the 2010 World Cup in South Africa.
- The number of football banning orders increased slightly to 3,248 on 19 November 2010 from 3,180 on 10 November 2009. This represents 1,025 new banning orders imposed during the period. Orders are time limited and expiring all the time.
- Banning orders work – since 2000 in the region of 92 per cent of individuals whose orders have expired are assessed by police as no longer posing a risk of football disorder.

The figures suggest that out of around 37 million attendances at professional games in England and Wales during the 2009–10 season, the amount of arrests per fan and per game are low.

Banning orders

The figures also show that the increased use of football banning orders (FBO), has successfully excluded and limited the movement of those convicted of football-related offences from stadiums and surrounding areas. The 1999, 2000 and 2006 Acts have strengthened the ability of the courts to make both domestic and international banning orders when individuals are convicted of 'football-related' criminal offences. It is important to note that they are essentially civil orders, but as with Anti-Social Behaviour Orders (ASBOs), their breach is a criminal offence.

---

138 See Taylor, N, 'Closed Circuit Television: The British Experience' (1999) Stanford Technology Law Review 11.
139 For more analysis see Pearson, G and Stott, C, *Football Hooliganism: Policing and the War on the English Disease* (2007) London: Pennant Books.

Their application can extend to, for example, police officers' refusing an individual fan the ability to travel abroad where the officer has 'reasonable suspicion' that the individual may be involved in hooligan activity.

Gough v Chief Constable of Derbyshire

Appeal by Gough and Smith ('the appellants') from a decision of the Divisional Court dismissing their appeals by way of case stated against banning orders for two years made against them under s 14B Football Spectators Act 1989 as amended by the Football Disorder Act 2000. The appellants had been convicted of violent offences in 1998 and 1990 respectively. In addition, each was the subject of a 'profile' prepared by the police that indicated repeated involvement in or near incidents of violence at or around football matches. By this appeal the appellants contended that: (i) the banning orders derogated from the positive rights on freedom of movement and freedom to leave their home country conferred on them by Art 1 and Art 2 Council Directive 73/148/EEC because it was not permissible to justify a banning order on public grounds, alternatively that no such grounds were made out on the evidence; (ii) the 2000 Act was contrary to Community law and therefore inapplicable insofar as it imposed mandatory restrictions on free movement within the Community on criteria that were not provided for or permitted by Community legislation; and (iii) it was contrary to the Community law principle of proportionality to ban an individual from travelling anywhere within the Community even if the relevant match or tournament was not taking place within the Community. The appellants further contended that the procedures for the imposition of banning orders infringed Art 6 and/ or Art 8 European Convention on Human Rights because: (a) only the civil standard of proof was required to be satisfied; (b) there were insufficient procedural safeguards appropriate to the 'criminal charge' that a notice of application for a banning order constituted; and (c) the geographical scope of the orders was unacceptably broad.

HELD: (1) The court was satisfied that there was a public policy exception to Art 2 of the Directive. There was no absolute right to leave one's country. (2) Although it might initially appear disproportionate to ban all foreign travel, the court was satisfied that such a reaction was unsound. Banning orders were only to be imposed where there were strong grounds for concluding that the individual had a propensity for taking part in football hooliganism. It was proportionate that those who had shown such a propensity should be subject to a scheme that restricted their ability to indulge in it. (3) Although the civil standard of proof applied, that standard was flexible and had to reflect the consequences that would follow if the case for a banning order were made out. This should lead magistrates to apply an exacting standard of proof which, in practice, would be hard to distinguish from the criminal one (see *B v Chief Constable of Avon and Somerset Constabulary* [2001] 1 WLR 340 and *R v Manchester Crown Court, ex parte McCann* [2001] 1 WLR 1084). (4) Banning orders were not 'criminal charges', yet the standard of proof to be applied was akin to the criminal standard. In such circumstances, the Art 6 challenge failed. (5) If a banning order were properly made, any interference with an individual's Art 8 rights would be justified under Art 8(2) because it was necessary for the prevention of disorder. (6) On the facts, and even though the correct standard of proof had not been applied, the case for a banning order on each of the appellants was amply made out. Appeals dismissed.[140]

Gough held that international banning orders under the Football Spectators Act 1989 as amended by the Football Disorder Act 2000 contravened neither European law on free movement of persons nor the European Convention on Human Rights. However, the feeling still continues that the civil

---

140 [2002] 2 All ER 985 CA (Civ Div). Also see *R v Winkler* [2004] EWCA Crim 1590; (2004) 168 JPN 720 (CA (Crim Div)).

liberties of football supporters that may have some football-related conviction are being restricted.[141] The application of the law has been reviewed.[142] The official view is that they have been a success.

Football (Disorder) Act 2000 – 'Report to Parliament, November 2005'

The combination of tough football banning orders and radical preventative measures have been universally well received by the police, both at home and abroad, by the football authorities, UEFA, FIFA and the overwhelming majority of fans who appreciate that they are the main beneficiaries when troublemakers are removed from their ranks. Football disorder remains a threat and major challenges lie ahead but the measures introduced in the wake of Euro 2000 are providing an effective means for preventing football disorder.[143]

One piece of research, however, has identified that guidelines concerning the granting of banning orders are often ignored.

James, M and Pearson, G, 'Football Banning Orders: Analysing their Use in Court'

The research revealed four main areas of concern with the procedures followed by courts when imposing FBOs that could mean that, despite the reported public order success of the 2006 World Cup Finals, many of the wrong people are still being targeted by the police in the ongoing campaign against football hooliganism.

First, the standard of proof held to be applicable by Lord Phillips MR in *Gough* was not being rigorously applied. Secondly, there was an over-reliance on evidence of a poor quality, particularly evidence of 'guilt by association' rather than 'guilt by commission'. Thirdly, there was no proper examination of the second test, merely an assumption that the respondent will be involved in future incidents of violence or disorder based on his having been previously involved in acts of 'hooliganism'. Finally, there was little or no individual consideration of either the appropriate duration of an FBO, or of the conditions attached to them.[144]

Spectator Racism in Sport

Racism in sport, as with racism generally in society, is an endemic problem in Britain.[145] Institutionalised racism has been accepted to exist in many areas of society.[146] The focus of this section will be on the regulation of spectator racism against those participating in sport. Racism in

---

141 Beckham, G, 'The Price Of Passion: The Banishment Of English Hooligans From Football Matches In Violation Of Fundamental Freedoms' (2001) 25 Hastings International and Comparative Law Review 41; Pearson, G, 'Legitimate Targets? The Civil Liberties of Football Fans' (1999) 4(1) Journal of Civil Liberties 37. For a review of regulatory frameworks for football hooliganism in other European countries, see Siekmann, R, Gardiner, S, Soek, J, Offers, M and Mojet, H, *Football Hooliganism with an EU Dimension: Towards an International Legal Framework*, Agis Programme 2003, Project Jai/203/Agis/138, October 2004, The Hague: TMC Asser Instituut.

142 Football (Disorder) Act 2000 – Report to Parliament, November 2005, http://tna.europarchive.org/20100413151441/ http://www.homeoffice.gov.uk/documents/Football-Disorder-2006.html.

143 Ibid, para 20.6.

144 James, M and Pearson, G, 'Football Banning Orders: Analysing their Use in Court' (2006) 70(6) Journal of Criminal Law 509–30.

145 For a number of perspectives on this issue, see McDonald, I and Carrington, B (eds), *'Race', Sport and British Society* (2001), London: Routledge, including Gardiner, S and Welch, R, 'Sport, racism and the limits of "colour blind" law', pp 133–51. Also see Burdsey, D (ed.) *Race, Ethnicity and Football: Persisting Debates and Emergent Issues* (2011), London: Routledge, including Gardiner, S and Welch, R, 'Football, Racism and the Limits of "Colour Blind" Law: Revisited'.

146 See MacPherson, W (Sir), *The Stephen Lawrence Inquiry: Report on the Inquiry by Sir William Macpherson of Cluny*, Cm 4262 (1999), London: HMSO. The report followed the public inquiry into the killing of Stephen Lawrence in South London in 1994. The report considered that institutionalised racism is 'not solely through the deliberate actions of a small number of bigoted individuals, but through a more systematic tendency that could unconsciously influence police performance generally' (para 6.5). Also see 'Amnesty attacks racism in criminal justice system', *The Guardian*, 25 July 2001.

social life can be brutally visible both in terms of physical attacks and a clear denial of the funda-mental freedoms accepted in contemporary liberal society. However, it also exists in the hidden interstices of society. Verbal racism is more insidious, but as all ethnic minority sportsmen will know in Britain, it is only too real. Racism has been a part of sport as long as sport has been played. The aetiology of spectator racism in sport is as complex as it is of racism generally in society. The focus will be on the problem in football, but other team and individual sports have also had a problem. For example, in 2008, Lewis Hamilton was the subject of racial abuse by spectators during pre-season Formula One tests in Spain.[147]

Hammond, D, *Foul Play: A Class Analysis of Sport*

The success of blacks in professional sports such as soccer has not, of course, eradicated racism either from the changing room or the terracing, but it has clearly made a difference. It is very difficult for racists to continually abuse blacks while supporting a team that is peppered with blacks, especially if the team is successful and the black players can be seen to be an integral part of that success.

Perhaps this effect should not be overestimated though. Terrace language still refers to 'our niggers' as opposed to 'theirs', and equally disturbing, when a team reverts to an all white line-up the abuse heaped on blacks playing for the opposing team increases. Blacks are undoubtedly still racially abused, albeit on a smaller scale, and they have still yet to make the breakthrough into senior positions on the coaching staff, and that management jobs are not available to blacks after their playing days are over must be a consideration before they take up serious sport in the first place. The effect of ignoring other opportunities to take up a sport that will eventually leave one uneducated and unemployed can be catastrophic.[148]

A major issue is what role the law has in addressing spectator racism in sport and what extra-legal policies should be developed.

Racism in football

English football has become, in terms of ethnicity, cosmopolitan. Over the last three or four decades, the participation of black players of Afro-Caribbean descent has dramatically increased. Many of these players have been second or third generation children of immigrants from the Caribbean who came to Britain in the 1950s and 1960s. Today, in English professional football, players of Afro-Caribbean descent are over-represented in relation to the general population. However, representa-tion by players from other ethnic minorities, for example those of Asian descent, is significantly lower than in the general population.[149] Black players have had to fight to achieve this prominence despite the dominant values within football culture.

As with the causes of football hooliganism generally, the causes of spectator racism are complex.[150] The *Bosman* decision has been a cause of this increasing cosmopolitanism with the

---

147 'Formula One chiefs threaten Spain after Hamilton racism row', *The Times*, 4 February 2008, www.timesonline.co.uk/tol/sport/ formula_1/article3306476.ece; and 'FIA will punish repeat of Lewis Hamilton racism', *Daily Telegraph*, 4 February 2008, www.telegraph.co.uk/sport/2290949/FIA -will-punish-repeat-of-Lewis-Hamilton-racism.html.
148 Hammond, D, *Foul Play: A Class Analysis of Sport* (1993), London: Ubique, p 52.
149 There are virtually no Asian professional footballers. See 'Asians can't play barrier', *The Guardian*, 10 February 1996 and 'Ooh, aah . . . Jaginder', *The Independent Magazine*, 17 August 1996.
150 See Greenfield, S and Osborn, G, 'When the whites come marching in' (1996) 6(2) MSLJ 315; Fleming, S and Tomlinson, A, 'Football, racism and xenophobia in England (I) Europe and the Old England'; Garland, J and Rowe, M, 'Football, racism and xenophobia in England (II) Challenging racism and xenophobia', in Merkel, U and Tokarski, W (eds), *Racism and Xenophobia in European Football Sports, Leisure and Physical Education Trends and Developments* (1996), Aachen: Meyer and Meyer Verlag, Vol 3; and Back, L et al, *Changing Face of Football: Racism, Identity and Multiculture in the English Game* (2001) London: Berg Publishers.

signing of more foreign players. English football has always had players from the other home coun-tries of the United Kingdom. It was not until the emergence of black players, during the 1960s, that the first manifestation of any real identifiable spectator reaction became evident. Some of these early players seem to have been grudgingly tolerated.[151] Perhaps it was not until the late 1970s, when the number of Afro-Caribbean players began to increase significantly, that they became 'visible' and began to represent a perceived threat. Sections of spectators, at some clubs more than others, began to react actively, through stereotyping racial abuse and 'monkey chants', and actions such as the throwing of bananas on to the ground.[152] It has been termed 'the English Disease', although it clearly is a worldwide phenomenon.[153] There is evidence that the racial nature of football hooliganism has increasingly become politicised and co-ordinated throughout Europe.[154] Legal and non-legal initia-tives have had some positive impact upon manifestations of spectator racism within football.[155]

The criminal offence of racist chanting has its origins in the Taylor Report, which considered that the provisions of the Public Order Act 1986 concerning 'threatening, abusive or insulting words or behaviour' did not adequately cover indecent or racist chanting. This was due to the need to have a clearly identifiable victim to establish liability, in that either another person believed 'unlawful violence will be used against him or another',[156] or the chanting was 'within the hearing or sight of a person likely to be caused harassment, alarm or distress'.[157] So s 3 of the Football Offences Act 1991 provided that it was an offence to engage or take part in chanting of an indecent or racialist nature at a designated football match. Subsection 2 provides that 'chanting' means the repeated uttering of any words or sounds in concert with one or more others; and 'of a racialist nature' means consisting of or including matter which is threatening, abusive or insulting to a person by reason of his colour, race, nationality (including citizenship) or ethnic or national origins. The offence is based on strict liability with no need to prove any intent to be racist on the defendant's part. No recognisable individual is needed, although the racial abuse will generally be directed at a particular player.

L'affaire Cantona

The Simmons/Cantona incident highlighted the limitation of the 1991 Act to chanting in concert with one or more others.[158] During the parliamentary progress of the legislation it was argued that to criminalise a single racist or indecent remark would have created 'too low' a threshold. 'L'affaire Cantona' in 1995 can be used to speculate that racial abuse and indifference has spread beyond the black/white demarcation that has been constructed in the 1960s to the 1990s.

---

151 It is interesting to compare Albert Johanneson, a South African, who played for Leeds United from 1960 to 1970 and Clyde Best, a Bermudian, who played for West Ham from 1967 to 1977. Johanneson's career petered out and, suffering from chronic alcoholism, he died in late 1995 in poverty in Yorkshire. In comparison, Best returned to the Caribbean at the end of his career and is a successful businessman.

152 Note the belated acknowledgment on the FA's part of its past inaction on responding effectively to this matter; see 'FA issues public apology for decades of racism', The Guardian, 4 July 2001.

153 There were, for example, a number of racist incidents in Italian football in the 1999–2000 and 2000–01 seasons; see Colantuoni, L, 'Italian update 2000' (2000), 3(4) Sports Law Bulletin 14; also see the FIFA anti-racism campaign launched in July 2001.

154 The crowd disorder which caused the abandoning of the international game between the Republic of Ireland and England in Dublin in early 1995 was seen as involving organised hooligan groups such as 'Combat 18'. See 'Troublemakers caught police on the hop', The Guardian, 16 February 1995.

155 It is important not to see this as a problem limited to football. A report compiled for the Rugby League Association showed levels of racial abuse by spectators. See p 586.

156 Public Order Act 1986, s 4, 'Fear or Provocation of Violence'.

157 Ibid, s 5, 'Harassment, Alarm or Distress'. An additional offence has been created with s 4A of the Public Order Act 1986, 'Intentional Harassment, Alarm or Distress', as substituted by s 154 of the Criminal Justice and Public Order Act 1994, again needing an identifiable victim.

158 See 'It takes two to chant, court decides', The Times, 23 January 1993 and Pendry, T, A Law with a Flaw, Kick It Again: Uniting Football Against Racism (1995), London: Commission for Racial Equality.

Gardiner, S, 'The law and hate speech: "Ooh aah Cantona" and the demonisation of "the Other"'

The Cantona incident in south London in early 1995 needs careful explanation. He was sent off after kicking out at a Crystal Palace player. He was walking along the touchline towards the exit to the dressing rooms when Matthew Simmons, a Crystal Palace supporter, ran down to the front of the crowd and 'verbally and digitally' abused Cantona ('Cantona hits fan, faces lengthy ban', *The Guardian*, 26 January 1995). He was reported as saying the immortal words: 'Fucking, cheating French cunt. Fuck off back to France, you motherfucker.' Cantona reacted by leaping over the advertising hoardings with a two-footed kick against Simmons' chest. He struck him a number of times before the two were parted by police, stewards and team officials.

Simmons' version of the outburst was rather different. He told the police after the event that he actually had walked eleven rows down to the front because he wanted to go to the toilet and said: 'Off! Off! Off! Go on, Cantona, have an early shower.' In court he said: 'The crowd was very noisy, everyone was cheering and shouting, everyone was pleased that he [Cantona] had been sent off, me included. Like any normal fan, I joined in with this and was just shouting "Off, off, off" and pointing towards the dressing rooms' ('"It was business as normal", says Cantona case accused', *The Guardian*, 1 May 1996).

Cantona was charged with common assault and pleaded guilty at his trial. He was initially given a two-week prison sentence by magistrates, justified at the time largely because 'he is a high-profile public figure looked up to by many young people' (*The Guardian*, 24 March 1995). This was commuted to 120 hours' community service teaching schoolchildren football skills, and he was also banned from playing for eight months by the English Football Association. Cantona's own obscure observation concerning the immense public interest in his case was: 'When seagulls follow a trawler, it is because they think sardines will be thrown into the sea' (Ridley 1995: 42).

As Redhead observes, the incident was 'caught clearly on camera and has been repeatedly shown via the international airwaves almost as many times as the Zapruder film of the JFK assassination in Dallas'. He compares it with the way that an incident involving Paul Ince was dealt with by the football authorities, one that was not clearly mediated by the TV cameras. Ince was charged with assaulting another Crystal Palace supporter, Dennis Warren, shortly after the Cantona incident. He was not given any ban before his trial and was acquitted on the charge of assault. Warren had four previous convictions for football violence and drunkenness, belonged to a right-wing fascist group and had been banned from acting as a manager in 1993 by Surrey Football Association for shouting instructions to his players to 'get the nigger' on the opposing team. The power of the video image and its ability to reify events and actions is well illustrated by the distinctions in the respective censuring of Cantona and Ince.

Simmons, over a year after the incident, was convicted of threatening behaviour ('Cantona tormentor jailed for court kick', *The Guardian*, 3 May 1996). At his trial he did, however, turn the tables on Cantona, although not targeting him as the victim: he launched his own drop-kick attack on the prosecuting lawyer, seconds after hearing he had been found guilty of provoking the Manchester United star. He threw himself at Jeffrey McCann, grabbing him around the neck, trying to haul him over a table and appearing to kick him in the chest. McCann had asked magistrates to bar Simmons from all football grounds. Six police officers rushed in to restrain Simmons, who then rushed at the press box shouting: 'I am innocent. I swear on the Bible. You press, you are scum.' Simmons was fined £500 for threatening behaviour, banned from all professional football grounds for 12 months, and sentenced to seven days in prison for contempt of court. During his trial there had been unsubstantiated claims that Simmons was linked with right-wing fascist groups.[159]

---

159 Gardiner, S, 'The law and hate speech: "Ooh aah Cantona" and the demonisation of "the other" ', in Brown, A (ed), *Fanatics! Power, Identity and Fandom in Football* (1998), London: Routledge. Also see 'The Kick that Stunned Football', *The Observer Sport Monthly*, 24 November 2004. Also see Ridley, I, 'Cantona: The Red and Black' (1995), London: Headline and Redhead, S, 'Post-fandom and the Millennial blues: The Transformation of Soccer Culture' (1997), London: Routledge.

Individualising racist chanting

This incident highlighted the issue of control of racist 'hate speech'. Is legislation the best answer to the xenophobia of the likes of Simmons? He was convicted under public order offences for racial hatred. He could not be charged under s 3 of the Football (Offences) Act 1991 for indecent and racist chanting because he fell outside the scope of this legislation due to his actions being solitary. At that time liability only occurred when, in a designated football match, 'words or sounds are chanted in concert with one or more others which are threatening, abusive or threatening to a person by reason of his colour, race, nationality or ethnic or national origins'. After the Cantona incident, there were calls for the legislation to be extended to include individual acts.

In 1995, a Labour Party report proposed that the offence should be individualised.[160] The Football Task Force interim report, *Eliminating Racism from Football*,[161] as one of its key recommendations asked the Government to 'amend the Football (Offences) Act 1991 as a matter of urgency to make it an offence for individuals to use racist comments inside football grounds'.

Football Task Force, *Eliminating Racism from Football*

5(a) 14. The introduction of the Football Offences Act may have contributed to this culture change by giving spectators more confidence to challenge unacceptable behaviour. Yet, this success should not obscure the fact that the Act is no longer fulfilling the purpose for which it was introduced. Rather, it should strengthen our resolve to amend it as it suggests that good legislation can be an effective deterrent against unacceptable behaviour.

5(a) 15. Kick It Out argues that the phrasing of the Act has 'significantly reduced the chances of the police mounting arrests that can be successfully prosecuted'. Home Office figures show that only 10 arrests were made during the last football season under this section of the Act.[162]

In 1998, the Home Office produced a *Review of Football-Related Legislation*.[163] Amongst a number of recommendations, it was suggested again that the offence should be able to be committed by a lone individual. Around this time there was some conjecture over whether spectator racism was increasing or decreasing. From the commencement of the Act in the early 1990s until early 1998, there were only about 180 convictions. In the 1998–99 season there were 33 convictions.[164] The most recently available official statistics concerning criminal conduct around designated football matches show that in the 2009–10 season, 31 of these arrests were for racist chanting, up from 23 two seasons before, which had been the lowest figure on record.

Section 3 of the 1991 Act has been little used, suggesting that it has been used primarily symbolically as an official indication that 'something was being done'. As Chambliss and Sideman argue, the way to identify legal symbolism is to measure the levels of enforcement.[165] If they are low, symbolism is likely. One of the major problems is the issue of detection and policing during matches, even though technologies such as closed circuit television cameras are used to aid identification of perpetrators during matches. Interestingly, around half of the convictions involved Premier League matches, which may say something about different levels of 'policing' of this offence between the Premier League and the Football League.

---

160 *A New Framework for Football: Labour's Charter for Football* (1995), London: Labour Party.

161 Football Task Force, *Eliminating Racism from Football* (1998), London.

162 Ibid, para 5.

163 *Review of Football-Related Legislation* (1998), London: Home Office – Operational Policing Policy Unit. Copy can be found at http://www.nationalarchives.gov.uk/ERORecords/HO/421/2/ppd/oppu/footb98.pdf; see Gardiner, S, 'New powers to fight football hooliganism' (1998), 1(6) Sports Law Bulletin 1.

164 In the 2002–03 season there were 78 arrests; in season 2003–04 there were 63 arrests.

165 Chambliss, W and Seidmann, R, *Law, Order and Power*, 2nd edn (1982), New York: John Wiley.

Convictions under s 3 Football Offences Act 1991 (*Statistics On Football Related Arrests & Banning Orders: Season 2009–10*, Home Office)	
2002–2003	78
2003–2004	63
2004–2005	51
2005–2006	55
2006–2007	41
2007–2008	23
2008–2009	36
2009–2010	31

The dominant discourse within the Football Association has been that the problem of racism is decreasing, if it has not been completely eradicated. There is, however, strong evidence that incidents of racist activity are still perpetuated by individuals and small groups that operate 'in complex and often contradictory ways . . . racist abuse in grounds occurs in an intermittent fashion'.[166] The location and form, and the expression of racism has changed – it is, however, unclear whether the extent of the problem has altered significantly. Caution is vital in alluding to the reduction of the problem.[167]

The offence was individualised with s 9 of the Football (Offences and Disorder) Act 1999. The effect of the amendment is that an individual who engages in such chanting on his own can commit the offence.[168] It seems, however, that the offence still must amount to 'chanting', albeit by an individual. A single abusive shout will not suffice.[169] A major question is whether or not the individualising of the offence would arguably be even harder to enforce, with police and ground stewards finding it difficult to identify the cries of a lone racist. As Parpworth argues:

> There is a certain futility in creating statutory offences, which are effectively moribund due to difficulties associated with detection.[170]

The future policing of this provision and the number of consequential convictions will be interesting to monitor. One case has given guidance on an unfortunately not uncommon chant in games between certain clubs. In *DPP v Stoke on Trent Magistrates' Court*[171] the court acquitted the defendant Ratcliffe, who admitted taking part together with a number of other Port Vale supporters in the chant 'You're just a town full of Pakis', directed at Oldham supporters, in a match between the two clubs. He was tried and acquitted on a submission at the end of the prosecution case that the words used were not of a racialist nature. The district judge's reasons included that the phrase had been 'mere doggerel' and amounted to no more than aimlessly stating that 'our town is better than your

---

166 Back, L, Crabbe, T and Solomos, J, 'Racism in football: patterns of continuity and change', in op. cit., fn 162, Brown (1998).
167 See Garland, J and Rowe, M, 'Policing racism at football matches: an assessment of recent developments in police strategies' (1999), 27(3) IJSLaw 251.
168 Gardiner, S, 'The continuing regulation of football supporters: the Football (Offences and Disorder) Act 1999' (1999) 2(4) SLB 1.
169 See Greenfield, S and Osborn, G, 'The Football (Offences and Disorder) Act 1999: amending s 3 of the Football (Offences) Act 1991' (2000), 5(1) Journal of Civil Liberties 55.
170 Parpworth, N, 'Football and racism: a legislative solution' (1993) SJ, 15 October.
171 *DPP v Stoke on Trent Magistrates' Court* [2004] 1 Cr App R 4; also see (2003) 6(5) SLB.

town'. On a prosecution appeal by way of case stated against an acquittal, the appeal was allowed and the case remitted to the District Judge with a direction that he should on the evidence convict Ratcliffe of the offence.

DPP v Stoke On Trent Magistrates' Court

The words 'of a racialist nature' meant, as provided by section 3(2)(b), that the chant consisted of, or included, matter that was threatening, abusive or insulting to a person, by reason of his colour, race, nationality or ethnic or national origins. It was immaterial whether persons of the racial group referred to in the alleged offending words were present so as to hear them or, if so present, were offended or affected in any way by them. (2) The word 'Paki' was in most contexts racially offensive. It went beyond a convenient and/or affectionate abbreviation of a description of a nationality such as 'Aussie' or 'Brit'. The use of the word had to be looked at in its context on a case by case basis. (3) On the facts found by the District Judge there was no doubt that R and his fellow Port Vale supporters were using the word as part of their chant in a racially derogatory or insulting sense. R's admitted behaviour fell squarely within the definition of racialist chanting in the Act.[172]

If convicted, the accused person can be fined, and, in addition to any other penalty, banned from attending football matches both in this country and abroad for a period of between two and ten years. Precise conditions can also be imposed on a case-by-case basis. Breach of a banning order is punishable by a maximum penalty of up to six months' imprisonment.

Non-legal approaches to regulating sports-related racism

There is a strong argument that the use of legislation can be seen as diverting attention and resources from educational and social policy initiatives, which might more successfully eliminate the causes of the problem. Football stadiums have become one of the most overtly regulated public spaces. There is an increasing danger that this regulatory approach to social problems by the use of the law will create increasingly anodyne environments where freedom of expression and movement is overtly suppressed through the law. Law is often made too hastily to deal with what is seen as a pressing problem. Panic law is invariably bad law. The alternative approach is the use of campaigns such as that conceived in 1993, when the Professional Footballers' Association and the Commission for Racial Equality (CRE) launched the 'Let's Kick Racism Out of Football' campaign.[173] The campaign has been periodically re-launched. In addition, many clubs have developed their own policies against racism with the 'Football in the Community' programme. Anti-racist fanzines have also developed as an informal method of campaigning.

The main objective of the 'Let's Kick Racism Out of Football' campaign was to 'encourage all those associated with the game of football to improve standards of behaviour, especially with reference to racial abuse, harassment, and the discrimination in and around grounds and to make grounds safe for spectators, and to motivate public opinion generally against all forms of racism associated with the game and other spheres of life'. In 1997, the campaign changed its name to 'Kick it Out' and became independent of the CRE (now incorporated within the Equality and Human Rights Commission).[174]

---

172 [2004] 1 Cr App R 4.
173 See Greenfield, S and Osborn, G, 'When the whites come marching in?' (1996) 6(2) MSLJ 330–31 for further details.
174 For further information see www.kickitout.org; also see Football Against Racism in Europe (FARE) – www.farenet.org.

Rugby league

The issue of racism has also been highlighted in other sports, including rugby league:

Long, J, Tongue, N, Spracklen, K and Carrington, B, *What's the Difference? A Study of the Nature and Extent of Racism in Rugby League*

Having accepted the challenge of trying to cast light on the nature and extent of racism in rugby league, we recognised that we were not going to get the answer but would unearth different shades of meaning. Discussing racism in the sport you love (which was how most of our respondents regarded rugby league) is uncomfortable, because for most of us it is one of those things that is 'not nice' and we would prefer it if it were not really there. That meant we felt we had to be especially careful with the questions we asked and the way they were presented in the surveys.

We cannot speculate on the views of those who did not respond, but the following quotes represent two of the most commonly held positions:

- I feel we could be highlighting a problem, which by and large does not exist. Our supporters are not moronic flag-waving National Front supporters (Club Official 102).
- We need to stop racism before it spreads. It is there in the game and there is no point hiding it (Club Official 89).

Our research suggests that the first of these views is probably the more frequently held, and there is a third set of people who flatly deny that there is any racism in rugby league. However, while our research confirmed that racism in professional rugby league is not on a par with what has been evidenced in professional soccer, there is a small but significant problem. Our evidence also suggests that although the intensity may vary, racism is evident throughout the game and should not be dismissed as simply being the preserve of a minority of rogue clubs. People on the inside refer to rugby league as the greatest game, which has been taken as the name of one of the fanzines. This kind of pride is obviously one of the game's great strengths, but can also encourage complacency, making it difficult to alert people to significant issues. It is important that people should be honest enough to recognise problems and seek to address them appropriately. It should be possible to appeal to the pride that fans have in the game to enlist their support in ridding the game of racism and setting an example for other sports to follow.

Among the supporters almost half had heard chanting against black players. While 87% feel that it is not acceptable for players to be abused because of the colour of their skin, that still leaves 13%; while 90% disagreed that black players are lazy, that still leaves 10%. There is still a message to be conveyed that while an individual player who happens to be black may be lazy (or have any number of other attributes, including positive ones), it is not because they are black that they are lazy.

Fewer club officials reported hearing chanting against black players, but a third were aware of it even at their own club and over half had witnessed racist behaviour at other clubs. Almost all clubs were named or included within a more general category so would be ill-advised to consider racism as just somebody else's problem. Many of the club officials (especially the chairmen) had stereotypical views of the attributes of ethnic minority players, most commonly relating to the athletic prowess of Afro-Caribbean players. Black players experiencing racism are rather ambivalent about that kind of stereotyping because some of it appears favourable to them. Other aspects about suitability only for certain positions may be very limiting.

Players were more aware of racism within the game than the coaches and other club officials. All the players interviewed acknowledged that there is racist chanting from the stands and terraces. They know that it is a small number but identified a significant problem. The players were also aware that racial abuse was not just confined to the stands and terraces. All the black players and some of the white players talked about the racial abuse they were aware of on the pitch. While this was considered to be a 'winding-up' tactic, the players felt there was no justification for it. Not surprisingly, players were reluctant to point the finger at their own team, but some of the dressing room jokes were not felt to be funny. Some coaches were also identified as adopting racist stereotypes.

It is important for it to be recognised that abuse because of the colour of a player's skin is racist and not just one of those things that can be laughed off. Clubs can and should do some-thing. On balance the feeling of club officials was that the anti-chanting campaigns had had a beneficial effect, and the supporters also thought they had been a good idea. However, beyond that, club officials identified very little that had been done to date to counter racism and promote the game within ethnic minority communities. There have been some notable excep-tions like the Keighley Classroom and the Batley free ticket scheme. But Asian and black people are still extremely rare among rugby league crowds. The players in particular saw the need for development initiatives to make sure that as many as possible be introduced to a great game and that talent be encouraged.

The black players we interviewed felt that when they encountered racism they just had to get on with the game, but did not see why they should have to accept it. Whether or not racist abuse was directed at them personally, they as black players were affected by it. There was also a feeling that many had been deterred along the way, deciding that if that was what the game was going to be about there were better directions they could go in. Of course, there are many reasons why people stop playing, but any sport should be concerned about an avoidable loss of talent. Moreover, experiencing racism like this may affect the form of black players, so it is in the interest of coaches and team mates to try to counter anything that has a detrimental effect on their players.

Not surprisingly, when confronted with racist chanting the majority of supporters ignored it. In the pressures of the crowd it is not easy for the individual to know what to do. Part of the 'Let's Kick Racism out of Football' campaign was to suggest to fans what they could do if they came across racist behaviour in football.

While beginning to question that it is, people do still want to see rugby league as a family sport and an environment in which racism is evident is not conducive to that image. If racism were to spread it could hit clubs in their pockets through lower attendances.

For the white players it was clear that rugby league is indeed very much a family game. Their families and network of family friends and social contacts had been instrumental in intro-ducing them to rugby league clubs. Lacking that kind of introduction, Asian and black players had had to find other routes into the game. To avoid missing out on talent in the various ethnic minority communities, rugby league needs to offer the kind of support that few youngsters will get from their networks of family and friends.

We have tried not to create a scare about 'a cancer sweeping through the game'. We are persuaded that such a conclusion would be unwarranted. However, we also believe it would be wrong for those in rugby league to shirk their responsibility and hide behind the protestations that there is no issue to address. Although racism is a problem in society at large, that is no reason for inaction within the game, which should instead acknowledge its social responsibility. There is an opportunity for rugby league to take an initiative for the good of the game and the communities that support it.[175]

---

175 See Long, J, Tongue, N, Spracklen, K and Carrington, B, *What's the Difference? A Study of the Nature and Extent of Racism in Rugby League* (1995), School of Leisure and Sports Studies, Leeds Metropolitan University, pp 43–45.

The report was a significant reason for the CRE in 1996 to launch an anti-racism campaign in rugby league.[176] The current manifestation can be found in the RFL's Respect policy.[177]

Regulation and criminalisation of other sports-specific hate speech

It is not only racist chanting that sportsmen and women are subject to which might amount to criminal liability. In 2010, Castleford Tigers Rugby League Club was fined £40,000 (reduced to £20,000 on appeal) by the Rugby Football League (RFL) for not taking enough measures to deal with a small minority of Castleford fans who took part in episodes of homophobic chanting aimed at Crusaders Rugby League Club's openly gay rugby league player, Gareth Thomas.[178] Those individuals identified as being involved were given bans from attending the ground. Such individuals could also incur criminal liability under part 3A of the Public Order Act 1986 as amended by s 74 of the Criminal Justice and Immigration Act 2008, by the creation of an offence of intentionally stirring up hatred on the grounds of sexual orientation. There are no reports of this offence being used against incidents of homophobic chanting at sports events.

In football, the 1991 Act has also been used to prosecute those involved in 'indecent' chanting under s 3 FOA, and this has included chanting seen as homophobic. This notably occurred in response to homophobic chanting targeted at the ex-Tottenham Player, Sol Campbell in September 2008 in a match between Portsmouth and Tottenham Hotspur. Five spectators were cautioned and four more pleaded guilty. Two other individuals charged, one adult and one teenage boy, were convicted and given three-year football banning orders. They had allegedly shouted 'gay boy' at Campbell. In an appeal hearing at Portsmouth Crown Court in September 2009, the convictions were overturned when the Court heard arguments that it could not be proved beyond reasonable doubt that either of these two were using the alleged words and that in fact those words did not constitute indecent chanting. The Judge concluded:

'Sol Campbell abusers found guilty by Portsmouth magistrates'

We can hear the crowd, we can hear the words 'gay boy' . . . We can't be sure that those words came from Mr Trow's mouth, we can't be sure that those words came from the boy's mouth . . . Even if they did come from either or both mouths it was a very brief intervention indeed and we can't be sure that what they did would be sufficient to be properly described as engaging or taking part in chanting.[179]

Under British law generally, a hate crime is any criminal offence that is motivated by hostility or prejudice based upon the victim's disability, race, religion or belief, sexual orientation or transgender. In UK football, another significant area of hate speech involves religious sectarianism, which has been particularly prevalent in Scotland between Catholic and Protestant affiliated teams.[180] Sectarianism became a 'hate crime' in Scottish law under s 74 of the Criminal Justice

176 Also note similar scheme in cricket, 'Clean Bowl Racism'; McDonald, I, 'Why we must hit racism for six', in *Hit Racism for Six: Race and Cricket in England Today* (1995), London: Roehampton Institute; McDonald, I and Sharda, U, *Anyone for Cricket?* (1999), London: Centre for New Ethnicities Research, UEL; Gardiner *et al*, *Sports Law*, 2nd edn (2001), London: Cavendish Publishing, pp 150–54; Williams, J, *Cricket and Race* (2001), London: Berg.

177 See http://www.giantsrl.com/theclub/respect_policy

178 'Castleford fined £40,000 for homophobic chants by fans', BBC Sport, 29 June 2010, http://news.bbc.co.uk/sport1/hi/rugby_league/super_league/castleford/8772418.stm.

179 'Sol Campbell's homophobic abusers found guilty by Portsmouth magistrates', *Daily Telegraph*, 15 May 2009, http://www.telegraph.co.uk/sport/football/teams/portsmouth/5331813/Sol-Campbells-homophobic-abusers-found-guilty-by-Portsmouth-magistrates.html.

180 'Seven Hearts fans are arrested over sectarian chants', *Edinburgh Evening News*, 28 November 2006, http://edinburghnews.scotsman.com/religiousissuesinscotland/Seven-Hearts-fans-are-arrested.2830580.jp.

(Scotland) Act 2003. This does not create a specific new offence but aggravates existing offences: where an individual commits an assault or public order offences such as breach of the peace, the courts are able to give a stiffer sentence if the act was motivated by religious hatred – just as would be the case with racial hatred. Under s 74, an offence is aggravated by religious prejudice where the conduct is aggravated by some form of malice or ill will based on the victim's membership, or perceived membership, of a religious group. Conviction can also lead to a Football Banning Order, which were introduced in Scotland by the Police, Public Order and Criminal Justice (Scotland) Act 2006.[181]

Key Points

- Sports venue safety is an international issue and major safety incidents have been reported worldwide.
- Sports venue disasters in the UK are the result of a complex interaction of legal and non-legal factors.
- Major venue disasters are matters of public safety and have been the subject of government inquiries.
- Although these factors have been identified repeatedly by these inquiries it is only in the last forty years that law has been used as a remedial measure.
- There is a wide range of actors in this area of law including owners, occupiers, neighbours, participants, spectators, police, local authorities and governing bodies.
- The main legal principle governing claims for compensation is negligence, which is based on a reasonable person standard.
- Football hooliganism as a social phenomenon has been subject to extensive regulation through specific legislation primarily criminalising conduct.
- Banning orders, which limit attendance at football matches, have been an additional civil law provision that is given to those convicted of football-related offences.
- There have been some civil libertarian concerns about the extent of restrictions imposed by banning orders.
- Spectator racism and other forms of abuse have been identified as a problem in a number of sports and have been subject to a range of legal and non-legal responses.

Key Sources

Alcock v Chief Constable of South Yorkshire (1991) 4 All ER 907.
Hartley, H, *Disaster Law; A Socio-Legal Perspective* (2001), London: Cavendish Publishing.
The Hillsborough Stadium Disaster (Final Report), Cm 962, London: HMSO.
Home Office Guidance on Football-Related Legislation, HC 34/2000.
Pearson, G and Stott, C, *Football Hooliganism: Policing and the War on the English Disease* (2007) London: Pennant Books.

---

181 For issues about the grounds for use of football banning orders in Scotland, see McArdle. D, 'Football, Sectarianism and Scots law: Walls v Brown' (2011) 9(1) World Sports Law Reports.

Index

A

accountability, self-regulation and 92–3
Acreman, L. 314–17
Adams, Tony 403
Adidas 349
adjudicative officials 15, 51–5
Adorno, T. 226
advertising 219, 220
    clean venue policy 345–50
    tattoo advertising 333
Advisory Conciliation and Arbitration Service
        (ACAS) 430, 435, 438–9
Afghanistan 39
age discrimination 461
agents 202, 396–7
    athletics 267–8
    boxing 269–70
    cricket 265
    football 188–90, 265–70, 396, 397
    regulation of sports agents 265–70
    rugby 265
agreements between undertakings 177–8
alcohol
    abuse of 403, 404
    alcohol-related sports sponsorship 219–20
    restrictions on trains and buses going to
        matches 546–7
alternative dispute resolution 138–42
    see also arbitration
Amateur Athletic Association (AAA) 241
Amateur Athletic Club 23
Amateur Swimming Association 536–40
amateurism 15, 70–1, 166
    professionalism and the end of amateurism
        212–18, 241
ambush marketing 329–35
    brand protection 343–4
    clean venue protection against 345–50
    Olympics and 330–1, 335–40, 341–2, 343,
        355–9
    other major sports events 340–3

Amsterdam Declaration on Sport 164
Anderson, J. 527
angling 15
arbitration 77, 138
    Court of Arbitration for Sport (CAS) 52–5,
        77, 82, 85, 138–9, 141, 142, 371,
        381
    judicial responses to 139–41
archery 13, 16, 19
Argentina 38
Armstrong, Chris 403
Armstrong, Lance 391
Arnaut, J.-L. 200
Arnaut Report 493
Arsenal Football Club 321
Association of Chief Police Officers (ACPO) 521
Association of Tennis Professionals (ATP) 289,
        298
associations of undertakings 177
    decisions of 177–8
Athens Olympics (2004) 317–18, 335–6
Atherton, Mike 60, 61, 63
athletics 15, 16, 23
    agents 267–8
    contract between regulator and regulation
        106–10
    corporate governance 241
    doping 106–10, 116, 182–6, 285, 364–5
        enhancing sport performance 384
        fair hearing right 379–81
        rule violations 373, 374–5
    marathon running 533
    professionalism in 212, 213–14
    technological doping 67–8
Atlanta Olympics (1996) 344, 350
Australia
    sports law in 85
    sports medical practitioners 512
    Sydney Olympics (2000) 141, 311, 348
    World Series Cricket 215
Australian Jockey Club (AJC) 131

B

badger baiting 20
Baldwin, R. 260
Bale, J. 46–7, 576
Bankowski, Z. 74
banning orders 577–9
Barcelona Olympics (1992) 348
Barnes, J. 22–3, 83–4, 85
Barr-Smith, A. 252–4
baseball 13, 72
basketball 52, 170–2
Bean, L. 331, 332
bear baiting 18, 20
Beck, John 433
Becker, D. 309, 312
Beckham, David 219
Bedford, David 321
Beijing Olympics (2008) 37–8, 210, 349
Beloff, Michael J. 64–6, 69, 85, 371
Benn, Nigel 423
Betfair 296–7, 298
betting *see* gambling
bias, rule against 132–4
billiards 117, 126, 180, 181
Birley, David 16, 22
Blake, A. 24–5, 27–8
Blissett, Gary 517–18
Bolton stadium disaster 30, 545–6
Bond, D. 239
Boon, G. 229
Botham, Ian 63, 403
Bower, T. 266
bowls 13, 19, 20
Bowyer, Lee 403, 522–3
boxing 7, 13, 129, 397, 423
    agents 269–70
    case for banning 526–31
    injuries to participants 508–9, 571
    review of decisions by adjudicative
        officials 53
    rules 23, 45–6, 529
    sex discrimination in 472–3
Boycott, Geoffrey 63
Boyes, S. 135–6, 270–1
Brackenridge, Celia 534, 540
Bradford stadium disaster 31, 545, 548, 549
Bradley, Graham 286–8
Brasch, R. 13–16
Brazil 41
Brearley, M. 60–2

Briatore, Flavio 64–5
Britannica Yearbook 24–5
British Amateur Weightlifters' Association
        (BAWLA) 105, 118
British Athletics Federation (BAF) 106–10,
        241, 364–5, 379–81
British Boxing Board of Control (BBBC) 129,
        508–9, 531, 571
British Darts Organisation (BDO) 11
British Horseracing Board (BHB) 256
British Medical Association (BMA) 527, 530
British Olympic Association (BOA) 33,
        116, 120
broadcasting of sport 24, 25, 203, 210, 212
    commodification of sport and 227
    competition and 245–6
        collective selling of TV rights 247–9
        property rights in televising sports
            events 246–7
        restrictions on selling of sports events
            249–54
    European Union (EU) law and
        196–7
        broadcast blackouts 197–8
        cross-territorial broadcasting 198
        joint and exclusive selling of
            broadcasting rights 197
        listing 198–9, 252
    World Series Cricket 215–18
Brown, Adam 235, 236, 237
Brown, W. M. 386
Bruce, Steve 405–6
BSkyB 24, 212, 226, 227, 228, 229, 245, 247,
        249
Buffham, Roger 286–7
bull baiting 18, 20
bullying 422
    see also harassment
burden of proof
    doping 377–8
    unfair dismissal 431
Burns Report 239
Bush, George W. 38

C

Cadbury Report 242
Caiger, A. 74
cam buck 17
Campbell, Beatrix 464
Campbell, Sol 588

Canada
  criminal liability for sports participant
    violence 519–20
  drug testing in 382
  sports law in 84, 85
  Vancouver Winter Olympics (2010) 311,
    312–13, 336, 352–5, 357–8
Cantona, Eric 403, 516–17, 566, 581–2
Carling, Will 212, 241
Carrington, B. 586–8
Carroll, Andy 403
Carter, Jimmy 39
celebrity players 219
Central Council of Physical Recreation (CCPR)
  30
certification 195–6
Chambers, Dwain 116
Chambliss, W. 583
characteristics of sport business 222–5
Charlish, P. 376
Chaudhary, V. 37–8, 462
cheating 50, 57–8
  cricket 55
    ball tampering 60–4
  criminalisation of 298–9
  drug use see doping
  football 65
  motor racing 64–5
  rugby 65
  technological doping 66–9
children and young people
  child abuse 533–4, 537
    definition 535–6
  football apprentices and scholars 298–399
  protection of 167, 533–4, 540–1
    development of effective child
      protection policy 536–40
  talent spotting 222
clean venue policy 345–50
club ball 17
coaches
  children and 533–4, 535, 537, 540–1
  liability for injuries to players 514
  screening of 540
Coakley, J. 5, 6, 26–7, 29
Coca-Cola 303
cock fighting 16, 20, 22
collective bargaining 399–402
collective selling of TV rights 247–9
Colombia 39

commercial rights 303–4
  licensing/merchandising 310–12
  ticketing 312–18
  see also advertising; intellectual property
    rights; sponsorship
commercialisation of sport 219–20
  sponsorship 195–6, 210, 212, 219–20
Commission for Racial Equality (CRE) 585
commodification of sport 225–7
Commonwealth Games 40
competition 222
  broadcasting and 245–6
    collective selling of TV rights 247–9
    property rights in televising sports
      events 246–7
    restrictions on selling of sports events
      249–54
Competition Commission (CC) 254
competition law 120–7
  European Union (EU) 116, 165–6,
    176–96
    applicability of Art 101 TFEU to sport
      176–9
    applicability of Art 102 TFEU to sport
      179–81
    commercial activities and 194–6
    reconciling regulatory and commercial
      functions 191–4
    sporting exception 182–8
    sports regulation and 188–91
  other competition law intervention into UK
    sport 254–6
confidentiality duty 408–9
conflict theory 26, 28–9
constructive dismissal 421–2, 429–30
consumerism, sport and 26
contemporary significance of sport 24–6
contests, sports as 8–9
contracts
  between regulator and regulation 106–10
  contractual relationships 105, 113
    affirming jurisdiction 105–6
    challenges 106–10
    extending justiciability 110–12
    nature of contractual nexus 106
    private law supervisory jurisdiction
      112–13
    contractual supervision of governing bodies
      117–18
  employment 397–8

apprentices and scholars 398–9
collective bargaining 399–402
disciplinary procedures 122–4, 141, 419, 435–9
duty of obedience 407
duty to maintain mutual trust and confidence 406–7
duty to provide work 405–6
duty to take reasonable care 407–8
exclusivity 408
express terms 402–4
health and safety issues 406
implied terms 404–9
maintaining confidentiality 408–9
remedies for unfair dismissal 440–1
remedies for wrongful dismissal 423–6, 427
restraint of trade 114–16, 120–7, 409–18
termination 418–22
unfair dismissal 426–35, 437–9
Olympic sponsorship 309–10
contributory negligence 514
Cooke, Paul 417
copyright 324–5
Cornelius, S. 52
Cornforth, John 504
corporate governance 201, 204, 241–2, 257
characteristics of sports governance 242–3
EU and 243–5
corruption 202, 259, 297–301
fixing of matches/races 272, 297–301
cricket 273–86, 297
football 272–3, 293
horse racing 286–8
increased criminalisation 298–9
memoranda of understanding 298
tennis 288–90
football 259–65, 272
hosting of major sporting events and 270–2
World Anti-Corruption Agency (WADA) 300–1
Cotonou Agreement 491
Council of Europe 'Fair Play Charter' 51
courts
appropriate relationship between sport and the courts 90
Court of Arbitration for Sport (CAS) 52–5, 77, 82, 85, 138–9, 141, 142, 371, 381

judicial review of sports governing bodies 93–105, 116
review of decisions by adjudicative officials 52
cricket 17, 21, 41
adjudicative officials 51
agents 265
'bodyline' tour 58–9
cheating 55
ball tampering 60–4
code of ethics 56–7
disciplinary procedures 123–4
employment in 395
contracts 399, 403, 408, 419
remedies for wrongful dismissal 424
unfair dismissal claims 428, 434, 439
gambling and 290, 291
injuries to spectators 566
liability to neighbours of cricket grounds 556–7, 559–62
match fixing 273–86, 297
patents and designs 323–4
playing culture 49
professionalism in 213, 215–18
rules 48, 56–7, 60, 62–3, 215
safety helmets 526
crime 34–5
prevention 35–7
Criminal Records Bureau (CRB) 540
critical theory 26, 27, 28–9
critical race theory 30
Cronje, Hansie 273, 274, 275–7, 285
Crown Prosecution Service (CPS) 520–3
Crozier, Adam 241
culture 75
cultural studies 226
rules of sports and playing culture 49–50
sport and 24–6
Curbishley, Alan 422
cyber squatting 333–4
cycling 147–9

D
damages
for negligence 515
for wrongful dismissal 425–6
dangerous sports 531–3
darts 11
database rights 325–9
Davies Report 252–3

Davydenko, Nikolay 288
De Knop, P. 77–9
de Pencier, J. 382
Deepak, R. 80
definitions of sport 4–5
    fundamental characteristics 9
    legal definition of sport 11–12
    recognition procedure 10–11
    social definition 5–9
Deloitte 229
Demetriou, M. 85
Department for Culture, Media and Sport
    (DCMS) 30, 31
design right 323–4
disability 476–7
    discrimination 468, 477
disciplinary procedures 122–4, 141, 419,
    435–9
discrimination 422, 448–9, 461–5
    age discrimination 461
    disability discrimination 468, 477
    EU law and 483–96
    harassment 422, 476, 477–80
        vicarious liability for 480–3
    positive 473
    unlawful 465–7
        direct discrimination 467–8
        indirect discrimination 469–73
    see also racial discrimination;
            religious discrimination; sex
            discrimination; sexual orientation
            discrimination
dismissal
    constructive 421–2, 429–30
    summary 418
    unfair 426–7, 437
        claiming 429
        continuity of employment and 427–9
        grievance procedures and 429–30
        meaning of unfair dismissal 430–5
        remedies 440–1
    wrongful 419–21
        remedies 423–6, 427
dis-play 7
dog fighting 22
dominant position 179–81, 222
doping 204
    anti-doping institutions 369–71
        UNESCO Convention against Doping in
        Sport 369, 370

World Anti-Doping Code 6, 365, 369,
    371–90
    athletics 106–10, 116, 182–6, 285, 364–5
        enhancing sport performance 384
        fair hearing right 379–81
        rule violations 373, 374–5
    banned substances 381–2
    enhancing sport performance 382–4
    EU law and 182–6, 365–8
    fair hearings 378–81
    future 390–1
    greyhound racing 95, 133
    health risk to athlete 384–7
    horse racing 102, 103
    human rights issues 390
    Olympics 369, 370
    proof of 377–8
    rugby 434
    rule violations 373–7
    sanctions 387–90
    swimming 365
    tennis 376
    therapeutic use exception 377
    whistle-blowing 388
Dow Chemical Company 308
Downes, S. 213–14, 241
drugs 386–7, 391, 403, 404, 434
    see also doping
Duthie, M. 313–14
duty of care, negligence and 502

E

Eastham, George 410
Ecclestone, Bernie 65
economic dimension of sport 202, 210,
    220–2
    characteristics of sport business 222–5
    commercialisation of sport 219–20
        sponsorship 195–6, 210, 212, 219–20
    commodification of sport 225–7
    measures to promote financial probity 240
education programmes 526
Elias, Norbert 27, 28, 528
Elliott, Paul 504
employment in sport 210
    contracts of employment 397–8
        apprentices and scholars 398–9
        collective bargaining 399–402
        disciplinary procedures 122–4, 141,
        419, 435–9

duty of obedience 407
duty to maintain mutual trust and
    confidence 406–7
duty to provide work 405–6
duty to take reasonable care 407–8
exclusivity 408
express terms 402–4
formation and terms of 397–8
health and safety issues 406
implied terms 404–9
maintaining confidentiality 408–9
remedies for unfair dismissal 440–1
remedies for wrongful dismissal 423–6,
    427
restraint of trade 114–16, 120–7,
    409–18
termination 418–22
unfair dismissal 426–35, 437–9
transfer of players *see* transfer systems
who is an employee 394–6
employment tribunals 426–7
endorsement 195–6
England and Wales Cricket Board 41, 56
English Defence League (EDL) 466, 478
Eriksson, Sven-Goran 263
Escobar, Andres 39
ethics in sport 50–1, 56
    hosting of major sporting events and 270–2
European Sponsorship Association (ESA) 344
European Sports Charter 11
European sports model 200–1
European Union (EU) 9, 146, 147–51, 205–6
    broadcasting of sport and 196–7
        broadcast blackouts 197–8
        cross-territorial broadcasting 198
        joint and exclusive selling of
            broadcasting rights 197
        listing 198–9, 252
    competition law 116–17, 165–6, 176–96
        applicability of Art 101 TFEU to sport
            176–9
        applicability of Art 102 TFEU to sport
            179–81
        commercial activities and 194–6
        reconciling regulatory and commercial
            functions 191–4
        sporting exception 182–8
        sports regulation and 188–91
    discrimination and 483–96
    doping and 182–6, 365–8

football transfer system and 79–80,
    157–60, 168, 415–17, 441–58
free movement of persons principles 146,
    151, 153–60, 168–72, 173, 205,
    441–58, 485–96
Independent European Sports Review
    199–201
Lisbon Treaty 203–5
sexual orientation discrimination and
    474–5
social inclusion and sport 33–4
sports governance and 243–5
trade unions and 402
White Paper on Sport (2007) 201–3
Europeanisation 223
exclusivity 408
expertise, self-regulation and 90–1

F
fair hearing right 128–32
    doping cases 378–81
fairness 9, 56
    procedural fairness 93
Fallon, Kieren 288
Farrington, David 36
Farrow, S. 269
Fashanu, John 272, 475
Fashanu, Justin 475
Fédération Internationale de Football
    Associations (FIFA) 37, 38, 77, 80,
    334
    EU competition law and 160–1, 188–90
    regulation of sports agents 265–70
    transfer rules 415–17, 451–4
Felix, A. 38–9, 41
feminist theories of sport 29–30
Ferdinand, Rio 404
figurational theory 27–8
financial corruption *see* corruption
financial stability 240
fixing of matches/races 272, 297–301
    cricket 273–86, 297
    football 272–3, 293
    gambling and 274, 287, 288–90, 298–9
    horse racing 286–8
    increased criminalisation 298–9
    memoranda of understanding 298
    tennis 288–90
Flood, J. 74
football 72

agents 188–90, 265–70, 396, 397
applicability of EU law 147, 150–1
    competition law 188–91
    free movement of persons 151–76,
        441–58, 485–96
arbitration procedures 140–1
banning orders 577–9
broadcasting of 245–6
    broadcast blackouts 197–8
    collective selling of TV rights 247–9
    cross-territorial broadcasting 198
    joint and exclusive selling of
        broadcasting rights 197
    property rights in televising events
        246–7
certification procedure 196
cheating 65
child protection policies 541
club membership of leagues and
        associations 124–6
commodification of 226
corruption 259–65, 272
dominance problems 222
employment in 394
    apprentices and scholars 398–9
    collective bargaining 399–402
    confidentiality duty 408–9
    disciplinary procedures 141, 435–6
    duty of obedience 407
    duty to maintain mutual trust and
        confidence 406–7
    duty to provide work 405–6
    exclusivity 408
    express terms in contracts 403–4
    grievance procedures 430
    referees 395–6
    remedies for wrongful dismissal 424,
        425–6
    restraint of trade 115, 409–18
    termination 419–21
    unfair dismissal claims 428, 438, 439
fair hearing right and 128–9
gambling and 291, 293–4
globalisation and 38–9
history 6, 13, 17, 19, 21
hooliganism 22, 75, 76, 435, 547, 548–9,
        574–9
injuries to players in
    civil liability 501, 502, 504, 505,
        511–12, 513, 515

criminal liability 516–17, 517–19,
        522–3
judicial review and 97–8, 100–2, 104
match fixing 272–3, 293
measures to promote financial probity 240
nationality rules 154–7, 441–58, 485–96
origins of modern sport 23
politics and 41
professionalism in 212
quotas of national players 173–4
racial discrimination in 462, 467–8
    harassment 478–80
    spectator racism 580–5
    vicarious liability for harassment 480–3
regulation 227–30
rules 47, 48–9, 138
sex discrimination in 463–4
sportsmanship 55–6
stadiums 552
    disasters 30–1, 544–52, 571–4, 575
    local authority licensing 555
talent spotting 222
trade marks 320, 321
training
    compensation for training of young
        players 174–5
    contracts for apprentices and scholars
        398–9
transfer system 115, 121–2, 229–30,
        410–18
    European Union (EU) and 79–80,
        157–60, 168, 415–17, 441–58
World Cup 41, 194–5, 215
    ambush marketing 342–3
Football Association (FA) 23, 97, 100–2, 104,
        121, 124–5
Burns Report 239
disciplinary procedures 435–6
equality policy 465
fair hearing right and 128–9
racial harassment and 478–9
restraint of trade and 115
rule against bias and 133
spectator racism and 583–4
transfer rules 411–14
Football Association of Wales (FAW) 97, 124
Football Licensing Authority (FLA) 555
Football Task Force 230–7, 583
Foster, Ken 73, 81, 82–3, 224–5
Foucault, Michel 74

France
- compensation for training of young players 174–5
- violence in 36

Fraser, David 49–50, 60

fraud
- horse racing 119

Frey, J. H. 39

functionalism 26, 27

G

Gallard, William 220

gambling 22, 290–5
- match/race fixing and 274, 287, 288–90, 298–9
- principles of UK gambling legislation 295–7
- Sports Betting Integrity Unit 299–300

garden leave 405–6

Gardiner, S. 38–9, 41, 50, 219–20, 255–6, 296–7, 447–9, 454–8, 481–3, 582

Gardner, R. 383

Gascoigne, Paul 261

Gasser, Sandra 116

Gaved, M. 244–5

Gay Olympics 358–9

gay people see sexual orientation discrimination

genetic engineering 68

Giddins, Ed 403, 419, 423

Giggs, Ryan 440

Giles, C. 313–14

Gleneagles Agreement 40, 41

globalisation 38, 223
- football and 38–9
- globalisation of sports law 77–83

go-karting 563

Goldman, B. 384–5

golf 19
- injuries in 504–5
- use of golf carts 68–9, 477

Gould, Bobby 478

governance issues see corporate governance

governing bodies 89–90, 142–4, 167, 202
- alternative dispute resolution and 138–42
- contractual relationships 105, 114
  - affirming jurisdiction 105–6
  - challenges 106–10
  - extending justiciability 110–12
  - nature of contractual nexus 106
  - private law supervisory jurisdiction 112–13
- gambling and 290
- judicial review of 93–105, 116
- liability for injuries to players 508–11
- self-regulation and
  - accountability 92–3
  - appropriate relationship between sport and the courts 90
  - efficiency 91–2
  - expertise 90–1
  - mandate 92
  - procedural fairness 93
- substantive rights against
  - contract and private law supervision 117–18
  - evaluation of case law 120, 126–7
  - human rights issues and 134–8
  - natural justice 127–8, 134
  - proportionality 119–20
  - relevant considerations 118–19
  - restraint of trade and competition law 120–7
  - right to fair hearing 128–32
  - rule against bias 132–4
- see also individual bodies

government and the state
- direct state intervention in sport 30–1
- indirect state intervention in sport 31–7
- using authority to persuade 37–41

Grace, W. G. 23

Graham, George 262–3

Gramsci, Antonio 226

Grant, Helen 527

Gray, Andy 464, 536–40

Gray, J. 267–8, 296–7

Grayson, Edward 70, 71, 83, 212

Green, N. 247–8

Greenfield, S. 217, 576

Greig, Tony 123–4, 215–17

greyhound racing 94–5
- doping 95, 133

grievance procedures 429–30

Grimberg, H. 508

gymnastics 535–6

H

Haaland, Alf-Inge 501

Haigh, G. 215

Hammond, D. 580

handball 17, 172
harassment 422, 476, 477–80
　vicarious liability for 480–3
Hargreaves, J,. 8–9, 25–6
Haslar Report 527
Havelange, Joao 38
health and safety issues 406, 570–1
health risks 384–7
　see also injuries
hearings, fair see fair hearing right
hegemony 226
Heiberg, Gerhard 330
Helsinki Declaration on Sport 164, 165–6
Henderson, P. 352–5
Hickson, Paul 533–4, 537
Higgins, John 299
Higgot, R. 80
Hill, Damon 321
Hillsborough disaster 31, 231, 544, 549–52,
　567, 571–4, 575
history of sports 13–16, 27–8
　contemporary significance of sport 24–6
　historical perspectives on sports regulation
　　16–21
　origins of modern sport 22–4
　rules of sports 22–3, 45–6
hockey 14
Holt, R. 58–9
hooliganism 22, 75, 76, 435, 547, 548–9,
　574–9
Horkheimer, M. 226
horse racing 13, 16
　competition law and 255–6
　doping 102, 103
　fraud 119
　gambling and 291, 294, 295–6
　injuries to jockeys 503
　judicial review 98–100
　natural justice and 127–8
　nature of contractual nexus 106
　race fixing 286–8
　review of decisions by adjudicative officials
　　52
　self-regulation 93
　stadiums 552
　three-day eventing as dangerous sport
　　531–2
　women trainers in 110–11
Horseracing Regulatory Authority 119, 120
Howman, David 376

Hoyzer, Robert 272–3
Huizinga, J. 6–7
human rights issues
　Beijing Olympics (2008) and 37–8
　doping and 390
　governing bodies and 134–8
　sexual orientation and 474
Hunt, A. 74
Hunter, Martin 67
hunting 13, 15, 16, 17
Hylton, K. 30

I
Ibrox disaster 31, 546, 548
ice hockey 49–50, 567
ice skating 54–5, 535
Illingworth, Ray 403, 408
Ince, Paul 58
Independent European Sports Review 199–201
Independent Football Commission 237–9
Indian Cricket League (ICL) 218
Indian Premier League (IPL) 218
industrial action 399–402
injunctions for wrongful dismissal 423–5
injuries 50, 385
　children 535–6
　civil liability for 500–1, 568–71
　　damages 515
　　defences 514
　　negligence 501–3
　　potential defendants 503–14
　　trespass to the person 501
　criminal liability for 515–16
　　consent defence 519–20
　　environs of the sports field 516–17
　　off-the-ball incidents 517, 522, 566
　　on-the-ball incidents 517–19, 523
　　prosecutorial discretion 520–5
　duty to take reasonable care 407–8
　psychiatric 571–4
　risk management 526
　　case for banning boxing 526–31
　　dangerous sports 531–3
　to spectators 516–17, 564–7
　unfair dismissal and 434–5
integrity of sports 9
intellectual property rights 318
　copyright 324–5
　database rights 325–9
　passing off 320–1

patents and designs 323–4
special protection for Olympic rings 319
trade marks 319–20, 321–3
International Amateur Boxing Association
527–8
International Association of Athletics
Federations (IAAF) 77, 116, 213–14
International Chamber of Commerce (ICC)
344
International Cricket Council (ICC) 123–4,
215, 275
match fixing and 282–5
International Cycling Union (UCI) 147–9
International Motorcycling Federation (FIM)
191
International Olympic Committee (IOC) 37,
77, 79, 213
ambush marketing and 343, 349
corruption and 270–2
doping and 369, 370
International Tennis Federation (ITF) 124, 140,
289
international trade 178
Internet, ambush marketing and 333–4
intersex 476
investment in sport 228

J
Jagodic, T. 309
James, M. 501, 579
Jardine, Douglas 58–9
Jarvie, G. 29
Jennings, A. 270
Jockey Club 93, 286–8, 295–6, 298
contract and private law supervision
117–18
extending justiciability 110–11
judicial review 98–100, 102–4
natural justice and 127–8
private law supervisory jurisdiction 112–13
proportionality of penalties 119–20
Jones, Mark 131
Jordan, Michael 348
judicial review 93–105, 116
judo 13, 168–9, 472
juridification of sport 73–7

K
karate 13
Karolyi, Bela 535–6

Kashmiri, Faisal 269
Kaufmann-Kohler, G. 390
Keane, Roy 501
Keegan, Kevin 409–10, 422, 426
Kerr, T. 85
Késenne, S. 222
Keys, Richard 464
Kick it Out campaign 585
King Commission 276–7
Klatz, R. 384–5
Knight, Alan 440
Korda, Petr 140
Kwon, Gyehyun 305

L
labour market 223–4
see also employment in sport; transfer
systems
Lamb, Allan 63–4
Lang Report (1969) 547
Lantos, Tom 38
Larive Report (1994) 163
Latta, V. 531–2
Le Roux, R. 277
Leaman, O. 57–8
legal definition of sport 11–12
legal positivism 27
Lewis, Adam 85
Li Ning 349
licensing
Olympic merchandising 310–12
stadiums and other venues 554–5
Lisbon Treaty 203–5
listing of events 198–9, 252
Little, G. 132–3
local authority licensing of stadiums and other
venues 554–5
localisation 78–9
Loncle, François 38
London Olympics (2012) 31, 32, 72, 310,
319, 336, 337–40, 351
Long, J. 586–8
Longmore, A. 48–9
Los Angeles Olympics (1984) 307
Lowen, D. 337–40
Luschen, Gunther 57

M
McArdle, D. 576
Macari, Lou 419–21

Macaulay, Stewart 76
McIntosh, Peter 57–8
Mackay, D. 213–14, 241
McKelvey, S. M. 344
MacLaurin, Lord 241
McLintock, Frank 262
McVicar, J. 34–5
Maguire, J. 29
Malcolm, Devon 403, 408
Malik, Salim 274, 275, 276
Malinverni, G. 390
Manchester United 226, 311
marathon running 533
Marcuse, H. 226
Martin, Casey 68–9, 477
Marylebone Cricket Club (MCC) 323–4
Mason, T. 290–5
match fixing *see* fixing of matches/races
maternity rights 483–4
May, Tim 274, 275
Mayhew, Henry 22
Meca-Medina, David 365
media *see* broadcasting of sport
mediation 77
medical practitioners
    liability for injuries to players 512–14
    negligence by 571
Meenaghan, T. 306, 329
Meier, K. 6
Melbourne Park 47
merchandising
    Olympics 310–12
Merson, Paul 403
Michener, J. 7
Miettinen, S. 494–6
Mitten, M. J. 82
Modahl, Diane 106–10, 241, 364–5, 379
Moelwyn Hughes Report (1946) 545–6
money laundering 202, 316
Monnington, T. 39–41
Monopolies and Mergers Commission (MMC)
    228
Moore, Brian 65
moral panics 75–6
morality clauses 310
Morris, P. 132–3, 161
Morrow, S. 161
Moscow Olympics (1980) 39–40
motor boat racing 562–3
motor racing 526

cheating 64–5
injuries to participants 509–10
injuries to spectators 564–6
rules 47–8
motorcycling 191–4
Mouritz, A. 357–8
Moynihan, Colin 40
Mungham, G. 74
Munroe, Hector 39
Murdoch, Rupert 212, 213
Murphy, M. 67–8
Murray, James 527
Mutu, Adrian 391, 404

N

Nafziger, J. A. R. 79, 81, 82
National Baseball League (NBL; USA) 221
National Basketball Association (NBA; USA)
    221, 333
national dimension to sport 223
National Football League (NFL; USA) 221
National Greyhound Racing Club (NGRC)
    95
National Hunt Committee (NHC) 106
National Lottery funding for sports 11
nationality rules in football 154–7, 441–58,
    485–96
natural justice 127–8, 134
negligence 556, 558, 559
    civil liability for sports participant violence
        501–3
        damages 515
        defences 514
        potential defendants 503–14
    contributory 514
    medical 571
    by police 571–4
New Zealand Rugby Football Union (NZRFU)
    111
Newell, Mike 263
Nice Declaration on Sport 166–8
Nike 348
Novacek, Karel 124
nuisance 556, 559, 563–4

O

Office of Fair Trading 254–6
Ohuruogu, Christine 373
Olympics 6, 23, 215
    ancient 13, 14

Athens Olympics (2004) 317–18, 335–6
Atlanta Olympics (1996) 344, 350
Barcelona Olympics (1992) 348
Beijing Olympics (2008) 37–8, 210,
    349
  Cityscape programme 350–5
  clean venue policy 345–50
  commercial rights 303–4
  corruption and 270–2
  injuries to participants 508
  intellectual property rights 318–29
    copyright 324–5
    database rights 325–9
    passing off 320–1
    patents and designs 323–4
    special protection for Olympic rings
      319
    trade marks 319–20, 321–3
  International Olympic Committee (IOC)
    37, 77, 79, 213
    ambush marketing and 343, 349
    corruption and 270–2
    doping and 369, 370
  licensing/merchandising 310–12
  London Olympics (2012) 31, 32, 72, 310,
    319, 336, 337–40, 351
  Los Angeles Olympics (1984) 307
  marketing plan 305–6
  Moscow Olympics (1980) 39–40
  Olympic Charter 81–2
  Rio Olympics (2016) 355–7
  Salt Lake City Winter Olympics (2002) 270,
    271, 306, 344, 350–1
  sponsorship 303, 304–7
    ambush marketing and 330–1, 335–40,
      341–2, 343, 355–9
    benefits to sponsors 308–9
    contracts 309–10
    distribution of funds 307–8
    domestic sponsors 308
    domestic suppliers and providers 310
  Sydney Olympics (2000) 141, 311, 348
  ticketing 312–18
  Vancouver Winter Olympics (2010) 311,
    312–13, 336, 352–5, 357–8
Opie, H. 82, 84–5, 86, 510–11
Osborn, G. 217, 576
Ougaard, M. 79
Oulmers, Abdelmajid 190
ownership issues 223

P

Pack Report (1997) 163
Packer, Kerry 212, 213, 215
Parrish, R. 162–3, 494–6
passing off 320–1
patents 323–4
Pearson, G. 579
Peru 38
Phillips, Kristie 535
Piau, Laurent 188–91
Pistorius, Oscar 67–8, 477
play 7, 8, 13
police
  crowd management and 547, 550, 551,
    567
  negligence by 571–4
politics, sport and 39–41
pools 291, 293–4
Popplewell Report 548, 575
power, sport and 25–6
pregnancy and maternity rights 483–4
Premier League (PL) 39, 100, 140, 197,
    198, 218, 222, 227–9, 234,
    236, 237, 239, 240, 246,
    247
  transfer rules 414–15, 453
procedural fairness 93
Procter, Mike 123–4
Procter & Gamble 308
Professional Footballers' Association (PFA)
    399–402
professionalism and the end of amateurism
    212–18
profit maximisation 220
proof *see* burden of proof; standard of
    proof
property rights in televising sports events
    246–7
proportionality principle 119–20
prosthetic limbs 67–8, 477
psychiatric injuries 571–4
public schools 23
Purse, Darren 475
Python Games 14

Q

Qayyum Report 276
Queensberry Rules 23, 46, 529
quotas of national players in football teams
    173–4

R

race fixing *see* fixing of matches/races
race theories of sport 29–30
racial discrimination 461–3, 465–6
    direct discrimination 467–8
    harassment 477, 478–80
        vicarious liability for 480–3
    indirect discrimination 470, 471
    spectator racism 579–80
        football 580–5
        non-legal approaches to regulation of
            585
        racist chanting 582, 583–5
        rugby 586–8
Ratcliffe, Kevin 478
ratting 22
raves 75
Reagan, Ronald 41
Reasbeck, Nicola 522–3
recognition procedure for sports 10–11
recreational activity distinguished from
        sport 6
Redhead, Steve 74, 75, 76
Reebok 348
referees *see* umpires/referees
regulation of sports 38, 70–3, 86–7, 257
    agents 265–70
    competition law 120–7
        European Union (EU) 116–17, 165–6,
            176–96
    direct state intervention in sport 30–1
    globalisation of sports law 77–83
    governing bodies 89–90
    historical perspectives 16–21
    indirect state intervention in sport 31–7
    juridification of sport 73–7
    models 220–1, 224–5, 227–30
    origins of modern sport 22–4
    restraint of trade 114–16, 120–7,
        409–18
    self-regulation *see* self-regulation
    sports law 83–6
    see also rules of sports
Reid, F. 333–5
religion
    'muscular Christianity' 23, 24
    sport and 5, 13, 14, 18, 19–20, 22
religious discrimination 465–6
    harassment 478, 479
    sectarianism 588–9

remedies
    unfair dismissal 440–1
    wrongful dismissal 423–6, 427
reservation systems 221
restraint of trade 114–16, 120–7, 409–18
revenue sharing 221
Revie, Don 133
Rice, Condoleezza 38
Richards, Dean 65
Richards, Renée 475
Rigozzi, A. 390
Rio Olympics (2016) 355–7
risk management 526
    case for banning boxing 526–31
    dangerous sports 531–3
Rix, Graham 534
Robins, D. 35–7
Robinson, L. 358
Rogge, J. 245
roller derbies 7
Ronaldo, Cristiano 219
Rous, Stanley 294
rowing 53–4
Rubie, Safi 269
rugby 6, 23
    adjudicative officials 51
    agents 265
    cheating 65
    doping 434
    employment in
        contracts 397–8
    fair hearing right and 131–2
    injuries to players in 504, 505–7, 510–11
    playing culture 49
    professionalism in 212–13, 241
    racial discrimination in 468
    spectator racism 586–8
    trade marks 320
    transfer system 417
Rugby Union 23
Rugby Union Football Committee (RFU)
        212
rules of sports 9, 44–5, 215
    adjudicative officials 15, 51–5
    changes 47–9
    cheating *see* cheating
    ethics in sport and 50–1, 56
    history 22–3, 45–6
    increasing conformity of playing rules
        46–7

playing culture and 49–50
  sportsmanship 55–7, 70
  violations 49–50
Rusedski, Greg 376
Ryan, Joan 535–6

S

sado-masochism 6
salaries of sportspeople 210
  caps 221, 222
  equal pay for women 484–5
Salt Lake City Winter Olympics (2002) 270,
      271, 306, 344, 350–1
Samaranch, Juan Antonio 271
Samsung 305
Santos, B. 76
Saunders, Dean 504
Schmitz, J. K. 331
Scholar, Irving 260, 261
Scholes, Paul 440
Schumacher, Michael 48
Seidmann, R. 583
self-regulation
  accountability 92–3
  appropriate relationship between sport and
      the courts 90
  efficiency 91–2
  expertise 90–1
  mandate 92
  procedural fairness 93
Semenya, Caster 66, 476
sex discrimination 448, 463–4, 465
  direct discrimination 467
  indirect discrimination 469–73
sexual misconduct 403–4
  child abuse 533–4, 537
    definition 535–6
sexual orientation discrimination 468,
      474–5
  harassment 477, 479
  spectator homophobia 588
Shankly, Bill 38
Sheard, K. 528–30
Sheringham, Teddy 262
shooting 15, 21
Shortt Report (1924) 545
Simon, R. 46, 384
Sinclair, D. 90
Singer, R. 5
Slusher, H. 5

Smith, Michael 500
Smoldon, Ben 506
snooker 117, 126, 180, 181
Snow, Jon 123–4
social definition of sport 5–9
social inclusion, sport and 33–7
social value of sport 201–2, 204
socialism 220–1
sociology of sport 26–7
  critical analysis 28–9
  feminist and race theories of sport 29–30
  figurational theory 27–8
South Africa
  ambush marketing in 340–1, 342–3
  apartheid regime 40, 41, 111
Spackle, K. 586–8
spectators 210, 223
  banning orders 577–9
  crowd management 547, 549–52, 567–8
  homophobia 588
  injuries to 516–17, 564–7
  racism 579–80
    football 580–5
    non-legal approaches to regulation of
      585
    racist chanting 582, 583–5
    rugby 586–8
  sectarianism 588–9
  stadium disasters 30–1
    Parliamentary enquiries 544–52
  violence in sport 34–5, 38–9, 75, 76
    hooliganism 22, 75, 76, 435, 547,
      548–9, 574–9
Spink, P. 161
sponsorship 195–6, 210, 212, 219–20, 303,
      304–7
  ambush marketing 329–35
    brand protection 343–4
    clean venue protection against 345–50
    Olympics and 330–1, 335–40, 341–2,
      343, 355–9
    other major sports events 340–3
  benefits to sponsors 308–9
  contracts 309–10
  distribution of funds 307–8
  domestic sponsors 308
  domestic suppliers and providers 310
  Olympics 303, 304–7
    ambush marketing and 330–1, 335–40,
      341–2, 343, 355–9

benefits to sponsors 308–9
contracts 309–10
distribution of funds 307–8
domestic sponsors 308
domestic suppliers and providers 310
Sport England 10, 31, 32
Sport Northern Ireland 31
Sport Scotland 31
Sport Wales 31
Sports and Recreation Alliance (SRA) 30, 33
Sports Betting Integrity Unit 299–300
Sports Coach UK 33
Sports Council 30, 31, 40
recognition procedure for sports and
10–11
Sports Resolutions 139
sportsmanship 55–7, 70
stadiums and other venues 47
all-seater stadiums 551
clean venue policy 345–50
crowd management 547, 549–52,
567–8
injuries to spectators 516–17, 564–7
local authority licensing 554–5
neighbours 555–64
occupiers' and owners' liability 552–4
spectator hooliganism 22, 75, 76, 435,
547, 548–9, 574–9
stadium disasters 30–1, 571–4, 575
Parliamentary enquiries 544–52
standard of proof
doping 377–8
Stanislaus, Roger 403
state see government and the state
Stephens, K. 325–9
Sterling, Paul 468
Stern, David 241
Stevens, Matt 386
Stone, G. 7
Stransky, Joel 397–8
Straw, Jack 90
Stretford, Peter 141, 269
strike action 399–402
Strinati, D. 227
Stringer, Korey 513–14
Sugar, Alan 261, 262
summary dismissal 418
surfing 51
Sutcliffe, S. 527–8
swimming 16

child abuse by coaches 533–4, 537
child protection policy 536–40
doping 365
technological doping 66
Sydney Olympics (2000) 141, 311, 348
symbolic interactionism 26, 27
Szymanski, Stefan 220, 240

T
take-overs 95–7, 228–9
talent spotting 222
TalkSport 320–1
tattoo advertising 333
taxation 260, 395
Taylor, Gordon 264
Taylor, Jonathan 85
Taylor Report (1989) 31, 47, 231, 544,
549–52, 567, 575
technology
adjudicative officials and 51, 53–4
technological doping 66–9
televised sport see broadcasting of sport
Temple, Cliff 534
tennis 17, 19, 23
adjudicative officials 51
arbitration procedures 140
disciplinary procedures 124
doping 376
match fixing 288–90
professionalism in 213
sponsorship 195
Test and County Cricket Board (TCCB)
123–4
Tethong, Kalon T C 38
Thatcher, Margaret 39, 40, 41
Thomas, Gareth 475, 588
Thorpe, Ian 321
ticketing for sports events 194–5
Olympics 312–18
ticket reselling 313–17
tobacco advertising 220
Tongue, N. 586–8
Topley, Don 274
Tottenham Hotspur 260–2, 320
town greens 11–12
trade
international 178
restraint of 114–16, 120–7, 409–18
trade marks 319–20, 321–3
passing off 320–1

trade unions 399–402

training

compensation for training of young
players 174–5

contracts for apprentices and scholars
398–9

sports training policies 167

see also coaches

transfer systems 221

basketball 170–2

football 115, 121–2, 229–30, 410–18

European Union (EU) and 79–80,
157–60, 168, 415–17, 441–58

rugby 417

transsexuality 475–6

trespass to the person 501

tug of war 14

U

UK Anti-Doping (UKAD) 371

UK Sport 31–2

ultra vires 118

umpires/referees 15, 51–5

employment status 395–6

liability for injuries to players 506–8

racial discrimination and 467–8

retirement 461

undertakings 177

agreements between 177–8

UNESCO Convention against Doping in Sport
369, 370

unfair dismissal 426–7, 437–9

claiming 429

continuity of employment and 427–9

grievance procedures and 429–30

meaning of unfair dismissal 430–5

remedies 440–1

United Parcel Service (UPS) 310

United States of America

agent regulation in 267–8

Atlanta Olympics (1996) 344, 350

child protection policies 536

economic dimension of sport 221

gambling in 297

Los Angeles Olympics (1984) 307

Salt Lake City Winter Olympics (2002) 270,
271, 306, 344, 350–1

sports medical practitioners 512, 513–14

trade mark law 321–3

Uzzell, John 518

V

Valcke, Jerome 343

Vancouver Winter Olympics (2010) 311,
312–13, 336, 352–5, 357–8

Venables, Terry 261, 262

venues *see* stadiums and other venues

vicarious liability

for harassment 480–3

for negligence 505–6

village greens 11–12

violence in sport 34–5, 38–9, 75, 76, 403,
434, 435, 500

civil liability for sports participant violence
500–1, 568–71

damages 515

defences 514

negligence 501–3

potential defendants 503–14

trespass to the person 501

criminal liability for sports participant
violence 515–16

consent defence 519–20

environs of the sports field 516–17

off-the-ball incidents 517, 522, 566

on-the-ball incidents 517–19, 523

prosecutorial discretion 520–5

spectators 34–5, 38–9, 75, 76

hooliganism 22, 75, 76, 435, 547,
548–9, 574–9

Vukelj, J. 333

W

Wachmeister, A. M. 250

Waddle, Chris 261

Warne, Shane 274, 275

water skiing 502

Watson, Michael 508–9, 571

Watt, Steve 527

Waugh, Mark 274, 275

Weatherill, S. 80–1, 186, 368–9

weightlifting 105, 118

Welch, R. 386–7, 400–2, 447–9, 454–8,
481–3, 488–90

Welsh Rugby Football Union (WRFU) 131–2,
134

Wembley Stadium 47

Wheatley Report (1971) 548

whistle-blowing 388, 404, 408

Whittington, Craig 403

Wilander, Matts 124

Williams, J. 463–4
Williams, R. 260–1
Williams, Tom 65
Wimbledon Lawn Tennis Tournament 23
win maximisation 220, 222–3
Wise, Dennis 403, 422, 438
Wolfenden Report (1960) 30
women
    boxing and 530
    equal pay 484–5
    feminist theories of sport 29–30
    as horse racing trainers 110–11
    pregnancy and maternity rights 483–4
    see also sex discrimination
Woodgate, Jonathan 403
Woodhouse, C. 83, 85
Woods, Tiger 219
World Anti-Corruption Agency (WADA)
    300–1
World Anti-Doping Code 6, 365, 369,
    371–2
    banned substances 381–2
    fair hearings 378–81
    proof of doping 377–8
    rule violations 373–7

    sanctions 387–90
    therapeutic use exception 377
    whistle-blowing 388
World Cup (football) 41, 194–5, 215
    ambush marketing 342–3
World Federation of the Sporting Goods
    Industry (WFSGI) 348
World Professional Billiards and Snooker
    Association (WPBSA) 117, 126, 180,
    181
World Series Cricket 215–18
World Wrestling Entertainment (WWE) 8
World Wrestling Federation (WWF) 8
wrestling 7, 8, 14
wrongful dismissal 419–21
    remedies 423–6, 427

Y
yachting 15
young people see children and young people

Z
Ziege, Christian 425–6
Zimbabwe 41
Zmeskal, Kim 535–6

Nunslinger

About the Author

Stark Holborn is the pseudonym of a thrilling new voice in fiction. But he – or she – knows to keep friends close ... and secrets closer.